Engineering Drawing

With an Introduction to AutoCAD

About the Author

Prof. Dhananjay A Jolhe is a Faculty in the Department of Industrial Engineering, Shri Ramdeobaba Kamla Nehru Engineering College, Nagpur, and has over 12 years of teaching experience in engineering. After completing a B. E degree in Production Engineering from Amravati University and an M.Tech degree in Industrial Engineering from Nagpur University, he adopted teaching profession with a great zeal.

During his prolific career, Prof. Jolhe has taught in AISSMS College of Engineering, Pune, Late Vasantdada Polytechnic, Nagpur, and Government Polytechnic, Yavatmal. Besides teaching, Prof. Jolhe has handled prestigious consultancy projects for Midland Diesel Services Pvt. Ltd., Nagpur, and Sun-Ind Systems Pvt. Ltd., Pune, and has also guided many industry-oriented undergraduate/post-graduate projects. His areas of specialization include methods engineering, ergonomics, performance and productivity improvement, process engineering and manufacturing planning.

Prof. Jolhe has published several research papers in various national and international journals and is also a life member of ISTE and a member of The Institution of Engineers (India). He actively takes part in attending conferences, workshops, cultural activities and enjoys drawing and painting in his spare time.

Engineering Drawing

With an Introduction to AutoCAD

Dhananjay A Jolhe

Department of Industrial Engineering
Shri Ramdeobaba Kamla Nehru Engineering College
Nagpur

Mc Graw Hill

McGraw Hill Education (India) Private Limited

Published by McGraw Hill Education (India) Private Limited,
Anjana Complex No: 5/90 A, Butt Road, St. Thomas Mount, Chennai – 600016, Tamil Nadu, India.

Engineering Drawing with an Introduction to AutoCAD

23rd reprint 2026

ISBN (13): 978-0-07-064837-1
ISBN (10): 0-07-064837-9

24 25 26 27 28 RAH 30 29 28 27 26

Typeset at The Composers, 260, C.A. Apt., Paschim Vihar, New Delhi 110 063 and,
Printed and Bound in India at Rahul Print O Pack, Z-57, Okhla Phase 2, New Delhi-110020

Visit us at: www.mheducation.co.in.
Toll free in India: 1800 103 5875
Write to us at: support.india@mheducation.com
CIN: U80302TN2010PTC111532

To my beloved parents & respected teachers—
Who carved me from a raw stone
and
To my dear students—The sole motivation behind this book

Visual Walkthrough

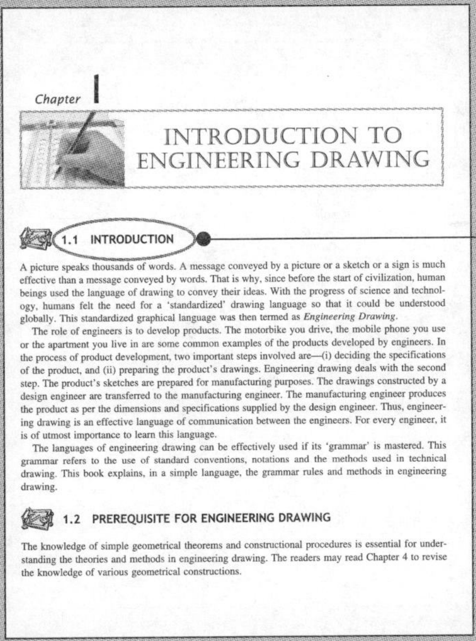

Chapter 1

INTRODUCTION TO ENGINEERING DRAWING

1.1 INTRODUCTION

A picture speaks thousands of words. A message conveyed by a picture or a sketch or a sign is much effective than a message conveyed by words. That is why, since before the start of civilization, human beings used the language of drawing to convey their ideas. With the progress of science and technology, humans felt the need for a 'standardized' drawing language so that it could be understood globally. This standardized graphical language was then termed as *Engineering Drawing*.

The role of engineers is to develop products. The motorbike you drive, the mobile phone you use or the apartment you live in are some common examples of the products developed by engineers. In the process of product development, two important steps involved are—(i) deciding the specifications of the product, and (ii) preparing the product's drawings. Engineering drawing deals with the second step. The product's sketches are prepared for manufacturing purposes. The drawings constructed by a design engineer are transferred to the manufacturing engineer. The manufacturing engineer produces the product as per the dimensions and specifications supplied by the design engineer. Thus, engineering drawing is an effective language of communication between the engineers. For every engineer, it is of utmost importance to learn this language.

The languages of engineering drawing can be effectively used if its 'grammar' is mastered. This grammar refers to the use of standard conventions, notations and the methods used in technical drawing. This book explains, in a simple language, the grammar rules and methods in engineering drawing.

1.2 PREREQUISITE FOR ENGINEERING DRAWING

The knowledge of simple geometrical theorems and constructional procedures is essential for understanding the theories and methods in engineering drawing. The readers may read Chapter 4 to revise the knowledge of various geometrical constructions.

Every chapter starts with a noteworthy **INTRODUCTION** highlighting the necessity and coverage of the chapter. It enables the readers to step into the chapter smoothly.

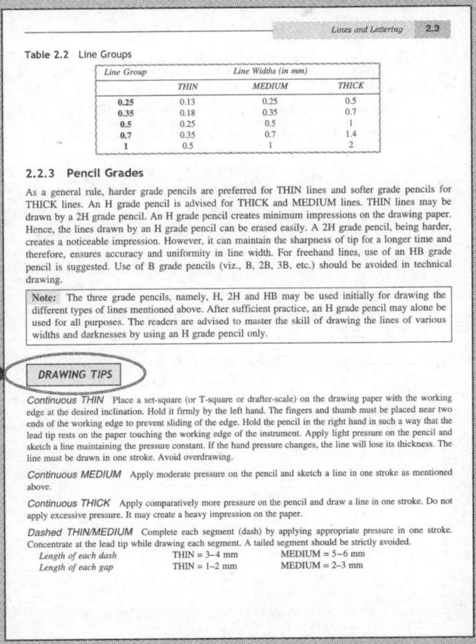

Lines and Lettering 2.3

Table 2.2 Line Groups

Line Group	Line Widths (in mm)		
	THIN	MEDIUM	THICK
0.25	0.13	0.25	0.5
0.35	0.18	0.35	0.7
0.5	0.25	0.5	1
0.7	0.35	0.7	1.4
1	0.5	1	2

2.2.3 Pencil Grades

As a general rule, harder grade pencils are preferred for THIN lines and softer grade pencils for THICK lines. An H grade pencil is advised for THICK and MEDIUM lines. THIN lines may be drawn by a 2H grade pencil. An H grade pencil creates minimum impressions on the drawing paper. Hence, the lines drawn by an H grade pencil can be erased easily. A 2H grade pencil, being harder, creates a noticeable impression. However, it can maintain the sharpness of tip for a longer time and therefore, ensures accuracy and uniformity in line width. For freehand lines, use of an HB grade pencil is suggested. Use of B grade pencils (viz., B, 2B, 3B, etc.) should be avoided in technical drawing.

Note: The three grade pencils, namely, H, 2H and HB may be used initially for drawing the different types of lines mentioned above. After sufficient practice, an H grade pencil may alone be used for all purposes. The readers are advised to master the skill of drawing the lines of various widths and darknesses by using an H grade pencil only.

DRAWING TIPS

Continuous THIN Place a set-square (or T-square or drafter-scale) on the drawing paper with the working edge at the desired inclination. Hold it firmly by the left hand. The fingers and thumb must be placed near two ends of the working edge to prevent sliding of the edge. Hold the pencil in the right hand in such a way that the lead tip rests on the paper touching the working edge of the instrument. Apply light pressure on the pencil and sketch a line maintaining the pressure constant. If the hand pressure changes, the line will lose its thickness. The line must be drawn in one stroke. Avoid overdrawing.

Continuous MEDIUM Apply moderate pressure on the pencil and sketch a line in one stroke as mentioned above.

Continuous THICK Apply comparatively more pressure on the pencil and draw a line in one stroke. Do not apply excessive pressure. It may create a heavy impression on the paper.

Dashed THIN/MEDIUM Complete each segment (dash) by applying appropriate pressure in one stroke. Concentrate at the lead tip while drawing each segment. A tailed segment should be strictly avoided.

Length of each dash	THIN = 3–4 mm	MEDIUM = 5–6 mm
Length of each gap	THIN = 1–2 mm	MEDIUM = 2–3 mm

DRAWING TIPS provided at appropriate places not only enhance the drawing skills but are also helpful in saving time and improve accuracy of drawings.

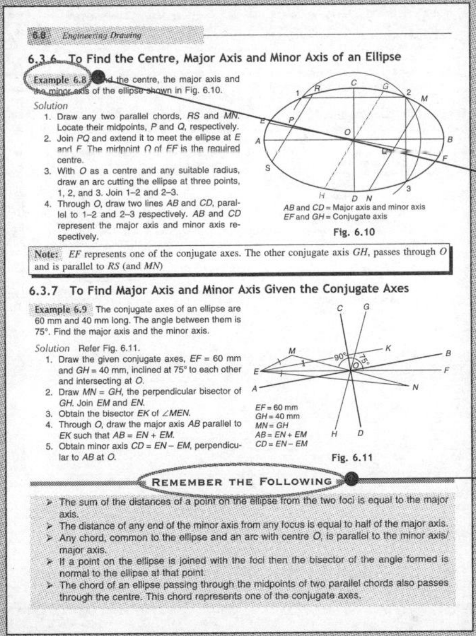

6.8 Engineering Drawing

6.3.6 To Find the Centre, Major Axis and Minor Axis of an Ellipse

Example 6.8 Find the centre, the major axis and the minor axis of the ellipse shown in Fig. 6.10.

Solution

1. Draw any two parallel chords, RS and MN. Locate their midpoints, P and Q, respectively.
2. Join PQ and extend it to meet the ellipse at E and F. The midpoint O of EF is the required centre.
3. With O as a centre and any suitable radius, draw an arc cutting the ellipse at three points, 1, 2, and 3. Join 1–2 and 2–3.
4. Through O, draw two lines AB and CD, parallel to 1–2 and 2–3 respectively. AB and CD represent the major axis and minor axis respectively.

AB and CD = Major axis and minor axis
EF and GH = Conjugate axis

Fig. 6.10

Note: EF represents one of the conjugate axes. The other conjugate axis GH, passes through O and is parallel to RS (and MN)

6.3.7 To Find Major Axis and Minor Axis Given the Conjugate Axes

Example 6.9 The conjugate axes of an ellipse are 60 mm and 40 mm long. The angle between them is 75°. Find the major axis and the minor axis.

Solution Refer Fig. 6.11.

1. Draw the given conjugate axes, EF = 60 mm and GH = 40 mm, inclined at 75° to each other and intersecting at O.
2. Draw $MN = GH$, the perpendicular bisector of GH. Join EM and EN.
3. Obtain the bisector EK of $\angle MEN$.
4. Through O, draw the major axis AB parallel to EK such that $AB = EN + EM$.
5. Obtain minor axis $CD = EN - EM$, perpendicular to AB at O.

EF = 60 mm
GH = 40 mm
$MN = GH$
$AB = EN + EM$
$CD = EN - EM$

Fig. 6.11

REMEMBER THE FOLLOWING

- The sum of the distances of a point on the ellipse from the two foci is equal to the major axis.
- The distance of any end of the minor axis from any focus is equal to half of the major axis.
- Any chord, common to the ellipse and an arc with centre O, is parallel to the minor axis/major axis.
- If a point on the ellipse is joined with the foci then the bisector of the angle formed is normal to the ellipse at that point.
- The chord of an ellipse passing through the midpoints of two parallel chords also passes through the centre. This chord represents one of the conjugate axes.

The sections and subsections are accompanied by **Example(s)** to explain the theoretical concepts presented in that section/subsection.

REMEMBER THE FOLLOWING is the sum-up of the important points at the end of appropriate sections. It helps memorize the key facts and prepare for viva-voce.

Visual Walkthrough

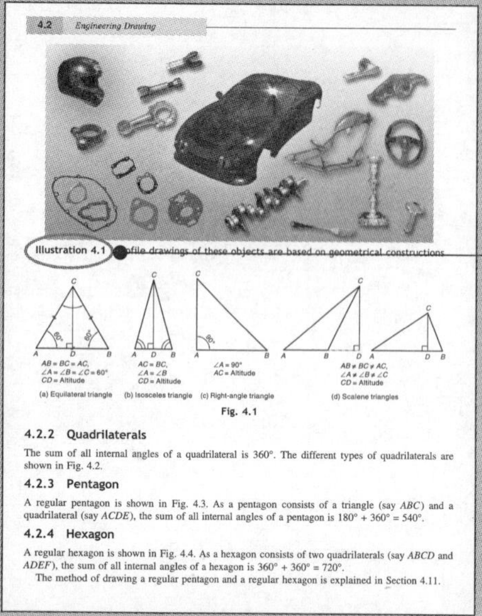

Illustration 4.1 Profile drawings of these objects are based on geometrical constructions

AB = BC = AC, ∠A = ∠B = ∠C = 60°, CD = Altitude — (a) Equilateral triangle; AC = BC, ∠A = ∠B, CD = Altitude — (b) Isosceles triangle; ∠A = 90°, AC = Altitude — (c) Right-angle triangle; AB ≠ BC ≠ AC, ∠A ≠ ∠B ≠ ∠C, CD = Altitude — (d) Scalene triangles

Fig. 4.1

4.2.2 Quadrilaterals

The sum of all internal angles of a quadrilateral is 360°. The different types of quadrilaterals are shown in Fig. 4.2.

4.2.3 Pentagon

A regular pentagon is shown in Fig. 4.3. As a pentagon consists of a triangle (say *ABC*) and a quadrilateral (say *ACDE*), the sum of all internal angles of a pentagon is 180° + 360° = 540°.

4.2.4 Hexagon

A regular hexagon is shown in Fig. 4.4. As a hexagon consists of two quadrilaterals (say *ABCD* and *ADEF*), the sum of all internal angles of a hexagon is 360° + 360° = 720°.

The method of drawing a regular pentagon and a regular hexagon is explained in Section 4.11.

Photographic **Illustrations** are used to show applications and real-life relevance.

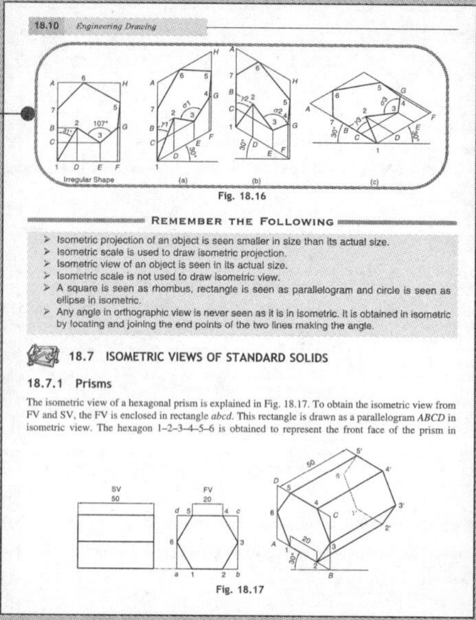

Fig. 18.16

Remember the Following

- Isometric projection of an object is seen smaller in size than its actual size.
- Isometric scale is used to draw isometric projection.
- Isometric view of an object is seen in its actual size.
- Isometric scale is not used to draw isometric view.
- A square is seen as rhombus, rectangle is seen as parallelogram and circle is seen as ellipse in isometric.
- Any angle in orthographic view is never seen as it is in isometric. It is obtained in isometric by locating and joining the end points of the two lines making the angle.

18.7 ISOMETRIC VIEWS OF STANDARD SOLIDS

18.7.1 Prisms

The isometric view of a hexagonal prism is explained in Fig. 18.17. To obtain the isometric view from FV and SV, the FV is enclosed in rectangle *abcd*. This rectangle is drawn as a parallelogram *ABCD* in isometric view. The hexagon 1–2–3–4–5–6 is obtained to represent the front face of the prism in

Fig. 18.17

A **STEP-BY-STEP APPROACH** improves imagination, thereby boosting the visualization capabilities of the students.

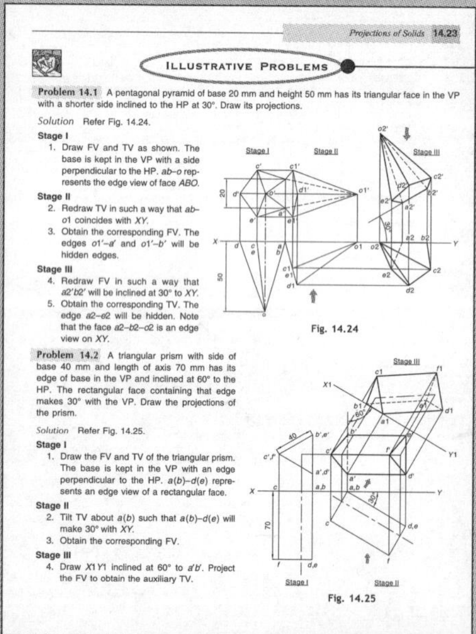

Illustrative Problems

Problem 14.1 A pentagonal pyramid of base 20 mm and height 50 mm has its triangular face in the VP with a shorter side inclined to the HP at 30°. Draw its projections.

Solution Refer Fig. 14.24.

Stage I

1. Draw FV and TV as shown. The base is kept in the VP with a side perpendicular to the HP. *ab–o* represents the edge view of face *ABO*.

Stage II

2. Redraw TV in such a way that *ab–o1* coincides with *XY*.
3. Obtain the corresponding FV. The edges *o1′–a′* and *o1′–b′* will be hidden edges.

Stage III

4. Redraw FV in such a way that *a2′b2′* will be inclined at 30° to *XY*.
5. Obtain the corresponding TV. The edge *a2–e2* will be hidden. Note that the face *a2–b2–c2* is an edge view on *XY*.

Fig. 14.24

Problem 14.2 A triangular prism with side of base 40 mm and length of axis 70 mm has its edge of base in the VP and inclined at 60° to the HP. The rectangular face containing that edge makes 30° with the VP. Draw the projections of the prism.

Solution Refer Fig. 14.25.

Stage I

1. Draw the FV and TV of the triangular prism. The base is kept in the VP with an edge perpendicular to the HP. *a(b)–d(e)* represents an edge view of a rectangular face.

Stage II

2. Tilt TV about *a(b)* such that *a(b)–d(e)* will make 30° with *XY*.
3. Obtain the corresponding FV.

Stage III

4. Draw *X1Y1* inclined at 60° to *a′b′*. Project the FV to obtain the auxiliary TV.

Fig. 14.25

ILLUSTRATIVE PROBLEMS, arranged in the order of simple to tough, help students prepare for university examinations. It includes problems on all the different topics in that chapter.

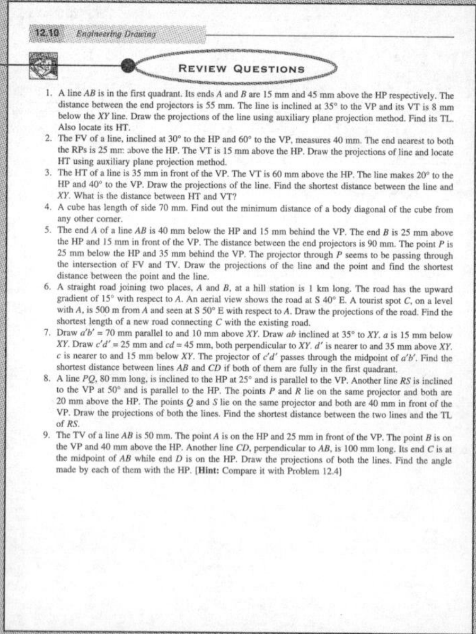

Review Questions

1. A line *AB* is in the first quadrant. Its ends *A* and *B* are 15 mm and 45 mm above the HP respectively. The distance between the end projectors is 55 mm. The line is inclined at 35° to the VP and its VT is 8 mm below the *XY* line. Draw the projections of the line using auxiliary plane projection method. Find its TL. Also locate its HT.
2. The FV of a line, inclined at 30° to the HP and 60° to the VP, measures 40 mm. The end nearest to both the RPs is 25 mm above the HP. The VT is 15 mm above the HP. Draw the projections of line and locate HT using auxiliary plane projection method.
3. The HT of a line is 35 mm in front of the VP. The VT is 60 mm above the HP. The line makes 20° to the HP and 40° to the VP. Draw the projections of the line. Find the shortest distance between the line and *XY*. What is the distance between HT and VT?
4. A cube has length of side 70 mm. Find out the minimum distance of a body diagonal of the cube from any other corner.
5. The end *A* of a line *AB* is 40 mm below the HP and 15 mm behind the VP. The end *B* is 25 mm above the HP and 15 mm in front of the VP. The distance between the end projectors is 90 mm. The point *P* is 25 mm below the HP and 35 mm behind the VP. The projector through *P* seems to be passing through the intersection of FV and TV. Draw the projections of the line and the point and find the shortest distance between the point and the line.
6. A straight road joining two places, *A* and *B*, at a hill station is 1 km long. The road has the upward gradient of 15° with respect to *A*. An aerial view shows the road at S 40° E. A tourist spot *C*, on a level with *A*, is 500 m from *A* and seen at S 50° E with respect to *A*. Draw the projections of the road. Find the shortest length of a new road connecting *C* with the existing road.
7. Draw *a′b′* = 70 mm parallel to and 10 mm above *XY*. Draw *ab* inclined at 35° to *XY*. *a* is 15 mm below *XY*. Draw *c′d′* = 25 mm and *cd* = 45 mm, both perpendicular to *XY*. *d′* is nearer to and 35 mm above *XY*. *c* is nearer to and 15 mm below *XY*. The projector of *c′d′* passes through the midpoint of *a′b′*. Find the shortest distance between lines *AB* and *CD* if both of them are fully in the first quadrant.
8. A line *PQ*, 80 mm long, is inclined to the HP at 25° and is parallel to the VP. Another line *RS* is inclined to the VP at 50° and is parallel to the HP. The points *P* and *R* lie on the same projector and both are 20 mm above the HP. The points *Q* and *S* lie on the same projector and both are 40 mm in front of the VP. Draw the projections of both the lines. Find the shortest distance between the two lines and the TL of *RS*.
9. The TV of a line *AB* is 50 mm. The point *A* is on the HP and 25 mm in front of the VP. The point *B* is on the VP and 40 mm above the HP. Another line *CD*, perpendicular to *AB*, is 100 mm long. Its end *C* is at the midpoint of *AB* while end *D* is on the HP. Draw the projections of both the lines. Find the angle made by each of them with the HP. [**Hint:** Compare it with Problem 12.4]

Ample number of **REVIEW QUESTIONS** at the end of the chapters provide good practice and are designed to enhance the thinking capabilities of the students.

Visual Walkthrough

GREY COLOUR is used to indicate (1) Auxiliary Construction, (2) Alternate Solution, (3) Additional Information, (4) Direction Sense, etc. GREY-COLOURED lines and texts are not the parts of the solution, but they may be needed for better understanding and/or for indicating to the students the need of some supportive constructions.

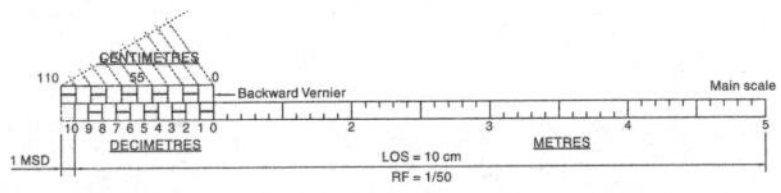

Fig. 5.5

Auxiliary Construction

Alternate Solution

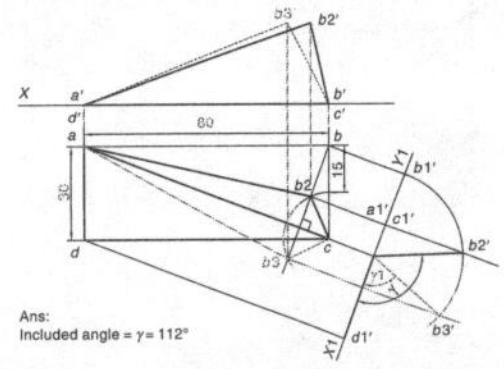

Fig. 13.37

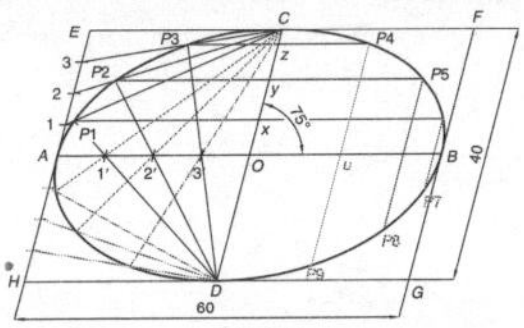

Fig. 6.7

Additional Information

Direction Sense

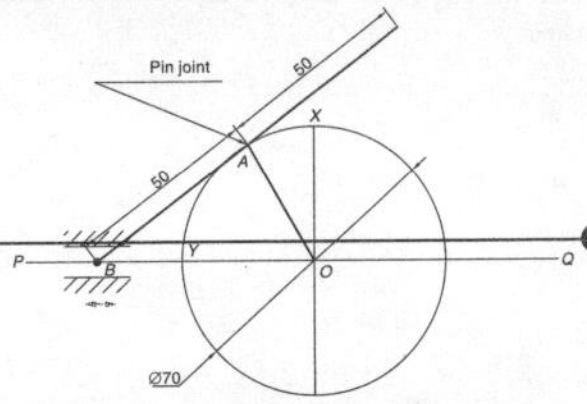

Fig. 7RQ.1

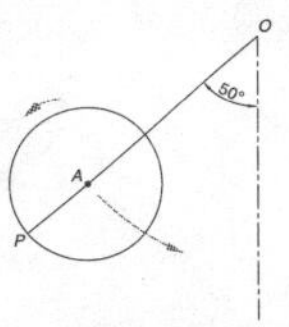

Fig. 7RQ.2

CONTENTS

FOREWORD

I have a great sense of happiness and pride in introducing this book on *Engineering Drawing* written by Prof. Dhananjay A Jolhe. Prof. Jolhe has been teaching this subject for the last thirteen years and has earned a reputation of being an excellent teacher in the subject due to his unique teaching style.

The subject of Engineering Drawing is often found to be difficult to understand by the fresh engineering students. It involves complex methods which demand for a good degree of imagination and skills. In this book, the author has simplified all the complexities. The entire subject is handled in a highly commendable style, maintaining the flow, lucidity and conceptual clarity. It covers the syllabi of Indian Universities and effectively explains the fundamental principles in a straight forward manner, easy to keep in mind by the students.

I have witnessed the untiring efforts made by Prof. Jolhe in making this book the most authoritative and updated book on the subject. I am sure that this comprehensive textbook will be highly beneficial to the students, the faculty and the practicing professional.

August 7, 2007

Dr. S. T. Deshmukh ***Ph. D. (Mechanical Engineering)***
Director, Shri Ramdeobaba Kamla Nehru Engineering College, Nagpur
(Ex-Vice Chancellor, SGB Amravati University &
Ex-Director, Visvesvaraya National Institute of Technology, Nagpur)

PREFACE

Drawing is a human being's way of expressing his thoughts and ideas with the help of pictures. I have great pleasure in presenting this book on *Engineering Drawing*—an engineer's way of expressing his thoughts and ideas!

What made me write this book

Engineering drawing is a prime subject in any engineering curriculum. It is all about the graphical language used by engineers. My experiences showed that most of the first-year engineering students have a great deal of difficulty in understanding the subject due to its unique graphical nature. Teachers, too, find it difficult to transfer the 'graphical theories' to the minds of students as it involves a lot of imagination and mental visualization of various concepts.

One has to assimilate the theoretical knowledge, develop one's imagination and acquire sufficient drawing skills to complete the course in engineering drawing. Theoretical knowledge covers the principles, methods and conventions practiced in technical drawing. Imagination is a must to develop the visualization capabilities for better understanding. And, lastly, one needs good drafting skills to transfer his/her mental picture on a sheet of paper. However, no single book available in the market covers these three aspects together. In the initial stages of my career, I strongly felt the need for a well-structured book on the subject. And, it was precisely at this time when my students complemented me on the notes and problems I used to dictate spontaneously in the classroom. All this invoked in me the inspiration of writing a book on this subject. Then, for the next few years, I started collecting and compiling my notes, and thus, the initial manuscript of the book came into being.

The biggest challenge was to compile this voluminous subject using a minimum of words. In my attempts at simplifying the difficult concepts, I had to spend many of my waking hours twisting and trembling and had to bend my mind in all possible ways to come up with an easy and lucid approach to this intriguing topic! After a long battle between pen and paper, the present volume finally took shape.

Objectives of this book

This book is written keeping in mind the three requirements of the subject as mentioned above, viz., knowledge, imagination and drawing skill. With its extensive coverage, the step-by-step approach and handy drawing tips, the book would help students to meet these three requirements. Lucidity and simplicity of the language is maintained throughout. The smooth flow of the topics enhance the understanding of the students. Accurate and precise line diagrams are a major strength of the book. A few photographic illustrations are added at appropriate places to explain the real-life relevance.

In the last few decades, this subject has undergone many changes. With the eye-glaring advances in computer technology, the manual work of drafting is now advantageously done by computers. This transformation has compelled the universities to update the subject for Computer Aided Drafting (CAD). A chapter on CAD, is therefore, provided to give an exhaustive insight to computerized drawing.

Who can benefit

The book would be helpful to students of engineering, polytechnics, higher secondary schools, B.Sc. (Engineering), architecture, graduation-level examinations (like AMIE), ITI, and many other technical examinations. I believe it will prove to be a good resource material for teachers, especially those who are in the early stages of their career. It would be equally helpful to professionals and practicing engineers working in the field of design and manufacturing.

Organization

The book follows unique language and standardized abbreviations. Hence, readers are advised to proceed in the sequence in which the chapters appear. Chapters 1 to 4 cover the prerequisite concepts needed to know engineering drawing. The readers may go quickly through them. Chapter 5 explains the basic proportions and precise engineering scales. Chapters 6 and 7 may be read later and to the depth specified in the syllabus as they deal with the engineering curves and loci of points in mechanisms. Chapters 8 to 17 follow a logical sequence and cover the core topics of engineering drawing. Readers should go sequentially through them to understand the methods and principles of projections. Chapters 18 and 19 explain the principles of pictorial projections, namely, isometric projection and perspective projection, and thus, provide insight for 3D drawing. Chapter 20 develops the sense of interpretation by testing the imagination capabilities of the readers. Chapter 21 provides useful hints for freehand drawing and may be read through quickly. Chapter 22 exhaustively deals with 2D drawing using the computerized package AutoCAD. At the end, a comprehensive question bank (chapter-wise) is provided to help students prepare for viva-voce.

Web Supplement

Readers are suggested to go through the Walkthrough which explains the key features of the book and helps them to understand the contents in a better way. Instructor resources contain the solution manual and PowerPoint presentations which can be accessed at https://connect.mheducation.com. Student resources contain abbreviations, symbols and notations and quiz which can be accessed at www.mheducation.co.in. The detailed instructions for accessing the online resources are printed on the cover.

The book uses the latest BIS standards. Equipped with hundreds of Solved Examples and Illustrative Problems, I am sure that this book will prove to be a full-fledged textbook for fresh engineering students.

Acknowledgements

Genius minds, skilled hands and the blessings of the Almighty are necessary for making any project successful. I am fortunate that I got all these in the making of this book. I express my cordial thanks to the esteemed reviewers—

Dr H V Ramakrishnan
MGR University, Chennai

Prof D Kingsly Jeba Singh
SRM Institute of Science and Technology, Chennai

Prof S Sundar
MGR University, Chennai

Prof P K Devan
Jerusalem College of Engineering, Chennai

Prof V Ananda Krishnan
School of Mechanical Engineering, SASTRA University, Thanjavur

Prof K R Srinivasan
Mepco Schlenk Engineering College, Madurai

Dr V V Subha Rao
JNTU College of Engineering, Pulivendula

Dr R Sivasubramanian
Coimbatore Institute of Technology, Coimbatore

Prof N Suresh
MVJ College of Engineering, Bangalore

Prof E Vijaya Krishna Rapaka
Pondicherry Engineering College, Pondicherry

Dr S Vijayarangan
Dr Mahalingam College of Engineering and Technology, Pollachi

Prof Chetan Patel
C K Pithawalla College of Engineering and Technology, Surat

Prof R S Deshmukh
Vidyawardhini's College of Engineering, Thane

Prof S V Chaudhari
Rajiv Gandhi Institute of Technology, Mumbai

Prof Sukanta Sarkar
Heritage Institute of Technology, Kolkata

Prof Pradyot Kumar Dey
Saroj Mohan Institute of Technology, Hoogly

Dr B Dash
Kalinga Institute of Industrial Technology, Bhubaneswar

Dr S K Srivastava
Madan Mohan Malviya Engineering College, Gorakhpur

Prof Manish Kewalramani
BITS, Pilani

Prof Y S Kokate
Government Engineering College, Jalgaon

Dr S M Shashidara
Sidhaganga Institute of Technology, Tumkur

Prof Suresh B
Globus Engineering College, Bhopal

Prof P S Bharti
Guru Govind Singh I P University, Delhi

Prof Nitin R Patel
G H Patel College of Engineering and Technology, Vallabh Vidyanagar

Prof M K Satyarthi
Dehradun Institute of Technology, Dehradun

for their valuable feedback and suggestions.

I express my gratitude to the Management of Shri Ramdeobaba Sarvajanik Samiti, Nagpur, for their constant encouragement. I am highly obliged to Dr S T Deshmukh for his valuable guidance and his kindness for writing the Foreword for the book. Dr S S Limaye, Dr S V Gole and Dr V S Deshpande (all from Shri Ramdeobaba Kamla Nehru Engineering College, Nagpur) deserve credit for their motivation. I am thankful to Dr D J Tidke (Yeshwantrao Chavan College of Engineering, Nagpur), Dr R D Askhedkar (KDK College of Engineering, Nagpur), Dr S G Patil (Ram Meghe

Institute of Technology and Research, Badnera), Prof J D Golhar (Government Polytechnic, Sakoli), Dr R V Kulkarni (Indira College of Engineering and Management, Pune), Dr P J Awsare and Dr A S Padalkar (both from Sinhgad College of Engineering, Pune), Dr P M Padole and Dr A M Kuthe (both from Visvesvarya National Institute of Technology, Nagpur) and Prof D H Joshi (AISSMS College of Engineering, Pune) for their esteemed support. I highly appreciate the cooperation rendered by Mr Harshal Deshmukh (ADCC InfoCAD, Nagpur).

I am grateful to my colleagues, present and past, for their precious suggestions and encouragement. My students deserve a special place in my heart for 'inspiring' the author in me.

It was impossible to complete this arduous task without the valuable support of my family members. Mrs Jayshri, my better half, performed the assiduous duty of composing many line diagrams and checking the proofs. I have no words to express my thanks to her as she stood strongly beside me even during her tough days of motherhood. My brother Nilesh shouldered all the family responsibilities during the peak of this project. Bhushan, my brother, took untiring efforts in developing excellent photographic illustrations. His valuable contribution in perspective projection enhanced the chapter to a great extent. My little daughter, Devanshi, showed great wisdom and sense and allowed me to work peacefully on the book.

Optimizing the book in terms of volume, price and content was a great challenge. I must thank Mrs Vibha Mahajan (McGraw-Hill Education) and Mr Rakesh Malhotra (The Composers) for meeting this challenge in a most effective way without compromising the quality of the book. Lastly, I would thank all the staff at McGraw-Hill Education, who were involved with this project at its various stages, for their constant support and cooperation.

Suggestions and feedback to improve the text will be highly appreciated. Please feel free to write me at **jolheda@knec.edu**.

August 15, 2007

DHANANJAY A JOLHE

 ABBREVIATIONS, SYMBOLS AND NOTATIONS USED

Abbreviations

2D	Two-dimensional
3D	Three-dimensional
AIP	Auxiliary Inclined Plane
AVP	Auxiliary Vertical Plane
BIS	Bureau of Indian Standards
BV	Bottom View
CAD	Computer Aided Drafting
CG	Centre of Gravity
COI	Curve of Intersection (or Interpenetration)
CP	Central Plane
EL	Elevation Length
FRP	Frontal Reference Plane
FV	Front View
GL	Ground Level or Ground Line
GP	Ground Plane
HL	Horizon Line
HP	Horizontal Plane/Horizon Plane
HRP	Horizontal Reference Plane
HT	Horizontal Trace
IS	Indian Standards
ISO	International Standard Organization
LC	Least Count
LHSV	Left Hand Side View
LOH	Line of Heights
LOI	Line of Intersection (or Interpenetration)
LOS	Length of Scale
MSD	Main Scale Division
NURBS	Non-Uniform Rational B-Spline
OSNAP	Object SNAP
PL	Plane Length
POI	Point of Intersection
POP	Plane of Projection
PP	Profile Plane
PPP	Perspective Picture Plane
PRP	Profile Reference Plane
RF	Representative Fraction
RHSV	Right Hand Side View
RP	Reference Plane
RV	Rear View
S	Station point
SP	Special Publication (of BIS)
SV	Side View
SVL	Side View Length
TL	True Length
TV	Top View
UCS	User Coordinate System
VP	Vanishing Point
VP	Vertical Plane
VSD	Vernier Scale Division
VT	Vertical Trace
WCS	World Coordinate System

Symbols

α	Apparent inclination of line with the HP

β	Apparent inclination of line with the VP
c	Constant of spiral
D	Diameter of base of cylinder, Diameter of generating circle
d	Distance of a point in front of / behind the VP
e	Eccentricity of conics
ϕ	Inclination of line with the VP
ϕ_p	Inclination of plane with the VP
h	Height of point above / below the HP
n	Convolution of spiral
R	Radius of directing circle, Slant height of cone
r	Radius of the base of cone (or cylinder), Radius vector of spiral
r_g	Greatest radius of spiral
r_s	Shortest radius of spiral
x	Distance between the end projectors of a line
X	Distance between the projectors through the traces of a line
θ	Angle subtended by the directing arc, Vectorial angle of spiral, Inclination of line with the HP, Included angle of the development sector of cone
θ_p	Inclination of plane with the HP
ψ	Inclination of line with the PP

See **Table 3.2** for Abbreviations and Symbols used in dimensioning.
See **Table 5.2** for Abbreviations of units of length.

Notations

A	Point *A* in space or on Development
a	TV of point *A*
a'	FV of point *A*
a''	SV of point *A*
h	Projection of HT on *XY*
v	Projection of VT on *XY*
O	Origin or pole point in isometric
A_0	Projection of point *A* on LOH
a_0	Projection of A_0 on the PPP

XY, *X*1*Y*1, *X*2*Y*2, etc. Reference projection lines

Chapter 1

INTRODUCTION TO ENGINEERING DRAWING

1.1 INTRODUCTION

A picture speaks thousands of words. A message conveyed by a picture or a sketch or a sign is much effective than a message conveyed by words. That is why, since before the start of civilization, human beings used the language of drawing to convey their ideas. With the progress of science and technology, humans felt the need for a 'standardized' drawing language so that it could be understood globally. This standardized graphical language was then termed as *Engineering Drawing*.

The role of engineers is to develop products. The motorbike you drive, the mobile phone you use or the apartment you live in are some common examples of the products developed by engineers. In the process of product development, two important steps involved are—(i) deciding the specifications of the product, and (ii) preparing the product's drawings. Engineering drawing deals with the second step. The product's sketches are prepared for manufacturing purposes. The drawings constructed by a design engineer are transferred to the manufacturing engineer. The manufacturing engineer produces the product as per the dimensions and specifications supplied by the design engineer. Thus, engineering drawing is an effective language of communication between the engineers. For every engineer, it is of utmost importance to learn this language.

The languages of engineering drawing can be effectively used if its 'grammar' is mastered. This grammar refers to the use of standard conventions, notations and the methods used in technical drawing. This book explains, in a simple language, the grammar rules and methods in engineering drawing.

1.2 PREREQUISITE FOR ENGINEERING DRAWING

The knowledge of simple geometrical theorems and constructional procedures is essential for understanding the theories and methods in engineering drawing. The readers may read Chapter 4 to revise the knowledge of various geometrical constructions.

1.3 DRAWING INSTRUMENTS AND ACCESSORIES

To ensure perfection in drawing, a set of instruments and accessories is required. This section explains these instruments.

1.3.1 Drawing Sheets and Papers

Drawing sheets and papers are the 'canvases' on which drawings are composed by pencils or pens. Drawing sheets are available in standard sizes. Indian Standards (IS) for drawing sheets and drawing boards as recommended by the Bureau of Indian Standards (BIS) are shown in Table 1.1. Each higher numbered sheet is half in size of the immediate lower numbered sheet, Fig. 1.1, i.e., width of the A0 sized sheet is equal to the length of the A1 sized sheet, width of the A1 sized sheet is equal to the length of A2 sized sheet and, so on. For drawing practice in schools and colleges, an A2 size (popularly called a *half-imperial* size) (and sometimes, A1 size) sheet is recommended.

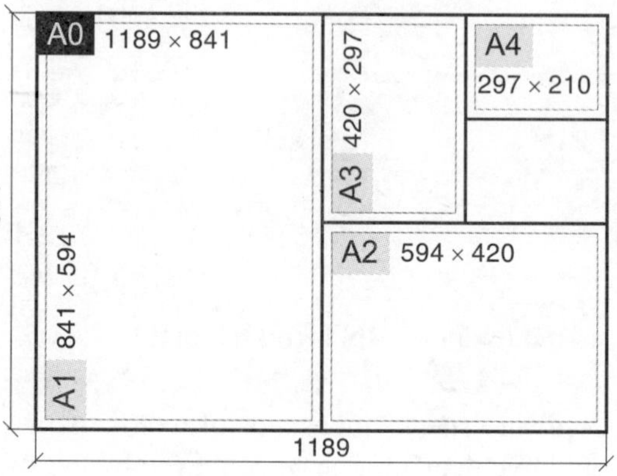

Fig. 1.1 Drawing sheet sizes

Table 1.1 Recommended Sizes of Drawing Sheets and Drawing Boards

Drawing Sheet (IS 10711:2001)		*Drawing Board (IS 1444:1989)*	
Designation	*Size (mm) Length × Width*	*Designation*	*Size (mm) Length × Width*
A0	1189 × 841	D0	1270 × 920
A1	841 × 594	D1	920 × 650
A2	594 × 420	D2	650 × 470
A3	420 × 297	D3	500 × 350
A4	297 × 210		

A3 and A4 sized drawing sheets are usually referred as to *drawing papers*. Drawing papers may be used for homework. The sketchbooks of thick and good quality drawing papers are recommended for classroom use. A0 size sheets are used to construct big drawings in the industry.

1.3.2 Drawing Board

Drawing boards are used to support a drawing sheet or paper. They are made up of soft wooden platens fastened together by two cross plates (battens), Fig. 1.2. The working surface of the board is planned perfectly. A shorter edge of the board carries a hard ebony strip fitted in a groove. This straight ebony edge, perfectly lined up with the edge of the drawing board, provides the guide for the T-square.

The standard sizes of drawing boards, corresponding to the sizes of drawing sheets, are shown in Table 1.1. For first-year engineering students, the use of D2 size drawing board (commonly called *half size* drawing board) is recommended.

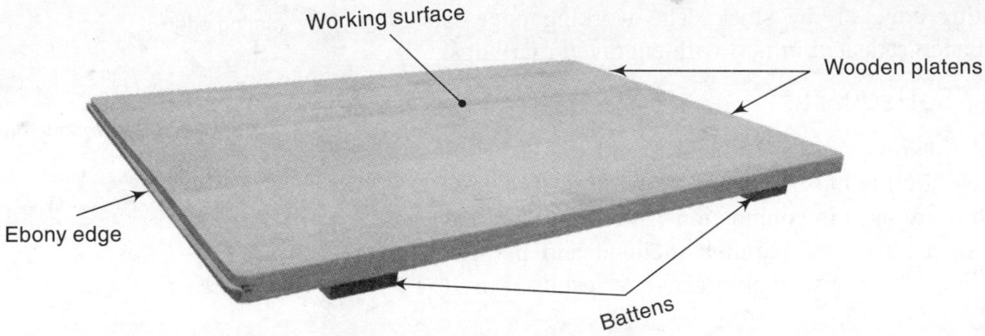

Fig. 1.2 Drawing board

1.3.3 Mini Drafter

A mini drafter is a portable device used to draw parallel, inclined and perpendicular lines speedily. It is mounted on a drawing board at the top left corner. A drafter consists of a scale, a scale screw, a scale plate, steel bars, a bar plate and a clamping mechanism, Fig. 1.3. An L-shaped scale is graduated in mm along both the arms. It also carries a degree scale for angle measurement. The scale is joined to a clamping mechanism by means of steel bars, the bar plate and the scale plate in such a way that it can be moved to the desired location on the drawing board.

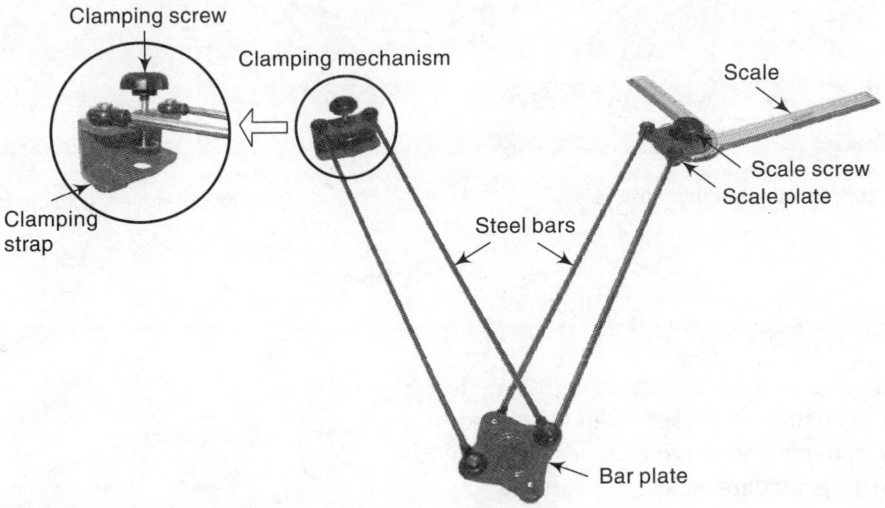

Fig. 1.3 Mini drafter

A mini drafter with a transparent plastic scale is recommended for school and college students.

1.3.4 T-square

A T-square is a T-shaped device used to draw straight horizontal lines. It consists of a stock and a blade joined together at right angles, Fig. 1.4. The inner edge of the stock, called *mating edge*, is made perfectly smooth and straight. It mates with and slides along the ebony edge of the drawing board. The upper edge of the blade, called *working edge*, is perfectly straight and set exactly at 90° to the mating edge of the stock. The working edge is beveled and graduated in mm with engraved markings.

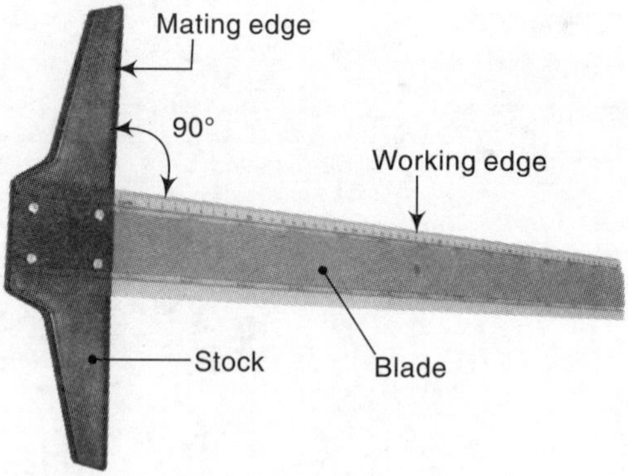

Fig. 1.4 T-square

1.3.5 Set-squares

Two set squares—(i) 45° set-square and (ii) 30°– 60° set-square, are the most common drawing instruments. Often they are used in conjunction with each other and with T-square to draw parallel, inclined and perpendicular lines. They give highly accurate results if used skillfully.

The set-squares are made up of transparent acrylic. Two edges of each set-square are perfectly set at right angles. The *working edges* are beveled and engraved with mm or inch markings. The hypotenuse edge is beveled but not engraved.

A protractor is usually included in a 45° set-square, Fig. 1.5(a). The 30°– 60° set-square may include French curves in it, Fig. 1.5(b).

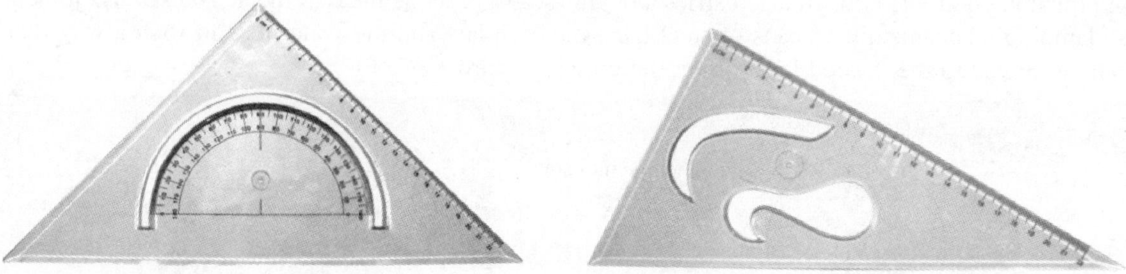

45° set-square with protractor
(a)

30°–60° set-square with curve
(b)

Fig. 1.5 Set-squares

1.3.6 Protractor

Protractor is used to draw and measure the angles. It is available separately or as merged in 45° set-square. A medium-sized transparent protractor capable of measuring up to 1° is recommended.

1.3.7 Roller Scale

A roller scale is a handy device used to draw parallel and inclined lines. It consists of a broad scale that includes a protractor mounted on a roller, Fig. 1.6. The accuracy of this device is not comparable with the accuracy of a T-square and drafter. However, it is a speedy device and may be used for practice in classrooms.

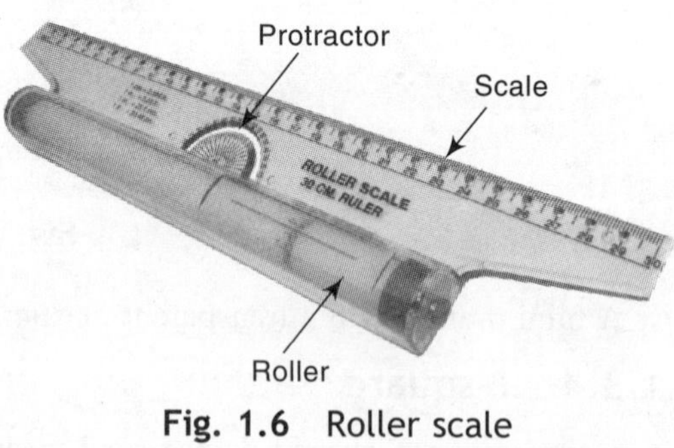

Fig. 1.6 Roller scale

1.3.8 Compasses

Compasses are used to draw circles or arcs. Good quality steel compasses are recommended to ensure accuracy in engineering drawing. Two sizes of compasses—(i) large compass and (ii) small spring bow compass are in common use.

A large compass consists of a needle leg and a pencil leg hinged together at upper ends, Fig. 1.7(a). The two legs carry, respectively, a needle point and a pencil point at their lower ends. The

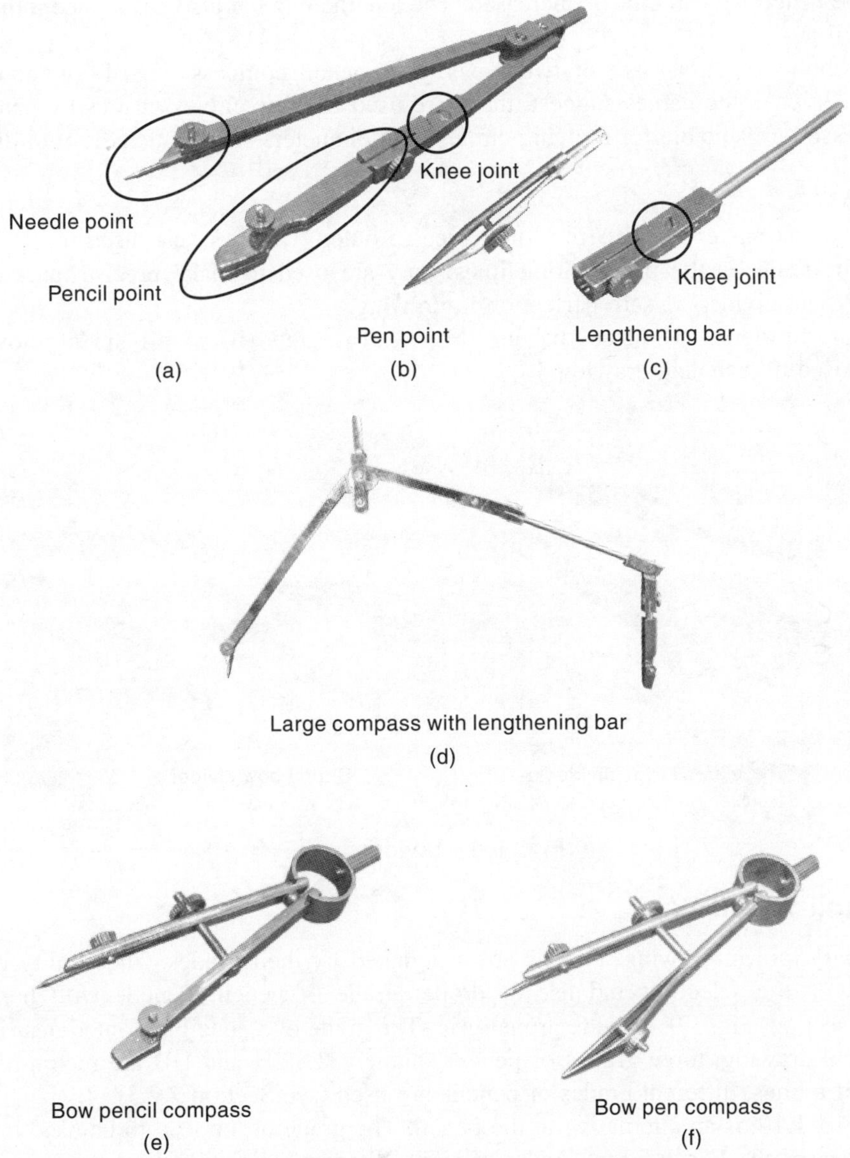

Fig. 1.7 Compasses and accessories

pencil leg has a knee joint which permits the leg to bend through the required angle so that the pencil point can be set perpendicular to the paper. A well-sharpened lead stick is fixed at pencil point. The pencil point can be interchanged with a pen point, Fig. 1.7(b). The pen point is used to draw circles or arcs in ink.

A large compass can be conveniently used to draw circles having a diameter larger than 25 mm. Lengthening bar, Fig. 1.7(c), is used to draw circles of diameter greater than 150 mm. The bar is fitted in place of a pencil point. The pencil point is then attached to the lengthening bar, Fig. 1.7(d). The length of the pencil leg can thus be increased. The lengthening bar also has a knee joint similar to that on the pencil leg.

Small spring bow compasses are of two types: bow pencil compass, Fig. 1.7(e) and Bow pen compass, Fig. 1.7(f). As the names suggest, these are used to draw circles or arcs by pencil or pen. The bow compasses are suitable for drawing circles with diameters smaller than 25 mm diameters.

1.3.9 Dividers

Dividers are used to transfer lengths from one place to other. They are also used to set-off desired distance from the scale on the paper. Sometimes, they are used to make precise markings on the drawing. Heavy steel dividers ensure perfection in drawing.

Two sizes of dividers—(i) large divider, Fig. 1.8(a), and (ii) small spring bow divider, Fig. 1.8(b), are used in technical drawing.

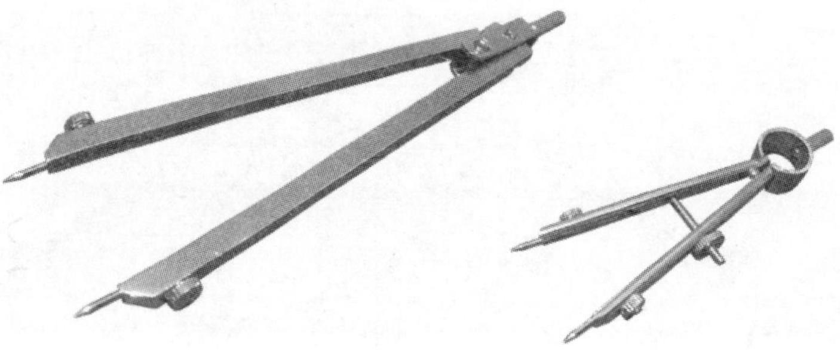

Large divider (a)   Spring bow divider (b)

Fig. 1.8 Dividers

1.3.10 Pencils/Lead Pens

Pencil is a primary tool in drawing. Pencils are designated by their grades. The quality of drawing largely depends on the selection and use of proper grade of pencil. Pencils with hexagonal or triangular cross-section, Fig. 1.9, provide proper grip. The grade of a pencil is printed near its blocked end. For technical drawing, three grades of pencils, namely, H, 2H and HB are recommended. For different types of a lines, different grades of pencils are used (see Section 2.2.3).

A lead pen, Fig. 1.10, is an alternative to the pencil. The grade of the lead to be used in lead pens must be ensured properly. For different grades of leads, different colours of lead pens may be used.

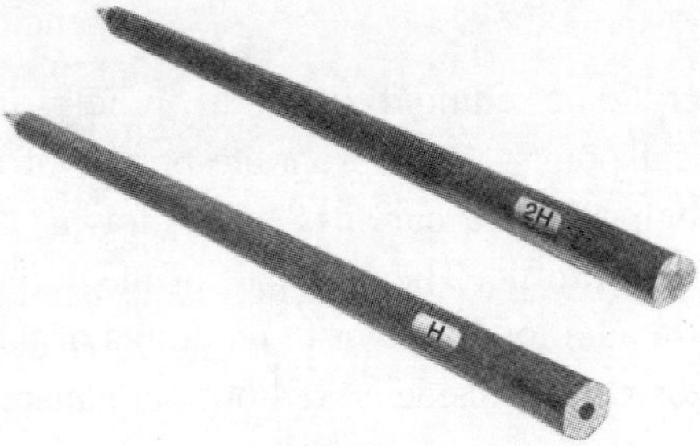

Fig. 1.9 Pencils

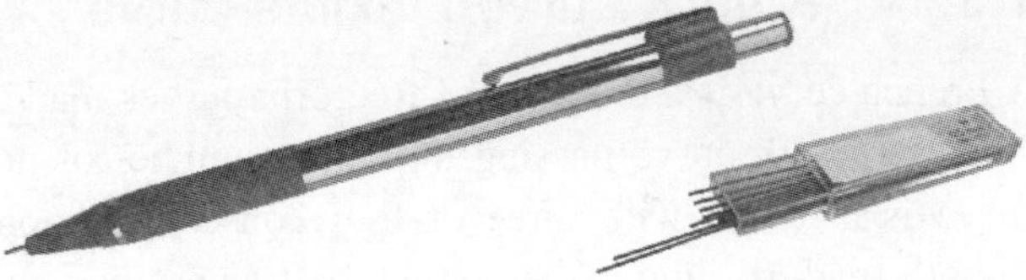

Fig. 1.10 Lead pen and lead box

1.3.11 Lead Sticks

Lead sticks, Fig. 1.11, are used with compasses. They are available in different grades. HB and H grades are frequently needed for technical drafting. The end of lead sticks must be sharpened properly using sandpaper.

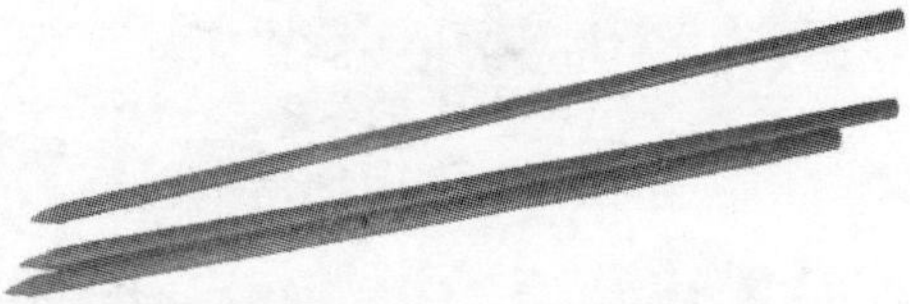

Fig. 1.11 Lead sticks

1.3.12 Pencil Sharpener

A pencil sharpener is a device used to mend the pencils. It conveniently removes the wooden shell covering the lead. A common hand-held sharpener, Fig. 1.12(a), is recommended.

A table-mounted pencil sharpener, Fig. 1.12(b), is faster in performance. It is costly and used in drafting sections of the companies. The sharpeners should not be used to sharpen the lead end.

Fig. 1.12 Pencil sharpeners

Fig. 1.13 Eraser

1.3.13 Eraser

An eraser, Fig. 1.13, is used to erase an unwanted part of the pencil drawing. A non-dusting good quality eraser is recommended.

1.3.14 French Curve/Flexible Curve

A French curve is a template of freeform curves made up of acrylic or celluloid, Fig. 1.14. It helps to draw a smooth curve passing through a number of non-collinear points. An appropriate profile of a curve is matched with three or four consecutive points through which a curve is to be drawn. A smooth freeform line is then drawn by tracing the pencil along the profile. The next part of the curve is drawn in a similar way by using the next two or three points in addition to the last two points of the previous curve. French curves are available separately or may be carved inside a 30°–60° set-square.

Fig. 1.14 French curves

Fig. 1.15 Flexible curve

A flexible curve is an alternative to the French curve. It consists of a flexible non-elastic metallic wire covered with smooth rubber or plastic coating that can be bent to the desired shape, Fig. 1.15. Flexible curves may have mm on inch markings enabling for the length measurement of the curve. They are available in 30 cm, 40 cm, 50 cm and 60 mm sizes. A thick aluminum wire used in electric transmission may be used as a cheapest alternative to a flexible curve.

French curves or flexible curves are frequently used to draw engineering curves (Chapter 6), loci of points (Chapter 7), sections of solids (Chapter 15), development curves (Chapter 16) and curves of intersections of solids (Chapter 17).

1.3.15 Circle Template

A transparent circle template made up of acrylic is used to draw circles of different radii quickly. The common circle templates have circles from 2 mm diameter to 30 mm diameter on them, Fig. 1.16. Each circle has four quadrant marks on its circumference which are used to locate the circle along the centrelines. The circle templates should only be used to draw circles of diameters smaller than 5 mm. For bigger circles, compasses are more accurate.

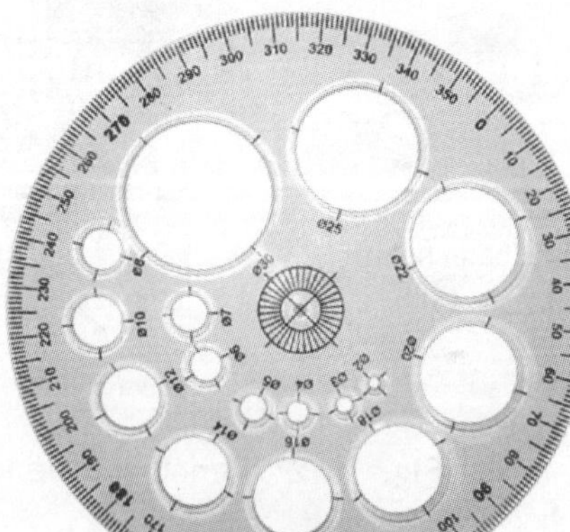

Fig. 1.16 Circle template

1.3.16 Lettering Set-squares

Small sized transparent set-squares without any graduations on their edges, Fig. 1.17, may be used for lettering purposes. The three edges of each of the set-squares are beveled. Some lettering set-squares carry holes and slots on them which help to draw horizontal and vertical guide lines.

Fig. 1.17 Lettering set-squares

1.3.17 Lettering Template

Lettering template is a plastic plate on which letters are carved, Fig. 1.18. It may be used for double stroke Gothic lettering (Section 2.3.4). For single-stroke lettering, the use of lettering template is not recommended.

Fig. 1.18 Lettering template

1.3.18 Drawing Clips, Pins and Adhesive Tape

Drawing clips, pins and adhesive tape are used to fix drawing paper/sheet on the drawing board. Drawing clips, Fig. 1.19(a), are used to clamp drawing sheet corners along drawing board edges. To fix the corners of the sheet on the surface of the board, we use drawing pin, Fig. 1.19(b), or adhesive tape, Fig. 1.19(c). Pins pierce the sheet and the board creating holes on them. Adhesive tapes are free

Drawing clips (a) | Drawing pins (b) | Adhesive tape (c)

Fig. 1.19 Drawing clips, drawing pins and adhesive tape

from this drawback. A crepe paper adhesive tape is recommended as it does not scratch the paper when removed. For plastic adhesive tape, a paper piece may be kept between the sheet and the tape to avoid sticking of the tape to the sheet.

1.3.19 Instrument Box

A wide variety of instrument boxes are available in the market. A typical instrument box contains the set of drawing instruments frequently needed, like a large compass, bow pencil compass, bow pen compass, large divider, spring bow divider, pencil point, pen point, lengthening bar, inking pen, screw driver, lead sticks, etc. An instrument box provides a place for each instrument and ease in carrying them.

1.3.20 Sheet Container

A sheet container, Fig. 1.20, is used to store and carry drawing sheets. Made up of plastic, the container has a detachable lid and belt. An expandable sheet container may be used to hold sheets of larger sizes.

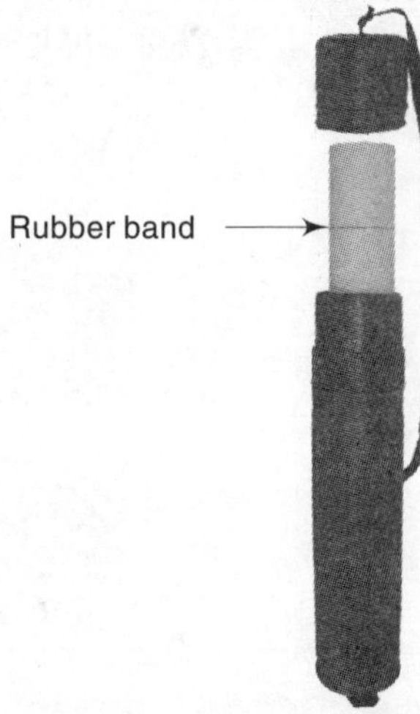

Fig. 1.20 Sheet container

1.3.21 Sandpaper

Sandpaper (or sandpaper block) is used to sharpen the pencil lead and lead sticks. Fine grade wood sandpaper, should be preferred.

1.3.22 Paper Napkins or Handkerchief

Paper napkins or a small handkerchief may be used to clean the drawing sheet and drawing instruments frequently. A cotton handkerchief can be advantageously used to remove eraser crumbs from the sheet.

1.4 PRACTICAL LESSONS

Before the start of drawing work, the drafting table and other drawing instruments should be cleaned properly. The user should also clean his or her hands. This helps to keep the drawing work clean.

1.4.1 Clamping a Drawing Sheet on Drawing Board and Setting the Drafter

This lesson explains how to clamp a drawing sheet and drafter to the drawing board and related setting.

Refer Fig. 1.21.

1. Place a drawing board on a table top or any other suitable surface. A table with an adjustable inclined surface is preferred. A specially designed drafting table (with a drawing board as a table top) may be used.

   The ebony edge of the board should be on your left-hand side if you are working with a T-square.
2. Place the drawing sheet on the drawing board. All the drawing sheets, except A4 size, are positioned horizontally. An A4 size paper is positioned vertically. If you are working with an A2 (or smaller size) sheet on D1 size drawing board, the preferred location for the sheet is the bottom right part of the drawing board. This location reduces the hand and trunk movements to

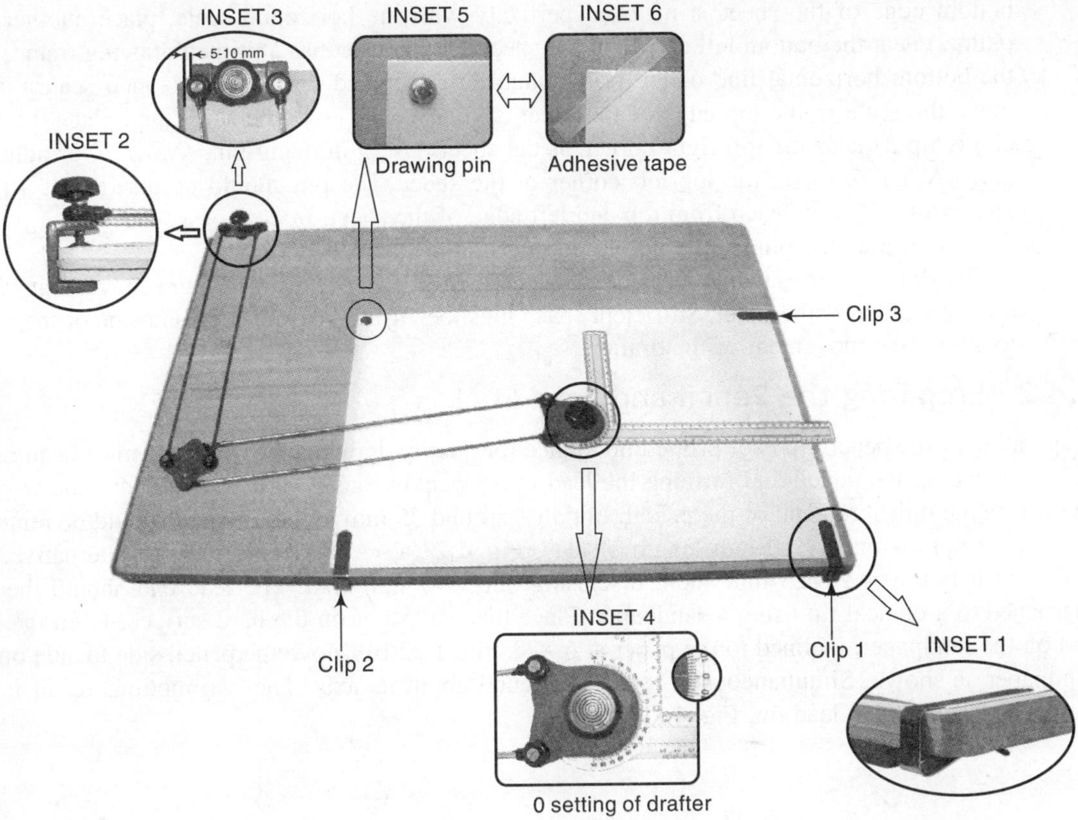

Fig. 1.21 Clamping the drawing sheet and drafter

a minimum. The space on the drawing board above the drawing sheet may be used to place frequently needed drawing instruments, like, set-squares, compasses, pencils, eraser, etc.

The bottom and right edges of the sheet should be approximately 1 cm each from the corresponding edges of the board.

3. Fix a drawing clip (Clip 1) at bottom right corner of the board. See *INSET 1* for proper clip placement.
4. Loosen the clamping screw of the mini drafter. Carry the drafter gently over the board and place its claming strap over the top left corner of the board such that two of the inner faces of the strap will mate with the corresponding faces of the top edge of the board, *INSET 2*. The distance of the clamp from the left edge of the board may be 5 mm to 10 mm, *INSET 3*. Tighten the clamping screw gently till the strap takes a firm grip on the board.
5. Move the drafter scale to the centre of the sheet. Loosen the scale screw and match the 0 degree mark on the degree scale with the mark on the scale plate, *INSET 4*. You must look directly from above the 0 degree mark to avoid the parallax error. Tighten the scale screw gently.
6. Move the drafter scale near the bottom edge of the sheet. Match the edge with the horizontal scale of the drafter. The sheet may be moved up and down pivoting about the Clip 1. Once the

bottom edge of the sheet is matched perfectly with the horizontal scale, place another clip (Clip 2) near the bottom left corner of the sheet. (If the sheet has a printed drawing frame, then the bottom horizontal line of the frame should be matched with the horizontal scale.) Now, move the scale to the top edge of the sheet, sliding gently over the sheet, and place the third clip (Clip 3) near the top right corner of the sheet. Use a drawing pin, *INSET 5*, or adhesive tape, *INSET 6*, to fix the top left corner of the sheet. The pin should be inserted at a point approximately 1 cm each from top and left edge of the sheet. In case of a sheet with a printed drawing frame, the pin should be placed outside the frame.

The drafter and drawing sheet clamped in such a way permit maximum movement of the drafter scale over the sheet. Sufficient space must be ensured on the left-hand side of the board to allow free movement of the drafter.

1.4.2 Preparing the Pencil and Lead Sticks

Preparation of the pencil tip is of prime importance for quality drawing. The students must acquire the skill of mending the pencil and forming the lead tip. A penknife may be used to remove the wooden shell from the unlettered end of the pencil. Initially, around 35 mm length of shell should be removed to uncover approximately 10 mm length of lead, Fig. 1.22(a). A sharpener is good alternative to a knife but it removes 20–25 mm shell, disclosing only 5–7 mm lead. The lead end should then be sharpened to a conical tip using a sandpaper. Place the sandpaper on the hard surface. Keep the lead end on the sandpaper, inclined to the paper at 6°–7°, Fig. 1.22(b). Move the pencil side to side on the sandpaper as shown. Simultaneously, rotate the pencil about its axis. The two motions result in the formation of a conical lead tip, Fig. 1.22(c).

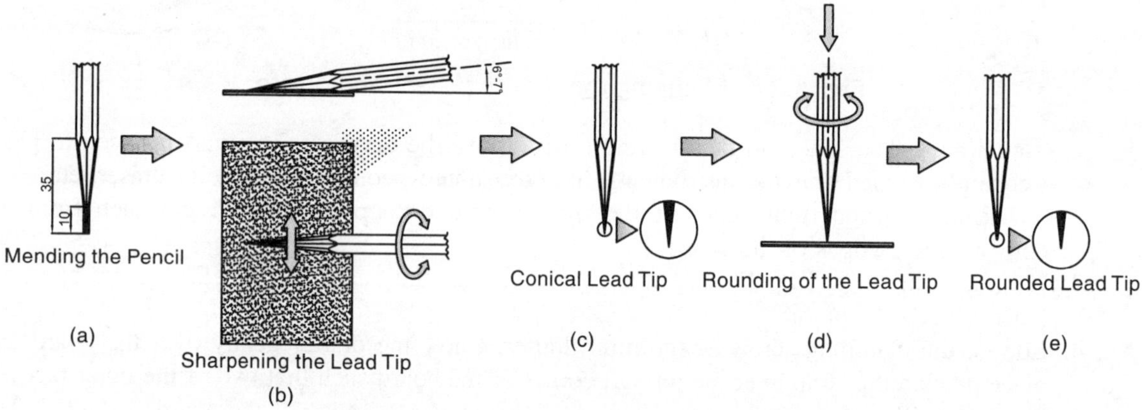

Fig. 1.22 Steps in pencil preparation

The sharp conical tip may scratch the drawing sheet. Further, it may break partially resulting in uneven lines. This can be avoided by smoothing the sharp tip. Hold the pencil perpendicular against a hard surface (say, reverse of the sandpaper) with the tip resting on the surface, Fig. 1.22(d). Rotate the pencil gently about its axis and simultaneously, apply little pressure axially. The sharp lead tip will be converted to a rounded tip, Fig. 1.22(e), suitable for drawing lines of uniform thicknesses.

The lead sticks to be used in compasses may be sharpened using sandpaper in a similar way. Usually, a lead stick is not sharpened to a conical shape but on one side. An inclined cut may be given by holding the lead at 20°–25° to the sandpaper and then moving the lead side to side slowly. The lead need not to be rotated. It gives the elliptical tip, Fig. 1.23(a). The tip is then tapered by cutting sideways on the sandpaper, Fig. 1.23(b). The tip may be then slightly rounded by providing an end cut, Fig. 1.23(c).

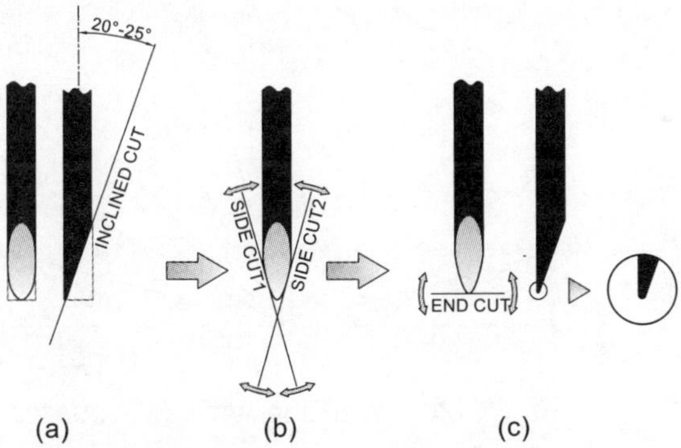

Fig. 1.23 Steps in lead preparation

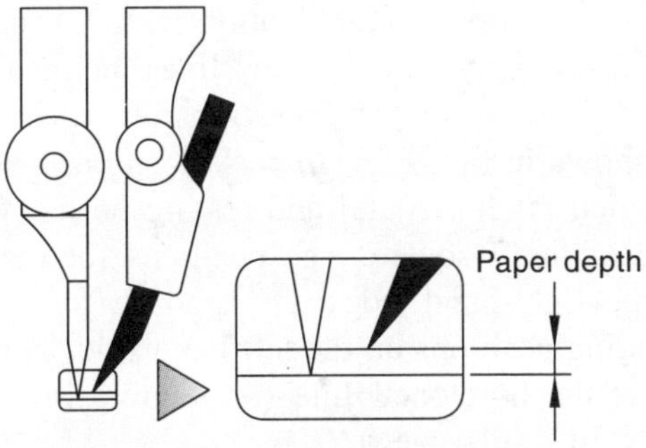

Fig. 1.24 Compass preparation

Once the pencil tip or lead tip is formed, the tip should be cleaned by a paper napkin to remove fine lead particles.

1.4.3 Preparing the Compass

The compasses should be prepared properly to ensure perfection in circles and arcs drawing. Loosen the screw of the pencil point of the compass. Insert a lead stick of appropriate length and prepared with tip as explained above. Note that, the cut-out end of the lead is on the outer side of the compass, Fig. 1.24. Adjust the needle and lead so that the needle tip extends slightly more than the lead tip. (The extended part of the needle tip gets inserted in the paper while drawing circles or arcs.) Tighten the screw gently.

The lead stick may be first fixed in the pencil point and then sharpened as mentioned above.

1.4.4 Working with Pencil

The pencil should be gripped at an approximate distance of 35 mm from the lead tip, Fig. 1.25. Depending on the precision required, the gripping point may be lowered or raised with respect to the lead tip. The inclination of the pencil with the paper plays an important role in the quality of lines. The pencil is usually held inclined at about 60° with the paper. The slope of the pencil should be in the direction of the stroke of the line. The angle made by the pencil with the paper may vary slightly as the hand moves from one end to other end. The hand strokes needed

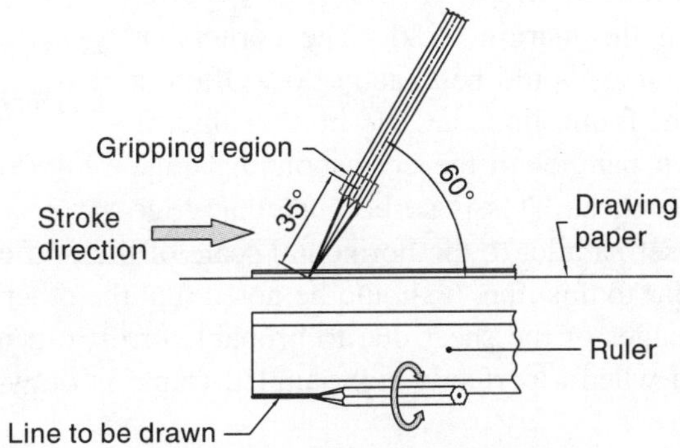

Fig. 1.25 Working with pencil

to draw horizontal, vertical and inclined lines are explained in Section 2.2.5. For horizontal lines, the pencil should slope up toward the right-hand side. For vertical lines, it should slope up toward the user. The pencil may be rotated slightly while drawing a line to ensure the uniformity in line thickness. In instrumental drawing, the wrist movements should be smaller than the elbow or shoulder movement.

1.4.5 Working with Set-squares

The set-squares, in combination with T-square, can be conveniently used to draw lines inclined at 15°, 30°, 45° and so on. The positions of the set-squares are shown in Fig. 1.26. In each position, a side of a set-square is horizontal and resting on the working edge of the T-square. The positions for the angles on the right-hand sides are opposite to the corresponding positions on the left-hand side. The angles below the horizontal line (0° degree line) can be drawn in similar ways.

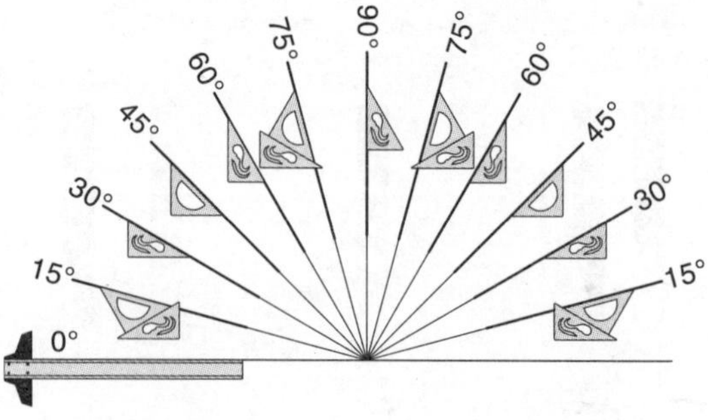

Fig. 1.26 Working with set-squares

1.5 DRAWING MARGINS AND TITLE BLOCK

As a standard practice, sufficient margins should be kept on all the sides of the drawing sheet. It prevents the actual drawing getting damaged due to spoilage at the sheet edges. The margin widths at the four sides of A2 size (trimmed) sheet are shown in Fig. 1.27. The margins at the top, bottom and right-hand sides are 10 mm each. The margin at the left-hand side is 20 mm. More margin width is needed on the left-hand side to provide space for filing. A thick drawing frame should be drawn after fixing the margin width. The corners of the frame should be exactly 90°. Often, a longer frame line, say the bottom line, is drawn parallel to the corresponding edge of the sheet. This is so because that edge was set parallel to the horizontal scale of the drafter. The vertical frame lines are then drawn perpendicular to this line. It should be noted that the other frame lines may not be parallel to the corresponding edges of the sheet due to probable error in trimming the sheet. Obviously, this error is compensated when a perfectly right-angled frame is drawn. The drawing should be drawn inside the frame only.

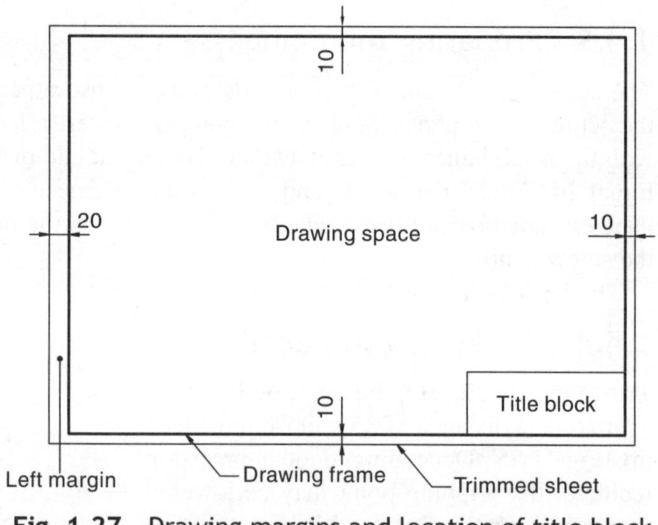

Fig. 1.27 Drawing margins and location of title block

The horizontal and vertical frame lines should be used as horizontal reference and vertical reference respectively during the entire drawing. The 0 setting of the drafter should be ensured frequently by matching its scales with the frame lines.

The title block is an important part of the drawing. It is located at the bottom right corner of the frame attached to the frame lines, Fig. 1.27. The title block varies greatly in size, contents and structure. However, it typically includes information like, name of the organization, name of the designer or draftsman, drawing title, scale of the drawing, etc. The projection method symbol is also included in the title block.

The title block, commonly adopted in engineering colleges is depicted in Fig. 1.28. Each row is of 9 mm width. Lettering of 7 mm height (see Section 2.3.2) is done to write the necessary information.

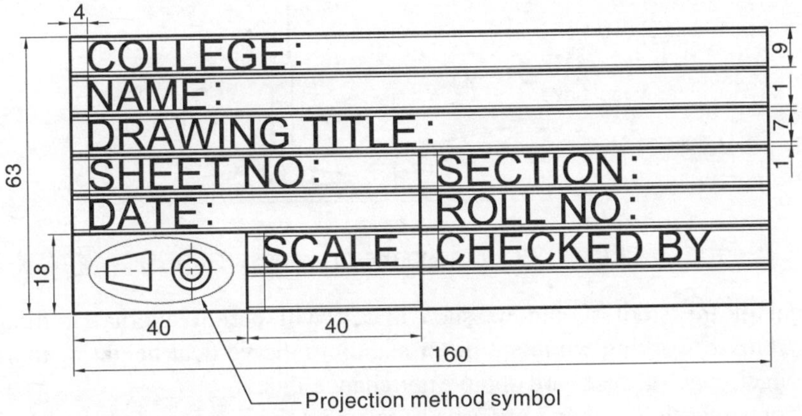

Fig. 1.28 Title block

1.6 ERGONOMIC DRAWING SET-UP

It may take hours to complete a drawing. Often, starters take more times to complete a drawing work than the experts. Working on big drawing sheets (A2 or higher sizes) demand for considerable body movements resulting in stress in the body. If proper care is not taken, it may lead to serious injuries. Therefore, it is extremely necessary to have a comfortable drawing set-up that will create minimum stress while working. The ergonomic working arrangement, Fig. 1.29, will not only reduce physiological stress but also make drawing enjoyable. The set-up is highly recommended for professional draftsmen.

Different persons have different body dimensions. Further, dimensions of males and females vary greatly. The dimensions shown in Fig. 1.29, are for an average Indian adult male, compatible with college students and professionals. (The dimensions for female are enclosed in [ ].) School students may use slightly smaller dimensions.

1. The longest edge of the drawing board nearer to the user should be 96 cm [92 cm] high (or slightly below elbow height) from the ground. Height adjustability of ±7 cm is recommended.
2. The drawing board should be ideally inclined at 30°, sloping downward toward the user. Angular adjustability of ±10° about the nearest edge is recommended. The downward slope thus obtained reduces the eye focus and trunk and hand movements. It also minimizes the distance between the eyes and the drawing, thereby improving the visibility.

Horizontal work surfaces for larger drawing sheets should be strictly avoided.

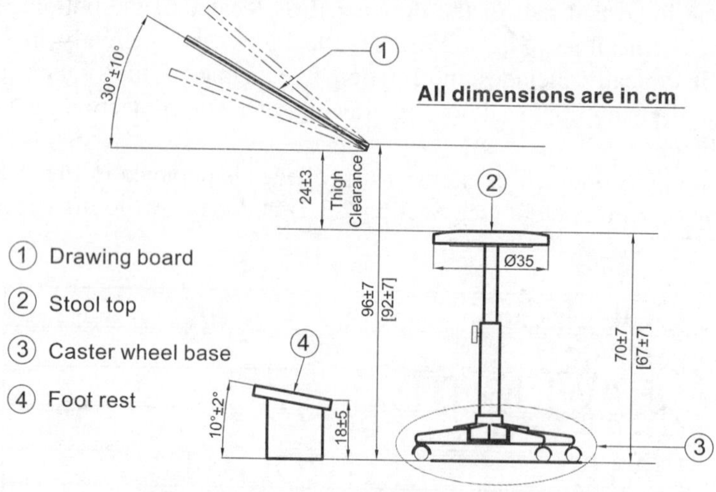

Fig. 1.29 Ergonomic drawing set-up

3. The height of the stool should be such that it will permit alternate sitting and standing. Whether you are working while sitting or standing, the vertical height of the elbow from the nearest longer edge of the board should not change much.

   The stool height of 70 cm [67 cm] (measured from the same ground level), with adjustability of ±7 cm, will permit sit-stand work posture. The circular stool top of around 35 cm diameter and well cushioned to absorb the stresses created in the buttock area should be preferred. A stool with a five-caster wheel base permits user mobility. A three-leg fixed base may be preferred if the user is unable to touch the ground with his/her feet in sitting position.
4. The space between the top of the stool and the nearest longer edge of the board should be sufficient for thigh movement. Thigh clearance of 24 cm (±3 cm) is sufficient.
5. The space below the drawing surface should be enough to permit leg movements for relaxation. Feet support 18 cm (with ±5 cm adjustability) high from the ground and inclined at 10° (with ±2° adjustability) to the ground is recommended.
6. The organization of drawing instruments and accessories is of prime importance. Provide the space for everything and keep everything in the allotted place. It reduces the time in searching.
7. Instruments which you hold by your left hand (e.g., set-squares, circle template, French curve, pencil sharpener, etc.) should be located on the left-hand side of the drawing board. Similarly, the instruments operated by the right hand (e.g., pencil, compasses, eraser, etc.) should be placed on the right-hand side of the board.
8. As far as possible, use the drawing board of the size compatible with the size of the drawing sheet you have chosen.
9. Lighting plays important role in precise drawing work. Insure proper lighting on the drawing sheet. Adjust light sources in such a way that the reflections from drawing sheet, plastic and steel instruments will be minimized as best as possible.
10. To minimize the strain in eyes and neck, use 20-20-20 principle. That is, after every 20 minutes, look 20 feet ahead for 20 seconds.

1.7 BIS STANDARDS

The BIS is the National Standards Body formed by the Government of India on 1 April 1987, replacing Indian Standard Institution (ISI) existing earlier. The objective of BIS is to foster the industrial and commercial growth of the country by developing globally acceptable standards for products. It works in association with other standard-developing organizations worldwide, in particular with the International Standard Organization (ISO).

BIS has recommended and published various standards for technical drawings. These standards are available in the form of IS codes and Special Publication (SP) 46: 2003. The readers are strongly encouraged to see and adopt these standards in drawing practice. This book uses the following ISs:

IS 1444: 1989	ENGINEER'S PATTERN DRAWING BOARD— SPECIFICATION
IS 10711: 2001	TECHNICAL PRODUCT DOCUMENTATION SIZES AND LAYOUT OF DRAWING SHEETS
IS 3221: 1966	SETS FOR DRAWING INSTRUMENTS
IS 10713: 1983	SCALES
IS 10714: 2001	LINES
IS 9609: 2001	LETTERING
IS 15021: 2001	PROJECTION METHODS
IS 10714: 1983	SECTIONS AND OTHER CONVENTIONS
IS 11669: 1986	GENERAL PRINCIPLES OF DIMENSIONING ON TECHNICAL DRAWINGS

Wherever ISs are not available, relevant international standards may be adopted.

TIPS FOR GOOD QUALITY DRAWING

1. Sharpen the tip of the pencil from time to time by using a penknife and sandpaper.
2. Sharpen the lead tip inserted in the compass frequently by sandpaper.
3. Use a proper grade of the pencil and/or lead, i.e., H, 2H or HB as the case may be.
4. Avoid frequent use of eraser.
5. Complete a line, circle or arc in one stroke only. Avoid overdrawing.
6. Maintain constant hand pressure while drawing a particular line, circle or arc.
7. Check frequently the 0 setting of the drafter scale.
8. Don't use a drafter to draw measured inclinations. Use a protractor for this purpose.
9. While moving the drafter scale from one point to another, care should be taken that it does not rub with the drawing sheet.
10. Use a bow compass to draw smaller circles or arcs. A circle template should only be used to draw circles or arcs having a diameter less than 5 mm.
11. Draw smooth curves (e.g., engineering curves, loci of points, sections of solids, development, curves of intersection, etc.,) initially very lightly by freehand and then use the French curve to make them sufficiently thick and uniform.
12. Use a paper napkin or clean handkerchief to clean away the rubbed particles from drawing sheet.
13. Avoid the contact of drawing instruments with drawing sheet except during their actual use.
14. Your drawing sheet gets stained by dirt on the drawing instruments, drawing board and your hands. Keep all these always clean.
15. Protect your drawing sheet from all external factors which may spoil or make it dirty.
16. Before placing the drawing sheet inside the container, roll it properly and place a rubber-band over it.

Chapter 2

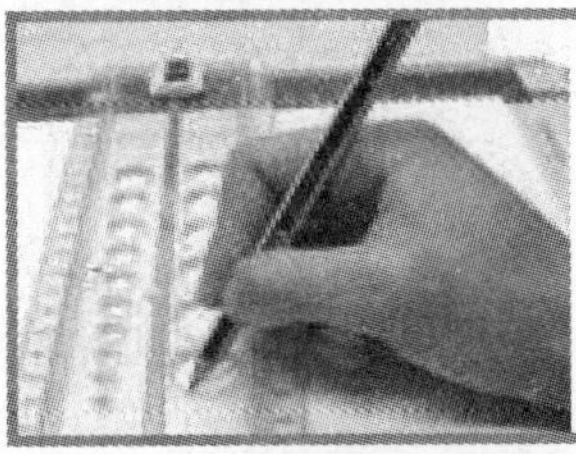

LINES AND LETTERING

2.1 INTRODUCTION

Lines and lettering are two important aspects of technical drawing. Lines are used to construct a drawing. Lettering is used to provide some specific information on it. Thus, lines and lettering, together are necessary for a meaningful technical drawing. This chapter deals with the various types of lines, their applications and the art of lettering.

2.2 LINES

Lines are like the alphabet of a drawing language. As the alphabet are used to form meaningful words, various types of lines are used to construct meaningful drawings. Each line in a drawing is used in a specific sense. Therefore, it must be drawn using some standard conventions. The conventions for the lines refer to the styles and uses of various types of lines. A line may be straight, curved, continuous or segmented. It may be thin or thick. A segmented line may consist of dashes or dots and gaps. To ensure appropriate thickness, a proper grades of pencils should be used.

2.2.1 Types of Lines

The basic types of lines, mentioned by BIS (SP 46: 2003), are shown in Table 2.1.

2.2.2 Line Width

Line width means the thickness of a line. Three grades of lines, viz., NARROW, WIDE and EXTRA-WIDE (referred hereafter as THIN, MEDIUM and THICK respectively) are in use. The proportions between THIN, MEDIUM and THICK lines are 1: 2: 4. The common line groups based on line widths are mentioned in Table 2.2.

The line group 0.25 is the most preferred line group for pencil drawing. These line widths can be easily obtained by varying the hand pressure.

Table 2.1 Types of Lines

S. No.	*Line Type*	*Representation*	*Width**	*Applications*
1	Continuous NARROW		THIN (0.13 mm)	*A.* Construction lines, *B.* Projection lines, *C.* Dimension lines, *D.* Extension lines, *E.* Leader lines, *F.* Section (Hatching) lines, *G.* Outlines of revolved sections, *H.* Imaginary lines of intersection
2	Continuous WIDE		MEDIUM (0.25 mm)	*A.* Visible outline of sectioned surface, *B.* Reference lines in projection, *C.* Ground Lines
3	Continuous EXTRA-WIDE		THICK (0.5 mm)	*A.* Visible outlines, *B.* Lines of special importance
4	Dashed NARROW		THIN	Hidden lines or edges
5	Dashed WIDE		MEDIUM	Hidden lines or edges
6	Long Dashed Dotted NARROW (Chain NARROW)		THIN	*A.* Centerlines, *B.* Lines of symmetry, *C.* Cutting planes
7	Long Dashed Dotted WIDE (Chain WIDE)		MEDIUM	Cutting planes (at ends & change of direction)
8	Long Dashed Double Dotted NARROW (Phantom NARROW)		THIN	*A.* Locus lines, *B.* Alternative and extreme positions of movable parts, *C.* Outlines of adjacent parts
9	Continuous Freehand NARROW		THIN	Short break line
10	Continuous Zigzag NARROW	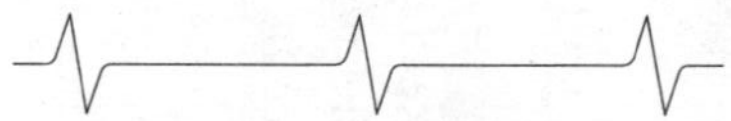	THIN	*A.* Long break line, *B.* Limits of partial or interrupted views

The NARROW, WIDE & EXTRA-WIDE lines are respectively referred as THIN, MEDIUM & THICK lines in this book

*Based on line group 0.25. See Table 2.2.

Table 2.2 Line Groups

Line Group	*Line Widths (in mm)*		
	THIN	*MEDIUM*	*THICK*
0.25	0.13	0.25	0.5
0.35	0.18	0.35	0.7
0.5	0.25	0.5	1
0.7	0.35	0.7	1.4
1	0.5	1	2

2.2.3 Pencil Grades

As a general rule, harder grade pencils are preferred for THIN lines and softer grade pencils for THICK lines. An H grade pencil is advised for THICK and MEDIUM lines. THIN lines may be drawn by a 2H grade pencil. An H grade pencil creates minimum impressions on the drawing paper. Hence, the lines drawn by an H grade pencil can be erased easily. A 2H grade pencil, being harder, creates a noticeable impression. However, it can maintain the sharpness of tip for a longer time and therefore, ensures accuracy and uniformity in line width. For freehand lines, use of an HB grade pencil is suggested. Use of B grade pencils (viz., B, 2B, 3B, etc.) should be avoided in technical drawing.

Note: The three grade pencils, namely, H, 2H and HB may be used initially for drawing the different types of lines mentioned above. After sufficient practice, an H grade pencil may alone be used for all purposes. The readers are advised to master the skill of drawing the lines of various widths and darknesses by using an H grade pencil only.

DRAWING TIPS

Continuous THIN Place a set-square (or T-square or drafter-scale) on the drawing paper with the working edge at the desired inclination. Hold it firmly by the left hand. The fingers and thumb must be placed near two ends of the working edge to prevent sliding of the edge. Hold the pencil in the right hand in such a way that the lead tip rests on the paper touching the working edge of the instrument. Apply light pressure on the pencil and sketch a line maintaining the pressure constant. If the hand pressure changes, the line will lose its thickness. The line must be drawn in one stroke. Avoid overdrawing.

Continuous MEDIUM Apply moderate pressure on the pencil and sketch a line in one stroke as mentioned above.

Continuous THICK Apply comparatively more pressure on the pencil and draw a line in one stroke. Do not apply excessive pressure. It may create a heavy impression on the paper.

Dashed THIN/MEDIUM Complete each segment (dash) by applying appropriate pressure in one stroke. Concentrate at the lead tip while drawing each segment. A tailed segment should be strictly avoided.

Length of each dash	THIN = 3–4 mm	MEDIUM = 5–6 mm
Length of each gap	THIN = 1–2 mm	MEDIUM = 2–3 mm

Long Dashed Dotted THIN/MEDIUM Maintain constant hand pressure for each long dash. Hold the pencil vertical for 'dot' and rotate it gently with appropriate hand pressure. To save time, dots are usually drawn as 'short dashes' by maintaining rhythm with the long dashes.

Length of long dash	THIN = 8–10 mm	MEDIUM = 10–12 mm
Length of dot (short dash)	THIN = 2 mm	MEDIUM = 3 mm
Length of gap	THIN = 2 mm	MEDIUM = 3 mm

Long Dashed Double Dotted THIN Obtain the constant width of dashes and dots. Dots are usually drawn as 'short dashes'.

Length of dash	= 8–10 mm
Length of dot (short dash)	= 2 mm
Length of gap	= 2 mm

Continuous Freehand THIN Draw a smooth wavy form line by freehand. Avoid sharp corners. Use a rounded pencil tip.

Continuous Zigzag THIN Draw a zigzag line by interrupting a continuous line at regular intervals. Use a set-square initially for drawing the zigzags. After sufficient practice, draw them freehand.

Length of straight segment	= 20–25 mm
Length of zigzag	= 6–8 mm
Height of zigzag	= 8–10 mm

Note: The lengths of dashes, dots, gaps, zigzags, etc., mentioned above are approximate and for guidelines only.

2.2.4 Application of Various Lines

The applications of various types of lines shown in Table 2.1 are explained below. See Fig. 2.1.

1A. Construction Lines These are used for construction of geometrical features. These are supporting lines and do not represent the main part or edges of the object.

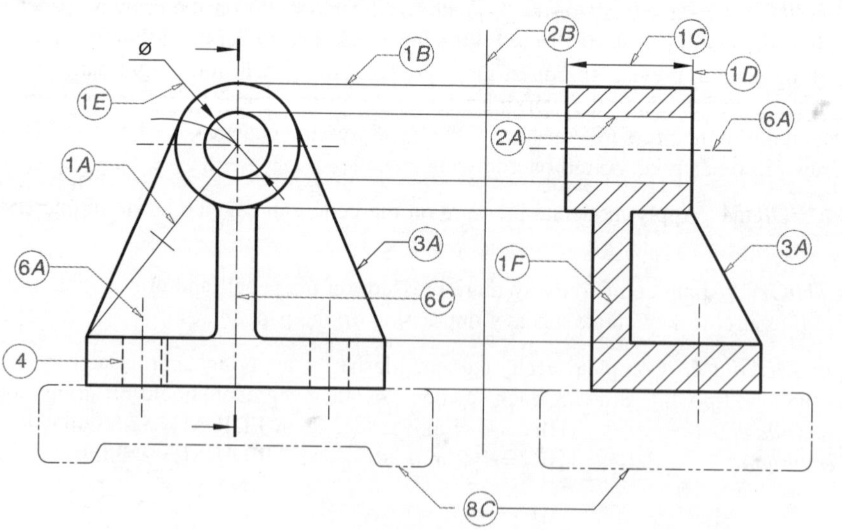

(a)

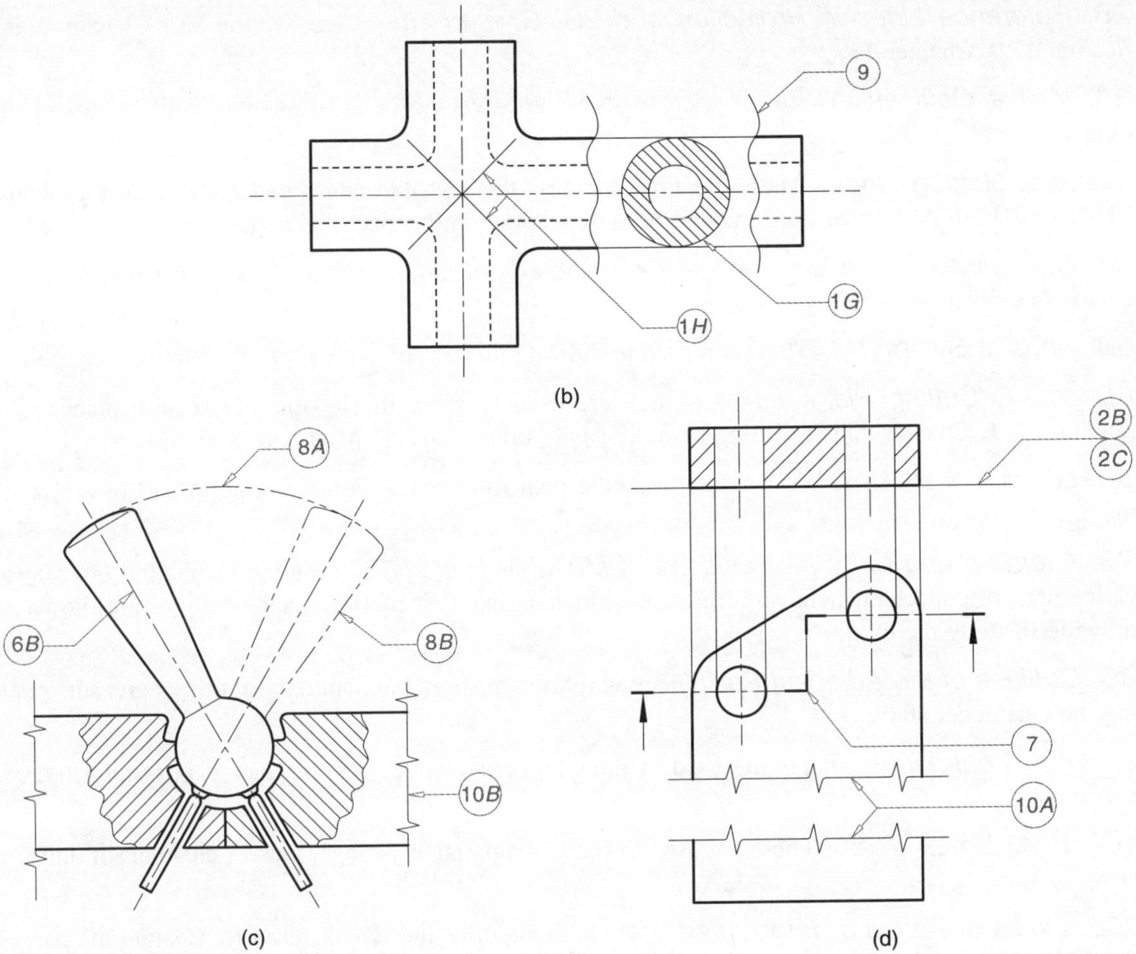

Fig. 2.1

1B. Projection Lines These are used to project a view of the object. See Section 8.2, Chapter 8 for detail.

1C. Dimension Lines, 1D. Extension Lines and 1E. Leader Lines These are used to provide the dimensions on a drawing. See Section 3.2, Chapter 3.

1F. Section (Hatching) Lines These are used to show sectioned surfaces. See Section 9.7.2, Chapter 9.

1G. Outlines of Revolved Section The revolved section is used to show the cross section of a bar along its length. See Section 9.7.4, Chapter 9.

1H. Imaginary Lines of Intersection The imaginary lines of intersections of two surfaces or two solids need to be shown in many drawings.

2A. Visible Outlines of Sectioned Surface These are used to indicate the outline (other than exterior outline) of the sectioned surface.

2B. Reference Lines in Projection and 2C. Ground Line See Section 9.2, Chapter 9 and Section 13.9, Chapter 13.

3A. Visible Outlines These are used to show outer visible boundaries and visible edges of the object.

4 and 5. Hidden Lines These are used to show the invisible edges and features of the object. THIN or MEDIUM hidden lines may be used depending on the size of drawing.

6A. Centerlines These are used to indicate the axis of holes, cylinders (or cylindrical features), cones (or conical features), spheres, etc.

6B. Lines of Symmetry These are used to indicate the axis of symmetry of a symmetrical object.

6C and 7. Cutting Plane Lines These are used to show the location of section planes. See Section 9.7.1, Chapter 9. The cutting plane lines are drawn MEDIUM at ends and corners.

8A. Locus Lines These are used to show the path followed by a moving point/part of a mechanism.

8B. Alternate and Extreme Positions of Movable Parts The rotating, oscillating or reciprocating parts of a mechanism have different positions during their motion. Such positions are shown on drawing to study the motions.

8C. Outlines of the Adjacent Part These are used to show the boundary of other parts surrounding the part under study.

9. Short Break Lines These are used to show moderate length bars or channels of uniform cross section.

10A. Long Break Lines These are used to show comparatively longer bars or channels of uniform cross section.

10B. Limits of Partial or Interrupted Views It signifies the 'break' used to separate the part of an object from a relatively less important part.

2.2.5 Line Strokes

The quality of drawing depends on your drafting skills. Drafting skills can be improved by understanding and practicing line strokes. Line strokes refer to the directions of drawing straight and curved lines, Fig. 2.2. Horizontal lines are drawn from left to right, vertical and inclined lines are drawn from top to bottom. Curved lines (e.g., arcs of circles) are also drawn from left to right or top to bottom. Right (or upper) half of a circle is drawn clockwise while left (or lower) half is drawn anticlockwise.

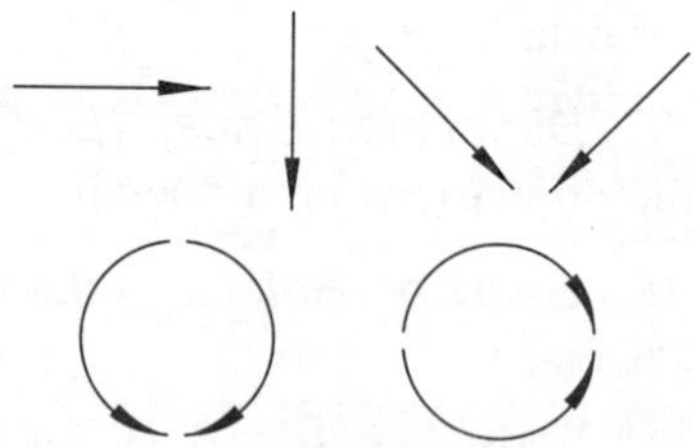

Fig. 2.2

Practice of the line strokes is extremely important for freehand drawing.

Note: Left-handed persons may reverse the strokes for horizontal line and the upper half and lower half of a circle.

2.3 LETTERING

Lettering is an art of writing text on a drawing by using alphabets, numerals and symbols. Texts are necessary to provide specific information, like dimensions, notes, special instructions, etc. The text should be clear and concise. Two types of lettering are commonly used—(1) single stroke, and (2) double stroke. Single stroke or double stroke letters may be vertical or inclined, Fig. 2.3. The line width of a double stroke letter is greater than that of a single stroke letter.

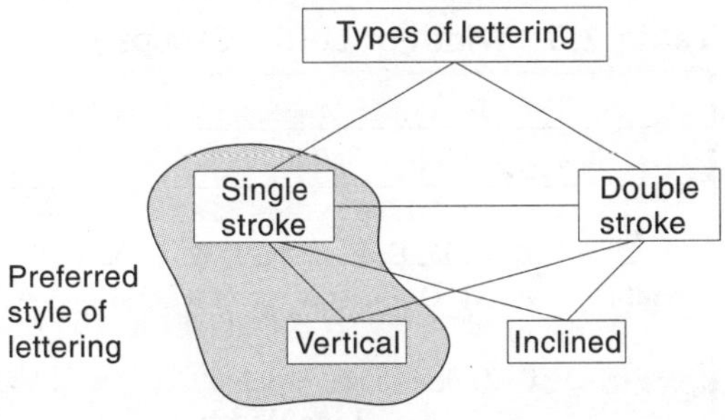

Fig. 2.3

BIS (SP46: 2003) has suggested the use of Type A and Type B lettering. The line width of Type A lettering is always less than that of Type B lettering. Hence, they may be treated equivalent to single stroke and double stroke lettering respectively. BIS has set very scrupulous dimensions for both the letterings. Interested readers may refer SP 46:2003 for these standards.

2.3.1 Lettering Rules

Before we study the different types of lettering, let's discuss about the general rules of lettering.

1. Draw letters as simple as possible. Artistic or cursive lettering should be strictly avoided.
2. Draw letters symmetrical about the vertical axis or horizontal axis. Asymmetric letters like, F, R, Z, 4, etc., may be drawn as they are.
3. Round-off the sharp corners wherever necessary, e.g., D, P, S, etc.
4. Draw all letters legible and uniform.
5. The height of all the letters in one line should be the same.
6. Use single stroke vertical CAPITAL letters as much as possible.

Note:	The word letter is used for alphabet, numeral, symbol, punctuation mark, etc.

2.3.2 Height and Width of Letters

The letters may have different heights depending on their purposes. BIS (SP 46: 2003) has recommended the heights of letters as: 1.8 mm, 2.5 mm, 3.5 mm, 5 mm, 7 mm, 10 mm, 14 mm and 20 mm. Large-sized letters are used for main titles and headings, medium-sized letters for subtitles and important notes and small-sized letters for dimensions and general notes. The height of letters bears direct relationship with the size of drawing, i.e., large-sized letters for larger drawings and small-sized letters for smaller drawings. Larger letters are preferred for ink lettering. For pencil lettering, smaller letters are suitable. The readers are advised to use letters of 10 mm, 7 mm and 5 mm height to write titles, subtitles and notes/dimensions respectively on the pencil drawing.

The body height of lowercase letters is taken as 0.7 times the height of capital letters, Fig. 2.4. The tail and the stem of the lowercase letters are drawn 0.3 times the height of a capital letter. Thus, the total height of a lowercase letter is the same as that of capital letters.

Fig. 2.4

The height-to-width ratio varies from letter to letter. Most of the letters follow the ratio 7 : 5 or 7 : 6. The letters I and 1 are the narrowest while the letter W is the widest. Table 2.3 shows the width of various letter groups.

Table 2.3 Width of Letter Groups

		Preferred Height		
	Letter Group	*10 mm*	*7 mm*	*5 mm*
Width	I , 1	5 mm	3 mm	2.5 mm
	B, C, D, E, F, G, H, J, K, L, N, P, R, S, U, Z	7 mm	5 mm	3.5 mm
	A, M, O, Q, T, V, X, Y (TOM-Q-VAXY)	8 mm	6 mm	4 mm
	W	12 mm	8 mm	6 mm
	0, 2, 3, 4, 5, 6, 7, 8, 9	6 mm	4 mm	3 mm
	Line Width	0.7 mm	0.5 mm	0.35 mm

2.3.3 Line Width

The line width of a letter depends on its height. Large-sized letters have more line thickness than small-sized letters. The appropriate line widths for the letters of different heights are shown in Table 2.3, Fig. 2.5.

10 MM LETTERING, LINE WIDTH 0.7 MM

7 MM LETTERING, LINE WIDTH 0.5 MM

5 MM LETTERING, LINE WIDTH 0.35 MM

Fig. 2.5

2.3.4 Styles of Lettering

As already mentioned, lettering should be simple, legible and uniform. One such style, most popular among engineers, is called the *Gothic* style of lettering. Gothic lettering has a uniform line width for all the parts of a letter. It may be single stroke or double stroke and vertical or inclined.

Single Stroke Vertical Gothic Lettering

This is the most common and preferred lettering style. 'Single stroke' refers to the thickness obtained in one stroke of a pencil or ink pen. It does not mean that the pencil or pen should not be lifted while completing a particular letter. The letters are drawn upright.

Figure 2.6 shows the alphabets, numerals, symbols and punctuation marks drawn in single stroke vertical gothic style (height = 7 mm, line width = 0.5 mm). The width of various characters may be noted carefully.

Figure 2.7 shows a sample lettering using this style.

Fig. 2.6 Single stroke vertical Gothic letter set

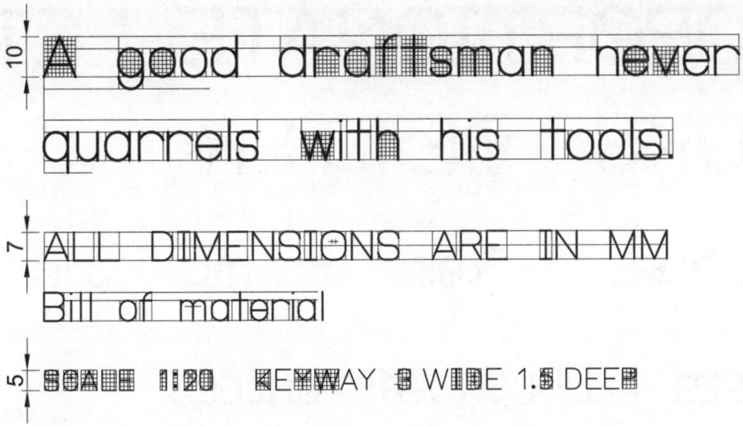

Fig. 2.7

Single Stroke Inclined Gothic Lettering The inclined letters are sloped to the right at 75° from the horizontal. The inclinations of all the letters should be the same. Figure 2.8 shows a sample lettering of this style.

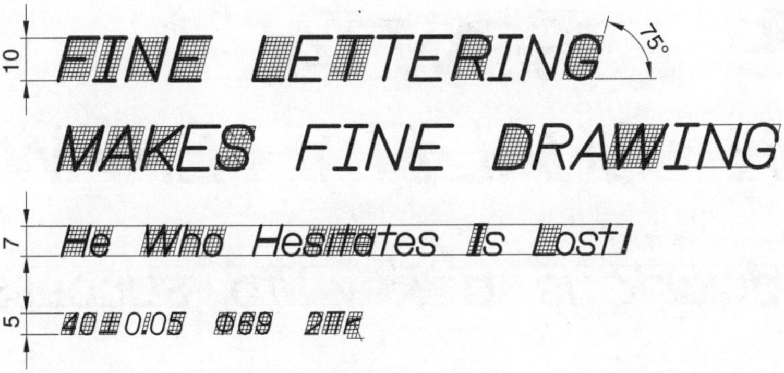

Fig. 2.8

Double Stroke Vertical Gothic Lettering This style is preferred for ink drawings. The lettering template, Fig. 1.18, is used to draw the outline of the letter. The letters are then filled in with ink. Obviously, double stroke letters are thicker than single stroke letters. They are drawn comparatively larger than single stroke letters. The line width varies from 0.1 to 0.2 of the height of the letters. The sample lettering is shown in Fig. 2.9.

Double Stroke Inclined Gothic Lettering When thicker letters, mentioned in the previous paragraph, are drawn inclined at 75° to the horizontal, the style is called double stroke inclined lettering. See Fig. 2.10 for samples.

2.3.5 Lettering Practice

Quite a good amount of practice is necessary for ensuring perfection in lettering. To start with, lettering may be done with instruments, i.e., lettering set-squares (Fig. 1.17) or specially designed

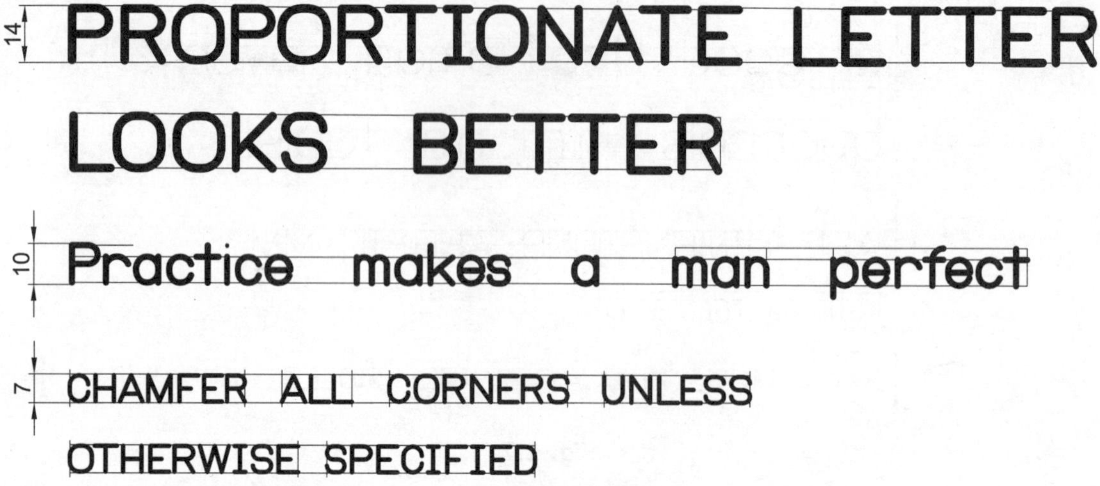

Fig. 2.9

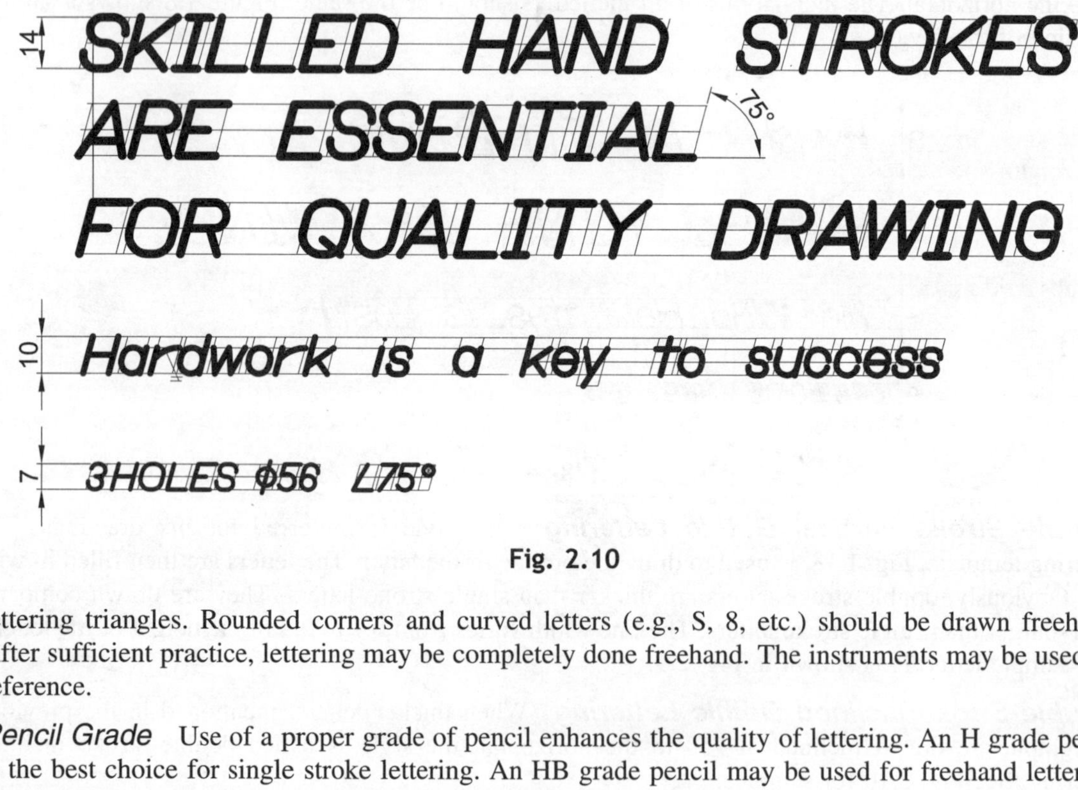

Fig. 2.10

lettering triangles. Rounded corners and curved letters (e.g., S, 8, etc.) should be drawn freehand. After sufficient practice, lettering may be completely done freehand. The instruments may be used for reference.

Pencil Grade Use of a proper grade of pencil enhances the quality of lettering. An H grade pencil is the best choice for single stroke lettering. An HB grade pencil may be used for freehand lettering. A pencil with a finely rounded tip gives a better result.

Hand Strokes Practice of line strokes as mentioned in Section 2.2.5 is extremely essential to ensure the speed in freehand lettering. The horizontal lines in the letters are drawn from left to right. The vertical or inclined lines are drawn downwards. The curves in the letter are drawn clockwise if they bend to right. An anticlockwise stroke is preferred if the curve bends to the left, Fig. 2.11. The reversed strokes should not be used in any case.

Fig. 2.11

Use of Grid/Guide Lines Initially, the grid as shown in Fig. 2.6 may be used for lettering practice. It ensures the proportion of each letter. Each grid cell is 1 mm × 1 mm. The grid lines should be very thin. Guide lines provide an alternative to a grid. Three horizontal guide lines for capital letters and four horizontal guidelines for lowercase letters, Fig. 2.7, may be used initially. Vertical guide lines may be drawn to determine letter widths and spacing. After sufficient practice, two horizontal guide lines (for capital letters and lowercase letters), Fig. 2.9, should be used.

Spacing The distances between two letters in a word may not be necessarily the same. The adjacent letters in a word are so placed that the background areas between them are seen approximately equal. Figure 2.12(a) and (b) show the letters with equal distances and with equal background areas respectively. The spacing between words may be taken equal to the height of the letters.

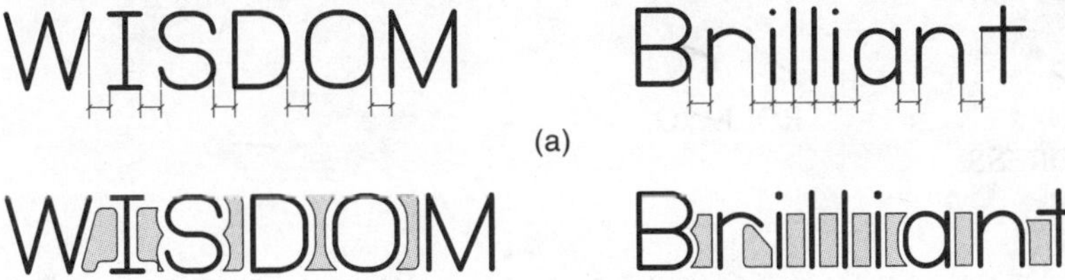

(b)

Fig. 2.12

Fractions and Indices Lettering While lettering a fraction, keep the height of the numerator and denominator equal to 3/4th of the height of a non-fractioned number. The spacing between division bar and the numerator or denominator should be such that the total height of fraction will be twice of that of a non-fractioned number, Fig. 2.13(a).

The height of index may be taken as half of the height of a base letter, Fig. 2.13(b).

Normal, Compressed and Expanded Letters The normal, compressed and expanded letters are shown in Fig. 2.14. Normal letters, as the name suggests, have normal proportions and spacing.

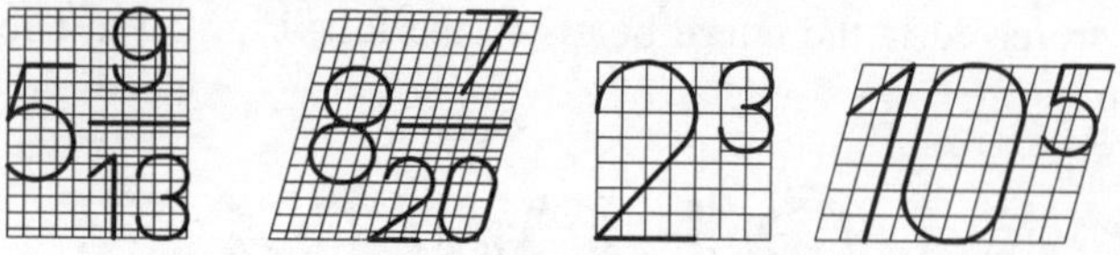

(a) (b)

Fig. 2.13

normal LETTERS
compressed LETTERS
extended LETTERS

Fig. 2.14

They should be preferred as much as possible. Compressed letters have narrowed proportions (i.e., more height-to-weight ratio) and spacing. They are preferred when the available space is small. Extended letters, on the other hand, have widened proportions (i.e., lesser height-to-weight ratio) and spacing. They are used to utilize a large available space. Compressed and expanded letters may be used to distinguish a sentence from other sentences.

Review Questions

1. Letter each of the following sentences using (i) grid (ii) three/four guide lines and (iii) two guide lines. Use 7 mm single stroke vertical gothic letters.
   (a) INDIA IS MY COUNTRY.
   (b) Never say die!
   (c) #519, Currey Road (E), Mumbai 400 012
2. Using 7 mm single stroke inclined gothic letters, write the following. Use two guide lines.
   Engineering is about the application of science to satisfy human needs in the most economical way. The needs of human beings are unlimited, while the resources are limited. The real challenge, therefore, is to fulfill unending needs of mankind with scarce resources under changing economic, social and environmental conditions.
3. Write your personal information in the following format. Use three guide line, 7 mm single stroke vertical gothic letters.
   NAME:
   COLLEGE:
   CLASS: ROLL NO:
   HOME ADDRESS:
   PIN:
   PHONE NO:
4. Write in freehand the following information in 5 mm vertical gothic style lettering (single stroke) using three/four guide lines.
   "There is a rhythm in nature. Our body, mind and breath have rhythms. Our soul also exhibits rhythm. If all these rhythms are not matched, we feel disturbed. We need to harmonize these rhythms to feel enlightened. The supreme spiritual goal of life, should, therefore, be to synchronize the rhythms of the body, the mind, the soul and the nature for divine joy."

Chapter 3

DIMENSIONING

3.1 INTRODUCTION

A drawing without dimensions is meaningless. Dimensions are necessary to show the exact size of an object. *Dimensioning* refers to the act of giving dimensions, i.e., length, width, height, diameter, etc., of the object. This information is provided by giving numeric values to various features of the object on the drawing. A *feature* is an individual characteristic such as a flat or cylindrical surface, a slot or a groove, a taper, a shoulder, a screw thread, etc.

BIS (SP 46: 2003) defines dimension as *a numerical value expressed in appropriate units of measurement and indicated graphically on technical drawings with lines, symbols and notes.*

The important aspects of dimensioning are as follows:

Units of Measurement On technical drawing we need to show lengths and angles. The most convenient unit for length is millimetre. In civil engineering and architectural drawing, inch or foot is often used as a unit of length. Angles are shown in degrees.

Symbols Symbols are incorporated to indicate specific geometry wherever necessary.

Notes Notes are provided to give specification of a particular feature or to give specific information necessary during the manufacturing of the object.

3.2 ELEMENTS OF DIMENSIONING

A line on the drawing whose length is to be shown is called an *object line.* The object line is essentially an outline representing the feature(s) of the object. While showing an angle, the two lines forming the angle will be the object lines.

Dimensioning is often done by a set of elements, which includes extension lines, dimension lines, leader lines, arrowheads and dimensions. These are shown in Fig. 3.1.

Extension Line An *extension line* is a short line drawn perpendicular to an object line. These lines start immediately or a few millimetres from the ends of object lines and extend a few millimetres beyond a dimension line.

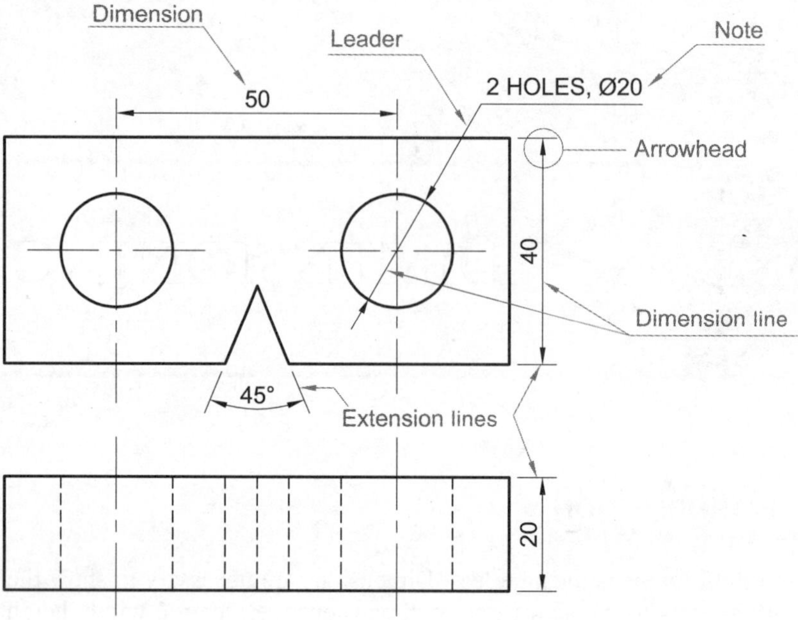

Fig. 3.1

Extension lines may be used to show an angle due to space constraint. In such a case, extension lines are drawn parallel to and at the ends of object lines.

Dimension Line A *dimension line* is drawn between two extension lines parallel to the object line. As a rule, there must be one and only one dimension line between any two extension lines. One dimension line represents one dimension. While dimensioning an angle, a curved dimension line is drawn by drawing a suitable arc having its centre at the vertex of the angle.

Leader Line A *leader line* (or *leader*) is a line which connects a note or a dimension with the feature to which it applies. Leaders are drawn at suitable angles, preferably 30°, 45° or 60°, and is never drawn horizontal or vertical. One end of the leader carries an arrowhead which connects it to the outline of the object. A dot is used instead of an arrowhead, if the leader ends inside the object, Fig. 3.2(b). The other end of the leader is made horizontal. A note or dimension is placed above the horizontal portion of the leader, Fig. 3.1.

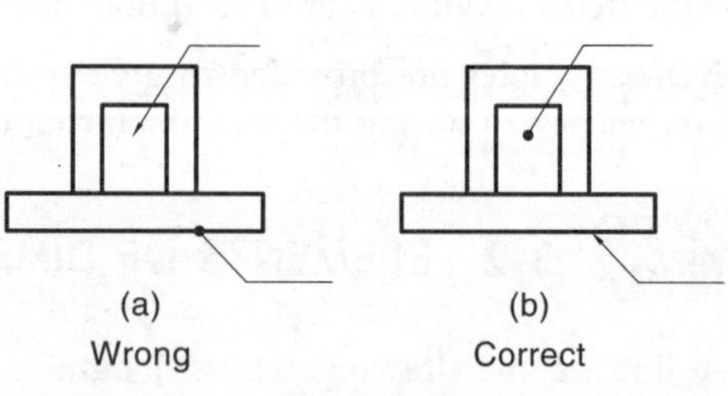

Fig. 3.2

Leaders are frequently used to indicate the diameter or radius of a circular feature.

Arrowheads An *arrowhead* is drawn at each end of a dimension line. The tip of an arrowhead touches the extension line. An arrowhead is also drawn at the end of a leader, which points out the feature of an object. The various styles of drawing an arrowhead are shown in Fig. 3.3. The arrowhead may be open, Fig. 3.3(a), closed, Fig. 3.3(b), or closed and filled, Fig. 3.3(c). The angle formed

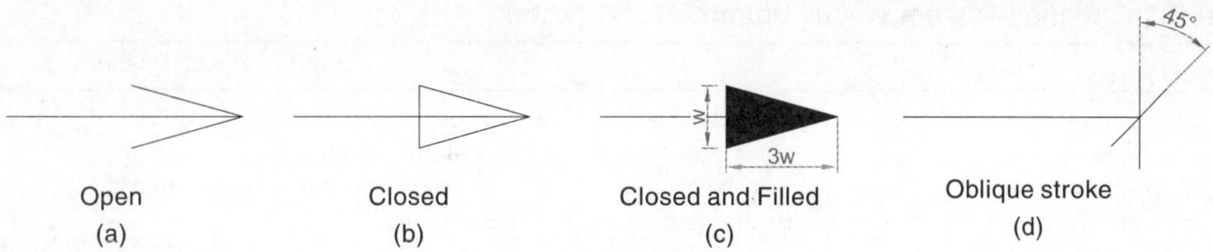

Fig. 3.3

by the barbs of the arrowhead usually varies from 15° to 90°. Sometimes, an oblique stroke drawn at 45° to the extension line, Fig. 3.3(d), is used instead of an arrowhead.

The closed and filled arrowhead, Fig. 3.3(c), is most commonly adopted. It is in the form of an isosceles triangle having a height three times of its base. The space inside the triangle is uniformly filled in. Readers may use this type of arrowhead as a standard practice.

The size of an arrowhead should be proportionate to the length of the dimension line. Too small or too large arrowheads should be avoided.

Dimension A *dimension* is a numeric value of length or angle expressed in a specified unit of measurement. Dimensions are placed near the middle and above dimension lines or at the centre of dimension lines by breaking them. Since all the dimensions of a drawing are expressed in the same unit (i.e., mm, cm or in), the unit is not written after the dimension figure. Instead, a note ALL DIMENSIONS IN MM is written at a prominent place (preferably on the left hand side of the title block) on the drawing sheet. The dimension text should be same for all the dimensions on a drawing and should have a suitable size.

3.3 SYSTEMS OF DIMENSIONING

For placing the dimensions on a drawing, one of the two systems mentioned below is adopted.

3.3.1 Aligned System

In the aligned system, dimensions are placed perpendicular to the dimension line so that they may be read from the bottom or right-hand side of the drawing sheet. As shown in Fig. 3.4, all horizontal and inclined dimensions can be read from the bottom, whereas vertical dimensions can be read from the right-hand side of the drawing sheet. Dimensions are placed at the middle and on top of the dimension lines.

3.3.2 Unidirectional System

In the unidirectional system, dimensions are placed in such a way that they can be read from the bottom edge of the drawing sheet. As shown in Fig. 3.5, all horizontal dimensions are placed at the middle and on top of the dimension lines while vertical and inclined dimensions are inserted by breaking the dimension lines at the middle.

Table 3.1 summarizes the differences in the two systems of dimensioning. It should be noted that dimensioning using leader lines is same in both the systems. In this book, the aligned system of dimensioning has been adopted throughout.

Table 3.1 Aligned System versus Unidirectional System

Aligned System	*Unidirectional System*
• Dimensions are placed perpendicular to dimension lines.	• Dimensions are always placed vertically irrespective of dimension lines.
• Horizontal and inclined dimensions can be read from the bottom of the drawing. Vertical dimensions can be read from the right-hand side of the drawing.	• All dimensions can be read from the bottom of the drawing.
• All dimensions are placed above the midpoint of dimension lines.	• Horizontal dimensions are placed above the midpoint of dimension lines. Vertical and inclined dimensions are placed at the middle of dimension lines by breaking them.

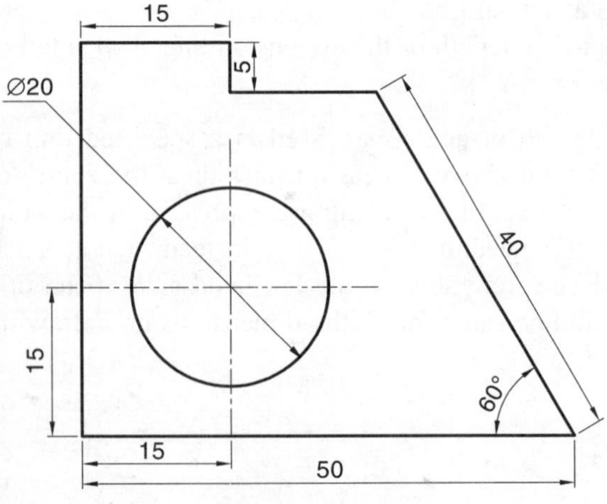

Fig. 3.4

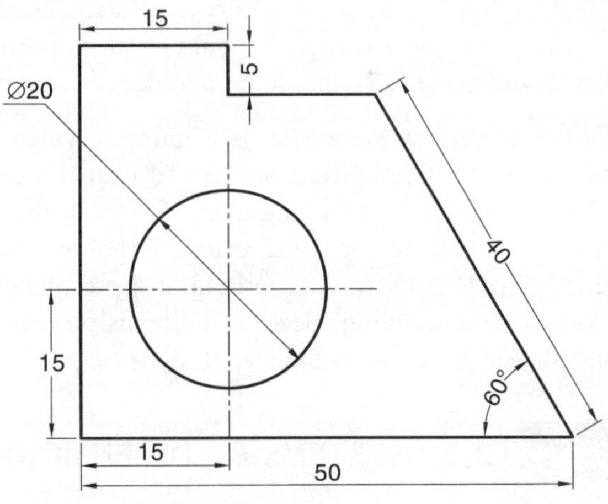

Fig. 3.5

3.4 RULES OF DIMENSIONING

The purpose of dimensioning is to provide a clear and complete description of an object. A complete set of dimensions will permit only one interpretation needed to manufacture the part. Good dimensioning is identified by characteristics like clearness, completeness, readability and accuracy. The following rules must be adopted to achieve these characteristics.

1. Between any two extension lines, there must be one and only one dimension line bearing one dimension.
2. As far as possible, all the dimensions should be placed outside the views, Fig. 3.6(a). Inside dimensions are preferred only if they are clearer and more easily readable, Fig. 3.6(b).
3. All the dimensions on a drawing must be shown using either Aligned System or Unidirectional System. In no case should, the two systems be mixed on the same drawing.
4. The same unit of length should be used for all the dimensions on a drawing. The unit should not be written after each dimension, but a note mentioning the unit should be placed below the drawing, Fig. 3.7.

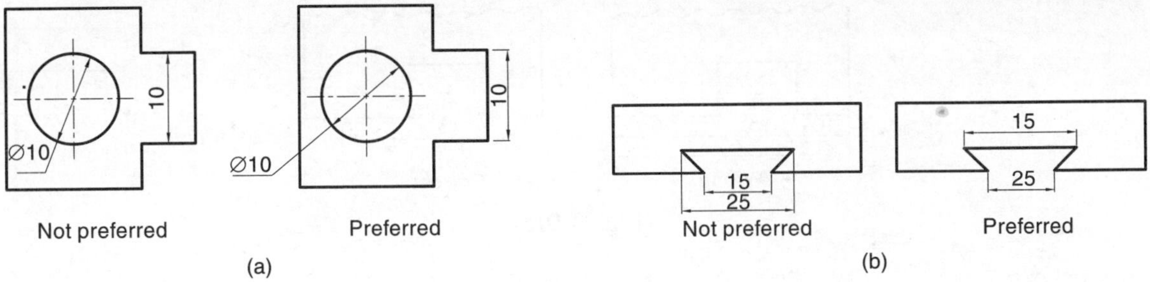

Fig. 3.6

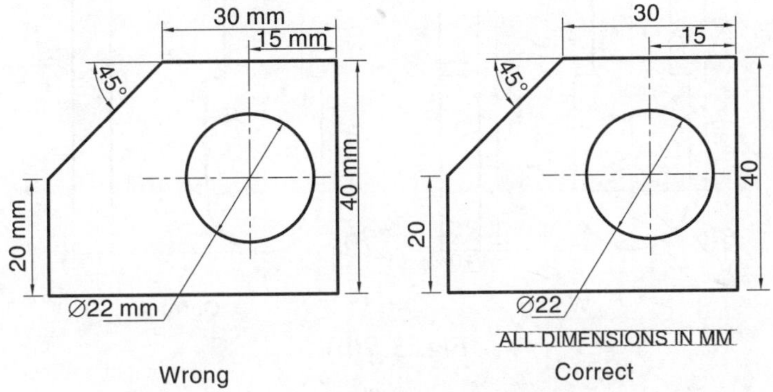

Fig. 3.7

5. Dimension lines should not cross each other. Dimension lines should also not cross any other lines of the object. However, extension lines may cross each other or outlines of the object, Fig. 3.8.

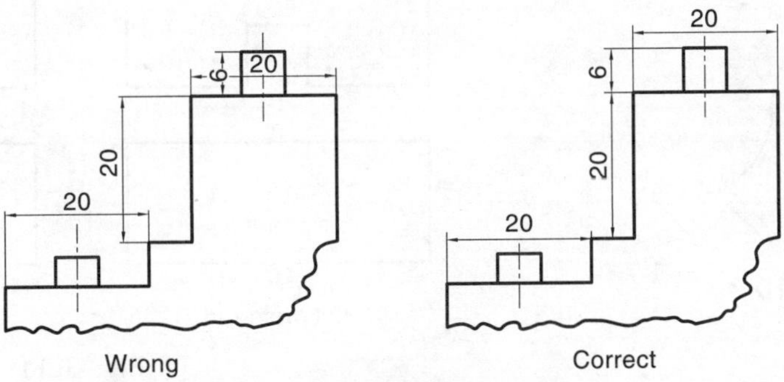

Fig. 3.8

6. All dimensions must be given. As far as possible, there should not be need for calculation, assumption or direct measurement for any dimension.
7. Each dimension should be given only once. No dimension should be redundant, i.e., no dimension should be repeated directly or indirectly, Fig. 3.9(a). If a particular dimension is mentioned, directly or indirectly, in one view, it should not be repeated in other views, Fig. 3.9(b).

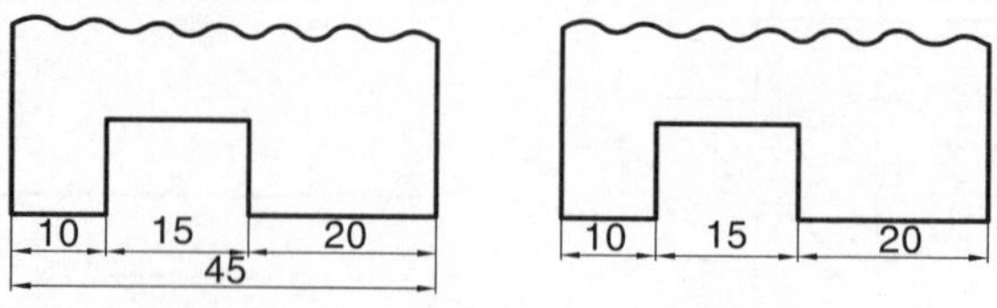

Wrong Correct

Fig. 3.9(a)

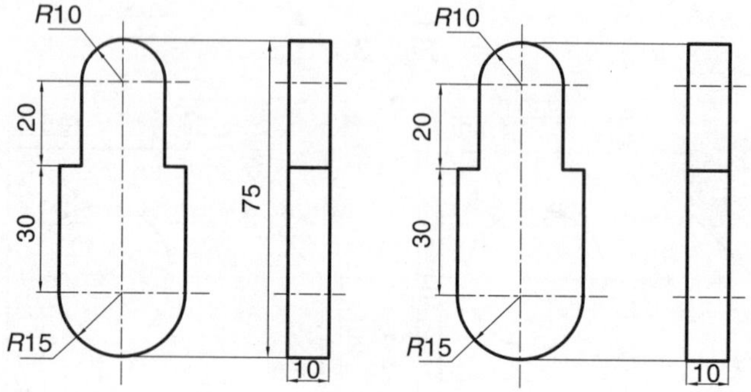

Wrong Correct

Fig. 3.9(b)

8. Do not use an outline or a centreline as a dimension line. A centreline may be extended to serve as an extension line, Fig. 3.9(b).
9. When it is necessary to place a dimension within a sectioned area, leave a blank space for the dimension, Fig. 3.10.

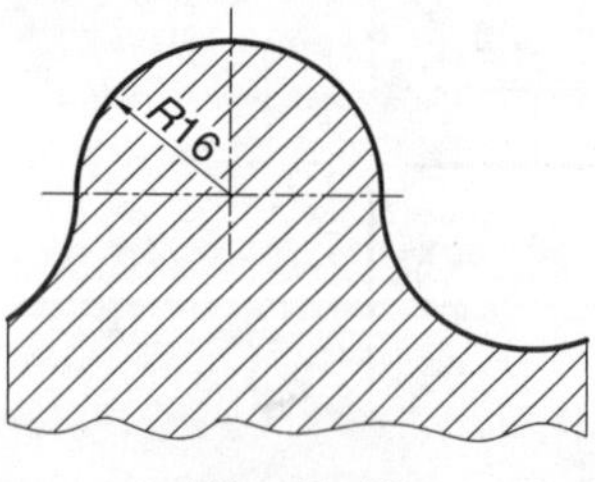

Fig. 3.10

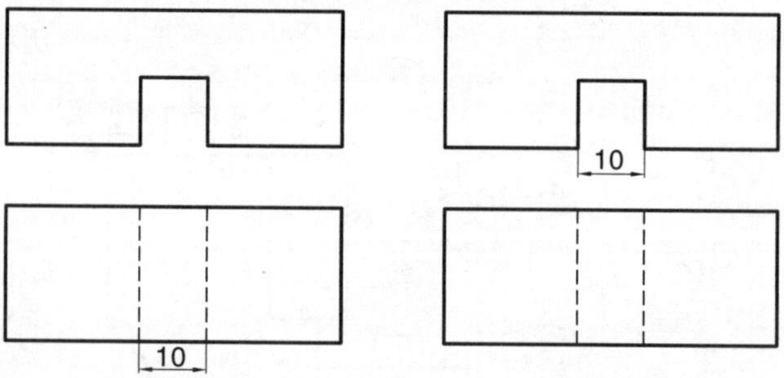

Not preferred Preferred

Fig. 3.11

10. Avoid dimensioning hidden lines, Fig. 3.11.
11. Keep dimension lines 6–8 mm away from the object line and also from each other.
12. If the space between two extension lines is too narrow to mark arrowheads and the dimension then one of the following ways, depending on space availability, should be adopted, Fig. 3.12(a).
    (i) Draw arrowheads touching the outsides of the extension lines and pointing toward each other. Place the dimension above the dimension line.
    (ii) Draw arrowheads as in (i) above and place the dimension at one end of the dimension line outside of the extension line.

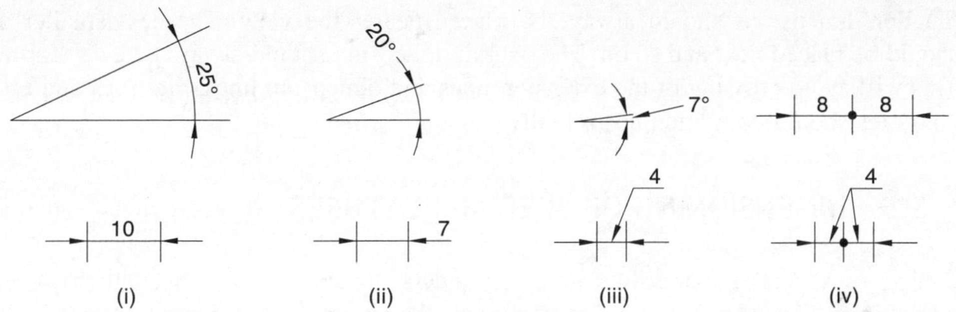

Fig. 3.12(a)

(iii) Draw arrowheads as in (i) above and place the dimension at the end of the leader which terminates on the dimension line.

(iv) For two consecutive dimensions, replace two intermediate arrowheads by a dot and place the dimensions as in (i) or (iii) above, depending on the space availability.

Refer Fig. 3.12(b) for illustration.

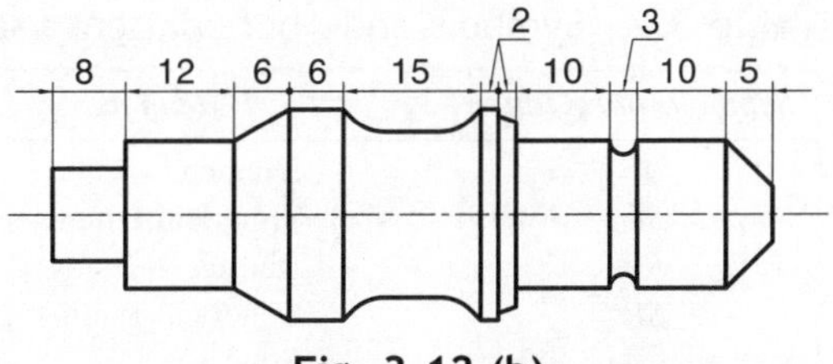

Fig. 3.12 (b)

13. For dimensions in series, adopt any one of the following ways.

(i) Chain dimensioning (Continuous dimensioning) All the dimensions are aligned in such a way that an arrowhead of one dimension touches tip-to-tip the arrowhead of the adjacent dimension. The overall dimension is placed outside the other smaller dimensions, Fig. 3.13(a).

(ii) Parallel dimensioning (Progressive dimensioning) All the dimensions are shown from a common reference line. Obviously, all these dimensions share a common extension line. This method is adopted when dimensions have to be established from a particular datum surface, Fig. 3.13(b).

(iii) Combined dimensioning When both the methods, i.e., chain dimensioning and parallel dimensioning are used on the same drawing, the method of dimensioning is called combined dimensioning, Fig. 3.13(c).

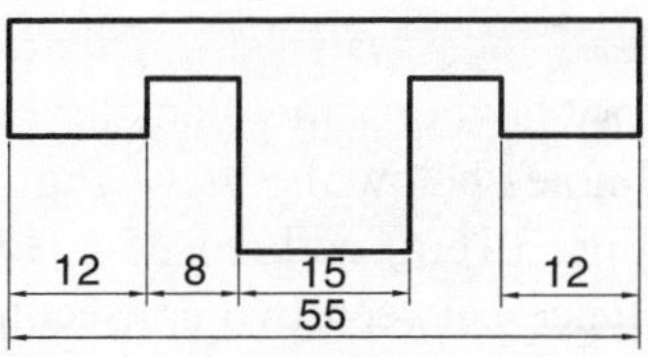

Fig. 3.13(a)

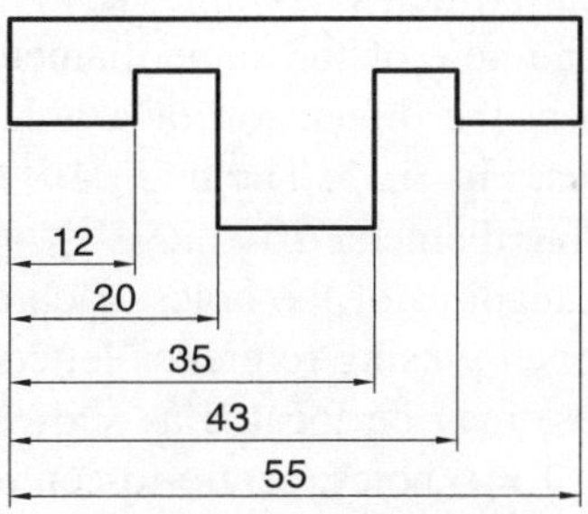

Fig. 3.13(b)

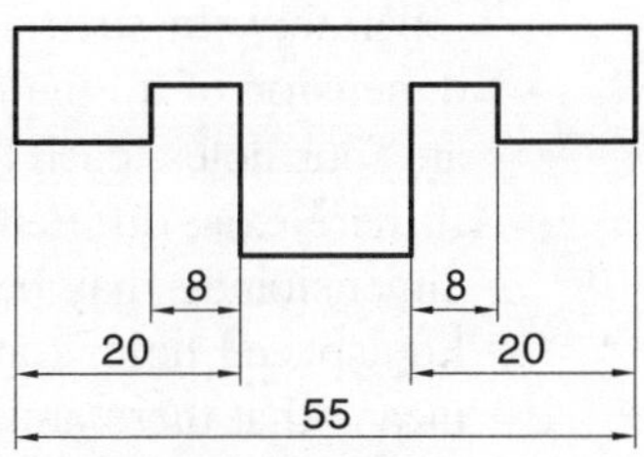

Fig. 3.13(c)

14. Smaller dimensions should always be placed nearer the view. The next smaller dimension should be placed next and so on. The overall dimension should always be away form the view. This will avoid crossing of the extension lines and dimension lines, Fig. 3.13 and Fig. 3.20(a).
15. All notes should be written horizontally.

3.5 DIMENSIONING OF SPECIAL FEATURES

Dimensioning of special features like holes, cylinders, tapers, threads, etc., are explained in the following sections. The specific symbol must precede the dimension to represent the particular feature. The symbols and abbreviations used for various features are given in Table 3.2.

Table 3.2 Symbols and Abbreviations used in Dimensioning

Symbol/Abbreviation	*Meaning*	*Symbol/Abbreviation*	*Meaning*
ϕ	Diameter	LG	Long
$S\phi$	Spherical Diameter	CSK	Countersunk
R	Radius	C'BORE	Counterbore
SR	Spherical Radius	SF or S'FACE	Spotface
□ or SQ	Square	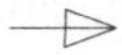	Conical Taper
CYL	Cylinder or Cylindrical		Flat taper
PCD	Pitch Circle Diameter	M	Metric Thread
EQ SP	Equispaced		

3.5.1 Dimensioning of Circular Features

1. A circle should be dimensioned by giving its diameter instead of radius. The dimension indicating a diameter should always be preceded by the symbol ϕ, Fig. 3.14. A leader may be used if the space available inside the circle is insufficient to accommodate the dimension, Fig. 3.14(b) and (c).

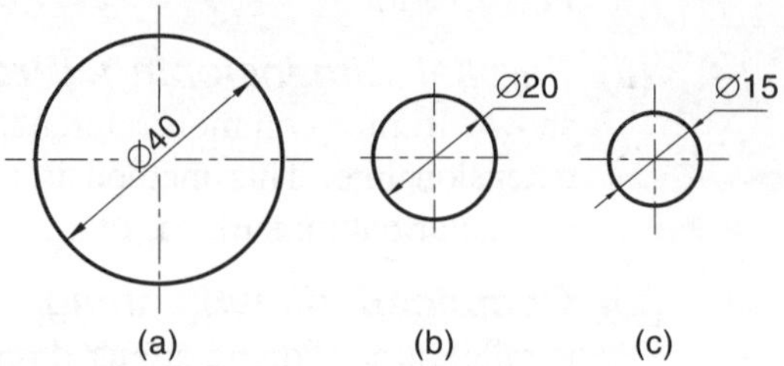

Fig. 3.14

2. Circular holes should be dimensioned in the view in which they appear as circles. The holes should always be located by their centrelines.
   If there are more than one hole of the same diameter, each hole need not to be dimensioned separately. In such a case, the dimension of a hole with a note will give an idea about the dimension of all the holes, Fig. 3.15. The note '4 × ϕ20' or '4 HOLES, ϕ20' means that there are four holes, each having diameter 20.
   If there exist different categories of the holes, each category having same diameter holes then dimensioning may be done by using reference letters and notes below the view, Fig. 3.15(c).
3. Equispaced holes (circles) may be located as shown in Fig. 3.16(a) and (b). '5 × 18 (= 90)' means that there are 5 + 1 = 6 holes, centre-to-centre distance between two consecutive holes = 18 and distance between centres of first and last hole = 90. The break lines may be used if there are a large number of holes on the uniform cross-sectioned area, Fig. 3.16(b).

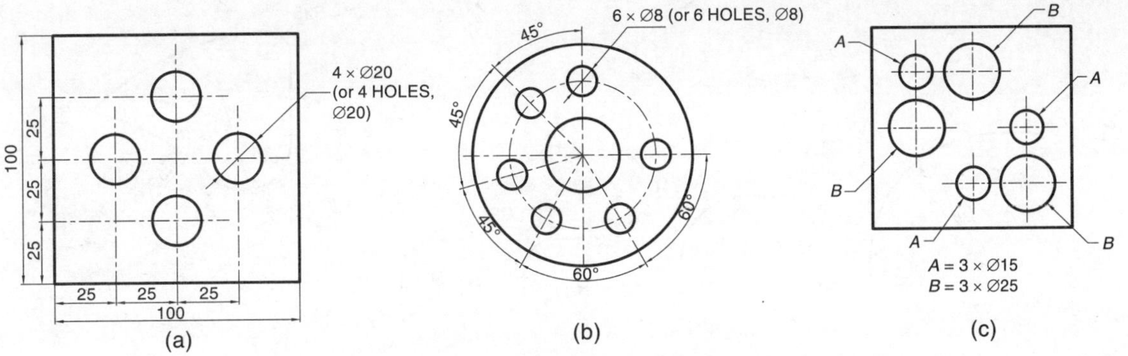

Fig. 3.15

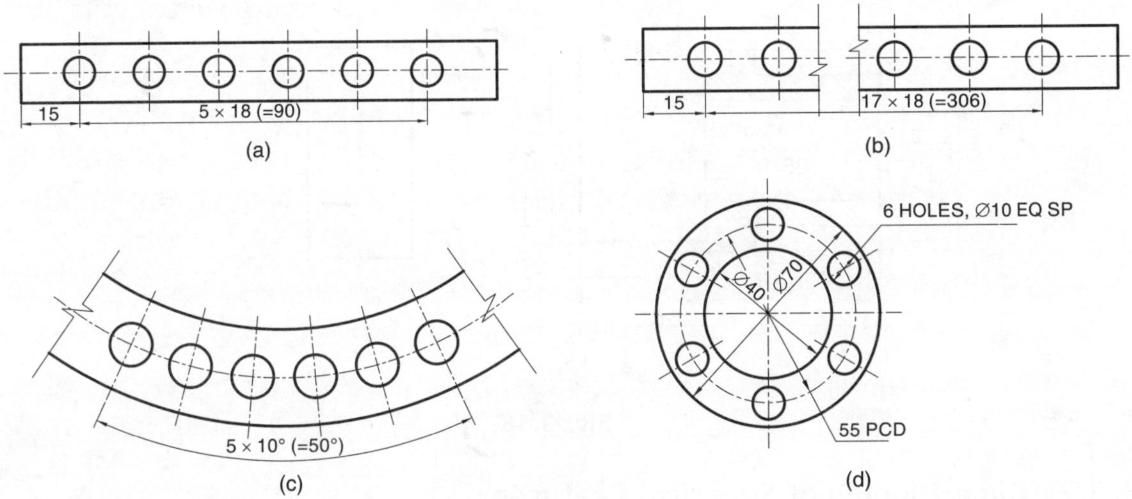

Fig. 3.16

In case of angular spacing of holes, the angular distance between two consecutive holes may be used to locate them as shown in Fig. 3.16(c).

Equispaced holes on a pitch circle should be dimensioned as shown in Fig. 3.16(d).

4. An arc should be dimensioned by giving its radius. The dimension indicating radius should be preceded by symbol *R*, Fig. 3.17. As far as possible, the centre of the arc should be marked by a cross. The dimension line should pass through the centre of the arc. A leader may be used if the space is insufficient, Fig. 3.17(b) and (c).

   If the radius of an arc is too large or too small to mark its centre on the space available, the centre mark may be omitted, Fig. 3.17(d).

5. Cylindrical features should be dimensioned by giving their diameters. As far as possible, they should be dimensioned in the views in which they appear as rectangles, Fig. 3.18(a).

   A cylinder may be dimensioned as shown in Fig. 3.18(b). Obviously, length is measured parallel to the axis.

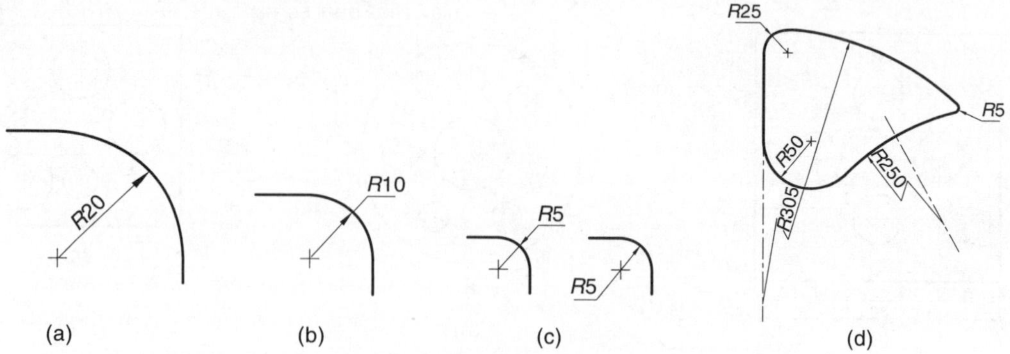

Fig. 3.17

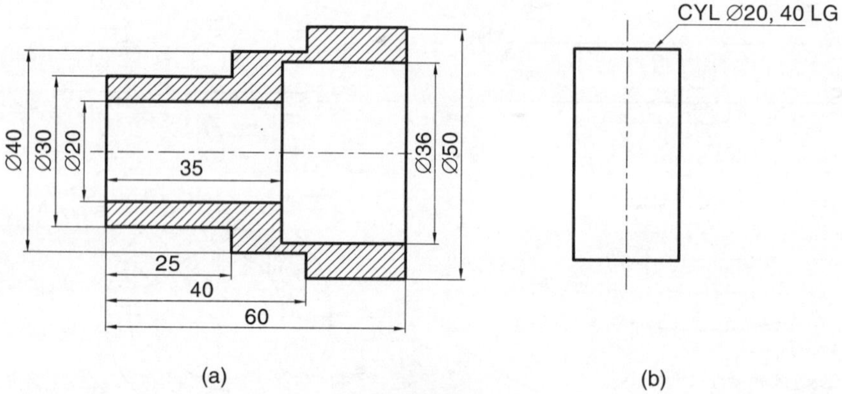

Fig. 3.18

3.5.2 Dimensioning of Spherical Features

Spherical features may be dimensioned by giving either the radius or diameter of a sphere. The symbols *SR* or *Sϕ* must precede the dimension for radius or diameter respectively, Fig. 3.19.

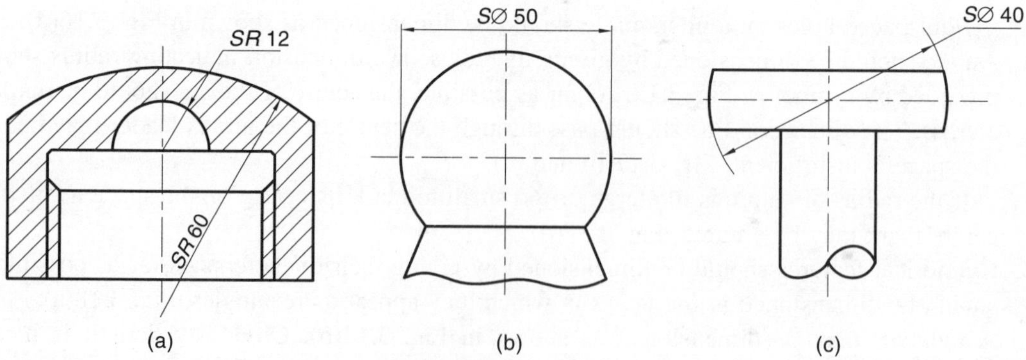

Fig. 3.19

3.5.3 Dimensioning of Conical and Tapered Features

1. Conical features are dimensioned in either of the following ways:
   (i) By giving the two diameters and the perpendicular distance between them, Fig. 3.20(a).
   (ii) By giving one of the diameters, distance between the end faces (i.e., length of taper) and taper using conical taper symbol, Fig. 3.20(b). The taper is calculated by taking the ratio of the difference between the diameters of the end faces and the length of taper.
   (iii) By giving one of the diameters, length of taper and taper angle, Fig. 3.20(c).

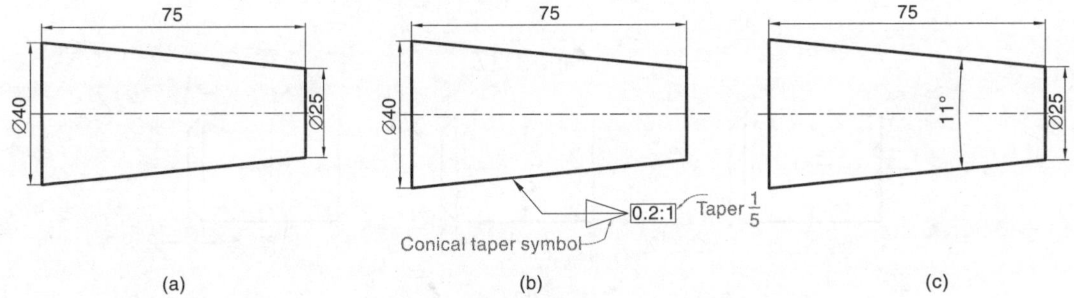

Fig. 3.20

2. The flat tapered features are dimensioned in either of the following ways:
   (i) By giving the height of one side, distance between flat ends (i.e., length of taper) and taper using flat taper symbol, Fig. 3.21(a). The taper is calculated by taking the ratio of the difference between the heights of two flat ends and the length of the taper.
   (ii) By giving the height of one side, length of taper and slope of the tapered face, Fig. 3.21(b).

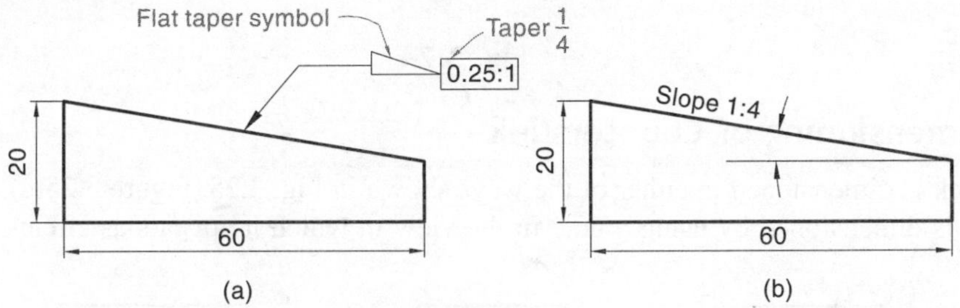

Fig. 3.21

3.5.4 Dimensioning of Square Features

Square features (e.g., a rod of square cross-section) are dimensioned using symbol □ or *SQ* as shown in (i) or (ii), Fig. 3.22(a). If the true shape of the square is not seen in the view, then cross lines are used to indicate the square cross-section, Fig. 3.22(b).

3.5.5 Dimensioning of Chamfered Features

1. The external chamfers are dimensioned in either of the ways shown in Fig. 3.23.
2. The internal chamfers are dimensioned in either of the ways shown in Fig. 3.24.

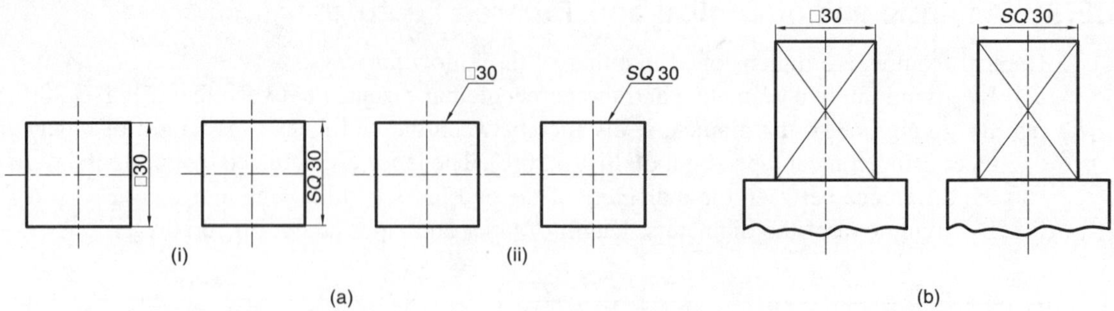

Fig. 3.22

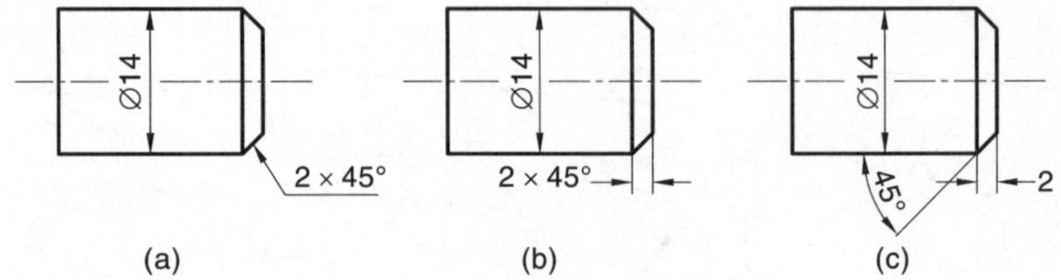

Fig. 3.23

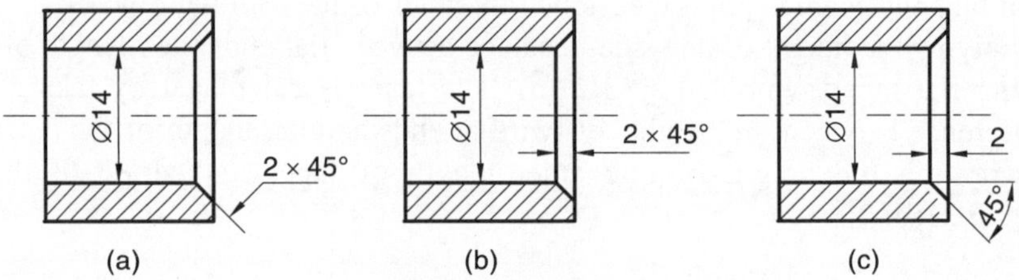

Fig. 3.24

3.5.6 Dimensioning of Countersunk

A countersunk is dimensioned in either of the ways shown in Fig. 3.25. Figure 3.25(c) explains how a countersunk is dimensioned by using a note in the view in which it appears as circles.

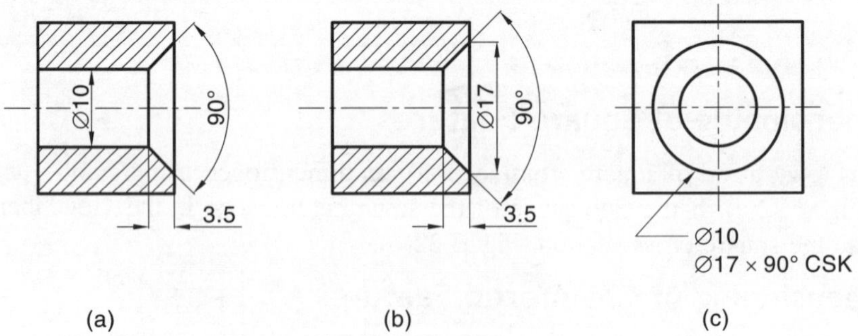

Fig. 3.25

3.5.7 Dimensioning of Screw Threads

1. External metric threads are dimensioned by giving the threaded length and nominal diameter preceded by symbol '*M*', Fig. 3.26(a).
2. Internal metric threads are dimensioned by giving the threaded length, depth of drilled hole before threading and nominal diameter preceded by symbol '*M*', Fig. 3.26(b).

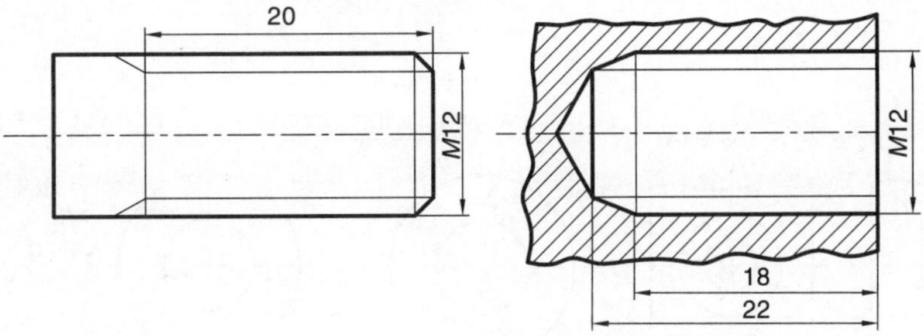

(a) (b)

Fig. 3.26

3.6 USE OF NOTES

As already explained, notes are used in technical drawings to give specifications of particular features or some specific information. A note may be a general sentence applied to the entire or some part of the drawing, or a note may be a specific sentence applied to a particular feature. General notes are written at a prominent place on the drawing sheet. The height of the letters is kept between 4 mm to 8 mm, preferably 6 mm. Underlining is avoided.

Specific notes are connected by leaders to the features they imply. These notes must have a proper syntax. The height of the letters is kept between 3 mm to 4 mm. The use of notes in dimensioning of some specific feature is explained below.

1. Circular hole Fig. 3.27(a): A hole of diameter 16, drilled to the depth of 25.

2. Countersunk Fig. 3.25(c): A countersunk of root diameter 10, top diameter 17 and included angle 90°.

3. Spot face Fig. 3.27(b): A spot face of diameter 22 on a hole of diameter 10.

4. Counterbore Fig. 3.27(c): A counterbore of root diameter 10, top diameter 20 and depth 10.

5. Keyway Fig. 3.27(d).

6. Saw cut Fig. 3.27(e): A saw cut of width 2.

7. Repeated features Fig. 3.27(f): Five slots, each of width 16 and depth 6.

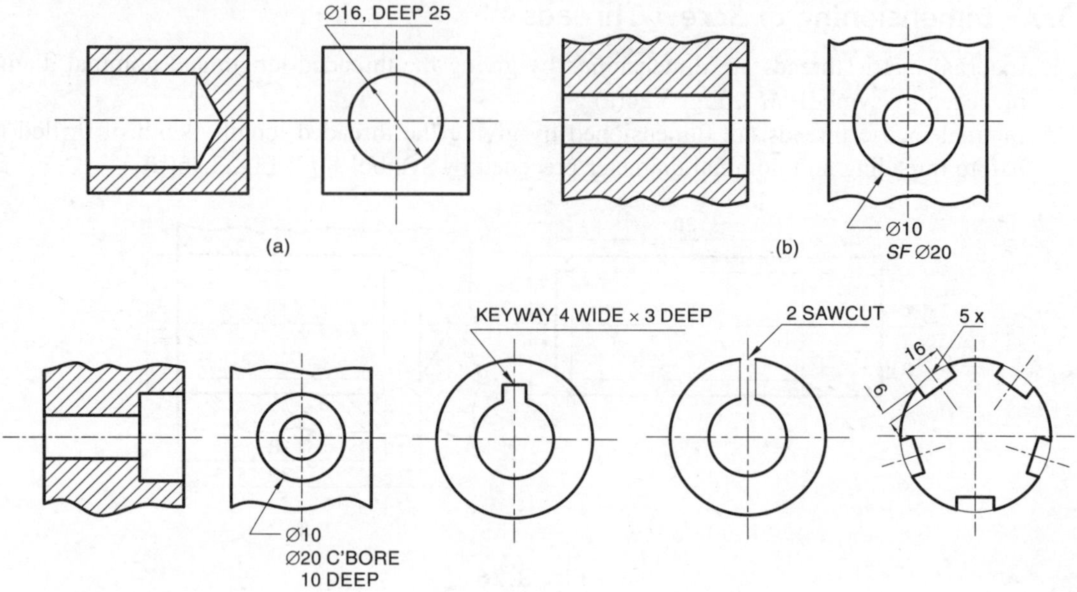

Fig. 3.27

ILLUSTRATIONS

Figures 3.28 to 3.30 show the illustrations of dimensioning based on the rules discussed in previous sections. In each case, Fig. (a) shows the wrong and Fig. (b) shows the correct way of dimensioning. Wrong dimensioning is marked as 'X' and corrected dimensioning is shown by '√'.

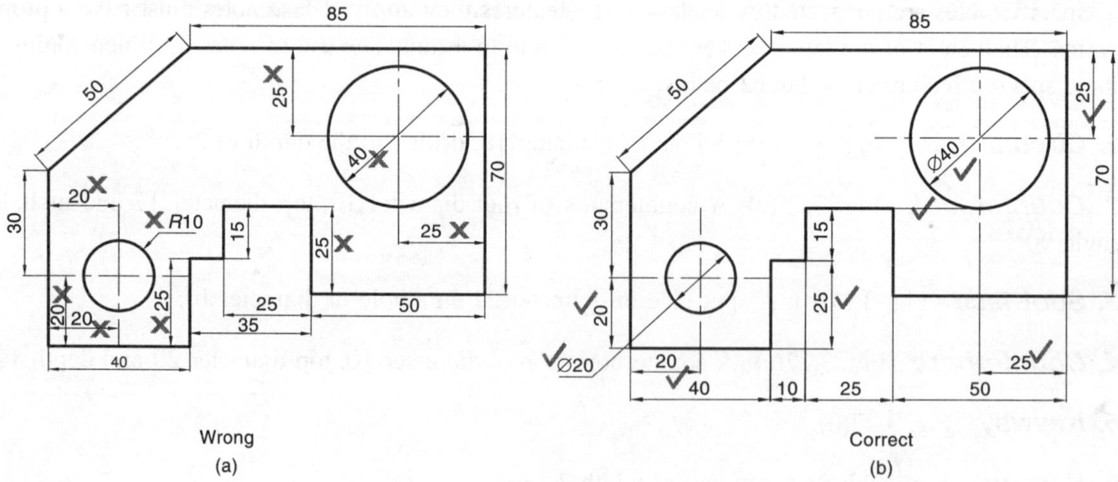

Fig. 3.28

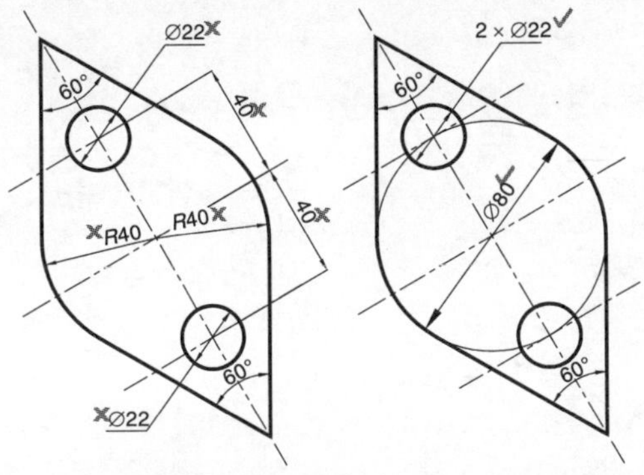

Wrong (a) Correct (b)

Fig. 3.29

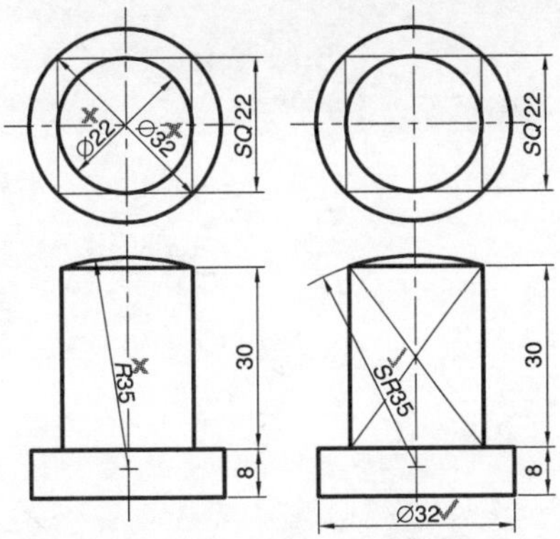

Wrong (a) Correct (b)

Fig. 3.30

REVIEW QUESTIONS

1. Identify the mistakes in dimensioning in Fig. 3RQ.1. Redraw the figure and correct the dimensioning.

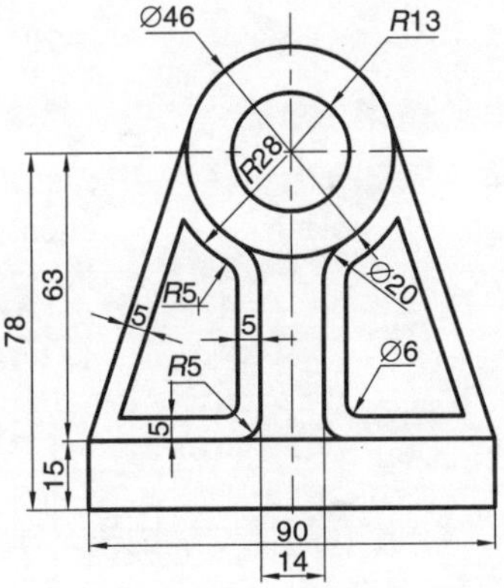

Fig. 3RQ.1

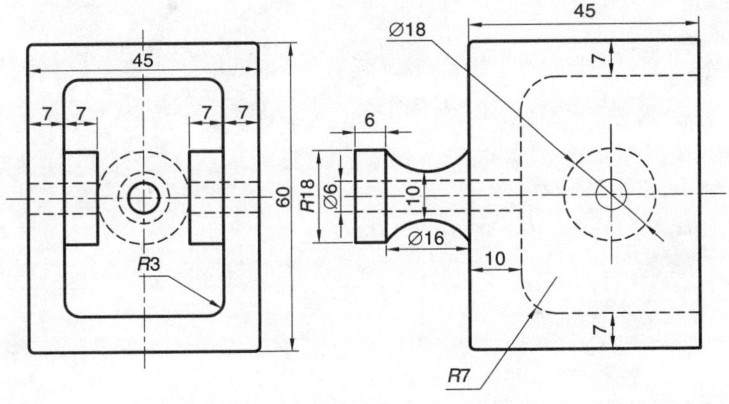

Fig. 3RQ.2

2. Correct the mistakes in dimensioning in Fig. 3RQ.2.
3. Identify the mistakes in dimensioning in Fig. 3RQ.3 and correct them.

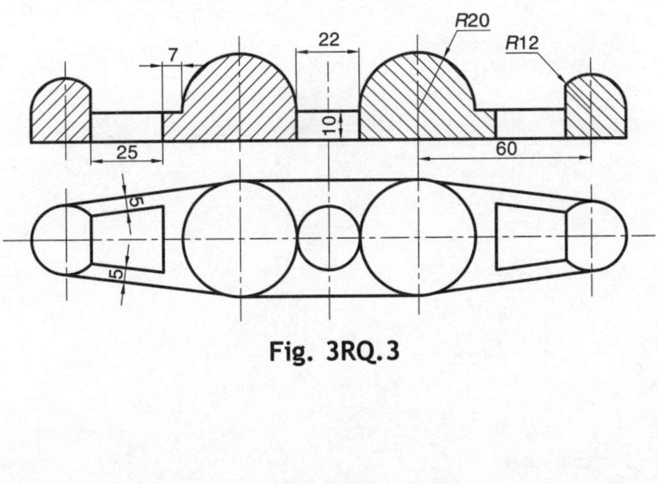

Fig. 3RQ.3

Chapter 4

GEOMETRICAL CONSTRUCTIONS

4.1 INTRODUCTION

Geometrical constructions serve as the basic building block of engineering drawing. This chapter reviews the most common and important geometrical exercises that are necessary in technical drawings. The geometrical exercises reviewed in this chapter are the following:

1. To bisect a line/an arc
2. To draw a perpendicular to a line
3. To divide a line
4. To bisect an angle
5. To trisect a right angle
6. To divide a circle
7. To find the centre of an arc/a circle
8. To draw a normal and a tangent to arc(s)/circle(s)
9. To construct regular polygons
10. To draw an arc/a circle passing through three given points
11. To draw parallel lines
12. To construct an angle equal to a given angle
13. To draw an arc/a circle tangent to line(s)/arc(s)
14. To draw reverse or ogee curves

These constructional methods are useful in drawing many objects like crankshafts, rocker arms, connecting rods, car bodies, motorbike frames, steering wheels, gaskets, etc., *Illustration 4.1*.

4.2 BASIC GEOMETRICAL SHAPES

The basic polygonal and circular shapes learnt by the readers in school-level geometry are mentioned in the following sections, without their constructional procedures.

4.2.1 Triangles

The sum of all internal angles of a triangle is 180°. The different types of triangles are shown in Fig. 4.1.

Illustration 4.1 Profile drawings of these objects are based on geometrical constructions

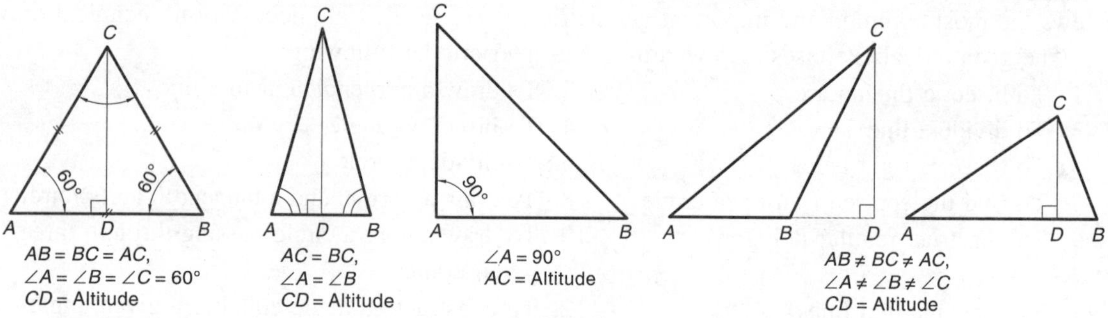

(a) Equilateral triangle (b) Isosceles triangle (c) Right-angle triangle (d) Scalene triangles

Fig. 4.1

4.2.2 Quadrilaterals

The sum of all internal angles of a quadrilateral is 360°. The different types of quadrilaterals are shown in Fig. 4.2.

4.2.3 Pentagon

A regular pentagon is shown in Fig. 4.3. As a pentagon consists of a triangle (say *ABC*) and a quadrilateral (say *ACDE*), the sum of all internal angles of a pentagon is 180° + 360° = 540°.

4.2.4 Hexagon

A regular hexagon is shown in Fig. 4.4. As a hexagon consists of two quadrilaterals (say *ABCD* and *ADEF*), the sum of all internal angles of a hexagon is 360° + 360° = 720°.

The method of drawing a regular pentagon and a regular hexagon is explained in Section 4.11.

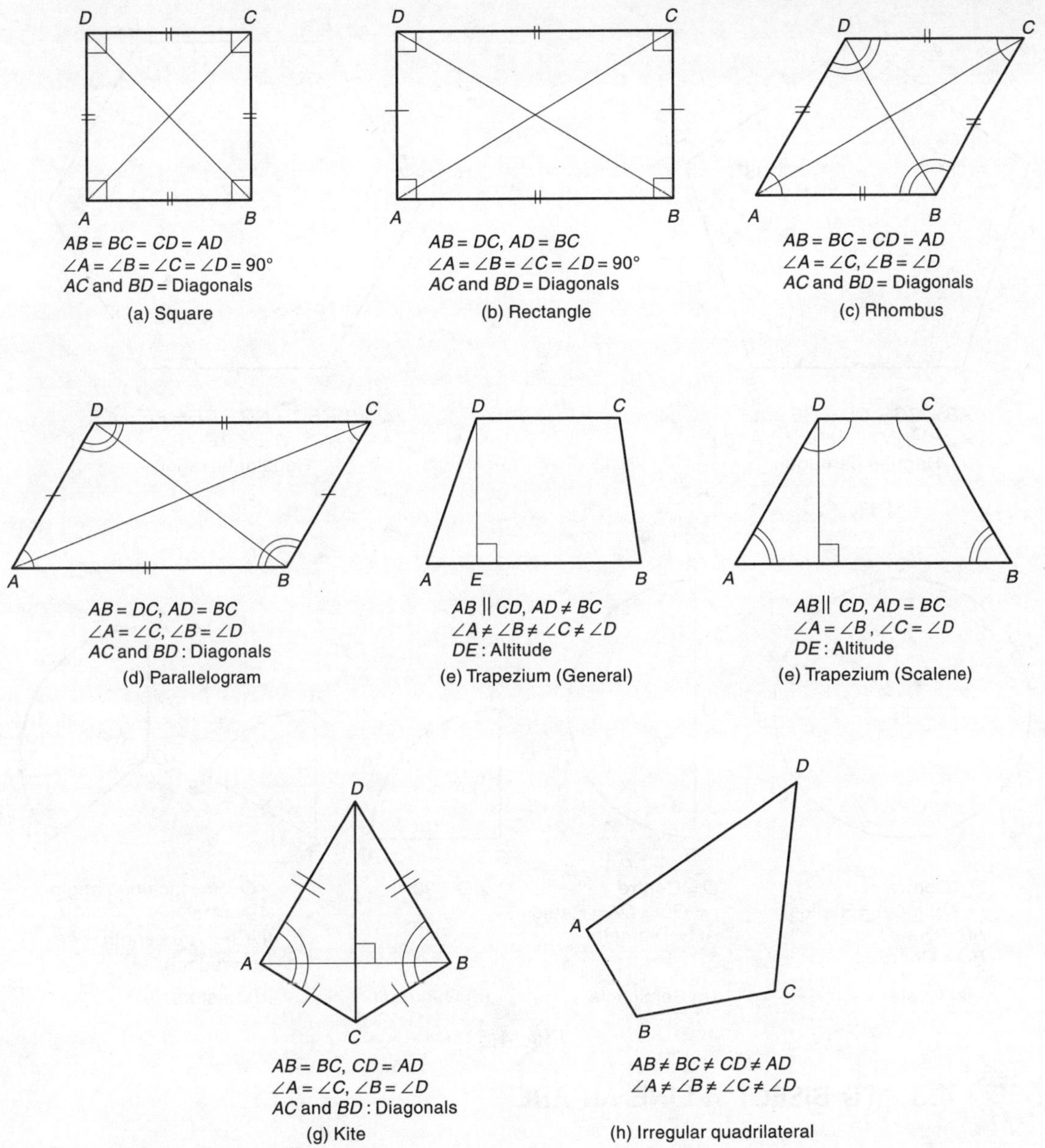

$AB = BC = CD = AD$
$\angle A = \angle B = \angle C = \angle D = 90°$
AC and BD = Diagonals
(a) Square

$AB = DC$, $AD = BC$
$\angle A = \angle B = \angle C = \angle D = 90°$
AC and BD = Diagonals
(b) Rectangle

$AB = BC = CD = AD$
$\angle A = \angle C$, $\angle B = \angle D$
AC and BD = Diagonals
(c) Rhombus

$AB = DC$, $AD = BC$
$\angle A = \angle C$, $\angle B = \angle D$
AC and BD : Diagonals
(d) Parallelogram

$AB \parallel CD$, $AD \neq BC$
$\angle A \neq \angle B \neq \angle C \neq \angle D$
DE : Altitude
(e) Trapezium (General)

$AB \parallel CD$, $AD = BC$
$\angle A = \angle B$, $\angle C = \angle D$
DE : Altitude
(e) Trapezium (Scalene)

$AB = BC$, $CD = AD$
$\angle A = \angle C$, $\angle B = \angle D$
AC and BD : Diagonals
(g) Kite

$AB \neq BC \neq CD \neq AD$
$\angle A \neq \angle B \neq \angle C \neq \angle D$
(h) Irregular quadrilateral

Fig. 4.2

4.2.5 Circle/Semicircle/Quadrant/Sector

Figure 4.5 shows a circle, a semicircle, a quadrant and sectors.

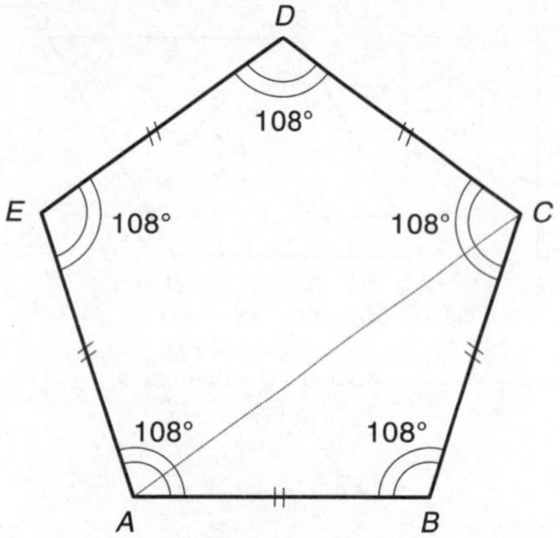

$AB = BC = CD = DE = AE$
$\angle A = \angle B = \angle C = \angle D = \angle E = 180°$
Regular pentagon

Fig. 4.3

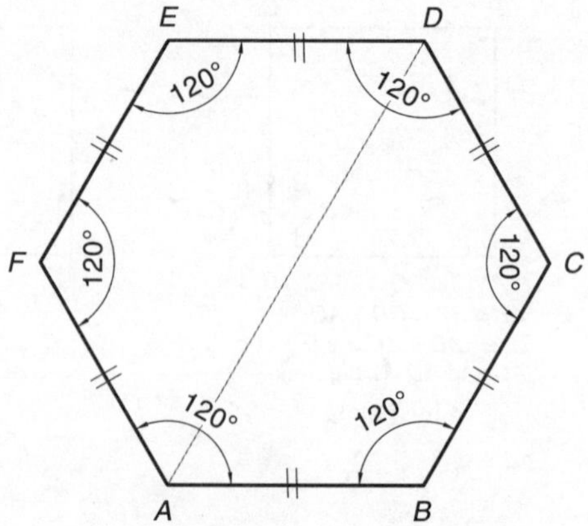

$AB = BC = CD = DE = EF = AE$
$\angle A = \angle B = \angle C = \angle D = \angle E = \angle F = 120°$
Regular hexagon

Fig. 4.4

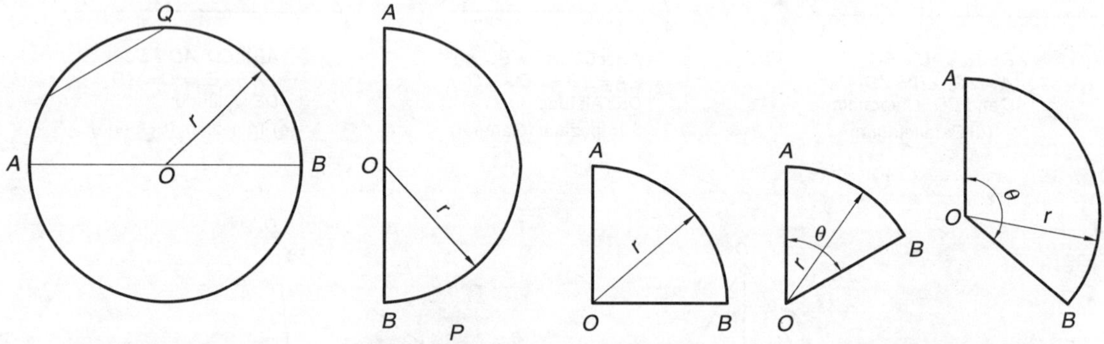

O = Centre
$r = OB = OA$ = Radius
AB = Diameter
PQ = Chord
(a) Circle

O = Centre
$r = OB = OA$ = Radius
AB = Diameter
(b) Semicircle

$\angle O = 90°$
(c) Quadrant

$\angle O = \theta$ = Included angle
AB = Arc
$l(AB)$ = Arc Length = $r.\theta$
(θ in radian)
(d) Sectors

Fig. 4.5

4.3 TO BISECT A LINE/AN ARC

Example 4.1 To bisect a given straight line AB.

Solution Refer Fig. 4.6.

1. With A as centre and radius greater than half of AB, mark two arcs, one on each side of AB.
2. With B as centre and same radius, mark two arcs intersecting the previous arcs at C and D.
3. Join CD. CD is the perpendicular bisector of AB.

Example 4.2 To bisect a given arc AB.

Solution Refer Fig. 4.7.

Follow the same procedure as explained in Example 4.1. CD is the bisector of arc AB. It will pass through the centre O (produced if necessary).

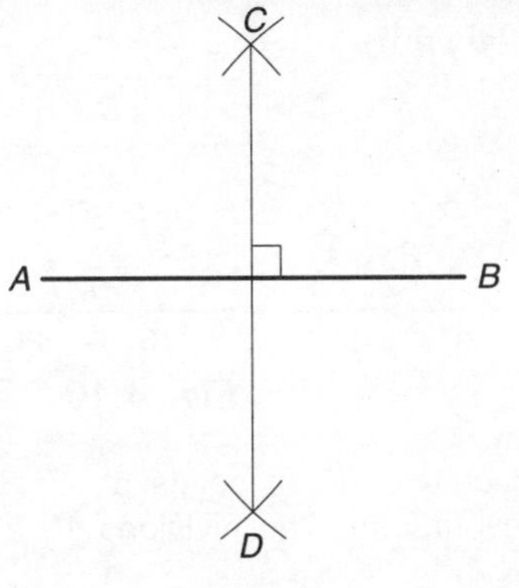

Fig. 4.6

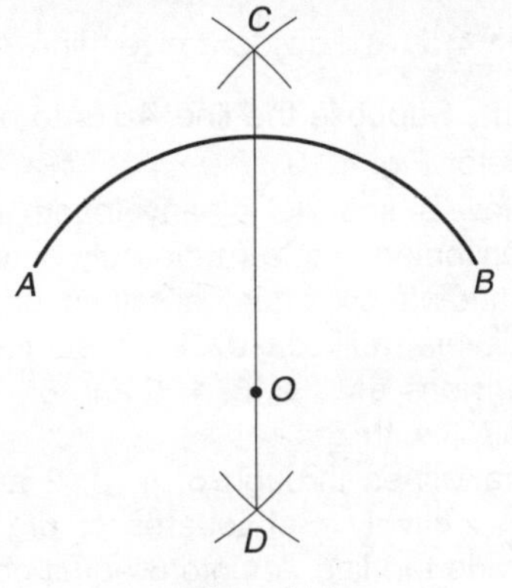

Fig. 4.7

4.4 TO DRAW A PERPENDICULAR TO A LINE

Example 4.3 To draw a perpendicular to a given line AB from a point P anywhere on it.

Solution Refer Fig. 4.8.

1. With P as centre and any convenient radius r_1, mark two arcs cutting AB at C and D. Produce AB if necessary.
2. With C and D as the centres and radius $r_2 > r_1$, mark two arcs intersecting each other at Q.
3. Join QP. QP is perpendicular to AB.

Example 4.4 To draw a perpendicular to a given line AB from a point P outside it.

Solution Refer Fig. 4.9.

1. With P as centre and any convenient radius, mark two arcs intersecting AB at C and D.
2. With C and D as centres and radius > $\left(\frac{1}{2} CD\right)$, mark two arcs intersecting each other at E.
3. Join PE for the required perpendicular.

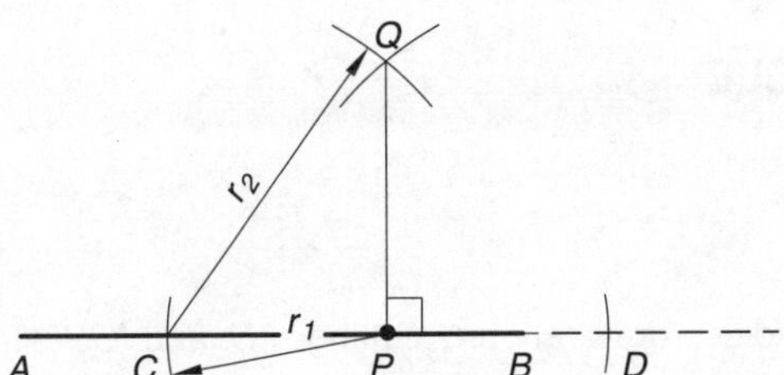

Fig. 4.8

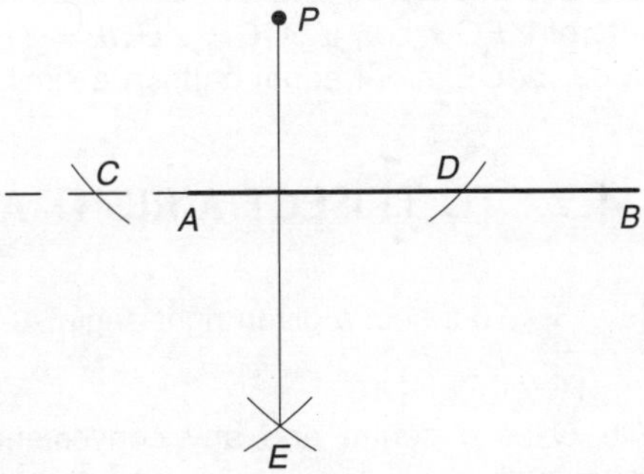

Fig. 4.9

4.5 TO DIVIDE A LINE

Example 4.5 To divide a given line *AB* into any number of equal parts.

Solution Suppose the line *AB* is to be divided into 6 equal parts. Refer Fig. 4.10.

1. Draw a line *AC* of any length inclined to *AB* at some convenient angle (preferably between 20° and 40°).
2. Mark off six equal divisions on *AC* by cutting arcs of suitable radii consecutively starting from *A*. Number these divisions as 1, 2, 3, 4, 5 and 6.
3. Join 6 with *B*.
4. Draw lines through 5, 4, 3, 2 and 1 parallel to 6–*B* and cutting *AB* at points 5′, 4′, 3′, 2′and 1′ respectively. Set-squares or drafter may be used for this purpose. The divisions 1′, 2′, 3′, 4′, 5′ divide the line *AB* into 6 equal parts.

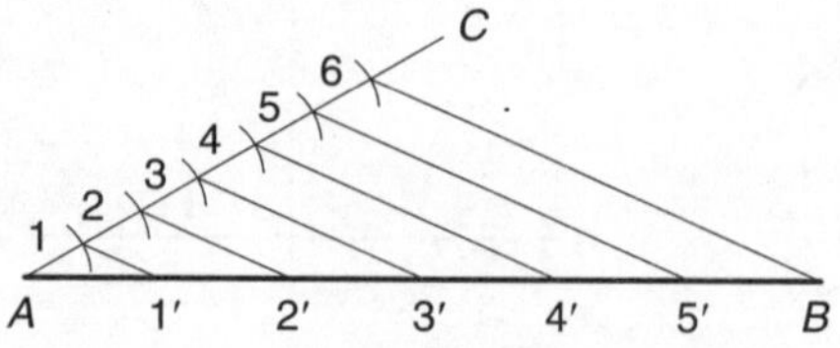

Fig. 4.10

4.6 TO BISECT AN ANGLE

Example 4.6 To bisect a given angle *AOB*.

Solution Refer Fig. 4.11.

1. With *O* as centre and any convenient radius, mark arcs cutting *OA* and *OB* at *C* and *D* respectively.
2. With *C* and *D* as centres and same or any other convenient radius, mark two arcs intersecting each other at *E*.
3. Join *OE*. *OE* is the bisector of ∠*AOB*, i.e., ∠*AOE* = ∠*EOB*.

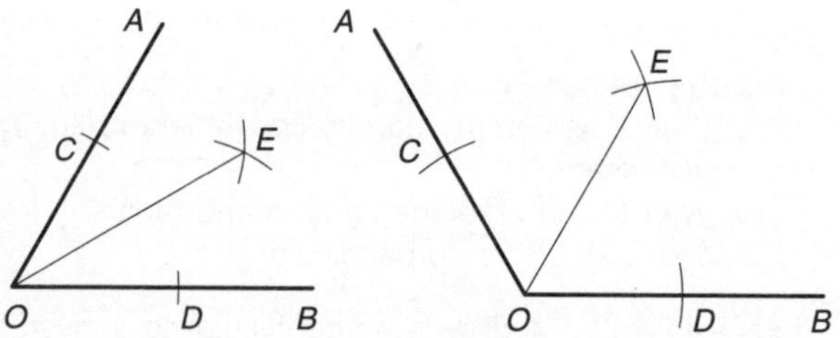

Fig. 4.11

Example 4.7 To divide a given angle into 2^i equal parts, *i* being a whole integer number.

Solution Let ∠*AOB* to be divided into $2^3 = 8$ equal parts. Refer Fig. 4.12.

1. Divide ∠*AOB* into 2 equal parts by drawing the bisector *OE* as explained in Example 4.6.
2. Divide ∠*EOB* into 2 equal parts by drawing the bisector *OF* using the same method.
3. Further divide ∠*EOF* and ∠*FOB* by drawing bisectors *OG* and *OF* respectively. Thus, we get 4 equal parts of ∠*EOB*, i.e., ∠*EOG* = ∠*GOF* = ∠*FOH* = ∠*HOB*.
4. Divide ∠*AOE* into 4 equal parts in a similar way. ∠*AOB* is now divided into 8 equal parts.

4.7 TO TRISECT A RIGHT ANGLE

Example 4.8 To trisect a given right angle *AOB*.

Solution Refer Fig. 4.13.

1. With *O* as a centre and any convenient radius, draw an arc cutting *AO* and *OB* at *C* and *D* respectively.

2. With C and D as the centres and same radius, mark two arcs cutting the arc CD at E and F respectively.
3. Join OF and OE. OF and OE trisect $\angle AOB$, i.e., $\angle AOF = \angle FOE = \angle EOB$.

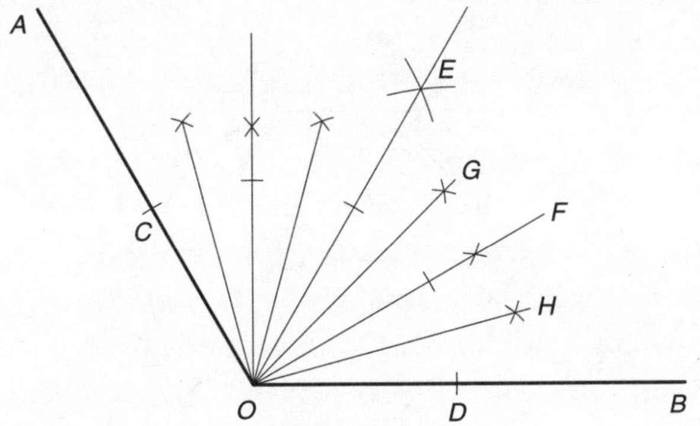

Fig. 4.12

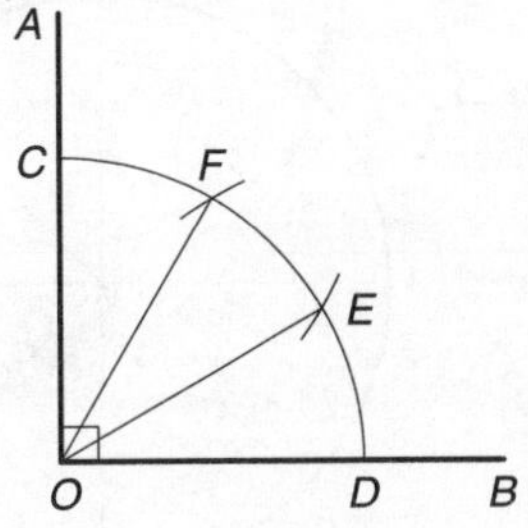

Fig. 4.13

4.8 TO DIVIDE A CIRCLE

Example 4.9 To divide a given circle into 12 equal parts.

Solution

Method 1: Refer Fig. 4.14(a).

Draw the diameters 1–7, 2–8, 3–9, 4–10, 5–11 and 6–12 having an angle of 30° between them as shown. These diameters divide the circle into 12 equal parts.

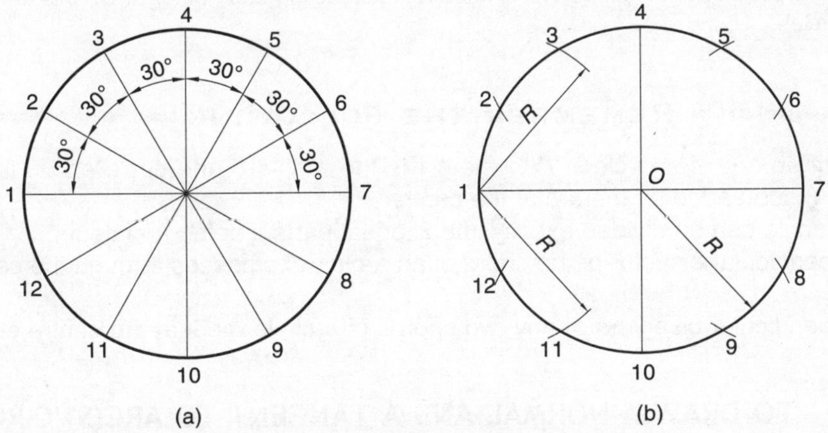

Fig. 4.14

Method 2: Refer Fig. 4.14(b).

1. Draw the two diameters 1–7 and 4–10, perpendicular to each other.
2. With 1 as a centre and radius = R (= radius of the circle), cut two arcs at 3 and 11 on the circle.
3. Similarly, with 4, 7 and 10 as the centres and the same radius, cut arcs on the circle respectively at 2 and 6, 5 and 9, and 8 and 12. The points 1, 2, 3, etc., give 12 equal divisions of the circle.

Example 4.10 To divide a given circle into 8 equal parts.

Solution Refer Fig. 4.15.

Draw the diameters 1–5, 2–6, 3–7 and 4–8, each inclined to the adjacent at 45°. These diameters give 8 equal parts of the circle.

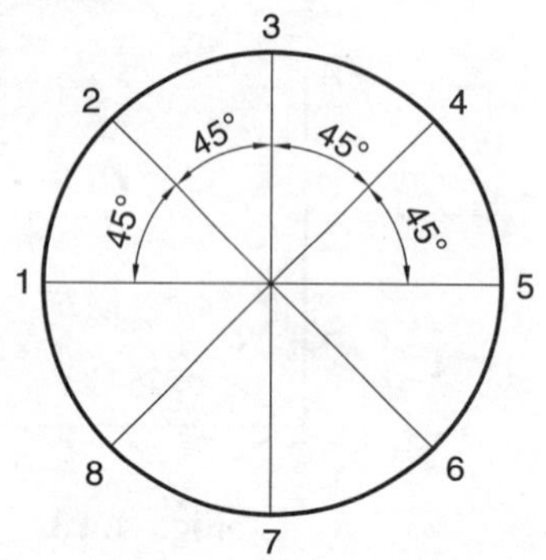

Fig. 4.15

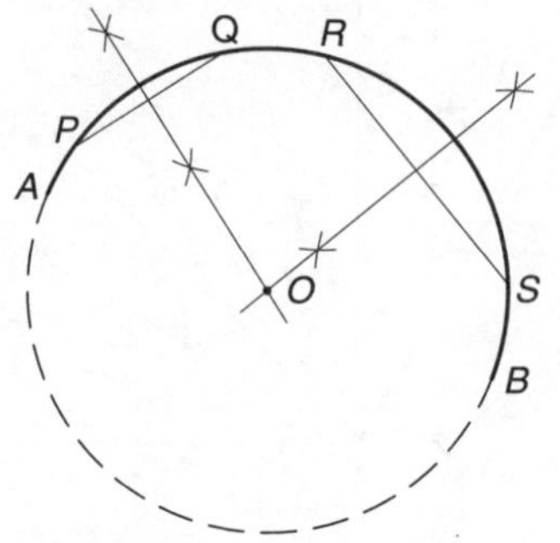

Fig. 4.16

4.9 TO FIND THE CENTRE OF AN ARC/A CIRCLE

Example 4.11 To find the centre of an arc *AB* (or circle).

Solution Refer Fig. 4.16.

1. Draw two chords *PQ* and *RS* of any convenient length in arc *AB*.
2. Draw the perpendicular bisectors of *PQ* and *RS*, intersecting each other at *O*. *O* is the centre of arc *AB* (or circle).

REMEMBER THE FOLLOWING

- Length of an arc of a circle = $r.\theta$, where *r* is the radius of the circle and θ is the angle (in radian) subtended by the arc at the centre.
- A given angle can be divided exactly into 2^i equal parts, *i* being an integer.
- The perpendicular bisector of the chord of an arc always passes through the centre of the arc.
- The perpendicular bisectors of any two chords of a circle meet at the centre of the circle.

4.10 TO DRAW A NORMAL AND A TANGENT TO ARC(S)/CIRCLE(S)

Example 4.12 To draw a normal and a tangent to a given arc *AB* (or a circle) at a point *P* on it.

Solution

Method 1: Refer Fig. 4.17(a).

1. Find the centre *O* of the arc/circle as explained in Example 4.11.
2. Join *O* with *P*. *OP* is the required normal.
3. At *P*, draw a perpendicular *ST* to *OP*. *ST* is the required tangent.

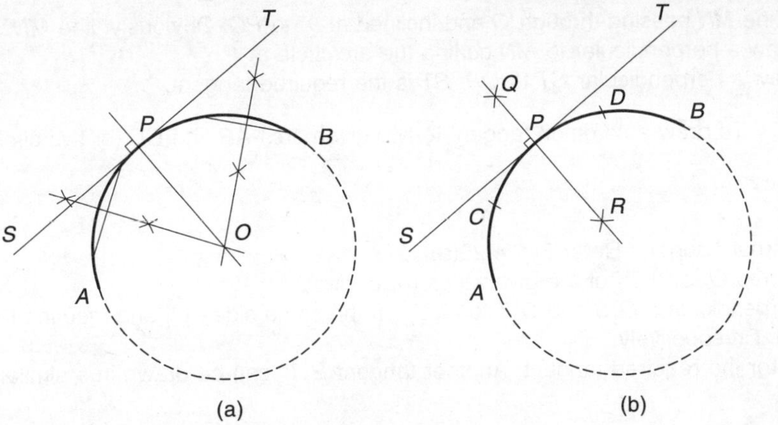

Fig. 4.17

Solution

Method 2: Refer Fig. 4.17(b).

1. With centre *P* and any convenient radius, mark off two arcs cutting the arc/circle at *C* and *D*.
2. Obtain *QR*, the perpendicular bisector of arc *CD*. *QR* is the required normal.
3. Draw the perpendicular *ST* to *QR* for the required tangent.

Example 4.13 To draw a tangent to a given arc *AB* (or a circle) from a point *P* outside it.

Solution Refer Fig. 4.18.

1. Join the centre *O* with *P* and locate the midpoint *M* of *OP*.
2. With *M* as a centre and radius = *MO*, mark an arc cutting the circle at *Q*.
3. Join *P* with *Q*. *PQ* is the required tangent.
   Another tangent *PQ′* can be drawn in a similar way.

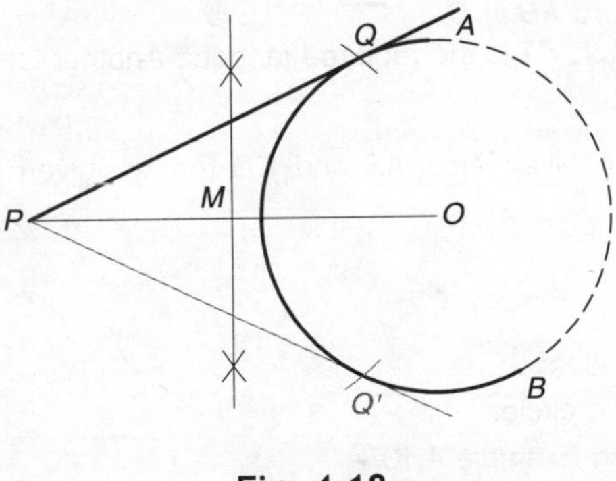

Fig. 4.18

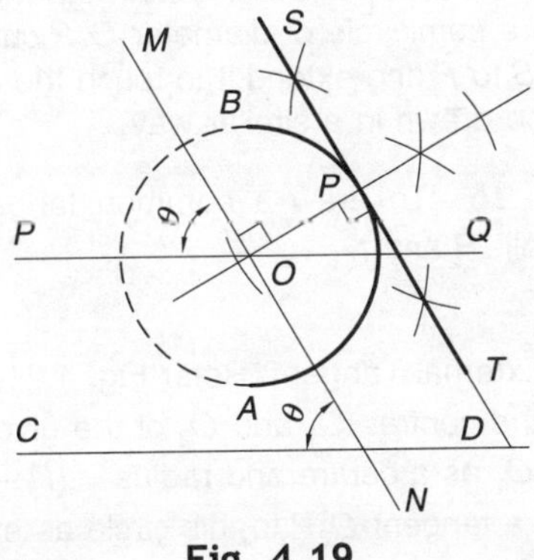

Fig. 4.19

Example 4.14 To draw a tangent to a given arc *AB* (or circle) and inclined to a given line *CD* at a given angle θ.

Solution Refer Fig. 4.19.

1. Draw a line *PQ* passing through the centre *O* of the arc *AB* (or circle) and parallel to *CD*.

2. Draw a line *MN* passing through *O* and inclined at $\theta°$ to *PQ*. Obviously, line *MN* will make $\theta°$ to *CD*.
3. At *O*, draw a perpendicular to *MN* cutting the arc/circle at *P*.
4. At *P*, draw a perpendicular *ST* to *OP*. *ST* is the required tangent.

Example 4.15 To draw a common tangent to two given arcs *AB* and *CD* (or two circles) of equal radius *R*.

Solution

Case (a): External Tangent: Refer Fig. 4.20(a).

1. Join centres O_1 and O_2 of the given arcs (or circles).
2. Draw perpendiculars O_1S and O_2T to O_1O_2 on the same side of it and meeting the arcs *AB* and *CD* at *S* and *T* respectively.
3. Join *ST* for the required tangent. Another tangent *S′T′* can be drawn in a similar way.

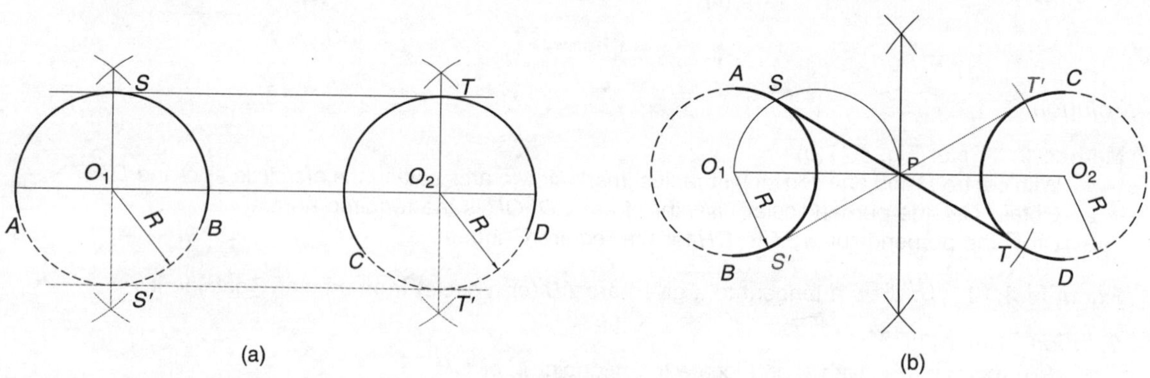

Fig. 4.20

Case (b): Internal Tangent: Refer Fig. 4.20(b).

1. Join centres O_1 and O_2. Obtain the midpoint *P* of O_1O_2.
2. Draw a semicircle of diameter O_1P cutting the arc *AB* at *S*.
3. Join *S* to *P* and extend it to touch the arc *CD* at *T*. *ST* is the required tangent. Another tangent *S′T′* can be drawn in a similar way.

Example 4.16 To draw a common tangent to two given arcs *AB* and *CD* (or two given circles) of unequal radii, *R* and *r*.

Solution

Case (a): External Tangent: Refer Fig. 4.21(a).

1. Join the centres O_1 and O_2 of the given arcs/circles.
2. With O_1 as a centre and radius = $(R - r)$, draw a circle.
3. Draw a tangent O_2P to this circle as explained in Example 4.13.
4. Join O_1P and produce it to meet arc *AB* at *S*.
5. Draw O_2T parallel to O_1S on the same side of O_1O_2 cutting the arc *CD* at *T*.
6. Join *ST*. *ST* is the required tangent.
   Another tangent *S′T′* can be drawn in a similar way.

Case (b): Internal Tangent: Refer Fig. 4.21(b).

1. Join the centres O_1 and O_2.

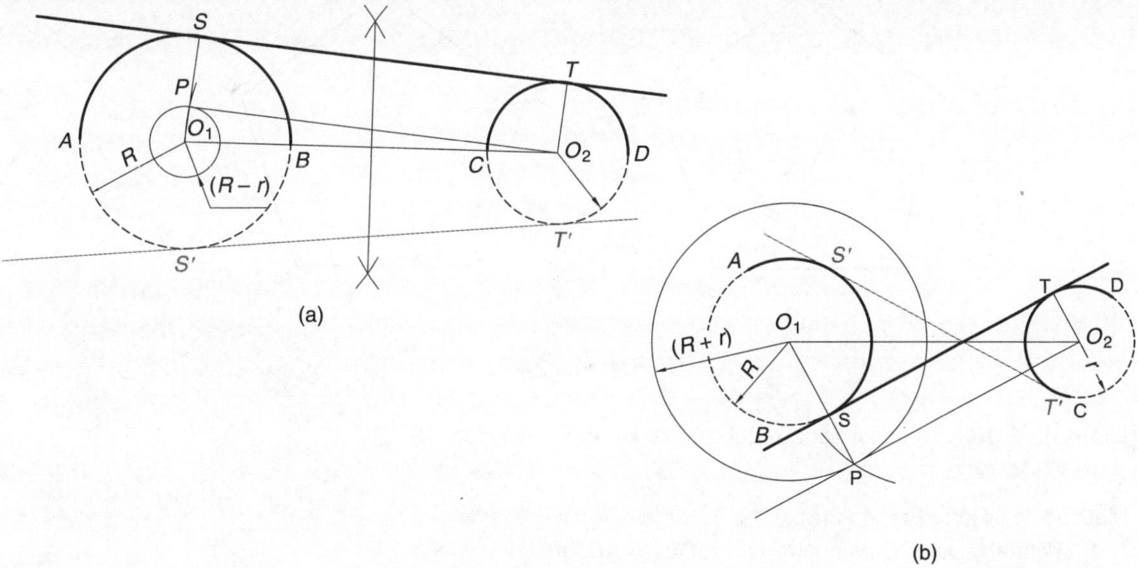

Fig. 4.21

2. With O_1 as centre and radius = $(R + r)$, draw a circle.
3. Draw a tangent O_2P to this circle.
4. Join O_1P to cut arc *AB* at *S*.
5. Draw O_2T parallel to O_1S on the other side of O_1O_2 cutting the arc *CD* at *T*.
6. Join *ST*. *ST* is the required tangent. Another tangent will pass through *S′T′*.

4.11 TO CONSTRUCT REGULAR POLYGONS

Example 4.17 To construct a regular pentagon of known side *AB*.

Solution

Method 1: Refer Fig. 4.22(a).

1. Draw a line *AB* of given length.
2. Draw *BC* and *AE* such that $\angle ABC = \angle EAB = 108°$ and $BC = EA = AB$.
3. With *C* and *E* as the centres and radius = *AB*, draw two arcs cutting each other at *D*.
4. Join *D* with *C* and *E*. *ABCDE* is the required pentagon.

Method 2: Refer Fig. 4.22(b).

1. Draw a line *AB* of given length.
2. Construct an isosceles triangle *ABO* such that $\angle ABO = \angle BAO = 54°$.
3. Draw a circle with *O* as centre and radius = *OA*.
4. On the circle, locate points *C*, *D* and *E* by marking off the arcs consecutively with centres *B*, *C* and *D* and radius *AB*.
5. Join *BC*, *CD*, *DE* and *EA* for the required pentagon.

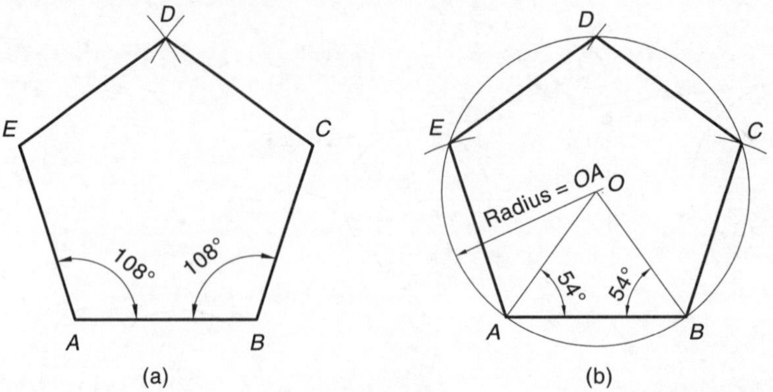

Fig. 4.22

Example 4.18 To construct a regular hexagon of known side *AB*.

Solution

Method 1: Refer Fig. 4.23(a).

1. With any point *O* as centre and radius = *AB*, draw a circle.
2. Starting from any point (say *A*) on the circle, mark off the five arcs of radius = *AB* consecutively cutting the circle at *B*, *C*, *D*, *E* and *F*.
3. Join *A*, *B*, *C*, *D*, *E* and *F* for the required hexagon.

Method 2: Refer Fig. 4.23(b).

1. Draw a line *AD* = 2(*AB*).
2. Through *A* and *D*, draw lines at 60° on either sides of *AB*.
3. On these lines, locate points *B*, *F* and *C*, *E* by marking off the arcs with *A* and *D* as centres and radius = *AB*.
4. Join *A*, *B*, *C*, *D*, *E* and *F*.

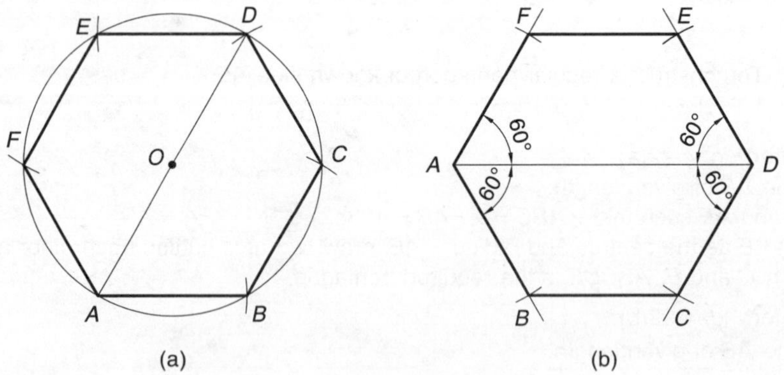

Fig. 4.23

Note: In Fig. 4.23, *AD* may be drawn at required inclination (i.e., horizontal, vertical or inclined) as per the desired inclinations of the sides of the hexagon.

Example 4.19 To draw any regular polygon of known side *AB*.

Solution Refer Fig. 4.24.

1. Draw a line *AB* of given length.
2. At *B*, erect perpendicular *BC* = *AB*. Join *AC*.
3. Obtain perpendicular bisector of *AB* intersecting *AB* at *M*.
4. Locate the point 4 at the intersection of *AC* and the bisector.
5. With centre *A* (or *B*) and radius = *AB*, mark off an arc to cut the bisector at 6.
6. Obtain the midpoint 5 of points 6 and 4.
7. On the bisector, mark points 7, 8, 9, etc., such that 6–7 = 7–8 = 8–9 = 5–6. The basic framework to construct any polygon is now ready.

Figure 4.25 explains how to construct a polygon of any number of sides using the framework shown in Fig. 4.24.

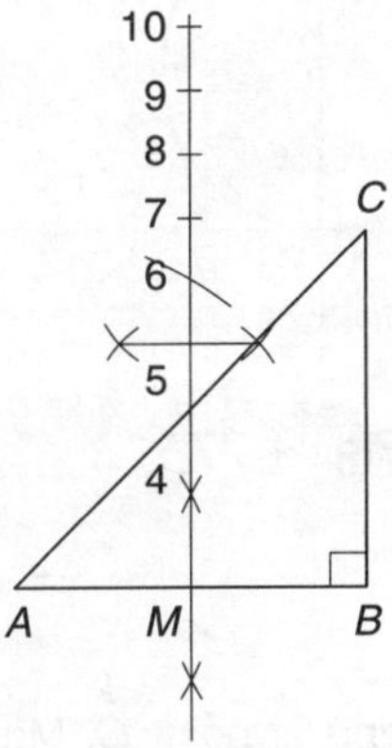

Fig. 4.24

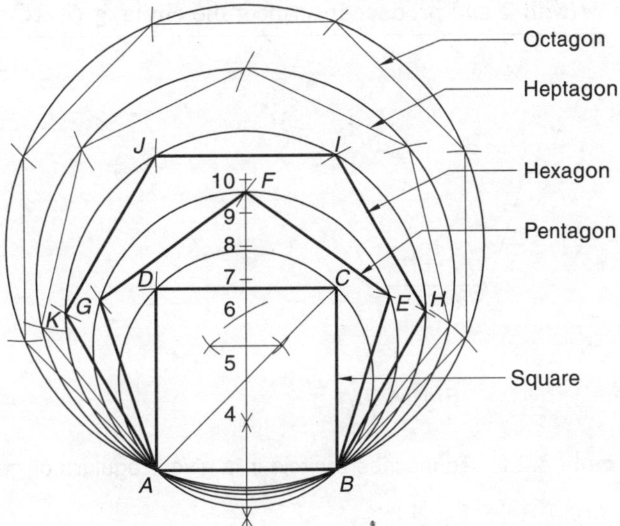

Fig. 4.25

Square With 4 as a centre and radius 4*A*, draw a circle. With *A* and *B* as centres and radius = *AB*, mark off the arcs cutting the circle at *D* and *C* respectively. Join *ABCD* for the required square.

Pentagon With 5 as centre and radius 5*A*, draw a circle. Mark off the arcs successively cutting the circle at *E*, *F* and *G*, with radius = *AB* and centres *B*, *E* and *F* respectively. Join *ABEFG* for the required pentagon.

Hexagon With 6 as centre and radius 6*A*, draw a circle. Mark off the arcs successively cutting the circle at *H*, *I*, *J* and *K*, with radius = *AB* and centres *B*, *H*, *I* and *J* respectively. Join *ABHIJK* for the required hexagon.

The polygons like heptagon, octagon, etc., can be drawn in a similar way.

Example 4.20 To inscribe a regular polygon in a circle of known diameter *AB*.

Solution Let the polygon to be inscribed be a pentagon.
Refer Fig. 4.26.

1. Draw a circle of diameter *AB*.
2. Divide *AB* into the same number of equal parts as the number of sides of the polygon, i.e., 5 in this case. Number the divisions as 1, 2, 3 and 4.
3. With *A* and *B* as the centres and radius = *AB*, mark two arcs intersecting each other at *M*.
4. Join *M*–2 and produce it to meet the circle at *C*. Join *AC*. *AC* represents one of the sides of the required pentagon.
5. Locate points *D*, *E* and *F* on the circle by marking off the arcs of radius *AC* and centres *C*, *D* and *E* respectively.
6. Join *CDEFA* for the required pentagon.

Note: Divide *AB* into 6 equal parts for a hexagon, 7 equal parts for a heptagon and so on. Always join *M* with 2 and produce it to meet the circle at *C*. *AC* always represents a side of the polygon.

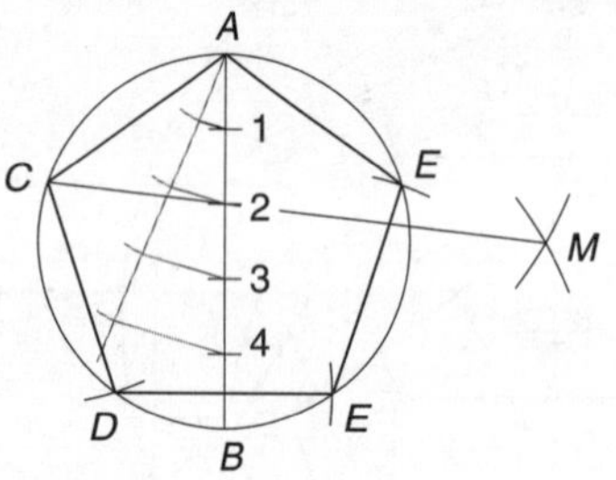

Fig. 4.26

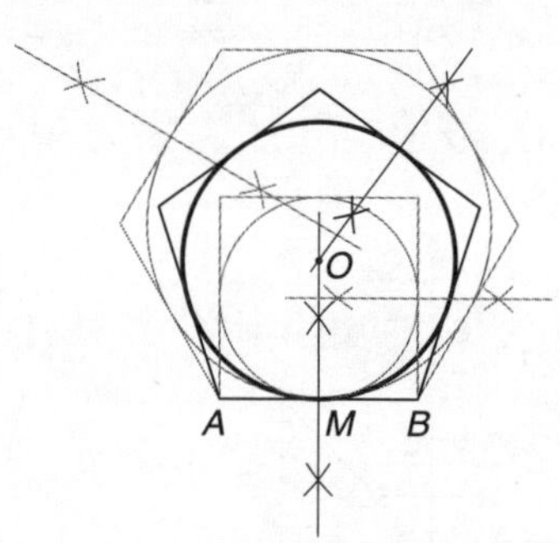

Fig. 4.27

Example 4.21 To inscribe a circle in a given regular polygon.

Solution Refer Fig. 4.27.

1. Draw perpendicular bisectors of any two sides of the polygon meeting at point *O*. Mark point *M* at the intersection of a bisector and the corresponding side (say *AB*).
2. With *O* as centre and radius = *OM*, draw the required circle. It is tangential to all the sides of the polygon.

4.12 TO DRAW AN ARC/A CIRCLE PASSING THROUGH THREE GIVEN POINTS

Example 4.22 To draw an arc (or a circle) passing through three given non-collinear points *A*, *B* and *C*.

Solution Refer Fig. 4.28.

1. Join *AB* and *BC*.
2. Draw perpendicular bisectors of *AB* and *BC* intersecting each other at point *O*. *O* is the centre of the required arc/circle.
3. With *O* as centre and radius = *OA*, draw the required arc/circle.

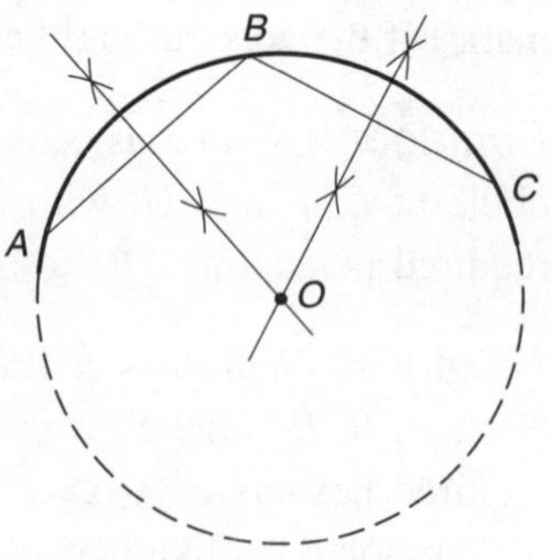

Fig. 4.28

4.13 TO DRAW PARALLEL LINES

Example 4.23 To draw a line passing through a point *P* and parallel to the given line *AB*.

Solution Refer Fig. 4.29.

1. With *A* as centre and radius = *AP*, draw an arc cutting *AB* at *M*. *AB* may be produced if necessary.
2. With *B* as centre and the same radius, draw an arc *ON*, cutting *AB* at *N*.
3. With *N* as centre and radius = *PM*, mark an arc cutting arc *ON* at *Q*.
4. Join *PQ*. *PQ* is parallel to *AB*.

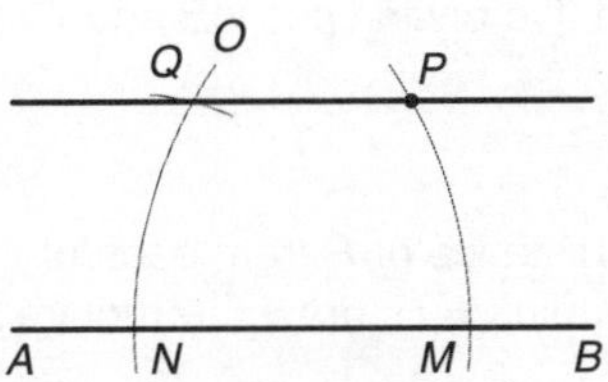

Fig. 4.29

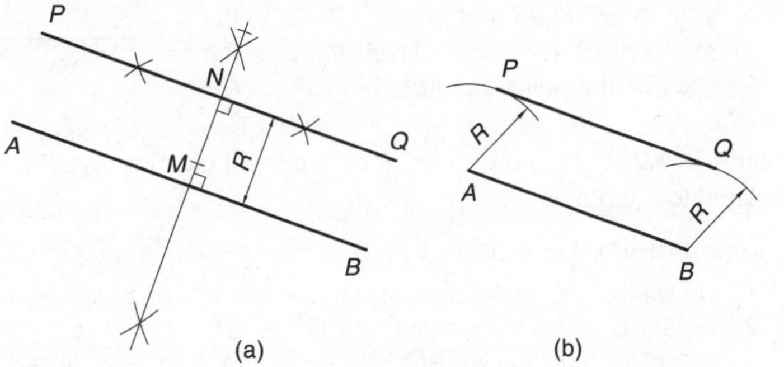

Fig. 4.30

Example 4.24 To draw a line parallel to a given line *AB* and at a given distance *R* from it.

Solution

Method 1: Refer Fig. 4.30(a).

1. Draw a perpendicular bisector of the line *AB*, cutting it at *M*.
2. Set off *MN* = *R*. Draw *PQ* perpendicular to *MN* at *N*. *PQ* is parallel to *AB*.

Method 2: Refer Fig. 4.30(b).

1. With centres *A* and *B* and radius = *R*, draw two arcs on the same side of *AB*.
2. Draw a line *PQ* tangent to both the arcs. *PQ* is parallel to *AB*.

4.14 TO CONSTRUCT AN ANGLE EQUAL TO A GIVEN ANGLE

Example 4.25 To construct an angle equal to a given angle, $\angle AOB$.

Solution Refer Fig. 4.31.

1. With *O* as centre and any convenient radius, draw an arc cutting *OA* and *OB* at *C* and *D* respectively.
2. Draw any line *PQ*. With *P* as centre and the same radius, draw an arc *EF* cutting *PQ* at *E*.
3. With *E* as centre and radius = *CD*, mark an arc cutting *EF* at *G*.
4. Join *PG*. $\angle GPQ$ is the required angle.

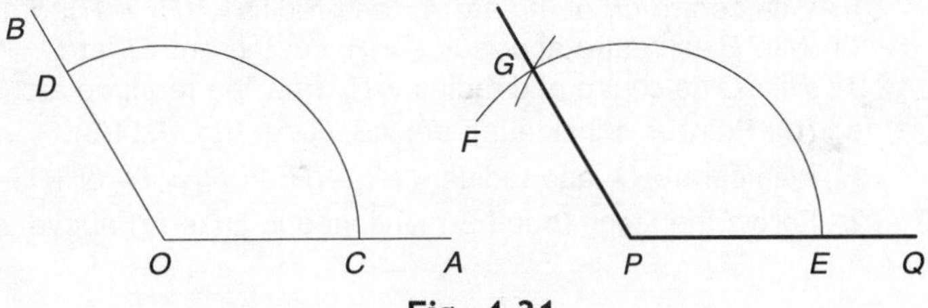

Fig. 4.31

4.15 TO DRAW AN ARC/A CIRCLE TANGENT TO LINE(S)/ARC(S)

Example 4.26 To draw an arc (or a circle) of given radius *R* passing through a given point *P* and tangent to a given line *AB*.

Solution Refer Fig. 4.32.

1. Draw a line *CD* parallel to *AB* at a distance of *R* from *AB*, as explained in Example 4.24.
2. With *P* as centre and radius = *R*, cut *CD* at *O*.
3. With *O* as centre and radius = *R*, draw the required arc (or circle), which touches the line *AB* at a point, say *M*.

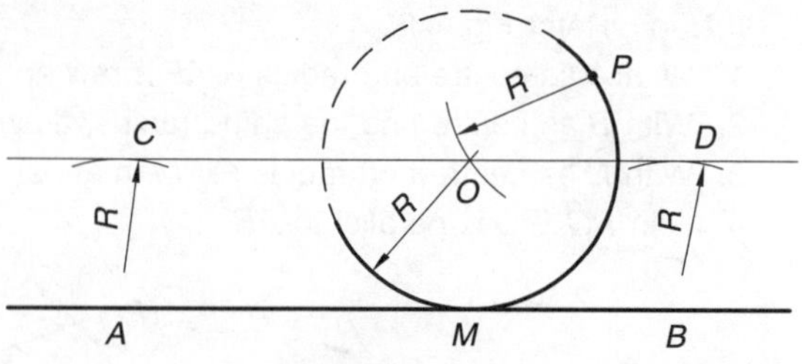

Fig. 4.32

Example 4.27 To draw an arc (or a circle) of given radius *R* tangent to two given lines *AB* and *CD* inclined to each other.

Solution Refer Fig. 4.33.

1. Draw lines *PQ* and *RS* parallel to *AB* and *CD* respectively and at a distance of *R* from each of them.
2. Locate *O* at the intersection of *PQ* and *RS*. With *O* as centre and radius = *R*, draw the required arc (or circle) touching *AB* and *CD*, each at a point, say *M* and *N*.

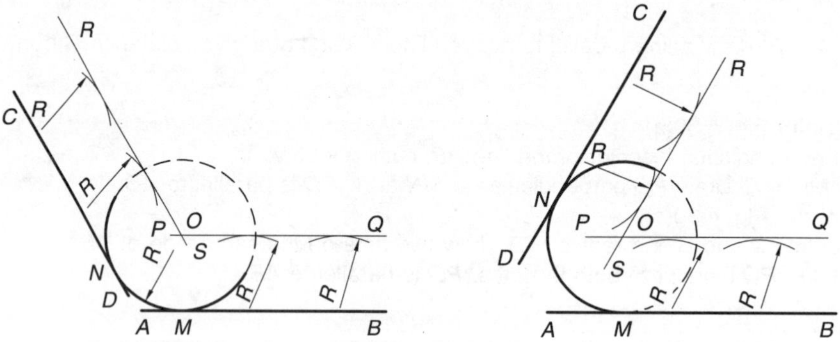

Fig. 4.33

Example 4.28 To draw an arc (or a circle) of given radius *R*, passing through a given point *P* and tangent to a given arc *AB*.

Solution

Case (a): Point *P* is outside the arc *AB*. Refer Fig. 4.34(a).

1. With centre O_1 of the arc *AB* and radius = $(R_1 + R)$, draw an arc *EF*.
2. With *P* as centre and radius = *R*, cut the arc *EF* at *O*.
3. With *O* as centre and radius = *R*, draw the required arc (or circle) touching arc *AB* at a point, say *M*.

Case (b): Point *P* is inside the arc *AB*. Refer Fig. 4.34(b).

1. With centre O_1 and radius = $(R_1 - R)$ [if $R_1 > R$] or $(R - R_1)$ [if $R > R_1$], draw an arc *EF*.
2. Follow the steps 2 and 3 mentioned in case (a) above.

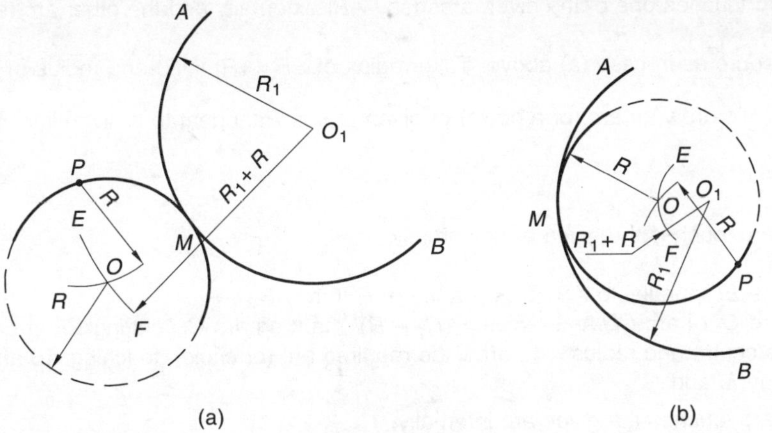

Fig. 4.34

Example 4.29 To draw an arc (or a circle) of given radius R tangent to two given arcs AB and CD.

Solution

Case (a): The arc touches both the given arcs externally.

Refer Fig. 4.35(a).

1. With centre O_1 of arc AB, draw an arc EF of radius = $(R_1 + R)$.
2. With centre O_2 of arc CD, draw an arc GH of radius = $(R_2 + R)$, cutting the arc EF at O.
3. With centre O and radius = R, draw the required arc (or circle), touching each of the arcs AB and CD at a point, say M and N.

Case (b): The arc touches both the given arcs internally.

Refer Fig. 4.35(b).

Repeat the procedure as in case (a) above. Take radius of $EF = (R_1 - R)$ and radius of $GH = (R_2 - R)$.

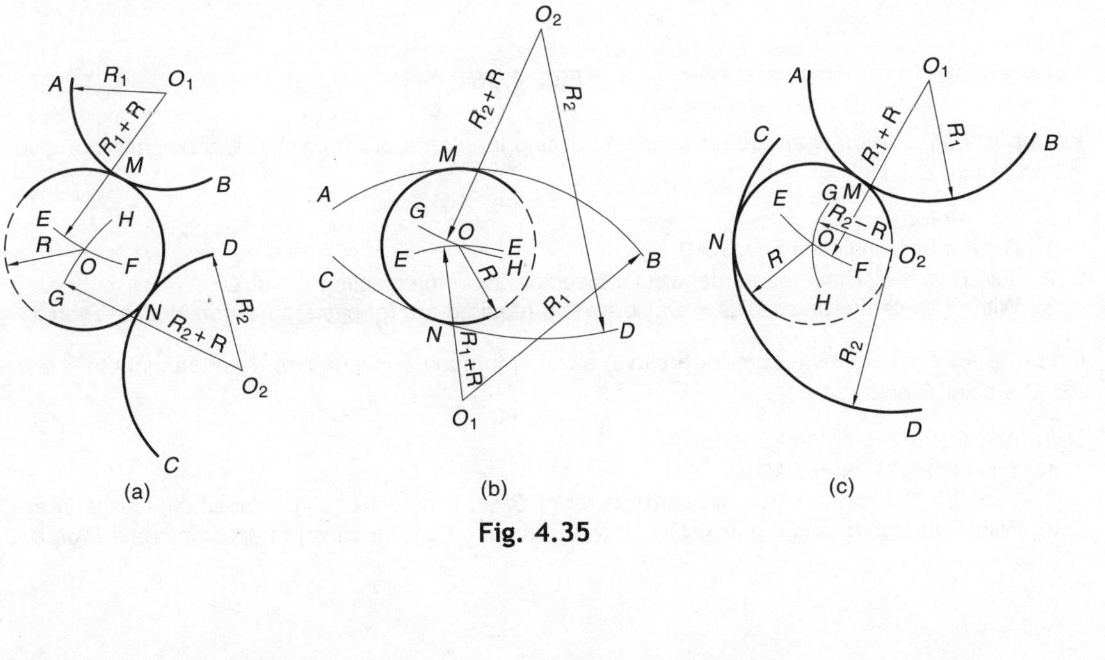

Fig. 4.35

Case (c): The arc touches one of the given arcs (say *AB*) externally and the other arc (say *CD*) internally. Refer Fig. 4.35(c).
Repeat the procedure as in case (a) above. Take radius of $EF = (R_1 + R)$ and radius of $GH = (R_2 - R)$.

Example 4.30 To draw an arc (or a circle) of given radius *R* tangent to a given line *AB* and a given arc *CD*.

Solution

Case (a): The arc touches the given arc externally.
Refer Fig. 4.36(a).

1. Draw a line *EF* parallel to *AB* at a distance of *R* from *AB*.
2. With centre O_1 of arc *CD* and radius = $(R_1 + R)$, mark an arc *GH* cutting *EF* at *O*.
3. With *O* as centre and radius = *R*, draw the required arc (or circle), touching *AB* and arc *CD*, each at a point, say *M* and *N*.

Case (b): The arc touches the given arc internally.
Refer Fig. 4.36(b).
Repeat the procedure as in case (a) above. Take radius of $GH = (R_1 - R)$.

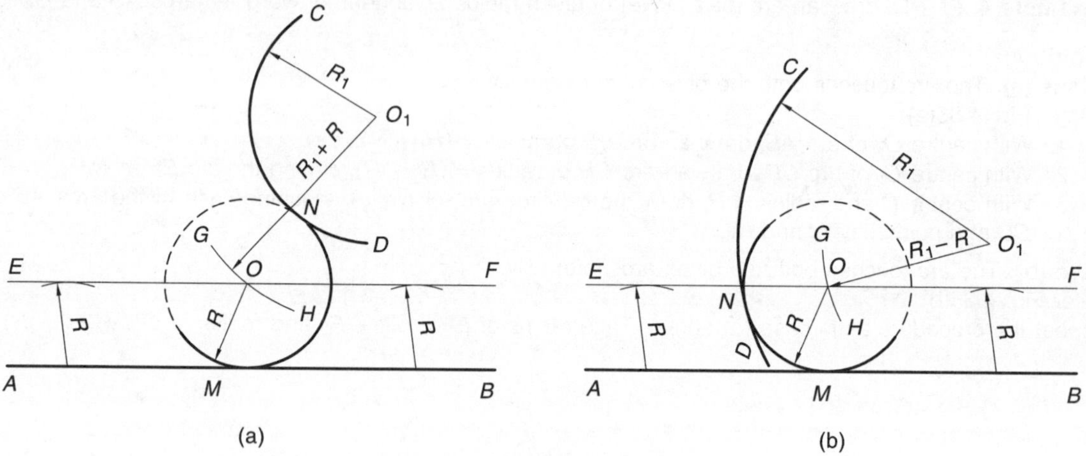

Fig. 4.36

Example 4.31 To draw an arc (or a circle) passing through a given point *P* and tangent to a given line *AB* at a point *C* on it.

Solution Refer Fig. 4.37.

1. Draw a perpendicular *CD* to *AB*.
2. Join *C* with *P*. Draw the perpendicular bisector of *CP* intersecting *CD* at *O*.
3. With *O* as centre and radius = *OC*, draw the required arc (or circle) to accommodate *P* on it.

Example 4.32 To draw an arc (or a circle) passing through a given point *P* and tangent to a given arc *AB* at a point *C* on it.

Solution Refer Fig. 4.38(a) and (b).

1. Join centre O_1 of arc *AB* with *C*.
2. Join *CP*. Obtain the perpendicular bisector of *CP* to intersect O_1C (produced if necessary) at *O*.
3. With *O* as centre and radius = *OC*, draw the required arc (or circle) to accommodate *P* on it.

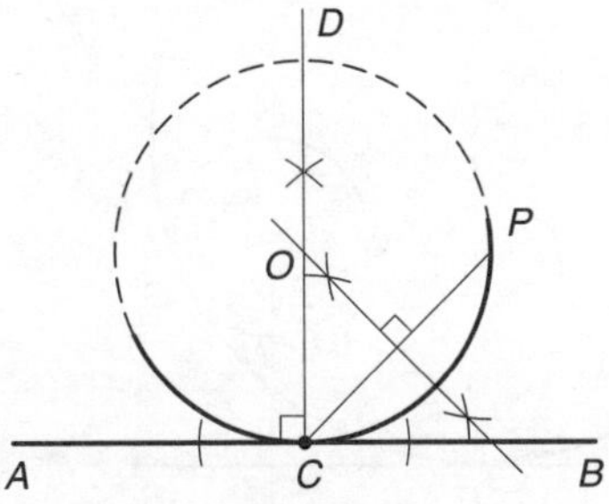

Fig. 4.37

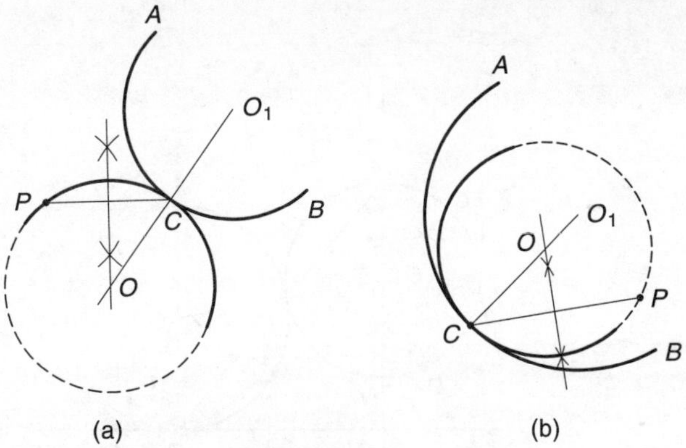

Fig. 4.38

Example 4.33 To draw an arc (or a circle) tangent to a given line *AB* and a given arc *CD* at a point *E* on it.

Solution Refer Fig. 4.39(a) and (b).

1. Join centre O_1 of arc *CD* with *E*. At *E*, draw a tangent to arc *CD* intersecting *AB* at *F*.
2. Obtain a bisector of $\angle EFB$ to intersect O_1E (produced if necessary) at *O*.
3. With *O* as centre and radius = *OE*, draw the required arc (or circle), which touches the line *AB* at a point, say *M*.

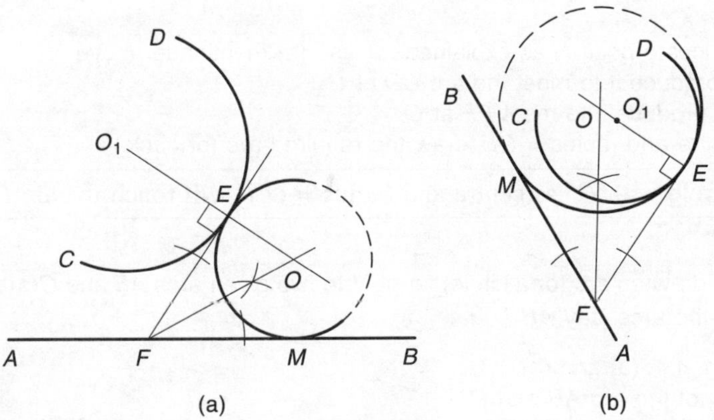

Fig. 4.39

Example 4.34 To draw an arc (or a circle) tangent to a given arc *CD* and a given line *AB* at a given point *E* on it.

Solution

Case (a): The arc touches the given arc externally.

Refer Fig. 4.40(a).

1. Draw perpendicular *EF* to *AB*.

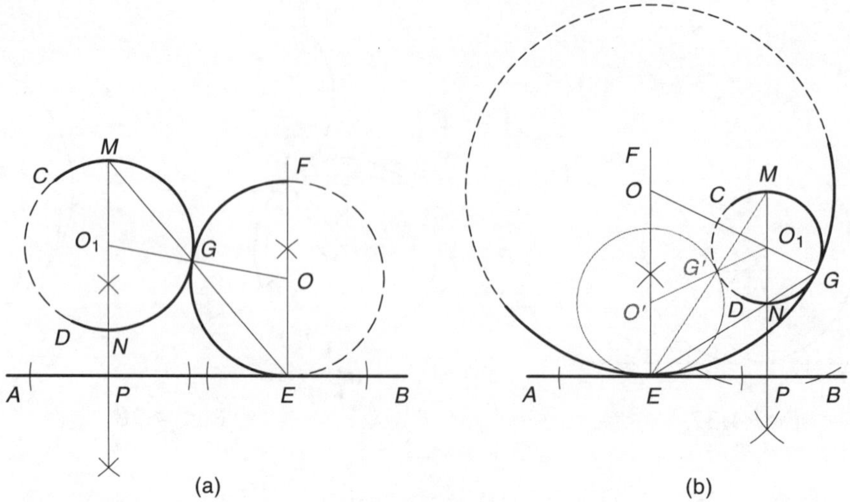

Fig. 4.40

2. From centre O_1 of arc *CD*, draw perpendicular on *AB*, cutting the arc at *N* and the line *AB* at *P*. Produce PO_1 to meet the arc *CD* at *M*.
3. Join *ME* and mark point *G* at its intersection with the arc *CD*.
4. Join O_1G and produce it to meet *EF* at *O*.
5. With *O* as centre and radius *OE*, draw the required arc (or circle).

Case (b): The arc touches the given arc internally.
Refer Fig. 4.40(b).

1. Draw *EF* and locate point *N* as explained in case (a) mentioned above.
2. Join *NE* and produce it to meet the arc *CD* at *G*.
3. Join GO_1 and produce it to meet *EF* at *O*.
4. With *O* as centre and radius = *OE*, draw the required arc (or circle).

Note: Another circle with O' as centre and radius = $O'E$ will touch the arc *CD* externally.

Example 4.35 To draw an arc (or a circle) tangent to two given arcs *AB* and *CD* (or two given circles) at a point *P* on one of the arcs, say *AB*.

Solution Refer Fig. 4.41(a) and (b).

1. Join centre O_1 of the arc *AB* with *P*.
2. Draw a line through centre O_2 of the arc *CD* parallel to O_1P and intersecting the arc *CD* at *E* (or *E′*).
3. Join *E* (or *E′*) with *P*. Locate *G* (or *G′*) at the intersection of *PE* (or *PE′*), produced if necessary, with the arc *CD*.
4. Join O_2G (or O_2G') and produce it if necessary to mark its intersection with O_1P (produced) at *O* (or *O′*). *O* (or *O′*) is the centre of the required arc/circle.
5. With *O* (or *O′*) as centre and radius = *OP* (or *O′P*) draw the required arc (or circle).

Example 4.36 To draw a smooth continuous curve of circular arcs passing through any number of non-collinear points, say *A, B, C, D* and *E*.

Solution Refer Fig. 4.42.

1. Join *AB, BC, CD* and *DE*.

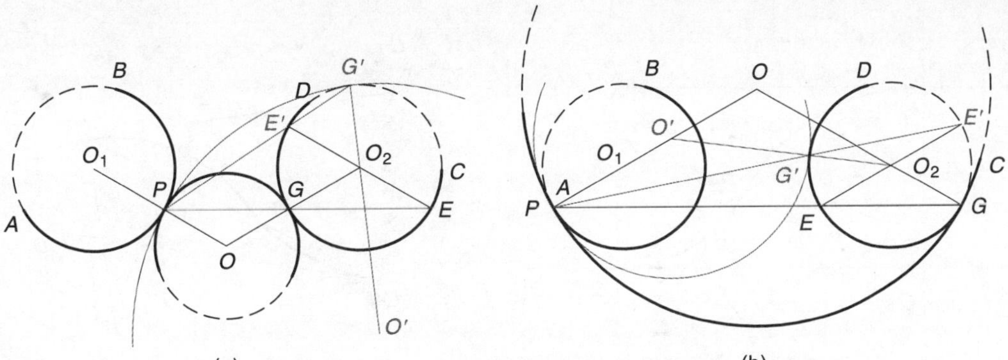

(a) (b)

Fig. 4.41

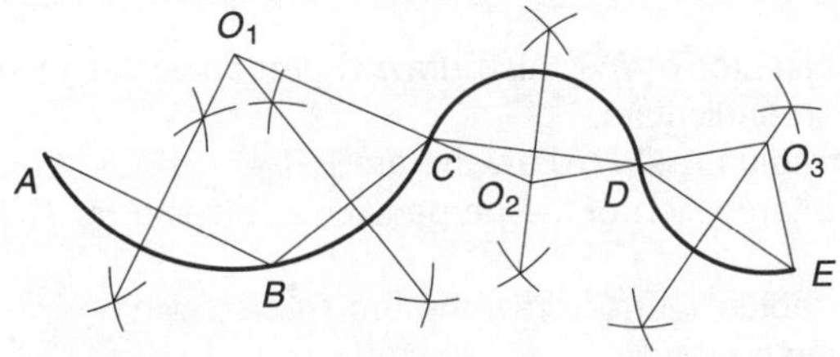

Fig. 4.42

2. Draw perpendicular bisectors of *AB* and *BC* to meet at O_1.
3. With O_1 as a centre and radius = O_1A, draw an arc *ABC*.
4. Join O_1C. Draw the perpendicular bisector of *CD* to meet O_1C produced at O_2.
5. With O_2 as centre and radius = O_2C, draw the arc *CD*.
6. Join O_2D. Draw the perpendicular bisector of *DE* to meet O_2D produced at O_3.
7. With O_3 as centre and radius = O_3D, draw the arc *DE*.

The above procedure may be repeated for any number of given points. Note that each arc is tangent to the arc that follows it.

4.16 TO DRAW REVERSE OR OGEE CURVES

The reverse (or ogee) curve is a curve composed of two consecutive tangent circular arcs that curve in opposite directions.

Example 4.37 To draw a reverse curve tangent to two parallel or inclined lines *AB* and *CD* at given points (say *P* and *Q*) on them.

Solution Refer Fig. 4.43(a) and (b).

In Fig. 4.43(a), the two lines *AB* and *CD* are parallel to each other. In Fig. 4.43(b), the two lines are inclined to each other.

1. Join *P* with *Q*. On *PQ*, mark any point *R* at which the curve is supposed to change the direction.

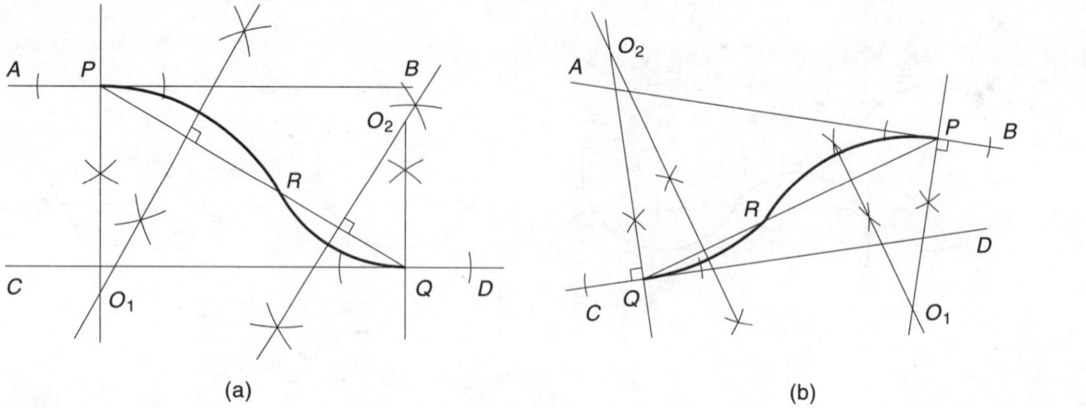

Fig. 4.43

2. Draw a perpendicular bisector of PR. Also draw a perpendicular to AB at P. Mark point O_1 at the intersection of these perpendiculars.
3. With O_1 as centre and radius = O_1P, draw the arc PR.
4. Locate point O_2 at the intersection of the perpendicular bisector of RQ and the perpendicular to CD at Q.
5. With O_2 as centre and radius = O_2Q, draw the arc RQ.
   PRQ is the desired reverse curve.

Example 4.38 To draw a reverse curve tangent to three intersecting lines AB, BC and CD.

Solution Refer Fig. 4.44.

1. Mark point R anywhere on BC at which the curve is supposed to change the direction.
2. Mark P on AB and Q on CD such that $BP = BR$ and $CR = CQ$.
3. Draw a perpendicular to AB at P and to BC at R. Mark O_1 at their intersections.
4. With O_1 as a centre and radius = O_1P, draw the arc PR.
5. Draw a perpendicular to CD at Q to meet O_1R produced at O_2.
6. With O_2 as centre and radius = O_2Q, draw the arc RQ. PRQ is the desired reverse curve.

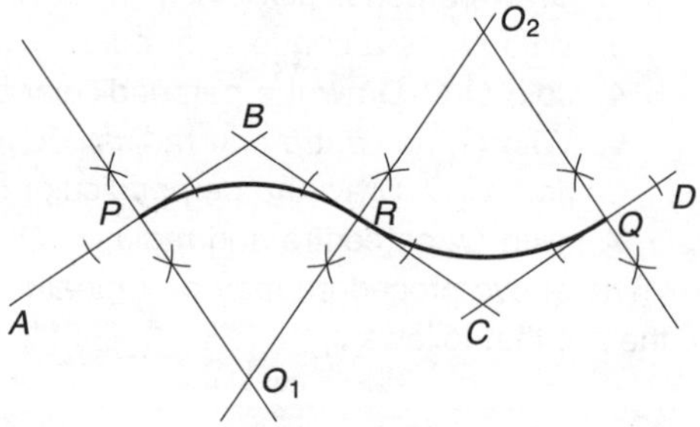

Fig. 4.44

Illustrative Problems

Problem 4.1 Draw three circles of diameter 50 mm, each tangent to other two.

Solution Refer Fig. 4.45.

1. With any point O_1 as centre and radius = 25 mm, draw a circle.
2. Locate O_2 such that O_1O_2 = 50 mm. Draw second circle with O_2 as centre and radius = 25 mm.
3. Mark-off two arcs with O_1 and O_2 as the centres and radius = 50 mm, meeting each other at O_3. Draw third circle with O_3 as a centre and radius = 25 mm.
   The three circles touch each other.

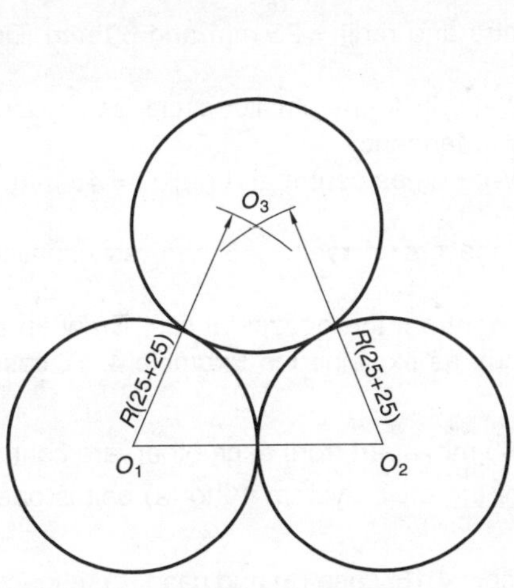

Fig. 4.45

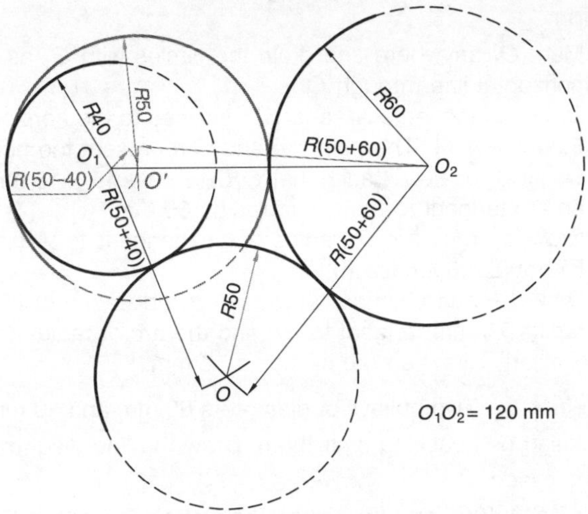

Fig. 4.46

Problem 4.2 Draw two arcs of radii 40 mm and 60 mm having their centres 120 mm apart. Draw a third arc of radius 50 mm tangent to both the arcs.

Solution Refer Fig. 4.46.

This problem is similar to Example 4.29, Fig. 4.35(a) and (c). Two possibilities exist: (i) the third arc touches both the given arcs externally, (ii) the third arc touches one of the given arcs externally and the other arc internally. Therefore, adopt steps as mentioned in Example 4.29, case (a) and case (c).

Problem 4.3 Redraw Fig. 4.47.

Solution

1. Draw O_2O_3 = 60 mm. Mark O_1 at the midpoint of O_2O_3.
2. With O_1 as centre and radii = 15 mm and 45 mm, draw two circles. Locate O_4 and O_5 at the intersection of the smaller circle and O_2O_3.
3. With O_2 and O_3 as the centres and radius = 15 mm, draw two semicircles.
4. With O_4 and O_5 as the centres and radius = 30 mm, draw two semicircles.

Problem 4.4 Redraw the spanner shown in Fig. 4.48.

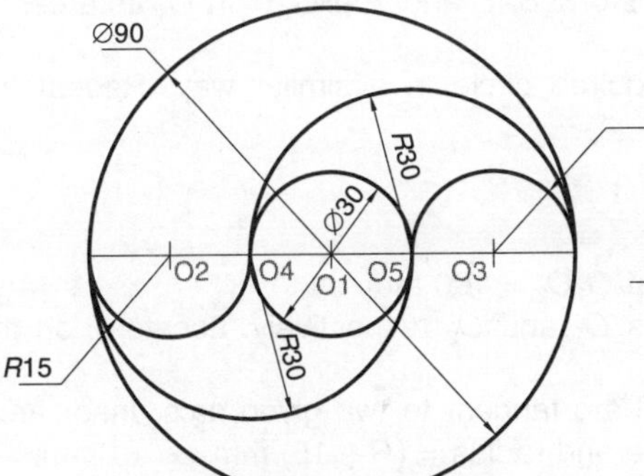

Fig. 4.47

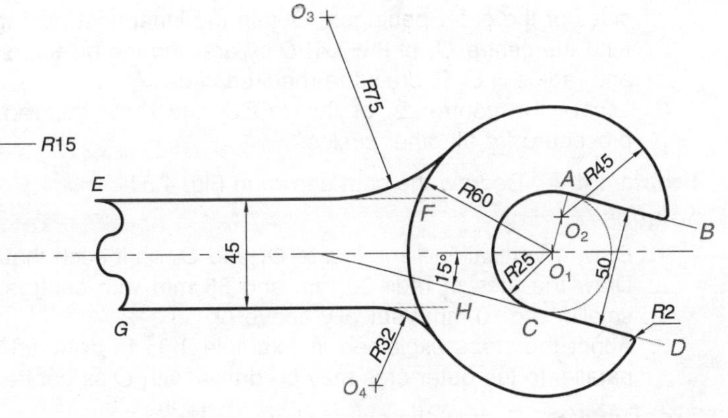

Fig. 4.48

Solution

1. Mark O_1 anywhere and draw the circles with O_1 as centre and radii = 25 mm and 60 mm. Draw a horizontal line through O_1.
2. Draw the tangents *AB* and *CD*, inclined to the horizontal at 15°, to the smaller circle, as explained in Example 4.14. The points *A* and *C* represent the points of tangency.
3. On AO_1, locate O_2 such that $O_1O_2 = 60 - 45 = 15$ mm. With O_2 as centre and radius = 45 mm, draw an arc tangent to the arc of radius 60 mm.
4. Draw a small arc of radius 2 mm tangent to *AB* and the arc of radius 45 mm, as explained in Example 4.30, case (b).
5. Draw *EF* and *GH* parallel to and at a distance of 22.5 mm from the horizontal line. Draw an arc of radius 75 mm tangent to *EF* and the arc of radius 60 mm, as explained in Example 4.30, case (a). Similarly, draw an arc of radius 32 mm.

Problem 4.5 Two pulleys of diameters 60 mm and 30 mm, 80 mm apart from each other, are connected by a closed belt passing over them. Draw the line diagrams of the drive system if the (a) belt is open (b) belt is crossed

Refer Fig. 4.49(a) and (b). Follow the steps explained in Example 4.16, case (a) and case (b) respectively.

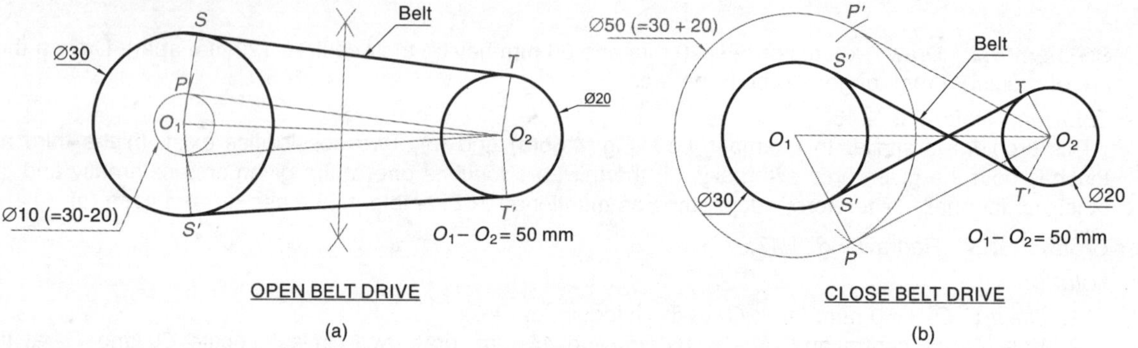

Fig. 4.49

Problem 4.6 Redraw the arrangement shown in Fig. 4.50.

Solution

1. Draw the outer pentagon of side 60 mm. Draw the inner pentagon by joining the midpoints of the sides of the outer pentagon. Obtain the innermost pentagon in a similar way.
2. Find the centre O_1 of the ΔABC by drawing the bisectors of $\angle BAC$ and $\angle ABC$. With O_1 as a centre and radius = O_1D, draw the required circle.
3. Locate the centre O_2 of the ΔEDO and draw the required circle in a similar way. Repeat the procedure for all other circles.

Problem 4.7 Redraw the cam shown in Fig. 4.51.

Solution

1. Draw a vertical line and locate O_1 and O_2 on it such that $O_1O_2 = 100$ mm.
2. Draw the arcs of radii 20 mm and 35 mm with centres O_1 and O_2 respectively. Locate *P* on the smaller arc 10 mm vertically above O_1.
3. Adopt the steps explained in Example 4.35 to draw an arc tangent to two given arcs. Inner arcs, parallel to the outer arcs may be drawn with *O* as centre and radius = $(R - 15)$ mm.

Problem 4.8 Redraw the object shown in Fig. 4.52.

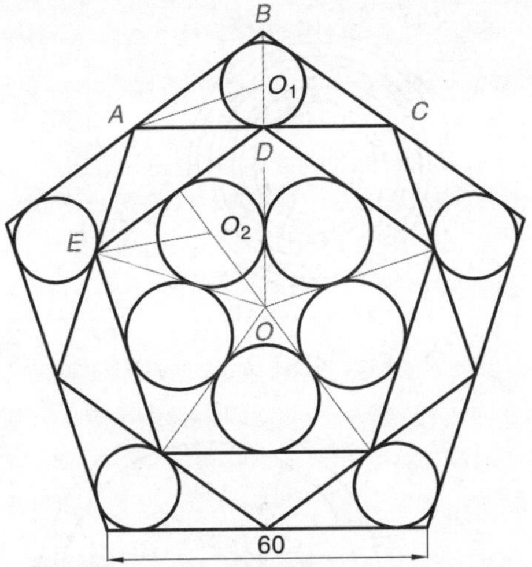

The corners of each inner pentagon lie at the midpoints of the sides of the outer pentagon.

Fig. 4.50

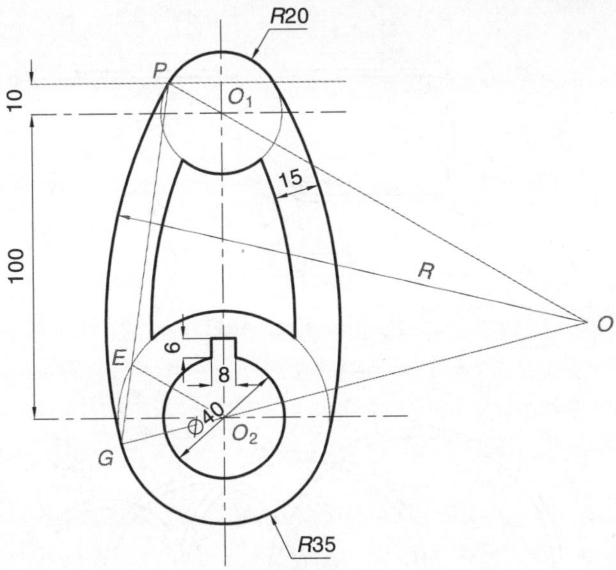

Fig. 4.51

Solution

1. Draw a vertical line and locate *P*, *Q* and *R* on it at given distances.
2. With *P* as centre and radii = 5 mm and 10 mm, draw two circles.
3. With *Q* as centre and radii = 12 mm and 20 mm, draw two circles.
4. With *R* as centre and radius = 6 mm, draw a circle. Draw line *AB* parallel to and at a distance of 3 mm from the vertical line.
5. Draw an arc of radius 10 mm tangent to the circle of radius 10 mm and the circle of radius 20 mm as explained in Example 4.29, case (a).
6. Draw an arc of radius 40 mm tangent to the circle of radius 20 mm and the line *AB* as explained in Example 4.30, case (a).
7. Draw the remaining half in a similar way. The construction of internal details is simple and need not be explained.

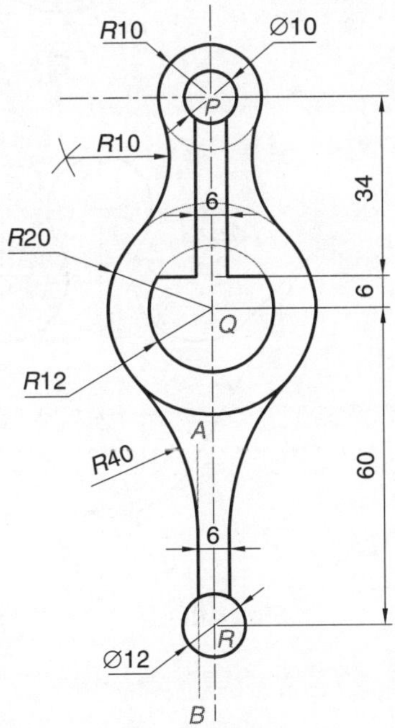

Fig. 4.52

Review Questions

1. Redraw the drawing clip shown in Fig. 4RQ.1.
2. Redraw the coil shown in Fig. 4RQ.2.
3. Redraw the object shown in Fig. 4RQ.3.
4. Redraw the steering wheel shown in Fig. 4RQ.4.
5. Redraw the object shown in Fig. 4RQ.5.
6. Redraw the Geneva cam shown in Fig. 4RQ.6.
7. Redraw the Fig. 4RQ.7.
8. Redraw the Fig. 4RQ.8.

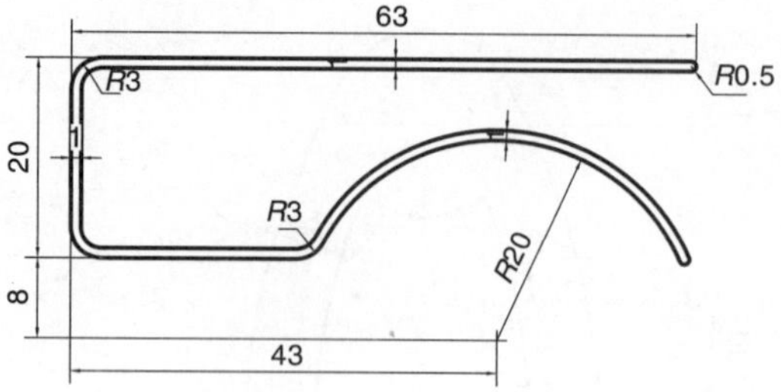

Fig. 4RQ.1

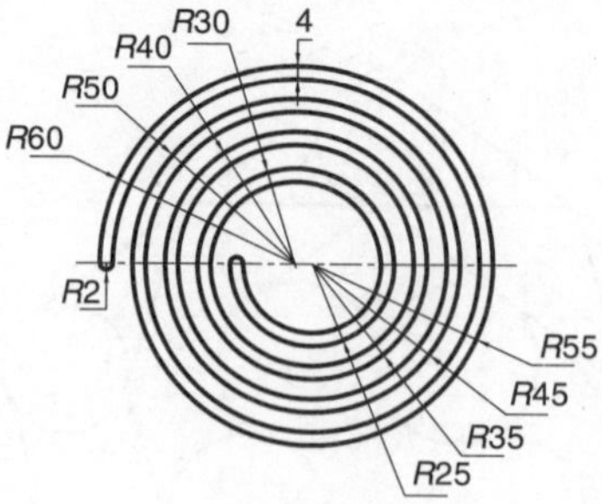

Fig. 4RQ.2

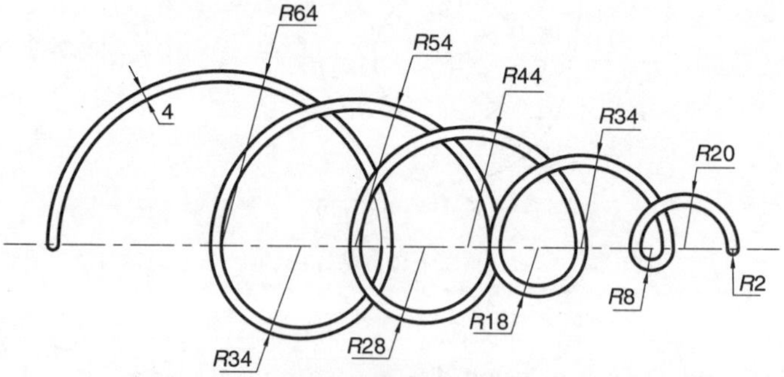

Fig. 4RQ.3

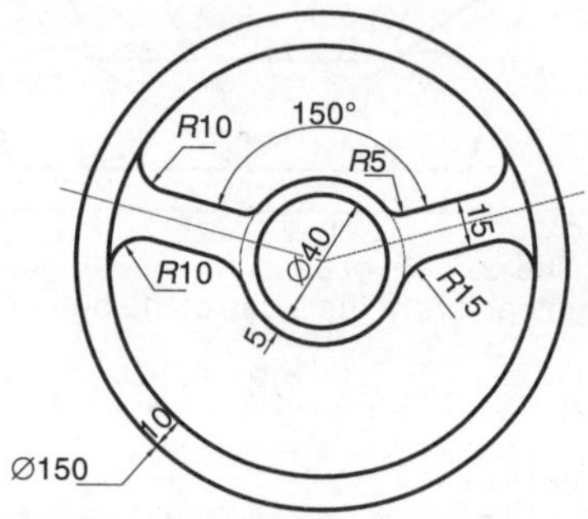

Fig. 4RQ.4

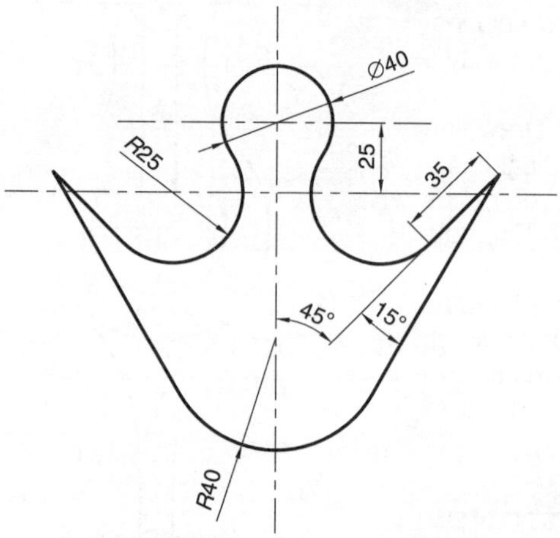

Fig. 4RQ.5

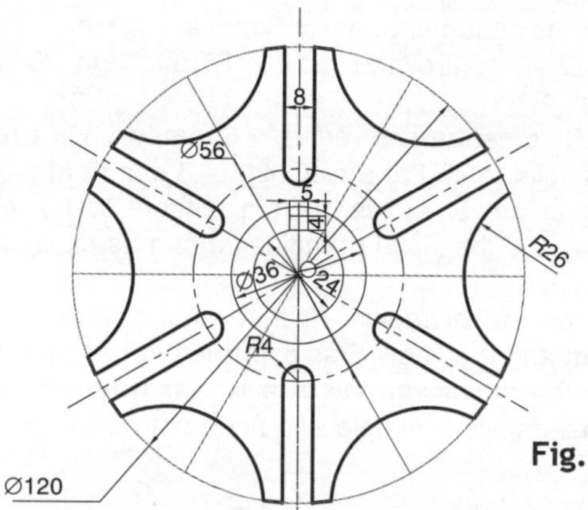

Fig. 4RQ.6

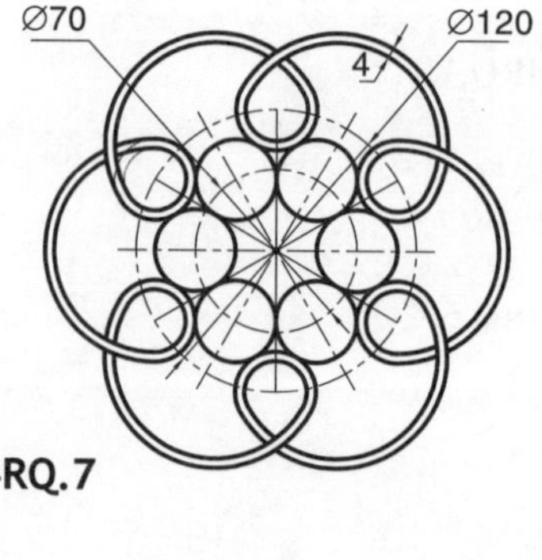

Fig. 4RQ.7

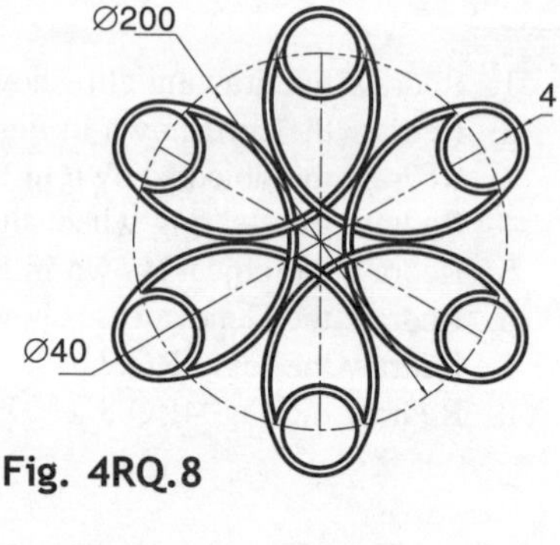

Fig. 4RQ.8

Chapter 5

SCALES

5.1 INTRODUCTION

Objects around us vary greatly in size. An object may be as small as a wristwatch gear or as huge as a ship. While drawing these objects on paper, one needs to enlarge or reduce them depending on their actual sizes. Clearly, smaller objects need to be enlarged while larger objects need to be reduced. Some objects can also be drawn exactly as their actual sizes on a given size of paper. The proportion by which the drawing of a given object is enlarged or reduced is called the *scale* of the drawing.

5.2 REPRESENTATIVE FRACTION

The scale of a drawing is indicated by a ratio, called the *Representative Fraction* (RF) or *Scale Factor*. RF is a ratio of the length of an object on a drawing to the actual length of the object.

i.e., RF = (Length on drawing)/(Actual length)

If a 1.5 m long steel bar is shown by a 15 cm long line on a drawing then, RF = 15 cm/1.5 m = 15 cm/150 cm = 1/10.

Note that while calculating RF, both the lengths should have same units. All other dimensions of the object should be drawn to the same RF.

The terms 'scale' and 'RF' are synonymous. The scale is most commonly expressed in the format $X:Y$ while RF is expressed in the format X/Y. In case of the steel bar mentioned above, the scale will be 1:10.

The scale must invariably be mentioned on the drawing. It is written in the format: SCALE $X:Y$, by letters of appropriate height. If the scale is the same for all the objects on a drawing sheet, it is written in the title block or above the title block. If different objects are drawn to different scales on a sheet then the scale for each object is mentioned below the drawing of that object. In such cases, the scale may be enclosed in a rectangle of appropriate size.

5.2.1 Enlarging or Enlargement Scales

As already mentioned, when smaller objects are to be drawn, they often need to be enlarged. The scales used in such cases are called *enlarging scales*. Obviously, the length of an object on the drawing is more than the corresponding actual length of the object. Enlarging scales are mentioned in the format $X : 1$, where X is greater than 1. Clearly, RF > 1.

Enlarging scales are used for objects like screws and gears used in small electronic gadgets, wristwatch parts, resistors, transistors, ICs, etc., *Illustration 5.1*.

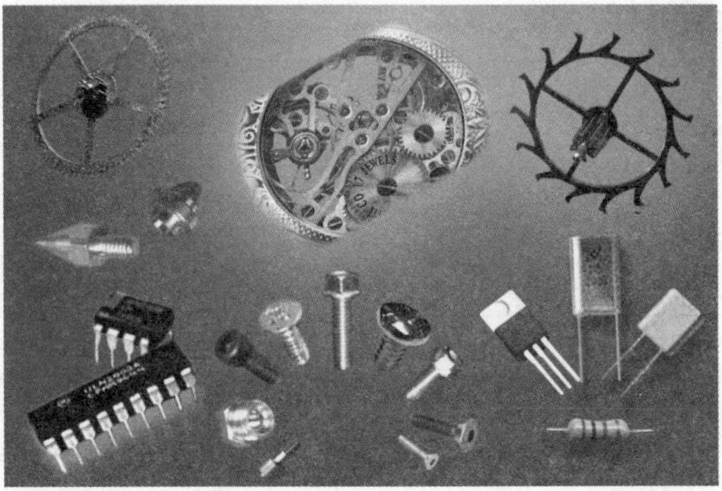

Illustration 5.1 These objects are drawn to an enlarging scale

5.2.2 Reducing or Reduction Scales

When huge objects are to be drawn, they are reduced in size on the drawing. The scales used for these objects are called *reducing scales*. It is clear that the length of the object on the drawing is less than the actual length of the object. Reducing scales are mentioned in the format $1 : Y$, where Y is greater than 1. Hence, RF < 1.

Objects like multistoreyed buildings, bridges, boilers, huge machinery, ships, aeroplanes, etc., are drawn to reducing scales, *Illustration 5.2*.

5.2.3 Full Scale

When an object is drawn on the sheet to its actual size, it is said to be drawn to *full scale*. As the length on the drawing is equal to the actual length of the object, the full scale is expressed as 1:1. Obviously, for full scale, RF = 1.

Illustration 5.3 shows some common objects that may be drawn to full scale.

The scales recommended for technical drawing by BIS (SP 46:2003) are given in Table 5.1.

Illustration 5.2 These objects are drawn to a reducing scale

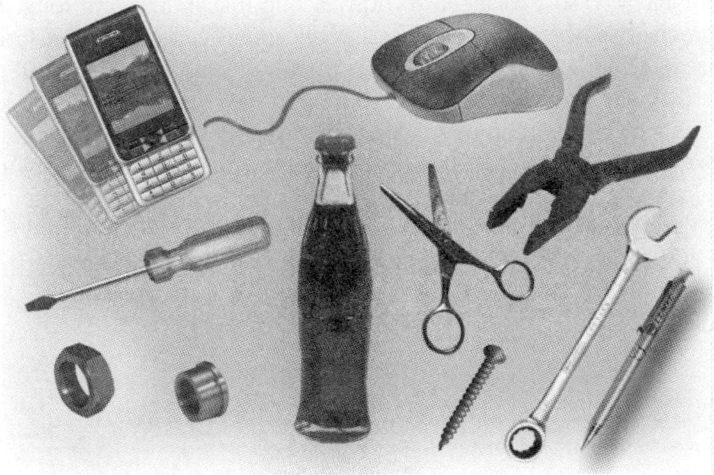

Illustration 5.3 These objects may be drawn to full scale

Table 5.1 BIS Recommended Scales

Category	*Format*	*Recommended Scales**		
Enlarging Scale	$X : 1$ $(X > 1)$	50:1	20:1	10:1
		5:1	2:1	
Full Scale	1 : 1	1:1		
Reducing Scale	$1 : Y$ $(Y > 1)$	1:2	1:5	1:10
		1:20	1:50	1:100
		1:200	1:500	1:1000
		1:2000	1:5000	1:10000

*Intermediate scales may be used in exceptional cases where recommended scales cannot be applied for functional reasons.

REMEMBER THE FOLLOWING

- RF = X/Y, where X = length on drawing and Y = actual length of the object

  $= (\sqrt{X^2})/(\sqrt{Y^2})$, where X^2 = area on drawing and Y^2 = actual area

  $= (\sqrt[3]{X^3})/(\sqrt[3]{Y^3})$, where X^3 = volume on drawing or model and Y^3 = actual volume
- Enlargement Scale: $X : 1$ ($X > 1$)
- Reduction Scale: $1 : Y$ ($Y > 1$)
- Full Scale: 1:1

5.3 TYPES OF SCALES

An engineer has to precisely show very large distances on a drawing sheet while planning big projects. This is especially needed for surveying, planning and mapping of civil engineering projects like constructions of bridges, dams, roads and railways. A very high level of precision and accuracy cannot be achieved by using ordinary enlarging or reducing scales. For example, to show a distance of 593 km on a scale of RF = $1/10^7$, we need to draw a line that is 5.93 cm long. It is not possible to show this distance precisely since an ordinary measuring rule is capable of measuring up to 0.1 cm (or 0.05 cm in some cases). Often an engineer has to compare distances measured in different systems of units or find out the distance exactly equivalent to a particular distance measured in some other unit. Both these difficulties can be overcome by using special types of engineering scales. These scales enable not only to set off the required distances and angles precisely on a drawing sheet but also to compare lengths measured in different units.

The following scales are used by engineers:

1. Plain Scales
2. Vernier Scales
3. Diagonal Scales
4. Comparative or Corresponding Scales
5. Scale of Chords

5.4 UNITS OF LENGTH AND THEIR CONVERSION

Before we proceed to the various types of scales, let us see the various units of length and their subdivisions. The SI unit of length is metre. However, metre is too large a unit to show on the drawing sheet. Therefore, the smaller divisions of metre, i.e., centimetre or millimetre are conveniently used as units of length on a drawing. Most often, the millimetre is used as a drawing unit since it can be measured precisely by an ordinary measuring rule.

Table 5.2 shows the various units of length and their relationships.

5.5 CONSTRUCTION OF SCALES: GENERAL PROCEDURE

All the scales (except the scale of chords) are constructed by drawing a line of length equivalent to the actual distance to be represented. This length is called *length of scale* (LOS). LOS is calculated by the formula

$$\text{LOS} = \text{RF} \times \text{Maximum distance to be represented}$$

Table 5.2 Units of Length

Unit	*Abbreviation*	*Relationships*
		Metric Units
Millimetre	mm	
Centimetre	cm	= 10 mm
Decimetre	dm	= 10 cm = 10^2 mm
Metre	m	= 10 dm = 10^2 cm = 10^3 mm
Decametre	dam	= 10 m = 10^2 dm = 10^3 cm = 10^4 mm
Hectometre	hm	= 10 dam = 10^2 m = 10^3 dm = 10^4 cm = 10^5 mm
Kilometre	km	= 10 hm = 10^2 dam = 10^3 m = 10^4 dm = 10^5 cm = 10^6 mm
		Imperial Units
Inch	in	
Foot	ft	= 12 in
Yard	yd	= 3 ft = 36 in
Furlong	fur	= 220 yd = 660 ft = 7920 in
Mile	mi	= 8 fur = 1760 yd = 5280 ft = 63360 in
Nautical Mile (International)	nmi	= 6080 ft
	Imperial to Metric Conversion	
	Imperial	Metric
	in	= 2.54 cm
	yd	= 0.91 m
	mi	= 1.61 km
	nmi	= 1.85 km

Note: In architectural and civil engineering drawing, foot and inch are indicated by the symbols ' and " respectively. For example, 3 ft 4 in = 3'4".

LOS is usually calculated in terms of centimetre or millimetre. If the maximum distance to be represented is not known, it may be taken equal to the maximum measurement (rounded off to the higher whole number) to be made with the help of the scale. In the absence of any data, LOS may be assumed 15 to 30 cm.

Thus, to construct scales, we need the following information:

1. RF of the scale
2. Unit of measurement
3. Maximum distance to be represented

The general procedure to construct the scales (except the scale of chords) is explained below. The procedure for the scale of chords is explained separately.

1. Calculate RF, if not given.
2. Calculate LOS.
3. Draw a line = LOS. Divide this line into the required number of equal parts. The divisions thus obtained are called *main divisions.* Each main division will indicate the main unit of measurement, say metre.
4. Mark zero (0) at the end of the first main division. Number the main divisions rightward from zero.

5. Divide the first main division into the required number of equal parts. The *subdivisions* thus obtained will indicate subunits of the main unit, say decimetre. Number the subdivisions leftward from zero. Write the main unit (say METRE) below the right end of the scale and the sub-unit (say DECIMETRE) below the first main division. RF should also be mentioned below the scale.

The plain scales and vernier scales are drawn as 3–4 mm thick bars. The subdivision (and also the main divisions) may be darkened alternately to differentiate between two adjacent subdivisions (or main divisions). One may draw small, thick horizontal lines across the alternate subdivisions or main divisions instead of darkening them. This is illustrated in the examples. This avoids confusion during measurement and improves the readability of scales.

The steps 1 to 5 give the common procedure for all the scales. The scales other than plain scales need some additional constructions.

5.6 PLAIN SCALES

A plain scale is used to indicate the distances in a unit and its immediate subdivision, e.g. m and dm, or yards and feet. Plain scales are simple in construction. These are constructed by the procedure explained in the previous section.

Example 5.1 Construct a plain scale of RF = 1/100 to read metres and decimetres and long enough to measure 10 metres. Show a distance of 7.6 metres on it.

Solution

$$RF = \frac{1}{100}$$

$$LOS = RF \times \text{maximum distance to be measured}$$

$$= \frac{1}{100} \times (10 \times 100)\text{ cm} = 10\text{ cm}$$

Refer Fig. 5.1.

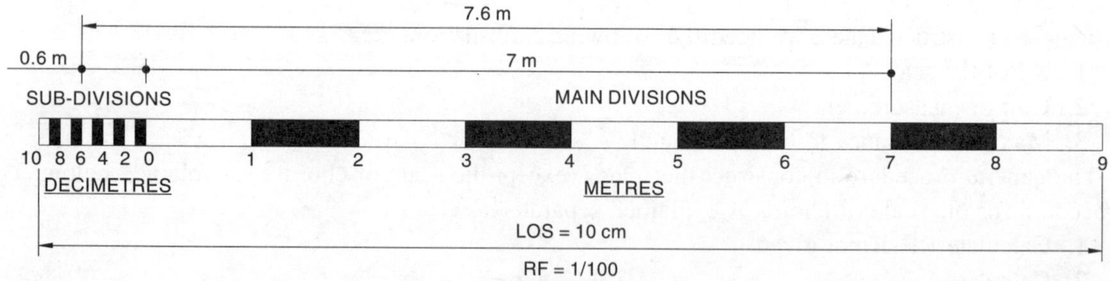

Fig. 5.1

Draw a 10 cm long line. Divide it into 10 equal parts. Each main division will indicate 1 metre. Mark zero (0) at the end of the first main division and number the main divisions on the right of zero as 1, 2, 3, ..., 9. Now, divide the first main division into 10 equal parts. Each subdivision will represent 1 decimetre. Number the subdivisions on the left of zero as 1, 2, 3 ..., 10. The distance of 7.6 metres can be shown in two parts, i.e., 7 metre + 0.6 metre. 7 metre is shown on the main divisions and 0.6 metre (i.e., 6 decimetres) on the subdivisions.

Example 5.2 Construct a plain scale of 1: 60000 to read kilometres and hectometres and long enough to show 7.5 kilometres. Show on this scale the distances 0.4 kilometres, 3.9 kilometres, and 6.2 kilometres.

Solution

$$\text{RF} = \frac{1}{60000}$$

$$\text{LOS} = \frac{1}{60000} \times 7.5 \text{ km}$$

$$= \left(\frac{1}{60000}\right) \times 7.5 \times 1000 \times 100 \text{ cm} = 12.5 \text{ cm}$$

Refer Fig. 5.2.

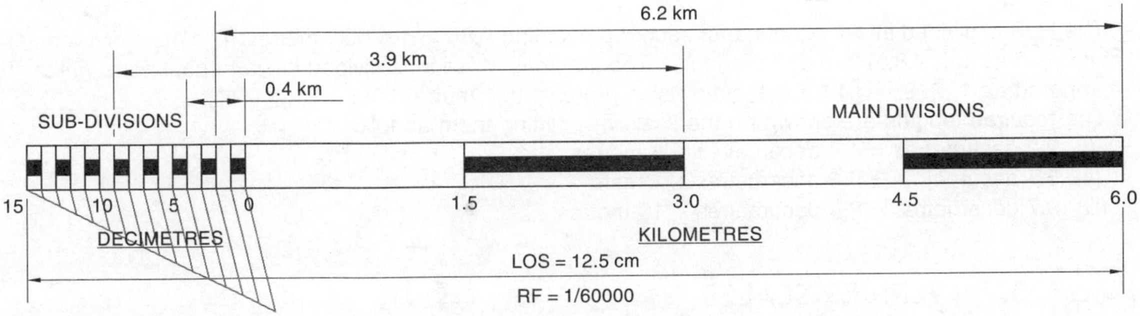

Fig. 5.2

Draw a 12.5 cm long line and divide it into 5 equal parts. Each main division will indicate 7.5/5 = 1.5 kilometres. Mark zero at the end of the first main division and number the other main divisions as 1.5, 3.0, 4.5 and 6.0. Divide the first main division into 15 equal parts so that each subdivision will indicate 1 hectometre. Number the subdivisions leftward as 1, 2, 3, ..., 15. Show the distances 0.4 kilometre (= 4 hectometres), 3.9 kilometres (= 3 kilometres + 9 hectometres) and 6.2 kilometres (= 6 kilometres + 2 hectometres) as indicated on the figure.

Note that, in this problem we have not divided the LOS into 10 equal parts. Had it been done, a main division would have been equal to 0.75 kilometre. Further, one subdivision, obtained after dividing the main division into 10 equal parts, would have shown 0.75 hectometre. This would have posed a difficulty in measurement. Therefore, the main divisions and sub-divisions should be obtained in such a way that one subdivision will indicate a whole number unit of length.

Example 5.3 A rectangular garden of area 196 m^2 is shown on a map by a similar rectangle of 4 cm^2. Construct a plain scale to read up to a single metre and long enough to measure up to 9.8 decametres. Show the distances of (i) 2.2 decametres (ii) 5.7 decametres and (iii) 9.7 decametres.

Solution Given, $4 \text{ cm}^2 = 196 \text{ m}^2$

i.e., $2 \text{ cm} = 14 \text{ m}$

$$\therefore \quad \text{RF} = \frac{2 \text{ cm}}{14 \text{ m}} = \frac{2}{(14 \times 100)} = \frac{1}{700}$$

$$LOS = \frac{1}{700} \times 9.8 \times 10 \times 100 = 14 \text{ cm}$$

Refer Fig. 5.3.

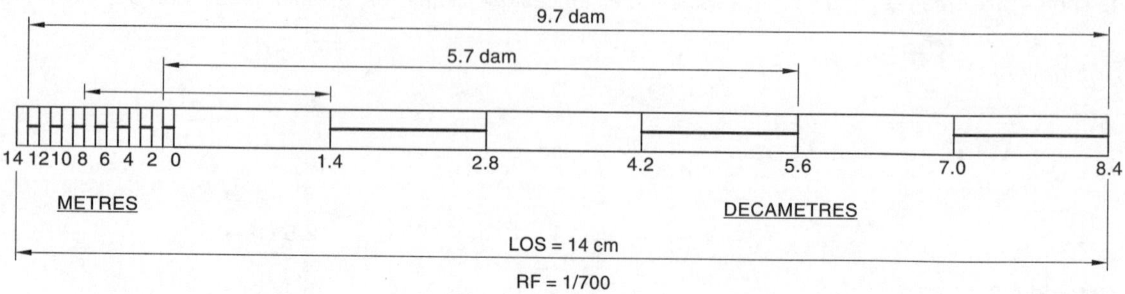

Fig. 5.3

The LOS is divided into 7 equal parts, each representing 9.8/7 = 1.4 decametres. The main divisions are numbered as 1.4, 2.8, 4.2, 5.6, 7.0 and 8.4. The first main division is divided into 14 equal parts which are numbered as 1, 2, 3, ..., 14. Each subdivision represents 1 metre.

The required lengths are shown on the scale by splitting them as follows:

(i) 2.2 decametres = 1.4 decametres + 8 metres
(ii) 5.7 decametres = 5.6 decametres + 1 metre
(iii) 9.7 decametres = 8.4 decametres + 13 metres

5.7 VERNIER SCALES

A vernier scale is used to indicate the distances in a unit and its immediate two subdivisions, e.g., m, dm and cm or yards, feet and inches. Obviously, vernier scales are more precise than plain scales.

A vernier scale consists of two parts—a main scale and a vernier. The main scale is similar to a plain scale. It shows length in a unit and its immediate subunit. However, unlike plain scales, all the main divisions on the main scale are subdivided into an equal number of subdivisions. The vernier is an auxiliary scale constructed above the first main division of the main scale. Its length is either more or less by a fixed amount than that of a main division. The vernier is divided into the same number of equal divisions as that on the first main division of the main scale. A subdivision on the main scale is called a *main scale division* (MSD), and that on the vernier scale is called a *vernier scale division* (VSD). Usually, the length of the vernier is more or less by one MSD than the length of the first main division on the main scale. However, it depends on the *least count* (LC) of the scale. LC is the minimum length that can be measured precisely by a given vernier scale.

$$LC = MSD - VSD \text{ (if } MSD > VSD)$$
$$= VSD - MSD \text{ (if } VSD > MSD)$$

The above relationships are used to calculate the length of a vernier. The LC must be mentioned as a fraction of MSD. For example, if the MSD of a scale represents 1 mm and the LC of 0.1 mm is expected on a scale then the length of the vernier is obtained as below:

$$MSD = 1 \text{ mm}$$

$$LC = 0.1 \text{ mm} = \frac{1}{10} \text{ MSD}$$

(i) Assuming MSD > VSD,

$$LC = MSD - VSD$$

$$\frac{1}{10}\ MSD = MSD - VSD$$

i.e., $$VSD = MSD - \frac{1}{10}\ MSD$$

i.e., $$10\ VSD = 9\ MSD$$

$\therefore$ Length of vernier = 9 MSD

This length must be divided into 10 equal parts so that LC = 0.1 mm.

(ii) Assuming VSD > MSD,

$$LC = VSD - MSD$$

$$\frac{1}{10}\ MSD = VSD - MSD$$

i.e., $$VSD = \frac{1}{10}\ MSD + MSD$$

i.e., $$10\ VSD = 11\ MSD$$

$\therefore$ Length of vernier = 11 MSD

This length must be divided into 10 equal parts so that LC = 0.1 mm.

There are two types of vernier scales:

(i) Forward vernier or Direct vernier
(ii) Backward vernier or Retrograde vernier

The constructions of both the types of verniers are explained in the following sections.

5.7.1 Forward Vernier Scales

If MSD > VSD then the vernier scale is called a *forward vernier scale*. Obviously, LC = MSD – VSD. In a forward vernier scale, the VSDs and MSDs are numbered in the same direction as that of the main divisions on a main scale.

Example 5.4 Construct a forward vernier scale of RF = 1/50 to read centimetres and long enough to measure 5 metres.

Solution We need to construct a forward vernier scale to read lengths in centimetres, decimetres and metres.

$$LOS = \left(\frac{1}{50}\right) \times 5 \times 100 = 10 \text{ cm}$$

Refer Fig. 5.4.

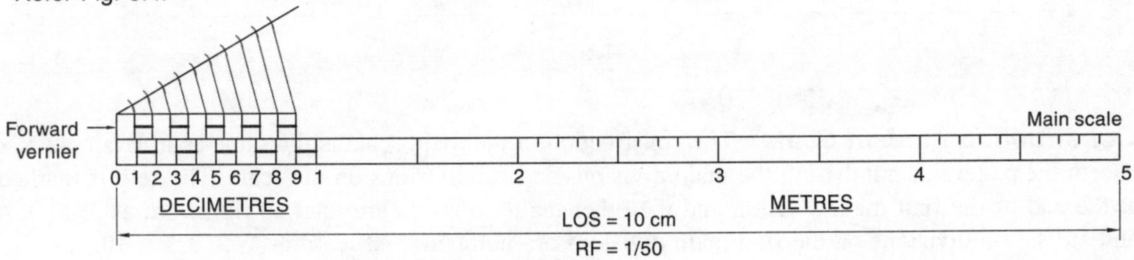

Fig. 5.4

Construction of Main Scale Draw a 10 cm long line and divide it into 5 equal parts. Each division will represent 1 metre. Mark zero at the start of the first division and number all the divisions as 1, 2, 3, 4 and 5. Divide all the divisions into 10 equal parts so that each subdivision (i.e., MSD) will represent 1 decimetre. Number the subdivisions on the first division rightward as 1, 2, 3, ..., 9. Write METRES below the right end and DECIMETRES below the first division of the scale.

Construction of Forward Vernier The LC = 1 cm and MSD represents 1 decimetre.

i.e., $$\text{LC} = 1 \text{ cm} = \frac{1}{100} \text{ MSD}$$

$\therefore$ $$\text{LC} = \text{MSD} - \text{VSD}$$

$\therefore$ $$\left(\frac{1}{10}\right) \text{MSD} = \text{MSD} - \text{VSD}$$

i.e., $$10 \text{ VSD} = 9 \text{ MSD}$$

$\therefore$ $$\text{Length of vernier} = 9 \text{ MSD}$$

Draw a vernier of length equal to 9 MSD above the first main division, as shown. The length of the vernier will represent 9×1 dm = 9 dm. Divide this length into 10 equal parts so that each VSD will represent 9/10 = 0.9 dm. Mark zero at the start of the vernier and 9, 18, 27, ..., 90 at subsequent subdivisions. Write CENTIMETRES above the vernier. Note that LC = 1 dm – 0.9 dm = 0.1 dm = 1 cm.

5.7.2 Backward Vernier Scales

If VSD > MSD then the vernier scale is called a *backward vernier scale*. The LC is obtained by the relation LC = VSD – MSD. In a backward vernier scale, the VSDs and MSDs are numbered in the direction opposite to that of the main divisions on the main scale.

Example 5.5 Construct a backward vernier scale for the data given in Example 5.5.
Refer Fig. 5.5.

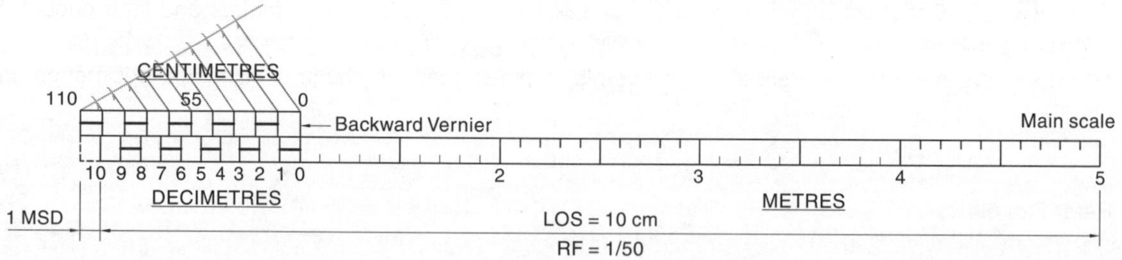

Fig. 5.5

Construction of Main Scale The construction of the main scale is the same as in Example 5.5, except the pattern of numbering the main divisions and subdivisions on the scale. The zero is marked at the end of the first main division and the other main divisions are marked rightward as 1, 2, 3, 4 and 5. The subdivisions on the first main divisions are numbered leftward as 1, 2, 3, ..., 10.

Construction of Backward Vernier In this case,

$$LC = VSD - MSD$$

$$\therefore \quad \left(\frac{1}{10}\right) MSD = VSD - MSD$$

i.e., $$10\ VSD = 11\ MSD$$

$$\therefore \quad \text{Length of vernier} = 11\ MSD$$

Draw a vernier of length equal to 11 MSD, starting from the zero mark on the main scale. The length of the vernier will represent 11 × 1 dm = 11 dm. After dividing this length into 10 equal parts, one VSD will represent 11/10 = 1.1 dm. Mark zero at the right end of the vernier and number the other subdivisions leftward as 11, 22, 33, …, 110. Note that LC = 1.1 dm – 1 dm = 0.1 dm = 1 cm.

> **Note:** The MSDs and VSDs are always numbered in the same direction. The 0th mark on the main scale and the vernier is always the same.

Example 5.6 On a map, the distance of 11 kilometres is shown by a 22 cm long line. Find the RF. Construct the forward vernier scale and backward vernier scale of this RF to read decametres and measure up to 4 kilometres. On both the scales, show the following distances: (i) 0.35 km (ii) 1.19 km (iii) 2.57 km.

Solution $$RF = \frac{22\ \text{cm}}{11\ \text{km}} = \frac{22}{(11 \times 1000 \times 100)} = \frac{1}{50000}$$

$$\therefore \quad LOS = \left(\frac{1}{50000}\right) \times 4 \times 1000 \times 100 = 8\ \text{cm}$$

(a) Forward Vernier Scale Refer Fig. 5.6(a).

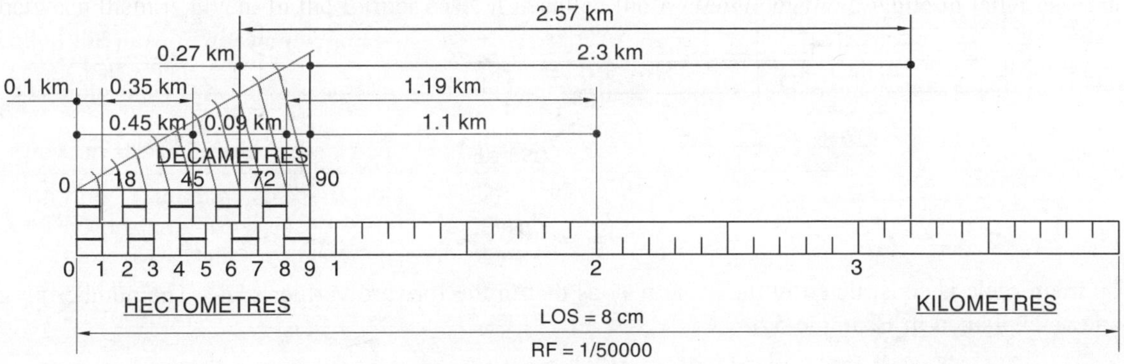

Fig. 5.6(a)

Construct the main scale as shown. Divide the LOS into 4 equal parts to show 1 kilometre by one division. Each main division is then divided into 10 equal parts to represent 1 hectometre.

$$MSD = 1\ \text{hm}$$

$$\text{LC} = 1 \text{ dam} = \frac{1}{10}\text{MSD}$$

$$\text{LC} = \text{MSD} - \text{VSD}$$

$$\frac{1}{10}\text{MSD} = \text{MSD} - \text{VSD}$$

i.e., $$10 \text{ VSD} = 9 \text{ MSD}$$

$\therefore$ $$\text{Length of vernier} = 9 \text{ MSD}$$

Construct a vernier of length = 9 MSD above the first main division of the main scale as shown. Divide the vernier length into 10 equal parts so that each VSD will represent 0.9 hm = 9 dam. Number the VSDs as shown.

To Show the Distances

Split up the given distances into two parts as shown below:

(i) 0.35 km = 0.45 km – 0.1 km
(ii) 1.19 km = 0.09 km + 1.1 km
(iii) 2.57 km = 0.27 km + 2.3 km

Note that the first part of each distance is in the multiple of 0.09 km, i.e., LC. On the scale, mark each part, adjoining to other, between appropriate divisions/subdivisions so that their addition or subtraction will give the required distance.

(b) Backward Vernier Scale Refer Fig. 5.6(b).

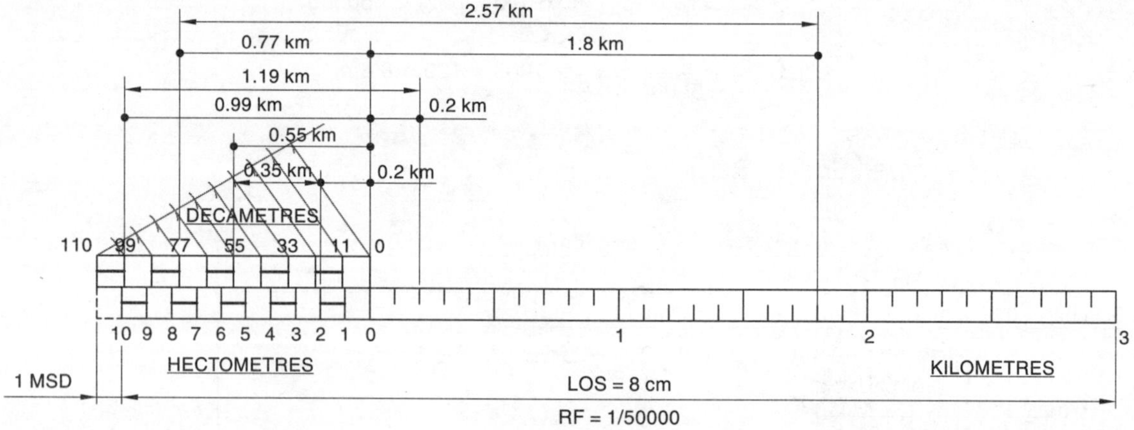

Fig. 5.6(b)

The main scale is constructed in the same way as that in the forward vernier scale. The numbering is done as explained in Example 5.5.

$$\text{LC} = \text{VSD} - \text{MSD}$$

i.e,. $$\frac{1}{10}\text{MSD} = \text{VSD} - \text{MSD}$$

i.e., $$10 \text{ VSD} = 11 \text{ MSD}$$

$\therefore$ $$\text{Vernier length} = 11 \text{ MSD}$$

Draw a vernier of length = 11 MSD and divide it into 10 equal parts so that each VSD = 1.1 hm = 11 dam. Number the VSDs as shown.

To Show the Distances Split up the given distances as shown below:

(i) 0.35 km = 0.55 km – 0.2 km

(ii) 1.19 km = 0.99 km + 0.2 km

(iii) 2.57 km = 0.77 km + 1.8 km

The first part of each distance is always the multiple of 0.11 km. Here also, the two parts of each distance are shown adjoining to each other.

Example 5.7 Construct a vernier scale of LC 2 mm. The LOS is 20 cm. Show the following distances on it: (i) 13.4 cm (ii) 2.8 cm.

Solution Refer Fig. 5.7.

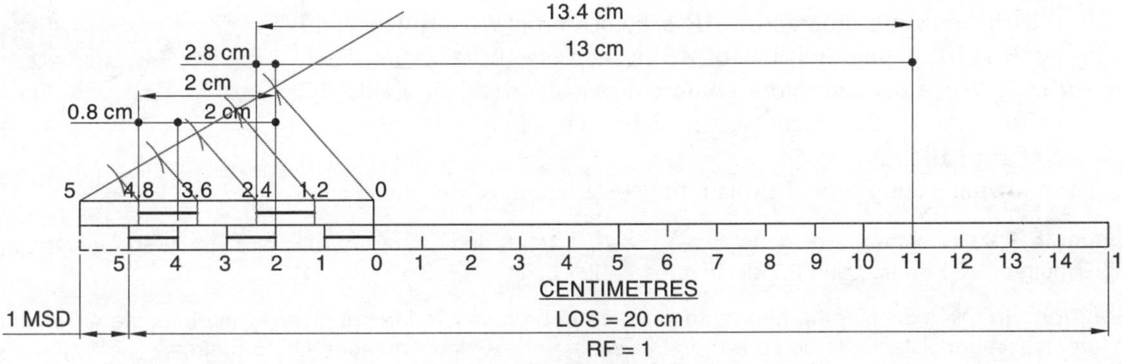

Fig. 5.7

Draw a 20 cm long line and divide it into 20 equal parts. Each main division will represent 1 cm. In this case, we need to show only two units, i.e., cm and mm and hence we need not divide any further main divisions on the main scale. The main divisions will represent MSDs.

Now, $\text{MSD} = 1 \text{ cm}$

$$\text{LC} = 2 \text{ mm} = \frac{1}{5}\text{ MSD}$$

For backward vernier,

$$\text{LC} = \text{VSD} - \text{MSD}$$

i.e., $$\left(\frac{1}{5}\right)\text{MSD} = \text{VSD} - \text{MSD}$$

i.e., $$5 \text{ VSD} = 6 \text{ MSD}$$

Therefore, draw a vernier = 6 MSD and divide it into 5 equal divisions. Each VSD will represent (6 × 1 cm) /5 = 1.2 cm. The LC = 1.2 cm – 1 cm = 0.2 cm = 2 mm.

The placement of zero and numbering of MSDs and VSDs should be observed carefully.

To show the distance of 13.4 cm, indicate 13 cm on the main scale and 0.4 cm on vernier. Similarly, to show the distance of 2.8 cm, indicate 2 cm on the main scale and 0.8 cm on the vernier.

5.8 DIAGONAL SCALES

Similar to vernier scale, a diagonal scale is also used to indicate the distances in a unit and its immediate two subdivisions. The diagonal scales are better than vernier scales—any distance can be measured easily on them. In addition, their constructions are simpler and there is no need of calculating the length of the vernier. However, diagonal scales need more space than vernier scales.

A diagonal scale consists of a plain scale and a diagonal construction.

5.8.1 Principle of Diagonal Scale

The construction of a diagonal scale is based on the principle of similarity of triangles. Let line *AB* represent any length, say 1 cm, Fig. 5.8. To divide line *AB* into 10 equal parts, draw a line *BC*, of any length, perpendicular to *AB* and complete the rectangle *ABCD*. Draw diagonal *BD*. Now divide *BC* into 10 equal parts. Through 1, 2, 3, …, 9, draw lines parallel to *AB* intersecting *BD* at 1′, 2′, 3′, …, 9′ respectively. From the geometry of the figure, it is clear that triangles *B*–1–1′, *B*–2–2′, *B*–3–3′, …, *BCD* are similar triangles.

As $B\text{–}5 = \tfrac{1}{2}(BC)$, $5\text{–}5' = \tfrac{1}{2}(AB)$

Similarly $1\text{–}1' = 0.1(AB)$, $2\text{–}2' = 0.2(AB)$, $3\text{–}3' = 0.3(AB)$, and so on.

Thus, each horizontal line above *AB* becomes progressively longer in length by (0.1)*AB*, giving divisions of *AB* in multiples of 0.1(*AB*). If the line *AB* needs to be divided into *n* number of equal parts then divide *BC* into *n* equal parts, so that each horizontal line above *AB* will be in the multiple of 1/*n* (*AB*).

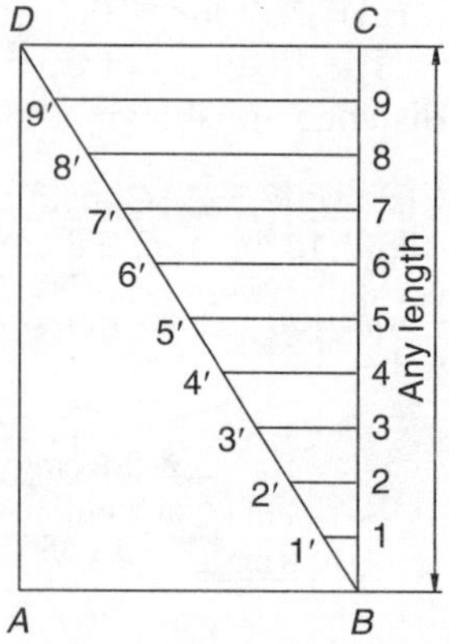

Fig. 5.8

The following examples will explain the construction of diagonal scales.

Example 5.8 Construct a diagonal scale of RF = 2/125 and LC of 1 centimetre. Show the lengths of 5.99 metres, 3.31 metres and 2.7 decimetres on it.

Solution In this example, the maximum distance to be measured is not given. Therefore, we will round off the maximum distance to be shown on this scale to next whole number, i.e., 6 metres.

$$\therefore \qquad \text{LOS} = \left(\frac{2}{125}\right) \times 6 \times 100 = 9.6 \text{ cm}$$

Refer Fig. 5.9.

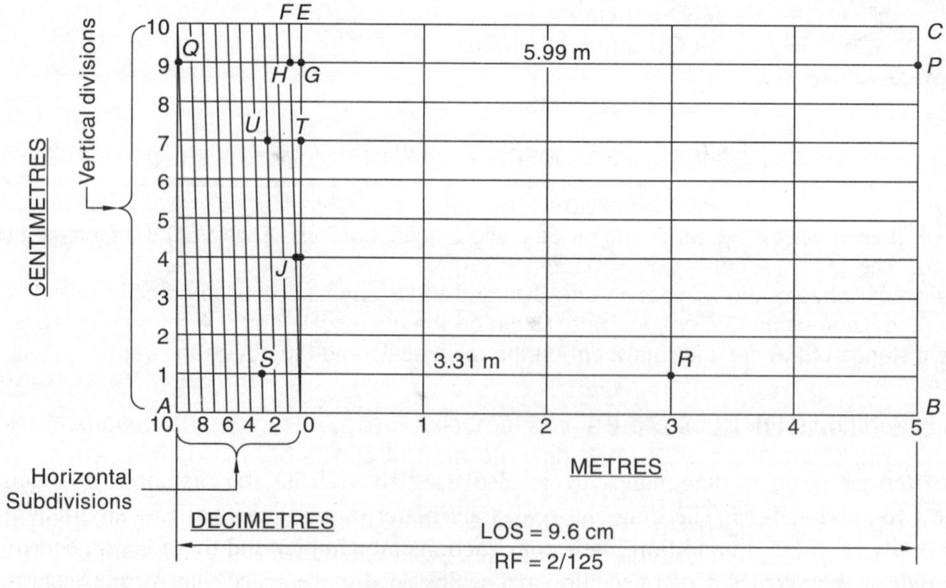

Fig. 5.9

Draw a line AB = 9.6 cm and divide it into 6 equal parts so that each division will represent 1 metre. Mark zero at the end of the 1st division and number the remaining divisions as 1, 2, 3, 4 and 5. Divide the first division into 10 equal parts so that each subdivision will show 1 decimetre. Number the subdivisions leftward as 1, 2, 3, ..., 10. To obtain the LC of 1 cm, we need to divide each subdivision into 10 equal parts. This is achieved by diagonal construction explained below.

Through A, erect a vertical line AD of any suitable length. Complete rectangle $ABCD$. Draw vertical lines through each division. Divide AD into 10 equal vertical divisions and number them as 1, 2, 3, ..., 10, starting from A and ending at D. Through all these divisions, draw horizontal lines ending on BC. Now join the 10th vertical division (i.e., D) with the 9th horizontal subdivision. Through all remaining horizontal subdivisions, draw lines parallel to diagonal D–9 as shown.

Note that $\Delta 0\text{–}EF$ can be compared to ΔBCD in Fig. 5.8. Obviously, each horizontal line within $\Delta 0\text{–}EF$ will be 0.1 dm (i.e., 1 cm) longer than the horizontal line below it. For example, the lengths GH and IJ will be equal to 0.9 dm and 0.4 dm respectively.

To Show the Distances

(i) 5.99 metres, i.e., 5 metres 9 decimetres and 9 centimetres
Look at the 5 m division (i.e., 5th main division), 9 dm division (i.e., 9th horizontal division) and 9 cm division (i.e., 9th vertical division). Locate point P where the vertical through the 5 m division meets the horizontal through the 9 cm division and locate point Q where the diagonal through the 9 dm division meets the same horizontal. The length PQ represents 5.99 metres.

(ii) 3.31 metres, i.e., 3 metres, 3 decimetres and 1 centimetre
Look at the 3 m division, 3 dm division and 1 cm division. Locate point R at the intersection of vertical through the 3 m division and horizontal through the 1 cm division. Locate point S at the intersection of the diagonal through the 3 dm division and the horizontal through the 1 cm division. The length RS = 3.31 metres.

(iii) 2.7 decimetres, i.e., 0 metre, 2 decimetres and 7 centimetres
Look at the 0 m division, 2 dm division and 7 cm division. Mark points T and U respectively where the vertical through 0 m division meets the horizontal through 7 cm division and diagonal through the 2 dm division meets to the same horizontal. TU = 2.7 decimetres.

Example 5.9 Draw a full-size diagonal scale to show 0.1 millimetre and long enough to measure up to 5 centimetres. Show on this scale the following distances: (i) 0.1 millimetre (ii) 2.35 centimetres (iii) 4.89 centimetres.

Solution In this case, RF = 1.

∴ LOS = maximum distance to be measured = 5 cm

Refer Fig. 5.10.

Draw a horizontal 5 cm long line AB and divide it into 5 equal parts. Divide the first division into 5 equal parts, each part representing 2 millimetres. Through A, draw a vertical and mark off 20 equal divisions, ending at D. Number all the main divisions, subdivisions and vertical divisions as shown. Complete rectangle $ABCD$. Through each main division, draw verticals. Draw a horizontal through each vertical division. Now join D with the 8 mm division and draw diagonals through other subdivisions parallel to $D8$.

To Show the Distances

(i) 0.1 millimetres, i.e., 0 centimetre 0 millimetre and 1(1/10) millimetre.
Locate point P at the intersection of the vertical through the 0 cm division and the horizontal through the 1(1/10) mm division. Locate point Q at the intersection of the diagonal through the 0 mm division and the horizontal through the 1(1/10) mm division. PQ = 0.1 mm.

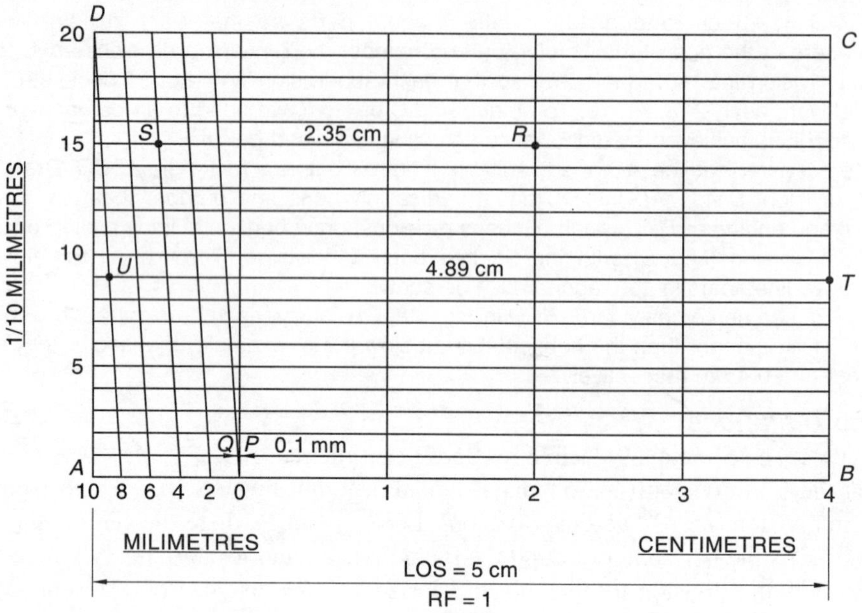

Fig. 5.10

(ii) 2.35 centimetres, i.e., 2 centimetres 3 millimetres and 5(1/10) millimetres, i.e., 2 centimetres, 2 millimetres and 15(1/10) millimetres.

Locate point *R* and *S* respectively at the intersections of the vertical through the 2 cm division and the horizontal through the 15(1/10) mm division and the diagonal through the 2 mm division and the horizontal through the 15(1/10) mm division. *RS* = 2.35 cm.

(iii) 4.89 centimetres, i.e., 4 centimetres, 8 millimetres and 9(1/10) millimetres

Locate points *T* and *U* where the horizontal through the 9(1/10) mm division meets the vertical through the 4 cm division and the diagonal through the 8 mm division respectively. *TU* = 4.89 cm.

Note: In this example, we may divide the first main division into 10 equal parts instead of 5 parts. *AD*, then, must be divided into 10 equal parts.

Example 5.10 The dimensions of an ancient tower, Qutub Minar, are as follows:

Height = 79 yards and 1 foot

Bottom diameter = 15 yards 2 feet and 3 inches

Top diameter = 3 yards

If the height is represented by a 29 ¾ inch long line on the drawing, find RF. Draw a diagonal scale of this RF long enough to show the diameters of the tower.

Solution RF = (29 ¾)/79 yards 1 foot = 29.75/(79 × 3 × 12 + 12) = 1/96

Let the maximum distance to be shown = 16 yards. Then

$$\text{LOS} = \left(\frac{1}{96}\right) \times 16 \times 3 \times 12 = 6 \text{ inches}$$

Refer Fig. 5.11.

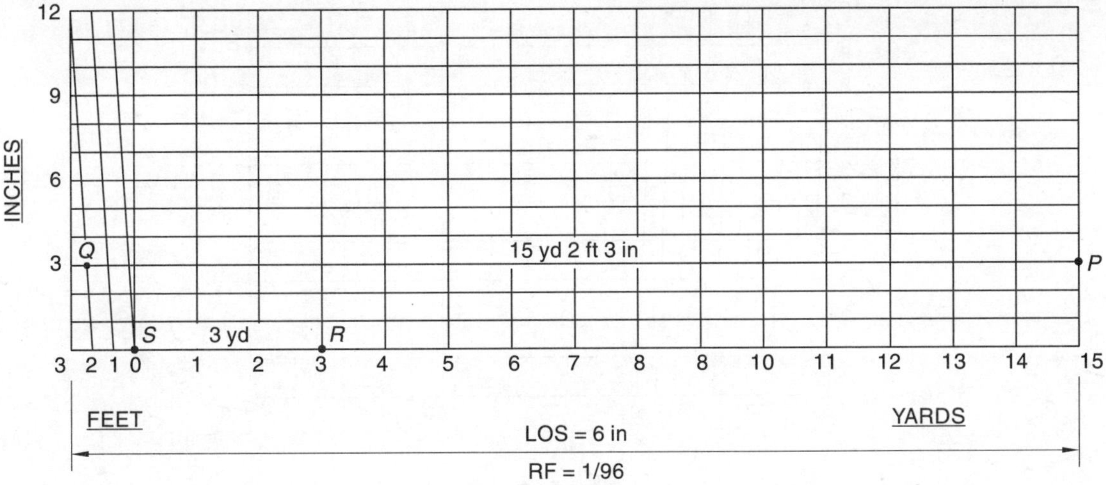

Fig. 5.11

Draw a 6 inch long line and divide it into 16 equal parts. Each part will represent 1 yard. The first division should now be divided into 3 equal subdivisions, each showing 1 foot.

Erect a vertical at the 3 ft division and set off 12 equal divisions on it. Each vertical division will represent 1 inch. Complete the diagonal construction as shown.

Both the diameters of the tower are shown on the scale.

PQ = bottom diameter = 15 yards 2 feet 3 inches

RS = top diameter = 3 yards

Example 5.11 A tunnel on the Konkan Railway route has a size of 640 m × 10 m × 10 m. It is represented on a model by the volume of 27 cm^3. Find RF. Devise a diagonal scale of this RF to read up to 300 metres. Show the distances of 299 metres, 171 metres and 9 metres on it.

Solution The volume of 64000 m^3 is represented by 27 cm^3.

$$\text{RF} = \sqrt[3]{27}\ \text{cm}^3/\sqrt[3]{64000}\ \text{m}^3 = 3\ \text{cm}/40\ \text{m} = 3/4000$$

$$\therefore \quad \text{LOS} = \left(\frac{3}{4000}\right) \times 300 \times 100 = 22.5\ \text{cm}$$

Refer Fig. 5.12.

Construct the scale as shown. Note how the distances are marked on the scale. On the scale, PQ = 299 m, RS = 171 m and TU = 9 m.

5.9 COMPARATIVE OR CORRESPONDING SCALES

Comparative scales consist of two scales of the same RF, constructed separately or one above the other. As the name suggests, these scales are used to compare the distances expressed in different systems of unit; e.g., kilometres and miles, centimetres and inches, etc. The two scales may be plain scales or vernier scales or diagonal scales. Accordingly, the comparative scales may be called plain comparative scales, vernier comparative scales or diagonal comparative scales.

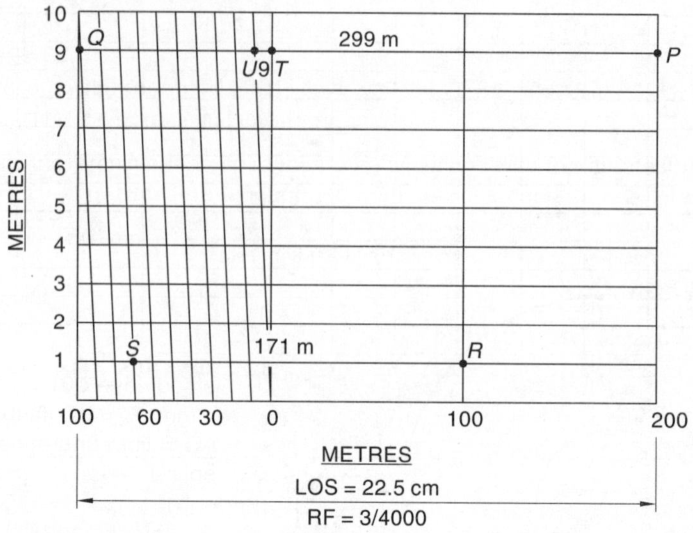

Fig. 5.12

Example 5.12 Construct plain comparative scales of RF = 1/625000 to read up to 50 kilometres and 40 miles. On these scales, show the

(i) kilometres equivalent to 18 miles.
(ii) miles equivalent to 50 kilometres.

Solution We have to construct two plain scales: kilometre scale and mile scale. Refer Fig. 5.13.

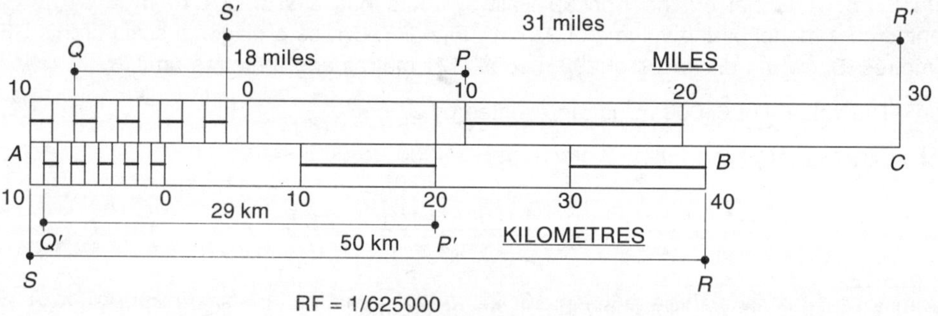

Fig. 5.13

(a) Kilometre Scale

$$\text{LOS} = \frac{1}{625000} \times 50 \times 1000 \times 100 = 8 \text{ cm}$$

Draw an 8 cm long line *AB* and construct a plain scale to represent kilometres.

(b) Mile Scale

$$\text{LOS} = \frac{1}{625000} \times 40 \times 1760 \times 3 \times 12 = 4 \text{ in}$$

Draw a 4 in long line *AC* and construct a plain scale to represent mile above the kilometre scale.

To find the equivalent distances

(i) On the mile scale, find the distance equal to 18 miles, i.e., PQ. With the help of a divider, mark $P'Q' = PQ$ on the kilometre scale such that P' will coincide with the appropriate main division. Find the length represented by $P'Q'$. $P'Q' = 29$ km.

$\therefore$ 18 miles = 29 km

(ii) On the kilometre scale, find the distance equal to 50 km, i.e., RS. With the help of a divider, find the distance on the mile scale equivalent to RS, i.e., $R'S'$. $R'S' = 31$ miles.

$\therefore$ 50 km = 31 miles

Example 5.13 The distance between Delhi and Agra is 200 km. A train covers this distance in 4 hours. Construct plain comparative scales to measure time up to a single minute. Take RF = 1/200000. Find the distance covered by the train in 42 minutes.

Solution Speed of the train = 200/4 = 50 km/h. As we have to find the distance covered by the train in 42 minutes, we will construct the scale for more than 42 minutes, say 60 minutes, i.e., 50 km.

$$\therefore \quad \text{LOS} = \frac{1}{200000} \times 50 \times 1000 \times 100 = 25 \text{ cm}$$

We have to construct two plain scales: kilometre scale and minute scale.
Refer Fig. 5.14.

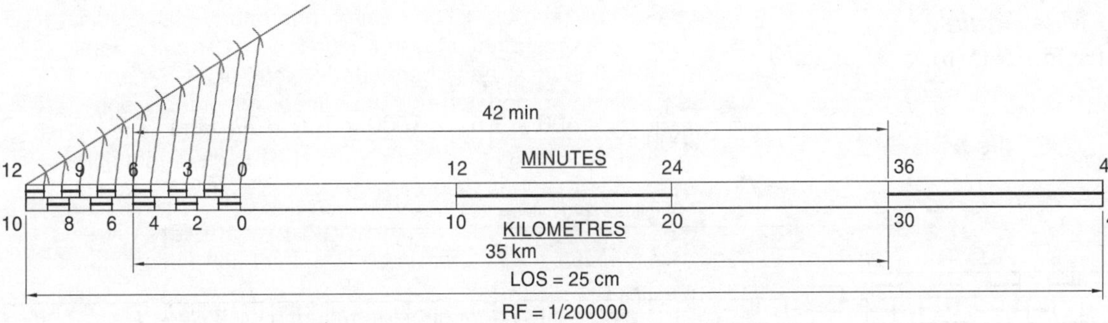

Fig. 5.14

(a) Kilometre Scale Draw a 25 cm long line to represent the distance of 50 km. Divide it into 5 equal parts. Each main division represents 10 kilometres. Divide the first division into 10 equal parts.

(b) Minute Scale As the LOS is the same for both the scales, construct the minute scale above the kilometre scale. Each main division represents 12 minutes. Divide the first division into 12 equal parts.

Show 42 minutes on the minute scale. Find the corresponding length on the kilometre scale. This length, i.e., 35 kilometres, is the distance covered by the train in 42 minutes.

Example 5.14 Construct the vernier comparative scales to read up to a single kilometre and mile and long enough to measure 600 kilometres and 400 miles. Take scale factor as 1:3000000. Show on the scale, a length of 457 km, and its equivalent distance in miles.

1 mile = 1.61 kilometres

Solution We have to construct two vernier scales: kilometre scale and mile scale.

(a) Kilometre Scale

Refer Fig. 5.15(a).

$$\text{LOS} = \frac{1}{3000000} \times 600 \times 1000 \times 100 = 20 \text{ cm}$$

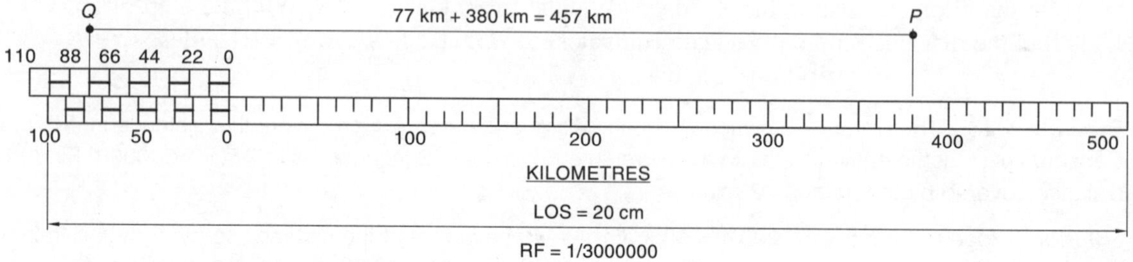

Fig. 5.15(a)

Draw a 20 cm long line and construct a vernier scale as shown. Note that LC = VSD – MSD = (110/10) – (100/10) = 1 km.

The distance of 457 km (= *PQ*) is marked on the scale.

(b) Mile Scale

Refer Fig. 5.15(b).

$$\text{LOS} = \frac{1}{3000000} \times 400 \times 1.61 \times 1000 \times 100 = 22.5 \text{ cm}$$

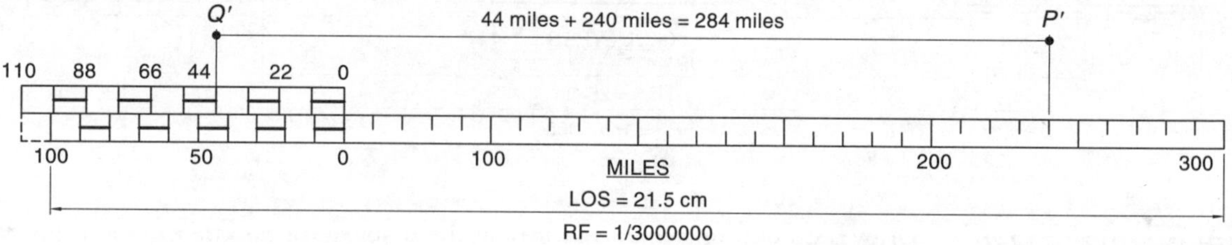

Fig. 5.15(b)

Draw a 21.5 cm long line and construct a vernier scale as shown. In this case, LC = (110/10) – (100/10) = 1 mile.

To show a distance equivalent to 457 km on the mile scale, locate points P' and Q' above it such that $P'Q' = PQ$ and the verticals through P' and Q' coincide exactly with an MSD and a VSD respectively. The distance represented by $P'Q'$ is the distance in miles equivalent to 457 km, i.e., 284 miles.

Example 5.15 A drawing is drawn in inch units to a scale 5/8 of full size. Construct a diagonal scale showing 1/8 inch divisions and to measure up to 12 inches. Draw a comparative scale showing centimetres and millimetres and long enough to read 24 centimetres. Show $7\frac{3}{8}''$ on the inch scale and its equivalent distance on the comparative scale.

Solution

(a) Inch Scale Refer Fig. 5.16(a).

$$\text{LOS} = \frac{5}{8} \times 12 = 7(1/2) \text{ inches}$$

Construct the inch scale as shown. PQ = 7¾ inches

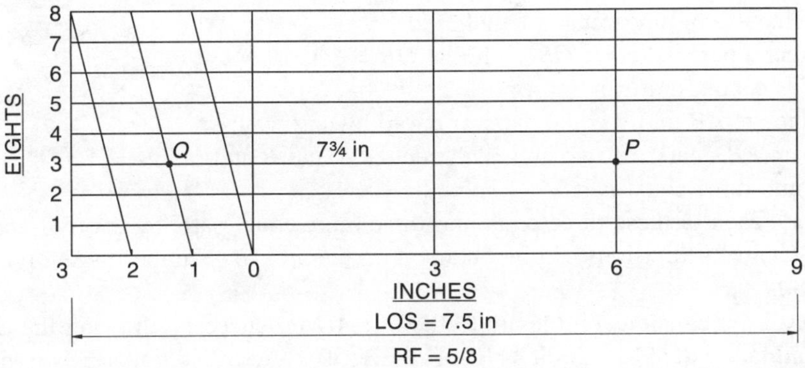

Fig. 5.16(a)

(b) Centimetre Scale Refer Fig. 5.16(b).

$$\text{LOS} = \frac{5}{8} \times 24 = 15 \text{ cm}$$

Draw the centimetre scale as shown. On this scale, draw line $P'Q' = PQ$. The line $P'Q'$ shows the length equivalent to 7¾ inches, i.e., 18.7 cm.

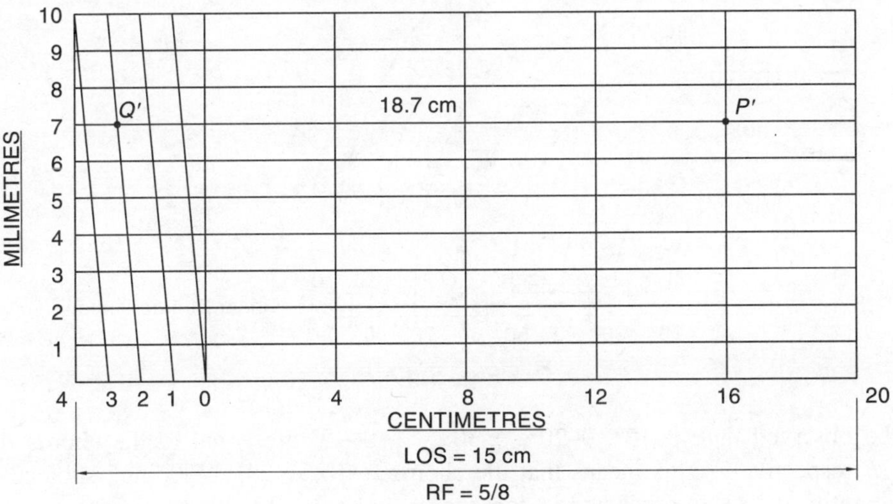

Fig. 5.16(b)

5.10 SCALE OF CHORDS

The scale of chords is used to set off or measure angles without the aid of a protractor. As the name suggests, it measures angles by comparing the angles subtended by chords of an arc at the centre of the arc.

The construction of a scale of chords is very simple. See Fig. 5.17.

1. Draw a line *AO* of any suitable length.
2. At *O*, erect a perpendicular *OB* such that *OB* = *OA*.
3. With *O* as centre, draw an arc *AB*.
4. Divide the arc *AB* into 9 equal parts in the following way:
   (i) On arc *AB*, mark off two arcs with centres *A* and *B* and radius = *AO*. This will divide arc *AB* into three equal parts.
   (ii) Divide each of these three parts into three more equal parts by the trial-and-error method. Thus, a total of 9 divisions can be obtained on the arc *AB*. Number these divisions as 10, 20, 30, …, 80.
5. Transfer all the divisions on the arc to the line *AO* produced by drawing the arcs with *A* as a centre and radii equal to chords *A*–10, *A*–20, *A*–30, …, *AB*. Note that *B* is transferred to *C* on *AO* produced.
6. Construct the *Linear Degree Scale* by drawing the rectangle below *AC*. Distinctly mark the divisions in the rectangle. Mark zero (0) below *A* and number the divisions subsequently as 10°, 20°, 30°, … 90°. Each division on the linear degree scale may be divided into two parts to read degrees in the multiple of 5°. The angles can be measured to 1° by dividing each division into 10 parts on a comparatively longer degree scale.

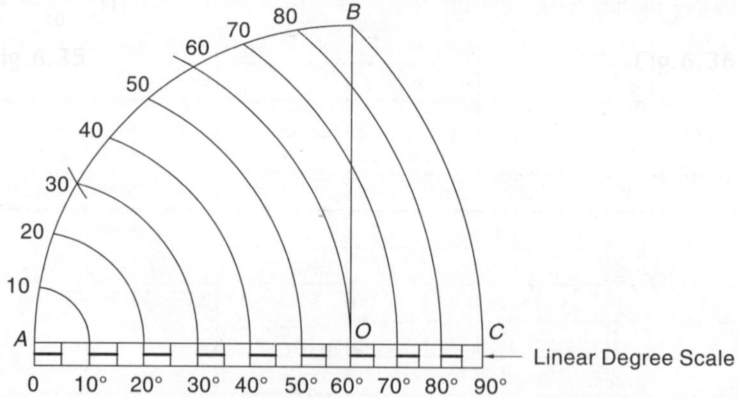

Fig. 5.17

It must be observed that, 0–10°, 0–20°, 0–30°, …, 0–90° are equal to the chords *A*–10, *A*–20, *A*–30, …, *AB* respectively. This means that the chords *A*–10, *A*–20, *A*–30, etc., subtend angles 10°, 20°, 30°, etc., at centre *O*. In other words, the chords *A*–10, 10–20, 20–30, …, 80–*B* on arc *AB* will subtend 10° each at centre *O*. It may be noted that the chord *A*–60 which subtends 60° at *O*, is equal to the radius of the arc *AB*. Another interesting fact that must be noted in relation to the scale of chords is that the divisions 0–10°, 10°–20°, 20°–30°, …, 80°–90° are not equal but decrease gradually from *A* to *C*.

The scale of chords gives approximate measurements for the angles other than 30°, 60° and 90° since the divisions on the arc are obtained by approximation.

The following examples will explain how to construct and measure the angles with the help of a scale of chords.

Example 5.16 Construct the angles of 25°, 53° and 125° by an aid of the scale of chords.

Solution Refer Fig. 5.18.

Draw any line *PQ* and mark point *O* anywhere on it. With *O* as centre and *OA* (from the scale of chords, Fig. 5.21) as a radius, draw a semicircle *AC*.

(i) *Angle 25°* With *A* as centre and radius = 0–25° (from the scale of chords), draw an arc cutting the semicircle at point *D*. Join *D* with *O*. $\angle AOD = 25°$.

(ii) *Angle 53°* With *A* as centre and radius = 0–53° (from the scale of chords), draw an arc cutting the semicircle at point *E*. The 53° mark can be obtained on the linear degree scale by dividing the 50°–60° division into 10 equal parts. Join *E* with *O*. $\angle AOE = 53°$.

(iii) *Angle 125°* The angle 125° can be constructed in two ways:

(a) With *A* as centre and radius = 0–90°, draw an arc cutting the semicircle at point *B*. Now, with *B* as centre and radius equal to 0–35°, mark another point *F* on the semicircle. Join *F* with *O*. $\angle AOF = \angle AOB + \angle BOF = 90° + 35° = 125°$.

(b) With *C* as centre and radius equal to 0–55°, mark point *F* on the semicircle. Join *F* with *O*. $\angle AOF = 180° - \angle COF = 180° - 55° = 125°$.

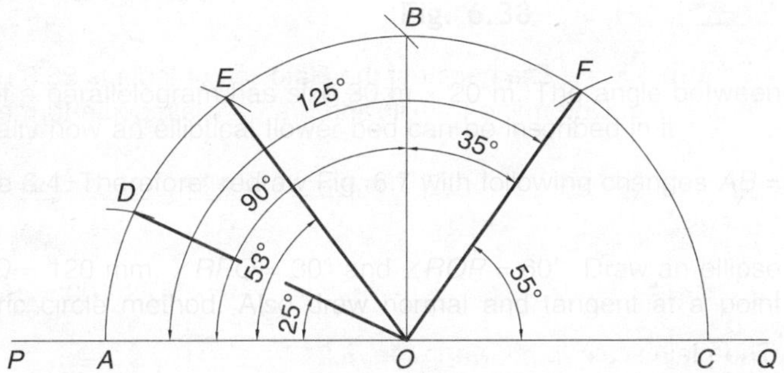

Fig. 5.18

Example 5.17 Measure $\angle PQR$ shown in Fig. 5.19 by means of the scale of chords.

Solution

1. With *Q* as centre and radius = *AO* (from the scale of chords, Fig. 5.17), draw an arc *ST* cutting *PQ* at *S* and *RQ* at *T*.
2. Find the length equivalent to the length of the chord *ST* on the linear degree scale with the help of a divider, by matching one end at the zero mark, as shown in Fig. 5.20. The corresponding length 0–48° gives the angle. Thus, $\angle PQR = 48°$.

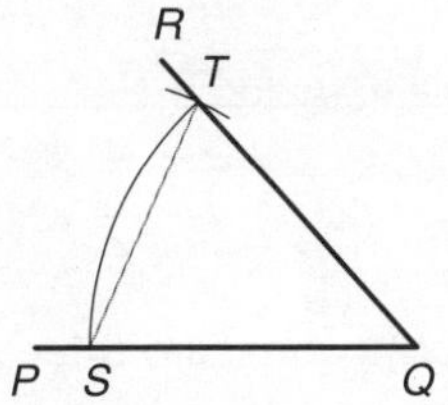

Fig. 5.19

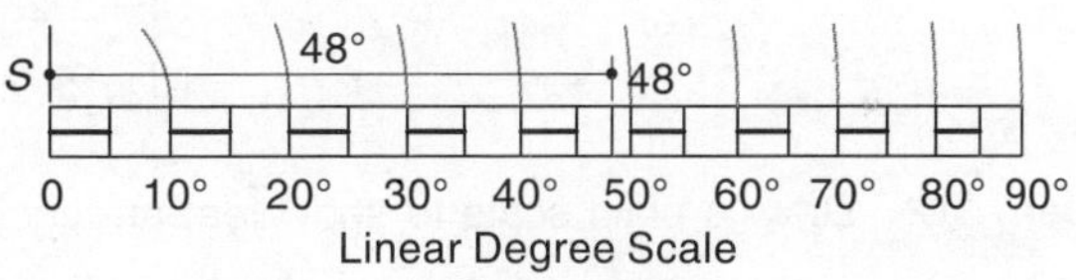

Fig. 5.20

Remember the Following

- LOS = RF × maximum distance to be represented
- A plain scale indicates the distances in a unit and its immediate subdivision.
- A vernier scale and diagonal scale indicate the distances in a unit and its immediate two subdivisions.
- Forward vernier scale: MSD > VSD
- Length of forward vernier: LC = MSD – VSD (VSDs and MSDs are numbered in the same direction as that of the main divisions on main scale)
- Backward vernier scale: VSD > MSD
  Length of backward vernier: LC = VSD – MSD (VSDs and MSDs are numbered in the direction opposite to that of the main divisions on the main scale)
- Comparative scales consist of two scales of same RF. They are used to compare the distances shown in two different systems of unit.
- A scale of chords is used to construct or measure angles.

Illustrative Problems

Problem 5.1 The height of the Gateway of India is 25.3 metres. It is shown as 10 cm in the elevation on a drawing. Determine the RF and draw a plain scale to measure up to 40 metres.

Solution

$$RF = \frac{10 \text{ cm}}{25.3 \text{ m}} = \frac{1}{253}$$

$$LOS = \frac{1}{253} \times 40 \times 100 = 15.8 \text{ cm}$$

The plain scale is shown in Fig. 5.21.

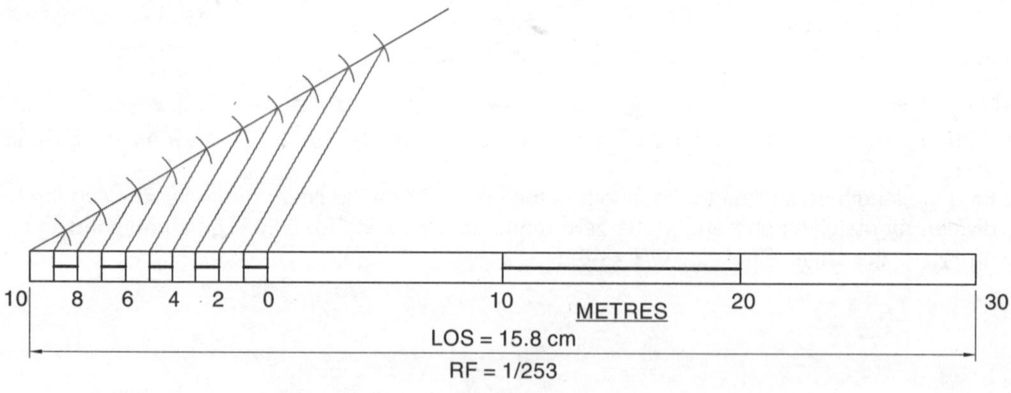

Fig. 5.21

Problem 5.2 Draw a plain scale to show feet and inches and long enough to measure 8 feet.

Solution In this problem, RF is not given. Therefore we will assume LOS = 6 inches. The scale is shown in Fig. 5.22.

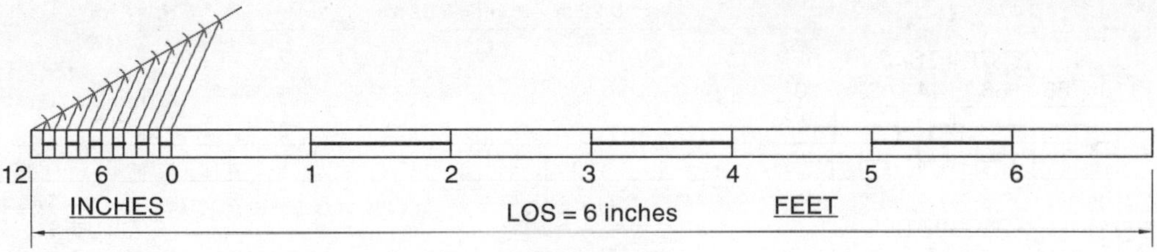

Fig. 5.22

Problem 5.3 Construct a vernier scale to read centimetres and to measure up to 4 metres, having a scale factor of 1/25. Mark a distance of 2.52 metres on it.

Solution

$$LOS = \frac{1}{25} \times 4 \times 100 = 16 \text{ cm}$$

LC = 0.02 m. If each MSD represents 1 dm (i.e., 0.1 m) then the length of the vernier can be found out as below:

$$LC = VSD - MSD$$

$$\frac{1}{5} MSD = VSD - MSD$$

i.e., $6 \text{ MSD} = 5 \text{ VSD}$

Refer Fig. 5.23(a). The construction of a vernier and numbering pattern of VSDs may be observed carefully. The distance of 2.52 m is marked on the scale. It should be noted that the 0th mark on vernier coincides with the 5th subdivision on the main scale.

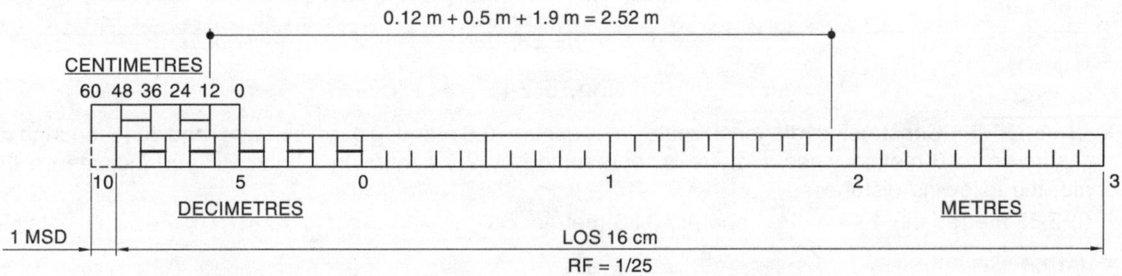

Fig. 5.23(a)

The vernier scale may be drawn as in Fig. 5.23(b). In this case, LC is considered to be 0.01 m and therefore, length of vernier = 11 MSD. The 0th mark on the vernier now coincides with the 0th mark on the main scale.

Note: The readers may construct either a backward vernier or a forward vernier scale if not specifically mentioned in the problem.

Problem 5.4 Construct a vernier scale of 2:1 to measure up to 1/10 millimetre and long enough to measure 60 millimetres. Mark off: (i) 19.9 mm and (ii) 52.5 mm on it.

Solution

$$LOS = \frac{2}{1} \times \frac{60}{10} = 12 \text{ cm}$$

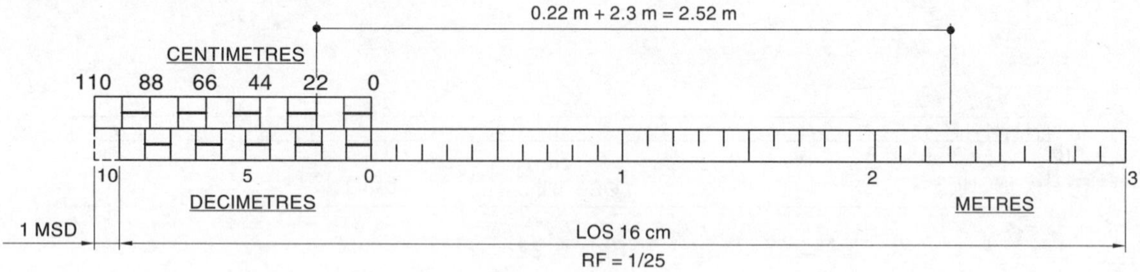

Fig. 5.23(b)

$$LC = \frac{1}{10} \text{ mm}$$

$$1 \text{ MSD} = 1 \text{ mm}$$

$\therefore$ Length of vernier = 11 MSD

Figure 5.24 shows the vernier scale with the required distances marked on it.

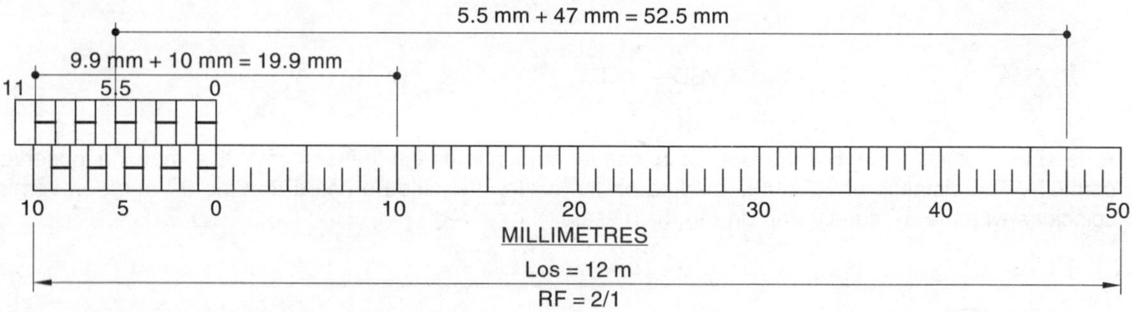

Fig. 5.24

Problem 5.5 Construct a diagonal scale to measure 0.01 and 0.1 of a metre and long enough to measure up to 6 metres when 1 metre is represented by 2.5 centimetres. Find RF and indicate on the scale, the following distances:

(i) 5.55 metres, (ii) 4.44 metres and (iii) 3.33 metres

Solution

$$RF = \frac{2.5 \text{ cm}}{1 \text{ m}} = \frac{1}{40}$$

$$LOS = \frac{1}{40} \times 6 \times 100 = 15 \text{ cm}$$

The diagonal scale is shown in Fig. 5.25.

Problem 5.6 On the map of Nagpur city, a straight road from the Zero mile to the airport, 9 km long, is shown by a 14 cm long line. A flyover bridge on this road starts at 300 m and ends at 2.1 km from the Zero mile. The distances of other important places, from the Zero mile, on this road are: Big Bazar—1.15 km, Sai *Mandir*—6.32 km. Construct a diagonal scale to show:

(i) length of flyover bridge
(ii) distance between the Zero mile and Big Bazar
(iii) distance between the Big Bazar and Sai *Mandir*

Solution The maximum distance to be represented is 9 km. Therefore, we will take LOS = 14 cm. The diagonal scale is shown in Fig. 5.26.

Length of flyover bridge: 2.1 km – 0.3 km = 1.8 km = *AB*

Distance between the Zero mile and Big Bazar = 1.15 km = *CD*

Distance between the Big Bazar and Sai *Mandir* = 6.32 km – 1.15 km = 5.17 km = *EF*

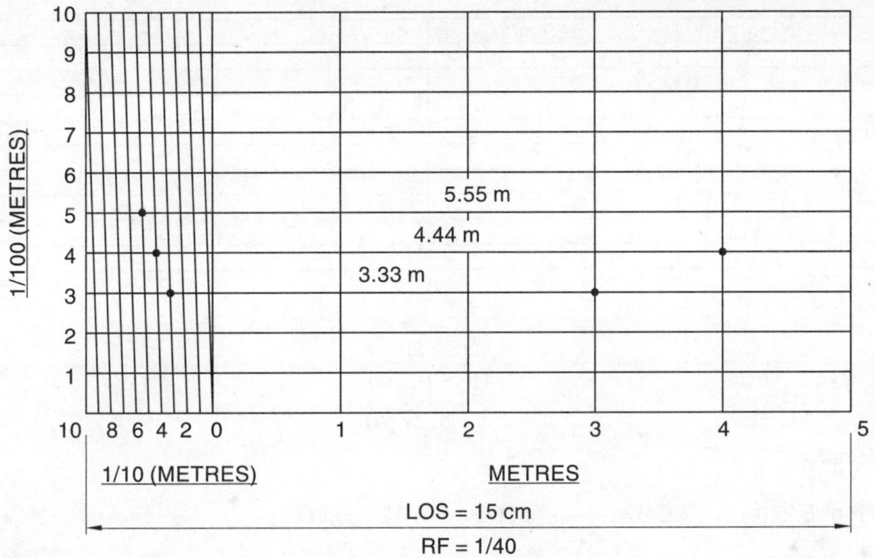

Fig. 5.25

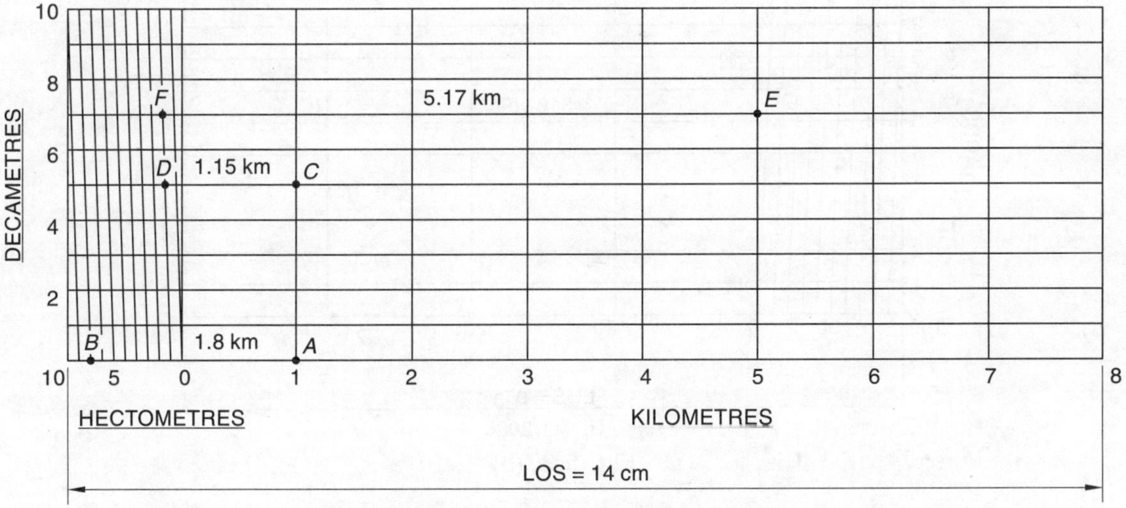

Fig. 5.26

Problem 5.7 The length of the Khandala tunnel on the Mumbai–Pune expressway is 330 m. On the road map, it is shown by a 16.5 cm long line. Construct a scale to show metres and to measure up to 400 m. Show the length of a 289 metre long bridge on the expressway. Construct another scale to read the equivalent length in yards and measure up to 500 yards.

Solution RF = 16.5 cm/330 m = 1/2000

(a) Metre Scale

Refer Fig. 5.27(a).

$$\text{LOS} = \frac{1}{2000} \times 400 \times 100 = 20 \text{ cm}$$

On the scale, *PQ* = length of the bridge = 289 m

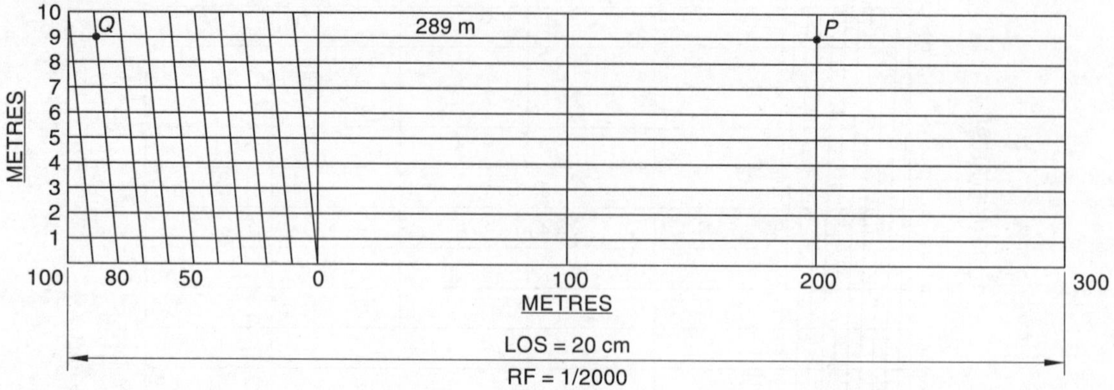

Fig. 5.27(a)

(b) Yard Scale

Refer Fig. 5.27(b). $\text{LOS} = \dfrac{1}{2000} \times 500 \times 3 \times 12 = 9$ in

On the scale, $P'Q' = PQ$ = length of the bridge = 316 yards.

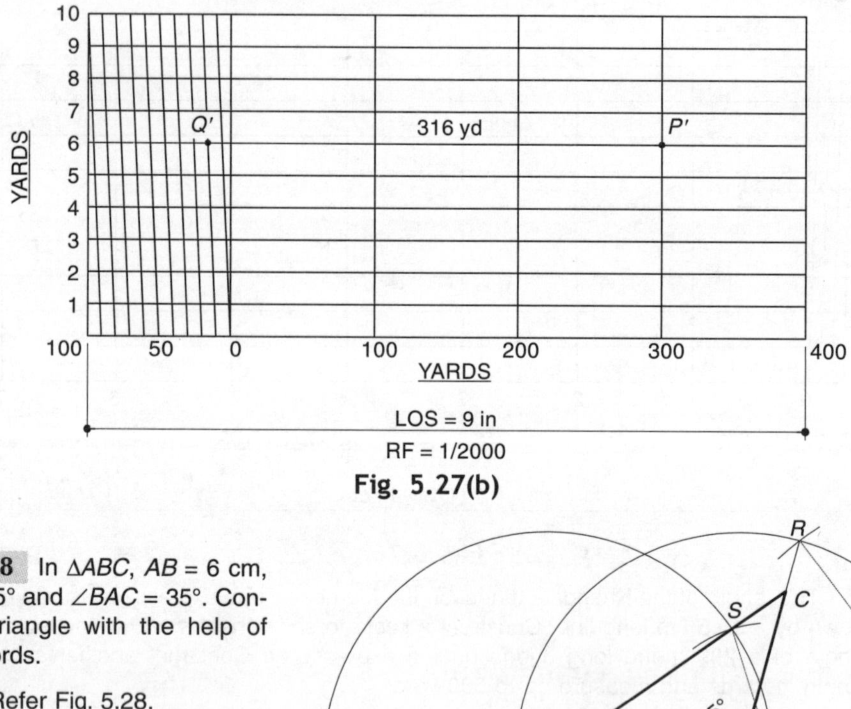

Fig. 5.27(b)

Problem 5.8 In ΔABC, $AB = 6$ cm, $\angle ABC = 105°$ and $\angle BAC = 35°$. Construct the triangle with the help of scale of chords.

Solution Refer Fig. 5.28.

1. Draw a line $AB = 6$ cm.
2. With B as centre and radius OA (from the scale of chords, Fig. 5.17), draw a semicircle cutting AB (produced if necessary) at P and Q.

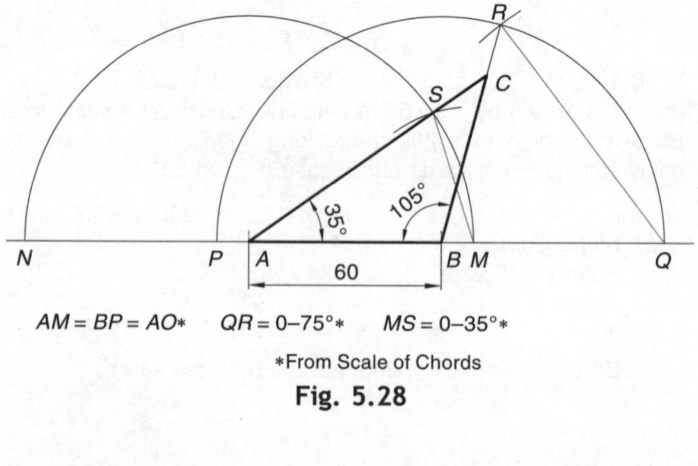

Fig. 5.28

3. With Q as centre and radius 0–75° (from the scale of chords), mark an arc cutting the semicircle at R. Join BR. $\angle ABR = 180° - 75° = 105°$.
4. With A as centre and radius OA (from the scale of chords), draw a semicircle cutting AB (produced if necessary) at M and N.
5. With M as centre and radius 0–35°, mark an arc cutting the latter semicircle at S. Join AS. $\angle MAS = 35°$.
6. Produce AS to meet BR at point C. ΔABC is the required triangle.

Problem 5.9 Draw all the possible quadrilaterals with the following dimensions:

$AB = 7$ cm, $BC = 4$ cm, $CD = 7.5$ cm, $AD = 8.5$ cm and $\angle DAB = 85°$.

Measure the remaining angles of the quadrilaterals by means of the scale of chords.

Solution The two possible quadrilaterals with given dimensions are shown in Fig. 5.29(a) and (b).

To measure angles of quadrilateral in Fig. 5.29(a)

$\angle ABC$ Draw an arc with B as a centre and radius = OA (from the scale of chords, Fig. 5.17) cutting AB and BC produced at $A1$ and $C1$ respectively. Find the length on the linear degree scale, Fig. 5.29(c), equivalent to chord $A1$–$C1$, Fig. 5.29(c). $A1$–$C1$ = 0–87°. ∴ $\angle ABC = 87°$.

$\angle BCD$ Draw an arc with C as centre and radius = OA (from the scale of chords) cutting BC produced and CD at $B1$ and $D1$ respectively. Match chord $B1$–$D1$ on the linear degree scale, Fig. 5.29(c) As $B1$–$D1$ extends beyond the length of the linear degree scale, locate point P on $B1$–$D1$ exactly above the 90° mark. Now, mark point Q on $B1$–$D1$ such that $B1$–Q = P–$D1$. Find the degree mark with which point Q coincides, i.e., 40°. $B1$–$D1$ = ($B1$–P) + ($B1$–Q) = 90° + 40° = 130°. ∴ $\angle BCD = 130°$

$\angle ADC$ Draw an arc with D as a centre and radius = OA (from the scale of chords) cutting AD and DC at $A2$ and $C2$ respectively. Match the chord $A2$–$C2$ on the linear degree scale and find the equivalent length. $A2 - C2$ = 0–58° ∴ $\angle ADC = 58°$

To measure angles in the quadrilateral in Fig. 5.29(b)

$\angle ABC$ and $\angle ADC$ can be measured in the same way as explained in relation to Fig. 5.29(a). $\angle ABC = 20°$ and $\angle ADC = 25°$.

To measure $\angle BCD$ internally, first measure it externally in the same way as explained in relation to $\angle BCD$ in Fig. 5.29(a). Obviously, $\angle BCD$ (internal) = 360° – $\angle BCD$ (external) = 360° – 130° = 230°.

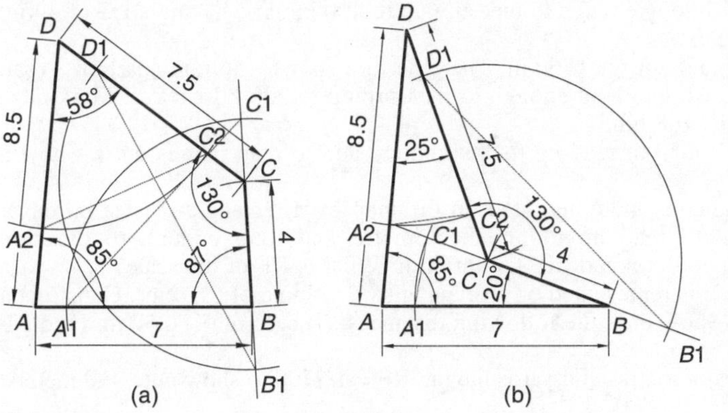

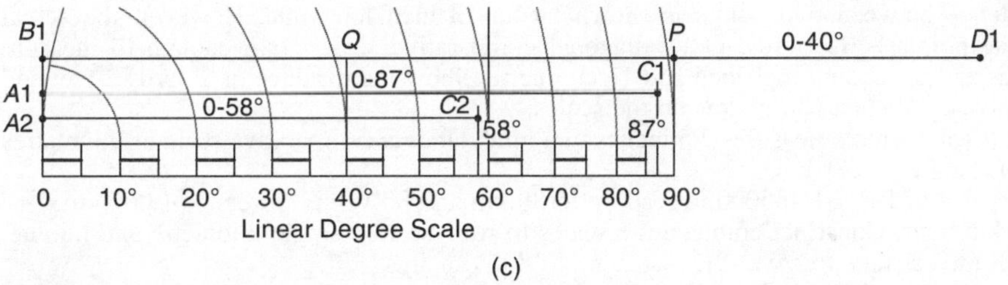

Fig. 5.29

Review Questions

1. Draw a scale of 10 centimetres = 3 decametres to show decametres and metres. Show the lengths of 33 metres and 11 metres on it.
2. Draw a vernier scale of RF = 1/5 to read decimetres, centimetres and millimetres and to measure up to 6 decimetres. Show the lengths of 5.73 dm, 2.99 dm and 0.49 dm.
3. Construct a vernier scale of RF = 1/500 to show decametres, metres and decimetre and to measures up to 4 decametres. Show the lengths of 0.0393 km and 0.0001 km.

4. Draw a vernier scale of RF = 1/24 to read yards, feet and inches and to measure up to 4 yards. Show lengths representing (i) 2 yards 2 feet 10 inches (ii) 1 foot 3 inches.
5. A map of size 500 cm × 50 cm represents an area of 6250 square kilometres. Construct a vernier scale to measure kilometres, hectometres and decametres and long enough to measure up to 7 kilometres. Indicate on this scale a distance of 5.55 kilometres.
6. Draw a vernier scale of 1 : 72 to read inches and long enough to measure 12 yards. Show the following distances on it:
(i) 1 yard 1 foot and 1 inch, (ii) 7 yards 2 feet and 9 inches, and (iii) 10 yards 10 inches.
7. An area of 4000 square kilometres is represented by a map of size 200 cm × 80 cm. Draw a scale to measure the distance up to a single decameter. Mark on it the following distances: (i) 0.09 km (ii) 6 km 4 hm and 6 dam.
8. An area of 144 cm^2 on a map represents an area of 36 km^2 on the field. Find the RF of the scale and draw the diagonal scale to show km, hm and dam and to measure up to 10 km. Indicate on this scale a distance of (i) 7 km (ii) 5 hm and 6 dam.
9. In a dam layout, a line of 33 cm in length represents a distance of 660 m. Prepare an approximate scale for the layout to read up to a single metre and mark a distance to measure 373 metres. Also show a distance of 93 metres. Draw a diagonal scale.
10. An aeroplane is travelling at a speed of 360 km/h. Draw a diagonal scale to represent 6 km by 2 cm and show a distance up to 60 km. Find the RF of the scale. Find the distance covered by the aeroplane in 7 minutes 48 seconds and show it on the scale.
11. A distance of 25.4 cm on a map represents the actual distance of 508 km in a field. What is the RF of the scale? Draw a diagonal scale of this RF long enough to measure up to 400 km and having a LC of 4 km. Show on the scale a distance of 272 km.
12. The distance between Nagpur and Chandrapur is 156 km. The cities are shown 156 mm apart on a road map. Draw a diagonal scale with this RF and long enough to measure up to 200 kilometres. Mark on it the following distances: (i) 109 km (ii) 168 hm.
13. Construct a diagonal scale of RF = 1/6250 to read up to 1 kilometre and to read metres on it. Show a length of 653 metres on it.
14. A forest, measuring 130000 sq. kilometres, is represented on the map by a rectangle of size 80 cm × 65 cm. Construct a diagonal scale to read up to one hectometre and long enough to measure 70 kilometres. Show the distances (i) 46.2 km and (ii) 0.6 km on it. What is RF of the scale?
15. The volume of a water tank is 64 m^3. It is represented on a drawing by a volume of 512 cm^3. Construct a diagonal scale to measure up to 7 m. Show on it the following distances: (i) 6.23 m (ii) 0.57 m. Find RF of scale.
16. Construct comparative diagonal scales of metres and yards having RF = 1/2700 to show upto 400 meters. 1 meter = 1.0936 yards.
17. On a map, the distance between two points is shown by an 18 inch long line. However, the actual distance between the points is 15 yards. Draw diagonal comparative scales long enough to measure 5 yards and 3 metres and to read up to 1 inch and 1 centimetre. Show the distance of 2 yards 2 feet and 2 inches and its equivalent distance in metres on the scales.
18. Calculate the RF of a scale which measures 2.5 inches to a mile. Draw a comparative scale of kilometres to read up to 10 km. 1 mile = 1.61 km.
19. Draw comparative scales of RF = 1/485000 to read up to 80 km and 80 versts. 1 verst = 1.067 km.
20. A car travels at 40 km/hour. Construct comparative scales to read up to a single kilometre and minute. How much time will the car take to cover the distance of 28 kilometres?
21. A car is travelling at a speed of 60 km/h. A 4 cm long line represents the distance traveled by the car in two hours. Construct a suitable comparative scale up to 10 hours. The scale should be able to read the distance traveled by the car in one minute. Show the time required to cover 234 km and also the distance traveled by the car in 4 hours and 24 minutes on the scale.
22. Construct a scale of chords showing 5° divisions and with its aid set off angles of 25°, 40°, 55° and 155°.
23. Draw a quadrilateral *ABCD* having sides AB = 6 cm, BC = 9.5 cm, CD = 4.2 cm and $\angle ABC$ = 89° and measure its remaining angles with the aid of a scale of chords.
24. Draw a trapezium of parallel sides 4 cm and 5.5 cm and the altitude 6 cm. Measure all angles with the aid of a scale of chords.
25. Draw a triangle having sides 8 cm, 9 cm and 10 cm and measure its angles with the aid of a scale of chords.

Chapter 6

ENGINEERING CURVES

6.1 INTRODUCTION

Engineering curves are used in designing certain objects. Designers provide specific profiles of the objects to meet their functional or aesthetic or ergonomic requirements. Therefore, it is important for engineers to study various engineering curves and their applications.

A wide variety of engineering curves are used in design practice. However, this chapter deals with a few common engineering curves like conic sections, cycloids, trochoids, spirals, involutes and helixes. All these curves satisfy specific mathematical equations. The following sections explain the properties, methods of drawing and applications of common engineering curves.

6.2 CONIC SECTIONS

Conic sections (or conics), as the name suggests, are the sections of a right circular cone obtained by cutting the cone in different ways. Depending on the position of the cutting plane relative to the axis of cone, three conic sections—ellipse, parabola and hyperbola—can be obtained, Fig. 6.1.

An *ellipse* is obtained when a section plane *A–A*, inclined to the axis cuts all the generators of the cone.

A *parabola* is obtained when a section plane *B–B*, parallel to one of the generators cuts the cone. Obviously, the section plane will cut the base of the cone.

A *hyperbola* is obtained when a section plane *C–C*, inclined to the axis cuts the cone on one side of the axis. A *rectangular hyperbola* is obtained when a section plane *D–D*, parallel to the axis cuts the cone.

> **Note:** A *circle* is also a conic section. It is obtained when a cutting plane parallel to the base cuts all the generators of the cone.

A conic is defined as the curve traced by a point moving in a plane such that the ratio of its distances from a fixed point and a fixed line is always constant. The fixed point is called the *focus* and the fixed line the *directrix*, (Fig. 6.2). The ratio is called the *eccentricity* and is denoted by *e*.

Thus, e = (Distance of a point from focus)/(Distance of a point from directrix)

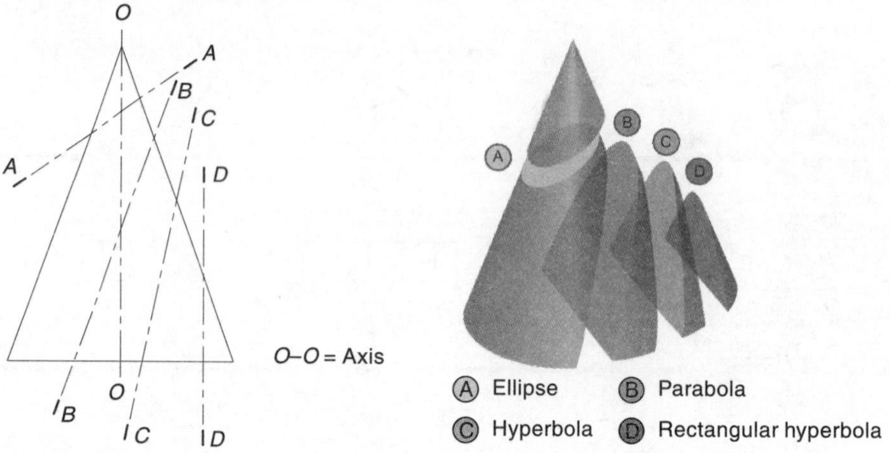

Fig. 6.1

For an ellipse, e is less than 1. For a parabola, it is equal to 1 and for a hyperbola, it is greater than 1.

Other important terms related to conics are as follows:

Axis The line passing through the focus and perpendicular to the directrix is called the axis.

Vertex The point at which the curve intersects the axis is called the vertex.

Latus Rectum The chord of a conic perpendicular to the axis and passing through the focus is called the *latus rectum*, Fig. 6.3, Fig. 6.12 and Fig. 6.18.

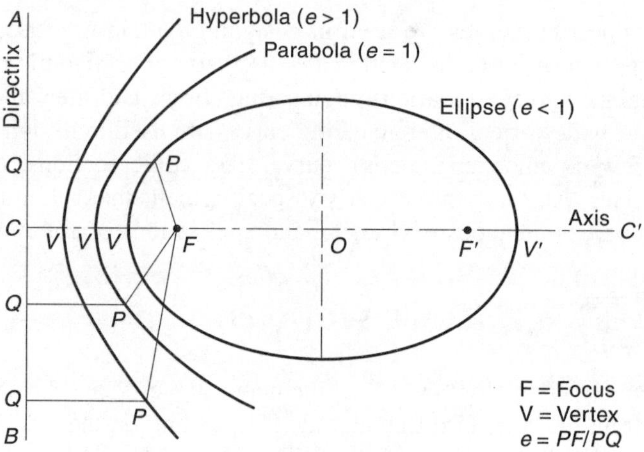

Fig. 6.2

REMEMBER THE FOLLOWING

- For ellipse, $e < 1$
- For parabola, $e = 1$
- For hyperbola, $e > 1$

6.3 ELLIPSE

An ellipse is a conic whose eccentricity is less than 1. It is defined as a closed curve traced by a point moving in a plane such that the sum of its distances from two fixed points in the same plane is always the same. The fixed points represent the foci. As shown in Fig. 6.3, an ellipse has two foci (F and F'),

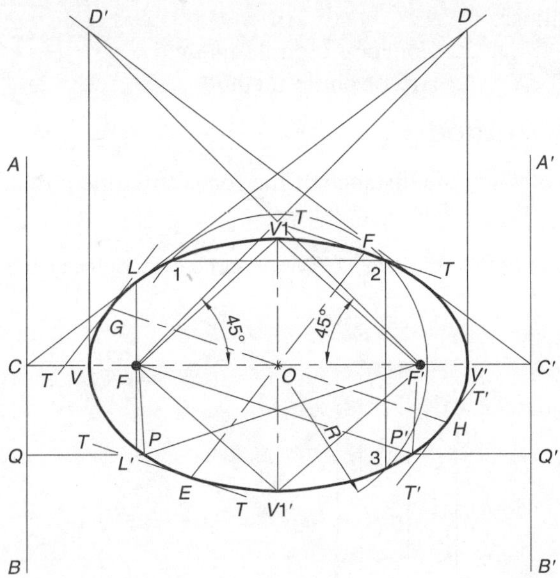

e = PF/PQ = PF/P′Q′ < 1
F & E′ = FOCI
AB & AB′ = Directrices
V–V1′ = Major Axis
V1–V1′ = Minor Axis
O = Centre
V, V′, V1 & V1′ = Vertices
EF & GH = Conjugate Axis
T–T = Tangent to Ellipse at E
T′–T′ = Tangent to Ellipse at G
T–T || GH & T′–T′ || EF
PF + PF′ = V1F + V1F′ = P′F + P′F′ = VF + VF′ = Major Axis
V1F = V1F′ = V1′F = V1′F′ = 1/2 (Major Axis)
Slope of CD = Slope of C′D′ = e
LL′ = Latus Rectum

Fig. 6.3

two directrices (*AB* and *A′B′*), two axes (*V–V′* and *V*1–*V*1′) and four vertices (*V*, *V′*, *V*1 and *V*1′). The two axes are called the *major axis* and *minor axis*. The major axis passes through the foci and terminates on the curve at either ends. The minor axis is a perpendicular bisector of the major axis terminating on the curve at either ends. The point of intersection of the major axis and minor axis is called the *centre*, *O*. Any chord passing through the centre is called the *diameter* of the ellipse. Two diameters, each of which is parallel to the tangents (to the curve) at the extremities of the other, are called *conjugate diameters* or *conjugate axes*, *EF* and *GH*. Obviously, the midpoints of the conjugate axes coincide with the centre *O* of the ellipse. If an arc, with centre *O* and any convenient radius, is drawn, cutting the ellipse at 1, 2 and 3 then 1–2 is parallel to the major axis and 2–3 is parallel to the minor axis. The chord *L–L′* represents the *latus rectum*. As per definition, *PF* + *PF′* = *P′F* + *P′F′* = *V*1–*F* + *V*1–*F′* = *V*1′–*F* + *V*1′–*F′* = *VF* + *VF′* = *V′F* + *V′F′* = Major axis. Obviously, *V*1–*F* = *V*1–*F′* = *V*1′–*F* = *V*1′–*F′* = 1/2 (major axis). A perpendicular through point *D*, which lies at the intersection of the line of slope *e* through *C* and the line at 45° through *F*, meets *CC′* at *V′*.

Elliptical curves find application in architectural and engineering designs, like arches, bridges, elliptical gears, fancy lamps, bullet nose, stuffing box, etc., *Illustration* 6.1.

Illustration 6.1

The following methods are used to construct an ellipse.

1. Focus-Directrix or Eccentricity method
2. Concentric circle method
3. Oblong method
4. Arc of circle method

6.3.1 Focus-Directrix or Eccentricity Method

This is a general method for constructing any conics when the distance of the focus from the directrix and its eccentricity is given.

Example 6.1 Draw an ellipse if the distance of focus from the directrix is 70 mm and the eccentricity is 3/4.

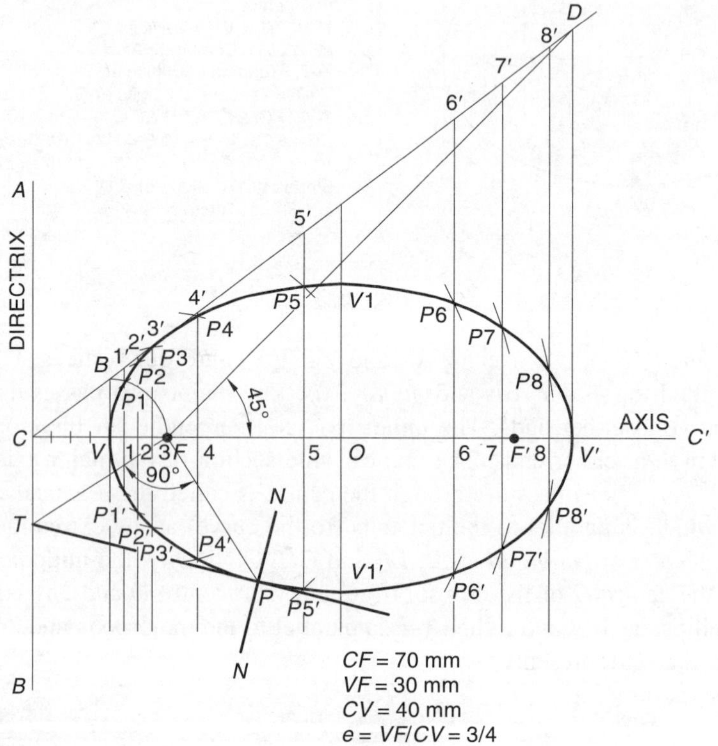

Fig. 6.4

Solution Refer Fig. 6.4.

1. Draw the directrix *AB* and axis *CC′* as shown.
2. Mark *F* on *CC′* such that *CF* = 70 mm.
3. Divide *CF* into 3 + 4 = 7 equal parts and mark *V* at the fourth division from *C*. Now, *e* = *FV*/*CV* = 3/4
4. At *V*, erect a perpendicular *VB* = *VF*. Join *CB*.
5. Through *F*, draw a line at 45° to meet *CB* produced at *D*. Through *D*, drop a perpendicular *DV′* on *CC′*. Mark *O* at the midpoint of *V*–*V′*.
6. Mark a few points, 1, 2, 3, … on *V*–*V′* and erect perpendiculars though them meeting *CD* at 1′, 2′, 3′ …. Also erect a perpendicular through *O*.
7. With *F* as a centre and radius = 1–1′, cut two arcs on the perpendicular through 1 to locate *P*1 and *P*1′. Similarly, with *F* as a centre and radii = 2–2′, 3–3′, etc., cut arcs on the corresponding perpendiculars to locate *P*2 and *P*2′, *P*3 and *P*3′, etc. Also, cut similar arcs on the perpendicular through *O* to locate *V*1 and *V*1′.

8. Draw a smooth closed curve passing through V, $P1$, $P2$, $P3$, ..., $V1$, ..., V', ...,$V1'$, ... $P3'$, $P2'$, $P1'$.
9. Mark F' on CC' such that $V'F' = VF$.

Note: The vertex V' can be located in different ways than mentioned in Step 5 above. As we know, $(V'F/V'C) = 3/4$, i.e., $V'F/(V'F + FC) = 3/4$, i.e., $V'F/(V'F + 70) = 3/4 \Rightarrow V'F = 210$ mm.

6.3.2 Concentric Circle Method

This method is applicable when the major axis and minor axis of an ellipse are given.

Example 6.2 Draw an ellipse having the major axis of 70 mm and the minor axis of 40 mm.

Solution Refer Fig. 6.5.

1. Draw the major axis AB = 70 mm and minor axis CD = 40 mm, bisecting each other at right angles at O.
2. Draw two circles with AB and CD as diameters. Divide both the circles into 12 equal parts and number the divisions as A, 1, 2, 3, ... 10, B and C, 1′, 2′, 3′ ... 10′, D.
3. Through 1, draw a line parallel to CD. Through 1′, draw a line parallel to AB. Mark $P1$ at their intersection.
4. Obtain $P2$, $P4$, $P5$, etc., in a similar way.
5. Draw a smooth closed curve through A–$P1$–$P2$–C–$P4$–$P5$–B–$P6$–$P7$–D–$P9$–$P10$–A.

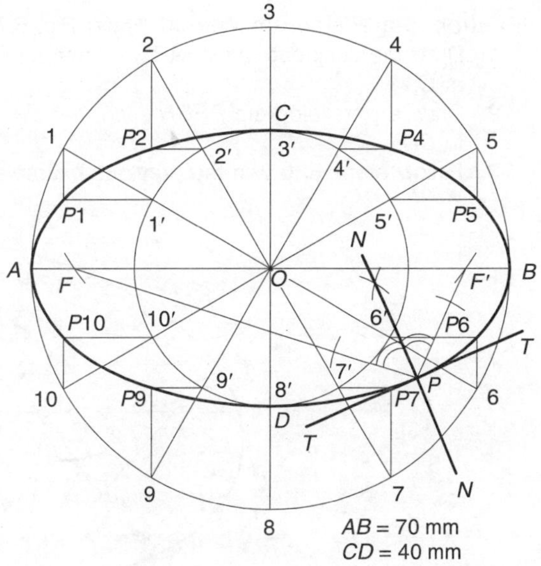

Fig. 6.5

6.3.3 Oblong Method

This method is applicable when the major axis and minor axis or the conjugate axes with the angle between them is given. In the former case, it is called the *rectangle method*, while in latter case, it is called the *parallelogram method*.

Example 6.3 Draw an ellipse with a 70 mm long major axis and a 45 mm long minor axis.

or

Draw an ellipse circumscribing a rectangle having sides 70 mm and 45 mm.

Solution **Rectangle Method:** Refer Fig. 6.6.

1. Draw the major axis AB = 70 mm and minor axis CD = 45 mm, bisecting each other at right angles at O.
2. Draw a rectangle $EFGH$ such that $EF = AB$ and $FG = CD$.
3. Divide AO and AE into same number of equal parts, say 4. Number the divisions as 1, 2, 3 and 1′, 2′, 3′, starting from A.
4. Join C with 1, 2 and 3.
5. Join D with 1′ and extend it to meet C–1 at $P1$. Similarly, join D with 2′ and 3′ and extend them to meet C–2 and C–3 respectively to locate $P2$ and $P3$.

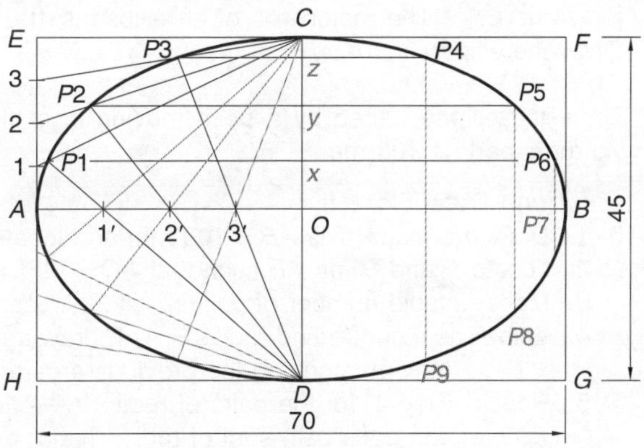

Fig. 6.6

6. Obtain other points in the remaining three quadrants in a similar way. *Alternatively*, other points can be obtained by drawing lines parallel to *AB* and *CD*, through the points *P*1, *P*2, *P*3, etc. For example, draw *P*1–*P*6 parallel to *AB* such that *P*1–*x* = *x*–*P*6. Similarly, *P*2–*y* = *y*–*P*5, *P*3–*z* = *z*–*P*4 and *P*4–*u* = *u*–*P*9.
7. Join *P*1, *P*2, *P*3, etc., to obtain the ellipse.

Example 6.4 Draw an ellipse having conjugate axes of 60 mm and 40 mm long and inclined at 75° to each other.

Solution **Parallelogram Method:** Refer Fig. 6.7.

1. Draw the conjugate axes, *AB* = 60 mm and *CD* = 40 mm, inclined at 75° to each other and bisecting at *O*.
2. Draw a parallelogram *EFGH* such that *EF* is parallel and equal to *AB*, and *FG* is parallel and equal to *CD*.
3. Follow steps 3 to 7 in the previous example.

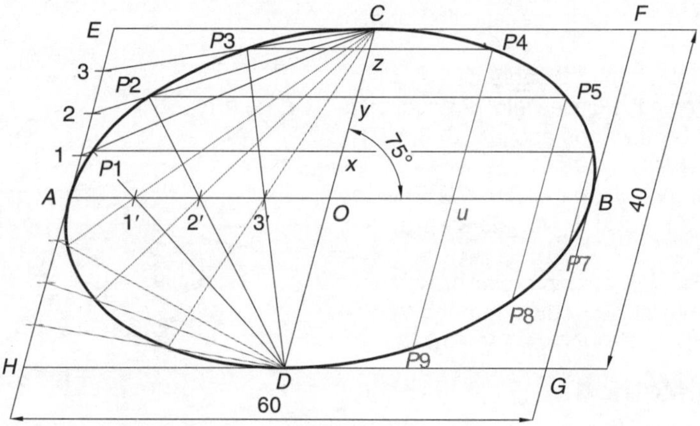

Fig. 6.7

6.3.4 Arcs of Circle Method

This method is applicable when the major axis and minor axis are known or the major axis and the distance between the foci is known. This method is based on the definition of the ellipse.

Example 6.5 The major axis of an ellipse is 100 mm long and the distance between its foci is 70 mm. Draw the ellipse.

or

Draw the ellipse traced by a point moving in a plane such that the sum of its distances from the foci, 70 mm apart, is 100 mm.

Solution Refer Fig. 6.8.

1. Draw the major axis *AB* = 100 mm and locate its midpoint *O*.
2. Locate *F* and *F*′ on *AB* such that *FO* = *OF*′ = 70/2 = 35 mm.
3. Mark suitable number of points, 1, 2, 3, ... on *AB* between *F* and *F*′.
4. With *F* as a centre and radius = *A*–1, draw arcs on either sides of *AB*. With *F*′ as a centre and radius = *B*–1, draw arcs cutting the previous arcs at *P*1 and *P*1′. Note that *A*–1 + *B*–1 = *AB* = major axis.
5. Repeat Step 4, for the pairs of radii = (*A*–2, *B*–2), (*A*–3, *B*–3), etc., to obtain points (*P*2, *P*2′), (*P*3, *P*3′), etc. In each pair, sum of radii = major axis. Therefore, *P*1–*F* + *P*1–*F*′ = *P*2–*F* + *P*2–*F*′ = *P*3–*F* + *P*3–*F*′ = ... = major axis.

6. Draw a smooth curve through *A–P*1–*P*2–*P*3 ... *B* ... *P*3′–*P*2′–*P*1′.

Note: If the minor axis *CD* is given instead of the distance between the foci, then locate the foci *F* and *F′* by cutting the arcs on major axis with *C* as a centre and radius = ½ (major axis) = *OA*.

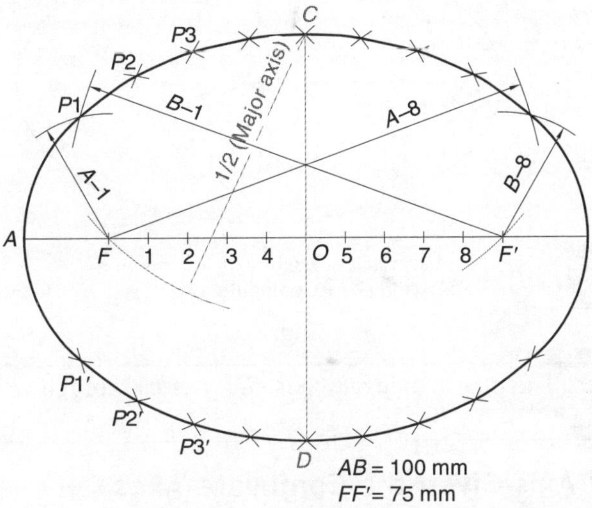

Fig. 6.8

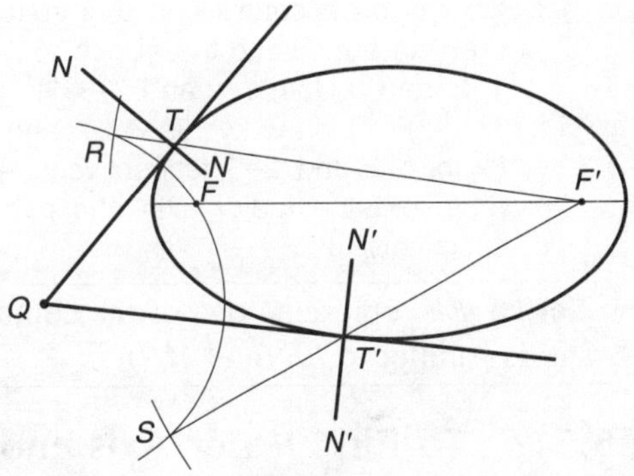

Fig. 6.9

6.3.5 Tangent and Normal to Ellipse

At a Point on the Ellipse There are two methods to draw a tangent and normal at a point on the ellipse: (i) General Method, and (ii) Bisector Method. The general method is common to all the conics and is described in Section 6.6.

Bisector Method It is based on the property of an ellipse that the bisector of an angle formed by joining a point on the curve to the foci is normal to the ellipse at that point.

Example 6.6 Draw the tangent and normal to the ellipse of Example 6.2, at any point *P* on it.

Solution Refer Fig. 6.5.

First obtain the foci *F* and *F′* by cutting the arcs on major axis with *C* as a centre and radius = *OA*.

1. Join *P* with *F* and *F′*.
2. Obtain *N–N*, the bisector of ∠*FPF′*. *N–N* is the required normal.
3. Draw *T–T* perpendicular to *N–N* at *P*. *T–T* is the required tangent.

From a Point outside the Ellipse

Example 6.7 Draw the tangent and normal to the ellipse shown in Fig. 6.9, from a point *Q* outside it.

Solution Refer Fig. 6.9.

1. With *Q* as a centre and radius = *QF*, draw an arc.
2. With *F′* as a centre and radius = major axis, draw an arc cutting the previous arc at *R* and *S*.
3. Join *RF′* and *SF′*, cutting the ellipse at *T* and *T′* respectively.
4. Join *QT* and *QT′* to represent the required tangents. Draw *N–N* and *N′–N′*, perpendicular to *QT* and *QT′* at *T* and *T′* respectively for the required normals.

6.3.6 To Find the Centre, Major Axis and Minor Axis of an Ellipse

Example 6.8 Find the centre, the major axis and the minor axis of the ellipse shown in Fig. 6.10.

Solution

1. Draw any two parallel chords, *RS* and *MN*. Locate their midpoints, *P* and *Q*, respectively.
2. Join *PQ* and extend it to meet the ellipse at *E* and *F*. The midpoint *O* of *EF* is the required centre.
3. With *O* as a centre and any suitable radius, draw an arc cutting the ellipse at three points, 1, 2, and 3. Join 1–2 and 2–3.
4. Through *O*, draw two lines *AB* and *CD*, parallel to 1–2 and 2–3 respectively. *AB* and *CD* represent the major axis and minor axis respectively.

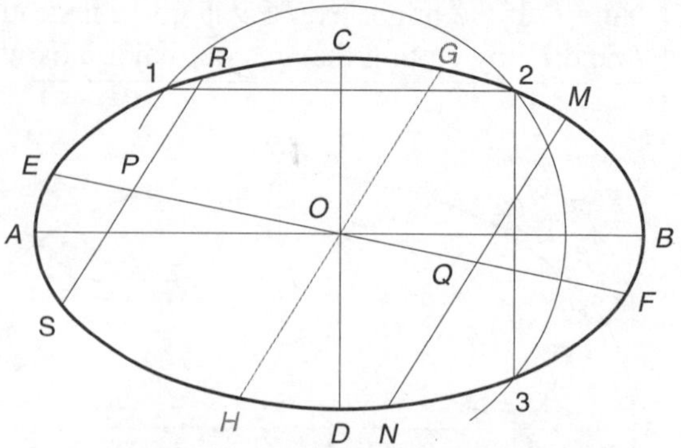

AB and *CD* = Major axis and minor axis
EF and *GH* = Conjugate axis

Fig. 6.10

Note: *EF* represents one of the conjugate axes. The other conjugate axis *GH*, passes through *O* and is parallel to *RS* (and *MN*)

6.3.7 To Find Major Axis and Minor Axis Given the Conjugate Axes

Example 6.9 The conjugate axes of an ellipse are 60 mm and 40 mm long. The angle between them is 75°. Find the major axis and the minor axis.

Solution Refer Fig. 6.11.

1. Draw the given conjugate axes, *EF* = 60 mm and *GH* = 40 mm, inclined at 75° to each other and intersecting at *O*.
2. Draw *MN* = *GH*, the perpendicular bisector of *GH*. Join *EM* and *EN*.
3. Obtain the bisector *EK* of ∠*MEN*.
4. Through *O*, draw the major axis *AB* parallel to *EK* such that *AB* = *EN* + *EM*.
5. Obtain minor axis *CD* = *EN* – *EM*, perpendicular to *AB* at *O*.

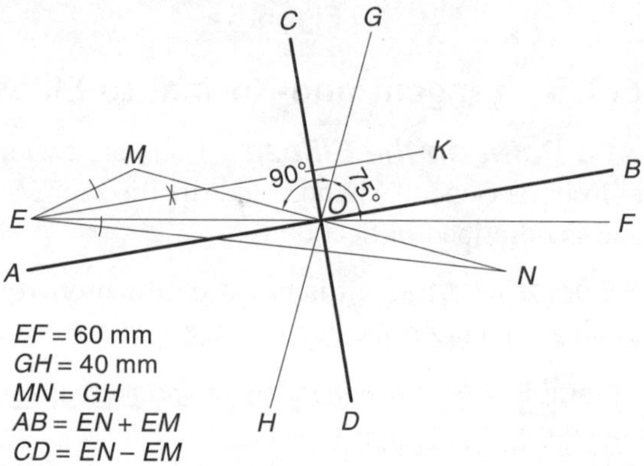

Fig. 6.11

REMEMBER THE FOLLOWING

- The sum of the distances of a point on the ellipse from the two foci is equal to the major axis.
- The distance of any end of the minor axis from any focus is equal to half of the major axis.
- Any chord, common to the ellipse and an arc with centre *O*, is parallel to the minor axis/major axis.
- If a point on the ellipse is joined with the foci then the bisector of the angle formed is normal to the ellipse at that point.
- The chord of an ellipse passing through the midpoints of two parallel chords also passes through the centre. This chord represents one of the conjugate axes.

6.4 PARABOLA

A parabola is a conic whose eccentricity is equal to 1. Unlike an ellipse, it is an open-end curve with a focus (F), a directrix (AB) and an axis (CC'), Fig. 6.12. Any chord (say MM') perpendicular to the axis is called a *double ordinate*. The double ordinate passing through the focus, i.e., LL' represents the *latus rectum*. The double ordinate passing through the ends of the parabola, i.e., RR' is called the *base*. The half of the double ordinate, i.e. RK is called the *ordinate*. The shortest distance of the vertex from any ordinate, i.e., VK is known as the *abscissa*. A line joining the midpoints G and H of any two parallel chords EE' and FF' respectively, is parallel to the axis. A perpendicular to the axis through point D, which lies at the intersection of the line of slope e (=1) through C and the line at 45° through F, meets the axis at V.

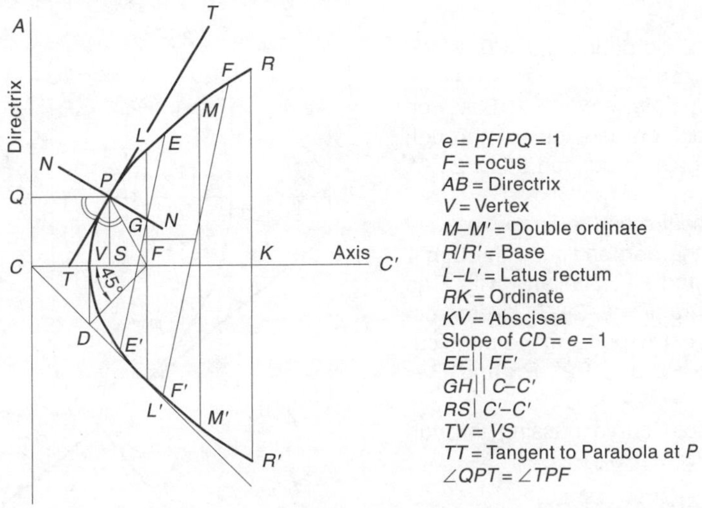

Fig. 6.12

If, through any point P on the parabola, a perpendicular PS is drawn on the axis then the line TP (where T is a point on the axis such that $TV = VS$), is a tangent to the parabola at P. The tangent at any point P on the parabola is a bisector of the angle between the line PF and PQ (PQ being parallel to the axis), i.e., $\angle QPT = \angle TPF$.

The parabolic curves are used on light reflectors, solar concentrators, telecommunication dishes, sound reflectors, parabolic mirrors, cantilever beams, missile trajectory, etc., *Illustration* 6.2. The movements of objects in space under the influence of gravity follow a parabolic path.

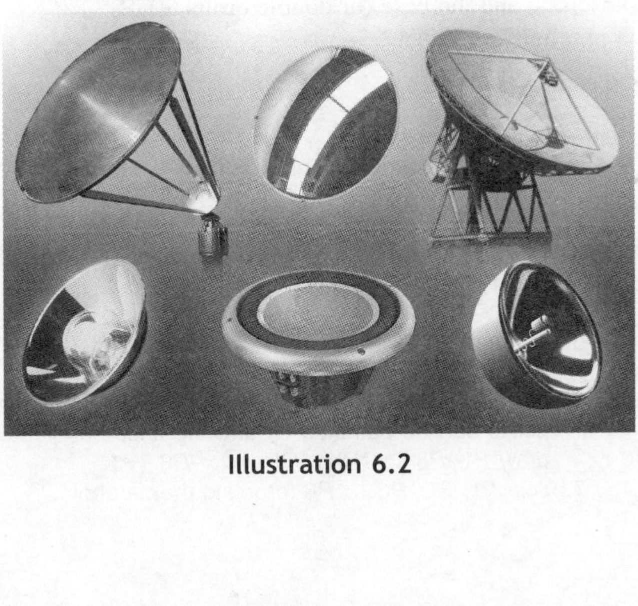

Illustration 6.2

A parabola can be constructed by following methods:

1. Focus-Directrix or Eccentricity Method
2. Rectangle Method
3. Parallelogram Method
4. Tangent Method

6.4.1 Focus-Directrix or Eccentricity Method

This method is similar to that for an ellipse.

Example 6.10 Draw a parabola if the distance of the focus from the directrix is 60 mm.

Solution Refer Fig. 6.13.

1. Draw directrix *AB* and axis *CC′* as shown.
2. Mark *F* on *CC′* such that *CF* = 60 mm.
3. Mark *V* at the midpoint of *CF*. Therefore, *e* = *VF*/*VC* = 1.
4. At *V*, erect a perpendicular *VB* = *VF*. Join *CB*.
5. Mark a few points, say, 1, 2, 3, ... on *VC′* and erect perpendiculars through them meeting *CB* produced at 1′, 2′, 3′, ...
6. With *F* as a centre and radius = 1–1′, cut two arcs on the perpendicular through 1 to locate *P*1 and *P*1′. Similarly, with *F* as a centre and radii = 2–2′, 3–3′, etc., cut arcs on the corresponding perpendiculars to locate *P*2 and *P*2′, *P*3 and *P*3′, etc.
7. Draw a smooth curve passing through *V*, *P*1, *P*2, *P*3 ... *P*3′, *P*2′, *P*1′.

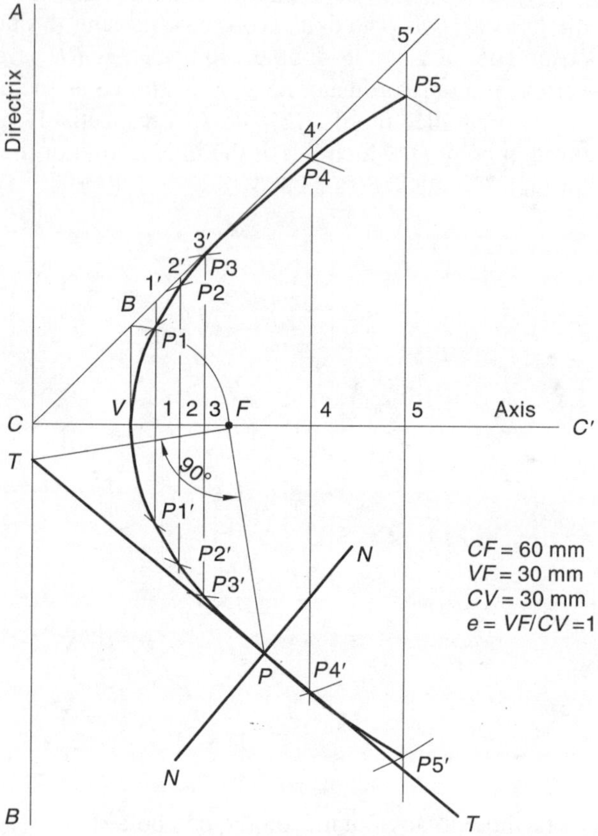

Fig. 6.13

6.4.2 Rectangle Method

This method is applicable when the axis (or abscissa) and the base (or double ordinate) of a parabola are given.

Example 6.11 Draw a parabola having an abscissa of 30 mm and the double ordinate of 70 mm.

Solution Refer Fig. 6.14.

1. Draw the double ordinate *RS* = 70 mm. At midpoint *K* erect a perpendicular *KV* = 30 mm to represent the abscissa.
2. Construct a rectangle *RSMN* such that *SM* = *KV*.
3. Divide *RN* and *RK* into the same number of equal parts, say 5. Number the divisions as 1, 2, 3, 4 and 1′, 2′, 3′, 4′, starting from *R*.
4. Join *V*–1, *V*–2, *V*–3 and *V*–4.
5. Through 1′, 2′, 3′ and 4′, draw lines parallel to *KV* to meet *V*–1 at *P*1, *V*–2 at *P*2, *V*–3 at *P*3 and *V*–4 at *P*4, respectively.
6. Obtain *P*5, *P*6, *P*7 and *P*8 in the other half of the rectangle in a similar way. *Alternatively*, these points can be obtained by drawing lines parallel to *RS* through *P*1, *P*2, *P*3 and *P*4. For example, draw *P*1–*P*8 such that *P*1–*x* = *x*–*P*8.
7. Join *P*1, *P*2, *P*3 ... *P*8 to obtain the parabola.

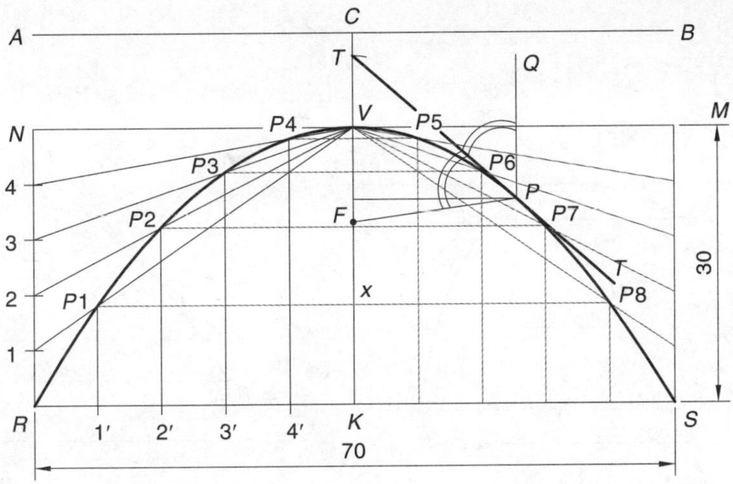

Fig. 6.14

6.4.3 Parallelogram Method

This method is similar to rectangle method. It is adopted when the axis and the base are inclined to each other.

Example 6.12 Draw a parabola of base 100 mm and axis 50 mm if the axis makes 70° to the base.

or

Inscribe a parabola in a parallelogram of sides 100 mm × 50 mm and with an included angle of 70°.

Solution Refer Fig. 6.15.

1. Draw the base *RS* = 100 mm and through its midpoint *K*, draw the axis *KV* = 50 mm, inclined at 70° to *RS*.
2. Draw a parallelogram *RSMN* such that *SM* is parallel and equal to *KV*.
3. Follow steps 3 to 7 of the previous example.

6.4.4 Tangent Method

This method is applicable when the base (or double ordinate) and the axis (or abscissa) or the base and the inclinations of tangents at open ends of the parabola with the base are given.

Example 6.13 Draw a parabola if the base is 70 mm and the tangents at the base ends make 60° to the base.

Solution Refer Fig. 6.16.

1. Draw the base *RS* = 70 mm. Through *R* and *S*, draw the lines at 60° to the base, meeting at *L*.
2. Divide *RL* and *SL* into the same number of equal parts, say 6. Number the divisions as 1, 2, 3 ... and 1′, 2′, 3′, ... as shown.
3. Join 1–1′, 2–2′, 3–3′, ...
4. Draw a smooth curve, starting from *R* and ending at *S* and tangent to 1–1′, 2–2′, 3–3′, etc., at *P*1, *P*2, *P*3, etc., respectively.

Note: A perpendicular to *RS* from *L* cutting the curve at *V* represents the axis of the parabola. As 3–3′ is midway of *LK*, *LV* = *VK* = abscissa. Therefore, if abscissa is given instead of inclination of the tangents, then construct Δ*RSL* such that *LK* = 2 (Abscissa). Steps 2 to 4 then may be followed to obtain the required parabola.

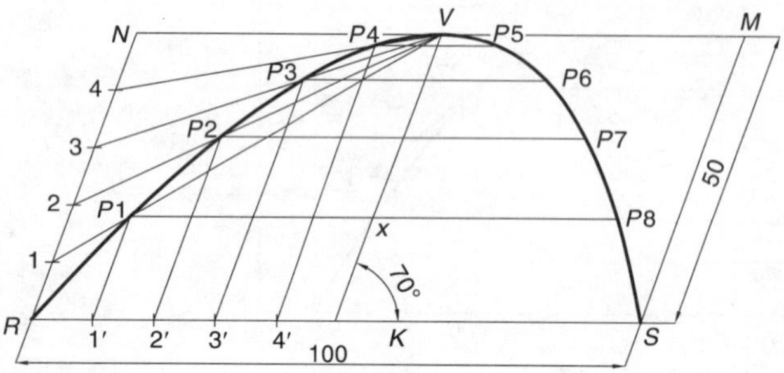

Fig. 6.15

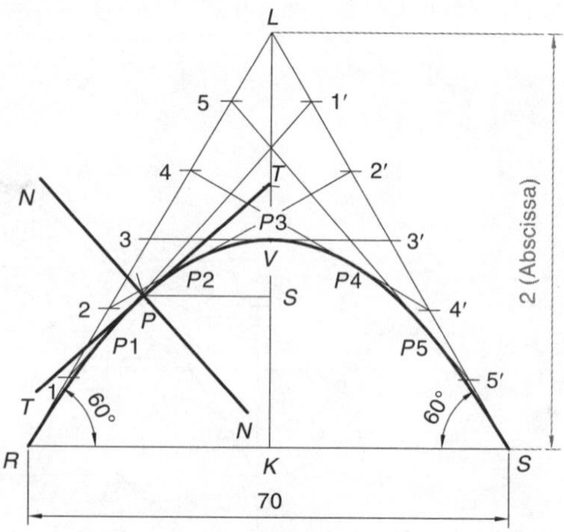

Fig. 6.16

6.4.5 Tangent and Normal to Parabola

At a Point on the Parabola Three methods may be adopted to draw a tangent and a normal at a point on the parabola—(i) General method, (ii) Bisector method, and (iii) Ordinate method.

Bisector Method: It is based on the property of a parabola that the tangent at any point *P* on the curve is a bisector of the angle formed between *PF* and *PQ*, *PQ* being parallel to the axis.

Example 6.14 Draw the tangent and normal to the parabola shown in Fig. 6.12 at any point *P* on it.

Solution

1. Join *PF*. Draw *PQ* parallel to the axis.
2. Draw the bisector *T–T* of ∠*FPQ* to represent the required tangent.
3. Draw normal *N–N* perpendicular *T–T* at *P*.

Ordinate Method: This method is very simple and applicable when the focus and directrix of a parabola are unknown.

Example 6.15 Draw the tangent and normal to the parabola of Example 6.13 at a point 20 mm from the vertex.

Solution Refer Fig. 6.16.

First locate point *P* on the curve 20 mm vertically below *V*.

1. Draw the ordinate *PS*. On *LK*, mark *T* such that *TV* = *VS*.
2. Join *TP* and extend to obtain tangent *T–T*.
3. Draw normal *N–N* perpendicular to *T–T* at *P*.

From a Point outside the Parabola

Example 6.16 Draw the tangent and normal to the parabola shown in Fig. 6. 17 from a point *Q* outside it.

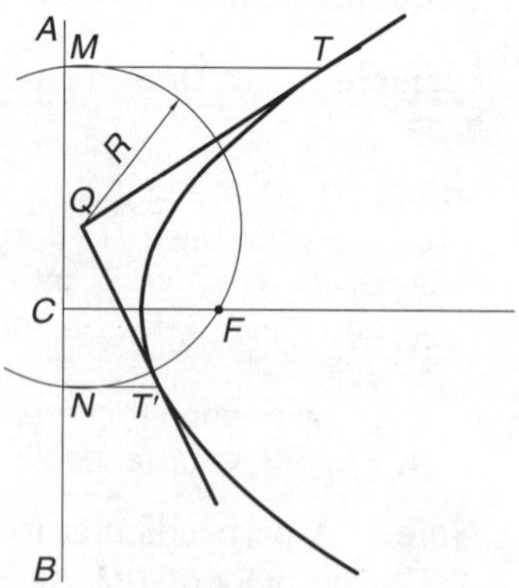

Fig. 6.17

Solution

1. With *Q* as a centre and radius = *QF*, draw an arc cutting the directrix at *M* and *N*.
2. From *M* and *N*, draw lines parallel to the axis cutting the curve at *T* and *T′*.
3. Join *QT* and *QT′* for the required tangents. Normals may be drawn perpendicular to the tangents.

6.4.6 To Find Focus and Directrix of Parabola

Example 6.17 Find the focus and directrix of the parabola in Example 6.11.

Solution Refer Fig. 6.14.

1. At any point *P*, draw tangent *T–T* to the curve using ordinate method.
2. Draw *PQ* parallel to the axis.
3. Through *P*, draw a line cutting the axis at *F* such that ∠*TPF* = ∠*TPQ*. *F* is the focus of parabola.
4. On *KV* produced, locate *C* such that *VF* = *VC*. Through *C*, draw directrix *AB* perpendicular to *KV*.

REMEMBER THE FOLLOWING

- ➢ The tangent at any point on the parabola is a bisector of the angle between the line joining that point with the focus and perpendicular from that point to the dirctrix.
- ➢ If an ordinate through any point on the parabola meets the axis at *S* and the tangent at that point meets the axis at *T*, then *TV* = *VS* (*V* being the vertex).
- ➢ A line joining the midpoints of any two parallel chords of the parabola is parallel to the axis.

6.5 HYPERBOLA

A hyperbola is a conic whose eccentricity is greater than 1. It is defined as a curve traced by a point moving in a plane such that the difference between its distances from two fixed points in the same plane is always the same. The fixed points represent the foci. Like a parabola, it is also an open-end curve. As shown in Fig. 6.18, the hyperbolas exist in a pair. It has two foci (*F* and *F′*), two directrices (*AB* and *A′B′*), an axis (*CD*) and two vertices (*V* and *V′*).

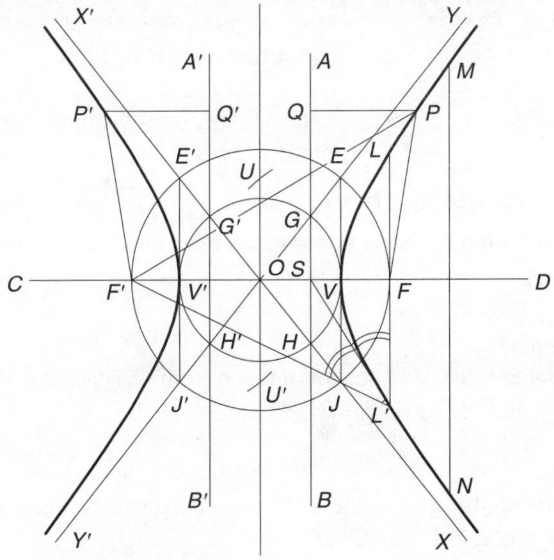

e = *PF*/*PQ* = *P′F′*/*P′Q′* > 1
F & *F′* = FOCI
AB & *A′B′* = Directrices
CD = Axis
O = Centre
V & *V′* = Vertices
V–V′ = *PF′–PF* = Transverse Axis
U–U′ = Conjugate Axes
X–X′ & *Y–Y′* = Asymptotes
MN = Double Ordinate
L–L′ = Latus Rectum
∠*F′L′S* = ∠*SL′F*

Fig. 6.18

The line $V–V'$ represents *transverse axis* of the hyperbola. As per definition, $PF'–PF = VF'–VF = V–V'$, i.e., the difference of the distances of a point on the curve from the two foci is always equal to transverse axis. The midpoint of the transverse axis is called the *centre O*. The two lines, $X–X'$ and $Y–Y'$, intersecting at O are called as *asymptotes*. If a circle is drawn with centre O and radius = OF then the asymptotes pass through the ends of the chords EJ and $E'J'$ (perpendicular to the axis and passing through vertices V and V' respectively) of the circle. The asymptotes also pass through the points of intersection of the circle of diameter $V–V'$ with the directrices AB and $A'B'$, i.e., G, H, G', H'. The hyperbola if produced at ends approaches nearer and nearer to the asymptotes but never touches them. Any chord, say MN, perpendicular to the axis represents *double ordinate* of the hyperbola. *Abscissa* is then the distance of the nearest vertex from the given ordinate. The *conjugate axis U–U'* is a line perpendicular to the axis at O such that $UV = U'V' = FO = F'O$. The perpendicular chord LL' through the focus represents *latus rectum.* If an end, say L', of the *latus rectum* is joined with the other focus, i.e., F', then the bisector of the angle between that line and the *latus rectum*, i.e., $\angle FL'F'$, passes through the intersection of directrix AB with the axis, i.e., $\angle F'L'S = \angle SL'F$.

If the asymptotes are perpendicular to each other then the hyperbola is called *rectangular hyperbola* or *equilateral hyperbola*. In case of rectangular hyperbola, the product of distances of any point on the curve from the asymptotes is always constant. Theoretically, it represent Boyle's law*, PV = Constant.

Hyperbolic curves are applied in designing cooling towers, hyperbolic mirrors, flower vases, curved wooden objects, etc., *Illustration* 6.3. The theory of hyperbola is useful in deciding the location of a ship in long-range navigation.

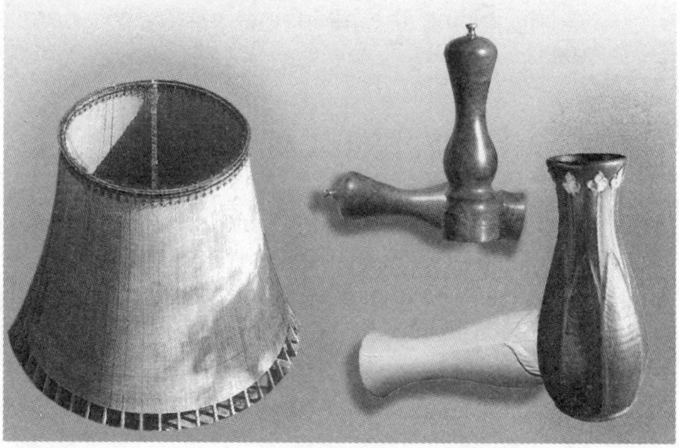

Illustration 6.3

The following methods are used to construct the hyperbola:

1. Focus-Directrix or Eccentricity Method
2. Arc of Circle Method
3. Rectangle or Abscissa-Ordinate Method
4. Asymptote Method

6.5.1 Focus Directrix or Eccentricity Method

Example 6.18 Draw a hyperbola of $e = 3/2$ if the distance of the focus from the directrix = 50 mm.

Solution Refer Fig. 6.19.

1. Draw directrix AB and axis CC' as shown.
2. Mark F on CC' such that CF = 50 mm.
3. Divide CF in to 3 + 2 = 5 equal parts and mark V at second division from C. Now, $e = VF/VC = 3/2$.
4. Follow steps 4 to 7 of Example 6.10.

6.5.2 Arc of Circle Method

This method is applicable when the length of the transverse axis and the distance between foci are given. It is based on the definition of hyperbola.

*The volume (V) of a gas in a closed container is inversely proportional to its absolute pressure (P) provided that the temperature is constant.

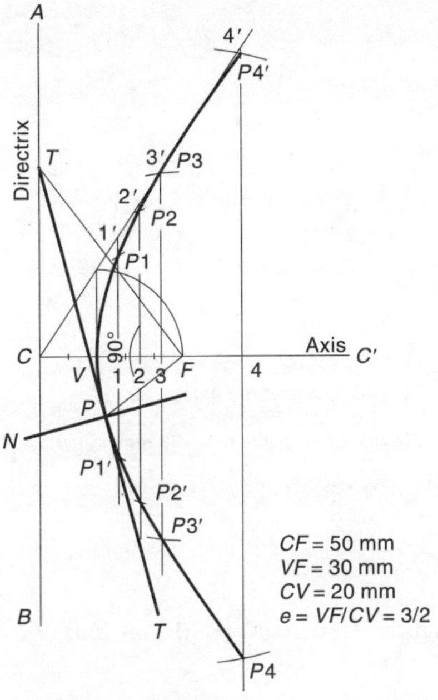

Fig. 6.19

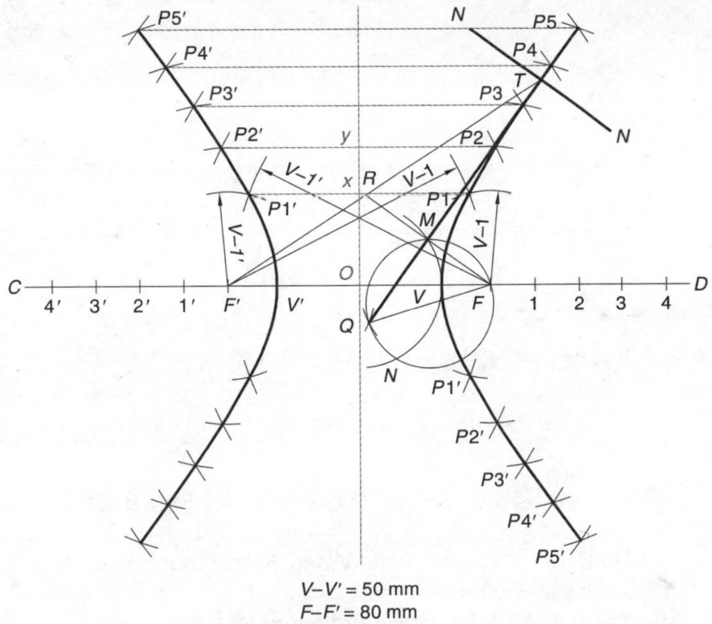

Fig. 6.20

Example 6.19 Draw a hyperbola if the transverse axis is 50 mm and the distance between the foci is 80 mm.

or

Draw the hyperbola traced by a point *P* moving in plane such that the difference of its distances from the foci, 80 mm apart, is 50 mm.

Solution Refer Fig. 6.20.

1. Draw axis *CD* and on it mark *V–V′* = 50 mm and *F–F′* = 80 mm such that *VF* = *V′F′*.
2. On *CD*, mark a few points, 1, 2, 3, 4 between *F* and *D*.
3. With *F* as a centre and radius =*V*–1, draw two arcs on either side of *CD*. With *F′* as a centre and radius = *V′*–1, draw two arcs cutting the previous arcs at *P*1 and *P*1′. Note that (*V′*–1) – (*V*–1) = transverse axis.
4. Repeat step 3, for the pairs of radii = (*V*–2, *V′*–2), (*V*–3, *V′*–3) to obtain points (*P*2, *P*2′), (*P*3, *P*3′), etc. In each pair, difference of radii = Transverse Axis. Therefore, (*V′*–*P*1) – (*V*–*P*1) = (*V′*– *P*2) – (*V*–*P*2) = (*V′*– *P*3) – (*V*–*P*3) = … = Transverse Axis.
5. Draw a smooth curve through *V*, *P*1, *P*2, *P*3 … *P*1′, *P*2′, ….
6. To obtain the other half of hyperbola, mark a few points 1′, 2′, 3′, 4′ between *F′* and *C′* and repeat the similar procedure. *Alternatively*, draw a conjugate axis though *O* and then draw *P*1- *P*1″, *P*2-*P*2″, etc., parallel to *CD* such that *P*1–*x* = *x*–*P*1″, *P*2–*y* = *y*–*P*2″, etc.

6.5.3 Rectangle or Abscissa-Ordinate Method

This method is applicable when the abscissa, double ordinate and the transverse axis are known.

Example 6.20 Draw a hyperbola having the double ordinate of 100 mm, the abscissa of 60 mm and the transverse axis of 160 mm.

Solution Refer Fig. 6.21.

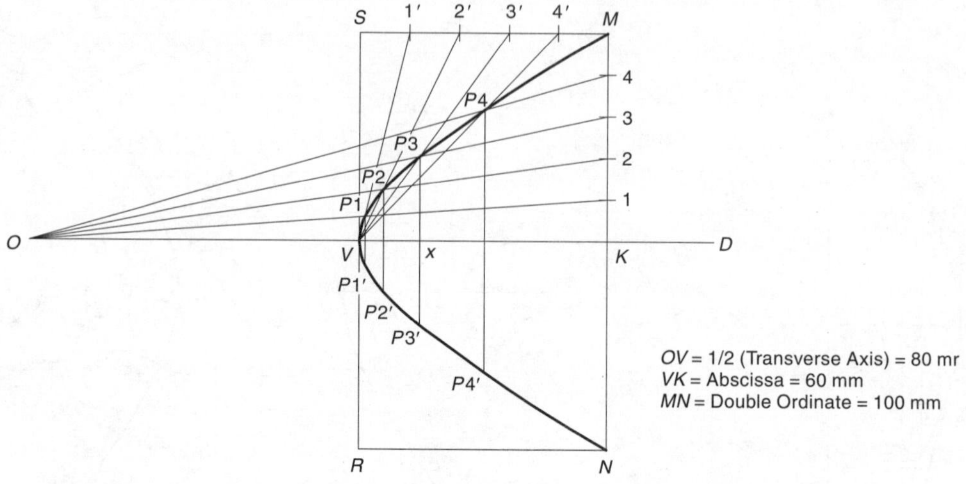

Fig. 6.21

1. Draw axis *OD* and mark *V* and *K* on it such that *OV* = 1/2(Transverse Axis) = 80 mm and *VK* = Abscissa = 60 mm.
2. Through *K*, draw double ordinate *MN* = 100 mm.
3. Construct rectangle *MNRS* such that *NR* = *VK*.
4. Divide *MK* and *MS* into the same number of equal parts, say 5. Number the divisions as shown.
5. Join *O*–1, *O*–2, *O*–3, etc. Also join *V*–1′, *V*–2′, *V*–3′, etc. Mark *P*1, *P*2, *P*3, etc., at the intersections of *O*–1 and *V*–1′, *O*–2 and *V*–2′, *O*–3 and *V*–3′, etc., respectively.
6. Obtain *P*1′, *P*2′, *P*3′, etc., in other half in a similar way. *Alternatively*, draw *P*1–*P*1′, *P*2–*P*2′, *P*3–*P*3′, etc., such that *P*3–*x* = *x*–*P*3′ and likewise.

6.5.4 Asymptote Method

This method is applicable when the angle between the asymptotes and the distances of a point on the hyperbola from the two asymptotes are given. Obviously, a rectangular hyperbola is obtained if the asymptotes are at right angles to each other.

Example 6.21 Draw a rectangular hyperbola if a point on it is 70 mm and 85 mm from the asymptotes.

Solution Refer Fig. 6.22.

1. Draw the asymptotes *OX* and *OY*, perpendicular to each other.
2. Draw *EF* parallel to and 70 mm from *OX*. Also, draw *GH* parallel to and 85 mm from *OY*. Mark *P* at the intersection of *EF* and *GH*.
3. On *PF*, mark a few points, 1, 2, 3, etc. Also mark 6, 7, 8, etc., on *PG*.
4. Join *O*–1, *O*–2, *O*–3, … , *O*–6, *O*–7, *O*–8, etc. Mark 1′, 2′, 3′, … 6′, 7′, 8′, etc., at the intersection of these lines with *GH* and *EF* as shown.
5. Through 1, draw a line parallel to *OY* and through 1′, draw a line parallel to *OX*, meeting each other at *P*1.
6. Follow step 5 in relation to points (2, 2′), (3, 3′), etc., to obtain *P*2, *P*3, etc.
7. Obtain *P*6, *P*7, *P*8, etc., in a similar way.
8. Draw a smooth curve through *P*, *P*1, *P*2, *P*3, …, *P*8.

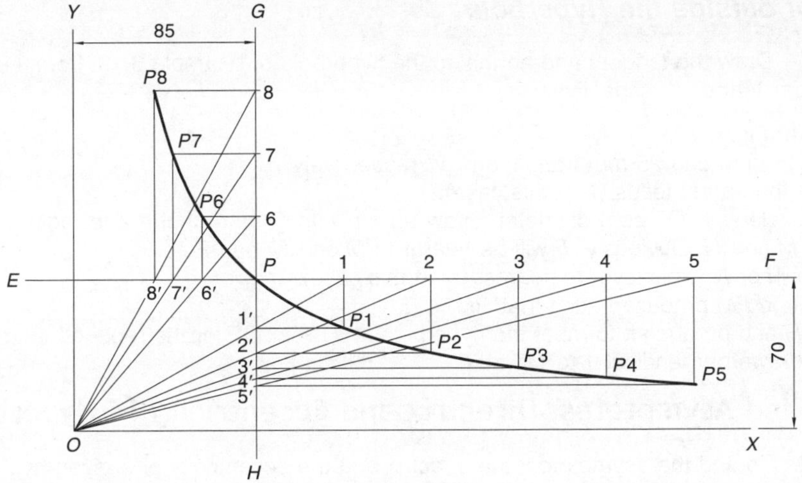

Fig. 6.22

Example 6.22 The asymptotes of a hyperbola are inclined at 60° to each other. Draw the hyperbola if a point on it is 30 mm and 45 mm from the two asymptotes.

Solution Refer Fig. 6.23.

1. Draw the asymptotes *OX* and *OY*, inclined at 60° to each other.
2. Draw *EF* parallel to and 30 mm from *OX*. Also draw *GH* parallel to and 45 mm from *OY*. Mark *P* at their intersection.
3. Follow steps 3 to 8 of the previous example.

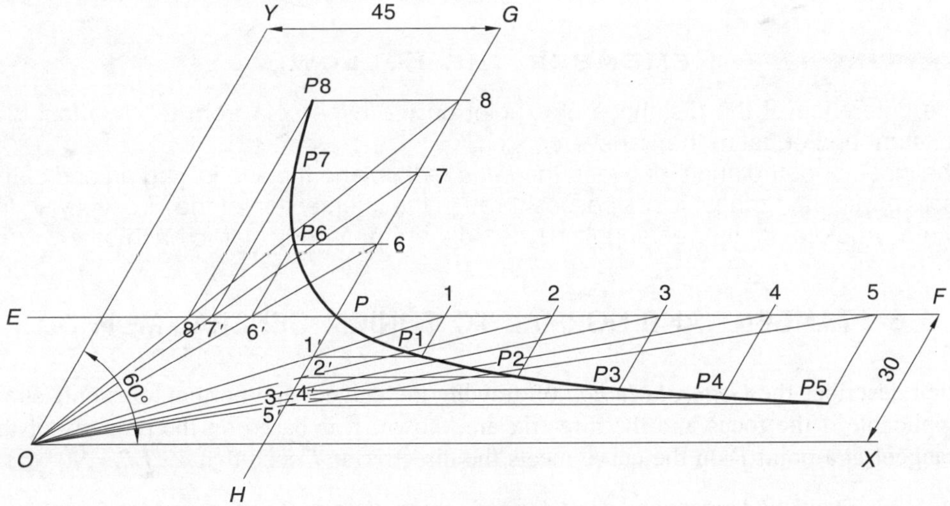

Fig. 6.23

6.5.5 Tangent and Normal to Hyperbola

At a Point on the Hyperbola The general method, explained in Section 6.6, is adopted to draw the tangent and normal at a point on the hyperbola.

From a Point outside the Hyperbola

Example 6.23 Draw the tangent and normal to the hyperbola of Example 6.19, from the point Q, 20 mm and 25 mm from V and V' respectively.

Solution Refer Fig. 6.20.
First locate Q, 20 mm and 25 mm from V and V' respectively.

1. Join Q with nearest focus (F in this case).
2. Draw a circle with QF as a diameter. Draw an arc with O as a centre and radius = OV, cutting the circle at M and N. Obviously, F will be nearer to M and N than F'.
3. Join F to M or N, whichever is nearest (M in this case).
4. Locate R on FM produced such that $RM = FM$.
5. Join F'–R and produce it to meet the hyperbola at T. Join QT for the required tangent. Normal N–N may be drawn perpendicular to QT at T.

6.5.6 To Find Asymptotes, Directrix and Eccentricity of Hyperbola

Example 6.24 To find the asymptotes, the directrix and the eccentricity of a given hyperbola.

Solution Refer Fig. 6.18.

To find asymptotes Draw a circle with O as a centre and radius = OF. Draw the chord EJ of this circle, passing through V and perpendicular to the axis. Join OE and OJ and extend them to represent the asymptotes.

To find directrix Draw a circle with O as a centre and radius = OV, intersecting the asymptotes at G and H. The line AB passing through G and H represents the directrix.

To find eccentricity Mark any point P on the curve. Draw a perpendicular PQ to the directrix. Then, $e = PF/PQ$.

REMEMBER THE FOLLOWING

- The difference of the distances of a point on the hyperbola from the two foci is always constant and equal to the transverse axis.
- The bisector of the angle between the *latus rectum* and the line joining an end of the *latus rectum* with the farthest focus passes through the intersection of the directrix with the axis.
- The asymptotes of the rectangular hyperbola are perpendicular to each other.

6.6 TANGENT AND NORMAL TO CONICS: GENERAL METHOD

This section describes the *General Method* of drawing the tangent and normal to a conic at a point on it. It is applicable if the focus and the directrix are known. It is based on the property of the conics that the tangent at a point P on the curve meets the directrix at T such that $\angle TFP = 90°$.

Example 6.25 Draw the tangent and normal to the conics, at point P on them, of the Examples 6.1, 6.10 and 6.18 (Figs 6.4, 6.13 and 6.19 respectively).

Solution

1. Join P with F.
2. Draw FT perpendicular to PF cutting the directrix at T.
3. Draw a line T–T passing through P for the required tangent.
4. Draw N–N, perpendicular to TT at P, to represent the required normal.

REMEMBER THE FOLLOWING

- If a triangle *PFT* is formed such that the points *P* and *T* are on the conic and directrix respectively and $PF \perp FT$, then *TP* is tangent to the conic.

6.7 CYCLOIDAL CURVES

The cycloidal curves include cycloids and trochoids.

A *cycloid* is a curve generated by a point on the circumference of a circle rolling along a straight line without slipping. The rolling circle is called a *generating circle* and the straight line is called a *directing line* or *base line*. The point on the generating circle which traces the curve is called the *generating point*. The cycloid is called the *epicycloid* when the generating circle rolls along another circle outside it. *Hypocycloid*, opposite to the epicycloid, is obtained when the generating circle rolls along another circle inside it. The other circle along which the generating circle rolls is called the *directing circle* or the *base circle*. Obviously, for one revolution of the generating circle of diameter *D*, the length of the directing line or directing circle covered will be equal to πD. If *R* is the radius of the directing circle, then $\pi D = R\theta$, where θ is the angle in radian, subtended by the directing arc at its centre.

If the normal at the point *P* on the cycloid intersects the directing line (or directing circle) at *N* and the normal to the directing line (or directing circle) at *N* meets the locus of the centre of generating circle at *C*, then *CP* = radius of the generating circle. This property is used to draw the tangent and normal to the cycloids.

The *trochoid* is a curve generated by a point outside or inside the circle rolling along a straigth line without slipping. If the point is outside the circle, the curve obtained is called the *superior trochoid*. On the contrary, the curve is an *inferior trochoid* if the point is inside the circle. If the generating circle rolls outside the directing circle, the resulting trochoid is called an *epitrochoid*. The trochoid is a *hypotrohoid* when the generating circle rolls inside the directing circle. The epitrochoid may be a *superior epitrochoid* or *inferior epitrochoid* depending on whether the generating point is outside or inside the generating circle. The same thing applies to *superior hypotrohoid* and *inferior hypotrohoid*. The detail classification of a cycloidal curve is shown in Table 6.1.

The cycloidal curves are extensively used in designing the various mechanisms. They find applications in designing the profiles of special purpose gears and racks, hydraulic gear pumps, cycloidal gear boxes, cycloidal cams, etc., *Illustration* 6.4.

The cycloids and trochoids are drawn by assuming various positions of the generating circle along the directing line or directing circle.

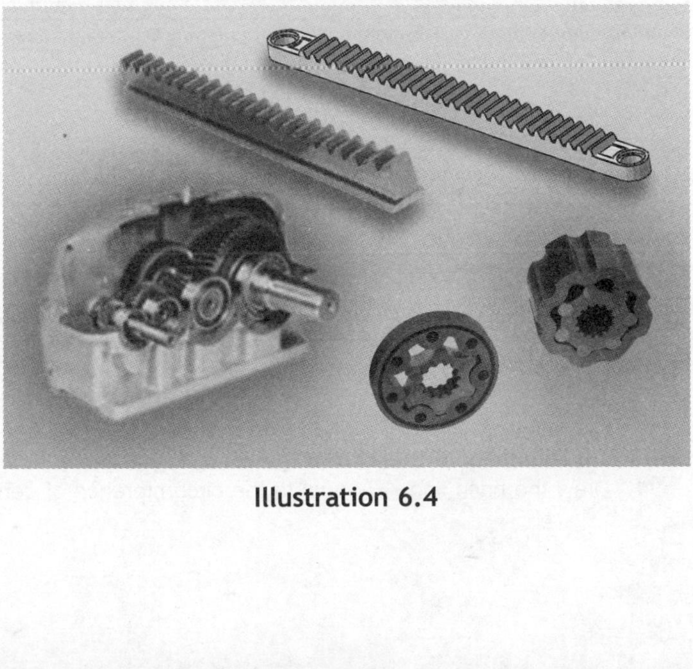

Illustration 6.4

Table 6.1 Classification of Cycloidal Curve

		Generating Circle		
		On the directing line	*Outside the directing circle*	*Inside the directing circle*
Generating Point	*On the generating circle*	Cycloid	Epicycloid	Hypocycloid
	Outside the generating circle	Superior Trochoid	Superior Epitrochoid	Superior Hypotrochiod
	Inside the generating circle	Inferior Trochoid	Inferior Epitrochoid	Inferior Hypotrochiod

6.7.1 Cycloid

Example 6.26 A wheel of diameter 60 cm rolls on a straight horizontal road. Draw the locus of a point *P* on the periphery of the wheel, for one revolution of the wheel, if *P* is initially (a) on the road (b) farthest from the road.

Solution

(a) Point *P* initially on the road, Fig. 6.24(a).

1. Draw the base line *P′–P″* equal to the circumference of generating circle, i.e., $\pi \times 60$ cm = 188 cm.
2. Draw the generating circle with *C* as a centre and radius = 30 cm, tangent to *P′–P″* at *P′*. Point *P* is initially at *P′*.
3. Draw *C–C″* parallel and equal to *P′–P″* to represent the locus of the centre of the generating circle.
4. Obtain 12 equal divisions on the circle. Number the divisions as 1, 2, 3, etc., starting from *P′* as shown. Through 1, 2, 3, etc., draw lines parallel to *P′–P″*.
5. Obtain 12 equal divisions on *C–C″* and name them as *C*1, *C*2, *C*3, etc.
6. With *C*1, *C*2, *C*3, etc. as the centres and radius = *CP′* = 30 mm, cut the arcs on the lines through 1, 2, 3, etc., to locate respectively *P*1, *P*2, *P*3, etc.
7. Join *P′*, *P*1, *P*2, *P*3, etc. by a smooth curve.

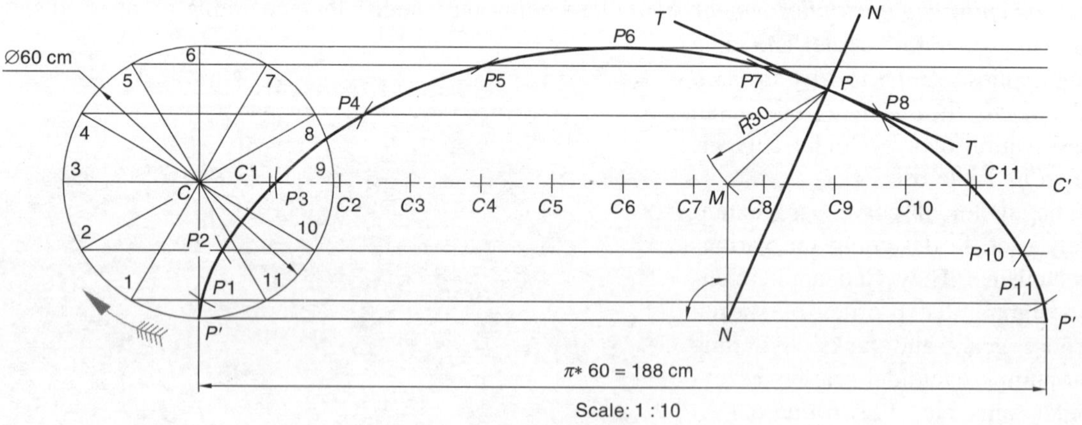

Fig. 6.24(a)

(b) Point *P* initially farthest from the road, Fig. 6.24(b).

1. Draw the base line *AB* equal to the circumference of generating circle, i.e., 188 cm.

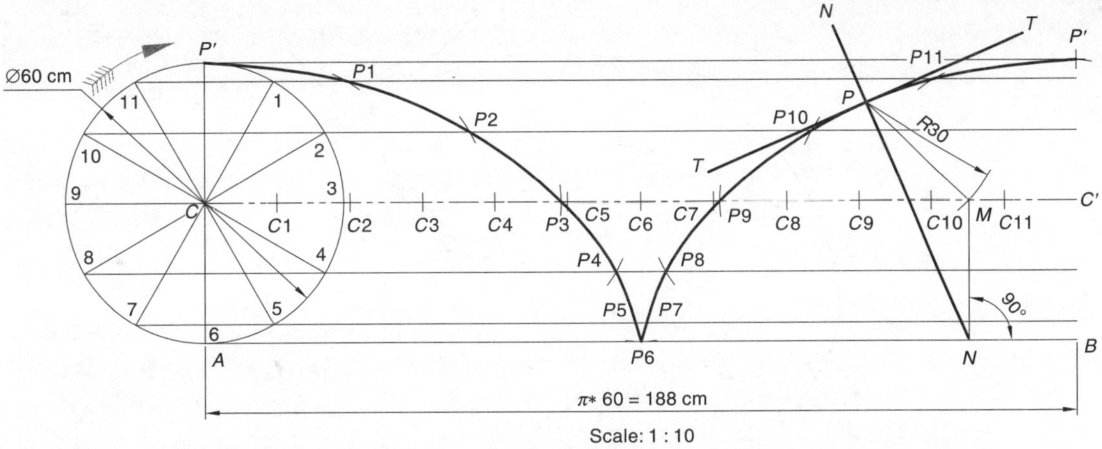

Fig. 6.24(b)

2. Draw the generating circle with C as a centre and radius = 30 cm, tangent to AB at A. Mark the generating point P', diametrically opposite to A. Draw P'–P'' parallel and equal to AB.
3. Repeat steps 3 to 7 as in (a) above.

Note: If two arcs are obtained with the same centre on a particular line, consider the arc which best describes the position of P based on the direction of rotation of the wheel.

6.7.2 Epicycloid

Example 6.27 Draw an epicylcoid if a circle of 40 mm diameter rolls outside another circle of 120 mm diameter for one revolution.

Solution Length of the arc of directing circle = $\pi D = R\theta$

∴ Included angle of the arc, $\theta = (\pi D/R)$ radian

$= (D/R \times 180)$ degree [since, π radian = 180°] = 40/60 × 180 = 120°

Refer Fig. 6.25.

1. With O as a centre and radius = 60 mm, draw the directing arc P'–P'' of the included angle 120°.
2. Produce OP' and locate C on it such that CP' = radius of generating circle = 20 mm. With C as centre and radius = CP', draw a circle.
3. With O as a centre and radius = OC, draw an arc C–C'' such that $\angle COC''$ = 120°. Arc C–C'' represents the locus of centre of generating circle.
4. Divide the circle into 12 equal parts. With O as a centre and radii = O–1, O–2, O–3, etc., draw the arcs through 1, 2, 3, etc., parallel to arc P'–P''.
5. Obtain 12 equal divisions on arc C–C'' by dividing $\angle COC''$ into 12 equal parts. Name the divisions as $C1$, $C2$, $C3$, etc.
6. With $C1$, $C2$, $C3$, etc., as the centres and radius = CP', draw the arcs cutting the arcs through 1, 2, 3, etc., to locate respectively $P1$, $P2$, $P3$, etc.
7. Join P', $P1$, $P2$, $P3$, etc., by a smooth curve.

6.7.3 Hypocycloid

Example 6.28 A circle of diameter 40 mm rolls inside another circle of radius 60 mm. Draw the hypocycloid traced by a point on the rolling circle initially in contact with the directing circle for one revolution.

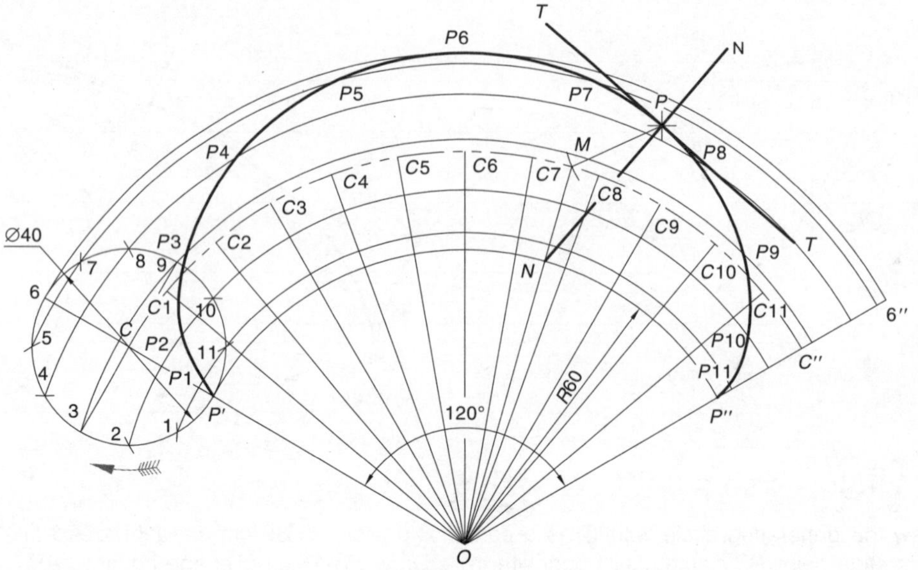

Fig. 6.25

Solution Included angle of the arc, $\theta = (D/R \times 180) = 40/60 \times 180 = 120°$. Refer Fig. 6.26.

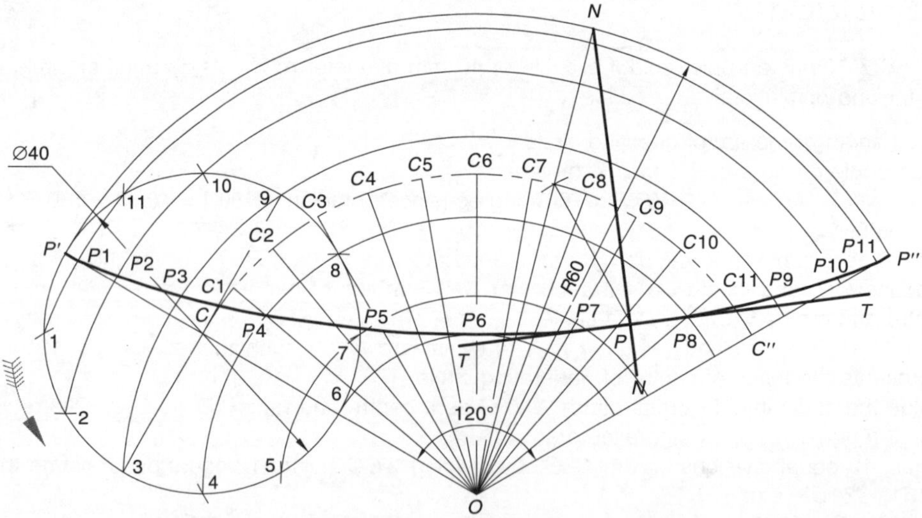

Fig. 6.26

1. With O as a centre and radius = 60 mm, draw the directing arc P'–P'' of included angle 120°.
2. On OP', locate C such that CP' = 20 mm. With C as a centre and radius = CP', draw a circle.
3. Follow steps 3 to 7 of the previous example.

Note: If $D = R$, then the hypocycloid is a straight line having length equal to $2R$. See Problem 6.10, Fig. 6.41.

6.7.4 Tangent and Normal to Cycloids

Example 6.29 Draw the tangent and normal to the cycloid, epicycloid and hypocycloid of the Examples 6.26, 6.27 and 6.28 respectively, at any point *P* on them.

Solution Refer Fig. 6.24, 6.25, 6.26.

1. With *P* as a centre and radius = *CP′* (i.e., radius of generating circle), cut an arc on *C–C″* at *M*.
2. From *M*, draw a normal *MN* to *P′–P″*. In case of epicycloid and hypocycloid, this can be done by joining *MO* and then locating *N* at the intersection of *P′–P″* and *MO* (produced it necessary).
3. Join *NP* for the required normal. Draw tangent *T–T* perpendicular to *NP* at *P*.

6.7.5 Superior Trochoid and Inferior Trochoid

Example 6.30 A circle of diameter 60 mm rolls along a straight line without slipping. Draw the locus of point *P*, 45 mm from the centre of the circle for one revolution.

Solution As the generating point is outside the circle, the curve obtained will be a superior trochoid. Refer Fig. 6.27.

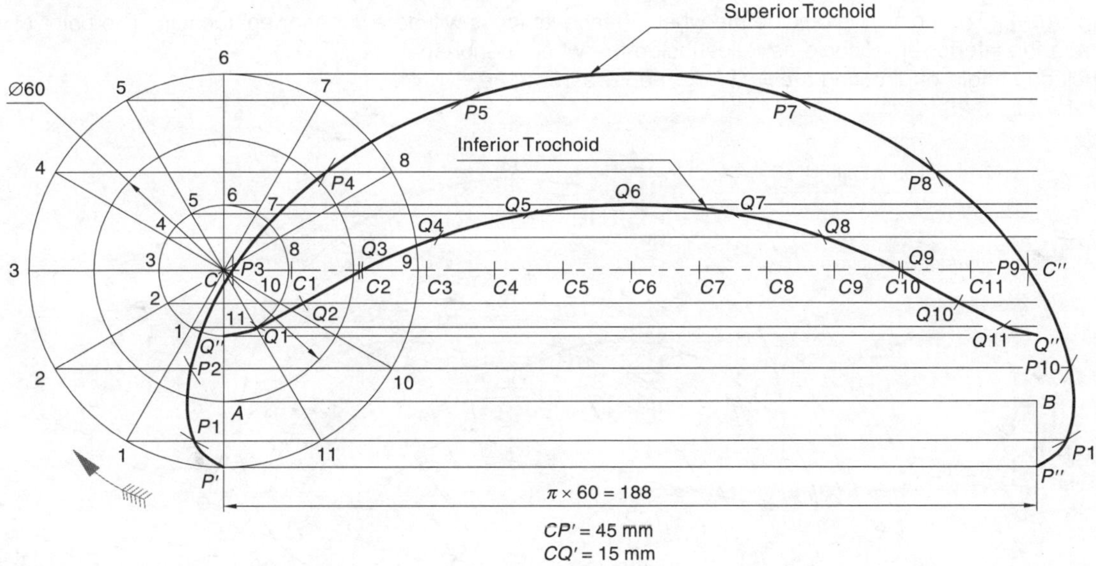

Fig. 6.27

1. Draw $AB = \pi \times D = 188$ mm to represent the directing line.
2. With centre *C* and radius = *CA* = 30 mm, draw a circle tangent to *AB* at *A*.
3. Locate *P′* on *CA* produced such that *CP′* = 45 mm. With centre *C* and radius *CP′*, draw a circle. Divide this circle into 12 equal parts and number the divisions as 1, 2, 3, etc., as shown.
4. Through 1, 2, 3, etc., draw lines parallel to *AB*.
5. Draw *C–C″* parallel and equal to *AB* and obtain 12 equal divisions, *C*1, *C*2, *C*3, etc., on it.
6. With *C*1, *C*2, *C*3, etc., as the centres and radius = *CP′*, cut the arcs on the lines through 1, 2, 3, etc., to locate respectively *P*1, *P*2, *P*3, etc.
7. Join *P′*, *P*1, *P*2, *P*3, etc., by a smooth curve.

Example 6.31 In a mechanism, a wheel of diameter 60 mm rolls along a straight guide way. A pin is driven perpendicularly in the face of the wheel at a point 15 mm from the centre of the wheel. Draw the locus of the pinhead for one revolution of the wheel.

Solution As the generating point is inside the generating circle, the curve obtained will be an inferior trochoid.

Refer Fig. 6.27.

1. Draw *AB* and the circle with centre *C* and radius = *CA*, as explained in the previous example.
2. Locate *Q′* on *CA* such that *CQ′* = 15 mm. With centre *C* and radius *CQ′*, draw a circle. Obtain 12 equal divisions, 1, 2, 3, etc., on this circle.
3. Follow steps 4 to 7 of the previous example, in a similar way, to obtain *Q*1, *Q*2, *Q*3, etc., and the required curve.

6.7.6 Superior Epitrochoid and Inferior Epitrochoid

Example 6.32 A wheel of diameter 12 cm rolls above the periphery of a wheel-sector of radius 15 cm. A 15 cm long lever, *PQ*, is fastened to the wheel radially such that *CP* = 11 cm, *CQ* = 4 cm (*C* being the centre of the wheel). Trace the loci of points *P* and *Q* for one complete revolution of the wheel.

Solution The point *P* is outside the wheel, hence its locus will be a superior epitrochoid. The point *Q* will trace the inferior epitrochoid as it lies inside the wheel periphery.

Included angle of directing arc = $D/R \times 180 = 12/15 \times 180 = 144°$.

Refer Fig. 6.28.

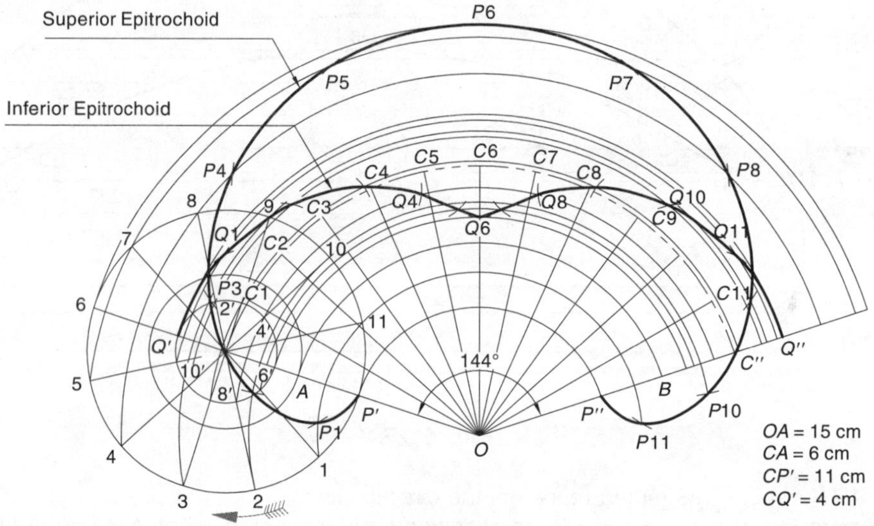

Fig. 6.28

1. With *O* as a centre and radius = *OA* = 15 cm, draw an arc *AB* of included angle 144°.
2. Mark *C* on *OA* produced such that *CA* = 6 cm. With *C* as a centre and radius = *CA*, draw a circle.
3. On *CO* (produced) locate *P′* and *Q′* such that *CP′* = 11 cm and *CQ′* = 4 cm.
4. With *C* as a centre and radii = *CP′* and *CQ′*, drawn two circles. Obtain 12 equal divisions on each of them and number them as 1, 2, 3, etc., and 1′, 2′, 3′, etc., as shown.
5. With *O* as a centre and radius = *OC*, draw an arc *C*–*C″*. Obtain 12 equal divisions *C*1, *C*2, *C*3, etc., on it.

To Draw Superior Epitrochoid

6. Draw arcs through 1, 2, 3, etc., with *O* as a centre. With *C*1, *C*2, *C*3, etc., as the centres and radius = *CP*', draw the arcs cutting the arcs through 1, 2, 3, etc., at points *P*1, *P*2, *P*3, etc., respectively. Join *P*′, *P*1, *P*2, *P*3, ... by a smooth curve.

To Draw Inferior Epitrochoid

7. Draw the arcs through 1′, 2′, 3′, etc., with *O* as a centre. With *C*1, *C*2, *C*3, etc., as the centres and radius = *CQ*′, draw the arcs cutting the arcs through 1′, 2′, 3′, etc., at point *Q*1, *Q*2, *Q*3, etc., respectively. Join *Q*′, *Q*1, *Q*2, *Q*3, ... by a smooth curve.

Note: While numbering the divisions on the rolling circle, observe its direction of rotation. In the above example, the generating circle rotates in clockwise direction. Therefore *P*′ will occupy positions 1, 2, 3, etc., in clockwise sense. Similarly *Q*′ will assume position 1′, 2′, 3′, etc., clockwise from *Q*′.

6.7.7 Superior Hypotrochoid and Inferior Hypotrochoid

Example 6.33 A circle of diameter 15 cm rolls inside another circle of radius 25 cm. The points *P* and *Q* are respectively 11.5 cm and 3.5 cm from the centre *C* of the smaller circle, but on the opposite sides of *C*. Draw the locus of *P* and *Q* for one revolution. How will the locus of *Q* appear, if ∠*PCQ* = 90°?

Solution The locus of *P* will be a superior hypotrochoid. The locus of *Q* will be an inferior hypotrochoid.

Included angle of directing arc = $D/R \times 180 = 15/25 \times 180 = 108°$

Refer Fig. 6.29.

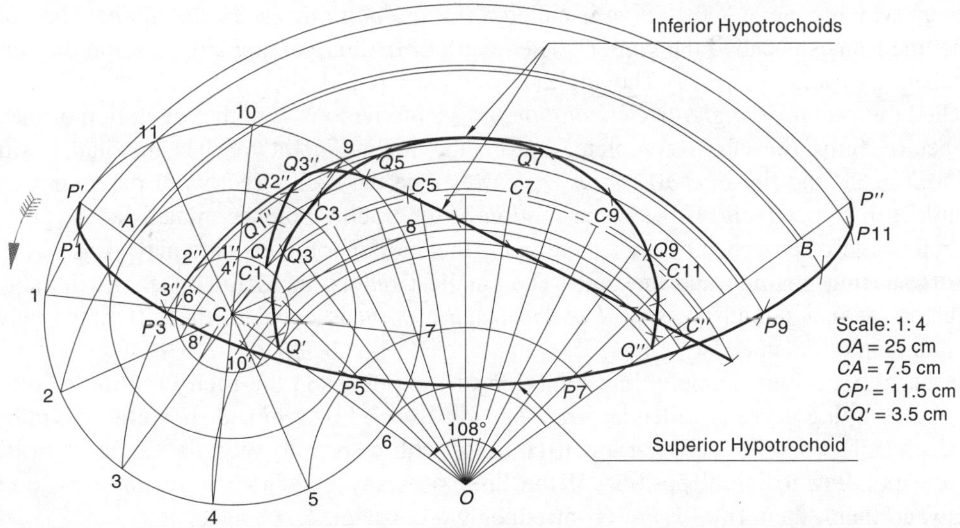

Fig. 6.29

1. With *O* as a centre and radius = *OA* = 25 cm, draw an arc *AB* of included angle 108°.
2. Mark *C* on *OA* such that *CA* = 7.5 cm. With *C* a as centre and radius = *CA*, draw a circle.
3. On *CO* (produced) locate *P*′ and *Q*′ such that *CP*′ = 11.5 cm and *CQ*′ = 3.5 cm.
4. Follow steps 4 and 5 of the previous example.
5. To obtain Superior Hypotrochoid and Inferior Hypotrochoid, follow steps similar to steps 6 and 7 of the previous example.

6. To obtain the locus of Q when $\angle PCQ = 90°$, locate Q such that $\angle P'CQ = 90°$. ($CQ = CQ'$). Number the divisions on the circle through Q as 1″, 2″, 3″, etc., using the direction sense. Obtain $Q1''$, $Q2''$ $Q3''$, etc., by following the procedure similar to that for $Q1$, $Q2$, $Q3$, etc. The smooth curve through Q, $Q1''$, $Q2''$, $Q3''$, etc., will represent another inferior hypotrochoid.

Note: If $D = R$, then the hypotrocoid is an ellipse. See Problem 6.12, Fig. 6.43.

REMEMBER THE FOLLOWING

- Directing arc angle, $\theta = (D/R \times 180)°$, where, D is the diametre of generating circle and R is the radius of the directing circle.
- If $D = R$ then the hypocycloid is a straight line.
- If $D = R$ then the hypotrocoid is an ellipse.

6.8 SPIRALS

A *spiral* is a curve traced by a point moving along a line in one direction, while the line is rotating in a plane about one of its ends or any point on it or on its extension. The curve is similar to somewhat that we get when the pencil leg of a compass is moved continuously toward the needle leg while drawing a circle. The spiral is a result of two simultaneous motions—linear motion of the point and rotary motion of the line. These two motions may or may not be uniform.

The point which generates the curve is called a *tracing point* or *generating point*. The point about which the line rotates is called the *pole, O*. The length of the line joining any point on the curve to the pole is called the *radius vector, r*. The angle between any radius vector and the initial position of the line is called the *vectorial angle, θ*. *Convolution, n*, is synonymous with the revolution of the line, i.e., the number of turns the curve completes before the tracing point reaches its final position. The *greatest radius*, r_g, and the *shortest radius*, r_s, correspond the radius vectors of maximum length and minimum length respectively. If the linear motion of the tracing point terminates at the pole then the shortest radius will be zero. On the other hand, the motion of the point may cease at any point between its starting position and the pole. The smallest radius, in such a case, will be equal to the radius vectors at that point. The *travel of the tracing point* is equal to the difference between the greatest radius and the smallest radius.

When the two motions, namely, linear motion of the point and the rotary motion of the line, are uniform, the resulting curve is called an *Archimedean spiral*. In Archimedean spiral, the radius vector goes on decreasing (or increasing) at a constant rate with respect to vectorial angle. If r_0 is a radius vector corresponding to initial position of the line, r_1 is any other radius vector, θ is the vectorial angle between them, then, $(r_0 - r_1) \propto \theta$. Introducing a constant, c, we have,

$$r_0 - r_1 = c\,\theta$$

i.e.,

$$c = (r_0 - r_1)/\theta$$

The constant c is called the *constant of the curve*. In fact, c is equal to the difference between any two radius vectors divided by the angle (in radian) between them. c, thus denotes the *radial increment* per unit vectorial angle. c is used to draw the normal to the Archimedean spiral. The normal at any point on the spiral is the hypotenuse of the right-angled triangle having other two sides equal to the radius vector at that point and the constant of the curve.

The spirals are used on the spiral springs in watches and toys, turbine casings, scroll discs of lathe chucks, spiral cams, *Illustration* 6.5.

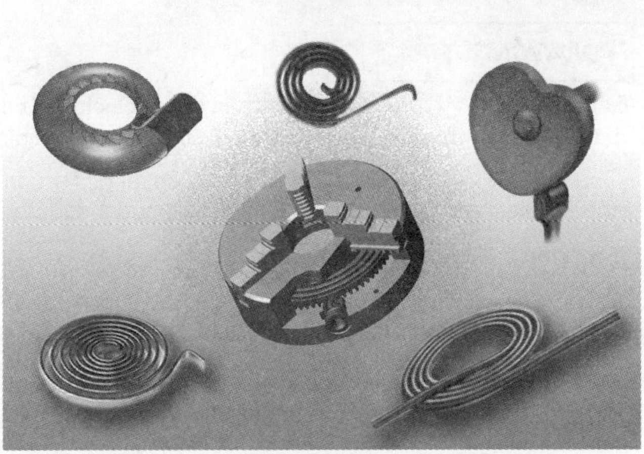

Illustration 6.5

Example 6.34 A 120 mm long link *OA* rotates about *O* at uniform angular velocity. *A* point *P*, initially at *A*, moves along *AO* at a uniform rate and reaches *O*, during one revolution of the link. Draw the locus of point *P* for one revolution of the link. Draw the tangent and normal to the curve at a point 50 mm from *O*.

Solution The point *P* will trace the Archimedean spiral.

Given, r_g = 120 mm, r_s = 0, n = 1

∴ Travel of tracing point = $r_g - r_s$ = 120 – 0 = 120 mm.

Refer Fig 6.30.

1. With *O* as a centre and radius = *OA* = 120 mm, draw a circle. Obtain 12 equal divisions *A*1, *A*2, *A*3, etc., on the circle.
2. Divide the travel of the tracing point, i.e., *OA*, into 12 equal divisions and number them as 1, 2, 3, etc., starting from *A*.
3. As the link moves from position *OA* to *OA*1, the point *P* will move through distance *A*–1. Therefore, with *O* as a centre and radius = *O*–1, draw an arc cutting *O*–*A*1 at *P*1.
4. With *O* as a centre and radii = *O*–2, *O*–3, etc., cut the arcs on *O*–*A*2, *O*–*A*3, etc., respectively to locate *P*2, *P*3, etc.
5. Join *A*, *P*1, *P*2, *P*3, ..., *P*11, *O* by a smooth curve.

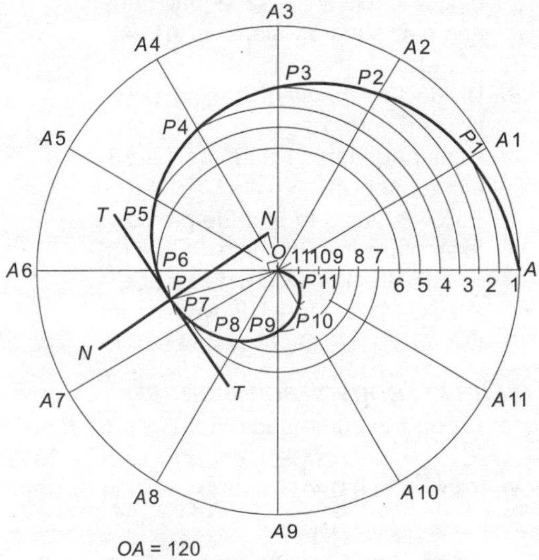

Fig. 6.30

To Draw Tangent and Normal

First locate *P* on the curve such that *OP* = 55 mm.

Measure *O*–*P*3 and find constant of curve, *c*.

$$c = [(OA) - (O\text{–}P3)]/(\pi/2) = [120 - 90]/(\pi/2) = 19 \text{ mm.}$$

6. Join *OP*. Draw *ON* perpendicular to *OP* such that *ON* = *c*.
7. Join *NP*. *NP* gives the required normal.
8. Draw *T*–*T* perpendicular to *NP* for the required tangent.

Notes:

1. The number of divisions to be obtained on the travel of tracing point is equal to the product of convolution and the number of divisions on the circle. In the above example, n = 1. Therefore, number of divisions on the link = 1 × 12 = 12.
2. c can be obtained by a general formula:

   $$c = (r_g - r_s)/n\ (2\pi)$$

   In the above example, r_g = 120 mm, r_s = 0 and n = 1. Therefore, c = (120 – 0)/1(2π) = 19 mm.

DRAWING TIP

To locate *P*1, *P*2, … *P*6, draw the arcs in an anticlockwise direction. But, to locate *P*7, *P*8, … *P*11, draw the arcs in a clockwise direction. This saves time and ensures accuracy.

Example 6.35 Draw the Archimedean spiral of 1½ convolutions with the greatest radius of 100 mm and the smallest radius of 20 mm. Draw the tangent and normal to the curve at a point 62 mm from the pole.

Solution Given, r_g = 100 mm, r_s = 20 mm, n = 1½

∴ Travel of tracing point = $r_g - r_s$ = 100 – 20 = 80 mm

Refer Fig. 6.31.

1. Draw a line *OA* = 100 mm. locate *B* on *OA* such that *OB* = 20 mm.
2. With *O* as a centre and radii = *OA* and *OB*, draw two circles. Divide bigger circle into 12 equal parts and name the divisions as *A*1, *A*2, *A*3, etc.
3. Divide the travel of tracing point, i.e., *AB* into 18 (=1.5 × 12) divisions and number them as 1, 2, 3, etc. as shown.
4. Follow steps 3 to 5 of the previous example. While locating *P*12, *P*13, … *P*18, it should be noted that *O*–*A*12, *O*–*A*13, … *O*–*A*18 overlap with OA, *O*–*A*1, … *O*–*A*6 respectively.

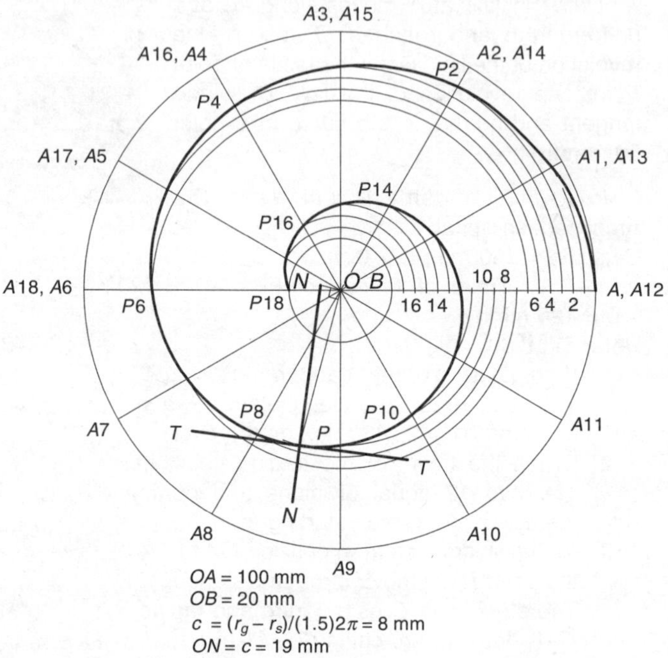

Fig. 6.31

To Draw Tangent and Normal

Locate *P* on the curve such that *OP* = 62 mm. Find *c*.

$$c = (r_g - r_s)/n(2\pi) = (100 - 20)/1.5\,(2\pi) = 8 \text{ mm}$$

Now, follow steps 6 to 8 of the previous example.

REMEMBER THE FOLLOWING

- In an Archimedean spiral, the linear motion of the tracing point and the rotary motion of the line are uniform.
- The travel of the tracing point = $r_g - r_s$
- $c = (r_0 - r_1)/\theta = (r_g - r_s)/n(2\pi)$
- If a triangle *PON* is drawn such that the point *P* is on the spiral and *ON* = c and *PO* ⊥ *ON*, then *PN* is normal to the spiral.

6.9 INVOLUTES

An *involute* is a curve traced by the free end of a thread unwound from a circle or a polygon, in such a way that the thread is always tight and tangential to the circle or the sides of the polygon. In other words, it is a curve traced by a point on a straight line when it rolls tangentially along a circle or a polygon without slipping. Thus, an involute is the reverse of a cycloid. Depending on whether the involute is traced over a circle or a polygon, the involute is called an *involute of circle* or *involute of polygon*. The normal to an involute of a circle is always tangent to the circle. The involute of a polygon is a series of tangential circular arcs of different radii and centres.

The involute profiles are used on gear teeth, centrifugal pump casings, etc., *Illustration* 6.6.

Illustration 6.6

6.9.1 Involute of Circle

Example 6.36 Draw the involute of a circle, 40 mm in diameter. Also draw the tangent and normal at a point on the curve at a distance of 100 mm from the centre of the circle.

or

A thread is unwound from a cylindrical reel, 40 mm in diameter. Draw the locus of the free end of the thread for one turn.

Solution Refer Fig. 6.32.

1. With *O* as a centre and radius = *OP* = 20 mm, draw a circle.
2. Draw a line *PQ* = $\pi \times 40$ = 126 mm, tangent to the circle at *P*.
3. Divide the circle into 12 equal parts and number the divisions as 1, 2, 3, etc.
4. Divide *PQ* into 12 equal parts and number the divisions as 1′, 2′, 3′, etc.
5. Draw the tangents to the circle at point 1, 2, 3, etc. On these tangents, locate points *P*1, *P*2, *P*3, etc. such that 1–*P*1 = *P*–1′, 2–*P*2 = *P*–2′, 3–*P*3 = *P*–3′, etc.
6. Join *P*, *P*1, *P*2, *P*3 ..., *Q* by a smooth curve.

To Draw Tangent and Normal

First locate point *M* on the curve such that *OM* = 100 mm.

7. Join *OM*.
8. Draw a semicircle with *OM* as a diameter, cutting the circle at *N*.
9. Join *NM* for the required normal. Draw *T*–*T*, perpendicular to *NM* at *M*.

Note: The tangents to the circle at 1, 2, 3, etc., i.e., *P*1–1, *P*2–2, *P*3–3, etc. are, normal to the involute at *P*1, *P*2, *P*3, etc., respectively.

6.9.2 Involute of Polygon

Example 6.37 Draw the involute of a pentagon of 25 mm side.

Solution Refer Fig. 6.33.

1. Draw the given pentagon *ABCDE*.
2. Produce *BA*, *CB*, *DC*, *ED* and *AE* and on them, locate *P*1, *P*2, *P*3, *P*4 and *P*5 respectively such that *A*–*P*1 = *AB* = 25 mm, *B*–*P*2 = 2(*AB*), *C*–*P*3 = 3(*AB*), *D*–*P*4= 4(*AB*) and *E*–*P*5 = 5(*AB*).
   Alternatively, draw an arc with *A* as a centre and radius = *AB*, to cut *BA* produced at *P*1. Similarly, with *B*, *C*, etc., as the centres and radii = *B*–*P*1, *C*–*P*2, etc., cut off the arcs on *CB* produced, *DC* produced, etc., respectively to locate *P*2, *P*3, etc.
3. Join *E*, *P*1, *P*2, ... *P*5 to obtain the desired involute.

Note: The involute obtained consists of a series of tangential circular arcs drawn with centres, *A*, *B*, *C*, *D* and *E* and radii = *AB*, 2(*AB*), 3(*AB*), 4(*AB*) and 5(*AB*) respectively.

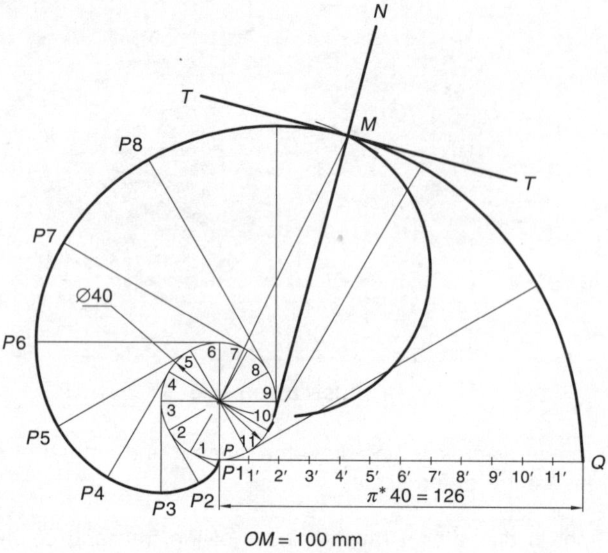

Fig. 6.32

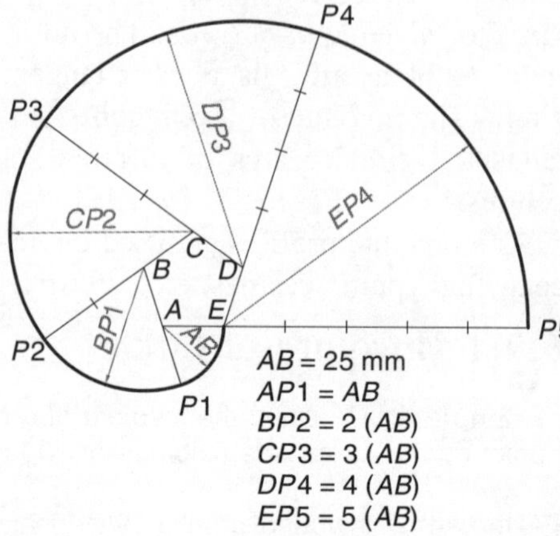

Fig. 6.33

REMEMBER THE FOLLOWING

> ➤ A tangent to the circle at any point on it is always normal to its involute.

6.10 HELIXES

A *helix* is a curve traced by a point moving along a line in one direction while the line is revolving about another line parallel or inclined to it, such that both the motions are uniform. If the axis of revolution is parallel to the line, then the helix obtained is called the *helix of the cylinder*. Obviously, the curve is obtained along the curved surface of a cylinder. If the axis of revolution is inclined to the line, the helix is called the *helix of cone*, as it is generated along the curved surface of the cone. This is illustrated in Fig. 6.34. The distance moved by the point, measured parallel to the axis of revolution, during one complete revolution of the line is called the *pitch* of the helix.

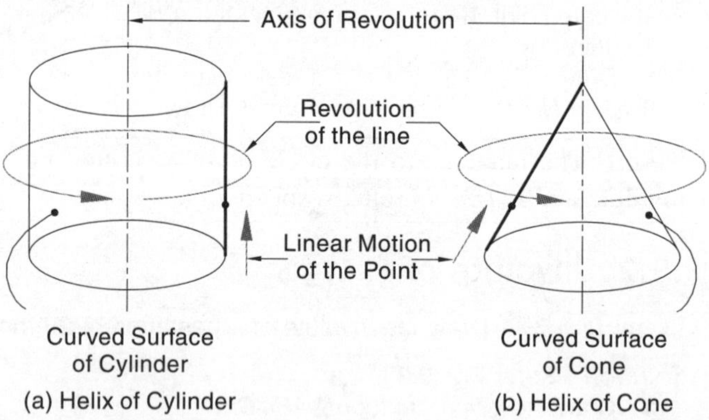

Fig. 6.34 Generation of Helix

As the helix is space curve, the two views FV and TV (i.e., front view and top view, see Section 9.3) are necessary to specify helixes completely, especially for the helix of cone. It should be noted that the helix of cone is seen as an Archimedean spiral in the view that shows the true shape of the base of the cone.

Helixes are the most common engineering curves. These are widely employed on screw threads, bolts, helical springs, conical spring, drilling tools, lead screws of lathe, power screws of screw-jack, screw conveyors, spiral staircases, etc., *Illustration* 6.7.

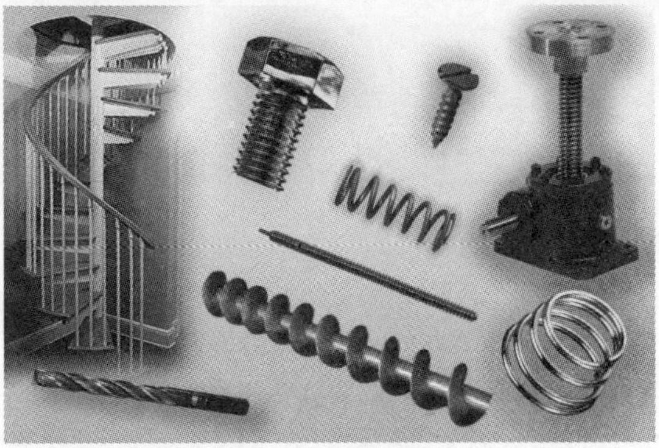

Illustration 6.7

6.10.1 Helix of Cylinder

Example 6.38 Draw a helix for one turn, upon a cylinder of 40 mm diameter and a height of 80 mm. The pitch of the helix is 60 mm.

Solution Refer Fig. 6.35

1. Draw the TV and FV of the given cylinder. The TV is a circle of diameter 40 mm and the FV is a rectangle of 1′–7′–7″–1″ of 80 mm height.
2. Divide the circle into 12 equal parts and project the division points 2, 3, 4, etc., to 2′, 3′, 4′, etc., in FV.
3. In F*V*, draw *p*′*q*′ parallel and equal to 1′–7′ such that 1′*p*′ = pitch = 60 mm. Obtain 12 equal divisions, namely, *a*′, *b*′, *c*′, etc., on 1′*p*′.
4. Through 2′, 3′, 4′, etc., draw vertical generators. Through *a*′, *b*′, *c*′, etc., draw horizontal lines to intersect the generators though 2′, 3′, 4′, etc., at *P*2′, *P*3′, *P*4′, etc., respectively.
5. Join 1′, *P*2′, *P*3′, *P*4′, ... *P*′ by a smooth curve. Note that the part of the curve form *P*7′ to *P*′ is invisible and is shown by a dashed line.

6.10.2 Helix of Cone

Example 6.39 Draw a helix upon a cone of base diameter 60 mm and a height of 60 mm for one turn. The pitch of the helix is equal to the height of the cone.

Solution Refer Fig. 6.36.

1. Draw the TV and FV of the cone as shown. TV is seen a circle of centre *O* and diameter = 60 mm. The triangle *O*′1′7′ of height = 60 mm will represent the FV.
2. Obtain 12 equal divisions 1, 2, 3, 4, etc., of the circle. Join 1, 2, 3, 4, etc., with *O*.
3. Project 1, 2, 3, 4, etc., to 1′, 2′, 3′, 4′, etc., in FV and join them with *O*′.

Method 1:

4. Divide *O*′1′ in to 12 equal parts and name the divisions as *a*′, *b*′, *c*′, ... etc.
5. Through *a*′, *b*′, *c*′, etc., draw horizontal lines to meet *O*′–2′, *O*′–3′, *O*′–4′, etc., respectively at *P*2′, *P*3′, *P*4′, etc.
6. Project *P*2′, *P*3′, *P*4′, etc., to *P*2, *P*3, *P*4, etc., on *O*–2, *O*–3, *O*–4, etc., respectively.
7. Join 1′, *P*2′, *P*3′, *P*4′, ... *O*′ and 1, *P*2, *P*3, *P*4, ... *O* to obtain the FV and TV of the required helix.

Method 2:

4. Divide *O*–1 into 12 equal parts and number the divisions as 2′, 3′, 4′, etc.
5. With *O* as a centre and radii = *O*–2′, *O*–3′, *O*–4′, etc., draw the arcs to obtain *P*2, *P*3, *P*4, etc., as in Archimedean spiral.

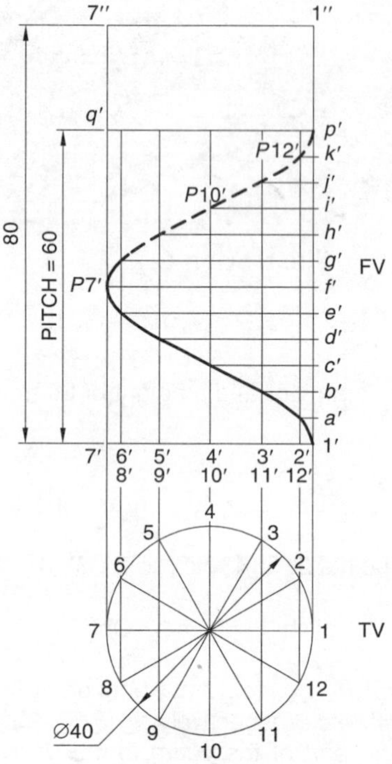

Fig.6.35

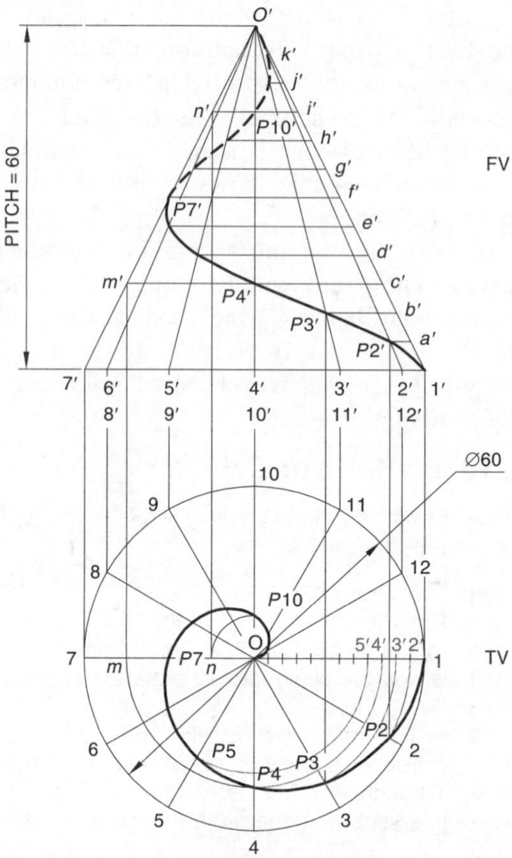

Fig.6.36

6. Project *P*2, *P*3, *P*4, etc., to *P*2′, *P*3′, *P*4′, etc., on *O*′–2′, *O*′-3′, *O*′–4′, etc., respectively. (The points *P*4 and *P*10 should be first projected to *m* and *n* and then to *m*′ and *n*′ as shown.)
7. Join 1, *P*2, *P*3, *P*4, ... *O* and 1′, *P*2′, *P*3′, *P*4′, ... *O*′ to obtain TV and FV of the required helix. The part of the helix form *P*7′ to *O*′ in FV is hidden and hence shown by a dashed line.

Remember the Following

➢ If a cone has its base parallel to the HP then its helix is seen as an Archimedean spiral in TV.

Illustrative Problems

Problem 6.1 The major axis and minor axis of an ellipse are 70 mm and 45 mm long respectively. Construct half of the ellipse by oblong method and the other half by concentric circle method.

Solution Refer Fig. 6.37.

Follow steps similar to those explained in Example 6.2 and Example 6.3.

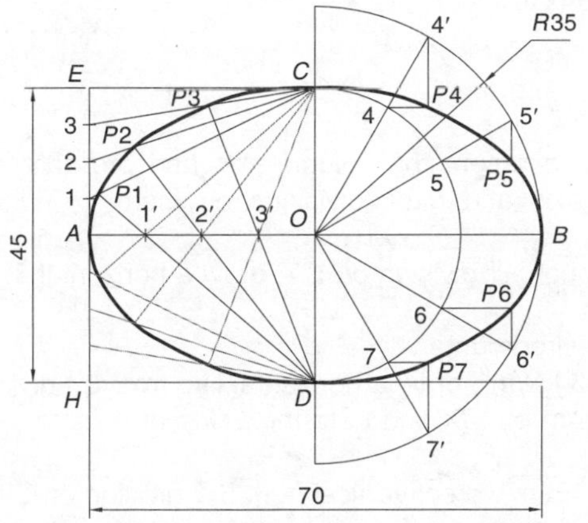

Fig. 6.37

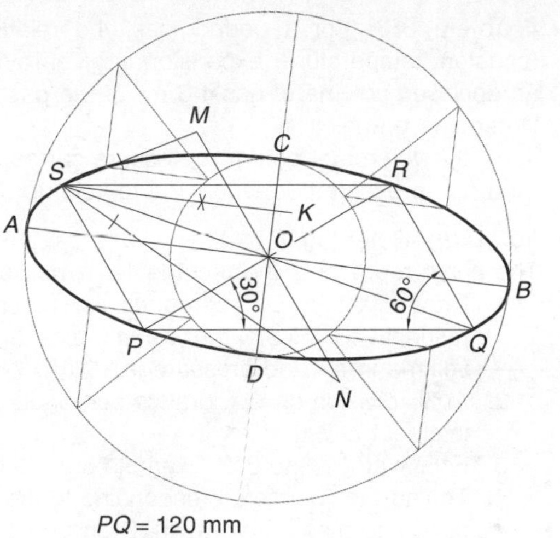

Fig. 6.38

Problem 6.2 A plot of land in the shape of a parallelogram has size 30 m × 20 m. The angle between the two adjacent sides is 60°. Show graphically how an elliptical flower bed can be inscribed in it.

Solution This problem is similar to Example 6.4. Therefore, redraw Fig. 6.7 with following changes AB = 30 m, CD = 20 m and $\angle COB = 60°$.

Problem 6.3 Draw a triangle PQR with PQ = 120 mm, $\angle RPQ = 30°$ and $\angle RQP = 60°$. Draw an ellipse circumscribing P, Q and R by the concentric circle method. Also draw normal and tangent at a point 30 mm from the major axis.

Solution Refer Fig. 6.38.

1. Draw the given ΔPQR.
2. Draw a parallelogram $PQRS$, such that RS is equal and parallel to PQ, and PS is equal and parallel to QR.
3. Join SQ. SQ and PR now represent the conjugate axes.
4. Obtain the major axis AB and the minor axis CD, as explained in Example 6.9.
5. Construct the required ellipse by concentric circle method as explained in Example 6.2.
6. To obtain the tangent and normal at a given point, first obtain the foci F and F', such that $CF = CF' = AO$. Then, adopt the procedure explained in Example 6.6.

Problem 6.4 A ball is thrown from the ground level at an inclination of 60° to the horizontal. The ball returns to the ground at a point 10 m from the point of throw. Trace the path of the ball. Name the curve.

Solution This problem is similar to Example 6.13. Take RS = 8 m and follow similar steps.

Problem 6.5 On a cricket ground, the ball thrown by a fielder reaches the wicket-keeper following parabolic path. Maximum height achieved by the ball above the ground is 30 m. Assuming the point of throw and the point of catch to be 1 m above the ground, draw the path of the ball. The distance between the fielder and the wicket-keeper is 70 m.

Solution This problem is similar to Example 6.11. Take double ordinate, RS = 70 m and abscissa, KV = 30 − 1 = 29 m. Follow similar steps. Take a suitable scale. The tangent method may also be adopted as explained in Example 6.13.

Problem 6.6 For a perfect gas, the relation between the pressure *P* and volume *V* in isothermal (constant temperature) expansion is given by PV = constant. Draw the curve of isothermal expansion of an enclosed volume of gas if 3 m^3 of the gas correspond to a pressure of 4 kN/m^2.
Determine graphically,

(i) the volume of gas at a pressure corresponding to 3 kN/m^2.
(ii) the pressure corresponding to volume of 4.5 m^3.

Solution Refer Fig. 6.39.
The curve represents the rectangular hyperbola.

1. Draw *OX* and *OY*, perpendicular to each other to represent the volume-axis and pressure-axis respectively. Scale the volume-axis and pressure-axis and mark divisions on them to indicate volume in m^3 and pressure in kN/m^2.
2. At 3rd division on *OX*, draw a perpendicular *GH*. Through 4th division on *OY*, draw a horizontal *EF* to intersect *GH* at *P*.
3. Follow steps 3 to 8 of Example 6.21 to obtain the desired curve.
4. To find the volume corresponding to the pressure of 3 kN/m^2, draw a horizontal line from 3rd division on *OY* to meet curve at *m*. Drop perpendicular from m on *OX* and note the value of volume at its intersection with *OX*.
5. To find the pressure corresponding to the volume of 4.5 m^3, erect vertical at $(4.5)^{th}$ division on *OX* to meet the curve at *n*. Find the value of the pressure at the intersection of the horizontal through *n* and *OY*.

Problem 6.7 Points *P* and *Q* are 70 mm apart. *A* point *R* is moving in the plane of *P* and *Q* such that the difference of its distances from *P* and *Q* is always 30 mm. Draw the curve traced by point *R*.

Solution This problem is similar to Example 6.19. *P* and *Q* represent the two foci.

Problem 6.8 A wheel of 60 mm diameter, rolls downward on a vertical wall for half revolution and then on the horizontal floor for the remaining half revolution without slipping. Draw the locus of a point *P* on the circumference of the wheel, the initial position of which is the contact point with the wall. Name the curve.

Solution Refer Fig. 6.40.

1. Draw $PQ = \pi D/ 2 = 94$ mm to represent the wall.
2. With *C* as a centre and radius = $CP = 30$ mm, draw a circle tangent to *PQ* at *P*.
3. Divide the circle into 12 equal divisions 1, 2, 3, etc. Draw vertical lines through 1, 2, 3, etc.
4. Draw a vertical line $C–C' = PQ$ to represents the locus of centre. Divide it into 6 equal parts and name the divisions as *C*1, *C*2, *C*3, etc.
5. Obtain *P*1, *P*2, ... *P*6 in a similar way as explained in Example 6.26.
6. After half revolution, the wheel will touch the floor at *R*. Draw $RS = \pi D/2 = 94$ mm to represent the floor.
7. Draw $C'–C'' = RS$ and obtain 6 equal divisions, *C*7, *C*8, *C*9, etc., on it.
8. Draw the horizontal lines through 7, 8, 9, etc.
9. Obtain *P*7, *P*8, *P*9, etc., in a similar way.
10. Draw a smooth curve through *P*, *P*1, *P*2, *P*3, ... *P*″. The curve represents a cycloid.

Problem 6.9 A motorcycle wheel has 0.5 m diameter. Draw the locus of a point on its circumference for one complete revolution of the wheel when it passes over a segmental arched culvert of radius 1.50 m at a speed of 25 km/hr. Name the curve.

Solution The problem is similar to Example 6.27. Here, the diameter of generating circle, $D = 0.5$ m and the radius of directing circle, $R = 1.5$ m.

$\therefore$ Included angle of the directing arc = $D/R \times 180 = 60°$.

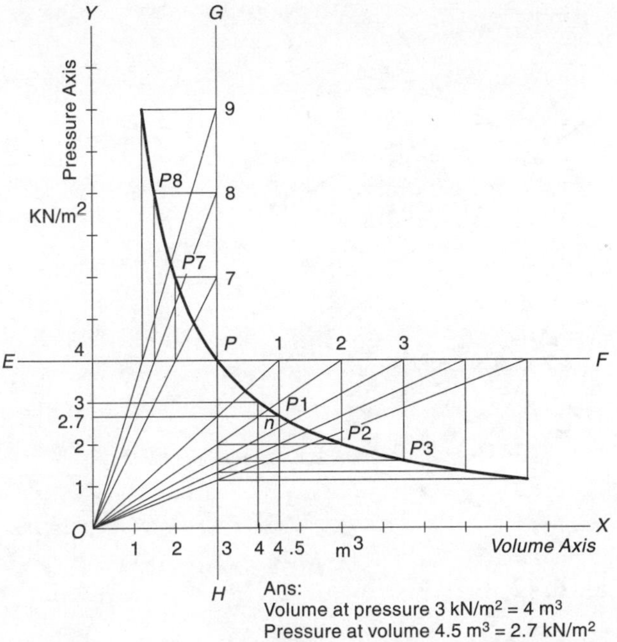

Fig. 6.39

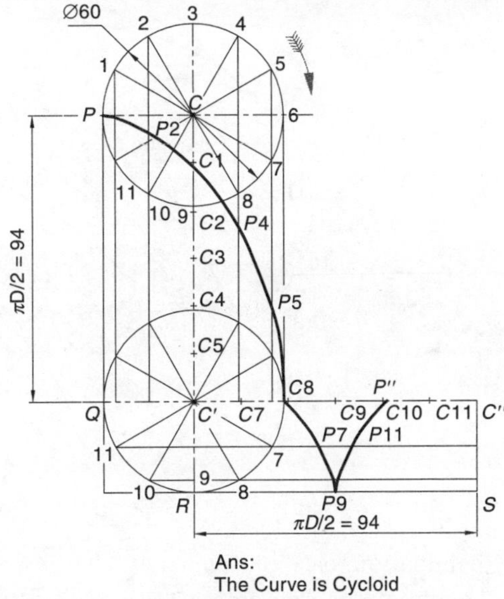

Fig. 6.40

Problem 6.10 Prove that the hypocycloid is a straight line if the diameter of generating circle is equal to the radius of the directing circle.

Solution Refer Fig. 6.41.

Given, diameter of generating circle, D = radius of directing circle, R

$\therefore$ Directing arc angle = $D/R \times 180 = 180°$

1. With O as a centre and radius = $OP' = R$, draw semicircle to represent the directing arc.
2. On OP', mark C such that $CP' = R/2$. Draw the generating circle with C as a centre and radius = CP'.
3. Follow procedure as explained in Example 6.28 to draw the required hypocycloid.
   The hypocycloid obtained is a straight line P'–P'' passing through O. The length of P'–P'' = $2R$.

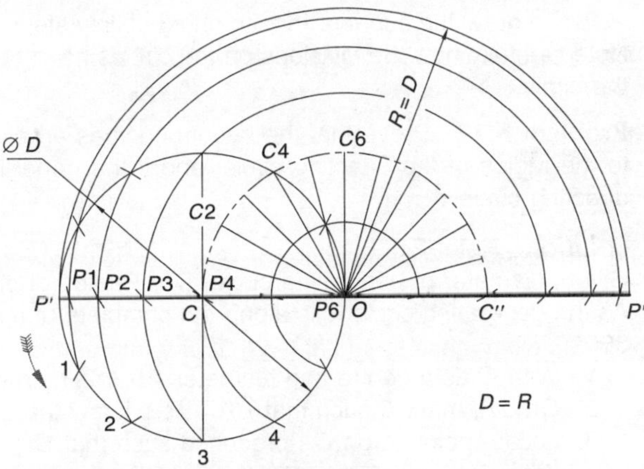

Fig. 6.41

Problem 6.11 A circle of diameter 40 mm rolls outside another circle of radius 75 mm. A point P is 30 mm from the centre of the rolling circle and is rigidly fixed to it. Draw the locus of P when the rolling circle completes one revolution along the bigger circle. The point P is initially away from the centre of the bigger circle.

If the rolling circle rolls inside the bigger circle, how will the locus of P appear? Assume P near to the centre of the bigger circle.

Solution Refer Fig. 6.42.

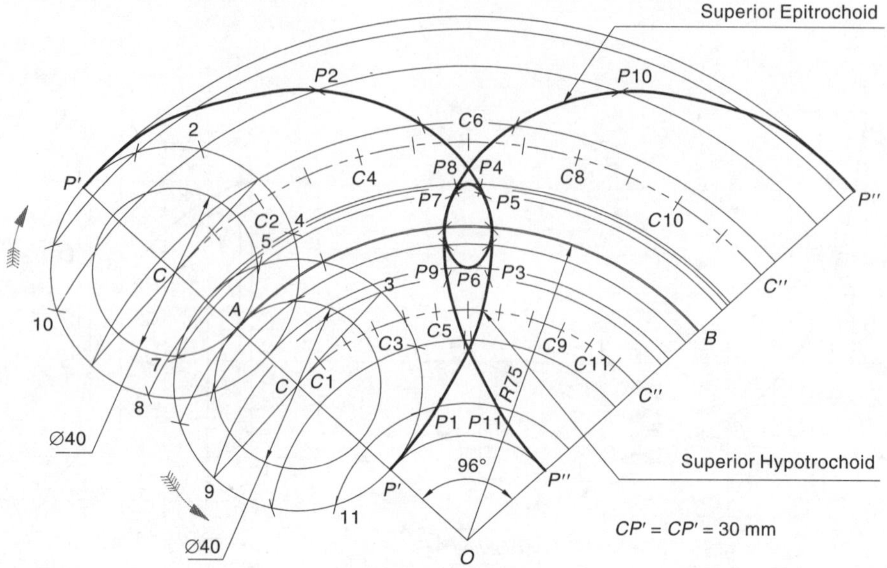

Fig. 6.42

Length of directing arc = $D/R \times 180 = 40/75 \times 180 = 96°$. When the rolling circle will roll outside the directing arc, the locus of P will be a superior epitrochoid. The locus will be a superior hypotrochoid when the rolling circle will roll inside the directing arc.

1. To draw the superior epitrochoid, follow steps similar to Example 6.32. The point P' is located away from O.
2. To draw the superior hypotrochoid, follow steps as in Example 6.33. The point P' is located near O.

Note carefully how the divisions on the circles have been numbered considering the direction of rotation of the circle.

Problem 6.12 Prove that the hypotrochoid is an ellipse if the diameter of the generating circle is equal to the radius of the directing circle; and if the generating circle rolls along the complete periphery of the directing circle.

Solution Refer Fig. 6.43.

Given, diameter of generating circle, D = Radius of directing circle, R

As the generating circle rolls along the complete periphery of the directing circle, the directing arc angle = 360°.

1. With O as a centre and diameter $AB = 2R$, draw the directing circle.
2. On OA, mark C such that $CA = R/2$. Draw the generating circle with C as a centre and radius = CA.
3. Locate point P' on CA produced such that $CP' = x > D/2$.
4. With C as a centre and radius = CP', draw a circle. Obtain 12 equal divisions 1, 2, 3, etc., on this circle.
5. With O as a centre and radius = OC, draw a circle and obtain 24 equal divisions, $C1$, $C2$, $C3$, etc., on it.
6. Follow the procedure explained in Example 6.33 to obtain the desired curve. The superior hypotrochoid, thus, obtained is the ellipse of major axis $P'–P'' = 2x + D$ and minor axis $P6–P18 = 2x – D$.

In a similar way, we can prove that, if $D = R$, then the inferior hypotrochoid of any point Q' ($CQ' = y < D/2$), is also an ellipse. The major axis and minor axis in that case, will be $Q'–Q'' = D + 2y$ and $Q6–Q18 = D – 2y$, respectively.

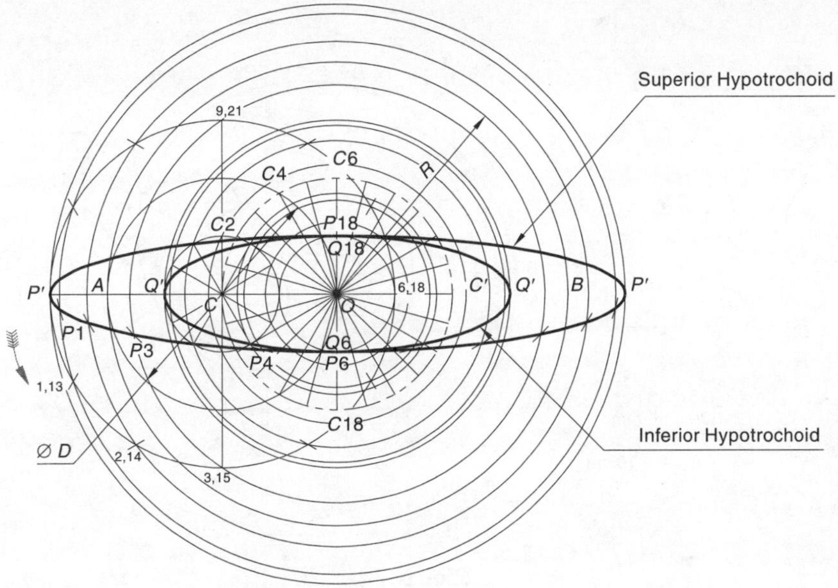

$D = R$
$CP' = x > (D/2)$
$CQ' = y < (D/2)$
$P' - P'' = 2x + D$, $P6 - P18 = 2x - D$
$Q' - Q'' = D + 2y$, $Q6 - Q18 = D - 2y$

Fig. 6.43

Problem 6.13 Draw a triangle *AOB* with *OA* = 30 mm, *OB* = 50 mm and ∠*AOB* = 120°. Draw an Archimedean spiral passing through points *A* and *B* with *O* as a pole. Complete the curve starting from *O*. Also draw tangent and normal to the curve at a distance of 27 mm from *O*.

Solution Refer Fig. 6.44.

Draw the given Δ*AOB* as shown. *OA* and *OB* represent two radius vectors of the spiral. When *OA* rotates to *OB*, i.e., through 120^0, point *A* moves to *B*.

∴ Radial increment for rotation through 1° = (*OB*–*OA*)/120 = 20/120°

∴ Radial increment for rotation through 30°, i.e., 1 division on the circle
= 20/120 × 30 = 5 mm.

In other words, the tracing point will move through 5 mm along the line when it turns through 30°. Therefore, for one convolution, the total distance moved by an initial radius vector,

r_g = 5 × 12 (or 20/120° × 360°) = 60 mm.

Once the point has reached *A*, it will need (30/5) × 30° = 180° rotation to reach at *O*. Therefore the initial radius vector will make 180° with *OA*.

1. Draw the initial radius vector *OP* = 60 mm in line with *OA*.
2. With *O* as centre and radius = *OP*, draw a circle. Obtain 12 equal divisions 1′, 2′, 3′, etc., on the circle.
3. Obtain 12 equal divisions 1, 2, 3, etc., on *OP*.
4. Follow the procedure explained in Example 6.34 to obtain the required spiral. Note that *P*2 and *P*6 will coincide with *B* and *A* respectively.

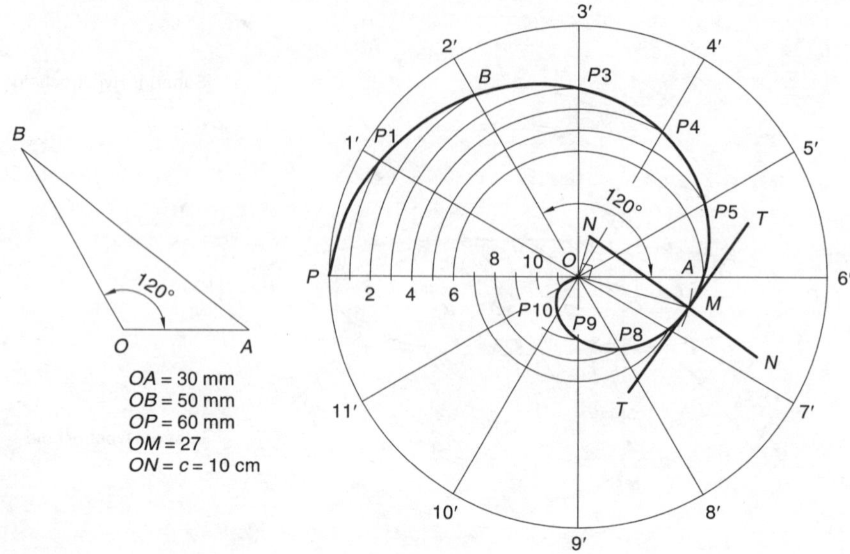

Fig. 6.44

To Draw Tangent and Normal

First locate the given point on the spiral by cutting arc with O as a centre and radius = 27 mm. Find out the constant of curve.

$c = (OB - OA)/(2/3\pi) = OP/2\pi = 9.54 \approx 10$ mm.

Now follow the steps similar to those explained in Example 6.34.

Problem 6.14 Fig. 6.45 shows a thick disc formed partly from a circle and a part of right regular pentagon. The disc is held fixed. An inelastic string of length 150 mm is fixed at point *A* on the disc and its free end is wound round the disc by turning clockwise (the string is held tight during winding). Draw the locus of the free end of the string.

Solution

1. Join *AO* and *OD*. Divide the arc *AD* into suitable number of equal parts, say 4 and name the division as *G*, *F* and *E* as shown.
2. At *A*, draw a tangent *AP* = 150 mm to the arc. Locate *D′* on *AP* such that *AD′* = length of arc *AD* = $30 \times [(144/180) \times \pi]$ = 75 mm. Divide *AD′* into 4 equal parts and name the divisions as *G′*, *F′* and *E′*.
3. Between *D′* and *P*, locate *C′* and *B′* such that *D′–C′* = *C′–B′* = *DC* = 35 mm.
4. Draw the tangents to the arc at *G*, *F*, *E* and *D*. With *G*, *F*, *E* and *D* as the centres and radii = *G′P*, *F′P*, *E′P* and *D′P*, draw the arcs to cut the corresponding tangents at *P*1, *P*2, *P*3 and *P*4 respectively.
5. Locate *P*5 and *P*6 respectively on *DC* produced and *CB* produced such that *C–P*5 = *C′P* and *B–P*6 = *B′P*.
6. With *B* as a centre and radius = *B–P*6, draw an arc to meet *AB* at *P*7.
7. Join *P*, *P*1, *P*2, ... *P*7 by smooth curve.

Problem 6.15 A line *PQ* = 120 mm long rolls without slipping on the periphery of a semicircle of diameter *AB* 70 mm, as shown in Fig. 6.46. Initially, the line is tangent to the circle at *A* such that *AP* = 100 mm. Draw the loci of ends of the line. Name the curves.

Solution The line *PQ* will always roll tangentially along the semicircle.

Circumference of semicircle = $\pi \times 70/2$ = 110 mm.

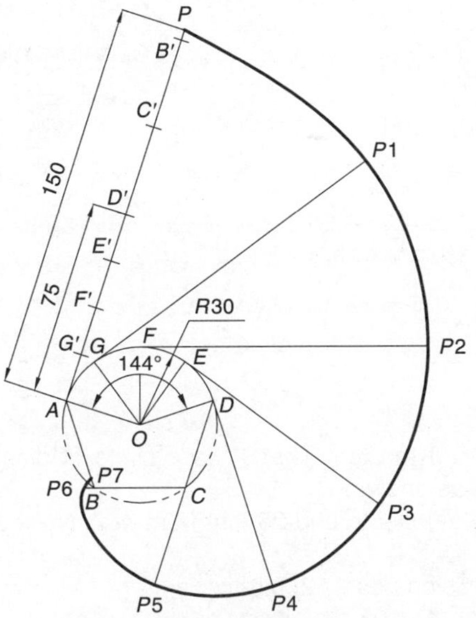

Fig. 6.45

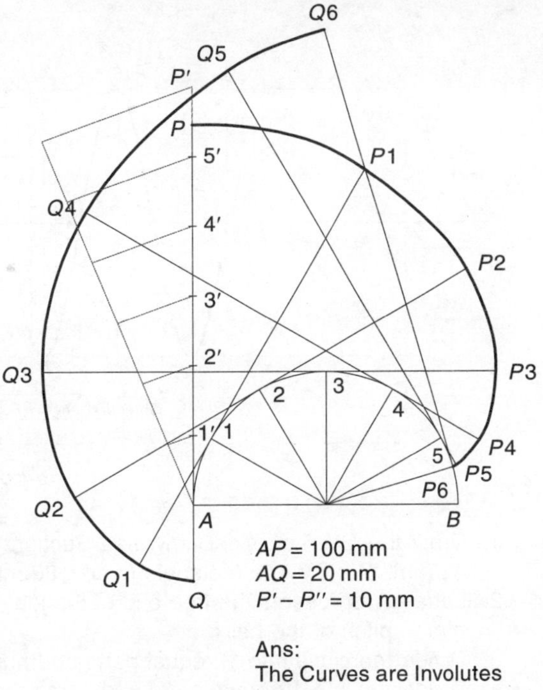

Fig. 6.46

1. Mark P' on AP produced such that P–P' = 10 mm (= circumference of the semicircle – AP).
2. Divide the semicircle into 6 equal parts and number the divisions as 1, 2, 3, etc. Also divide AP' into 6 equal parts and number the divisions as 1′, 2′, 3′, etc.
3. At 1, 2, 3, etc., draw tangents to the circle and on them locate $P1$, $P2$, $P3$, etc., respectively, such that 1–$P1$ = 1′–P, 2–$P2$ = 2′–P, 3–$P3$ = 3′–P, etc. To locate $P6$, draw an arc cutting the semicircle with 5 as a centre and radius = 5–$P5$. Join P, $P1$, $P2$, etc., for the required curve.
4. Produce $P1$–1, $P2$–2, $P3$–3, etc., and on them locate $Q1$, $Q2$, $Q3$, etc., respectively such that $P1$–$Q1$ = $P2$–$Q2$ = $P3$–$Q3$ = 120 mm. To locate $Q6$, draw a tangent at $P6$ and measure $P6$–$Q6$ = 120 mm on it. Join Q, $Q1$, $Q2$, etc., by a smooth curve.

The curves thus obtained represent involutes.

Problem 6.16 A cylindrical job of 45 mm diameter and 80 mm length is held horizontally in a chuck on lathe. The job is to be threaded for the length of 50 mm by a single point V–threading tool. The job rotates at the rate of 40 RPM and the feed of tool is 1 m/min. Draw the locus of the point traced by tool tip on the surface of the job, when the tool tip moves axially from the free end of the job towards the chuck. Name the curve.

Solution The tool tip is moving axially along the curved surface of the cylindrical workpiece while the workpiece is rotating about its axis. Obviously, the curve traced by the tool tip on the workpiece will be the helix of cylinder. To draw the curve, we will first find the pitch.

Pitch = Axial advancement of the tool during one rotation of the workpiece
= (Rate of axial advancement of the tool)/ RPM
= Feed/RPM = $[(1 \times 1000)\ \text{mm/min}]/40\ \text{min}^{-1}$ = 25 mm.

Therefore the helix will take 2 turns for the threaded length of 50 mm.

Refer Fig. 6.47.

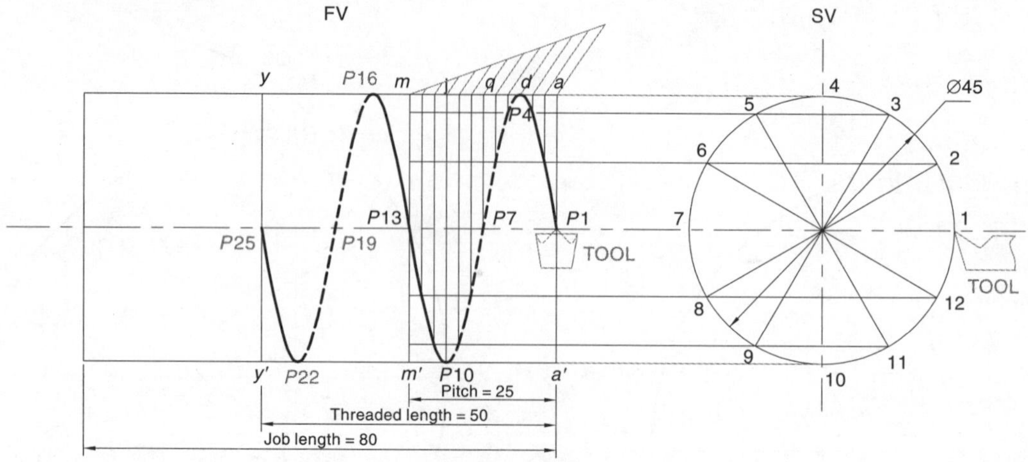

Fig. 6.47

1. Draw the SV (i.e., side view, see Section 9.3) and FV of the job. The SV is a circle of diameter 45 mm. The FV is a rectangle of size 80 mm × 45 mm as shown.
2. Let *a–a′* represents the free end of the job. Draw *m–m′* parallel to and 25 mm from *a-a′*. Now, *am* = *a′m′* = pitch of the helix.
3. Divide the circle into 12 equal parts and number the divisions as 1, 2, 3, etc.
4. Divide *am* into 12 equal parts and name the divisions as *b*, *c*, *d*, etc.
5. Obtain the points *P*1, *P*2, *P*3, etc., in a similar way as explained in Example 6.38. Draw a smooth curve through these points. Obtain another turn of the helix between *m–m′* and *y–y′* by locating *P*14, *P*15, *P*16, etc., in a similar way.

Review Questions

1. Draw an ellipse by focus-directrix method when the distance of the focus from the directrix is equal to 60 mm and the eccentricity is 2/3.
2. In a triangle *ABC*, *AB*, *AC* and *AC* are 100 mm, 55 mm and 70 mm, respectively. Draw an ellipse such that *A* and *B* are foci and *C* is a point on the curve. Find directrix and eccentricity of ellipse.
3. An artificial satellite is orbiting around the earth. The major axis of its orbit is 40,000 km and the minor axis is 30,000 km. Draw the orbit of the satellite and show the position of the earth centre, assuming that it is on one of the foci. Also draw the tangent and normal to the orbit at a point 10,000 km away from the earth centre.
4. A stone is thrown from a 7 m high building and at its highest flight the stone just crosses a 14 m high palm tree. Trace the path of the stone, till it touches the ground. The distance between the building and the palm tree is 4 m.
5. An artillery gun fires a bombshell from surface to a target, 15 km away. The bomb shell achieves a maximum height of 5 km. Draw the path traced by the shell, selecting a suitable scale. Name the curve.
6. Draw a parabola having a base of 80 mm and an axis equal to 80 mm by the tangent method.
7. A perfect gas follows the law *PV* = constant. At a pressure of 3 N/cm^2 absolute, the volume of the gas being 2 m^3. Draw the graph of *P* versus *V* for the pressure range of 1 N/cm^2 absolute to 10 N/cm^2 absolute. Name the curve.

8. Draw the path traced out by a point on a circumference of the circle but opposite to the contact point. The circle rolls without slipping vertically downwards for the distance equal to its perimeter. The diameter of the circle is 40 mm. Name the curve.
9. Draw a circle of 40 mm diameter. The diameter *AB* is vertical with end *A* at top. Trace the curve generated by the end *A* when the circle rolls without slipping on a horizontal line for three-fourth rotation and then on the vertical line for its next half rotation. Name the curve traced by end *A*.
10. Trace the locus of the point on the circumference of the rolling circle of 40 mm diameter rolling on circle of same diameter for one complete revolution. Name the curve.
11. A circle of radius 30 mm rolls along a straight path for half of its rotation and then along a concave path of radius 120 mm for the remaining half rotation. Draw the locus of point *P* which is initially opposite to the contact point. The starting point and end point of the concave path are in line with the straight path.
12. A wheel of a vehicle has outer diameter of 0.75 m. The vehicle passes over a small bridge having the radius of curvature 1.5 m. Draw the locus of the tip of the inflating valve of tube for one revolution of the wheel. The tip of the valve is 0.1 m inside the periphery of the wheel. Name the curve.
13. Draw the half convolution of an Archimedean spiral with a minimum radius of 25 mm and a radial increment of 6 mm for each 30°.
14. A circular disc of an 80 mm diameter *AB* rotates with uniform angular velocity about its centre. The point *P* which is at *A*, moves with uniform linear velocity and reaches the point *B*, when the disc completes one revolution. Trace the path of point *P* moving from *A* to *B*.
15. A thin rod *PR* of 120 mm length revolves about point *Q* on it, 20 mm from end *P*. A point *S* located on *PR* at 20 mm distance from end *R* moves along the rod and reaches point *P* during the period the rod completes one revolution. Draw the path of the point *S* if both the motions are uniform. Name the curve. Draw a tangent and a normal at any convenient point on the curve.
16. A circular disc of diameter 2 m is mounted centrally on the 0.4 m diameter shaft. The disc rotates about the axis of the shaft at the speed of 60 RPM. Simultaneously, a point *P* on the outer periphery of the disc moves radially toward the shaft at the velocity of 0.8 m/s. Trace the path of point *P* for one revolution of the disc. Name the curve. Draw tangent and normal to the curve at a point 0.7 m from the pole. List any three important terms associated with this curve.
17. Draw the path of the end of the 140 mm long thread when it is wound on a half hexagon of side 25 mm. Name the curve.
18. One end *Q* of the inelastic string *PQ*, 150 mm long, is attached to the circumference of a half circular half hexagonal disc of 49 mm diameter. Draw the curve traced out by the other end *P* of the string when it is completely wound round the circumference of the disc, keeping the string always tight. Take the initial position of string tangent at the midpoint *Q* of circular portion.
19. An inelastic string of 120 mm length has its one end attached to the circumstance of a circular disc with a 50 mm diameter. Draw the curve traced out by the other end of the string when it is completely wound round the disc keeping the string always taut. Draw the tangent and normal to the curve at a point 70 mm from the centre of the circular disc. Name the curve.
20. Draw a helix of one revolution around the cone, given the pitch = 75 mm, the diameter = 60 mm and the height of a cone = 80 mm, when the starting point is present on the base.

Chapter 7

LOCI OF POINTS

7.1 INTRODUCTION

A locus* is a path traced by a point moving in space according to a specific geometric condition. The study of loci of points is most important in engineering, especially in designing the mechanisms and analyzing design related problems. Therefore, every engineer must thoroughly learn the methods of obtaining the various loci as explained in this chapter.

7.2 SOME STANDARD LOCI

Most of the geometrical curves are standard loci as they satisfy some conditions. The conditions are the laws governing the motion or constraints restricting the movement of a point. They may be expressed in terms of mathematical equations. Straight lines and circles are most common examples of loci. The engineering curves studied in Chapter 6 satisfy specific conditions and therefore, are loci of points. Depending on the conditions the points follow, loci have different shapes. If a point moves in a plane, then the locus obtained is a *line curve* or a *2D curve*. On the other hand, a point traces a *space curve* or a *3D curve* when it moves in space not in a particular plane. Line, circle, parabola, hyperbola, ellipse, cycloids, spirals and involutes are the examples of line curves. Helixes are space curves.

7.3 GENERAL EXAMPLES ON LOCI

This section explains the procedures of drawing the loci of points following some general conditions.

Example 7.1 Draw the locus of a point *P* equidistant from a fixed straight line *AB* and a fixed point *F*.

Solution Refer Fig. 7.1.

1. From *F*, draw perpendicular *FC* to *AB*. Mark the midpoint *P* of *FC*. *P* will lie on the curve since *CP* = *FP*.

**Plural* loci

2. Mark a few points 1, 2, 3, etc., on *PF* and draw verticals through them.
3. With *F* as a centre and radius = *C*–1, mark off arcs on the vertical through 1, cutting it at *P*1 and *P*1′.
4. With *F* as a centre and radii = *C*–2, *C*–3, etc., mark off arcs on verticals through 2, 3, etc., cutting them at *P*2, *P*2′, *P*3, *P*3′, etc.
5. Join *P*, *P*1, *P*2, *P*3, *P*1′, *P*2′, *P*3′, etc., as shown for the desired locus.

Note: The locus obtained in the above example represents the parabola. Compare this example with Example 6.10.

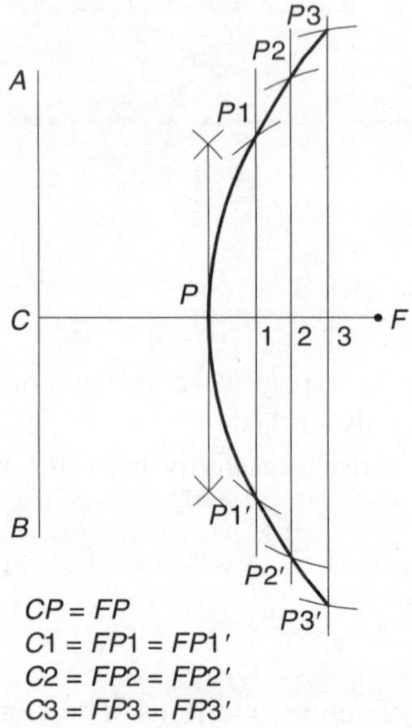

Fig. 7.1

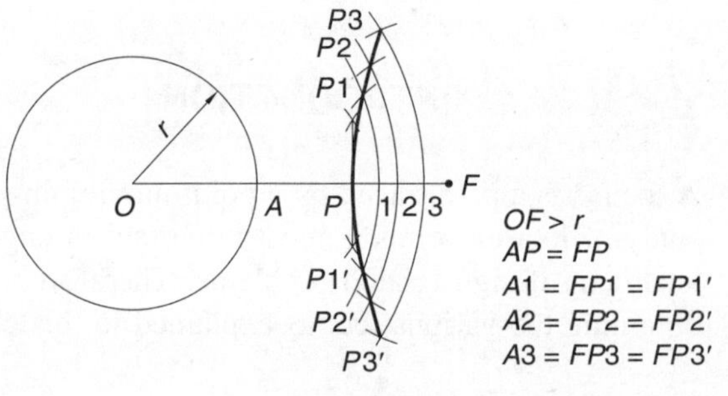

Fig. 7.2

Example 7.2 Draw the locus of a point *P* equidistant from a fixed circle (of radius *r* and centre *O*) and a fixed point *F*.

Solution Refer Fig. 7.2.

1. Join *OF* and mark point *A* at its intersection with the circle. Locate the midpoint *P* of *AF*. *P* will lie on the curve as *AP* = *FP*.
2. Mark a few points 1, 2, 3, etc., on *PF* and through them, draw arcs with *O* as a centre.
3. With *F* as a centre and radius *A*–1, cut arcs on the arc through 1. Name the points as *P*1 and *P*1′.
4. With *F* as a centre and radii = *A*–2, *A*–3, etc., cut arcs on arcs through 2, 3, etc., intersecting them at *P*2, *P*2', *P*3, *P*3', etc.
5. Join *P*, *P*1, *P*2, *P*3, *P*1′, *P*2′, *P*3′, etc., as shown for the desired locus.

Example 7.3 Draw the locus of a point *P* equidistant from a fixed straight line *AB* and a fixed circle (of radius *r* and centre *O*).

Solution Refer Fig. 7.3.

1. From *O*, draw perpendicular *OC* on *AB*. Mark point *D* at its intersection with the circle. Locate the midpoint *P* of *CD* As *CP* = *DP*, point *P* will lie on the curve.
2. Mark a few points 1, 2, 3, etc., on *PD* and erect verticals through them.

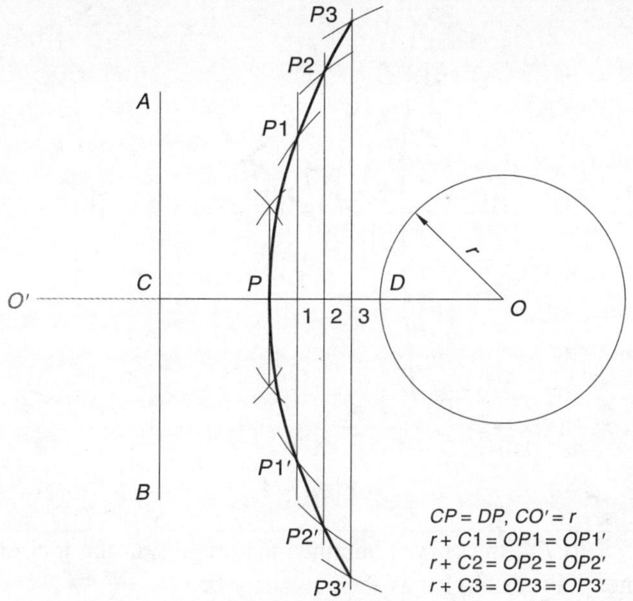

Fig. 7.3

3. With *O* as a centre and radius = (*C*–1) + *r*, cut the arcs on the vertical through 1. Name the points as *P*1 and *P*1′.
4. With *O* as a centre and radii = (*C*–2) + *r*, (*C*–3) + *r*, etc., cut arcs on verticals through 2, 3, etc., to locate points *P*2, *P*2′, *P*3, *P*3′, etc.
5. Join *P*, *P*1, *P*2, *P*3, *P*1′, *P*2′, *P*3′, etc., to obtain the desired curve.

DRAWING TIP

The distances *r* + (*C*–1), *r* + (*C*–2), etc., can be easily measured if point *O*′ is marked on the extension of *OC* such that *CO*′ = *r*. Now *O*′1 = *r* + (*C*–1), *O*′2 = *r* + (*C*–2) and so on.

Example 7.4 Draw the locus of a point *P* equidistant from two given circles (of radii *r* and *R* and centres *O*1 and *O*2 respectively).

Solution Refer Fig. 7.4.

1. Join *O*1–*O*2 and mark points *C* and *D* at its intersection with the circles. Locate the midpoint *P* of *CD* Point *P* will lie on the curve.
2. Mark a few points 1, 2, 3, etc., on *PD* and through them, draw arcs with *O*1 as centre.
3. With *O*2 as a centre and radius = (*C*–1) + *R*, intercept the arc through 1 at *P*1 and *P*1′.
4. With *O*2 as a centre and radii = (*C*–2) + *R*, (*C*–3) + *R*, etc., cut the arcs through 2, 3, etc., to obtain points *P*2, *P*2′, *P*3, *P*3′, etc.
5. Join *P*, *P*1, *P*2, *P*3, *P*1′, *P*2′, *P*3′, etc., to obtain the desired curve.

Note: To measure the distances (*C*–1) + *R*, (*C*–2) + *R*, etc., *C*–*O*2′ = *R* may be drawn.

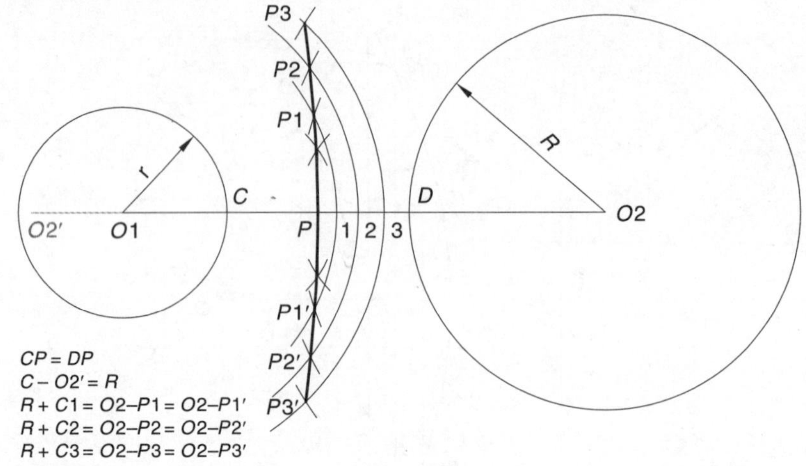

Fig. 7.4

> **Note:** In examples 7.1 to 7.4, the curves obtained also represent the loci of centres of the circles touching the given line, point or circles as the case may be.

Example 7.5 Draw a circle touching two given circles (of radii *r* and *R* and centres *O*1 and *O*2 respectively) and a given straight line *AB*.

Solution The centre of required circle must be equidistant from two given circles and a given straight line. Therefore, it is the combination of Example 7.3 and Example 7.4.

Refer Fig 7.5.

1. Draw the locus of a point equidistant from any one circle (say, of radius *r* and centre *O*1) and straight line *AB*, using the steps mentioned in Example 7.3.
2. Draw the locus of a point equidistant from both the circles, using steps mentioned in Example 7.4.
3. Locate point *O* at the intersection of two loci obtained in steps 1 and 2 above. *O* is the centre of the required circle.
4. Join *O*–*O*1 and mark point *M* at its intersection with the circle. With *O* as a centre and radius = *OM*, draw the required circle.

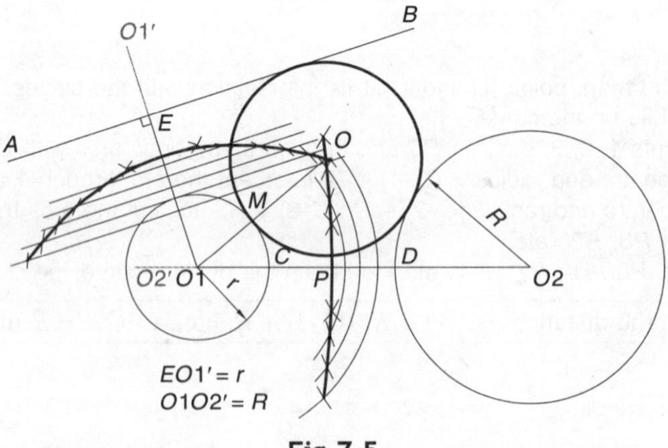

Fig 7.5

7.4 SIMPLE ARRANGEMENTS/MECHANISMS

In this section, we will see the problems on loci of the points in simple arrangements or mechanisms. The common method is to draw different possible positions of the arrangement/mechanism and locate the point(s) of interest in each position. In some cases, we need to find the starting and ending positions or extreme positions of the arrangement. The desired locus is then obtained by joining all the intermediate positions of the point with the extreme positions. This is illustrated in the following examples.

Example 7.6 A pendulum of a clock, 100 mm long, oscillates through 60°. During one cycle of oscillation, a point *P* moves from the moving end to the pivoted end at uniform velocity. Draw the locus of point *P* for one oscillation. Assume initial position of the pendulum to be vertical.

Solution Refer Fig. 7.6.

1. Draw *OA* = 100 mm to represent the initial vertical position of the pendulum. The end *O* is pivoted and end *A* is free to oscillate.
2. With *O* as a centre and radius = *OA*, draw an arc and locate the extreme positions *OA′* and *OA″* of the pendulum. $\angle AOA' = \angle AOA'' = 60/2 = 30°$. (It is assumed that the pendulum moves first to left, then to right and again to left).
3. During one cycle of oscillation, pendulum moves through 120° (= 30° + 60° + 30°). We need to divide this angle into 12 equal parts. However, since angle of 60° (i.e., $\angle A'OA''$) is retraced, we divide it into 6 equal parts. Number all the intermediate positions as *A*1, *A*2, ..., *A*12.
4. Divide *OA* into 12 equal parts and number the divisions as 1, 2, ..., 11 as shown.
5. For the initial vertical position of the pendulum, i.e., *OA*, point *P* lies at *A*. As soon as the pendulum moves to position *O*–*A*1, point *P* will move towards *O* through distance *A*–1. Therefore, cut arc on *O*–*A*1 with *O* as a centre and radius *O*–1 to locate point *P*1.
6. As the pendulum acquires position *O*–*A*2, point *P* moves through distance *A*–2 towards *O*. Therefore, locate point *P*2 on *O*–*A*2 by cutting an arc with *O* as a centre and radius *O*–2.
7. Locate point *P*3, *P*4, etc., in a similar way. Point *P*12 will lie at *O*. Note that the pendulum reverses the direction at *O*–*A′* and *O*–*A″*.
8. Draw a curve through *P*, *P*1, *P*2, ..., *P*12. The curve shows sharp corners at *P*3 and *P*9 since it changes the direction through these points.

Note: The locus obtained in the above example is an Archimedean spiral.

Example 7.7 Figure 7.7 shows an arm *AB* of a giant wheel rotating clockwise about an axis passing through the midpoint *O*. *A* gondola is attached at point *P* on link *AP*. The link *AP* remains vertical for the vertical positions of *AB*. However, due to centrifugal force, it starts deflecting outward and reaches the maximum deflection through 30° when *AB* becomes horizontal. Draw the locus of the point *P* for one complete rotation of the wheel. *AB* = 20 m, *AP* = 2 m. Take a suitable scale.

1. *AB* represents one of the positions of the wheel arm. To decide the other position, draw a circle with *O* as a centre and radius = *OA*. Divide this circle into 12 equal parts. Mark the divisions as *A*1, *A*2, ..., *A*11.
2. The link *AP* will start deflecting as it leaves the vertical position. It shows maximum deflection (i.e., 30°) when *AB* is horizontal. Therefore, as *AB* rotates through one division, *AP* will get deflected through 30/3 = 10°. Draw *AP* = 2 m inclined at 10° to vertical.
3. Draw *A*1–*P*1 and *A*2–*P*2 inclined to vertical at 20° and 30° respectively.
4. As the arm turns from *O*–*A*2 to *O*–*A*5, the angle of deflection of *AP* gradually approaches zero. Therefore, obtain points *P*3 and *P*4 in the same way as that of *P*1 and *P* respectively.
5. Obtain *P*6, *P*7, ..., *P*10 in a similar way. *P*5 and *P*11 will lie vertically below *A*5 and *A*11 respectively.
6. Obtain the required locus by joining the points *P*, *P*1, *P*2, ..., *P*11 by a smooth curve.

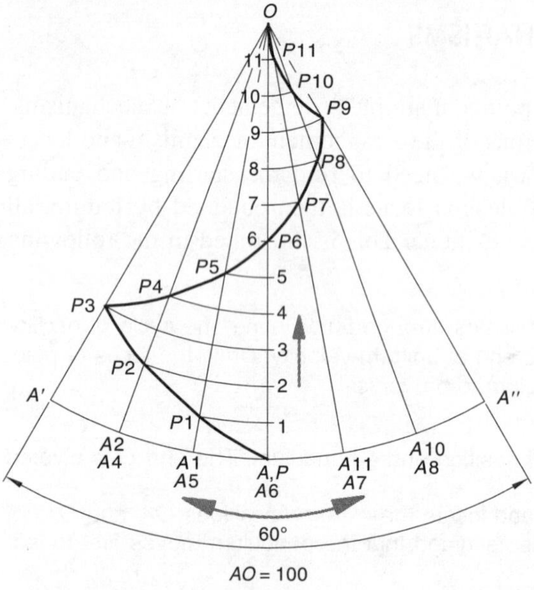

Fig. 7.6

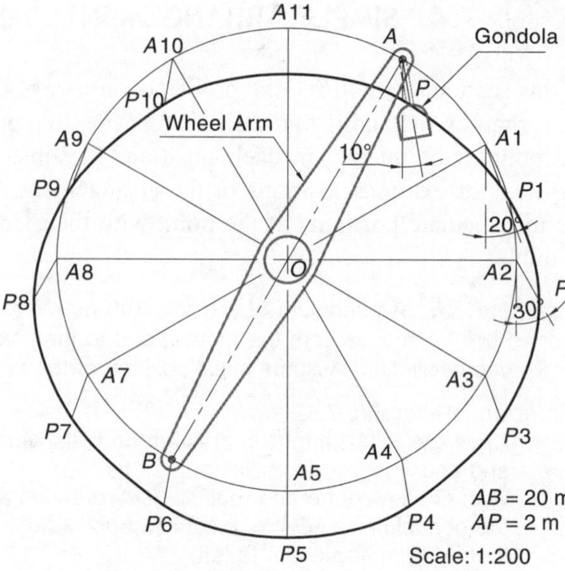

Fig. 7.7

Example 7.8 A 3 m long ladder is resting vertically on a wall. The end *A* is on the wall and the end *B* is on the floor. Draw the locus of point *P*, 0.5 m from end *A*, if the ends *A* and *B* slide along the wall and floor respectively until the ladder becomes horizontal.

Solution Refer Fig. 7.8.

1. Draw the ladder *AB* = 3 m resting vertically on the wall. Draw *BC* perpendicular to *AB* to represent the floor. Locate point *P* on *AB* at 0.5 m from *A*.
2. Divide *AB* into 6 equal parts and mark divisions as *A*1, *A*2, ..., *A*5.
3. With *A*1 as a centre and radius = *AB*, mark off an arc on *BC* cutting at *B*1. Join *A*1–*B*1 and locate *P*1 on it at 0.5 m from *A*1.
4. Obtain *A*2–*B*2, *A*3–*B*3, etc., and locate on them *P*2, *P*3, etc., in a similar way explained in Step 3 above.
5. Join *P*, *P*1, *P*2, ..., *P*6 by a smooth curve to represent the required locus.

Example 7.9 A circular disc of diameter *AB* =120 mm rotates about its centre with uniform angular velocity. *A* point *P*, which is at *A*, moves with uniform linear velocity and reaches the point *B*, when the disc completes one revolution. Trace the locus of point *P* moving from *A* to *B*.

Solution Refer Fig. 7.9. It is assumed that the disc rotates in clockwise direction.

1. Draw a circle of diameter *AB* = 120 mm (centre *O*). Divide it into 12 equal parts. Mark divisions as 1, 2, 3, ..., 11. Join 1–7, 2–8, 3–9, 4–10 and 5–11.
2. Divide *AB* into 12 equal parts. Mark divisions as 1′, 2′, 3′, ..., 11′.
3. With *O* as a centre and radius = *O*–1′, cut the arc on 1–7 at *P*1.
4. Obtain the other points *P*2, *P*3, ..., *P*11 by cutting the arcs on 2–8, 3–9, ..., 5–11 with *O* as a centre and radii = *O*–2′, *O*–3′, ..., *O*–11′ respectively.
5. Join *P*, *P*1, *P*2, ..., *P*11, *B* to obtain the desired curve.

Note that point *P*6 will coincide with *O*. Also, point *P*3 coincides with point *P*9.

Note: The locus obtained in the above example is an Archimedean spiral.

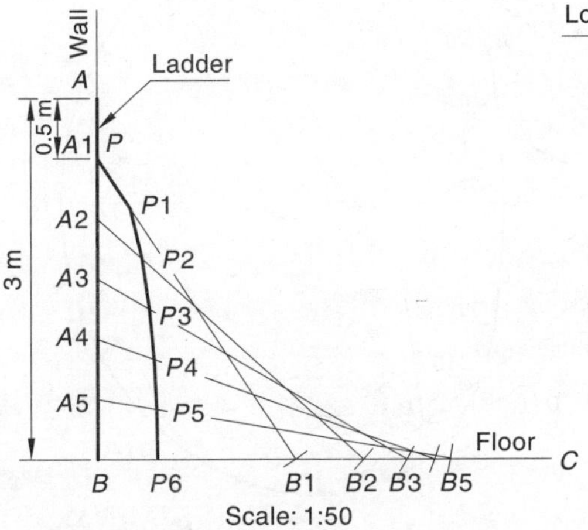

Fig. 7.8

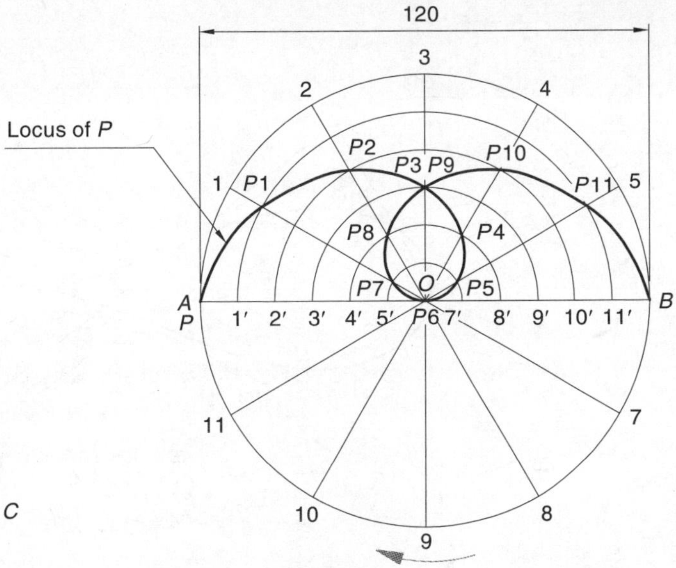

Fig. 7.9

7.5 FOUR-BAR MECHANISM

The *four-bar mechanism* is a very common type of mechanism. It has four elements, which permit definite motions in relation to each other. The elements are called *links*. A link may be a rod, a cam, a rigid frame or a sliding element. One of the links is often a fixed link (rigid frame), *Illustration* 7.1. A link connected to a fixed link and capable of rotating or oscillating about its pivoted end is called a *crank*. A link which connects two cranks, or a crank and another link is called a *connecting rod*.

The following examples illustrate the methods of obtaining loci of points in a four-bar mechanism.

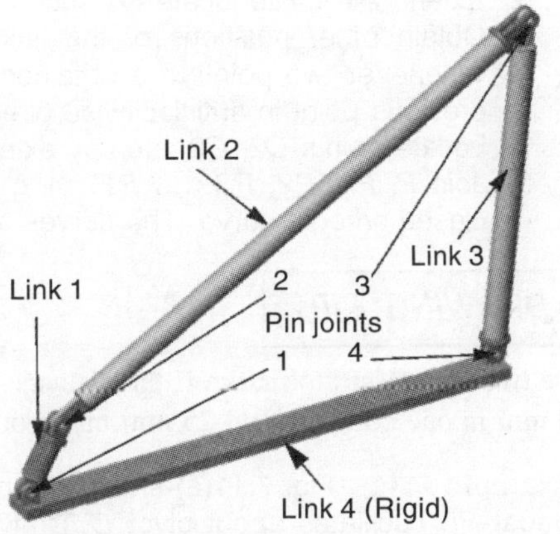

Illustration 7.1 Four Bar Mechanism

Example 7.10 In a mechanism shown in Fig. 7.10, cranks *AB* and *CD* rotate in opposite directions. Draw the locus point *P* on the connecting rod *BD* and of point *Q* on the extension of *BD* *AB* = *CD* = 50 cm, *AC* = *BD* = 150 cm, *BP* = 50 cm and *DQ* = 25 cm.

Solution

1. With *A* as a centre and radius = *AB*, draw a circle to represent the locus of *B*.
2. With *C* as a centre and radius = *CD*, draw a circle to represent the locus of *D*
3. Divide any one circle (say, locus of *B*) into 12 equal parts. Number the divisions as *B*1, *B*2, *B*3, ..., *B*11.

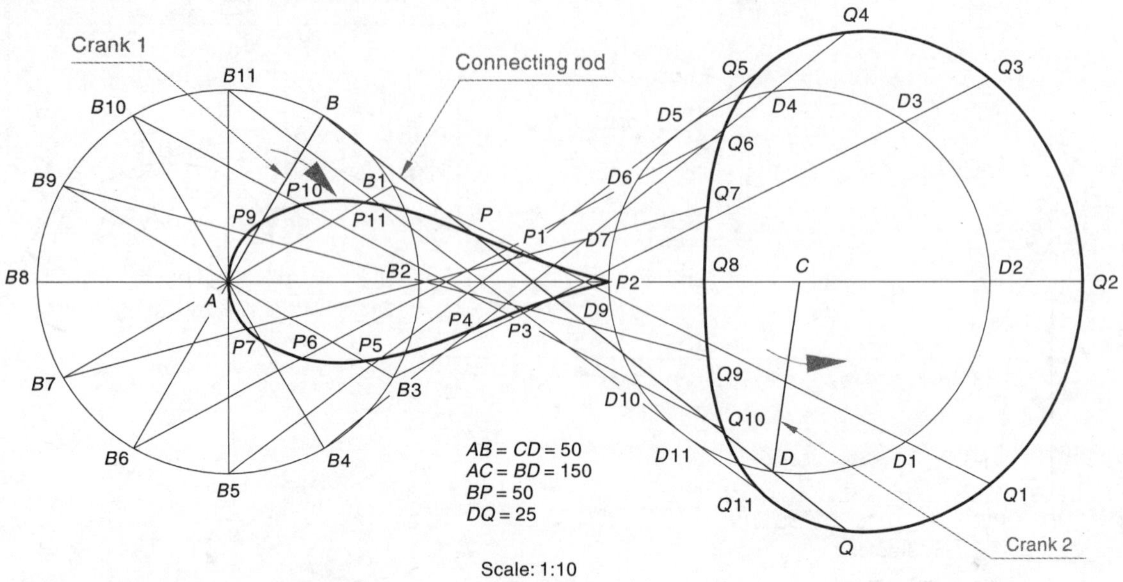

Fig. 7.10

4. Assuming that *AB* rotates in a clockwise direction, *CD* will rotate in an anticlockwise direction. With *B*1 as a centre and radius = *BD*, cut an arc on a locus of *B* at point *D*1. Join *B*1–*D*1. It represents a new position of *BD* Mark *P*1 on *B*1–*D*1 such that *B*1–*P*1 = 50 cm.
5. Extend *B*1–*D*1 to locate *Q*1 such that *D*1–*Q*1 = *DQ*.
6. Obtain other positions of the link *BD*, namely, *B*2–*D*2, *B*3–*D*3, etc., as mentioned in Step 4. Whenever two points are obtained for the same position, select the point which is nearest to the previous point in anticlockwise direction. Mark points *P*2, *P*3, etc., in each case.
7. Locate points *Q*2, *Q*3, etc., by extending *B*2–*D*2, *B*3–*D*3, etc., as mentioned in Step 5.
8. Join *P*, *P*1, *P*2, *P*3, ..., *P*11 by a closed smooth curve. Join *Q*, *Q*1, *Q*2, *Q*3, ..., *Q*11 by another closed smooth curve. The curves represent required loci.

DRAWING TIP

Use two compasses to mark off the distances *BP* and *DQ* in each position of the mechanism. Set the distance of 50 mm in one compass and 25 mm in the other compass.

Example 7.11 Fig. 7.11(a) shows the mechanism of a sewing machine. Crank *OA* rotates about *O* and pedal *BD* oscillates about pivot *C*. Draw the locus of the midpoint *P* of the connecting rod *AB* for one revolution of the crank. *OA* = 5 cm, *AB* = 30 cm, *BC* = *CD* = 10 cm.

Solution Refer Fig. 7.11(b).

1. With *O* as a centre and radius = *OA*, draw a circle to represent the locus of *A*. Divide the circle into 8 equal parts and name the divisions as *A*1, *A*2, ..., *A*7.
2. With *C* as a centre and radius = *BC*, draw an arc to represent the locus of *B*.
3. With *A*, *A*1, *A*2, etc., as centres and radius = *AB*, cut the arcs at *B*, *B*1, *B*2, etc., on the locus of *B*.
4. Join *AB*, *A*1–*B*1, *A*2–*B*2, etc., and on each of them, mark midpoints *P*, *P*1, *P*2, etc.
5. Join *P*, *P*1, *P*2, etc., by a closed smooth curve for the desired locus.

Example 7.12 Two cranks *AB* and *CD*, rotating and oscillating about *A* and *C* respectively, are connected by a link *BD*, as shown in Fig. 7.12. Draw the locus of the midpoint of the link *BD* for one complete revolution of the crank *AB*. *AB* = 50 cm, *CD* = 80 cm and *BD* = 115 cm.

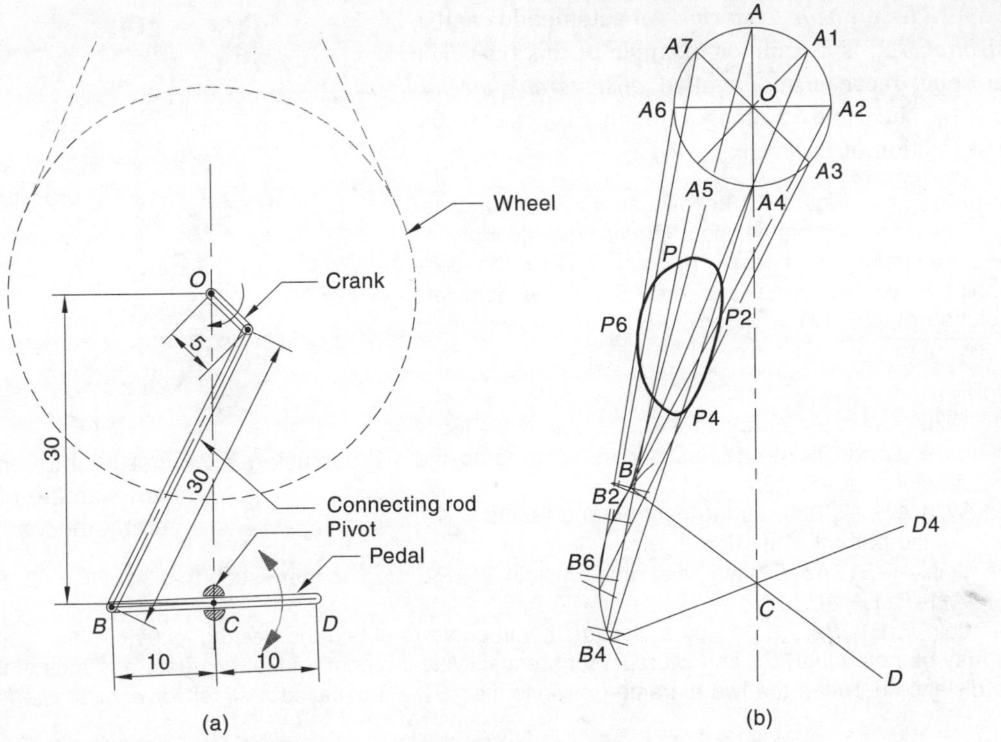

Fig. 7.11

Solution

1. With *A* as a centre and radius = *AB*, draw the locus of *B*. Divide it into 12 equal parts and number the divisions as *B*1, *B*2, ..., *B*11.
2. With *C* as a centre and radius = *CD*, draw an arc to represent the locus of *D*
3. With *B*1, *B*2, etc., as the centres and radius = *BD*, cut the arcs on the locus of *D* at *D*1, *D*2, etc.
4. Join *B*1–*D*1, *B*2–*D*2, etc., and mark midpoints *P*1, *P*2, etc., on them.
5. Draw a closed smooth curve through *P*, *P*1, *P*2, ..., *P*11 for the required locus.

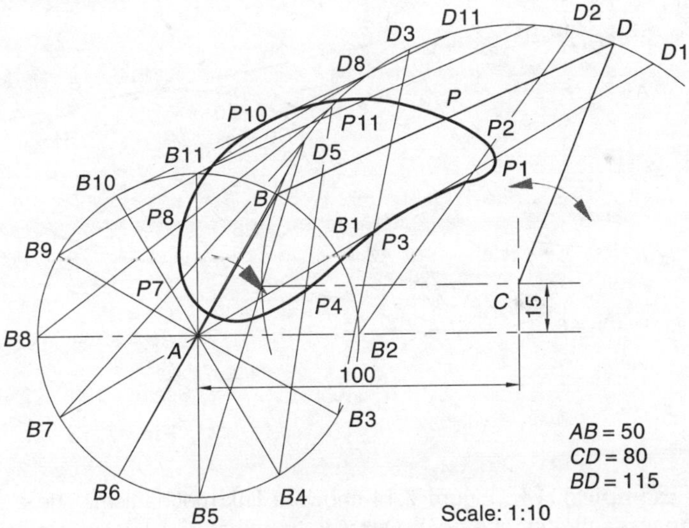

Fig. 7.12

7.6 SLIDER-CRANK MECHANISM

If one of the elements in the crank mechanism is a sliding element (e.g., piston), the mechanism is called a *slider crank mechanism*. An automobile engine, *Illustration* 7.2, is a common example of this type. The slider-crank mechanism is called *offset crank mechanism* if the slider moves along a line that is offset to the axis of rotation of the crank.

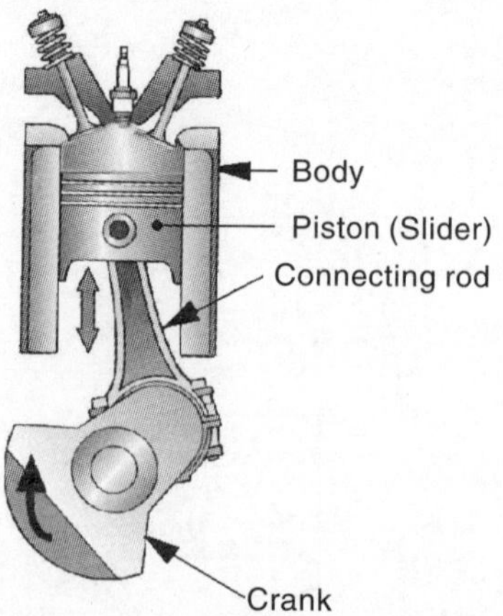

Illustration 7.2 Automobile engine—An example of slider crank mechanism

Example 7.13 Figure 7.13 shows an IC engine mechanism. The crank *OA* rotates about *O*, while the slider moves along the straight line passing through *O*. Draw the locus of point *P* on the connecting rod *AB* for one complete revolution of *OA*. *OA* = 20 cm, *AB* = 90 cm and *AP* = 40 cm.

Solution

1. With *O* as a centre and radius = *OA*, draw the locus of *A*. Divide it into 12 equal parts and name the divisions as *A*1, *A*2, ..., *A*11.
2. With *A*1, *A*2, etc., as the centres and radius = *AB*, cut the path of *B* at *B*1, *B*2, etc.
3. Join *A*1–*B*1, *A*2–*B*2, etc., and obtain points *P*1, *P*2, etc., on them such that *A*1–*P*1 = *A*2–*P*2 = ... = *A*11–*P*11 = *AP*.
4. Join *P*, *P*1, *P*2, ..., *P*11 by a closed smooth curve to obtain the desired locus.

It may be noted that, *B*2 and *B*8 represent respectively the right and left extreme positions of the slider. The distance between the two extreme positions, i.e., *B*2–*B*8 is called a *slider travel* or *stroke length*.

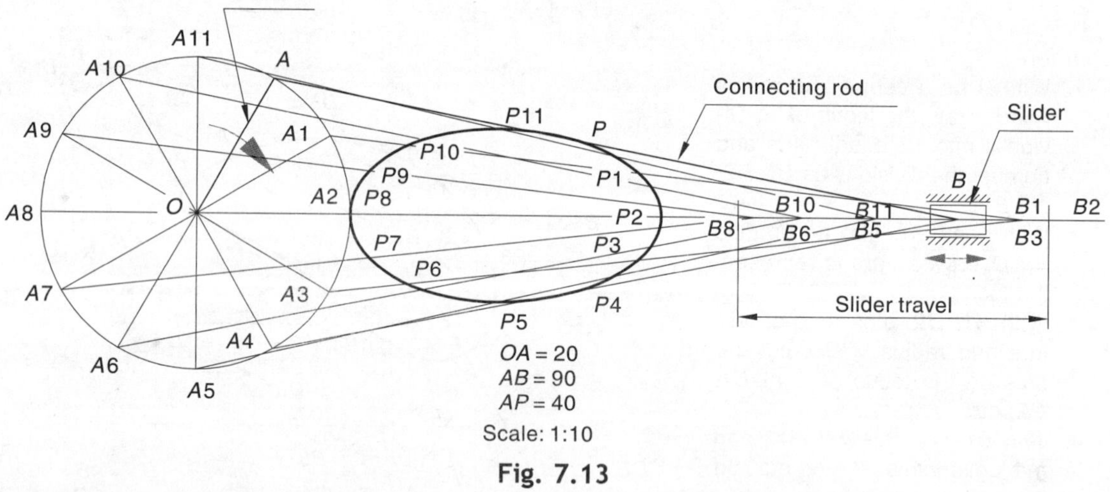

Fig. 7.13

Example 7.14 Figure 7.14 shows a link mechanism. The crank *AB* rotates about *A*. Link *PBC* always passes through the point *D* (being trunnion). Draw loci for points *P* and *C*.

Solution

1. Obtain 8 positions of *AB* by dividing the circle into 8 equal parts. Number the divisions as *B*1, *B*2, ..., *B*7.
2. Join *B*1, *B*2, ..., *B*7 to *D* and extend them to locate *C*1, *C*2, ..., *C*7 such that *B*1–*C*1 = *B*2–*C*2 = ... = *B*7–*C*7 = 150 cm.

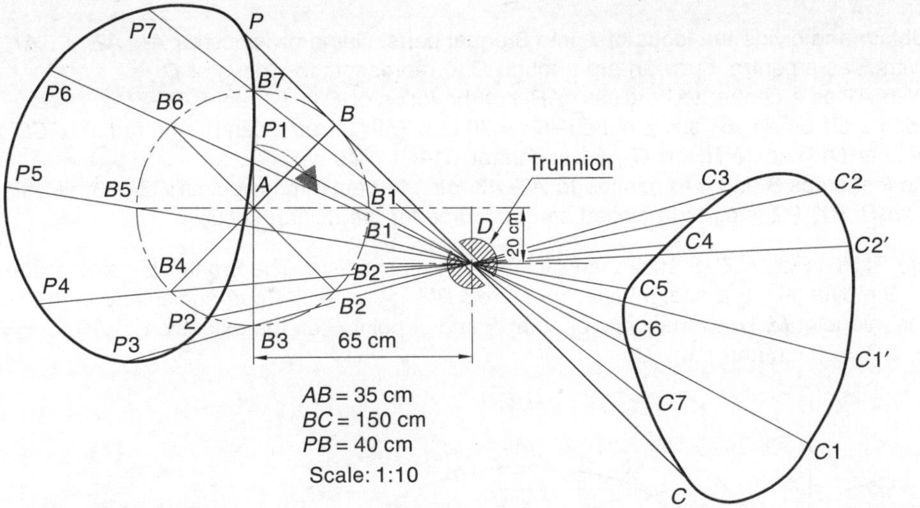

Fig. 7.14

3. The distance between *C*1 and *C*2 is too large. To locate intermediate points between them, mark *B*1′ and *B*2′ anywhere between *B*1 and *B*2. Join *B*1′ and *B*2′ to *D* and extend them to locate *C*1′ and *C*2′ respectively such that *B*1′–*C*1′ = *B*2′–*C*2′ = 150 cm.
4. Extend *B*1–*C*1, *B*2–*C*2, ..., *B*7–*C*7 to locate *P*1, *P*2, ..., *P*7 such that *B*1–*P*1 = *B*2–*P*2 = ... = *B*7–*P*7 = 40 cm.
5. Join *C*, *C*1, *C*1′, *C*2′, *C*2, etc., by a closed smooth curve. Also, join *P*1, *P*2, *P*3, etc., by another closed smooth curve. The two curves represent the required loci.

Example 7.15 Figure 7.15 shows a steam engine valve gear mechanism. Draw the locus of the point *P* for one complete revolution of the crank *OA*. Take *OA* = 45 cm, *AB* = 150 cm, *BC* = *CD* = 70 cm, *CP* = 40 cm and *FD* = 115 cm.

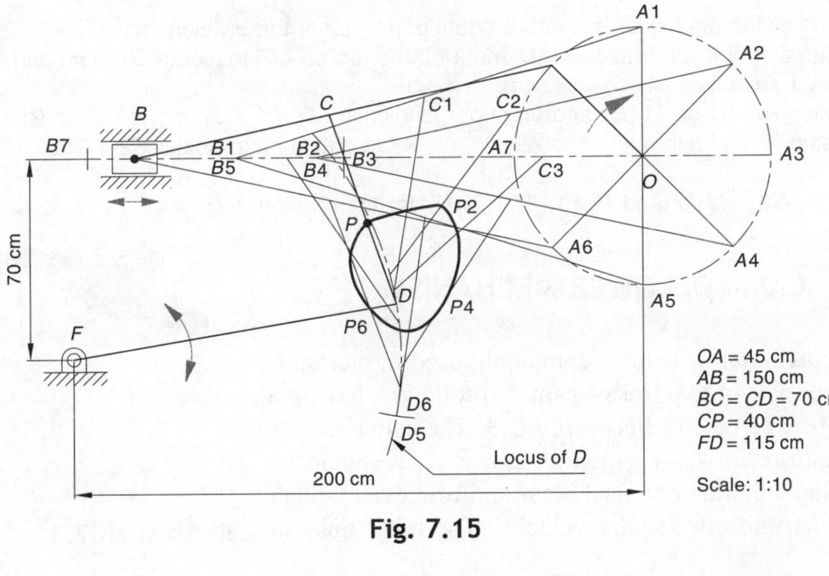

Fig. 7.15

Solution

1. Obtain and divide the locus of *A* into 8 equal parts. Name divisions as *A*1, *A*2, ..., *A*7.
2. With *F* as a centre, draw an arc through *D* to represents the locus of *D*
3. With *A*1 as a centre and radius = *AB*, cut the locus of *B* at *B*1. Join *A*1–*B*1.
4. Locate *C*1 on *A*1–*B*1 such that *B*1–*C*1 = 70 cm. With *C*1 as a centre and radius = *CD*, cut the locus of *D* at *D*1. Locate *P*1 on *C*1–*D*1 such that *C*1–*P*1 = 40 cm.
5. Repeat steps 3 and 4 in relation to *A*2, *A*3, etc., to obtain more points *P*2, *P*3, etc.
6. Join *P*, *P*1, *P*2, etc., by a closed smooth curve for the desired locus.

Example 7.16 Figure 7.16 shows an offset crank mechanism. The crank *OA* rotates about *O* and the slider at *B* moves along a straight line *QR*. *A* rod *PM* is connected perpendicularly to the connecting rod *AB* at the midpoint *M*. Draw the locus of point *P* and of point *C* on the extension of *AB*. *OA* = 38 cm, *AB* = 140 cm, *BC* = 30 cm and *PM* = 20 cm.

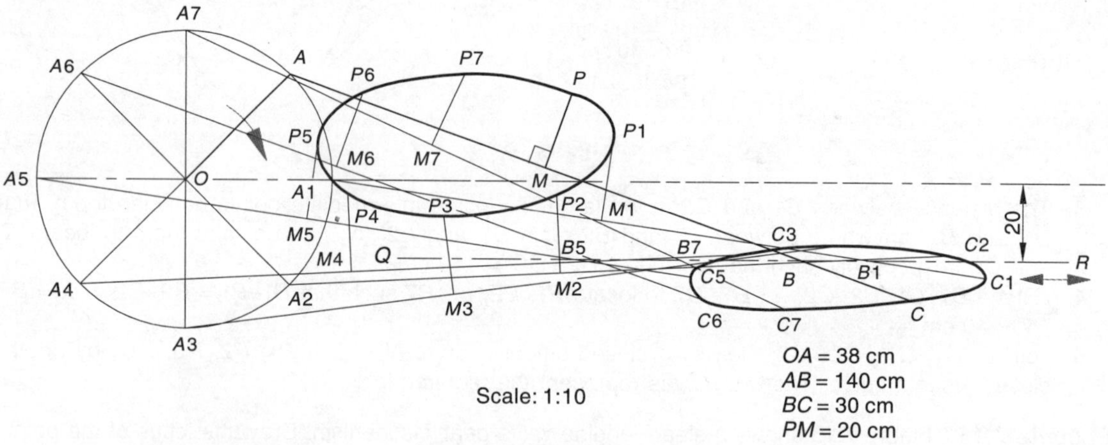

Fig. 7.16

Solution

1. Obtain and divide the locus of *A* into 8 equal parts. Name the divisions as *A*1, *A*2, ..., *A*7.
2. With *A*1 as a centre and radius = *AB*, mark off the arc on *QR* to locate *B*1. Join and extend *A*1–*B*1 to locate *C*1 such that *B*1–*C*1 = 30 cm.
3. Locate midpoint *M*1 of *A*1–*B*1 and erect perpendicular *M*1–*P*1 = 20 cm to locate *P*1.
4. Repeat steps 2 and 3 in relation to *A*2, *A*3, ..., *A*7 to obtain more points *C*2, *C*3, ..., *C*7 and *P*2, *P*3, ..., *P*7.
5. Join *C*, *C*1, *C*2, ..., *C*7 and *P*, *P*1, *P*2, ..., *P*7 for the required loci.

7.7 CAM-FOLLOWER MECHANISM

A *cam-follower mechanism* is most commonly used in mechanical devices. It consists of two links—cam and follower, having a sliding contact between them, *Illustration* 7.3. The cam converts rotary motion into reciprocating motion. However, it should be noted that the linear motion obtained is not uniform even though the cam rotates at uniform angular velocity. The other links in

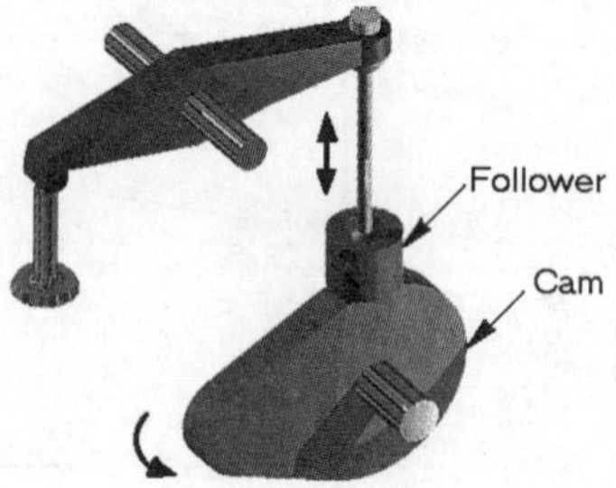

Illustration 7.3 Cam-follower mechanism

the mechanism have some definite set of motions depending on the cam-follower relationship. The maximum travel of the follower due to cam is called *cam throw*.

The following example illustrates the loci of points in the cam-follower mechanism.

Example 7.17 Figure 7.17 shows a cam-follower mechanism. The cam rotates about *C* at a uniform angular velocity and the follower moves between *D* and *D′*. Two links *OA* and *OB* are pin joint to the end *O* of the follower. The links *OA* and *OB* pass through two independent trunnions *T* and *T′* respectively. *A* point *P* which is initially at *A*, moves at a uniform velocity along *AO* and reaches to *P′* during one reciprocation of the follower. Draw the locus of *P* and of *B* for one cycle of cam rotation. *OA* = 120 mm, *OB* = 60 mm, *AP′* = 80 mm and *CO′* = 60 mm.

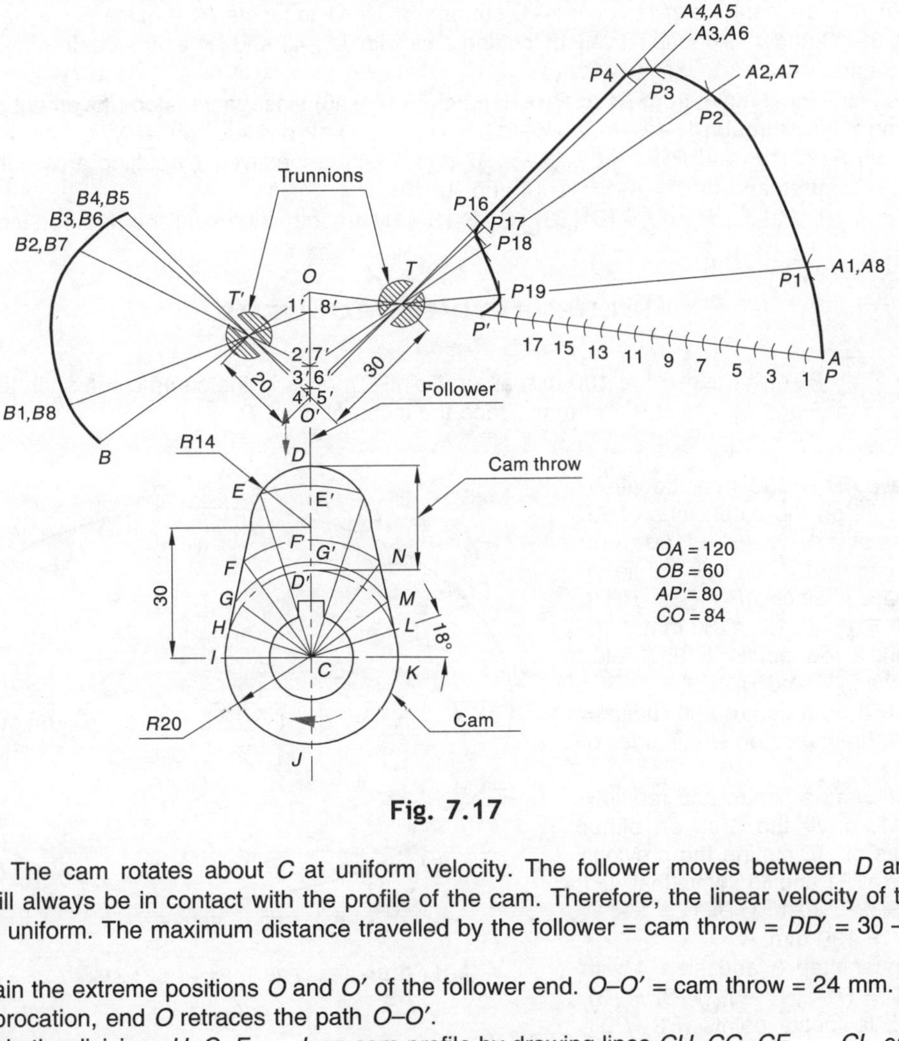

Fig. 7.17

Solution The cam rotates about *C* at uniform velocity. The follower moves between *D* and *D′*. The follower will always be in contact with the profile of the cam. Therefore, the linear velocity of the follower will not be uniform. The maximum distance travelled by the follower = cam throw = *DD′* = 30 – 20 + 14 = 24 mm.

1. Obtain the extreme positions *O* and *O′* of the follower end. *O–O′* = cam throw = 24 mm. During one reciprocation, end *O* retraces the path *O–O′*.
2. Obtain the divisions *H*, *G*, *F*, ..., *L* on cam profile by drawing lines *CH*, *CG*, *CF*, ..., *CL*, each making an angle of 18° with the adjacent line. These 10 equi-angular divisions correspond to half revolution (i.e., *K–D–I*) of the cam. For the other half revolution (i.e., *I–J–K*), there will not be any movement of the follower since the cam profile is semicircular.

3. With C as centre, draw arcs through $H(L)$, $G(M)$, $F(N)$ and $E(Q)$, meeting CO at D', G', F' and E'.
4. On O–O', locate points 1′ (8′), 2′ (7′), 3′ (6′) and 4′ (5′) such that O–1′ (8′) = DE', O–2′ (7′) = DF', O–3′ (6′) = DG' and O–4′ (5′) = DD'. 4′ (5′) will coincide with O'.

   When the cam rotates through 18°, i.e., D to E, the follower end O will move to 1′. If the cam further rotates through 18°, i.e., E to F, the end O will reach to 2′. The positions 4′, 5′ ..., 8′ will be assumed in a similar way.
5. Join 1′ (8′)–T and extend it to obtain $A1(A8)$ such that 1′ (8′)–$A1(A8)$ = OA. Obtain 2′ (7′)–$A2(A7)$, 3′(6′)–$A3(A6)$ and 4′(5′)–$A4(A5)$ in a similar way.
6. Join 1′ (8′)–T' and extend it to obtain $B1(B8)$ such that 1′ (8′)–$B1(B8)$ = OB. Obtain $B2(B7)$, $B3(B6)$ and $B4(B5)$ in a similar way.
7. Divide AP' into (10 × 2 =) 20 equal parts and number the divisions as 1, 2, 3, ..., 19.
8. With $A1$ as a centre and radius = A–1, cut arc on 1′–$A1$ to locate $P1$. Locate $P2$, $P3$ and $P4$ on 2′–$A2$, 3′–$A3$ and 4′–$A4$ respectively by cutting arcs with $A2$, $A3$ and $A4$ as the centres and radii = A–2, A–3 and A–4.
9. The point P will move from $P4$ to $P16$ along 4′(5′)–$A4(A5)$ since there is no movement of follower for cam rotation through H–I–J–K–L. $P4$–$P16$ = (10 + 2 =) 12 divisions on AP', i.e., $A4$–$P16$ = A–16.
10. Obtain $P17$, $P18$ and $P19$ on 6′–$A6$, 7′–$A7$ and 8′–$A8$ respectively by cutting arcs with $A6$, $A7$ and $A8$ as centres and radii = A–17, A–18 and A– 19.
11. Join P, $P1$, $P2$, ..., P' and B, $B1(B8)$, ..., $B4(B5)$ by smooth curves for the required loci.

ILLUSTRATIVE PROBLEMS

Problem 7.1 Points A and B are 100 mm apart. Point P moves in the same plane such that sum of its distances from A and B is always 130 mm. Trace the locus of point P.

Solution Refer Fig. 7.18.

1. Draw AB = 100 mm. Locate P and P' on the extensions of AB such that $AP = BP'$ = (130–100)/2 = 15 mm. P and P' will lie on the locus since $AP + PB = BP' + P'A$ = 15 + 115 = 130 mm.
2. Mark a few points 1, 2, 3, etc., between A and B.
3. With A as a centre and radius = P–1, draw arcs on either sides of AB.
4. With B as a centre and radius = P'–1, draw the arcs on either sides of AB cutting the previous arcs at $P1$ and $P1'$. Note that $AP1 + BP1 = AP1' + BP1' = P–1 + P'–1$ = 130 mm.
5. Repeat step 3 and step 4 with radii = (P–2, P'–2), (P–3, P'–3), etc., to locate points ($P2$, $P2'$), ($P3$, $P3'$), etc.
6. Join P, $P1$, $P2$, ... etc., by a closed smooth curve.

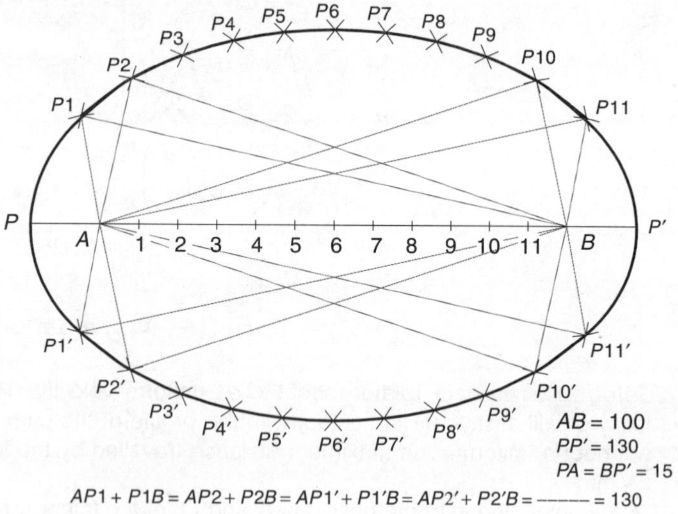

Fig. 7.18

Note: The curve obtained in above example represents an ellipse. See Section 6.3.4.

Problem 7.2 A 100 mm long link *AB* is oscillating about its midpoint. The angle of oscillation is 150° and the rate is 300° per second. A point *P*, initially at *A* on the link, moves along the link (to and fro) at the rate of 200 per second. Assuming both the motions taking place simultaneously, draw the locus of point *P* for a period of one second.

Solution Refer Fig. 7.19.

1. Draw *AB* = 100 mm assuming it is initially vertical. Locate the midpoint *O* of *AB*.
2. Obtain the extreme positions *A*3–*B*3 and *A*9–*B*9 of the link *AB* such that ∠*A*3–*O*–*A*9 = 150°.
3. Mark 6 equal divisions on arc *A*3–*A*–*A*9 and obtain intermediate position of *AB* as *A*1–*B*1, *A*2–*B*2, *A*7–*B*7 and *A*8–*B*8.
4. Mark 6 equal divisions on *AB* and number them as 1, 2, ..., 11.
5. As *AB* moves to *A*1–*B*1, *P* will move form *A* to 1. Therefore, mark *P*1 on *A*1–*B*1 by cutting an arc with *O* as a centre and radius = *O*–1.
6. Obtain *P*2, *P*3, ..., *P*11 in a similar way. *P*3 and *P*9 will coincide with *O*. Also, *P*6 will coincide with *B*.
7. Join *P*, *P*1, *P*2, ..., *P*11 by a closed smooth curve.

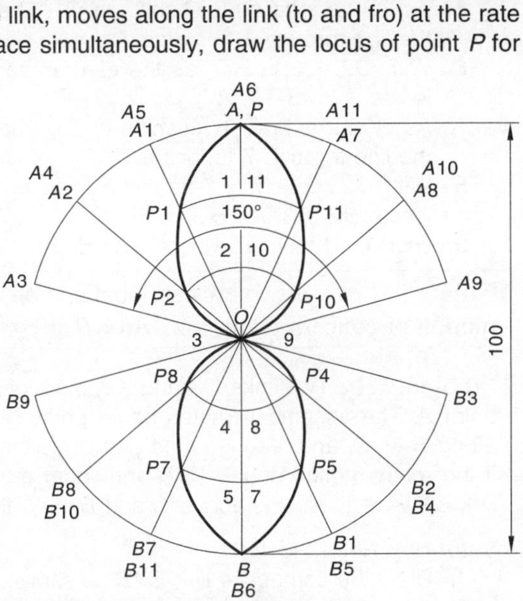

Fig. 7.19

Problem 7.3 A 100 mm long thin rod *AB*, revolves uniformly about its midpoint *O* while its midpoint *O* is also moving linearly and covers a distance equal to the length of the rod during one complete revolution of the rod. Draw the loci of ends *A* and *B*.

Solution Refer Fig. 7.20.

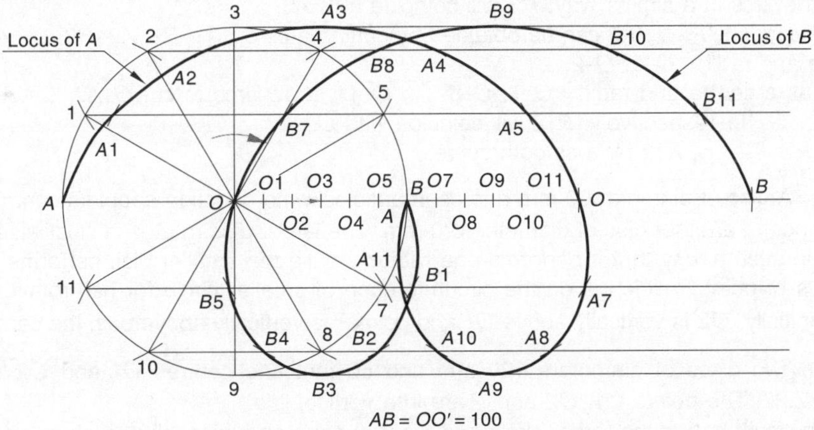

Fig. 7.20

1. Draw *AB* = 100 mm assuming it is initially horizontal. Locate the midpoint *O*.
2. Draw a circle with *AB* as a diameter and mark 12 equal divisions 1, 2, ..., 11 on it.
3. Draw *O*–*O*′ = *AB* and mark 12 equal divisions *O*1, *O*2, ..., *O*11 on it.

4. Through 1(5), 2(4), 3, 6(B), 7(11), 8(10) and 9 draw the lines parallel to *O–O′*.
5. As *OA* turns to *O*–1, *O* shifts to *O*1. Therefore, with *O*1 as a centre and radius = *OA*, cut an arc on the line through 1 to locate *A*1.
6. With *O*2, *O*3, ..., *O′* as the centres and radius = *OA*, cut arcs on the lines through 2, 3, ..., *A* to locate *A*2, *A*3, ..., *A′*.
7. As *OB* turns to *O*–7, *O* shifts to *O*1. Therefore, with *O*1 as a centre and radius = *OB*, cut an arc on the line through 7 to locate *B*1.
8. With *O*2, *O*3, ..., *O′* as the centres and radius = *OB*, cut arcs on the lines though 8, 9, ..., *B* to locate *B*2, *B*3, ..., *B′*.
9. Join *A*, *A*1, *A*2, ... *A*11, *A′* and *B*, *B*1, *B*2, ... *B*11, *B′* by smooth curves.

Note: Wherever two arcs are obtained on the same line, consider the arc which best describes the motion of concern point, viz., *A* or *B*.

Problem 7.4 Two links *OA* and *AB*, each of length 50 mm, are connected to each other at right angle at point *A*. The assembly rotates about point *O* in a clockwise direction. The point *P*, initially at *B*, moves along *B–A–O*, and reaches *O* in one complete revolution of the composite link. Draw the locus of point *P* if the rotary motion of link *OAB* and linear motion of point *P*, both are uniform. Assume that, initially, the link *OA* is vertical, *A* is above *O* and *B* is on the left side of *OA*.

Solution Refer Fig. 7.21.

1. Draw the composite link *OAB* as shown. *OA* = *AB* = 50 mm.
2. With *O* as a centre, draw two circles passing through *A* and *B* to represent the loci of *A* and *B* respectively.
3. Divide the locus of *A* into 12 equal parts and name divisions as *A*1, *A*2, ..., *A*11.
4. With *A*1, *A*2, etc., as the centres and radius = *AB*, mark arcs on the locus of *B* to locate points *B*1, *B*2, etc. Join *A*1–*B*1, *A*2–*B*2, etc.
5. Obtain 12 equal divisions on the composite link, i.e., 6 divisions on each link *AB* and *OA*. Number the divisions as 1, 2, ..., 11.
6. With *B*1 as a centre and radius = *B*–1, mark an arc cutting *A*1–*B*1 at *P*1. Obtain *P*2, *P*3, *P*4, *P*5 by cutting the arcs in a similar way. *P*6 will coincide with *A*6.
   Alternatively, *P*1, *P*2..., *P*5 can be obtained by cutting arcs on *A*1–*B*1, *A*2–*B*2, ..., *A*5–*B*5 with *O* as a centre and radii = *O*–1, *O*–2, ..., *O*–5.
7. With *O* as a centre and radii = *O*–7, *O*–8, ..., *O*–11, draw arcs to cut *O*–*A*7, *O*– *A*8, ..., *O*–*A*11 at *P*7, *P*8, ..., *P*11 respectively. *P*12 will coincide with *O*.
8. Join *P*, *P*1, *P*2, ..., *P*12 by a smooth curve.

Problem 7.5 A disc of diameter 60 mm rotates in anticlockwise direction about its centre *O*2 which is at the circumference of another disc of diameter 120 mm. The larger disc rotates in clockwise direction about its centre *O*1 in such a way that it performs one rotation while the smaller disc performs two revolutions. Draw the locus of point *P* which is on the circumference of smaller circle for half rotation of larger disc. Assume that, initially, *O*2 is vertically above *O*1 and point *P* is vertically above both the centres *O*1 and *O*2.

Solution The two discs of diameters 120 mm and 60 mm and centres *O*1 and *O*2 respectively are shown in Fig. 7.22. The points *O*1, *O*2 and *P* are in a vertical line.

1. Divide the right half of the larger circle into 6 equal parts and name the divisions as *C*1, *C*2, ..., *C*6. When the larger disc will rotate, *O*2 will assume positions *C*1, *C*2, ..., *C*6 sequentially.
2. Divide the smaller circle into 6 equal parts and number the divisions as 1, 2, ..., 6 (6 will coincide with *P*). During the half-revolution of the larger disc, the smaller disc will perform one revolution.

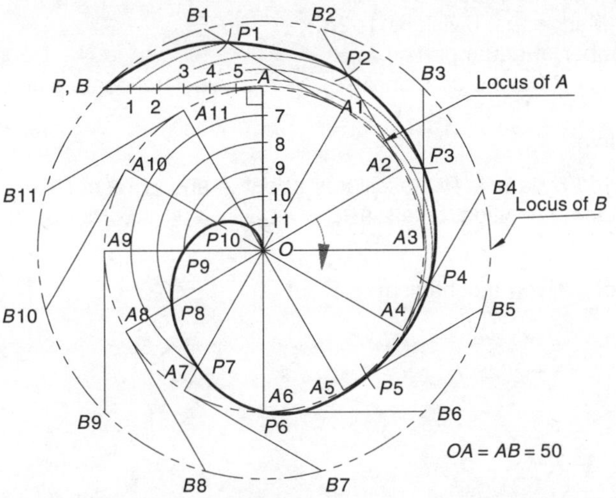

Fig. 7.21

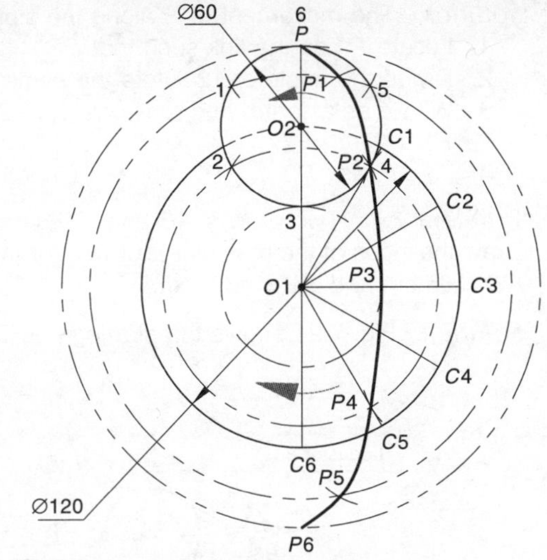

Fig. 7.22

3. With $O1$ as a centre, draw the circles through $P(6)$, 1(5), 2(4) and 3.
4. With $C1$, $C2$, ..., $C6$ as the centres and radius = O_2P, cut the arcs on circles through 1, 2, ..., 6 respectively to locate points $P1$, $P2$, ..., $P6$. Whenever, two arcs are obtained, select the arc which is nearer to $O1$–$O2$. This is because the smaller disc rotates in an anticlockwise direction.
5. Draw a smooth curve through P, $P1$, $P2$, ..., $P6$ for the required locus.

Problem 7.6 A slotted link shown in Fig. 7.23 swings on pivot A through an angle 120°. During one swing from left to right at uniform velocity (angular), a point P moves at uniform speed from position P to P'. Draw locus of P for one swing of link. Show clearly all construction lines.

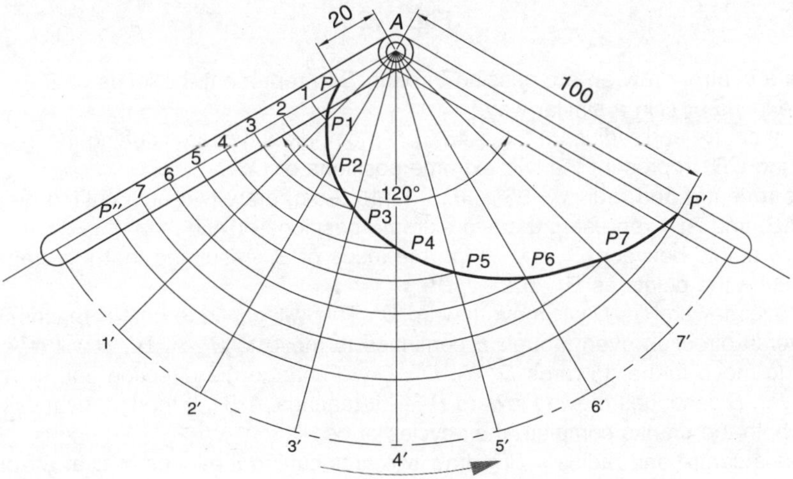

Fig. 7.23

Solution The movement of *P* along the slotted link = 100–20 = 80 mm.

1. Locate *P″* on the link such that *PP″* = 80. Mark equal divisions 1, 2, ..., 7 on *PP″*.
2. Divide the angle of 120° into the same number of equal parts.
3. With *A* as a centre and radii = *A*–1, *A*–2, ..., *A*–7 cut the arcs on *A*–1′, *A*–2′, ..., *A*–7′ to locate points *P*1, *P*2, ..., *P*7.
4. Join *P*, *P*1, *P*2, ..., *P*7, *P′* by a smooth curve.

Problem 7.7 Two cranks *AB* and *CD*, connected by a link *BD*, oscillates about *A* and *C* respectively. Draw the locus of the midpoint *P* of *BD* For the starting position, take ∠*ABD* = ∠*CDB* = 90°, *AB* = 52.5 cm, *CD* = 65 cm and *BD* = 45.5 cm.

Solution Fig. 7.24 shows the starting position of a given mechanism.

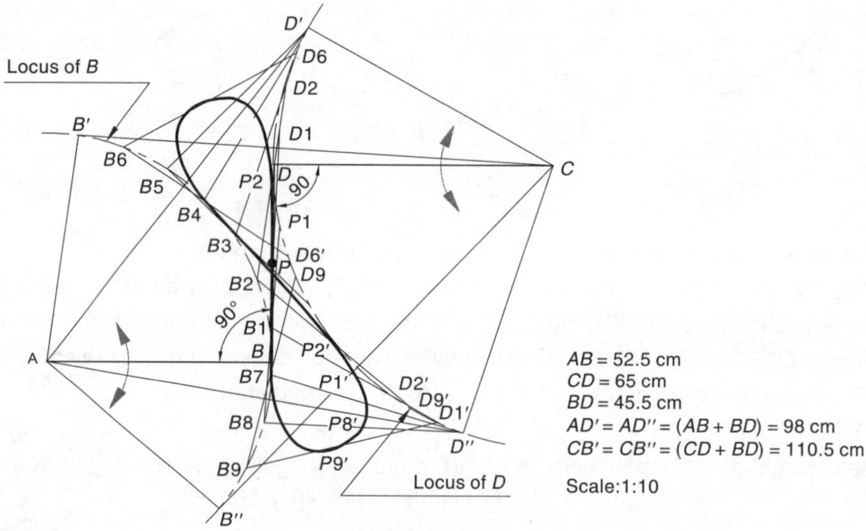

Fig. 7.24

1. With *A* as a centre, draw an arc passing through *B* to represent the locus of *B*.
2. Obtain the locus of *D* in a similar way.
3. With *A* as a centre and radius = 52.5 + 45.5 = 98 cm, draw two arcs cutting the locus of *D* at *D′* and *D″*. *CD′* and *CD″* represent the two extreme positions of *CD*
4. With *C* as a centre and radius = 65 + 45.5 = 110.5 cm, draw two arcs cutting the locus of *B* at *B′* and *B″*. *AB′* and *AB″* represent the two extreme positions of *AB*.
5. Take a few points between *B′* and *B″* on the locus of *B*. Assuming that the crank *AB* first moves upward, name the points as *B*1, *B*2, ..., *B*9.

   As *B* moves toward *B′*, *D* will move toward *D′*. This will continue until *D* reaches to *D′*. After that, *D* will reverse direction even though *B* continues to move to *B′*. At *B′*, *B* will reverse the direction forcing *D* to move further towards *D″*. At *D″*, *D* will change the direction and start moving towards *D′*. However, *B* continues moving toward *B″* till it reaches to *B″*. It then starts moving towards *B′*. In this way, both the cranks complete their cycles of oscillation.
6. With *B*1 as a centre and radius = *BD*, draw two arcs cutting the locus of *D* at *D*1 and *D*1′. Join *B*1–*D*1 and *B*1–*D*1′ and locate their midpoints *P*1 and *P*1′.
7. Repeat Step 6 in relation to *B*2, *B*3, ..., *B*9 to obtain *P*2, *P*2′, *P*3, *P*3′ ..., *P*9, *P*9′.
8. Join *P*, *P*1, *P*2, ..., *P*9′ in a proper sequence by a closed smooth curve. The direction of movement of *BD* must be observed while joining these points.

Problem 7.8 As seen in Fig. 7.25, *AD* and *DB* are two equal-sized portions of a folding door hinged or pin jointed at *D* Span *CB* of the door is 150 cm. The end *B* is fixed and the end *A* is allowed to move along the line *BC*. Draw the locus of the midpoint *P* of *AD* for a complete movement of the folding door.

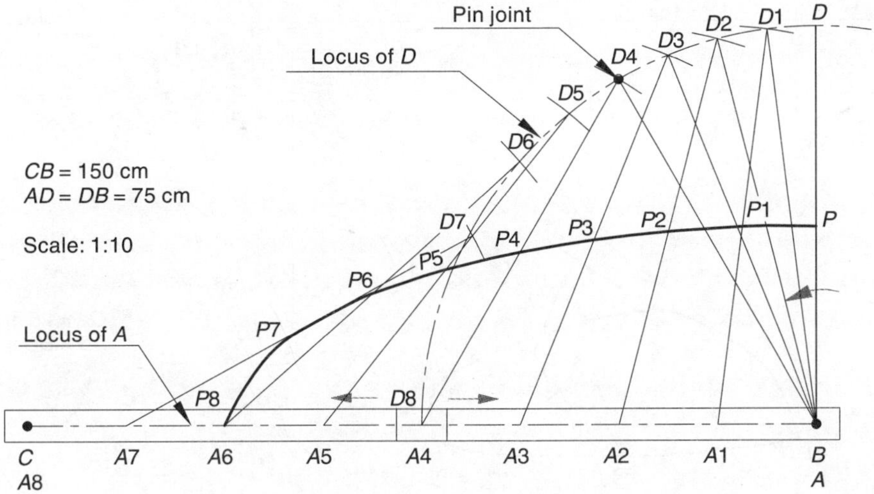

Fig. 7.25

Solution

1 Draw *A*(*B*)*D* = 75 cm perpendicular to *CB* to represent the initial position of door. Locate the midpoint *P* of *AB*.
2. With *B* as a centre, draw an arc passing through *D* to represent the locus of *D BC* represents the locus of *A*.
3. Obtain any number (say 8) of equal divisions *A*1, *A*2, ..., *A*7 on *BC*.
4. With *A*1, *A*2, ..., *A*7 as the centres and radius = *AD*, cut arcs on the locus of *D* at point *D*1, *D*2, ..., *D*7.
5. Join *A*1–*D*1, *A*2–*D*2, ..., *A*7–*D*7 and locate their midpoints *P*1, *P*2, ... *P*7. *P*8 coincides with *A*6.
6. Join *P*, *P*1, *P*2, ..., *P*8 by a smooth curve.

Problem 7.9 Figure 7.26 shows a crank *OA* connected to a slider through two links *AB* and *BC*. The crank rotates about *O* in a clockwise direction and the slider reciprocates through 64° along a curved guideway of radius 80 mm. For initial vertical position of *OA* (*A* above *O*), the slider is at mean position *C*. The slider first moves to right, reverses its direction at two ends of guideway and completes one cycle during one rotation of the crank. Assuming both the motions to be uniform, draw the locus of *B* for one rotation of the crank. *OA* = 25 mm, *AB* = *BC* = 90 mm.

Solution

1. Draw the locus of *A* and obtain 8 equal divisions *A*1, *A*2, ..., *A*7 on it.
2. Divide the angle of 64° into 4 equal parts and mark divisions as *C*1, *C*2, ..., *C*7 on the guideway.
3. As *A* moves to *A*1, the slider moves to *C*1. Therefore, with *A*1 and *C*1 as the centres and radius = 90 mm, mark two arcs meeting at *B*1.
4. Obtain *B*2, *B*3, ..., *B*7 by drawing the arcs with the centres (*A*2, *C*2), (*A*3, *C*3), ..., (*A*7, *C*7) and radius = 90 mm.
5. Join *B*, *B*1, *B*2, ..., *B*7 by a closed curve.

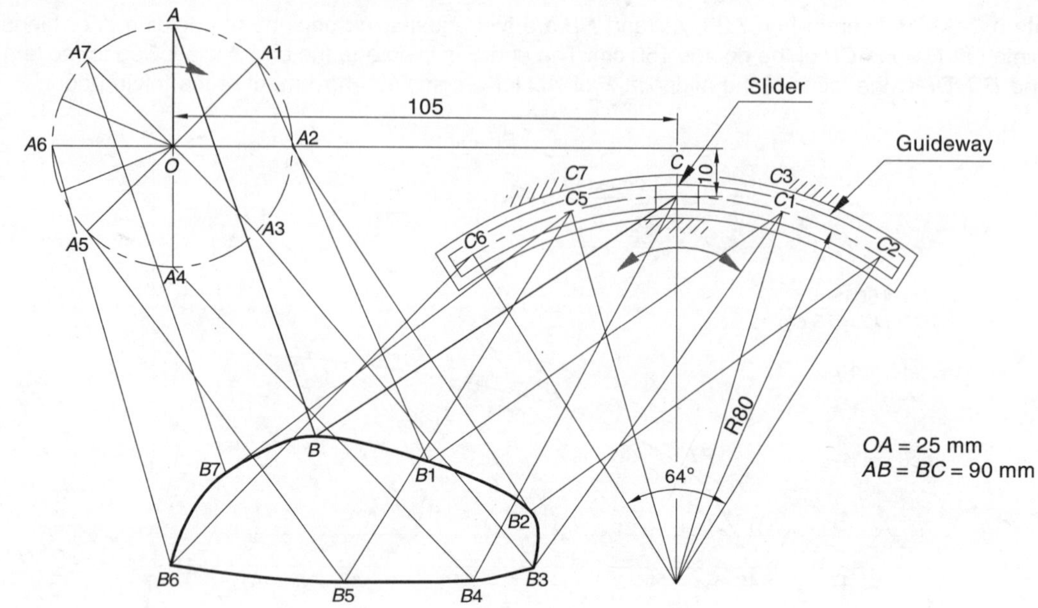

Fig. 7.26

Problem 7.10 Two cams pivoted at $O1$ and $O2$, as shown in Fig. 7.27, rotate in clockwise direction with a uniform and the same angular velocity. A common follower 400 mm long derives its motion from both the cams. Draw the locus of the end P of the follower for one complete rotation of the cams.

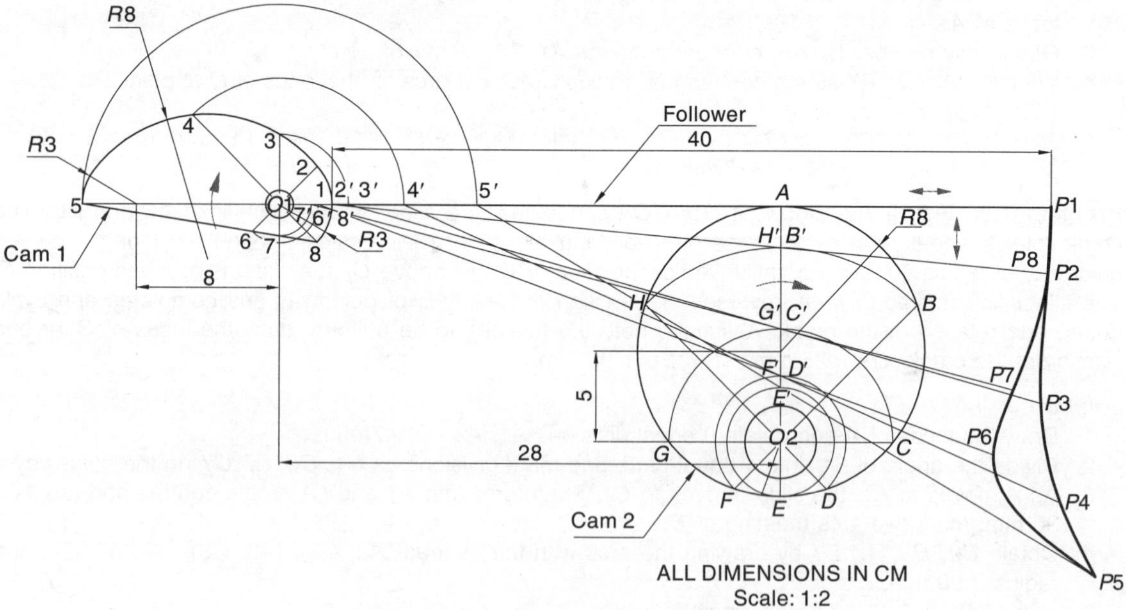

Fig. 7.27

Solution

1. Through $O1$, draw 8 lines to mark 8 divisions 1, 2, ..., 8 on cam 1. Each of these lines makes angle of 45° with the neighbouring two lines. Note that $O1$–5 is horizontal, which describes the initial position of cam 1.
2. Through $O2$, draw 8 lines in a similar way to mark 8 divisions A, B, C, ..., H on cam 2.
3. With $O1$ as a centre and radii = $O1$–2, $O1$–3, ..., $O1$–8, draw the arcs meeting 5–A at 2′, 3′, ..., 8′. 2′ and 8′ coincide with 1.
4. With $O2$ as a centre and radii = $O2$–B, $O2$–C, etc., draw the arcs meeting AE at B', C', etc.
5. Join 2′–B' and extend it to locate $P2$ such that 2′–$P2$ = 40 cm.
6. In a similar way, join 3′, 4′, ..., 8′ to C', D', ..., H' respectively and extend them to locate $P3$, $P4$, ..., $P8$ such that 3′–$P3$ = 4′–$P4$ = ... = 8′–$P8$ = 40 cm.
7. Join $P1$, $P2$, ..., $P8$ by a closed smooth curve.

REVIEW QUESTIONS

1. Figure 7RQ.1 shows a mechanism where crank OA oscillates between the points X and Y. OA is pin jointed to link BAC. Point B is constrained to slide along the line PQ. Plot the locus of point C for the given movement. OA = 35 mm, AB = 50 mm and AC = 50 mm.

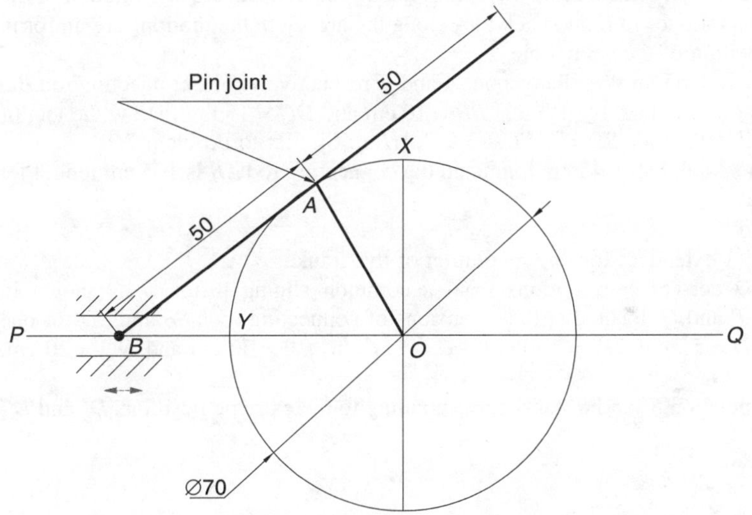

Fig. 7RQ.1

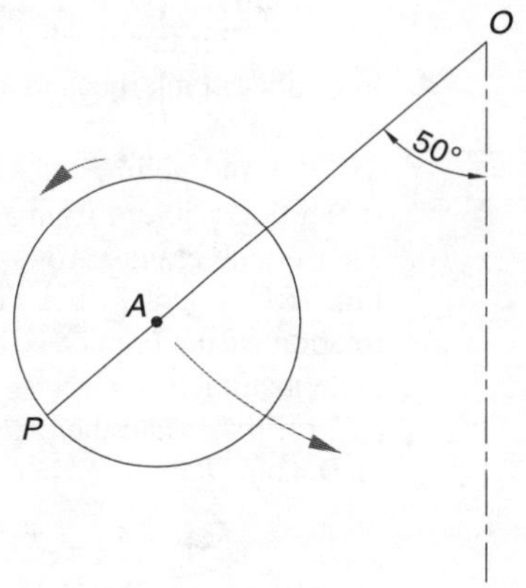

Fig. 7RQ.2

2. The link OA is 15 cm long and carries a circular disc of 5 cm radius. The end O is hinged while the disc can revolve about its centre A. The link turns uniformly to the right through 100° and at the same time the disc revolves uniformly in an anticlockwise direction through one complete revolution. Draw the locus of point P situated on the circumference of the disc. Refer Fig. 7RQ.2.
3. A crank OA rotates about its end O as centre. A rod AB slides over the curved surface of a shaft, whose axis is parallel to the axis of the crank. Plot the locus of the end B for one complete revolution of the crank OA. OA = 30 mm, AB = 120 mm, shaft diameter = 40 mm, OC = 80 mm where C is the centre of the shaft.

4. A circular disc of 100 mm diameter revolves clockwise about its centre with uniform angular velocity. A point *P*, situated initially at the end *A* of the chord *AB* (70 mm long), travels along the chord towards the end *B* with uniform velocity. As the disc completes one revolution, the point *P* reaches the end *B*. Trace the path of the point *P*.
5. The end *A* of a rod *AB* rotates about *O*, while end *B* slides along a straight line, Fig. 7RQ.3. A crank *CQ* oscillates about *Q*. Draw the locus of the end point *E* of the connecting link *CDE* for one revolution of crank *OA*. Given *AB* = 150 cm, *AD* = 90 cm, *CD* = 75 cm, *DE* = 15 cm, *OA* = 45 cm, *CQ* = 120 cm and *OQ* = 225 cm. Take a suitable scale.

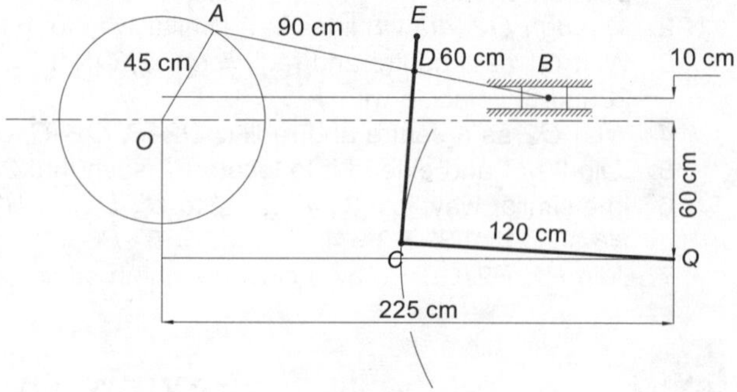

Fig. 7RQ.3

6. *PO* is a 50 mm long rod. It rotates about its end *O* with a speed of one revolution per second, while *O* moves along a straight line *OB* towards *B* with a speed of 120 mm per second. Draw the path traced out by the end *P* for one complete revolution of the rod to full-size scale. In the starting position, assume the rod *PO* to be lying along the extension of the line *BO*. Show all construction lines.
7. A semicircle of diameter *AB* = 120 mm rotates in its own plane about point *A*. During one rotation of the semicircle, a point *P*, initially at *A* moves to *B* and back to *A* along the arc. Both the motions are uniform. Draw the locus of *P* for one rotation of the semicircle.
8. Two cranks *AB* = 52.5 cm and *CD* = 65 mm oscillate about *A* and *C* respectively. The connecting rod *BD* = 45.5 cm has points *P* and *Q* at its extensions such that *BP* = 10 cm and *DQ* = 15 mm. Draw the loci of *P* and *Q*. For the starting position, take ∠*ABD* = ∠*CDB* = 90°. [*Hint:* Similar to Problem 7.7.]
9. In a slider crank mechanism, the crank *OA* is 45 cm long, and the connecting rod *AB* is 105 cm long. Plot the locus of
   (i) the mid-point *P* of *AB*, and
   (ii) a point 60 cm from *A* on *BA* extended, for one revolution of the crank.
10. Two equal cranks *AB* and *CD* derive their motions from a common sliding piston *S* as shown in Fig. 7RQ.4. Draw the locus of *P* and *Q*, located at the extensions of connecting rods *SB* and *SD* for one rotation of the cranks. *AB* = *CD* = 55 cm, *DS* = 150 cm, *AC* = 117 cm, *BP* = 30 cm and *DQ* = 20 cm. Take a suitable scale.
    [*Hint:* First locate the extreme position *S′* and *S″* of *S* corresponding to the extreme positions *D′* and *D″* of *D* Then *BS* = *B′S′* = *B″S″*.]

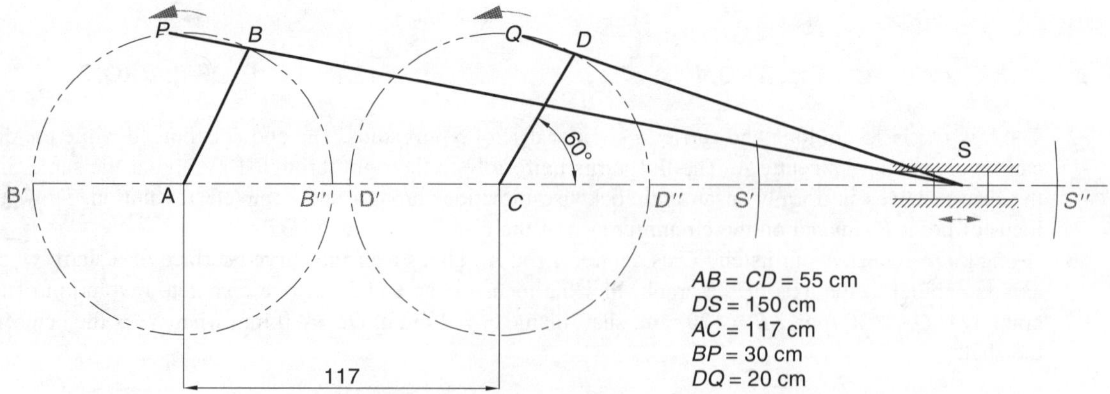

Fig. 7RQ.4

Chapter **8**

THEORY OF PROJECTION

8.1 INTRODUCTION

In engineering drawing, the word 'projection' means an image or the act of obtaining the image of an object. Technical people often refer to the image as a *view*. Engineers use various techniques to construct the views of an object. These techniques are grouped under various methods of projection. This chapter reviews these methods of projection and the important terms and the conventions associated with them.

8.2 PROJECTION SYSTEM

To understand the concept of projection, look at an object kept in front of an illuminating bulb, as shown in Fig. 8.1. The light rays from the bulb strike the object and create its shadow on the screen. The image thus obtained represents a view of the object. The view appears larger than the object since the light rays are divergent.

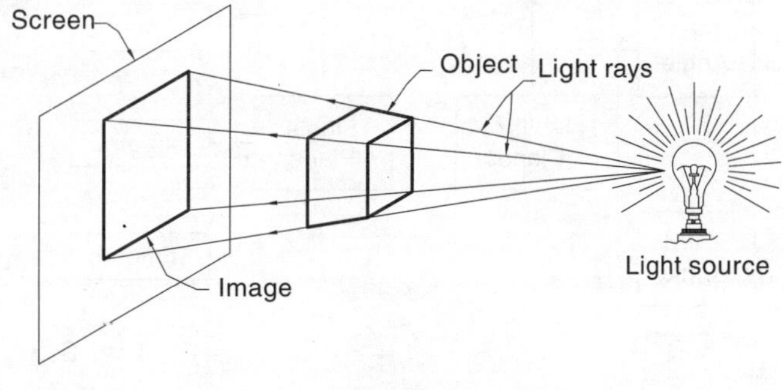

Fig. 8.1

The projection system used in engineering drawing, similar to that shown in Fig. 8.1, is depicted in Fig. 8.2. The light source is replaced by a person—called *observer*—looking toward the object. The lines of sight of the observer create the view of the object on the screen. The screen is referred as *plane of projection* (POP). The lines of sight are called *projection lines* or

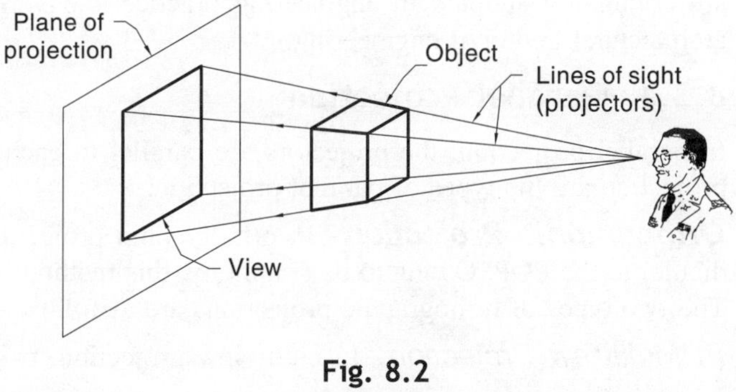

Fig. 8.2

projectors. The view (i.e., projection) of the object is formed on the POP when the points of intersections of the projectors and the POP are joined in a proper sequence. Thus, the object, the observer and the POP are three basic elements of the projection system. It should be noted that the object might be real or imaginary, i.e., in one's mind.

8.3 PROJECTION METHODS

Depending on the relationship between the projectors and POP and the number of POPs used for the projections, the projection methods are classified as shown in Fig. 8.3.

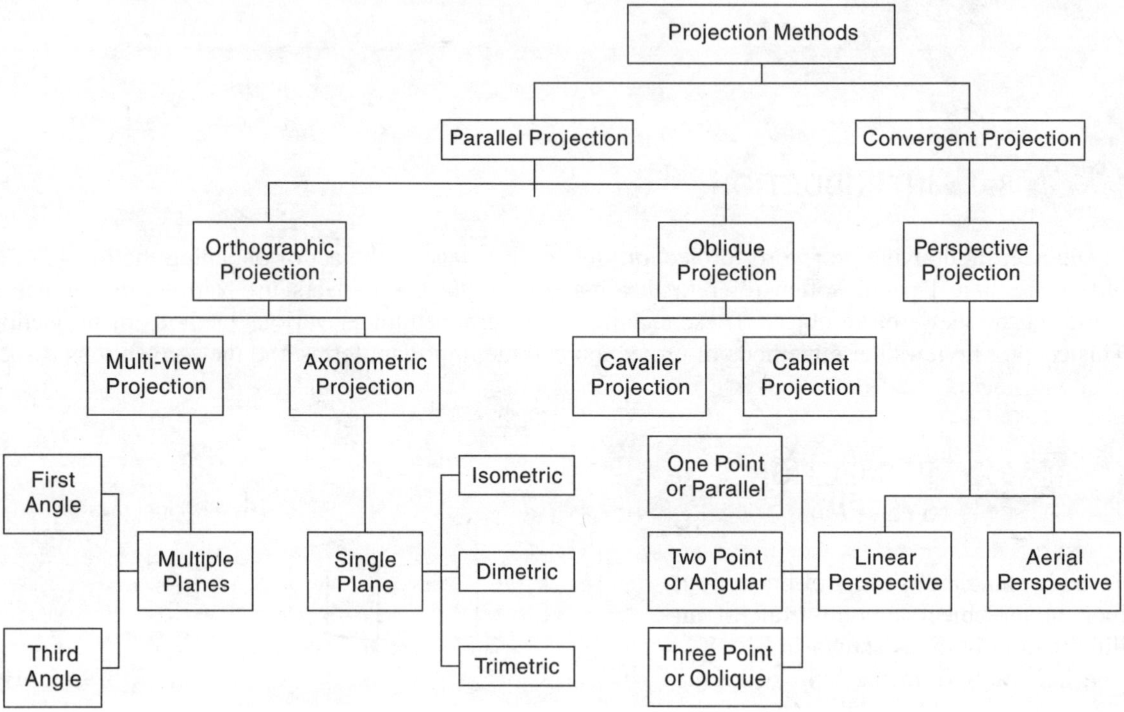

Fig. 8.3

Parallel projection methods, particularly, multiview orthographic projection and isometric projection are commonly adopted in engineering practice. Convergent projection methods find application in architectural and civil engineering.

8.3.1 Parallel Projection

In parallel projection, the projectors are parallel to each other. Orthographic projection and oblique projection are the types of parallel projection.

Orthographic Projection In orthographic projection, mutually parallel projectors are perpendicular to the POP. Owing to its simplicity, this method is widely used in all engineering professions. The two types of orthographic projections are as follows:

(i) Multiview Projection In multiview projection, two or more views of an object are drawn on

different POPs. The object is oriented in such a way that two of its dimensions will be visible in any one view. It is explained in detail in Chapter 9.

(ii) Axonometric Projection In axonometric projection, only one view showing all the three dimensions of an object is drawn on a POP. The orientation of the object is kept in such a way that its three mutually perpendicular edges will remain inclined to the POP.

(a) Isometric Projection If the three mutually perpendicular edges of an object make equal inclinations with the POP, the axonometric projection is called isometric projection, Fig. 8.4(a). An *isometric scale* is used to determine the lengths of foreshortened edges. Isometric projection method is discussed in Chapter 18.

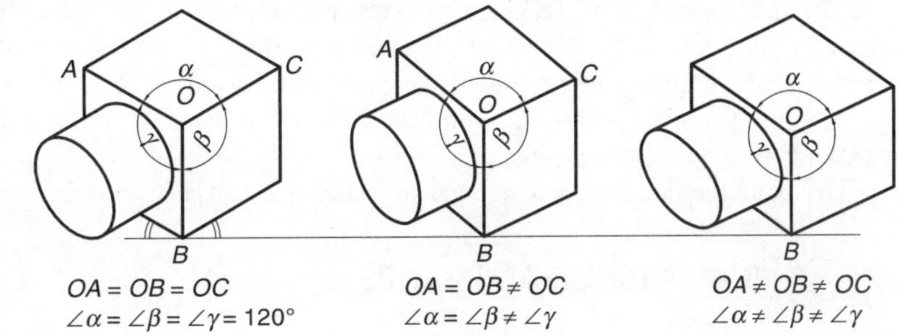

Fig. 8.4

(b) Dimetric Projection If two of the three mutually perpendicular edges of an object are equally inclined to the POP, the axonometric projection is called diametric projection, Fig. 8.4(b). Two different *diametric scales* are used to determine the lengths of foreshortened edges.

(c) Trimetric Projection If all of the three mutually perpendicular edges of an object make different inclinations with the POP, the axonometric projection is called trimetric projection, Fig. 8.4(c). Three different *trimetric scales* are used to find the lengths of foreshortened edges.

Oblique Projection In oblique projection, mutually parallel projectors are inclined (oblique) to the POP at 30°, 45° or 60°. Unlike axonometric projection, one of the faces of the object is kept parallel to the POP. The face parallel to the POP is called *principal face*. Obviously, the projection of the principal face will give its true shape and size. The edges perpendicular to the principal face are drawn inclined to the horizontal. These lines are called *receding lines* and the angle made by them with the horizontal is called *receding angle*.

(i) Cavalier Projection In cavalier projection, the receding lines are drawn to their actual lengths, Fig. 8.5(a).

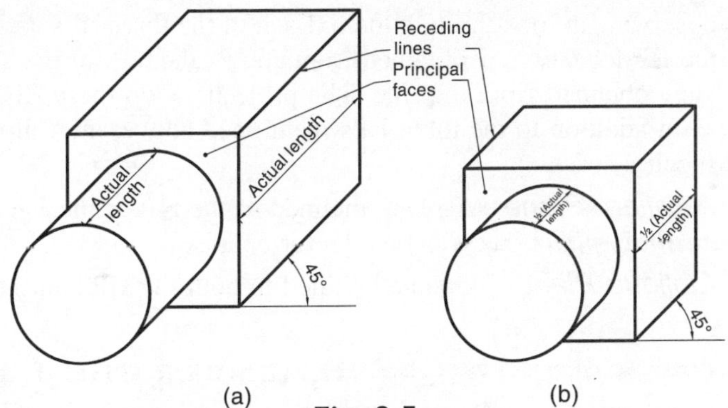

Fig. 8.5

(ii) Cabinet Projection In cabinet projection, the receding lines are drawn to half of their actual lengths, Fig. 8.5(b).

8.3.2 Convergent Projection

In convergent projection, the projectors are not parallel to each other but converge to a point, called *station point*. The station point essentially coincides with the observer's eye. The view is obtained on a POP—called *picture plane*—situated between the object and the observer. The parallel edges of the object are seen to be converging at a point, called *vanishing point*. The object appears smaller and smaller as its distance from the observer increases. The most common type of convergent projection is called *perspective projection*.

Linear Perspective In linear perspective, the size of the object seen bears constant ratio with its distance from the observer. In other words, the ratio at which more distant objects decrease in size is constant. Linear perspective uses one or two or three vanishing points to obtain the perspective view of an object.

Linear perspective projection is discussed in Chapter 19.

Aerial Perspective In aerial perspective, the effect of atmosphere is taken into account while drawing the view of an object. As the distance between an object and the station point increases, the contrast between the object and its background decreases. Therefore, the illusion of depth is created by softening contours and reducing the colour contrasts. Aerial perspective is widely used in artistic drawing.

The axonometric projection, oblique projection and perspective projection are called *pictorial projections*.

8.4 PRINCIPAL PLANES

A POP is a plane on which a particular view is projected. In multiview orthographic projections, we need different POPs to draw different views of an object. Three such planes, perpendicular to each other, are called *principal planes* or *reference planes* (RP). These are as follows:

Horizontal Plane A plane parallel to the ground (or horizon) is called *horizontal plane* (HP) or *horizontal reference plane* (HRP).

Vertical Plane A plane perpendicular to the ground and intersecting the HP is called *vertical plane* (VP) or *frontal reference plane* (FRP).

Profile Plane A plane perpendicular to the HP and the VP and intersecting both of them is called *profile plane* (PP) or *profile reference plane* (PRP).

It should be noted that the RPs are imaginary only. They are assumed to be transparent so that the observer can look through them. Each of the three RPs acts as a POP for the corresponding view, e.g., the HP for the view obtained from above, the VP for the view obtained from front and the PP for the view obtained from the side. The projections on these RPs are explained in Chapter 9.

In addition to the three RPs mentioned above, the following planes are also used as POP in some specific cases:

Auxiliary Plane A plane inclined to the HP or the VP and perpendicular to an other RP is called *auxiliary plane*. See Chapter 12 for details.

Oblique Plane A plane inclined to both the HP and the VP is called *oblique plane*.

REMEMBER THE FOLLOWING

- Projections mean the views of the object.
- In parallel projection, the projectors are parallel to each other.
- In convergent projection, the projectors converge to a point.
- In isometric projection, an isometric scale is used.
- In dimetric projection, dimetric scales are used.
- In trimetric projection, trimetric scales are used.
- In oblique projection, the receding lines make 30° or 45° or 60° with the horizontal.
- A POP is a plane on which a particular view is projected.
- Three RPs used in multiview orthographic projections are the HP, the VP and the PP.
- A plane inclined to both the HP and the VP is called an oblique plane.

Chapter 9

MULTIVIEW ORTHOGRAPHIC PROJECTIONS

9.1 INTRODUCTION

Multiview orthographic projection is a method of drawing two or more views of an object on the RPs placed at right angles to each other. The word 'ortho' means perpendicular. In this projection, the projectors are perpendicular to the POP and parallel to each other. Different views of an object are obtained by viewing it from different directions. Any one view gives two dimensions. Two views together give three dimensions. Though multiview projection is a type of orthographic projection, many people essentially call it orthographic projection.

9.2 MULTIVIEW PROJECTION SYSTEM

The three RPs required to obtain the views in multiview projections are the HP, the VP and the PP, Fig. 9.1 (see Section 8.4 for detail). The HP and the VP make four quadrants. The position of an object in space can be determined by these quadrants, i.e., the object can be in the first quadrant or in the second quadrant or in the third quadrant or in the fourth quadrant. The line at which the HP and the VP meet is called *horizontal reference line* and denoted by *XY*. The line at which the HP (or the VP) and the PP meet is called the *profile reference line* and is denoted by *X*1*Y*1. After the views are obtained, the HP is rotated about *XY* in the *clockwise direction* to bring it in plane with the VP. The PP is rotated about *X*1*Y*1 *away* from the object. The views of an object are now assumed to be in one

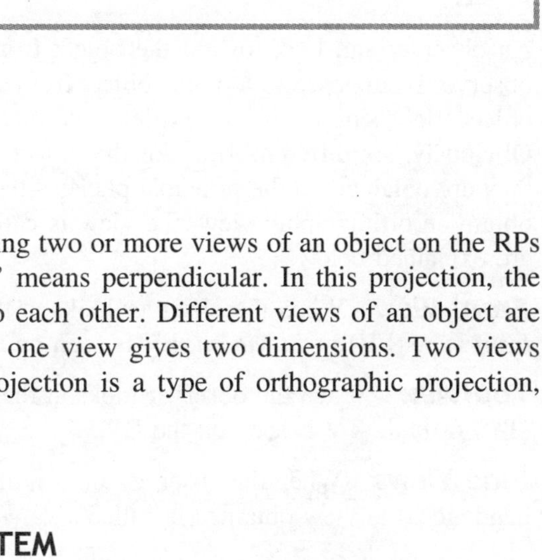

Fig. 9.1 Three principal planes

plane and can be drawn on a drawing paper. Two views of an object are obtained on the HP and the VP. The third view is obtained on the PP.

REMEMBER THE FOLLOWING

- The HP is rotated in the *clockwise* direction.
- The PP is rotated *away* from the object.

9.3 ORTHOGRAPHIC VIEWS

An observer can look toward the object from any direction. However, in multiview projection, the observer is supposed to look the object from six principal directions, i.e., front of the object, top of the object, right side of the object, left side of the object, back of the object and bottom of the object. Obviously, six different views of the object are obtained. These views are called *principal views* as they are obtained on the principal planes—the VP, the HP and the PP. If an auxiliary plane is used to obtain an orthographic view, the view is called an *auxiliary view*. The principal orthographic views are explained below.

Front View When the observer looks at the object from the front, the view obtained is called the *front view* (FV) or *Elevation*. FV is seen on the VP.

Top View When the observer looks at the object from above, the view obtained is called *top view* (TV) or *plan*. TV is seen on the HP.

Side Views When the observer looks at the object from side, i.e., from his left-hand side or right-hand side, the view obtained is called *side view* (SV). SV is seen on the PP.

Left-Hand Side View When the observer views the object from his left-hand side, the view obtained is called *left-hand side view* (LHSV).

Right Hand Side View When the observer views the object from his right-hand side, the view obtained is called as *right-hand side view* (RHSV).

For longer objects of uniform cross section (e.g., long pipe, spline shaft, etc.), the SV is usually referred as *end view*.

Bottom View When the observer looks to the object from below, the view obtained is called *bottom view* (BV) or *bottom plan*.

Rear View When the observer looks to the object from back, the view obtained is called *rear view* (RV) or *back view* or *rear elevation*.

The FV, TV and either LHSV or RHSV are usually drawn in orthographic projection. The other views are added if they are extremely essential.

Note: As per BIS (SP46: 2003), the FV, TV, LHSV, RHSV, BV and RV should be referred as the *view from the front*, the *view from above*, the *view from the left*, the *view from the right*, the *view from below* and the *view from the rear* respectively. However, the terms FV, TV, LHSV, etc., are very popular and their use is continued in this book.

REMEMBER THE FOLLOWING

- FV is seen on the VP.
- TV is seen on the HP.
- LHSV and RHSV are seen on the PP.

9.4 METHODS OF MULTIVIEW PROJECTION

The object can be placed in any one of the four quadrants. However, in multiview orthographic projections, the object is placed in either first quadrant or third quadrant. Accordingly, the method is called *first-angle method of projection* or *third-angle method of projection.* Each of these methods is represented by a conventional symbol, usually drawn in title block or below the views.

9.4.1 First-angle Projection Method

In first-angle projection, an object is placed in the first quadrant, i.e., above the HP and in front of the VP, Fig. 9.2(a). The views of the object are projected by drawing parallel projectors from the object to the POP. The observer looks at the object from the front (i.e., direction *X*) to obtain FV on the VP. Similarly, to get TV on the HP and LHSV on the PP, the observer looks at the object from the above (i.e., direction *Y*) and from the left side (i.e., direction *Z*) respectively. Once the views are obtained, the RPs are unfolded so that the views are placed at their proper locations. Note that the HP is rotated *clockwise* about *XY* while the PP is rotated *away* from the object about *X*1*Y*1. Therefore, TV is placed below FV and LHSV is placed on the right side of FV, Fig. 9.2(b). To obtain RHSV, the observer views the object from right side (i.e., direction *W*) and the PP is located on the side of the object opposite to the observer. The PP, when rotated away from the object, will show RHSV on the left side of the FV.

In the first angle method of projection, the object is placed between the observer and the POP, Fig. 9.2(c). The readers must observe the relative positions of the various views.

Symbol of First-angle Projection Method The first-angle projection method is indicated by the symbol shown in Fig. 9.2(d). It shows the two views of a frustum of a cone.

9.4.2 Third-angle Projection Method

In third-angle projection, an object is placed in the third quadrant, i.e., below the HP and behind the VP, Fig. 9.3(a). The observer looks at the object through the POP to obtain its views. The RPs are rotated as in first-angle method, i.e., the HP in *clockwise* direction and the PP *away* from the object. Obviously, TV is placed above FV, LHSV on the left side of FV and RHSV on the right side of FV, Fig. 9.3(b). In third-angle method of projection, the POP exists between the object and the observer, Fig. 9.3(c).

Symbol of Third-angle Projection Method The third-angle projection method symbol is shown in Fig. 9.3(d).

It should be noted that the views in both the methods are same. It is only their locations which changed.

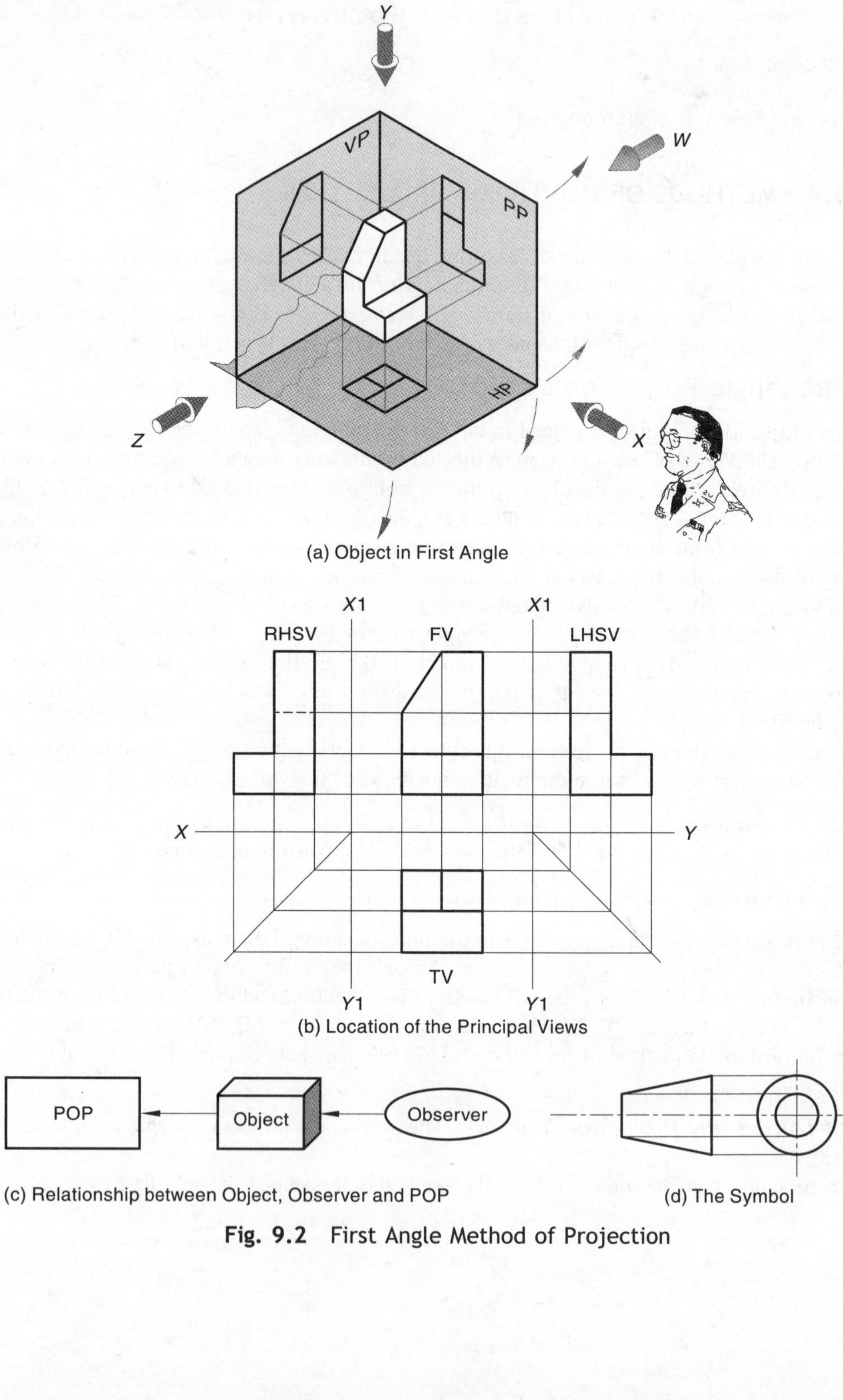

(a) Object in First Angle

(b) Location of the Principal Views

(c) Relationship between Object, Observer and POP

(d) The Symbol

Fig. 9.2 First Angle Method of Projection

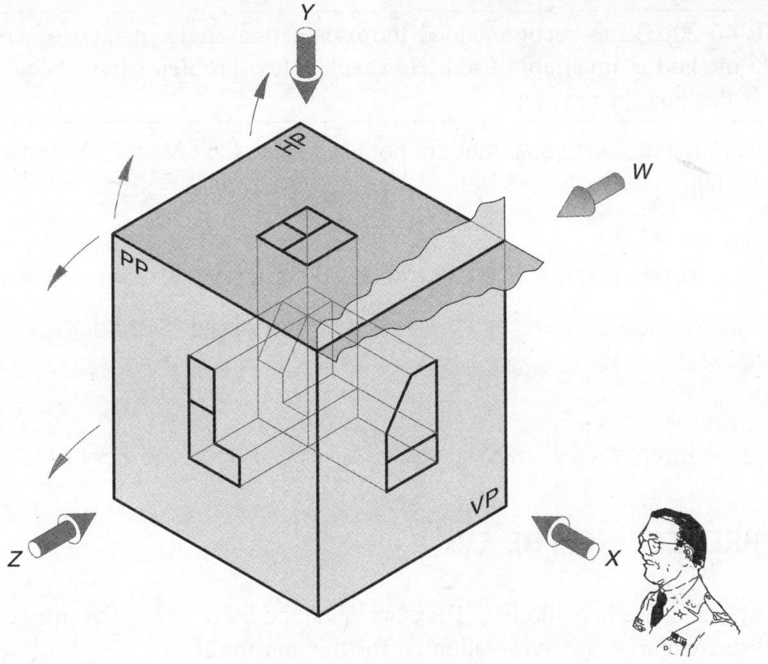

(a) Object in Third Angle

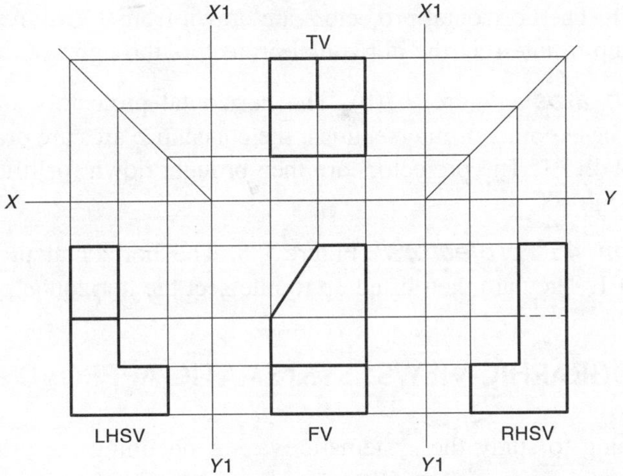

(b) Location of the Principal Views

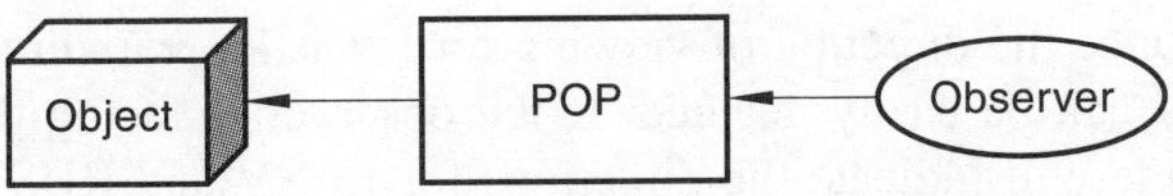

(c) Relationship between Object, Observer and POP

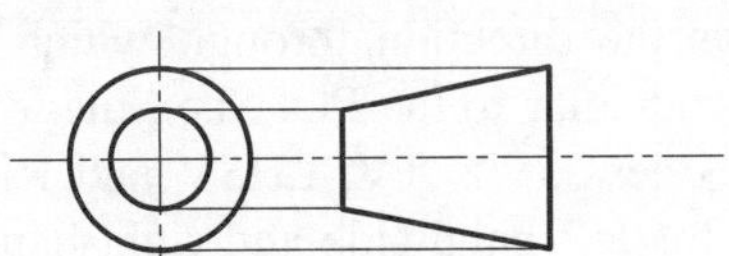

(d) The Symbol

Fig. 9.3 Third Angle Method of Projection

Note: BIS (SP 46-2003) has recommended the use of first-angle method of projection. In this book, first-angle method is invariably used. However, a few problems have been solved by third-angle method for the sake of practice.

The second quadrant and fourth quadrant are not used since the FV and TV come on the same side of *XY* and may overlap.

REMEMBER THE FOLLOWING

- In First Angle Method,
  - FV is *above XY*
  - TV is *below XY*
  - LHSV is on the *right side* of FV
  - RHSV is on the *left side* of FV
- In Third Angle Method,
  - FV is *below XY*
  - TV is *above XY*
  - LHSV is on the *left side* of FV
  - RHSV is on the *right side* of FV

9.5 PROJECTING THE SVs

The SVs are always placed alongside FV. They are obtained by drawing the projectors from FV and TV. One of the three techniques may be adopted for this purpose.

(i) Projecting across meter line Figure 9.6(c). A meter line is drawn from the intersection of *XY* and *X*1*Y*1 at 45° to *XY*. The horizontal projectors are drawn from TV to meet the meter line. The projectors are then lifted up to intersect the horizontal projectors through FV.

(ii) Projecting through arcs Figure 9.7(b). The horizontal projectors are drawn from TV to intersect *X*1*Y*1. Through these points of intersections, the concentric arcs are drawn with the centre at the intersection of *XY* and *X*1*Y*1. The projectors are then brought down (or lifted up) to intersect the horizontal projectors through FV.

(iii) Projecting through 45° projectors Figure 9.8. The horizontal projectors from TV are turned through 45° at *X*1*Y*1. They are then lifted up to intersect the horizontal projectors through FV.

9.6 ORTHOGRAPHIC VIEWS: SYSTEMATIC APPROACH

In this section we are going to study the systematic way of obtaining the orthographic views of a object. The object may be real or imaginary. Often, we are given with the pictorial (usually isometric) view of an object with the front direction of viewing, as shown in Fig. 9.4. The arrow marked *X* shows the direction through which the object is viewed to obtain FV. Note that this direction is perpendicular to the POP, i.e., the VP. Once the direction of viewing for FV is known, directions for other views, viz. TV, LHSV and RHSV can be easily decided. If the observer is facing the object, then his left-hand side and right-hand side will indicate the directions for LHSV and RHSV respectively. The direction of viewing for TV will obviously be from top of the object. In Fig. 9.4, the directions for TV, LHSV and RHSV are shown by arrows marked as *Y*, *Z* and *W* respectively. Each of these directions is perpendicular to the corresponding POP, i.e., the PP (for LHSV and RHSV) and

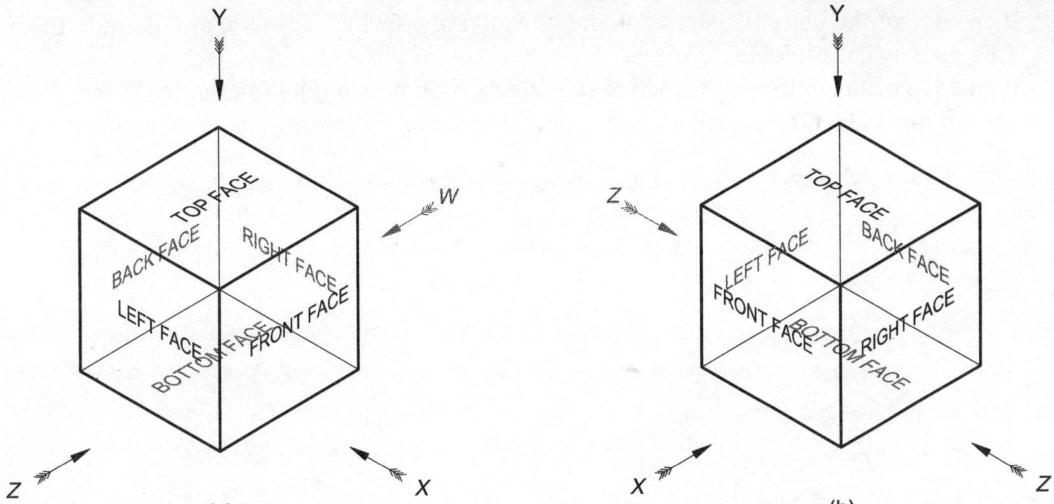

(a) (b)

Fig. 9.4

the HP (for TV). In majority of the problems, only one arrow for FV is given. However, if no arrow for front direction is given, then the direction which shows maximum details of the object should be chosen for FV. Figure 9.4(a) and (b) explain how different directions for FV can be chosen for the same object. Figure 9.4 also explains the front face, left face, right face, top face, back face and bottom face of the object. In this case, the front face, left face, right face and back face are vertical (i.e., parallel to the VP or the PP) and top face and bottom face are horizontal (i.e., parallel to the HP). Such faces are called *perpendicular* faces. However, this may not be the case always. The faces of the object may be *inclined* (i.e., inclined to either HP or VP), *oblique* (i.e., inclined to both the HP and VP), or *curved* as shown in Fig. 9.5. To obtain the projections of various faces of an object, the following rules must be observed:

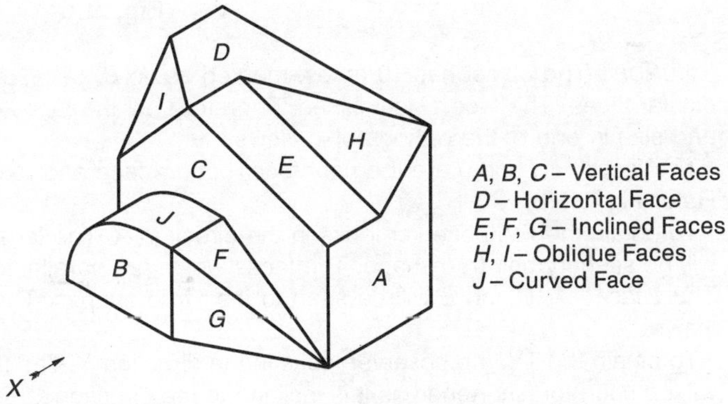

Fig. 9.5

1. If a face is perpendicular to the direction of viewing, its true shape and size will be seen in that view.
2. If a face is parallel to the direction of viewing, it is seen as a line in that view. This view is called the *line view* or *edge view*.
3. If a face is inclined to the direction of viewing, its true shape and size will not be seen in any view.
4. If an edge of the object is perpendicular to the direction of viewing, its actual length will be seen in that view.

5. If an edge of the object is parallel to the direction of viewing, it is seen as a point in that view. This view is called *point view*.
6. If an edge of the object is inclined to the direction of viewing, its foreshortened length will be seen in that view. The foreshortened length is obtained by locating the end points of the edge.

Example 9.1 For the object shown in Fig. 9.6(a), draw FV, TV and LHSV.

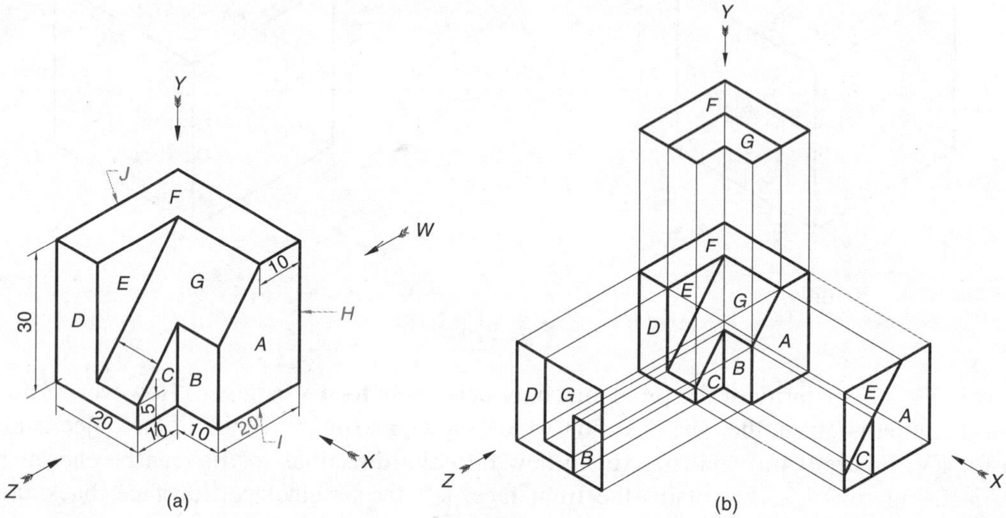

Fig. 9.6

Solution The object has 10 faces, marked as *A*, *B*, *C*, ..., *J*. Except face *G*, all other faces are perpendicular faces. The face *G* is inclined. Therefore, all the faces other than face *G* will show their true shape and size in one of the orthographic views.

The faces *H*, *I* and *J* are the right face, bottom face and rear face respectively and not visible. Refer Fig. 9.6(b).

To obtain the FV, observer looks in the direction *X*. The faces which are perpendicular to the direction *X* will be seen in their true shape. The faces which are parallel to the direction *X* will be seen as edge views. Thus, faces *A*, *C* and *E* will be seen to their true shapes. The faces *B*, *D*, *F* and *G* will be seen as edge views.

To obtain the TV, the observer looks in the direction *Y*. The face *F* will be seen in true shape. The face *G* will be seen foreshortened as it is inclined to the direction *Y*. The faces *A*, *B*, *C*, *D*, *E*, *H* and *J* will be seen as edge views.

To obtain the LHSV, the observer looks in the direction *Z*. The faces *B* and *D* will be seen as their true shapes. The face *G* will be seen as foreshortened. The faces *A*, *C*, *E*, *F*, *J* and *I* will be seen as edge views.

The three orthographic views are shown in Fig. 9.6(c). The LHSV is drawn on the right-hand- side of FV since we are following the first-angle method of projection.

Example 9.2 Draw the FV, TV and RHSV of the object shown in Fig. 9.7(a).

Solution The object has 11 faces, *A*, *B*, ..., *K*. In FV (direction *P*), the faces *B* and *D* will be seen in their true shapes. Faces *A*, *C*, *E*, *F* and *G* will be seen as edge views. In TV (direction *R*), the faces *C* and *G*

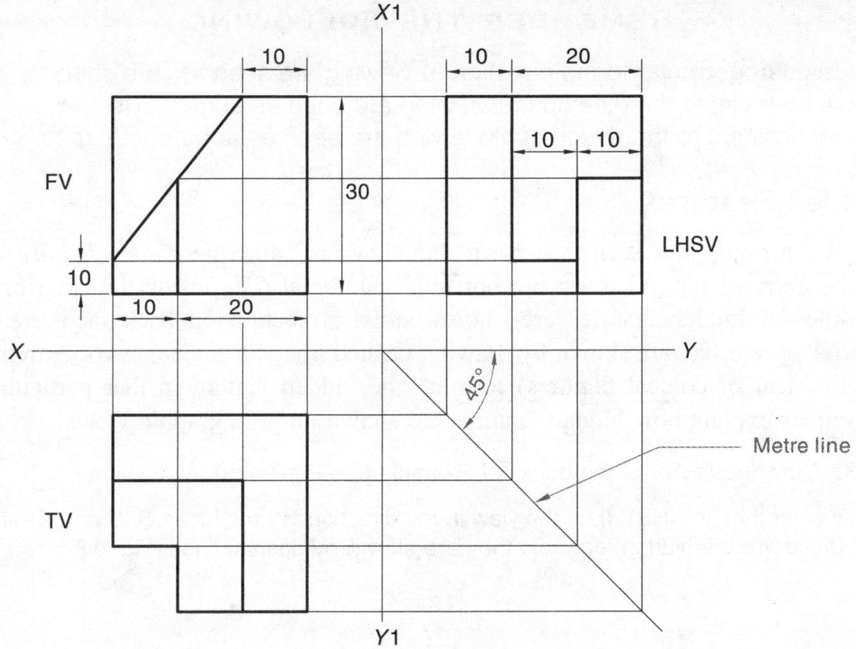

Fig. 9.6(c)

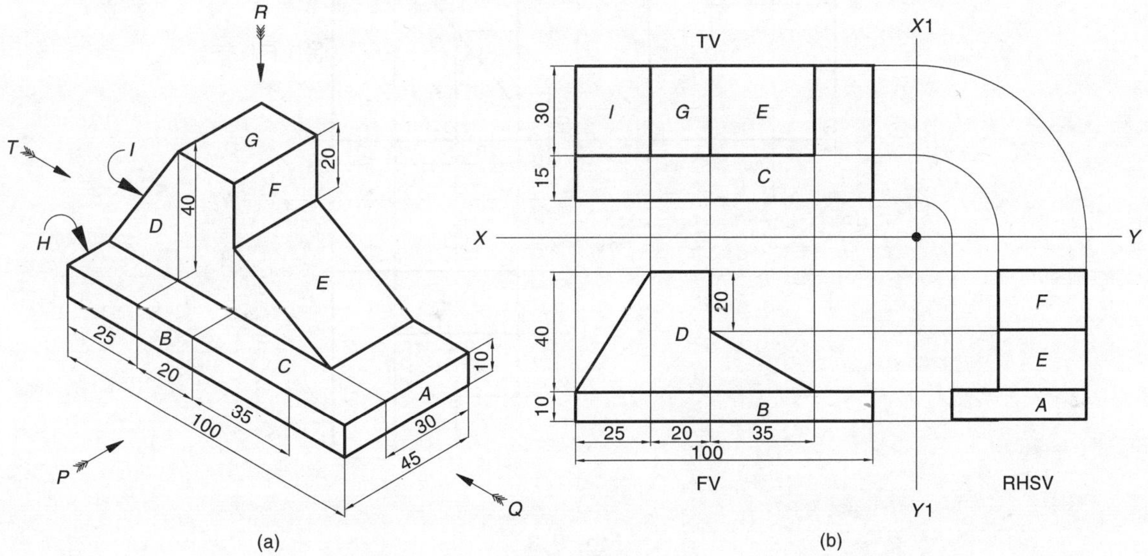

Fig. 9.7

will be seen in true shapes. The faces *E* and *I* will be seen as apparent shapes. In RHSV (direction *Q*), the faces *A* and *F* will be seen as true shapes. The face *E* will be seen as an apparent shape.

The views are shown in Fig. 9.7(b) using the third-angle method.

REMEMBER THE FOLLOWING

- The faces perpendicular to the direction of viewing are seen as true shapes.
- The faces parallel to the direction of viewing are seen as edge views.
- The faces inclined to the direction of viewing are seen as apparent shapes.

9.6.1 Hidden Features

The features of the object not seen in a particular view are called as *hidden features*. The hidden features may be external (i.e., visible from outside) or internal (i.e., inside the exterior walls of the object). Examples of hidden features are—holes, slots, projection on back face, etc. The hidden features, internal or external, are shown by drawing dashed lines for the edges (or extreme generators in case of cylindrical or conical features) forming the hidden feature in that particular view. The following examples explain how hidden features are shown on orthographic views.

Example 9.3 Draw the RHSV of the object of Example 9.1, Fig. 9.6(a).

Solution It is clear that, in RHSV (i.e., the view in the direction *W*) the faces *B*, *G* and *D* will not be seen. However, as these are the hidden features, they are shown by dashed lines, Fig. 9.8.

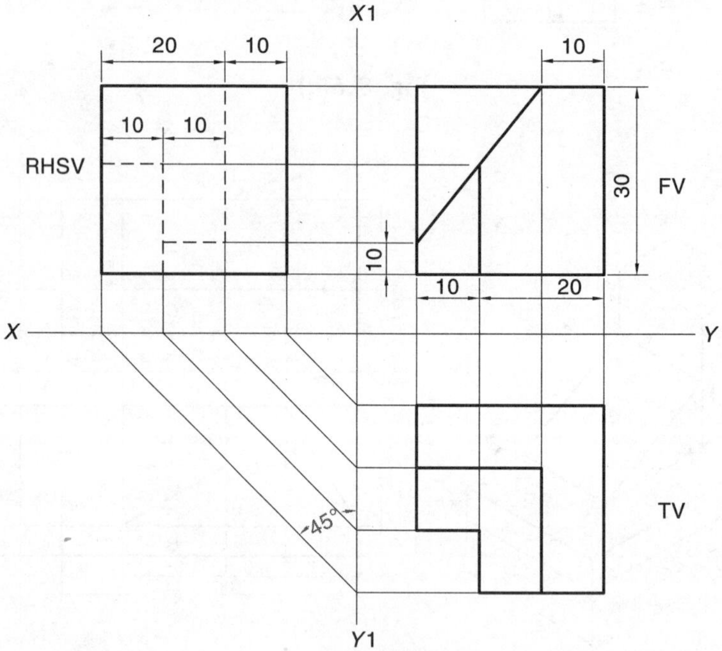

Fig. 9.8

Example 9.4 Draw the LHSV of the object shown in Fig. 9.7(a).

Solution In the LHSV (direction *T*), the faces *A*, *E* and *F* are the hidden features. The LHSV is shown in Fig. 9.9.

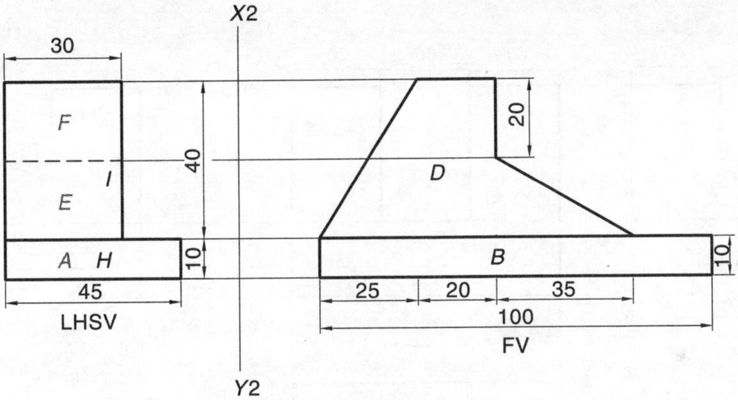

Fig. 9.9

Example 9.5 For the object shown in Fig. 9.10(a), draw FV (in direction *X*), TV, LHSV and RHSV.

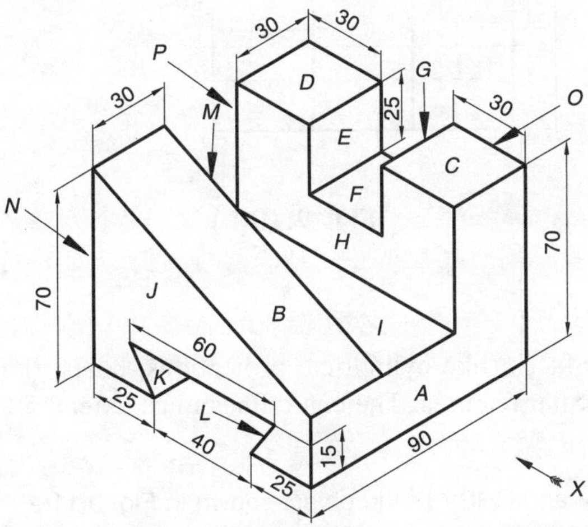

Fig. 9.10(a)

Solution With reference to Fig. 9.10(a), the faces that will be seen as true shapes, apparent shapes and hidden faces in different views are shown in the following table:

View	*Faces Seen To True Shapes*	*Faces Seen To Apparent Shapes*	*Hidden Faces*
FV	*A*	*B*	*E*, *G*, *P*, *N*, *K* and *L*
TV	*D*, *F*, *C* and *I*	*B*	*K* and *L*
LHSV	*J* and *H*—partially visible	…	*M*, *O* and *H*—partially hidden
RHSV	*O* and *M*—partially visible	…	*J*, *H* and *M*—partially hidden

Figure 9.10(b) shows the required four views. Please note carefully how hidden lines are drawn for the hidden faces.

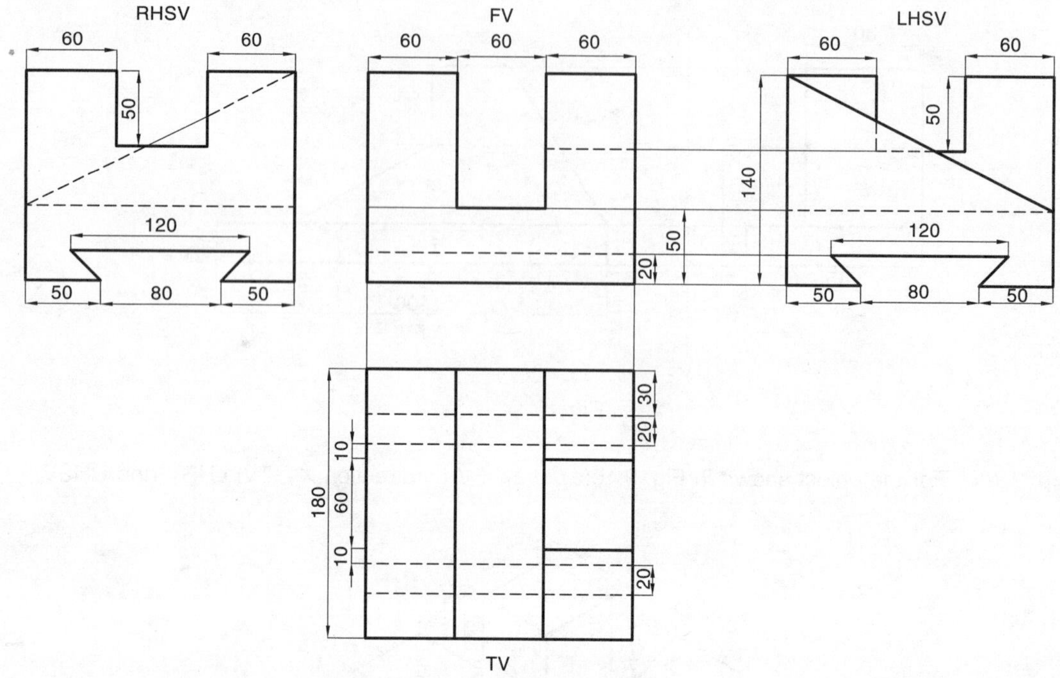

Fig. 9.10(b)

9.6.2 Circular Features

The objects having circular faces (like cylindrical projections, holes, flanges, etc.) are characterized by the centrelines of the circular features. The centrelines must extend 5 to 8 mm beyond the features and represent.

Example 9.6 Draw FV, TV and RHSV of the object shown in Fig. 9.11(a).

Solution The object has a cylindrical projection on the front face and a vertical hole. Fig. 9.11(b) shows its three views. Note how centrelines are used to indicate the circular features. Also observe the dashed lines for the hole.

9.6.3 Precedence of Lines

Wherever visible line, hidden line and centrelines overlap, the following precedence rules should be observed:

1. A visible line has precedence over a hidden line and a centreline, i.e., visible line should only be drawn if it overlaps with a hidden line and/or centreline.
2. A hidden line has precedence over a centreline, i.e., a hidden line should only be drawn if it overlaps with a centreline.
3. If a visible line or a hidden line precedes a centreline, the ends of the centreline should be drawn to show its existance.

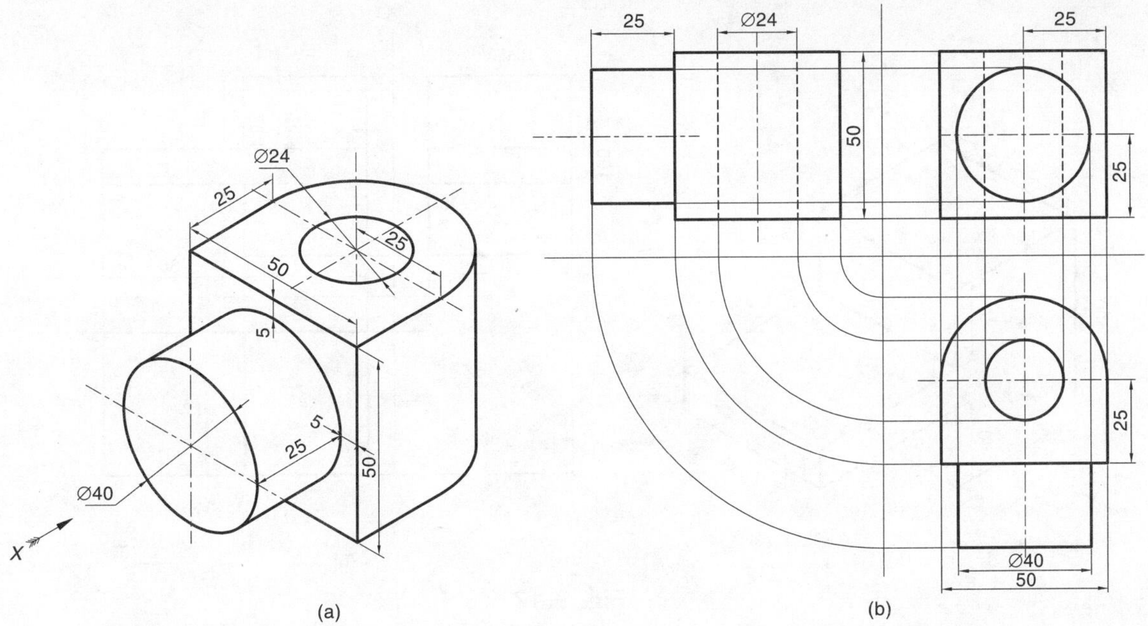

Fig. 9.11

REMEMBER THE FOLLOWING

- The hidden features of the object are shown by dashed lines.
- The circular features are indicated by the centrelines.

The procedure to obtain orthographic views of a complex object is explained step by step in the following two sets of examples. The first set includes Examples 9.7 to 9.14 and the second set includes Example 9.15 to 9.18. In each set, the object considered in each higher numbered example is obtained by adding some new features in the object of the previous example. The examples explain the use of dashed lines and centrelines to show the hidden features and circular features respectively.

Example 9.7 Draw the three principal views of the object shown in Fig. 9.12(a).

Solution As per the direction of viewing for FV, the FV, TV and RHSV are shown in Fig. 9.12(b).

Example 9.8 Draw the FV, TV and RHSV of the object shown in Fig. 9.13(a).

Solution See Fig. 9.13(b) for required TV, FV and RHSV. Note how centerlines are added in the views to indicate circular features.

Example 9.9 From the pictorial view of the object shown in Fig. 9.14(a), draw its FV, TV and RHSV.

Solution The required views are shown in Fig. 9.14(b).

Example 9.10 From the pictorial view of the object shown in Fig. 9.15(a), draw its three principal views.

Solution Refer Fig. 9.15(b) for the three principal views.

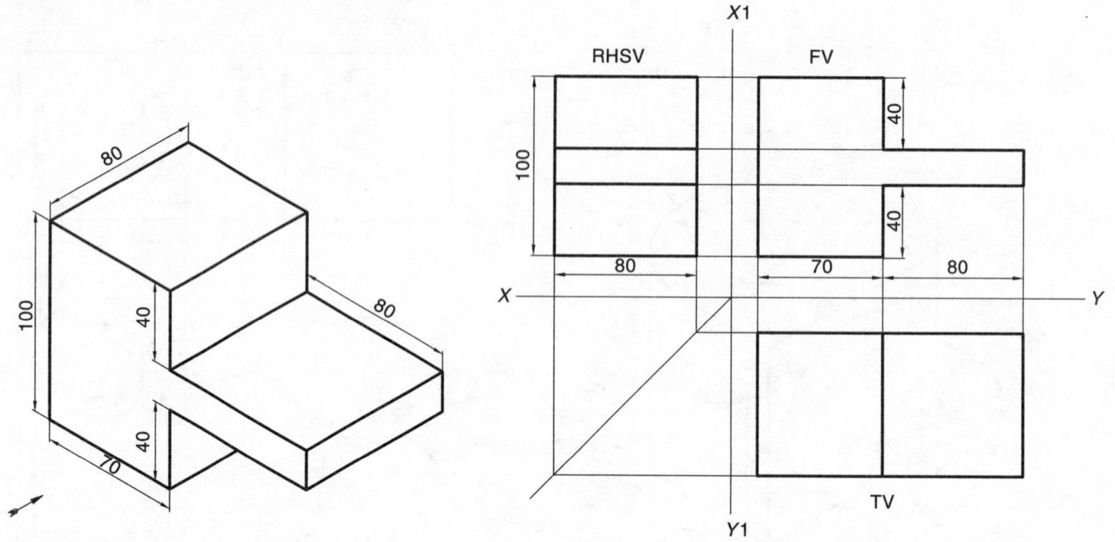

(a) (b)

Fig. 9.12

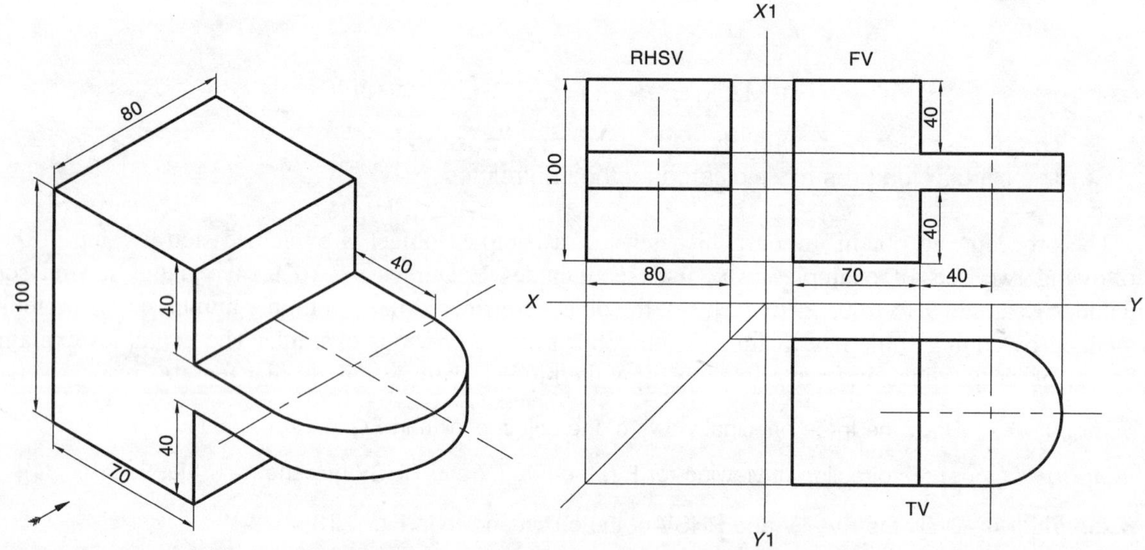

(a) (b)

Fig. 9.13

Example 9.11 Figure 9.16(a) shows the pictorial view of an object. Draw its following views: (a) FV, (b) TV and (c) RHSV

Solution Figure 9.16(b) shows the FV, TV and RHSV of the object. Note that the TV shows two dashed lines. Observe the object carefully to understand why and how these hidden lines are drawn.

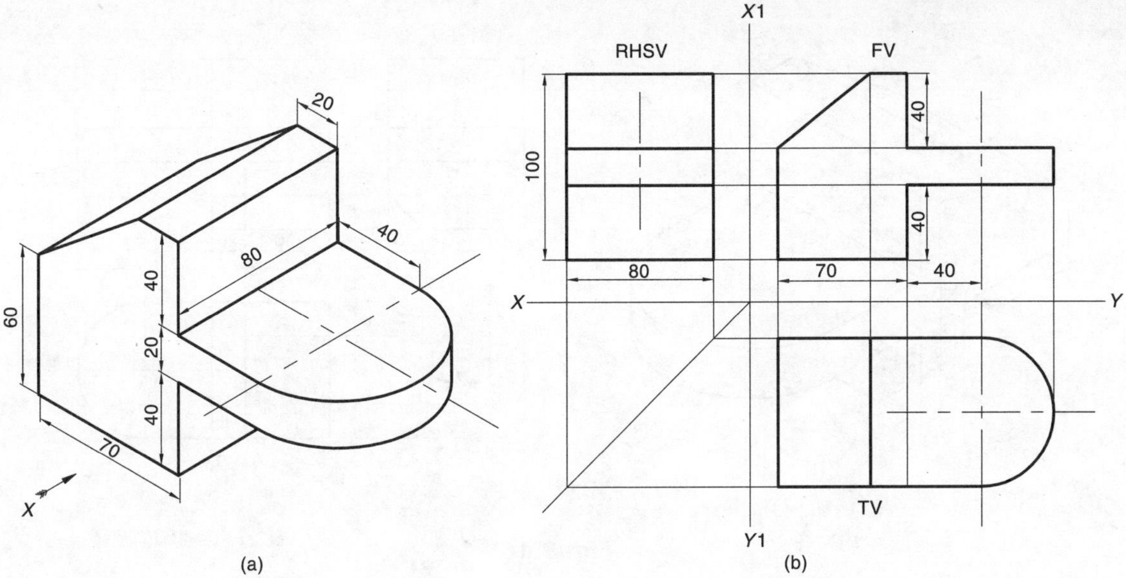

Fig. 9.14

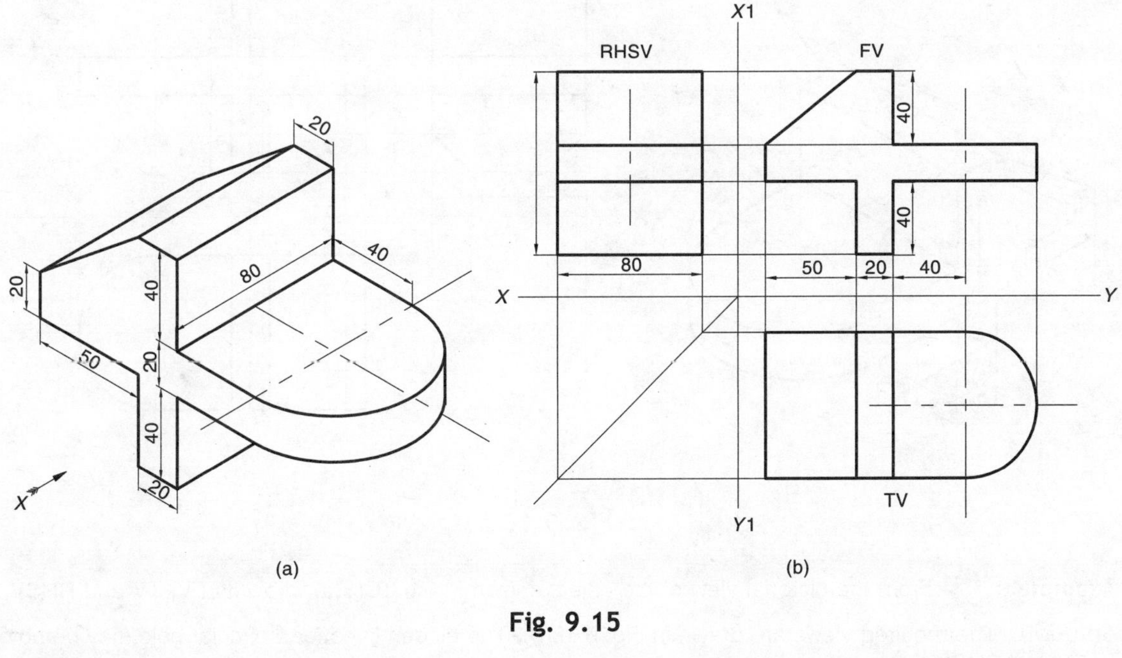

Fig. 9.15

Example 9.12 From the pictorial view of the object shown in Fig. 9.17(a), draw its three views.

Solution Figure 9.17(b) shows the required three views. Carefully note the hidden lines in TV and RHSV.

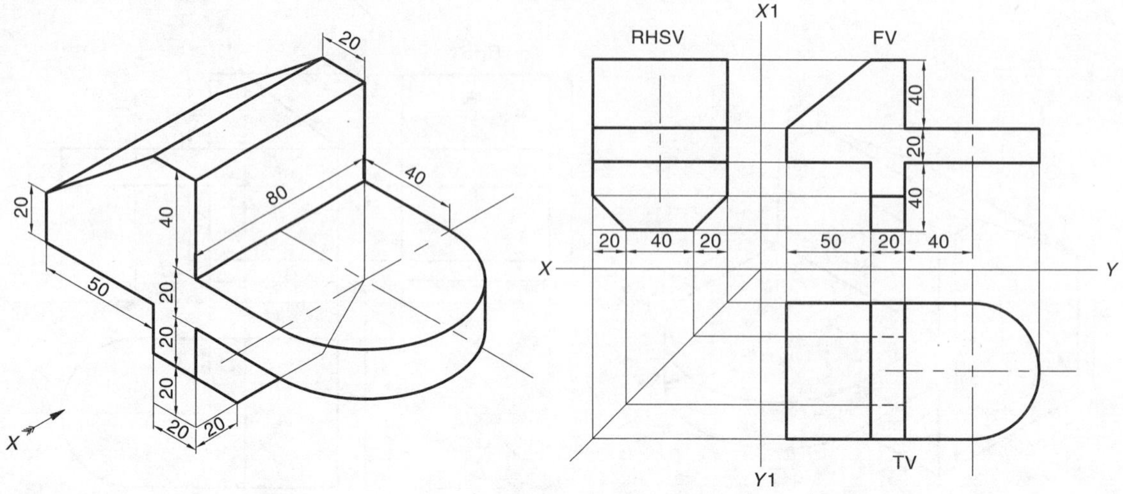

(a) (b)

Fig. 9.16

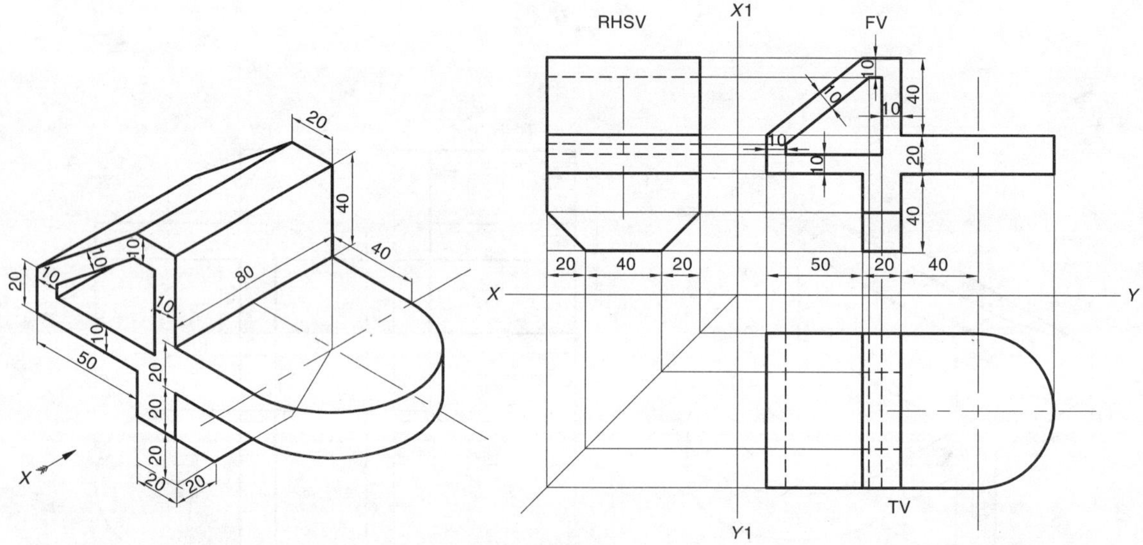

(a) (b)

Fig. 9.17

Example 9.13 From the pictorial view of the object shown in Fig. 9.18(a), draw its FV, TV and RHSV.

Solution The required views are drawn in Fig. 9.18(b). The hidden lines for a circular hole may be noted in FV and RHSV.

Example 9.14 Draw the FV, TV and RHSV of the object, pictorial view of which shown in Fig. 9.19(a).

Solution See Fig. 9.19(b) for the required views. Observe all the hidden lines in FV, TV and RHSV and relate them with the corresponding features in pictorial view.

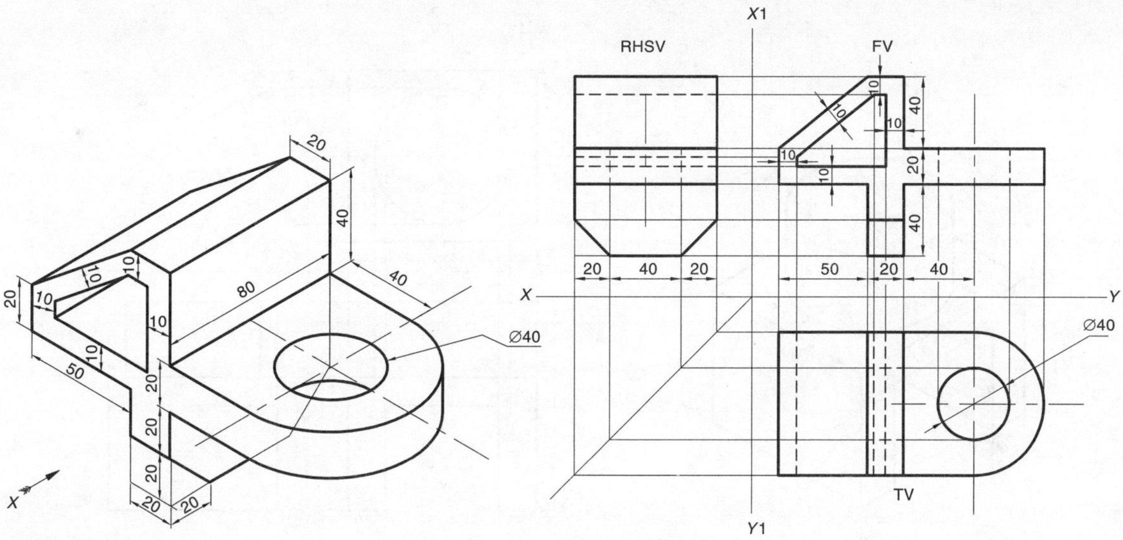

(a) (b)

Fig. 9.18

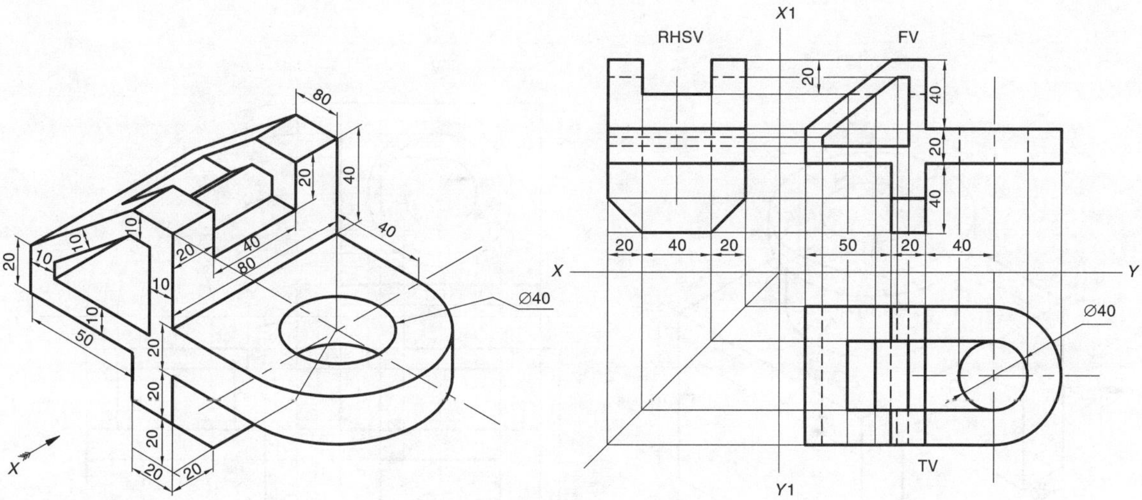

(a) (b)

Fig. 9.19

Example 9.15 Draw the FV, TV and RHSV of the object shown in Fig. 9.20(a). Use third-angle method.

Solution See Fig. 9.20(b) for the required views.

Example 9.16 Using third-angle method, draw the FV, TV and RHSV of the object shown in Fig. 9.21(a).

Solution Refer Fig. 9.21(b) for required FV, TV and RHSV.

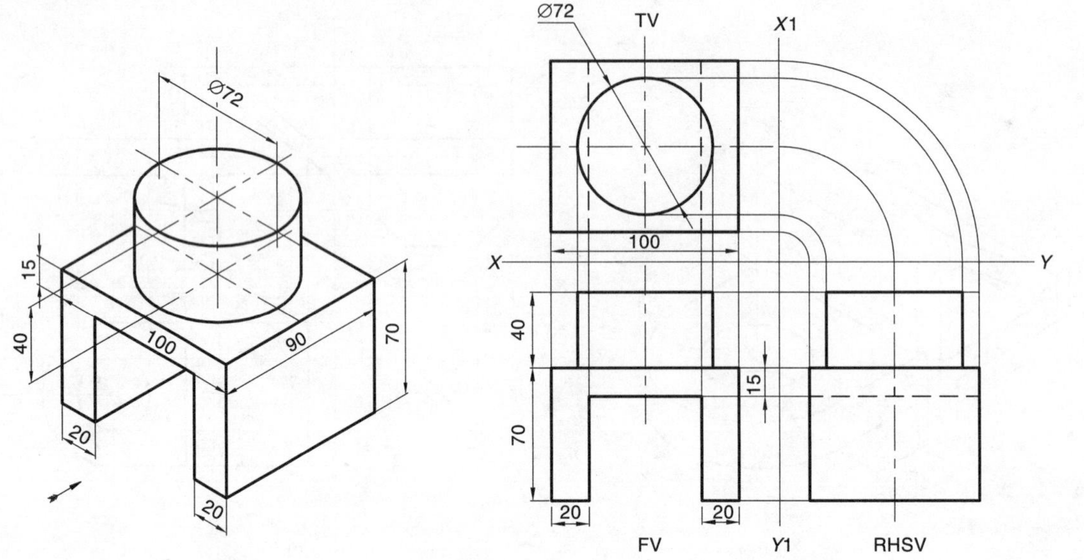

(a) (b)

Fig. 9.20

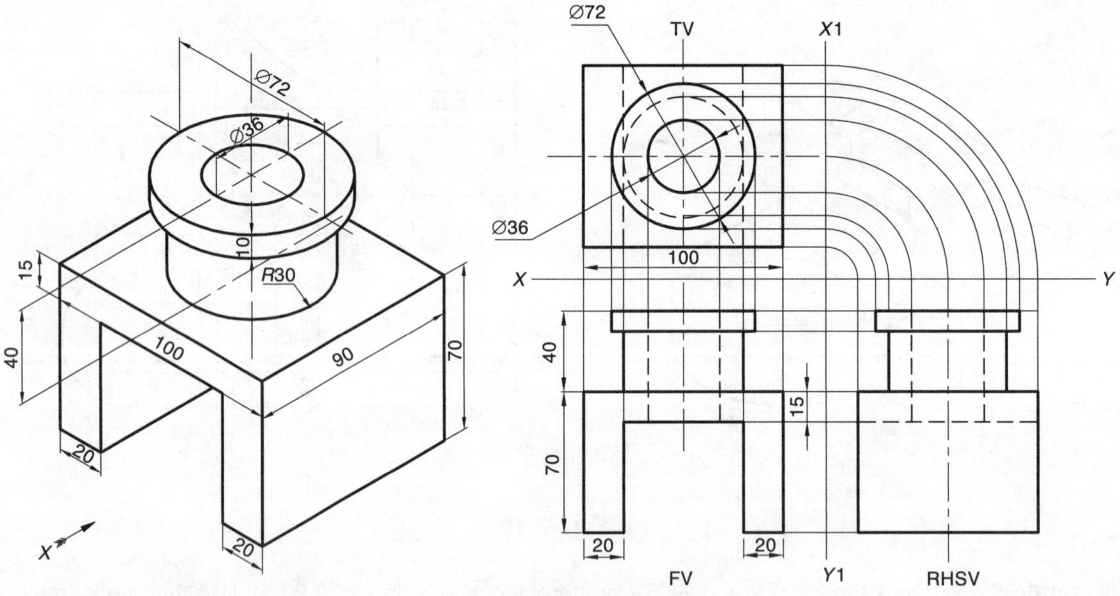

(a) (b)

Fig. 9.21

Example 9.17 Figure 9.22(a) shows the pictorial view of an object. Using third-angle method, draw its FV, TV and RHSV.

Solution The TV, FV and RHSV are shown in Fig. 9.22(b). Note how a centreline is added in FV and RHSV to indicate a circular feature.

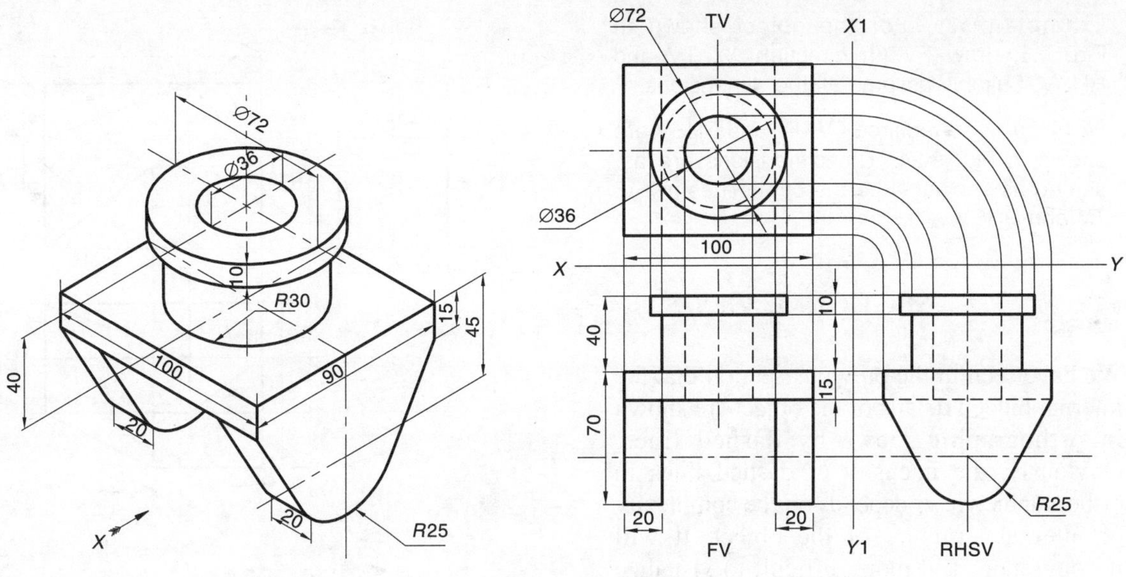

(a) (b)

Fig. 9.22

Example 9.18 Figure 9.23(a) shows the isometric view of an object. Draw the following views by the third-angle method:

(i) FV in the direction of '*X*', (ii) TV, and (iii) RHSV

Solution Refer Fig. 9.23(b) for the required views. Note all the hidden lines and obtain their correspondence with hidden features.

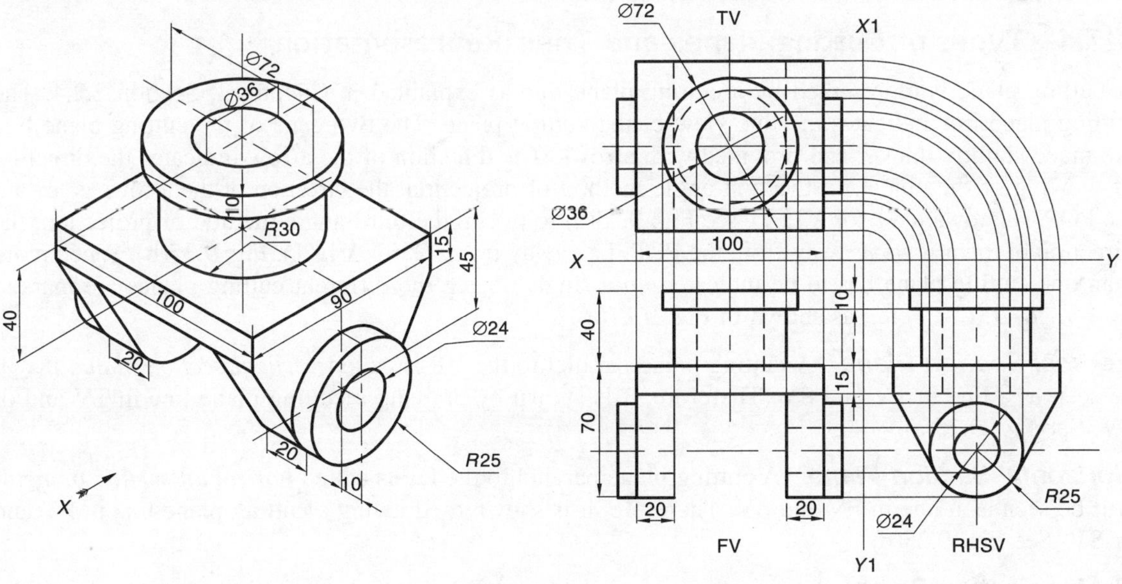

(a) (b)

Fig. 9.23

Example 9.19 For the object shown in Fig. 9.5, draw FV (in direction *X*), TV and RHSV. Suitably assume all the dimensions.

Solution The required FV, TV and RHSV are shown in Fig. 9.24. The dimensions are assumed as shown. Note the centrelines in FV, TV and RHSV.

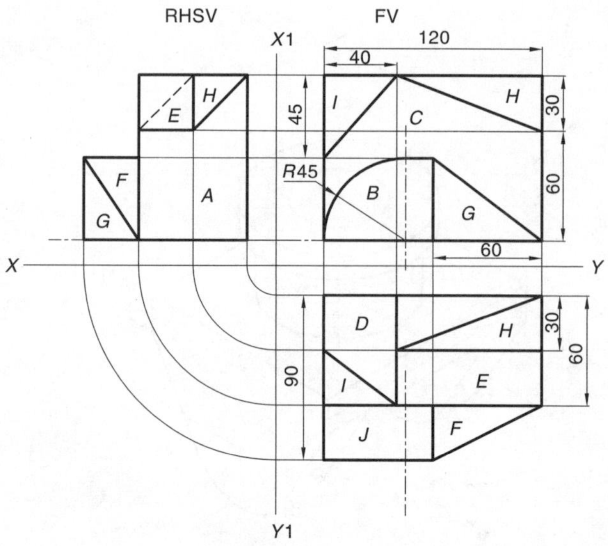

Fig. 9.24

9.7 SECTIONAL VIEWS

We have seen in the previous section that the internal hidden details of the object are shown in orthographic views by dashed lines. Obviously, the intensity of dashed lines in orthographic views depends on the complexity of internal structure of the object. It will become more and more difficult to visualize the shape of the object as the number of dashed lines in orthographic views goes on increasing. Also, the numbers of dashed lines make the drawing unnecessarily complicated and confusing to interpret. Therefore, the general practice is to draw sectional views for complex objects in addition to or instead of simple orthographic views. A sectional view, as the name suggests, is obtained by taking the section of the object along a particular plane. An imaginary cutting plane is used to obtain the section of the object. The part of the object between the observer and the imaginary cutting plane is assumed to be removed and the view of the cut object thus obtained is called the *sectional view*.

9.7.1 Types of Cutting Planes and Their Representation

A cutting plane is represented by a cutting plane line as explained in Chapter 2, Section 2.2.4. The cutting plane line indicates the line view of the cutting plane. The two ends of the cutting plane line are made slightly thicker and provided with arrows. The direction of the arrow indicates the direction of viewing of the object. In the first-angle method of projection, the direction of the arrows is toward the POP, i.e., toward *XY* (or *X*1*Y*1), see Fig. 9.25(a) to (e). In the third-angle method of projection, the direction of the arrows is away from the POP, i.e., away from *XY* (or *X*1*Y*1), Fig. 9.35(b). When more than one cutting plane has to be indicated on a single object, the different cutting planes are marked as *A–A*, *B–B*, *C–C*, etc., as shown in Fig. 9.27(a).

Vertical Section Plane A cutting plane parallel to the VP is called *vertical section plane*. It will be seen as a line in TV and SV. Therefore, it is shown by drawing a cutting plane line in TV and or SV. See Fig. 9.25(a).

Horizontal Section Plane A cutting plane parallel to the HP is called *horizontal section plane*. It will be seen as a line in FV and SV. Therefore, it is shown by drawing a cutting plane line in FV and or SV. See Fig. 9.25(b).

Profile Section Plane A cutting plane parallel to the PP is called *profile section plane*. It will be seen as a line in FV and TV. Therefore, it is shown by drawing a cutting plane line in FV and or TV. See Fig. 9.25(c).

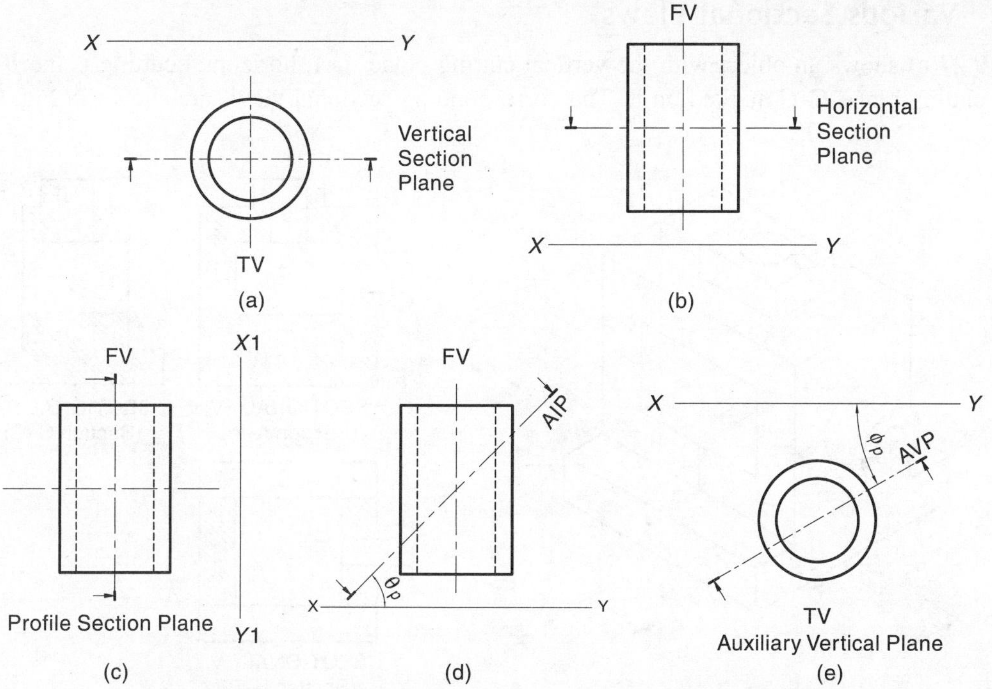

Fig. 9.25 Types of cutting planes and their representation

Auxiliary Section Planes A cutting plane inclined to either HP or VP is called *auxiliary section plane*. Two types of auxiliary planes are as given below:

Auxiliary Inclined Plane A plane inclined to the HP and perpendicular to the VP is called *auxiliary inclined plane* (AIP). It is shown by a cutting plane line in FV. See Fig. 9.25(d).

Auxiliary Vertical Plane A plane inclined to the VP and perpendicular to the HP is called *auxiliary vertical plane* (AVP). It is shown by a cutting plane line in TV. See Fig. 9.25(e).

Oblique Section Plane A cutting plane inclined to both the HP and VP is called *oblique section plane*. None of the principal views of the object will show the line view of the oblique section plane. Such a section plane can be shown by a cutting plane line in the auxiliary view of the object.

9.7.2 Hatching of the Sections

The surface created by cutting the object by a section plane is called as *section*. The section is indicated by drawing the hatching lines (section lines) (Chapter 2, Section 2.2.4) within the sectioned area. The hatching lines are drawn at 45° to the principal outlines or the lines of symmetry of the section, Fig. 9.26. The spacing between hatching lines should be uniform and in proportion to the size of the section.

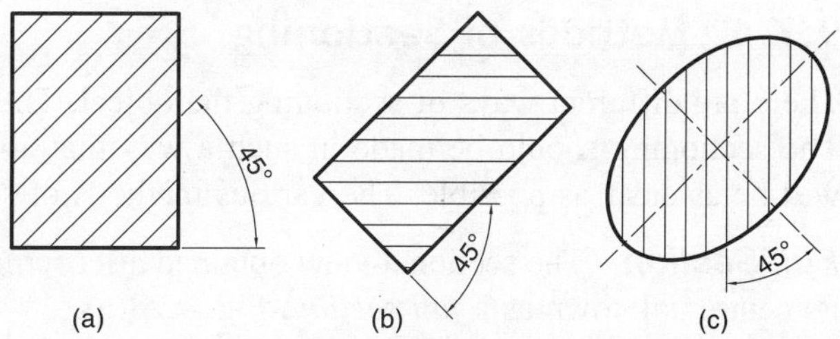

Fig. 9.26

9.7.3 Various Sectional Views

Figure 9.27(a) shows an object with the vertical cutting plane *A–A*, horizontal cutting plane *B–B* and profile cutting plane *C–C* marked on it. The corresponding sectional views are shown in Fig. 9.27(b)

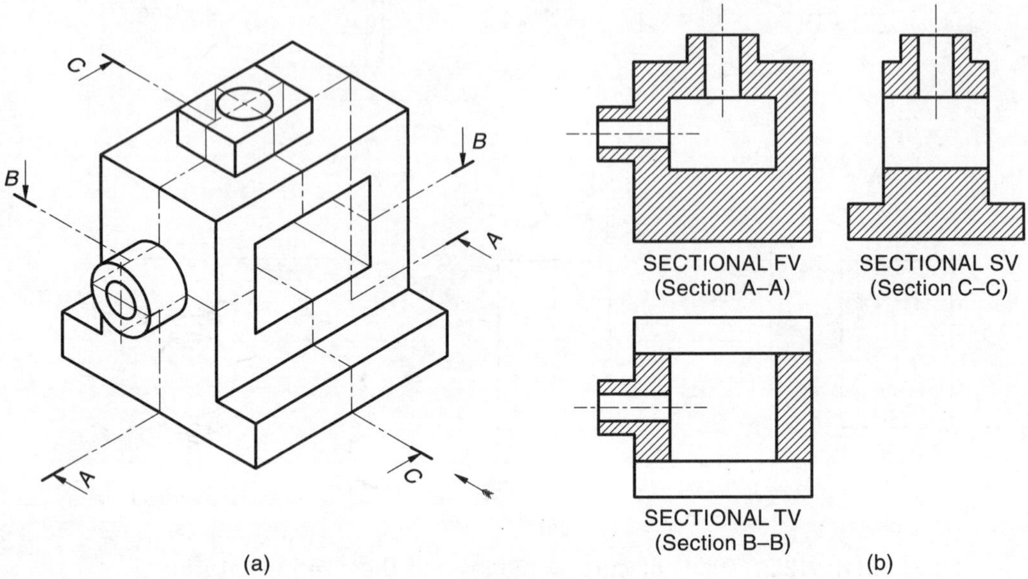

Fig. 9.27

Sectional FV When an object is cut by a vertical cutting plane or AVP, the FV obtained is called *sectional* FV or *sectional elevation.*

Sectional TV When an object is cut by a horizontal cutting plane or AIP, the TV obtained is called *sectional* TV or *sectional plan.*

Sectional SV When an object is cut by a profile cutting plane or AIP or AVP, the SV obtained is called *sectional* SV or *sectional end view.*

Sectional Auxiliary View A sectional view of an object showing the true shape of the section when it is cut by an auxiliary cutting plane is called *sectional auxiliary view.*

Sectional Oblique View A sectional view of an object showing the true shape of the section when it is cut by an oblique cutting plane is called *sectional oblique view.*

9.7.4 Methods of Sectioning

There are different ways of sectioning the object. The object is sectioned by considering its features. The sectioning should be made in such a way that all the complicated internal features of the object will be as clear as possible. The various methods of sectioning are explained below.

Full Section The sectional view obtained after removing the front-half portion of an object through its centre is known as a *full section*, Fig. 9.28(a).

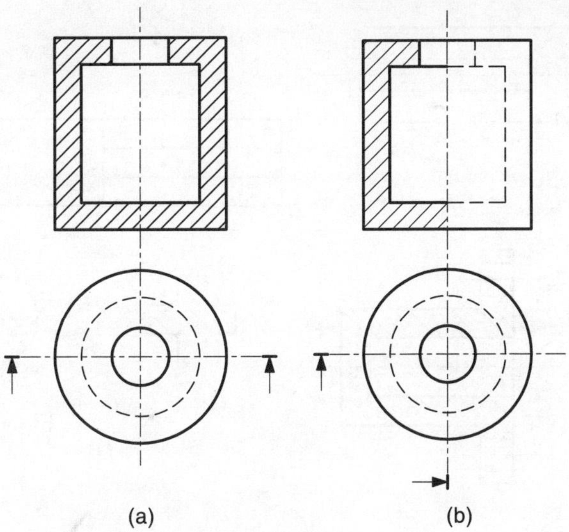

Fig. 9.28

Half Section The sectional view obtained after removing the front quarter portion by means of two cutting planes at right angles to each other is known as *half section*, Fig. 9.28(b).

Offset Section The sectional view obtained by a cutting plane in a zigzag way so as to reveal the maximum details of the object is known as an *offset section*, Fig. 9.29.

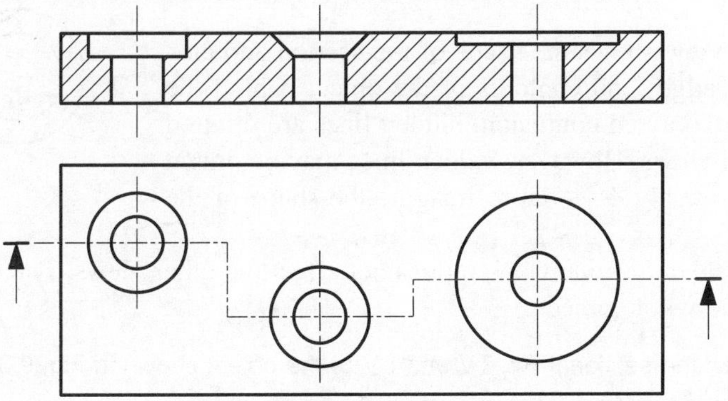

Fig. 9.29

Revolved Section A *revolved section* is used to show the uniform shape of the object from end to end, Fig. 9.30.

Removed Section A *removed section* is used to show the variable shape of the object from end to end, Fig. 9.31.

Aligned Section An *aligned section* is used to show the shape of features that do not align with the vertical and horizontal centrelines of the object, Fig. 9.32.

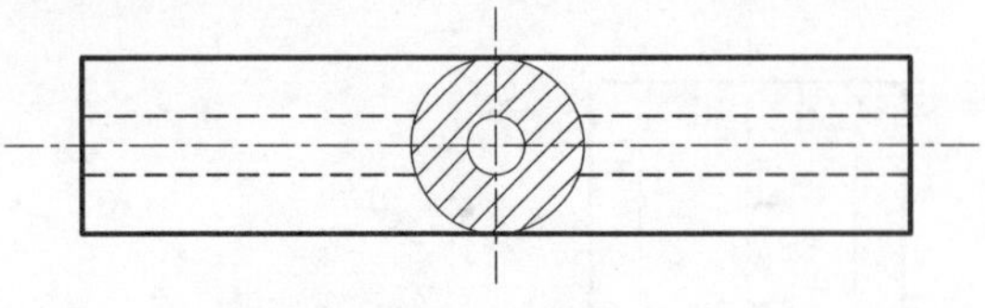

Fig. 9.30

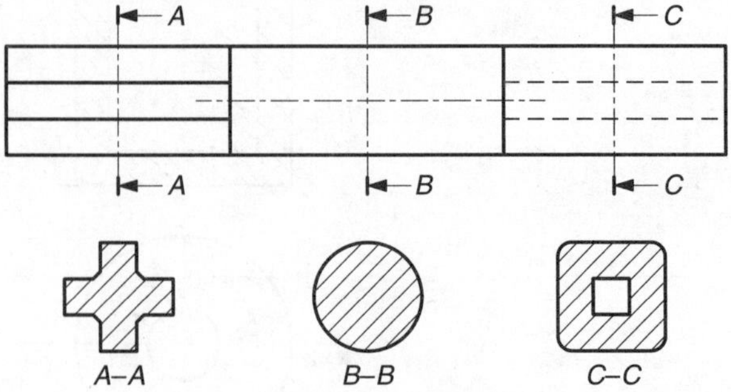

Fig. 9.31

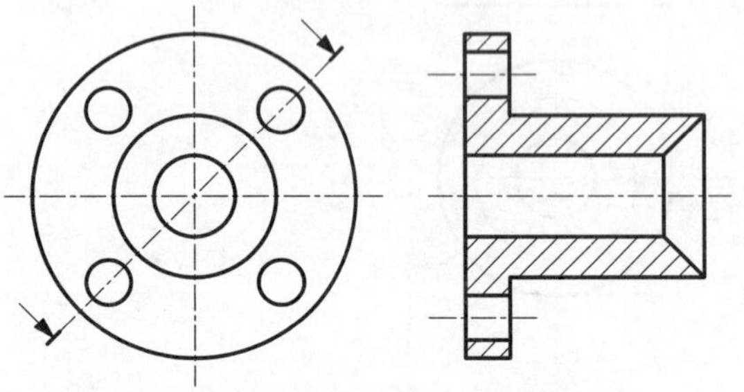

Fig. 9.32

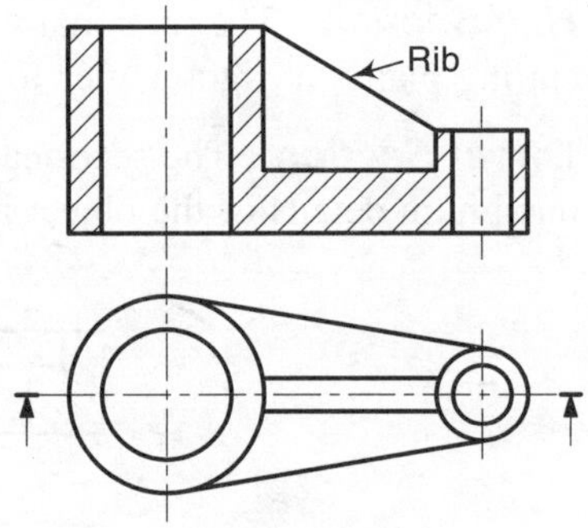

Fig. 9.33

Ribs and Other Standard Parts in Section When a cutting plane passes longitudinally through the centre of the ribs, spokes, webs or other standard parts, they are not shown sectional because it gives a wrong impression of the thickness or of the other details, Fig. 9.33.

The following points are to be remembered while drawing the sectional view:

- The sectional view shows the shape of the section and also all the visible edges and contours of the object behind the section plane. To avoid confusion, hidden lines are omitted from sectional views. However, hidden lines may be drawn if they are extremely essential to imagine the shape of the object.
- If a section is taken for one view, it does not affect the other views. The other views are drawn considering the whole object.

Example 9.20 Draw the sectional FV, TV and SV of the object shown in Fig. 9.34(a).

Solution The object is cut by cutting plane *A–A* as shown. This will give a full sectional view. As indicated by the direction of arrows on the cutting plane line, the FV will be sectional. The three views of the object, namely, sectional FV, TV and LHSV are shown in Fig. 9.34(b). The cutting plane line *A–A* is also shown in TV. As already explained, in the first-angle method, the arrows of cutting plane line are pointed toward *XY*, i.e., toward the other view. In the third-angle method, the arrows on the cutting plane line in one view (say TV) will be pointing away from other view (say FV).

Example 9.21 For the object shown in Fig. 9.35(a), draw:

(i) sectional FV (ii) TV (iii) LHSV

Use the third-angle method of projection.

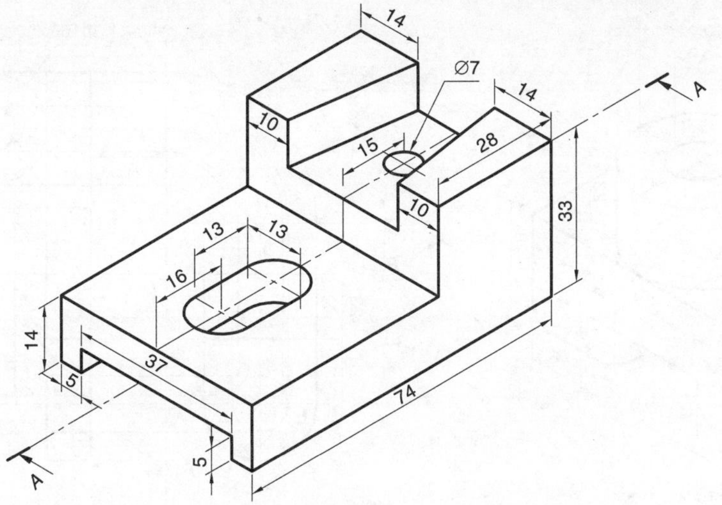

(a)

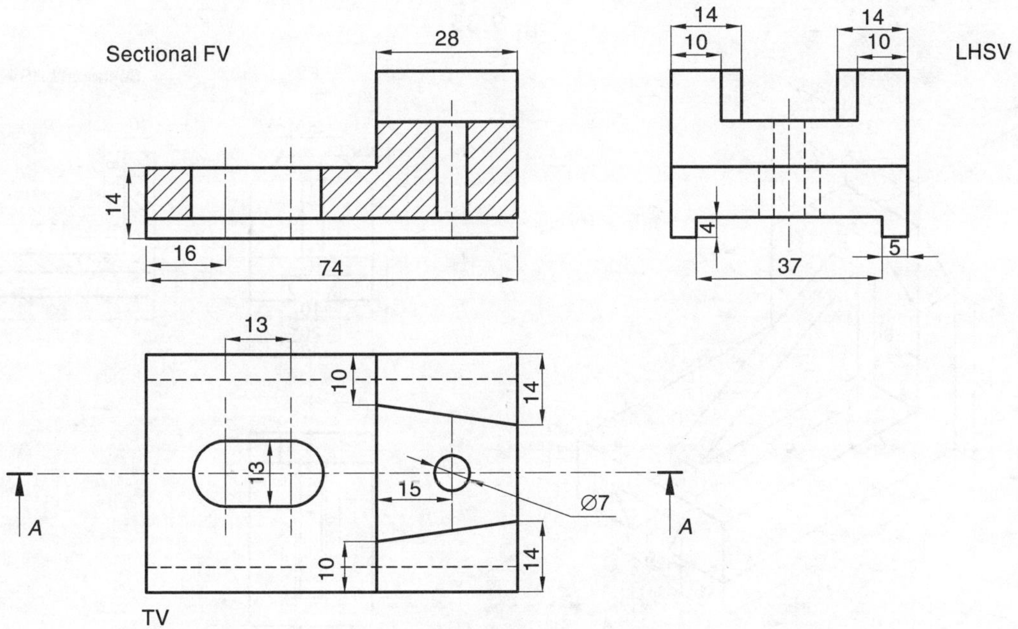

(b)

Fig. 9.34

Solution The three views are shown in Fig. 9.35(b). As it is the third-angle method, the direction of the arrows on the cutting plane line is away from the other view.

Example 9.22 For the object shown in Fig. 9.36(a), draw the FV (direction *X*), sectional SV and TV.

Solution The object has a triangular rib as shown. The rib is being cut by a cutting plane longitudinally. Therefore, as already explained, the rib is not shown sectional in LHSV. The three views are shown in Fig. 9.36(b).

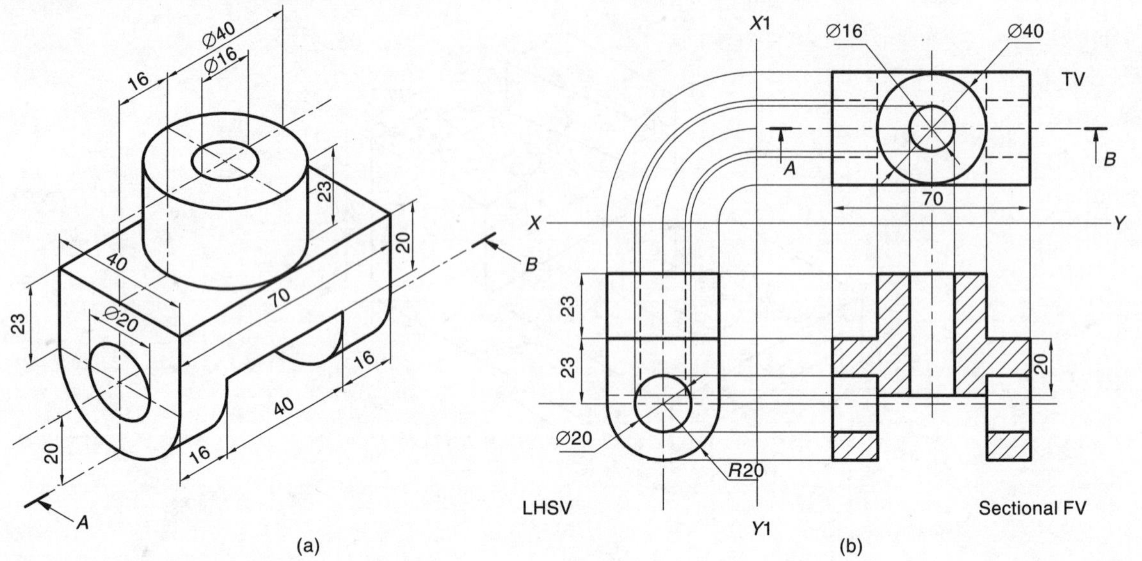

Fig. 9.35

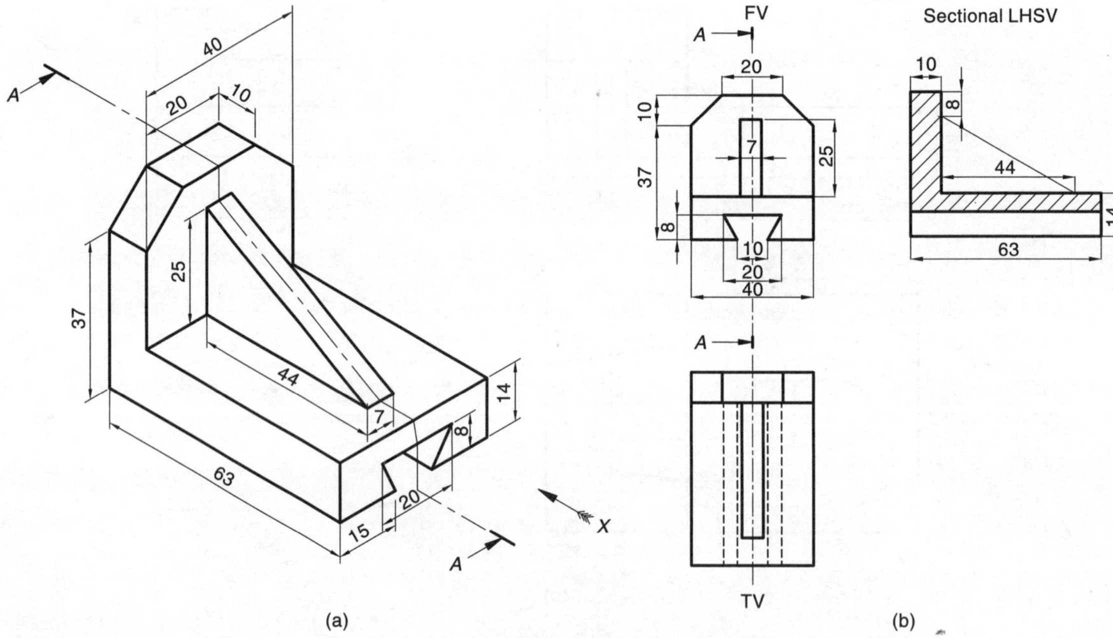

Fig. 9.36

Example 9.23 Figure 9.37(a) shows the pictorial view of a 'shaft support'. Using the first-angle method of projection, draw the following views.

(a) Sectional elevation—Section *A–A* (b) Plan

Show all dimensions.

Solution Figure 9.37(b) shows the sectional elevation and plan.

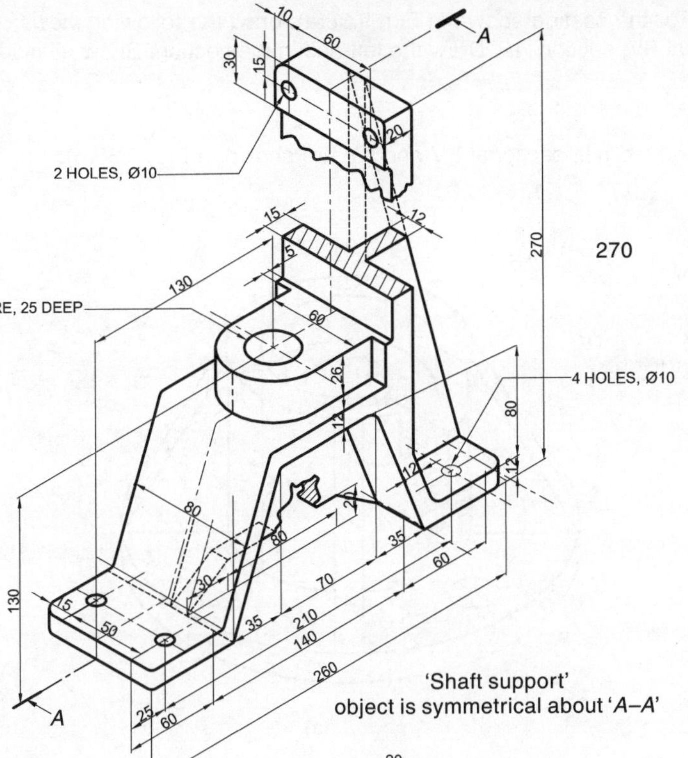
2 HOLES, Ø10
Ø30 BORE, 25 DEEP
4 HOLES, Ø10
270
A
A
'Shaft support'
object is symmetrical about 'A–A'

(a)

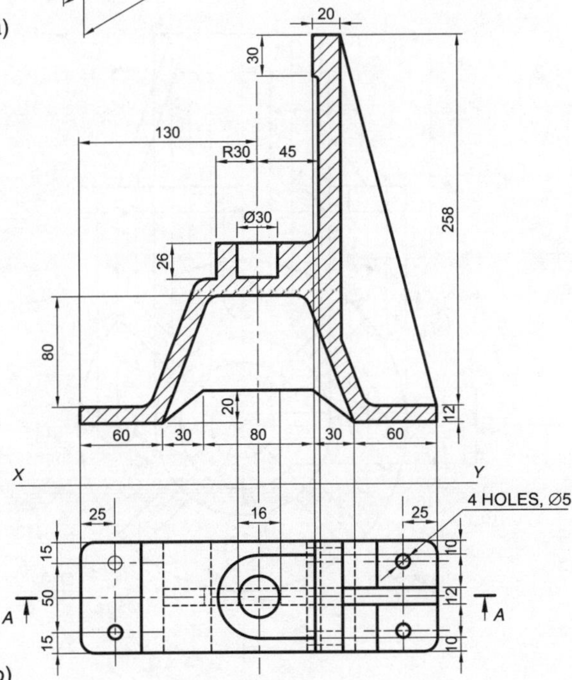
X
Y
4 HOLES, Ø5
R30
Ø30
A
A

(b)

Fig. 9.37

Example 9.24 For the casting shown in Fig. 9.38(a), draw the following views:

(i) Half-sectional FV, section *AB*. Draw the left-half in the section. Show all hidden lines in the right half.

(ii) TV

Give eight important dimensions.

Solution The required half-sectional FV and TV are shown in Fig. 9.38(b).

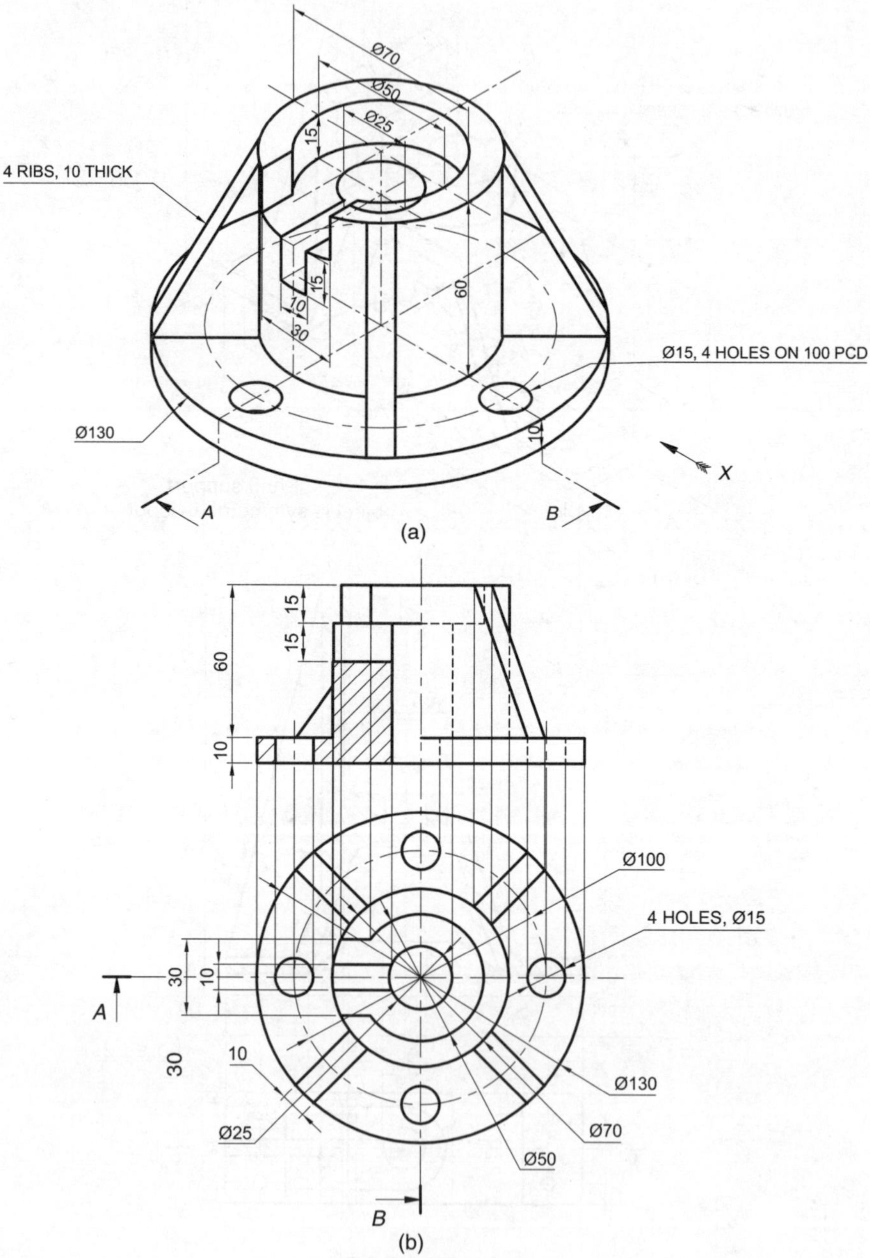

Fig. 9.38

ILLUSTRATIVE PROBLEMS

Problem 9.1 For the object shown in Fig. 9.39(a), draw: (i) FV (ii) TV (iii) SV. Dashed lines are used to indicate hidden edges.

Solution Figure 9.39(b) shows the FV, TV and SV of the object.

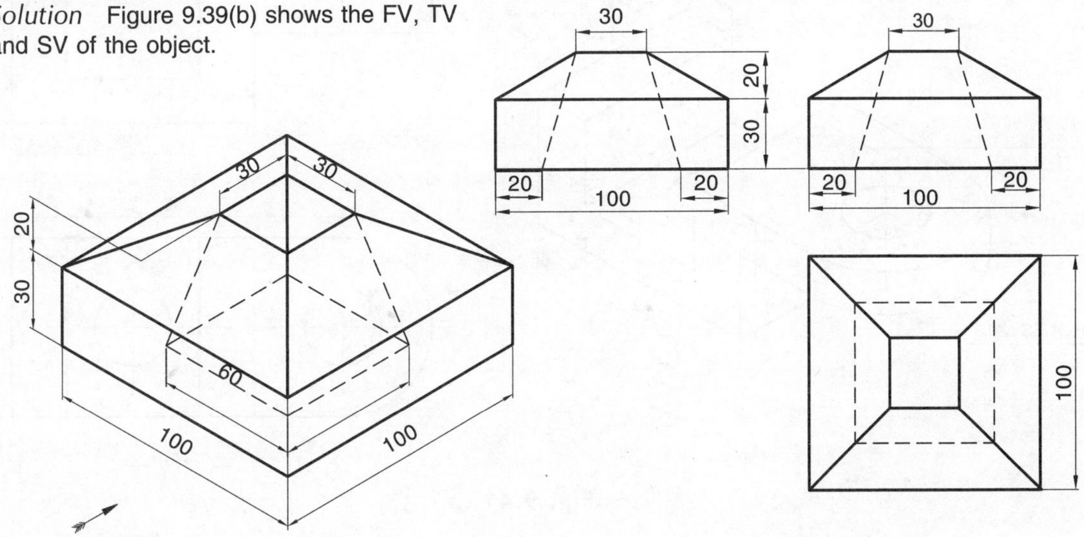

(a) (b)

Fig. 9.39

Problem 9.2 Figure 9.40(a) shows an object formed of square sectioned steel bar. Draw its three principal views.

Solution The required views are shown in Fig. 9.40(b).

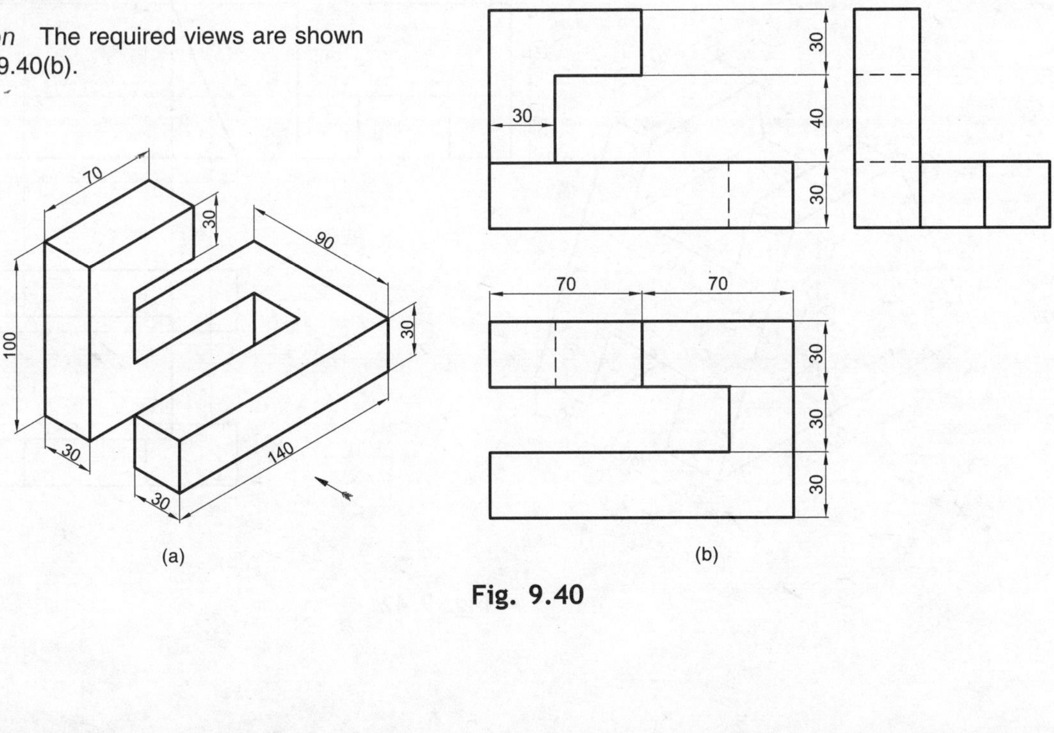

(a) (b)

Fig. 9.40

Problem 9.3 Figure 9.41(a) shows a pictorial view of an object. Draw its: (a) FV in specified direction and (b) TV.

Solution The FV and TV are shown in Fig. 9.41(b).

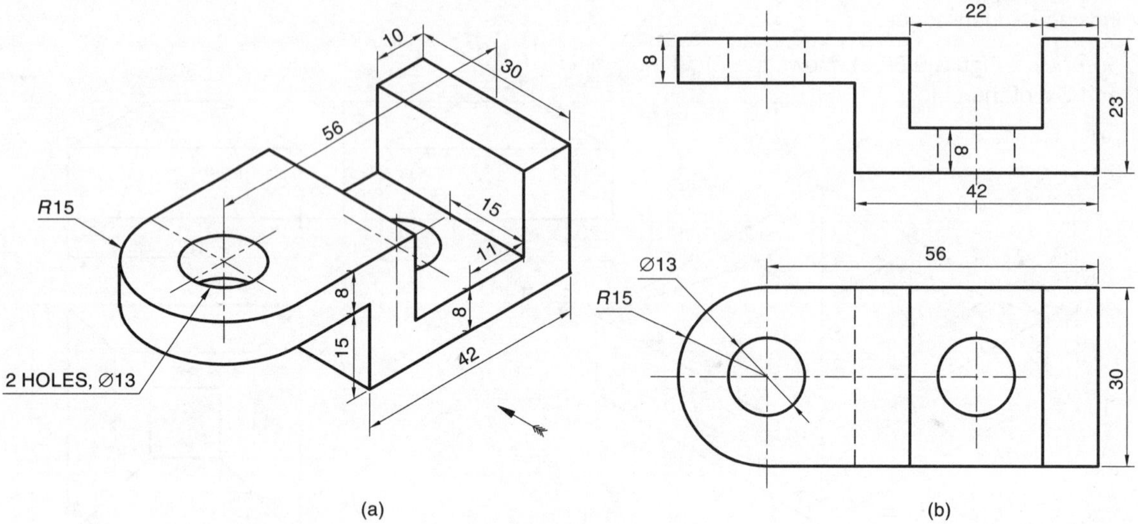

Fig. 9.41

Problem 9.4 A carpenter has created a wooden pattern shown in Fig. 9.42(a). Obtain its FV, TV and RHSV.

Solution See Fig. 9.42(b) for the TV, FV and RHSV of the pattern.

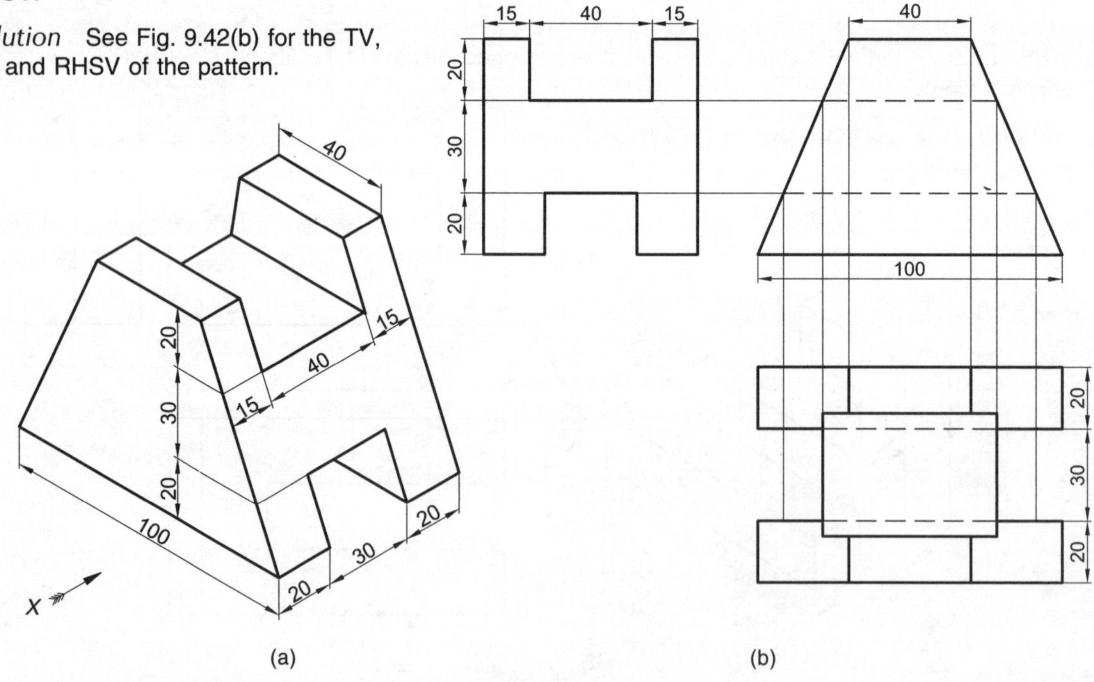

Fig. 9.42

Problem 9.5 For the object shown in Fig. 9.43(a), draw FV and TV.

Solution The FV and TV are shown in Fig. 9.43(b).

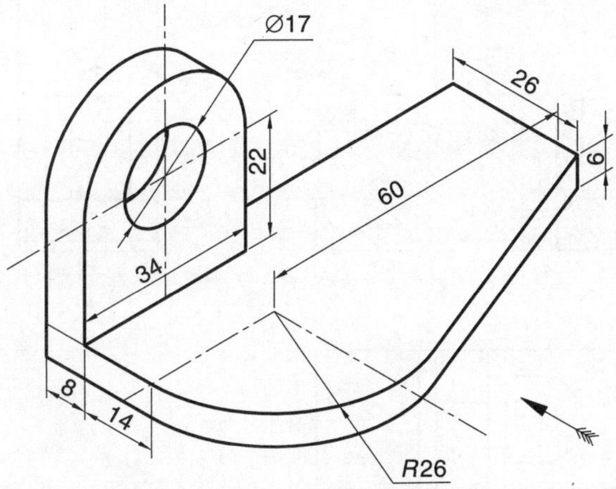

(a)

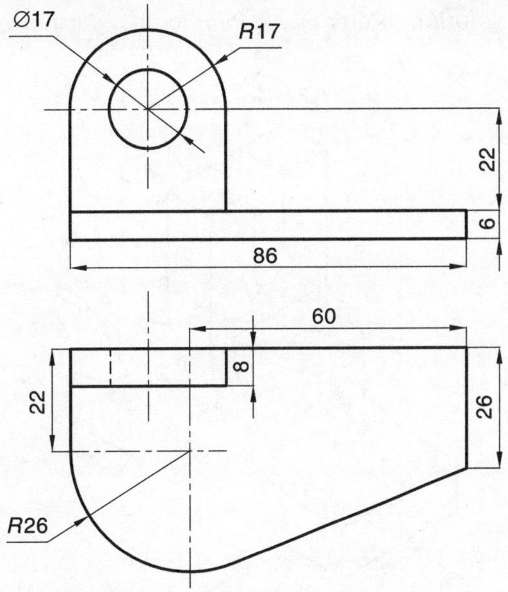

(b)

Fig. 9.43

Problem 9.6 Draw the FV and TV of the object shown in Fig. 9.44(a) using the third-angle method.

Solution See Fig. 9.44(b) for the required views.

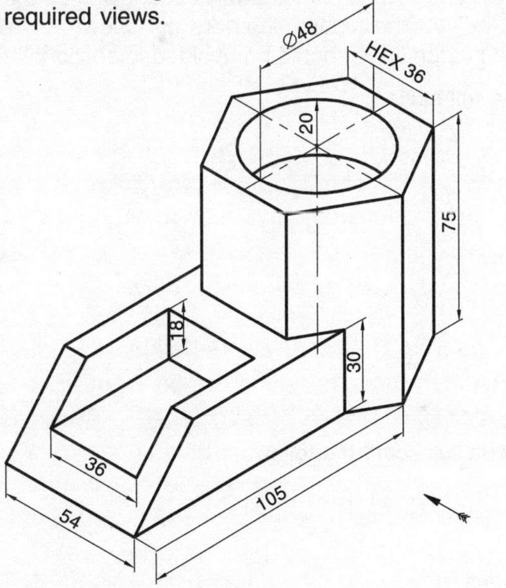

(a)

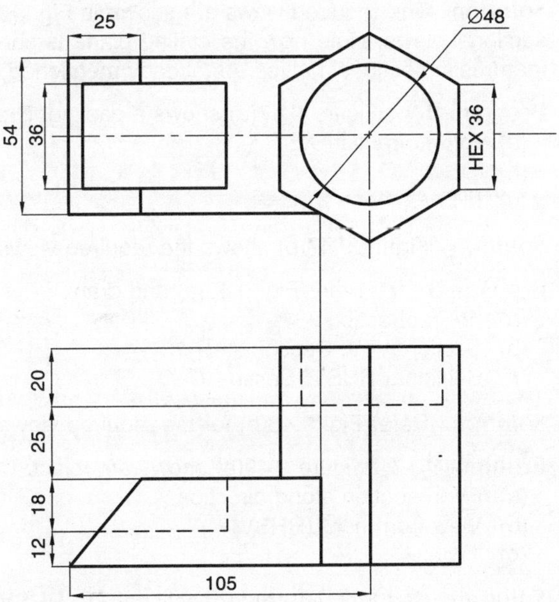

(b)

Fig. 9.44

Problem 9.7 Draw the Sectional FV, TV and LHSV of the object shown in Fig. 9.45(a).

Solution Refer Fig. 9.45(b) for the required views.

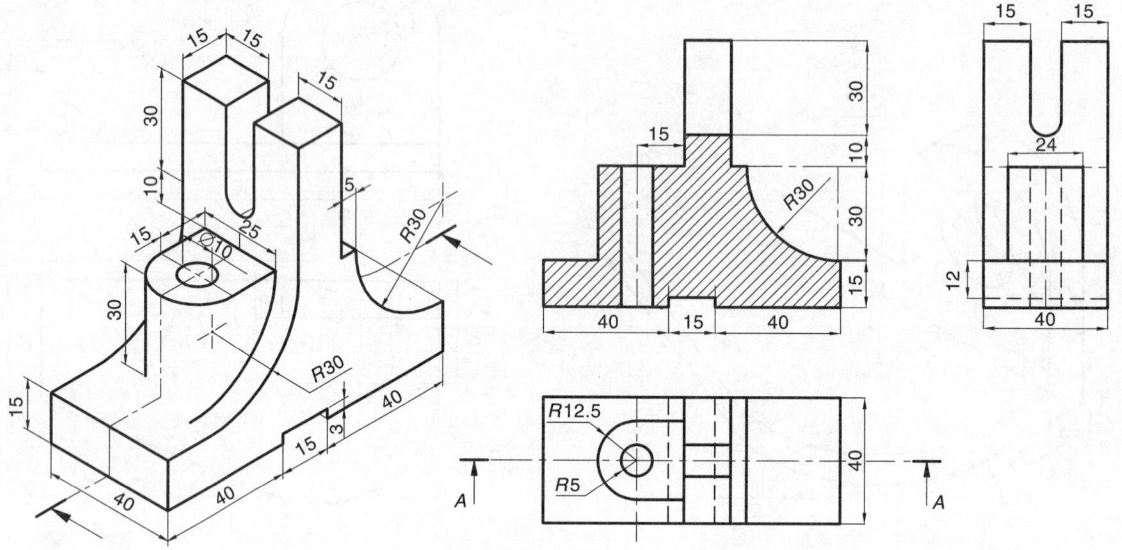

(a) (b)

Fig. 9.45

Problem 9.8 Refer Fig. 9.46(a). Draw the half-sectional FV, half-sectional RHSV and TV.

Solution The required views are shown in Fig. 9.46(b). The cutting plane, in this case, gives us the half-sectional views. Note how the cutting plane is shown in TV. The hidden lines are not shown for hidden features in sectional halves. As already mentioned, the hidden lines should be avoided in sectional views.

Problem 9.9 Figure 9.47(a) shows a casting. Draw a full scale
- (a) FV in direction *X*
- (b) TV
- (c) LHSV

Solution Figure 9.47(b) shows the required views.

Problem 9.10 Refer Fig. 9.48(a) and draw:
- (a) FV in direction *X*
- (b) Sectional TV, Section *A–B*
- (c) Sectional RHSV, Section *C–D*

Solution Refer Fig. 9.48(b) for the required views.

Problem 9.11 Figure 9.49(a) shows an object. Draw to full scale the following:
- (a) FV in section along direction *X*
- (b) View from right (RHSV)
- (c) TV

Solution See Fig. 9.49(b) for sectional FV, RHSV and TV.

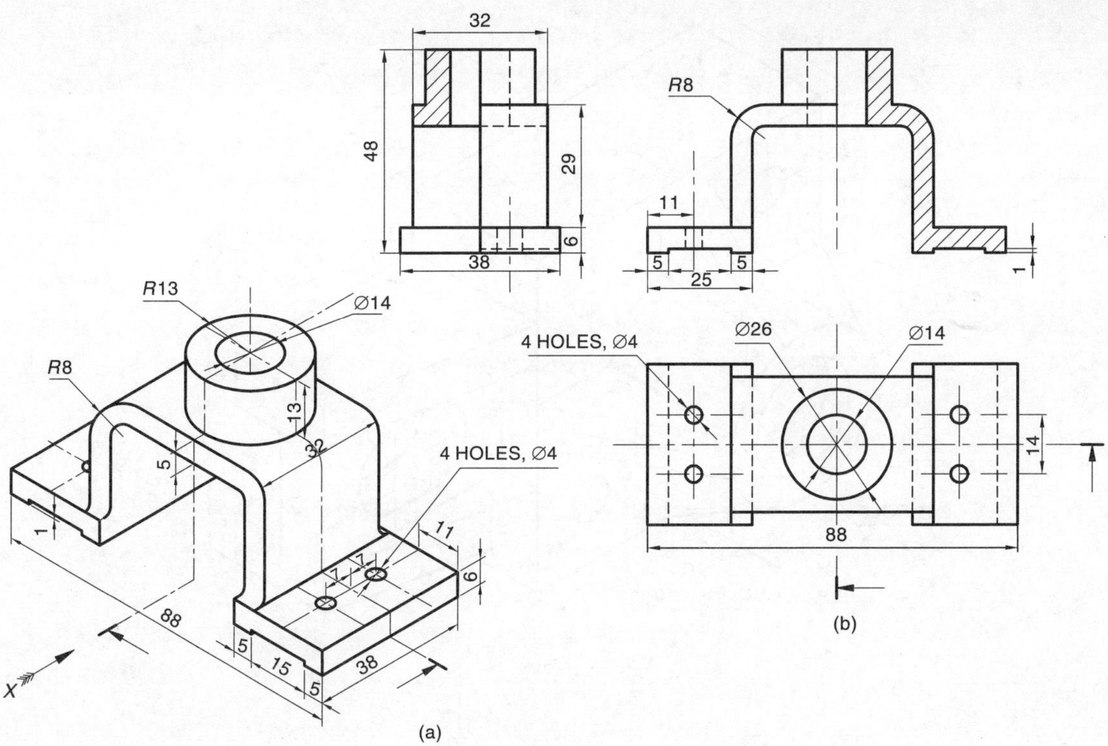

Fig. 9.46

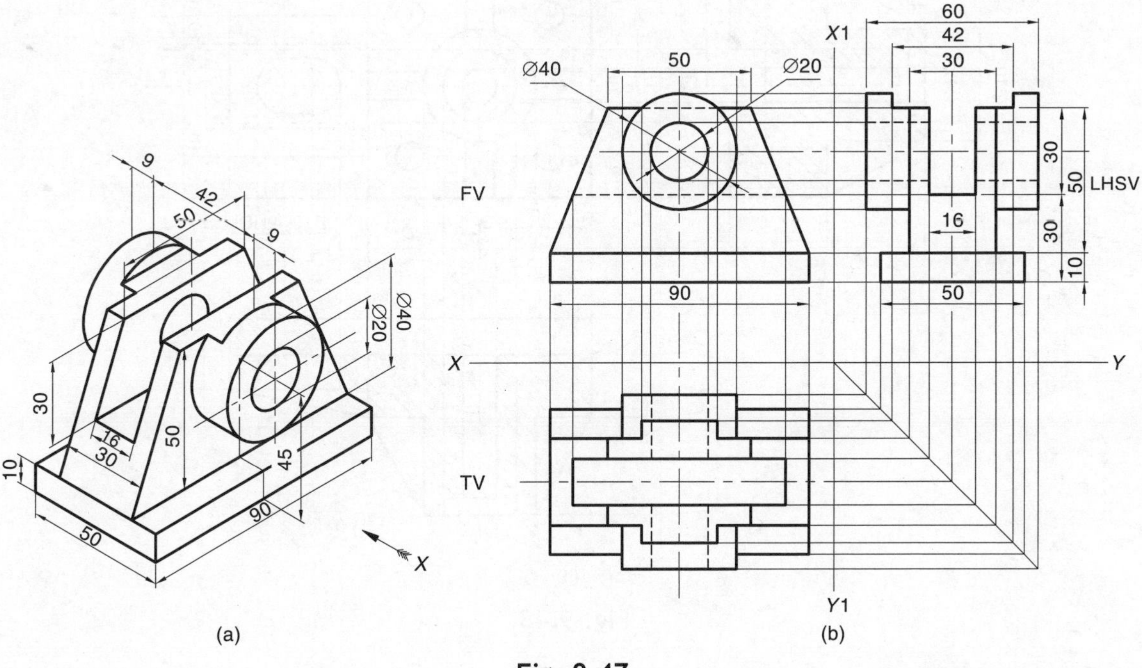

Fig. 9.47

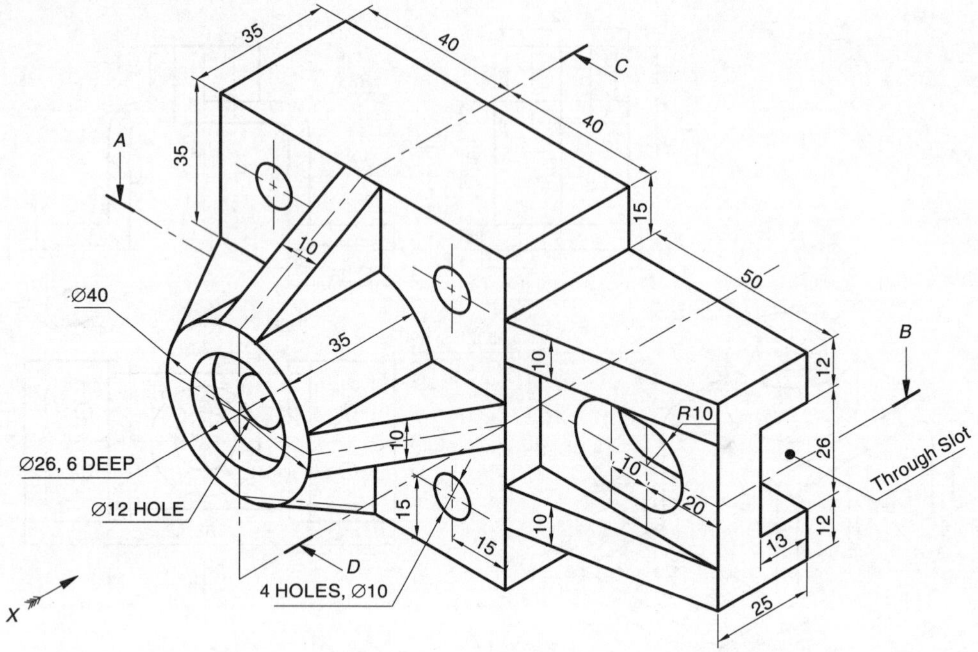
35
40
C
40
A
35
15
10
50
Ø40
35
B
12
R10
10
26
Through Slot
Ø26, 6 DEEP
10
20
Ø12 HOLE
15
10
12
15
13
D
4 HOLES, Ø10
25
X

(a)

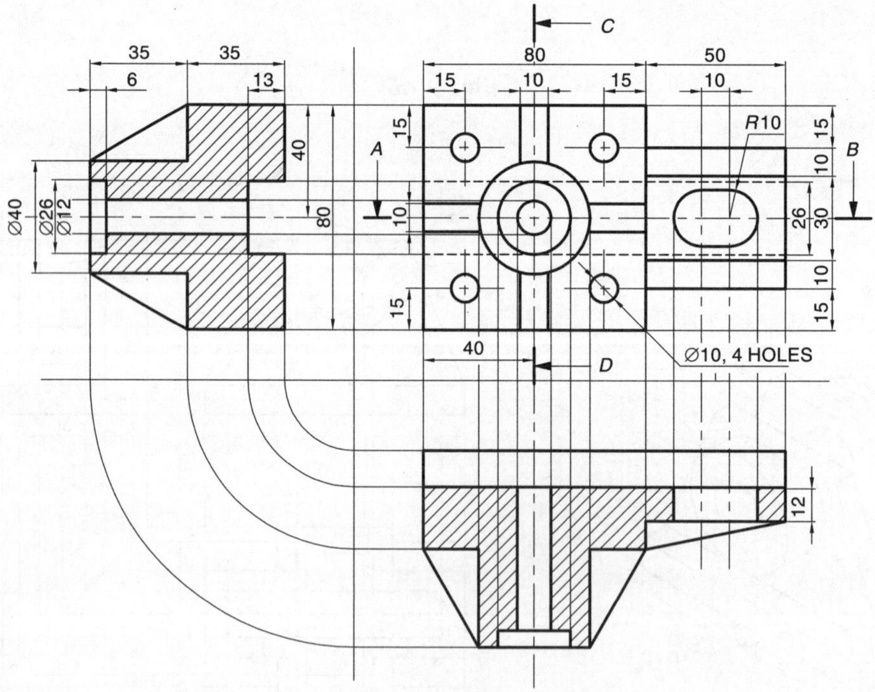
C
35
35
80
50
6
13
15
10
15
10
R10
40
15
15
A
10
B
Ø40
Ø26
Ø12
80
10
26
30
10
15
15
40
D
Ø10, 4 HOLES
12

(b)

Fig. 9.48

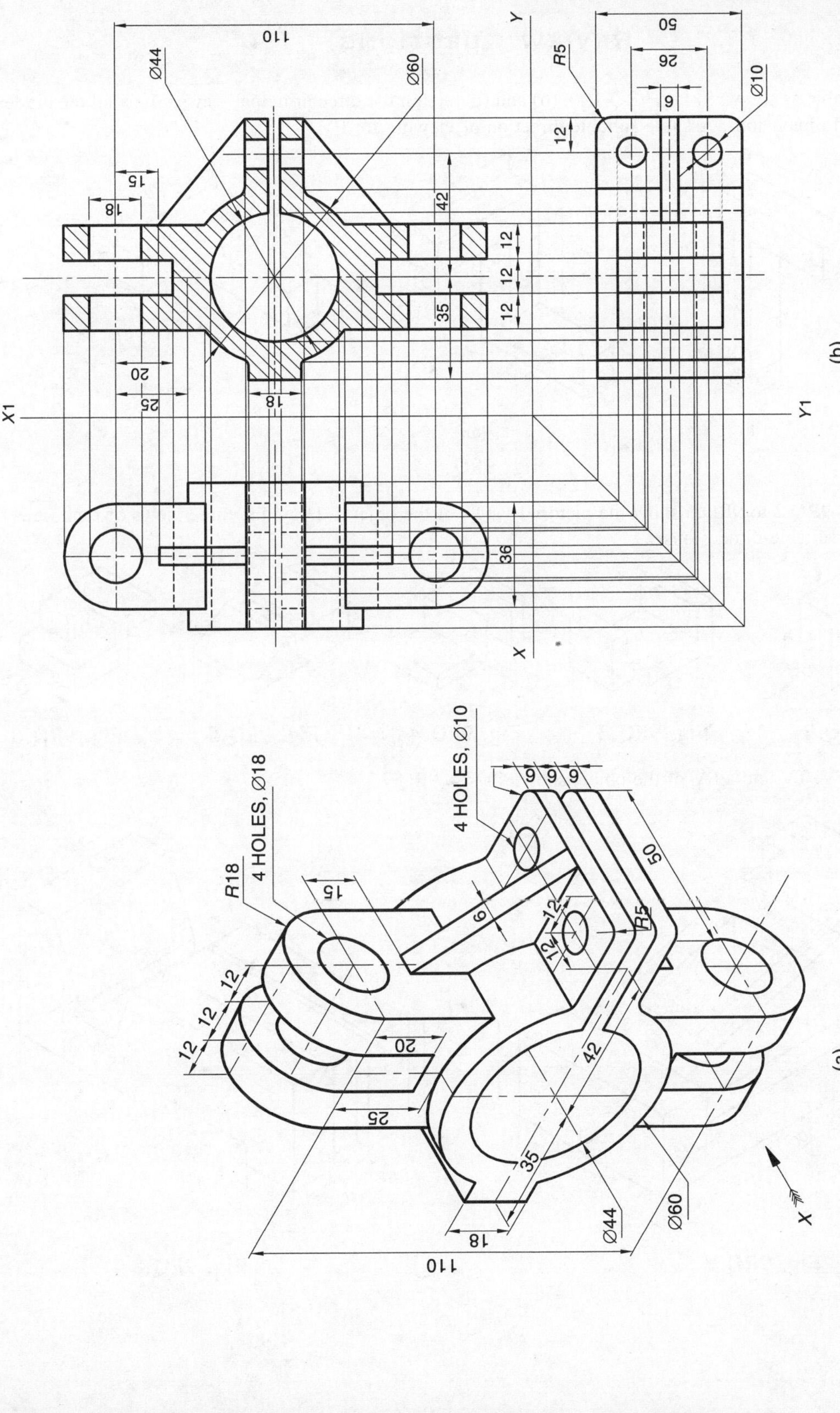
110
Ø44
Ø60
18
15
20
25
42
35
36
12
12
12
X1
Y1
X
Y
R5
50
26
9
12
Ø10
(b)
R18
4 HOLES, Ø18
4 HOLES, Ø10
9
9
9
15
6
12
14
R5
50
12
12
12
20
42
25
35
18
Ø44
Ø60
110
X
(a)

Fig. 9.49

REVIEW QUESTIONS

1. For the objects shown in Fig. 9RQ.1(a), (b) and (c), obtain the three principal views. Show all the hidden lines and dimensions. Assume suitable direction of viewing for FV.

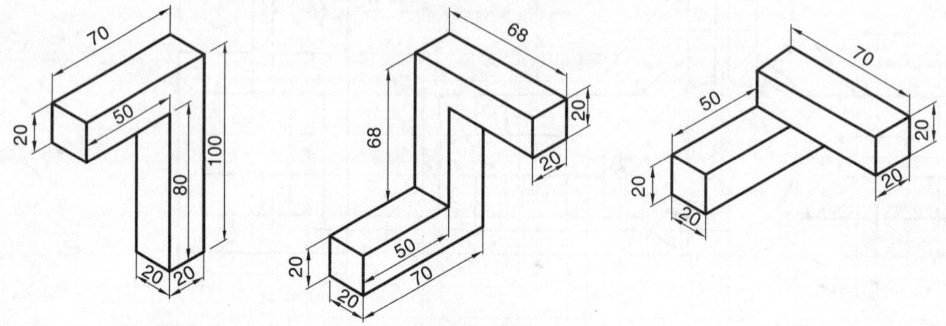

(a) (b) (c)

Fig. 9RQ.1

2. The Fig. 9RQ.2 to 9RQ.6 show the pictorial views of the objects. Draw the three views of each object. Assume suitable dimensions.

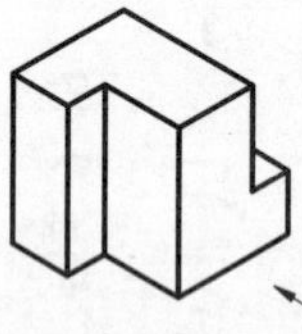

Fig. 9RQ.2

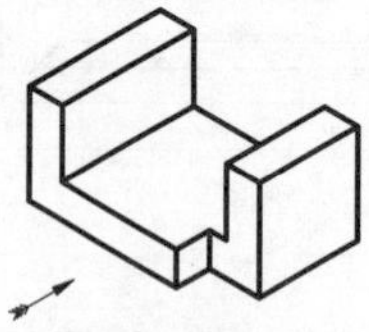

Fig. 9RQ.3

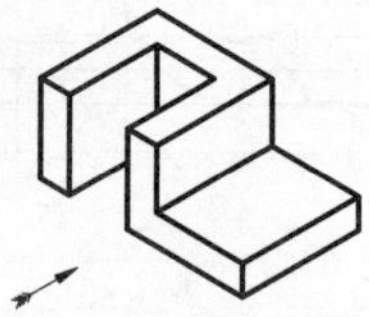

Fig. 9RQ.4

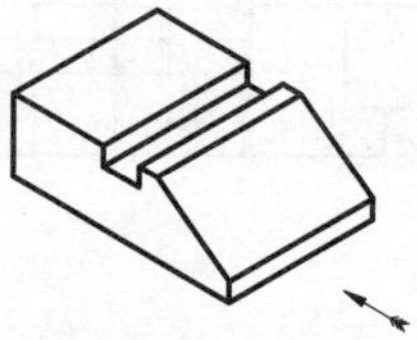

Fig. 9RQ.5

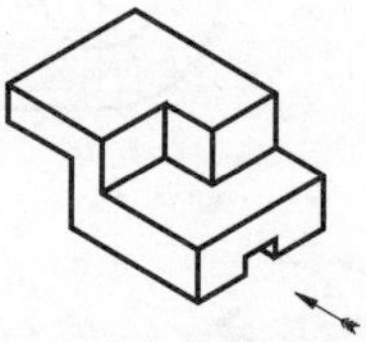

Fig. 9RQ.6

3. Obtain FV, TV and a SV of the object shown in Fig. 9RQ.7.

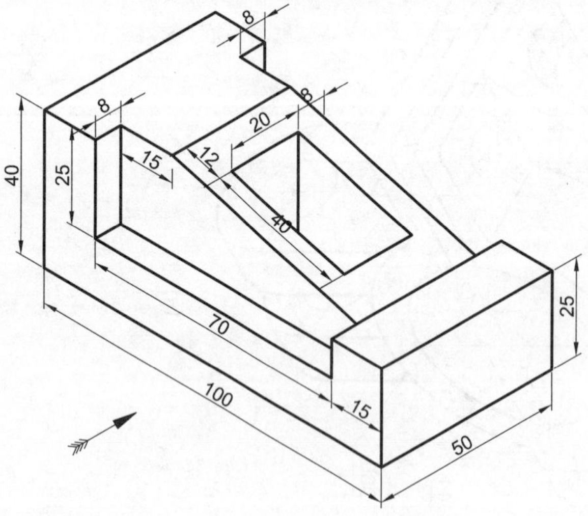

Fig. 9RQ.7

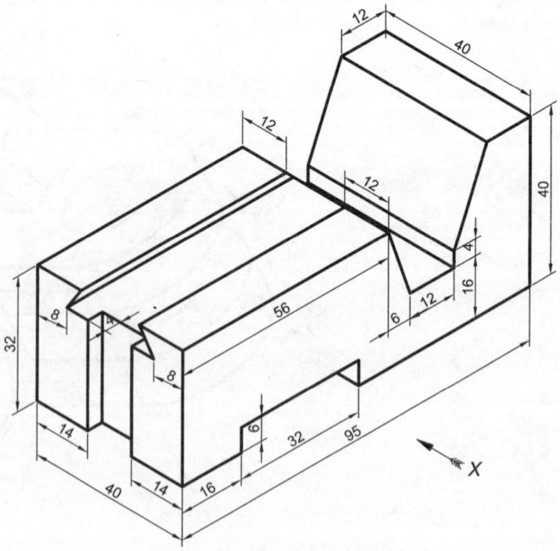

Fig. 9RQ.8

4. For the object shown in Fig. 9RQ.8, draw the following views:
   (i) FV in direction of arrow *X*
   (ii) SV from the left
   (iii) TV
   Show all the hidden lines in all the views.
5. Construct FV, TV and LHSV of the object shown in Fig. 9RQ.9. Use the third-angle method of projection.
6. For the object shown in Fig. 9RQ.10, draw FV, TV and RHSV.

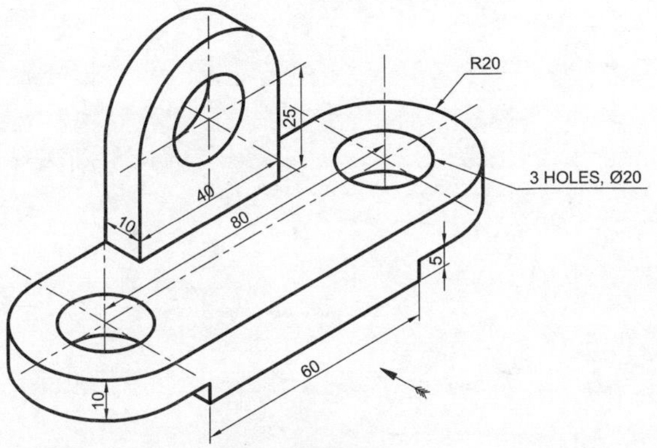

Fig. 9RQ.9

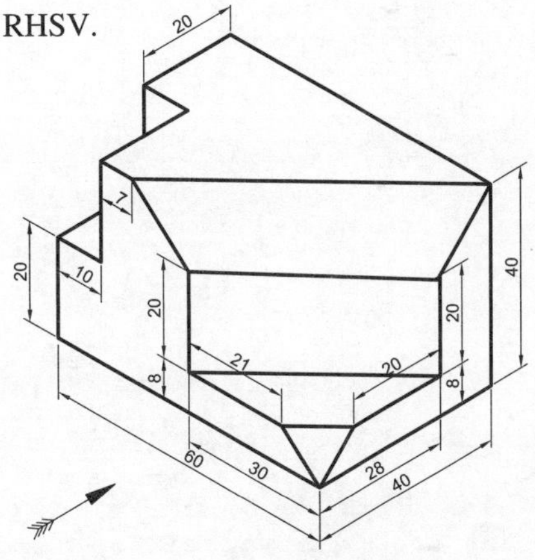

Fig. 9RQ.10

7. Draw FV, TV and LHSV for the object shown in Fig. 9RQ.11.
8. Draw the three principal views of the object shown in Fig. 9RQ.12.

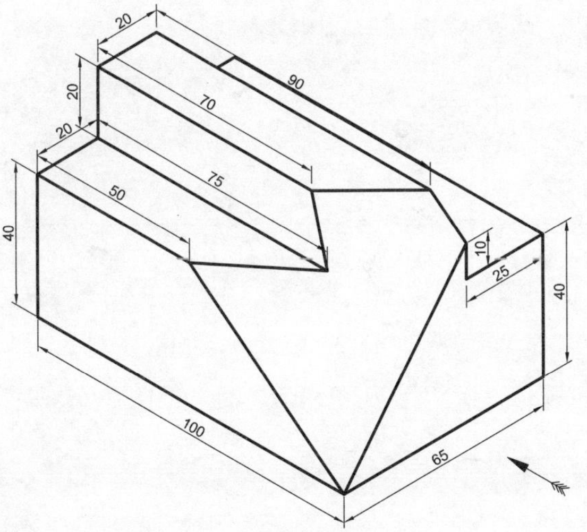

Fig. 9RQ.11

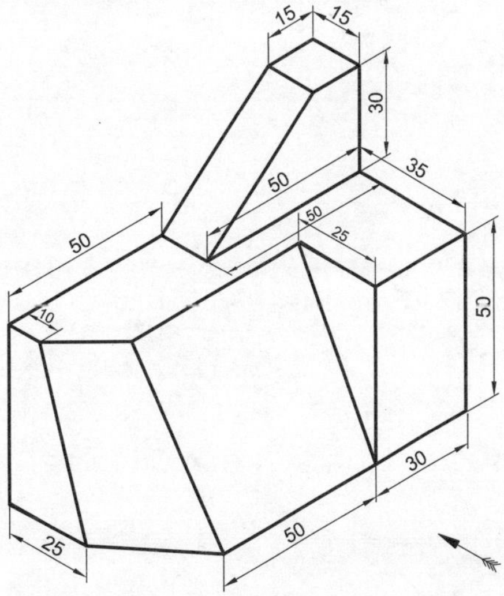

Fig. 9RQ.12

Chapter 10

PROJECTIONS OF POINTS

10.1 INTRODUCTION

A point represents a location in space. It is a dimensionless geometrical entity which has simply position but no magnitude. A point is obtained wherever two straight or curved lines intersect each other. A point is also obtained at the intersection of three mutually inclined or perpendicular planes. A point is usually represented by a dot or a very small circle.

In fact, projections of points have no practical significance. However, it serves the basis for projections of lines, projections of planes and projections of solids. Hence, readers must go through this topic very carefully as the subsequent chapters are based on it.

10.2 POSITIONS OF A POINT

In the conventional coordinate system, the position of a point in space is denoted by its three coordinates, viz. x, y and z. In engineering drawing, two RPs, i.e., the HP and the VP, as explained in Section 9.2, are used to indicate the position of a point in space. The PP, being an arbitrary plane, is rarely used to specify the point's position. The given point may be situated in any one of the four quadrants as shown in Fig. 10.1. The point may also lie on either of the RPs or both the RPs.

The distances of a point from the HP and the VP are necessary to determine its position in space. Just as the coordinates (x, y) are used in the Cartesian coordinate system, we may use parameters (h, d) to indicate the position of the point in space—h indicates the height of the point above/below the HP, d indicates the distance of the point in front of/behind the VP. These parameters may be suffixed by a small alphabet for that point. For example, to indicate the point P in space, parameters (h_p, d_p) may be used. The space-coordinates h_p and d_p may be prefixed by a (+) or (–) sign to indicate whether the point is above the HP/in front of the VP or below the HP/behind the VP as illustrated in Fig. 10.1.

The positions of a point may be as follows:

1. A point in the first quadrant, i.e., above the HP and in front of the VP (e.g., Point A)
2. A point in the second quadrant, i.e., above the HP and behind the VP (e.g., Point B)
3. A point in the third quadrant, i.e., below the HP and behind the VP (e.g., Point C)

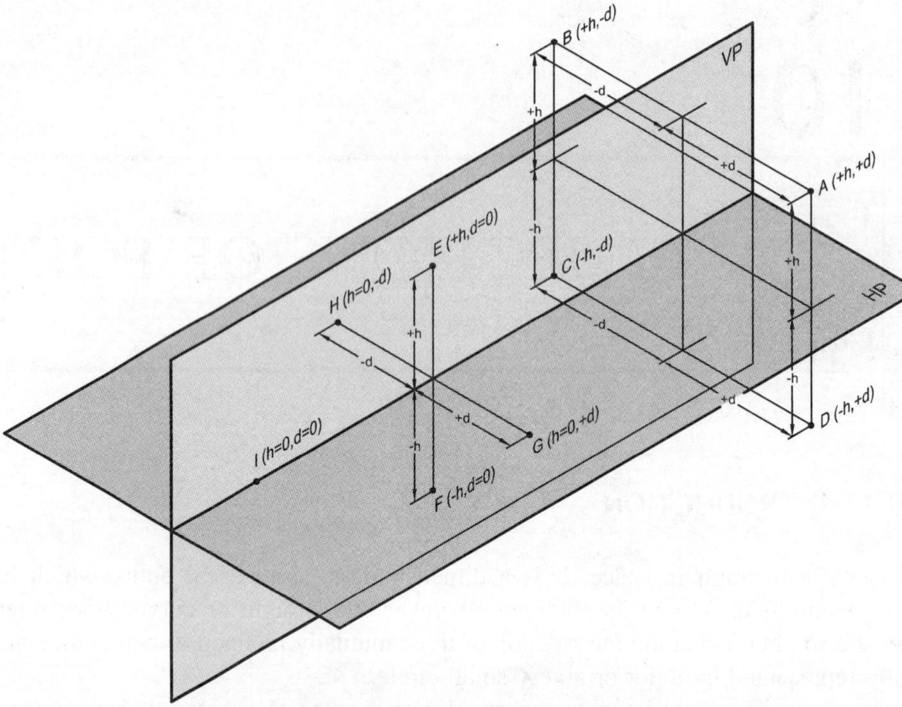

Fig. 10.1 Positions of a point

4. A point in the fourth quadrant, i.e., below the HP and in front of the VP (e.g. Point *D*)
5. A point in the VP and above the HP (e.g. Point *E*)
6. A point in the VP and below the HP (e.g. Point *F*)
7. A point in the HP and in front of the VP (e.g. Point *G*)
8. A point in the HP and behind the VP (e.g. Point *H*)
9. A point in both the RPs (e.g. Point *I*)

Note: Sometimes, a third parameter p is used to indicate the distance of a point from the PP. For example, p_a denotes the distance of point *A* from the PP.

10.3 NOTATION SYSTEM

The notation system refers to the standard rules for designating the FV, TV and SVs. These rules are applicable everywhere in engineering drawing. Hence, it should be understood properly. The notations to be followed are as given:

1. The TV of a point *P* shall be indicated by p
2. The FV of a point *P* shall be indicated by p'
3. The SV of a point *P* shall be indicated by p''

Hereafter, these notations are followed in all the chapters.

10.4 PROJECTIONS OF POINTS: SYSTEMATIC APPROACH

10.4.1 A Point in the First Quadrant

Example 10.1 Draw the projections of the point *A* which is 50 mm above the HP and 30 mm front of the VP.

Solution Given, $h_a = +50$, $d_a = +30$

Refer Fig. 10.2.

As h_a and d_a both are (+), the point *A* is in the first quadrant. Therefore, FV of the point will be seen above *XY* at a distance of 50 mm and TV will be seen below *XY* at a distance of 30 mm.

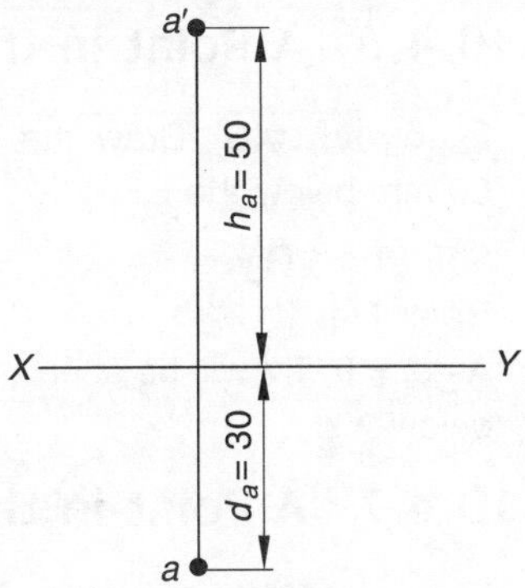

Fig. 10.2

10.4.2 A Point in the Second Quadrant

Example 10.2 Draw the projections of the point *B* which is 50 mm above the HP and 30 mm behind the VP.

Solution Given, $h_b = +50$, $d_b = -30$

Refer Fig. 10.3.

As h_b is (+) and d_p is (–), the point *B* lies in the second quadrant. Therefore, FV and TV, both will be seen above *XY* at a distance of 50 mm and 30 mm respectively. This is because when the HP is rotated in a clockwise direction about *XY*, the TV on the HP will go up on the side of the FV.

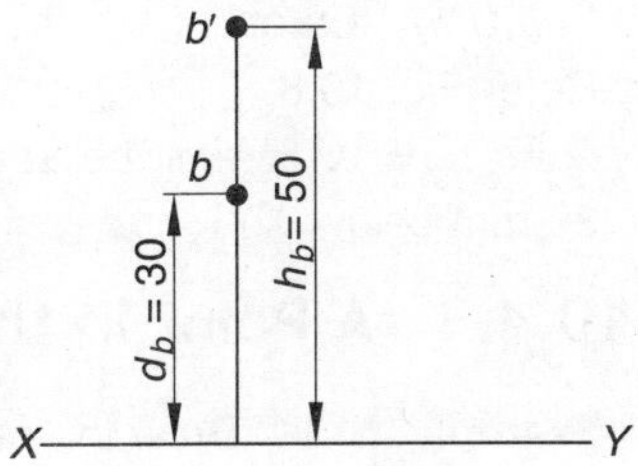

Fig. 10.3

10.4.3 A Point in the Third Quadrant

Example 10.3 Draw the projections of the point *C*, 50 mm below the HP and 30 mm behind the VP.

Solution Given, $h_c = -50$, $d_c = -30$

Refer Fig. 10.4.

As h_c and d_c both are (–), the point *C* is in the third quadrant. Therefore, FV will be seen 50 mm below *XY* and TV will be seen 30 mm above *XY*.

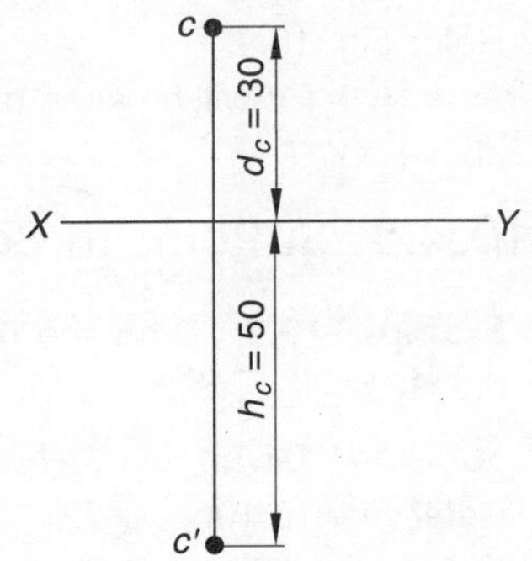

Fig. 10.4

10.4.4 A Point in the Fourth Quadrant

Example 10.4 Draw the projections of the point *D* which is 50 mm below the HP and 30 mm in front of the VP.

Solution Given, $h_d = -50$, $d_d = +30$

Refer Fig. 10.5.

As h_d is (–) and d_d is (+), the point *D* lies in the fourth quadrant. Therefore, FV and TV both will be seen below *XY* at a distance of 50 mm and 30 mm respectively. When the HP is rotated in a clockwise direction about *XY*, the TV on the HP will go down on the side of the FV.

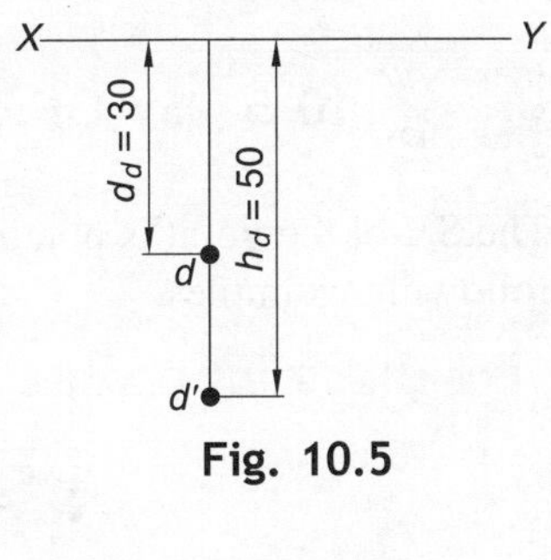

Fig. 10.5

10.4.5 A Point in the VP and Above the HP

Example 10.5 Draw the projections of the point *E* in the VP and 50 mm above the HP.

Solution Given, $h_e = +50$, $d_e = 0$

Refer Fig. 10.6.
As $h_e = +50$, FV will be seen above *XY*. As $d_e = 0$, TV will be seen on *XY*.

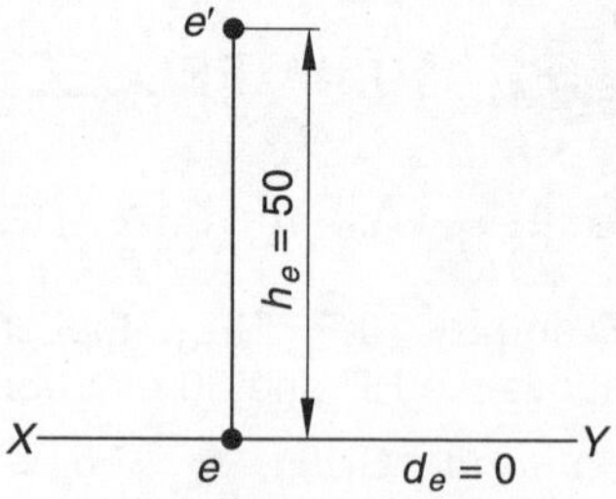

Fig. 10.6

10.4.6 A Point in the VP and Below the HP

Example 10.6 Draw the projections of the point *F* in the VP and 50 mm below the HP.

Solution Given, $h_f = -50$, $d_f = 0$
Refer Fig. 10.7.
As $d_f = 0$, TV will be seen on *XY*. As $h_f = -50$, FV will be seen 50 mm below *XY*.

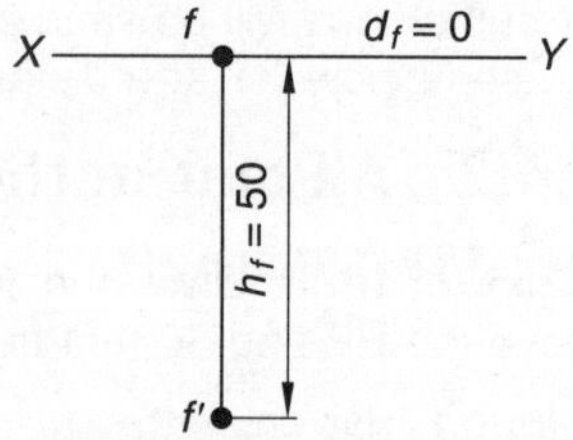

Fig. 10.7

10.4.7 A Point in the HP and in Front of the VP

Example 10.7 Draw the projections of the point *G* which is in the HP and 30 mm in front of the VP.

Solution Given, $h_g = 0$, $d_g = +30$
Refer Fig. 10.8.
As $h_g = 0$, FV will be seen on *XY*. As $d_g = +30$, TV will be seen 30 mm below *XY*.

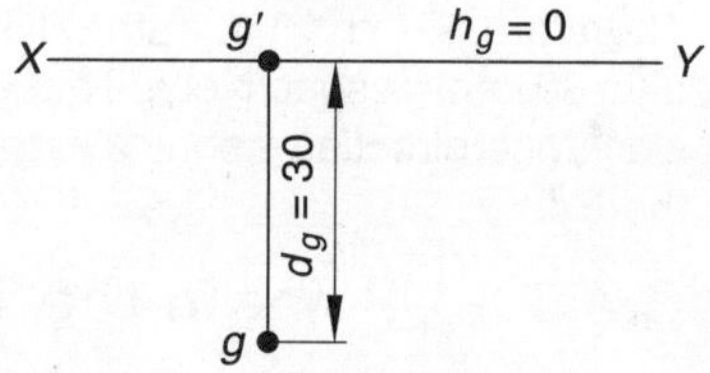

Fig. 10.8

10.4.8 A Point in the HP and Behind the VP

Example 10.8 Draw the projections of the point *H* which is in the HP and 30 mm behind the VP.

Solution Given, $h_h = 0$, $d_h = -30$
Refer Fig. 10.9.
As $h_h = 0$, FV will be seen on *XY*. As $d_h = -30$, TV will be seen 30 mm above *XY*.

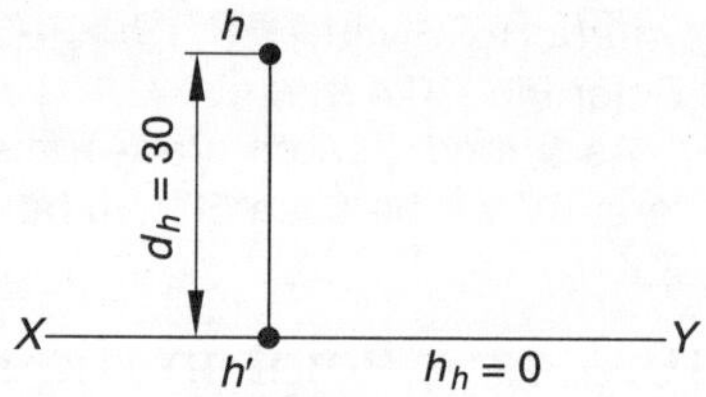

Fig. 10.9

10.4.9 A Point in Both the RPs

Example 10.9 Draw the projections of the point *I* which lies in both the RPs.

Solution Given, $h_i = 0$, $d_i = 0$
Refer Fig. 10.10.
If the point *I* lies in both the RPs then it lies at the intersection of the two RPs, i.e., on *XY*. Hence, its FV and TV both will coincide on *XY*.

Fig. 10.10

10.5 SV OF THE POINT

The SV of the point is obtained by projecting the FV and TV with respect to *X*1*Y*1 as explained in the following examples.

Example 10.10 Draw the LHSV of the point *A* mentioned in Example 10.1.

Solution The LHSV of the point is shown in Fig. 10.11. As already mentioned in the previous chapter, SV is always drawn to the side of FV. Here, the LHSV of the point is drawn to the right side of FV, because the point is in first quadrant. *X*1 *Y*1 may be taken arbitrarily at any suitable distance from FV and TV.

Example 10.11 Draw the LHSV of the point *c* mentioned in Example 10.3.

Solution The LHSV of the point *c* is drawn in Fig. 10.12. It should be noted that the LHSV is drawn to the left side of FV as point *c* is in the third quadrant.

Example 10.12 Draw the RHSV of the point *E* mentioned in Example 10.5.

Solution The RHSV will be seen on the left side of FV as shown in Fig. 10.13. As the point *E* is in the VP, its SV will be on *X*1 *Y*1.

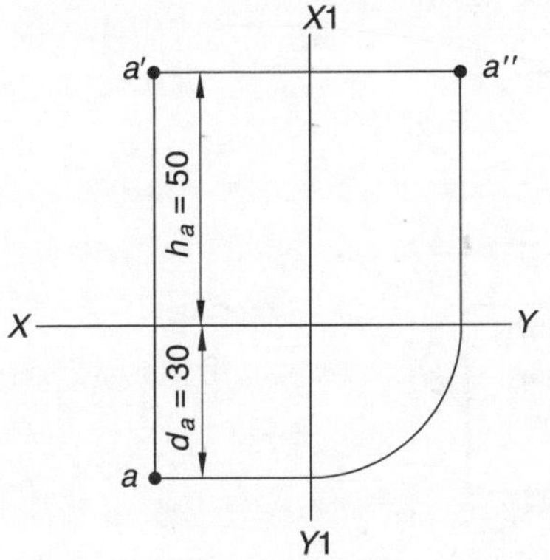

Fig. 10.11

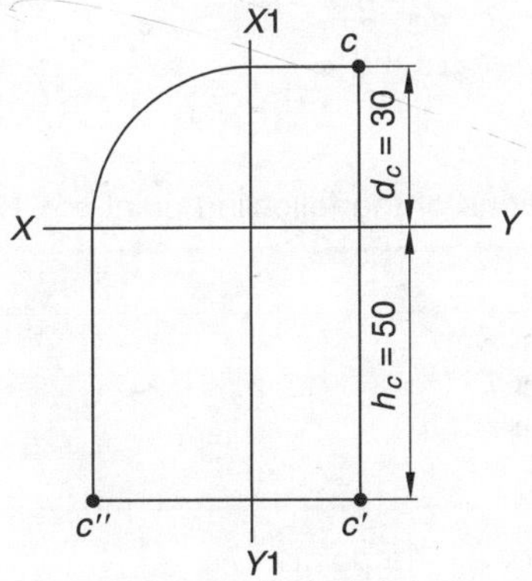

Fig. 10.12

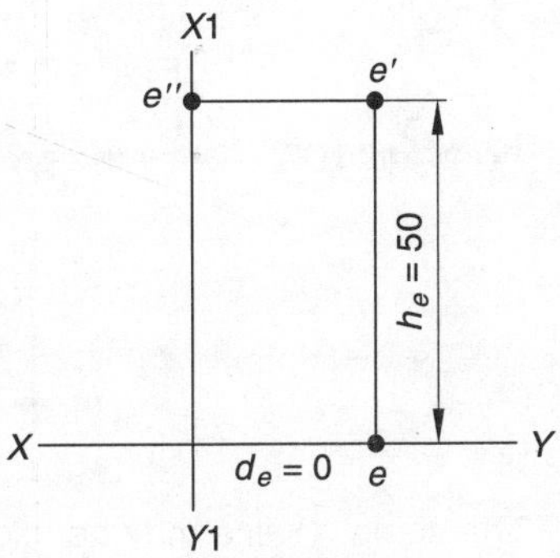

Fig. 10.13

REMEMBER THE FOLLOWING

- If *h* is (+) then the FV of the point will be above *XY*.
- If *h* is (–) then the FV of the point will be below *XY*.
- If *d* is (+) then the TV of the point will be below *XY*.
- If *d* is (–) then the TV of the point will be above *XY*.
- If $h = 0$ then the FV and SV of the point will be on *XY*.
- If $d = 0$ then the TV and SV of the point will be on *XY* and *X*1 *Y*1 respectively.
- If a point is in the second quadrant, its FV and TV lie above *XY*.
- If a point is in the fourth quadrant, its FV and TV lie below *XY*.

ILLUSTRATIVE PROBLEMS

Problem 10.1 Draw the projections of the following points:

(a) *A* (+30 mm, +25 mm) (b) *B* (+28 mm, –22 mm)

(c) *C* (–30 mm, –28 mm) (d) *D* (–25 mm, +40 mm)

The same *XY* line may be used for all the points.

Solution The projections of all the above points are shown in Fig. 10.14. The procedure is explained below:

(a) Point *A* lies in the first quadrant. It's FV *a*′ is 30 mm above *XY* and its TV *a* is 25 mm below *XY*.

(b) Point B lies in the second quadrant. It's FV b' and TV b are therefore 28 mm and 22 mm above XY respectively.

(c) Point C lies in the third quadrant. Its TV c' is 28 mm above XY and the FV c' is 30 mm below XY.

(d) Point D lies in the fourth quadrant. Its FV d' and TV d are 25 mm and 40 mm below XY respectively.

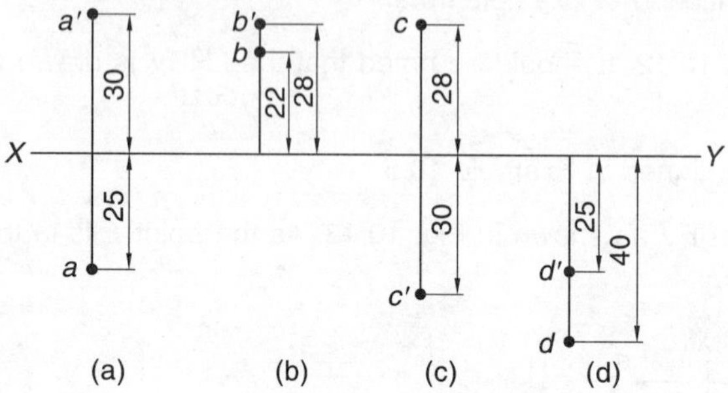

Fig. 10.14

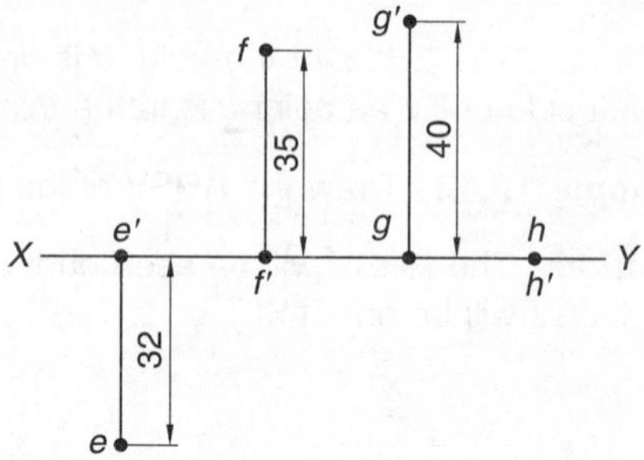

Fig. 10.15

Problem 10.2 Draw the projections of the following points:

	h	d
Point E	0	+32 mm
Point F	0	–35 mm
Point G	+40 mm	0
Point H	0	0

The same XY line may be used for all the points.

Solution The required projections are drawn in Fig. 10.15.

Problem 10.3 Draw the FV, TV and RHSV of the following points:

(i) Point P lies in the HP and 22 mm behind the VP.

(ii) Point Q lies in the VP and 32 mm below the HP.

(iii) Point R lies 32 mm below the HP and 22 mm behind the VP.

Solution Refer Fig. 10.16 for the required projections of all the points.

Problem 10.4 The FVs of two points P and Q coincide at 30 mm above XY. Their TVs are 30 mm below and 10 mm above XY respectively. Draw the three views of each point and determine the distance between them.

Solution Refer Fig. 10.17.

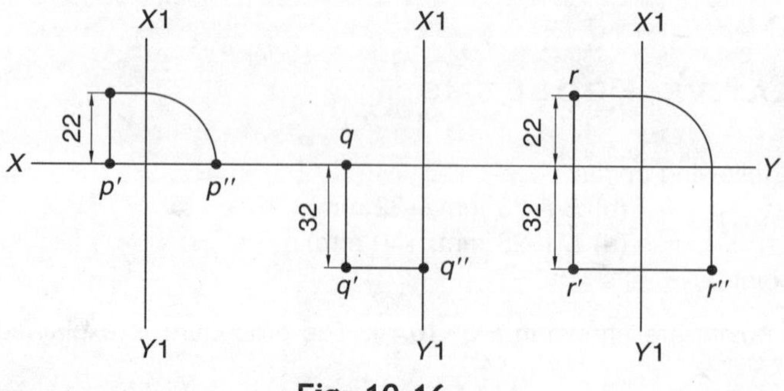

Fig. 10.16

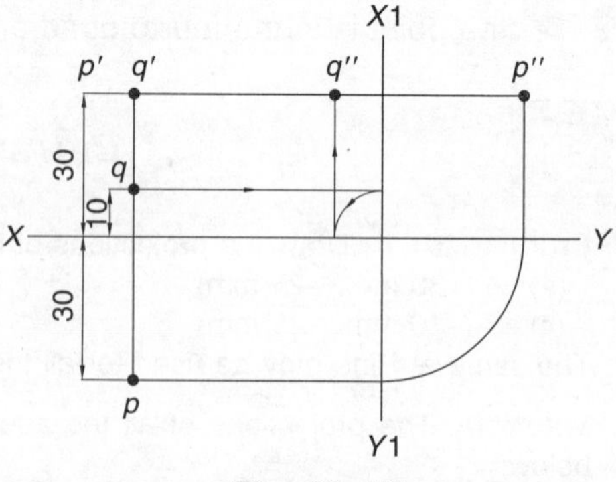

Fig. 10.17

p' and q' are coinciding at 30 mm above XY. p and q are 30 mm below and 10 mm above XY respectively. Carefully, note how their SVs are obtained. The distance between P and Q is given by pq (or $p'' - q''$). Obviously, $pq = 30 + 10 = 40$ mm.

REVIEW QUESTIONS

1. Draw the projections of the following points:
   Point M (+55 mm, –35 mm), Point N (–35 mm, +55 mm), Point O (–55mm, +35 mm), Point P (+35 mm, –55 mm), Point Q (+55 mm, 0), Point R (–35 mm, 0), Point S (0, +35 mm), and Point T (0, –55 mm)
2. An electric pole is 10 m high. A mighty storm bent it in such a way that its tip is now at a distance half of its original distance from the ground. Draw the projections of the pole tip if it is 3 m from a wall of a building.
3. An electric bulb is hanging from the centre of the ceiling of a room having floor area 12 m × 8 m. Draw the projections of the bulb if the length of the wire connecting the bulb to the ceiling is 1 m. The height of the room is 4 m.
4. A stick is struck in the ground making an angle of 30° to the ground. Draw the projections of the free end of the stick if the length of the stick above the ground is 1.5 m and the distance of the end from a wall is 2.5 m.
5. Identify the positions of the points shown in Fig. 10RQ.1.

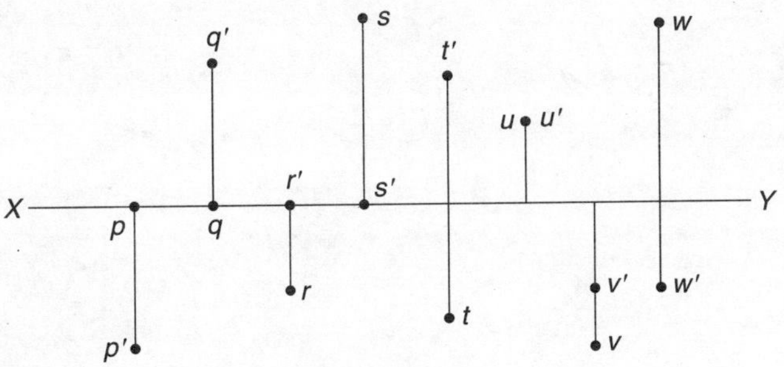

Fig. 10RQ.1

6. In which quadrant are the following points located?
   (i) a' 30 mm above XY and a 10 mm above a'
   (ii) b' 25 mm above XY and b 35 mm below b'
7. Two points M and N lie in the VP. The point M is above the HP and the point N is 40 mm below the HP. The perpendicular distance between their projectors is 60 mm. The line joining m' and n' makes 60° with XY. Draw the projections of the points. Find the height of point M from the HP.
8. A point A is 20 mm above the HP and 50 mm in front of the VP. Another point B is 40 mm below the HP and 15 mm behind the VP. The distance between the projectors of the points, measured parallel to XY, is 75 mm. Draw the projections of the points. Draw lines joining their FVs and TVs.

Chapter 11

PROJECTIONS OF LINES

11.1 INTRODUCTION

A straight line is the shortest distance between any two points in space. It is a one-dimensional entity, i.e., it has only length and no thickness. A line represents the locus of a point moving along a fixed path in space. As a line consists of a number of points, its projections are drawn by joining the projections of any two points on the line (preferably the end points) or on the extension of the line. A straight line may have different orientations in space. It may be parallel or inclined to either or both the RPs. It may be perpendicular to either of the RPs. It may be contained by either or both the RPs.

11.2 POSITIONS OF STRAIGHT LINES

For the sake of projections, straight lines are classified into the following categories based on their inclinations with the RPs.

1. Line parallel to both the RPs
    - Case (i): Line away from both the RPs
    - Case (ii): Line in the HP and away from the VP
    - Case (iii): Line in the VP and away from the HP
    - Case (iv): Line contained by both the RPs
2. Line perpendicular to either of the RPs
    - Case (i): Line perpendicular to the HP and away from the VP
    - Case (ii): Line perpendicular to the HP and in the VP
    - Case (iii): Line perpendicular to the VP and away from the HP
    - Case (iv): Line perpendicular to the VP and in the HP
3. Line inclined to one RP and parallel to the other
    - Case (i): Line inclined to the HP, parallel to the VP and away from the VP
    - Case (ii): Line inclined to the HP and in the VP
    - Case (iii): Line inclined to the VP, parallel to the HP and away from the HP
    - Case (iv): Line inclined to the VP and in the HP

4. Line inclined to both the RPs (Oblique line)
   Case (i): h_a less than h_b and d_a less than d_b
   Case (ii): h_a less than h_b and d_a greater than d_b
   Case (iii): h_a greater than h_b and d_a less than d_b
   Case (iv): h_a greater than h_b and d_a greater than d_b
   (*A* and *B* being the two ends of the line.)
5. Line parallel to (or contained by) the PP
   Case (i): Line parallel to the PP and the HP
   Case (ii): Line parallel to the PP and the VP
   Case (iii): Line parallel to the PP and inclined to the HP and the VP

The above categorization considers that the line fully lies in any one of the four quadrants. However, a particular line may lie partly in two or three quadrants. Such a line will intersect one, two or all the three RPs. Even if the line lies fully in one quadrant, its endpoint(s) may lie on the HP, the VP or the PP. It should be noted that the procedure to obtain the projections is same irrespective of whether the line lies in one quadrant or more than one quadrants. This is illustrated with the help of solved examples in later sections.

11.3 TERMS USED IN PROJECTIONS OF LINES

Before we proceed for the procedural aspect of the projections of a line, the following terms must be understood.

True Length (TL) The actual length of a line is called its *true length*.

Plan Length (PL) or Top View Length The apparent length of a line seen in TV is called the *plan length* or *top view length*. If a line is parallel to the HP, its PL will be equal to TL. If a line is inclined to the HP, its PL will be shorter than TL.

Elevation Length (EL) or Front View Length The apparent length of a line seen in FV is called the *elevation length* or *front view length*. If a line is parallel to the VP, its EL will be equal to TL. If a line is inclined to the VP, its EL will be shorter than TL.

Side View Length (SVL) The apparent length of a line seen in SV is called its *side view length*. If a line is parallel to the PP, its SVL will be equal to TL. If a line is inclined to the PP, its SVL will be shorter than TL.

Inclinations with the RPs The inclination of a line with an RP is the angle which the line makes with its projection on that RP.

Inclination with the HP (θ) It is the true angle that a line makes with its projection on the HP. It is measured along the plane containing the line and perpendicular to the HP. It is indicated by θ.

Inclination with the VP (ϕ) It is the true angle that a line makes with its projection on the VP. It is measured along the plane containing the line and perpendicular to the VP. It is indicated by ϕ.

Since the HP and the VP are perpendicular to each other, sum of θ and ϕ never exceeds 90°.

Inclination with the PP (ψ) It is the true angle the line makes with its projection on the PP. It is measured along the plane containing the line and perpendicular to the PP. It is indicated by ψ.

Apparent Angle with the HP (α) It is the angle which an oblique line seems to be making with the HP in FV. It is the angle between FV and *XY*. It is indicated by α. α corresponds to θ and is always greater than θ.

Apparent Angle with the VP (β) It is the angle which an oblique line seems to be making with the VP in TV. It is the angle between TV and *XY*. It is indicated by β. β corresponds to ϕ and is always greater than ϕ.

Traces of the Line The points of intersection of the line (or its extension) with the RPs are called *traces* of the line. A line may have *horizontal trace* or *vertical trace* or both or none.

Horizontal Trace (HT) The point of intersection of the line (or its extension) with the HP is called the *horizontal trace* of the line.

Vertical Trace (VT) The point of intersection of the line (or its extension) with the VP is called the *vertical trace* of the line.

The HT and VT are explained in detail in Section 11.9.

Point View of the Line The view of a line seen as a point (i.e., when the views of two ends coincide) is called the *point view*.

REMEMBER THE FOLLOWING

- PL ≤ TL
- EL ≤ TL
- SVL ≤ TL
- $(\theta + \phi) \leq 90°$
- $\alpha > \theta$
- $\beta > \phi$
- If $\theta = \phi$ then $\alpha = \beta$

The following sections explain the step-by-step procedures with the help of examples, to draw the projections of lines of different categories.

11.4 LINE PARALLEL TO BOTH THE RPs

11.4.1 Line Away from Both the RPs

Example 11.1 Draw the projections of a line *AB* that is 50 mm long and is parallel to both the HP and the VP. The line is 40 mm above the HP and 25 mm in front of the VP.

Solution Refer Fig. 11.1.

The line *AB* is parallel to both the VP and the HP. So, its FV and TV, will be parallel to *XY* and both will show the TL (= 50 mm). If a line is parallel to both the HP and the VP, it must be perpendicular to the PP. Therefore, point *A* and point *B* will coincide in SV of the line. Hence, the LHSV is a point view.

11.4.2 Line in the HP and Away from the VP

Example 11.2 A line *AB*, 50 mm long, is in the HP and parallel to the VP. Draw the three views of the line if it is 25 mm in front of the VP.

Solution Refer Fig. 11.2.

The line *AB* is in the HP and parallel to the VP. So, it's FV and TV both will be parallel to *XY* and will show the TL. As the line is on the HP, its FV will be seen along *XY*. The LHSV is seen as a point view on *XY*.

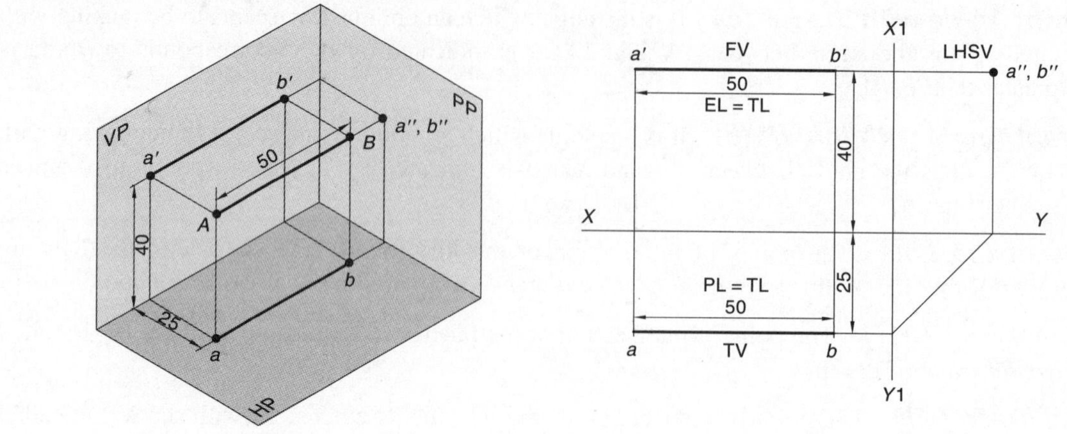

Fig. 11.1

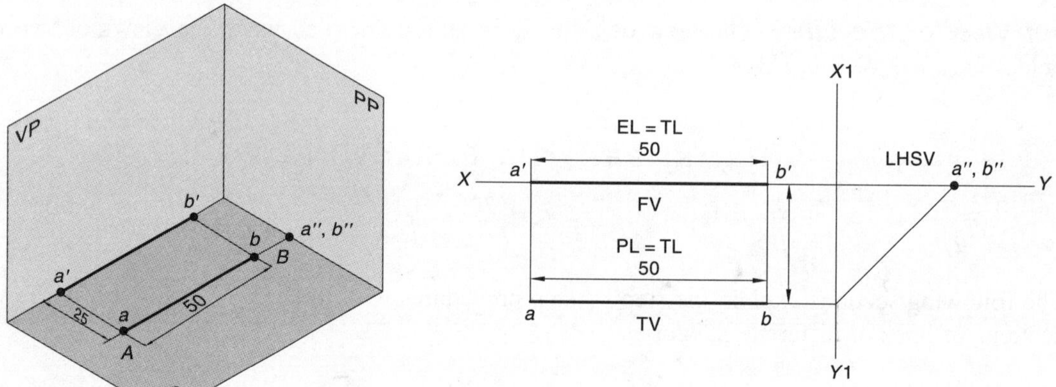

Fig. 11.2

11.4.3 Line in the VP and Away from the HP

Example 11.3 A line *AB*, 50 mm long, is in the VP and parallel to the HP. Draw the three views of the lines if its distance above the HP is 40 mm.

Solution Refer Fig. 11.3.

The FV and TV both will be parallel to *XY* and will show the TL. TV will be seen along *XY*. The LHSV is seen as a point view on *X*1 *Y*1.

11.4.4 Line Contained by Both the RPs

Example 11.4 A line *AB*, 50 mm long, is contained by both the HP and the VP. Draw its projections.

Solution Refer Fig. 11.4.

If the line is contained by both the RPs, it definitely lies on the intersection of the two RPs, i.e., on *XY*. Hence its FV and TV, both are seen along *XY*. SV is seen as a point view at the intersection of *XY* and *X*1 *Y*1.

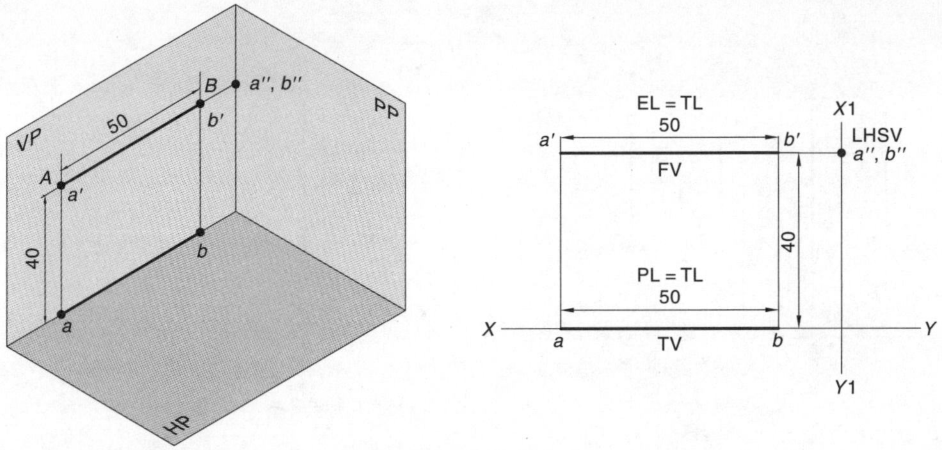

Fig. 11.3

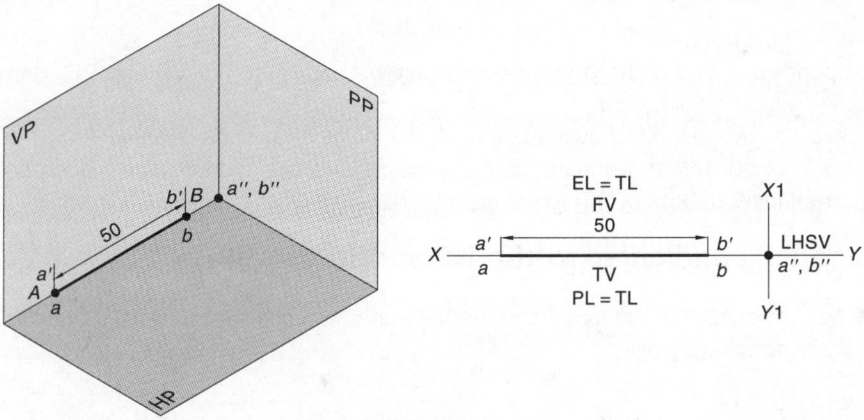

Fig. 11.4

REMEMBER THE FOLLOWING

- If a line is parallel to both the RPs, its TV and FV are seen parallel to *XY* and both are equal to the TL of the line.
- If a line is parallel to both the RPs, its SV is seen as point view.
- If a line is parallel to both the RPs and in one RP, its projection on the other RP is seen on *XY*.

11.5 LINE PERPENDICULAR TO EITHER OF THE RPs

11.5.1 Line Perpendicular to the HP and Away from the VP

Example 11.5 A line *AB*, 50 mm long, is perpendicular to the HP and 25 mm in front of the VP. Draw its projections if the end nearest to the HP is 10 mm above the HP.

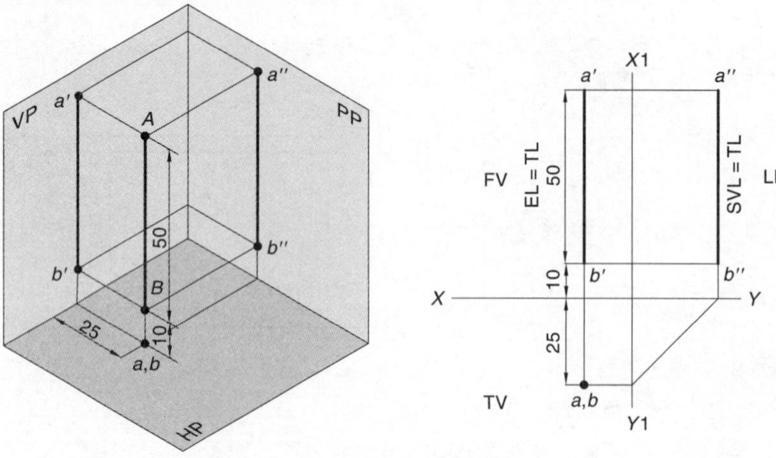

Fig. 11.5

Solution Refer Fig. 11.5.

If a line is perpendicular to the HP, it will automatically be parallel to the VP and PP. Hence, its FV will show the TL. TV will be a point view.

Wherever two (or more) points overlap, the visible point should be marked first. For example, in Fig. 11.5, TV is marked as *a,b*. It means that *a* is visible and *b* is hidden. The hidden point(s) may be enclosed in parenthesis (), e.g., *a*(*b*).

11.5.2 Line Perpendicular to the HP and in the VP

Example 11.6 A line *AB*, 50 mm long, is in the VP and perpendicular to the HP. Draw its projections if the end *B* is 10 mm above the HP.

Solution Refer Fig. 11.6.

FV will be perpendicular to *XY* and show the TL. TV will be a point view on *XY*.

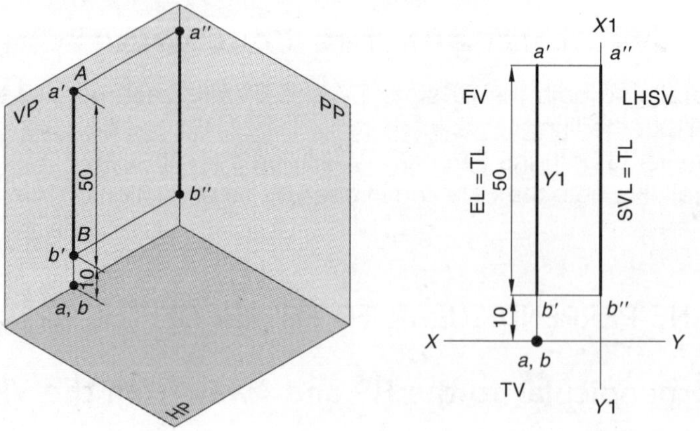

Fig. 11.6

11.5.3 Line Perpendicular to the VP and Away from the HP

Example 11.7 A line *AB*, 50 mm long, is perpendicular to the VP and is 40 mm above the HP. Draw its projections if the nearest end is 10 mm in front of the VP.

Solution Refer Fig. 11.7.

As the line *AB* is perpendicular to the VP, its TV will show the TL. FV will be a point view.

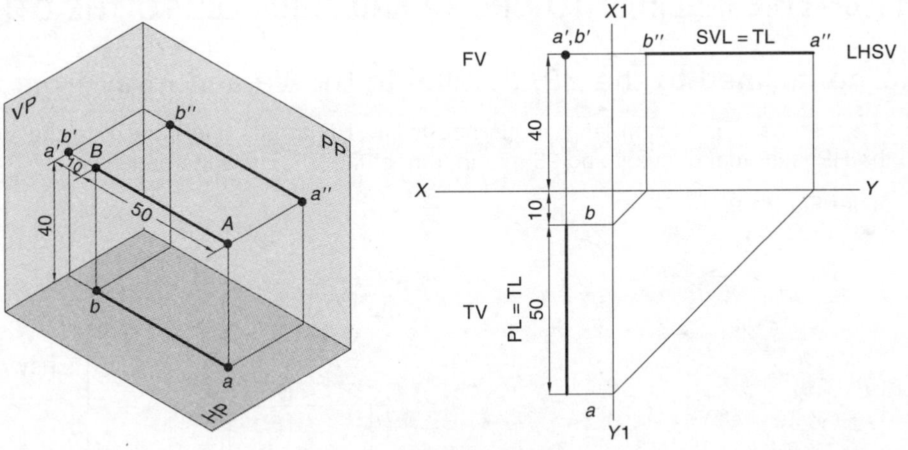

Fig. 11.7

11.5.4 Line Perpendicular to the VP and in the HP

Example 11.8 A line *AB*, 50 mm long, is in the HP and perpendicular to the VP. Draw its projections if the end *B* is 10 mm in front of the VP.

Solution Refer Fig. 11.8.

TV will be same as in the previous example. FV will be a point view on *XY*.

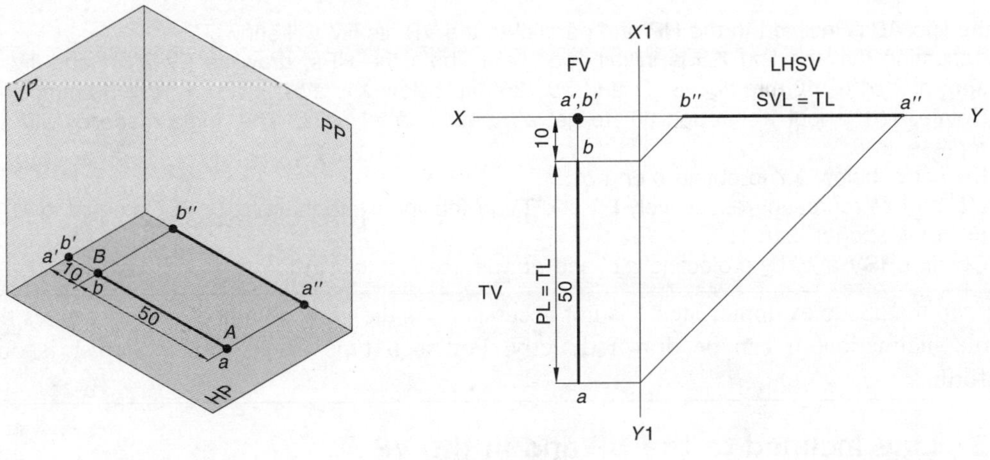

Fig. 11.8

REMEMBER THE FOLLOWING

If a line is perpendicular to a particular RP then
- it is automatically parallel to the other RP
- its view on that RP is always a point view

11.6 LINE INCLINED TO ONE RP AND PARALLEL TO THE OTHER

11.6.1 Line Inclined to the HP, Parallel to the VP and Away from the VP

Example 11.9 A line *AB*, 50 mm long, is inclined to the HP at 30° and parallel to the VP. The end nearest to the HP is 40 mm above it and 25 mm in front of the VP. Draw the projections.

Solution Refer Fig. 11.9.

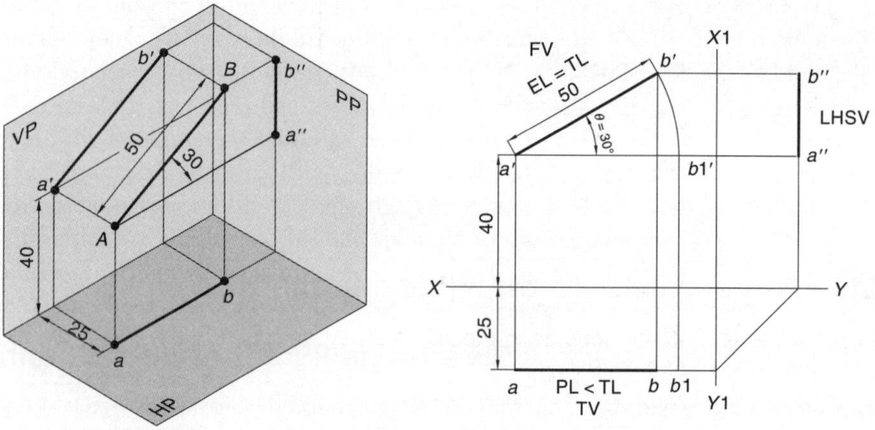

Fig. 11.9

As the line *AB* is inclined to the HP and parallel to the VP, its FV will show TL.

1. Assuming that the line *AB* is initially parallel to both the RPs, draw its FV *a′b*1′ and TV *ab*1 as shown. *a′b*1′ is 40 mm above *XY* and *ab*1 25 mm below *XY*. *a′b*1′ = *ab*1 = TL = 50 mm.
2. Rotate *a′b*1′ about *a′* through 30° to get *a′b′*. *a′b′* = *a′b*1′ = TL. The angle made by *a′b′* with *XY* represents θ.
3. Project *b′* below *XY* to obtain *b* on *ab*1.
   a′b′ and *ab* represent respectively FV and TV of the line. Note that *a′b′* (= EL) is equal to TL and *ab* (= PL) is shorter than TL.
4. Obtain LHSV *a″b″* by projecting *a′b′* and *ab* with respect to *X*1 *Y*1.

Note: In the above example, Step 1 is not necessary. As the view obtained in Step 2 gives the TL and true inclination, it can be drawn directly. For such type of problems, Step 1 is omitted henceforth.

11.6.2 Line Inclined to the HP and in the VP

Example 11.10 A line *AB*, 50 mm long, is inclined at 30° to the HP and in the VP. The end nearest to the HP is 40 mm above the HP. Draw the projections.

Solution Refer Fig. 11.10.

The line *AB* is in the VP and $\theta = 30°$. $h_a = +\ 40$ mm.

1. Draw FV *a′b′* = TL, inclined at 30° to *XY*. *a′* is 40 mm above *XY*.
2. Project *a′b′* on *XY* to obtain *ab*. *a′b′* and *ab* represent respectively FV and TV of the line.

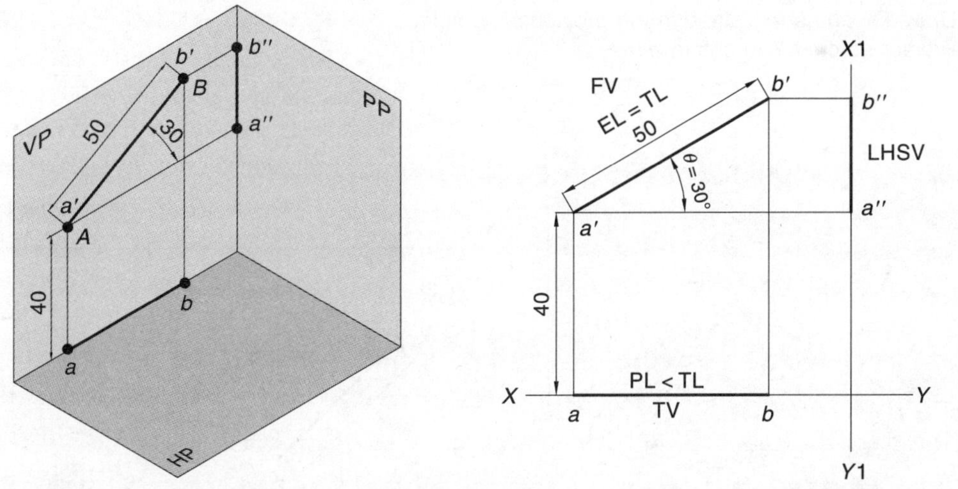

Fig. 11.10

11.6.3 Line Inclined to the VP, Parallel to the HP and away from the HP

Example 11.11 A line *AB*, 50 mm long, is inclined at 45° to the VP and parallel to the HP. The nearest end of the line is 25 mm in front of the VP. Draw the projections of the line if it is 40 mm above the HP.

Solution Refer Fig. 11.11.

1. Draw TV *ab* = TL, inclined at 45° to *XY*. *a* is 25 mm below *XY*.
2. Project *ab* above *XY* to obtain *a′b′*. *ab* and *a′b′* represent respectively TV and FV of the line.

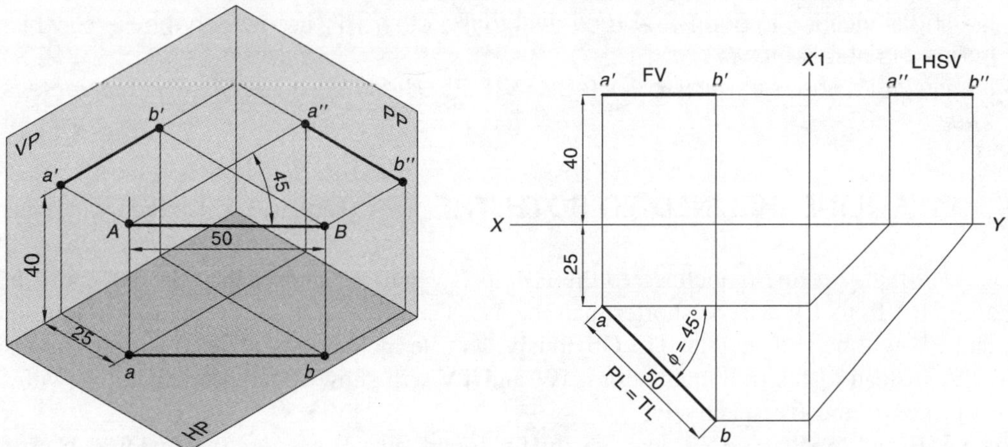

Fig. 11.11

11.6.4 Line in the HP and Inclined to the VP

Example 11.12 A line *AB*, 50 mm long, lies in the HP and makes an angle of 45° to the VP. Its end *A* is nearer to the VP and 25 mm in front of it. Draw the projections.

Solution Refer Fig. 11.12.

1. Draw TV *ab* as explained in the previous example.
2. Project *ab* on *XY* to obtain *a′b′*.

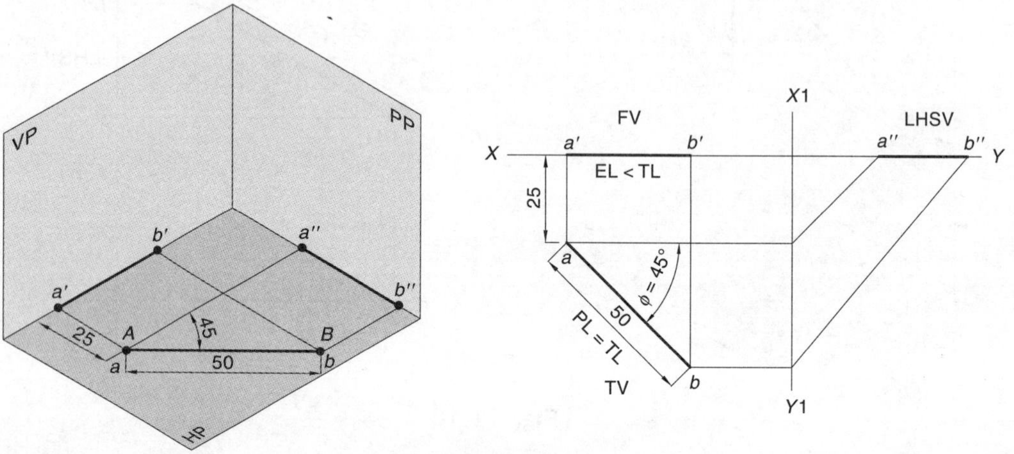

Fig. 11.12

Remember the Following

- If a line is parallel to a particular RP, its projection on that RP gives TL.
  - If a line is parallel to the HP, its TV will give TL.
  - If a line is parallel to the VP, its FV will give TL.
  - If a line is parallel to the PP, its SV will give TL.
- If a line is inclined to one RP and parallel to the other RP, its view on the RP to which it is inclined is parallel to *XY*.
- If a view of a line is parallel to *XY* (or *X*1 *Y*1), its other view gives TL. *The converse is also true.*

11.7 LINE INCLINED TO BOTH THE RPs (OBLIQUE LINE)

We have seen that if a line is inclined to the HP, its TV will be shorter than the TL and if a line is inclined to the VP, its FV will be shorter than the TL. Therefore, if a line is inclined to both the RPs, its TV and FV will be shorter than TL. Obviously, its true inclinations θ and ϕ will not be visible in FV and TV. Instead of the true inclinations, FV and TV will show apparent inclinations with the HP and the VP, i.e., α and β respectively.

Knowing θ and ϕ, PL and EL can easily be found out. However, the major concern in the projections of the oblique line is to obtain its apparent inclinations, α and β. This can be achieved in two stages as mentioned below.

Stage 1 Refer Fig. 11.13.

Assuming that a line (say $AB1$ = TL) is inclined to the HP at $\theta°$ and parallel to the VP, draw its projections $a'–b1'$ and $ab1$. $ab1$ will show PL. If the line is made inclined to the VP at any angle (keeping θ unchanged) then TV will no longer remain parallel to XY. It will get tilted through a specific angle. In such a case, if the TV is tilted about one of its endpoints (say a), its other end (i.e., $b1$) will trace a circle. This circle represents the locus of that point (i.e., $B1$) in TV. Note that, in FV, this circle is seen as a line parallel to XY. This line represents the locus of that point (i.e., $B1$) in FV. It is shown by $f–f$.

Now, suppose $ab1$ is tilted about a through, say $\beta1°$, in such a way that $b1$ occupies the new position b on the circle. ab now represents the TV of the line inclined to both the RPs. $\beta1$ will give the apparent angle between the line and the VP. Let the real angle corresponding to $\beta1$ be $\phi1$.

As soon as $b1$ moves to b, $b1'$ moves to b' along $f–f$. This is so because the circular path of $b1$ in TV is represented by linear path $f–f$ in FV. $a'b'$ now represents the FV of the line inclined to both the RPs. Let the angle made by $a'b'$ with XY is $\alpha1°$. $\alpha1°$ represents the apparent angle between the line and the HP.

Note that ab and $a'b'$ represent the final TV and final FV respectively of a line AB which is inclined to both the HP and the VP. To obtain these views, we must know TL, θ and ϕ. However, in this stage, ϕ was unknown.

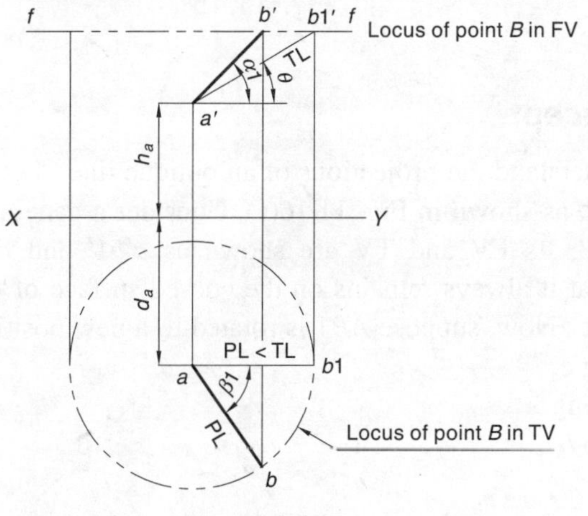

Fig. 11.13

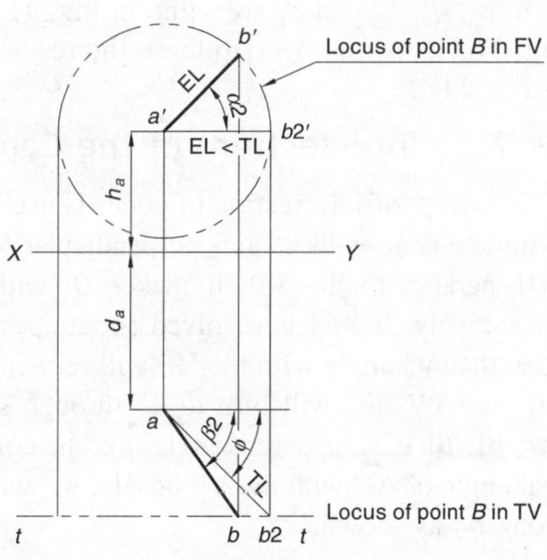

Fig. 11.14

Stage 2 Refer Fig. 11.14.

Assuming that a line (say $AB2$ = TL = $AB1$ in Stage 1) is inclined to the VP at $\phi°$ and parallel to the HP, draw its projections $ab2$ and $a'–b2'$. $a'–b2'$ will show EL. If the line is made inclined to the HP at any angle (keeping ϕ unchanged) then FV will get tilted through a specific angle. In such a case, if the FV is tilted about one of its endpoints (say a'), its other end (i.e., $b2'$) will trace a circle. This circle represents the locus of $B2$ in FV. In TV, this circle is seen as a line parallel to XY. This line represents the locus of $B2$ in TV. It is shown by $t–t$.

Now, suppose $a'b2'$ is tilted about a' through, say $\alpha2°$, in such a way that $b2'$ occupies new position b' on the circle. $a'b'$ now represents the FV of the line inclined to both the RPs. $\alpha2$ will give the apparent angle between the line and the HP. Let the real angle corresponding to $\alpha2$ be $\theta2$.

As soon as $b2'$ moves to b', $b2$ moves to b along *t–t*. *ab* now represents the TV of the line inclined to both the RPs. Let the angle made by *ab* with *XY* be $\beta 2°$. $\beta 2°$ will represent the apparent angle between the line and the VP.

$a'b'$ and *ab* represent the final FV and final TV respectively of a line *AB* which is inclined to both the HP and the VP. To obtain these views, we must know TL, ϕ and θ. However, in this stage, θ was unknown.

In Stage 1 (Fig. 11.13), we have obtained the FV and TV of line *AB* inclined at $\theta°$ to the HP and $\phi 1°$ to the VP. Similarly, in Stage 2 (Fig. 11.14), we have obtained the FV and TV of line *AB* inclined at $\theta 2°$ to the HP and $\phi°$ to the VP. Note that, in both the stages, the line *AB* has same TL. We knew θ in Stage 1 and ϕ in Stage 2. If $\theta = \theta 2$ and $\phi 1 = \phi$ then $\alpha 1 = \alpha 2$ and $\beta 1 = \beta 2$. If end *A* is at same distances from the HP and the VP in both the stages the end *B* will assume same positions in both the stages. As all the parameters, namely, TL, θ, ϕ, h_a, d_a, h_b and d_b are same in Fig. 11.13 and Fig. 11.14, we can overlap these figures as shown in Fig. 11.15.

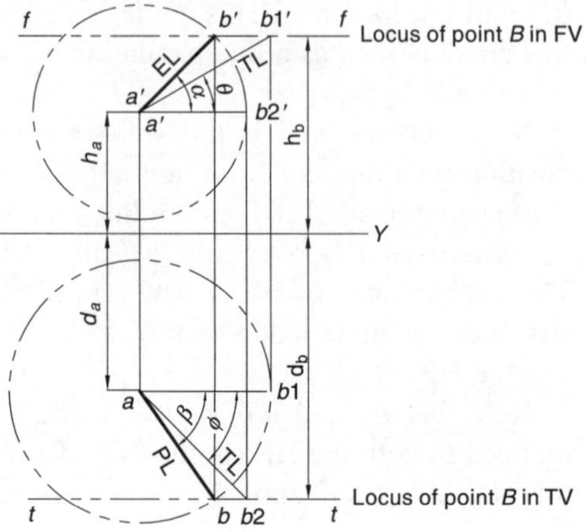

Fig. 11.15

11.7.1 Intersections of the Cones Concept

The concept of intersection of cones is useful to understand the projections of an oblique line. Let us assume a cone with its axis perpendicular to the HP, as shown in Fig. 11.16(a). Consider a generator *AB*1 parallel to the VP. It makes $\theta°$ with the HP. Its FV and TV are shown as $a'b1'$ and *ab*1 respectively. If *AB*1 is revolved about apex *A* so that it always remains on the curved surface of the cone then its angle with the HP will remain constant. Now, suppose *AB*1 is rotated to a new position *AB* then TV *ab*1 will turn to *ab* through some angle, say, $\beta 1$. $\beta 1$ is an apparent angle. Let the corresponding real angle of AB with the VP be $\phi 1°$. $b1'$ will shift to b' along *f–f* as shown.

Now, consider another cone with its axis perpendicular to the VP as shown in Fig. 11.16(b). The generator *AB*2 is parallel to the HP. It makes $\phi°$ with the VP. Its TV and FV are shown as *ab*2 and $a'b2'$ respectively. If *AB*2 is rotated along the curved surface of the cone so that it occupies a new position *AB* then FV $a'b2'$ will turn to $a'b'$ through some angle, say, $\alpha 2$. $\alpha 2$ is an apparent angle. Let the corresponding real angle of *AB* with the HP be $\theta 2°$. *b*2 will shift to *b* along *t–t* as shown.

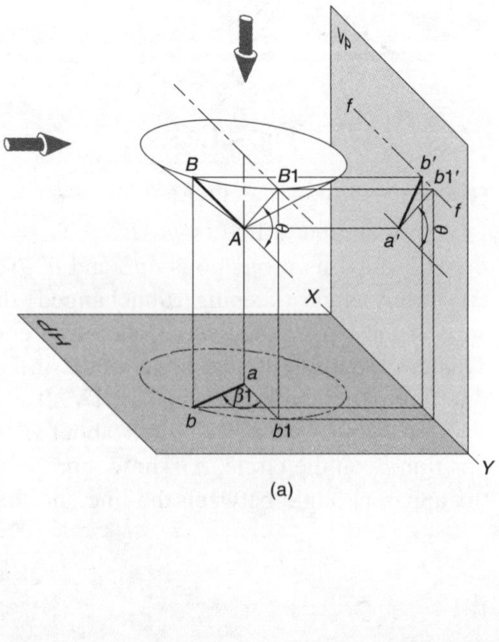

(a)

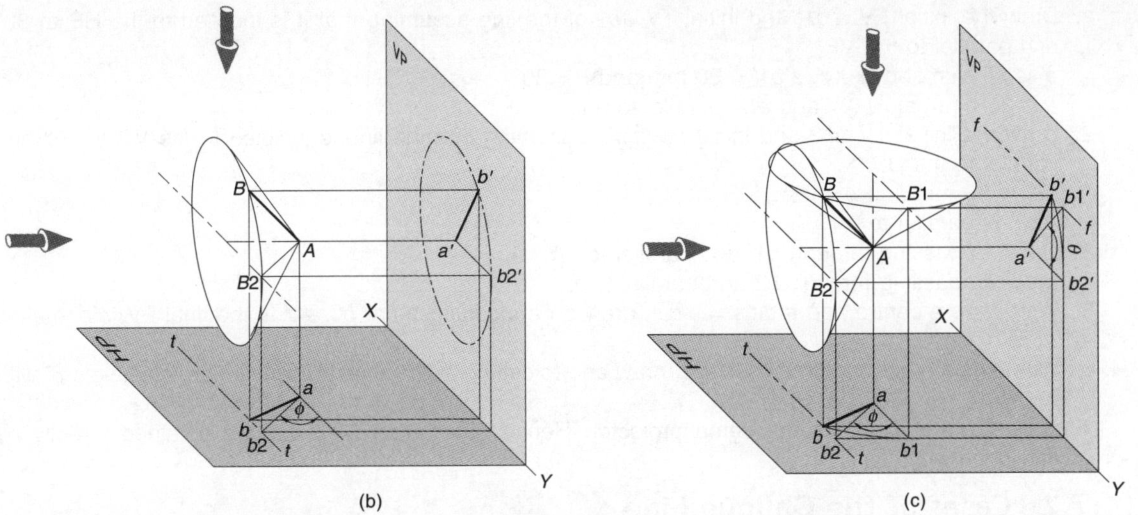

Fig. 11.16

If *AB* is same in both the cases, i.e., *AB* = *AB*1 = *AB*2, then it will lie at the intersection of the two cones, as shown in Fig. 11.16(c). It is the line which makes $\theta°$ with the HP and $\phi°$ to the VP.

The projections of an oblique line is further explained in the following example.

Example 11.13 A line *AB*, 50 mm long, is inclined to the HP at 30° and to the VP at 45°. The point *A* is 20 mm above the HP and 35 mm in front of the VP. Draw the projections of the line. Assume that the end *A* is nearer to both the RPs than end *B*.

Given: TL = 50 $\theta = 30°$ $\phi = 45°$ $h_a = +20$ $d_a = +35$

Solution Refer Fig. 11.17.

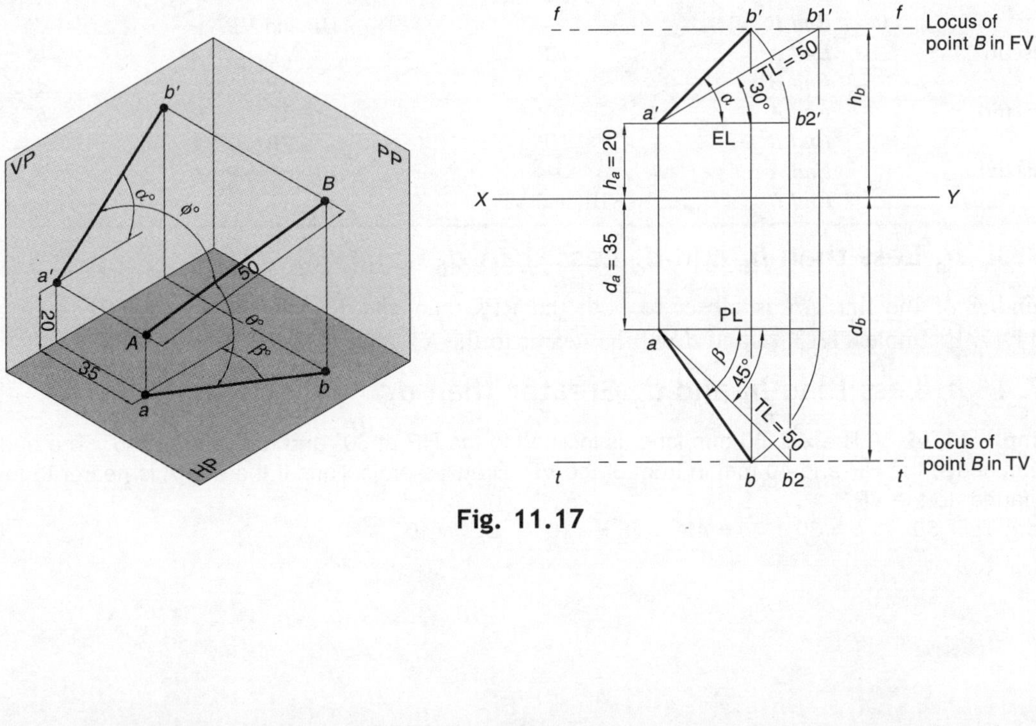

Fig. 11.17

1. Draw the initial FV $a'b1'$ and initial TV $ab1$ of the line assuming that it is inclined to the HP at 30° and parallel to the VP.
   a' is 20 mm above XY, $a'b1' = 50$ mm and $\theta = 30°$.
   a is 35 mm below XY and $ab1$ parallel to XY.
2. Draw the initial TV $ab2$ and initial FV $a'b2'$ assuming that the line is inclined to the VP at 45° and parallel to the HP.
   $ab2 = 50$ mm and $\phi = 45°$.
   $a'b2'$ is parallel to XY.
3. Draw f–f passing through $b1'$ and parallel to XY.
4. Draw t–t passing through $b2$ and parallel to XY.
5. With a' as a centre and radius = $a'b2'$, draw an arc cutting f–f at b'. $a'b'$ is the final FV. $a'b'$ makes $\alpha°$ with XY.
6. With a as a centre and radius = $ab1$, draw an arc cutting t–t at b. ab is the final TV. ab makes $\beta°$ with XY.

Note that b' and b lie on the same projector. Hence, after Step 5, b can be obtained directly by projecting b' on t–t.

11.7.2 Cases of the Oblique Line

An oblique line may have different orientations in space depending on the values of θ and ϕ. All the possible orientations of the oblique line can be studied with the help of the following four cases:

Case (i): h_a less than h_b and d_a less than d_b
Case (ii): h_a less than h_b and d_a greater than d_b
Case (iii): h_a greater than h_b and d_a less than d_b
Case (iv): h_a greater than h_b and d_a greater than d_b

The above cases are summarized in Table 11.1.

Table 11.1 Cases of the Oblique Line

		Nearer to	*Away from*	*Remark*
Case(i)	***End A***	HP and VP	—	$h_a < h_b$
	End B	—	HP and VP	$d_a < d_b$
Case(ii)	***End A***	HP	VP	$h_a < h_b$
	End B	VP	HP	$d_a > d_b$
Case(iii)	***End A***	VP	HP	$h_a > h_b$
	End B	HP	VP	$d_a < d_b$
Case(iv)	***End A***	—	HP and VP	$h_a > h_b$
	End B	HP and VP	—	$d_a > d_b$

11.7.3 h_a Less than h_b and d_a Less than d_b

The end A of the line AB is closer to both the RPs than end B. Such a line will be seen as in Fig. 11.17, Example 11.13. a' and a will be nearer to the XY than b' and b respectively.

11.7.4 h_a Less than h_b and d_a Greater than d_b

Example 11.14 A line AB, 50 mm long, is inclined to the HP at 30° and to the VP at 45°. The end A is 10 mm above the HP and 40 mm in front of the VP. Draw its projections if the end A is nearer to the HP and farther to the VP.

Given: TL = 50 $\quad \theta = 30° \quad \phi = 45° \quad h_a = +10 \quad d_a = +40$

Solution Refer Fig. 11.18.

The projections may be obtained by adopting the steps mentioned in Example 11.13. As the point *A* is nearer to the HP than point *B*, *a′b*1′ is drawn in such a way that *b*1′ will be away from *XY*. Similarly, as the point *B* is nearer to the VP than point *A*, *ab*2 is drawn in such a way that *b*2 will be near to *XY*. Therefore, *t–t* is closer to *XY*. The remaining procedure is the same as in the previous example.

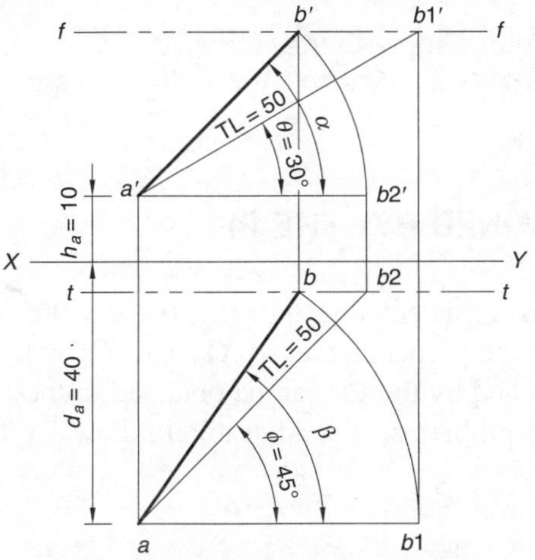

Fig. 11.18

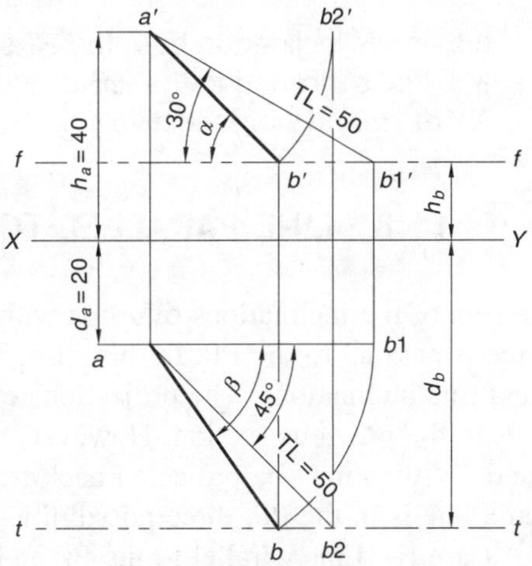

Fig. 11.19

11.7.5 h_a Greater than h_b and d_a Less than d_b

Example 11.15 A line *AB*, 50 mm long, has its end *A* at 40 mm above the HP and 20 mm in front of the VP. The end *B* is closer to the HP but away from the VP. Draw the projections of the line if it is inclined to the HP at 30° and to the VP at 45°.

Given: TL = 50 $\theta = 30°$ $\phi = 45°$ $h_a = +40$ $d_a = +20$

Solution Refer Fig. 11.19.

As the point *B* is closer to the HP than point *A*, *a′b*1′ is drawn in such a way that *b*1′ will be nearer to *XY*. Therefore, *f–f* is closer to *XY*. Also, as the point *B* is away from the VP than point *A*, *ab*2 is drawn in such a way that *b*2 will be farther to *XY*. The remaining procedure is the same as in Example 11.13.

11.7.6 h_a Greater than h_b and d_a Greater than d_b

Example 11.16 A line *AB*, 50 mm long, has its end *A* away from the HP and the VP than end *B*. The line is inclined to the HP at 30° and to the VP at 45°. Draw the projections if end *A* is 35 mm above the HP and 50 mm in front of the VP.

Given: TL = 50 $\theta = 30°$ $\phi = 45°$ $h_a = +35$ $d_a = +50$

Solution Refer Fig. 11.20.

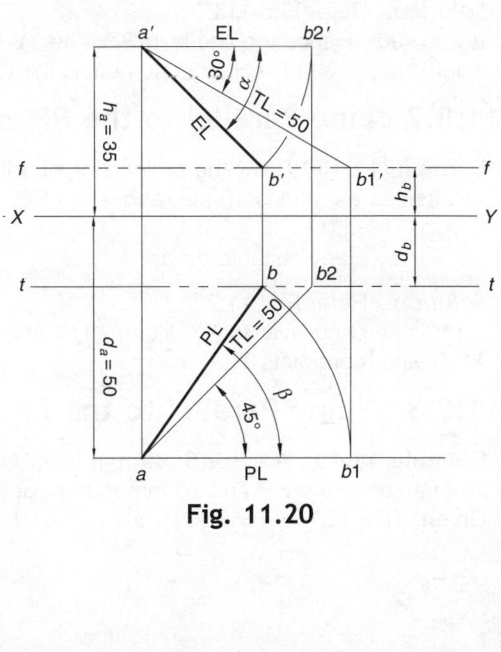

Fig. 11.20

As the point A is away from the HP than point B, $a'b1'$ is drawn in such a way that a' will be away from XY. Therefore, f–f is closer to XY. Also, as the point A is farther to the VP than point B, $ab2$ is drawn in such a way that a will be away from XY. Hence, t–t is closer to XY.

REMEMBER THE FOLLOWING

- If a line is inclined to both the RPs, its FV and TV are seen shorter than TL.
- If a line is inclined to the HP at $\theta°$ and to the VP at $\phi°$, its FV and TV are seen inclined to XY at $\alpha°$ and $\beta°$ respectively.

11.8 LINE PARALLEL TO (OR CONTAINED BY) THE PP

If the sum of the inclinations of a line with the HP and the VP is equal to 90°, i.e., $\theta + \phi = 90°$, then the line is parallel to the PP. In this case, TV and FV will be perpendicular to XY. The SV will give TL and true inclinations. The projections of the line contained by the PP can be obtained in the same way as in the previous section. However, for such type of problems, it is advisable to draw SV first. FV and TV then may be projected back from the SV.
When a line is in the PP, three possibilities exist:

Case (i): Line parallel to the PP and the HP

Case (ii): Line parallel to the PP and the VP

Case (iii): Line parallel to the PP and inclined to the HP and the VP

Case (i) and Case (ii) above are similar to Case (iii)/Case (iv) and Case (i)/Case (ii) of Category 2 respectively. All the three cases are explained below with the help of examples.

11.8.1 Line Parallel to the PP and the HP

Example 11.17 Draw the projections of a line AB, 50 mm long, which lies in the PP and parallel to the HP. Its nearest end is 10 mm in front of the VP. Assume any suitable distance of the line above the HP.
Given: TL = 50 $\theta = 0$ $\phi = 90°$ h_a = any suitable distance $d_b = +10$

Solution Refer Fig. 11.21.
$\theta + \phi = 90°$. Hence the line is in PP. The TV is perpendicular to XY, along $X1Y1$ and denotes TL. FV is a point view on $X1Y1$. LHSV is perpendicular to $X1Y1$ and represents TL.

11.8.2 Line Parallel to the PP and the VP

Example 11.18 Draw the projections of a line AB, 50 mm long, which lies in the PP and parallel to the VP. Its nearest end is 10 mm above the HP. Assume any suitable distance of the line in front of the VP.
Given: TL = 50 $\theta = 90°$ $\phi = 0$ $h_b = +10$
d_a = any suitable distance

Solution Refer Fig. 11.22.
FV is perpendicular to XY, along $X1Y1$ and denotes TL. TV is a point view on $X1Y1$. LHSV is parallel to $X1Y1$ and represents TL.

11.8.3 Line Parallel to the PP and Inclined to the HP and the VP

Example 11.19 A line AB, 50 mm long, is inclined at 30° to the HP and 60° to the VP. Its end A is 25 mm above the HP and 20 mm in front of the VP. Draw its projections.
Given: TL = 50 $\theta = 30°$ $\phi = 60°$ $h_a = +25$ $d_a = +20$

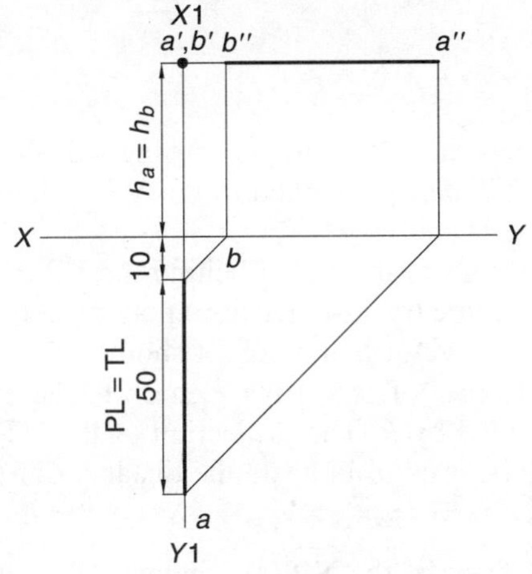

Fig. 11.21

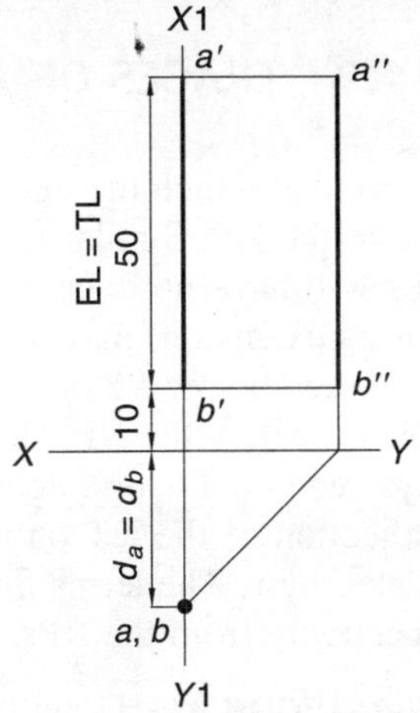

Fig. 11.22

Solution As $\theta + \phi = 90°$, the line is parallel to (or in) the PP.

Method 1: Refer Fig. 11.23(a).

1. Assuming the line inclined at 30° to the HP and parallel to the VP, draw its FV *a′b*1′ and TV *ab*1 as shown.
2. Assuming the line inclined at 60° to the VP and parallel to the HP, draw its TV *ab*2 and FV *a′b*2′ as shown.
3. Draw *f–f* and *t–t*.
4. With *a′* as a centre and radius = *a′b*2′, draw an arc meeting *f–f* at *b′*. Join *a′b′* for the final FV.
5. With *a* as a centre and radius = *ab*1, draw an arc meeting *t–t* at *b*. Join *ab* for the final TV.
   Note that the arcs *b*2′*b′* and *b*1*b* are tangent to *f–f* and *t–t* respectively. Hence $\alpha = \beta = 90°$

Method 2: Refer Fig. 11.23(b).

As the line is in the PP, its SV will give TL and true inclinations. Hence, first draw SV *a″b″* as shown. Then obtain its FV *a′b′* and TV *ab* by projecting the SV on *X*1*Y*1.

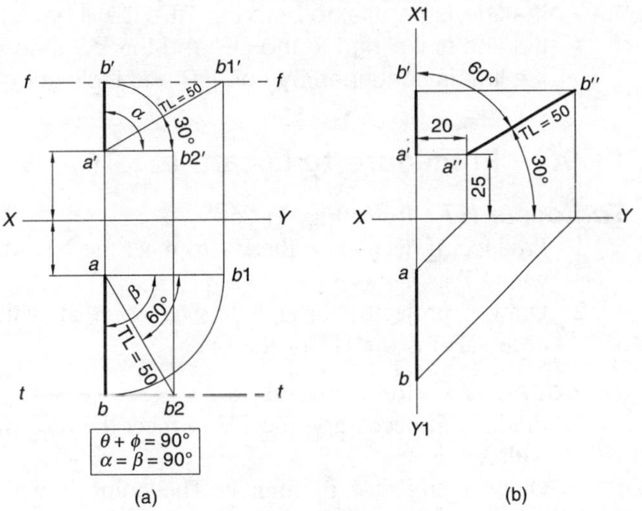

Fig. 11.23

Remember the Following

- If $\theta + \phi = 90°$, the line lies in the PP.
- If a line is in the PP then
  - its SV gives TL and true inclinations
  - $\alpha = \beta = 90°$

11.9 TRACES OF A LINE

A trace is a point at which the line or its extension meets the HP or the VP. A line will show an HT if it is inclined to the HP. Similarly, a line will show a VT if it is inclined to the VP. A line parallel to both the RPs will have no trace.

A line (or its extension) may meet the HP either in front of the VP or behind the VP. Accordingly, its HT will be seen below *XY* or above *XY*. Similarly, a line (or its extension) may meet the VP either above the HP or below the HP. Hence, its VT will be above or below *XY*. It should be noted that the HT is always seen on TV or extension of TV, whereas the VT is always seen on FV or extension of FV. The projection of the HT on the *XY* line is indicated by *h*. The projection of the VT on the *XY* line is indicated by *v*. The terms *h*-HT and *v*-VT may be used to indicate the distances of the HT and the VT respectively from the RPs.

Sign Conventions *h*-HT will be (+) if HT is in front of the VP (i.e., below *XY*) and (–) if it is behind the VP (i.e., above *XY*). Similarly, *v*-VT will be (+) if VT is above the HP (i.e., above *XY*) and (–) if it is below the HP (i.e., below *XY*).

REMEMBER THE FOLLOWING

- If a line is parallel to both the RPs it will have no trace.
- If a line is inclined to the HP and the VP then it will have both HT and VT.
- If a line is contained by one RP and inclined to the other than its trace will be seen on the *XY* line.

11.9.1 Procedure to Locate the Traces

To Locate HT Refer Fig. 11.25.

1. Produce, if necessary, the FV to meet the *XY*. Mark the point of intersection of FV (produced) with *XY* as *h*.
2. Draw a projector through *h*. The point at which this projector meets the TV (produced if necessary) is the HT of the line.

To Locate VT Refer Fig. 11.26.

1. Produce, if necessary, the TV to meet the *XY*. Mark the point of intersection of TV (produced) with *XY* as *v*.
2. Draw a projector through *v*. The point at which this projector meets the FV (produced if necessary) is the VT of the line.

11.9.2 Traces of the Line Parallel to Both the RPs

If a line is parallel to both the RPs then it will have no trace.

11.9.3 Traces of the Line Perpendicular to an RP

If a line *AB* is perpendicular to the HP, it will have only HT which is seen overlapping on TV *a*(*b*). Similarly, if a line *CD* is perpendicular to the VP, its VT will be seen overlapping on FV *c*′(*d*′), Fig. 11.24.

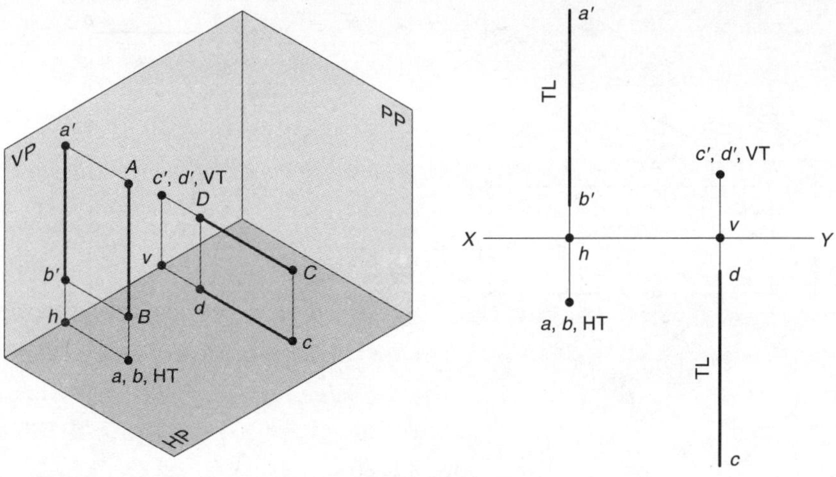

Fig. 11.24

11.9.4 Traces of the Line Inclined to One RP and Parallel to Other

Line Inclined to the HP and Parallel to the VP If a line *AB* is inclined to the HP and parallel to the VP then it will have only HT, Fig. 11.25. Produce *a′b′* to meet *XY* at *h*. Project *h* on *ab* produced to locate HT. If a line lies in the VP then its HT will be on *XY*. *h* will coincide with HT.

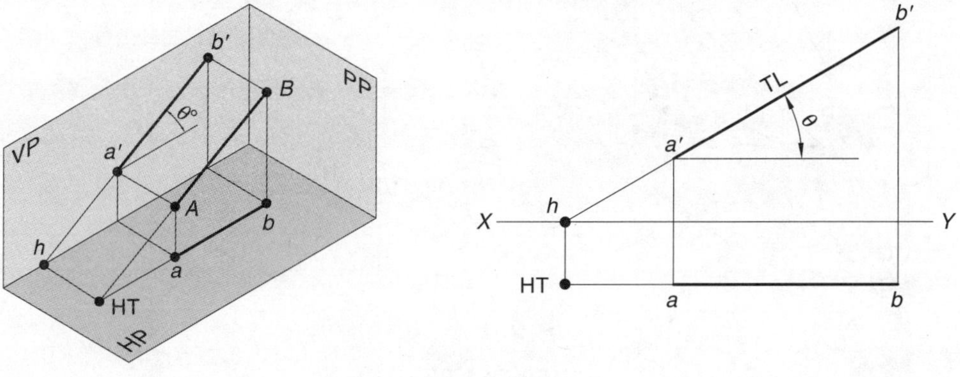

Fig. 11.25

Line Inclined to the VP and Parallel to the HP If a line *AB* is inclined to the VP and parallel to the HP then it will have only VT, Fig. 11.26. Extend *ab* to meet *XY* at *v*. Project *v* to VT on *a′b′* produced. If a line lies in the HP then its VT will coincide with *v* on *XY*.

11.9.5 Traces of the Line Inclined to Both the RPs

If the ends of line *AB* are away from both the RPs then the traces are obtained as in Fig. 11.27. Extend FV *a′b′* to meet *XY* at *h*. Project *h* to HT on TV *ab* produced. Mark *v* at the intersection of *XY* and TV *ab* produced. Project *v* to VT on FV *a′b′* produced. Note that, in the present case, VT is on the VP below the HP.

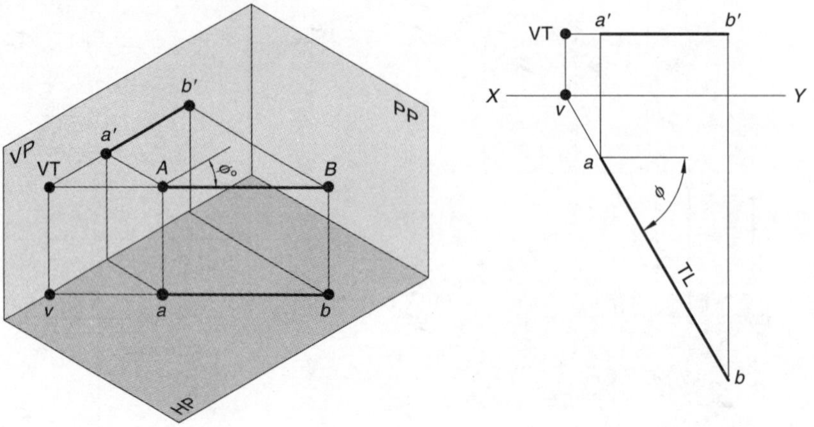

Fig. 11.26

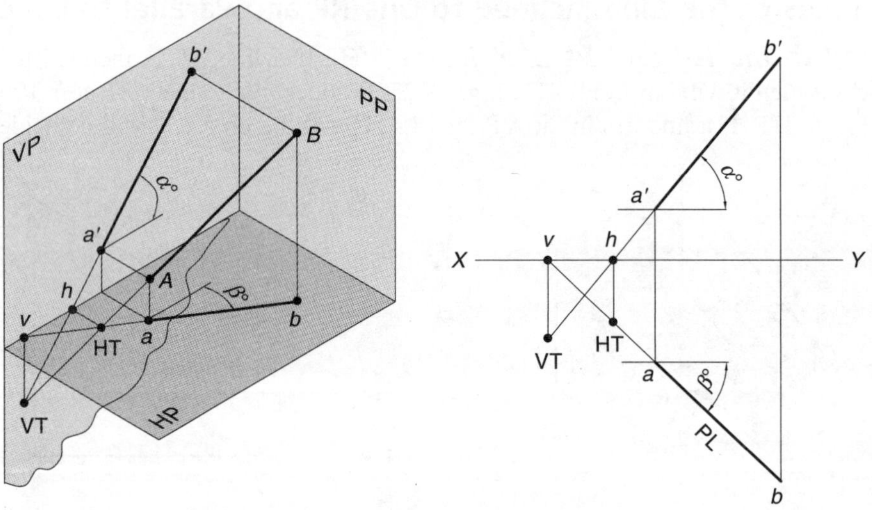

Fig. 11.27

If the end *A* of a line *AB* is in both the RPs then its HT and VT will coincide with *a* and *a′* on the *XY* Fig. 11.28. If the end *A* of a line *AB* is in the VP and the end *B* in the HP then its VT will coincide with *a′* and its HT with *b*, Fig. 11.29.

11.9.6 Traces of the Line Contained by the PP

First draw the SV-*a″b″*, Fig. 11.30. SV is then extended to meet *X*1*Y*1 and *XY* at VT and *h″* respectively. *h″* is then projected through an arc on TV, i.e., *ba* produced, to obtain HT. Note that HT is on extended TV whereas VT is on extended FV.

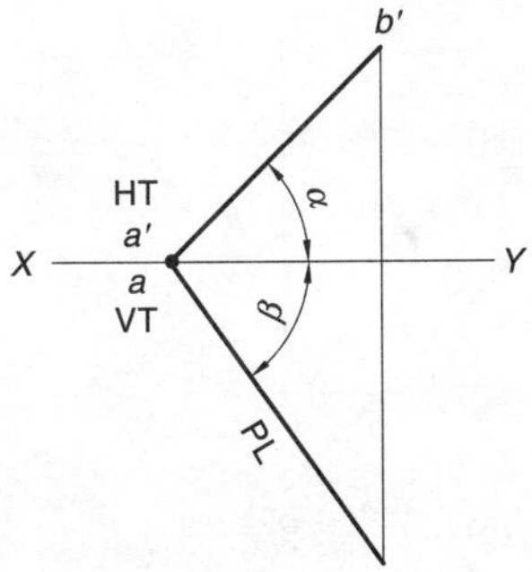

Fig. 11.28

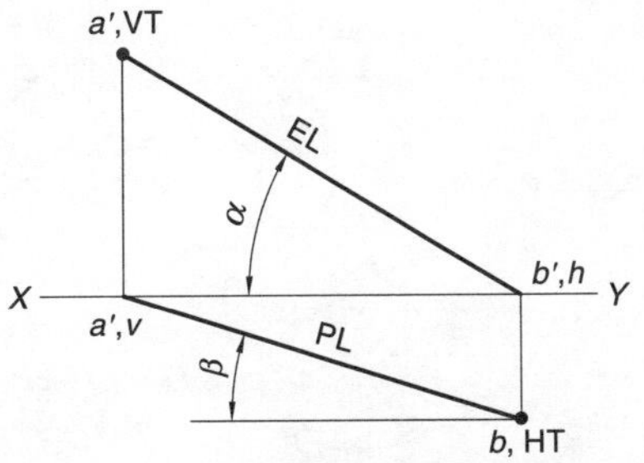

Fig. 11.29

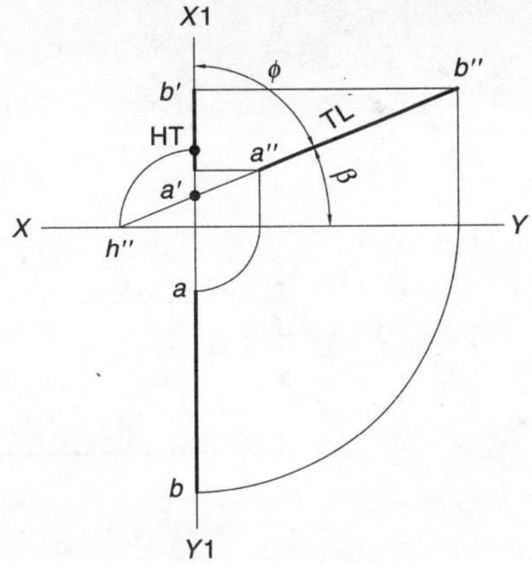

Fig. 11.30

11.10 GENERALISATION OF PROJECTIONS OF LINES

We will now see the general procedure to draw the projections of an oblique line. Though it has already been discussed in Section 11.7, we will revise it here to draw the projections and HT and VT. The procedure can be applied to any line having any position with respect to the HP and the VP, i.e., category 2 to category 5. The projections are obtained for a line *AB* whose TL, θ, ϕ, h_a and d_a are given.

Refer Fig. 11.31(a) for steps 1–3 below:

1. Mark *a′* and *a* at a distance of h_a and d_a from *XY*.
2. Draw *a′b*1′ equal to TL and inclined at $\theta°$ to *XY*.
3. Project *a′b*1′ below *XY* to obtain *ab*1 parallel to *XY*. It represents PL.

Refer Fig. 11.31(b) for steps 4–5 below:

4. Draw *ab*2 equal to TL and inclined at $\phi°$ to *XY*.
5. Project *ab*2 above *XY* to obtain *a′b*2′ parallel to *XY*. It represents EL.

Refer Fig. 11.31(c) for steps 6–8 below:

6. Draw *f–f* through *b*1′ and *t–t* through *b*2 parallel to *XY*.
7. With point *a′* as a centre and radius *a′b*2′, draw an arc cutting *f–f* at *b′*. Join *a′b′* to represent the FV of line *AB*.
8. With point *a* as a centre and radius *ab*1, draw an arc cutting *t–t* at *b*. Join *ab* to represent the TV of line AB.

Refer Fig. 11.31(d) for steps 9–12 to locate HT and VT.

9. Extend *b′a′* to meet *XY* at *h*.
10. Extend *ba* to meet *XY* at *v*.
11. Project *h* on extended *ba* to locate HT.
12. Project *v* on extended *b′a′* to locate VT.

Figure 11.31(d) shows 15 terms: TL, PL, EL, θ, ϕ, α, β, *h*–HT, *v*–VT, h_a, d_a, h_b, d_b, *x* and *X*.

The term '*x*' is used to indicate the distance between the end projectors of the line, i.e., the projectors through *A* and *B*. The term '*X*' is used to indicate the distance between the projectors passing through HT and VT.

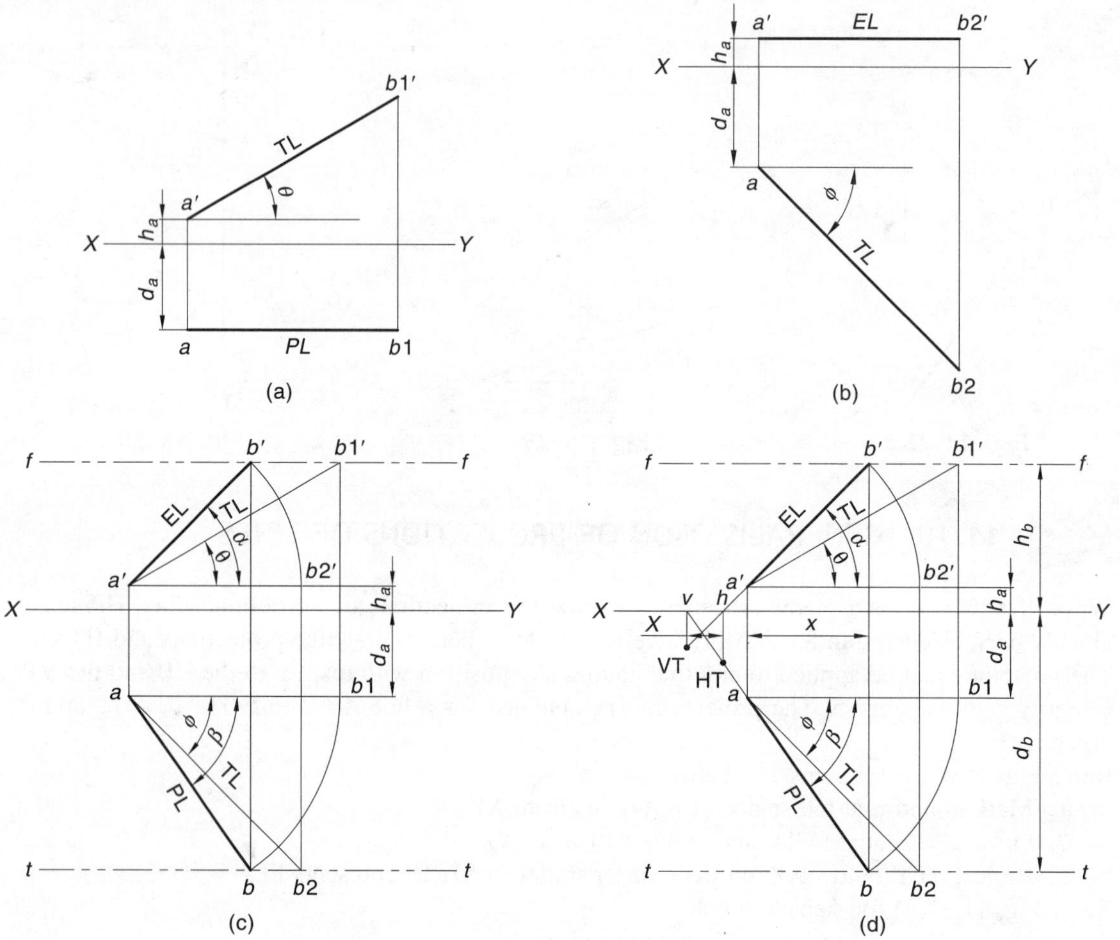

Fig. 11.31

The projectors through any point, say P, is represented by $\widehat{P}$. Thus, $\widehat{\text{HT}}$ and $\widehat{\text{VT}}$ mean the projectors through HT and VT respectively. The terms $\widehat{A}$-$\widehat{B}$ and $\widehat{\text{HT}}-\widehat{\text{VT}}$ denote the perpendicular distances between the respective projectors and may be used in place of x and X respectively.

In addition to the above 15 terms, few more, like $\widehat{A}-\widehat{\text{HT}}$, $\widehat{B}-\widehat{\text{VT}}$, etc., may be added. The distances of the ends of a line from the PP, i.e., p_a and p_b may also be given sometimes.

11.11 GENERALISATION: VARIOUS CASES

In Section 11.7 (Examples 11.13 to 11.16) we have seen various cases of projections of an oblique line lying fully in the first quadrant. If the line lies fully in the third quadrant or partly in two or three quadrants then the projections will be seen in different ways. For example, if a line is in the third quadrant, its FV will be below XY and TV will be above XY. Table 11.2 shows general models for various cases of the oblique line.

Table 11.2 Oblique Lines in the First and Third Quadrants

		Case (i) $h_a < h_b$ $d_a < d_b$	Case (ii) $h_a < h_b$ $d_a > d_b$	Case (iii) $h_a > h_b$ $d_a < d_b$	Case (iv) $h_a > h_b$ $d_a > d_b$
***Line inclined to both the RPs* (Category 4)**	*Line in the first quadrant*	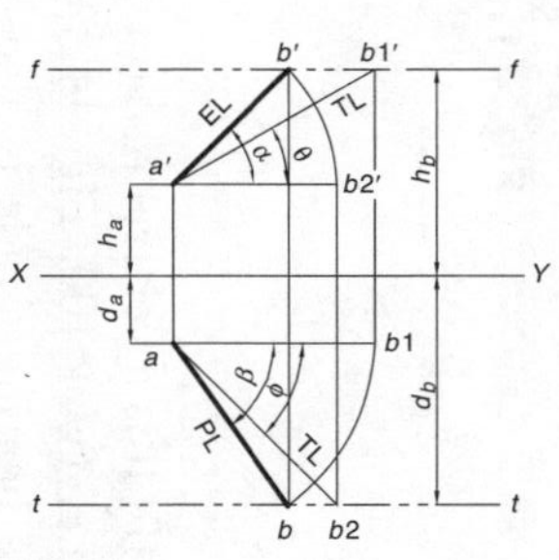	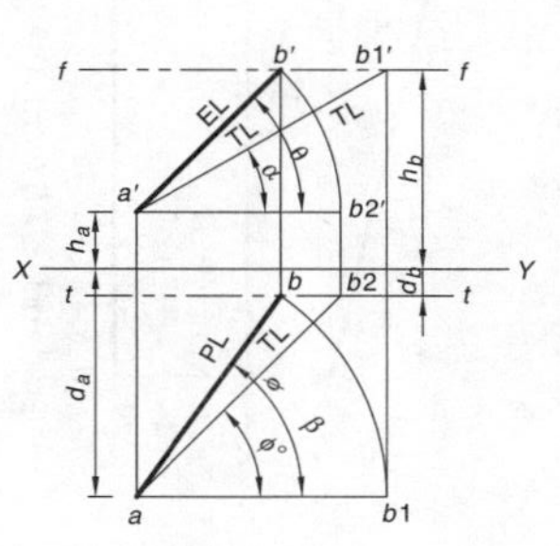	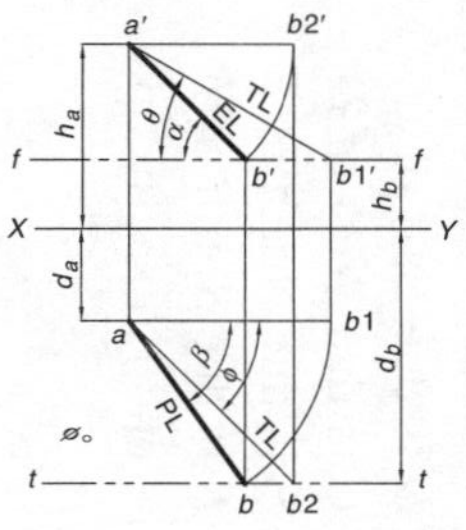	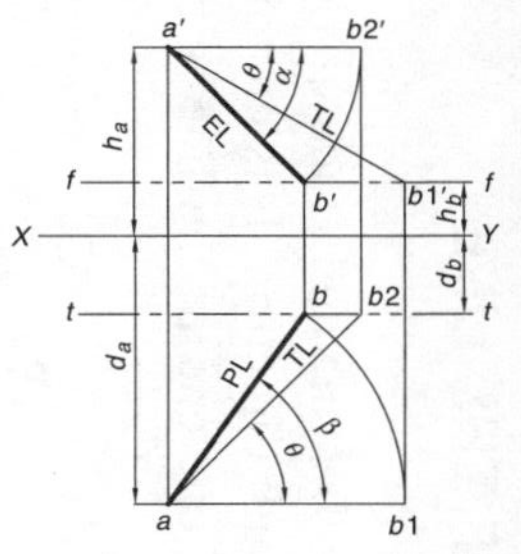
	Line in the third quadrant	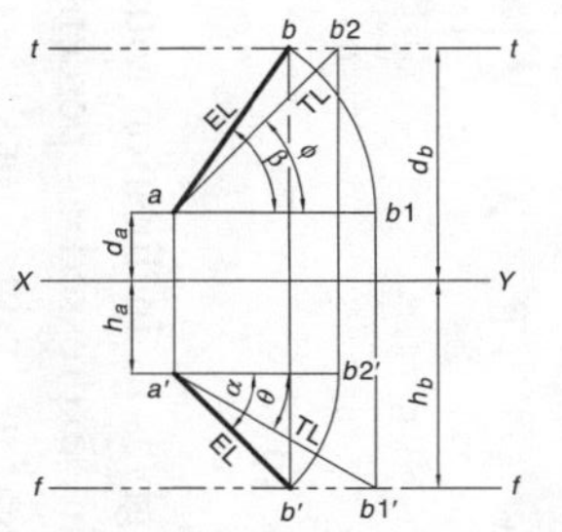	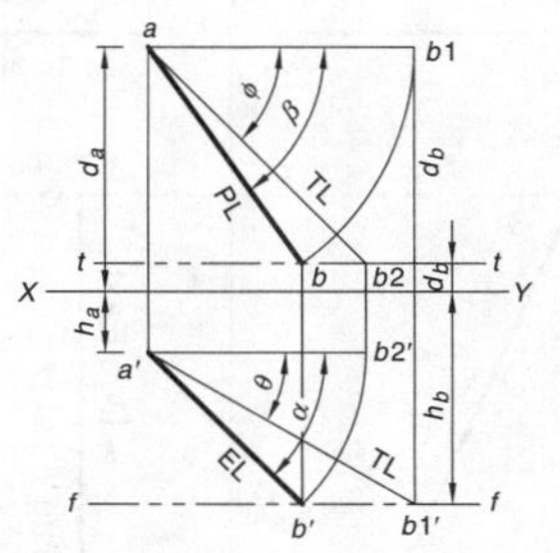	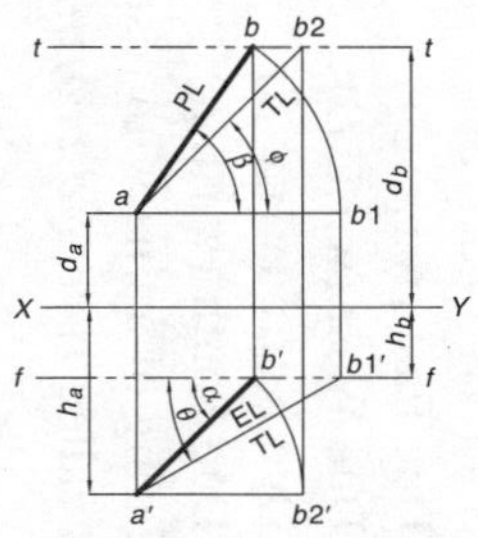	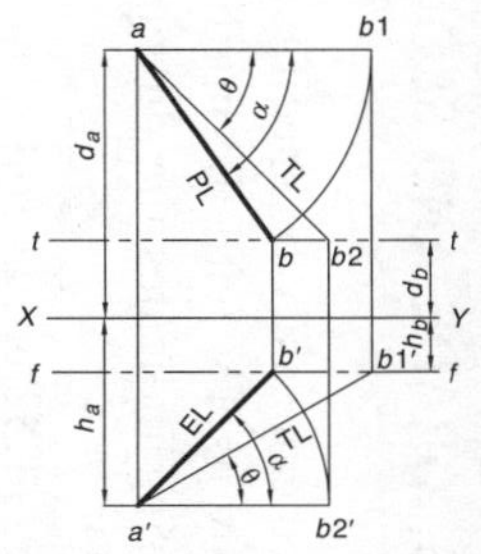

11.12 BEARING, GRADE AND SLOPE OF THE LINE

The orientation of a line in space can easily be specified by its bearing and grade or slope. *Bearing* of a line is the acute angle made by its TV with the north or south direction. It is customary to assume north vertically upward. A bearing indicates the direction of one end of the line with respect to the other.

The bearings of the lines in Fig. 11.32 are as follows:

		Bearings	*Meaning*
(a)	Line *AB*	N 45° E (w.r.t. *A*)	*B* is due 45° East of North of *A*
		S 45° W (w.r.t. *B*)	*A* is due 45° West of South of *B*
(b)	Line *CD*	Due East (w.r.t. *C*)	*D* is due East of *C*
		Due West (w.r.t. *D*)	*C* is due West of *D*
(c)	Line *EF*	Due North (w.r.t. *E*)	*F* is due North of *E*
		Due South (w.r.t. *F*)	*E* is due South of *F*

It should be noted that the bearing of a line with respect to one end is exactly opposite to that with respect to the other end. This is called *reversed bearing*.

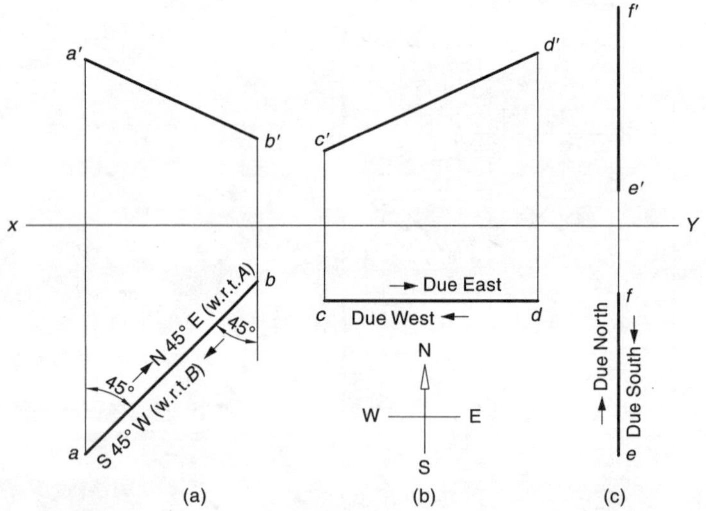

Fig. 11.32

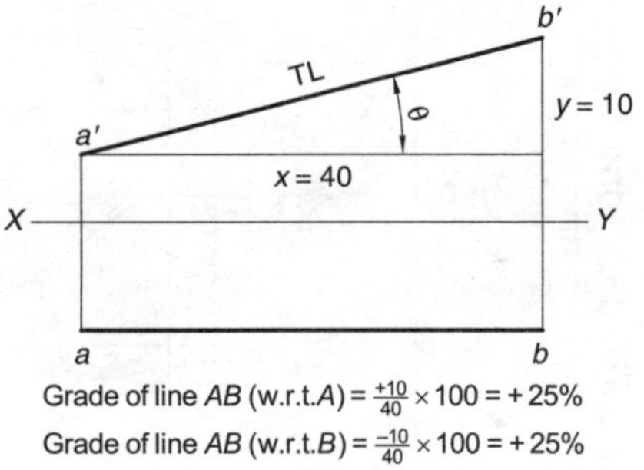

Fig. 11.33

Grade (or gradient) of a line gives its inclination with the HP. It is a vertical rise (or fall) of the line per unit horizontal advancement, expressed as percentage, i.e. $(y/x)*100$, Fig. 11.33. However, in many cases, gradient is expressed as 'y in x' or '$y : x$'. Like bearing, grade is also expressed with respect to an end of the line. The vertical rise (i.e., upward grade) with respect to a particular end is taken positive while vertical fall (i.e., downward grade) is taken negative. Obviously, gradients of a line with respect to two ends will have the same magnitude, but opposite signs.

Slope is synonymous with grade. It may be expressed in terms of 'y/x' (i.e., $\tan\theta$) or simply θ. As the grade or slope gives true inclination of the line, it is always shown in FV representing TL.

REMEMBER THE FOLLOWING

- Bearing is always shown in TV.
- Grade or slope is always shown in FV representing TL.

11.13 ANGLES OF DEPRESSION AND ELEVATION

If an observer is looking toward the object situated below his eye level, the angle made by his rays of sight with the horizontal is called the *angle of depression.* If the object is situated above the eye level of the observer, the similar angle is called the *angle of elevation*, Fig. 11.34. It should be noted that the angle of depression and angle of elevation represent the negative grade and positive grade respectively of a line joining the eyes of the observer with the object with respect to the eyes of the observer.

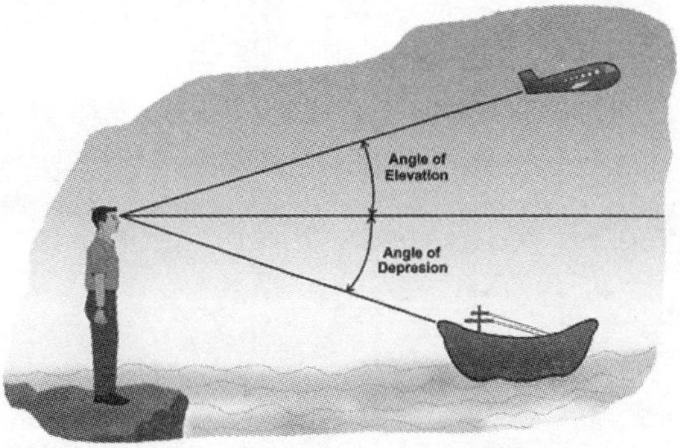

Fig. 11.34

Example 11.20 Two straight roads *AB* and *AC* are 2 km and 1.4 km long respectively. *AB* bears N 40° E on a downward slope of 30°. *AC* bears S 35° E on a downward grade of 15°. Draw the projections. Find TL, bearing and grade of the new road joining *B* to *C*.

Given: *AB*: TL = 2 km, Bearing = N 40° E, Grade = –30°
AC: TL = 1.4 km, Bearing = S 35° E, Grade = –15°

Solution Refer Fig. 11.35.

1. Mark *a* and *a′*, at suitable distances, below and above *XY* respectively.
2. Draw *a′b*1′ = 2 km and *a′c*1′ = 1.4 km making 30° and 15° respectively to *XY*. Note that *AB* and *AC* has downward grade with respect to *A*.
3. Project *b*1′ and *c*1′ below *XY* to obtain *ab*1 and *ac*1 parallel to *XY*. *ab*1 and *ac*1 give PLs of *AB* and *AC* respectively.
4. Rotate *ab*1 to *ab* to make 40° with the vertical. Similarly, rotate *ac*1 to *ac* to make 35° with the vertical. *ab* and *ac* gives required TVs.
5. Project *b* and *c* on f_b–f_b and f_c–f_c respectively to obtain desired FVs—*a′b′* and *a′c′*.
6. Join *c′b′* and *cb*. Rotate *cb* to obtain *cb*2 parallel to *XY* and then project *b*2 to *b*2′ on f_b–f_b. Join *c′b*2′. Measure θ. *c′b*2′ and θ gives TL and grade of *CB*.
7. Measure β, i.e., angle made by *cb* with the vertical. It gives the bearing of *BC*, i.e., N β° E.

Example 11.21 A car is moving in the direction of N 20° E along a straight road *CD*, 100 m long, with upward gradient of 1 in 4. A man at the top of a tower observed the car initially at *C* at an angle of depression of 45° and at a bearing of S 50° E. When the car reached *D*, the man observed it at N 80° E. The foot of the tower and point *C* are on the ground level. Draw the projections of the road and find the height of the tower.

Solution Refer Fig. 11.36.

1. Mark *c′* on *XY* and *c* at a suitable distance below *XY*.
2. Draw a line *c′d*1′ = 100 m with grade 1 in 4 as shown. Obtain *cd*1 parallel to *XY*.
3. Rotate *cd*1 to *cd* to make 20° with the vertical. *cd* gives the TV of the road.

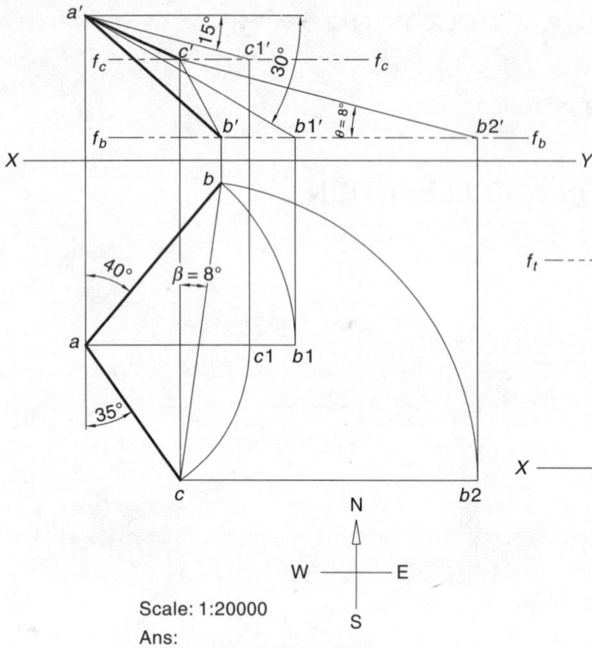

Scale: 1:20000

Ans:
TL of $BC = c'b2' = 127$ mm = 2.54 km
Bearing of BC = N 8° E
Grade of BC = +15° (w.r.t. B)

Fig. 11.35

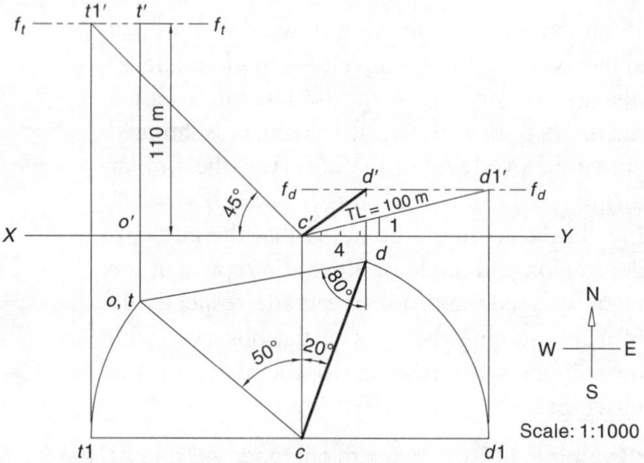

Scale: 1:1000

Ans: Height of tower = $t'o'$ = 110 mm = 110 m

Fig. 11.36

4. Project d to d' on f_d–f_d. $c'd'$ gives the FV of the road.
5. Through c, draw a line of reversed bearing N 50° W (i.e., 50° to vertical). Through d, draw a line of reversed bearing S 80° W (i.e., 80° to vertical). The two lines meet at $t(o)$.
6. Rotate ct to $ct1$ parallel to XY. Through c', draw a line at 45° to XY to intersect the projector through $t1$ at $t1'$.
7. Project t on f_t–f_t to locate t'. Measure $t'o'$ to get the height of the tower.

Illustrative Problems

Problem 11.1 A straight line AB, 60 mm long, makes an angle of 25° to the HP and 55° to the VP. The end A is in the VP and 20 mm above the HP. Draw the projections of the line AB.

Given: TL = 60 $\theta = 25°$ $\phi = 55°$ $d_a = 0$ $h_a = +20$

Solution Refer Fig. 11.37.

1. Locate a' 20 mm above XY and a on XY. Draw $a'b1'$ = TL, at 25° to XY. Obtain $ab1$ along XY.
2. Draw $ab2$ = TL, at 55° to XY. Obtain $a'b2'$ parallel to XY. Draw t–t and f–f parallel to XY.
3. With a as centre and radius = $ab1$, draw an arc cutting t–t at b. Join ab.
4. With a' as centre and radius = $a'b2'$, draw an arc cutting f–f at b'. Join $a'b'$.
   ab and $a'b'$ represent the TV and FV of the line AB.

Problem 11.2 A line BC, 80 mm long, is inclined at 45° to the HP and 30° to the VP. Its end B is in the HP and 40 mm in front of the VP. Draw its projections and determine its traces.

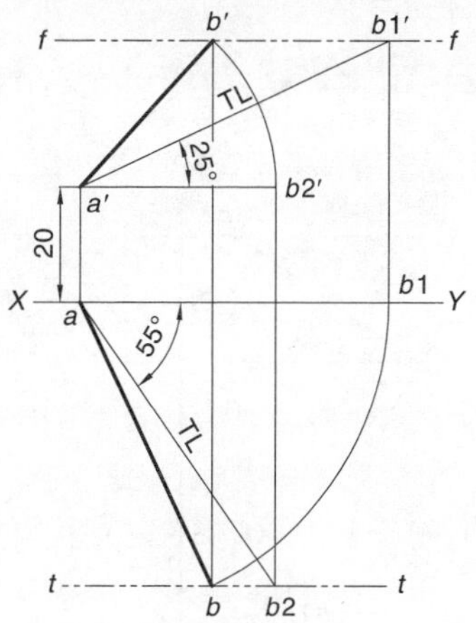

Fig. 11.37

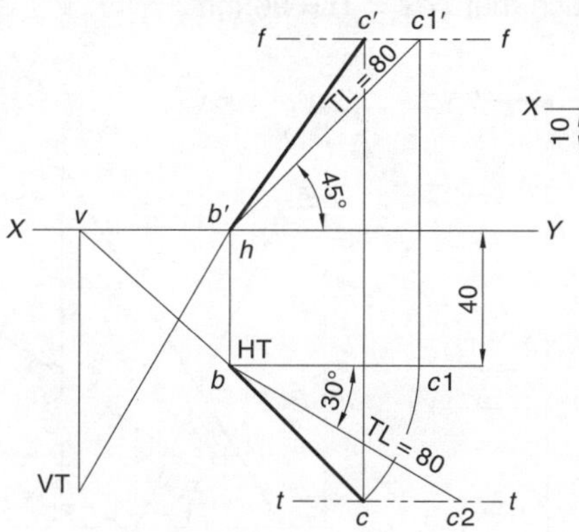

Fig. 11.38

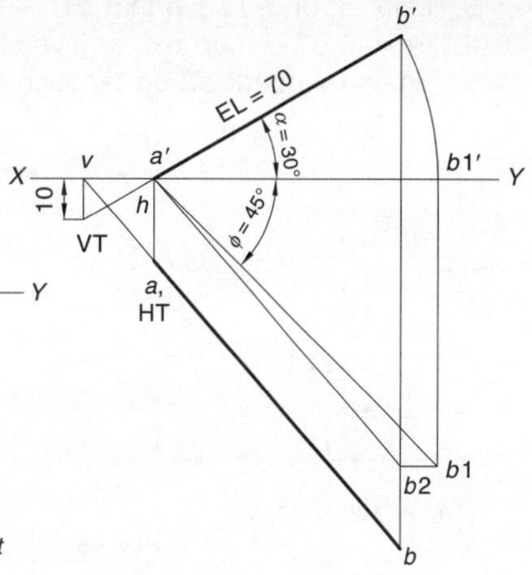

Fig. 11.39

Given: TL = 80 $\theta = 45°$ $\phi = 30°$ $h_b = 0$ $d_b = +40$

Solution Refer Fig. 11.38.

1. Locate *b′* on *XY* and *b* 40 mm below *XY*. Draw *b′c*1′ = TL, at 45° to *XY*. Obtain *bc*1 parallel to *XY*.
2. Draw *bc*2 = TL, at 30° to *XY*. Draw *f–f* through *c*1′ and *t–t* through *c*2.
3. Locate *c* on *t–t* such that *bc* = *bc*1. Project *c* to *c′* on *f–f*.
4. Join *b′c′* and *bc* to represent final projections of line *BC*.
5. As point *B* is on the HP, it represents the HT. Therefore, mark *h* at *b′* and HT at *b*.
6. Produce *cb* to meet *XY* at *v*. Project *v* on *c′b′* produced to locate VT.

Problem 11.3 FV of a line measures 70 mm and makes an angle of 30° with *XY*. The end *A* is in the HP and the VT of the line is 10 mm below *XY*. The line is inclined at 45° to the VP. Draw the projections of the line and find its TL and true inclinations with the HP. Also locate the HT.

Given: EL = 70 $\alpha = 30°$ $h_a = 0$ *v*-VT= –10 $\phi = 45°$

Solution Refer Fig. 11.39.

1. Mark *a′* on *XY* and draw *a′b′* = EL = 70 mm at 30° to *XY*.
2. With *a′* as centre and radius = *a′b′*, draw an arc to intersect *XY* at *b*1′. Project *b*1′ to meet the 45° line through *a′* at *b*1. *a′b*1 is the TL of the line.
3. Project *b′* to meet the locus through *b*1 at *b*2. *a′b*2 is the TV but not according to the conditions stated in the problem.
4. Locate VT 10 mm below *XY* on *b′a′* produced. Obtain *v* on *XY*.
5. Through *v*, draw a line parallel to *a′b*2. Project *a′* and *b*2 on this line to get *a* and *b*. *ab* is the final TV. HT coincides with *a*.

Problem 11.4 A line *CD*, 90 mm long, measures 72 mm in FV and 65 mm in TV. Draw the two views of the line if it fully lies in the first quadrant. Find the true inclinations of the line. Assume point *C* at suitable distances from the RPs.

Given: TL = 90 EL= 72 PL= 65

Solution Refer Fig. 11.40.

1. Locate *c′* and *c* at suitable distances from *XY*. Draw *cd*1 = PL = 65 mm parallel to *XY*.
2. With *c′* as a centre and radius = TL = 90 mm, cut an arc on the projector through *d*1. Join *c′d*1′. Measure θ.

3. Mark d' on f–f such that $c'd'$ = EL = 72 mm. $c'd'$ is final FV.
4. Project d' to d on t–t. cd gives final TV.
5. To find ϕ, mark $d2$ on t–t such that $cd2$ = TL= 90 mm.

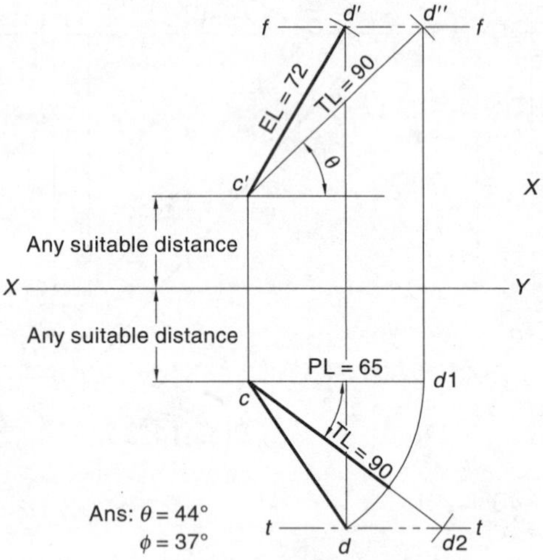

Fig. 11.40

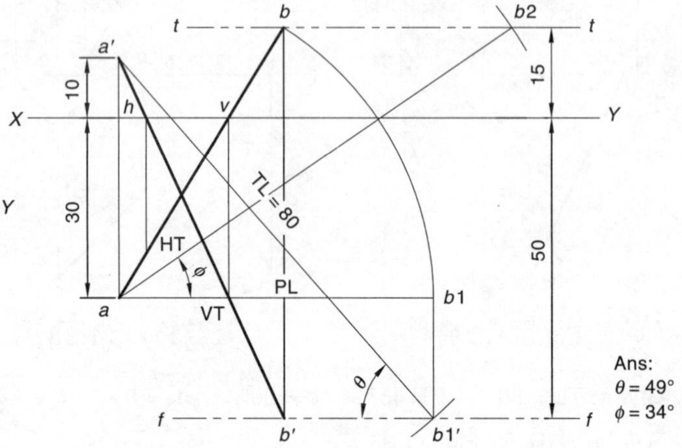

Fig. 11.41

Problem 11.5 The end A of line AB is 10 mm above the HP and 30 mm in front of the VP. The end B is 50 mm below the HP and 15 mm behind the VP. The length of the line is 80 mm. Draw the projection and locate the traces. What are the inclinations of the line with the RPs?

Given: $h_a = +10$ $d_a = +30$ $h_b = -50$ $d_b = -15$ TL = 80

Solution Refer Fig. 11.41.

1. Locate a' 10 mm above and a 30 mm below XY. Draw f–f 50 mm below XY. Locate $b1'$ on it such that $a'b1'$ = TL = 80 mm.
2. Obtain $ab1$ parallel to XY by projecting $b1'$.
3. Draw t–t 15 mm above XY. With a as a centre and radius = $ab1$, cut an arc on t–t at b. ab gives TV.
4. Project b on f–f to obtain b'. $a'b'$ gives FV.
5. Locate HT and VT as shown. Mark off TL $ab2$ to obtain ϕ.

Problem 11.6 The TV of a line CD measures 80 mm and makes an angle of 55° with XY. End C is in the VP and the HT of the line is 25 mm above XY. The line is inclined at 30° to the HP. Draw the projections of line CD. Determine its TL, true inclination with the VP, and the VT.

Given: PL = 80 $\beta = 55°$ $d_c = 0$ h-HT = +25 $\theta = 30°$

Solution Refer Fig. 11.42.

1. Mark c on XY and draw cd = PL = 80 mm inclined at 55° to XY. Extend dc and locate HT 25 mm above XY on it.
2. Draw HT-$d1$ = HT-d parallel to XY.
3. Obtain h and draw h–$d1'$ inclined at 30° to XY meeting $\widehat{D1}$ at $d1'$.
4. Draw f–f and obtain d' on it by projecting d. Join hd'.
5. Project c on hd' to locate c'. $c'd'$ represents the final FV.
6. To find TL and ϕ, obtain $cd2$ as shown. As c is on XY, c' gives VT.

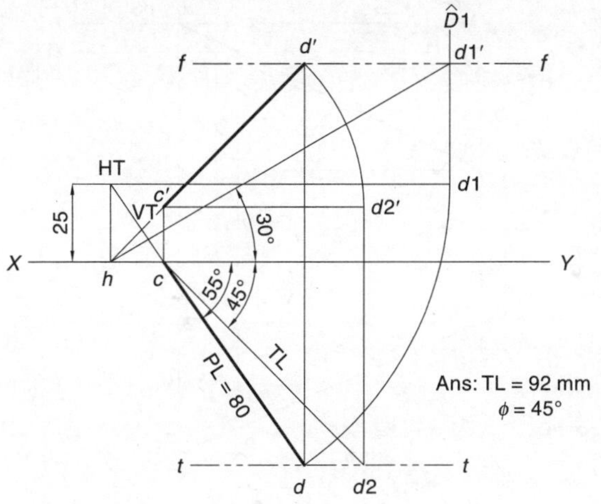

Fig. 11.42

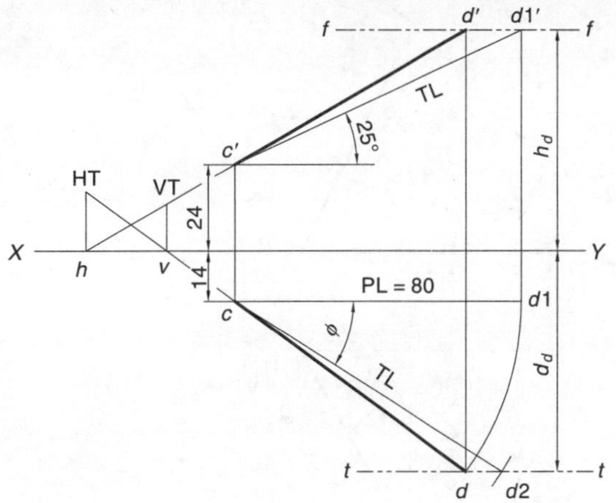

Fig. 11.43

Problem 11.7 A line *CD*, inclined at 25° to the HP, measures 80 mm in TV. The end *C* is in the first quadrant and 24 mm and 14 mm from the HP and the VP respectively. The end *D* is at equal distances from both the RPs. Draw the projections, find TL and true inclination with the VP. Locate the traces.
Given: $\theta = 25°$ PL = 80 $h_c = +24$ $d_c = +14$ $h_d = d_d$

Solution Refer Fig. 11.43.

1. Locate *c*′ 24 mm above and *c* 14 mm below *XY*. Draw *cd*1 = PL = 80 mm parallel to *XY*.
2. Through *c*′ draw a line inclined at 25° to *XY* intersecting the projector through *d*1 at *d*1′. *c*′*d*1′ = TL. Measure the distance of *d*1′ from *XY*. It gives h_d.
3. Draw *t*–*t* below *XY* at a distance of $h_d (= d_d)$. Rotate *cd*1 about *c* to get *d* on *t*–*t*. *cd* represents the final TV.
4. Project *d* on *f*–*f* to get *d*′. *c*′*d*′ gives the final FV.
5. To find ϕ, locate *d*2 on *t*–*t* such that *cd*2 = TL. Locate HT and VT as shown.

Problem 11.8 A line *EF* is contained by a plane perpendicular to the HP and inclined at 60° to the VP. The line is inclined to the HP at 45°. The length of the line is 65 mm. The end *F* is on the HP and 20 mm in front of the VP. Draw the projections of the line and locate its traces. What is the inclination of the line with the VP?
Given: $\beta = 60°$ $\theta = 45°$ TL = 65 $h_f = 0$ $d_f = +20$

Solution Refer Fig. 11.44.

As the line *EF* lies in the plane perpendicular to the HP and inclined to the VP at 60°, the angle made by PL with *XY* is 60°.

1. Mark *f*′ on *XY* and *f* 20 mm below *XY*.
2. Draw *f*′ *e*1′ = 65 mm inclined at 45° to *XY*.
3. Project *e*1′ to obtain *f*–*e*1 parallel to *XY*. *f*–*e*1 represents PL.
4. Rotate *f*–*e*1 till it makes 60° to *XY*. *fe* thus obtained gives TV.
5. Project *e* on *f*–*f* to locate *e*′. *f*′ *e*′ gives FV.
6. Locate HT and VT as shown.
7. To find ϕ, mark off *f*–*e*2 = TL = 65 mm.

Problem 11.9 A line *AB* measures 95 mm. The projectors through its VT and the end *A* are 35 mm apart. The end *A* is 25 mm above the HP and 15 mm in front of the VP. The VT is 8 mm above the HP. Draw the projections of the line and determine the HT and inclinations of the line with the HP and the VP.

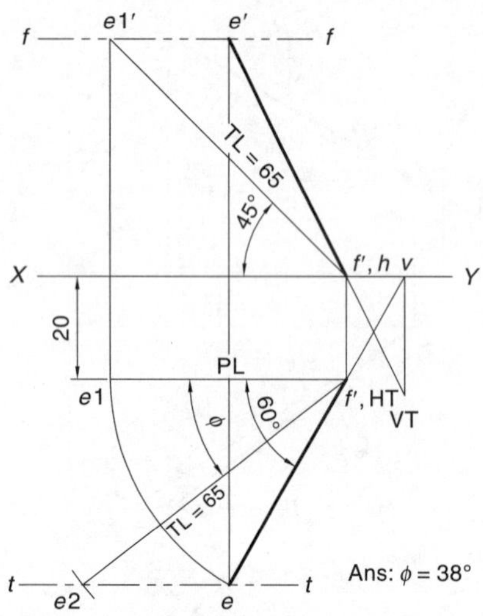

Fig. 11.44

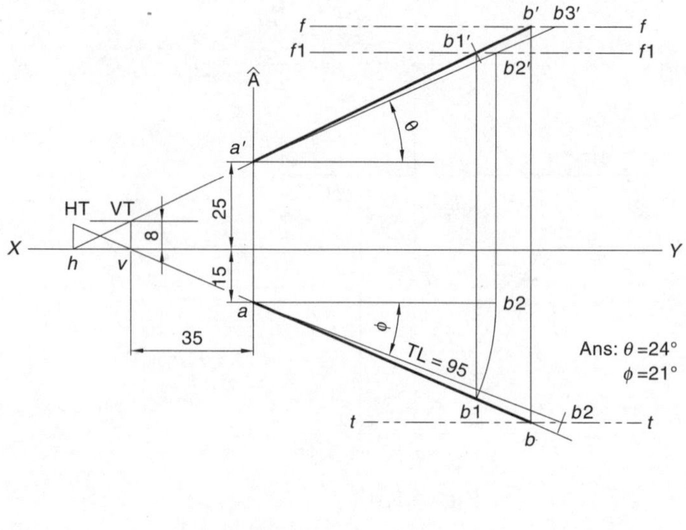

Fig. 11.45

Given: TL = 95 $\quad \widehat{VT}-\widehat{A} = 35 \quad h_a = +25 \quad d_a = +15 \quad$ v-VT = +8

Solution Refer Fig. 11.45.

1. Locate *a′* and *a* respectively 25 mm above and 15 mm below *XY*.
2. Locate *v* 35 mm from *A* on *XY*. Obtain VT 8 mm above *XY*.
3. Join VT-*a′* and mark *b*1′ arbitrarily anywhere on its extension. Project *b*1′ on *va* produced to locate *b*1. *a′–b*1′ and *ab*1 represent the FV and TV of a line *AB*1 ≠ *AB*.
4. Rotate *ab*1 to *ab*2 parallel to *XY*. Project *b*2 on *f*1–*f*1 to locate *b*2′.
5. Join *a′–b*2′ to give TL of *AB*1. Measure θ.
6. Locate *b*3′ on *a′–b*2′ (produced if necessary) such that *a′–b*3′ = TL = 95 mm.
7. Locate *b′* on the intersection of *a′b*1′ (produced if necessary) and *f–f*. Project *b′* on *ab*1 (produced if necessary) to locate *b*. *a′b′* and *ab* represent FV and TV of *AB*.
8. To find φ, locate *b*4 on *t–t* such that *a–b*4 = TL = 95 mm. Locate HT as shown.

Problem 11.10 The FV and TV of a line *PQ* are inclined at 50° and 25° respectively to *XY*. The end *Q* is 20 mm in front of the VP. The distance between the projectors through *P* and *Q* is 65 mm. The distance between the traces, measured parallel to *XY* is 95 mm. Draw the projections, locate the traces and find TL of the line. Also find the true inclinations.

Given: $\alpha = 50° \quad \beta = 25° \quad d_q = +20 \quad x = 65 \quad X = 95$

Solution Refer Fig. 11.46.

1. Draw $\widehat{P}$ and $\widehat{Q}$, 65 mm apart from each other.
2. On $\widehat{Q}$, locate *q*, 20 mm below *XY*. Draw *pq* inclined at 25° to *XY*.
3. Extend *pq* and locate *v*. Draw $\widehat{HT}$, 95 mm from $\widehat{VT}$, and locate *HT* at its intersection with *pq*.
4. Mark *h* and through it draw a line at 50° to *XY*. Mark *p′*, *q′* and *VT* on the corresponding projectors.
5. To find TL and θ, rotate *pa* to *pa*1 parallel to *XY* and project *q*1 to *q*1′ on *f–f*. *p′q*1′ = TL.
6. To find φ, mark *q*2 on *t–t* such that *pq*2 = TL.

Problem 11.11 A straight line *PQ*, equally inclined to the HP and the VP, has its end *P* in front of the VP and 20 mm above the HP. End *Q* is behind the VP and 40 mm below the HP. A point on this line is in the VP and 10 mm below the HP. Draw the projections and find TL and inclination of the line with the HP, if the distance between the projectors of the ends is 60 mm.

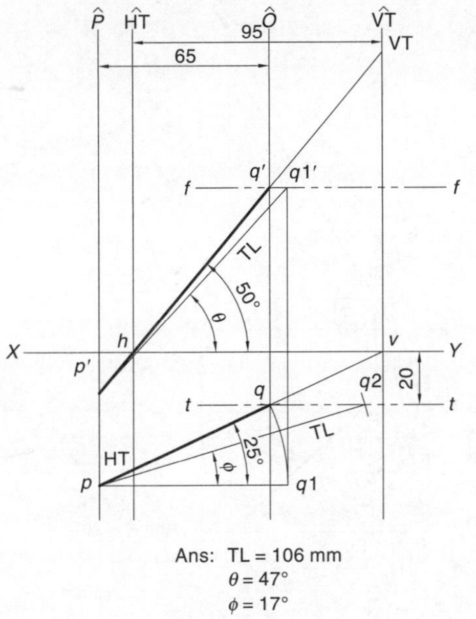

Fig. 11.46

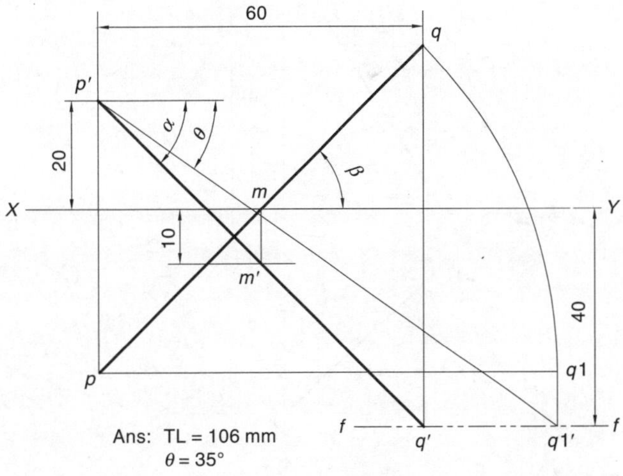

Fig. 11.47

Given: $\theta = \phi \quad h_p = +20 \quad (d_p = +ve) \quad h_q = -40 \quad (d_q = -ve) \quad h_m = -10 \quad d_m = 0 \quad x = 60$

Solution Let *M* be the point on *PQ* in the VP and 10 mm below the HP.

Refer Fig. 11.47.

1. Locate *p′* and *q′* respectively 20 mm above and 40 mm below *XY* such that the distance between their projectors is 60 mm.
2. Join *p′q′* and mark *m′* on it 10 mm below *XY*. Project *m′* to *m* on *XY*. *p′q′* makes $\alpha°$ to *XY*.
3. As $\theta = \phi$, $\alpha = \beta$. Therefore, through *m*, draw a line at $\beta°$ to *XY* (sloping opposite to *p′q′*). Locate *p* and *q* on corresponding projectors.
4. Rotate *pq* to obtain *pq*1 parallel to *XY*. Project *q*1 on *f–f* to locate *q*1′. *p′q*1′ gives TL and θ.

Problem 11.12 A line *AB*, 100 mm long, is inclined at 50° to HP. The end *A* is 10 mm above the HP and end *B* is 65 mm in front of the VP. Draw projections of the line if its FV measures 90 mm. Locate traces and find the inclination of the line with the VP.

Given: TL = 100 $\quad \theta = 50° \quad h_a = +10 \quad d_b = +65 \quad$ EL = 90

Solution **Method 1:** Refer Fig. 11.48(a).

1. Locate *a′* 10 mm above *XY* and draw *a′b*1′ = TL = 100 mm inclined at 50° to *XY*.
2. Obtain *a*1–*b*1, along *XY* to represent PL.
3. Locate *b′* on *f–f* such that *a′b′* = EL = 90 mm.
4. Rotate *a*1–*b*1 to locate *b*2 on $\hat{B}$. Join *a*1–*b*2.
5. Locate *b*, 65 mm below *XY* on $\hat{B}$. Draw *ab* parallel and equal to *a*1–*b*2.
6. Locate traces as shown.
7. To find ϕ, draw *ab*3 = TL.

Method 2: Refer Fig. 11.48(b).

1. Locate *a*1′, 10 mm above *XY* and draw *a*1′*b′* = TL = 100 mm inclined at 50° to *XY*.

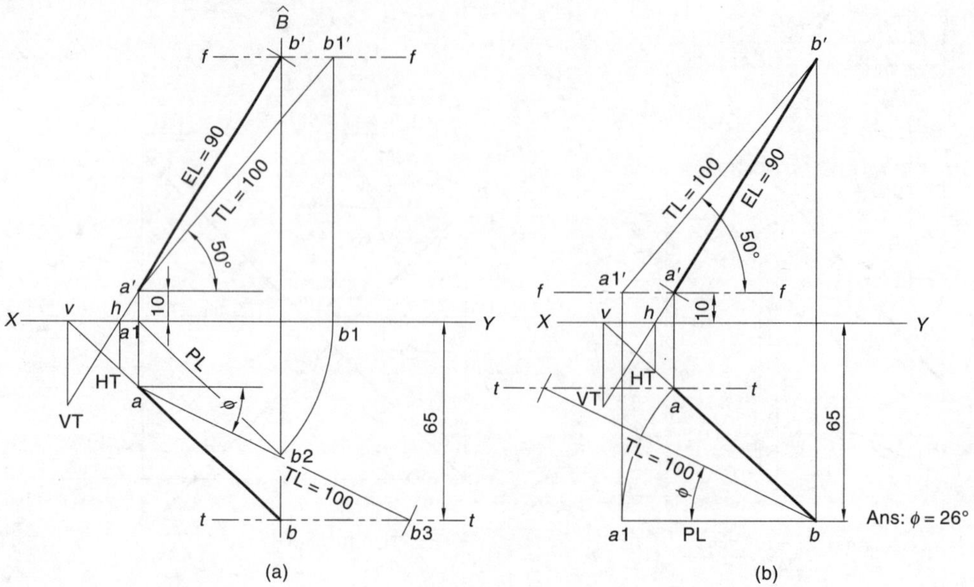

Fig. 11.48

2. Draw *f–f* and on it, and locate *a′* such that *a′b′* = EL = 90 mm.
3. Project *b′* to obtain *b*, 65 mm below *XY*. Project *a*1′ to obtain *a*1 and draw *a*1–*b* parallel to *XY*. *a*1–*b* = PL.
4. Mark *a* on the projector through *a′* such that *ab* = *a*1–*b*.
5. Locate traces and find ϕ as shown.

Problem 11.13 A line *PQ* = 120 mm has its end *Q*, 20 mm above the HP and 15 mm in front of the VP. Draw the projections of the line if its TV and SV measure 95 mm and 110 mm respectively.

Given: TL = 120 $h_q = +20$ $d_q = +15$ PL = 95 SVL = 110

Solution Refer Fig. 11.49.

1. Locate *q′* and *q* respectively, 20 mm above and 15 mm below *XY*. Draw *qp*1 = PL= 95 mm parallel to *XY*.
2. With *q′* as a centre and radius = TL = 120 mm, cut an arc on the projector through *p*1. Join *p*1′*q′*.
3. Obtain *q″* in SV by projecting *q′* and *q*. With *q″* as a centre and radius = SVL = 110 mm, cut an arc at *p″* on the horizontal projector though *p*1′. *p″q″* represents final SV.
4. In TV, locate *p* on the projector through *p″*, such that *qp* = *qp*1. *pq* represents the final TV.
5. Obtain *p′* in FV by projecting *p* on *f–f*. *p′q′* represents final FV.

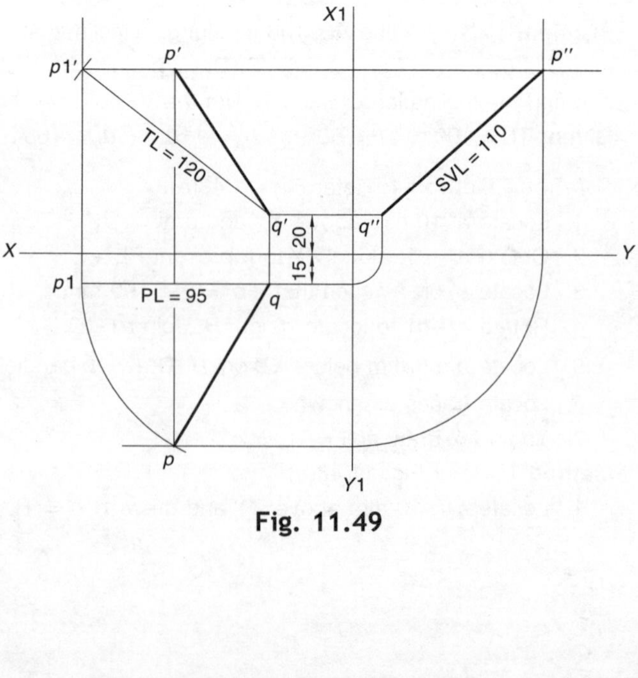

Fig. 11.49

Problem 11.14 The end *P* of a line *PQ* is in the third quadrant whereas the end *Q* is in the first quadrant. The ends *P* and *Q* are respectively 22 mm and 14 mm from the VP. The distance between the end projectors is 70 mm. The line makes 40° to the HP and its HT is 15 mm behind the VP. Draw the three views, determine TL and locate VT.

Given: $d_p = -22$ (h_p = –ve) $d_q = +14$ (h_q = +ve) $x = 70$ $\theta = 40°$ h-HT = –15

Solution Refer Fig. 11.50.

1. Draw $\hat{P}$ and $\hat{Q}$ 70 mm apart from each other.
2. On $\hat{P}$ and $\hat{Q}$, locate *p*, 22 mm above, and *q*, 14 mm below *XY* respectively. Join *pq*.
3. On *pq*, locate HT 15 mm above *XY*. Obtain *h*. Along *XY*, draw *h*–*q*1 = HT-*q*.
4. Through *h*, draw a line at 40° to *XY* intersecting the projector through *q*1 at *q*1′. *h*–*q*1′ gives TL of the line HT–*Q*.

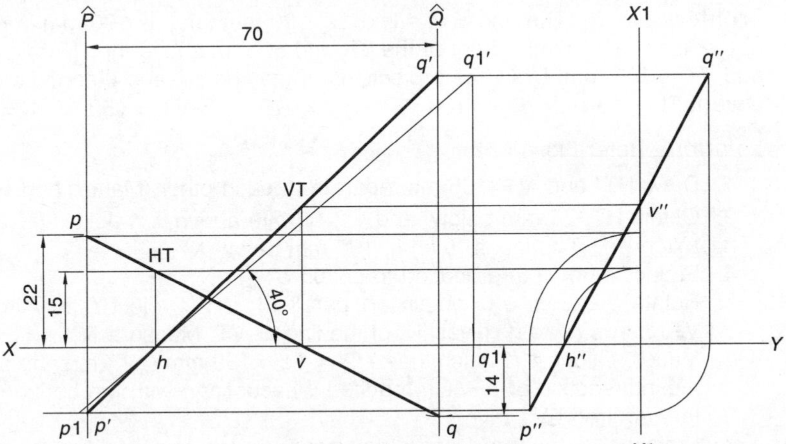

Ans: TL = *p*1′*q*1′ = 103 mm

Fig. 11.50

5. Project *q*1′ to *q*′on $\hat{Q}$. Join *h*–*q*′. It gives FV of the line HT–*Q*.
6. Extend *q*′*h* to meet $\hat{P}$ at *p*′. *p*′*q*′ is now the required FV.
7. Locate *v* and VT as shown.
8. Obtain SV-*p*″*q*″ by projecting *p*′ and *q*′ and *p* and *q* as shown. Carefully note how *p*′ and *p* are projected to obtain *p*″. *h*″ and *v*″ may be marked in SV in a similar way.
9. To obtain TL, extend *q*1′–*h* to meet the horizontal projector through *p*′ at *p*1′. *p*1′*q*1′ = TL.

Problem 11.15 An end of a line, measuring 70 mm in FV, is on the HP. FV of the line makes 30° to *XY* and the VT is 15 mm below the HP. Draw the projections of the line if it is inclined at 30° to the VP. Find TL and *θ*. Also locate the HT.

Given: EL = 70 $h_a = 0$ $\alpha = 30°$
v-VT= –15 $\phi = 30°$

Solution Refer Fig. 11.51.

1. Mark *a*′ on *XY* and draw *a*′*b*′ = EL = 70 mm at 30° to *XY*.
2. Obtain *a*′*b*1′ = *a*′*b*′ along *XY*.
3. Mark *a*1 anywhere below *XY* on the projector through *a*′. Through *a*1, draw a line at 30° to *XY* meeting the projector through *b*1' at *b*1. Now *a*1*b*1 = TL.

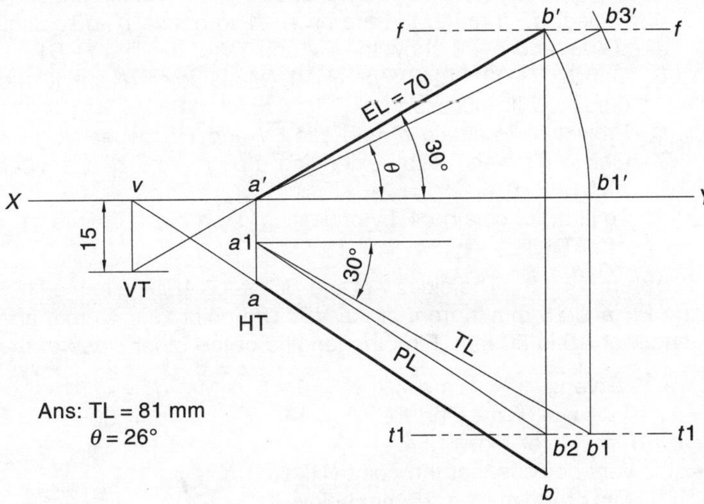

Ans: TL = 81 mm
θ = 26°

Fig. 11.51

4. Project *b′* on t_1–t_1 to locate *b*2. *a*1*b*2 gives the PL but not the final TV.
5. Extend *b′a′* and locate VT such that *v*-VT = 15 mm.
6. Though *v*, draw a line parallel to *a*1–*b*2 and mark *a* and *b* on it on corresponding projectors. *ab* is the final TV.
7. To find θ, obtain *b*3′ on *f*–*f* such that *a′b*3′ = TL.
8. As *a′* is on *XY*, HT will coincide with *a*.

Problem 11.16 The end *E* of a line *EF*, 130 mm long, is 100 mm in front of the VP. The HT and the VT of the line are 75 mm in front of the VP and 50 mm above the HP respectively. The distance between HT and VT is 105 mm. Draw the projections of the line *EF* and determine its angles with the HP and the VP.
Given: TL = 130 d_e = +100 *h*-HT = +75 *v*-VT = +50 *X* = 105

Solution Refer Fig. 11.52.

1. Draw $\widehat{HT}$ and $\widehat{VT}$ 105 mm apart from each other. Mark *h* and *v*.
2. Obtain HT, 75 mm below, and VT, 50 mm above *XY*. Join *h*-VT and *v*-HT.
3. Extend *v*-HT to locate *e* on it, 100 mm below *XY*.
4. Project *e* on VT-*h* produced to obtain *e′*.
5. Rotate *ev* about *e* to obtain *ef*1 parallel to *XY*. Project *f*1 to *f*1′ on the horizontal projector through VT. Join *e′f*1′. *e′f*1′ gives TL of the line *E*–VT. Measure θ.
6. Mark *f*2′ along *e′f*1′ such that *e′f*2′ = TL = 130 mm (*e′f*1′ may be produced if necessary). Locate *f′* at the intersection of *e′*-VT (produced if necessary) with the horizontal projector through *f*2′. *e′f′* gives the required FV.
7. Project *f′* on *ev* (produced if necessary) to locate *f*. *ef* gives the required TV.
8. To find ϕ, obtain *f*3 on *t*–*t* such that *e*–*f*3 = TL = 130 mm.

Problem 11.17 A straight line *CD*, laying fully in the first quadrant, is inclined at 30° to the VP and 45° to the HP. Its LHSV measures 50 mm. The midpoint *P* of the line is 35 mm from both the RPs. Draw the three views of the line and find its TL.
Given: ϕ =30° θ = 45° SVL = 50 mm $h_p = d_p$ = +35
As *P* is the midpoint of *CD*, *p″d″* = ½ (SVL) = 25 mm.

Solution Refer Fig. 11.53.

1. Mark *p′*, 35 mm above, and *p*, 35 mm below *XY*.
2. Assuming a line *P*–*D*1 of any length, draw *p′d*1′ inclined at 45° to *XY*. Obtain *pd*1.
3. Draw *p*–*d*2 (= *p′d*1′) inclined at 30° to *XY*. Obtain *p′d*2′.
4. Project *d*2 through the arc on *f*1–*f*1 to obtain *p′*–*d*3′. Similarly, project *d*1 on *t*1–*t*1 to obtain *p*–*d*3. *p′*–*d*3′ and *p*–*d*3 show the FV and TV of the line *P*–*D*1.
5. Obtain *p″*–*d*3″, LHSV of *P*–*D*1. Mark point *d″* on it such that *p″d″* = 25 mm (*p″*–*d*3″ may be produced if necessary).
6. Project *d″* to obtain *d′* and *d* in FV and TV respectively.
7. Obtain *c′*, *c* and *c″* by extending *d′p′*, *dp* and *d″p″* respectively such that *p′c′* = *d′p′*, *pc* = *dp* and *p″c″* = *d″p″*.
8. To find TL, obtain *d*4′ by projecting *d′* on *p′d*1′. Locate *c*1′ on *d*4′*p′* produced such that *p′c*1′ = *p′d*4′. *c*1′*d*4′ = TL.

Problem 11.18 The sides *AB* and *BC* of a Δ*ABC* lie in the HP and the VP respectively. The point *A* is in the PP and 25 mm in front of the VP. The point *C* is 40 mm above the HP and 50 mm from the PP. The length of *AB* is 80 mm. Find the lengths of the other sides of the triangle.

Given:	Line *AB*: p_a = 0	d_a = +25	TL = 80
	Line *BC*: h_c = +40	p_c = 50	

Solution Refer Fig. 11.54.

It is very obvious that the point *B* lies on *XY*.

1. On *X*1*Y*1, mark *a* 25 mm below *XY*.
2. With *a* as a centre and radius = 80 mm, cut an arc on *XY* at *b*. *ab* represents TV of *AB*.
3. As *AB* lies in the HP, *a′b′* will lie on *XY*.

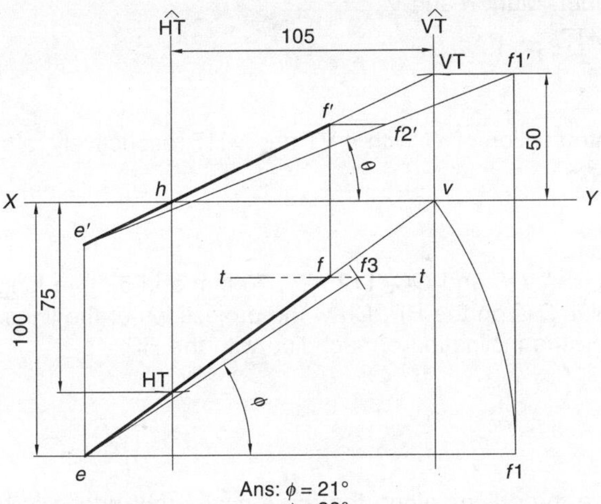

Ans: $\phi = 21°$
$\phi = 33°$

Fig. 11.52

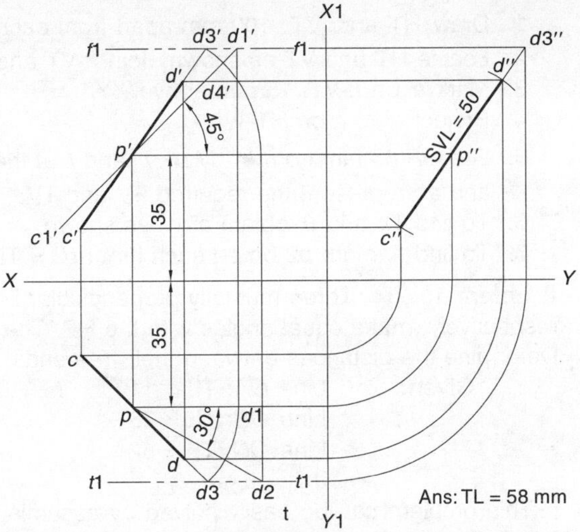

Ans: TL = 58 mm

Fig. 11.53

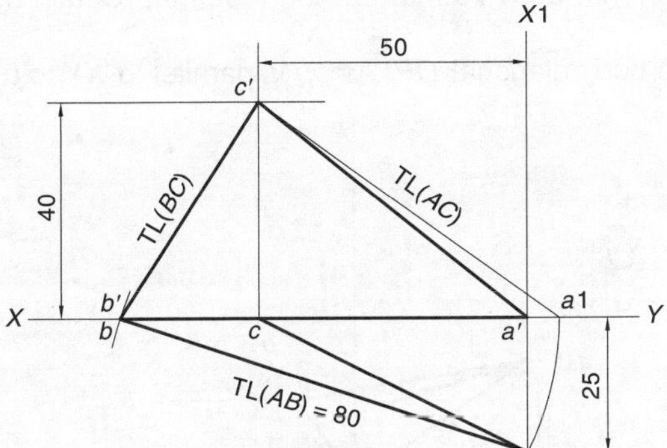

Ans: TL(*BC*) = 48 mm
TL(*AC*) = 89 mm

Fig. 11.54

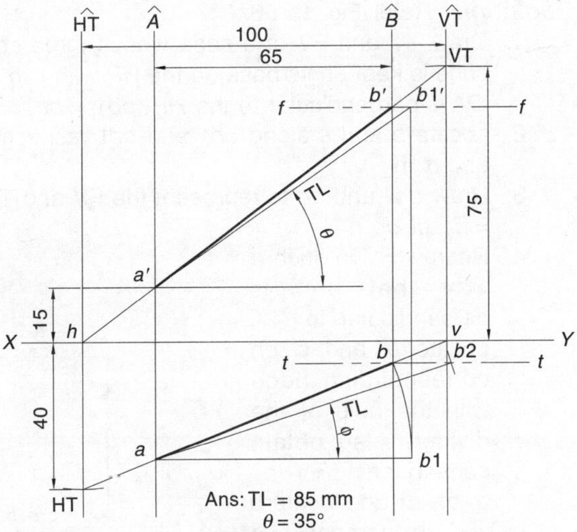

Ans: TL = 85 mm
$\theta = 35°$
$\phi = 18°$

Fig. 11.55

4. Locate *c*′ 40 mm above *XY* and 50 mm from *X*1*Y*1. *b*′*c*′ gives FV of *BC*.
5. As *BC* lies in the VP, *bc* will lie on *XY*. Obviously, *b*′*c*′ gives TL of *BC*.
6. Join *a*′*c*′ and *ac*.
7. Mark *a*1 on *XY* such that *ca* = *ca*1. *c*′*a*1 will give TL of *AC*.

Problem 11.19 The projectors through the HT and VT of a line are 100 mm apart while those through its ends are 65 mm apart. An end of the line is 15 mm above the HP. The HT is 40 mm in front of the VP and the VT is 75 mm above the HP. Draw the FV and TV of the line and find its TL. Also find the inclinations the line makes with the RPs.

Given: $X = 100$ $x = 65$ $h_a = +15$ h-HT = +40 v-VT= +75

Solution Refer Fig. 11.55.

1. Draw $\widehat{HT}$ and $\widehat{VT}$, 100 mm apart from each other. Mark *h* and *v*.
2. Locate HT and VT as shown. Join *h*-VT and *v*-HT.
3. Mark *a′* on *h*-VT, 15 mm above *XY*.
4. Project *a′* to *a* on HT-*v*.
5. Draw $\hat{B}$ 65 mm from $\hat{A}$. Mark *b′* and *b* at the intersection of $\hat{B}$ with *h*-VT and *v*-HT respectively. *a′b′* and *ab* represent the required FV and TV.
6. To find TL and θ, obtain *a′b1′* as shown.
7. To find ϕ, mark *b2* on *t–t* such that *ab2* = TL.

Problem 11.20 Three mutually perpendicular lines, *OA*, *OB* and *OC*, 112 mm, 76 mm and 52 mm long respectively, make equal angles with the HP. The point *O* is on the HP. Draw the projections of the lines. Determine the distances between their free ends. Find the inclination of each line with the HP.

Given: Line *OA*: TL = 112 $h_o = 0$
Line *OB*: TL = 76
Line *OC*: TL = 52
$\theta_{OA} = \theta_{OB} = \theta_{OC}$

This problem can be easily solved by assuming the three lines along the three concurrent edges of a cube. The three edges will make equal inclinations with the HP when the body diagonal through the common corner is vertical.

Solution Refer Fig. 11.56.

1. Draw TV and FV of a cube whose three concurrent edges are *OA* = *OB*1 = *OC*1 = 112 mm. The cube is kept on its base on the HP with two adjacent sides *OB*1 and *OC*1 equally inclined to the VP. *OA* is perpendicular to the HP. *ob*1 = *oc*1 = *o′a′* = TL = 112 mm.
2. Locate *b* and *c* along *ob*1 and *oc*1 respectively such that *ob* = 76 mm and *oc* = 52 mm. Obtain *b′* and *c′* in FV.
3. Draw *o′p′* and *op* to represent the FV and TV of the body diagonal *OP*. As *op* is parallel to *XY*, *o′p′* = TL of *op*.
4. Redraw FV in such a way that *o′p′* is perpendicular to *XY*. Locate *b′* and *c′* on corresponding edge with the help of the divider. Also obtain corresponding TV- *o*–*a*–*b*1–*c*1 and locate *b* and *c* on respective edges.
5. Join *a′b′* and *a′c′*. Obtain *a*1′*b′*, *a*2′*c′* and *b2′c′* to represent the TLs of *AB*, *AC* and *BC*.
6. Measure the angle made by *o′a′* with *XY*, i.e. θ_{OA}. Since, all the three lines *OA*, *OB* and *OC* make equal angles with the HP, $\theta_{OA} = \theta_{OB} = \theta_{OC} = 35°$.

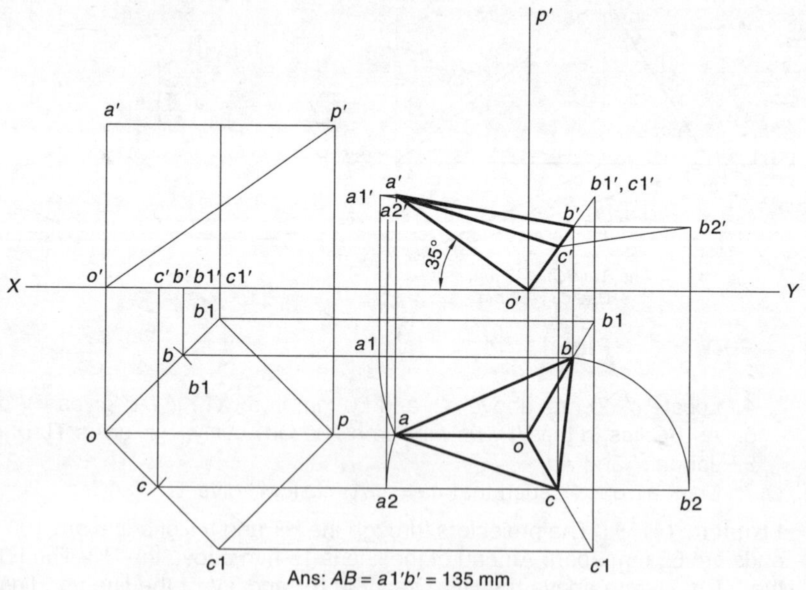

Ans: $AB = a1'b' = 135$ mm
$AC = a2'c' = 123$ mm
$BC = b2'c' = 92$ mm
$\theta_{OA} = \theta_{OB} = \theta_{OC} = 35°$

Fig. 11.56

Problem 11.21 A pipeline from point *A*, running due north-east has a downward gradient of 1 in 5. Another point *B* is 12 m away from and due east of *A* and on the same level. Find the length and slope of a pipeline from *B* which runs due 15° east of north and meets the pipeline from *A*.

Solution Refer Fig. 11.57.

1. Draw *ab* = 12 m at suitable distance below and parallel to *XY*. Draw a line through *a*, inclined at 45° to *XY* and another line through *b*, inclined at 15° to the vertical, both meeting at *c*.
2. Rotate *ac* to *ac*1 parallel to *XY*.
3. Project *ab* to draw *a′b′* at a suitable distance above and parallel to *XY*. Through *a′*, draw a line of negative grade of 1 in 5 to meet the projector through *c*1 at *c*1′. *a′c*1′ gives *TL* of *AC*.
4. Project *c* to *c′* on *f–f*. Join *a′c′* and *b′c′*.
5. To obtain the inclination and *TL* of *BC*, rotate *bc* to *bc*2 and project *c*2 to *c*2′ on *f–f*. *b′c*2′ = *TL* of *BC*. Measure θ.

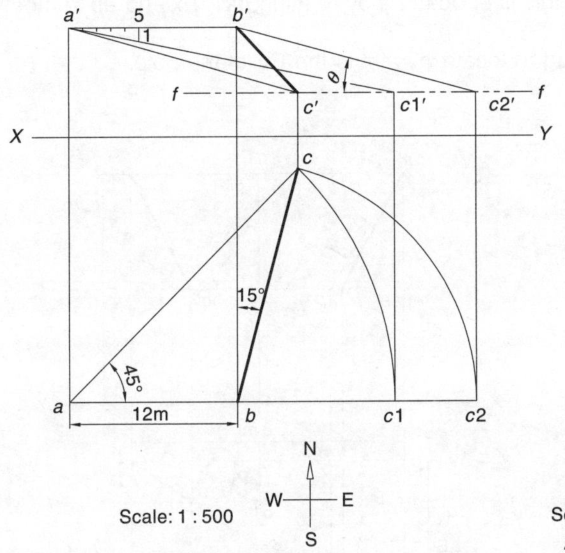

Scale: 1 : 500

Ans: *BC* = 35 mm = 17.5 mm
Slope of *BC* = θ = 15°

Fig. 11.57

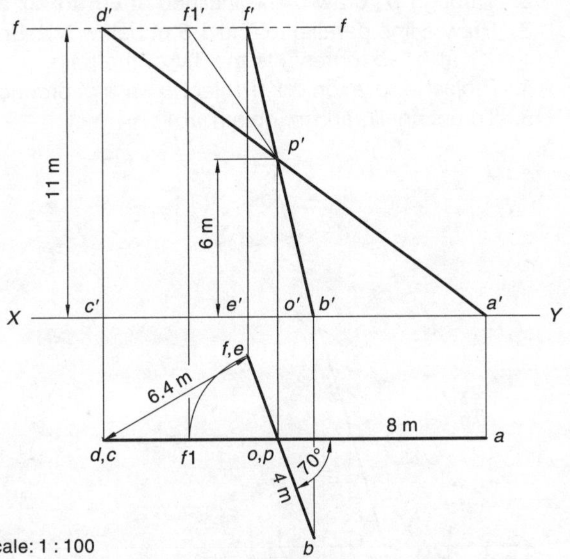

Scale: 1 : 100

Ans: Distance between the bulbs = *df* = 64 mm = 6.4 m
Distance between bulb *D* & pole top = *d′p′* = 83 mm = 8.3 m
Distance between bulb *F* & pole top = *f*1′*p′* = 60 mm = 6 m

Fig. 11.58

Problem 11.22 Two electric lamp posts, each 11 m high, produce shadows *oa* and *ob* of lengths 8 m and 4 m respectively on the ground, of a 6 m high pole, *OP*. The angle between the shadows is 70°. Determine graphically the distance between the bulbs and also from the pole top to each bulb. Take a suitable scale.

Solution Refer Fig. 11.58.

1. At suitable distances below *XY*, draw the TVs of the two shadows, *oa* and *ob*. Draw one of the shadows, say *oa*, parallel to *XY*. Point *o*(*p*) represents TV of the pole *OP*. ∠*aob* = 70°.
2. Project *a*, *b* and *o* to *a′*, *b′* and *o′* on *XY*. Also project *p* to *p′* such that *o′p′* = 6 m. *o′a′* and *o′b′* represent FVs of the shadows. *o′p′* gives FV of the pole.
3. Draw *f–f* 11 m above *XY*. Join *a′p′* and extend it to meet *f–f* at *d′*. Similarly, join *b′p′* and extend it to obtain *f′*.

4. Draw verticals from *d′* and *f′* to meet *XY* at *c′* and *e′* respectively. *c′d′* and *e′f′* represent the FVs of posts *CD* and *EF* respectively.
5. Project *d′*(*c′*) on *ao* produced to obtain *d*(*c*). Similarly, obtain *f*(*e*) on *bo* produced.
6. As *d′f′* is parallel to *XY*, *df* gives the true distance between the bulbs. Also, as *dp* is parallel to *XY*, *d′p′* gives the distance between bulb *D* and pole top.
7. To obtain the distance between bulb *F* and pole top, obtain *f*1′*p′*.

Problem 11.23 A point on the pole is 1 m above the floor and 1 m in front of a wall; while the lower end is on the floor, 1.2 m from the same wall. It leans against a corner of the wall and is inclined to the ground at 60°. Draw its projections and decide the length of the pole. Take a suitable scale.

Solution Let *P* be a point on the pole *AB*.
Refer Fig. 11.59.

1. Draw *p′* 1 m above and *p* 1 m below *XY*.
2. Through *p′*, draw a line inclined at 60° to *XY* and meeting *XY* at *a*1′. Obtain *pa*1 parallel to *XY*.
3. Draw a line parallel to and 1.5 m below *XY*. On this line, obtain *a* by rotating *pa*1. Extend *ap* to meet *XY* at *b*. *ab* represents the TV of the pole.
4. Project *a* to *a′* on *XY*. Project *b* on *a′p′* produced to locate *b′*. *a′b′* is the FV of the pole.
5. To obtain TL and ϕ, obtain *ab*1′.

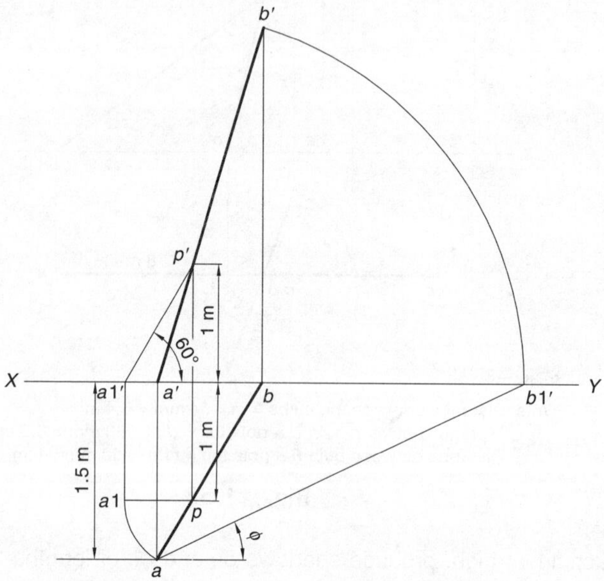

Scale: 1 : 20
Ans: Length of Pole = *ab*1′ = 174 mm = 3.48 m
ϕ = 26°

Fig. 11.59

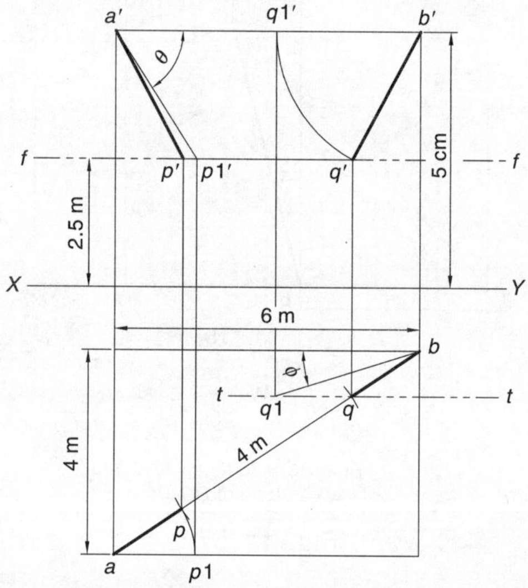

Scale: 1 : 100
Ans: Length of each rope = *bq*1 = 30 mm = 3 m
Angle of rope with floor = θ = 57°
Angle of rope with longer wall = ϕ = 17°

Fig. 11.60

Problem 11.24 A room has a floor area of 6 m × 4 m and height 5 m. A steel rod of negligible diameter and length 4 m is suspended from the two opposite corners of the ceiling by two non-elastic ropes attached to two ends of the rod in such a way that the rod hung horizontally at the midway of the height of the room. Determine graphically the length of each rope and the angles made by them with the floor and one of the longer walls.

Solution Refer Fig. 11.60.

1. Draw a rectangle of 6 m × 4 m below *XY* to represent TV of the room. Take longer sides parallel to *XY*.
2. Project TV to obtain FV above *XY*. The rectangle in FV has a longer side along *XY* and height = 5 m.
3. In TV, join opposite corners *a*–*b*. Along *ab*, mark *p* and *q* such that *ap* = *bq* and *pq* = 4 m. *pq* represents TV of the rod. *ap* and *bq* represent TVs of the ropes.
4. In FV, mark *a′* and *b′* at appropriate corners. Draw *f*–*f* 2.5 m above *XY* and on it to locate *p′* and *q′* by projecting *p* and *q*.
5. Join *a′p′* and *b′q′* to represent FVs of the ropes.
6. To obtain TL and ϕ of the rope, obtain *bq*1 as shown.
7. To obtain θ, obtain *a′p*1′.

Problem 11.25 In a rectangular room, a peg is driven at the centre of the floor. Another peg is driven at the midpoint of the common edge between the two mutually perpendicular walls. The minimum length of the thread connecting these two pegs is 5.5 m. The thread makes 30° with the floor. The TV of the thread makes 40° with a longer wall. Find graphically the size of the room.

Solution Refer Fig. 11.61.

1. Mark *p*1′ on *XY* and *p*1 at a suitable distance below *XY* to represent the FV and TV of the peg at the centre of the floor.
2. Draw *p*1′–*p′* = 5.5 m inclined at 30° to *XY*. Obtain *p*1–*p* parallel to *XY*.
3. Rotate *p*1–*p* to *p*1–*p*2 such that it will make 40° to the vertical, i.e., 50° to *XY*. *p*1–*p*2 gives the TV of the thread.
4. Project *p*2 to *p*2′ on *f*–*f*. Join *p*1′–*p*2′ to give the FV of the thread.
5. From *p*2, drop perpendiculars on *p*1–*p* and *p*1′–*p*1 at *a* and *b* respectively. Also, locate *c* at the intersection of *p*2′–*p*2 and *XY*. As the points *a*, *b* and *p*2′ represent the midpoints of corresponding edges, length of the room = 2 (*p*2–*a*), width of the room = 2 (*p*2–*b*) and height of the room = 2 (*p*2′–*c*).

Problem 11.26 A room is 7 m long, 5 m wide and 4 m high. A chandelier hangs at the centre of the ceiling and 1.5 m below it. A thin straight wire connects the chandelier to a nail in one of the corner edges of the room. The nail is 1 m above the floor. Draw the projections and find TL of the wire. What will be the slope of the wire?

Solution Refer Fig. 11.62.

1. Draw a rectangle *a*(*a*1)–*b*(*b*1)–*c*(*c*1)–*d*(*d*1) of size 7 m × 5 m below *XY*. Take any side, say length, parallel to *XY*.
2. Obtain FV–*a′*(*d′*)–*b′*(*c′*)–*b*1′(*c*1′)–*a*1′(*d*1′). *a′*–*a*1′ = 4 m.
3. Locate *c* at the centre of TV and project it to *c′*, 1.5 m below *a*1′–*b*1′.
4. Locate *n* at a corner in TV and project it to *n′*, 1 m above *XY*.
5. Join *cn* and *c′n′* to represent the TV and FV of the wire respectively.
6. To obtain TL and θ, obtain *c′n*1′ as shown.

Problem 11.27 A soldier on a 700 m high hill observed an enemy's fighter plane at an angle of elevation of 55° and at a bearing of N 65° W. The plane is still in air at a height of 1800 m from the ground. The soldier informed about the plane to his army base, located on the ground, seen at an angle of depression of 20° and at a bearing of S 35° E. The army fired a missile that could travel at 300 m/s. How much time will the missile take to hit the enemy's plane?

Solution Refer Fig. 11.63.

1. Draw *h′* 700 m above and *h* at a suitable distance below *XY* to represent the FV and TV of the top to the hill.
2. Draw *f*–*f* 1800 m above *XY*. Through *h′*, draw a line at 55° to *XY*, meeting *f*–*f* at *p*1′.
3. Obtain *hp*1 parallel to *XY* and rotate it to *hp* to make 65° to the vertical. Project *p* to *p′* on *f*–*f*.

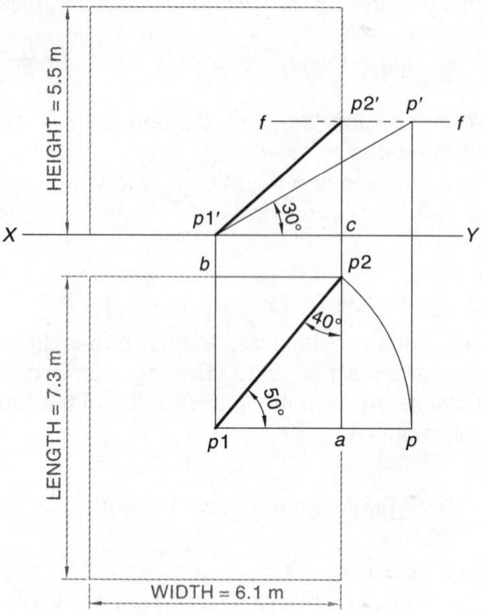

Scale: 1 : 100

Ans: Size of room = 7.3 m × 6.1 m × 5.5 m

Fig. 11.61

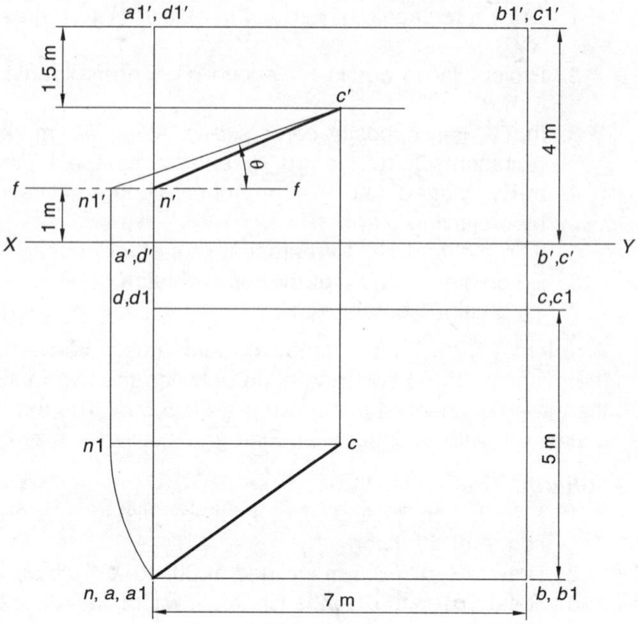

Scale: 1 : 100

Ans: TL = $n1'c'$ = 45 mm = 4.5 m

θ = 19°

Fig. 11.62

4. Through *h'*, draw a line at 20° to *XY* to locate *a*1′ on *XY*.
5. Obtain *ha*1 parallel to *XY* and rotate it to *ha* to make 35° to the vertical. Project *a* to *a'* on *XY*.
6. Join *a'p'*. Obtain TL of *AP* as shown.

The time taken by the missile to hit the plane = (TL of *AP*)/(Speed of the missile) = 3180/300 = 10.6 s

Problem 11.28 A 2.5 m wide and 1.5 m high picture frame is to be fixed on a wall railing by two straight wires attached to the top corners. The frame is to make an angle of 30° with the wall and the wires are to be fixed to a hook on the wall on the centreline of the frame and 2 m above the railing. Find the length of wires and the angle between them.

Solution Refer Fig. 11.64.

1. Draw SV of the frame *a″*(*b″*)–*c″*(*d″*) = 1.5 m, inclined at 30° to *X*1 *Y*1 as shown.
2. Project SV to obtain FV- *a′b′c′d′*. *a′b′* = *c′d′* = 2.5 m.
3. Locate *h″* on *X*1*Y*1 2 m above *XY*. Project *h″* to *h′*, centrally above *a′b′*.
4. Join *h″*–*a″*(*b″*), *h′*–*a′* and *h′*–*b′*.
5. Rotate *h″*–*a″*(*b″*) to *h″*–*a*1″ (*b*1″) on *X*1 *Y*1. Project *a*1″(*b*1″) to *a*1′ and *b*1′ on *a′d′* and *b′c′* respectively. Join *h′*–*a*1′ and *h′*–*b*1′. *h′*–*a*1′ = *h′*–*b*1′ = TL of wire. Measure ∠*a*1′–*h′*–*b*1′.

Problem 11.29 Pune City Development Corporation wishes to connect two tourist places, namely, the Parvati hill and the Sarasbaug (the garden) by a ropeway. The proposed way will start from the Ganapati Temple in the garden and end at the peak of the hill. The hill is 200 m high and the plateau of the garden is 10 m below the bottom level of the hill. The distance between the two places, in aerial view, is 750 m. The hill is due 20° west of the south of the temple.

(i) Find the length of the ropeway and its slope with the ground.
(ii) If the slope of the ropeway should not exceed 12°, how far will the start of the way be located from the temple?

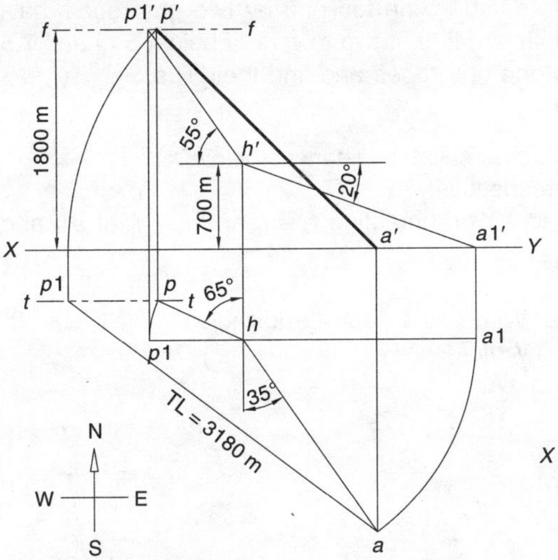

Scale: 1 : 10000

Ans: Missile will take h10.6 s to hit plane

Fig. 11.63

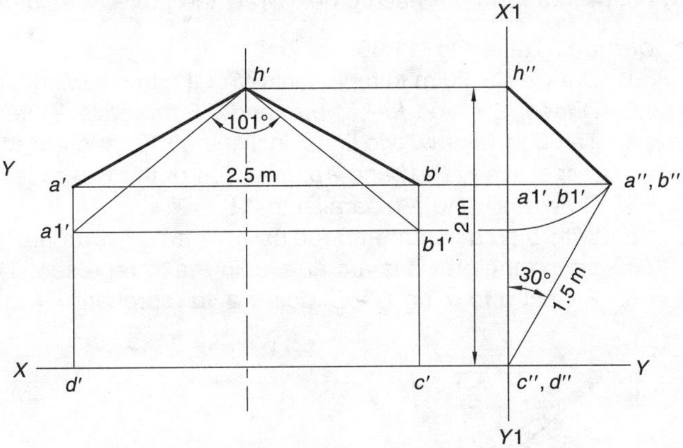

Scale: 1 : 20

Ans: Length of wire = $h'a1'$ = 81 mm = 1.62 m

Angle between wires = 101°

Fig. 11.64

Solution Refer Fig. 11.65.

1. Draw f_h–f_h and f_t–f_t 200 m above and 10 m below XY respectively.
2. Mark t' on f_t–f_t and t at suitable distances below XY. Draw th = 750 m, inclined at 20° to vertical as shown. th gives TV of the ropeway.
3. Project h to h' on f_h–f_h. Join $h't'$ for FV of the ropeway.
4. Find TL–h'–$t1'$ and θ as shown.
5. Through h', draw a line at 12° to XY meeting f_t–f_t at $t2'$. Project $t2'$ to $t2$ on h–$t1$ produced. $t1$–$t2$ gives the minimum distance between the temple and the start of the ropeway if the slope of the ropeway should not exceed 12°.

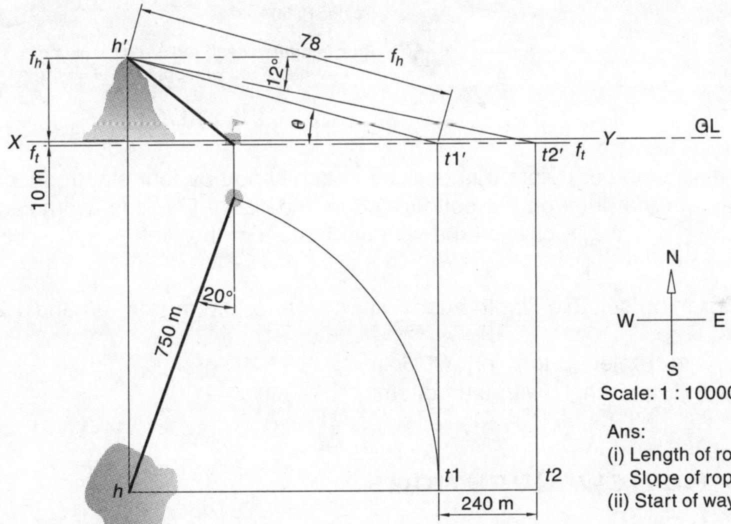

Scale: 1 : 10000

Ans:

(i) Length of rope-way = $h' - t1'$ = 78 mm = 780 m

Slope of rope-way = θ = 16°

(ii) Start of way from temple = $t1 - t2$ = 24 mm = 240 m

Fig. 11.65

Problem 11.30 A 20 m high telecommunication tower is tied at the top end by two guy ropes, having angles of depression of 30° and 40°. Other ends of the ropes are tied at two towers of height 5 m and 7.5 m and 14 m apart from each other. Draw the projections of the guy ropes and find their TLs.

Solution Refer Fig. 11.66.

1. Draw *o′t′* = 20 m to represent FV of the tower. Mark *t*(*o*) at suitable distances below *XY*.
2. Draw $f_a - f_a$ and $f_b - f_b$, 5 m and 7.5 m above *XY* respectively.
3. Through *t′*, draw two lines, inclined at 30° and 40° to *XY* and meeting $f_a - f_a$ and $f_b - f_b$ at *a*1′ and *b′* respectively. *t′a*1′ and *t′b′* give TLs of the two ropes.
4. Draw *t*–*a*1 and *t*–*b* parallel to *XY*.
5. With *b* as a centre and radius = 14 m, draw an arc. With *t* as a centre and radius = *t*–*a*1, cut off an arc on the previous arc at *a*. Join *t*–*a* to represent TV of TA.
6. Project *a* to *a′* on $f_a - f_a$. Join *t′a′* to represent FV of TA.

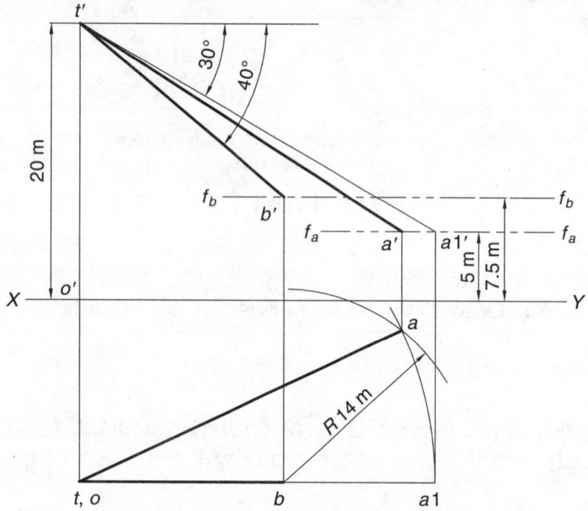

Scale: 1 : 100

Ans: TA = *t′a*1′ = 300 mm = 30 m
TB = *t′b′* = 194 mm = 19.4 m

Fig. 11.66

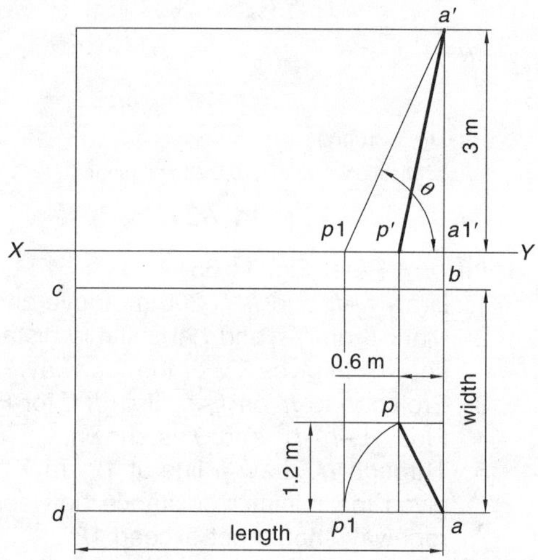

Scale: 1 : 50

Ans: Length of each rod = *a′p*1′ = 66 mm = 3.3 m
Angle of rod with bottom = θ = 66°

Fig. 11.67

Problem 11.31 A rectangular metallic tank of height 3 m is to be strengthened by four stay rods, each connecting the top corner of the tank to the point on the bottom, 0.6 m and 1.2 m from the two adjacent walls. Determine graphically the length and angle of each rod with the bottom of the tank.

Solution Refer Fig. 11.67.

1. Draw TV of the tank *abcd* assuming suitable length and width. Locate *p*, 0.6 m from *ab* and 1.2 m from *ad*. Join *ap*.
2. Obtain FV such that *a*1′–*a′* = 3 m. Project *p* to *p′* on *XY*. Join *a′p′*.
3. Obtain *a′*–*p*1′ as shown to find TL and angle with the bottom.

REVIEW QUESTIONS

1. A 90 mm long line *AB* is inclined at 40° to the HP. The end *A* is 12 mm above the HP and the end *B* is 52 mm in front of the VP. Draw projections of the line if its FV measures 76 mm. Locate traces.

2. The ends of a line *CD* are on the same projector. The end *C* is 25 mm below the HP and 15 mm behind the VP. The end *D* is 55 mm above the HP and 35 mm in front of the VP. Determine the TL and traces of *CD* and its inclinations with the RPs.
3. The TV and FV of a line *RM* measure 60 mm and 75 mm respectively. The line is 80 mm long. Draw its projections and indicate grade and bearing with respect to *R*.
4. A line *PQ* is in the first quadrant. Its ends *P* and *Q* are 16 mm and 48 mm in front of the VP respectively. The distance between the end projectors is 60 mm. The line is inclined at 30° to the HP and its HT is 10 mm above the *XY* line. Draw the projections of the line *PQ* and find its TL and locate its VT.
5. The perpendiculars from the point *A* on the HP and the VP are 60 mm and 15 mm long respectively. The perpendiculars from another point *B* on the HP and the VP are 20 mm and 35 mm long respectively. The length of the line joining *AB* is 80 mm. Draw the projections of the line. Both the points lie in the first quadrant.
6. A line *PQ* has its end *P*, 10 mm behind the VP and 20 mm below the HP. Its end *Q* is 30 mm behind the VP and 40 mm below the HP. The distance between the end projectors is 40 mm. Draw the projections of line *PQ*, find its TL and inclinations with the HP and the VP. Locate its traces.
7. A line *AB* measures 100 mm. The projectors through its VT and the end *A* are 40 mm apart. The point *A* is 30 mm below the HRP and 20 mm behind the FRP. The VT is 10 mm above the HRP. Draw the projections of the line and determine its HT and inclinations with the FRP and the HRP.
8. A straight line *RS*, equally inclined to the HP and the VP, has its end *R* in front of the VP and 18 mm above the HP. End *S* is behind the VP and 38 mm below the HP. A point on this line is in the VP and 10 mm below the HP. Draw the projections and find TL and inclination of the line with the HP. The distance between projectors of the ends is 56 mm.
9. An 85 mm long line makes 20° to the HP and 40° to the VP. Its midpoint is 15 mm from both the RPs. Draw the projections of the line.
10. A line has its end in the HP and the other end at the intersection of the HP and the PP. The midpoint of the line is 55 mm above the HP and 46 mm in front of the VP. The TV of the line makes 30° to *XY*. Draw the projections and find the TL of the line.
11. The TV of a 75 mm long line *CD* measures 50 mm. *C* is 50 mm in front of the VP and 15 mm below the HP. *D* is 15 mm in front of the VP and is above the HP. Draw the FV of *CD* and find its inclinations with the HP and the VP. Also show its traces.
12. The end *E* of a straight line *EF* is 12 mm above the HP. The distance between the end projectors of the line is 75 mm and that between the projectors through the traces is 100 mm. If the plan and the elevation of the line both make 35° with the *XY* line, obtain the projections of the line and find
    (i) TL of the line and (ii) inclination of the line with the HP and the VP
13. The TV of a line *MN* measures 75 mm and makes an angle of 55° with *XY*. The end *M* is in the VP and the HT of the line is 18 mm above *XY*. The line is inclined at 35° to the HP. Draw the projections of the line *MN* and determine its TL, true inclination with the VP, and traces.
14. The TV of an 80 mm long line *AB* measures 70 mm, while the length of its FV is 55 mm. Its one end *A* is in the HP and 15 mm in front of the VP. Draw the projections of *AB* and determine its inclinations with the HP and the VP.
15. A line *MN* is in the first quadrant. Its ends *M* and *N* are 15 mm and 45 mm in front of the VP respectively. The distance between the end projectors is 55 mm. The line is inclined at 35° to the HP and its HT is 8 mm above the *XY*. Draw the projections of the line. Find its TL. Also locate its VT.
16. The distance between the projectors of HT and VT of a line *AB* is 40 mm. The HT of the line is 20 mm behind the FRP and VT is 40 mm below the HRP. The end *A* of the line is 10 mm below the HRP. Draw the projections of line *AB*, assuming the end *B* in the fourth quadrant. The line is 120 mm long. Also find the inclination of the line with the FRP and the HRP.
17. Draw the projections and locate the traces of an 80 mm long line *RS* whose end *R* is 16 mm below the HP and 20 mm behind the VP and the end *S* is in the first quadrant. The line is inclined at 55° to the HP and 35° to the VP.
18. A straight line *CD* is inclined at 30° to the VP and 45° to the HP. Its LHSV measures 45 mm. The midpoint *P* of the line is 55 mm in front of the VP and 50 mm above the HP. Draw the three views of the line and find its TL.

19. A line *EF* is inclined at 60° to the VP and 30° to the HP. Its end *E* is 25 mm from the HP and 20 mm from the VP. The FV of the line is 55 mm long. Draw the projections of *EF* if it fully lies in the third quadrant. Also draw SV, find TL and locate traces.
20. Two lines *AB*, 70 mm long, and *BC*, 40 mm long, are perpendicular to each other. *AB* is inclined at 30° to the HP whereas *BC* is parallel to the HP and inclined at 45° to the VP. Draw the projections of both the lines and determine the angle made by *AB* with the VP.
21. The distance between the end projectors of a line *AB* is 70 mm and the projectors through the traces are 110 mm apart. The TV and FV make 40° and 60° to *XY* respectively. The end *A* is 10 mm above the HP. Draw the projections of the line and determine the
    (i) TL of the line (ii) angles wiht the HP and the VP (iii) traces
22. Line *AB*, 80 mm long, has its end *A*, 15 mm above the HP and HT, 15 mm in front of the VP. It is inclined to the VP at 35° and its length is 65 mm. Draw its projections and mark
    (i) its angle with the HP, (ii) location of VT, (iii) distance of *A* from the VP, (iv) distances of *B* from the HP and the VP
23. A line segment *CD* is placed in the third quadrant such that point *C* is 12 mm from the HP and point *D* is 50 mm from the VP. Distance between the projectors of *C* and HT is 15 mm. Length of the FV of the line is 80 mm. The line is contained in the vertical plane that makes an angle 30° with *XY*. Draw projections of the line. Determine traces, TL and inclinations of the line segment with the RPs.
24. A line *RS*, 75 mm long, shows its TV 55 mm long. The line is inclined at 28° to the VP. The end *R* is 80 mm above the HP whilst the VT is 10 mm below the HP. Draw the projections of the line if end *S* is nearer to both the RPs than end *R*. Locate the HT. What is the inclination of the line with the HP?
25. Line *PQ* is 150 mm long. The end *P* is 15 mm below the HP. The end *Q* is in first quadrant. Its HT and VT are respectively 50 mm behind the VP and 35 mm above the HP. FV of the line shows an apparent angle of 30° with the HP. Draw the projections of the line.
26. A line *AB* = 80 mm lies fully in the first quadrant. Its FV and TV each makes 45° to *XY*. The end *A* is nearer to and 15 mm from the VP. The end *B* is nearer to and 25 mm above the HP. Draw the projections. Find the true inclinations.
27. Two lines, *AB* and *CD*, each 80 mm long, are parallel to the PP. The distance between the end projectors of *AB* and that of *CD* is 45 mm. The ends *A* and *C* are on the HP and 60 mm in front of the VP. The ends *B* and *D* are nearer to the VP. Draw the projections of the line if *AB* makes 30° and *CD* makes 60° to the HP. Find the length *BD*.
28. The elevation of a line *AB* is 75 mm and is inclined to line *XY* at 45°. The end *A* is 25 mm above the HP and the end *B* is 10 mm behind the VP. Draw its projections if the length of the line is 95 mm and the end *B* is in the third quadrant. Find the inclination of the line with the HP and the VP and also the traces.
29. A straight line segment, 100 mm long, measures 80 mm in the plan and 70 mm in elevation. The midpoint *M* is situated 36 mm above the HP and 46 mm in front of the VP. Draw the TV and FV of the line. Also locate the traces.
30. A straight line makes an angle of 30° with the HP and 60° with the VP. One end of the line is in the HP and 40 mm from the VP. The other end lies in the VP. Draw the projections of the line. Also find the TL of the line and the height of the end in the VP.
31. The projectors of the ends of line *PQ* are 90 mm apart. *P* is 20 mm above the HP whereas *Q* is 45 mm behind the VP. The HT and VT of the line coincide with each other on *XY*, between the two ends of the projectors and 35 mm away from the projector of the end *P*. Draw the projection and find the TL of the line.
32. Two points *A* and *B* are 6.5 m and 10 m above the ground level. They are connected by road and are seen at angles of depression of 60° and 45° respectively from a point *O* on a hill, 18 m above the ground level. *A* is due 15° north of east and *B* is due 30° west of south of *O*. Find the length of the connecting road.
33. Two poles *AB* and *CD* are respectively 5 m and 9 m high and are standing at the opposite corners of a rectangular plot of 8 m × 6 m. Determine the actual distance between the top ends of poles *B* and *D*. Assume the longer sides of the rectangular plot are parallel to the VP.
34. In a room, 6 m × 4 m × 3.5 m, the switch on the wall, of an electric bulb, is at a height of 1.5 m from the floor and 1.2 m from one of the shorter walls. The bulb is situated on the opposite wall, 0.5 m below the

ceiling and equidistant from the shorter walls. Determine the true distance, graphically, between the bulb and its switch.

35. A room is 8 m × 5 m × 4 m. A peg is driven at the centre of the roof. Another peg is driven on the common edge between the two mutually perpendicular walls. The minimum length of the thread connecting these two pegs is 5.5 m. Find graphically the height of the peg on the common edge above the ground.
36. The top and bottom of a wooden stool have the sizes 30 cm × 30 cm and 60 cm × 60 cm respectively. The height of the stool is 70 cm. It has four legs, each located at a corner. Find the length of a leg and its angle with the floor.
37. Two buildings are situated diagonally opposite to each other across the roads at a square. The width of each road is 30 m. The buildings are 40 m and 50 m high. Find the length of a television cable connecting the nearest corners of the two buildings.
38. A chimney of 1.8 m diameter and 26 m height is supported by a set of three non-elastic ropes. These ropes are attached on the outside of the chimney at 3 m from the top. They are anchored 4.5 m above the ground at a distance of 12 m from the axis of the chimney. Draw the projections of the ropes if the anchor points are due south, north-west and north-east of the chimney. Find TL and the slope with the ground of one of the ropes. Take a suitable scale.
39. The vertical poles *AB*, *CD* and *EF* are 5 m, 8 m and 12 m long respectively. Their ends are on the HP and lie at the corner of an equilateral triangle of 10 m side. Determine graphically the distance between the top ends of the poles, viz., *A*, *C* and *E*.
40. Three poles stand on the ground at the corners of an equilateral triangle of side 8 m. An electric lamp post of height 5 m, situated at the centre of the triangle, creates the shadows of the poles 4 m, 2.5 m and 1.5 m long. Find out the height of each pole.
41. A pan of weighing balance is attached by three chains from the three equispaced points on its circumference to a 40 cm hook above the centre of the pan. The flat pan has a diameter of 30 cm. Draw the projections and find the TLs of each chain. What is the inclination of the chain with the HP?
42. A man and a child are standing on the ground, 6 m from an electric pole. A bulb on the pole creates the shadows of the man and the child as 1.6 m and 0.8 m long respectively. The height of the pole is 8 m. Find the height of the man and the child.

    If the angle between the shadows is 110°, how far is the man standing from the child?
43. A crane has a vertical mast and a reach-arm. The mast can rotate about its own axis. The reach-arm is connected to the mast at one end and carries a hook at another end. The arm can swivel in a vertical plane about its pivoted end on the mast.

    The arm was initially set horizontal and parallel to a wall to pick a box. It then turned upward through 50°. The mast simultaneously rotated through 30° to place the box at the new location.

    Find graphically the distance moved by the box. The length of the arm is 5 m. Neglect the length of the hook.
44. The guy ropes of two poles, 15 m apart, are attached to a point 12 m above the ground on the corner of a building. The points of attachments on the poles are 8 m and 5 m above the ground. The inclinations of the ropes with the ground are 45° and 30° respectively. Draw the projections and find the distances of the poles from the building and the lengths of the guy ropes.
45. A straight road going uphill from a point *A*, due east to another point *B*, is 6 km long and has a slope of 22°. Another straight road from *B* due 35° east of north, to a point *C* is 3.5 km long but is on a level ground. Determine the length and slope of the straight road joining the points *A* and *C*.
46. An electric post of 10 m height is vertically mounted on the top of a hillock of height 30 m. Another pole of the same height is due 30° east of north of the first pole and is mounted vertically on the ground at a distance of 100 m from the latter. Find out the shortest length of the electric wire needed to connect the top of the first pole to the top of the second pole. Also find graphically the angle made by the wire with the ground.

Chapter 12

AUXILIARY PLANE PROJECTION METHOD

12.1 INTRODUCTION

Any plane perpendicular to an RP and inclined to the other RP is called an *auxiliary plane*. The view of an object obtained on an auxiliary plane is called an *auxiliary view*. In drawing practice, two auxiliary planes, viz., Auxiliary Inclined Plane (AIP) and Auxiliary Vertical Plane (AVP), are used. An AIP is a plane inclined to the HP and perpendicular to the VP. On the contrary, AVP represents a plane inclined to the VP and perpendicular to the HP. Obviously, AIP and AVP are seen as lines in FV and TV respectively. These lines are called *auxiliary reference lines* and are shown by $X1Y1$, $X2Y2$, etc. Auxiliary planes are used to obtain auxiliary views and true shapes of sections of solids.

The auxiliary plane projection method provides quick and accurate solutions to many projection problems. It is especially helpful in projections of planes and solids. This chapter explains the use of auxiliary plane projection method in solving problems on projections of lines. The application of this method in projections of planes and solids is explained in the corresponding chapters.

REMEMBER THE FOLLOWING

- AIP is seen as a line in FV.
- AVP is seen as a line in TV.

12.2 CONCEPT OF AUXILIARY PLANE PROJECTION METHOD

To understand the concept of auxiliary plane projection method, let us see Problem 11.6, Fig. 11.42. The projections, i.e., $c'd'$ and cd of the line CD are obtained as explained. To find TL of CD, $c'd'$ is rotated about c' so that $c'd2'$ becomes parallel to XY. $d2'$ is then projected to locate $d2$ on t–t. $cd2$ gives TL. Now, instead of drawing $c'd2'$ parallel to XY, if an auxiliary reference line $X1Y1$ is drawn parallel to $c'd'$, it would serve the same purpose. Drawing $c'd2'$ parallel to XY is the same as drawing $X1Y1$ parallel to $c'd'$ (since $c'd' = c'd2'$). This is shown in Fig. 12.1.

c' and d' are then projected on $X1Y1$ to locate $c1$ and $d1$ respectively. The distances of $c1$ and $d1$ from $X1Y1$ are same as those of c and d from XY respectively. Obviously, $c1$ is seen on $X1Y1$. As $c'd'$

is FV, $c1d1$ represents TV. This TV is obtained on the auxiliary reference line $X1Y1$ (AIP) and hence called *auxiliary* TV. Note the similarities between Fig. 11.42 and Fig. 12.1, as shown in Table 12.1.

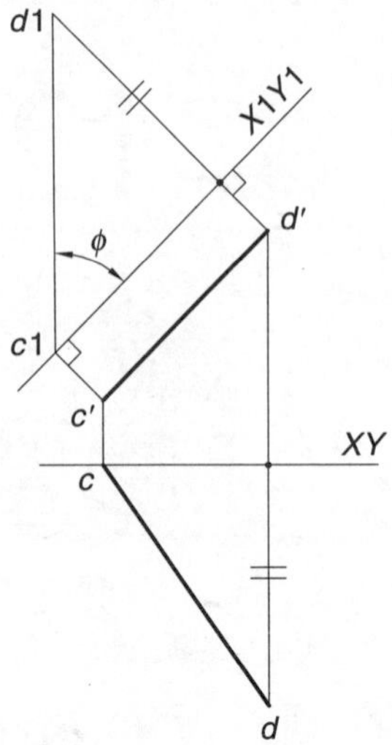

Fig. 12.1

Table 12.1

Fig. 11.42	*Fig. 12.1*
• $c'd2'$ is parallel to XY ($c'd2' = c'd'$). • $d2'$ is projected on XY to locate $d2$. • Distance of $d2$ from XY = Distance of d from XY. • c is on XY.	• $c'd'$ is parallel to $X1Y1$ ($c'd' = c'd2'$). • d' is projected on $X1Y1$ to locate $d1$. • Distance of $d1$ from $X1Y1$ = Distance of d from XY. • $c1$ is on $X1Y1$.

From the comparison shown in Table 12.1, it is clear that $cd2 = c1d1$ = TL of CD. Also, angle between $cd2$ and XY = angle between $c1d1$ and $X1Y1 = \phi$.

The following sections explain the application of auxiliary plane projection method to find TL, θ, ϕ and traces of a line and also, to decide the distance of a point from a line and the distance between two skew lines.

12.3 TRUE LENGTH, TRUE INCLINATIONS AND TRACES OF A LINE

Example 12.1 A line AB has its end A, 10 mm above the HP and 24 mm in front of the VP. End B is 55 mm above the HP and 50 mm in front of the VP. The distance between the end projectors is 45 mm. Draw the projections of the line and find the TL and true inclinations. Also locate the traces.

Solution Refer Fig. 12.2.

Locate a' and a, 10 mm above and 24 mm below XY respectively. Draw $\hat{B}$ at a distance of 45 mm from $\hat{A}$ and on it, locate b' and b, 55 mm above and 50 mm below XY respectively. Join $a'b'$ and ab.

To obtain the TL, θ, ϕ and traces, one may adopt the general method, Fig. 12.2(a), or auxiliary plane projection method, Fig. 12.2(b). In Fig. 12.2(a), $a'b'$ is turned about a' to make $a'b1'$ parallel to XY. $b1'$ is then projected on t–t to obtain TL $ab1$. Angle between $ab1$ and XY gives ϕ. To find θ, $b2'$ is obtained on f–f such that $a'b2'$ = TL. HT and VT are then located in the usual way.

Figure 12.2(b) makes use of auxiliary plane projection method. An auxiliary reference line $X1Y1$ (i.e., AIP) is set along $a'b'$. $a'b'$ is projected on $X1Y1$ to locate $a1b1$ such that the distances of $a1$ and $b1$ from $X1Y1$ are same as the distances of a and b from XY. $a1b1$ is the auxiliary TV representing TL. Note that $a1b1$ is on AIP. Therefore, the angle made by $a1b1$ with $X1Y1$ gives ϕ. The intersection of $a1b1$ produced with $X1Y1$ gives VT.

To find θ and HT, $X2Y2$ is set along ab. ab is then projected on $X2Y2$ and $a2'b2'$ is marked such that the distances of $a2'$ and $b2'$ from $X2Y2$ are equal to the distances of a' and b' from XY. $a2'b2'$ is auxiliary FV. As $a2'b2'$ is on AVP, its inclination and intersection (obtained when $a2'b2'$ produced) with $X2Y2$ give θ and HT respectively.

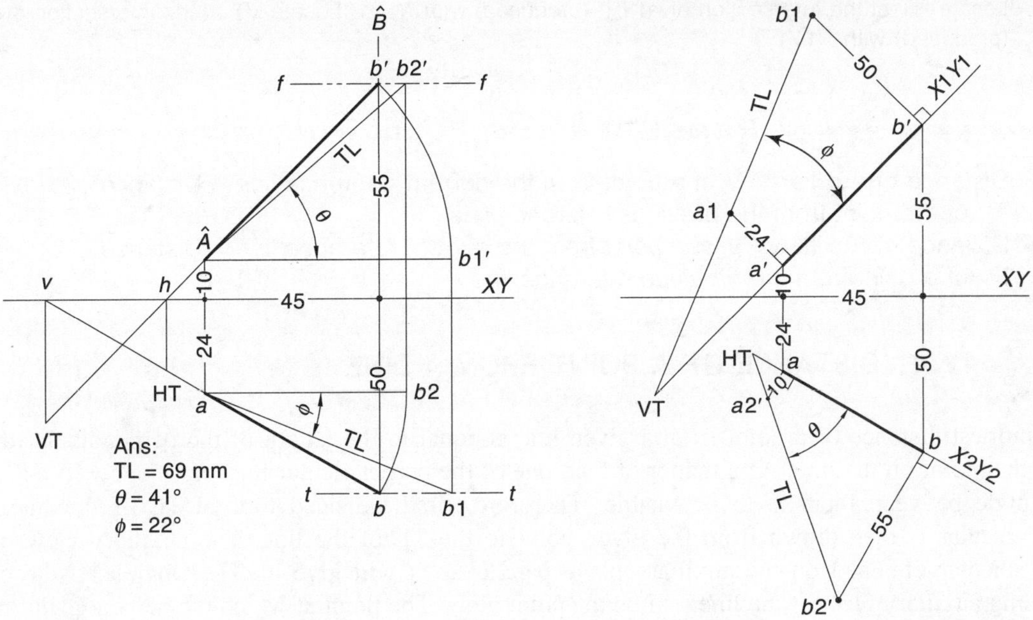

(a) (b)

Fig. 12.2

Table 12.2 shows the similarities between Fig. 12.2(a) and (b).

Table 12.2

Fig. 12.2(a)	*Fig. 12.2(b)*
• $a'b1'$ and $ab2$ are parallel to XY ($a'b1' = a'b'$ and $ab2 = ab$).	• $a'b'$ and ab are parallel to $X1Y1$ and $X2Y2$ respectively.
• Distance of $b1$ from XY = Distance of b from XY. Distance of $b2'$ from XY = Distance of b' from XY.	• Distances of $a1$ and $b1$ from $X1Y1$ = Distances of a and b from XY (respectively). Distances of $a2'$ and $b2'$ from $X2Y2$ = Distances of a' and b' from XY (respectively).
• $a'b2' = ab1$ = TL	• $a1b1 = a2'b2'$ = TL
• Angle between $a'b2'$ (i.e., TL) and $XY = \theta$	• Angle between $a2'b2'$ (i.e., TL) and $X2Y2 = \theta$
• Angle between $ab1$ (i.e., TL) and $XY = \phi$	• Angle between $a1b1$ (i.e., TL) and $X1Y1 = \phi$

Example 12.2 The EL and PL of a line *AB* are 25 mm and 55 mm respectively. The end *A* is 15 mm in front of the VP while the end *B* is 20 mm above the HP. The line lies fully in the first quadrant. Draw the projections of the line if its end projectors coincide. Find TL, true inclinations and locate traces.

Solution As the end projectors of the line coincide, the line is parallel to the PP. The projections are shown in Fig. 12.3. Auxiliary reference line $X1Y1$ is assumed to be coinciding with $a'b'$ (and ab).

1. Obtain auxiliary TV $a1b1$ such that the distances of $a1$ and $b1$ from $X1Y1$ are respectively equal to the distances of a and b from XY. $a1b1$ = TL. Angle between $a1b1$ and $X1Y1 = \phi$.
2. Obtain auxiliary FV $a1'b1'$ such that the distances of $a1'$ and $b1'$ from $X1Y1$ are respectively equal to the distances of a' and b' from XY. $a1'b1'$ = TL. Angle between $a1'b1'$ with $X1Y1 = \theta$.

3. Locate HT at the intersection of $a1'b1'$ (produced) with $X1Y1$. Locate VT at the intersection of $a1b1$ (produced) with $X1Y1$.

REMEMBER THE FOLLOWING

- Distance of Auxiliary TV of a point from the current reference line = Distance of previous TV of the point from the previous reference line
- Distance of Auxiliary FV of a point from the current reference line = Distance of previous FV of a point from the previous reference line

12.4 DISTANCE OF A POINT FROM A LINE

The shortest distance of a point from a given line is equal to the length of the perpendicular drawn from that point on the line. As a matter of fact, one of the perpendicular lines must show its TL if the real angle between them is to be visible. Therefore, first, we need to find TL of the line. The perpendicular is then drawn from the given point to the TL of the line. The auxiliary view of the perpendicular obtained on the auxiliary plane parallel to it will give its TL. Obviously, the corresponding auxiliary view of the line will be the point view. The point at which the perpendicular meets the line may be projected back in the original views. The following examples explain the use of the auxiliary plane projection method to find the distance of a point from a given line.

Example 12.3 Figure 12.4 shows the FVs and TVs of a line *AB* and point *P*. Find the shortest distance between the point and the line.

Solution

1. Draw an auxiliary reference line $X1Y1$ along any one of the views (say, $a'b'$). Obtain auxiliary TV $a1b1$ of the line to represent TL. Also obtain auxiliary TV $p1$ of the point.
   Distances of $a1$, $b1$ and $p1$ from $X1Y1$ = Distances of a, b and p from XY (respectively).
2. Draw auxiliary reference line $X2Y2$ perpendicular to $a1b1$. Project $a1$, $b1$ and $p1$ on $X2Y2$ to obtain $a2'$ ($b2'$) and $p2'$ respectively.
   Distances of $a2'$, $b2'$ and $p2'$ from $X2Y2$ = Distances of a', b' and p' from $X1Y1$ (respectively). Obviously, $a2'(b2')$ is obtained on $X2Y2$ and it represents the point view of line *AB*.
3. Join and measure $p2'$–$a2'(b2')$ for the shortest distance between the point *P* and the line *AB*.

12.5 DISTANCE BETWEEN TWO SKEW LINES

Two non-intersecting, non-parallel lines are called *skew lines*. Obviously, skew lines are non-coplanar. The shortest distance between any two skew lines is the length of the common perpendicular to them. To find the shortest distance between skew lines, we need to find the point view of any one line. The perpendicular from that point view on the corresponding auxiliary view of the other line gives the required distance.

If the FVs (or TVs) of the two lines are parallel to each other, then the distance between the FVs (or TVs) gives the shortest distance between the lines (Problem 12.5). If the point of intersection of FVs of two lines shares the common projector with the point of intersection of the TVs of the lines, then the lines are not skew lines. The case indicates two intersecting coplanar lines.

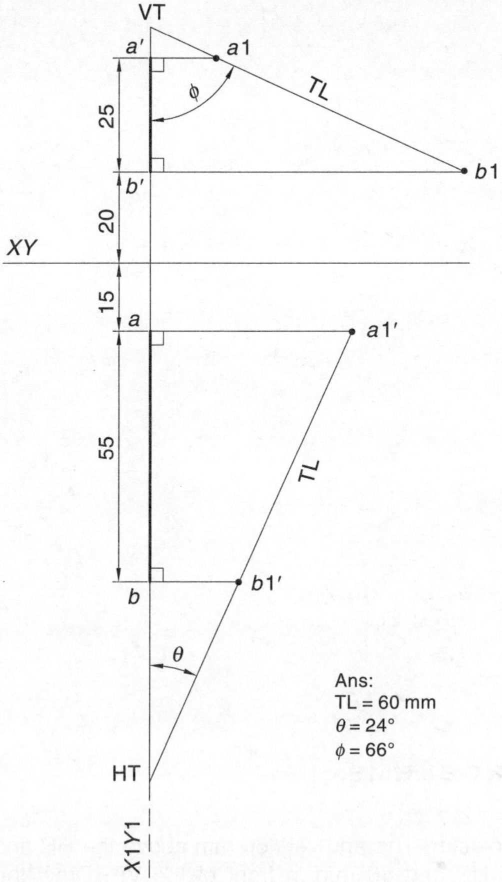

Fig. 12.3

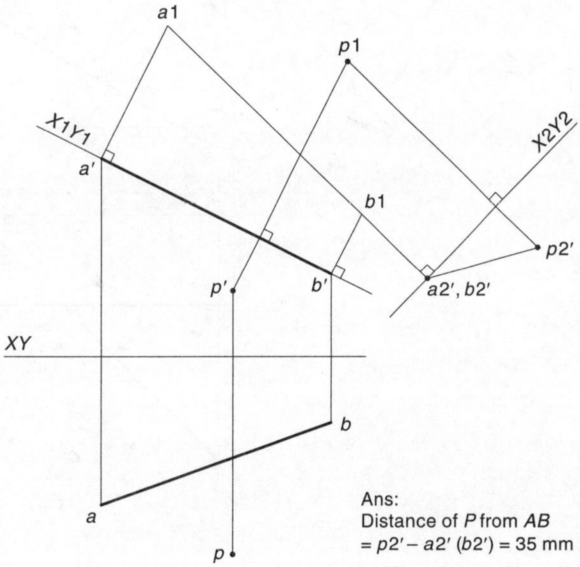

Fig. 12.4

Example 12.4 A line *AB* is inclined to the HP and parallel to the VP. The end *A* is 10 mm above the HP and 25 mm in front of the VP. The end *B* is 40 mm above the HP. Another line *CD* is inclined to the VP and parallel to the HP. The end *C* is 15 mm above the HP and 60 mm in front of the VP. The end *D* is 10 mm in front of the VP. Both the lines share common end projectors which are 50 mm apart. Draw the projections of the lines and find the shortest distance between them.

Solution Refer Fig. 12.5.

Draw the projections *a′b′* and *ab* of the line *AB* and *c′d′* and *cd* of the line *CD* as shown. *a′b′* shows TL of *AB* and *cd* shows TL of *CD*. To find the shortest distance between the two lines, we will obtain the point view of any one (say, line *AB*) of them.

1. Draw *X*1*Y*1 perpendicular to *a′b′*. Obtain point view *a*1*b*1 of *AB* and also the corresponding auxiliary TV *c*1*d*1 of *CD*.
2. From *a*1(*b*1), drop a perpendicular on *c*1*d*1, meeting it at *m*1. *a*1(*b*1)–*m*1 gives the shortest distance between the two lines.

Note: If *m*1 is projected to *m′* on *c′d′* and *m′n′* is drawn parallel to *X*1*Y*1, then *m′n′* will represent FV of the common perpendicular to both the lines. TV *mn* is obtained by projecting *m′* and *n′* to *m* and *n* on *cd* and *ab* respectively. *m′n′* is perpendicular to *a′b′* (i.e., TL of *AB*). Similarly, *mn* is perpendicular to *cd* (i.e., TL of *CD*).

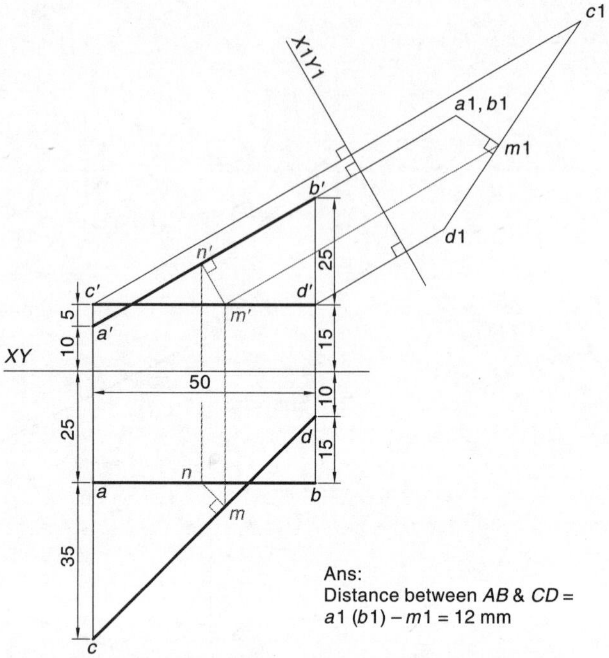

Fig. 12.5

ILLUSTRATIVE PROBLEMS

Problem 12.1 The ends of a line *AB* lie on the same projector. The end *A* is 60 mm above the HP and 30 mm behind the VP. The end *B* is 15 mm above the HP and 40 mm in front of the VP. Draw the projections of the line. Find its true inclinations and TL and locate the traces.

Solution Refer Fig. 12.6.

The FV *a′b′* and TV *ab* of the line are drawn as shown.

1. Assuming *X*1*Y*1 along *a′b′* (or *ab*), obtain auxiliary TV *a*1*b*1 to represent TL of the line. Measure ϕ, i.e., angle between *a*1*b*1 and *X*1*Y*1.
   Note that, *a*1 and *b*1 are marked on opposite sides of *X*1*Y*1 as *a* and *b* are on opposite sides of *XY*.
2. Project *ab* on *X*1*Y*1 to obtain auxiliary FV *a*1′*b*1′. Measure θ, i.e., angle between *a*1′*b*1′ and *X*1*Y*1. *a*1′*b*1′ = *a*1*b*1 = TL.
3. Locate VT at the intersection of *a*1*b*1 and *X*1*Y*1. Similarly, locate HT at the intersection of *a*1′*b*1′ produced and *X*1*Y*1.

Problem 12.2 Solve Problem 11.9 by auxiliary plane projection method.

Given: TL = 95 $\widehat{\text{VT}} = \hat{A}$ = 35 h_a = +25 d_a = +15 *v*-VT = + 8

Solution Refer Fig. 12.7.

1. Draw $\hat{A}$ and on it, mark *a′* and *a*, 25 mm above and 15 mm below *XY* respectively.
2. Draw *v*-VT at a distance of 35 mm from $\hat{A}$. *v*-VT = 8 mm. Joint VT-*a′* and *v*–*a*.
3. Through *a′*, set perpendicular *a′*–*a*1 to VT-*a′* such that *a′*–*a*1 = 15 mm.
4. Join VT-*a*1 and produce it to locate *b*1 such that *a*1*b*1 = TL = 95 mm.

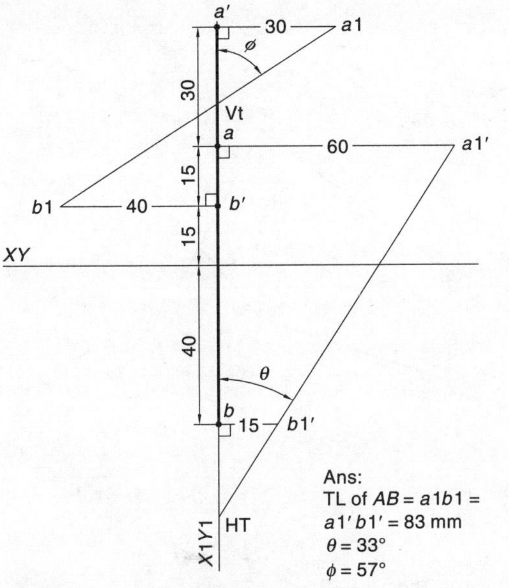

Fig. 12.6

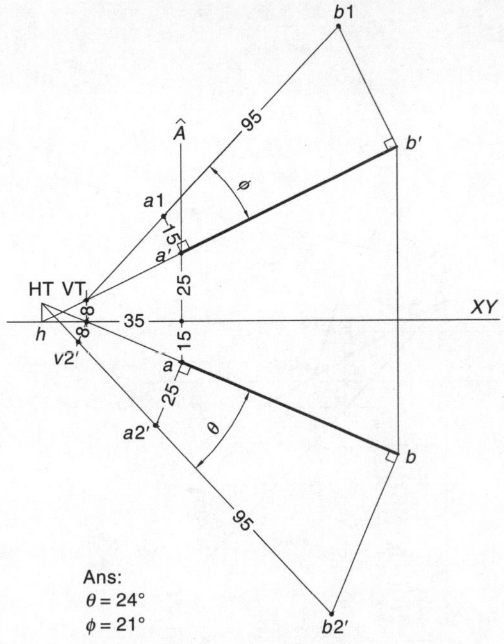

Fig. 12.7

5. Through *b*1, draw a perpendicular on VT-*a*′ produced to locate *b*′. *a*′*b*′ is the required FV. Measure the angle between *a*′*b*′ and *a*1*b*1, i.e., ϕ.
6. Project *b*′ to *v*–*a* produced to locate *b*. *ab* is the required TV.
7. To find θ and HT, draw perpendiculars *a*–*a*2′ and *b*–*b*2′ to *ab* such that *a*–*a*2′ = distance of *a*′ from *XY* and *b*–*b*2′ = distance of *b*′ from *XY*. Join *a*2′–*b*2′ and measure its angle with *ab*., i.e., θ. Produce *ba* and *b*2′–*a*2′ to meet at HT.

Problem 12.3 The end *A* of a line *AB* is 20 mm above the HP and 20 mm behind the VP. The end *B* is 15 mm below the HP and 45 mm in front of the VP. Elevation of the line measures 70 mm. The point *P* is 25 mm above the HP and 35 mm in front the VP. The projector through *P* lies between the projectors through *A* and *B* and at a distance of 25 mm from the projector through *A*. Draw the projections of the line and the point and find the shortest distance between them. Also draw the projections of the perpendicular from point *P* on the line *AB*.

Solution Refer Fig. 12.8.

The projections, *a*′*b*′ and *ab*, of line *AB* are drawn as shown. *a*′ and *a* will coincide. *p*′ and *p* represent the projections of point *P*. $\hat{P}$ is between $\hat{A}$ and $\hat{B}$ and at a distance of 25 mm from $\hat{A}$. To find the distance of *P* from *AB*, we will obtain the point view of *AB*.

1. Draw *X*1*Y*1 parallel to and at a suitable distance from any view (say, *a*′*b*′) of the line. Obtain auxiliary TVs—*a*1*b*1 of the line and *p*1 of the point. Note that *a*1 and *b*1 are marked on opposite sides of *X*1*Y*1. This is because, *a* and *b* are on opposite sides of *XY*. Also, observe that *p*1 and *b*1 are on the same side of *X*1*Y*1. *a*1*b*1 gives TL.
2. Draw *X*2*Y*2 perpendicular to *a*1*b*1 and obtain *a*2′, (*b*2′) and *p*2′ as mentioned in the previous example. *a*2′(*b*2′) is the point view of line *AB*.
3. Join *p*2′–*a*2′(*b*2′) to represent the shortest distance between *P* and *AB*.

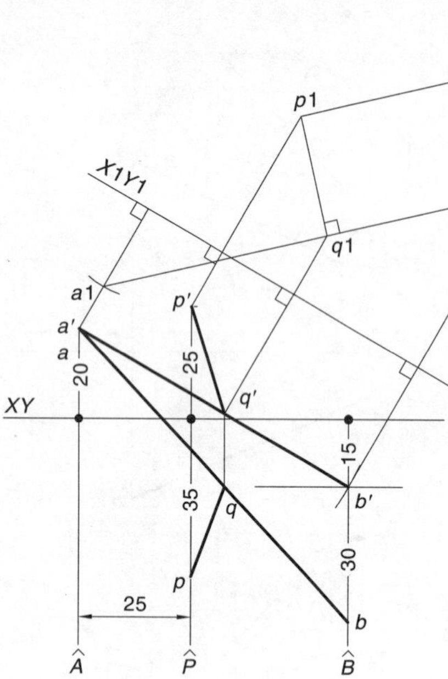

Fig. 12.8

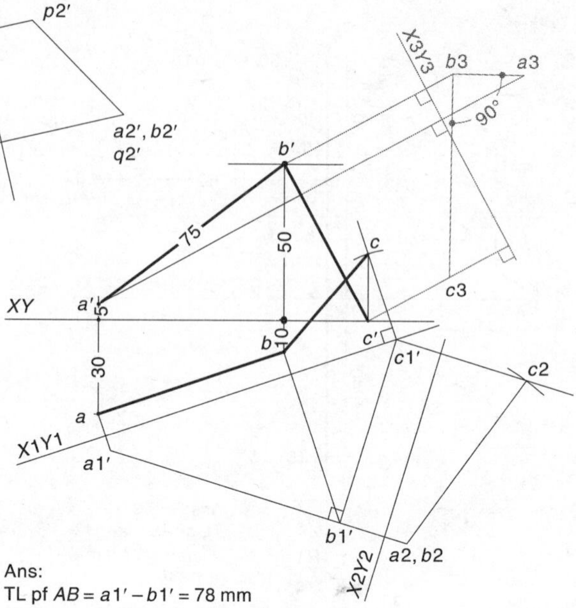

Ans:
TL pf $AB = a1' - b1' = 78$ mm
Distance of C from the VP $= c'c = 22$ mm

Fig. 12.9

4. From *p*1, drop perpendicular *p*1*q*1 on *a*1*b*1. *p*1*q*1 represents the auxiliary view of the perpendicular *PQ* to *AB*. (*q*2′ may be marked at *a*2′(*b*2′) such that *p*2′–*q*2′ = TL of *PQ*.)
5. Project *q*1 to *q*′ on *a*′*b*′ and then to *q* on *ab* as shown. Joint *p*′*q*′ and *pq* for the required projections of *PQ*.

Problem 12.4 Two lines *AB* and *BC* are perpendicular to each other. The length of *BC* is 65 mm whereas *AB* is seen as 75 mm in FV. The point *A* is 5 mm above the HP and 30 mm in front of the VP. The point *B* is 50 mm above the HP and 10 mm in front of the VP. The point *C* is on the HP. Draw the projections and find the TL of *AB*. What will be the distance of point *C* from the VP?

Solution Refer Fig. 12.9.

Draw *a*′*b*′ and *ab* as shown. As *C* is on the HP, *c*′ must be on *XY*. Since *AB* and *BC* are perpendicular, the real angle between them will be visible only if any one of them shows the TL.

1. Draw *X*1*Y*1 parallel to *ab* and obtain auxiliary FV *a*1′*b*1′. *a*1′*b*1′ gives TL of *AB*.
2. As *a*1′*b*1′ shows TL, the 90° angle between *AB* and *BC* must be marked in this view. Draw *b*1′*c*1′ perpendicular to *a*1′*b*1′. *c*1′ must be on *X*1*Y*1 (as *C* is on the HP).
3. Set *X*2*Y*2 perpendicular to *a*1′*b*1′. Obtain point view *a*2(*b*2) of *AB*.
4. With *a*2(*b*2) as a centre and radius = 65 mm (i.e., TL of *BC*), cut an arc on the projector through *c*1′ to locate *c*2. Join *b*2*c*2.
5. Through *c*1′, draw a perpendicular to *X*1*Y*1 and on it locate *c* such that the distance of *c* from *X*1*Y*1 = distances of *c*2 from *X*2*Y*2.
6. Project *c* to *c*′ on *XY*. Join *b*′*c*′ and *bc* for the FV and TV of *BC*.
   c′*c* gives the distance of *C* from the VP. It is very clear that the point *C* lies behind the VP.

Note: As a check, one may set *X*3*Y*3 parallel to *b*′*c*′ and obtain auxiliary views *a*3*b*3 and *b*3*c*3. *b*3*c*3 gives TL of *BC*. The angle between *a*3*b*3 and *b*3*c*3 = 90°.

Problem 12.5 Four poles, 3 m, 8 m, 11 m and 16 m high, are erected at the corners of a square plot of side 20 m. The two shorter poles are at the corners opposite to each other. Find the shortest distance between the two ropes, each connecting the tops of opposite poles.

Solution The two possible arrangements are shown in Fig. 12.10(a) and (b).

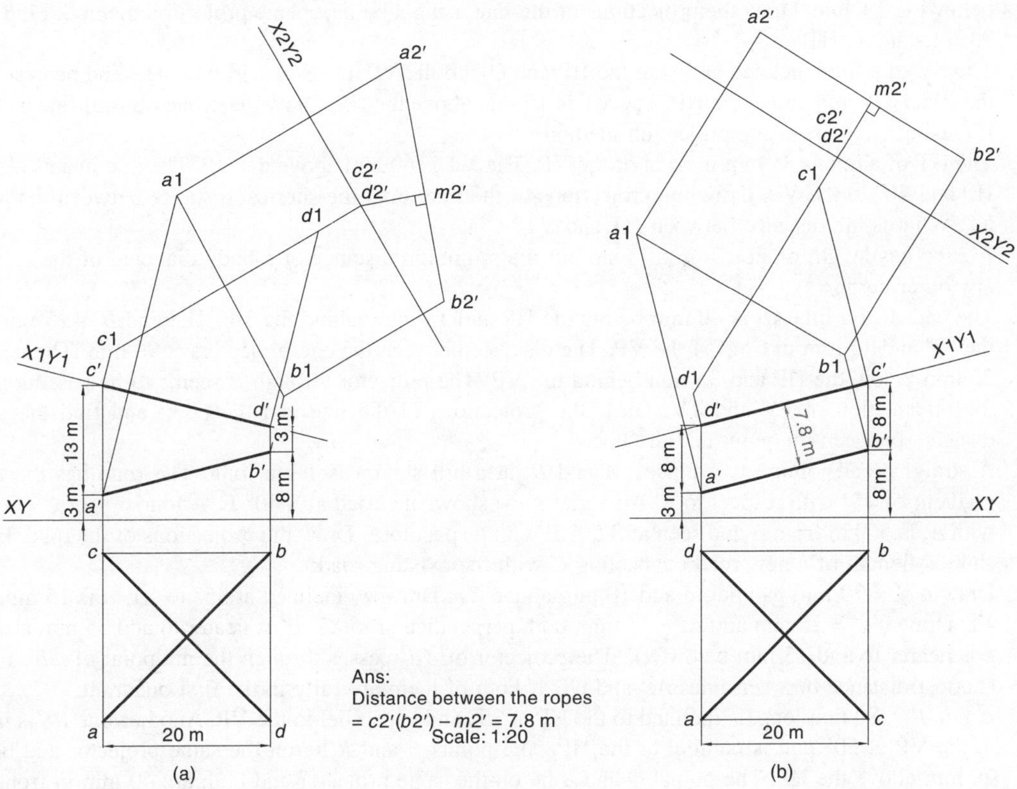

Fig. 12.10

1. Draw a square *adbc* of side 20 m. The corners *a*, *b*, *d* and *c* represent the TVs of the poles of height 3 m, 8 m, 11 m and 16 m respectively. Note that *a* is opposite to *b* and *c* is opposite to *d*. Join *ab* and *cd* to represent the TVs of the ropes.
2. Obtain FVs of the pole tops, viz, *a*′, *b*′, *c*′ and *d*′ at a distances of 3 m, 8 m, 16 m and 11 m respectively from *XY*. Join *a*′*b*′ and *c*′*d*′ to represent the FVs of the ropes.
3. Assuming *X*1*Y*1 along *c*′*d*′, obtain auxiliary TV *c*1*d*1 of *CD*. *c*1*d*1 gives TL of *CD*. Also, obtain auxiliary TV *a*1*b*1 of *AB*.
4. Draw *X*2*Y*2 perpendicular to *c*1*d*1. Obtain auxiliary FVs, *c*2′(*d*2′) and *a*2′*b*2′, of *CD* and *AB* respectively. *c*2′(*d*2′) is point view.
5. Draw perpendicular from *c*2′(*d*2′) on *a*2′*b*2′ to meet it at *m*2′. *c*2′(*d*2′)–*m*2′ gives the shortest distance between the ropes.

Note: In Fig. 12.10(b), *a*′*b*′ and *c*′*d*′ are parallel to each other. Hence, the distance between them will give the shortest distance between the ropes. In such cases, we need not to obtain the point view of a line.

Review Questions

1. A line *AB* is in the first quadrant. Its ends *A* and *B* are 15 mm and 45 mm above the HP respectively. The distance between the end projectors is 55 mm. The line is inclined at 35° to the VP and its VT is 8 mm below the *XY* line. Draw the projections of the line using auxiliary plane projection method. Find its TL. Also locate its HT.
2. The FV of a line, inclined at 30° to the HP and 60° to the VP, measures 40 mm. The end nearest to both the RPs is 25 mm above the HP. The VT is 15 mm above the HP. Draw the projections of line and locate HT using auxiliary plane projection method.
3. The HT of a line is 35 mm in front of the VP. The VT is 60 mm above the HP. The line makes 20° to the HP and 40° to the VP. Draw the projections of the line. Find the shortest distance between the line and *XY*. What is the distance between HT and VT?
4. A cube has length of side 70 mm. Find out the minimum distance of a body diagonal of the cube from any other corner.
5. The end *A* of a line *AB* is 40 mm below the HP and 15 mm behind the VP. The end *B* is 25 mm above the HP and 15 mm in front of the VP. The distance between the end projectors is 90 mm. The point *P* is 25 mm below the HP and 35 mm behind the VP. The projector through *P* seems to be passing through the intersection of FV and TV. Draw the projections of the line and the point and find the shortest distance between the point and the line.
6. A straight road joining two places, *A* and *B*, at a hill station is 1 km long. The road has the upward gradient of 15° with respect to *A*. An aerial view shows the road at S 40° E. A tourist spot *C*, on a level with *A*, is 500 m from *A* and seen at S 50° E with respect to *A*. Draw the projections of the road. Find the shortest length of a new road connecting *C* with the existing road.
7. Draw $a'b'$ = 70 mm parallel to and 10 mm above *XY*. Draw *ab* inclined at 35° to *XY*. *a* is 15 mm below *XY*. Draw $c'd'$ = 25 mm and *cd* = 45 mm, both perpendicular to *XY*. d' is nearer to and 35 mm above *XY*. *c* is nearer to and 15 mm below *XY*. The projector of $c'd'$ passes through the midpoint of $a'b'$. Find the shortest distance between lines *AB* and *CD* if both of them are fully in the first quadrant.
8. A line *PQ*, 80 mm long, is inclined to the HP at 25° and is parallel to the VP. Another line *RS* is inclined to the VP at 50° and is parallel to the HP. The points *P* and *R* lie on the same projector and both are 20 mm above the HP. The points *Q* and *S* lie on the same projector and both are 40 mm in front of the VP. Draw the projections of both the lines. Find the shortest distance between the two lines and the TL of *RS*.
9. The TV of a line *AB* is 50 mm. The point *A* is on the HP and 25 mm in front of the VP. The point *B* is on the VP and 40 mm above the HP. Another line *CD*, perpendicular to *AB*, is 100 mm long. Its end *C* is at the midpoint of *AB* while end *D* is on the HP. Draw the projections of both the lines. Find the angle made by each of them with the HP. [**Hint:** Compare it with Problem 12.4]

Chapter 13

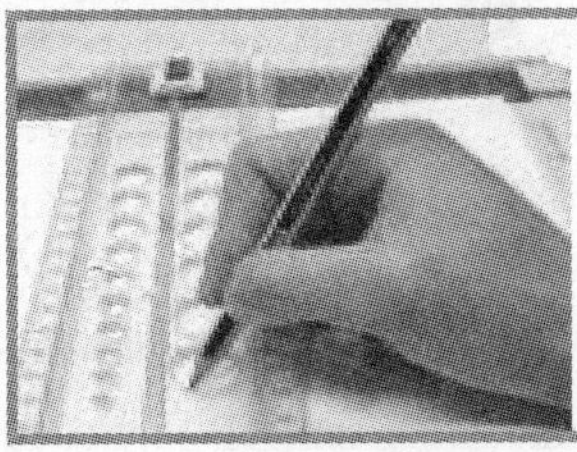

PROJECTIONS OF PLANES

13.1 INTRODUCTION

A plane is a two-dimensional geometrical entity. It has length and width but no thickness. For practical purposes, a flat face of an object may be treated as a plane. A plane which has limited extent is termed as a *lamina*. A plane can be located by: (i) three non-collinear points, (ii) a straight line and a point outside it, (ii) two parallel or intersecting straight lines, or (iv) traces of the lines.

This chapter deals with the projections of laminas of pre-defined shapes, e.g., triangular plane, square plane, rectangular plane, pentagonal plane, hexagonal plane, circular plane, semicircular plane, etc. These are already discussed in Section 4.2 (Figs 4.1 to 4.5). Sometimes, a given plane is composed of two or more planes mentioned above. Such planes are called *composite planes*, e.g., plane composed of a half hexagon and a semicircle, circular plane with hexagonal hole, etc.

13.2 POSITIONS OF PLANES

Depending on the inclinations with the RPs, a plane may have one of the following positions:

1. Plane parallel to an RP
   - Case (i): Plane parallel to the HP
   - Case (ii): Plane parallel to the VP
2. Plane inclined to one RP and perpendicular to the other RP
   - Case (i): Plane inclined to the HP and perpendicular to the VP (i.e., AIP).
   - Case (ii): Plane inclined to the VP and perpendicular to the HP (i.e., AVP).
3. Plane perpendicular to both the RPs
4. Plane inclined to both the RPs (i.e., oblique planes)
   - Case (i) $(\theta_p + \phi_p) \neq 90°$
   - Case (ii) $(\theta_p + \phi_p) = 90°$

13.3 TERMS USED IN PROJECTIONS OF PLANES

The following terms must be understood before we proceed for the step-by-step procedure of obtaining the projections of a plane.

True Shape The actual shape of a plane is called its *true shape*.

Inclination with the RPs The inclination of a plane with an RP is the acute angle the plane makes with that RP. It is always measured in a plane perpendicular to the given plane and the RP.

Inclination with the HP (θ_p) It is the acute angle the plane makes with the HP.

Inclination with the VP (ϕ_p) It is the acute angle the plane makes with the VP.

Traces of the Plane Just like a line, a plane also has traces. The traces of a plane are the lines of intersections of the plane with the RPs.

A plane may have a horizontal trace or vertical trace or both.

Horizontal Trace (HT) The real or imaginary line of intersection of a plane with the HP is called *horizontal trace* of the plane. HT is always located in the TV.

Vertical Trace (VT) The real or imaginary line of intersection of a plane with the VP is called *vertical trace* of the plane. VT is always located in the FV.

It should be noted that the plane has no trace on the RP to which it is parallel. For example, a plane parallel to the HP will have no HT. Similarly, a plane parallel to the VP will have no VT.

HT and VT of a plane (produced if necessary) meet at a point on the *XY*.

Perpendicular Planes The planes perpendicular to one or both the RPs are called *perpendicular planes*. The first three positions of the planes mentioned in the previous section represent perpendicular planes.

Oblique Planes The planes inclined to both the RPs are called *oblique planes*. The fourth position of the planes mentioned in the previous section represents oblique planes.

Line View or Edge View The view of a plane seen as a line is called *line view* or *edge view* of the plane. One view of a perpendicular plane is always an edge view. The edge view always represents the trace of the plane. For example, if a plane is perpendicular to the VP, then its FV will be an edge view representing VT of the plane. Similarly, TV of a plane perpendicular to the HP will be an edge view representing HT.

13.4 PLANE PARALLEL TO AN RP

If the given plane is parallel to an RP, it remains perpendicular to the other RP. In such a case, the view of the plane on the RP to which it is parallel gives the true shape. Another view is always an edge view parallel to *XY*.

13.4.1 Plane Parallel to the HP

If a plane is parallel to the HP, its TV gives the true shape. Therefore, TV should be drawn first. FV will be an edge view parallel to *XY*. SV will be perpendicular to *X*1*Y*1.

Example 13.1 A rectangle *ABCD* of size 30 mm × 20 mm is parallel to the HP and has a shorter side *AB* perpendicular to the VP. Draw its projections.

Solution Refer Fig. 13.1.

1. Draw TV *abcd*. The shorter side *ab* is drawn perpendicular to *XY*.
2. Project TV above *XY* to obtain FV *a′b′–c′d′*. *a′b′–c′d′* is an edge view parallel to *XY*.
3. Draw LHSV *a″d″–b″c″* by projecting TV and FV with respect to *X*1*Y*1. *a″d″–b″c″* is an edge view perpendicular to *X*1*Y*1.

The following points may be noted:

(i) As the plane is parallel to the HP, there is no HT.
(ii) FV of the plane represents the VT.

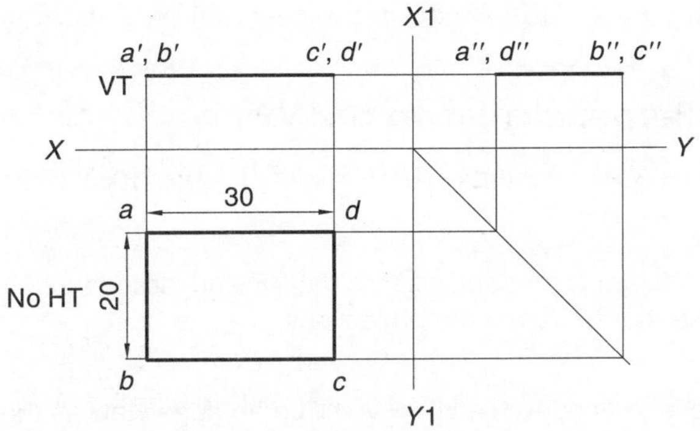

Fig. 13.1

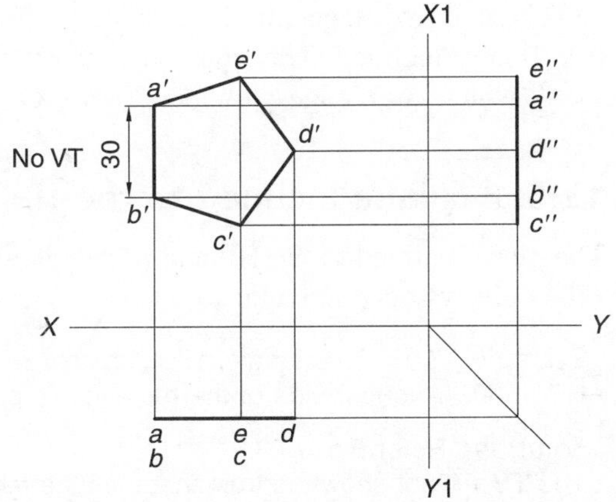

Fig. 13.2

13.4.2 Plane Parallel to the VP

If a plane is parallel to the VP, its FV gives the true shape and hence it should be drawn first. TV will be an edge view parallel to *XY*. SV will be parallel to *X*1*Y*1.

Example 13.2 A regular pentagon *ABCDE* of side 30 mm is parallel to the VP. The side *AB* is perpendicular to the HP. Draw the projections of the pentagon.

Solution Refer Fig. 13.2.

1. Draw FV *a′b′c′d′e′*. *a′b′* is perpendicular to *XY*.
2. Project FV below *XY* to obtain TV *ab–ec–d*. *ab–ec–d* is an edge view parallel to *XY*.
3. Draw LHSV *a″b″c″d″e″* by projecting TV and FV with respect to *X*1*Y*1. *a″b″c″d″e″* is parallel to *X*1*Y*1.

Following points may be noted:

(i) As the plane is parallel to the VP, there is no VT.
(ii) TV of the plane represents the HT.

REMEMBER THE FOLLOWING

- If a plane is parallel to an RP, it will be perpendicular to the other RP.
- If a plane is perpendicular to the HP, its TV will be an edge view.
- If a plane is perpendicular to the VP, its FV will be an edge view.
- If an edge view of the plane is parallel to *XY* (or *X*1*Y*1), another view gives the true shape.
- A plane will have no trace on the RP to which it is parallel.

13.5 PLANE INCLINED TO ONE RP AND PERPENDICULAR TO THE OTHER RP

If a plane is inclined to one RP and perpendicular to the other RP, none of its views will give the true shape. The view on the RP to which the plane is inclined will be smaller than the actual size of the plane. The view on the RP to which the plane is perpendicular will be a line view. Such problems can be solved in two stages. In the first stage, the given plane is assumed to be parallel to the RP to which it is finally inclined. The true shape can thus be obtained in one view. In the second stage, another view (which is an edge view parallel to *XY*) is tilted so as to make desired inclination with the first RP.

13.5.1 Plane Inclined to the HP and Perpendicular to the VP

The plane inclined to the HP and perpendicular to the VP represents AIP. FV of AIP gives its VT. Its HT is always perpendicular to *XY*.

Example 13.3 A rectangle *ABCD* of size 30 mm × 20 mm is perpendicular to the VP and inclined to the HP at 30°. A longer side of the rectangle is parallel to the VP. Draw the projections.

Solution Refer Fig. 13.3.
The TV will not show the true shape as the rectangle is inclined to the HP. FV will be an edge view as the rectangle is perpendicular to the VP. In Stage I, assume that the rectangle is parallel to the HP so that the true shape can be obtained in TV. FV of Stage I (which is an edge view parallel to *XY*) is then tilted in Stage II so that it will make θ_p = 30° to *XY*.

Stage I

1. Draw TV *abcd* assuming that the rectangle is parallel to the HP. *ad* is parallel to *XY*.
2. Project TV above *XY* to obtain FV *a′b′–c′d′*. *a′b′–c′d′* is an edge view parallel to *XY*.

Stage II

3. Redraw *a′b′–c′d′* as *a*1′*b*1′–*c*1′*d*1′ inclined at 30° *XY*. *a*1′*b*1′–*c*1′*d*1′ represents the final FV.
4. Draw the final TV *a*1*b*1*c*1*d*1 by projecting *a*1′*b*1′*c*1′*d*1′ and *abcd*.

Note that the FV represents the VT. To find HT, produce VT to meet *XY* at *h*. Then project *h* to meet the projectors through TV.

13.5.2 Plane Inclined to the VP and Perpendicular to the HP

The plane inclined to the VP and perpendicular to the HP represents AVP. TV of AVP shows its HT. Its VT is always perpendicular to *XY*.

Example 13.4 A regular pentagon *ABCDE* of side 30 mm is inclined at 45° to the VP and perpendicular to the HP. The side *AB* is perpendicular to the HP. Draw the projections of the pentagon.

Solution Refer Fig. 13.4.
As the pentagon is inclined to the VP, keep it parallel to the VP in Stage I. The true shape is thus obtained in FV. TV will be an edge view. In Stage II, tilt this TV to make ϕ_p = 45° to *XY*.

Stage I

1. Draw FV *a′b′c′d′e′* assuming that the pentagon is parallel to the VP. Keep *a′b′* perpendicular to *XY*.
2. Project FV below *XY* to obtain TV *ab–ce–d*. *ab–ce–d* is an edge view parallel to *XY*.

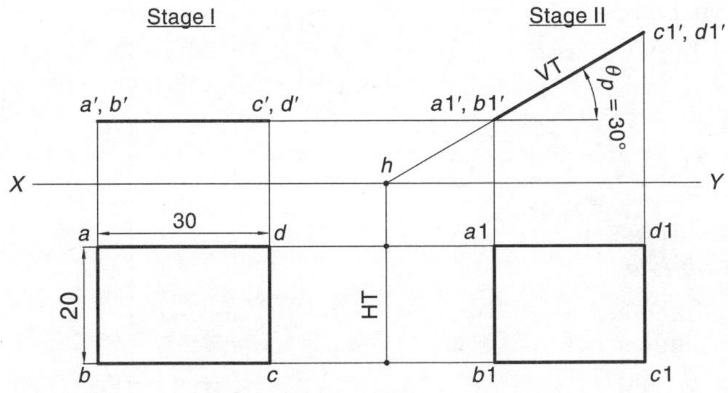

Fig. 13.3

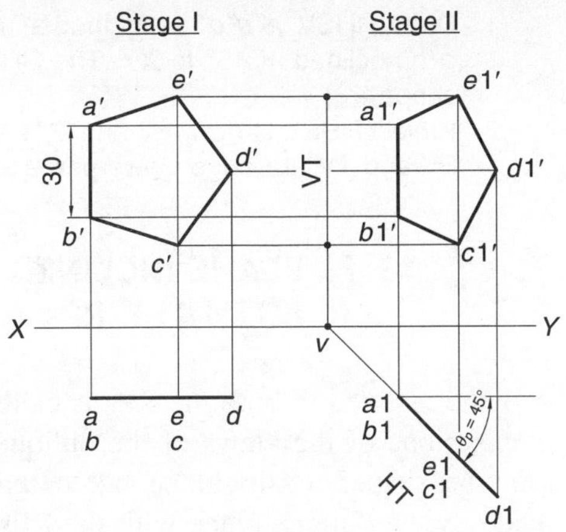

Fig. 13.4

Stage II

3. Redraw *ab–ce–d* as *a*1*b*1–*c*1*e*1–*d*1 inclined at 45° to *XY*. *a*1*b*1–*c*1*e*1–*d*1 represents the final TV.
4. Draw final FV *a*1′*b*1′*c*1′*d*1′*e*1′ by projecting *a*1*b*1–*c*1*e*1–*d*1 and *a*′*b*′*c*′*d*′*e*′.

Note that the TV represents the HT. To find VT, produce HT to meet *XY* at *v*. Then project *v* to meet the projectors through FV.

REMEMBER THE FOLLOWING

- If the FV of a plane is an edge view, then the angle between the FV and *XY* gives θ_p.
- If the TV of a plane is an edge view, then the angle between the TV and *XY* gives ϕ_p.
- If a plane is inclined to the HP and perpendicular to the VP, its HT will be a line perpendicular to *XY*.
- If a plane is inclined to the VP and perpendicular to the HP, its VT will be a line perpendicular to *XY*.
- The HT and the VT of a plane, produced if necessary, intersect at a point on *XY*.

13.6 PLANE PERPENDICULAR TO BOTH THE RPs

If a plane is perpendicular to both the RPs, then its FV and TV both will be seen as edge views perpendicular to *XY*. Such a plane is parallel to the PP and hence its true shape is seen in SV. Therefore for such problems, it is advisable to draw SV first.

Example 13.5 An equilateral triangle, side 60 mm, is perpendicular to both the HP and the VP. One of the corners of the triangle is on the HP and an edge through that corner is inclined at 45° to the HP. Draw the projections of the triangle.

Solution Refer Fig. 13.5.

As the triangle is perpendicular to both the RPs, it's SV should be drawn first. FV and TV both will be perpendicular to *XY*.

1. Draw RHSV $a''b''c''$ such that a'' is on XY and $a''b''$ inclined at 45° to XY. The RHSV gives true shape.
2. Project RHSV to draw FV and TV as shown. Both, FV and TV are edge views perpendicular to XY.

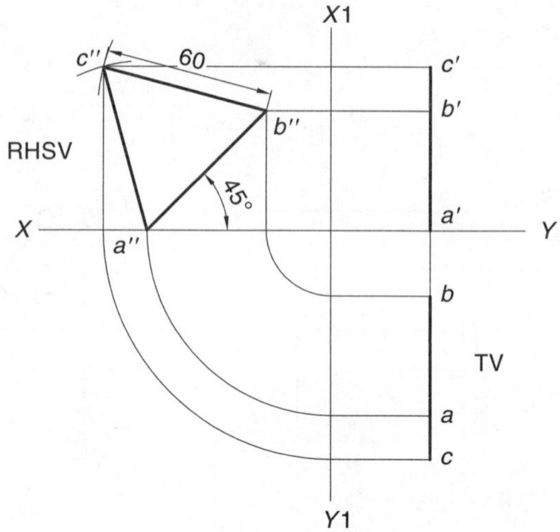

Fig. 13.5

13.7 PLANE INCLINED TO BOTH THE RPs

A plane inclined to both the RPs is called an *oblique plane*. None of the views of the oblique plane gives the true shape. It should be noted that the angles made by the oblique plane with the RPs (i.e., θ_p and ϕ_p) might not be directly given in the problem. Often, either of the inclinations, θ_p or ϕ_p, is given along with some other condition(s) that automatically pose the restriction on the other inclination.

There are two cases of the oblique planes: (i) $(\theta_p + \phi_p) \neq 90°$ and (ii) $(\theta_p + \phi_p) = 90°$. The procedure to obtain the projections in both the cases is same. In fact, we may not know initially to which case the given problem belongs to since both θ_p and ϕ_p are not mentioned. However, it should be noted that if $(\theta_p + \phi_p) = 90°$, then SV of the plane will be an edge view inclined at θ_p° to XY and ϕ_p° to $X1Y1$ (Example 13.8).

The problems on oblique planes are solved in three stages. In the first stage, the plane is often assumed to be parallel to one of the RPs so that the true shape can be obtained in one view. In the second stage, the given angle between the plane and the RP (i.e., either the HP or the VP) or some other condition mentioned in the problem is established. In the third stage, all other remaining conditions are satisfied.

Example 13.6 A rectangle $ABCD$ of size 30 mm × 20 mm is inclined to the HP at 30°. Its shorter side AB is parallel to the HP and inclined at 45° to the VP. Draw the projections of the rectangle.

Solution There are three conditions mentioned in the problem: (i) The rectangle is inclined to the HP at 30°, (ii) The shorter side AB is parallel to the HP. (iii) The shorter side AB is inclined at 45° to the VP. Note that, in this case θ_p is directly given. The other two conditions will automatically fix the value of ϕ_p. Refer Fig. 13.6.

As the rectangle is finally inclined to the HP, in Stage I, assume that it is parallel to the HP so that the TV will show the true shape. This will satisfy condition (ii) above. The shorter edge, which is finally inclined to the VP, should be kept perpendicular to the VP in Stage I. FV of Stage I (which is an edge view parallel to XY) is then tilted in Stage II so that it will make 30° to XY. This will satisfy condition (i) above. TV of Stage II is now rotated so that the shorter edge (which is perpendicular to the XY in Stage I and Stage II) will make 45° to XY. This will satisfy condition (iii) above.

Stage I

1. Draw TV $abcd$ assuming that the rectangle is parallel to the HP. ab is perpendicular to XY.
2. Project TV above XY to obtain FV $a'b'$–$c'd'$. $a'b'$–$c'd'$ is an edge view parallel to XY.

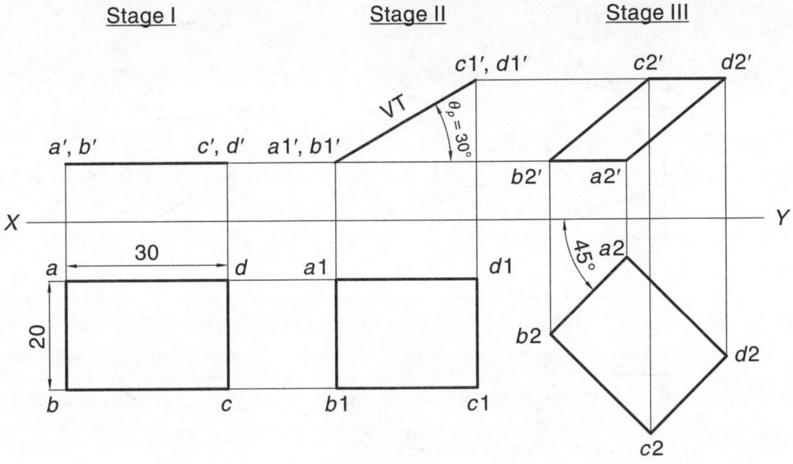

Fig. 13.6

Stage II

3. Redraw *a′b′–c′d′* as *a1′b1′–c1′d1′* inclined at 30° to *XY*.
4. Project *a1′b1′–c1′d1′* below *XY* to obtain *a1b1c1d1*.

Stage III

5. Redraw *a1b1c1d1* as *a2b2c2d2* such that *a2b2* makes 45° to *XY*. *a2b2c2d2* represents final TV.
6. Obtain final FV *a2′b2′c2′d2′* by projecting *a2b2c2d2* and *a1′b1′–c1′d1′*.

Note that *b2′a2′* is parallel to *XY*. Therefore, its other view, i.e., *b2a2* gives the TL and true inclination with the VP. It is always a good practice to check whether the final FV and final TV satisfy all the conditions mentioned in the problem or not.

Example 13.7 A regular pentagon *ABCDE* of side 30 mm has one of its edges parallel to the VP and inclined at 30° to the HP. The pentagon is inclined at 45° to the VP. Draw the projections.

Solution Three conditions given in the problem are: (i) an edge (say, *AB*) of the pentagon parallel to the VP, (ii) the edge *AB* inclined at 30° to the HP, and (iii) the pentagon inclined to the VP at 45°, i.e., $\phi_p = 45°$. The conditions (i) and (ii) will automatically fix the value of θ_p.

Refer Fig. 13.7.

In Stage I, assume that the pentagon is parallel to the VP. FV will then show the true shape. This will satisfy condition (i) above. The edge, which is inclined to the HP at 30°, i.e., *AB*, should be kept perpendicular to the HP in Stage I. TV of Stage I (which is an edge view parallel to *XY*) is then tilted in Stage II so that it will make 45° to *XY*. This will satisfy condition (iii) above. FV of Stage II is now rotated so that the edge *AB*, perpendicular to the HP in Stage I and Stage II, will make 30° to *XY*. This will satisfy condition (ii) above.

Stage I

1. Draw FV *a′b′c′d′e′* assuming that the pentagon is parallel to the VP. Draw *a′b′* perpendicular to *XY*.
2. Obtain TV *ab–ce–d* parallel to and below *XY*.

Stage II

1. Redraw *ab–ce–d* as *a1b1–c1e1–d1* inclined at 45° to *XY*.
2. Obtain FV *a1′b1′c1′d1′e1′* above *XY*.

Stage III

5. Redraw *a1′b1′c1′d1′e1′* as *a2′b2′c2′d2′e2′* such that *a2′b2′* makes 30° to *XY*. *a2′b2′c2′d2′e2′* represents the final FV.

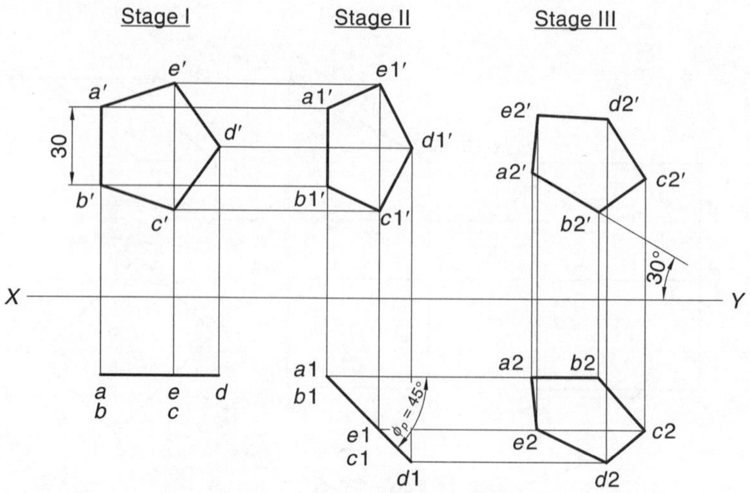

Fig. 13.7

6. Obtain final TV *a*2*b*2*c*2*d*2*e*2 by projecting *a*2′*b*2′*c*2′*d*2′*e*2′ and *a*1*b*1–*c*1*e*1–*d*1.

Note that *a*2*b*2 is parallel to *XY*. Therefore, its other view, *a*2′*b*2′ gives the TL and true inclination with the HP. The sequence in which given conditions are satisfied must be carefully observed.

To decide the first stage, some 'rules of thumb' are provided below.

Rule 1: If the plane is inclined to an RP, keep it parallel to that RP in the first stage.

Rule 2a: If an edge of the plane (or a line in the plane) lies in an RP, keep the entire plane in that RP in first stage.

Rule 2b: If an edge of the plane (or a line in the plane) is parallel to an RP, keep the entire plane parallel to that RP in first stage.

Rule 3: If a corner of a plane (or a point on the circumference of a circular plane) lies in an RP, keep the entire plane in that RP in the first stage.

Rule 4: If an edge of the plane (or a line in the plane) is parallel to an RP and inclined to the other RP, in the first stage, keep it perpendicular to the RP to which it is inclined.

Note: All the rules mentioned above are used in combination. Whenever two rules contradict each other, adopt the lower-numbered rule.

Example 13.8 A regular hexagon of side 25 mm is inclined at 60° to the HP and 30° to the VP. One of its edges is parallel to the VP. Draw the projections of the hexagon.

Solution In this case, $\theta_p = 60°$ and $\phi_p = 30°$, i.e., $(\theta_p + \phi_p) = 90°$. Therefore, SV will be an edge view showing both the angles. This problem can be solved by any one of the two methods explained below:

Method 1: This utilises the usual 3-stage approach.

Refer Fig. 13.8(a).

In Stage I, keep the hexagon parallel to the HP with an edge perpendicular to the VP (*Rule* 1 dominant to *Rule* 2*b*). Obtain the true shape in TV. In Stage II, rotate FV of Stage I through 60° about the edge which is perpendicular to the VP. In Stage III, rotate TV of Stage II so that the edge which was perpendicular to the VP in Stage I and Stage II, will now become parallel to the VP.

Stage I

1. Draw TV *abcdef* assuming the hexagon parallel to the HP. *ab* is drawn perpendicular to *XY*.
2. Obtain FV *a*′*b*′–*f*′*c*′–*e*′*d*′.

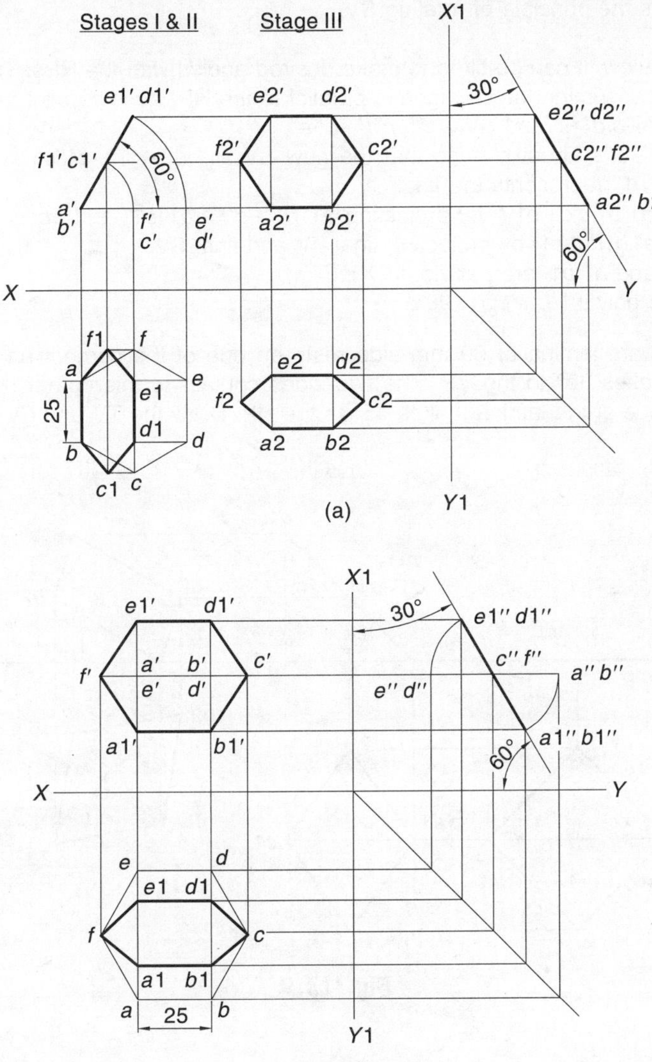

(a)

(b)

Fig. 13.8

Stage II

3. Rotate *a′b′–f′c′–e′d′* about *a′b′* through 60° and mark *e1′d1′* and *f1′c1′* on it.
4. Obtain TV *abc1d1e1f1*.

Stage III

5. Redraw *abc1d1e1f1* as *a2b2c2d2e2f2*. *a2b2* is parallel to *XY*. *a2b2c2d2e2f2* represents the final TV.
6. Obtain final FV *a2′b2′c2′d2′e2′f2′* from *a2b2c2d2e2f2* and *a′b′–f1′c1′–e1′d1′*.
7. Obtain SV *a2″b2″–c2″f2″–e2″d2″* by projecting final TV and final FV.

Note that *a2″b2″–c2″f2″–e2″d2″* is an edge view. Its angle with *XY* represents θ_p(= 60°) and angle with *X1Y1* represents ϕ_p(= 30°). Also note that *a2b2* and *a2′b2′* are parallel to *XY*, which means that the edge *AB* is parallel to both the RPs.

Method 2: This utilises the principle of rotating SV.
Refer Fig. 13.8(b).
As the SV is an edge view, it can be tilted to make desired angles with the RPs. This is explained below:

1. Draw TV *abcdef* assuming the hexagon is parallel to the HP. *ab* is parallel to *XY*.
2. Obtain FV *f′–a′e′–b′d′–c′* and SV *a″b″–c″f″–d″e″*.
3. Rotate *a″b″–c″f″–d″e″* about *c″f″* so that the new SV *a1″b1″–c″f″–d1″e1″* will make 60° with *XY*. *a1″b1″–c″f″–d1″e1″* represents the final SV.
4. Obtain final FV *a1′b1′c′d1′e1′f′* by projecting *a1″b1″–c″f″–d1″e1″* and *abcdef*.
5. Obtain final TV *a1b1cd1e1f* by projecting final FV and final SV.

Again note that *a1b1* and *a1′b1′* are parallel to *XY*.
Method 2 is applicable only if $(\theta_p + \phi_p) = 90°$.

Example 13.9 A square lamina of 50 mm side rests on one of the corners on the HP. The diagonal through that corner makes 30° to the VP. The two sides containing this corner make equal inclinations with the HP. The surface of the lamina makes 45° to the HP. Draw the TV and FV of the lamina.

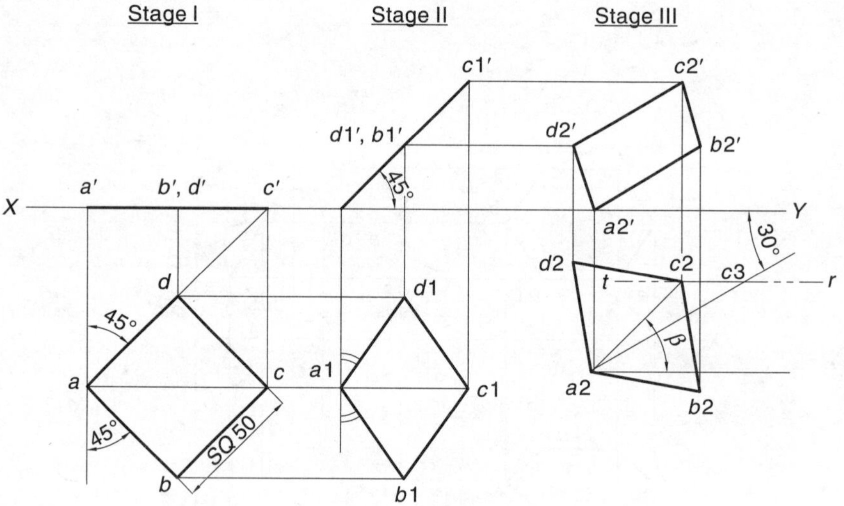

Fig. 13.9

Solution Refer Fig. 13.9.
In this case, it is necessary to draw the lamina in Stage I as a square of the true shape, resting on the HP, with its two concurrent edges inclined to the VP at an angle of 45° each (*Rule* 1 + *Rule* 3). This is so because the diagonal through the intersection of the two edges will be parallel to both the RPs. The inclination of the lamina with the HP then can be easily obtained in Stage II.

Stage I

1. Draw the TV *abcd* assuming the plane lying on the HP. Draw *ab* and *ad* inclined at 45° to *XY*. When the plane is tilted about *A*, keeping the diagonal *AC* parallel to the VP, the inclinations of *AB* and *AD* with the HP will remain equal.
2. Obtain FV *a′–b′d′–c′* along *XY*.

Stage II

3. Redraw *a′–b′d′–c′* as *a1′–b1′d1′–c1′* inclined at 45° with *XY*. Note that *a1′* is on *XY*.
4. Obtain TV *a1b1c1d1*.

Stage III

The diagonal *AC* makes 30° to the VP. *AC* is already inclined to the HP. Therefore, its TV will not show the true inclination of 30°. Instead, it will show an apparent inclination β° with *XY*. To obtain β, theory of projections of lines is used.

5. Draw *a*2*c*3 = *ac* at 30° to *XY*. Through *c*3 draw *t–t* parallel to *XY*. With *a*2 as a centre and radius = *a*1*c*1 (i.e., PL of *AC*) draw an arc to intersect *t–t* at *c*2. Now *a*2*c*2 represents the diagonal *AC* as seen in the TV.
6. Redraw *a*1*b*1*c*1*d*1 as *a*2*b*2*c*2*d*2. *a*2*b*2*c*2*d*2 represents the final TV.
7. Obtain final FV *a*2′*b*2′*c*2′*d*2′ by projecting *a*2*b*2*c*2*d*2 and *a*1′–*b*1′*d*1′–*c*1′.

Note that *a*2*c*2 is not the TL of *AC* and hence it will not show the true inclination.

Example 13.10 A semicircular plane of 60 mm diameter is inclined to the VP at 30°. Its straight edge is in the VP and inclined to the HP at 45°. Draw its three views.

Solution Refer Fig. 13.10.

In Stage I, the plane is kept in the VP with its straight edge perpendicular to the HP (*Rule* 1 + *Rule* 2a + *Rule* 4). Then, plane's inclination with the VP can be easily measured in Stage II.

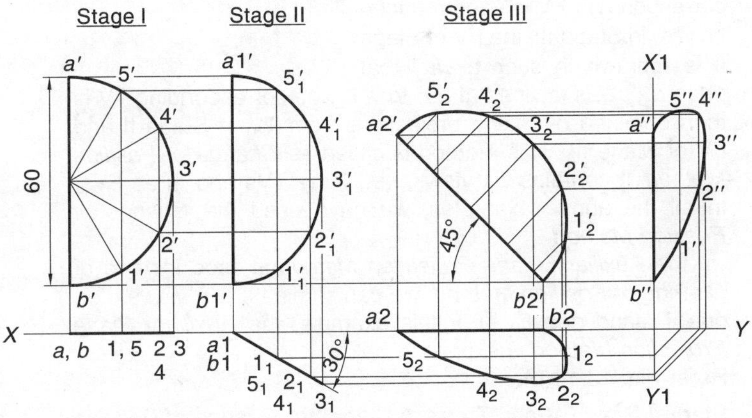

Fig. 13.10

Stage I

1. Draw the semicircle in FV. *a*′*b*′ is perpendicular to *XY*. Divide the semicircle into 6 equal parts and mark it as 1′, 2′, ..., 5′.
2. Draw TV *ab*–12345 on *XY*.

Stage II

3. Redraw TV *ab*–12345 as *a*1*b*1–$1_1 2_1 3_1 4_1 5_1$ inclined at 30° to *XY*. *a*1 must be on *XY*.
4. Draw FV *a*1′*b*1′–$1_1' 2_1' 3_1' 4_1' 5_1'$ as shown.

Stage III

5. Redraw *a*1′*b*1′–$1_1' 2_1' 3_1' 4_1' 5_1'$ as *a*2′*b*2′–$1_2' 2_2' 3_2' 4_2' 5_2'$ such that *a*2′*b*2′ makes 45° with *XY*. *a*2′*b*2′–$1_2' 2_2' 3_2' 4_2' 5_2'$ represents the final FV.
6. Draw final TV *a*2*b*2–$1_2 2_2 3_2 4_2 5_2$ by projecting *a*2′*b*2′–$1_2' 2_2' 3_2' 4_2' 5_2'$ and *a*1*b*1–$1_1 5_1$–$2_1 4_1$–3_1.
7. Draw the SV *a*″*b*″–1″2″3″4″5″ by projecting final FV and final TV.

13.8 USE OF AUXILIARY PLANE PROJECTION METHOD

Auxiliary plane projection method reduces the steps in solving the problem. It avoids redrawing particular view in Stage II and Stage III. Instead of tilting (i.e., redrawing) a particular view in the next step, it is always easy to draw an auxiliary plane, which gives the same relation that would exist between redrawn view and the reference line *XY*. The next few examples explain the use of auxiliary projection method.

Example 13.11 A pentagon of 40 mm side is resting on one of its corners on the VP. The edge opposite to that corner makes an angle of 30° to the HP. The surface of the pentagon is inclined at 45° to the VP. Draw the projections.

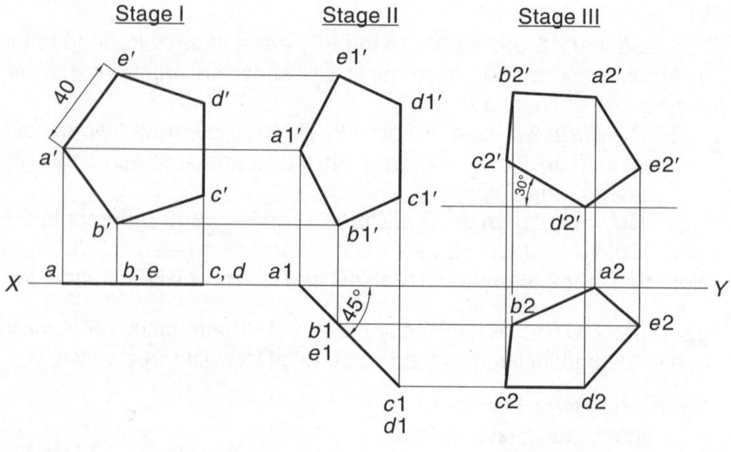

(a)

Solution This problem can be solved by the usual method as shown in Fig. 13.11(a). In Stage I, the plane is kept in the VP with a side perpendicular to the HP. In Stage II, the TV of Stage I is tilted (i.e., redrawn) through 45°. The corresponding FV is seen reduced in size. In Stage III, the FV of Stage II is redrawn in such a way that edge *d2′c2′* is inclined at 30° to *XY*. The corresponding TV is then obtained by taking projections from TV of Stage II and FV of Stage III. This method is called as *Change of Position Method.* It contains six views, i.e., three TVs and three FVs. In all the above examples, we have used the *Change of Position Method.*

If the *Auxiliary Plane Projection Method* is used instead of *Change of Position Method*, we can eliminate two views, i.e., one TV and one FV. For this example, the *Auxiliary Plane Projection Method* is explained below.
Refer Fig. 13.11(b).

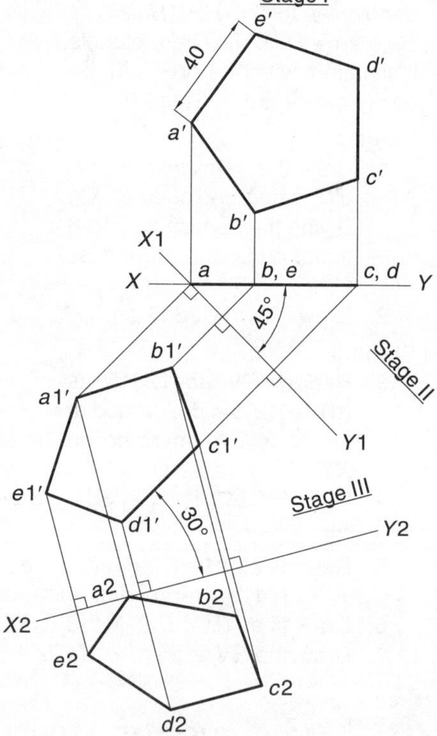

(b)

Fig. 13.11

Stage I Draw FV and TV as in Stage I of *Change of Position Method.* The FV gives the true shape and the TV is an edge view.

Stage II Draw an auxiliary reference line *X1Y1* passing through *a* and inclined at 45° to *a–be–cd.* Note that *X1Y1* makes same inclination with *a–be–cd* as *XY* makes with *a1–b1e1–c1d1* in Fig. 13.11(a). Thus, drawing auxiliary plane *X1Y1* in Fig. 13.11(b) is the same as tilting FV of Stage I in Stage II in Fig. 13.11(a).

Now project all points in TV, i.e., *a, b, c, d* and *e*, on *X1Y1*. (The projector must be perpendicular to *X1Y1*.) To obtain auxiliary FV *a1′b1′c1′d1′e1′*, take distances of points *a′, b′, c′, d′* and *e′* from *XY* and transfer them on corresponding projectors on *X1Y1*, measuring each distance from *X1Y1*, i.e. distance of *a1′* from *X1Y1* is equal to distance of *a′* from *XY*, distance of *b1′* from *X1Y1* is equal to distance of *b′* from *XY*, and so on.

Note that auxiliary FV *a1′b1′c1′d1′e1′* is same as FV of Stage II in Change of Position Method.

Stage III Draw another auxiliary reference line *X2Y2* inclined at 30° to *c1′d1′*. Project all the points of auxiliary FV, i.e., *a1′, b1′, c1′, d1′* and *e1′* on *X2Y2*. On these projectors mark points *a2, b2, …, e2* such that the distances of *a2, b2, …, e2* from *X2Y2* are respectively equal to distances of *a, b, …, e* from *X1Y1*. The view *a2b2c2d2e2* represents an auxiliary TV.

The auxiliary FV *a1′b1′c1′d1′e1′* and auxiliary TV *a2b2c2d2e2* are the final FV and final TV respectively. These are same as final FV and final TV of Fig. 13.11(a).

Thus, we have eliminated two views in the Auxiliary Plane Projection Method, i.e., TV of Stage II and FV of Stage III of *Change of Position Method.*

Example 13.12 A square *ABCD* of 40 mm side has its plane inclined at 30° to the VP. Its one side is inclined at 60° to the HP and parallel to the VP. Draw its projections.

Solution This problem is solved by the Auxiliary Plane Projection Method in Fig. 13.12(a).

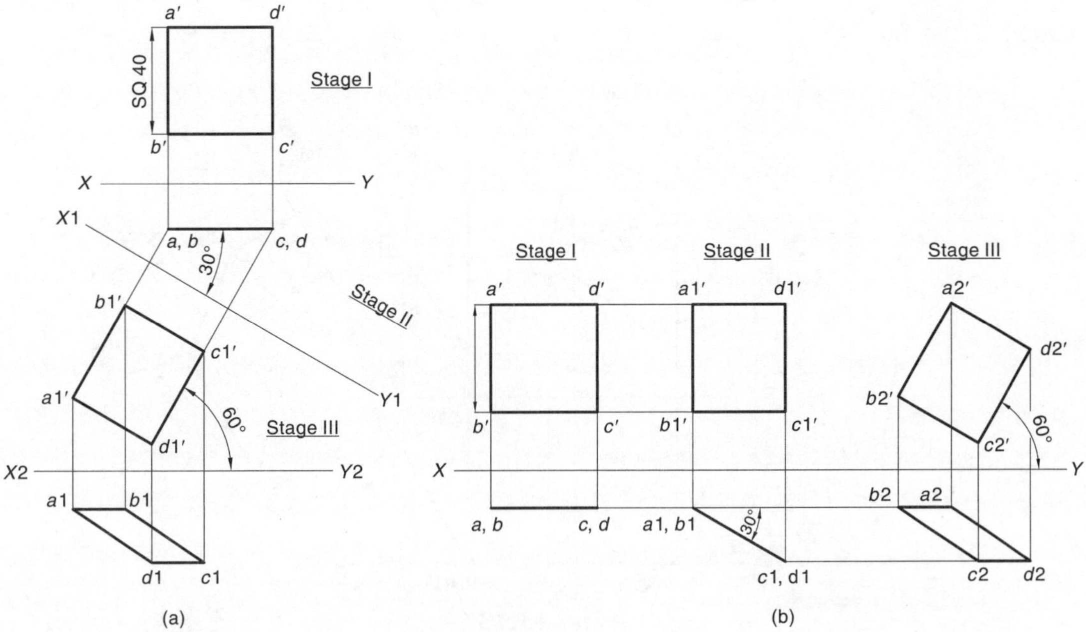

Fig. 13.12

Stage I Draw square *a′b′c′d′* to the true shape above *XY* and draw edge view *ab–cd* parallel to and below *XY* as shown.

Stage II Draw *X1Y1* inclined at 30° to *ab–cd*. Project points *a*, *b*, *c* and *d* on *X1Y1* and obtain points *a1′*, *b1′*, *c1′* and *d1′* such that distance of point *a1′* from *X1Y1* is equal to the distance of point *a′* from *XY*, distance of point *b1′* from *X1Y1* is equal to the distance of point *b′* from *XY*, and so on.

Stage III Draw *X2Y2* inclined at 60° to *c1′d1′*. Project points *a1′*, *b1′*, *c1′* and *d1′* on *X2Y2* and obtain *a1*, *b1*, *c1* and *d1* on these projectors. The distances of *a1*, *b1*, *c1* and *d1* from *X2Y2* are respectively equal to the distances of points *a, b, c* and *d* from *X1Y1*.

The views *a1′b1′c1′d1′* and *a1b1c1d1* represent final FV and final TV respectively.

Fig. 13.12(b) shows the solution to this problem by *Change of Position Method.*

13.9 CONCEPT OF GROUND LEVEL

Many times, the plane rests on the ground on its edge or on a corner or on a point on its curved edge. In such cases, it is customary to use the concept of Ground Level or Ground Line (*GL*). The *GL* is drawn parallel to and below *XY* at some suitable distance. The plane is then shown resting on *GL* as per the given conditions. The problem is then solved in the same way as if the plane is resting on the HP. Obviously, the third-angle method of projection is convenient for such problems. However, it can be solved by the first-angle method. In the latter case, *GL* is assumed along the HP.

Example 13.13 A kite has diagonals of 80 mm and 50 mm length. The diagonals intersect at a point 30 mm from an end of the major diagonal. The kite rests on the ground on one of its longer edges. The plane of the kite makes 60° with the ground while the edge on the ground makes 30° with a vertical wall. Draw the projections of the kite.

Solution Refer Fig. 13.13.

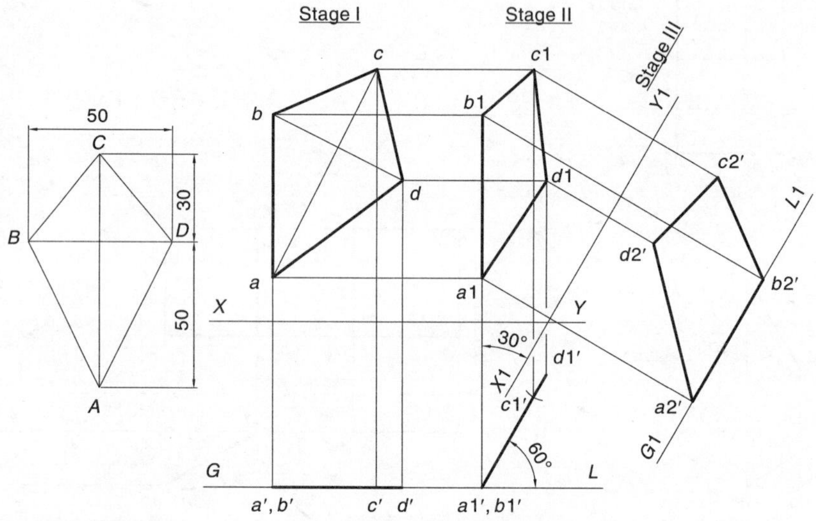

Fig. 13.13

This problem is solved by the third-angle method.

Stage I

1. Draw TV *abcd* to the true shape. *ab* is perpendicular to *XY*.
2. Draw *GL* below *XY* at a suitable distance. Obtain FV *a′b′–c′–d′* on *GL*.

Stage II

3. Redraw *a′b′–c′–d′* as *a1′b1′–c1′–d1′* inclined at 60° to *GL*.
4. Obtain the corresponding TV *a1b1c1d1*.

Stage III

5. Draw *X1Y1* inclined at 30° to *a1b1*. Obtain the auxiliary FV *a2′b2′c2′d2′*. Draw *G1L1* parallel to *X1Y1* at the same distance as that of *GL* from *XY*. Obviously, *a2′b2′* is seen on *G1L1*.

13.10 SUSPENDED PLANES

A plane may be suspended freely in air by attaching a string at any corner or a point along any edge. In such a case, the fact to be noted is that the imaginary line joining the point of attachment of the string to the centroid of the plane is always vertical. The locations of centroids of various planes are mentioned in Table 13.1.

Table 13.1 Centroids of Planes

Types of Planes	*Location of Centroid*
Triangles	Intersection of the medians
Quadrilaterals	Intersection of the bimedians
Regular polygons	Intersection of the perpendicular bisectors of the sides
Circle	Centre
Semicircle	(0.424 × Radius) from the centre along the radius perpendicular to straight edge

The TV of the plane suspended freely in air is always an edge view.

Example 13.14 A 45° set square, having longest side as 25 cm, is freely suspended from the midpoint of one of the shorter sides. The plane of the set square makes 60° with a vertical wall. Draw the two views of the set square.

Solution Refer Fig. 13.14.
First, draw the set-square *ABC* (*AB* = 25 cm) and locate its centroid *G*. *M* is the midpoint of *AC*.

Stage I

1. Draw FV *a′b′c′* of the set square to the true shape, assuming that it is parallel to the wall. *m′g′* should be vertical.
2. Obtain TV *a–b–c* parallel to *XY*.

Stage II

3. Rotate *a–b–c* about *b* through 60° to obtain *a*1–*b*1–*c*1.
4. Obtain the final FV *a*1′*b*1′*c*1′.

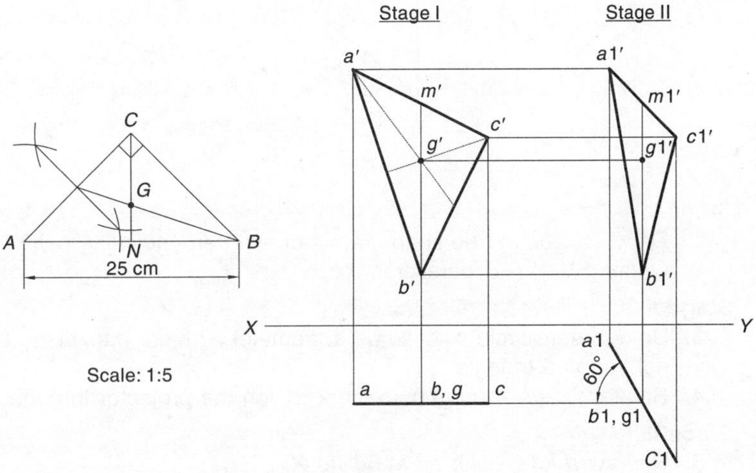

Fig. 13.14

13.11 INCLINATIONS OF A PLANE WITH THE RPs

When a plane is inclined to both the RPs, its true inclinations are not seen in the final projections. However, the true inclinations can be obtained from the final FV and final TV. If, the FV of a plane is an edge view, then the angle made by it with the corresponding reference line (i.e., *XY*, *X*1*Y*1, *X*2*Y*2, etc.) gives θ_p. Similarly, if the TV of a plane is an edge view then the angle made by it with the corresponding reference line gives ϕ_p. The edge views can be easily obtained by the auxiliary plane projection method, as explained in the following example.

Example 13.15 A triangular plate has sides 80 mm, 70 mm and 60 mm. Its TV is a right-angled triangle with one side as 80 mm making an angle of 60° with *XY*. Draw the projections of the plate. Find its inclinations with the RPs.

Solution Refer Fig. 13.15.

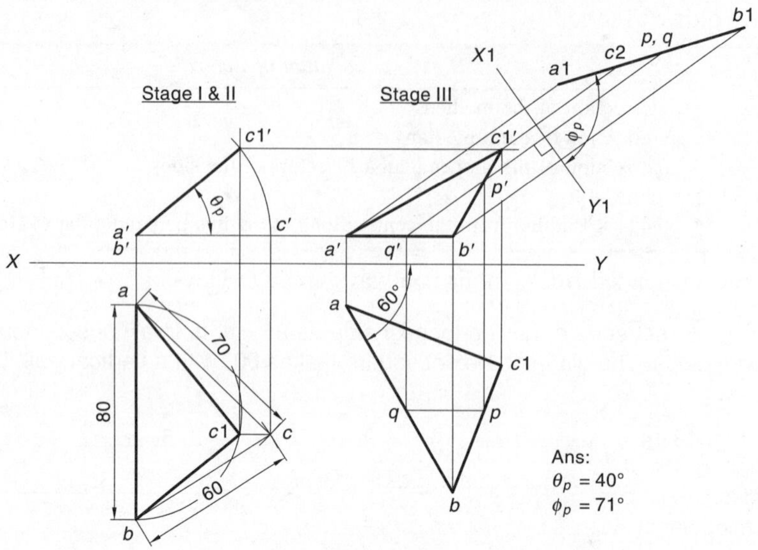

Fig. 13.15

Stage I

1. Draw TV *abc* to true shape. *ab* is drawn perpendicular to *XY*.
2. Obtain FV *a′b′–c′* parallel to *XY*.

Stage II

3. Draw a semicircle with *ab* as a diameter. Project *c* to *c*1 on the semicircle. *a–c*1*–b* represents the right-angled triangle.
4. Rotate *a′b′–c′* about *a′b′* to mark *c*1′ on the projector through *c*1.

Stage III

5. Redraw *a–c*1*–b* with *ab* at 60° to *XY*.
6. Obtain the required FV by projecting FV of Stage II and TV of Stage III.

The FV of Stage II, i.e., *a′b′–c*1′, is an edge view. So the angle between *a′b′–c*1′ and *XY* gives the inclination of the plate with the HP, i.e., θ_p. To obtain the plate's inclination with the VP, it is necessary to obtain TV as an edge view.

1. Draw a line *pq*, parallel to *XY*, anywhere in the final TV. Project *pq* to *p′q′* in the final FV. *p′q′* gives TL of *PQ*.
2. Draw *X*1*Y*1 perpendicular to *p′q′*. Project *a′*, *b′* and *c*1′ on *X*1*Y*1 and obtain points *a*1, *b*1 and *c*2 on these projectors. The distances of *a*1, *b*1 and *c*2 from *X*1*Y*1 are the same as the distances of *a*, *b* and *c*1 from *XY*.
3. Join *a*1, *c*2 and *b*1. The edge view thus obtained represents an auxiliary TV of the plane. Its angle with *X*1*Y*1 is the inclination of the plane with the VP, i.e., ϕ_p.

13.12 TRUE SHAPE OF THE PLANE

Sometimes, only final FV and final TV of an oblique plane are given. In such a case, we need to find the true shape of the plane. It should be noted that when any one of the views (i.e., FV or TV or SV) is an edge view parallel to the corresponding reference line, then another view gives the true shape. Hence to obtain true shape of the plane, we first need to obtain its edge view.

Example 13.16 Fig. 13.16(a) shows the FV and TV of a triangular plane. Obtain it's inclinations with the HP and the VP. Also, find the true shape of the plane.

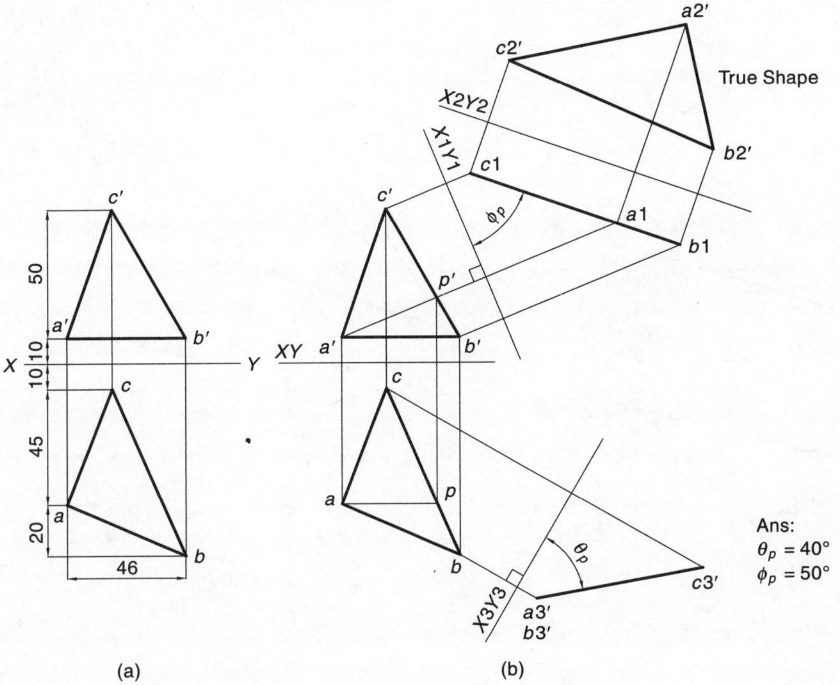

Fig. 13.16

Solution Refer Fig. 13.16(b).

1. Redraw the given views *abc* and *a′b′c′*. Draw a line *ap* in TV parallel to *XY*. Project point *p* above *XY* to obtain *p′*. Join *a′p′*. *a′p′* represents TL.
2. Draw *X*1 *Y*1 perpendicular to *a′p′*. Obtain edge view *c*1–*a*1–*b*1 by auxiliary plane projection method. The angle between this edge view and *X*1 *Y*1 is ϕ_p.
3. Draw *X*2 *Y*2 parallel to *c*1–*a*1–*b*1. Project points *c*1, *a*1 and *b*1 on *X*2 *Y*2 and locate points *c*2′, *a*2′ and *b*2′. The distances of *c*2′, *a*2′ and *b*2′ from *X*2 *Y*2 are respectively equal to the distances of *c′*, *a′* and *b′* from *X*1 *Y*1. The view *a*2′*b*2′*c*2′ represents the true shape.
4. To obtain the inclination of the plane with the HP (i.e., θ_p), we need to draw a line in the final FV parallel to *XY*. However, the line *a′b′* is already parallel to *XY*. Clearly, *ab* represents TL. Therefore, draw an auxiliary plane *X*3 *Y*3 perpendicular to *ab*.
5. Project points *a*, *b* and *c* on *X*3 *Y*3 and mark *a*3′, *b*3′ and *c*3′ on these projectors by auxiliary plane projection method. Obtain the edge view *a*3′*b*3′*c*3′. The angle between this edge view and *X*3 *Y*3 is θ_p.

13.13 DISTANCE OF A POINT FROM A PLANE

The shortest distance of a point from a given plane is the length of the perpendicular from that point on that plane. We need to obtain an edge view of the plane to find the length of the required perpendicular.

Example 13.17 Fig. 13.17(a) shows the FVs and TVs of a point *P* and a triangular plane *ABC*. Find the shortest distance between the point and the plane.

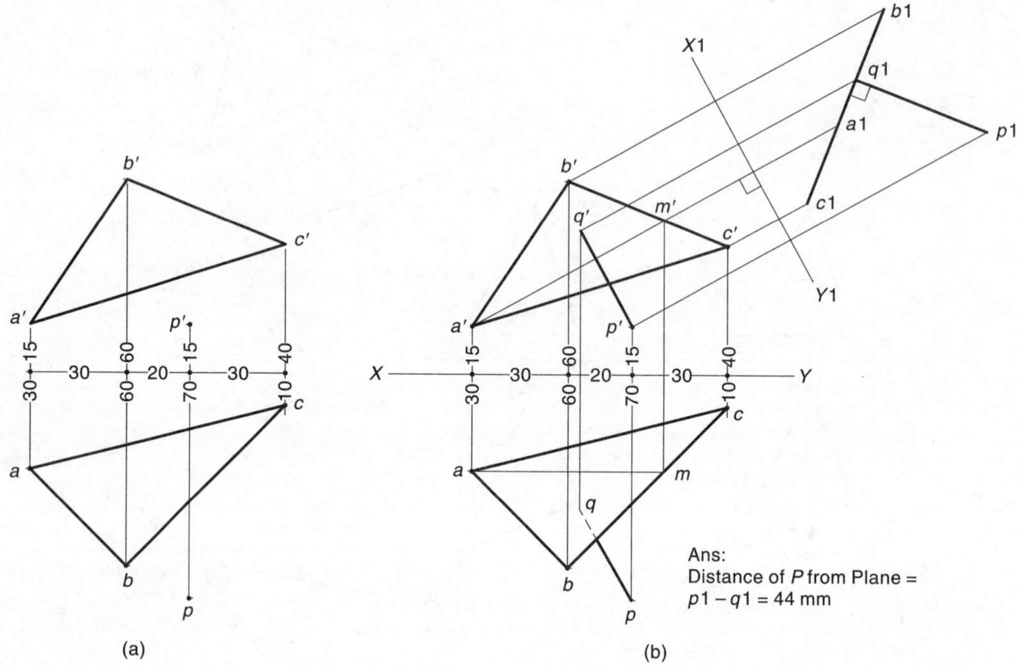

Fig. 13.17

Solution Refer Fig. 13.17(b).

1. In TV, draw *am* parallel to *XY*. Obtain *a′m′* in FV to represents TL of *AM*.
2. Draw *X*1 *Y*1 perpendicular to *a′m′*.
3. Project *a′*, *b′*, *c′* and *p′* on *X*1 *Y*1 to obtain auxiliary edge view *a*1*b*1*c*1 of the plane and auxiliary view *p*1 of the point.
4. Drop perpendicular *p*1*q*1 on *a*1*b*1*c*1. Measure *p*1*q*1 for the required distance.

Note: *q*1 may be projected to *q′* in FV and *q* in TV as shown. *p′q′* is parallel to *X*1*Y*1 (as *p*1*q*1 gives TL of *PQ*). *p′q′* and *pq* give FV and TV of the perpendicular drawn from the point on the plane. *pq* will be partly visible.

13.14 ANGLE BETWEEN TWO PLANES

The true angle between two given planes is the angle between their edge views. Obviously, we need to find edge views of both the planes. The point at which the edge views intersect (produced if necessary) represents the line of intersection (actual or imaginary) of the two planes.

Example 13.18 The FVs and TVs of two triangular planes are shown in Fig. 13.18(a). Find the true angle between them.

Solution Refer Fig. 13.18(b).

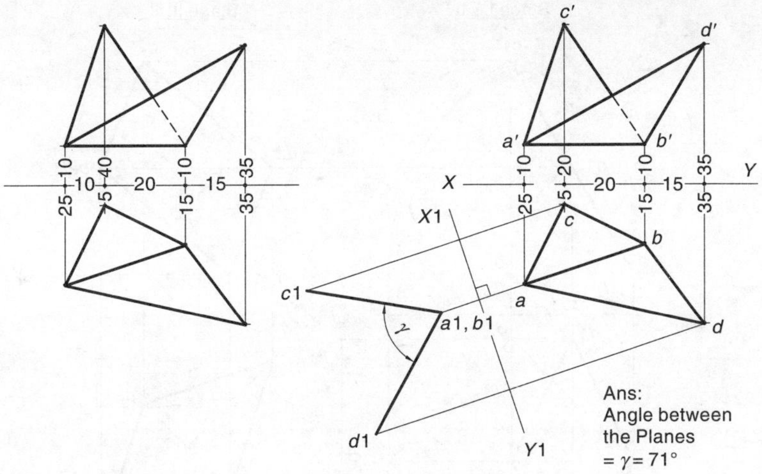

Fig. 13.18

a'b' and *ab* are the FV and TV of the common edge of the two planes. As *a'b'* is parallel to *XY*, *ab* gives TL.

1. Draw *X*1*Y*1 perpendicular to *ab*.
2. Project *a, b, c* and *d* on *X*1*Y*1 and obtain edge views *a*1*b*1–*c*1 and *a*1*b*1–*d*1 of the planes. Measure the angle between the edge views. Note that *a*1*b*1 represents the point view of the common edge of the two planes.

Illustrative Problems

Problem 13.1 A square of diagonal 70 mm is resting on the HP on one of its corners. In TV, the square is seen as a rhombus with a 70 mm major diagonal and a 35 mm minor diagonal. Draw the projections of the square if the diagonal which is parallel to the HP is inclined to the VP at 45°.

Solution Refer Fig. 13.19.

Stage I

1. Draw TV *abcd* to the true shape. *ac* is drawn parallel to *XY*.
2. Obtain FV *a'–b'd'–c'* on *XY*.

Stage II

3. Draw a rhombus *ab*1*c*1*d*1 such that *ac*1 = 35 mm. *b*1*d*1 (= *bd*) is perpendicular to *XY*.
4. Rotate *a'–b'd'–c'* about *a'* to mark *c*1′ on the projector through *c*1. Also, project *b*1*d*1 to *b*1′*d*1′ on *a'–c*1′.

Stage III

5. Redraw *ab*1*c*1*d*1 as *a*2*b*2*c*2*d*2 with *b*2*d*2 inclined at 45° to *XY*.
6. Obtain the required FV by projecting FV of Stage II and TV of Stage III. Note that, *d*2′–*b*2′ is parallel to the HP.

Problem 13.2 A hexagon with a 40 mm side has a side in the VP and is inclined at 60° to the HP. The side opposite the side in the VP is 50 mm in front of the VP. Draw the three views of the hexagon.

Solution Refer Fig. 13.20.

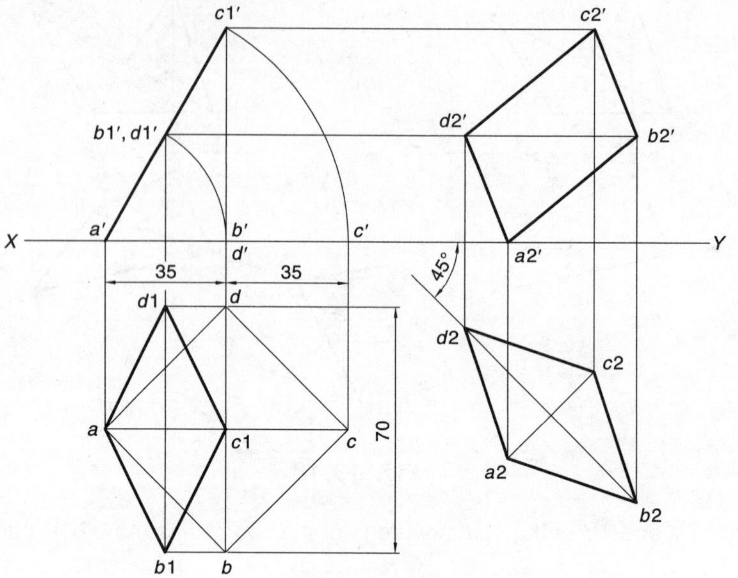

Fig. 13.19

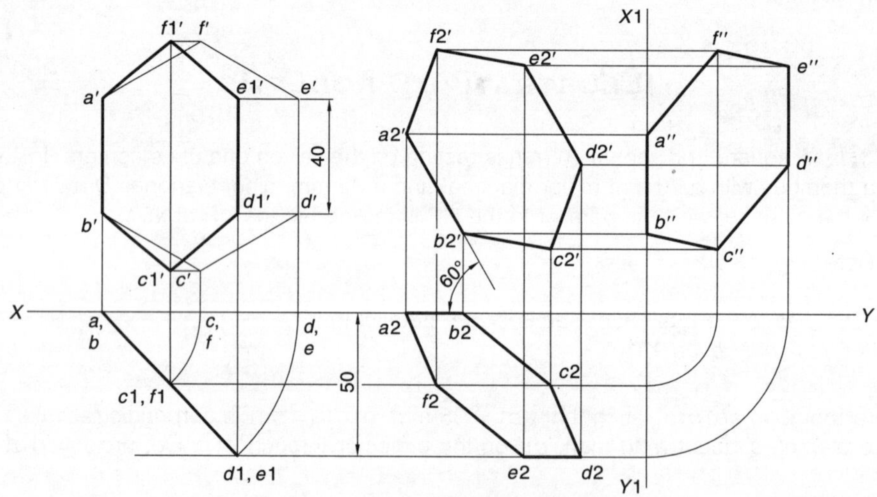

Fig. 13.20

Stage I

1. Draw FV *a′b′c′d′e′f′* to true shape. *a′b′* is drawn perpendicular to *XY*.
2. Obtain TV *ab–cf–de* on *XY*.

Stage II

3. Draw a line parallel to and 50 mm below *XY*. Rotate *ab–de* about *ab* to mark *d*1*e*1 on this line. Also, locate *c*1*f*1 on *ab–d*1*e*1.
4. Obtain FV *a′b′c*1′*d*1′*e*1′*f*1′.

Stage III

5. Redraw *a′b′c1′d1′e1′f1′* as *a2′b2′c2′d2′e2′f2′* with *a2′b2′* inclined at 60° to *XY*.
6. Obtain TV *a2b2c2d2e2f2* by projecting *a2′b2′c2′d2′e2′f2′* and *ab–c1f1–d1e1*.
7. Obtain SV *a″b″c″d″e″f″*.

Note that *a2b2* and *a″b″* are on *XY* and *X1Y1* respectively.

Problem 13.3 A hexagon of 30 mm side is resting on a corner in the HP, with its surface making an angle of 30° with the HP. The TV of the diagonal passing through that corner is inclined at 60° to the VP. Draw the three principal views.

Solution Refer Fig. 13.21.

Stage I

1. Draw TV *abcdef* and FV *a′b′c′d′e′f′*. *ad* is parallel to *XY*.

Stage II

2. Tilt FV about *a′* to obtain *a1′b1′c1′d1′e1′f1′* inclined at 30° to *XY*. Obtain TV *a1b1c1d1e1f1*.

Stage III

3. Draw *X1Y1* at 60° to *a1d1*. Obtain auxiliary FV *a2′b2′c2′d2′e2′f2′*.
4. Draw *X2Y2* perpendicular to *X1Y1* to obtain SV *a″b″c″d″e″f″*.

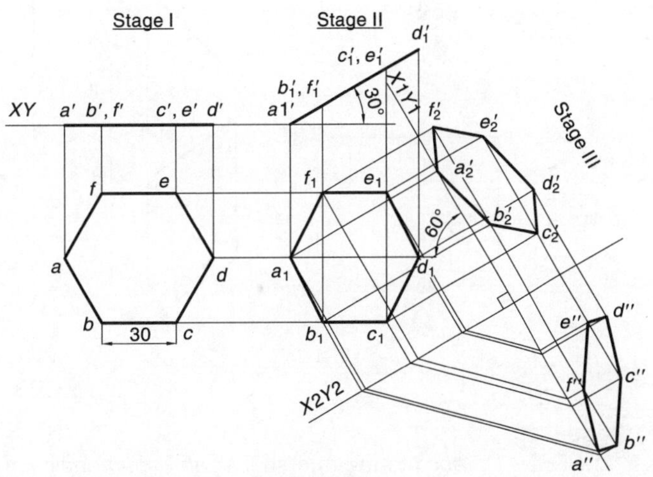

Fig. 13.21

Problem 13.4 A plane has VT of 20 mm length perpendicular to *XY*. The nearest end of the VT is 10 mm above *XY*. The HT of the plane measures 30 mm and is inclined at 30° to *XY*. The nearest end of the HT is 30 mm below *XY*. Draw the projections of the plane.

Solution The VT is perpendicular to *XY*. It means that the plane is perpendicular to the HP. As the HT is inclined to *XY*, the plane must be inclined to the VP (at $\phi_p = 30°$). Refer Fig. 13.22.

1. Draw VT = 20 mm perpendicular to *XY*, the lowest end being 10 mm above *XY*. Extend VT to meet *XY* at *v*.
2. Through *v*, draw a line inclined at 30° to *XY* and on it, locate *a*(*b*) 30 mm below *XY*. Also locate *c*(*d*) on it such that *a*(*b*)–*c*(*d*) = HT = 30 mm.
3. Obtain FV *a′b′c′d′* by projecting the ends of VT and HT. Obtain SV *a″b″c″d″* as shown.

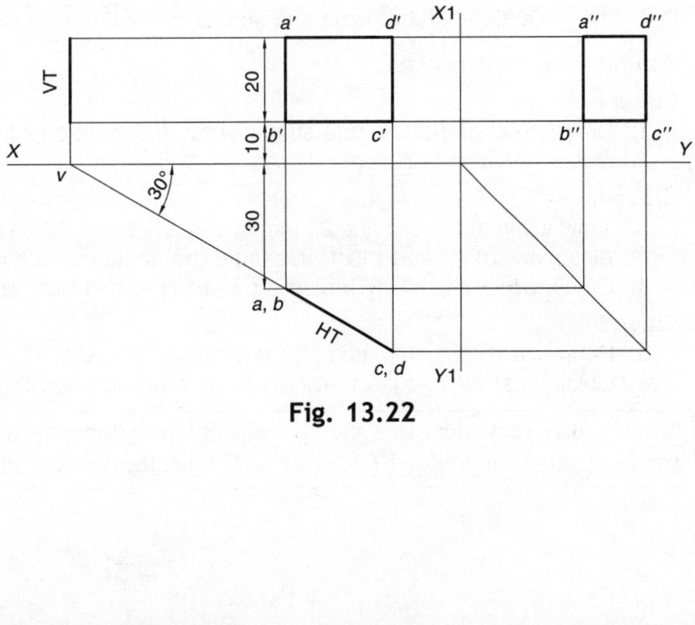

Fig. 13.22

Problem 13.5 A rhombus *ABCD* has its diagonals *AC* = 80 mm and *BD* = 50 mm. The side *AB* is in the HP and the side *BC* is in the PP. Draw the three views of the rhombus if it makes 45° with the HP.

Solution Refer Fig. 13.23.

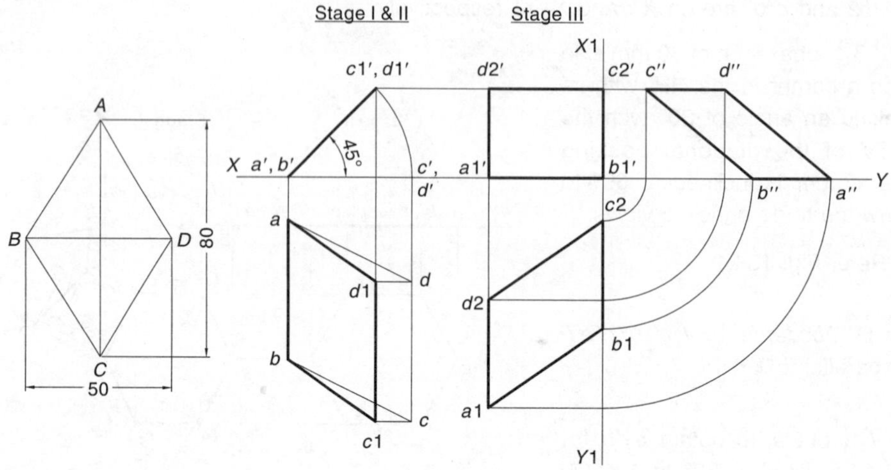

Fig. 13.23

Stage I

1. Draw TV *abcd* to the true shape. *ab* is perpendicular to *XY*.
2. Obtain FV *a′b′–c′d′* on *XY*.

Stage II

3. Rotate *a′b′–c′d′* about *a′b′* through 45° to obtain *a′b′–c1′d1′*.
4. Obtain the corresponding TV *ab–c1–d1*.

Stage III

5. Draw *X1Y1* to represent the PP. Redraw *ab–c1–d1* as *a1b1–c2–d2* with *b1–c2* on *X1Y1*.
6. Obtain the corresponding FV *a1′b1′c2′d2′*. Also project SV *a″b″c″d″*.

Problem 13.6 A regular hexagon of 30 mm side has a corner on the HP. The corner opposite to this corner is 25 mm above the HP. The TV of the diagonal through these corners is perpendicular to *XY*. Draw the projections of the plane and find its inclination with the VP.

Solution Refer Fig. 13.24.

Stage I

1. Draw TV *abcdef* to the true shape. *ad* is drawn parallel to *XY*.
2. Obtain FV *a′–b′f′–c′e′–d′*.

Stage II

3. Draw a line parallel to and 25 mm above *XY*. Mark *d1′* on this line by rotating *a′–b′f′–c′e′–d′* about *a′*. Also mark *b1′f1′* and *c1′e1′*. Measure the angle made by *a′–b1′f1′–c1′e1′–d1′* with vertical, i.e., ϕ_p.
4. Obtain *ab1c1d1e1f1* by projecting *a′–b1′f1′–c1′e1′–d1′* and *abcdef*.

Stage III

5. Redraw *ab1c1d1e1f1* such that *ad1* makes 90° with *XY*.
6. Obtain final FV *a′–b1′–c1′–d1′–e1′f1′* by projecting *ab1c1d1e1f1* and *a′–b1′f1′–c1′e1′–d1′* of Stage II.

Note: It is very clear that the above problem belongs to case $\theta_p + \phi_p = 90°$. Therefore, the angle made by edge view *a′–b1′f1′–c1′e1′–d1′* with the vertical gives ϕ_p.

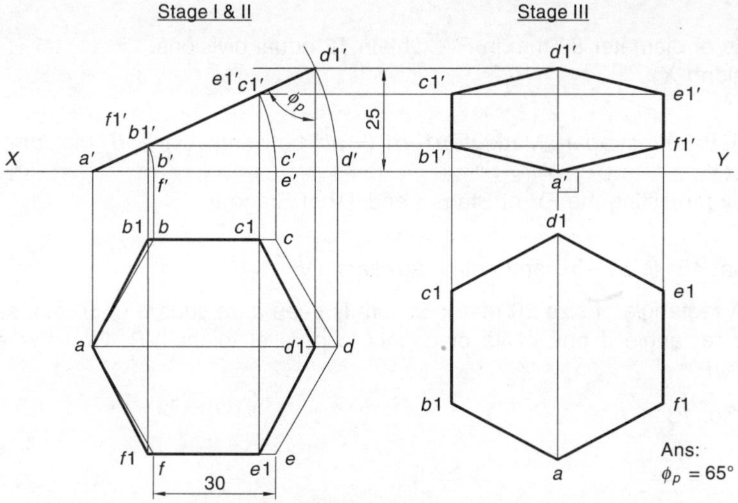

Fig. 13.24

Problem 13.7 A circular plate of negligible thickness and diameter 80 mm has a point *A* on its circumference in the VP. The surface of the plate is inclined to the VP in such a way that the FV is seen as an ellipse of 50 mm long minor axis. Draw the projections of the plate when FV of diameter *AB* makes 45° with the HP. Find inclination of the plate with the VP.

Solution Refer Fig. 13.25.

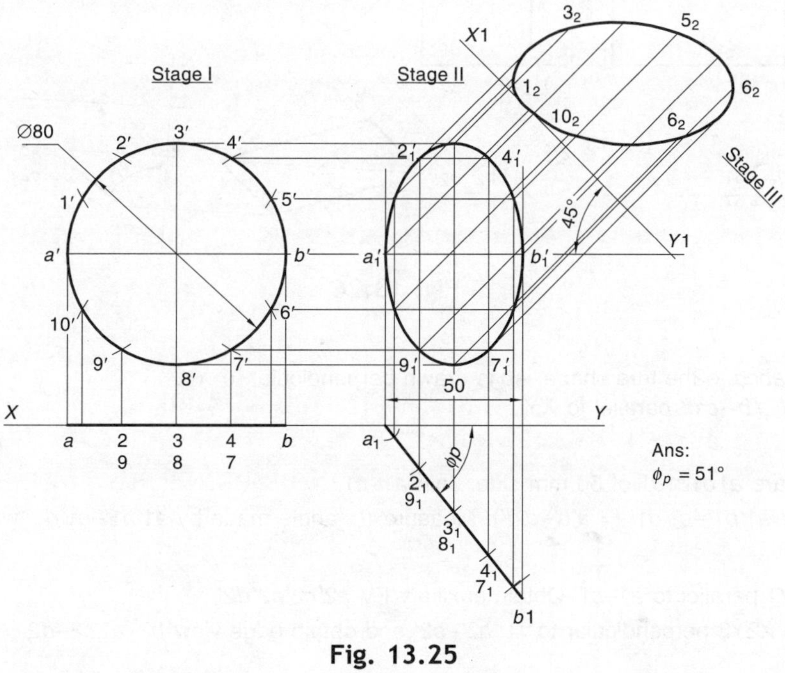

Fig. 13.25

Stage I

1. Draw a circle of diameter 80 mm in FV. Obtain 12 equal divisions.
2. Obtain TV along *XY*.

Stage II

1. Draw $\widehat{A}$ and $\widehat{B}$ 50 mm apart. Mark off *a*1–*b*1 (= *ab*) between $\widehat{A}$ and $\widehat{B}$. Measure the angle between *a*1–*b*1 and *XY*.
2. Obtain FV by projecting the FV of Stage I and TV of Stage II.

Stage III

1. Draw *X*1*Y*1 at 45° to *a*1′–*b*1′ and obtain auxiliary TV.

Problem 13.8 A rectangle of size 80 mm × 50 mm is seen as a square of 50 mm side in TV. Draw the projections of the rectangle if one of its diagonals is parallel to the VP. Find the angle made by the rectangle with the VP.

Solution Refer Fig. 13.26.

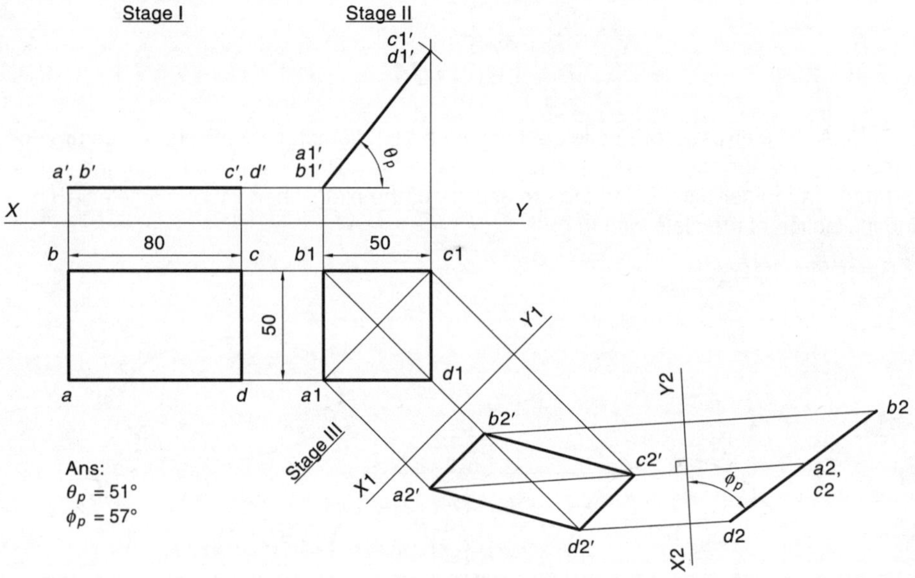

Fig. 13.26

Stage I

1. Draw TV *abcd* to the true shape. *ab* is drawn perpendicular to *XY*.
2. Obtain FV *a′b′*–*c′d′* parallel to *XY*.

Stage II

3. Draw square *a*1*b*1*c*1*d*1 of 50 mm side. Join *a*1–*c*1.
4. Obtain FV *a*1′*b*1′–*c*1′*d*1′ (= *a′b′*–*c′d′*). Measure θ_p, angle made by *a*1′*b*1′–*c*1′*d*1′ with *XY*.

Stage III

5. Draw *X*1*Y*1 parallel to *a*1–*c*1. Obtain auxiliary FV *a*2′*b*2′*c*2′*d*2′.

To find ϕ_p, set *X*2*Y*2 perpendicular to TL *a*2′–*c*2′ and obtain edge view *b*2–*a*2*c*2–*d*2.

Problem 13.9 A pentagonal plate *ABCDE* of side 36 mm is freely suspended from a point *M*, 12 mm from *B* along side *BC*. The plate is inclined to the VP in such a way that the projectors through *A* and *D* are seen 25 mm apart. Draw the projections of the plate.

Solution Refer Fig. 13.27(a).

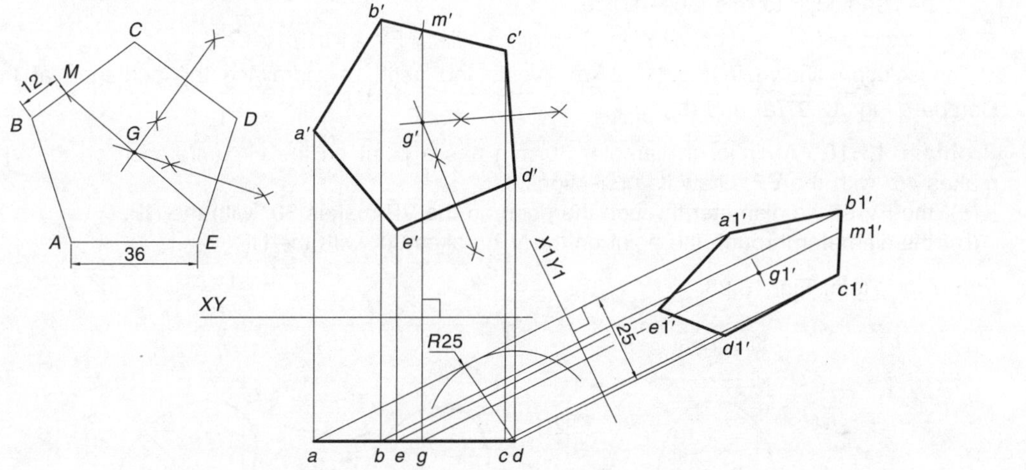

(a)

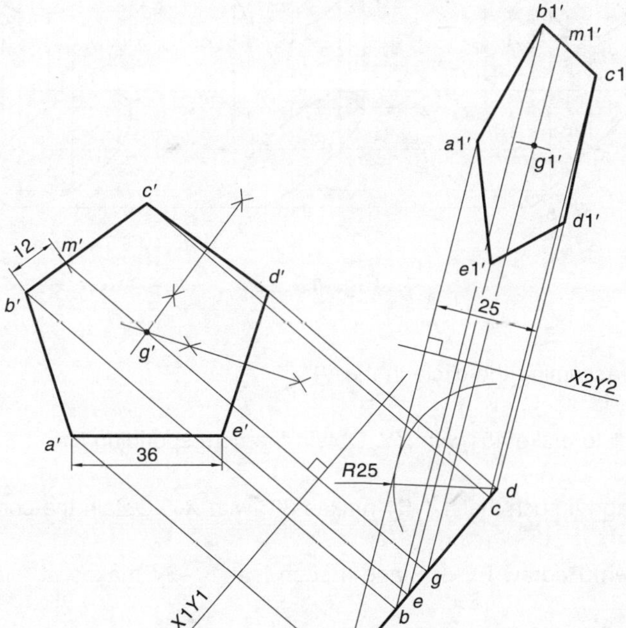

(b)

Fig. 13.27

First, we draw the given pentagon *ABCDE* and locate its centroid *G*. Point *M* is the point of attachment. When the plate is suspended from *M*, line *MG* should be vertical.

1. Draw FV *a′b′c′d′e′* to the true shape such that *m′g′* is vertical.
2. Obtain TV *a–b–e–c–d* parallel to *XY*.
3. With *d* as a centre, draw an arc of radius 25 mm. From *a*, draw a tangent to this arc. Draw *X*1*Y*1 perpendicular to this tangent line.
4. Project *a–b–e–c–d* on *X*1*Y*1 and obtain auxiliary FV *a*1′*b*1′*c*1′*d*1′*e*1′.

The solution shown in Fig. 13.27(b) avoids the need of redrawing the pentagon at the first step. Compare Fig. 13.27(a) and (b).

Problem 13.10 A circle of diameter 50 mm has a point on the circumference on the VP. The circle makes 45° with the VP. Draw its projections if

(a) the FV of the diameter through the point on the VP makes 30° with the HP.
(b) the diameter through the point on the VP makes 30° with the HP.

Solution Refer Fig. 13.28.

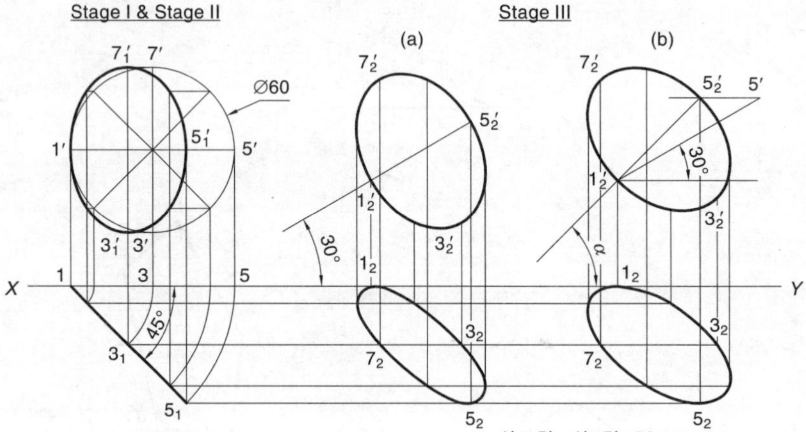

Fig. 13.28

Stage I

1. Draw FV and TV assuming the circle in the VP.

Stage II

2. Rotate TV about 1 to make 45° with *XY*. Obtain the corresponding FV.

Stage III (a)

3. Redraw FV of Stage II such that $1_2'–5_2'$ makes 30° with *XY*. Obtain the corresponding TV.

Stage III (b)

4. Obtain α as shown. Redraw FV of Stage II such that $1_2'–5_2'$ makes $\alpha°$ with *XY*. Obtain the corresponding TV.

Problem 13.11 A regular pentagonal plane *ABCDE* of 40 mm side has side *AB* in the HP making an angle of 15° with the VP. The plane makes an angle of 50° with the HP and the point *D* lies in the VP. Draw the projections of the plane and find its angle with the VP.

Solution Refer Fig. 13.29.

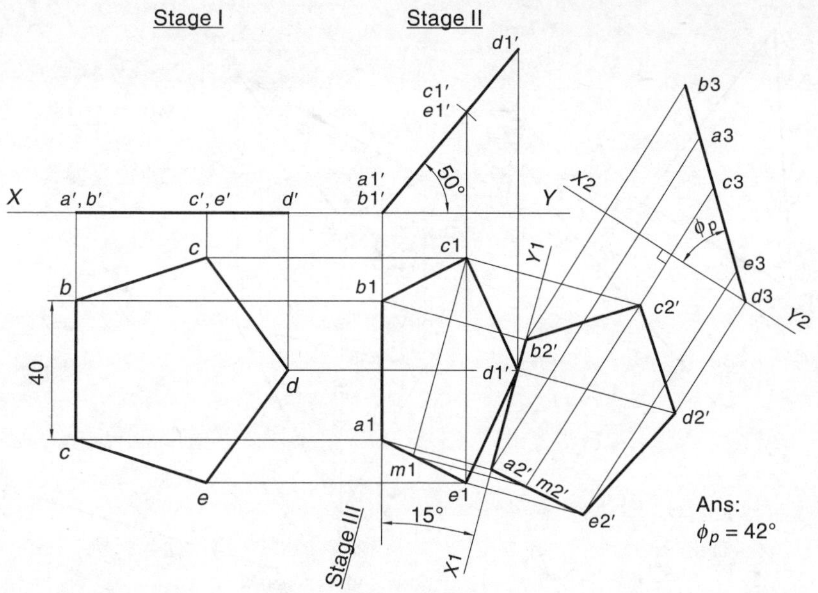

Fig. 13.29

Stage I

1. Draw TV *abcde* to the true shape. *ab* is perpendicular to *XY*.
2. Obtain FV *a′b′–c′e′–d′* on *XY*.

Stage II

3. Redraw *a′b′–c′e′–d′* as *a*1′*b*1′–*c*1′*e*1′–*d*1′ inclined at 50° to *XY*.
4. Obtain the corresponding TV *a*1*b*1*c*1*d*1*e*1.

Stage III

5. Draw *X*1*Y*1 through *d*1 inclined at 15° to *a*1*b*1. Obtain auxiliary FV *a*2′*b*2′*c*2′*d*2′*e*2′.

To find ϕ_p, draw *c*1–*m*1 parallel to *X*1*Y*1. Obtain its TL *c*2′–*m*2′. Set *X*2*Y*2 perpendicular to *c*2′–*m*2′and obtain the edge view *b*3–*a*3–*c*3–*e*3–*d*3.

Problem 13.12 The distances between the projectors of the corners *A* and *B*, *B* and *C* and *C* and *A* of a triangular thin plate *ABC* are respectively 20 mm, 25 mm and 45 mm. The corners *A*, *B* and *C* are respectively 20 mm, 10 mm and 45 mm above the HP and 25 mm, 60 mm and 15 mm in front of the VP. Draw the projections of the plate. Use auxiliary plane projection method and find the true shape and the true inclinations of the plate with the RPs.

Solution Refer Fig. 13.30.

The projections *a′b′c′* and *abc* are drawn as shown.

1. To find θ_p, draw *a′m′* parallel to *XY*. Obtain its TL *am*. Set *X*1*Y*1 perpendicular to *am* and obtain the edge view *b*1′–*a*1′–*c*1′.
2. To find ϕ_p, draw *an* parallel to *XY*. Obtain its TL *a′n′*. Set *X*2*Y*2 perpendicular to *a′n′* and obtain the edge view *b*2–*a*2–*c*2.
3. Set *X*3*Y*3 along *b*2–*a*2–*c*2 and obtain the auxiliary FV *a*3′–*b*3′–*c*3′ to represent the true shape.

Problem 13.13 The FV and TV of an ellipse are circles of 50 mm diameter each. Draw the true shape of the ellipse.

Solution Refer Fig. 13.31.

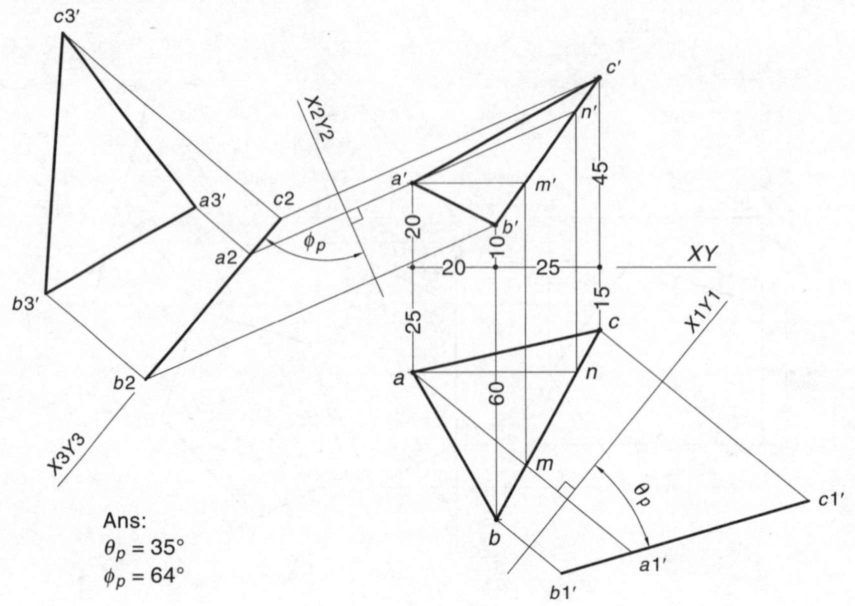

Fig. 13.30

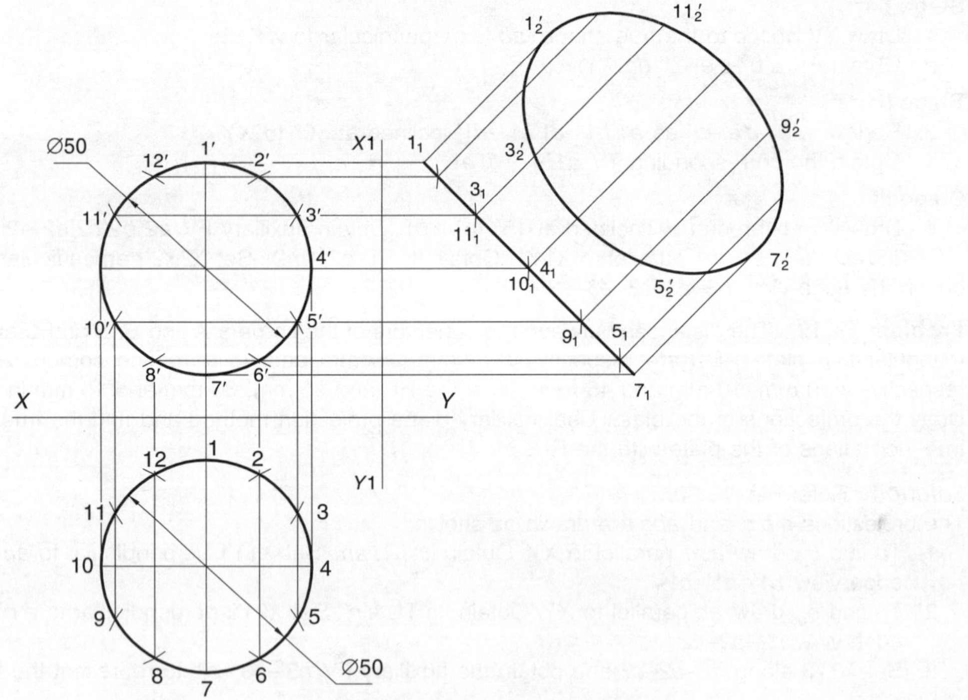

Fig. 13.31

1. Draw FV, a circle of 50 mm diameter and divide it into 12 equal parts.
2. Draw TV, another circle of 50 mm diameter and project the division points on it.
3. Draw *X*1*Y*1 perpendicular to 10′–4′. (10′–4′ gives TL.) Obtain auxiliary TV 1_1–7_1.
4. Assuming an auxiliary plane along 1_1–7_1, obtain auxiliary FV $1_2'$–$3_2'$–$5_2'$–$7_2'$–$9_2'$–$11_2'$ to represent the true shape of the ellipse.

Problem 13.14 A triangular plate *PQR* has *PQ* (= 80 mm) on the HP and parallel to the VP. Corner *R* is in the VP. TV *pqr* is seen as an equilateral triangle whereas FV *p′q′r′* is seen as a right-angled isosceles triangle. Draw the projections and find the true shape of the plate.

Solution Refer Fig. 13.32.

As *PQ* is on the HP and *R* in the VP, *p′q′* and *r* will be seen on *XY*. Further, *p′q′* and *pq* will show TL.

1. Draw *p′q′* = 80 mm on *XY*. Draw a semicircle with *p′q′* as a diameter. Locate *r′* at the midpoint of the semicircle. *p′r′q′* is a right-angled isosceles triangle and represents the FV.
2. Project *r′* to *r* on *XY*. Complete equilateral triangle *pqr* as shown (*pq* parallel to *XY*).
3. Draw *X*1*Y*1 perpendicular to *p′q′* and obtain the edge view *p″q″*–*r″*.
4. Assuming an auxiliary plane along *p″q″*–*r″*, obtain auxiliary FV *p*1′–*q*1′–*r*1′ to represent the true shape of the triangle.

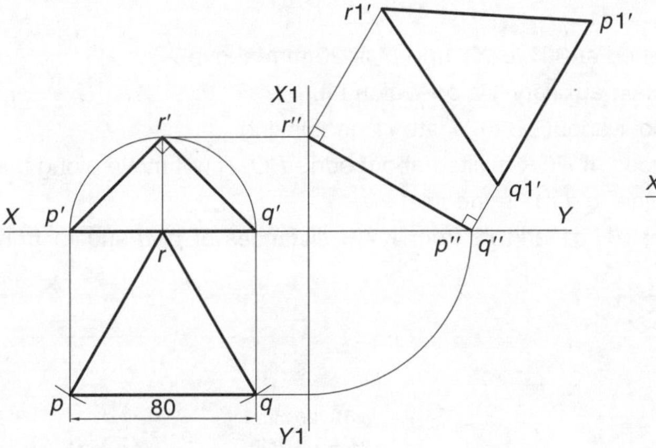

Fig. 13.32

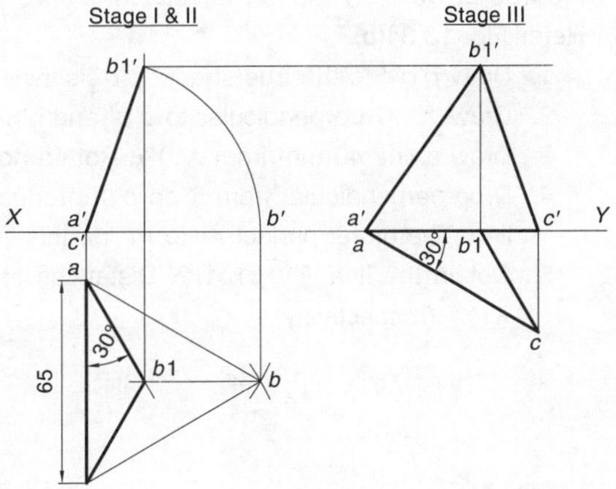

Fig. 13.33

Problem 13.15 An equilateral triangle *ABC*, with a 65 mm side has its base *AC* in the HP and is inclined at 30° to the VP. The corners *A* and *B* are in the VP. Draw its projections.

Solution Refer Fig. 13.33.

Stage I

1. Draw TV *abc* to the true shape. *ac* is drawn perpendicular to *XY*.
2. Obtain FV *a′c′*–*b′* on *XY*.

Stage II

3. Draw *a*–*b*1 at 30° to *ac*. *b*1 lies at the horizontal projector through *b*. Join *c*–*b*1.
4. Rotate *a′c′*–*b′* about *a′c′* to locate *b*1′ on the projector through *b*1.

Stage III

5. Redraw *a*–*b*1–*c* such that *a*–*b*1 is on *XY*. Obviously, *ac* will make 30° with *XY*.
6. Obtain FV *a′*–*b*1′*c′* by projecting FV of Stage II and TV of Stage III. Note that *a′c′* is on *XY*.

Problem 13.16 A triangle *PQR* has *PQ* = 80 mm, *QR* = 60 mm and *PR* = 120 mm. The side *PQ* is in the VP and makes 30° to the HP. Point *P* is 20 mm above the HP and point *R* is 40 mm in front of the VP. Draw the projections of the triangle.

Solution This problem is solved by two methods.

Method 1: *Change of Position Method*

Refer Fig. 13.34(a).

Stage I

1. Draw FV *p′q′r′* to the true shape. *p′q′* is perpendicular to *XY*.
2. Obtain TV *pq–r* along *XY*.

Stage II

3. Draw a line 40 mm below and parallel to *XY*. Rotate *pq–r* about *pq* to locate *r*1 on this line.
4. Project *r*1 to locate *r*1′ on the horizontal projector through *r′*.

Stage III

5. Redraw *p′q′r*1′ such that *p′q′* is inclined at 30° to *XY* and *p′* is 20 mm above *XY*.
6. Obtain the corresponding TV *p*1*q*1*r*2 as shown.

Method 2: *Auxiliary Plane Projection Method*

Refer Fig. 13.34(b).

1. Draw *p′q′r′* to the true shape. *p′q′* is inclined at 30° to *XY* and *p′* is 20 mm above *XY*.
2. Draw *X*1*Y*1 perpendicular to *p′q′* and obtain auxiliary TV *pq–r* along it.
3. Draw a line 40 mm from *X*1*Y*1. Rotate *pq*–r about *pq* to locate *r*1 on this line.
4. Drop perpendicular from *r′* on *p′q′* produced. If *PQR* is tilted about edge *PQ*, *R* will move along this line. Therefore, project *r*1 to *r*1′ on this line. *p′q′r*1’ is the final FV.
5. Obtain the final TV *p*1*q*1*r*2. Distances of *p*1, *q*1 and *r*2 from *XY* = distances of *p*, *q* and *r*1 from *X*1*Y*1 (respectively).

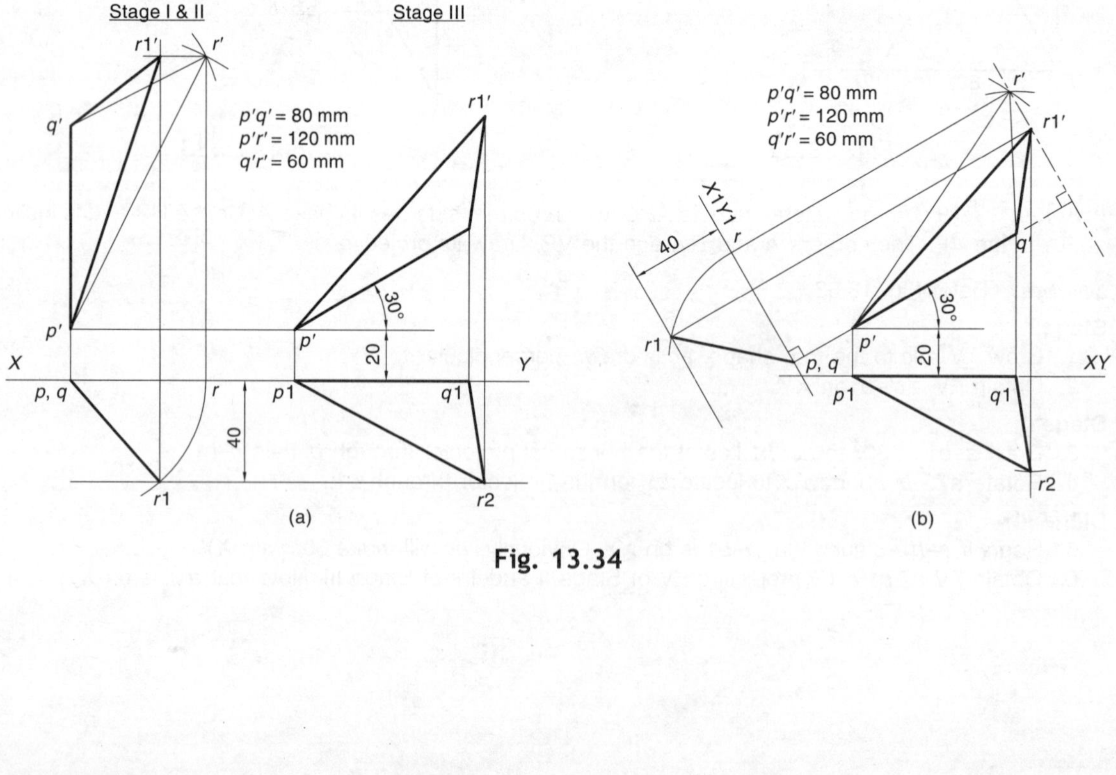

Fig. 13.34

Problem 13.17 An isosceles triangle *ABC* has its base *AB* in the VP and is inclined at 45° to the HP. The end *A* is near to and 25 mm above the HP. The plane of a triangle is inclined at 30° to the VP while its vertex *C* is on the HP. Draw the projections of the triangle if *AB* = 75 mm. Find the true shape of the triangle.

Solution Refer Fig. 13.35.

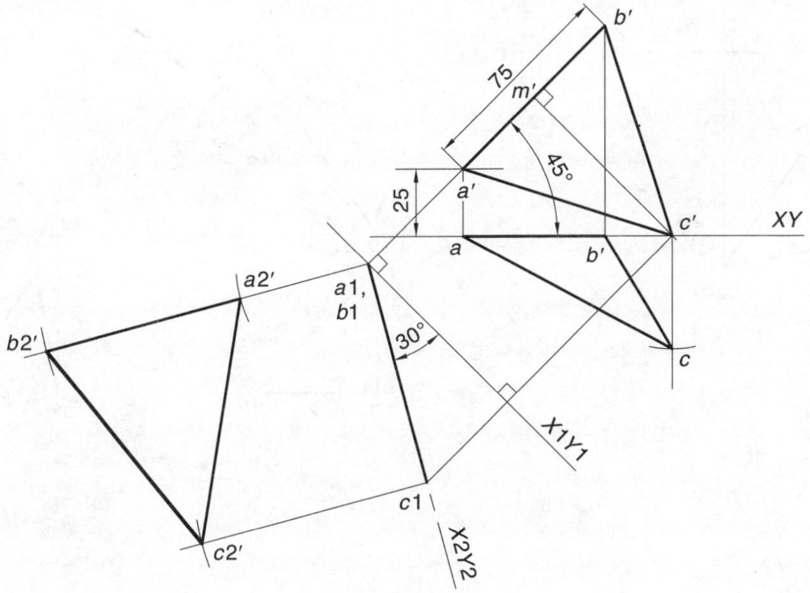

Fig. 13.35

We know the length of the base of the triangle. However, its FV can be easily obtained from the given data.

1. Mark *a′* at a point 25 mm above *XY*. Draw *a′b′* = 75 mm, inclined at 45° to *XY*.
2. Set a perpendicular to *a′b′* through midpoint *m′* to meet *XY* at *c′*. *a′b′c′* gives the final FV.
3. Project *a′b′c′* on *XY* to obtain the final TV. *a* and *b* will be on *XY* (as *AB* is in the VP). To locate *c*, we will first obtain the auxiliary TV.
4. Draw *X*1 *Y*1 perpendicular to *a′b′*. Project *a′*, *b′* and *c′* on *X*1 *Y*1 to obtain the auxiliary TV. *a*1 and *b*1 will be on *X*1 *Y*1. Draw *a*1*b*1–*c*1 at 30° to *X*1 *Y*1.
5. Complete the final TV *abc* by locating *c* such that (distance of *c* from *XY*) = (distance of *c*1 from *X*1 *Y*1).
6. To find the true shape, obtain the auxiliary FV *a*2′–*b*2′–*c*2′ by assuming *X*2 *Y*2 along the edge view *a*1*b*1–*c*1.

Problem 13.18 A 30°–60° set square has its shortest edge of 50 mm long in the HP. The TV of the set square is an isosceles triangle. The hypotenuse of the set square is inclined at 40° to the VP. Draw its projections and determine its inclination with the HP.

Solution Refer Fig. 13.36(a).

1. Draw TV *abc* to the true shape. *ac* is drawn at 40° to *XY*.
2. Draw *X*1 *Y*1 perpendicular to *ab*. Obtain FV *a*1′*b*1′–*c′* on *X*1 *Y*1.
3. Locate *c*1 on *bc* scuh that *bc*1 = *ba*. Complete the isosceles triangle *abc*1.

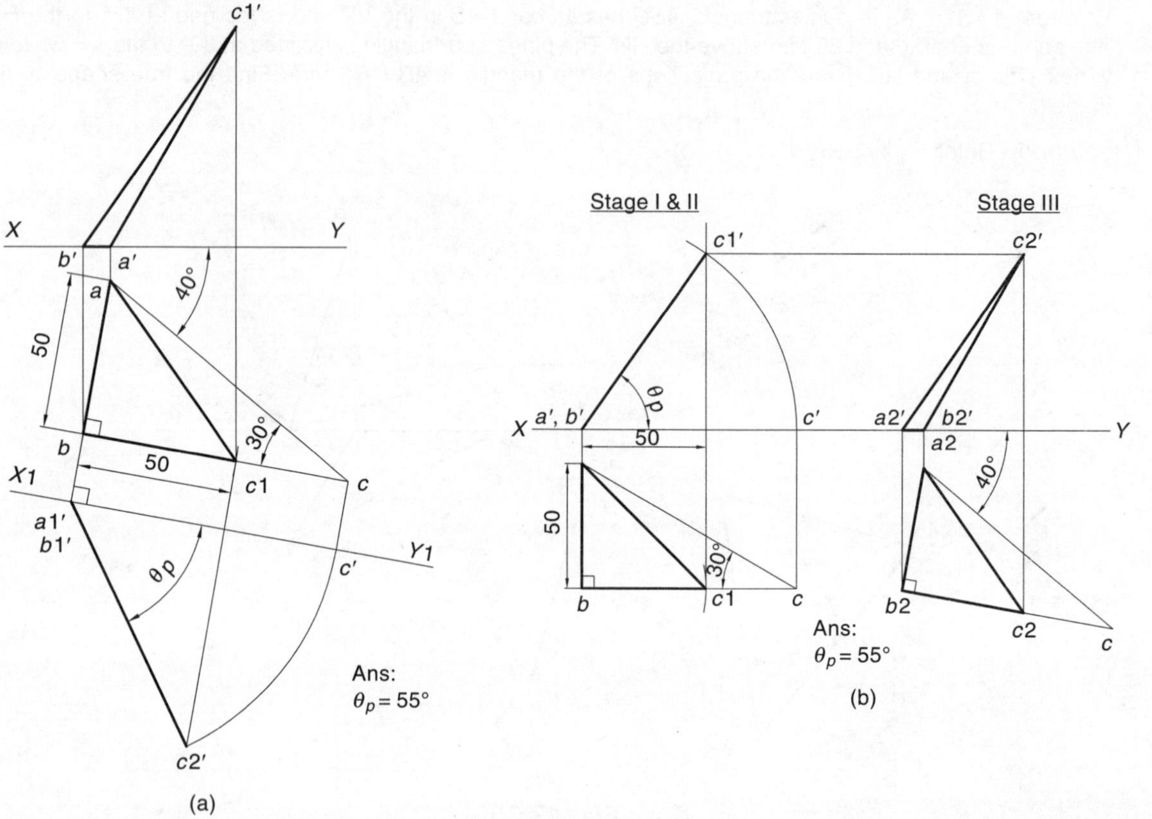

Fig. 13.36

4. Rotate $a1'b1'-c'$ about $a1'b1'$ to locate $c2'$ on the projector of $c1$. Measure the angle made by $a1'b1'-c2'$ with $X1Y1$.
5. Project $abc1$ on XY to obtain the auxiliary FV $a'b'c1'$.

See Fig. 13.36(b) for the stage wise solution.

Problem 13.19 A rectangular foil *ABCD* (*AB* = 80 mm, *BC* = 30 mm) is kept on the HP with *AB* parallel to the VP. The foil is bent along diagonal *AC* such that *BC* shows half of its TL in TV. Draw the projections of the foil and find the included angle.

Solution Refer Fig. 13.37.

1. Draw TV *abcd* to the true shape.
2. Obtain FV $a'd'-b'c'$ along *XY*.
3. Join *ac* and set $X1Y1$ perpendicular to it. Obtain auxiliary FV $b1'-a1'c1'-d1'$.
4. Drop a perpendicular from *b* on *ac*. When the foil is bent along *ac*, *b* will move along this line. With *c* as a centre and radius = 15 mm (= ½ *BC*), draw an arc cutting the perpendicular at *b*2. Join $a-b2-c$.
5. Project *b*2 on $X2Y2$. Rotate $a1'c1'-b1'$ about $a1'c1'$ till $b2'$ is obtained on the projector through *b*2. Measure angle γ, i.e., the included angle between $d1'-a1'c1'-b2'$.
6. Project *b*2 on *XY* and on this projector, locate $b2'$ such that (distance of $b2'$ from *XY*) = (distance of $b2'$ from $X1Y1$ in the auxiliary FV). Join $a'-b2'-c'$.

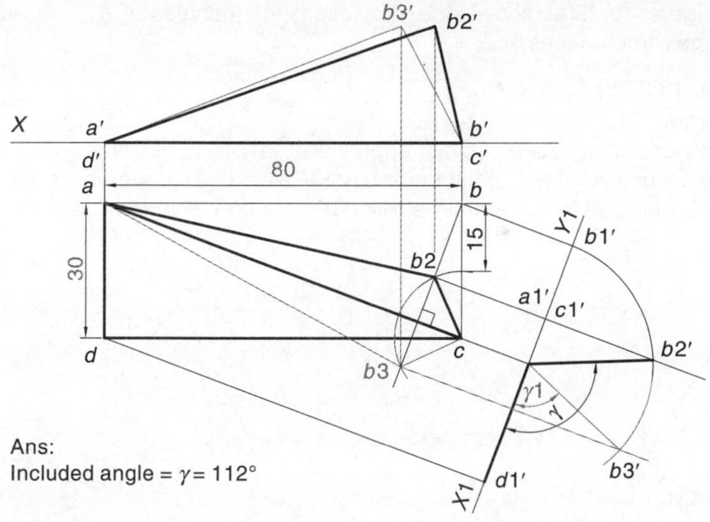

Fig. 13.37

> **Note:** Another point $b3$ can be obtained in TV such that $cb3 = \frac{1}{2} BC$. In that case, a'–$b3'$–c' will be the required FV and $\gamma 1$, the required included angle.

Problem 13.20 Two equal semicircular plates, each of radius 50 mm, are joined at right angles along their straight edges. The composite plate is kept on the HP such that its curved edges touch the HP. The straight edge is parallel to the HP and is inclined at 45° to the VP. Draw the projections of the plate.

Solution Refer Fig. 13.38.

Initially, we will assume that the straight edge is parallel to the HP and is perpendicular to the VP.

1. Draw FV h'–$1'$–c' of the composite plate. h'–$1'$ = $1'$–c' = 50 mm and $\angle h'$–$1'$–c' = 90°.
2. Draw two semicircles to represent the auxiliary views of the plates. Divide each of them into 6 equal parts. Transfer the division points to FV.
3. Obtain the TV by projecting the division points from FV and taking their distances from the auxiliary views. TV consists of two semi-ellipses, one each for a semicircle.
4. Draw $X1Y1$ at 45° to 1–2. Obtain the corresponding auxiliary FV. Note that $h1'$ and $c1'$ lie on $X1Y1$. Part of the curve $1_1'$–$a1'$–$c1'$–$e1'$–$2_1'$ will not be visible.

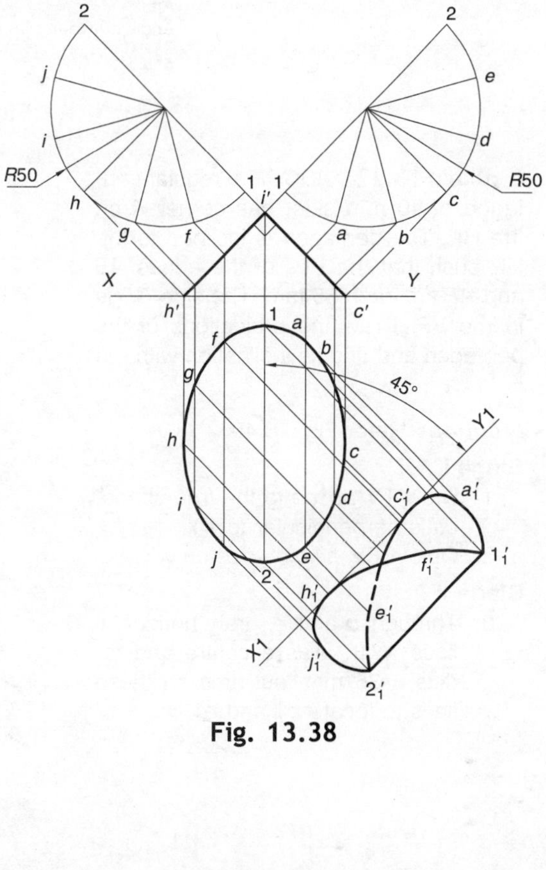

Fig. 13.38

Problem 13.21 Figure 13.39(a) shows the projections of triangles *ABC* and *ABD*. Find the angle between them and their true shapes.

Solution Refer Fig. 13.39(b).
It is clear that *a′b′* shows TL.

1. Draw *X*1*Y*1 perpendicular to *a′b′*. Obtain edge views, *a*1*b*1–*c*1 and *a*1*b*1–*d*1. Measure γ.
2. Assuming *X*2*Y*2 along *a*1*b*1–*c*1, obtain auxiliary FV *a*2′*b*2′*c*2′ to represent the true shape of *ABC*.
3. Assuming *X*3*Y*3 along *a*1*b*1–*d*1, obtain auxiliary FV *a*3′*b*3′*d*3′ to represent the true shape of *ABD*.

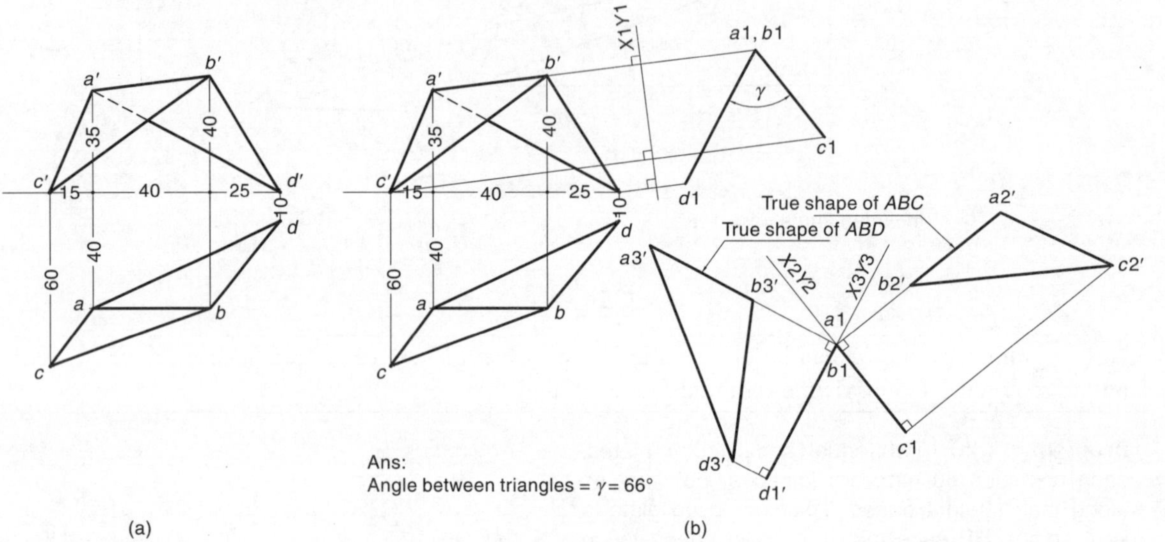

Fig. 13.39

Problem 13.22 *ABCDE*, a regular pentagon of 40 mm side, has corner *A* on the HP. The pentagon is inclined to the HP such that the PLs of the edges *AB* and *AE* are each 35 mm. The side *CD* is in the VP. Draw the projections of the pentagon and find its inclination with the HP.

Solution Refer Fig. 13.40.

Stage I

1. Draw TV *abcde* to the true shape. *cd* is perpendicular to *XY*.
2. Obtain FV *a′*–*b′e′*–*c′d′* on *XY*.

Stage II

3. Through *b* and *e*, draw horizontal lines. With *a* as a centre and radius = 35 mm, cut arcs on these lines to locate *b*1 and *e*1.

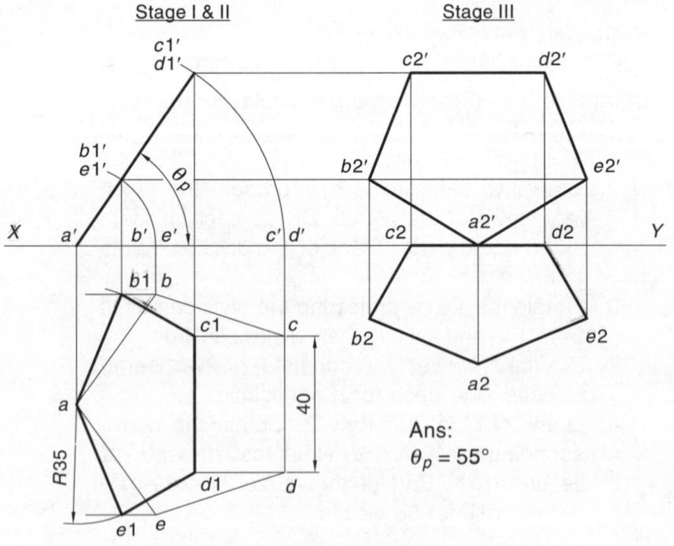

Fig. 13.40

4. Project $b1$ and $e1$ on XY. With a' as a centre, draw an arc through $b'(e')$ to intersect the projector through $b1(e1)$ at $b1'(e1')$.
5. With a' as a centre, draw another arc through c' (d'). Join a'–$b1'(e1')$ and produce it to meet this arc at $c1'(d1')$. Measure θ_p, i.e., the angle between a'–$c1'(d1')$ and XY.
6. Project $c1'(d1')$ to locate $c1$ and $d1$ as shown. Join a–$b1$–$c1$–$d1$–$e1$.

Stage III

7. Redraw a–$b1$–$c1$–$d1$–$e1$ as $a2$–$b2$–$c2$–$d2$–$e2$ such that $c2$–$d2$ is on XY.
8. Obtain the final FV $a2'$–$b2'$–$c2'$–$d2'$–$e2'$.

Problem 13.23 *ABCD* is a rhombus with diagonals AC = 115 mm and BD = 75 mm. The corner A is in the HP and the rhombus is made inclined to the HP such that the plan appears as a square. If the diagonal AC makes an angle of 25° with the VP, draw the projections of the plane and find its inclinations with the RPs.

Solution Refer Fig. 13.41.

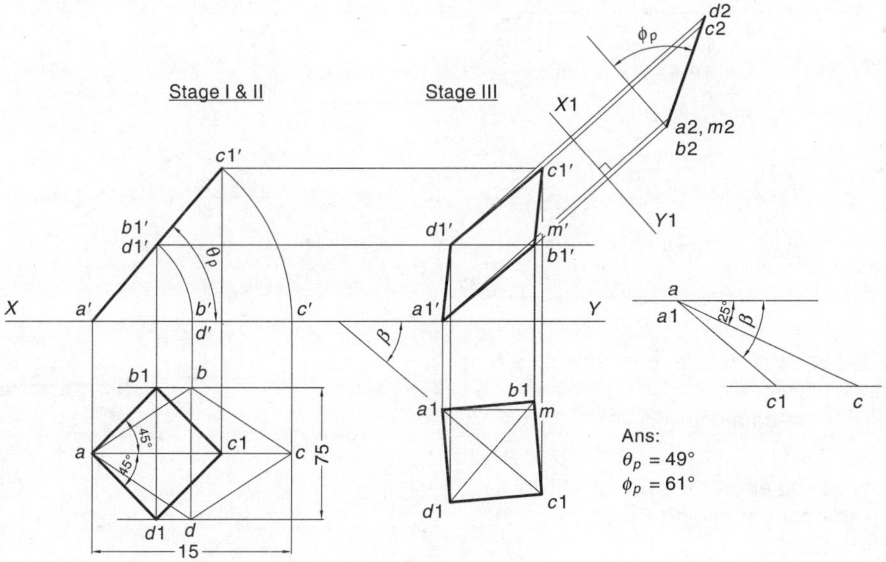

Fig. 13.41

Stage I

1. Draw TV *abcd* to true shape. *ac* is parallel to XY.
2. Obtain FV a'–$b'd'$–c' on XY.

Stage II

3. Draw a line through a, inclined at 45° to ac and meeting the horizontal line through b at $b1$. Locate $d1$ in a similar way. Complete square a–$b1$–$c1$–$d1$.
4. Project $b1$ and $e1$ on XY. With a' as a centre, draw an arc through b' (e') to intersect the projector through $b1(e1)$ at $b1'(e1')$.
5. Rotate a'–c' about a' to locate $c1'$ on the projector through $c1$. Obtain β as shown.

Stage III

6. Redraw a–$b1$–$c1$–$d1$ as $a1$–$b1$–$c1$–$d1$ with $a1$–$c1$ making β° with XY.
7. Obtain the final FV $a1'$–$b1'$–$c1'$–$d1'$.

To find ϕ_p, draw $a1$–m parallel to XY. Obtain its TL $a1'$–m'. Set $X1Y1$ perpendicular to $a1'$–m' and obtain the edge view $b2$–$a2(m2)$–$c2$–$d2$.

Problem 13.24 The edge *AB* of a symmetrical trapezium *ABCD* (*AB* = 70 mm, *CD* = 40 mm, and *BC* = *AD* = 50 mm) is in the VP. The edge *BC* is on the HP and the plane makes an angle of 45° with the VP. Obtain the projections of the plane and find its angle with the HP.

Solution Refer Fig. 13.42.

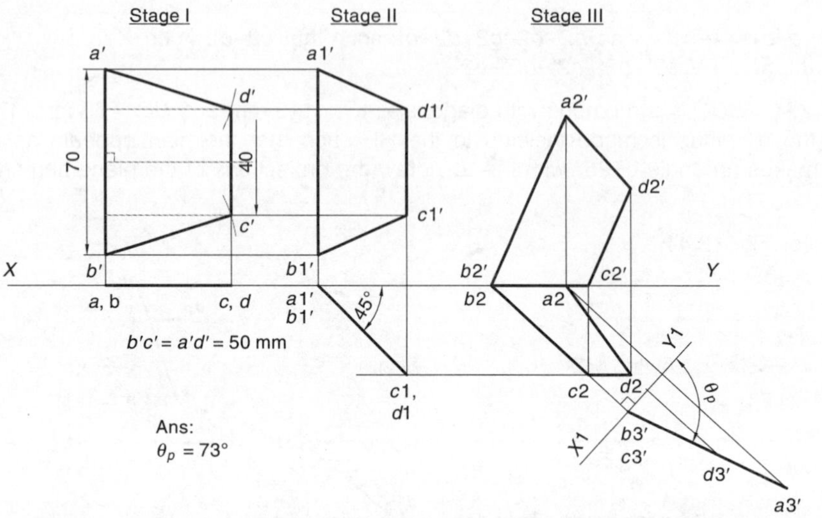

Fig. 13.42

Stage I

1. Draw FV *a′b′c′d′* to the true shape. *a′b′* is perpendicular to *XY*.
2. Obtain TV *ab–cd* along *XY*.

Stage II

3. Redraw *ab–cd* as *a*1*b*1–*c*1*d*1 at 45° to *XY*.
4. Obtain the corresponding FV *a*1′*b*1′*c*1′*d*1′.

Stage III

5. Redraw *a*1′*b*1′*c*1′*d*1′ as *a*2′*b*2′*c*2′*d*2′ with *b*2′*c*2′ on *XY*.
6. Obtain the final TV *a*2*b*2*c*2*d*2 as shown.

To find θ_p, set *X*1*Y*1 perpendicular to *b*2*c*2. (*b*2*c*2 shows TL.) Obtain the edge view *a*3′*d*3′–*b*3′*c*3′.

Problem 13.25 Draw a parallelogram *a′b′c′d′* (*a′b′* = *c′d′* = 20 mm, *b′c′* = *a′d′* = 16 mm, ∠*a′b′c′* = ∠*c′d′a′* = 75°). *a′b′* is on *XY*. Corresponding to *a′b′c′d′*, draw a rectangle *abcd* with *ab* inclined at 45° to *XY*. *a′b′c′d′* and *abcd* represent FV and TV of the blade of a hoe drawn to the scale of 1:10. A handle is attached to the blade at right angles at the midpoint of the edge *CD*. Another end of the handle rests on the ground. Find the length of the handle of the hoe. Also draw FV and TV of the handle.

Solution Refer Fig. 13.43.

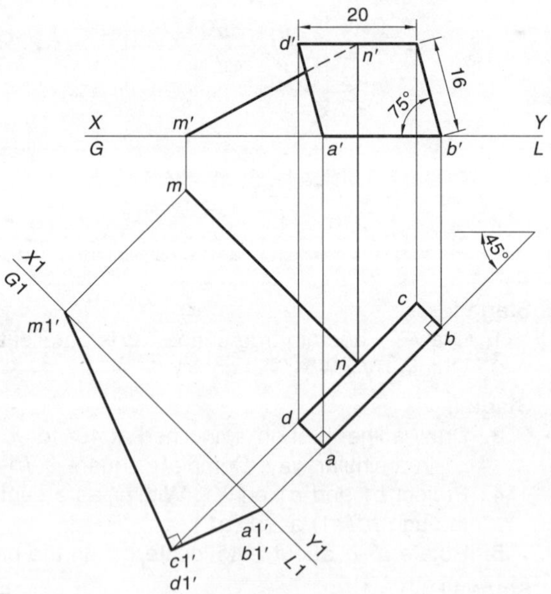

Scale 1:10
Ans : Length of handle = *m*1′*c*1′ = 44 cm

Fig. 13.43

As the handle is perpendicular to the blade, its TL will be seen when the blade will show the edge view.

1. Draw FV *a′b′c′d′* and TV *abcd* of the blade as shown. *GL* may be taken along *XY*.
2. *ab* shows TL. Draw *X*1*Y*1 perpendicular to it. Obtain the edge view of the blade *a*1′*b*1′–*c*1′*d*1′. Obviously, *a*1′*b*1′ will be on *X*1*Y*1 (*G*1*L*1).
3. Draw a perpendicular to *a*1′*b*1′–*c*1′*d*1′ at *c*1′*d*1′ to meet *X*1*Y*1 at *m*1′. *m*1′*c*1′ gives TL of the handle.
4. Locate *n* and *n′* at the midpoints of *cd* and *c′d′* respectively. Through *n*, draw *a* line parallel to *X*1*Y*1 and locate *m* on it on the projector through *m*1′. *mn* is the TV of the handle.
5. Project *m* to *m′* on *XY*. Join *m′n′* to represent FV of the handle. *m′n′* is partly visible.

Problem 13.26 A thin hexagonal plate of 35 mm side has a central equilateral triangular hole of side equal to that of the plate. The plate is kept in such a way that one of its edges is parallel to the ground and inclined at 30° to the VP. The plate makes 45° with ground. Draw the projections of the plate and the hole. A side of the hole is parallel to the ground.

Solution Refer Fig. 13.44.

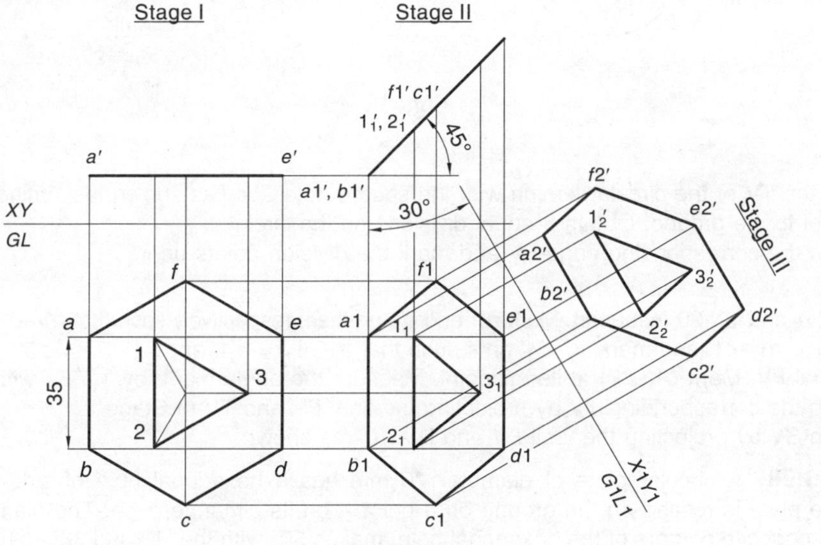

Fig. 13.44

Stage I

1. Draw a hexagon *abcdef* with an equilateral triangle 123 in it. *ab* and 1–2 are perpendicular to *XY*. Draw *a′e′*.

Stage II

2. Draw *a*1′*e*1′ (= *a′e′*) inclined at 45° to *XY*. Obtain *a*1–*b*1–*c*1–*d*1–*e*1–*f*1.

Stage III

3. Draw *X*1*Y*1 at 30° to *a*1*b*1 and obtain auxiliary FV *a*2′*b*2′*c*2′*d*2′*e*2′*f*2′ as shown.

Problem 13.27 A circular lamina of 60 mm diameter has a square hole of 30 mm side. A diagonal of the hole is parallel to the VP. The lamina is inclined to the ground such that the diagonal parallel to the VP measures 20 mm in TV. Draw the three views of the lamina. Find the inclination of the lamina with the ground.

Solution Refer Fig. 13.45.

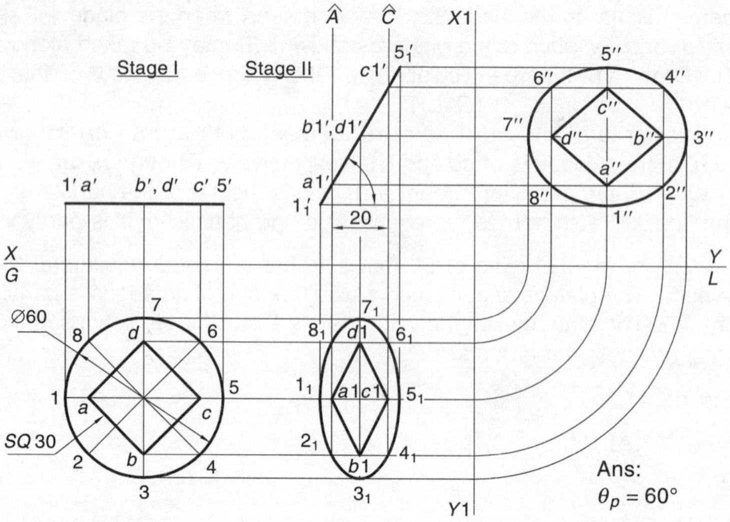

Fig. 13.45

Stage I

1. Draw the TV of the circular lamina with the square hole *abcd* as shown, assuming the lamina to be parallel to the ground. Obtain 8 equal divisions on the circle.
2. Obtain the corresponding edge-FV and mark the division points on it.

Stage II

3. Draw $\hat{A}$ and $\hat{C}$, 20 mm apart. Mark *a*1′ and *c*1′ on them respectively such that *a*1′–*c*1′ = *a*″*c*′.
4. Produce *a*1′–*c*1′ and mark $1_1'$–$5_1'$ on it such that *a*1′–$1_1'$ = *a*′1′ and *c*1′–$5_1'$ = *c*′5′. $1_1'$–$5_1'$ represents the final FV. Mark *b*1′(*d*1′) at its midpoint. Measure the angle made by $1_1'$–$5_1'$ with *XY* (*GL*).
5. Obtain the corresponding TV by projecting the final FV and TV of Stage I.
6. Obtain SV by projecting the final FV and final TV as shown.

Problem 13.28 A circular plate of diameter 70 mm has a hexagonal hole of side 28 mm, centrally located. The plate is resting on the ground on a point *A* on its circumference. The diameter *AB* (passing through two opposite corners of the hexagonal hole) makes 50° with the HP and 30° with the VP. Draw the projections.

Solution Refer Fig. 13.46.
This problem is solved by the third-angle method.

Stage I

1. Draw a circle of diameter 70 mm to represent the TV. Diameter *ab* is drawn parallel to *XY*. Also draw the hexagon inside the circle. The corners *c* and *f* of the hexagon lie on *ab*. Divide the circle into 8 equal divisions.
2. Obtain FV of the circle (with hexagon) along *GL*.

Stage II

3. Redraw FV as *a*1′–*b*1′ inclined at 50° to *GL*.
4. Obtain TV of the circle by projecting TV of Stage I and FV of Stage II.

Obtain β as shown.

Stage III

5. Draw *X*1*Y*1 inclined at β° to *a*1–*b*1. Obtain auxiliary FV *a*2′–$2_2'$*b*2′–$5_2'$ as shown. Note that *a*2′ is on *G*1*L*1.

Project the hexagon in each stage in a similar way.

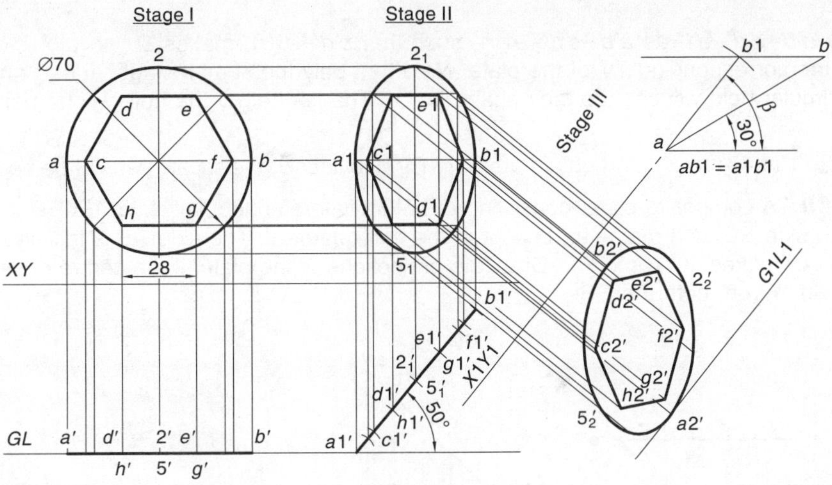

Fig. 13.46

Problem 13.29 A thin composite plate consists of a square *ABCD* of 60 mm sides with a semi-hexagon constructed on *CD* as a diagonal. A circular hole of diameter 40 mm and having its centre at the midpoint of *CD* is drilled in the plate. The plate is kept on the HP with *CD* perpendicular to the VP. The plate is then bent along *CD* such that the included angle is 50°. Draw the projections of the plate with the hole. Obtain an auxiliary FV on an AVP inclined at 45° to the VP.

Solution Refer Fig. 13.47.

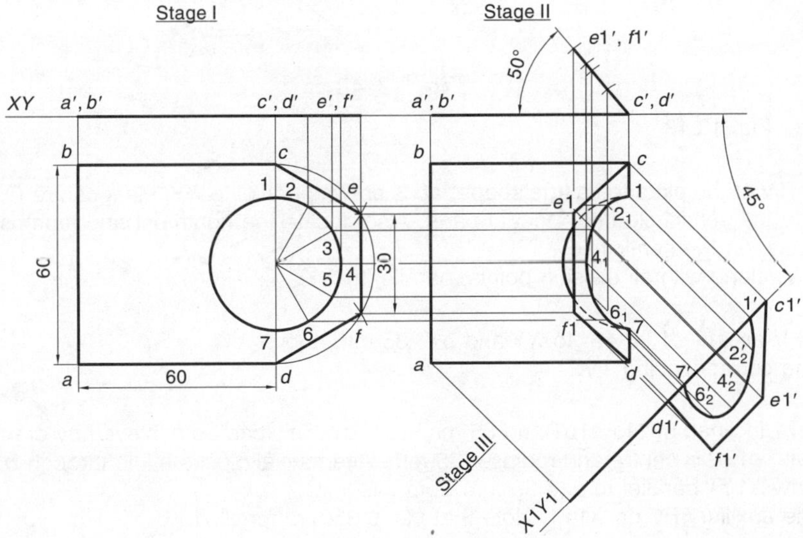

Fig. 13.47

Stage I

1. Draw TV *abcefd* of the composite plate to the true shape. *cd* is drawn perpendicular to *XY*. Draw a circular hole (centre at midpoint of *cd*) and divide its right half into 6 equal parts.
2. Obtain FV *a′b′–c′d′–e′f′* along *XY*.

Stage II

3. Redraw *a′b′–c′d′–e′f′* as *a′b′–c′d′–e1′f1′* such that *c′d′–e1′f1′* makes 50° to *a′b′–c′d′*.
4. Obtain the corresponding TV of the plate. Note that only the semi-hexagonal part and the right half of the circular hole will change their shape in TV. The left half of the hole will be partly visible.

Stage III

5. Draw *X*1 *Y*1 at 45° to *XY* and obtain auxiliary FV. Obviously, the square part will be seen along *X*1 *Y*1.

Problem 13.30 A composite plate, consisting of an equilateral triangular plate *ABC* (side 50 mm) and a semicircle with side *BC* as a diameter, is kept in the first quadrant. The side *AB* is inclined to HRP at 45° and the TV of *AB* makes 60° with FRP. Draw the projections of the plate, if the centre of semicircle is at a distance of 35 mm from both the RPs.

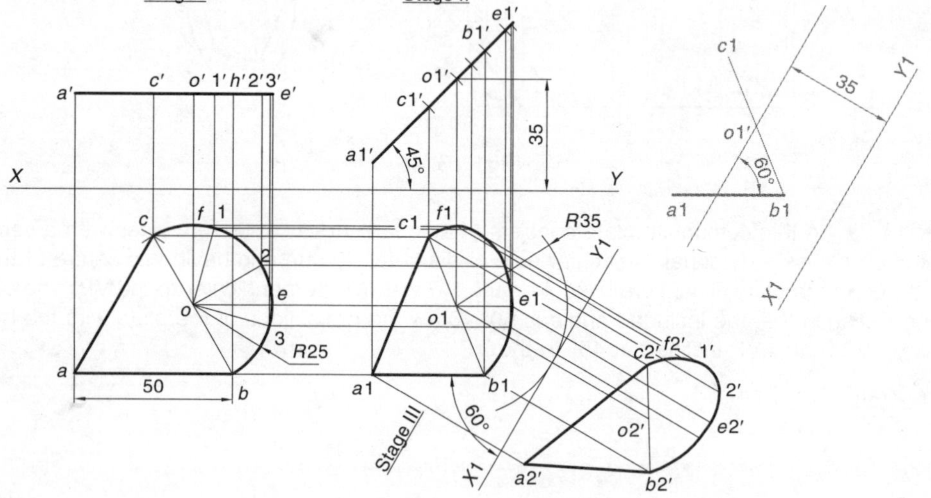

Fig. 13.48

Solution Refer Fig. 13.48.

Stage I

1. Draw the TV of the plate to its true shape. *ab* is drawn parallel to *XY*. Mark centre *O* of the semicircle and divide the semicircle into 4 equal parts. Also, locate the rightmost and topmost points, *e* and *f* respectively, on the semicircle.
2. Obtain FV, along with all division points, parallel to *XY*.

Stage II

3. Redraw FV as *a*1′–*e*1′ at 45° to *XY* and *o*1′, 35 mm above *XY*.
4. Obtain the corresponding TV.

Stage III

5. Draw *X*1 *Y*1 inclined 60° to *a*1*b*1 and 35 mm from *o*1. This can be achieved by drawing a tangent to the arc with *o*1 as a centre and radius = 35 mm. Alternatively, pass a line through *o*1 at 60° to *a*1*b*1. Then, draw *X*1 *Y*1 parallel to and 35 mm from this line.
   Obtain the auxiliary FV on *X*1 *Y*1. Note that *o*2′ is 35 mm form *X*1 *Y*1.

REVIEW QUESTIONS

1. A square of 50 mm side is seen as a rectangle of size 50 mm × 20 mm in TV. Draw the projections of the square if one of its sides is on the HP and at 45° to the VP.

2. A right-angled triangle with a shorter side of 40 mm and hypotenuse of 80 mm is inclined to the HP at 40°. Its shorter side is parallel to the HP and inclined to the VP at 30°. Draw the projections of the triangle.
3. A pentagonal plate of 35 mm side has one of its edges parallel to the VP and inclined at 45° to the HP. The plate is inclined at 60° to the VP. Draw the projections of the plate.
4. A trapezium plane of parallel sides 70 mm and 40 mm is resting on the HP on its longer edge. The plane makes 25° to the HP and a shorter side is parallel to the VP. Draw the projections of the plane if the distance between the parallel sides is 50 mm.
5. Draw the projections of a circle of diameter 70 mm if one of its diameters makes 30° to the HP and 45° to the VP.
6. A pentagon of side 35 mm has a corner in the VP. The perpendicular from that corner on the opposite edge makes 25° to the VP and 50° to the HP. Draw the projections.
7. A regular pentagonal lamina of 40 mm side is resting on the HP on one of its sides which is inclined at 45° to the VP. The plane of the lamina is inclined to the HP at 30°. Draw the TV, FV and LHSV.
8. The FV of a plane figure is a line inclined at 45° to *XY* and its TV is a regular hexagon of sides 30 mm with one side of it being parallel to *XY*. Draw FV and TV. Also find its true shape.
9. A regular hexagon of 40 mm side is resting on one of its sides on the HP having that side parallel to and 20 mm in front of the VP. It is tilted about that side so that its highest side rests in the VP. Draw the projections.
10. A rhombus having diagonals 150 mm and 60 mm is so placed that its smaller diagonal is parallel to both the RPs and the larger diagonal is inclined at 40° to the HP. Draw its projections. Also, find the angles made by the plane with the HP and the VP.
11. *ABC* is a thin triangular plate with an edge *AB* in the HP, and the point *A* is 10 mm in front of the VP. The distance between the projectors through *A* and *B* is 45 mm. The sides *AB*, *BC* and *AC* measure 70 mm, 80 mm and 60 mm respectively. The point *C* is 45 mm above the HP. Draw the projections of the plate and measure the angles of the plate with the HP and the VP.
12. A valve has a circular disc of 70 mm diameter. The disc is pivoted at the ends of the diameter *AB* which is parallel to the VP and inclined to the HP at 30°. Draw the projections of the disc if it is inclined to the VP at 30°. Find the angle made by the disc with the HP.
13. A semicircle of radius 38 mm is suspended freely from a point on its straight edge, 18 mm from a corner. The semicircle is inclined to the VP at 60°. Draw the projections of the semicircle.
14. A semicircle of diameter 80 mm is kept on the HP with its straight edge (i.e., diameter) parallel to both the planes. It is then tilted about one of the corners such that the straight edge remains parallel to the VP and the semicircle makes 30° to the HP. The semicircle is again tilted about the same corner such that the TV of the straight edge is seen perpendicular to *XY*. Draw the TV and FV of semicircle.
15. A thin pentagonal plate *ABCDE* of 35 mm side has a side *AB* in the HP and inclined at 30° to the VP. Draw its projections when the corner *D* is 50 mm above the HP. Determine the inclination of the plate with the HP.
16. A rhombus *PQRS* has diagonal *PR* = 90 mm and *QS* = 60 mm. Draw its projections, if *PR* makes 45° to the HP and *QS* makes 30° to the VP. Neglect its thickness.
17. The rhombus having diagonals 150 mm and 60 mm is so placed that its smaller diagonal is parallel to both the planes and the larger diagonal is inclined at 40° to the HP. Draw its projections. Also, find the angles made by the plane with the HP and the VP.
18. A circular plate of 70 mm diameter has a triangular hole of sides 25 mm at its centre. If a point *A* on the circumference of the plate is on the ground with the diameter *AB* making an angle 50° with the HP and 30° with the VP, draw the final projections of the plate and find the inclination of the plate with the VP. (One side of the triangular hole remains parallel to ground.)
19. A divider has 60 mm long legs. The angle between them is 30°. It is resting on the HP on the ends of its legs with the line joining those ends inclined at 45° to the VP. The head of the divider is 35 mm above the HP. Draw the three views of the divider and determine the angle made by its plane with the HP.
20. A triangle *ABC* rests on a corner *C* on the HP. Point *A* is 15 mm above the HP and 25 mm in front of the VP. Point *B* is 40 mm from both the RPs. The distance between the projectors of *A* and *B* is 50 mm. The sides *AC* and *BC* are 45 mm and 60 mm long respectively. Draw the projections and determine the true shape of the triangle.

21. An isosceles triangle *PQR* has base *PQ* of 50 mm and an altitude of 75 mm. *PQ* is parallel to the VP with *P* on the HP and *Q* is 25 mm above the HP. *R* is 50 mm above the HP. Draw the projections of the triangle. Find its inclinations with the RPs.
22. Determine the true shape of a plate by projecting auxiliary views if the FV of the plate is a regular pentagon *a′b′c′d′e′* of 25 mm side with side *a′b′* inclined at 35° to *XY*, *a′* being on *XY*. In the TV, *a*, *b*, *c*, *d*, and *e* are seen 10 mm, 25 mm, 35 mm, 50 mm and 30 mm below *XY* respectively.
23. Draw the true shape of a triangle *ABC* of which *a′b′c′* is an FV and *abc* is a TV. *a′b′c′* is an isosceles triangle of altitude 90 mm and *abc* is an equilateral triangle. The side *AB* is 80 mm and parallel to both the RPs.
24. A triangular plane *ABC* has a 60 mm long base *AB* and is on the ground inclined to the VP at 30°. Its altitude length is 80 mm. The plane is lifted on *AB* such that *AC* lies on a plane perpendicular to both the HP and the VP. Draw the projections of the plane. Find out the angles of inclination of the plane with the HP and the VP.
25. Draw the projections of a circle of 75 mm diameter having the end *A* of the diameter *AB* in the HP, the end *B* in the VP and the surface inclined at 30° to the HP and 60° to the VP.
26. A pentagonal plate of 60 mm edges has a corner on the HP and the side opposite to that corner is in the VP at a distance of 30 mm above the HP. It has a central equilateral triangular hole of 30 mm altitude length. The base of the triangle is parallel to the side of the plate in FRP. Draw the projections of the plate and find the angle of the plate with the HP.
27. Draw a rhombus having diagonals 100 mm and 60 mm, with the longer diagonal horizontal. The figure is the TV of a square with 100 mm long diagonals, with a corner on the ground. Draw its FV and determine the angle which its surface makes with the ground.
28. A thin, composite plate consists of a square *ABCD* of 50 mm sides with an additional semicircle constructed on *CD* as diameter. The circular hole of 30 mm diameter is made concentric with the semicircle. The side *AB* is in the VP and makes 30° with the HP and the surface of the plate makes 45° with the VP. Draw the projection.
29. Draw a rectangle of 50 mm × 30 mm dimensions with the longer side making an angle of 35° with *XY* in TV. Corresponding to this, draw another rectangle with the longer side making an angle of 65° with *XY* in the FV. These two views represent the FV and TV of a quadrilateral thin plate. Determine the true shape of the plate.
30. Two semicircular laminas of equal size (radius 30 mm) are connected along their base such that the included angle between them is 90°. The surface of one of the laminas makes 30° to the ground and the common edge is 45° to the VP. The combined object is resting on the common edge on the ground. Draw the projections.
31. Draw an ellipse of major axis *a′b′* = 80 mm and minor axis *c′d′* = 50 mm (*a′b′* perpendicular to *XY*). Draw another ellipse of major axis *cd* = 50 mm and minor axis *ab* = 30 mm. The ellipses represent two views of a lamina. Obtain true shape of the lamina.
32. Draw an isosceles triangle *p′q′r′* (*p′q′* is base, 60 mm long and perpendicular to *XY*; *s′r′* is altitude and 80 mm long). Draw a right-angled triangle *pq–r–s* (*pq–r* = 45 mm and ∠*s–pq–r* = 90°). These two triangles represent the FVs and TVs of two triangles *PSR* and *QSR*. Find the true shapes and the angle between the triangles.
33. Two regular pentagonal plates *ABCDE* and *AFGHI* of equal sizes are joined at *A* such that the included angle between them is 75°. The edges opposite to corner *A* are on the ground and make 30° with a vertical wall. Draw the projections of the plates. Find the length of a rod joining the centres of both the plates.
34. Draw a trapezium *p′q′r′s′* (*p′q′* = 85 mm and on *XY*, *r′s′* = 40 mm, *p′q′* parallel to and 50 mm from *r′s′*) and join *q′s′* to represent FVs of two triangles *PQS* and *QRS*. Two right angled triangles *pqs* (∠*pqs* = 90° and *qs* is inclined at 30° to *XY*) and *qrs* (∠*qrs* = 90°) represent TVs of the two triangles. Find the angle between the triangles.
35. A circle of diameter 80 mm is seen as an ellipse with a major axis of 80 mm and a minor axis of 50 mm in TV. Its FV is another ellipse with a major axis of 80 mm and a minor axis of 25 mm. A point on the circumference of the circle is on the HP and the point diametrically opposite to this point is in the VP. What will be the shortest distance of the centre of the circle from the HP?

Chapter 14

PROJECTIONS OF SOLIDS

14.1 INTRODUCTION

Any object having definite length, width and height is called a solid. In engineering drawing, solids are often represented by two or more orthographic views, i.e., FV, TV or SV. As seen in Chapter 9 any one orthographic view gives two dimensions, but two orthographic views together give three dimensions. In some cases, the projections are drawn on an auxiliary plane (i.e., auxiliary view) to make the description of the solid clearer. The study of the projections of a solid is very important in mechanical-design problems. The knowledge of projections of solids is essential in 3D modeling and animation. Projections of solids find wide applications in the construction industry.

14.2 BASIC SOLIDS

Basic solids are those which have predefined shapes. The basic solids are the constituent parts of any complex solid. Objects in the real world are made up of combinations of basic solids. In 3D modeling, the basic solids are called *solid primitives*. Solid primitives are combined in logical ways to obtain the desired 3D shape.

The two categories of basic solids are: polyhedra and solids of revolution.

Polyhedra are bounded by plane surfaces. *Solids of revolution* have curved outer faces.

14.2.1 Polyhedra

Polyhedra are sub-divided into three types—regular polyhedra, prisms and pyramids.

Regular Polyhedra In a *regular polyhedron*, all the faces are similar, equal and regular. The angles formed between the faces are also equal. Since all the edges are of same length, a regular polyhedron is expressed by length of any edge.

The following are the five regular polyhedra:

Tetrahedron A regular polyhedron having four equal equilateral triangular faces is called a *tetrahedron*, Fig. 14.1(a).

Cube A regular polyhedron having six equal square faces is called a *cube* or *hexahedron*, Fig. 14.1(b).

Octahedron A regular polyhedron having eight equal equilateral triangular faces is called an *octahedron*, Fig. 14.1(c).

Dodecahedron A regular polyhedron having twelve equal and regular pentagonal faces is called a *dodecahedron*, Fig. 14.1(d).

Icosahedron A regular polyhedron having twenty equal equilateral triangular faces is called an *icosahedron*, Fig. 14.1(e).

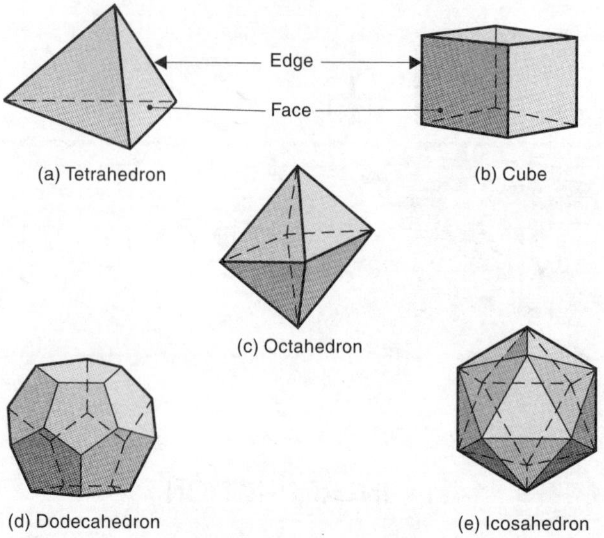

Fig. 14.1 Polyhedra

Prisms In a *prism*, there are two equal and similar end faces, parallel to each other, joined together by other rectangular faces. In some cases, the faces joining the end faces may be parallelograms instead of rectangles. In case of a vertical prism, the end faces may be called *base* or *top* depending on their position. The faces joining the end faces are called *side faces* or *lateral faces* or simply *faces*. The imaginary line joining the centres of the end faces is called the *axis* of the prism. A prism is called a *right-angled prism* if its axis is perpendicular to the end faces. If the axis is inclined to the end faces, the prism is called an *oblique prism*. Needless to say, the lateral faces of an oblique prism will be parallelograms. A *right regular prism* is the right-angled prism whose all lateral faces are equal rectangles. Obviously, the end faces of the right regular prism are regular polygons. This text deals only with right regular prisms, hence the word 'prism' henceforth stands for 'right regular prism'.

The prisms are expressed by the length of the side of the base and the length of the axis (i.e., height).

The different types of prisms are explained below:

Triangular Prism A prism having triangular end faces is called a *triangular prism*, Fig. 14.2(a).

Square Prism A prism having square end faces is called a *square prism*, Fig. 14.2(b).

Rectangular Prism A prism having rectangular end faces is called a *rectangular prism*, Fig. 14.2(c).

Pentagonal Prism A prism having pentagonal end faces is called a *pentagonal prism*, Fig. 14.2(d).

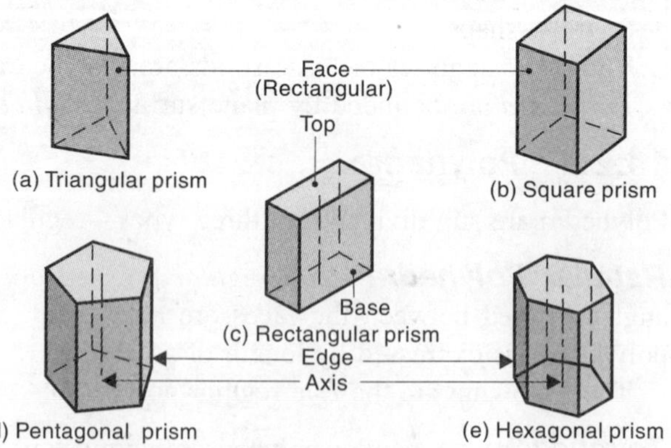

Fig. 14.2 Prisms

Hexagonal Prism A prism having hexagonal end faces is called a *hexagonal prism*, Fig. 14.2(e).

Pyramids In a *pyramid*, there is a polygonal face for the base which is connected at the edges to a number of triangular faces equal to the number of sides of the base. All the adjacent triangular faces are joined to each other at the common edge and all the triangular faces meet at a point. The point is called an *apex* of the pyramid. The triangular faces are called *slant faces* or *lateral faces* or simply *faces*. The edges of the slant faces meeting at the apex are called *slant edges*. The length of a slant edge is called the *slant height* of the pyramid. The imaginary line joining the centre of the base to the apex is called the *axis* of the pyramid. A pyramid is called a *right-angled pyramid* if its axis is perpendicular to the base. If the axis is inclined to the base, the pyramid is called an *oblique pyramid*. A *right regular pyramid* is the right-angled pyramid whose all slant faces are equal triangles. Obviously, the base of the right regular pyramid is a regular polygon. As this text deals only with right regular pyramids, the word 'pyramid' is used henceforth for 'right regular pyramid'.

The pyramid is specified by the length of the side of the base and the length of the axis or slant height.

The different types of pyramid are explained below:

Triangular Pyramid A pyramid having a triangular base is called a *triangular pyramid*, Fig. 14.3(a).

Square Pyramid A pyramid having a square base is called a *square pyramid*, Fig. 14.3(b).

Rectangular Pyramid A pyramid having a rectangular base is called a *rectangular pyramid*, Fig. 14.3(c).

Pentagonal Pyramid A pyramid having a pentagonal base is called a *pentagonal pyramid*, Fig. 14.3(d).

Hexagonal Pyramid A pyramid having a hexagonal base is called a *hexagonal pyramid*, Fig. 14.3(e).

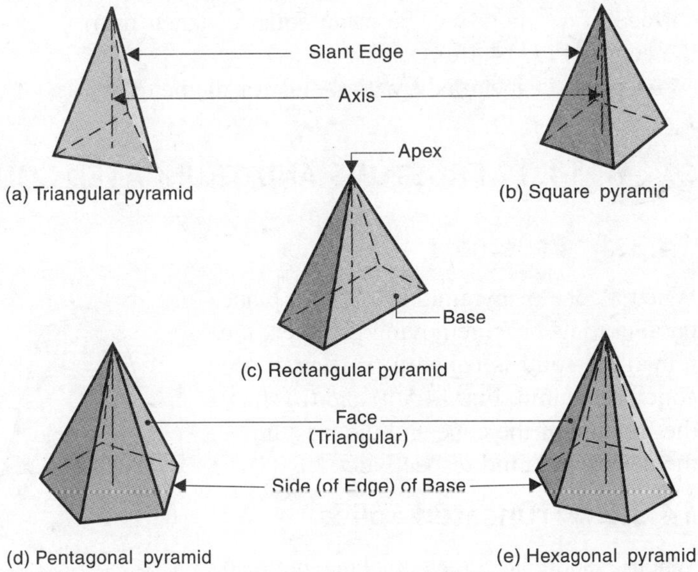

(a) Triangular pyramid (b) Square pyramid (c) Rectangular pyramid (d) Pentagonal pyramid (e) Hexagonal pyramid

Fig. 14.3 Pyramids

Solids of Revolution *Solids of revolution* are formed by the revolution of plane figures, like rectangles, triangles or semicircles about a fixed line.

Three most common solids of revolution are as follows:

Cylinder A *cylinder* is a solid generated by revolving a rectangle about one of its sides, keeping that side fixed. The fixed side, about which the rectangle revolves, is called the *axis* of the cylinder. The circles described by the sides perpendicular to the axis are called the *ends* or *bases*. The side of the rectangle parallel to the axis (and which revolves about the axis) is called the *generator*, Fig. 14.4(a).

A cylinder is specified by the radius (or diameter) of the base and the length of the axis or generator (i.e., height).

Cone A *cone* is a solid generated by revolving a right-angled triangle about one of its perpendicular sides, keeping that side fixed. The fixed side, about which the triangle revolves, is called the *axis* of the cone. The circle described by the side perpendicular to the axis is called the *base*. The side of the triangle inclined to the axis (and which revolves about the axis) is called the *generator*, Fig. 14.4(b). The length of the generator represents the *slant height* of the cone.

A cone is specified by the radius (or diameter) of the base and the length of the axis (i.e., height) or the slant height.

Sphere A *sphere* is a solid generated by revolving a semicircle about its diameter, keeping the diameter fixed. The mid-point of the diameter represents the *centre* of the sphere. Obviously, every point on the surface of a sphere will be at an equal distance from the centre, Fig. 14.4(c).

A sphere is specified by its radius (or diameter).

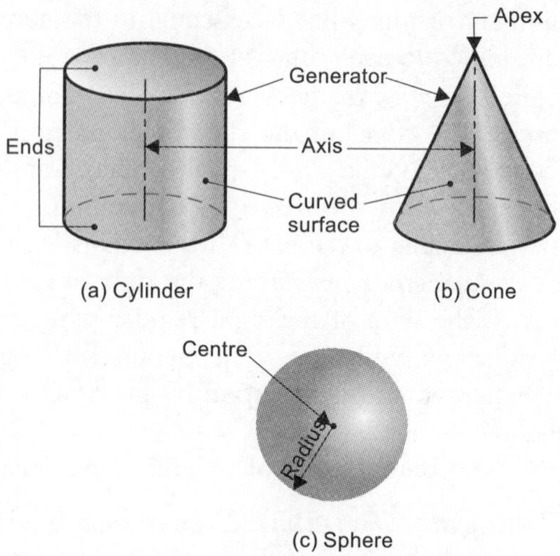

Fig. 14.4 Solids of Revolution

14.3 FRUSTUMS AND TRUNCATED SOLIDS

14.3.1 Frustums

When a cone or pyramid is cut by a plane parallel to its base, removing the apex, the remaining solid is called a *frustum* of the cone or pyramid. Fig. 14.5(a) and (b) show the frustum of the cone and the frustum of the square pyramid respectively.

14.3.2 Truncated Solids

When a solid is cut by a plane inclined to its base, it is said to be *truncated*. Figure 14.6 shows some of the truncated solids.

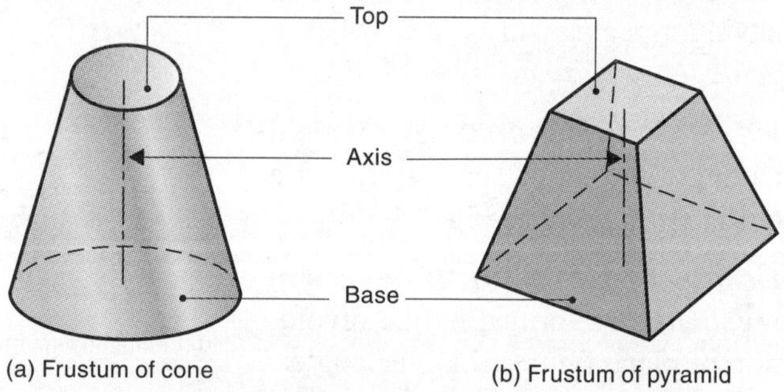

Fig. 14.5 Frustums of Cone and Pyramid

14.4 POSITIONS OF THE SOLIDS

The position of a solid in space is specified by the inclinations of its axis with the RPs. Therefore, a solid will have positions with respect to RPs same as that of a line. Depending on the orientation of its axis in space, a solid may have the following positions:

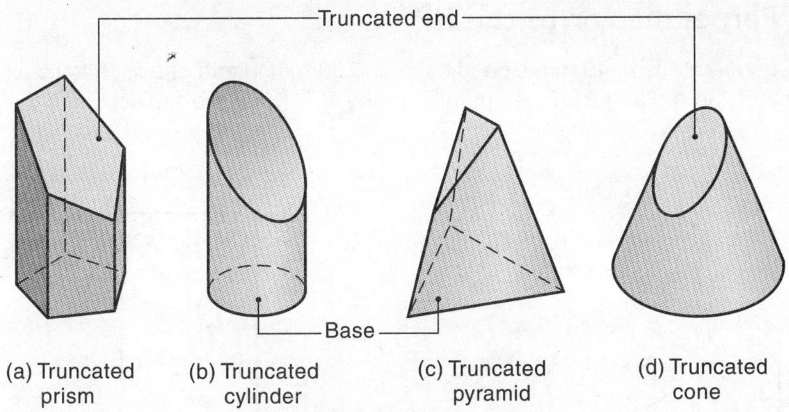

Fig. 14.6 Truncated Solids

1. Solid with axis perpendicular to an RP
   Case (i): Axis perpendicular to the HP
   Case (ii): Axis perpendicular to the VP
2. Solid with axis inclined to one RP and parallel to the other
   Case (i): Axis inclined to the HP and parallel to the VP
   Case (ii): Axis inclined to the VP and parallel to the HP
3. Solid with axis inclined to both the RPs
4. Solid with axis parallel to the PP
5. Solid with axis parallel to both the RPs

It should be noted that the above conditions can be obtained in different ways. Many times the inclinations of the axis of the solid are not given directly but they are expressed in terms of other parameters; e.g., angle made by an edge of the base with the HP or the VP, angle made by an edge of the face or slant edge (or generator in case of solids of revolution) with the HP or the VP, angle made by the base with the HP or the VP, angle made by the lateral face or slant face with the HP or the VP, etc. Sometimes, some other conditions are mentioned, e.g., a corner of the base of a pyramid in the HP, apex of the cone in the VP, freely suspended solid, etc. In fact, whatever the conditions mentioned in the problem, it automatically puts conditions on the axis and hence the given problem can be put into any one of the five categories mentioned above.

All the five categories mentioned above are discussed independently in the following sections.

14.5 SOLID WITH AXIS PERPENDICULAR TO AN RP

If the axis of a solid is perpendicular to one RP, it automatically remains parallel to the other. The base remains parallel to the RP to which the axis is perpendicular. In such a case, the view of the solid on the RP to which its axis is perpendicular is drawn first. This view will give the true shape of the base.

14.5.1 Axis Perpendicular to the HP

Example 14.1 A square prism, 40 mm side of base and 60 mm length of axis, has its axis perpendicular to the HP and one of the rectangular faces parallel to the VP. Draw the projections if the base is 10 mm above the HP.

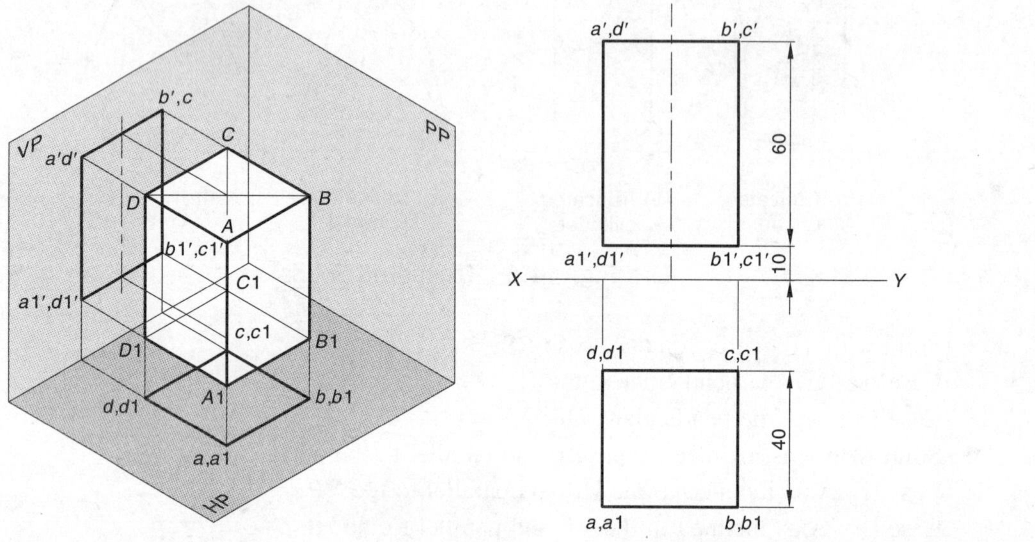

Fig. 14.7

Solution Refer Fig. 14.7.

As the axis of the prism is perpendicular to the HP, its TV must be drawn first. The solution may be obtained in the following steps:

1. Draw a square *a*(*a*1)–*b*(*b*1)–*c*(*c*1)–*d*(*d*1) of side 40 mm (at suitable distance below *XY*) to represent the TV. *ab* is parallel to *XY*.
2. Project TV above *XY* to obtain FV–*a*′(*d*′)–*b*′(*c*′)–*b*1′(*c*1′)–*a*1′(*d*1′) such that *a*′–*a*1′ = *b*′–*b*1′ = 60 mm. Note that *a*1′(*d*1′)–*b*1′(*c*1′) is an edge view of the base and is parallel to and 10 mm above *XY*. Show the axis in FV.

Example 14.2 Draw the projections of the square prism in Example 14.1 if one of its rectangular faces is inclined at 60° to the VP.

Solution Refer Fig. 14.8.

The above problem is similar to the previous one except that a rectangular face makes 60° with the VP. Therefore, the TV of previous problem should be rotated so that one side will make 60° to *XY*.

1. Draw TV *a*(*a*1)–*b*(*b*1)–*c*(*c*1)–*d*(*d*1) of side 40 mm such that *ab* is inclined at 60° to *XY*.
2. Project TV above *XY* to obtain an edge view of the base– *a*1′*b*1′*c*1′*d*1′ at a distance of 10 mm from *XY*.
3. Obtain the FV by drawing *b*′–*b*1′–*d*1′–*d*′ as shown. Also draw *a*′*a*1′ and *c*′*c*1′. Note that *c*′*c*1′is not visible and shown by dashed line in FV. Show the axis in FV.

14.5.2 Axis Perpendicular to the VP

Example 14.3 A triangular prism, 40 mm side of base and 60 mm length of axis, has its axis perpendicular to the VP. Draw the projections if one of the rectangular faces is parallel to the HP and 20 mm above the HP.

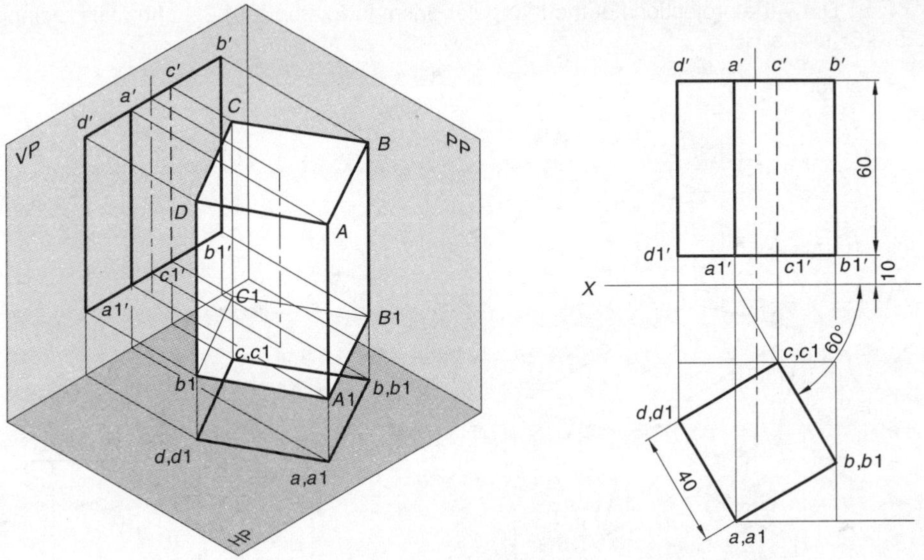

Fig. 14.8

Solution Refer Fig. 14.9.

As the axis of the prism is perpendicular to the VP, its FV will give the true shape of the base. Hence, FV must be drawn first.

1. Draw FV *a'a1'–b'b1'–c'c1'* of side 40 mm, at 20 mm above *XY*, such that *a'b'* is parallel to *XY*.
2. Project FV below *XY* to obtain TV of the base – *a1b1c1* (at suitable distance below *XY*). Note that *a1b1c1* is an edge view parallel to *XY*.
3. Obtain the TV by drawing *a–a1–b1–b* as shown. Show the axis in TV.

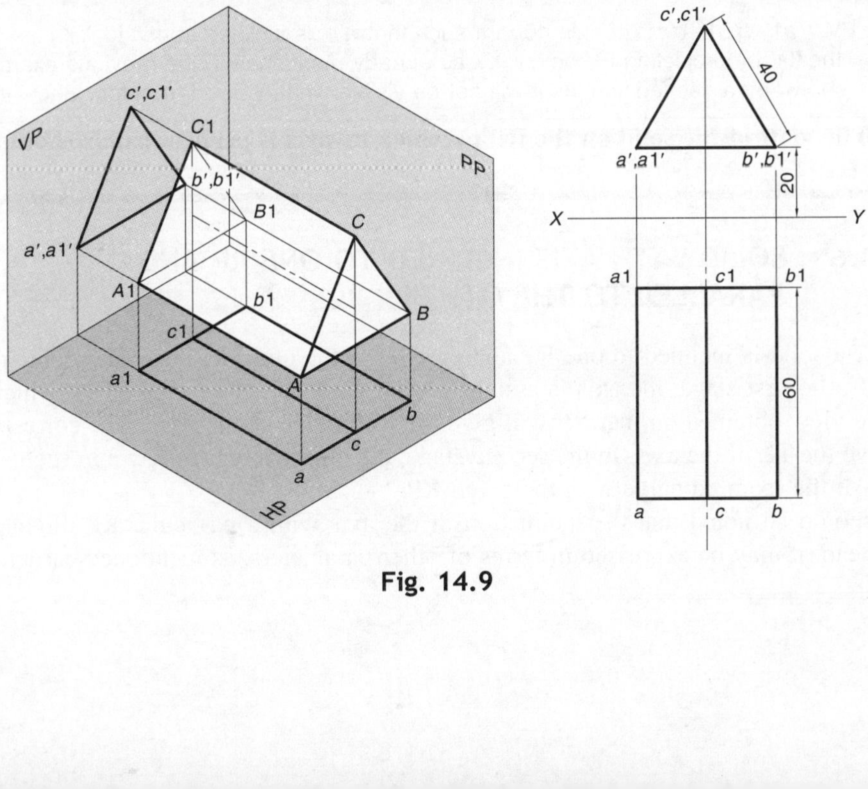

Fig. 14.9

Example 14.4 Draw the projections of the triangular prism in Example 14.3 if one of its rectangular faces is inclined at 45° to the HP.

Solution Refer Fig. 14.10.

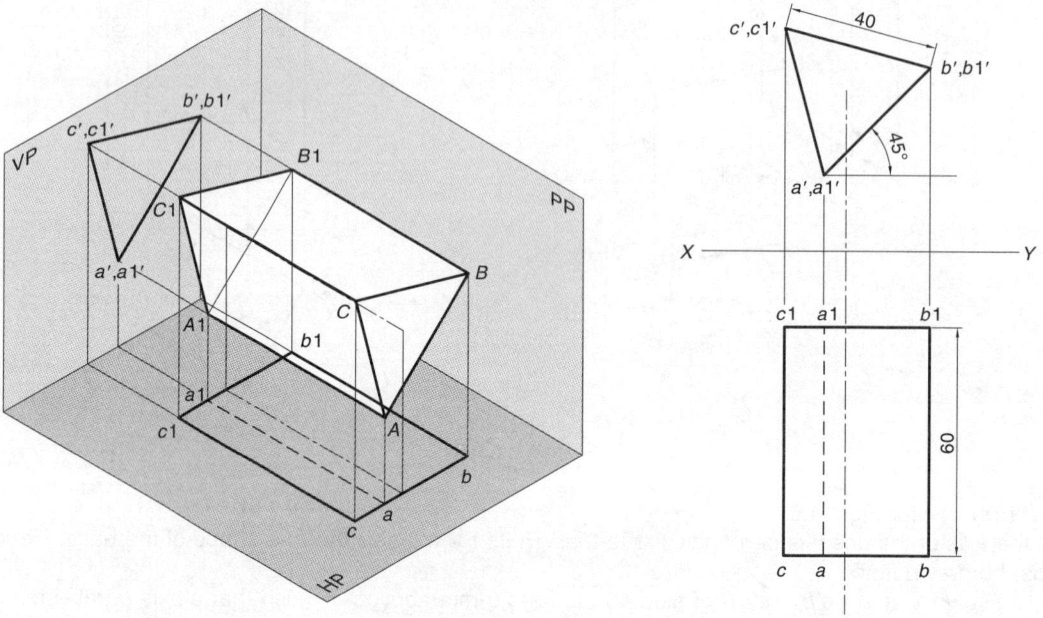

Fig. 14.10

The FV of the previous problem is tilted so that one of the rectangular faces of the prism will be inclined at 45° to the HP.

1. Draw FV *a′a*1′–*b′b*1′–*c′c*1′ of side 40 mm such that *a′b′* is inclined at 45° to *XY*.
2. Obtain the TV by projecting FV below *XY* as already mentioned in the previous example. Note that *aa*1 is shown by a dashed line, as it will not be visible when viewed from top. Show the axis in TV.

Rule 1: The view of the solid on the RP to which its axis is perpendicular should always be drawn first.

14.6 SOLID WITH AXIS INCLINED TO ONE RP AND PARALLEL TO THE OTHER

If the axis of a solid is inclined to one RP and parallel to the other RP then the problem is solved in two stages. In the first stage, the axis is assumed to be perpendicular to the RP to which it is finally inclined. The view obtained on that RP will give the true shape of the base. The corresponding other view will give the TL of the axis. In the second stage, the other view is redrawn in such a way that the axis will make the required angle with the given RP.

Here, it should be noted that the inclination of the axis with a particular RP might not be given directly. Instead, it may be expressed in terms of other parameters, as mentioned earlier.

14.6.1 Axis Inclined to the HP and Parallel to the VP

Example 14.5 A cone of diameter 60 mm and height 60 mm is resting on the HP on one of its generators. Draw its projections if its axis is parallel to the VP.

Solution Refer Fig. 14.11.

If the cone is resting on the HP on one of its generators, obviously its axis will be inclined to the HP. As the axis is inclined to the HP, assume it is initially perpendicular to the HP.

Stage I

The cone is kept on its base on the HP so that the axis will be perpendicular to the HP.

1. Draw a circle of diameter 60 mm to represent the TV of the cone. Mark apex o at the centre. Divide the circle into 12 equal parts and mark them as 1, 2, 3, ..., 12.
2. Draw a triangle 1′–7′–*o*′ of height 60 mm to represent FV of the cone. Project 1, 2, 3, etc., to 1′, 2′, 3′, etc., on 1′–7′ in FV.

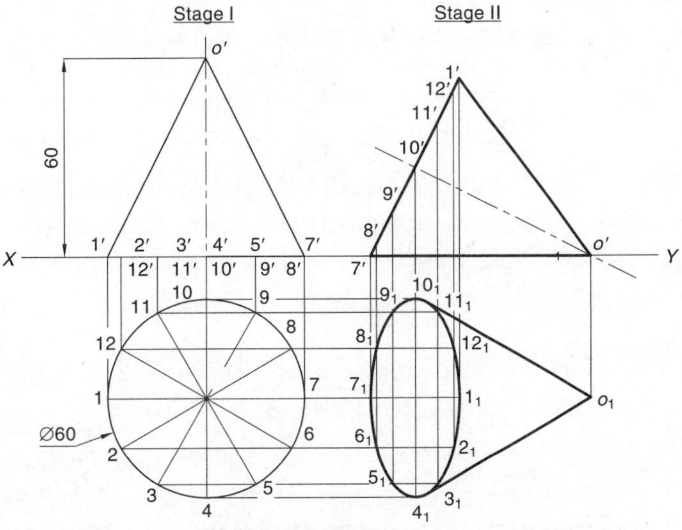

Fig. 14.11

Stage II

The cone is now tilted about a point on its circumference such that a generator will fall on the HP.

3. Redraw FV in such a way that edge 7′–*o*′ will coincide with *XY*. Relocate points 1′, 2′, 3′, etc., on 1′–7′ by using a divider.
4. Project 1′, 2′, 3′, etc., from FV to intersect the projectors through 1, 2, 3, etc., to obtain 1_1, 2_1, 3_1, etc. Join 1_1, 2_1, 3_1, etc., to obtain elliptical base. Also obtain o_1 in a similar way.
5. Join o_1 to the ellipse by drawing two tangent lines. The view represents the required TV.

Note: The tangent lines do not meet at 4_1 and 10_1. But they meet between 3_1 and 4_1 and 10_1 and 11_1.

14.6.2 Axis Inclined to the VP and Parallel to the HP

Example 14.6 A hexagonal prism of side of base 25 mm and length of axis 70 mm is resting on the HP on one of its rectangular faces. Draw its projections when its axis is inclined to the VP at 45°.

Solution Refer Fig. 14.12.

Note that the prism is resting on the HP on its rectangular face. Hence its axis will remain parallel to the HP. As the axis is inclined to the VP, in the first stage, it should be kept perpendicular to the VP.

Stage I

The prism is kept on its rectangular face on the HP with its axis perpendicular to the VP.

1. Draw FV *a*′*a*1′–*b*′*b*1′–*c*′*c*1′–*d*′*d*1′–*e*′*e*1′–*f*′*f*1′. It shows the true shape of the base. The line *a*′*a*1′–*b*′*b*1′ should be on *XY*.
2. Obtain corresponding TV *c*–*c*1–*f*1–*f*. It shows TL of the axis.

Stage II

The prism is now tilted so that the axis will make 45° with the VP.

3. Redraw the TV such that the axis will make 45° with *XY*.

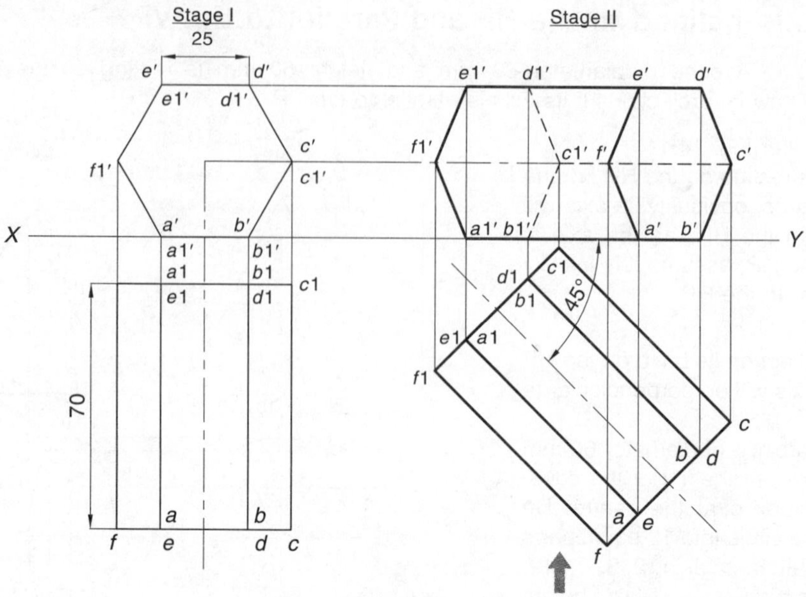

Fig. 14.12

4. Project TV to obtain FV. Note that the edges *c*′–*c*1′, *d*1′–*c*1′ and *b*1′–*c*1′ will not be visible and hence shown by dashed lines.

Note: The rules to decide the hidden lines/ features are discussed in Section 14.10.

Rule 2(a): If the axis of a solid is inclined to an RP, keep the solid in the first stage with the axis perpendicular to that RP.

14.7 SOLID WITH AXIS INCLINED TO BOTH THE RPs

If the axis of a solid is inclined to both the RPs then the problem is solved in three stages. As already mentioned, the inclinations of the axes may not be given directly. Instead, it may be indirectly mentioned by means some other parameters. If the inclinations are given directly then, in the first stage, the axis is assumed to be perpendicular to any one RP. The view obtained on that RP will give the true shape of the base. The corresponding other view will give the TL of the axis. In the second stage, the other view is redrawn so that the axis will make the required angle with the RP to which it was initially perpendicular. The corresponding next view is obtained in the second stage. In the third stage, the next view is redrawn so as to make the 'desired inclination' of the axis with the other RP. Here, the 'desired inclination' is the apparent inclination of the axis which is obtained by using the theory of projections of the lines. The view thus obtained satisfies all the conditions, i.e., inclinations with both the RPs, and hence represents the final view. This view is then projected to obtain the other corresponding final view.

If the inclinations are not given directly then the first stage must be decided carefully. Often an inclination of the axis with one RP is given and the inclination with the other RP is given in terms of the inclination of an edge or face of the solid. In such a case, the first stage is to keep the axis perpendicular to that RP with which its inclination is known. In the second stage, the required inclination with that RP is obtained. In the third stage, the other condition, viz., inclination of the face or inclination of an edge, is established. It must be remembered that, in the first stage, the solid is always kept in such a way that the true shape of the base and TL of the axis are visible. This helps to satisfy the condition on the axis (mentioned directly or indirectly) easily in the second stage. Note that one view in the second stage always gives TL of the axis (since it is simply redrawn from the first stage).

Other possibilities are explained with the help of examples.

Example 14.7 A triangular pyramid of edge of base *s* mm and length of axis *h* mm is resting on a side of base on the HP. The axis of the pyramid is inclined at $\theta°$ to the HP and $\phi°$ to the VP. Draw its projections.

Solution Refer Fig. 14.13.

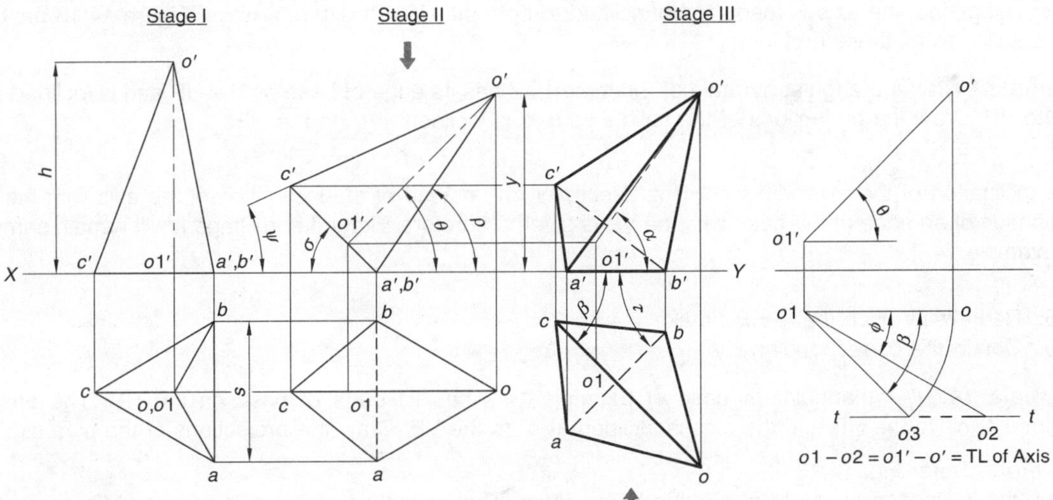

Fig. 14.13

In this problem, the inclinations of the axis with both the RPs are clearly mentioned. Therefore, obtain the inclination of the axis with the HP in the second stage. The inclination with the VP is established in the third stage by finding the corresponding apparent inclination.

Stage I

The pyramid is kept with its axis vertical. As the edge of the base is expected to be in the HP, the entire base is placed initially on the HP, *Rule 2a,* Chapter 13. An edge of the base must be perpendicular to the VP so that the solid can be tilted about that edge to make the required inclination of the axis with the HP.

1. Draw the TV– *abco*(*o*1) of the pyramid as shown. The true shape of the base is seen with side *ab* perpendicular to the VP.
2. Obtain the FV– *a*′(*b*′)–*c*′–*o*′. It shows the TL of the axis.

Stage II

The pyramid is tilted about the edge of the base, perpendicular to the VP, so that the axis will make the required angle with the HP.

3. Rotate FV about *a*′(*b*′) so that *o*′–*o*1′ makes $\theta°$ with *XY*.
4. Obtain the corresponding TV. Show axis *o*–*o*1 in TV.

Stage III

The pyramid is now turned, maintaining the edge *AB* in the HP and the inclination of the axis with the HP constant, in such a way that the axis will make $\phi°$ with the VP. The axis is now inclined to both the RPs, hence the true inclinations will not be seen in the TV and FV. Instead, the apparent inclinations will be seen. In other words, if the axis makes $\theta°$ to the HP and $\phi°$ to the VP, its FV and TV will be seen at $\alpha°$ and $\beta°$ to *XY* respectively. Therefore, we need to find angle β if the axis is expected to make $\phi°$ with the VP. The TV of the axis when turned through $\beta°$ will give the real inclination of $\phi°$.

The *External Construction* is used to find angle β. Draw *o*1′–*o*′ = TL of the axis, inclined at $\theta°$ to *XY*. Obtain *o*1–*o* parallel to *XY*. Then draw *o*1–*o*2 = TL of the axis, inclined at $\phi°$ to *XY*. Obtain *t*–*t*, the locus of *o*2. With *o*1 as centre and radius = *o*1–*o*, draw an arc cutting *t*–*t* at *o*3. Join *o*1–*o*3 and measure β.

5. Redraw TV such that *o*–*o*1 will make $\beta°$ with *XY*.
6. Obtain the corresponding FV. Locate axis *o*′–*o*1′ in FV. Note that *o*′–*o*1′ will make $\alpha°$ with *XY*. *a*′–*b*′ is seen on *XY*.

Example 14.7 can be expressed in different ways as in Example 14.8 to Example 14.14. Note that, in all these examples, the axis is made to be inclined to both the RPs in different ways. Figure 14.13 provides the solution to all these problems.

Example 14.8 A triangular pyramid of Example 14.7 has its edge of base on the HP and is inclined at $\tau°$ to the VP. Draw the projections of the solid if its axis is inclined at $\theta°$ to the HP.

Solution Refer Fig. 14.13.

The inclination of the axis with the HP is directly given. Instead of the inclination of the axis with the VP, inclination of an edge of the base with the VP is given. Therefore, Stage I and Stage II will remain same as in Example 14.7.

Stage III

5. Redraw TV such that *ab* will make $\tau°$ with *XY*.
6. Obtain the corresponding FV.

Example 14.9 A triangular pyramid of Example 14.7 has its edge of base on the HP. The base is inclined at $\sigma°$ to the HP and the axis is inclined at $\phi°$ to the VP. Draw the projections of the pyramid.

Solution Refer Fig. 14.13.

Here, the inclination of the axis with the VP is given. The inclination of the axis with the HP is indirectly mentioned by giving the inclination of the base with the HP. Therefore, follow Stage I and Stage III of Example 14.7. Find the apparent inclination of $\beta°$ using External Construction. Stage II is explained below:

Stage II

3. Rotate FV about *a*′(*b*′) so that *a*′(*b*′)–*c*′ makes $\sigma°$ with *XY*.
4. Obtain the corresponding TV. Show axis *o*–*o*1 in TV.

Example 14.10 A triangular pyramid of Example 14.7 has its edge of base on the HP and inclined at $\tau°$ to the VP. Draw the projections of the solid if its base is inclined at $\sigma°$ to the HP.

Solution Refer Fig. 14.13. This example is the combination of Example 14.8 and Example 14.9. Here, none of the inclinations is clearly mentioned. Therefore, obtain the inclination of the base in the second stage and the inclination of the base edge in the third stage. Follow Stage I of Example 14.7, Stage II of Example 14.9 and Stage III of Example 14.8.

Example 14.11 A triangular pyramid of Example 14.7 has its edge of base on the HP. The slant face through that edge is inclined to the HP at $\rho°$. Draw the projections of the solid if its axis is inclined at $\phi°$ to the VP.

Solution Refer Fig. 14.13.

Here, the inclination of the axis with the VP and the inclination of a slant face with the HP are given. Therefore, establish the inclination of a slant face in the second stage. Find β in the third stage. Follow Stage I and Stage III of Example 14.7.

Stage II

3. Rotate FV about $a'(b')$ so that $a'(b')$–o' makes ρ° with XY.
4. Obtain the corresponding TV. Show axis o–$o1$ in TV.

Example 14.12 A triangular pyramid of Example 14.7 has its edge of base on the HP and inclined at τ° to the VP. The slant edge opposite to the edge on the HP makes ψ° to the HP. Draw the two views of the pyramid.

Solution Refer Fig. 14.13.

Here, again, none of the axis inclinations is mentioned directly. Therefore, obtain the inclination of the slant edge in the second stage and the inclination of the base edge in the third stage. Follow Stage I of Example 14.7 and Stage III of Example 14.8.

Stage II

3. Rotate the FV about $a'(b')$ so that c'–o' makes ψ° with XY.
4. Obtain the corresponding TV. Show axis o–$o1$ in TV.

Example 14.13 A triangular pyramid of Example 14.7 has its edge of base on the HP. The axis of the solid makes θ° with the HP and the TV of the axis makes β° with XY. Draw the TV and FV of the pyramid.

Solution In this case, the inclination of the axis with the HP is given. The real inclination of the axis with the VP is not given but its apparent inclination with the VP is given. Obviously, we need not find β. Therefore, Stage I, Stage II and Stage III of Example 14.7 may be followed without using External Construction to obtain the solution depicted in Fig. 14.13.

Example 14.14 A triangular pyramid of Example 14.7 is resting on its edge of base on the HP. The edge makes τ° with the VP and the apex is y mm from the HP ($y < h$). Draw the projections of the pyramid.

Solution Again, none of the axis inclinations are clearly given. However the height of the apex from the HP creates the axis' inclination with the HP. Therefore, the height h must be established in the second stage. In the third stage, turn the edge on the HP to make τ° with the VP. Follow Stage I of Example 14.7 and Stage III of Example 14.8.

Stage II

3. Rotate FV about $a'(b')$ so that o' will come at y mm from XY.
4. Obtain the corresponding TV. Show axis o–$o1$ in TV.

A few more problems can be formed by taking the combinations of: σ and β, ψ and β, ψ and ϕ, ρ and β, ρ and τ, y and β and y and ϕ. In fact, there are numerous ways of putting the problems on projections of solids having inclinations of the axis with both the RPs.

The Examples 14.7 to 14.14 are provided to give readers an idea about how the axis of the given solid can be made inclined to both the RPs using various conditions. It should be remembered that we need not find the apparent inclinations, i.e., α or β, always.

The following examples will focus more light on the projections of the solids with oblique axes.

Example 14.15 A cone of base 60 mm diameter and height 80 mm is resting on a point on the circumference of base on the HP with its apex 55 mm above the HP. Draw its projections if its axis is inclined at 45° to the VP.

Solution Refer Fig. 14.14.

The problem contains three conditions: (i) A point (say A) on the circumference of the base on the HP, (ii) the apex O 55 mm above the HP, and (iii) the axis inclined to VP at 45° (i.e., ϕ = 45°). The first two conditions give the angle made by the axis with the HP, i.e.,θ. ϕ is directly given.

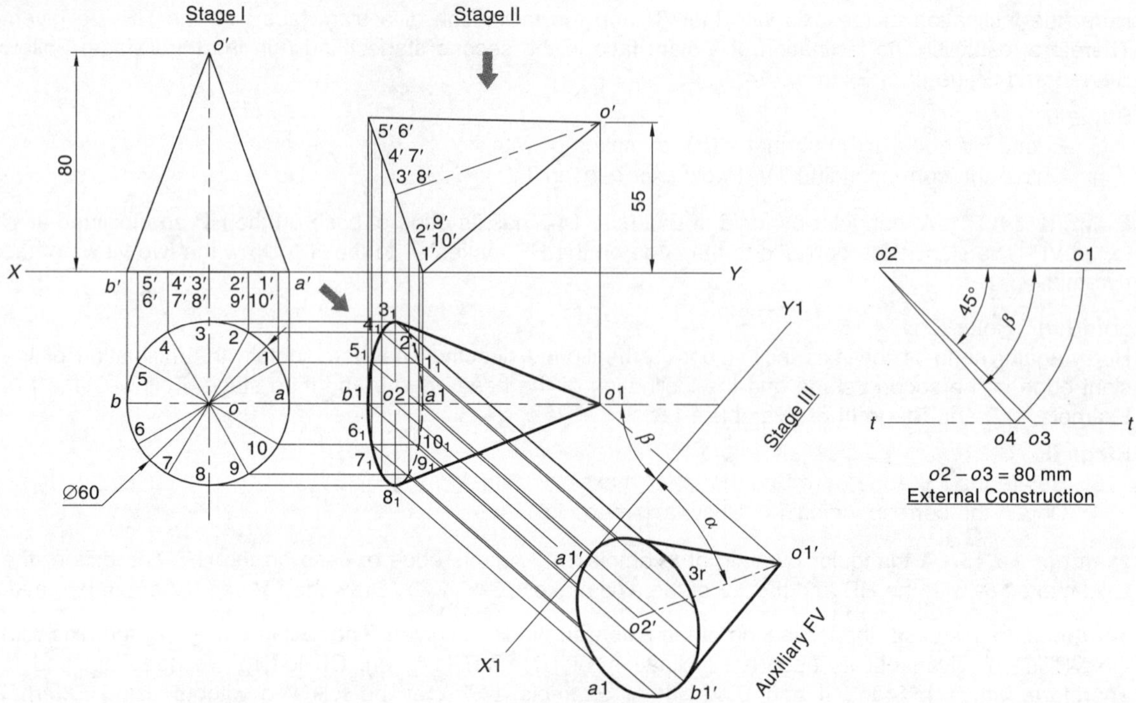

Fig. 14.14

Stage I

As a point on the circumference of the base is in the HP, keep the entire base of the solid in the HP.

1. Draw the TV of the cone. Divide it into 12 equal parts.
2. Produce the FV. Project 12 points on the base in the FV.

Stage II

Tilt the cone about the point in the HP so that the apex will come at a point of 55 mm above the HP.

3. Tilt FV about *a′* such that the apex *o′* will be 55 mm from *XY*.
4. Project FV below *XY* to obtain TV. It should be noted that the base is not seen from the top and hence part of base is shown by a dashed line.

Stage III

Turn the cone about the point in the HP, keeping the axis' inclination with the HP constant, so that the axis will make 45° to the VP. Obviously, we have to find the apparent inclination $\beta°$ corresponding to $\phi = 45°$. This is shown in *External Construction*. Draw *o*2–*o*3 (= TL of the axis = 80 mm) inclined at 45° to *XY*. Draw *t–t* parallel to *XY*. With *o*2 as a centre and radius = *o*2–*o*1 (= PL of axis Stage II), draw an arc cutting *t–t* at *o*4. The angle between *o*2–*o*4 and *XY* gives β.

Auxiliary projection method is used in this problem to obtain the final FV.

5. Draw an auxiliary reference line *X*1*Y*1 inclined at $\beta°$ to *o*1–*o*2.
6. Project TV on *X*1*Y*1 to obtain the auxiliary FV. Note that *a*1′ is seen on *X*1*Y*1. The invisible portion of the cone is shown by dashed lines.

The two views obtained in Stage III are the required views. The axis in auxiliary FV, i.e., *o*1′–*o*2′, will now be automatically inclined at $\alpha°$ to *X*1*Y*1.

Example 14.16 A pentagonal pyramid of edge of base 30 mm and length of axis 65 mm is resting on a corner of the base on the HP. The triangular face opposite to the corner on the HP is inclined to the HP at 45° with its shorter edge inclined to the VP at 60°. Draw its projections.

Solution Refer Fig. 14.15. The problem contains three conditions: (i) A corner (say *A*) of the base on the HP, (ii) A face (say *CDO*) opposite to the corner A inclined to the HP at 45° and (iii) A shorter edge (i.e., *CD*) of the face *CDO* inclined to the VP at 60°.

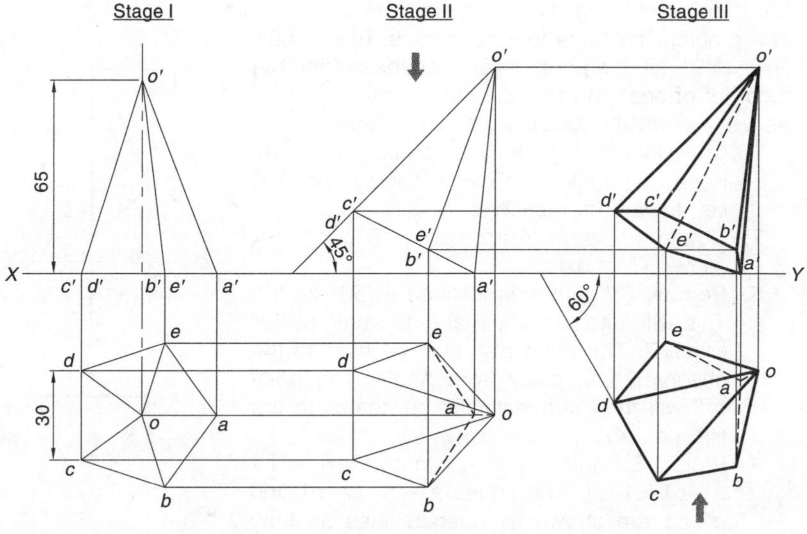

Fig. 14.15

Stage I

1. Draw TV and FV as shown. The base is in the HP with a side perpendicular to the VP. Note that, *c*′(*d*′)–*o*′ represents the edge view of triangular face *CDO*.

Stage II

2. Redraw FV in such a way that *c*′(*d*′)–*o*′ will be inclined to *XY* at 45° and point *a*′ will be on *XY*.
3. Obtain the corresponding TV. Note that *cd* is perpendicular to *XY*.

Stage III

4. Redraw TV in such a way that *cd* will be inclined to *XY* at 60°.
5. Obtain the corresponding FV.

Rule 2(b): In the first stage, keep the solid in such a way that the true shape of the base and TL of the axis will be visible.

Rule 3: If a solid rests on a corner or an edge of its base on the RP, keep the entire base on that RP in first stage.

14.8 SOLID WITH AXIS PARALLEL TO THE PP

This category of solid is the special case of the previous category, i.e., solid with axis inclined to both the RPs. If the sum of the angles made by the axis with the HP and with the VP is 90° (i.e., $\theta + \phi = 90°$) then the axis will be parallel to the PP. If the axis is parallel to the PP, the base of the solid will be perpendicular to the PP. Hence in SV, the base will be seen as an edge view and axis will show TL. This type of problem can be easily solved by the method explained in Section 14.7. If this method is followed, it can be shown graphically that $\alpha = \beta = 90°$. However, such problem can more easily be solved by considering, in the first stage, the axis of the solid perpendicular to any one RP and then, in the second stage, tilting the SV through desired angle.

Example 14.17 A triangular pyramid of base 40 mm side and length of axis 60 mm is lying in space in such a way that its axis is inclined at 60° to the HP and 30° to the VP. Draw its three views if the apex is toward the observer and a corner of base towards the HP.

Solution Refer Fig. 14.16.

The problem contains four conditions: (i) $\theta = 60°$, (ii) $\phi = 30°$, (iii) the apex towards observer, and (iv) a corner of base towards the HP.

As $\theta + \phi = 90°$, the axis is parallel to the PP.

1. Draw TV of triangular pyramid *abco* as shown. Keep *ab* parallel to *XY* and *c* away from *XY*, i.e., toward the observer.
2. Obtain FV *a′b′c′o′* and SV *a″b″c″o″*. SV shows TL of axis.
3. Redraw SV with axis inclined at 60° to *XY*. This will automatically make an angle of 30° with VP. The point *o*1″ must be near to the observer, i.e., away from *X*1*Y*1. The point *c*1″ will then automatically be nearer to the HP, i.e., *XY*.
4. Project SV and original TV to obtain new TV *a*1–*b*1–*c*1–*o*1. The edges *a*1–*c*1, *c*1–*b*1 and *c*1–*o*1 are shown by dashed lines as they are not visible from top.
5. Project SV and original FV to obtain new FV *a*1′–*b*1′–*c*1′–*o*1′. The edge *a*1′–*b*1′ is shown by a dashed line.

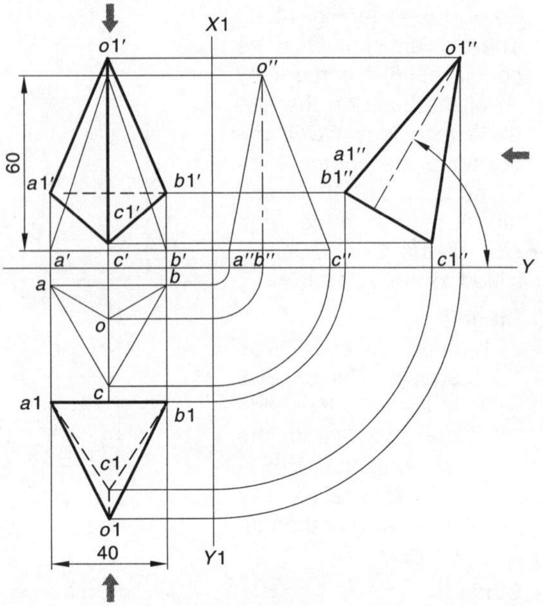

Fig. 14.16

14.9 SOLID WITH AXIS PARALLEL TO BOTH THE RPs

If the axis of a solid is parallel to both the RPs then it will be perpendicular to the PP. Hence, the view of the solid on the PP, i.e., SV will show the true shape of the base. Therefore, SV is drawn first. FV and TV show the TL of the axis. However, this type of problem can be solved by keeping the solid's axis perpendicular to any RP in the first stage and then making it parallel to *XY* in second stage.

Example 14.18 A square prism of base side 40 mm and length of axis 70 mm is resting on the HP on one of its longer edges with axis parallel to both the RPs. One of the rectangular faces is inclined at 30° to the HP. Draw its three views.

Solution Refer Fig. 14.17. The problem contains three conditions: (i) a longer edge on the HP, (ii) axis parallel to both the RPs, and (iii) a rectangular face inclined at 30° to the HP.

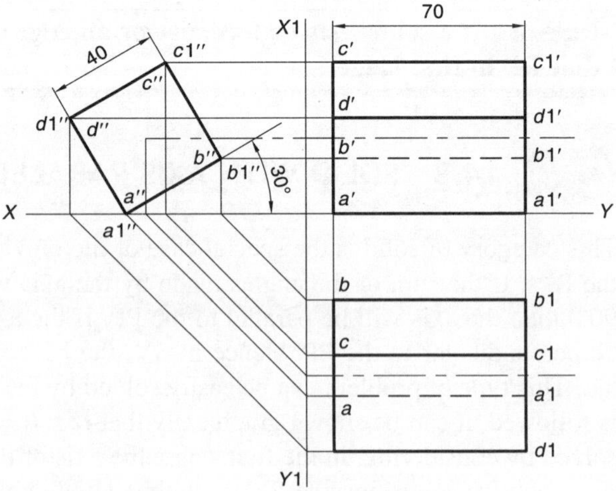

Fig. 14.17

1. Draw SV *a″a1″–b″b1″–c″c1″–d″d1″* such that *a″a1″* is on *XY* and edge *a″a1″–b″b1″* inclined at 30° to *XY*.
2. Draw FV *a′a1′c1′c′* by projecting the SV as shown. *b′b1′* is shown by a dashed line.
3. Draw TV *dd1b1b* by projecting SV and FV. *aa1* is shown by a dashed line.

Example 14.19 A square pyramid of side of base 40 mm and length of axis 60 mm is resting on its corner of base on ground with an edge of the base through that corner making an angle of 60° with the HP. The apex is away from the observer and the axis is parallel to the HP. Draw the projections if the axis is inclined to the VP at 20°.

Solution Refer Fig. 14.18.

This problem is solved by the third–angle method. As the pyramid is resting on ground, the concept of *GL* may be used as explained in Section 13.9.

Stage I

1. Draw *GL* below *XY* at suitable distance.
2. Draw FV *a′b′c′d′–o′* such that *a′* is on *GL* and *a′d′* inclined at 60° to *GL*. Note that the apex is away from the observer and hence edges *a′o′*, *b′o′*, *c′o′* and *d′o′* are shown by hidden lines.
3. Project FV above *XY* and draw TV *abcd–o*. The base *abcd* is parallel to and at some suitable distance from *XY*.

Stage II

4. Redraw TV as *a1–b1–c1–d1–o1* in such a way that *o1–o2* is inclined at 20° to *XY*.
5. Obtain final FV *a1′–b1′–c1′–d1′–o1′* by projecting the TV *a1–b1–c1–d1–o1* and the FV *a′b′c′d′–o′*.

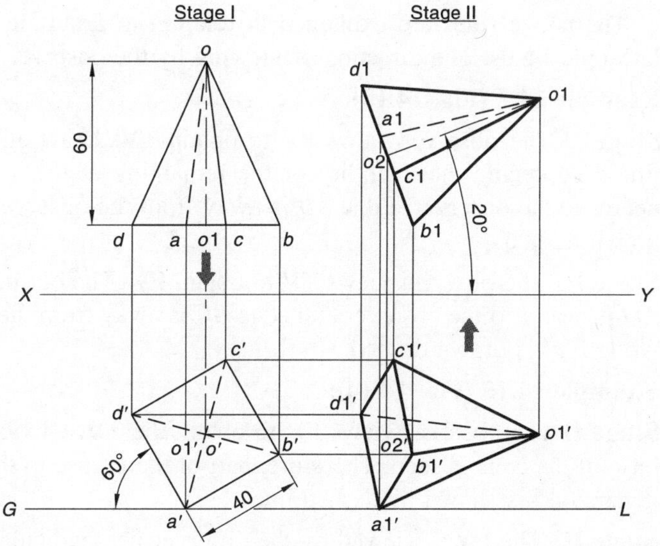

Fig. 14.18

14.10 RULES FOR DECIDING THE HIDDEN LINES

When a solid lies in the space with specific orientation, all its edges/features will not be visible in any one view. In such cases, dashed lines are used to show the invisible features. The following rules will help to decide the hidden lines.

1. The outer lines represent the boundary of the solid. These are always continuous lines.
2. Amongst the remaining lines, the lines nearer to the observer are visible. The lines farther from the observer, i.e., on the back side of the solid, will be invisible and drawn by dashed lines.

   To decide the nearness of the edges, the direction of viewing by the observer must be decided. The observer looks towards FV to obtain TV or SV and vice-versa. In the first angle method, the observer views the object from the end away from POP. In the third-angle method, the object is viewed from the end nearer to POP.

3. Two points are joined by a visible line if they are at the intersection of visible lines only. Similarly, two points are joined by a hidden line if they are formed at the intersection of hidden lines only.
4. A visible line or a hidden line may emerge from the intersection of two (or more) visible lines.
5. Only a hidden line may emerge from the intersection of two (or more) hidden lines only. A visible line never emerges from the intersections of two hidden lines only.
6. A hidden line may start and end at another hidden line or visible line. But, a straight visible line always starts and ends at another straight or curved visible line.
7. Follow the precedence rules explained in Section 9.6.3.

The above rules are explained in relation to Example 14.7, Example 14.15, Example 14.16 and Example 14.19. The direction of viewing by the observer is shown by an arrow in each case.

Example 14.7 (Fig. 14.13):

Stage II The observer views FV to obtain TV. Draw all the outlines, i.e., *a–o–b–c*, by continuous lines. To decide the visibility of the remaining edges, mark the direction of viewing. Edge *CO* is nearer to the observer. Edge *AB* is away from the observer. Hence, *co* is drawn continuous and *ab* is drawn dashed.

Stage III The observer views TV to obtain FV. The outlines *a′–b′–o′–c′* are drawn continuous. Edge *AO* is nearer to the observer and edge *BC* is away from the observer. Hence, *a′o′* is drawn continuous while *b′c′* is drawn dashed.

Example 14.15 (Fig. 14.14):

Stage II The observer views FV to obtain the TV. Obviously, only half of the circumference of the base of the cone is seen. Therefore, part of the ellipse to the right side of points of tangency (with the generators) is shown by dashed lines.

Stage III The FV is viewed by the observer perpendicular to *X*1*Y*1 as shown. The observer sees the entire base, hence no part in the auxiliary FV is shown hidden.

Example 14.16 (Fig. 14.15):

Stage II All the outlines, i.e., *o–b–c–d–e*, are shown by continuous lines. The edges *OC* and *OD* are nearer to the observer. Hence *oc* and *od* are continuous. The edges *AB* and *AE* lie on farther side of the object when viewed from the top. Hence *ab* and *ae* are dashed lines. The same thing applies to *oa*. It also satisfies Rule 5.

Stage III Join all the outer points by continuous lines. Amongst the other edges, *OB*, *OC*, *BC* and *CD* are seen nearer to the observer. Hence, *o′b′*, *o′c′*, *b′c′* and *c′d′* are shown continuous. Edge *OE* is farther, hence *o′e′* is hidden. *b′*and *a′* are at the intersections of continuous lines only. Therefore they are joined by continuous line.

Example 14.19 (Fig. 14.18):

This example is solved by the third-angle method of projection.

Stage I The observer views FV from above *XY* line to obtain the TV. *OC* is nearer to and *OA* is away from the observer. Therefore, *oc* is continuous and *oa* is hidden.

Stage II TV is viewed by the observer from below *XY*. *o*1–*d*1 is away from the observer. Hence, *o*1′–*d*1′ is hidden.

14.11 SUSPENDED SOLIDS

A solid may be suspended freely in air by attaching a string at some suitable point. The projections of such a solid should be treated as a special case. The interesting fact is that an imaginary line joining the point of attachment of the string to the centre of gravity (CG) of the solid is always vertical. Therefore, the location of CGs of the various solids should be known. Table 14.1 shows the location of CGs of basic solids.

Table 14.1 CGs of the Solids

Group of Solids	*Location of CG*
Pyramids (including Tetrahedron) and Cone	1/4 (Height) from base along the axis
Prisms (including Cube) and Cylinder	Midpoint of the axis
Sphere	Centre
Hemisphere	3/8 (Radius) from circular face along the perpendicular to the face at centre.

Example 14.20 A cone of base diameter 50 mm and a 70 mm long axis is freely suspended from a point on the rim of its base. Draw the FV and the TV when the plane containing its axis is perpendicular to the HP and makes an angle of 35° with the VP.

Solution Refer Fig. 14.19.

Stage I

1. Draw TV and FV of the cone as shown. The base is kept on the HP. Let the solid be suspended from point 5′.
2. Locate CG- g′ of the solid at a distance of ¼(70) = 17.5 mm from the base along the axis. Join 5′–g′.

Stage II

3. Redraw FV such that 5′–g′ becomes vertical.
4. Obtain the corresponding TV. Locate o–o1 in TV.

Stage III

5. Draw X1Y1 inclined at 35° to o–o1.
6. Project the TV and obtain the corresponding auxiliary FV. Draw the hidden portion properly.

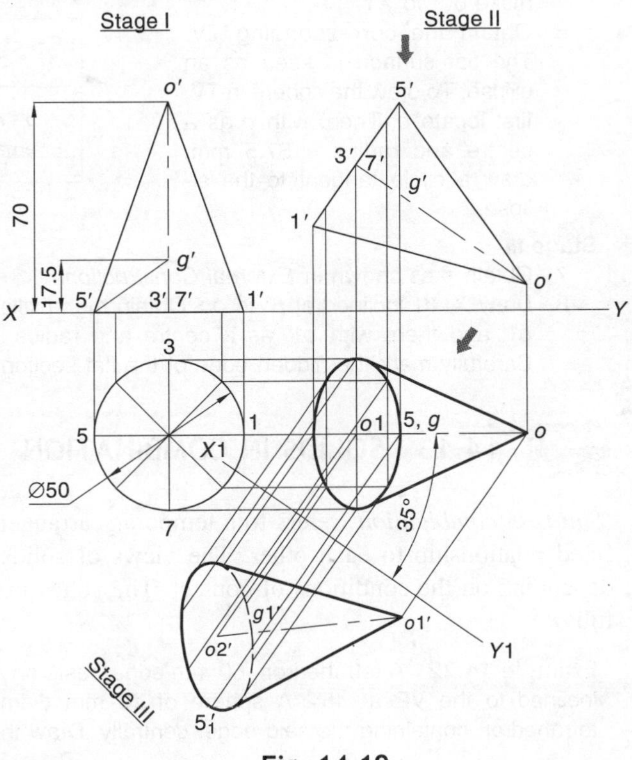

Fig. 14.19

14.12 PROJECTIONS OF SPHERE

The TV, FV and SV of a sphere is always the circle of radius equal to that of the sphere. However, a flat section on a sphere is seen as an ellipse when viewed in the direction inclined to that section. The circular face of a hemisphere also appears as an ellipse if it is inclined with the RP.

Example 14.21 A sphere of diameter 75 mm has a flat cut section of 54 mm diameter. The sphere rests on the HP on its curved surface such that the line joining the centre of the sphere with the centre of the flat surface makes 60° to the HP and 15° to the VP. Draw the projections of the sphere.

Solution Refer Fig. 14.20.

Stage I

1. Draw TV and FV of the sphere
2. In TV, draw a circle with *o* as a centre and radius = 27 mm to represent the flat cut section. Divide this circle into 8 equal parts.
3. In FV, the flat surface is seen as a line. Project the 8 divisions on this line.
4. Join the centre of the sphere to the centre of flat surface, i.e., *o′c′*.

Stage II

5. Redraw FV such that *o′c′* will make 60° to *XY*.
6. Obtain the corresponding TV. The flat surface is seen as an ellipse. To draw the sphere in TV, first locate *o*. Then, with *o* as a centre and radius = 37.5 mm, draw a circle tangent to the ellipse.

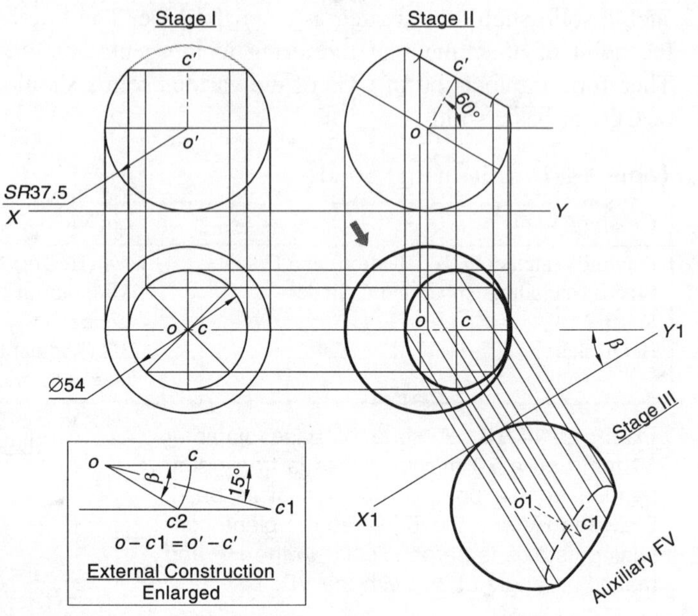

Fig. 14.20

Stage III

7. Obtain β as shown in *External Construction*.
8. Draw *X*1*Y*1 inclined at $\beta°$ to *oc*. Obtain the auxiliary FV of the sphere as shown. For sphere, locate *o*1′ and then, with *o*1′ as a centre and radius = 37.5 mm, draw an arc tangent to the ellipse. Carefully mark the hidden edge of the flat section.

14.13 SOLIDS IN COMBINATION

'*Solids in combination*' refers to a temporary arrangement in which two or more solids are kept in a fixed relationship to each other. The views of solids are seen overlapping or touching each other, depending on the conditions of contact. The solids in the arrangement may hide each other partly or fully.

Example 14.22 A tetrahedron, 60 mm edge, rests on a face of it on the ground with an edge of that face inclined to the VP at 45°. A sphere of 70 mm diameter placed on ground touches the face of the tetrahedron containing the said edge, centrally. Draw the projections of the combination.

Solution Refer Fig. 14.21.
This problem is solved by the third-angle method of projection.

Stage I

1. Draw the TV and FV of the tetrahedron. One of the faces of the tetrahedron is kept on the ground with a side perpendicular to the VP.

2. In FV, locate o' 35 mm each from GL and $a'(b')$–d'. With o' as a centre and radius = 35 mm, draw a circle to represent the sphere.
3. Project o' to o in TV. With o as a centre and radius = 35 mm, draw a circle to represent the TV of sphere. The part of the edge of the tetrahedron below the sphere will not be seen.

Stage II

4. As the edge of face on the ground is inclined to the VP at 45°, draw $X1Y1$ inclined to ab at 45°.
5. Obtain auxiliary FVs of both the solids. Draw the hidden lines properly.

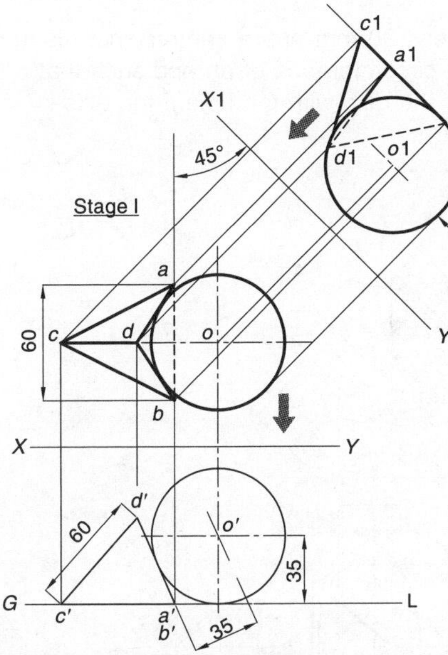

Fig. 14.21

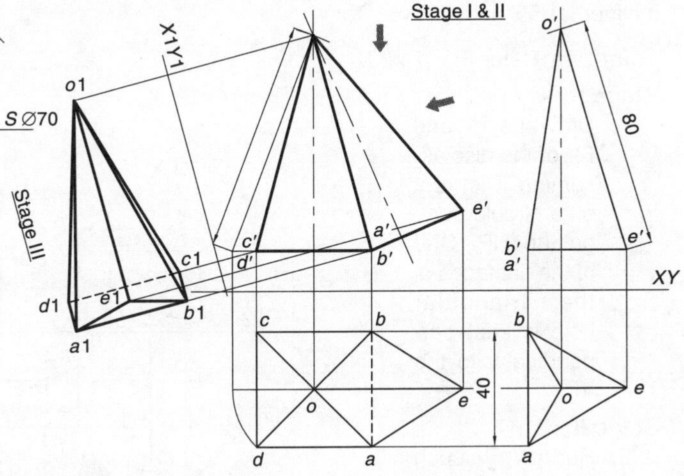

Fig. 14.22

14.14 COMPOSITE SOLIDS

When two or more solids are joined together in a fixed relationship, the resulting solid is called a '*composite solids*'. Their projections are obtained in the same way as that of solids in combination. Sometimes, in the first stage, the two (or more) constituent solids are drawn separately. Then, they are joined in the second stage as per the conditions mentioned in the problem. When a solid is subtracted from the other solid, the resulting solid may be treated as a composite solid. For example, a circular hole in a rectangular block, i.e., a cylinder subtracted from a rectangular prism.

Example 14.23 A square pyramid and a triangular pyramid share a common triangular face. The base side and slant height of the pyramids are 40 mm and 80 mm respectively. Draw the projections of the composite solid if the common face is horizontal and the axes of the pyramids are parallel to the VP. Assume triangular pyramid on upper side.

Solution Refer Fig. 14.22.

Stage I and II

1. Draw TVs and FVs of both the pyramids assuming that they are separate. The bases are kept

parallel to the HP. A side of base of each of the pyramid is kept perpendicular to the VP. Note that the lengths of sides of base and slant heights of both the pyramids are the same.

2. Pick the FV of the triangular pyramid and put it on the FV of the square pyramid such that the face *a*′(*b*′)–*o*′ is shared by both the FVs.
3. Project the new FV of the triangular pyramid below *XY* to obtain the TV of the composite solid.

Stage III

4. Draw *X*1*Y*1 parallel to *a*′(*b*′)–*o*′ on opposite side of the triangular pyramid.
5. Project the FV of the composite solid on *X*1*Y*1 to obtain auxiliary TV. Draw the hidden line properly.

Example 14.24 A circular disc of diameter 80 mm and thickness 30 mm has a centrally cut triangular hole of side 45 mm. The disc rests on the HP on a point on the circumference of an end such that a flat face of the hole makes 45° with the HP. Draw the projections of the disc with the hole if the axis is seen inclined at 55° in the TV.

Solution Refer Fig. 14.23.

Stage I

1. Draw the TV and FV of the disc assuming it is kept on a circular face on the HP. One of the flat faces of the triangular hole is kept perpendicular to the VP.

Stage II

2. Redraw FV such that a corner remains on *XY* and the flat face *a*′(*b*′)–*d*′(*e*′) makes 45° to *XY*.
3. Obtain the new TV by projecting the FV and the previous TV. Locate axis *o*–*o*1.

Stage III

4. Draw *X*1*Y*1 inclined at 55° to *o*–*o*1.
5. Obtain the auxiliary FV. Draw hidden lines properly.

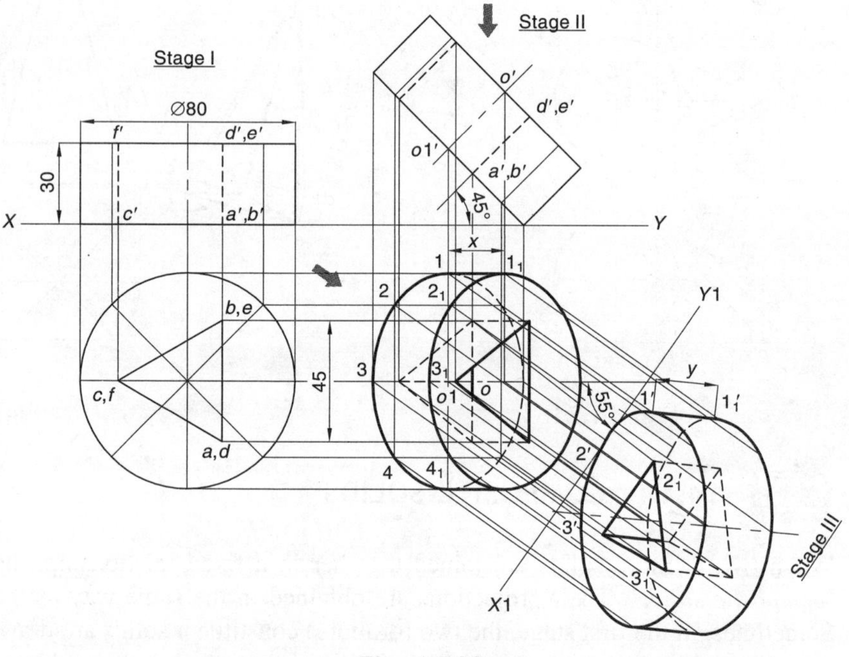

Fig. 14.23

DRAWING TIP

Once the projection of an end of a cylinder is drawn as an ellipse, the projection of the other end can be obtained by transferring all the points on that end through the desired distance along the specific direction. In the above example, the point 1, 2, 3, etc., can be transferred through distance '*x*' along the direction parallel to $1–1_1$ to obtain 1_1, 2_1, 3_1, etc., respectively. Similarly, points 1′, 2′, 3′, etc., can be shifted though distance '*y*' along the direction parallel to $1'–1_1'$ to locate $1_1'$, $2_1'$, $3_1'$, etc. The same procedure may be applied for the prisms.

ILLUSTRATIVE PROBLEMS

Problem 14.1 A pentagonal pyramid of base 20 mm and height 50 mm has its triangular face in the VP with a shorter side inclined to the HP at 30°. Draw its projections.

Solution Refer Fig. 14.24.

Stage I

1. Draw FV and TV as shown. The base is kept in the VP with a side perpendicular to the HP. *ab–o* represents the edge view of face *ABO*.

Stage II

2. Redraw TV in such a way that *ab–o*1 coincides with *XY*.
3. Obtain the corresponding FV. The edges *o*1′–*a*′ and *o*1′–*b*′ will be hidden edges.

Stage III

4. Redraw FV in such a way that *a*2′*b*2′ will be inclined at 30° to *XY*.
5. Obtain the corresponding TV. The edge *a*2–*e*2 will be hidden. Note that the face *a*2–*b*2–*o*2 is an edge view on *XY*.

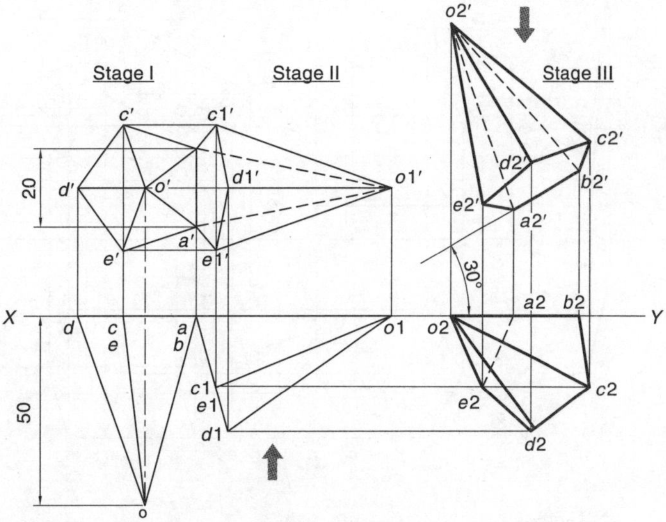

Fig. 14.24

Problem 14.2 A triangular prism with side of base 40 mm and length of axis 70 mm has its edge of base in the VP and inclined at 60° to the HP. The rectangular face containing that edge makes 30° with the VP. Draw the projections of the prism.

Solution Refer Fig. 14.25.

Stage I

1. Draw the FV and TV of the triangular prism. The base is kept in the VP with an edge perpendicular to the HP. *a*(*b*)–*d*(*e*) represents an edge view of a rectangular face.

Stage II

2. Tilt TV about *a*(*b*) such that *a*(*b*)–*d*(*e*) will make 30° with *XY*.
3. Obtain the corresponding FV.

Stage III

4. Draw *X*1*Y*1 inclined at 60° to *a*′*b*′. Project the FV to obtain the auxiliary TV.

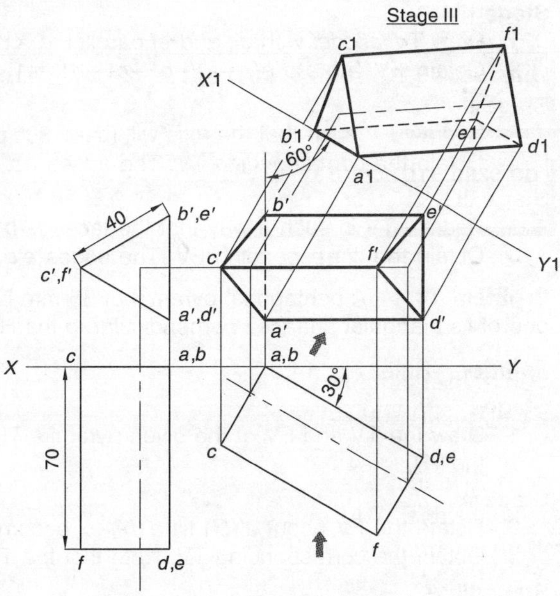

Fig. 14.25

Problem 14.3 The axis of a hexagonal prism (side of base 30 mm and height 60 mm) is inclined at 30° to the HP. Its two opposite rectangular faces are perpendicular to the HP and inclined to the VP at 45°. Draw its projections.

Solution Refer Fig. 14.26.

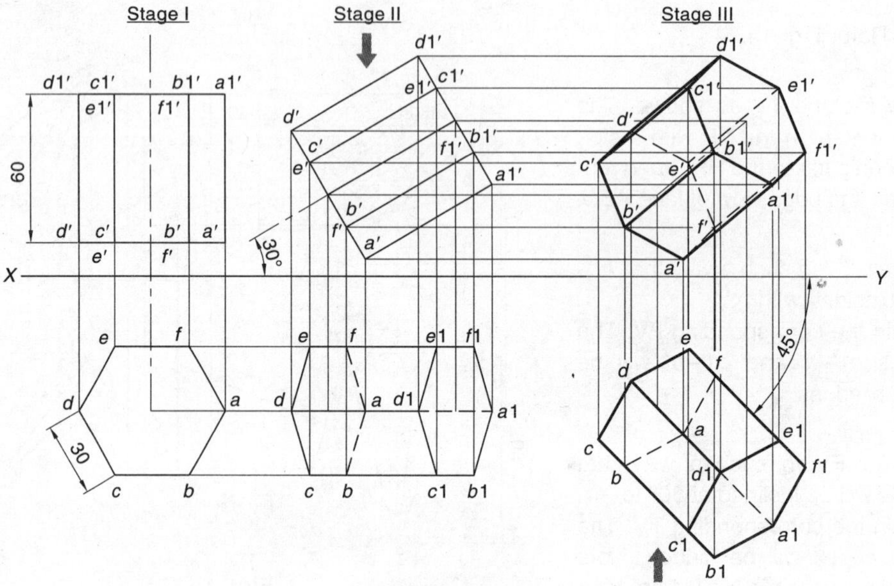

Fig. 14.26

Stage I

1. Draw TV *abcdef* with *cb* and *ef* parallel to *XY*.
2. Obtain FV *a′b′c′d′e′f′–a1′–b1′–c1′–d1′–e1′–f1′*.

Stage II

3. Redraw FV such that the axis will make 30° to *XY*.
4. Obtain the corresponding TV. The edges *ab*, *af* and *a–a*1 will be hidden edges.

Stage III

5. Redraw TV in such a way that the faces *c–b–b*1*–c*1 and *e–f–f*1*–e*1 will be inclined to *XY* at 45°.
6. Obtain the corresponding FV. The edges *e′d′*, *e′f′*, *a′f′*, *f′–f*1*′* and *e′–e*1*′* will be hidden edges.

Problem 14.4 A pentagonal pyramid of 35 mm base edge and 70 mm height is resting on the HP with one of its triangular surfaces perpendicular to the HP, and parallel and nearer to VP. Draw its projections.

Solution Refer Fig. 14.27

Stage I

1. Draw the TV and FV of the given pyramid. The base is kept on the HP with a side perpendicular to the VP.

Stage II

2. Rotate the FV about *a′*(*b′*) till *a′*(*b′*)–*o′* becomes vertical.
3. Obtain the corresponding TV. Note that the TV shows an edge view of face *ABO*.

Stage III

4. Draw *X*1 *Y*1 parallel and nearer to *abo*.
5. Project the TV on *X*1 *Y*1 and obtain auxiliary FV. Show the hidden edges properly.

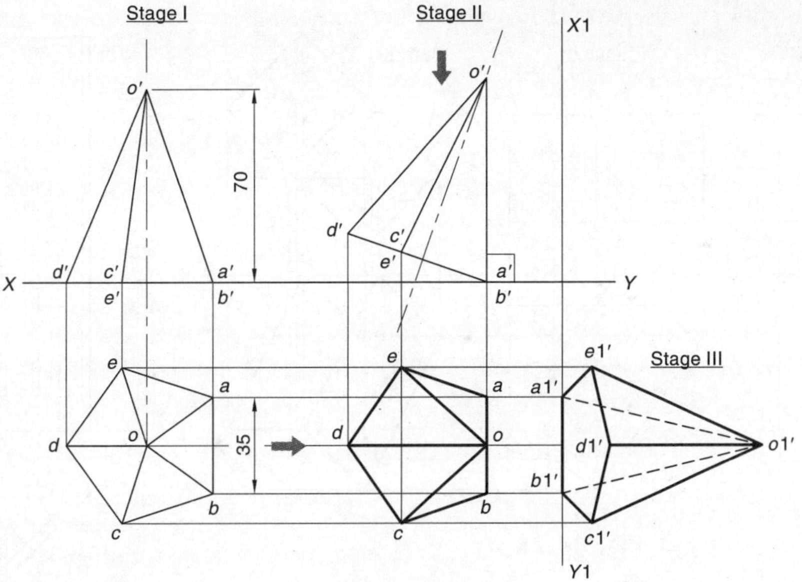

Fig. 14.27

Problem 14.5 A square prism, side of base 40 mm and length of axis 70 mm, has an edge of its base in the VP. The axis is making an angle of 55° with the VP and its elevation is making 45° with *XY*. Draw the projections of the solid.

Solution Refer Fig. 14.28.

Stage I

1. Draw the FV and TV of the prism. An end of the prism is kept in the VP with an edge perpendicular to the HP.

Stage II

2. Redraw TV such that the axis will make 55° with *XY* and the edge *a*(*b*) is on *XY*.
3. Obtain the corresponding FV. Locate axis *o*′–o1′.

Stage III

4. Redraw FV such that *o*′–o1′ will make 45° with *XY*.
5. Obtain the corresponding TV. Note that the edge *ab* is seen on *XY* in TV.

Problem 14.6 A door is in the form of a rectangular slab of size 180 cm × 76 cm × 5 cm. It is hinged at a longest side to a vertical side of the frame in a wall. The door has a hexagonal hole of side 20 cm, the centre of which is 50 mm from the top edge and of 38 mm from the longest edge. Draw the projections of the door with the hole if it makes 45° to the wall. The two opposite faces of the hole are vertical.

Solution Refer Fig. 14.29.

1. Draw FV *a*′–*b*′–*b*1′–*a*1′ of the door. *a*′–*a*1′ is drawn vertical. Locate the centre of the hexagonal hole 50 mm from *a*1′–*b*1′ and 38 mm from *a*1′–*a*′. Draw the hexagon as shown.
2. Obtain TV of the door. *a*–(*a*1)–*b*(*b*1) is drawn on *XY*. The hexagonal hole is represented by three dashed lines.
3. Turn *a*(*a*1)–*b*(*b*1) about *a*(*a*1) through 45° to obtain the new TV of the door. Also, locate dashed lines for the hole.
4. Project the TV above *XY* to obtain new FV. Also obtain the new FV of the hole as shown. Observe carefully how hidden lines are shown.

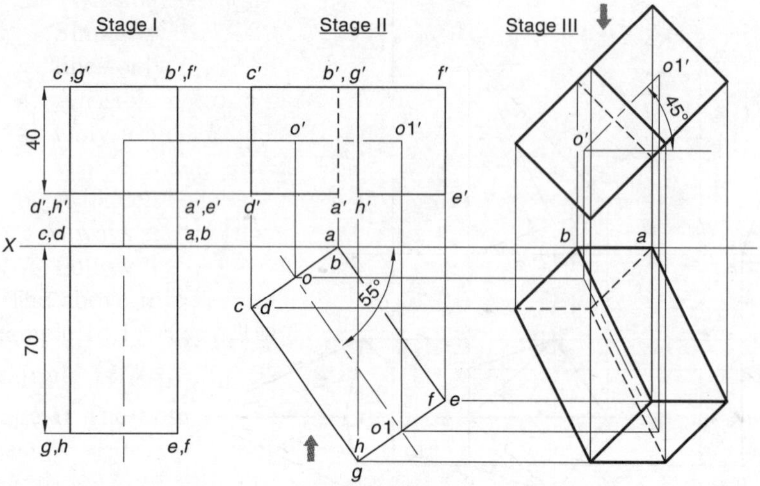

Fig. 14.28

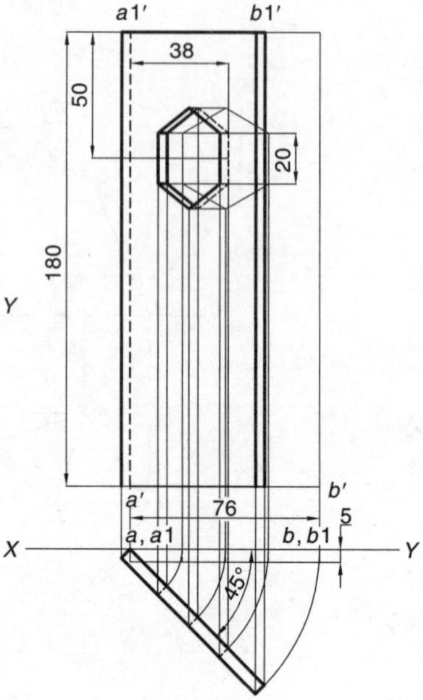

Fig. 14.29

Problem 14.7 A triangular pyramid having base side 45 mm and length of axis 75 mm is kept in the first quadrant such that its FV shows the true shape of a lateral face. The base edge of the lateral face is parallel to the HRP. Draw the two views of the solid. Measure the slant height of the pyramid.

Solution Refer Fig. 14.30.

Stage I

1. Draw the TV and FV of the triangular pyramid assuming the base parallel to the HRP and an edge of base perpendicular to the FRP. *a*′(*b*′)–*o*′ represents the edge view of face *ABO*.

Stage II

2. Redraw FV such that *a*1′(*b*1′)–*o*1′ becomes vertical.
3. Obtain the corresponding TV. *a*1–*o*1–*b*1 represents the edge view of face *ABO*.

Stage III

4. Rotate TV till *a*2–*o*2–*b*2 becomes parallel to *XY*.
5. Obtain the required FV. *a*2′–*b*2′–*o*2′ gives the true shape of the triangular face *ABO*. Measure slant height *o*2″–*b*2″.

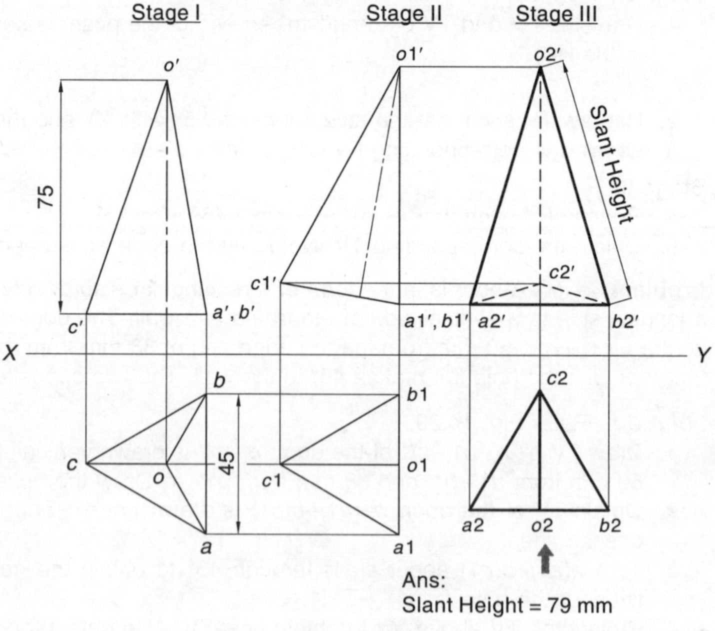

Fig. 14.30

> **Note:** In Stage II the face *ABO* is perpendicular to both the RPs. Hence its SV will give the true shape. Therefore one may directly obtain SV of the pyramid after Stage II to represent the required view.

Problem 14.8 A cylinder of base 60 mm diameter and height 80 mm has the midpoint of the axis 60 mm away from both the RPs. The axis is inclined at 30° to the VP and 60° to the HP. Draw the projections.

Solution Refer Fig. 14.31.

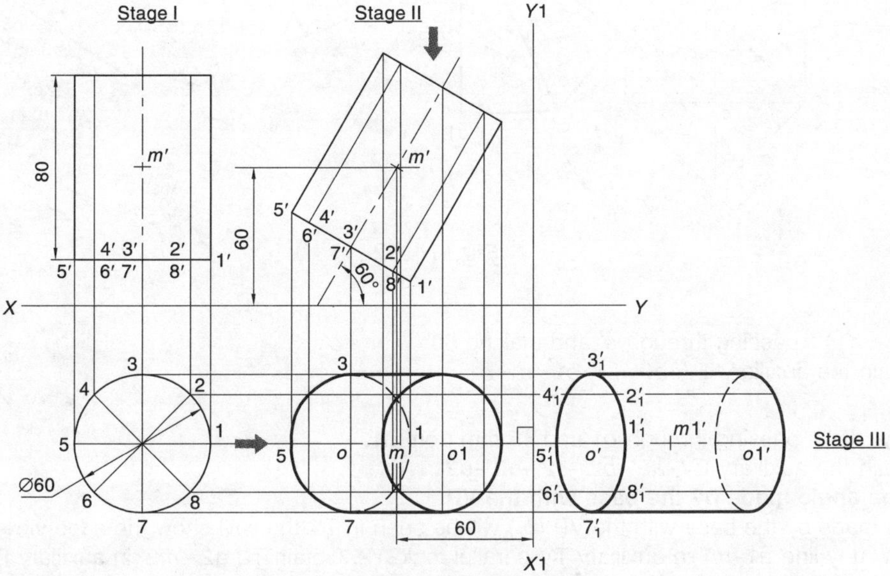

Fig. 14.31

Stage I

1. Draw TV and FV of the cylinder as shown. Obtain 8 division points in TV and FV.
2. Locate the midpoint *m′* of the axis.

Stage II

3. Redraw FV in such a way that the axis will make an angle of 60° to *XY* and *m′* 60 mm from *XY*.
4. Obtain the corresponding TV. Draw *o*–*o*1 and locate midpoint *m*.

Stage III

Since, $\theta + \phi = 90°$, the axis is parallel to the PP. Therefore, $\beta = 90°$.

5. Draw *X*1 *Y*1 inclined at $\beta = 90°$ to *o*–*o*1 and 60 mm from *m*.
6. Obtain auxiliary FV as shown. Note that *m*1′ is 60 mm from *X*1 *Y*1.

Problem 14.9 A square pyramid, 50 mm side of base and height 80 mm, has a corner of base on the HP and 45 mm in front of the VP. The slant edge through that corner makes an angle of 50° with the HP. The apex is in the VP. Draw the projections of the solid and find the angle made by its base with the VP.

Solution Refer Fig. 14.32.

Stage I

1. Draw TV and FV of the pyramid. The base is kept on the HP and two slant edges are parallel to the VP.

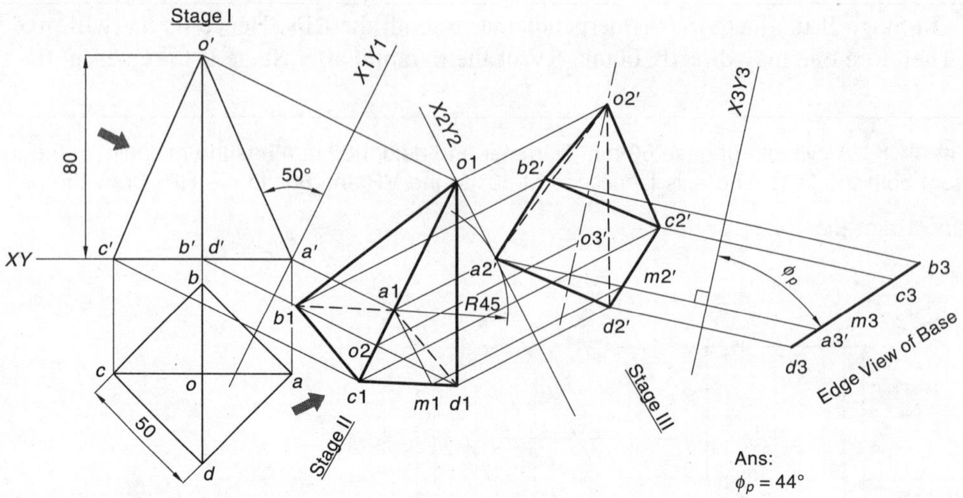

Fig. 14.32

Stage II

2. Draw $X1Y1$ passing through a' and making 50° with $a'o'$.
3. Obtain the auxiliary TV–$a1$– $b1$–$c1$– $d1$–$o1$.

Stage III

4. Draw $X2Y2$ passing through $o1$ and 45 mm from $a1$.
5. Obtain the auxiliary FV–$a2'$–$b2'$–$c2'$–$d2'$–$o2'$.

To find the angle made by the base with the VP:

The angle made by the base with the VP (ϕ_p) will be seen in TV that will show the edge view of the base.

1. Draw any line $a1$–$m1$ in auxiliary TV parallel to $X2Y2$. Obtain TL $a2'$–$m2'$ in auxiliary FV.
2. Draw $X3Y3$ perpendicular to $a2'$–$m2'$. Obtain auxiliary TV, i.e., edge view of the base as shown. Measure the angle between the edge view and $X3Y3$.

Problem 14.10 A frustum of triangular pyramid has base side 45 mm, top side 22 mm and height 40 mm. An edge of the base of the solid is on the HP and parallel to and 15 mm from the VP. The corresponding edge of the top is in the VP. Draw the two views of the solid.

Solution Refer Fig. 14.33.

Stage I

1. Draw the TV and FV of the frustum of the pyramid as shown. The base is kept on the HP with an edge perpendicular to VP.

Stage II

2. Tilt the FV about $a'(b')$ such that $d'(e')$ will fall in a vertical line 15 mm from $a'(b')$.
3. Obtain the corresponding TV.

Stage III

4. Redraw the TV such that ed is along XY. Obviously, ab will be 15 mm from XY
5. Obtain the final FV as shown. Carefully draw the hidden lines.

Problem 14.11 A pentagonal prism, base 20 mm side and axis 50 mm long is standing on a corner of the base on the ground with the longer edge containing that corner inclined at 45° to the HP and 30° to the VP. Another end of the edge is 25 mm from the VP. Draw its projections.

Solution Refer Fig. 14.34.

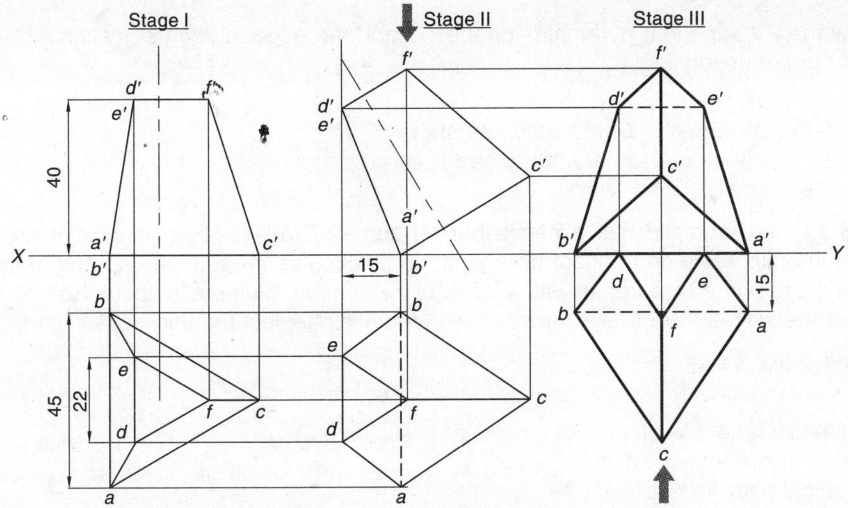

Fig. 14.33

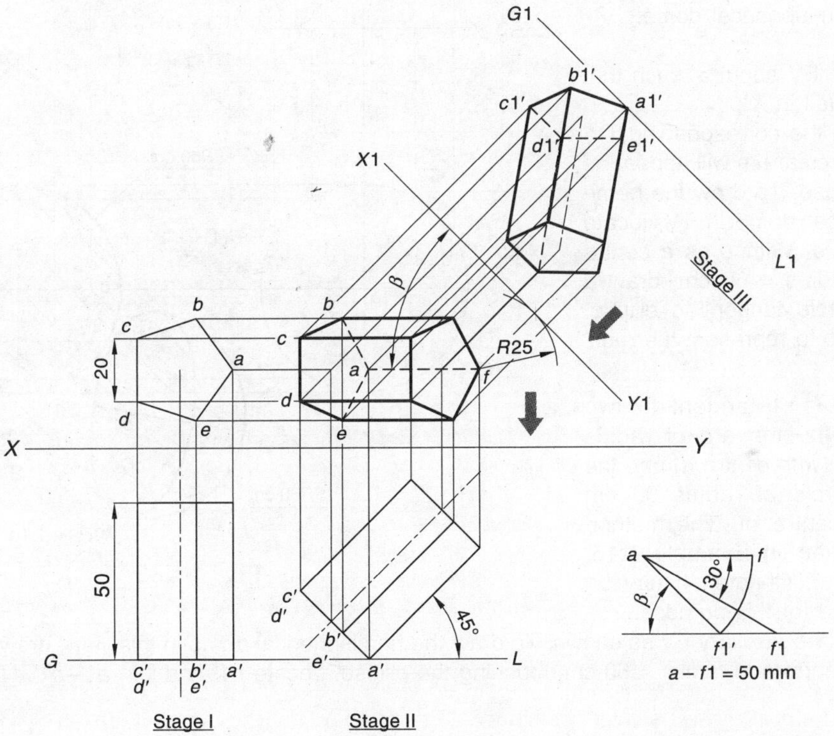

Fig. 14.34

This problem is solved by the third-angle method of projection.

Stage I

1. Draw the TV and FV of the prism. The base is kept on the ground. The rectangular face opposite the edge which is finally inclined to both the RPs is kept initially perpendicular to the VP.

Stage II

2. Redraw the FV such that *a′* remains on the *GL* and the edge through *a′* makes 45° to the *GL*.
3. Obtain the corresponding TV.

Stage III

4. Obtain β though *External Construction* as shown.
5. Draw *X*1*Y*1 inclined at β° to *af* and 25 mm from *f*.
6. Obtain the auxiliary FV as shown.

Problem 14.12 An umbrella has a hemispherical dome of radius 60 cm and a central rod of length 120 cm. The umbrella rests on the floor on a point on its circular rim and the grip-end of the rod. The rod is initially parallel to and 90 cm from a wall. A blow of air turned the umbrella about the grip-end so that the dome touches the wall. Draw the two views of the umbrella. Neglect the thickness of rod.

Solution Refer Fig. 14.35.

Stage I

1. Draw the TV and FV of the umbrella. The central rod is kept vertical with its grip-end *A* on the floor, i.e., *a′* on *XY*. Locate the centres *o* and *o′* of the hemispherical dome.

Stage II

2. Tilt the FV about *a′* such that *c′* will fall in *XY*.
3. Obtain the corresponding TV. The circular rim will appear as an ellipse. To draw the hemispherical dome in TV, locate centre *o*. With *o* as a centre and radius = 60 cm, draw a semicircle tangent to ellipse. Join *ab* to represent the rod.

Stage III

4. Draw *X*1*Y*1 tangent to two arcs, viz. the arc of radius 90 cm (with centre *a*) and the semicircle of radius 60 cm (with centre *o*). The method explained in Example 4.16, case (a), Chapter 4 may be adopted for this purpose.

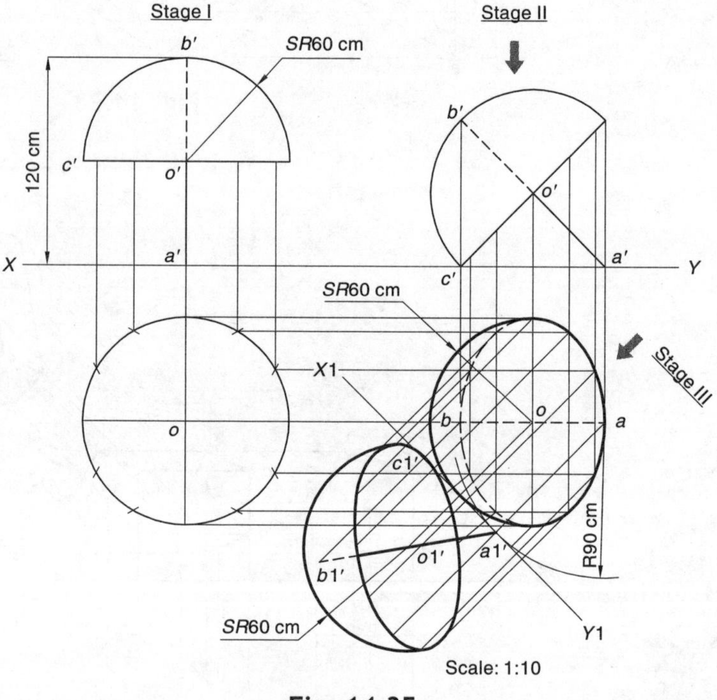

Fig. 14.35

5. Obtain the auxiliary FV as shown. To draw the hemispherical dome in this view, draw an arc with *o*1′ as a centre and radius = 60 cm, touching the ellipse. Locate *b*1′ and join *a*1′–*b*1′. Note that *c*1′ lies on *X*1*Y*1.

Problem 14.13 A square pyramid, having base *ABCD* and apex *O* is hung freely in the air with a thread tied at midpoint *P* of *OA*. Draw the projections when the axis of the pyramid makes 30° to the VP. Take *AB* = 60 mm and axis of the pyramid = 80 mm.

Solution Refer Fig. 14.36.

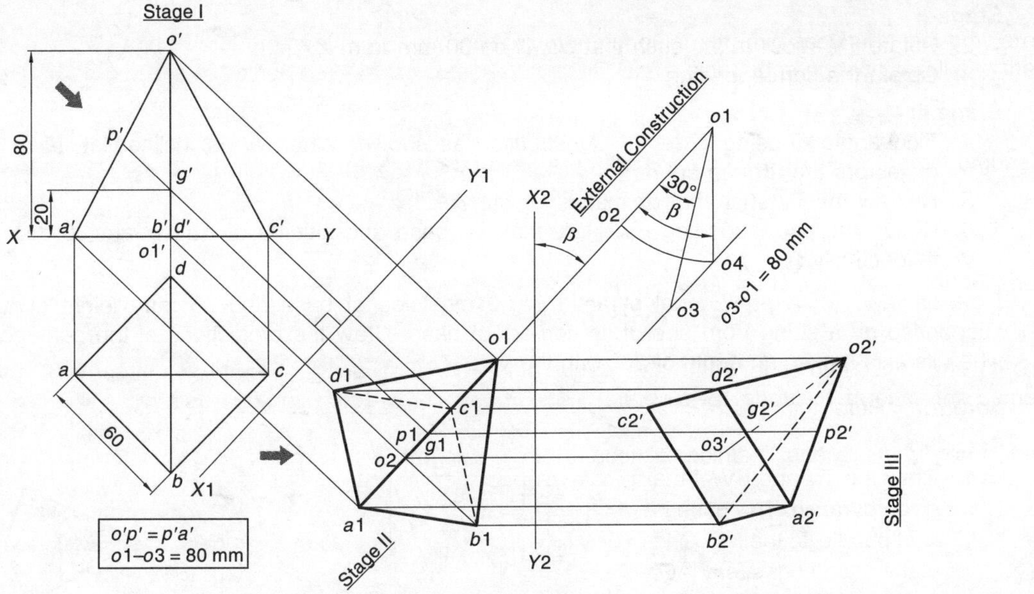

Fig. 14.36

Stage I

1. Draw the TV and FV as shown. The base may be kept parallel to the HP or on the HP. The edge *AO* is kept parallel to VP.
2. Locate *CG–g′* on the axis at ¼(80) = 20 mm from the base. Join midpoint *p′* of *a′o′* to *g′*.

Stage II

3. Draw *X*1 *Y*1 perpendicular to *p′g′*.
4. Obtain the auxiliary TV. Locate axis *o*1–*o*2.

Stage III

5. As the axis is inclined (at 30°) to the VP, obtain β as shown in *External Construction.*
6. Draw *X*2*Y*2 inclined at β° to *o*1–*o*2. Obtain auxiliary FV.

Problem 14.14 A tetrahedron of side 45 mm is resting on an edge on the HP such that the face containing that edge is seen as a triangle of base 35 mm and altitude 30 mm in FV. Draw the projections of the tetrahedron.

Solution Refer Fig. 14.37.

Stage I

1. Draw TV and FV of the tetrahedron. *A* face is kept on the HP with an edge of the face perpendicular to the VP.

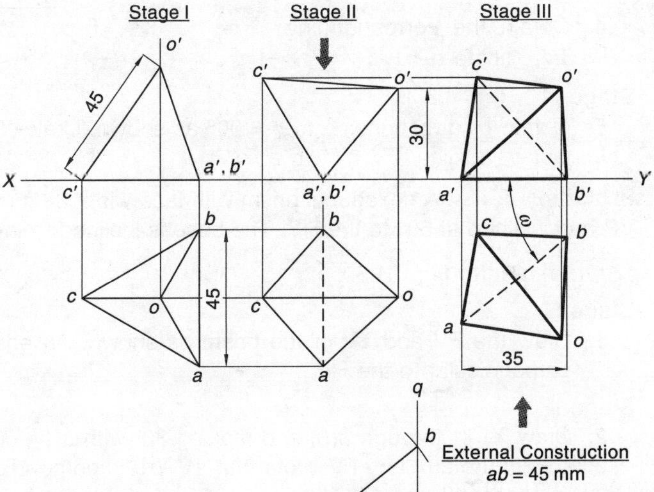

Fig. 14.37

Stage II

2. Rotate FV about a' (b') such that o' will be 30 mm from *XY*.
3. Obtain the corresponding TV.

Stage III

4. Find angle ω using *External Construction* as shown. When *ab* is inclined at $\omega°$ to *XY*, its end projectors are 35 mm apart.
5. Redraw the TV such that *ab* makes $\omega°$ with *XY*.
6. Obtain the corresponding FV. Note that the base and altitude of $\Delta a'b'o'$ are 35 mm and 30 mm respectively.

Problem 14.15 A pentagonal pyramid of 50 mm side of base and 85 mm height of axis is freely suspended by a string from one of its corners of base. Draw the projections of the pentagonal pyramid when its axis makes an angle of 30° with the VP.

Solution Refer Fig. 14.38.

Stage I

1. Draw the TV and FV of the given pyramid. The base is kept parallel to the HP. One of the slant edges, say *AO*, is kept parallel to the VP.
2. Locate *CG* g' on the axis at 85/4 = 21.25 ≈ 21 mm from the base. Join $a'g'$.

Stage II

3. Redraw the FV such that $a'g'$ becomes vertical. The axis is now inclined to the HP.
4. Obtain the corresponding TV. Locate *o*–*o*1.

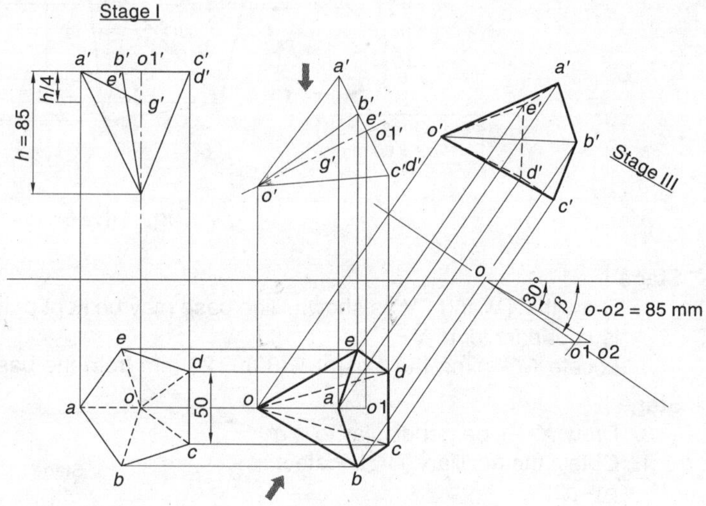

Fig. 14.38

Stage III

5. Obtain β corresponding to ϕ = 30° as shown. Draw *X*1*Y*1 inclined at $\beta°$ to *o*–*o*1.
6. Obtain auxliary FV $a'b'c'd'e'$–o'.

Problem 14.16 A hexagonal prism with face width 30 mm and height 70 mm has its edge of base in the VP and inclined at 60° to the HP. The base is inclined to the VP at 30°. Draw the FV and TV of the prism.

Solution Refer Fig. 14.39.

Stage I

1. Draw the FV and TV of the prism as shown. An end of the prism is kept in the VP with an edge perpendicular to the HP.

Stage II

2. Draw *X*1*Y*1 through *a*(*b*) and making 30° with *a*(*b*)–*d*(*e*).
3. Obtain the auxiliary FV. Note that *a*1′–*b*1′ is perpendicular to *X*1*Y*1 (since *a*(*b*) is the point view) and represents TL of *AB*. However, *AB* should be finally inclined at 60° to the HP.

Stage III

4. Draw *X*2*Y*2 inclined at 60° to the *a*1′–*b*1′.
5. Obtain the corresponding auxiliary TV. As *AB* lies in the VP, *a*2–*b*2 lies along *X*2*Y*2.

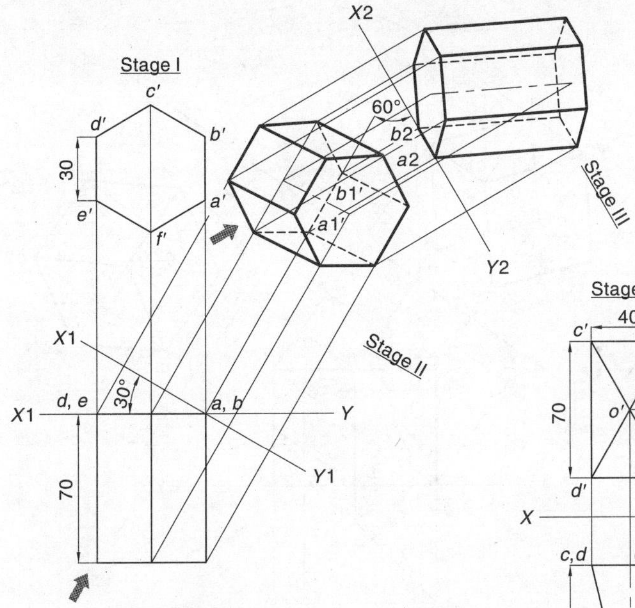

Fig. 14.39

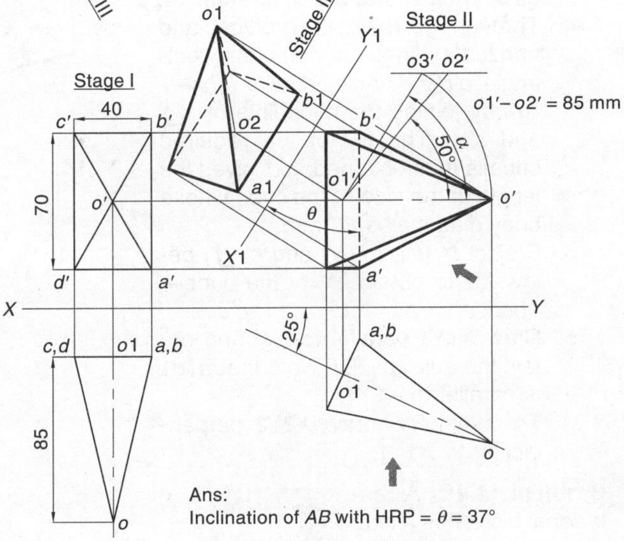

Fig. 14.40

Problem 14.17 A pyramid has rectangular base of size 70 mm × 40 mm and height 85 mm. Its longer edge of base is parallel to the FRP. The axis of pyramid is inclined at 25° to the FRP and 50° to the HRP. Draw the projections of the solid assuming the apex nearer to the observer. What is the inclination of the longer edge of the base with the HRP?

Solution Refer Fig. 14.40.

Stage I

1. Draw the FV and TV of the rectangular pyramid as shown. The base is kept parallel to the FRP with its longer edge perpendicular to the HRP.

Stage II

2. Redraw the TV such that the axis will make 25° with *XY*.
3. Obtain the corresponding FV. The axis *o*′–*o*1′ is seen parallel to *XY*.

Stage III

4. Obtain apparent inclination α of the axis as shown.
5. Draw *X*1*Y*1 inclined at α° to *o*′–*o*1′, i.e., parallel to *o*1′–*o*3′.
6. Obtain the auxiliary TV as shown. Measure θ, i.e., inclination of *AB* with the HRP.

Problem 14.18 Draw the three views of a cube of solid diagonal 85 mm long such that the TL of a solid diagonal is seen in both the FV and TV.

Solution Refer Fig. 14.41.

1. Draw TV–*apqr* and FV–*a′q′s′t′* of a cube assuming any length of side.
2. Join *a′s′* to represent the FV of a body diagonal. Note that *a′s′* gives the TL of the diagonal.
3. Locate *g′* on *a′s′* (produced if necessary) such that *a′g′* = 85 mm.
4. Through *g′*, draw the vertical and horizontal lines to complete rectangle *a′c′g′e′*. Also, draw *f′* (*h′*)–*b′* (*d′*) by joining the midpoints of *e′g′* and *a′c′*. The FV of the required cube is thus obtained. *g′c′* gives the length of the side of the cube whose body diagonal is 85 mm.
5. Project *b′* (*f′*), *d′* (*h′*) and *c′* (*g′*) below *XY* to obtain TV of the cube—*abcd*. *ab* = *bc* = *cd* = *da* = *g′c′*.
6. Draw *X*1*Y*1 parallel to *a′g′* and obtain the auxiliary TV. Note that *a*1*g*1 is parallel to *X*1*Y*1.

   To obtain SV, draw *X*2*Y*2 perpendicular to *X*1*Y*1.

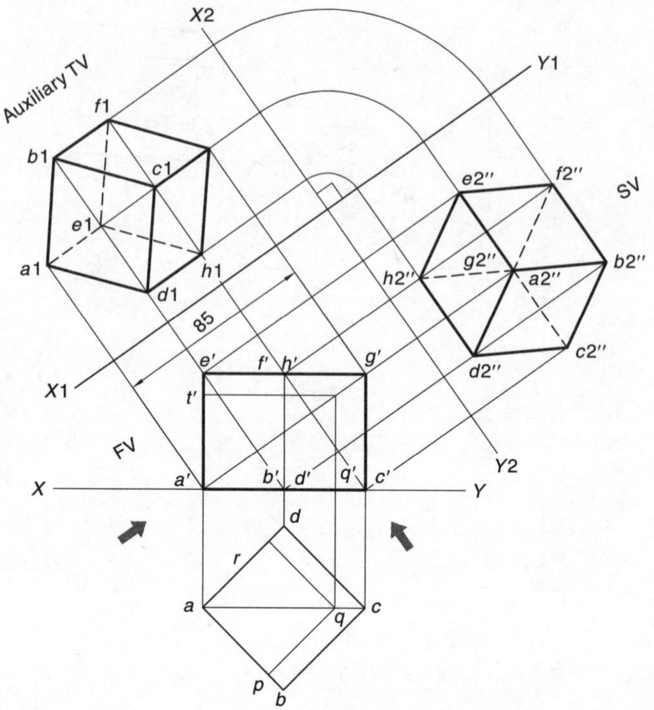

Fig. 14.41

Problem 14.19 A pentagonal block has a side of end 50 mm and thickness 25 mm. It has a centrally drilled circular hole of diameter 50 mm. A rectangular face of the block is parallel to the HP and the end faces are inclined at 30° to the VP. Draw the two views of the block with the hole if its corner is placed in the VP. Project the FV on a reference line inclined at 30° to *XY*.

Solution Refer Fig. 14.42.

Stage I

1. Draw FV and TV of the block showing the hole. An end is kept in the VP and a rectangular face is kept parallel to the HP.

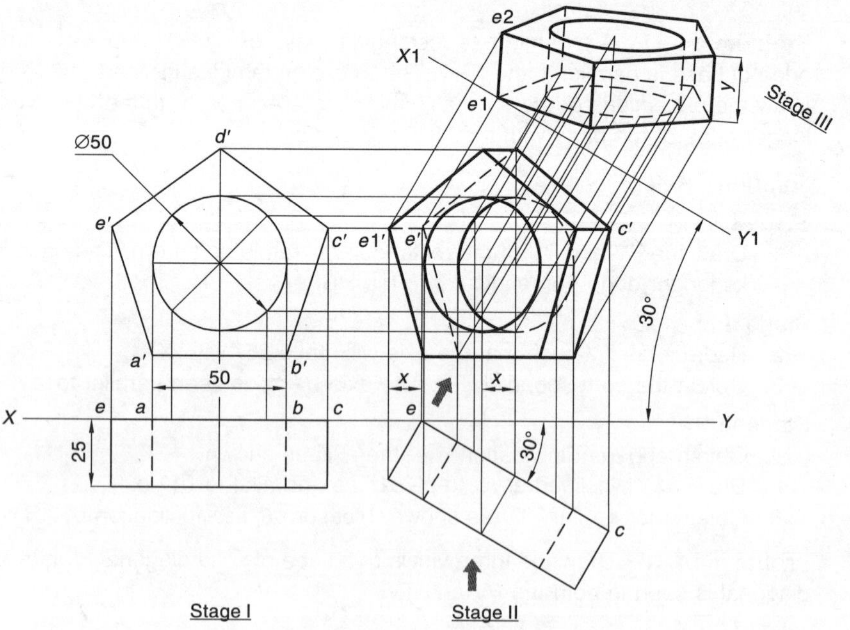

Fig. 14.42

Stage II

2. Rotate TV about *e* such that *ec* makes 30° to *XY*.
3. Obtain the corresponding FV. Carefully observe how the projection of the hole is drawn.

Stage III

4. Draw *X*1 *Y*1 inclined at 30° to *XY* and obtain auxiliary TV as shown. Note that *e*1 lies on *X*1 *Y*1.

DRAWING TIP

Always project one pentagonal face of the block/ prism. Another face is then obtained by shifting the points of the first face through distance *x* (or *y*) along *e′*–*e*1′ (or *e*1–*e*2). The same thing applies to the projections of the hole.

Problem 14.20 Three equal cones of base 50 mm diameter and axis 75 mm long are placed on the HRP on their bases, each touching the other two. A sphere of 40 mm diameter is placed centrally between them. Draw the three views of the arrangement and determine the height of the centre of the sphere above the HRP.

Solution Refer Fig. 14.43.

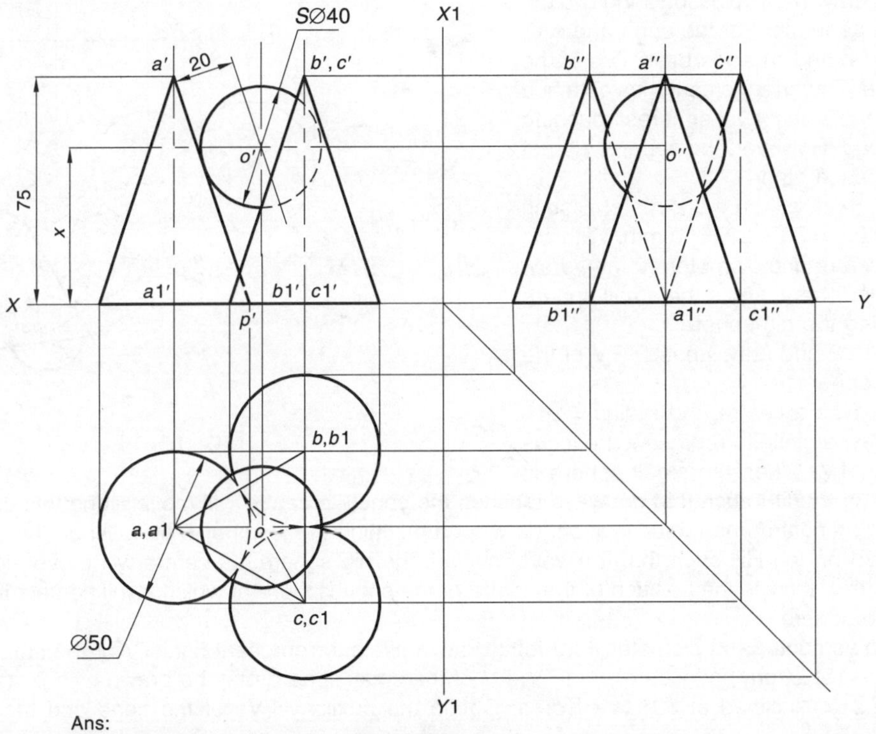

Ans:
Height of sphere centre above HRP = *x* = 52 mm

Fig. 14.43

1. Draw the TVs of the three cones tangent to each other. For this, draw an equilateral triangle *a*(*a*1)–*b*(*b*1)–*c*(*c*1) of side 50 mm. *b*(*b*1)–*c*(*c*1) is drawn perpendicular to *XY*. Now with *a*, *b* and *c* as the centres and radius = 25 mm, draw the three circles.
2. Find centre *o* of the triangle. With *o* as a centre and radius = 20 mm, draw a circle to represent the TV of the sphere. As the sizes of all the three cones are equal, the centre of the sphere will lie at the centre of the triangle.

3. Obtain the FVs of the cones.
4. Locate *o′* at the intersection of a line 20 mm from *a′p′* and the projector through *o*. With *o′* as a centre and radius = 20 mm, draw a circle to indicate the FV of the sphere. Clearly, the circle will be tangent to *a′p′*.
5. Obtain the SVs of the cones and the sphere by projecting their FVs and TVs. In SV, first locate *o″* and then draw a circle with *o″* as a centre and radius = 20 mm.

   Draw the hidden portions of the cones and the sphere properly in all the views.

Problem 14.21 A cone of diameter of base 70 mm and axis 80 mm long has its base on the HP. Two spheres *A* and *B* of diameter 60 mm and 40 mm respectively are also resting on the HP. All the three solids touch each other. A plane passing through the axis of the cone and the centre of the sphere *A* makes an angle of 60° with the VP. Draw the projections of the solids.

Solution Refer Fig. 14.44.

1. Draw TV and FV of the cone keeping its base on the HP.
2. With *a′* and *b*1′ as the centres and diameters = 60 mm and 40 mm respectively, draw two circles touching two extreme generators of the cone and *XY*.
3. Locate *a* and *b*1 and obtain TVs of the sphere. The arrangement thus obtained represents the two spheres touching the cone. However, the spheres do not touch each other.
4. In FV, mark *b*2′ on the locus of *B* such that *a′b*2′ = 30 + 20 = 50 mm. With *b*2′ as a centre and diameter 40 mm, draw a circle. It represents the small sphere touching the big sphere.
5. Obtain *b*2 and draw another TV of the small sphere.
6. With *o*1 as a centre and radius = *o*1–*b*1, draw a circle to represent the locus of *B* in TV. When the small sphere is rolled on the HP such that it always touches the cone, its centre will move along this circle.

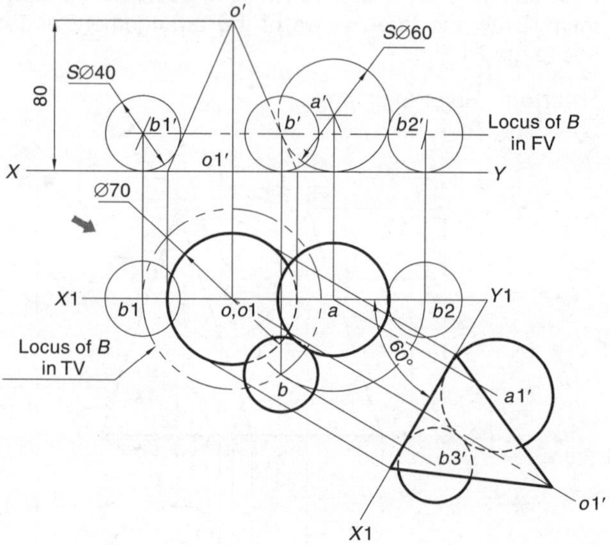

Fig. 14.44

7. With *a* as centre and radius = *a*–*b*2, draw an arc cutting the locus of *B* at *b*. When the small sphere is rolled on the HP such that it always touches the big sphere, its centre will move along this arc. Obviously, *b* gives the position of the centre of the small sphere at which it will contact the cone and the big sphere.
8. With *b* as centre and diameter = 40 mm, draw a circle to represent final TV of the small sphere.
9. Project *b* to *b′* on the locus of *B* in FV. FV of the small sphere may be drawn with *b′* as a centre.
10. Draw *X*1*Y*1 inclined at 60° to *o*1(*o*)–*a*. Obtain the auxiliary FVs of the cone and the spheres as shown.

    The hidden portions of the cone and the spheres are shown by a dashed line.

Problem 14.22 An open ended square prism formed out of thin metal sheet has one edge of 50 mm and height 60 mm. It is placed on the ground with its vertical faces equally inclined to the VP. A cone of 60 mm diameter and axis of 60 mm length is placed in the prism with the apex down. Mark the distance of the apex from ground.

The combination is tilted about the corner of the prism such that the common axis is inclined to the HP at 30° and the plan of the axis at 45° with *XY*. Draw the projections of the combination when the base of the cone is towards the observer.

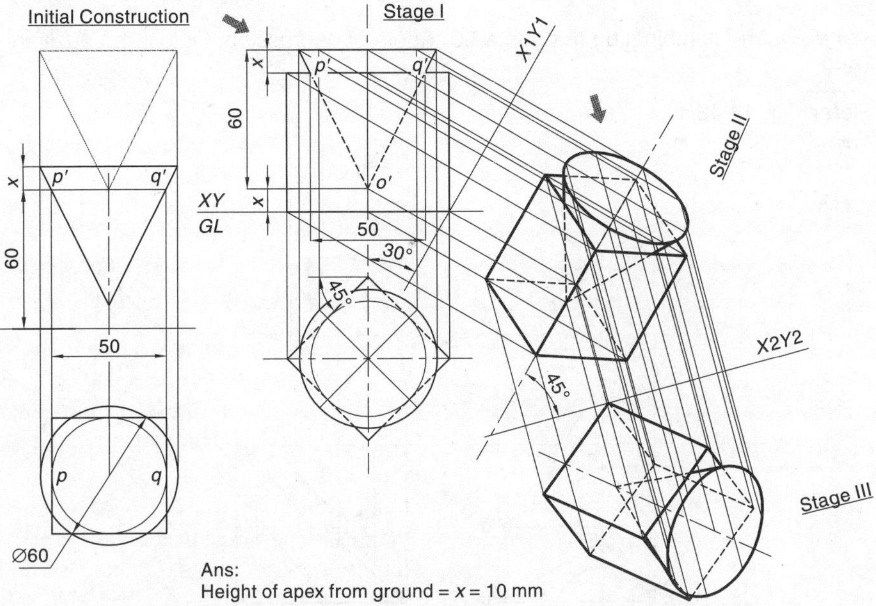

Fig. 14.45

Solution Refer Fig. 14.45.

When a cone of sufficiently bigger size is inserted in a hollow prism with the apex inside the prism, the curved surface of the cone remains tangent to the faces of the prism. The first task is therefore, to find the points of tangency between the cone and the prism. This is explained in *Initial Construction*.

Draw the TV and FV of the square prism assuming that a vertical face is parallel to the VP. Also, draw the TV and FV of the cone. The FV of the cone is drawn initially above the FV of the prism. The cone is then pushed down till it fits in the prism. As the base diameter of the cone is larger than the face-width of the prism, the cone will partly enter inside the prism. When the cone fully fits inside the prism the top edges of the prism will touch the curved surface of the cone. Obviously, these points of tangency, i.e., *p′* and *q′*, lie at the intersection of the generators of the cone and the vertical faces of the prism as shown.

Stage I

1. Draw the TVs and FVs of the prism and the cone as shown. The base of the prism is on the HP (ground) with vertical faces making 45° to the VP. In FV, locate the points of tangency *p′* and *q′* and draw the cone. Measure the height of the apex from the ground, i.e., *x*.

Stage II

2. Draw *X*1*Y*1 passing through a corner of the prism and making 30° with the axis.
3. Obtain auxiliary TVs of the arrangement.

Stage III

4. Draw *X*2*Y*2 inclined at 45° to the TV of axis.
5. Obtain the corresponding FV of the assembly. Note carefully how hidden lines are shown.

DRAWING TIP

The point of tangency *p′* and *q′* can directly be located in FV in Stage I as shown. *Initial Construction* is only for the sake of illustration.

Problem 14.23 A sphere of diameter 40 mm is placed on ground. A triangular pyramid, hollow and open from the base, is fitted on the sphere from the base side. The axis of the pyramid is vertical and a side of base makes 20° to the VP. Draw TVs and FVs of the solids. The pyramid has a base side of 75 mm and height 25 mm.

An observer views the combination through a 50° angle of depression. Obtain the auxiliary view as seen by the observer.

Solution Refer Fig. 14.46.

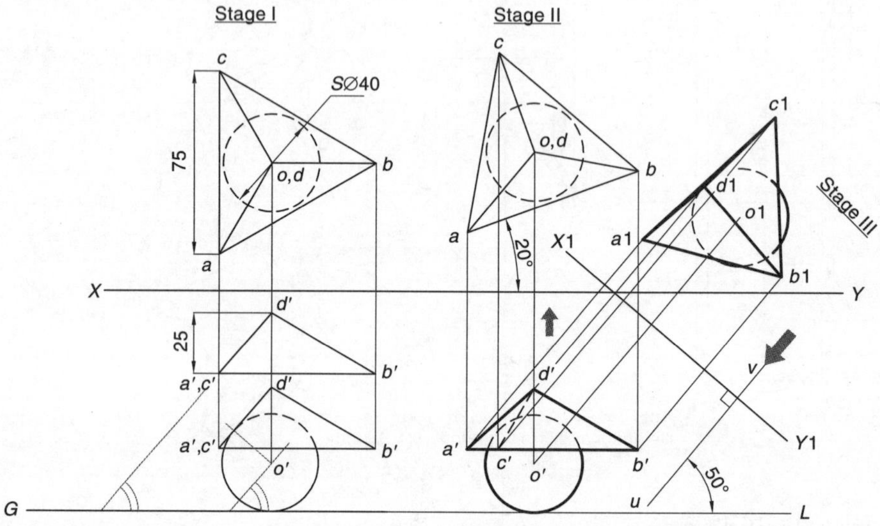

Fig. 14.46

The problem is solved by the third-angle method of projection

Stage I

1. Draw TVs and FVs of the solids. The base of the pyramid is kept parallel to the HP with a side perpendicular to the VP. FV of the pyramid is initially drawn above the FV of the sphere.
2. Move the FV of the pyramid down to fit it on that of the sphere. This is achieved by drawing *a*′ (*c*′)–*d*′ tangent to the circle as per the method explained in Example 4.14, Chapter 4.

Stage II

3. Rotate the TV so that *ab* makes 20° to *XY*.
4. Obtain the corresponding FV.

Stage III

5. Draw *uv* inclined at 50° to *GL*. It represents the direction of viewing by the observer.
6. Draw *X*1 *Y*1 perpendicular to *uv*.
7. Obtain the auxiliary TV as shown. Show the hidden portion properly.

Problem 14.24 A pentagonal pyramid of base 30 mm side and slant height 70 mm is resting on the HP on its base with one edge of the base perpendicular to the VP. A triangular pyramid, having a slant edge common with that of the pentagonal pyramid, is attached to the latter in such a way that the angle between the two attached triangular surfaces of the two solids is 60°. The base of the triangular pyramid is of 45 mm side. Draw the two views of the composite solid.

Solution Refer Fig. 14.47.

Stage I

1. Draw the TVs and FVs of the pentagonal pyramid and the triangular pyramid assuming that they are separate. The bases of both the solids are placed on the HP with a slant edge of each parallel to the VP. These slant edges are drawn nearer to each other.

Stage II

2. Pick the FV *a′o′f′* of the triangular pyramid and keep it on the FV *a′o′c′*(*d′*)*b′*(*e′*) of the pentagonal pyramid such that the edges coincide along *a′o′*.
3. Obtain the corresponding TV of the triangular pyramid.

Stage III

We need to measure the angle between the two attached triangular faces of the two solids, i.e., *OAB* and *OAF*. This is possible when both the faces are seen as edge views.

4. Set *X*1 *Y*1 perpendicular to *a′o′*.
5. Obtain the partial auxiliary TV as shown. It shows the edge views of the faces *OAB*, *OAF* and *OAG*.
6. Rotate *o*1–*f*1 about *o*1 such that ∠*b*1–*o*1–*f*2 = 60°. Also, rotate *o*1–*g*1 about *o*1 through the same angle to obtain *o*1–*g*2.
7. Draw *f*–*f* parallel to *X*1 *Y*1 and passing through *f′* (*g′*). As soon as points *f*1 and *g*1 move along the arcs in auxiliary TV, the points *f′* and *g′* will move long *f*–*f* in FV.
8. Project *f*2 and *g*2 back to locate *f*2′ and *g*2′ on *f*–*f*. Complete FV *o′*–*a′*–*f*2′–*g*2′.
9. Project *f*2′ and *g*2′ below *XY* to complete the required TV.

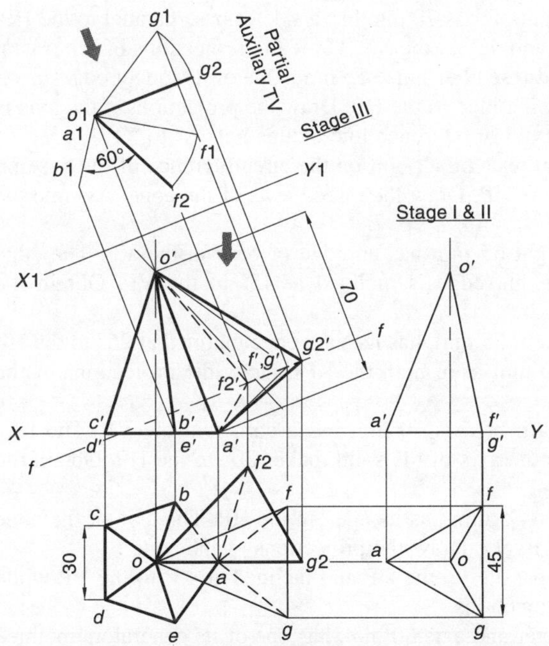

Fig. 14.47

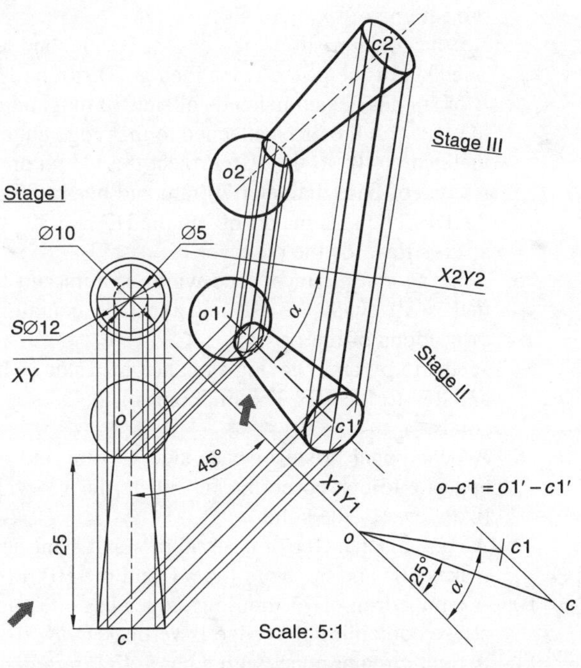

Fig. 14.48

Problem 14.25 A toggle switch consists of a conical rod attached to a spherical ball across a flat section. The ball has a diameter of 12 mm. The conical rod has diameters of 10 mm at the free end and 5 mm at the end attached to the ball. The length of the rod is 25 mm. The switch is turned about the centre of the ball such that the axis of the rod makes 45° to the VP and 25° to the HP. Draw the projections of the switch.

Solution Refer Fig. 14.48.

Stage I

1. Draw FVs and TVs of the two solids. The axis of the rod is kept perpendicular to the VP. FV of smaller end of the rod is projected in TV to obtain the flat section on the sphere.

Stage II

2. Draw $X1Y1$ inclined at 45° to oc.
3. Obtain the corresponding FV.

Stage III

4. As the axis is inclined at 25° to the HP, find apparent the inclination α as shown.
5. Draw $X2Y2$ inclined at α° to $o1'$–$c1'$, i.e., parallel to o–$c1$.
6. Obtain the required auxiliary TV.

Review Questions

1. A triangular prism of base side 45 mm and length of axis 75 mm has its edge of base on the HP and inclined at 50° to the VP. The face through that edge makes an angle of 30° to the HP. Draw the projections of the prism.
2. A square pyramid of base side 40 mm and slant height 70 mm has a corner of base on the HP. The slant edge through that corner makes 25° to the HP. The TV of that edge is seen at 75° to *XY*. Draw the projections of the pyramid.
3. A pentagonal prism of side of base 35 mm and length of axis 70 mm has a side of base parallel to the HP. The axis of the prism is inclined at 30° to the HP and 45° to the VP. Draw the projections of the prism.
4. A prism has hexagonal ends of side 35 mm and end-to-end distance 55 mm. One of its longer edges is on the HP with the faces attached to that edge equally inclined to the HP. Draw the projections if the axis is inclined at 40° to the VP. Project the FV on an auxiliary reference line inclined at 30° to *XY*.
5. A cone of base diameter 70 mm and height 85 mm rests on a point on the circumference of the base on the HP. The axis makes 60° to the HP and 30° to the VP. Draw the three views of the cone. Assume the apex is towards the observer.
6. A hexagonal prism of face width 35 mm and height 65 mm has an edge of base in the VP. The edge makes 50° with the HP and the face containing that edge is inclined at 45° to the VP. Obtain the projections of the prism.
7. A square pyramid having slant height = side of base = 55 mm, has its slant edge inclined at 25° to the HP and 45° to the VP. The midpoint of the axis is 60 mm from both the RPs. Draw the projections of the solids.
8. A pentagonal prism of base side 45 mm and length of axis 70 mm has a corner in the VP. The face apposite to that corner makes 50° to the VP while the axis of the solid makes 30° to the HP. Obtain the two views of the solid.
9. A cone of diameter of base 60 mm and slant height 75 mm has its apex in the HP. The axis of the cone makes 20° and 50° with the VP and the HP respectively. Draw the projections of the cone.
10. A tetrahedron of 75 mm long edges has one edge parallel to the HP and inclined at 45° to the VP while a face containing that edge is vertical. Draw its projections.
11. A right circular cone, with a base of 60 mm diameter and axis 80 mm, has one of its generators inclined to the HP at 30° and to the VP at 40°. Draw the projections of the cone if its apex is nearer to the VP.
12. A square pyramid, 50 mm side of base and height 80 mm has a corner of base on the HP and is 45 mm in front of the VP. The slant edge through that corner makes an angle of 50° with the HP. The apex is in the VP. Draw the projections of the solid and find the angle made by its base with the VP.
13. A hexagonal pyramid of base side 40 mm and height of axis 80 mm is tilted on its base edge (lying on the ground) such that the apex is away from the observer. The triangular face containing that edge appears as an isosceles triangle in the elevation with a 40 mm base and a 60 mm altitude. Draw its projections and find the inclination of the base of the pyramid with the HP.

14. A tetrahedron of side 50 mm in length rests on one of its edges in the HP, with the edge opposite to the edge in the HP making an angle of 45° with the HP and 30° with VP. Draw the projections.
15. A pentagonal pyramid has a corner of its base in the HP and triangular face opposite to it inclined at 45° to the HP. A slant edge within that triangular face is inclined at 30° to the VP. Draw the projections of the pyramid if the edge of its base is 30 mm and the axis is 65 mm long.
16. A regular pentagonal prism has base edge 25 mm and height 60 mm. One of the base edges of the prism makes 30° with the HP and 60° with the VP. The axis of the prism makes 45° with the HP. Draw the projections. Find the angle made by the axis with the VP. [**Hint:** In the first stage, draw TV and FV assuming the base parallel to the HP with a side perpendicular to the VP. In the second stage, establish the angle between the axis and the HP and then obtain SV. In the third stage, draw an auxiliary reference line inclined at 30° to the base edge in SV and obtain the auxiliary TV. For FV, draw another auxiliary reference line perpendicular to the first auxiliary reference line.]
17. A pentagonal pyramid has its corner of base in the VP. The slant edge through that corner makes 45° to the VP and 30° to the HP. The apex is toward the observer. Draw the projections. The side of base of the pyramid is 40 mm and the height is 70 mm.
18. A tetrahedron of side 50 mm has an edge in the VP. The edge opposite to the edge in the VP is perpendicular to the HP. Draw the two views of the tetrahedron.
19. A cylinder of diameter 50 mm and length of axis 60 mm is hung freely in air from a point on its circumference of an end. Draw its projections if the axis makes 40° to the VP.
20. A cone (diameter of base 80 mm and height 90 mm) is suspended by a string attached to the midpoint of one of its generators. Draw the projections of the solid when the axis makes 30° with the VP, the vertex being away from the observer. Find the inclination of the axis with the HP.
21. A hemispherical drum of radius 12 cm is hung freely at a point on the circumference of the circular face. Draw two views of the drum assuming the circular face to be perpendicular to the VP. An observer views the drum in a direction inclined at 35° to the VP. Obtain the auxiliary FV.
22. Draw the three views of a cube of 60 mm side resting on a corner on the HP such that the three edges through that corner make equal angles with the HP and one of the edges is parallel to the PP. [**Hint:** The three edges will make equal angles with the HP when the body diagonal through that corner will be perpendicular to the HP.]
23. A tetrahedron *ABCV* of 70 mm edges is resting with its edge *AB* on the ground. The face *ABV* is inclined to the HP such that its plan is a right-angled triangle. Draw the projections of the solid when its axis makes an angle of 30° with the VP and vertex *V* towards the observer.
24. A square pyramid of base 40 mm and height 70 mm has its slant edge in the VP and inclined to the HP at 45°. Draw the three views of the pyramid if the apex is in HP.
25. A square prism of base side 30 mm and longer edge 60 mm is situated in such a way that one end of a longer edge is on the HP and the other end is on the VP. Draw the projections when the axis is 45° to the VP and 30° to the HP.
26. A triangular prism of base side 40 mm and a 50 mm axis long is lying on the ground on one of its rectangular faces with the axis perpendicular to the VP. A cone of base diameter 40 mm and a 50 mm long axis is resting on the ground and is leaning centrally on a face of the prism, with its axis parallel to the VP. Draw the projections of the solids and project another FV on a reference line making 60° angle with *XY*.
27. A circular disc of 60 mm diameter and thickness 20 mm is kept on the ground on its flat face. A tetrahedron, having its face inscribed in the top of the disc, is placed on the disc in such a way that a side of the tetrahedron on the top of the disc is perpendicular to the VP. Draw the two views of the solids. The combination is viewed by an observer in the direction 30° to the HP. Obtain the auxiliary TV.
28. A square prism of side of base 45 mm and length of axis 75 mm is resting on the HP on a longer side with the faces equally inclined to the HP. The side on the HP is perpendicular to the VP. A triangular pyramid of base side 35 mm and length of axis 80 mm is resting on the HP on an edge of base such that the triangular face through that edge mates centrally with the face of the prism. Draw the two views of the combination. Project FV on a reference line inclined at 50° to *XY*.

Chapter 15

SECTIONS OF SOLIDS

15.1 INTRODUCTION

An object is difficult to visualize from its orthographic views if its internal structure is complicated. The views of such an object may have numerous hidden lines. In such a case, the concept of 'sectioning the object' helps to interpret and visualize the object easily. The object is assumed to be cut by an imaginary plane to reveal internal details. The imaginary plane which cuts the object is called the *cutting plane* (or *section plane*). The new imaginary face generated on the object is called the *section.* Readers are directed to refer Section 9.7 for details on the section planes, related conventions and various sectional views. This chapter deals with the methods of obtaining the sections of standard (and combined) solids in various positions. The study of sections of solids plays an important role in designing many machine parts and also in the interpenetration of the objects.

15.2 THEORY OF SECTIONING

Whenever a section plane cuts a solid, it intersects (and or coincides with) the edges of the solids. The point at which the section plane intersects an edge of the solid is called the *point of intersection* (POI). The POIs are located in one view and then projected in the desired view to draw the section. In case of the solids having a curved surface, viz., cylinder, cone and sphere, POIs are located between the cutting plane and the lateral lines. It should be noted that a flat section plane will never cut all the edges of a polyhedron, but only cuts some of them. A section plane will cut a minimum of three edges of the polyhedra, creating three POIs. The maximum number of POIs depends on the type of polyhedron, i.e., prism or pyramid, as shown in Table 15.1.

Table 15.1 Maximum POIs between a Section Plane and Polyhedron

Type of Solid	*Maximum POIs*
Prism (and Cube)	(Number of sides of base) + 2
Pyramid (and Tetrahedron)	(Number of sides of base) + 1

Types of section planes are explained in Section 9.7.1. In this chapter, five of them, namely, horizontal section plane, vertical section plane, profile section plane, AIP and AVP have been considered.

15.2.1 True Shape of a Section

A section will show its *true shape* when viewed in normal direction. Obviously, to find the true shape of a section, it must be projected on a plane parallel to the section plane. TV shows true shape of the section when a horizontal section plane cuts the object. FV and SV show true shapes when a vertical section plane and a profile section plane, respectively, cut the object. When the AIP cuts the object, the auxiliary TV shows the true shape of the section. Similarly, when the object is cut by AVP, the auxiliary FV will show the true shape of the section.

For polyhedra, the true shape of the section depends on the number of POIs. The shape of the section will be a polygon of the sides equal to the number of POIs. For a cylinder, the shape of the section will be circular, rectangular or elliptical depending on the position of the cutting plane. The section of a cone will be circular, elliptical, parabolic, hyperbolic or triangular depending on the cutting plane. The true shape of the section of a sphere is always a circle. The sections of prisms and pyramids are straight line segmented curves. The sections of cylinders and cones will mostly have smooth curves. The sections will consist of straight lines if the cutting plane includes two generators on the cylinder or cone.

The true shapes of the sections of the cylinder and cone, depending on the position of the cutting plane, are explained in Table 15.2.

Table 15.2 True Shapes of Sections of Cylinder and Cone

Solid	*Position of the Cutting Plane*	*True Shape of Section*
Cylinder	Perpendicular to the axis	Circle
	Inclined to the axis cutting all generators	Ellipse
	Parallel to the axis	Rectangle
Cone	Perpendicular to the axis	Circle
	Inclined to the axis cutting all generators	Ellipse
	Parallel to a generator	Parabola
	Inclined to and on one side of the axis	Hyperbola
	Parallel to the axis	Rectangular Hyperbola
	Passing through the axis or the apex	Triangle

Sometimes, an auxiliary view of the object showing the true shape of the section is also constructed.

15.2.2 Locating the Section Plane When the True Shape of the Section is Known

Locating the section plane when the true shape of the section is given is a reverse process. For polyhedra, the cutting plane must cut the solid at the points equal to the number of corners in the section. For example, if the true shape of a section of a cube is a hexagon, then the cutting plane must create 6 POIs in FV or TV. To locate the cutting plane, it is a usual practice to draw the true shape of the section in auxiliary view and then, projecting all the corners in FV or TV. For this, inclination of the cutting plane (with the HP or the VP) must be first decided. If the true shape of the section of a cylinder is an ellipse, then the minor axis of the ellipse will be equal to the diameter of the cylinder. The major axis will be equal to the length of the cutting plane between two farthest generators.

Similar logics can be applied to locate section planes on a cone if the true shape of the section is an ellipse, a parabola or a hyperbola.

The sections of prisms, cubes, pyramids, tetrahedrons, cylinders, cones, spheres and combined solids are explained in the following sections. The logic needed to decide the section plane when the true shape is known is explained in some of the examples.

REMEMBER THE FOLLOWING

- Maximum number of POIs: Prisms ⇒ (Number of sides of base) + 2, Pyramids ⇒ (Number of sides of base) + 1
- True shape of section: Horizontal Section Plane ⇒ TV, Vertical Section Plane ⇒ FV, Profile Section Plane ⇒ SV, AIP ⇒ Auxiliary TV, AVP ⇒ Auxiliary FV
- Section curve: Straight-line segmented ⇒ Prisms and Pyramids, Smooth curve ⇒ Cylinder, Cone (*Exception*- cutting plane including generators), Circle ⇒ Sphere

15.3 SECTIONS OF PRISMS AND CUBES

Example 15.1 A triangular prism with a base side of 50 mm and an axis length of 70 mm is resting on its rectangular face on the HP with the axis perpendicular to the VP. The prism is cut by a horizontal section plane passing through the axis. Draw FV and sectional TV of the prism.

Solution Refer Fig. 15.1.

1. Draw FV and TV of the prism as shown.
2. In FV, draw the section plane, parallel to *XY* and passing through the axis as shown. The direction of the arrowheads should be towards *XY* (since it is a first angle method of projection).
3. Locate POIs 1′, 2′, 3′ and 4′ in FV. 1′, 2′, 3′ and 4′ represent the intersections of the cutting plane with *a′c′*, *b′c′*, *b*1′*c*1′ and *a*1′*c*1′ respectively.
4. Project 1′, 2′, 3′ and 4′ to 1, 2, 3 and 4 on the corresponding edges in TV. Join 1–2–3–4 and hatch the area to indicate the section. 1–2–3–4 represents the true shape of the section (since the cutting plane is parallel to *XY*).

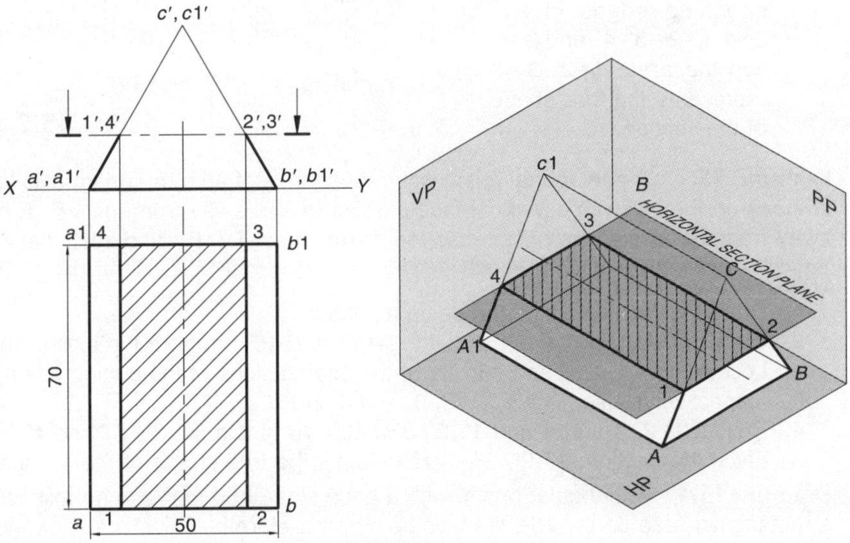

Fig. 15.1

Note: As indicated by the direction of arrowheads on the section plane, the lower half of the prism is viewed by the observer. The upper half is assumed to be removed. Hence, all the lines (i.e., $1'4'–c'c1'$ and $2'3'–c'c1'$) representing the upper half are drawn thin. In TV, line $c–c1$ need not be drawn. Only the retained part of the solid should be drawn thick.

Example 15.2 A square prism with a base side of 45 mm and an axis length of 90 mm is resting on its end on the HP. All the vertical faces are equally inclined to the VP. A vertical section plane passing through the midpoints of two adjacent sides of base cuts the prism. Draw TV and sectional FV of the prism.

Solution Refer Fig. 15.2.

1. Draw TV and FV of the prism as shown.
2. In TV, draw the section plane, parallel to *XY* and passing through the mid-points of *a*(*a*1)–*b*(*b*1) and *b*(*b*1)–*c*(*c*1), as shown.
3. Locate POIs 1, 2, 3 and 4 in TV at the intersections of the cutting plane with *ab*, *bc*, *b*1–*c*1 and *a*1–*b*1 respectively.
4. Project 1, 2, 3 and 4 to 1′, 2′, 3′ and 4′ on the corresponding edges in FV. Join 1′–2′–3′–4′ and section the area. 1′–2′–3′–4′ represents the true shape of the section.

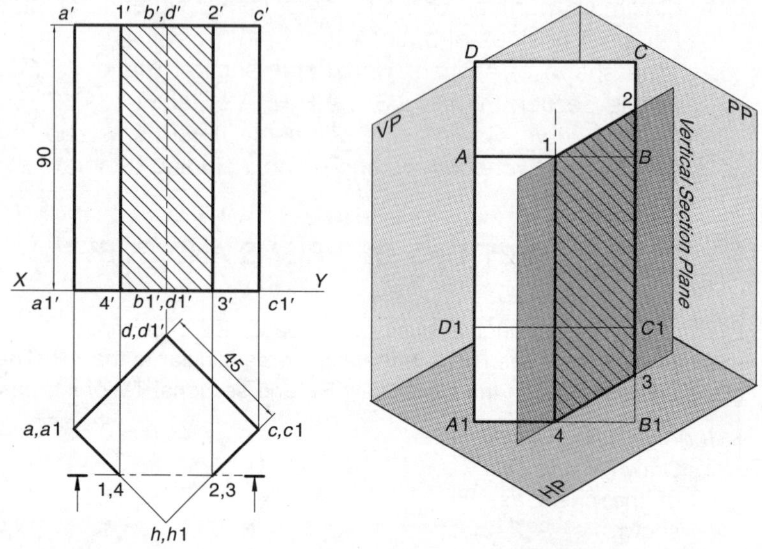

Fig. 15.2

Example 15.3 A pentagonal prism with a base side of 45 mm and an axis length of 90 mm is resting on its base on the HP with a vertical face parallel to and away from the VP. A profile section plane, 15 mm away from the axis of the prism, cuts the prism. Draw TV, FV and sectional SV of the prism.

Solution Refer Fig. 15.3.

1. Draw TV, FV and SV of the prism as shown.
2. Draw the section plane, parallel to *X*1*Y*1 and 15 mm from the axis of the prism.
3. Locate POIs 1, 2, 3 and 4 in TV at the intersections of the cutting plane with *ab*, *de*, *d*1*e*1 and *a*1*b*1 respectively. Also, locate 1′, 2′, 3′ and 4′ in FV.
4. Project 1, 2, 3 and 4 and 1′, 2′, 3′ and 4′ to obtain 1″, 2″, 3″ and 4″ in SV. Join 1″–2″–3″–4″ and hatch the section. 1″–2″–3″–4″ represents the true shape of the section.

Example 15.4 A triangular prism, with a base side of 50 mm and an axis length of 70 mm, is resting on a rectangular face on the HP, the axis being parallel to the VP. An AIP inclined at 45° to the HP cuts the prism. The cutting plane intersects the axis at a distance of 30 mm from one end of the prism. Draw FV, sectional TV and sectional SV of the prism.

Solution Refer Fig. 15.4.

1. Draw SV, FV and TV of the prism as shown.
2. In FV, draw the section plane, inclined at 45° to *XY* and intersecting the axis at 30 mm from an end of the prism, as shown.

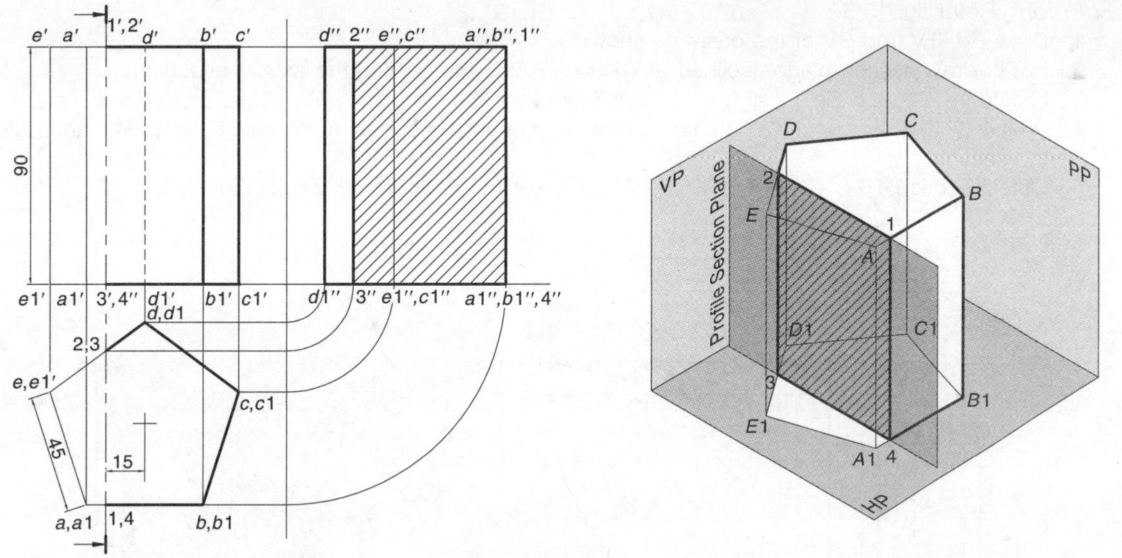

Fig. 15.3

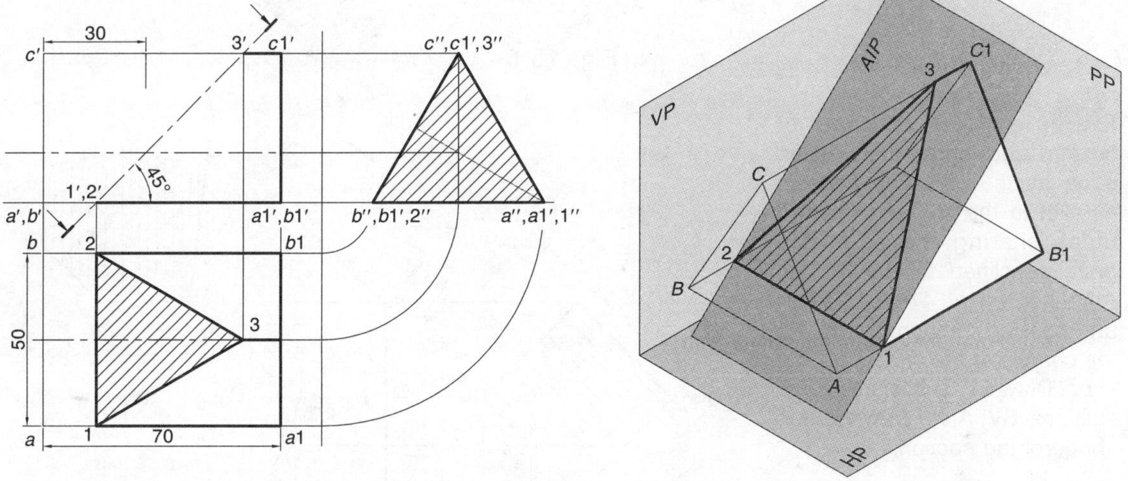

Fig. 15.4

3. Locate 1′, 2′ and 3′ in FV at the intersections of the cutting plane with *a′a*1′, *b′b*1′ and *c′c*1′ respectively.
4. Project 1′, 2′ and 3′ to 1, 2 and 3 on corresponding edges in TV. Join 1–2–3 and hatch the section.
5. Obtain section 1″–2″–3″ in SV by projecting POIs from FV and TV. 1″, 2″ and 3″ will obviously lie at *a*″, *b*″ and *c*″ respectively.

Example 15.5 A square prism, with a base side of 45 mm and an axis length of 90 mm, is resting on a longer edge on the HP. A rectangular face through that edge is inclined at 30° to the HP. The axis of the prism is perpendicular to the VP. An AVP inclined at 70° to the VP and passing through the midpoint of the axis cuts the prism. Draw TV, sectional FV and sectional SV of the prism.

Solution Refer fig. 15.5.

1. Draw FV, TV and SV of the prism as shown.
2. In TV, draw section plane, inclined at 70° to *XY* and intersecting the axis at midpoint.
3. Locate 1, 2, 3, etc., in TV at the intersections of the cutting plane with edges *ab*, *cb*, *c*–*c*1, etc.
4. Project 1, 2, 3, etc., to 1′, 2′, 3′, etc., on the corresponding edges in FV. Join these points and hatch the section.
5. Obtain section 1″–2″–3″–4″–5″–6″ in SV by projecting POIs from FV and TV.

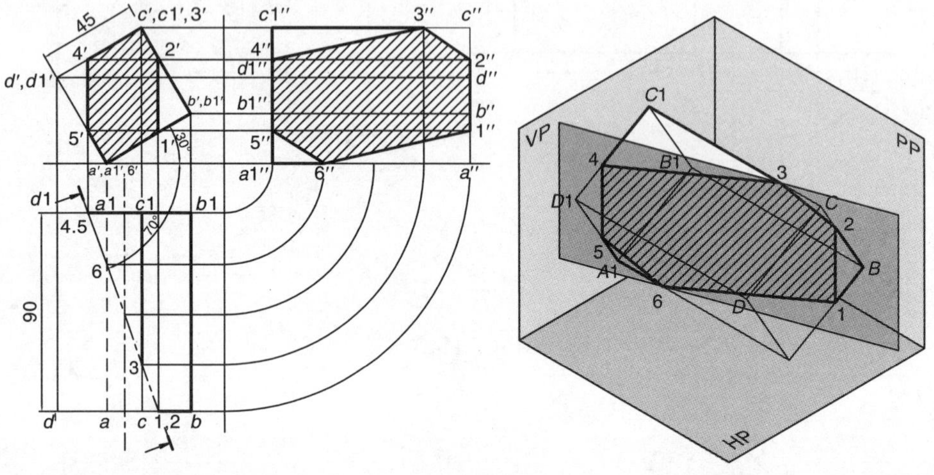

Fig. 15.5

Example 15.6 A cube of 50 mm side length rests on an edge on the HP. The edge is parallel to the VP and the two faces sharing the edge are equally inclined to the HP. An AIP, inclined at 47° to the HP and passing through one of the top corners of the cube, cuts the cube. Draw FV, sectional TV and sectional SV. Also, draw the true shape of the section.

Solution Refer Fig. 15.6.

1. Draw SV, FV and TV of the cube as shown.
2. In FV, draw the section plane passing through *c*1′ and inclined at 47° to *XY*.
3. Locate 1′, 2′, 3′, 4′ and 5′ in FV at the intersections of the cutting plane with the edges. (1′ coincides with *c*1′.)

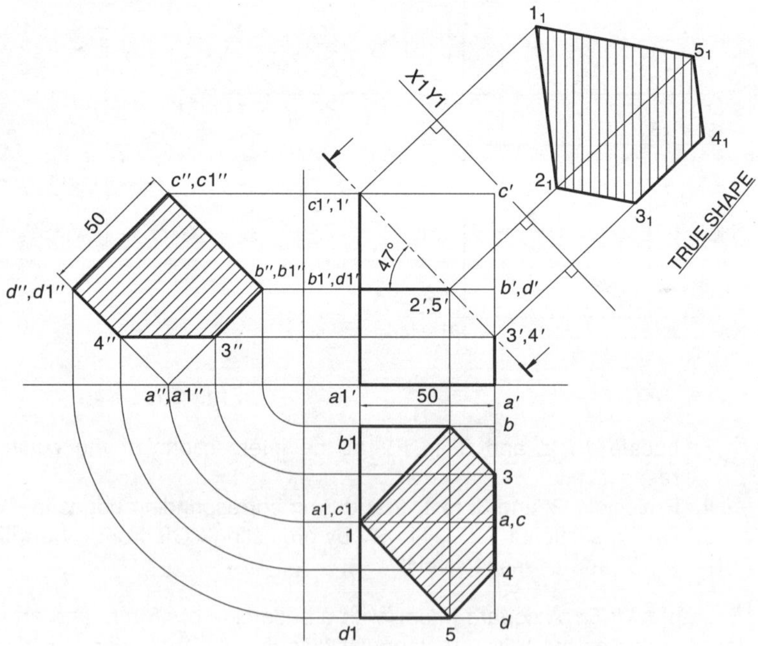

Fig. 15.6

4. Project 2′ and 5′ to 2 and 5 on the corresponding edges in TV. Project 1′, 3′ and 4′ to 1″, 3″ and 4″ on the corresponding edges in SV. (1″ coincides with *c*1″.)
5. Project 1″, 3″ and 4″ to 1, 3 and 4 in TV. (1 coincides with *c*1.) Join 1–2–3–4–5 and hatch the area.
6. Project 2 and 5 to 2″ and 5″ in SV. (2 and 5 coincide with *b*″ (*b*1″) and *d*″ (*d*1″) respectively.) Join 1″–2″–3″–4″–5″ and hatch the area.
7. To draw the true shape of the section, draw *X*1*Y*1 parallel to the cutting plane. Project 1′, 2′, 3′, 4′ and 5′ on *X*1*Y*1 and draw auxiliary view 1_1–2_1–3_1–4_1–5_1. (Distances of 1_1, 2_1, 3_1, 4_1 and 5_1 from *X*1*Y*1 = Distances of 1, 2, 3, 4 and 5 from *XY*.)

Example 15.7 A triangular prism with a base side of 50 mm and a 70 mm height stands on its base on the HP with a rectangular face perpendicular to the VP. It is cut by different AIPs such that the true shape of the section is

(i) an isosceles triangle of 42 mm base and 38 mm height
(ii) an isosceles triangle of maximum size
(iii) a trapezium of parallel sides of 50 mm and 22 mm

Locate the cutting plane and the draw FV, TV and the true shape of the section in each case.

Solution For the true shape of the section to be a triangle, the section plane must cut 3 edges of the prism. Similarly, the section plane must cut 4 edges for the section to be trapezium.
Draw TV and FV of the prism as shown in Fig. 15.7.

Case (i): *True shape: Isosceles triangle of* 42 mm *base and* 38 mm *height*
For the isosceles triangle of given size, the section plane must cut two adjacent edges of the top at points 42 mm apart. The third point can be located on the vertical edge (emerging from the intersection of the two top edges) such that the distance of that point from the line joining the first two points will be equal to the altitude of the triangle.

1. In TV, locate 1 and 2 such that 1–2 = 42 mm. Project 1 and 2 to 1′(2′) in FV.
2. With 1′(2′) as a centre and radius = 38 mm, cut an arc on the vertical edge at 3′. Draw the cutting plane *A–A* through 1′(2′)–3′.
3. Project 1′, 2′ and 3′ on the cutting plane *A–A* to obtain auxiliary view 1–2–3 revealing true shape of the section.

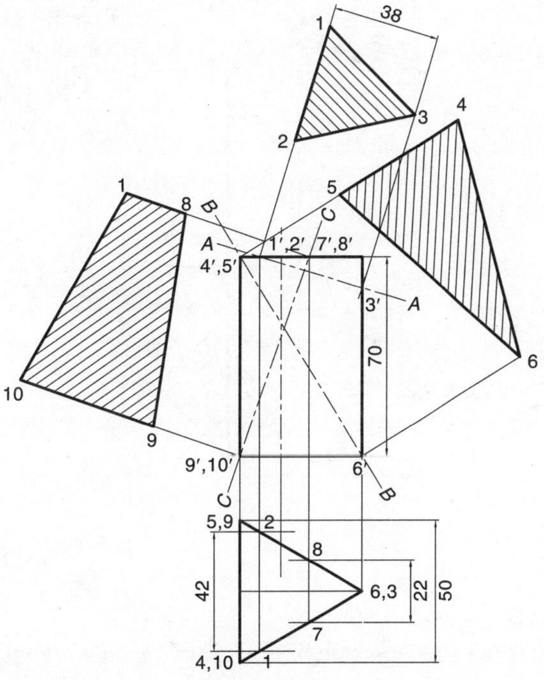

Fig. 15.7

Case (ii): *True shape: Isosceles triangle of maximum size*
For the maximum size of the isosceles triangle, the cutting plane must pass through a top edge and the base corner opposite to that edge.

1. Draw the cutting plane *B–B* through 4′(5′)–6′.
2. Project 4′, 5′ and 6′ on the cutting plane *B–B* to obtain the auxiliary view 4–5–6, indicating the true shape of the section.

Case (iii): *True shape: Trapezium of parallel sides 50 mm and 22 mm*
For trapezium, the cutting plane must cut both the ends of the prism. The distance between the intersecting points on each face should be equal to the parallel side of the trapezium. In this case, one of the parallel sides is 50 mm long. Hence, the cutting plane must pass through a base edge.

1. In TV, locate 7 and 8 on two adjacent sides such that 7–8 = 50 mm.
2. Project 7 and 8 to 7′(8′) in FV.
3. Draw the cutting plane *C–C* through 7′ (8′)–9′ (10′). Project 7′ (8′) and 9′ (10′) on *C–C* and obtain the true shape of the section 7–8–9–10.

Example 15.8 A square prism of 40 mm base side and 75 mm axis length is resting on its base on the HP with the faces equally inclined to the VP. It is cut by different AIPs such that the true shape of the section is

(i) an equilateral triangle of maximum size
(ii) an isosceles triangle of maximum size
(iii) an equilateral triangle of 40 mm side
(iv) an isosceles triangle of 30 mm base and 60 mm altitude

Draw the cutting plane, FV, sectional TV and true shape of the section in each case.

Solution For the true shape of the section to be a triangle, the section plane must cut 3 edges of the prism.

Draw TV and FV of the prism as shown in Fig. 15.8.

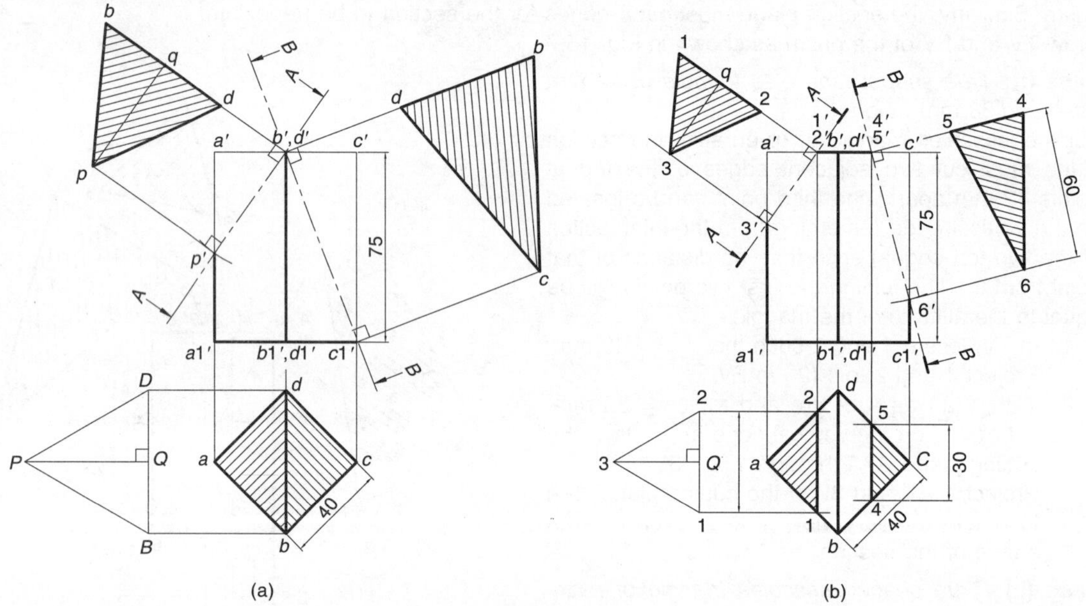

Fig. 15.8

Refer Fig. 15.8(a).

Case (i): *True shape: Equilateral triangle of maximum size.*

If the true shape of the section is an equilateral triangle of maximum possible size, the section plane must pass through two opposite corners of an end face. Obviously, the equilateral triangle will have a side equal to the distance between these corners.

1. Draw the equilateral triangle *BDP* such that *BD* = *bd*. Obtain the height *PQ* of the triangle.
2. Locate *p*′ on *a*′–*a*1′ such that *b*′(*d*′)–*p*′ = *PQ*. Draw the cutting plane *A–A* through *b*′(*d*′)–*p*′.
3. In TV, join *bd*. *abd* represents the hatched section area.
4. Project *b*′, *d*′ and *p*′ on the cutting plane *A–A* to obtain auxiliary TV *bdp*. It represents the true shape of the section.

Case (ii): *True shape: Isosceles triangle of maximum size.*
For the maximum size of the isosceles triangle, the base should be equal to the diagonal of the top of the prism and the altitude should be equal to the shortest distance between that diagonal and the opposite corner of the base.

1. Draw the cutting plane *B–B* through *b*′(*d*′)–*c*1′.
2. In TV, *bdc* represents the hatched section area.
3. Project *b*′, *d*′ and *c*1′ on the cutting plane *B–B* to obtain auxiliary TV *bdc* indicating the true shape of the section.

Refer Fig. 15.8(b).

Case (iii): *True shape: Equilateral triangle of 40 mm side.*
For an equilateral triangle of 40 mm side, the section plane must cut two adjacent edges of the top at the points 40 mm apart. The third point can be located on the vertical edge (emerging from the intersection of the two top edges) such that the distance of that point from the line joining the first two points will be equal to the altitude of the triangle.

1. In TV, locate 1 and 2 on *ab* and *ad* respectively such that 1–2 = 40 mm. Project 1 and 2 to 1′(2′) in FV.
2. Draw an equilateral triangle at 1–2–3 of 40 mm side as shown. Obtain the altitude 3–*Q* of the triangle.
3. With 1′(2′) as a centre and radius = 3–*Q*, cut an arc on *a*′–*a*1′ at 3′. Draw the cutting plane *A–A* through 1′(2′)–3′.
4. In TV, join 1–2. 1–2–*a* represents the hatched section area.
5. Project 1′, 2′ and 3′ on the cutting plane *A–A* to obtain auxiliary TV 1–2–3. It represents the true shape of the section.

Case (iv): *True shape: Isosceles triangle of 30 mm base and 60 mm altitude.*
For the given isosceles triangle, the section plane must cut two adjacent edges of the top at the points 30 mm apart. The third point can be located on the vertical edge in a similar way explained in Case (iii) above.

1. Locate 4 and 5 on *bc* and *cd* respectively such that 4–5 = 30 mm. Project 4 and 5 to 4′(5′) in FV.
2. With 4′(5′) as a centre and radius = 60 mm, cut an arc on *c*′–*c*1′ at 6′. Draw the cutting plane *B–B* through 4′(5′)–6′.
3. In TV, join 4–5. 4–5–6 represents the hatched section area.
4. Project 4′, 5′ and 6′ on the cutting plane *B–B* to obtain true shape 4–5–6.

Example 15.9 A square prism, base side 40 mm and a 75 mm axis length rests on its base on the HP with all the sides of the base equally inclined to the VP. Different AIPs cut the prism in such way that the true shape of the section is
(i) a rhombus of maximum size
(ii) a rhombus of longest diagonal 65 mm
(iii) a trapezium of parallel sides 50 mm and 15 mm
(iv) a pentagon of 25 mm base side and maximum altitude
Locate the cutting plane and draw FV and the true shape of the section in each case.

Solution The section plane must cut 4 edges of the prism for a quadrilateral true shape and 5 edges for a pentagonal true shape of the section.
Refer Fig. 15.9.
Draw TV and FV of the prism.

Case (i): *True shape: Rhombus of maximum size*
For the rhombus of maximum size, the cutting plane must pass through two opposite corners of the end faces. The longest diagonal of the rhombus will be equal to the shortest distance between these points, i.e., the solid diagonal of the prism. The shortest diagonal will, always, be equal to the diagonal of the end face.

1. Draw the cutting plane *A–A* through 1′–3′.
2. Locate 2′(4′) at the intersections of the cutting plane with the intermediate edges.
3. Locate 1, 2, 3 and 4 in TV at the corners.
4. Project 1′, 2′, 3′ and 4′ on the cutting plane *A–A* to obtain true shape of the section 1–2–3–4.

Case (ii): *True shape: Rhombus of longest diagonal 65 mm*

The cutting plane, in this case, will cut two opposite vertical edges such that the distance between the intersecting points will be 65 mm.

1. With any suitable point on an extreme vertical edge, say 5′, as a centre and radius = 65 mm, cut an arc at 7′ on another extreme vertical edge.
2. Draw the cutting plane *B–B* through 5′–7′. Locate 6′ (8′) at the intersections of the cutting plane with the intermediate vertical edges.

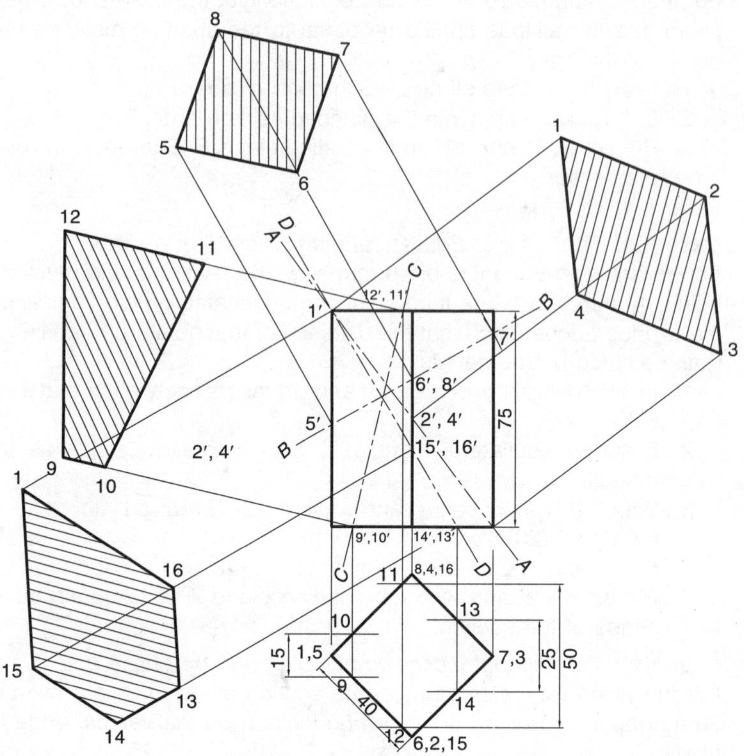

Fig. 15.9

3. In TV, 5, 6, 7 and 8 will be seen at the corners.
4. Obtain the true shape of the section 5–6–7–8 in a similar way explained in Case (i) above.

Case (iii): *True shape: Trapezium of parallel sides 50 mm and 15 mm*

The cutting plane must cut both the ends of the prism on one side of the axis. The lines joining the intersecting points on the corresponding faces will represent parallel sides of the trapezium.

1. In TV, locate 9, 10, 11 and 12 on two adjacent sides such that 9–10 = 15 mm and 11–12 = 50 mm.
2. Project 9, 10, 11 and 12 to 9′, 10′, 11′ and 12′. 9′ and 10′ lie on the bottom end while 11′ and 12′ lie on the top end.
3. Draw the cutting plane *C–C* through 9′ (10′)–12′(11′) and obtain the true shape of the section, 9–10–11–12, as explained in case (i) above.

Case (iv): *True shape: Pentagon of 25 mm base side and maximum altitude*

The cutting plane must pass through two edges of the base, two vertical edges and a corner of the top. The line joining the two intersecting points on the base will decide the base of the pentagon. The shortest distance between this line and the top corner will represent the altitude of the pentagon.

1. In TV, locate 13 and 14 on two adjacent sides such that 13–14 = 25 mm.
2. Project 13 and 14 to 14′(13′) on the bottom end of the prism.
3. Draw the cutting plane *D–D* through 14′(13′)–1′. Locate 15′(16′) at the intersections of the cutting plane and the vertical edges.
4. Mark 15 and 16 in TV. Obtain the true shape of the section 13–14–15–1–16 as explained earlier.

Example 15.10 A cube of 70 mm long edges has its vertical faces equally inclined to the VP. It is cut by an AIP in such a way that the true shape of the cut part is a regular hexagon. Determine the inclination of the cutting plane with the HP. Draw FV, sectional TV and true shape of the section.

Solution Refer Fig. 15.10.

1. Draw TV and FV of the cube as shown.
   As the true shape of the section is a hexagon, the cutting plane must cut the prism at 6 points. Obviously, the cutting plane will cut two edges of the top, two edges of the base and two vertical edges. The POIs at two vertical edges will be farthest from each other. These points will represent the two opposite corners of the hexagon and the distance between them will be equal to $b(b1)$–$d(d1)$.
2. Draw a line 3–6 = $b(b1)$–$d(d1)$. Draw a circle with 3–6 as a diameter. Inscribe a hexagon 1–2–3–4–5–6 in it as shown. Measure the distance between 1–2 and 4–5, i.e., PQ.
3. In FV, locate 3′ at the midpoint of $b'(d')$–$b1'(d1')$. With 3′ as a centre and radius = ½(PQ), cut arcs on $a'b'$ and $b1'c1'$ to locate 1′ and 4′ respectively. Join 1′–4′ for the required cutting plane. Measure θ.
4. Draw $X1Y1$ parallel to 1′–4′. Redraw hexagon 1–2–3–4–5–6 as 1_1–2_1–3_1–4_1–5_1–6_1 such that pq is parallel to $X1Y1$. Project all the corners of the hexagon in FV. 2′, 6′ and 5′ will coincide with 1′, 3′ and 4′ respectively.
5. Project 1′, 2′, 3′, etc., to 1, 2, 3, etc., on the corresponding edges in TV to obtain the section. 3 and 6 will coincide with $d(d1)$ and $b(b1)$ respectively.

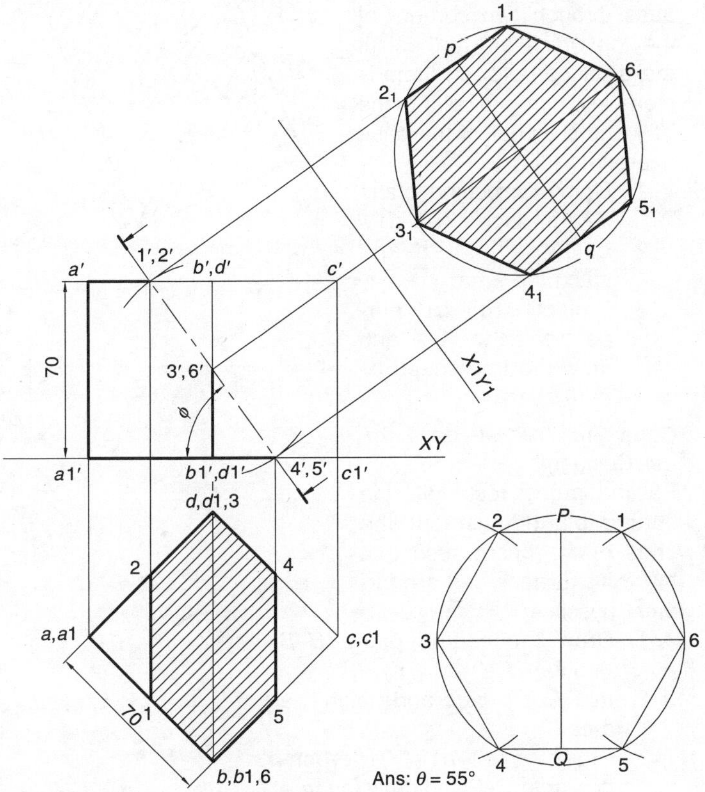

Fig. 15.10

> **Note:** The points 1′, 2′, 3′, 4′, 5′ and 6′ will be midpoints of the respective edges. The cutting plane is perpendicular to body diagonal $a1'$–c'.

Example 15.11 A hexagonal prism with end faces of 35 mm side and an 80 mm height is resting on one of its ends on the HP with two opposite rectangular faces parallel to the VP. Two AIPs cut it in such a way that the true shape of the section is

(i) a largest isosceles triangle (ii) a largest rectangle

Show the prism with the cutting planes and draw its sectional plan. Also, draw the true shapes of the sections.

Solution Refer Fig. 15.11.
Draw TV and FV of the prism as shown.

Case (i): *True shape: Largest Isosceles Triangle*

For the largest isosceles triangle, the cutting plane must pass through two corners of the top which are farthest (if the distance between them is measured perpendicular to the VP) and a corner of the base nearest to them.

1. Draw the cutting plane *A–A* through *c*′(*e*′)–*d*1′.
2. In TV, join *ced* and hatch the area.
3. Project *c*′(*e*′)–*d*1′ perpendicular to *A–A* and draw the true shape *c–e–d*1.

Case (ii): *True shape: Largest Rectangle*

For the largest rectangle, the cutting plane must cut the ends of the prism such that the POIs at each end are farthest possible.

1. Draw the cutting plane *B–B* through *c*′(*e*′)–*b*1′(*f*1′).
2. In TV, join *cefb* and hatch the area.
3. Project *c*′(*e*′)–*b*1′(*f*1′) perpendicular to *B–B* and draw the true shape *c–e–f*1–*b*1 as shown.

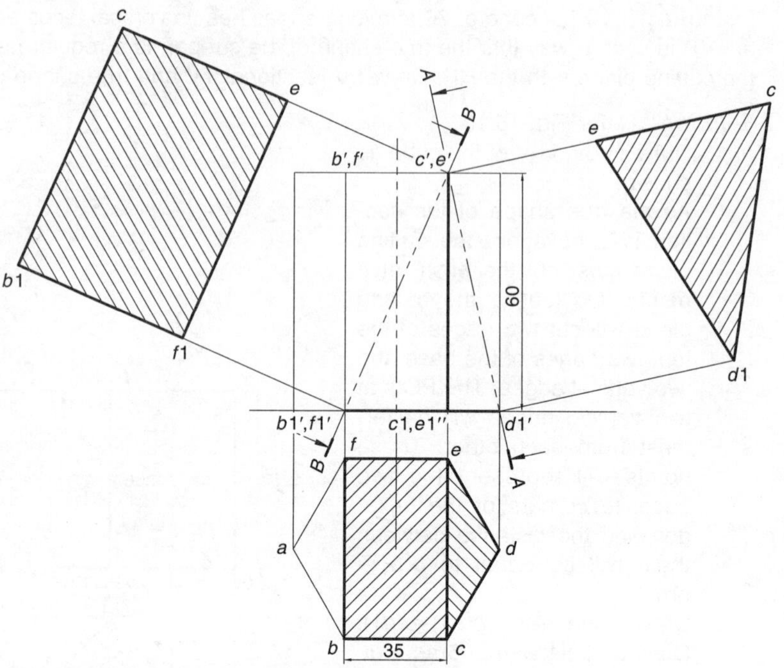

Fig. 15.11

Example 15.12 A hexagonal prism, having base parallel to the HP, is cut by an AIP such that the true shape of the section is a trapezium of maximum size. If the longest parallel side of the trapezium is 60 mm and the distance between two parallel sides is 75 mm, draw FV and sectional TV of the prism. Also, draw an auxiliary view showing the true shape of the section. What will be the dimensions of the prism? What will be the inclination of the cutting plane with the HP?

Solution The largest trapezium is obtained when the cutting plane passes through the farthest corners

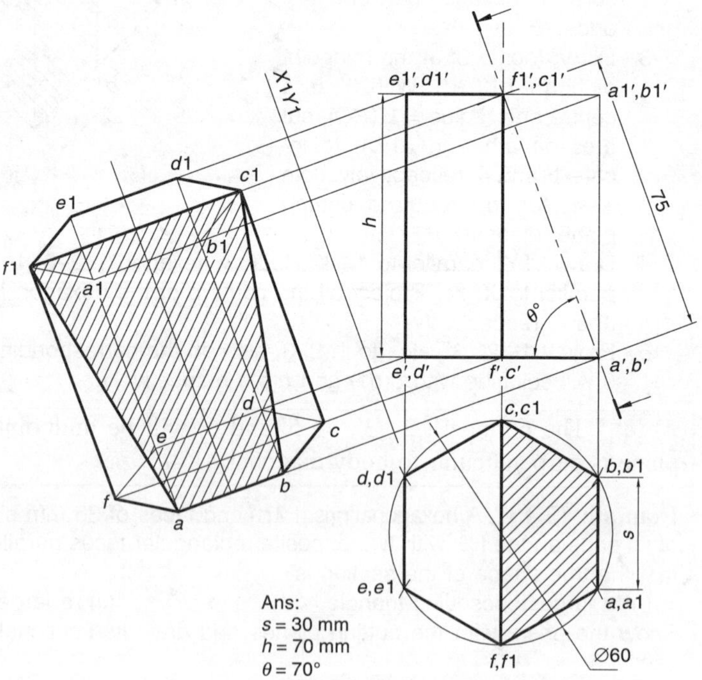

Fig. 15.12

of the top and a side of the base. Obviously, the parallel sides of the trapezium will be equal to the distance between the farthest top corners and the side of base. In this problem, to locate the AIP, two opposite vertical faces should be drawn perpendicular to the VP.

Refer Fig. 15.12.

1. Draw *c*(*c*1)–*f*(*f*1) = 60 mm perpendicular to *XY*. Draw a circle with *c*(*c*1)–*f*(*f*1) as a diameter. Inscribe a hexagon *a*(*a*1)–*b*(*b*1)–*c*(*c*1)–*d*(*d*1)–*e*(*e*1)–*f*(*f*1) inside the circle to represent TV of the prism. Measure *a*(*a*1)–*b*(*b*1) for the base side of the prism.
2. Project TV to obtain FV *a*′(*b*′)–*f*′(*c*′)–*e*′(*d*′) of the base of the prism. Draw the axis through *f*′(*c*′). With *a*′(*b*′) as a centre and radius = 75 mm, cut an arc on axis at *f*1′(*c*1′). Draw the top face *a*1′(*b*1′)–*f*1′(*c*1′)–*e*1′(*d*1′) and complete FV of the prism. Measure *a*′(*b*′)–*a*1′(*b*1′) for the height of the prism.
3. Draw the cutting plane through *a*′(*b*′)–*f*1′(*c*1′). Measure θ.
4. In TV, join *c*(*c*1)–*f*(*f*1) and hatch the area.
5. Draw *X*1*Y*1 parallel to the cutting plane and obtain the auxiliary TV showing the true shape of the section.

REMEMBER THE FOLLOWING

- If a cutting plane cuts 6 edges of a cube (i.e., 2 edges of top, 2 vertical edges and 2 edges of base) at their midpoints, the section will be a regular hexagon.

15.4 SECTIONS OF PYRAMIDS AND TETRAHEDRON

Example 15.13 A triangular pyramid with a base side of 50 mm and a slant height of 70 mm, rests on the base on the HP with a side of base perpendicular to the VP. It is cut by an AIP inclined at 30° to the HP and bisecting the axis and a profile section plane intersecting the AIP at the edge of the pyramid parallel to the VP. Draw FV, sectional TV and sectional SV.

Solution Refer Fig. 15.13.

1. Draw TV, FV and SV of the pyramid.
2. In FV, draw the cutting plane inclined at 30° to *XY* and passing through the midpoint of the axis. Locate POIs 1′, 2′ and 3′ as shown. Through 1′, draw a vertical cutting plane cutting the base at 4′ and 5′.
3. Project 1′, 2′, 3′, 4′ and 5′ to 1, 2, 3, 4 and 5 in FV and 1″, 2″, 3″, 4″ and 5″ in SV on the corresponding edges. (4″ and 5″ are projected from TV.). Join 1–2–3, 1″–2″–3″ and 1″–4″–5″ and hatch the areas.

Example 15.14 A square pyramid with a base side of 40 mm and a length of axis of 70 mm, has its axis parallel to both the RPs and the base edges equally inclined to both the RPs. Two cutting planes, an AIP and a vertical section plane, cut it. The AIP slopes towards the apex at 45° and passes through the midpoint of the axes. The vertical section plane is 17 mm away from the axis on the side opposite to the VP. Draw the sectional FV, sectional TV and sectional SV.

Solution Refer Fig. 15.14.

1. Draw SV, FV and TV of the pyramid.
2. In FV, draw cutting plane inclined at 45° to *XY*, sloping towards the apex and bisecting the axis. Locate POIs 1′, 2′, 3′ and 4′ as shown.
3. In TV, draw cutting plane parallel to *XY*, 17 mm away from the axis and nearer to observer. Locate POIs 5, 6 and 7.

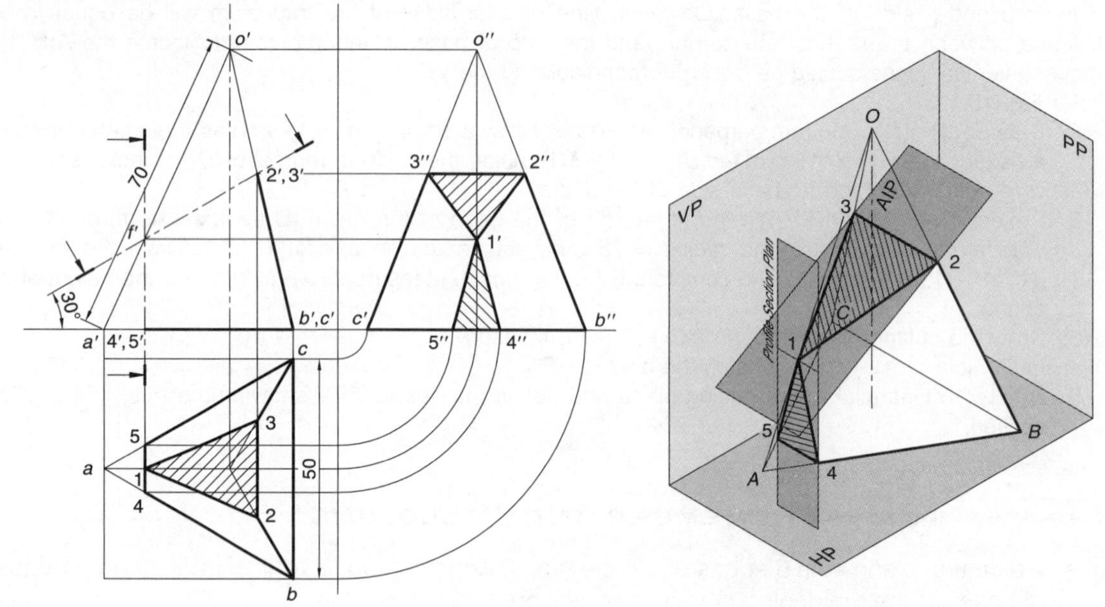

Fig. 15.13

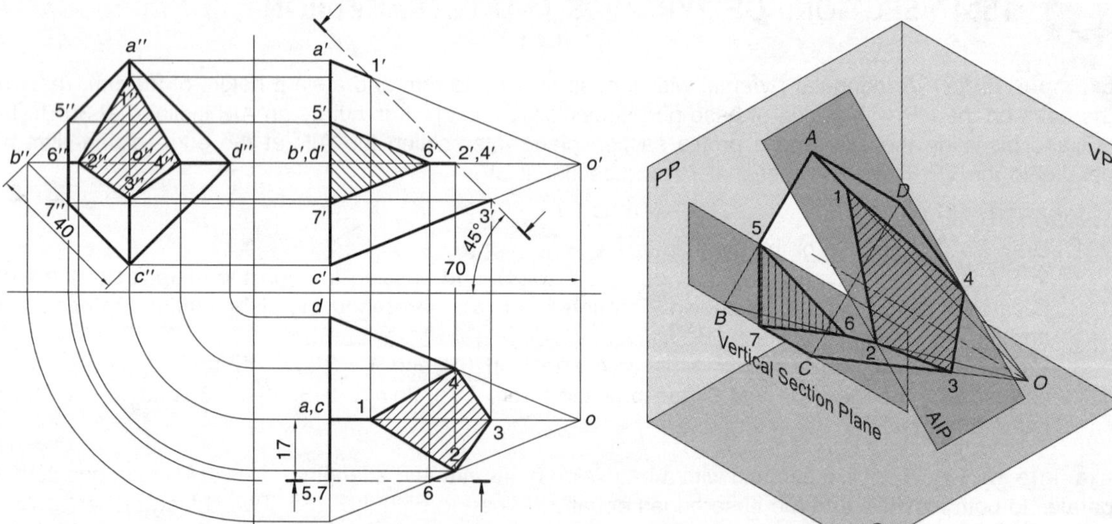

Fig. 15.14

4. Project 1′, 2′, 3′ and 4′ to 1, 2, 3, 4 in TV and 1″, 2″, 3″ and 4″ in SV on the corresponding edges. (2″ and 4″ are projected from TV.) Join 1–2–3–4 and 1″–2″–3″–4″ and section the areas.
5. Project 5 and 7 to 5″ and 7″ in SV and then to 5′ and 7′ in FV. Project 6 to 6′ in FV. Join 5′–6′–7′ and section the area.

Example 15.15 A tetrahedron of side 50 mm rests on a face on the HP. One of the edges other than those on the HP is parallel to the VP. Different section planes cut the tetrahedron in such a way that the true shape of the section is

(i) an isosceles triangle of base 18 mm and maximum height
(ii) an isosceles triangle of maximum base and 37 mm, height
(iii) an equilateral triangle of 18 mm side.

Draw FV and TV and locate the cutting planes. Also, draw true shape of the section in each case.

Solution For the true shape of the section to be a triangle, the section plane must cut 3 edges of the tetrahedron.

Draw TV and FV of the tetrahedron as shown in Fig. 15.15.

Case (i): *True shape: Isosceles triangle of 18 mm base and maximum height*

Solution For isosceles triangle of 18 mm base, the section plane must cut two adjacent edges of base at the points, 18 mm apart. For maximum altitude, the section plane must pass through the apex.

1. In TV, locate 1 and 2 on two adjacent sides such that 1–2 = 18 mm. Project 1 and 2 to 1′(2′) in FV.
2. In FV, mark 3′ at the apex. Draw the cutting plane *A–A* through 1′(2′)–3′.
3. Project 1′, 2′ and 3′ on the cutting plane *A–A* to obtain the true shape 1–2–3.

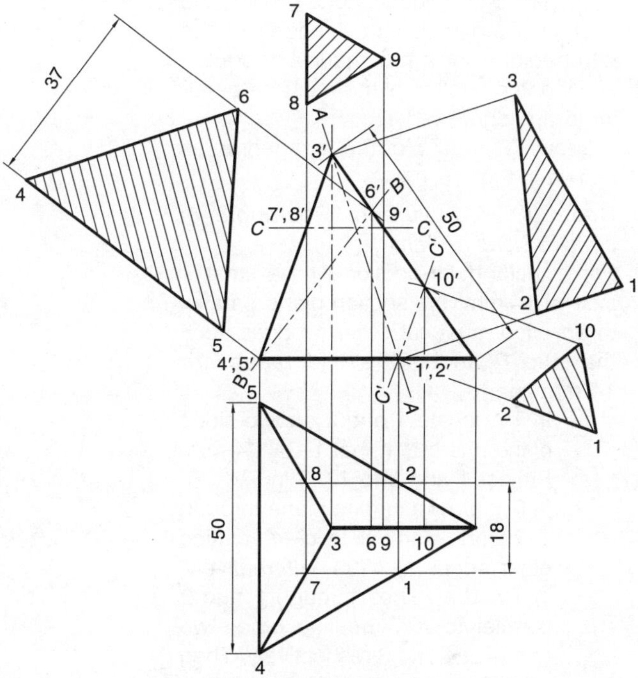

Fig. 15.15

Case (ii): *True shape: Isosceles triangle of maximum base and height 37 mm*

For a maximum base of the isosceles triangle, the cutting plane must pass through a base edge. For height of the triangle to be 37 mm, the cutting plane must pass through a point on the opposite edge such that the distance of that point from the base edge is equal to 37 mm.

1. In FV, locate 4′(5′) at the base corner. With 4′(5′) as a centre and radius = 37 mm, cut an arc on the opposite edge at 6′.
2. Draw the cutting plane *B–B* through 4′(5′)–6′.
3. Project 4′, 5′ and 6′ on the cutting plane *B–B* to obtain the true shape 4–5–6.

Case (iii) *True shape: Equilateral triangle of side 18 mm*

For an equilateral triangle, the cutting plane must cut parallel to any triangular face.

1. In TV, locate 7 and 8 such that 7–8 = 18 mm. Project 7 and 8 to 7′ (8′) in FV.
2. Through 7′ (8′), draw a cutting plane *C–C* parallel to base face intersecting other edge at 9′.
3. Project 7′ (8′) and 9′ on the cutting plane *C–C* to obtain the true shape of the section 7–8–9.

Note: Another cutting plane *C′–C′* through 1′(2′) and parallel to the face 3′–4′(5′) will also give section as an equilateral triangle, i.e., 1–2–10.

Example 15.16 A tetrahedron of 50 mm side is resting on a face on the HP with a side of the base face perpendicular to the VP. Different cutting planes cut the tetrahedron in such a way that the true shape of the section is

(i) a rectangle with smaller sides of 14 mm,
(ii) a square of possible size
(iii) a trapezium with parallel sides of 25 mm and 14 mm

Draw FV and TV and locate the cutting planes. Also, draw the true shape of the section in each case.

Solution For a quadrilateral section, the section plane must cut 4 edges of the tetrahedron. For a rectangular or square section, the section plane must be parallel to an edge.

Draw TV and FV of the tetrahedron as shown in Fig. 15.16.

Case (i): *True shape: Rectangle of smaller sides 14 mm*

For a rectangular section with a smaller side of 14 mm, the section plane parallel to an edge must cut other 4 edges such that the POIs on the two faces are 14 mm apart.

1. In TV, locate 1 and 2 on two sides of the base such that 1–2 = 14 mm. Project 1 and 2 to 1′(2′) in FV.
2. In FV, draw a cutting plane through 1′(2′) and parallel to *o′–c′*, cutting other edges at 4′(3′). *Alternatively,* in TV, draw lines through 1 and 2 parallel to *XY*, meeting other two edges at 4 and 3 respectively. Then project 4 and 3 to 4′(3′) in FV. The line 1′(2′)–4′(3′) will be parallel to *o′c′*.
3. Draw the cutting plane *A–A* through 1′(2′)–4′(3′).
4. Project 1′, 2′, 3′ and 4′ on the cutting plane *A–A* to obtain true shape 1–2–3–4.

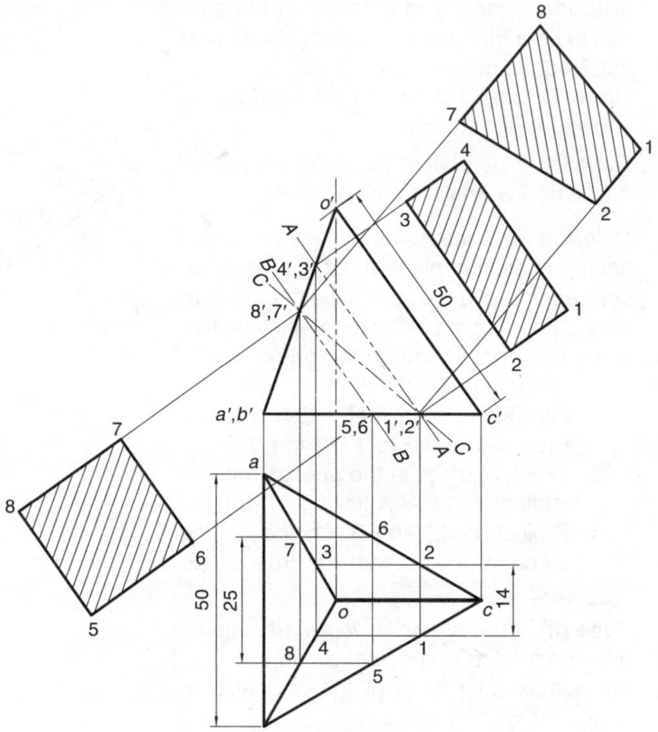

Fig. 15.16

Case (ii): *True shape: Square of possible size*

For a square shape of the section, the cutting plane parallel to an edge must cut other 4 edges such that each of the POIs is at equal distance from the nearest two. Obviously, the cutting plane must pass through the midpoints of the edges. The side of the square will be equal to half of the edge of the tetrahedron.

1. In TV, locate 5, 6, 7 and 8 at the midpoints of respective edges. Project 5, 6, 7 and 8 to 5′(6′) and 8′(7′) on the corresponding edges in FV.
2. Draw the cutting plane *B–B* through 5′(6′)–8′(7′). Note that, 5′(6′) and 8′(7′) are the midpoints of respective edges in FV and the cutting plane *B–B* is parallel to *o′–c′*.
3. Project 5′, 6′, 7′ and 8′ on the cutting plane *B–B* to obtain the square true shape 5–6–7–8.

Case (iii): *True shape: Trapezium with parallel sides of 25 mm and 14 mm*

For a trapezium of given size, the section plane must cut the base face at the points 14 mm apart and the other face at the points 25 mm apart.

1. In TV, locate 1 and 2 and 7 and 8 such that 1–2 = 14 mm and 7–8 = 25 mm. Project 1, 2, 7 and 8 to 1′(2′) and 8′(7′) in FV.
2. Draw a cutting plane *C–C* through 1′(2′)–8′(7′).
3. Project 1′(2′) and 8′(7′) on the cutting plane *C–C* to obtain the true shape of the section 1–2–7–8.

Remember the Following

- If a cutting plane is parallel to a face of the tetrahedron, the section will be an equilateral triangle.
- If a cutting plane is parallel to a side of the tetrahedron, the section will be a rectangle.
- If a cutting plane is parallel to a side of the tetrahedron and passes through the midpoints of other edges, the section will be a square of side equal to half of the side of the tetrahedron.

Example 15.17 A square pyramid with a base side of 45 mm and an axis length of 70 mm is resting on the base on the HP with the base sides equally inclined to the VP. It is cut by the different cutting planes such that the true shape of the section is

(i) an equilateral triangle of maximum possible size
(ii) an equilateral triangle of 30 mm side
(iii) a kite of smallest diagonal 35 mm and maximum possible longest diagonal
(iv) a pentagon of 30 mm base and 50 mm height

Draw FV and TV and the cutting planes. Also, draw the true shape of the section in each case.

Solution For the true shape to be a triangle, kite or pentagon, the cutting plane must cut 3, 4 or 5 edges of the pyramid.

Draw TV and FV of the pyramid as shown in Fig. 15.17.

Case (i): *True shape: Equilateral triangle of maximum possible size*

For the maximum size of an equilateral triangle, the section plane must cut the two farthest corners of the base. The third point, equidistant from the two corners, will lie on the opposite slant edge.

1. In TV, locate 1 and 2 at two opposite base corners. Draw equilateral triangle *ABC* such that *AB* is equal and parallel to 1–2. *CD* represents the height of the triangle.
2. Mark 1′(2′) in FV. With 1′(2′) as a centre and radius = *CD*, cut an arc on the slant edge at 3′.
3. Draw the cutting plane *A–A* through 1′(2′)–3′.
4. Project 1′, 2′ and 3′ on the cutting plane *A–A* to obtain the true shape 1–2–3.

Case (ii): *True shape: Equilateral triangle of 30 mm side*

For the equilateral triangle of 30 mm side, the section plane must cut two base edges at points 30 mm apart. The third point will be at a distance equal to the altitude of the triangle from the line joining the first two points.

1. In TV, locate 4 and 5 at two base sides such that 4–5 = 30 mm. Draw the equilateral triangle *MNO* such that *MN* is equal and parallel to 4–5. *OP* represents the height of the triangle.
2. Project 4 and 5 to 4′(5′) in FV. With 4′(5′) as a centre and radius = *OP*, cut an arc on the slant edge at 6′.
3. Draw the cutting plane *B–B* through 4′(5′)–6′.
4. Project 4′, 5′ and 6′ on the cutting plane *B–B* to obtain the true shape 4–5–6.

Case (iii): *True shape: Kite with smallest diagonal of 35 mm and maximum possible longest diagonal*

For a kite, the section plane must cut all the four slant edges of the pyramid. The lines joining POIs on two opposite edges will be equal to the diagonals of the kite. For the maximum possible longest diagonal, the cutting plane must pass through a base corner.

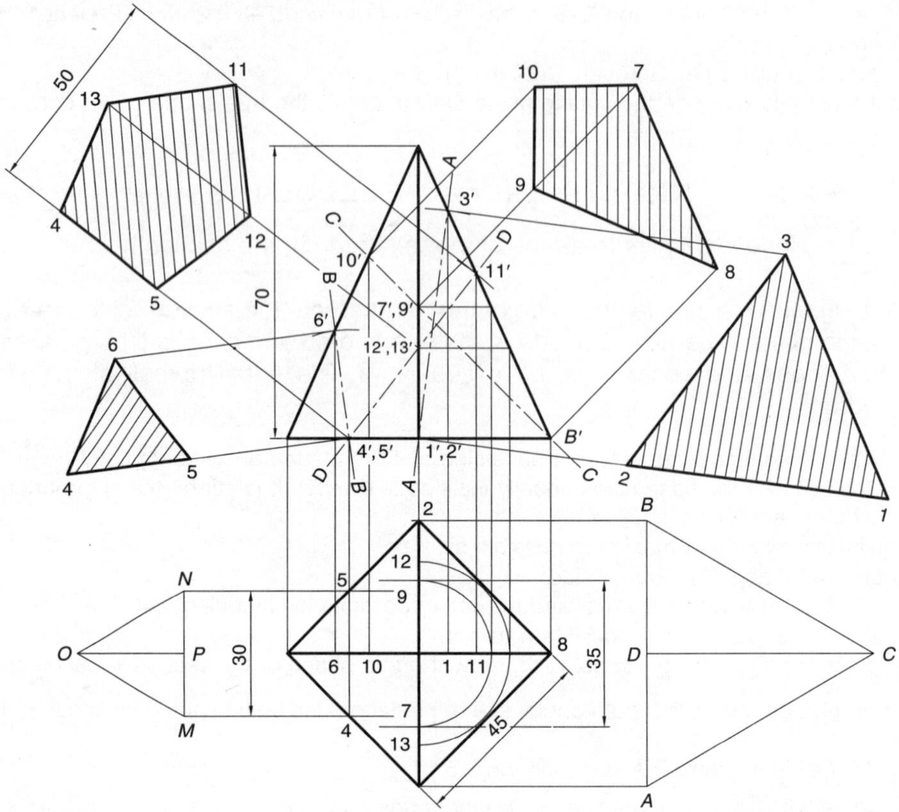

Fig. 15.17

1. In TV, locate 7 and 9 on the slant edges on either side of and equidistant from the axis such that 7–9 = 35 mm. Project 7 and 9 to 7′ and 9′ in FV as shown.
2. In FV, mark 8′ at a base corner. Draw a cutting plane *C–C* through 8′–7′ (9′) intersecting other slant edge at 10′.
3. Project 7′(9′), 8′ and 10′ on the cutting plane *C–C* to obtain the true shape of the section 7–8–9–10.

Case (iv): *True shape: Pentagon of 30 mm base and 50 mm height*

For pentagon, the section plane must cut two base edges and three slant edges. The distance between cutting points on the base will be equal to the base of the pentagon.

1. In TV, locate 4 and 5 on the base edges such that 4–5 = 30 mm. Project 4 and 5 to 4′(5′) in FV as shown.
2. With 4′(5′) as a centre and radius = 50 mm, cut an arc on the farthest slant edge at 11′. Draw a cutting plane *D–D* through 4′(5′)–11′ intersecting the other slant edges at 12′(13′).
3. Project 4′, 5′, 11′, 12′ and 13′ on the cutting plane *D–D* to obtain the true shape of the section 4–5–12–11–13.

Example 15.18 A square pyramid with a base side of 45 mm and a slant height of 70 mm is resting on the base on the HP with two base sides perpendicular to the VP. It is cut by two AIPs, sloping in opposite directions, such that the true shape of the section is

(i) a trapezium with parallel sides of 30 mm and 14 mm

(ii) a trapezium with smaller parallel sides of 20 mm and the distance between parallel sides being 36 mm

Locate the cutting planes and draw FV and sectional TV. Draw two sectional auxiliary FVs on the two auxiliary planes, each inclined at 45° to *XY* but sloping in opposite directions. Also, draw the true shapes of both the sections.

Solution Refer Fig. 15.18.

1. Draw TV and FV of the pyramid. *o′a′* does not represent TL (as *oa* is inclined to *XY*). Therefore, first rotate *oa* to *o*–*a*1 and then project *a*1 to *a*1′ in FV. With *a*1′ as a centre and radius = 70 mm, cut an arc on the axis to locate *o′*. Now, join *o′a′*.
2. In TV, locate 1, 2, 3 and 4 on the slant edges such that 1–2 = 30 mm and 3–4 = 14 mm.
3. Project 1, 2, 3 and 4 to 1′(2′) and 4′(3′) on the corresponding edges in FV. Draw the cutting plane through them. Project 1′(2′) and 4′(3′) on the cutting plane to obtain the true shape of the section.
4. In TV, locate 5 and 6 on the slant edges such that 5–6 =20 mm. Project 5 and 6 to 5′(6′) in FV.
5. With 5′(6′) as a centre and radius = 36 mm, cut the arc on the base at 8′(7′). Project 8′(7′) to 8 and 7 in TV.
6. Draw the cutting plane through 5′(6′)–8′(7′). Project 5′(6′) and 8′(7′) on the cutting plane to obtain the true shape of the section.
7. In TV, join 1–2–3–4 and 5–6–7–8 and hatch the areas.
8. Draw *X*1*Y*1 at 45° to *XY*. Project TV on *X*1*Y*1 to obtain auxiliary FV.
9. Draw *X*2*Y*2 at 45° to *XY* sloping in the direction opposite to *X*1*Y*1. Project TV on *X*2*Y*2 to obtain another auxiliary FV.

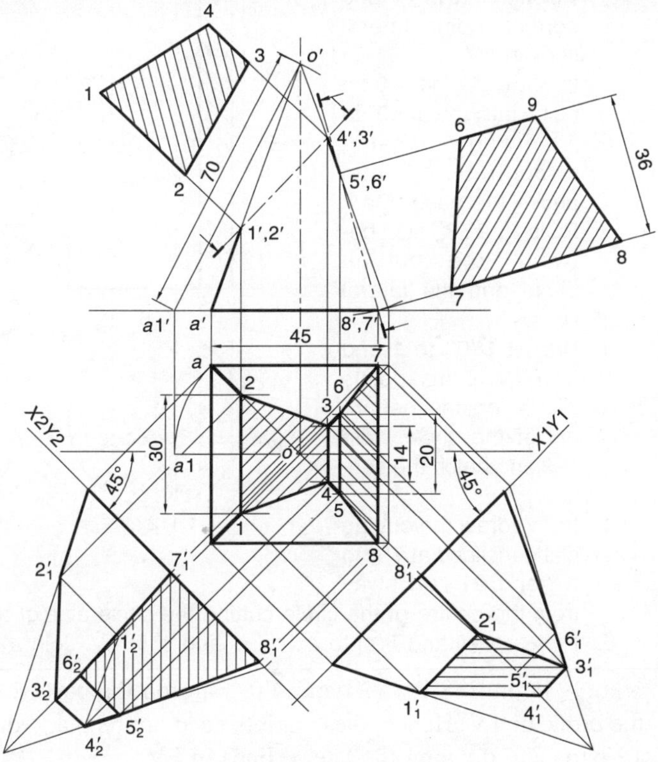

Fig. 15.18

15.5 SECTIONS OF CYLINDERS

Example 15.19 A cylinder with a 60 mm diameter and a 100 mm height stands on its base on the HP. It is cut by two section planes,

(i) an AIP inclined at 60° to the HP and intersecting an extreme generator at a point 36 mm from the base and,

(ii) an AVP inclined at 75° to the VP and 21 mm away from the axis of the cylinder.

Draw the sectional TV and sectional FV.

Solution Refer Fig. 15.19.

1. Draw TV and FV of the cylinder. Obtain 12 division points in TV and corresponding lateral lines in FV.
2. In FV, draw the cutting plane inclined at 60° to *XY* and passing through 5′, 36 mm above the base. Mark POIs 1′, 2′, 3′, etc., between the cutting plane and the lateral lines.
3. Project 1′(9′) to 1 and 9 in TV. Other points will lie on the periphery of the circle. Join 1–9 and hatch the section.
4. In TV, draw the cutting plane inclined at 75° to *XY* and 21 mm away from the centre of the circle cutting the circle at *a*(*d*) and *b*(*c*).
5. Project *a*(*d*) and *b*(*c*) to *a*′, *d*′, *b*′ and *c*′ in FV. Join *a*′–*b*′–*c*′–*d*′ and hatch the area.

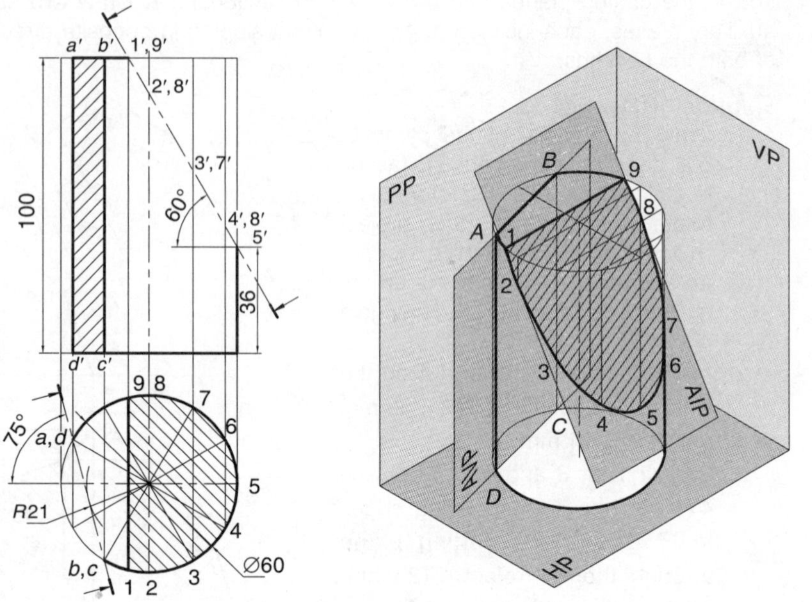

Fig. 15.19

Note: Point 2′(8′), 3′(7′) and 4′(6′) are on the curved surface of the cylinder. They are seen on the circle in TV. Hence, these points need not be marked. Also there is no need of dividing TV into 12 parts and drawing the lateral lines in FV.

Example 15.20 A horizontal cylinder (axis parallel to the VP) with a 60 mm diameter and 100 mm length is cut by two AIPs such the true shape of the section is

(i) an ellipse of maximum major axis

(ii) an ellipse of major axis 90 mm

Draw FV and SV and locate the cutting planes. Also, draw the true shapes of sections.

Solution Refer Fig. 15.20.

For the section to be an ellipse, the cutting plane inclined to the axis must cut all the generators.

Draw SV and FV of the cylinder as shown. Obtain 12 division points in SV and draw lateral lines in FV.

Case (i): *True shape: Ellipse of maximum major axis*

The cutting plane must pass through two opposite ends of the extreme generators.

1. Locate 1′ and 7′ at the opposite ends of farthest generators. Draw cutting plane *A*–*A* through 1′–7′. Mark 2′, 3′, 4′, etc., at the intersections of the cutting plane with the lateral lines.
2. Project 1′, 2′, 3′, etc., perpendicular to *A*–*A* and obtain the true shape of the section.

Case (ii): *True shape: Ellipse with a 90 mm major axis*

The length of the cutting plane between two extreme generators should be equal to 90 mm.

1. Mark 13′ (preferably near an end) on one of the extreme generators. With 13′ as a centre and radius = 90 mm, cut another extreme generator at 19′. Draw the cutting plane *B*–*B* through 13′–19′. Mark 14′, 15′, 16′, etc., at the intersections of *B*–*B* with the lateral lines.
2. Project 14′, 15′, 16′, etc., perpendicular to *B*–*B* and obtain the true shape of the section.

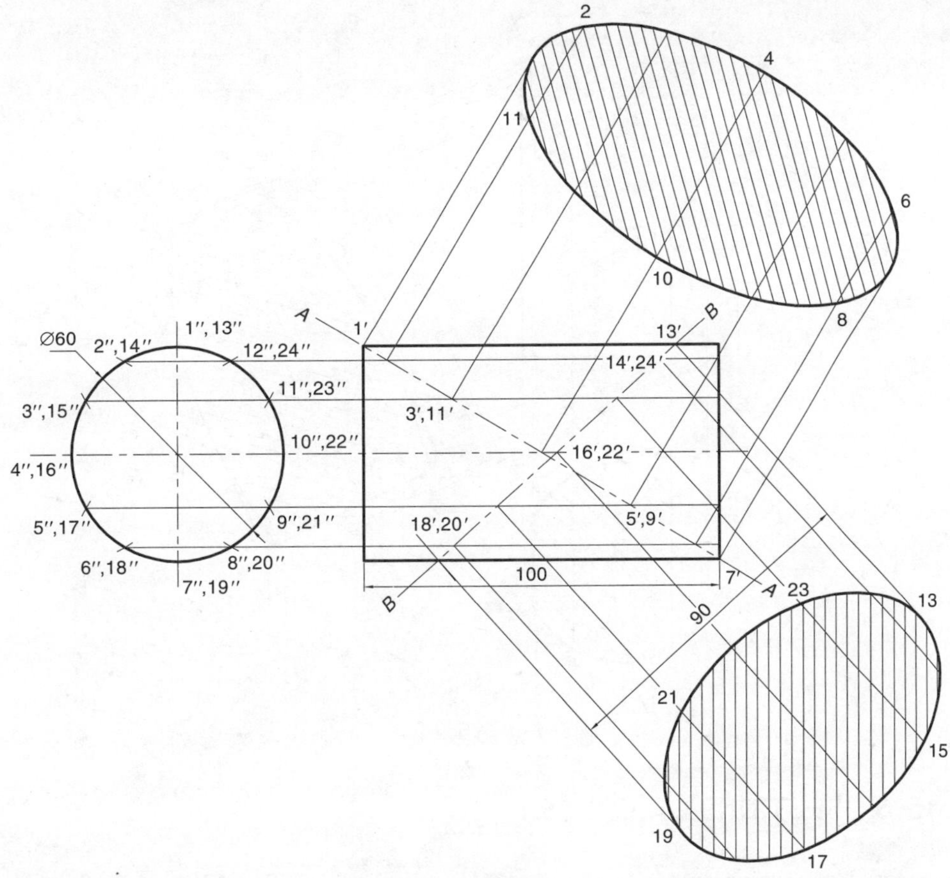

Fig. 15.20

Example 15.21 A cylinder with a diameter of 60 mm and an axis length of 90 mm stands on its base on the HP. An AIP inclined at 65° to the HP and intersecting the axis of the cylinder at a point 32 mm above the base cuts the cylinder. Draw FV, sectional TV and an auxiliary view showing the true shape of the section.

Solution Refer Fig. 15.21.

1. Draw the TV and FV of the cylinder. Obtain 12 division points in TV and corresponding lateral lines in FV.
2. In FV, draw the cutting plane inclined at 65° to *XY* and passing through point 4′(7′) on the axis, 32 mm from the base. Mark 1′, 2′, 3′, etc., at the intersections between the cutting planes and the lateral lines.
3. Project 1′(10′) and 5′(6′) to 1, 10, 5 and 6 on the circle in TV. (Other points need not be projected as they fall on the periphery of the circle.) Join 1–10 and 5–6 and hatch the area between them.
4. Draw *X*1 *Y*1 parallel to the cutting plane and project FV on it to obtain the auxiliary sectional TV. Note that the section 1–2–3–4–5–6–7–8–9–10 shows the true shape.

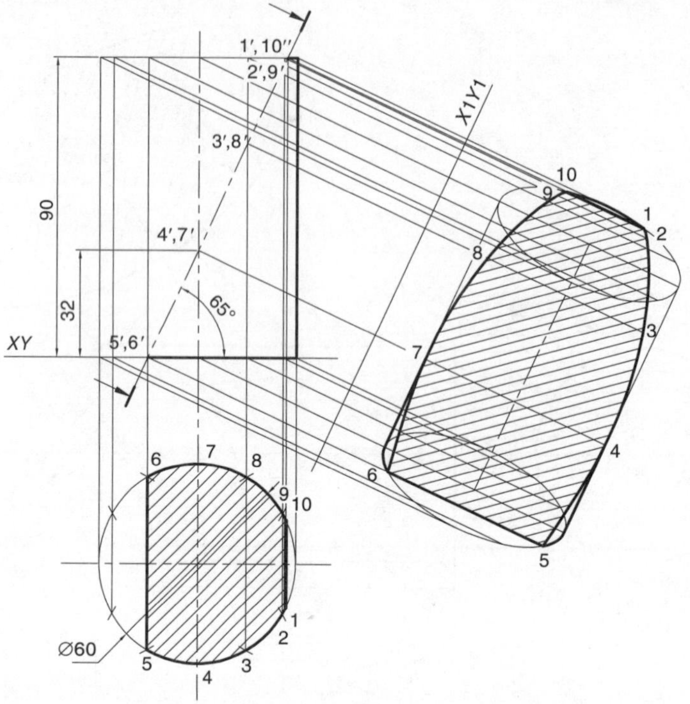

Fig. 15.21

15.6 SECTIONS OF CONES

The sections of a cone give special curves called *conic sections*. See Chapter 6 (Section 6.2) for detail.

Example 15.22 A cone with a base diameter of 75 mm and an axis length of 100 mm is lying in space with its axis parallel to both the RPs. An AVP inclined at 30° to the VP and passing through a point on the axis, 32 mm from the base cuts the cone. Draw TV, sectional FV and sectional SV. The part of the cone containing the apex is retained.

Solution Refer Fig.15.22.

1. Draw SV, FV and TV of the cone as shown. Divide SV into 12 equal parts and obtain the lateral lines in FV and TV.
2. In TV, locate the cutting plane inclined at 30° to *XY* and passing through axis, 32 mm away from the base. Mark 1, 2, 3, etc., at the intersections of the cutting plane with the lateral lines.
3. Project 1, 2, 3, etc., in FV and in SV on the corresponding lateral lines. 1 and 9 are projected to 1″ and 9″ in SV on the base and then to 1′ and 9′ in FV. Similarly, 2 and 8 are projected to 2′ and 8′ in FV and then to 2″ and 8″ in SV.
4. Join 1′, 2′, 3′, etc., and 1″, 2″, 3″, etc., and hatch the areas.

Example 15.23 A cone with a 70 mm base diameter and a 90 mm height stands on its base on the HP. It is cut by two AIPs in such a way that the true shapes of the sections are

(i) an ellipse of major axis 24 mm and
(ii) a parabola of axis 60 mm

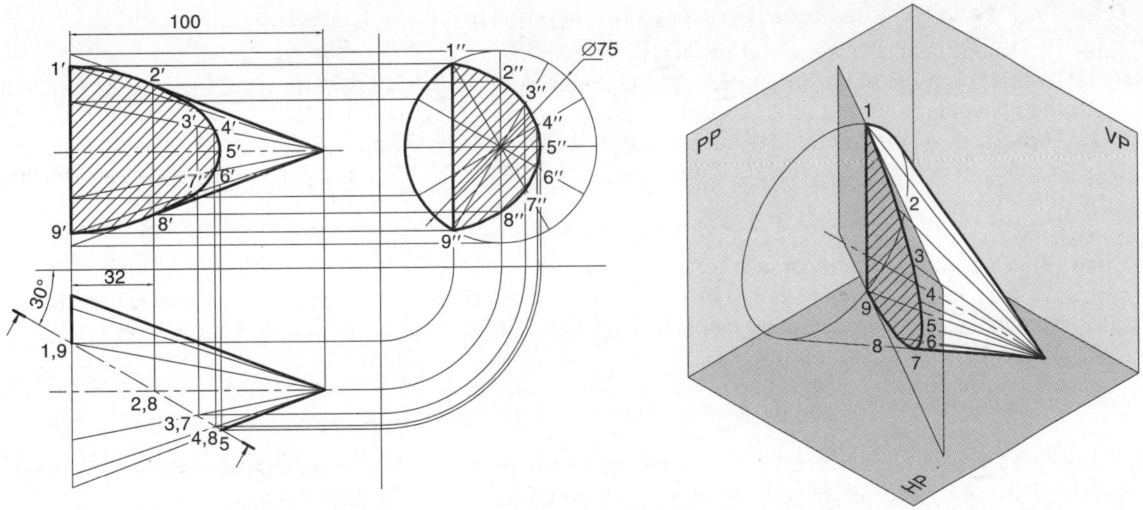

Fig. 15.22

Draw FV, cutting planes, sectional SV and true shapes of the sections, assuming the part of the cone between two cutting planes is retained.

Solution For a section to be an ellipse, the cutting plane must be inclined to the base and cut all the generators. For a section to be a parabola, the cutting plane must be parallel to a generator.
Refer Fig. 15.23.

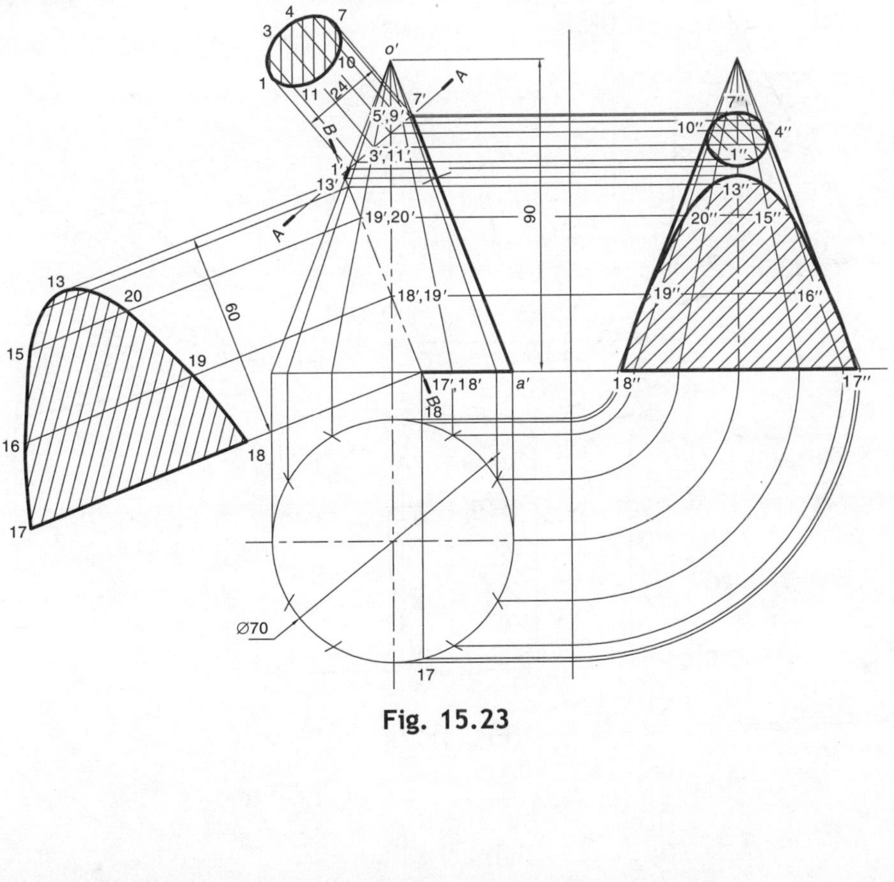

Fig. 15.23

Draw TV, FV and SV of the cone. Obtain 12 division points in TV and lateral lines in FV and SV.

Case (i): *True shape: Ellipse with a major axis of 24 mm*

1. Mark 1′ on a generator (preferably on the upper side). With 1′ as a centre and radius = 24 mm, cut the opposite generator at 7′. Draw the cutting plane *A–A* through 1′–7′.
2. Mark 2′, 3′, 4′, etc., at the intersections of *A–A* with other generators. Project 1′, 2′, 3′, etc., to 1″, 2″, 3″, etc., in SV on the corresponding generators. Join 1″, 2″, 3″, etc., by a smooth curve and section the area.
3. Project 1′, 2′, 3′, etc., on *A–A* and obtain the true shape of the section.

Case (ii): *True shape: Parabola with an axis of 60 mm*

1. On *o′a′*, locate *p′* such that *a′p′* = 60 mm. Project *p′* on the opposite generator to locate 13′. Through 13′, draw the cutting plane *B–B* parallel to *o′a′*, cutting the base at 17′ (18′).
2. Mark 14′, 15′, 16′, etc., at the intersections of *B–B* with the other generators. Project these points in SV on the corresponding generators. Join them and hatch the area.
3. Project 13′, 14′, 15′, etc., on *B–B* to obtain the section parabola.

Example 15.24 A cone with a 70 mm diameter of base and a 90 mm length of axis, rests on its base on the HP. It is cut by two AIPs in such a way that the true shapes of the sections are

(i) a hyperbola with a double-ordinate of 68 mm and 48 mm abscissa, and
(ii) an isosceles triangle with a 54 mm base.

Draw FV, cutting planes, sectional TV and true shapes of the sections. Assume the part of the cone between the two cutting planes is retained.

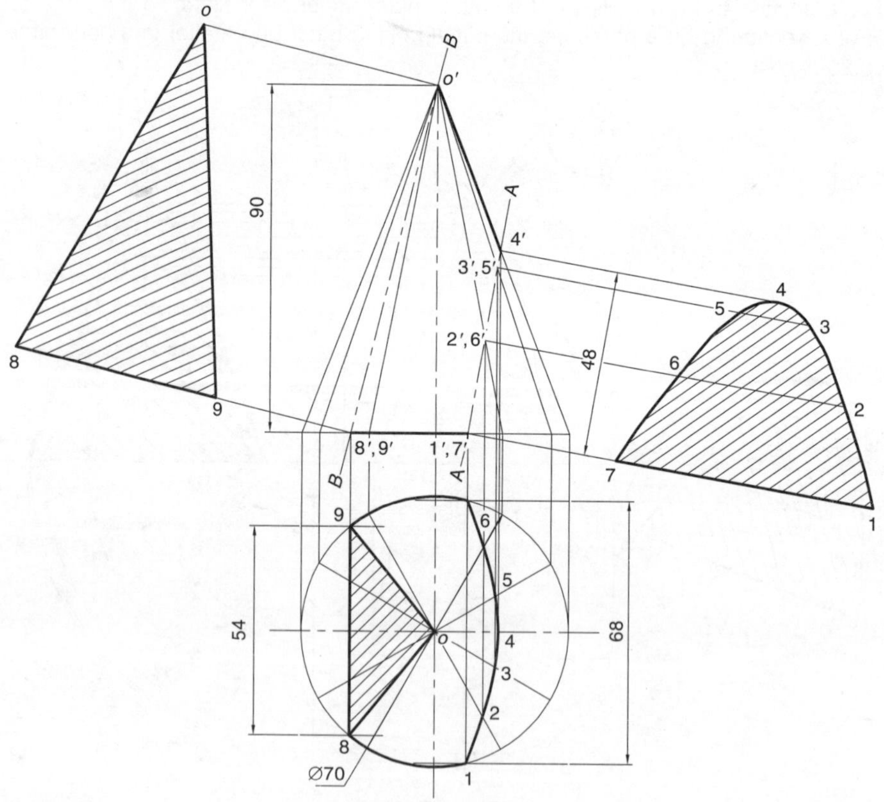

Fig. 15.24

Solution For a section to be a hyperbola, the cutting plane should be inclined to the axis and cut the cone on one side of the axis. If the cutting plane is inclined (or perpendicular) to the base and passes through the apex, then the section is an isosceles triangle.
Refer Fig. 15.24.
Draw TV and FV of the cone. Obtain 12 division points in TV. Draw the lateral lines in TV and FV.

Case (i): *True shape: Hyperbola with a 68 mm double-ordinate and a 48 mm abscissa*

1. In TV, locate 1 and 7 such that 1–7 = 68 mm. Project 1 and 7 to 1′(7′) in FV on the base.
2. With 1′(7′) as a centre and radius = 48 mm, cut an arc to locate 4′ on the generator at the same side of the axis. Draw the cutting plane *A–A* through 1′(7′)–4′.
3. Mark 2′, 3′, 5′ and 6′ at the intersections of *A–A* with the other lateral lines. Project 2′, 3′, 4′, etc., to 2, 3, 4, etc., on the corresponding lateral lines in TV. Join 1, 2, 3, etc., by a smooth curve.
4. Project 1′, 2′, 3′, etc., perpendicular to *A–A* and obtain a section hyperbola.

Case (ii): *True shape: Isosceles triangle with a 54 mm base*

1. In TV, locate 8 and 9 such that 8–9 = 54 mm. Project them to 8′(9′) in TV. Draw the cutting plane *B–B* through 8′(9′)–*o*′.
2. In TV, join 8–9–*o* and hatch the section.
3. Project 8′(9′) and *o*′ perpendicular to *B–B* to obtain the true shape.

Example 15.25 A cone with a 70 mm diameter of base and 90 mm length of axis, rests on its base on the HP. Two section planes—a profile section plane and a horizontal section plane—cut the cone. Both the section planes pass through the midpoint of an extreme generator. Draw FV, section planes, sectional TV and sectional SV. Also, draw an auxiliary TV on a plane parallel to the extreme generator of the cone at which the two cutting planes intersect.

Solution Refer Fig. 15.25.

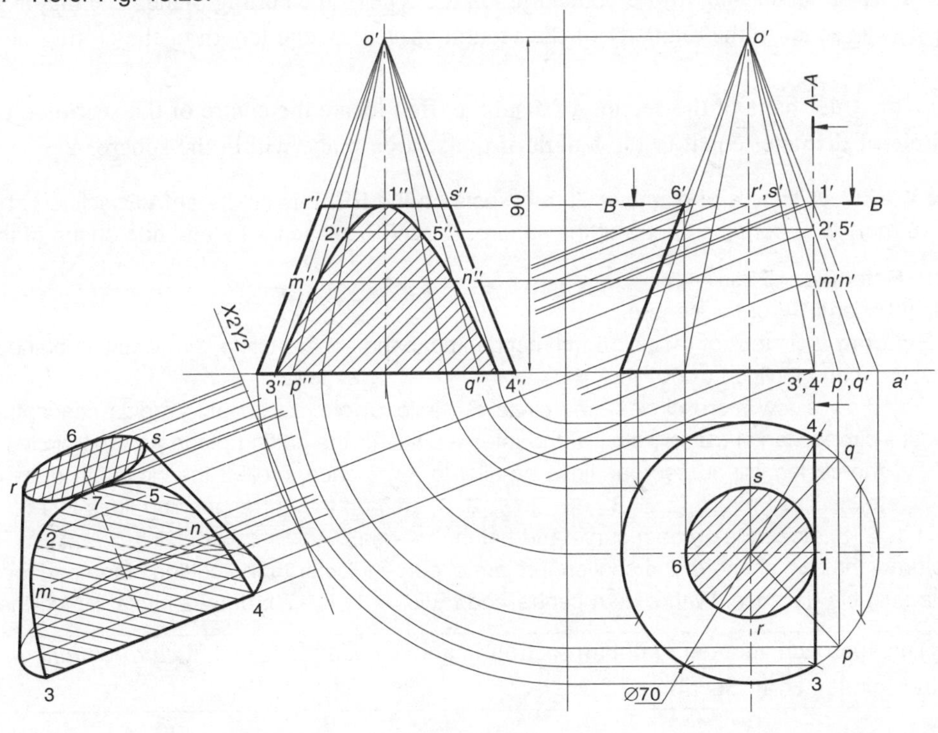

Fig. 15.25

As the profile cutting plane is parallel to the axis, the true shape of the section will be a rectangular hyperbola. For the horizontal section plane, the section will be a circle.

1. Draw TV, FV and SV of the cone. Obtain 12 division points in TV and the lateral lines in FV and TV.
2. Draw the profile section plane *A–A* and a horizontal section plane *B–B* through midpoint 1′ of *o′a′*, cutting the base at 3′(4′) and the other extreme generator at 6′ respectively.
3. Mark 2′(5′) at the intersections of *A–A* with lateral lines. Project 1′, 2′(5′) and 3′(4′) to 1″, 2″, 5″, 3″, and 4″ in SV. 3′(4′) are projected to 3 and 4 in TV and then to 3″ and 4″ in SV. Join 3″–2″–1″–5″–4″ by smooth curve and hatch the area to represent section hyperbola.
4. Mark *r′*(*s′*) at the intersections of *B–B* with intermediate lateral lines. Project *r′*(*s′*) to *r″*and *s″* in SV. Join *r″–s″*.
5. Project 6′ to 6 in TV. With o as a centre and radius = 0–6, draw a circle. Hatch the circle to represent the section. Also, join 3–4.
6. Draw *X*2*Y*2 parallel to *o′a′*. Project the FV on *X*2*Y*2 to obtain the auxiliary TV showing the sections.

Note: To ensure the accuracy in drawing a section hyperbola, two intermediate points *m″* and *n″* may be obtained. Draw lateral lines *o′–p′*(*q′*) and mark *m′*(*n′*) at their intersections with *A–A*. obtain *o″–p″* and *o″–q″* in SV. Project *m′*(*n′*) to *m″*and *n″*.

15.7 SECTIONS OF SPHERES

The section of a sphere when cut by any section plane is always a circle. However, in FV, TV or SV, the section may be seen as an ellipse depending on the type of the cutting plane. The major axis of the ellipse is always equal to the diameter of the section circle, i.e., the length of the cutting plane within the sphere.

To draw the true shape of the section of a sphere, first locate the centre of the section circle. Then, draw a circle of diameter equal to the length of the section plane within the sphere.

Example 15.26 A sphere of diameter 75 mm rests on the HP. It is cut by an AIP inclined at 50° to the HP and 18 mm away from the centre of the sphere. Draw FV, sectional TV and true shape of the section.

Solution Refer Fig. 15.26.

1. Draw FV and TV of the sphere.
2. In FV, draw a circle *A* of radius 18 mm concentric to the sphere-circle. Draw cutting plane tangent to this circle and inclined at 50° to *XY*.
3. In FV, draw a few more circles, say circle *B*, circle *C*, etc., of suitable radius concentric with the sphere-circle. Mark 1′, 2′, 3′, etc., at the intersections of the cutting plane and the circles.
4. In TV, the circles will be seen as lines parallel to *XY*. Hence, project the circles to draw lines *A–A*, *B–B*, etc., in TV. Project 1′, 2′, 3′, etc., to 1, 2, 3, etc., on the corresponding lines in TV.
5. Join 1, 2, 3, etc., by a smooth curve and hatch the area.
6. To draw the true shape of the section, project *o′* perpendicular to the cutting plane and locate *o* on it at a suitable distance. With *o* as a centre and radius = ½ (1′–7′), draw a circle. Hatch the circle.

Note: The approach adopted to obtain section in above example is called *cutting plane approach.* It is further explained in Section 17.3.2.

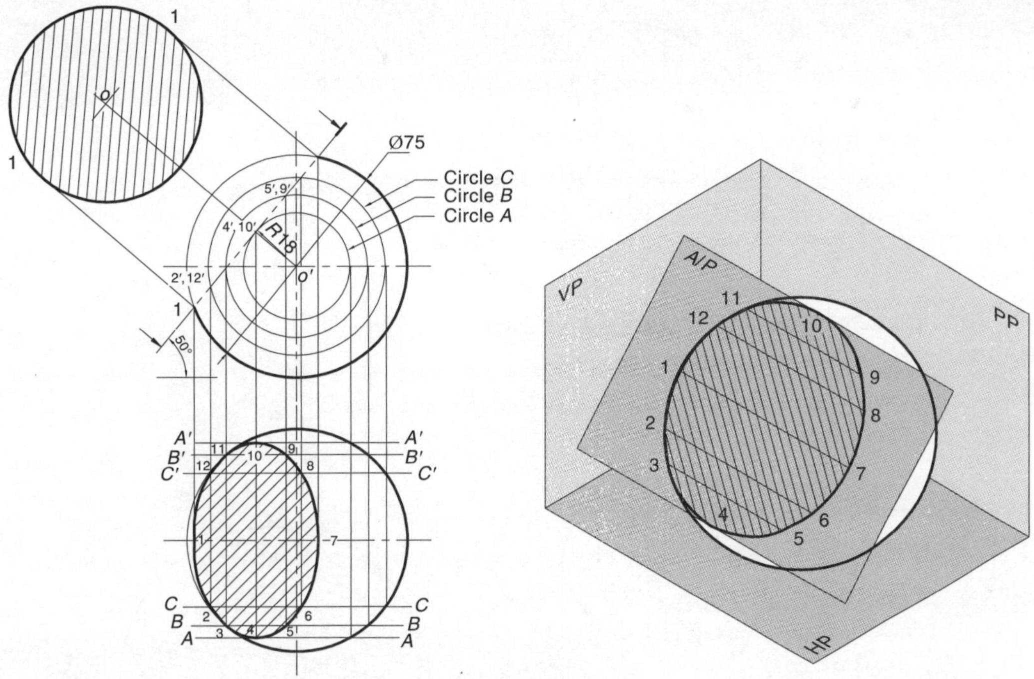

Fig. 15.26

Example 15.27 A sphere (diameter of 90 mm) cut by an AVP shows the section as an ellipse with a major axis of 90 mm and a minor axis of 30 mm in FV. Draw two views of the sphere showing the section. Also, draw and comment on the true shape of the section. Measure the inclination of the cutting plane with the VP.

Solution As the major axis of the ellipse is equal to the diameter of the sphere, the section plane must pass through the centre of the sphere.

Refer Fig. 15.27.

1. Draw FV and TV of the sphere.
2. In TV, draw two parallel lines, each on either side of the vertical axis at a distance of 15 mm from it. Locate 1 and 7 at the intersections of these lines with the circle. Draw the cutting plane through 1–7. Measure ϕ.
3. In TV, draw few circles, say circle *A* and circle *B*, etc., concentric with the sphere-circle. Mark 2, 3, 4, etc., at the intersections of the cutting plane and the circles.
4. In FV, draw lines *A–A*, *B–B*, *A′–A′* and *B′–B′* to represent the projections of the circles *A* and *B*. Project 1, 2, 3, etc., to 1′, 2′, 3′, etc., on the corresponding lines in FV. 1 and 7 are projected on the horizontal axis in FV.
5. Join 1′, 2′, 3′, etc., by a smooth curve and hatch the area.
6. To draw the true shape of the section, project *o* perpendicular to the cutting plane and locate *o*1 on it at a suitable distance. With *o*1 as a centre and radius = ½ (1–7), draw a circle. Hatch the circle.

As the section plane passes through the centre of the sphere, the true shape of the section is a circle of diameter equal to that of the sphere.

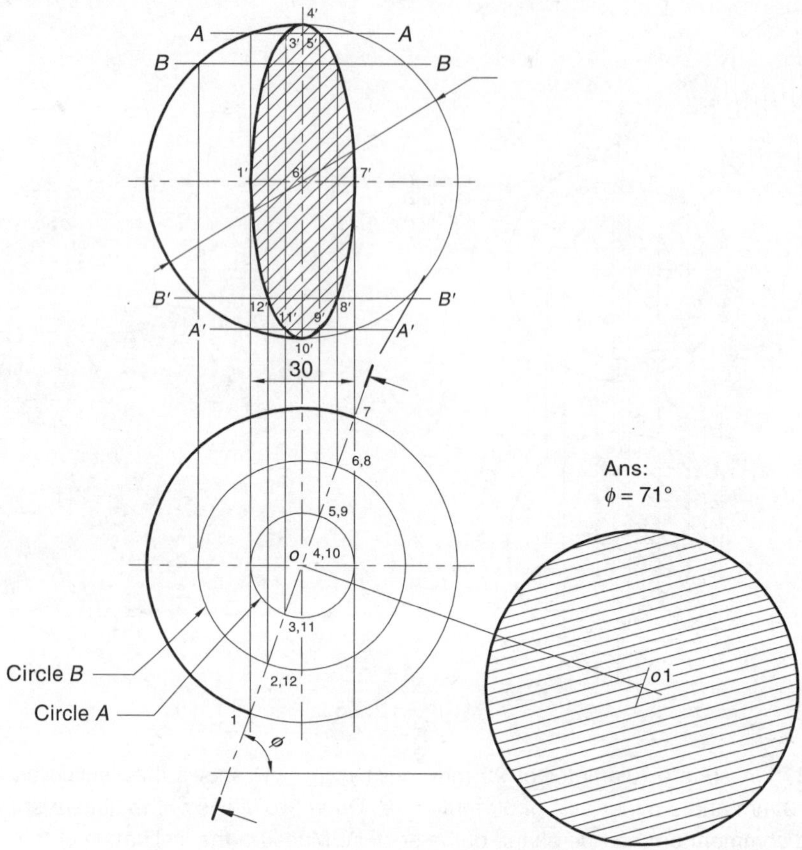

Fig. 15.27

15.8 SECTIONS OF SOLIDS IN COMBINATION AND COMPOSITE SOLIDS

The sections of the two solids touching each other or joined together can be obtained by considering each solid separately. The two sections must be hatched by the section lines sloping in opposite directions.

Example 15.28 A frustum of a pentagonal pyramid having a base edge of 50 mm, top edge of 30 mm and a height of 50 mm is placed on its base on the HP with a base edge *AB* perpendicular to the VP. A semicylinder of 25 mm radius is placed symmetrically on its flat face on the top of the frustum. The axis of the semicylinder is parallel to the VP. The end faces of the semicylinder lie on the planes drawn through *AB* and the corner of the base opposite to *AB*. The combination is cut by an AVP inclined at 54° to the VP and passing through *A*. Draw the sectional elevation and the true shape of the section.

Solution Refer Fig. 15.28.

1. Draw TVs and FVs of the frustum of the pyramid and the semicylinder. *ab* is drawn perpendicular to *XY*.

2. Draw the cutting plane passing through *a* and inclined at 54° to *XY*. Locate *c*, *d* and *e* at the intersections of the cutting plane with the edges of the frustum.
3. Project *c*, *d* and *e* to *c′*, *d′* and *e′* on the corresponding edges of the frustum in FV. Join *a′c′d′e′* and hatch the area.
4. Draw an end view of the semicylinder. Obtain 6 division points on it. Draw the corresponding lateral lines in FV and TV.
5. In TV, locate 1, 2, 3, etc., at the intersections of the cutting plane with the lateral lines. (1 and 6 coincide with *a* and *d* respectively.)

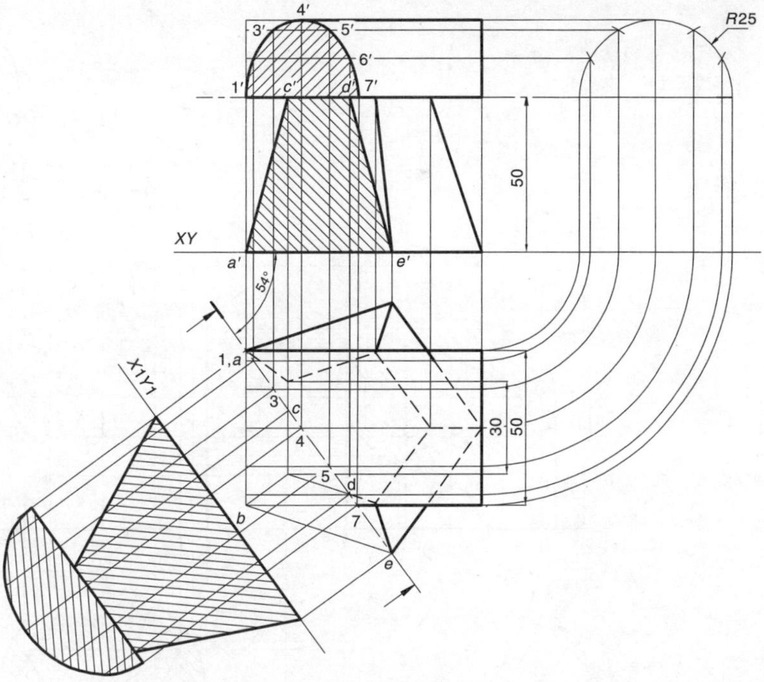

Fig. 15.28

6. Project 1, 2, 3, etc., to 1′, 2′, 3′, etc., on the corresponding lateral lines in FV. Join these points and hatch the area to indicate the section of the semicylinder.
7. Draw *X*1 *Y*1 parallel to the cutting plane. Project *a, c, d, e*, 1, 2, 3, etc., on it and draw the true shape of the section by the auxiliary plane projection method.

Example 15.29 The true shape of the section of a vertical cylinder is an ellipse with a major axis of 100 mm and a minor axis of 80 mm, when cut by an AIP. It has a coaxial equilateral triangular hole with 60 mm sides, a face of which is parallel to the VP. Draw the three views of the cut cylinder with the hole and mark the angle of inclination of the AIP. Show the true shape of the cut face.

Solution Refer Fig. 15.29.

We know that the diameter of a cylinder is equal to the minor axis of the section ellipse, i.e., 80 mm.

1. Draw TV, FV and SV of the cylinder. Also, draw TV, FV and SV of the hole. In TV, one side of a triangle is parallel to *XY*. In TV, obtain 12 division points and project them in FV and SV to draw lateral lines.
2. In FV, locate 1′ on an extreme generator, preferably near one end. With 1′ as a centre and radius = 100 mm, cut an arc at 7′ on the other extreme generator. Draw the cutting plane through 1′–7′. Measure θ. Mark 2′, 3′, 4′, etc., at the intersection of the cutting plane with the lateral lines. Also, mark *a′*, *b′* and *c′* at the intersection of the cutting plane and the edges of the triangular hole.
3. The points 1′, 2′, 3′, etc., will get projected on the circle in TV. Similarly, *a′*, *b′* and *c′* will be seen at the corners of the triangle. Hatch the area between the circle and the triangle.
4. Project 1′, 2′, 3′, etc., and *a′*, *b′* and *c′* on the corresponding lateral lines/edges in SV. Join 1″–4″–7″–10″ by a smooth curve. Join *a″*, *b″* and *c″* to form a triangle. Hatch the area between the curve and the triangle.
5. Project 1′, 2′, 3′, etc., and *a′*, *b′* and *c′* perpendicular to the cutting plane to obtain the true shape of the section.

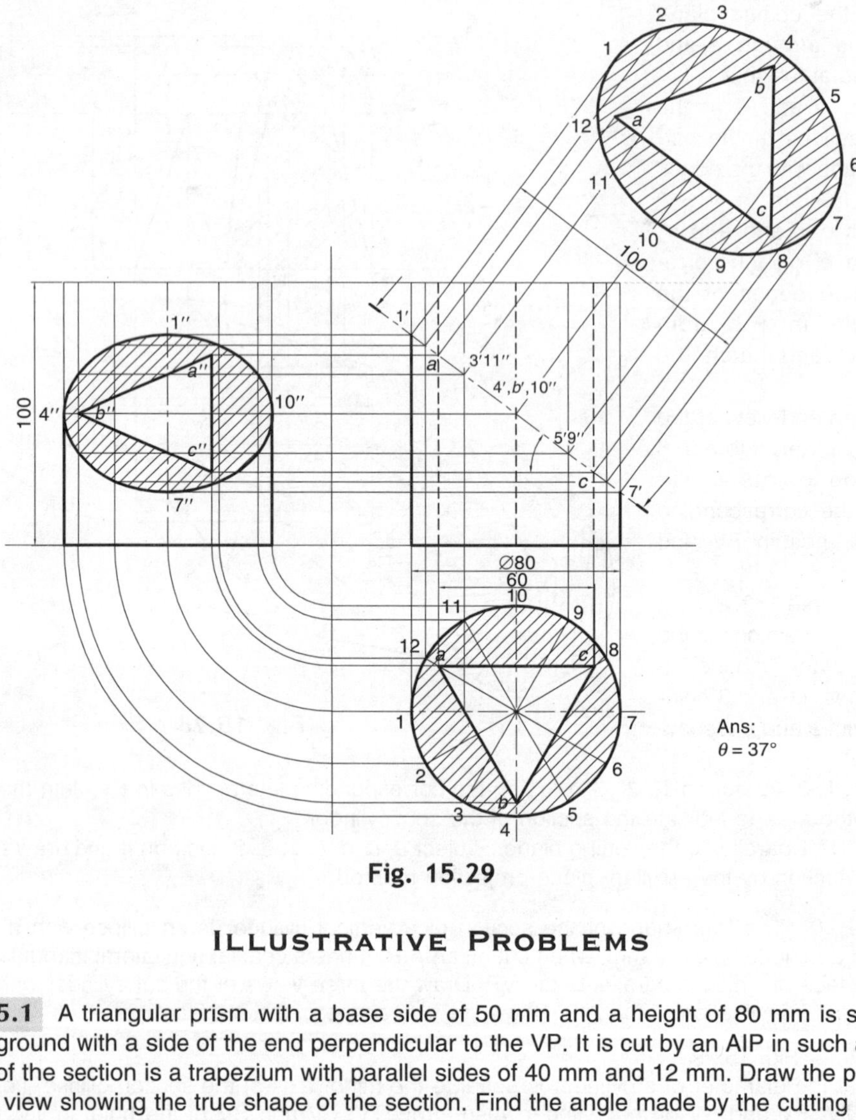

Fig. 15.29

Illustrative Problems

Problem 15.1 A triangular prism with a base side of 50 mm and a height of 80 mm is standing on its end on the ground with a side of the end perpendicular to the VP. It is cut by an AIP in such a way that the true shape of the section is a trapezium with parallel sides of 40 mm and 12 mm. Draw the projections and an auxiliary view showing the true shape of the section. Find the angle made by the cutting plane with the HP.

Solution Refer Fig. 15.30.

1. Draw TV and FV of the prism as shown. *a*(*a*1)–*b*(*b*1) is perpendicular to *XY*.
2. In TV, locate 1 and 2 and 3 and 4 such that 1–2 = 40 mm and 3–4 = 12 mm.
3. Project 1, 2, 3 and 4 to 1′, 2′, 3′ and 4′ on the corresponding edges in FV. Draw the cutting plane through 1′(2′)–4′(3′). Measure θ.
4. In TV, join 1–2–3–4 and hatch the area.
5. Draw *X*1 *Y*1 parallel to cutting plane. Project FV on *X*1 *Y*1 and draw the auxiliary view with true shape 1–2–3–4.

Problem 15.2 A square prism with a 110 mm long axis is resting on its base on the HP. The edges of the base are equally inclined to the VP. The prism is cut by an AIP passing through the midpoint of the

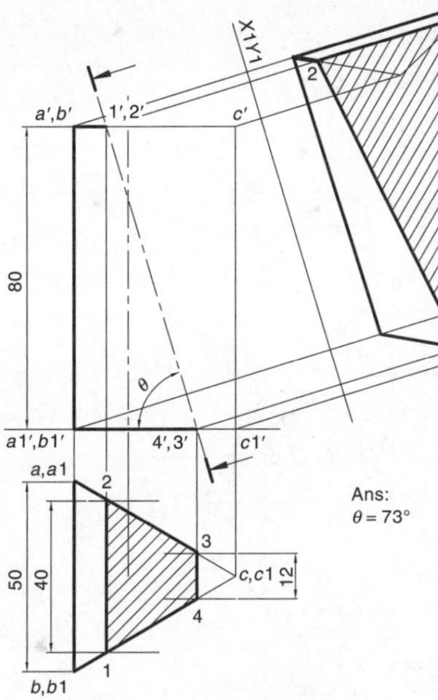

Fig. 15.30

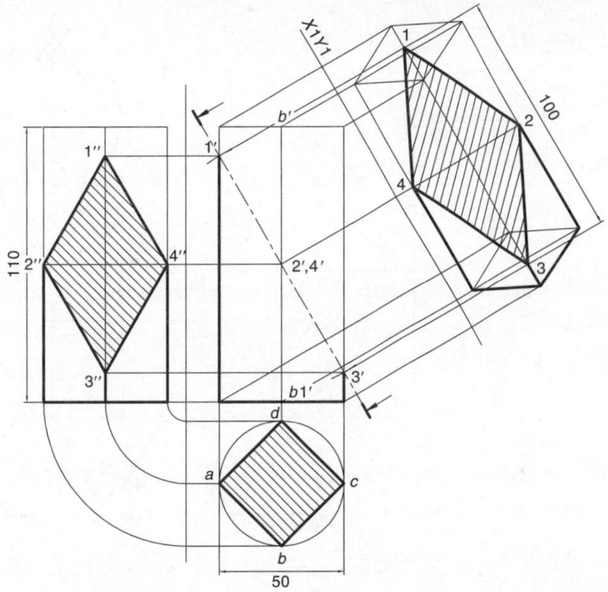

Fig. 15.31

axis in such a way that the true shape of the section is a rhombus having diagonals of 100 mm and 50 mm. Draw the three views showing section and an auxiliary view revealing the true shape of the section.

Solution Refer Fig. 15.31.

The length of the smallest diagonal of the rhombus will be equal to the diagonal of the base of the prism.

1. Draw a circle with a 50 mm diameter and inscribe a square *abcd* in it. It represents TV of the prism. Obtain FV and SV.
2. In FV, locate midpoint 2′(4′) of *b′*–*b*1′. With 2′(4′) as a centre and radius = ½ (100), cut arcs at 1′ and 3′ on the other sides of the prism. Draw the cutting plane through 1′–3′.
3. Project 1′, 2′, 3′ and 4′ to 1, 2, 3 and 4 in TV and 1″, 2″, 3″ and 4″ in SV. Join the points and hatch the areas.
4. Draw *X*1 *Y*1 parallel to the cutting plane and project FV to obtain an auxiliary view revealing the true shape of the section.

Problem 15.3 A cube of 40 mm side rests on a corner on the HP with the body diagonal through that corner perpendicular to the HP. It is cut by

(i) an AVP passing through the vertical body diagonal and inclined at 45° to the VP
(ii) a horizontal section plane passing through the midpoint of the vertical body diagonal

Draw the sectional views in each case.

Solution Refer Fig. 15.32.

1. Draw TV and FV of the cube assuming the base on the HP. In TV, all the sides are equally inclined to *XY*. Draw body diagonal *a*1′–*c*′.
2. Redraw FV such that *a*1′–*c*′ is vertical and *a*1′ on *XY*. Obtain the corresponding TV.

Case (i): *Cutting plane: AVP*

3. In TV, draw cutting plane through *c*(*a*1) and inclined at 45° to *XY*. Locate POIs 1 and 2.
4. Project 1 and 2 to 1′ and 2′ in FV. Join 1′–*a*1′–2′–*c*′ and hatch the area.

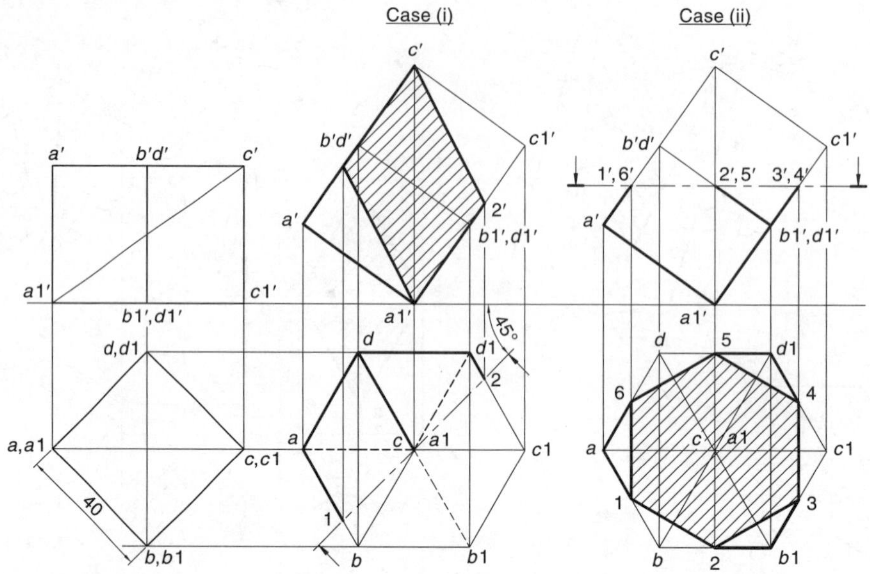

Fig. 15.32

Case (ii): *Cutting plane: Horizontal Section Plane*

3. In FV, draw a horizontal cutting plane through the midpoint of *c′*–*a*1′. Locate POIs 1′, 2′, 3′, etc.
4. Project 1′, 2′, 3′, etc., to 1, 2, 3, etc., in TV. Join 1–2–3–4–5–6 and hatch the area. The section 1–2–3–4–5–6 represents the true shape.

Note: Compare Case (ii) with Example 15.11.

Problem 15.4 A pentagonal prism with a 25 mm edge of base and a 60 mm long axis is resting on a corner on the HP such that the longer edge through that corner makes 60° to the HP and 30° to the VP. Another end of the edge is in the VP. An AVP inclined at 50° to the VP and passing through the corner on the HP cuts the solid. Draw TV and sectional FV. Also draw the true shape of the section.

Solution Refer Fig. 15.33.

1. Draw TV and FV of the prism assuming the base on the HP. Draw an edge of base perpendicular to *XY*.
2. Redraw FV with *a*1′ on *XY* and *a*1′–*a*′ making 60° to *XY*. Obtain the corresponding TV.
3. Redraw TV with *a* on *XY* and *a*–*a*1 perpendicular to *XY*. (As *A*–*A*1 is parallel to the PP, its plan and elevation will be perpendicular to *XY*.) Project the TV to obtain the corresponding FV.
4. In TV, draw cutting plane passing through *a*1 and inclined at 50° to *XY*. Locate 1, 2, 3, 4 and 5 at the intersections of cutting plane with the edges. (5 coincides with *a*.)
5. Project 1, 2, 3, etc., to 1′, 2′, 3′, etc., on the corresponding edges in FV. To project 3 to 3′, first mark it on *c*–*c*1 in intermediate TV. Then project it to 3′ in intermediate FV and then to 3′ in final FV as shown. Join the points and hatch the area.
6. Draw *X*1 *Y*1 parallel to the cutting plane and project 1, 2, 3, 4 and 5 to obtain the true shape of the section.

Problem 15.5 A hexagonal prism with a side of base of 25 mm and a 65 mm long axis, is resting on an edge of the base on the VP, its axis being inclined at 60° to the VP and parallel to the HP. An AVP inclined at 30° to the VP cuts the prism through the base. The section plane passes through a point on the axis at

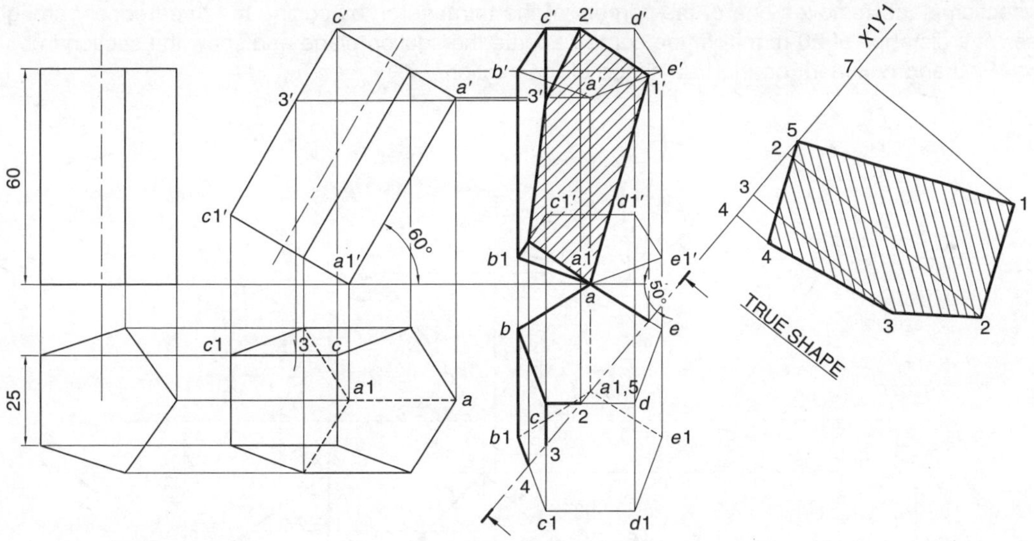

Fig. 15.33

a distance of 15 mm from the end away from the VP. Draw TV, sectional FV and the true shape of the section.

Solution Refer Fig. 15.34.

1. Draw FV and TV of the prism assuming the base on the VP.
2. Redraw TV such that *a*1(*b*1) is on *XY* and the axis makes 60° to *XY*. Obtain the corresponding FV.
3. Draw cutting plane inclined at 30° to *XY* and passing through a point on the axis, 15 mm from *c*(*f*).
4. Locate 1, 2, 3, etc., in TV at the intersections of the cutting plane with the edges.
5. Project 1, 2, 3, etc., to 1′, 2′, 3′, etc., on the corresponding edges in FV. Join these points and hatch the area.
6. Draw *X*1*Y*1 parallel to the cutting plane. Project 1, 2, 3, etc., on *X*1*Y*1 and draw the true shape 1′–2′–3′–4′–5′–6′.

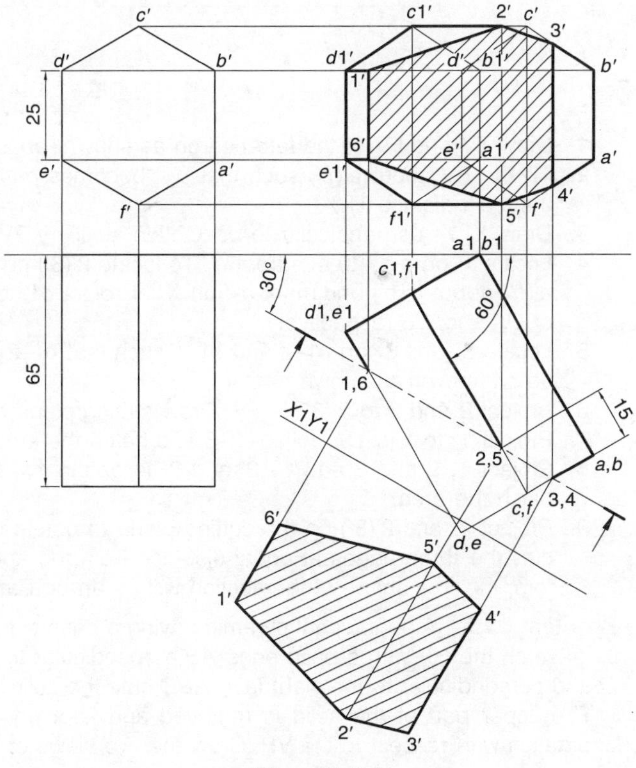

Fig. 15.34

Problem 15.6 A tetrahedron with a 45 mm side is kept in such a way that an edge is parallel to both the RPs. The edge opposite to the edge parallel to both the RPs is perpendicular to the VP. Draw FV and TV of the solid.

A section plane removes one of the corners of the tetrahedron by cutting the three edges through that corner at a distance of 20 mm from the corner. Locate the section plane and show the section in both the views. Find and comment on the true shape of the section.

Solution Refer Fig. 15.35.

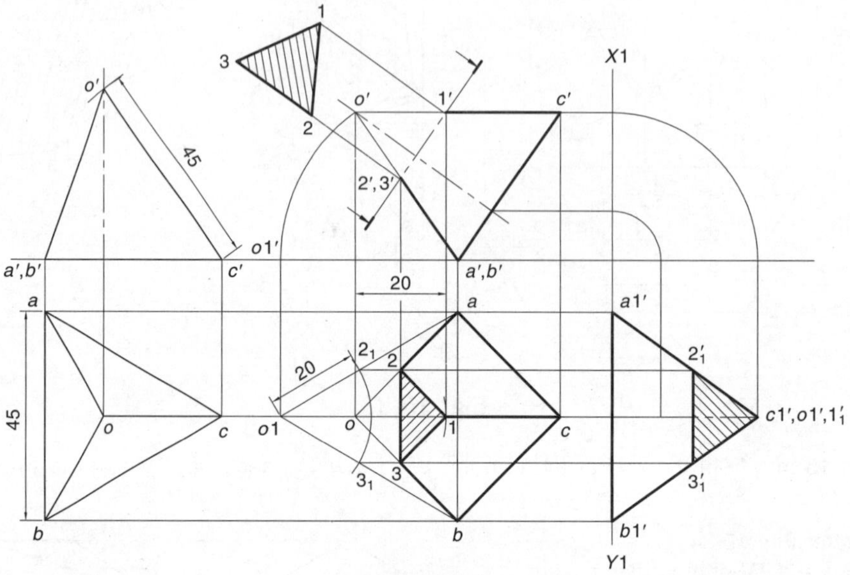

Fig. 15.35

1. Draw TV and FV of the tetrahedron as shown. *ab* is drawn perpendicular to *XY*.
2. Tilt the FV about *a′*(*b′*) such that *o′c′* becomes parallel to *XY*. Obtain the corresponding TV. Note that *oc* indicates TL.
3. Draw *X*1 *Y*1 perpendicular to *oc*. Obtain auxiliary FV.
4. Locate 1′ on *o′c′*, 20 mm from *o′*. To locate 2′(3′) on *o′*–*a′*(*b′*), first, find TL of *OA* and *OB*. Rotate *o′*–*a′*(*b′*) about *a′*(*b′*) and mark *o*1′ on *XY*. Project *o*1′ to *o*1 in TV. Join *o*1–*a* and *o*1–*b* to represent TLs of *OA* and *OB* respectively.
5. Locate 2_1 and 3_1 on *o*1–*a* and *o*1–*b* such that *o*1–2_1 = *o*1–3_1 = 20 mm. Project 2_1 and 3_1 to 2 and 3 on *oa* and *ob* as shown.
6. Project 2 and 3 to 2′(3′) in FV. Draw cutting plane through 1′–2′(3′).
7. Project 1′ to 1 in TV. Join 1–2–3 and hatch the area.
8. Project 1, 2 and 3 and 1′, 2′ and 3′ to obtain $1_1'$, $2_1'$ and $3_1'$ in auxiliary FV. Join $1_1'$–$2_1'$–$3_1'$ and hatch the area.
9. Project 1′ and 2′(3′) on the cutting plane to obtain the true shape of the section. The cutting plane cuts the three edges at equal distance from the apex. Hence, it is parallel to face *a′*(*b′*)–*c′*. Therefore, the true shape of the section will be an equilateral triangle.

Problem 15.7 A pentagonal pyramid having a base side of 45 mm and a slant length of 80 mm rests on its base on the HP with a base edge *AB* perpendicular to the VP. A section plane passing through corner *D* and perpendicular to the slant face *ABO* cuts the solid. Draw FV and sectional TV.

The upper part of the solid is removed and kept on its cut surface on the HP without changing its orientation with respect to the VP. Draw the two views of the part of the pyramid.

Solution Refer Fig. 15.36.

1. Draw TV and FV of the pyramid. *ab* is drawn perpendicular to *XY*.
2. In FV, draw the cutting plane passing through *d′* and perpendicular to *a′*(*b′*)–*o′*. Locate 1′, 2′, 3′, 4′ and 5′ at the intersections of the cutting plane with the edges of the pyramid. (4′ coincides with *d′*.)
3. Project 1′, 2′, 3′, 4′ and 5′ to 1, 2, 3, 4 and 5 on the corresponding edges in TV. Join 1–2–3–4–5 for the hatched section.
4. Redraw the upper part of the pyramid in such a way that 1′–4′ coincides with *XY*. Obtain the corresponding TV of the part of the pyramid. Note that 1–2–3–4–5 shows the true shape of the section.

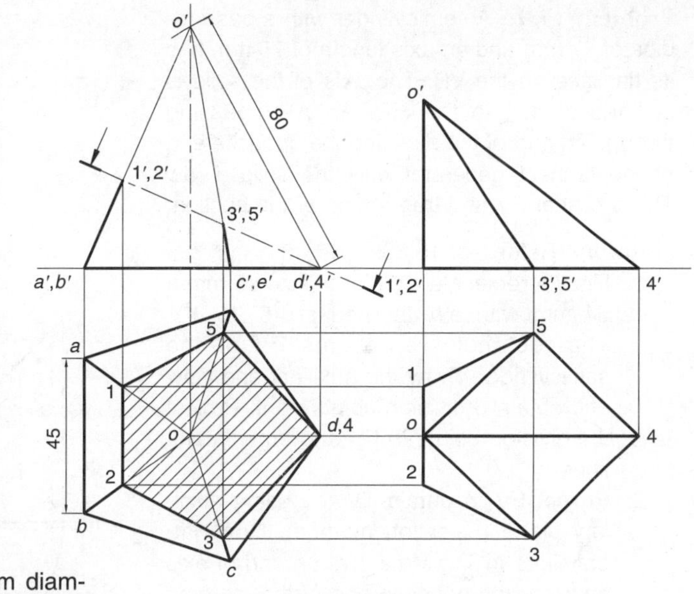

Fig. 15.36

Problem 15.8 A circular disc of 70 mm diameter and 40 mm thickness lies on its circular face on the HP. It is cut by two AIPs parallel to each other. Each of the cutting planes passes through an end of the axis and an end of the extreme generator. Draw FV, sectional TV and an auxiliary view showing the true shape of the sections.

Solution Refer Fig. 15.37.

1. Draw TV and FV of the disc. Obtain 12 division points in TV and draw the lateral lines in FV.
2. Mark 1′(7′) and 8′(14′) at the ends of the axis. Mark 4′ and 11′ at the opposite ends of extreme generators. Draw the cutting plane *A–A* through 1′(7′)–4′. Draw another cutting plane *B–B* through 8′(14′)–11′.
3. Mark 2′(6′) and 3′(5′) at the intersections of *A–A* with the lateral lines. Similarly, mark 9′(13′) and 10′(12′) at the intersections of *B–B* with the lateral lines.
4. Project 1′(7′) and 8′(14′) to 1(14) and 8(7) in TV. Points 2′(6′), 3′(5′), 9′(13′) and 10′(12′) will be seen on the periphery of the circle in TV. Join 8(7)–1(14) and hatch the area 1–4–7 to represent the section. Another half 8–11–14 represents the hidden section (and need not be hatched).
5. Draw *X*1*Y*1 parallel to *A–A*. Project FV on *A–A* and obtain the auxiliary TV showing the true shapes of the sections. Note that, only section 1–2–3–4–5–6–7 is visible. The other section 8–9–10–11–12–13 is invisible. Both the sections show their true shapes.

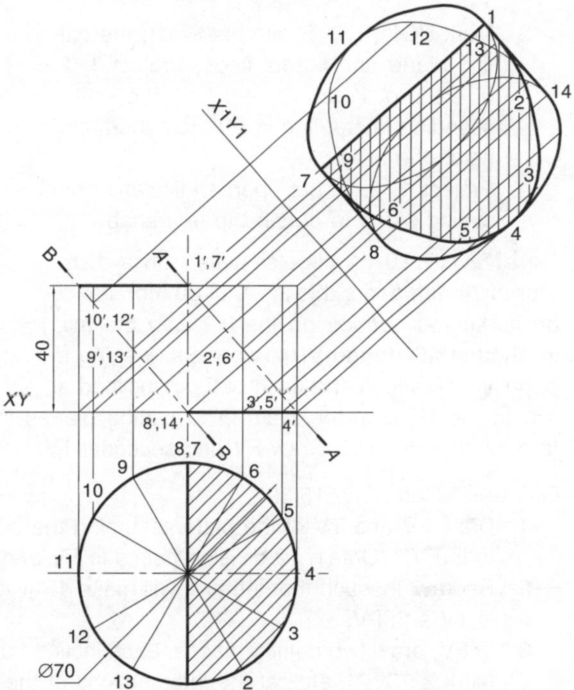

Fig. 15.37

Problem 15.9 A semicylinder with a base radius of 27 mm and an axis length of 75 mm has its flat face on the VP. The axis of the solid is inclined at 45° to the HP. An AVP passing through an end of the axis and the opposite end of the farthest generator cuts the solid. Draw TV, sectional FV and true shape of the section.

Solution Refer Fig. 15.38.

1. Draw a rectangle *a′b′c′d′* of size 75 mm × 54 mm with *a′b′* inclined at 45° to *XY*. The rectangle represents FV of the semicylinder. Draw the auxiliary end view and obtain 6 division points on it. Project the division points in FV and draw lateral lines.
2. Project FV to obtain TV (by using auxiliary plane projection method). Draw lateral lines in TV. Mark 1 at an end of axis and 5 at the opposite end of the extreme generator. Draw the cutting plane through 1–5.
3. Mark POIs 2, 3, 5, etc., between the cutting plane and lateral lines. Project 1, 2, 3, etc., to 1′, 2′, 3′, etc., on the corresponding lateral line in FV. Join them and hatch the area.
4. Project 1, 2, 3, etc., perpendicular to the cutting plane to obtain the true shape.

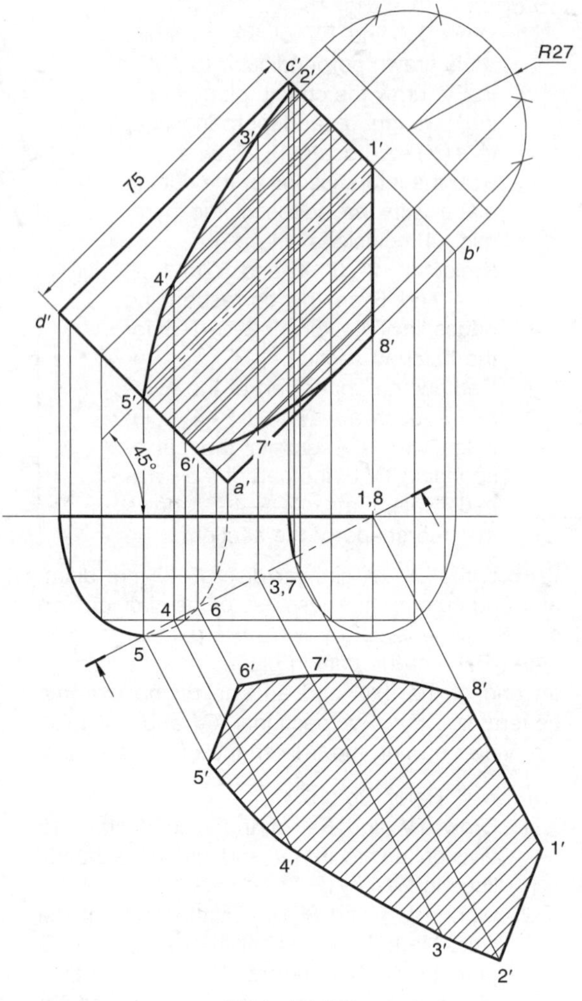

Fig. 15.38

Problem 15.10 A circular plate with a diameter of 74 mm and a thickness of 30 mm stands on its curved surface on the HP with the axis inclined at 45° to the VP. Two AIPs, leaning in opposite directions and each of them inclined at 45° to the HP, cut the plate. The cutting planes intersect each other at the midpoint of the generator farthest from the HP. Draw FV and sectional TV.

Solution Refer Fig. 15.39.

1. Draw FV and TV of the plate assuming the curved surface touching the HP and axis perpendicular to the VP. Obtain 12 division points in FV and TV.
2. Redraw TV such that the axis will make 45° with *XY*. Obtain the corresponding FV. Draw lateral lines in TV and FV.
3. In FV, draw two cutting planes, each inclined at 45° to *XY* and passing through midpoint 1′ of *a′*–*a*1′. Mark 2′, 3′, 4′, etc., at the intersections of the cutting planes with the lateral lines.
4. Project 1′, 2′, 3′, etc., to 1, 2, 3, etc., on the corresponding lateral lines in TV. Join 5–1–2–3–4 and 9–1–6–7–8 and hatch them to represent two sections.

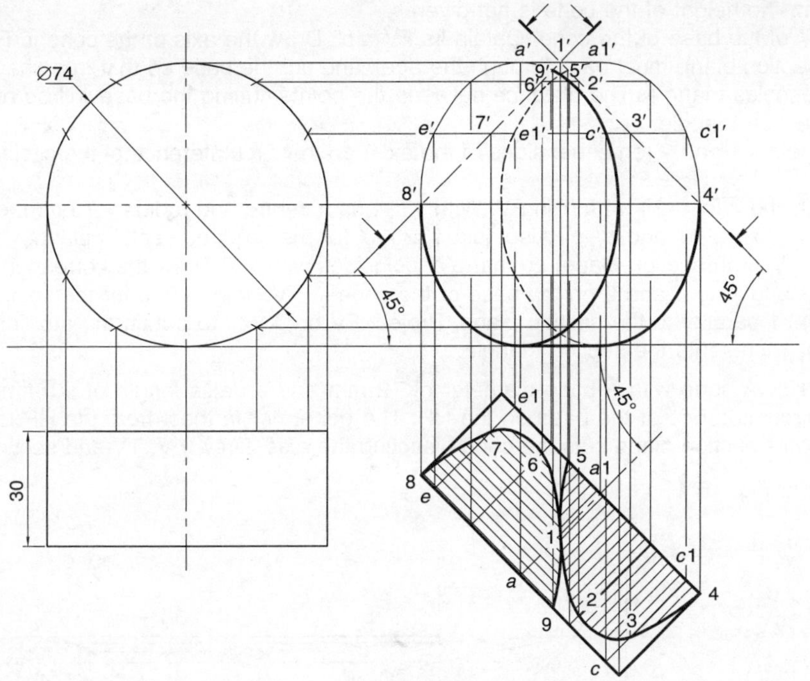

Fig. 15.39

Problem 15.11 A cone of diameter 80 mm is kept on the HP on one of its generators with the axis parallel to the VP. It is cut by an AIP such that the true shape of the section is an isosceles triangle with a base of 60 mm and an altitude of 75 mm. Draw FV, sectional TV and an auxiliary view showing the true shape of the section.

Solution Refer Fig. 15.40.

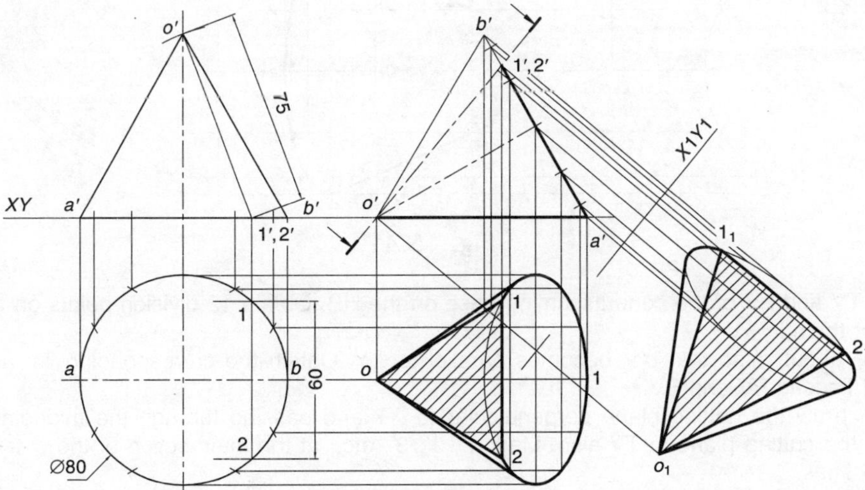

Fig. 15.40

In this problem, the height of the cone is not given.

1. Draw TV of the base of the cone. Obtain its FV $a'b'$. Draw the axis of the cone in FV.
   The section plane must pass through the apex and cut the base so that true shape of the section is an isosceles triangle. The distance between the points cutting the base will be equal to the base of the section triangle.
2. Locate points 1 and 2 (on either sides of the axis) on the circumference of the circle such that 1–2 = 60 mm.
3. Project 1 and 2 to 1′(2′) on $a'b'$ in FV. With 1′(2′) as a centre and radius = 75 mm, cut an arc on the axis at o'. Join a'–o' and b'–o'. Also, join 1′(2′)–o' for the required section plane.
4. Redraw FV (with section plane) so that $a'o'$ coincides with XY. Draw the corresponding TV.
5. Project 1′and 2′ to 1 and 2 on the base of the cone in TV. Join 1–2–o for the sectioned area.
6. Draw $X1Y1$ parallel to the section plane. Project FV on $X1Y1$ to obtain the auxiliary TV as shown. 1_1–2_1–o_1 represents the section triangle.

Problem 15.12 A cone with a base diameter of 72 mm and an axis length of 90 mm, is resting on a point on the circumference of the base on the HP. The generator farthest from the HP is parallel to both the RPs. A profile section plane cuts the cone bisecting the axis. Draw FV, TV and sectional SV.

Solution Refer Fig. 15.41.

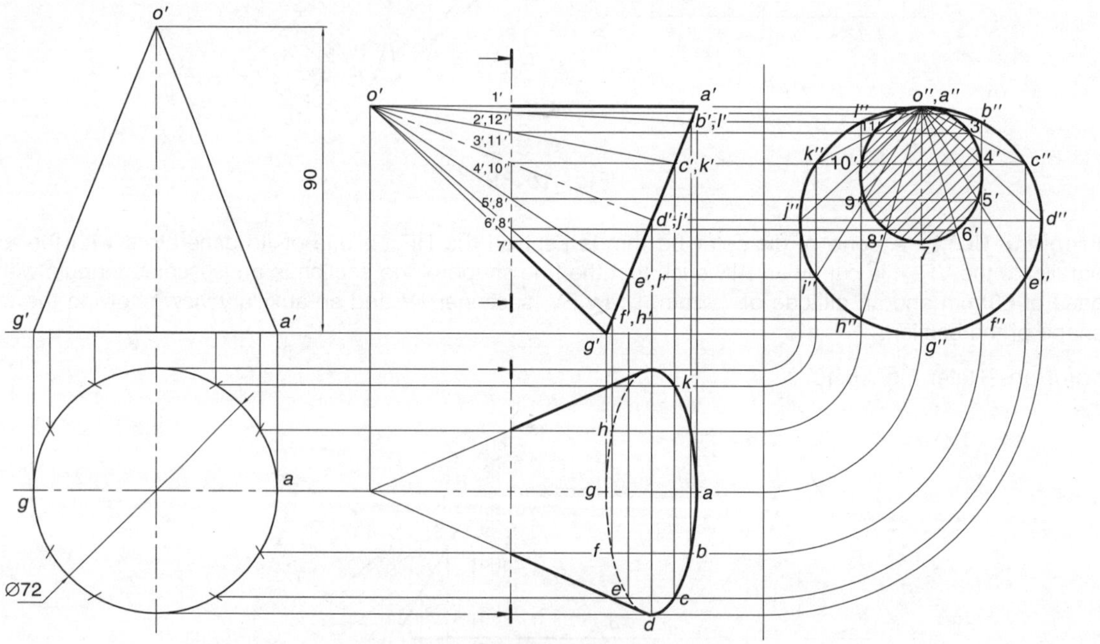

Fig. 15.41

1. Draw TV and FV of the cone assuming base on the HP. Obtain 12 division points on the circle and project them in FV.
2. Tilt FV about g' so that $o'a'$ becomes parallel to XY. Obtain the corresponding TV and SV. Draw lateral lines in FV and SV.
3. In FV, draw the cutting plane perpendicular to XY and passing through the midpoint of the axis. Show the cutting plane in TV also. Mark 1′, 2′, 3′, etc., at the intersection of the cutting plane and lateral lines.
4. Project 1′, 2′, 3′, etc., to 1″, 2″, 3″, etc, in SV on the corresponding lateral lines. Join 1″, 2″, 3″, etc., by a smooth curve and section the area.

Problem 15.13 A frustum of cone with the larger diameter of 90 mm, and a smaller diameter of 40 mm and a length of axis of 50 mm is kept on its larger base on the HP. Two AIPs, leaning in opposite directions, cut the solid. The cutting planes intersect along the centreline of the top face. Each of the cutting plane passes through the lowest end of the extreme generator. Draw the sectional views of the frustum.

Solution Refer Fig. 15.42.

1. Draw TV and FV of the frustum of the cone.
2. In FV, mark 1′(7′) at the centre of the top and and 4′and 10′ at the lowest ends of the extreme generators. Draw two cutting planes passing through 1′(7′)–4′ and 1′(7′)–10′.
3. In FV, draw lines *A–A* and *B–B* parallel to base. Mark 2′(6′) and 3′(5′) at the intersections of a cutting plane and *A–A* and *B–B* respectively. Lines *A–A* and *B–B* will be seen as circles in TV.
4. Project *A–A* and *B–B* in TV to draw the circle *A* and circle *B*.
5. Project 2′(6′) and 3′(5′) to 2, 6, 3 and 5 on the corresponding circle in TV. Also, project 1′(7′) on the top circle and 4′ on the base circle. Join 1–2–3–4–5–6–7 and hatch the area.
6. Obtain the section in the other half in a similar way.

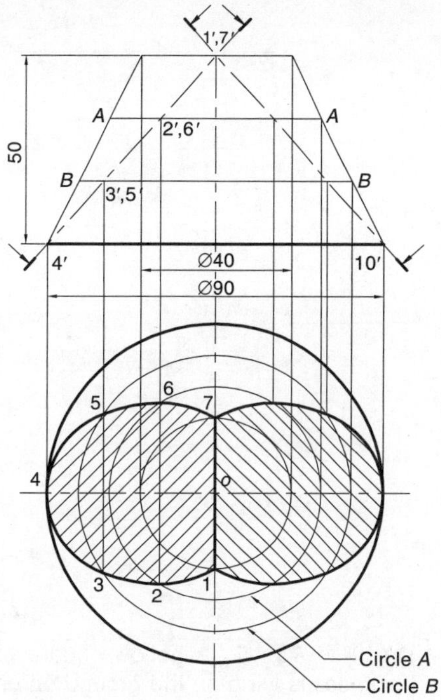

Fig. 15.42

> **Note:** The above problem can be solved in the usual way by drawing generators along the frustum of the cone. However, it is solved here by adopting cutting plane approach.

Problem 15.14 A hemisphere with a 65 mm diameter, lying on the ground on its flat face, is cut by an AVP so that the semiellipse seen in its FV has a 45 mm long minor axis and a 25 mm long half major axis. Draw the TV, sectional FV and true shape of the section.

Solution Refer Fig. 15.43.

1. Draw TV and FV of the hemisphere. In FV, draw a line parallel to and 25 mm above *XY*, cutting the semicircle at *a*′. Project *a*′ to *a* In TV. On the same projector, mark *b*′(*c*′) and *b* and *c* in FV and TV respectively, at the intersections with the base.
2. Draw two parallel lines $\widehat{B1}$ and $\widehat{C1}$, 45 mm apart. Mark *b*1 on $\widehat{B1}$ anywhere. With *b*1 as a centre and radius = *bc*, cut an arc at *c*1 on $\widehat{C1}$. Locate the midpoint *a*1 of *b*1–*c*1. Draw the perpendicular *a*1–*o*1 to *b*1–*c*1 such that *a*1–*o*1 = *ao*. With *o*1 as a centre and radius = 32.5 mm, draw a circle to represent the required TV of the hemisphere.
3. Draw the corresponding FV.
4. In TV, draw the cutting plane through *b*1–*c*1. Draw a few concentric circles in TV intersecting the cutting plane at 1, 2, 3, etc.
5. In FV, draw lines parallel to *XY* to represent the projections of the circles. Project 1, 2, 3, etc., to 1′, 2′, 3′, etc., on the corresponding lines in FV. *b*1 and *c*1 are projected on the base.
6. Join *b*1′–1′–2′–3′ ... *c*1′ and hatch the area for section. Note that, *b*1′–*c*1′ = 45 mm and *p*′–*a*1′ = 25 mm.

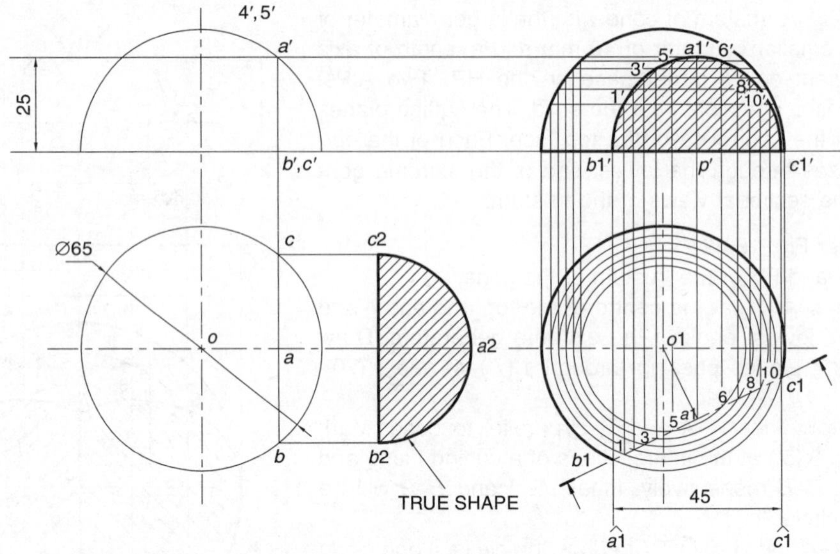

Fig. 15.43

Problem 15.15 A hollow square prism with a 50 mm base (outside), 75 mm length and 9 mm wall thickness is lying on the ground on one of its rectangular faces, with the axis inclined at 30° to the VP. A vertical section plane cuts the prism, intersecting the axis at a point 25 mm from one of its ends. Draw the TV and sectional FV of the prism.

Solution Refer Fig. 15.44.

1. Draw a rectangle of 75 mm × 50 mm size below *XY* with the longer side inclined at 30° to *XY*. Draw a smaller rectangle (by dashed lines) inside this rectangle such that all sides are parallel to and 9 mm away from the sides of the outside rectangle. The rectangles represent TV of the hollow prism. Draw the axis.
2. Draw *X*1*Y*1 parallel to the smaller edge, i.e., *a*(*d*)–*b*(*c*). Project *a*(*d*) and *b*(*c*) on *X*1*Y*1 to draw a square *a*1′–*b*1′–*c*1′–*d*1′. Draw another square (by dashed lines) inside this square having all the sides parallel to and 9 mm from the sides of the outside square. The squares represent the auxiliary end view of the prism.
3. Project the TV on *XY* and obtain FV by auxiliary plane projection method.

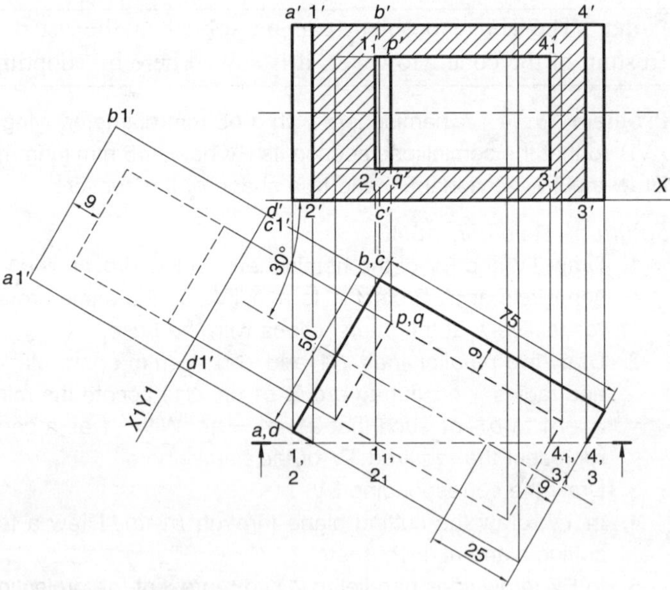

Fig. 15.44

4. In TV, draw cutting plane parallel to XY and cutting the axis at a point 25 mm from an end of the prism as shown. Mark 1(2) and 4(3) at the intersections of the cutting plane with the outer edges of the prism. $1_1(2_1)$ and $4_1(3_1)$ represent the similar points of intersections at the inner edges of the prism.
5. Project 1(2), 4(3), $1_1(2_1)$ and $4_1(3_1)$ to 1′, 2′, 4′, 3′, $1_1'$, $2_1'$, $4_1'$, and $3_1'$ on the corresponding edges in TV. Join 1′–2′, 3′–4′, $1_1'$–$2_1'$ and $3_1'$–$4_1'$. Hatch the area between 1′–2′–3′–4′ and $1_1'$–$2_1'$–$3_1'$–$4_1'$. Note that, the edge *p′q′* is visible in FV.

Problem 15.16 A cone with a base diameter of 70 mm and a height of 80 mm is placed coaxially on a circular disc with a diameter of 120 mm and thickness of 35 mm. An AIP cuts the combination of solids. The cutting plane bisects the cone axis and passes tangential to the base circle of the cone. Draw the projections and obtain the true shape of the section of the combination.

Solution Refer Fig. 15.45.

1. Draw TVs and FVs of the cone and the disc. In TV, obtain 12 division points on the smaller circle. Project the division points in FV and draw lateral lines on the cone.
2. In FV, draw the cutting plane through the midpoint 4′ of the axis of the cone and the corner 7′ of the triangle. Mark 1′, 2′, 3′, etc., at the intersections of the cutting plane with the lateral lines on the cone.
3. Project 1′, 2′, 3′, etc., to 1, 2, 3, etc., on the corresponding lateral lines in TV. Note, how point 4′ is projected. Join 1, 2, 3, etc., by a smooth curve and hatch the area.
4. In FV, the cutting plane cuts the disc at *a′*, *b′* and *c′*. In TV, *a*, *b* and *c* will be seen along the circle. Join *a–b* and hatch the area *a–b–c*.

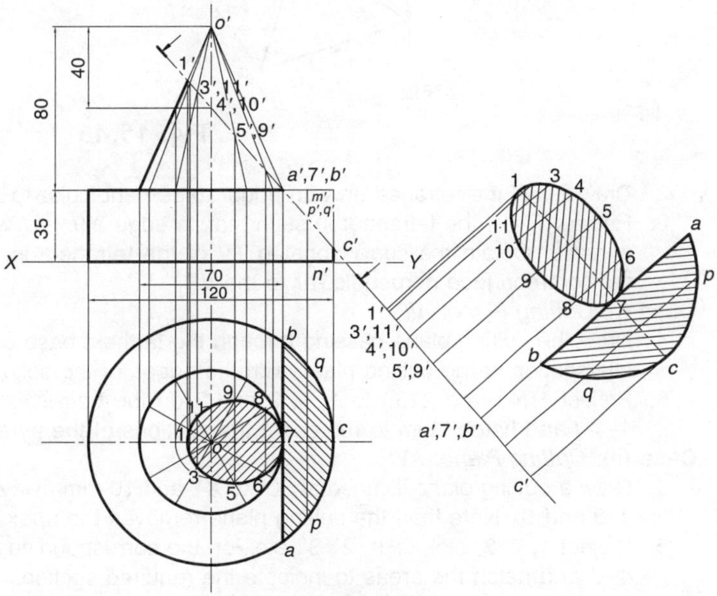

Fig. 15.45

5. Project 1′, 2′, 3′, etc., and *a′*, *b′* and *c′*, etc., perpendicular to the cutting plane and obtain the true shape of the section. *p* and *q* may be marked anywhere between *ac* and *bc* respectively to draw the curve in true shape of the section.

Problem 15.17 A pentagonal pyramid with a base side of 50 mm and a slant height of 50 mm, stands on its base on the HP. A tetrahedron of side 50 mm is attached to the pyramid such that the two solids share a common triangular face. The common face is perpendicular to the VP. The combination is cut by two section planes,

(i) an AIP passing through the farthest base corners of the pyramid and the tetrahedron,
(ii) an AVP inclined at 30° to the VP, 10 mm away from the axis of the pyramid and removing the apex.

Draw the projections with sections.

Solution Refer Fig. 15.46

1. Draw TV of the pyramid with edge *ab* perpendicular to *XY*. Obtain FV.

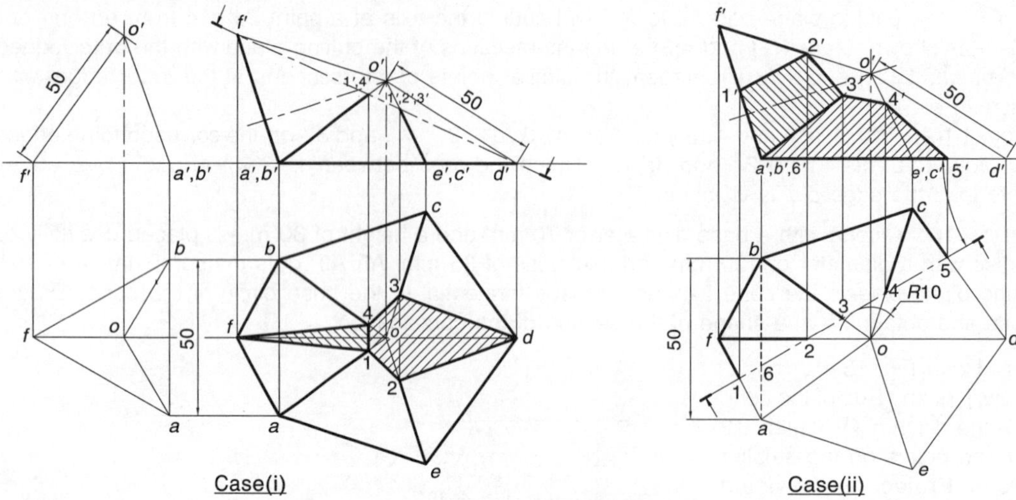

Fig. 15.46

2. Draw TV of the tetrahedron with edge *ab* perpendicular to *XY*. Obtain its FV.
3. Redraw FV of the tetrahedron such that its edge *a*′(*b*′)–*o*′ will coincide with the edge *a*′(*b*′)–*o*′ of the pyramid. Obtain the corresponding TV of the tetrahedron. Note that the edge *a*′(*b*′)–*o*′ represents the common face perpendicular to the VP.

Case (i): *Cutting Plane: AIP*

4. Draw the cutting plane passing through the farthest base corners *f*′–*d*′. Mark 1′(4′) and 2′(3′) at the intersection of the cutting plane with the edges of the solids.
5. Project 1′(4′) and 2′(3′) to 1, 4, 2 and 3 on the corresponding edges in TV. Join 1–2–*d*–3–4 and 1–4–*f* and hatch them to represent the sections of the pyramid and the tetrahedron respectively.

Case (ii): *Cutting Plane: AVP*

4. Draw a cutting plane inclined at 30° to *XY* and 10 mm away from *o*, intersecting the edges at 1, 2, 3, 4, 5 and 6. Note that, the cutting plane removes the apex.
5. Project 1, 2, 3, etc., to 1′, 2′, 3′, etc., on the corresponding edges in FV. Join 1′–2′–3′–6′ and 6′–3′–4′–5 and hatch the areas to indicate the required sections.

Problem 15.18 A conical bucket is made up of a thin metal sheet. Its top diameter is 350 mm and its bottom diameter is 200 mm. The height of the conical part is 300 mm. It is fitted with a cylindrical ring of 60 mm height at the bottom. The bucket is completely filled with water and is then tilted on a point of its bottom rim on the HP through 40°. Draw the projections showing the water surface in both the views when the bucket axis is parallel to the VP.

Solution Refer Fig. 15.47.

1. Draw TV and FV of the bucket assuming the rim of its base ring on the HP. Obtain 12 division points in TV and project the points on the base and top of the conical part in FV. *O*–*O* indicates the level of water in the bucket.
2. Redraw FV such that the axis makes 40° with the vertical. Note that, *a*1′ is on *XY*. Obtain the corresponding TV. Draw the lateral lines in FV and TV.
3. Through 1′, draw line *A*–*A* parallel to *XY*. *A*–*A* represents the new level of water when the bucket is tilted. Mark 2′, 3′, 4′, etc., at the intersections of *A*–*A* and the lateral lines.
4. Project 1′, 2′, 3′, etc., to 1, 2, 3, etc., on the corresponding line in TV. Join these points by a smooth curve to represent the level of water in TV.

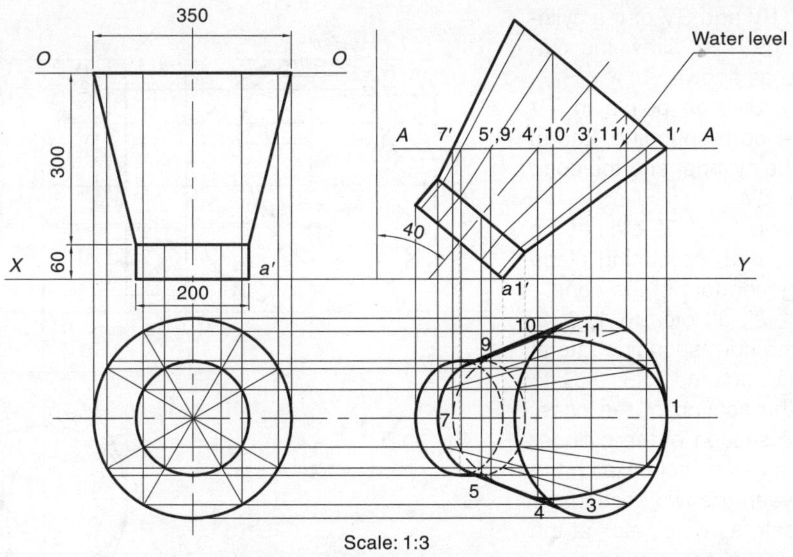

Fig. 15.47

Problem 15.19 Two equal size frustums of cones (larger end of 80 mm diameter, smaller end of 30 mm diameter and a height of 60 mm) are joined coaxially along their smaller ends. The composite solid is kept on a circular base on the HP. A vertical section plane nearer to the observer and 20 mm away from the axis of the solid cuts the solid. Draw TV and sectional FV.

Solution Refer Fig. 15.48.

1. Draw TV and FV of the solid.
2. In TV, draw cutting plane parallel to *XY*, 20 mm away from the axis and cutting the circle at 1 and 7.
3. In the region of ∠1–0–7, draw a few lateral lines, intersecting the cutting plane at 2, 3, 4, etc. (∠1–0–7 may be divided into the desired number of equal parts, say 6). Draw corresponding lateral lines in FV.
4. Project 1 and 7 to 1′ and 7′ on the base in FV. Project 2, 3, 4, etc., to 2′, 3′, 4′, etc., on the corresponding lateral lines in FV. Join 1′–2′–3′–4′–5′–6′–7′ by a smooth curve and hatch the region.
5. Draw the section in the upper half in a similar way.
   The two sections represent a pair of rectangular hyperbola.

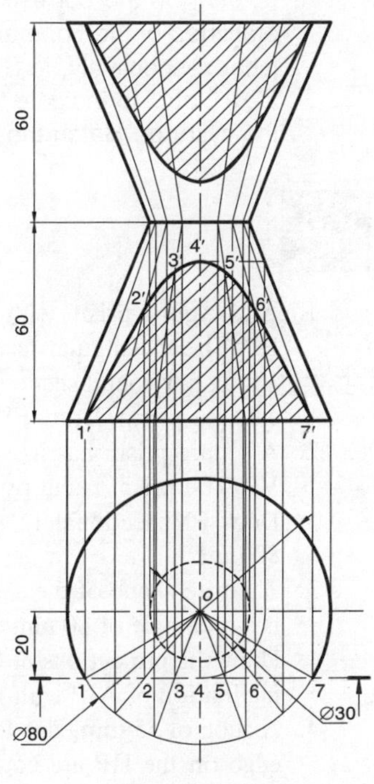

Fig. 15.48

Problem 15.20 A cylinder with a diameter of 80 mm and an axis length of 80 mm has a full length coaxial conical hole. The largest diameter of the hole is equal to the diameter of the cylinder. The apex of the conical hole lies on the base of the cylinder. The cylinder rests on its base on the HP. An AIP passing through the opposite ends of the two extreme generators of the cylinder cuts the solid into two halves. Draw FV, sectional TV and sectional SV of the solid.

Solution Refer Fig. 15.49.

1. Draw TV, FV and SV of the cylinder with the hole. Draw the cutting plane as shown.
2. Obtain 12 division points in TV and draw corresponding lateral lines on the cylinder and the cone in FV and SV.
3. In FV, locate 1′, 2′, 3′, etc., at the intersections of the cutting plane with the generators of the cone.
4. Project 1′, 2′, 3′, etc., to 1, 2, 3, etc., on the corresponding lateral lines in TV. Join 1, 2, 3, etc., to indicate the section of the cone. In TV, the section of the cylinder will be seen as a circle. Hatch the area between the two sections.
5. In FV, locate *a*′, *b*′, *c*′, etc., at the intersections of the cutting plane with the generators of the cylinder.
6. Project 1′, 2′, 3′, etc., and *a*′, *b*′, *c*′, etc., on the corresponding lateral lines of the cone and the cylinder respectively, in SV. Join 1″, 2″, 3″, etc., to indicate the section of the cone. Similarly, join *a*″, *b*″, *c*″, etc., to indicate the section of the cylinder. Hatch the area between the two sections.

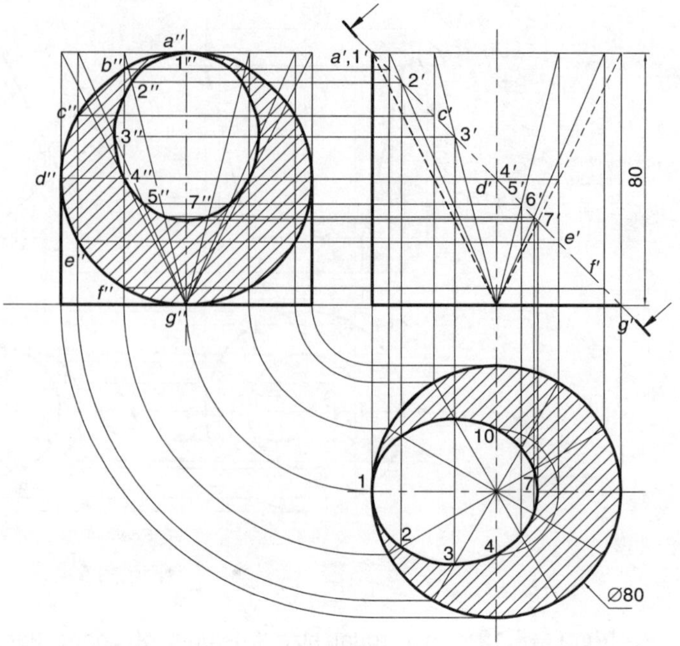

Fig. 15.49

Review Questions

1. A triangular prism with a base side of 45 mm and an axis length of 70 mm has an edge of base on the HP. The rectangular face which includes that edge is inclined at 25° to the HP and perpendicular to the VP. A horizontal section plane passing through the midpoints of the longest edges of the rectangular face cuts the prism. Draw FV and sectional TV.
2. A square prism has its shorter edge in the VP. Its axis is parallel to the HP and is inclined at 50° to the VP. The prism is cut by an AIP inclined at 45° to the HP and passing through the midpoint of the axis. Draw FV, sectional TV and sectional SV. The base side of the prism is 40 mm and its length of axis is 80 mm.
3. The true shape of the section of a vertical square prism resting on the HP on its base and cut by an AIP is a rectangle of 80 mm × 45 mm. The AIP cuts one of the side faces at a height of 20 mm from the base. Draw the projections of the prism with the section. Assume suitable height of the prism. What will be the inclination of AIP with the HP?
4. A cube of 55 mm edge length has an edge on the HP and at 60° to the VP. The two faces which share the edge on the HP are equally inclined to the HP. A vertical section plane cuts the cube into two equal halves. Draw TV and sectional FV.
5. A pentagonal prism with a base side of 30 mm and an axis length of 75 mm, is resting on a corner on the HRP with the longer edge through that corner inclined at 30° to the HRP. The rectangular face opposite to that edge has its smaller side inclined at 45° to the FRP. An AIP inclined at 45° to HRP cuts the prism at the midpoint of the axis. Draw FV and sectional TV.

6. A pentagonal prism with a 25 mm base side and 70 mm height is resting on its base on the HP with a side of base inclined at 40° to the VP. An AIP inclined at 65° to the HP and passing through the midpoint of the axis cuts the prism. Draw FV, sectional TV, sectional SV and the true shape of the section.
7. A hexagonal prism with a base side of 30 mm and an axis of 65 mm, is resting on an edge of the base on the HP with the axis inclined at 60° to the HP and parallel to the VP. An AVP inclined at 45° to the VP and passing through a point on the axis at a distance of 25 mm from the top end of the axis cuts the prism. Draw the sectional FV and true shape of the section.
8. A hexagonal block is resting on a rectangular face on the ground with the axis making 30° to the VP. The block is 50 mm thick and the distance between the opposite parallel faces is 75 mm. It is cut by an AIP inclined at an angle of 30° with the HP and bisecting the axis. Draw the projections with the section. Also, draw an auxiliary view showing the true shape of the section.
9. A triangular pyramid has a shorter edge on the HP and is parallel to the VP. The apex is on the VP. The triangular face formed by that edge and the apex makes 45° to the HP. Draw the projections of the pyramid. The base edge and the slant edge of the pyramid are 45 mm and 75 mm respectively.
An AVP passing through an edge of the base cuts the pyramid. Show the section in FV. Obtain the true shape of the section.
10. A tetrahedron with 70 mm long edges rests on its face on the HP with a side of that face perpendicular to the VP. The solid is cut by an AIP in such a way that the true shape of the section is a trapezoid of parallel sides 40 mm and 18 mm. Draw the elevation and sectional plan. Find the inclination of the cutting plane with the HP. Also, draw the auxiliary view showing the true shape of the section.
11. A square pyramid (42 mm base side and 72 mm long axis) rests on its longer side on the HP with the base sides equally inclined to the VP. The edge on the HP is inclined at 60° to the VP. A vertical section plane passing through a point on the axis, 26 mm from the base, cuts the solid. Draw TV and sectional FV.
12. A square pyramid, with a 50 mm base and a 75 mm long axis, is resting on the ground on one of its triangular faces. The top view of the axis makes 30° with the VP. It is cut by a horizontal section plane, the VT of which intersects the axis at a point 6 mm from the base. Draw FV and sectional TV.
13. A pentagonal pyramid has a triangular face on the ground. The axis of the pyramid is parallel to the VP. A horizontal section plane cuts the pyramid through the midpoint of the axis. Draw FV and sectional TV. The base side of the pyramid is 30 mm and the axis length is 65 mm.
14. A pentagonal pyramid, with a 35 mm base side and a 75 mm long axis has its base horizontal and an edge of the base parallel to the VP. It is cut by an AIP inclined at 60° to the HP and bisecting the axis. Draw FV and TV when the pyramid is tilted so that it lies on its cut face on the HP with the axis parallel to the VP. Show the shape of the section by dashed lines.
15. A pentagonal pyramid with a 55 mm base side and a 90 mm slant height, has its base on the HP with a side of base perpendicular to the VP. It is cut by a section plane whose VT is inclined at 60° to *XY* and intersecting the axis at 40 mm from its base. Draw FV, sectional TV, sectional SV and the true shape of the section.
16. A pentagonal pyramid, with a base side of 35 mm and an axis length of 65 mm, is resting on a side of base on the HP. The triangular face through that edge is inclined at 30° to the HP and perpendicular to the VP. The pyramid is cut by a horizontal cutting plane passing through two intermediate base corners. Draw FV and sectional TV.
17. A hexagonal pyramid with an axis length of 90 mm is cut by a section plane in such a way that the true shape of the section is a trapezium of parallel sides 48 mm and 32 mm. The section plane cuts the sides of the pyramid at their midpoints. The base of the pyramid is parallel to the HP.
Draw TV, FV and the cutting plane. Show the section in appropriate view. What is the inclination of the cutting plane with the HP?
18. A hexagonal pyramid *O–ABCDEF* (*O* being the apex) is kept on the ground on its base and is cut by a section plane which is perpendicular to the slant edge *OC* and intersecting the slant edge *OA* on a point

5 mm from A. Draw the projections of the pyramid showing the section. Take the side of the base of the pyramid as 40 mm and the axis to be 80 mm long.

19. A cylinder with a 55 mm base diameter and a 95 mm long axis, stands vertically on the ground. It is cut by an AIP such that the true shape of the section is an ellipse with major axis of 80 mm. Draw its FV, sectional TV and the true shape of the section. Determine the inclination of the section plane with the HP.
20. A cylinder has its axis horizontal and inclined at 60° to the VP. An AVP cuts it such that the true shape of the section is an ellipse with a major axis of 100 mm and a minor axis of 65 mm. Draw the TV, sectional FV and true shape of the section. The length of the cylinder is 105 mm.
21. A cylinder (base diameter of 60 mm and axis length of 85 mm) has its axis inclined at 35° with the HP and 55° with the VP. An AVP inclined at 45° to the VP cuts the cylinder into two equal halves. Draw TV, sectional FV and true shape of the section.
22. A semicylinder with a base radius of 35 mm and a height 75 mm stands on its base on the ground with its flat face parallel and nearer to the PP. Draw its TV and FV. A section plane passes through two opposite corners of the rectangle in FV. Draw the sectional SV and an auxiliary view showing the true shape of the section.
23. A cone with a base diameter of 60 mm and a height of 75 mm is resting on one of the generators on the HP. The generator is parallel to the VP. The cone is cut by a horizontal section plane 30 mm from the HP. Draw FV and sectional TV.
24. A cone with a base diameter of 75 mm and a slant height of 75 mm is resting on a point on the circumference of the base on the HP. The axis of the cone is inclined at 45° to the HP and parallel to the VP. The cone is cut by a section plane HT which passes through the midpoint of the axis and is seen parallel to an extreme generator in TV. Draw TV, sectional FV and true shape of the section of the cone. Assume that the apex of the cone is removed.
25. A cone with a base diameter of 70 mm and a height of 80 mm is lying on its generator with the axis parallel to the VP. It is cut by an AIP passing through the midpoint of its axis such that the true shape of the section is an ellipse with a major axis of maximum possible length. Draw the projections of the cut solid and the true shape of the section. The apex side part of the solid is kept and the upper side part is removed. Also, find the inclination of the cutting plane.
26. A cone of base diameter 75 mm and an axis length of 90 mm stands inverted on its apex on the HP, the base being parallel to the HP. It is cut by an AIP parallel to an extreme generator and passing through the centre of the base. Draw FV, sectional TV and an auxiliary TV showing the true shape of the section.
27. A sphere of a 110 mm diameter lies in the first quadrant touching both the RPs. An AIP inclined at 60° to the HP cuts the sphere in such a way that the true shape of the section is a circle of a 40 mm diameter. Draw FV and sectional TV of the sphere.
28. A water container is in the form of a hemispherical dome. It is installed in such a way that its axis makes 75° with the ground and is parallel to a vertical wall. The container is filled with water up to the highest possible level. Draw FV and TV of the dome showing the water level. The diameter of the dome is 100 cm.
29. A frustum of a cone, with a 75 mm base diameter, 50 mm top diameter and 80 mm axis, has a 30 mm diameter hole drilled coaxially through its flat faces. It is resting on its base on the ground and is cut by a section plane whose VT makes an angle of 60° with *XY* and bisects the axis. Draw its sectional TV and the true shape of section.
30. A cylinder with a 60 mm base diameter and a 100 mm long axis has a square hole of 30 mm side cut through it centrally. The axis of the hole coincides with that of the cylinder. The cylinder rests on a generator on the HP which is inclined at 30° to the VP. The faces of the hole are equally inclined to the HP. The cylinder is cut by a vertical section plane, HT of which passes through a point on the axis, 20 mm from one end. Draw TV and sectional FV assuming that the major portion of the cylinder is retained.

Chapter 16

THEORY OF DEVELOPMENT

16.1 INTRODUCTION

Development is a graphical method of obtaining the area of the surfaces of a solid. When a solid is opened out and its complete surface is laid on a plane, the surface of the solid is said to be developed. The figure thus obtained is called a *development of the surfaces of the solid* or simply *development*. It should be noted that every line on the development represents the true length of the corresponding line on the surface of the solid. Development of the solid, when folded or rolled, gives the solid. For example, when a piece of paper having the shape of a sector is rolled so that the extreme edges meet, we get a cone, Fig. 16.1. In the same way, when a rectangular sheet is rolled so that extreme edges meet, we get a cylinder, Fig. 16.2.

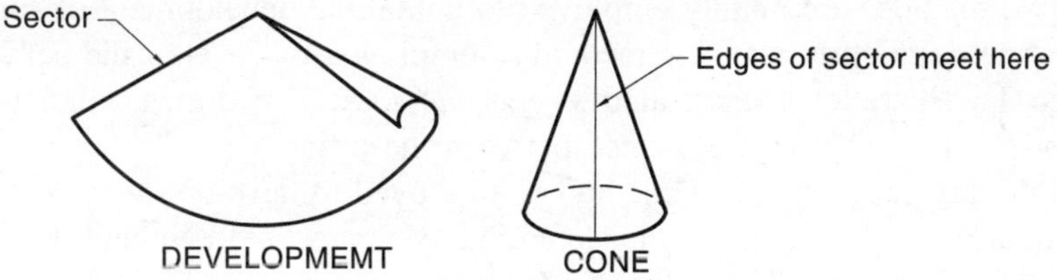

Fig. 16.1

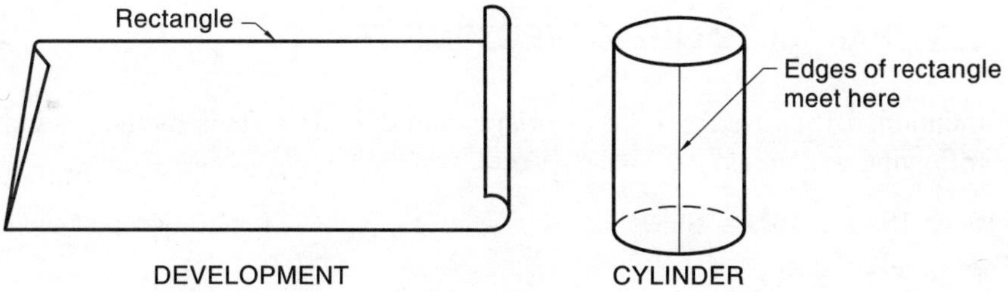

Fig. 16.2

The knowledge of development of surfaces of solids is required in designing and manufacturing of the objects. Practical applications of development occur in sheet metal work (e.g., manufacture of car hood, funnel of a sheet metal, etc.), pattern making in casting (e.g., manufacture of a hollow multi-piece pattern), design of piping in chemical industry and ducting in air conditioning. Some of the common sheet metal objects which employ the theory of development are shown in *Illustration 16.1.*

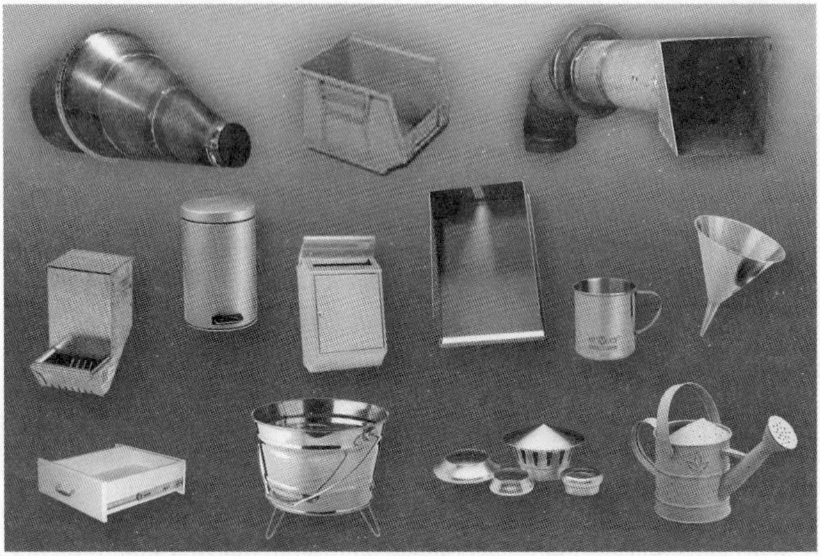

Illustration 16.1 Sheet metal objects

16.2 METHODS OF DEVELOPMENT

The following two methods are mainly employed to obtain the development of surfaces of solids:

1. **Parallel line development:** This method is employed to develop the surfaces of prisms and cylinders. Two parallel lines (called *stretch-out lines*) are drawn from the two ends of the solids and the lateral faces are located between these lines.
2. **Radial line development:** This method is employed to develop the surfaces of pyramids and cones. An arc of radius equal to the slant edge/generator is drawn and the lateral faces/curved face are marked properly inside the arc.

16.3 PARALLEL LINE DEVELOPMENT

As already mentioned it is used in case of prisms and cylinders. This method is explained with the help of the following examples.

Example 16.1 The Fig. 16.3(a) shows the FV of a cube of side 50 mm. Develop all the faces of the cube.

Solution Refer Fig. 16.3(b).

A cube has six equal square faces. To obtain the development, draw two parallel stretch-out lines, one each from the top and bottom face. Draw four lateral faces 1, 2, 3 and 4 between these lines as shown. The top face 5 and bottom face 6 can be drawn attached to any one lateral face. Note that the sides of all the faces in the development are equal to 50 mm.

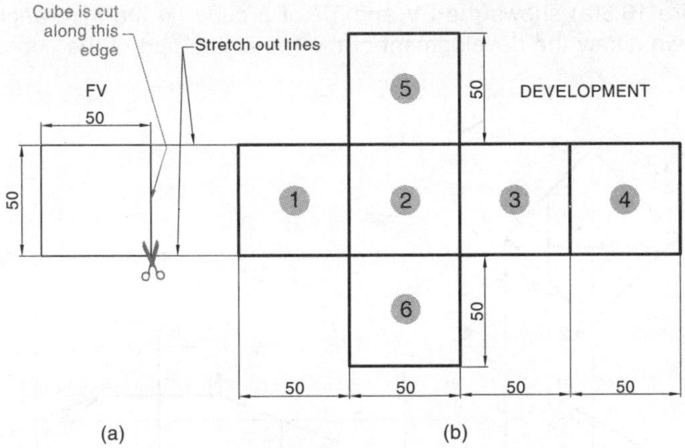

Fig. 16.3

Example 16.2 The Fig. 16.4(a) shows the FV and TV of a rectangular prism of base 40 mm × 35 mm and height 70 mm. Develop all the faces of the prism.

Solution Refer Fig. 16.4(b).

A rectangular prism has four rectangular side faces and two equal rectangular end faces. Two opposite side faces will be of same size. To obtain the development, draw stretch-out lines and locate the four side faces 1, 2, 3 and 4 between them as shown. The side faces 1 and 3 have the same size, i.e., 70 mm × 40 mm. The other two side faces, i.e., 2 and 4 will have size 70 mm × 35 mm each. The end faces 5 and 6 can be drawn attached to any one side face. Each of them will have size 40 mm × 35 mm.

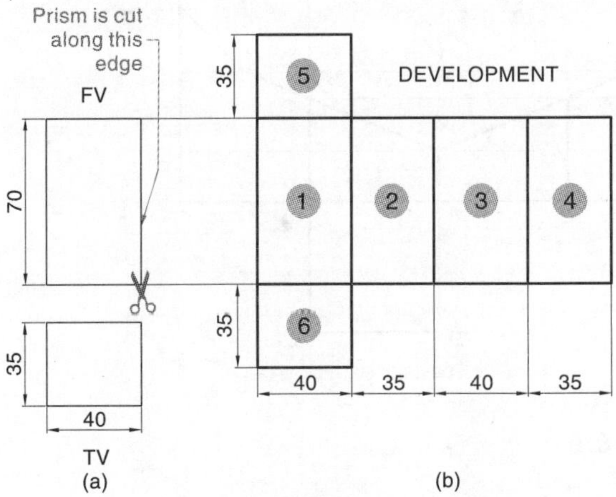

Fig. 16.4

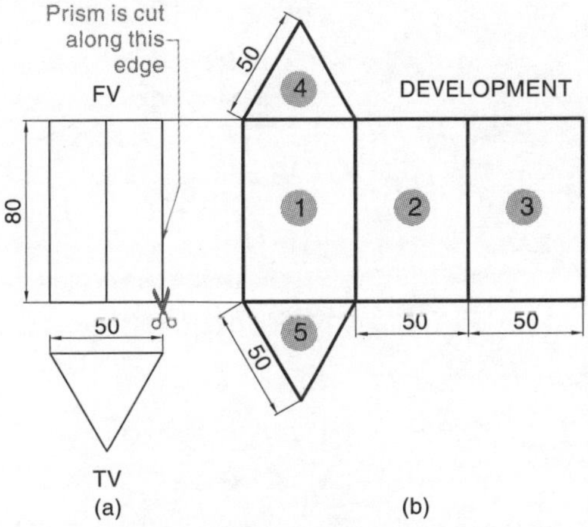

Fig. 16.5

Example 16.3 The two views of a triangular prism of side of base 50 mm and length of axis 80 mm are shown in Fig. 16.5(a). Develop the prism.

Solution Refer Fig. 16.5(b).

A triangular prism has three equal rectangular lateral faces and two equal triangular end faces. In a development, the three lateral faces, 1, 2 and 3, are drawn between the stretch-out lines. The end faces 4 and 5 are attached to a lateral face. All the faces show their true shapes.

Example 16.4 Figure 16.6(a) shows the FV and TV of a cube (in the third-angle method of projection) cut by an AIP as shown. Draw the development of the remaining part of the cube.

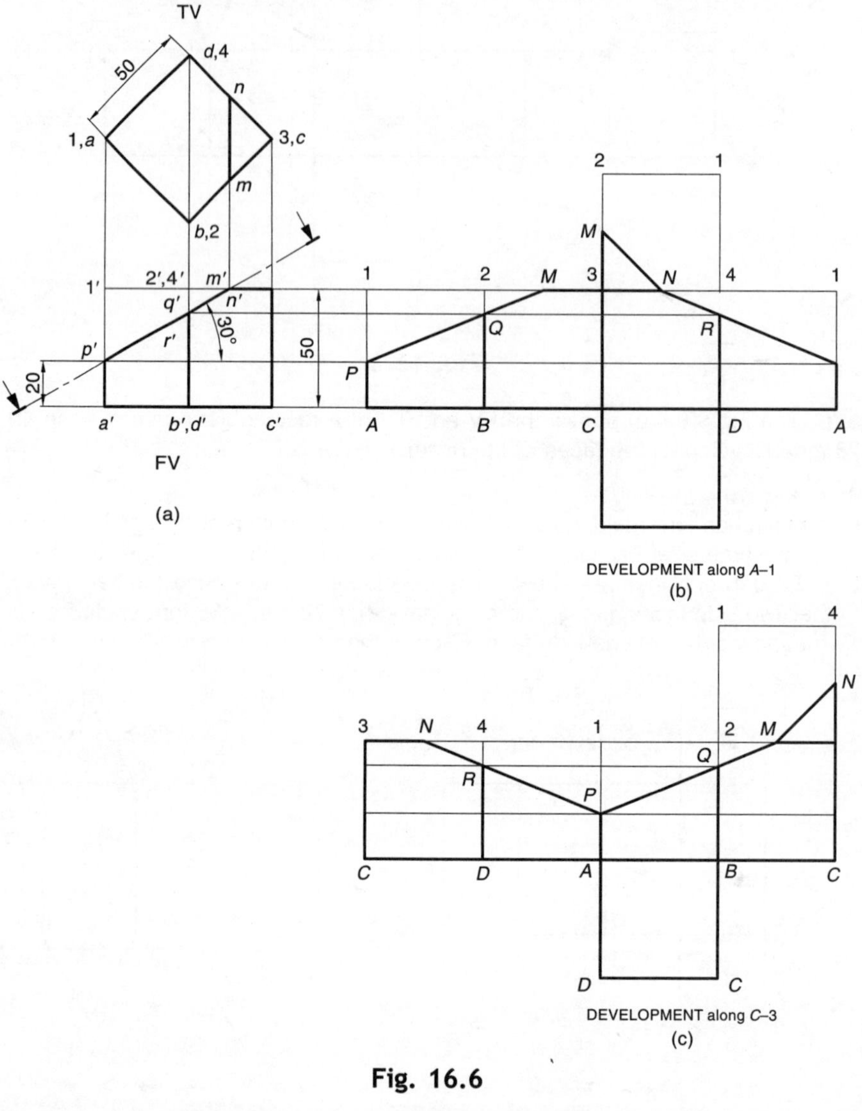

Fig. 16.6

Solution Refer Fig. 16.6(b). It shows the development along edge *A*–1.

1. Locate points *p′*, *q′*, *r′*, *m′* and *n′* at the intersection of the cutting plane with the edges.
2. Draw the stretch-out lines *A*–*A* and 1–1 directly in line with *a′c′* and 1′3′ respectively.
3. Assuming the cube to be whole, draw four squares for the vertical faces (i.e., *A*–*B*–2–1, *B*–*C*–3–2, *C*–*D*–4–3 and *D*–*A*–1–4), one square for the top (i.e., 3–4–1–2) and another for the bottom (i.e., *C*–*D*–*A*–*B*) as shown to represent the development.
4. Project *p′* to *P* on 1–*A* in development. Similarly, project *q′* (*r′*) to *Q* and *R* on 2–*B* and 4–*D* respectively. The projector lines must be parallel to stretch-out lines.

5. The line 2′(4′)–3′ does not represent the TLs of the respective edges. TV shows the TLs of these edges. Hence, project *m*′ (*n*′) to *m* and *n* in TV between 3–2 and 3–4 respectively. Now, 3–*m* and 3–*n* respectively give the true distances of points *M* and *N* from corner 3. Therefore, mark *M* and *N* in the development such that 3–*M* = 3–*m* and 3–*N* = 3–*n*. Note that *M* is on 3–2 and *N* is on 3–4. As the edge 3–2 appears twice in the development, *M* will also appear twice.
6. Join the points located in the development in the correct sequence, i.e. *P–Q–M–3–M–N–R–P–A–D–A–B–C–B–A–P*. Show this curve by thicker lines. The folding lines, i.e., *QB*, 3–*C*, 3–*N*, etc., may also be thickened. Keep the other lines thin since they do not lie on the actual development.

Figure 16.6(b) shows the development along the edge *A*–1. If the solid is opened along the edge *C*–3, its development will be seen as in Fig. 16.7(c). Both the developments are same though their shape is different. When a cut solid is opened along different edges, the developments are seen different. The solid should be opened along the edge which will give its one-piece development.

Example 16.5 Figure 16.7(a) shows a cylinder cut by an AIP. Draw the development of truncated cylinder.

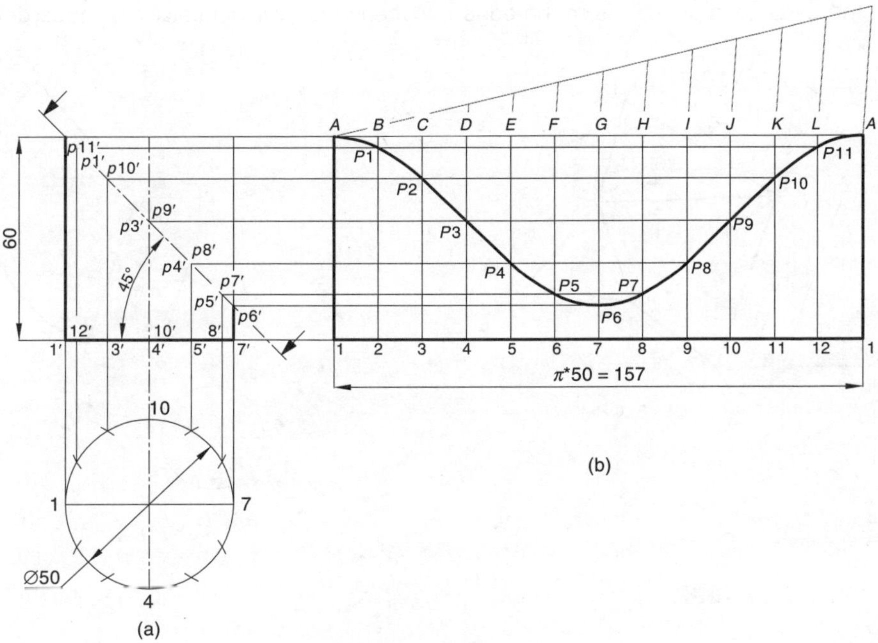

Fig. 16.7

Solution Refer Fig. 16.7(b).

1. Divide the circle in TV into 12 equal parts. Project the division points to the FV and draw the generators. Mark points *p*1′, *p*2′, *p*3′, etc., at the intersection of the AIP and the generators.
2. Draw the development of the lateral surface of the whole cylinder. The length of the line 1–1 is equal to $\pi \times 50$ = 157 mm (circumference of the circle). Divide the length of 157 mm into 12 equal parts. Draw lines 2–*B*, 3–*C*, 4–*D*, etc.
3. Draw horizontal lines through points *p*1′, *p*2′, *p*3′, etc., to cut the corresponding generators (i.e., 2–*B*, 3–*C*, *D*–4, etc.) in points *P*1, *P*2, *P*3, etc. Draw a smooth curve through these points. The figure *A–P*1*–P*2*–P*3 … *P*11*–A*–1–1*–A* is the required development.

16.4 RADIAL LINE DEVELOPMENT

The developments of pyramids and cones are obtained by this method. The following examples explain the radial line development method.

Example 16.6 Figure 16.8(a) shows the two views of a triangular pyramid of base side 50 mm and slant height 85 mm. Obtain the development of the pyramid.

Solution Refer Fig. 16.8(b).

A triangular pyramid has three equal lateral triangular faces and an equilateral triangular base face. To draw the development, first draw *OA* parallel and equal to slant height *o′a′*. Then, with *O* as a centre and radius = *OA*, draw an arc. Obtain the three sides of the base of the pyramid inside this arc. This is done by cutting the arcs of radius 50 mm, subsequently with the centres *A*, *B* and *C* on the bigger arc. Join *AB*, *BC* and *CA*. Also join these sides with *O* to obtain faces 1, 2 and 3 in development. Attach the base face 4 to any one of the lateral faces as shown.

Note that the pyramid is opened from the edge *o′a′*, hence *OA* will appear twice in the development.

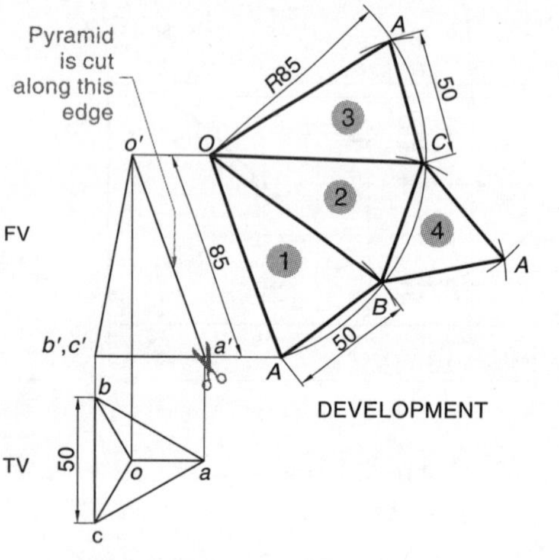

(a) (b)

Fig. 16.8

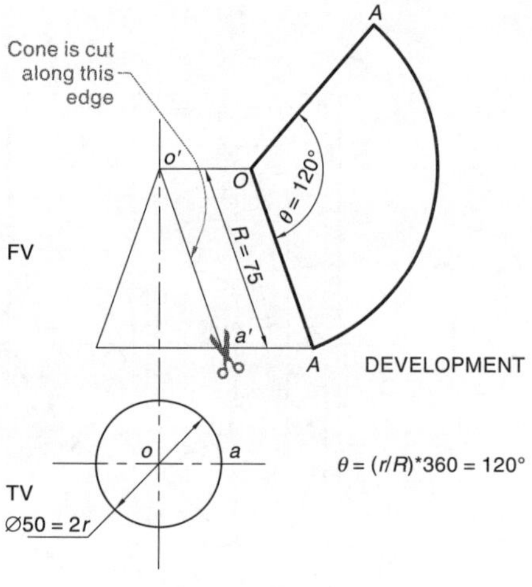

(a) (b)

Fig. 16.9

Example 16.7 Figure 16.9(a) shows the TV and FV of a cone of base diameter 50 mm and slant height 75 mm. Draw the development of its curved surface.

Solution Refer Fig. 16.9(b).

When the curved surface of a cone is opened and laid on a plane, it shows the shape of a sector. The included angle of the sector depends on the slant height, *R* and the radius of the base of the cone, *r*. The radius of the sector will be equal to the slant height of the cone. The length of the arc will be equal to the circumference of the base of the cone, i.e., $2\pi r$. If θ is the included angle (in radian) of the sector, then, $R\theta = 2\pi r$.

i.e., $\theta = 2\pi(r/R)$

i.e., θ (in degree) = $360(r/R)$

Therefore, the first step is to find the included angle of the sector, θ. In this example, θ = 360 (25/75) = 120°. Then draw a line *OA*, parallel and equal to an extreme generator *o′a′*. With *O* as a centre and radius

= *OA*, draw an arc of included angle 120° to complete the sector. As the cone is opened from the edge *o′a′*, *OA* will appear twice in the development.

Note: If $R = 2r$ then $\theta = 180°$, i.e., if the slant height of a cone is equal to its diameter of base then its development is a semicircle of radius equal to the slant height.

Example 16.8 A cone of base diameter 40 mm and slant height 60 mm is kept on the ground on its base. An AIP inclined at 45° to the HP cuts the cone through the midpoint of the axis. Draw the development.

Solution Refer Fig. 16.10.

1. Draw FV and TV as shown. Locate the AIP.
2. Divide the TV into 12 equal parts and draw the corresponding lateral lines (i.e., generators) in FV. Mark points *p*1′, *p*2′, *p*3′, ..., *p*12′ at the points of intersections of the AIP with generators of the cone.
3. Obtain the included angle of the sector. θ = (20/60)* 360 = 120°.
4. Draw *O*–1 parallel and equal to *o′*–7. Then draw sector *O*–1–1–*O* with *O* as a centre and included angle 120°.
5. Divide the sector into 12 equal parts (i.e., 10° each). Draw lines *O*–2, *O*–3, *O*–4, ..., *O*–12.
6. Project points *p*1′, *p*2′, *p*3′, ..., *p*12′ from FV to corresponding lines in development and mark points *P*1, *P*2, *P*3, ..., *P*12 respectively. Join all these points by a smooth freehand curve.

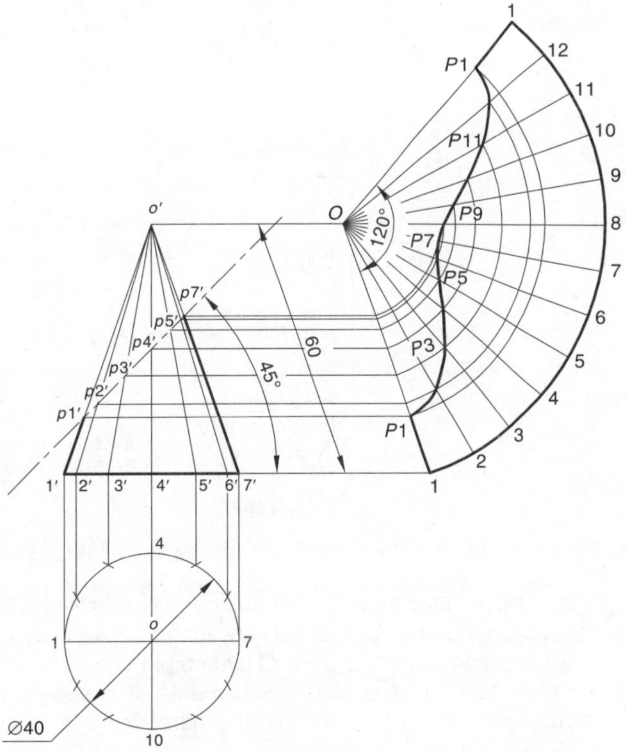

Fig. 16.10

Example 16.9 A hexagonal pyramid of side of base 60 mm and length of axis 140 mm is kept on the ground on its base. It is cut by an AIP inclined at 45° to the base and cutting the axis at 94 mm from the apex. Draw the development of lateral surfaces of the pyramid.

Solution Refer Fig. 16.11.

1. Draw TV and FV of the pyramid. Indicate AIP as shown.
2. Mark the points of intersections of AIP with the slant edges of the pyramid as 1′, 2′, etc. The AIP cuts base at points *p′* and *q′*.
3. Project *p′* and *q′* to *p* and *q* respectively in TV.
4. Draw a line *OA* parallel and equal to *o′d′*. Note that *o′d′* represents the slant length. With *O* as a centre and radius = *OA*, draw an arc *AW* of any length.
5. On arc *AW*, mark off points *B*, *C*, *D*, *E*, *F* and *A* such that *AB* = *BC* = *CD* = *DE* = *EF* = *FA* = 60 mm.
6. Join *B*, *C*, *D*, *E*, *F* and *A* with *O*. The six triangles thus obtained represent the lateral faces of the pyramid.
7. Project points 1′, 2′, etc., from FV to corresponding edges in development and mark them as 1, 2, etc.

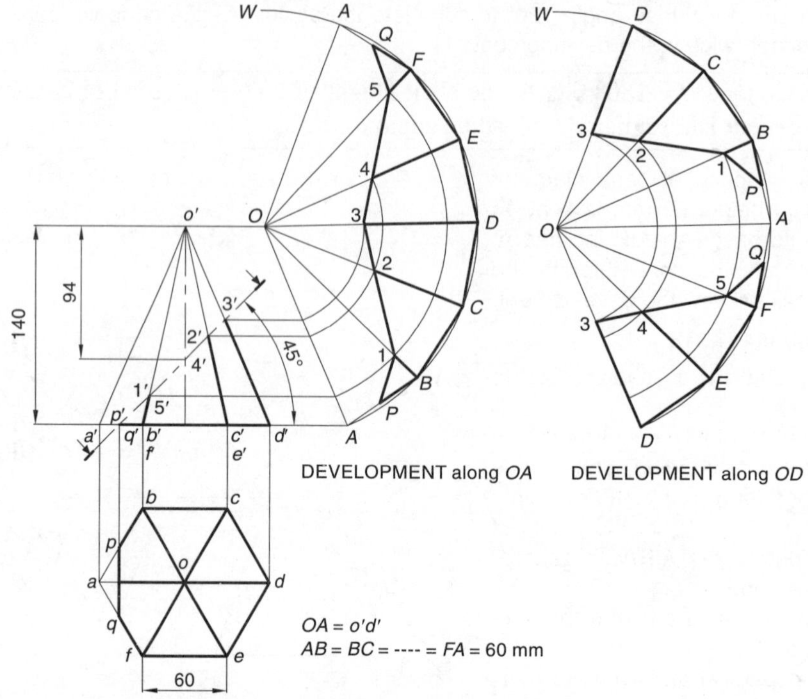

Fig. 16.11

8. The points *p* and *q* lie on *ab* and *af* respectively. To locate these points in development, mark *P* and *Q* on *AB* and *AF* respectively such that *AP* = *ap* and *AQ* = *aq*.
9. Join points *P*–1–2 ... 5–*Q* by straight line segments to obtain the required development.

Figure 16.11 shows two developments of the same pyramid: (i) Development along *OA*, and (ii) The development along *OD*. The development along *OD* is seen in two pieces. Hence, it should be avoided as explained in Example 16.4.

Note: In case of cone and cylinder, the development curve is a smooth freehand curve. In case of prism and pyramid, the development curve is a straight-line segmented curve.

16.5 ANTI-DEVELOPMENT

Anti-development is the reverse process of development. In this case, the developed surface of a solid is given and one has to draw the solid. Many times, the development of a truncated or cut solid is given and the solid has to be drawn. The method to obtain anti-development is essentially same as that of development. The following examples deal with anti-development.

Example 16.10 Figure 16.12(a) shows the development of a cut cylinder of height 170 mm. Draw the solid from development.

Solution The cut cylinder obtained from the given development is shown in Fig. 16.12(b).

1. Enclose the given development in rectangle 1–1–1′–1′ as shown.
2. Find the diameter of the cylinder, i.e., $157/\pi = 50$ mm.

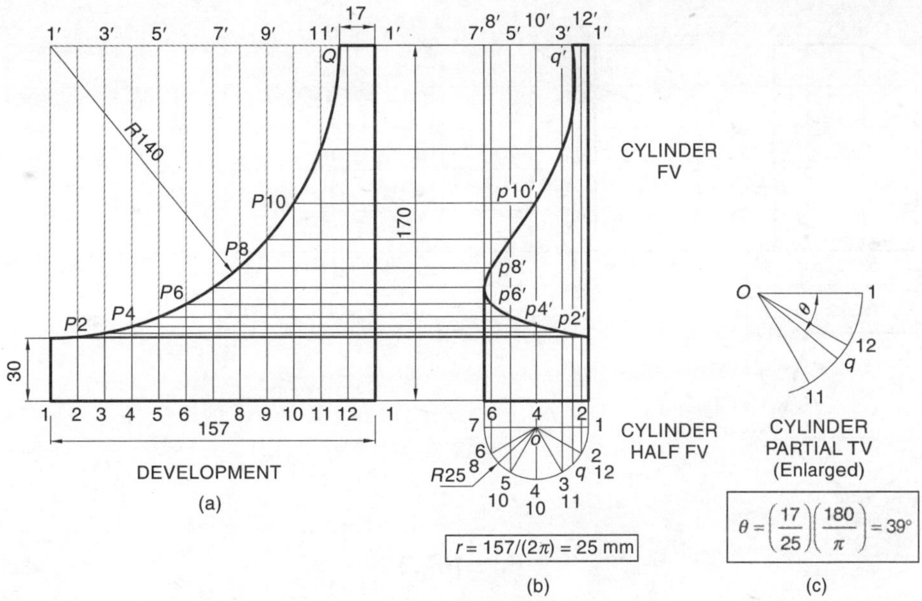

Fig. 16.12

3. Draw FV and half TV of the cylinder as shown. Full TV is not necessary since 6 divisions of the semicircle will serve the purpose of 12 divisions of the circle as shown.
4. Divide the length 1–1 in the development into 12 equal parts and draw vertical lines through each point, viz., 2–2′, 3–3′, 4–4′, ..., 12–12′. Locate the points of intersections of these vertical lines with the arc and mark them as *P*1, *P*2, *P*3, ..., *P*12.
5. Divide half TV into 6 equal parts and obtain the corresponding lateral lines in FV.
6. Projects points *P*1, *P*2, *P*3, ..., *P*11 from development to corresponding lateral lines in FV and mark these points as *p*1′, *p*2′, *p*3′, ..., *p*11′.

   Point *Q* lies between 11′–12′. First locate it between 11–12 in half TV in such a way that 12′–*Q* in development = 12–*q* in half TV. Project *q* from half TV to *q*′ in FV exactly in between 11′–12′.
7. Join points *p*1′, *p*2′, *p*3′, ..., *q*′ by smooth curve. The cut cylinder thus obtained represents the required anti-development.

Note: Point *Q* can be accurately located in TV as shown in Fig. 16.12(c). If $\angle 1\text{–}o\text{–}q = \theta$ (radian), then the length of arc $1\text{–}q = r^*\theta = 1'\text{–}Q$ in development. Therefore $25^*\theta = 17 \Rightarrow \theta = 39°$. However, for small distance 12′–*Q* in development, arc $12\text{–}q \approx 12'\text{–}Q$.

Example 16.11 A regular pentagonal prism of side 40 mm and length of axis 75 mm is kept on the ground on its base with one of its rectangular faces away from the observer and parallel to the VP. A thread is wound around the prism starting from the nearest corner of the base and is brought back to the top of the same vertical edge. Find the minimum length of the thread and show it in FV and SV.

Solution Refer Fig. 16.13.

1. Draw TV of the prism with one edge parallel to *XY* and a corner nearest to the observer. Obtain FV and SV.
2. Draw development *A*–*A*–*A*1–*A*1 of the whole prism as shown.
3. Draw a straight line *A*1–*A* in development. *A*1–*A* represents the minimum length of the thread. This is because the shortest distance between any two points is the length of straight line joining them. Note that *A*1 and *A* represent two ends of the same vertical edge of the prism.

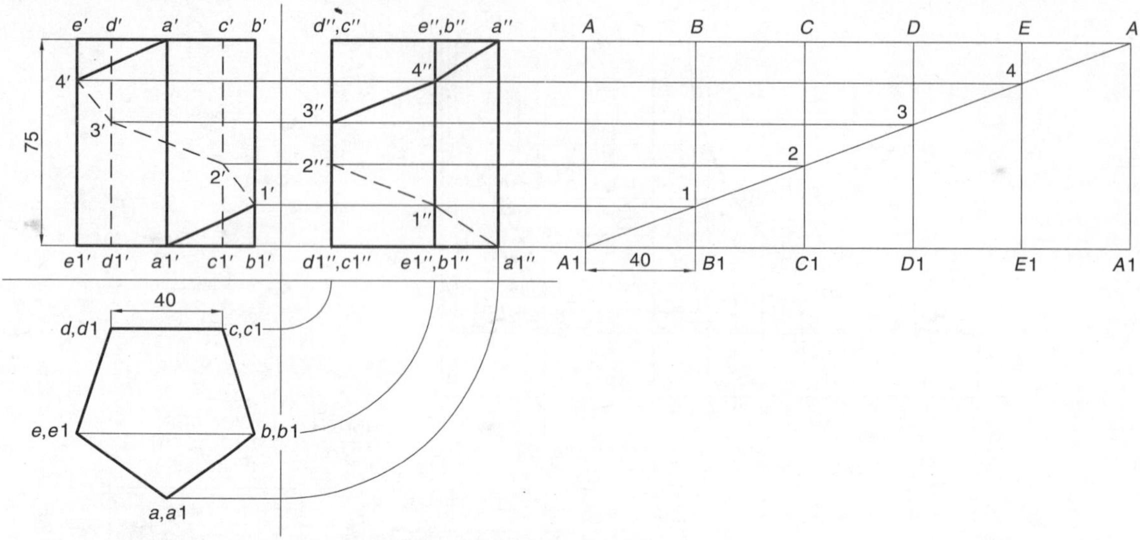

Fig. 16.13

4. Locate points of intersection of the thread with vertical lines through *B*, *C*, *D* and *E*. Mark them as 1, 2, 3 and 4.
5. Project points 1, 2, 3 and 4 on respective edges in FV and SV. Join *a*1′–1′–2′–3′–4′–*a*′ and *a*1″–1″–2″–3″–4″–*a*″. Points 1′–2′–3′–4′ are joined by dashed lines as the part of thread is invisible from the front. In SV, *a*1″–1″–2″ is hidden.

Example 16.12 A pentagonal pyramid of base side 30 mm and length of axis 60 mm is kept on the ground on its base. A thread is wound around the pyramid in such a way that it starts from a corner of the base and comes back to the same corner after completing one revolution by the shortest route. Draw the development of the pyramid and show the thread in FV and TV.

Solution Refer Fig. 16.14.

1. Draw TV and FV of the pyramid as shown. *o*′*b*1′ is the slant height of the pyramid. To obtain *o*′*b*1′, rotate *ob* to *ob*1 parallel to *XY*. Project point *b*1 to *b*1′ in FV.
2. Draw *OA* parallel and equal to *o*′*b*1′. Obtain development *O–ABCDEA* by radial line method.

   Let the thread be wound along the pyramid, starting from point *A*. It will complete one round along all the faces of the pyramid and then will come back to *A* again. The shortest path taken by the thread is obtained by a straight line joining *A–A* in the development.
3. Mark points 1, 2, 3 and 4 at the intersections of *A–A* with *OB*, *OC*, *OD* and *OE* respectively.
4. Project the points 1, 2, 3 and 4 from development to FV on corresponding slant edges. Mark these points as *p*1′, *p*2′, *p*3′ and *p*4′.

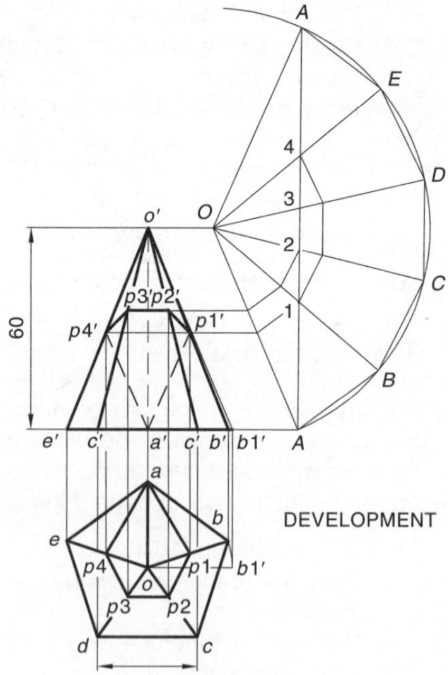

Fig. 16.14

5. Join points $p1'$, $p2'$, $p3'$, $p4'$ and a' by straight-line segments to form a closed loop. This curve represents the path of the thread in FV. Note that $p1'$–a'–$p4'$ is shown by a dashed line.
6. Project $p1'$, $p2'$, $p3'$ and $p4'$ from FV to corresponding edges in TV and mark $p1$, $p2$, $p3$ and $p4$. Join $p1$, $p2$, $p3$, $p4$ and by a straight-line segments to represent the thread in TV.

ILLUSTRATIVE PROBLEMS

Problem 16.1 A hexagonal prism of side of base 20 mm and length of axis 50 mm is kept on the ground on its base such that two opposite sides of the base are parallel to the VP. It is cut by an AIP inclined at 45° to the HP and passing through one of the top corners of the prism. Draw the development of the cut prism.

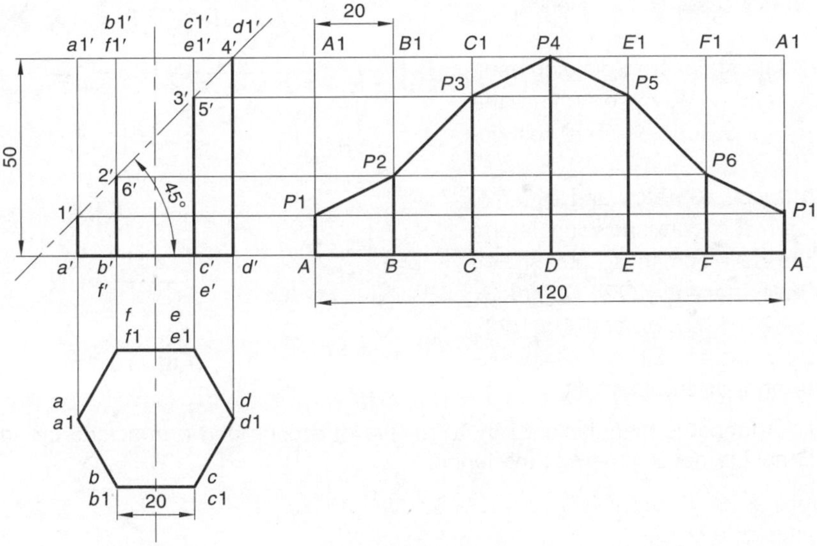

Fig. 16.15

Solution Refer Fig. 16.15.

1. Draw FV and TV as shown. Locate the AIP.
2. Mark points 1′, 2′, 3′, 4′, 5′ and 6′ at the intersections of the AIP with vertical edges of the prism.
3. Draw the development *A–A–A*1–*A*1 of the complete prism. Mark points *B*, *C*, *D*, *E* and *F* such that *AB* = *BC* = *CD* = *DE* = *EF* = *FA* = 20 mm. Draw lines *BB*1, *CC*1, *DD*1, *EE*1 and *FF*1 all parallel to *AA*1.
4. Project points 1′, 2′, 3′, ..., 6′ from FV to corresponding edges in development and mark points *P*1, *P*2, *P*3, ..., *P*6. Join these points by straight-line segments. The area *A–B–C–D–E–F–A–P*1–*P*6–*P*5–*P*4–*P*3–*P*2–*P*1–*A* represents the required development.

Problem 16.2 A cone of base diameter 60 mm and slant height equal to the base diameter is resting on its base on the HP. It is cut by two section planes: (i) an AIP inclined at 45° to the HP and passing through a point on the axis 14 mm from the apex, and (ii) an curved plane of radius 30 mm, as shown in Fig. 16.16(a). Develop the intermediate portion of the cone.

Solution Refer Fig. 16.16(b).

1. Draw half TV of cone and obtain 6 equal divisions on it. Obtain corresponding lateral lines in FV.
2. Mark the points of intersections of the AIP with the generators as *p*1′, *p*2′, *p*3′, etc. Similarly, mark the points of intersections of the curved section plane with the generators as *q*1′, *q*2′, *q*3′, etc. The generator *o*′–*m*′ can be drawn in FV by locating m at the midpoint of arc 4–5 in TV. (Clearly, ∠4–*o*–*m* = ∠*m*–*o*–5.)
3. Draw a sector, i.e., semicircle in development. In this case, $R = 2r$. Hence, $\theta = 180°$.
4. Obtain 12 lateral lines on development. Draw *OM* and *OM*′ by bisecting the angles, ∠4–*O*–5 and ∠9–*O*–10 respectively.
5. Project *p*1′, *p*2′, *p*3′, etc., and *q*1′, *q*2′, *q*3′, etc., on the corresponding lateral lines in the development to obtain *P*1′, *P*2′, *P*3′, etc., and *Q*1′, *Q*2′, *Q*3′, etc.
6. Join *P*1′, *P*2′, *P*3′, etc., and *Q*1′, *Q*2′, *Q*3′, etc., by two smooth curves to represent the area of development.

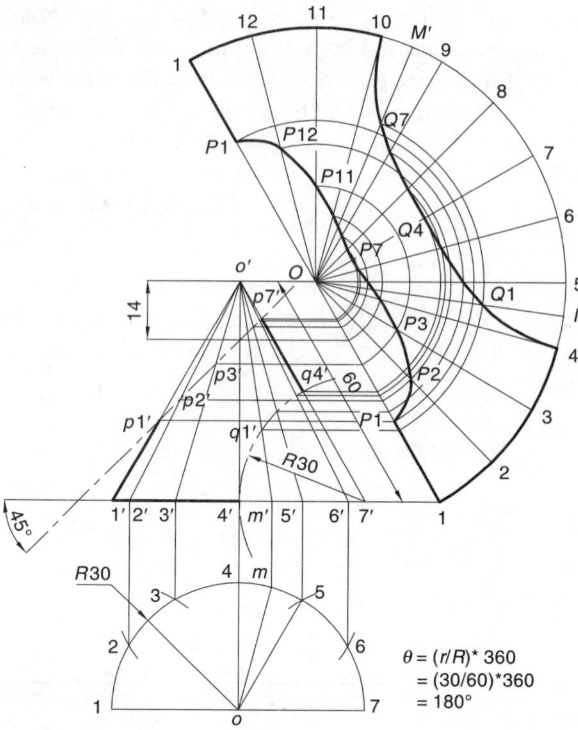

(a) (b)

Fig. 16.16

Problem 16.3 A funnel is manufactured by a frustum of a cone and a truncated cylinder as shown in Fig. 16.17(a). Draw the development of the funnel.

Solution Refer Fig. 16.17(b).

Part *A* is a frustum of a cone.

1. Obtain the apex *o*′ by extending *a*′*d*′ and *b*′*c*′. Measure length *o*′*a*′.
2. Obtain the included angle of development. $\theta = [30/(o'a')]* 360 = [30/75]* 360 = 144°$.
3. Draw a sector *O*–*A*–*A*–*O* such that *O*–*A* = *o*′*a*′ and ∠*AOA* =144°.
4. Project point *c*′(*d*′) from FV to *D* on *O*–*A* in development. Draw arc *DD*. Note that *a*′*b*′ and *d*′*c*′ are parallel to each other and hence the arcs *AA* and *DD* are concentric.

Part *B* is a truncated cylinder.

5. Draw the half TV of the cylinder and divide it into 4 equal parts.
6. Obtain lateral lines in FV. Locate the points of intersections of the cutting plane with the lateral lines and mark them as 1′, 2′, 3′, ..., 8′.
7. Draw the development 1–*C*–*C*–1 of cylinder assuming that it is not cut. Note that the length 1–1 = π* 20 = 63 mm. Divide length 1–1 into 8 equal parts and mark divisions as 2, 3, ..., 8.
8. Through points 2, 3, ..., 8 on development, set vertical lines.
9. Project points 1′, 2′, 3′, ..., 8′ from FV on the corresponding vertical lines in the development. Mark points *P*1, *P*2, *P*3, ..., *P*8.
10. Join the points *P*1, *P*2, *P*3, ..., *P*8 by a freehand smooth curve. *C*–*P*1–*P*2–*P*3–*P*4–*P*5–*P*6–*P*7–*P*8–*P*1–*C*–*D*–*C* represents the required development.

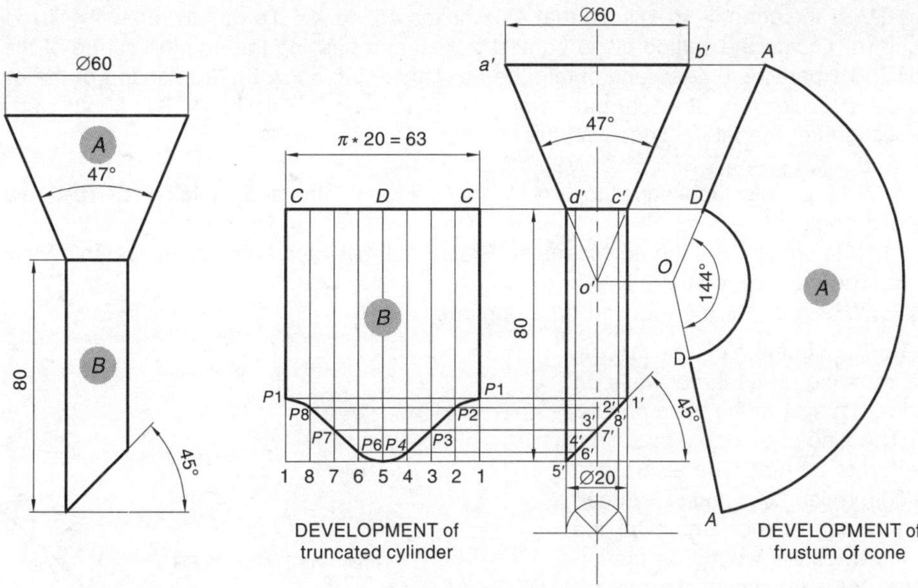

(a) (b)

Fig. 16.17

Problem 16.4 A cone of base diameter 50 mm and axis 75 mm long has a point on its circumference of the base in the VP and the generator through that point is inclined at 45° to the VP and parallel to the HP. It is cut by a vertical section plane which is parallel to that generator. The cutting plane passes through the centre of the base. Develop the part of the truncated cone containing the apex.

Solution Refer Fig. 16.18.

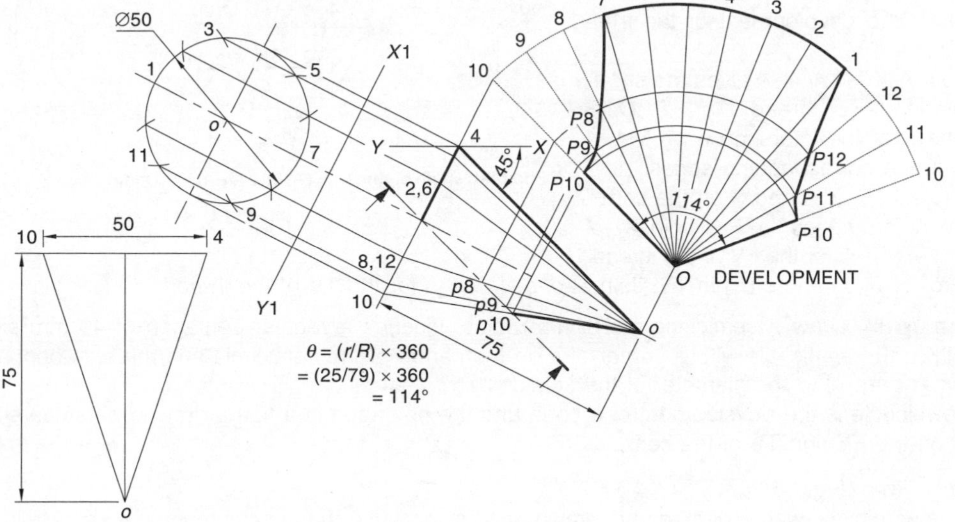

Fig. 16.18

1. Draw TV of the cone 4–10–*o* such that 4–*o* makes 45° to *XY*. To do this, draw Δ4–10–*o* separately as shown. Locate the cutting plane parallel to 4–*o* and passing through the centre of the base.
2. Draw *X*1*Y*1 parallel to 4–10 and obtain the auxiliary FV to show the true shape of the base.
3. Divide the circle into 12 equal parts and obtain 12 lateral lines in TV. Mark *p*8, *p*9, etc., at the intersections of the lateral lines with the cutting plane.
4. Find θ. $\theta = [25/(4–o)] \times 360° = [25/79] \times 360° = 114°$.
5. Draw *O*–10 parallel and equal to *o*–4. With *O* as a centre and radius = *O*–10, draw an arc of included angle 114°.
6. Obtain 12 lateral lines in the development. Project *p*8, *p*9, etc., in the development to locate *P*8, *P*9, etc., on the respective lateral lines.
7. Join *P*8, *P*9, etc., for the required development.

Problem 16.5 A frustum of a hexagonal pyramid is standing on its larger base on the ground with a side of the base parallel to the VP. The side of the base is 35 mm and of the top is 20 mm. The axis of the frustum is 60 mm long. An end of a thread is attached to one of the corners of the base and the thread is wound on the lateral surface, following shortest path, so that it will pass through the opposite corner of the top and then brought back to the same corner of the base. Determine the shortest length of the thread required and show the path followed by the thread in FV and TV.

Solution Refer Fig. 16.19.

1. Draw TV and FV of the frustum. A side of the base is drawn parallel to *XY*.
2. Draw the development of the frustum.
3. Join *A*–4–*A*. *A*–4–*A* gives the shortest length of thread. Mark *P*, *Q*, *R* and *S* at the intersection of *A*–4–*A* with the corresponding edges.
4. Project *P*, *Q*, *R* and *S* on the corresponding edges in FV. Join *a*′–*p*′ (*s*′)–*q*′(*r*′)–4′ for the FV of the thread.
5. Project *p*′(*s*′) and *q*′(*r*′) in TV. Join *a*–*p*–*q*–4–*r*–*s*–*a* for the TV of the thread.

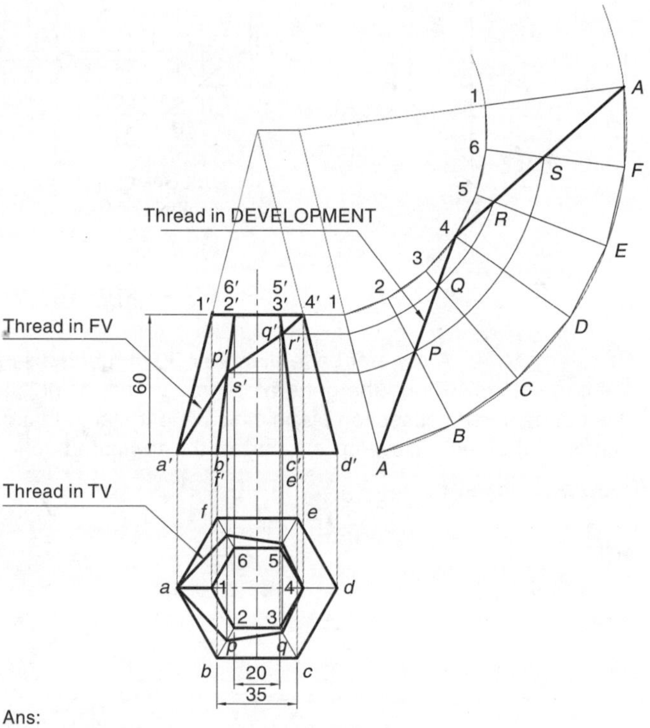

Ans:
Shortest length of thread = (*A*–4) + (4–*A*) = 98 mm

Fig. 16.19

Problem 16.6 Draw a semicircle of 70 mm radius. Inscribe a regular pentagon of 40 mm sides symmetrically in the semicircle with a corner of it on the centre of the semicircle and the side opposite to the said corner parallel to the diameter of the semicircle.

The semicircle is the development of a cone and the pentagon is a figure drawn on its curved surface. Show it on the FV and TV of the cone.

Solution Refer Fig. 16.20.

1. The semicircle with a pentagon is drawn as shown. Since the development is a semicircle of radius = 70 mm, the cone will have slant height = base diameter = 70 mm.
2. Draw TV and FV of the cone.

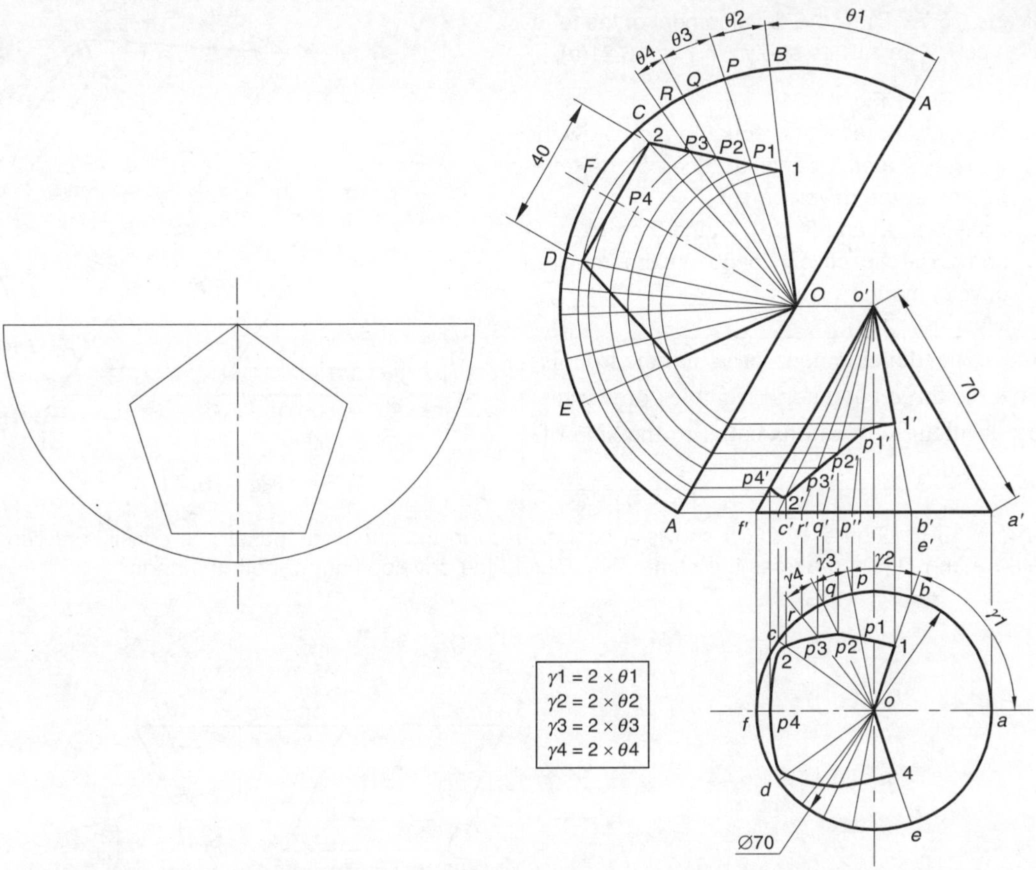

Fig. 16.20

3. In development, draw the lines joining centre O with each corner of the pentagon, i.e., OB, OC, OD and OE.
4. The point B, C, D and E will be seen as b, c, d and e respectively in TV.
   Let $\angle AOB = \theta 1$ and $\angle aob = \gamma 1$. Then, we have $R^* \theta 1 = r^* \gamma 1$.
   i.e., $\gamma 1 = (R/r)^* \theta 1 = (70/35)\ ^* \theta 1 = 2^* \theta 1$.
   Therefore, locate b such that $\angle aob = 2^* \theta 1$. The points c, d and e may be located in a similar way.
5. Project b, c, d and e to b', c', d' and e' in FV. Join them with o' to obtain the corresponding lateral lines.
6. Project 1, 2, 3 and 4 from the development to FV on the corresponding lateral lines.
7. Locate few points $P1$, $P2$, etc., along 1–2 in the development. Join O with $P1$, $P2$, etc., and extend them to meet the arc at P, Q, etc.
8. Obtain p, q, etc., in TV and p', q', etc., in FV as explained in steps 4 and 5.
9. Obtain $p1'$, $p2'$, etc., in FV by projecting $P1$, $P2$, etc., from the development on the corresponding lateral lines.
10. The extreme generator $o'f'$ is represented by OF in the development. Mark $P4$ at its intersection with the edge of the pentagon and project it to $p4'$ on $o'f'$.
11. Join all the points by smooth curve.
12. Project all the points in TV for the required curve. Note that $o'1'$, o–1 and o–4 are straight-line segments.

Problem 16.7 Draw the development of the tetrahedron cut by an AIP as shown in Fig. 16.21(a).

Solution Refer Fig. 16.21.

1. Draw *OC* parallel and equal to *o′c′*. Draw the three equilateral triangular faces of the tetrahedron in the development.
2. Project 1′, 2′ and 3′ to 1, 2 and 3 on *OC*, *OA* and *OB* respectively to obtain the required development.

> **Note:** The development of a tetrahedron is always the three equilateral triangles drawn inside a semicircle of radius equal to the side of the tetrahedron.

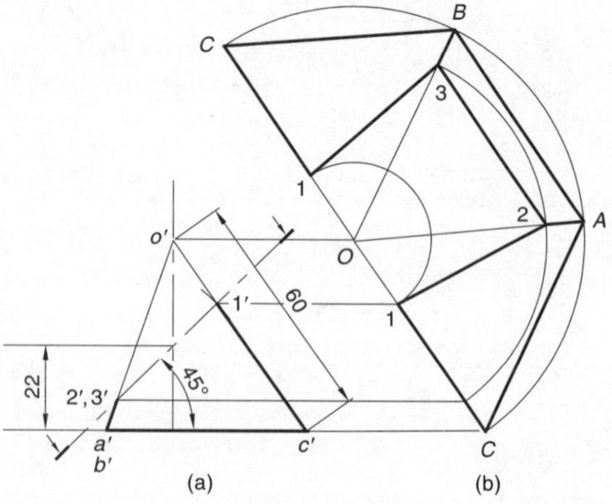

Fig. 16.21

Problem 16.8 Figure 16.22(a) shows a hopper used in the chemical industry. It consists of two parts labeled *A* and *B* joined across the plane *X–X*. Obtain the development of both the parts.

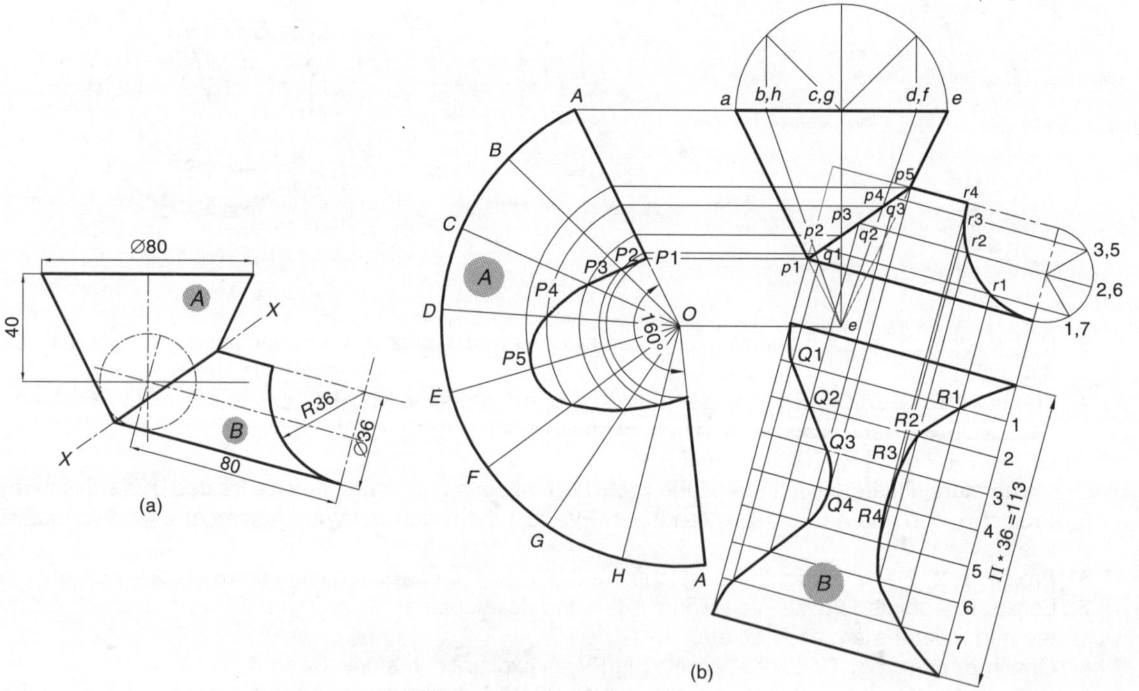

Fig. 16.22

Solution Refer Fig. 16.22(b).

Part *A* is a truncated cone.

1. Locate the apex *o* by extending *a–p*1 and *b–p*5. Measure slant height *ao*.

2. Find θ. $\theta = (40/ao) \times 360° = (40/90) \times 360° = 160°$.
3. Draw *OA* parallel and equal to *oa*. Draw an arc of radius = *OA* and included angle 160°.
4. Obtain the 8 lateral lines on the cone and development. Mark *p*1, *p*2, etc., at the intersection of the lateral lines with the cutting plane.
5. Project *p*1, *p*2, etc., in the development on the corresponding lateral lines to locate *P*1, *P*2, etc.

Part *B* is a cylinder cut by two section planes at two ends.

6. Obtain the 8 lateral lines on the cylinder and its development. Locate *q*1, *q*2, etc., and *r*1, *r*2, etc., at the intersections of the lateral lines and the section planes.
7. Project these points on the corresponding lines in the development.

Problem 16.9 Figure 16.23(a) shows the FV and TV of a sheet metal object. Develop its lateral face.

Solution The development is shown in Fig. 16.23(b).

From the FV and TV, it is clear that the portion *a*′–1′–*m*′(*n*′)–*p*′(*q*′) is flat whereas the portion *a*′–1′–4′–*d*′ is cylindrical.

1. Draw a rectangle *A*–*G*–*G*1–*A*1 of size 63 mm × 80 mm to represent the development of the cylindrical portion.
2. Obtain six equal divisions on semicircle *a*–*d*–*g*. Obtain the lateral lines *a*′–1′, *b*′–2′, *c*′–3′ in FV. Project 1′, 2′, etc., in the development on the corresponding lateral lines.
3. To draw the development of the flat portion, draw *AP* = *GQ* = 10 mm and then locate *M* and *N* as shown. Draw the arcs *M*–1 and *N*–7 by locating their centres as shown.

Problem 16.10 A square pyramid, side of base 60 mm and height 90 mm, is placed on the HP on its base with the sides of the base equally inclined to the VP. A hole of diameter 40 mm is cut through the pyramid. The axis of the hole is perpendicular to the VP and cuts the axis of the pyramid 35 mm above the base. The solid is further cut by an AIP inclined at 30° to the HP and passing through the two opposite corners of the base.

Draw the development of cut pyramid showing the holes on it. Also obtain the TV.

Solution Refer Fig. 16.24.

1. Draw the TV and FV of the pyramid. The hole and cutting plane are located as shown.
2. Mark the intersection of *O*–*b*′ with the circle as 1′ and 7′.
3. Draw *O*–*m*′ and *O*–*q*′ tangent to circle at 4′ and 10′ respectively. Draw a few more lines, say *O*–*n*′ and *O*–*t*′, intersecting the circle at 3′, 5′, 2′ and 6′ respectively.
4. Project *m*′, *n*′ and *t*′ in TV on *ab*. Join *m*, *n* and *t* with *o*.
5. Draw the development of the pyramid. Draw lateral lines *OM*, *ON* and *OT* such that *a*′–*M* = *am*, *MN* = *mn* and *NT* = *nt*.
6. Project 1′, 2′, etc., in the development on the corresponding lateral lines. Obtain other points in the development in a similar way to complete two closed curves.
7. Project *p*′ to *P* in development. Join *B*–*P*–*D*.
8. Project 1′, 2′, etc., and *p*′ in TV on the corresponding lateral lines to obtain closed curves. Note how 1′ and 7′ are projected to 1 and 7 in TV.

Problem 16.11 Figure 16.25(a) shows the two views of a domestic dust pan. Develop all the surfaces of the pan.

Solution Refer Fig. 16.25(b).

The pan consists of four faces—*A*, *B*, *C*1 and *C*2. The faces *C*1 and *C*2 are similar. The face *A* shows the true shape i.e., development in TV.

1. To obtain the true shape of face *B*, obtain the TLs of its edges. Rotate *p*′–*t*′(*u*′) to *p*′–*t*1′(*u*1′) parallel to *XY*. Project *t*1′ (*u*1′) on the loci of *t* and *u*. Join *p*–*t*1–*u*1–*q* for the true shape of face *B*.

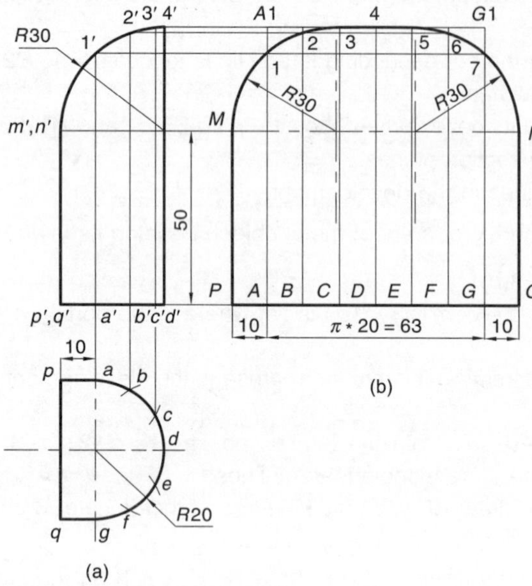

Fig. 16.23

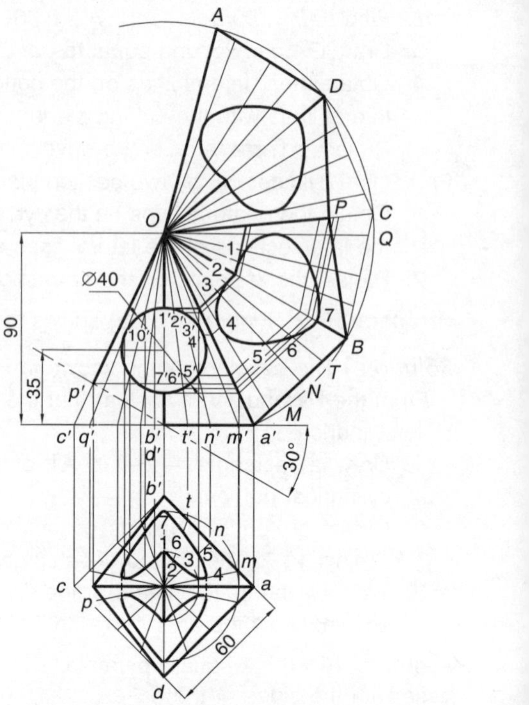

Fig. 16.24

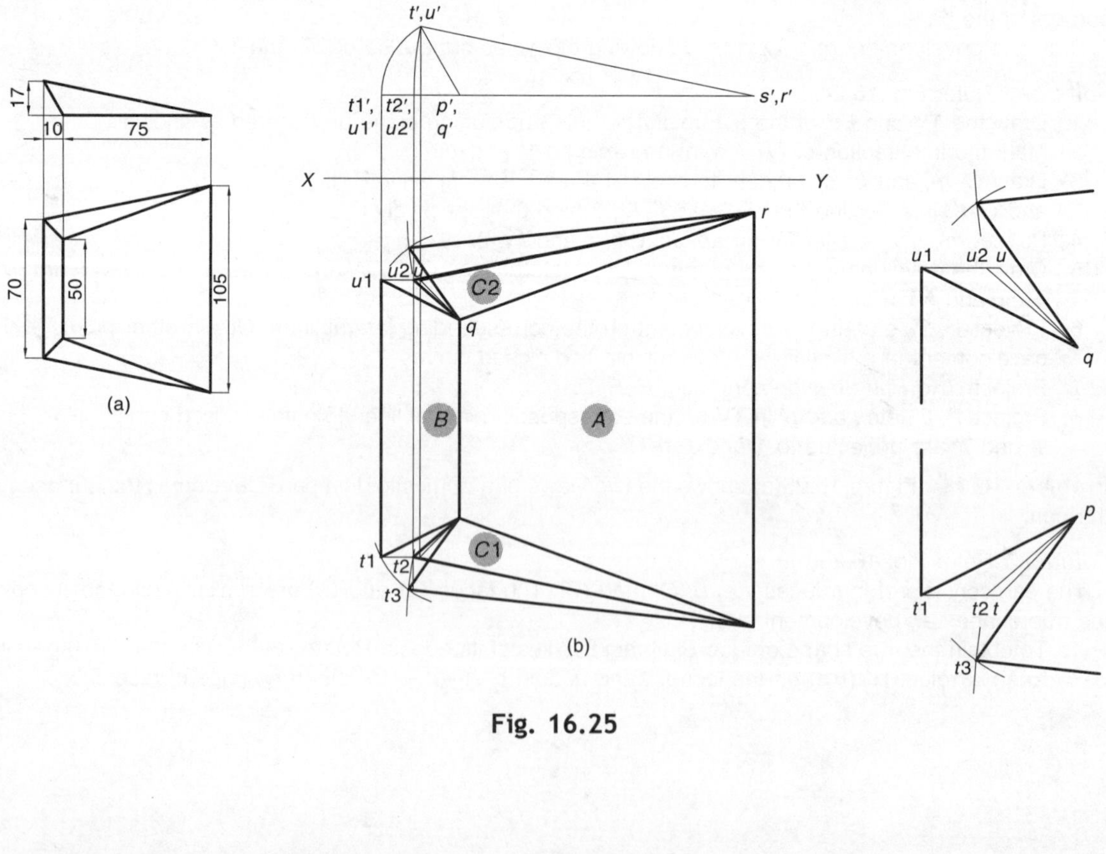

Fig. 16.25

2. Rotate s'–$t'(u')$ to s'–$t2'(u2')$ parallel to *XY*. Project $t2'$ to $t2$ on the locus of t in TV. Join s–$t2$ for the TL of ST.
3. With p as a centre and radius = p–$t1$, draw an arc. With s as a centre and radius = s–$t2$, draw another arc cutting the previous arc at $t3$. Join $t3$ to p and s. s–p–$t3$ gives the true shape of $C1$. Obtain true shape of face $C2$ in a similar way.

Problem 16.12 A pentagonal pyramid, base side 56 mm and length of axis 90 mm, has a corner of base in the VP. The slant edge through that corner is inclined to the VP at 60° and parallel to the HP. The solid is cut by two section planes: (i) an AVP inclined at 30° to the VP and passing through the midpoint of axis, and (ii) profile section plane passing through the corners of the base nearer to the VP (other than that in the VP). Develop the intermediate portion of the pyramid.

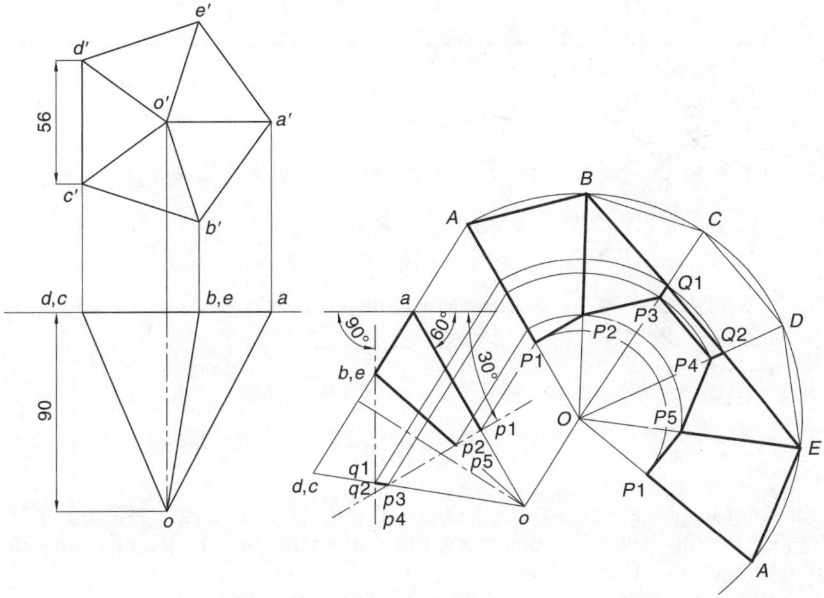

Fig. 16.26

Solution Refer Fig. 16.26.

1. Draw FV and TV of the pyramid as shown.
2. Redraw FV such that *ao* makes 60° to *XY*.
3. Locate the cutting planes as per the conditions given in the problem. Mark $p1$, $p2$, etc. and $q1$ and $q2$ at the intersections of the cutting planes with the edges of the pyramid.
4. Draw *OA* parallel and equal to *oa*. Obtain the development of the pyramid. Locate $P1$, $P2$, etc., and $Q1$ and $Q2$ on the corresponding edges.

Problem 16.13 A cylinder is standing on its base on the HP. A pentagonal hole is cut through the cylinder. The axis of the hole is perpendicular to the VP and bisects the axis of the cylinder. The base diameter and the height of cylinder are 70 mm and 90 mm respectively. The hole has a face width of 30 mm. Draw the development of the cylinder. Assume a flat face of the hole perpendicular to the HP.

Solution Refer Fig. 16.27.

1. Draw the TV and FV of the cylinder. Show the pentagonal hole in FV.
2. Draw the development of the cylinder. The length of the rectangle = $\pi \times 70$ = 220 mm.

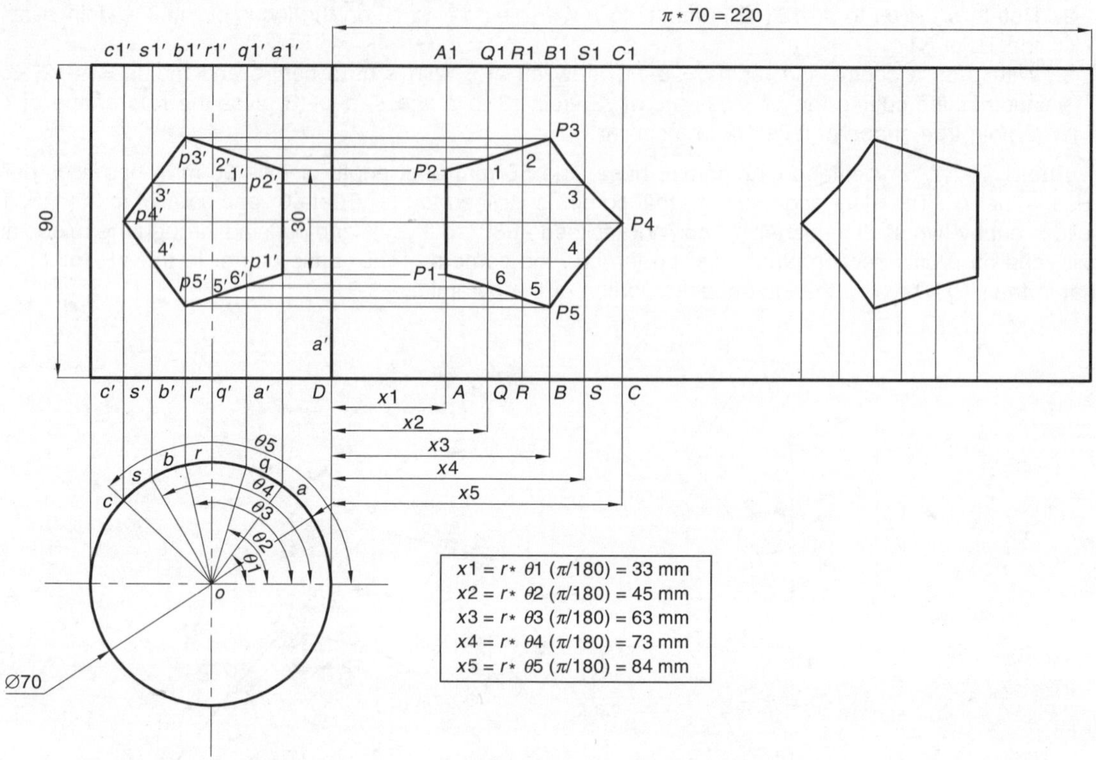

Fig. 16.27

3. In FV, draw lateral lines a'–$a1'$, b'–$b1'$ and c'–$c1'$ through the corners $p1'$, $p2'$, $p3'$, $p4'$ and $p5'$ of the pentagon. Locate few more points on the pentagon, say, 1', 2', etc., and draw lateral lines through them, say, q'–$q1'$, r'–$r1'$, etc.
4. Project a', q', r', etc., to a, q, r, etc., in TV. Join these points to o.
5. In the development, draw lateral lines A–$A1$, Q–$Q1$, etc., such that $DA = x1 = r^* \theta1(\pi/180) = 33$ mm, $DQ = x2 = r^* \theta2(\pi/180) = 45$ mm, etc.
6. Project $p1'$, $p2'$, 1', 2', etc., from FV to the development on the corresponding lateral lines. Join $P1$, $P2$, 1, 2, etc., by a smooth curve. Note that $P1$–$P2$ is a straight line segment.
7. Obtain a similar curve for the other side of the cylinder.

Problem 16.14 A frustum of a cone, with an 80 mm base diameter, 40 mm top diameter and 70 mm axis is kept on the base on the HP. A thread is wound around the curved surface of the frustum starting from the point on the base nearest to the observer. The thread, after taking a turn around the frustum, returns to the initial point. Find out the minimum possible length of the thread. Show the thread in FV and TV of the frustum.

Solution Refer Fig. 16.28.

1. Draw TV and FV of the frustum as shown. Locate apex O. Measure slant height Od'.
2. Find θ. $\theta = [40/(Od')] \times 360° = [40/146] \times 360° = 99°$. Draw the development of the frustum. Join A–A by a straight line. A–A represents the minimum possible length of the thread.
3. Obtain 12 equal divisions in the development. Mark 1, 2, 3, etc., at the intersection of A–A with the lateral lines.

4. Obtain 12 lateral lines in TV and FV. Project 1, 2, 3, etc., to 1′, 2′, 3′ in FV on the corresponding lateral lines.
5. Join *a*′–1′–2′–3′, etc., by a smooth curve. Note that curve 3′–4′–5′–6′–7′–8′–9′ is hidden and shown by a dashed line.
6. Project 1′, 2′, 3′, etc., to 1, 2, 3, etc., in TV. Join these points by a smooth curve.

Problem 16.15 A solid cylinder with 40 mm diameter of base and 80 mm height is resting on the ground with the axis making 60° with the ground. It is cut by a section plane such that the true shape of the section is an ellipse of major axis 70 mm and minor axis 40 mm. Draw the sectional TV and develop of the remaining part of the solid.

Solution Refer Fig. 16.29.

1. Draw the FV of the cylinder with axis inclined at 60° to *XY*. Draw the auxiliary TV on *X*1*Y*1.
2. As the true shape of the section is an ellipse of major axis = 70 mm, the length of the section plane across the cylinder must be 70 mm. Therefore, with any point, say *a*′ on 1′–$1_1'$ as a centre and radius = 70 mm, cut an arc on 7′–$7_1'$ at *g*′. Draw the cutting plane passing through *a*′–*g*′.
3. Obtain 12 lateral lines in FV. Mark *b*′, *c*′, etc., at the intersection of the cutting plane with the lateral lines.
4. Draw the TV below *XY*. Draw lateral lines in TV. Locate *a*, *b*, etc., on the corresponding lateral lines in TV to obtain the section.
5. Draw the development. Length of rectangle = $\pi \times 40$ = 126 mm. Obtain 12 lateral lines on it.
6. Project *a*′, *b*′, etc., in the development on the corresponding lateral lines.

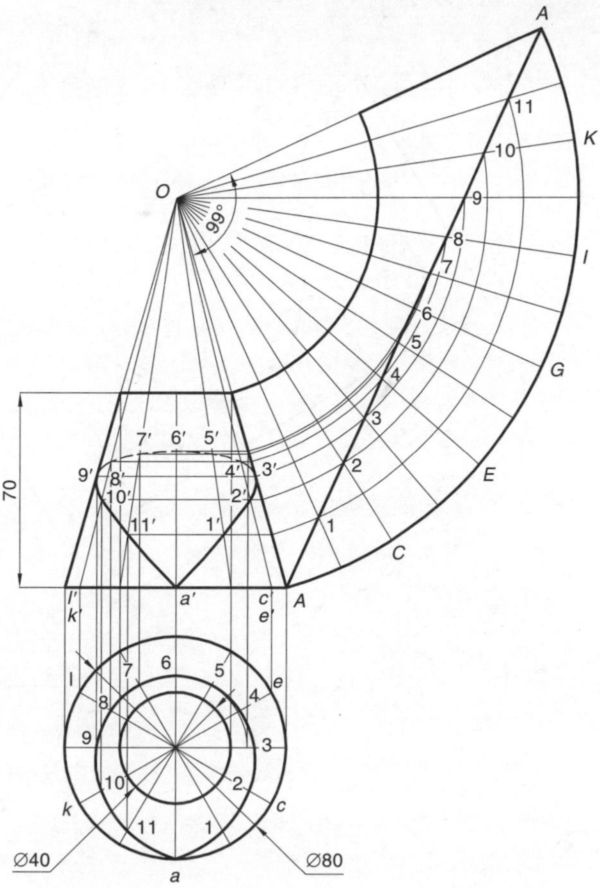

Ans:
Length of thread = *A*–*A* = 221 mm

Fig. 16.28

Remember the Following

- The development shows the TLs of all the edges of the solid.
- The development of a cone is a sector of the included angle, $\theta = 360\ (r/R)$, where *r* and *R* are the radius of base and slant height of the cone respectively.
- The development of a cone having its slant height equal to the diameter of base is a semicircle of radius equal to the slant height.
- The development of cylinder and cone is smooth curve.
- The development of prism and pyramid is straight-line segmented curve.

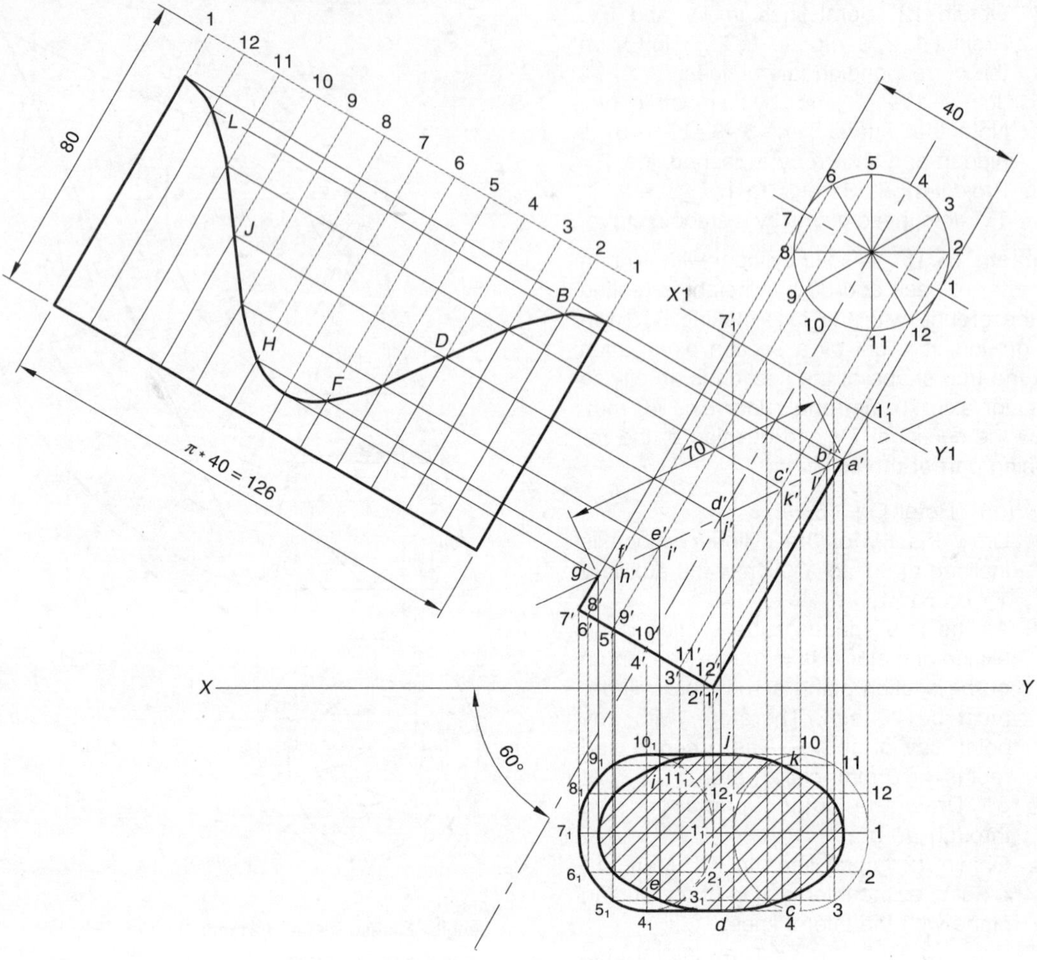

Fig. 16.29

Review Questions

1. A cone frustum has 75 mm base diameter, 35 mm top diameter and a 65 mm height. It is resting on its base on the ground and is cut by a section plane perpendicular to the VP, parallel to an end generator and passing through the top end of the axis. Draw the development of the frustum.
2. A hexagonal prism with a 35 mm base side and 80 mm height is resting on one of its ends on the HP with two opposite rectangular faces parallel to the VP. An AIP cuts the solid in such a way that the true shape of the section is the largest rectangle. Draw the development of the lateral surfaces of the prism.
3. A conical bucket is made up of a thin metal sheet. Its top diameter is 350 mm and its bottom diameter is 200 mm. The height of the conical part is 300 mm. It is fitted with a cylindrical rim of 60 mm height at the bottom. Draw the development of the bucket.
4. An ice-cream company wishes to print a paper to be wrapped around an ice-cream cone. The paper when wrapped should extend 5 mm from the base for packing purpose. For pasting purposes, an overlap of 2 mm is expected at mating lateral edges of the paper. Decide and draw the optimum size and shape of

the paper using the theory of development. The cone has a diameter of base 35 mm and length of axis 90 mm.

5. A circus tent is in the form of an octagonal pyramid. The height of the tent is 28 m. The base of the tent has to be inscribed in a circle of 120 m diameter. Develop the lateral surface of the tent. Take a suitable scale.
6. A hexagonal pyramid *O–ABCDEF* (*O* being the apex) is kept on the ground on its base and is cut off by a section plane which is perpendicular to the slant edge *OC* and intersecting the slant edge *OA* on a point 5 mm from *A*. Draw the development of the pyramid.
7. A pentagonal prism is resting on a corner on the HRP with the longer edge through that corner inclined at 30° to the HRP. The rectangular face opposite to that edge has its smaller side inclined at 45° to the FRP. An AIP inclined at 60° to the HRP cuts the prism at the midpoint of the axis. Draw the development of the prism.
8. A hollow right circular cone made of paper is opened out and the development is a semicircle of 50 mm radius. A full circle of the largest possible size is drawn in ink inside this semicircle and the paper is folded back to its shape of cone. Draw the TV and FV of the cone keeping it in simple position and show the ink lines in these views.
9. Figure 16RQ.1 shows the development of a solid. All the triangles are equilateral triangles. Draw the two views of the solids. Name the solid.

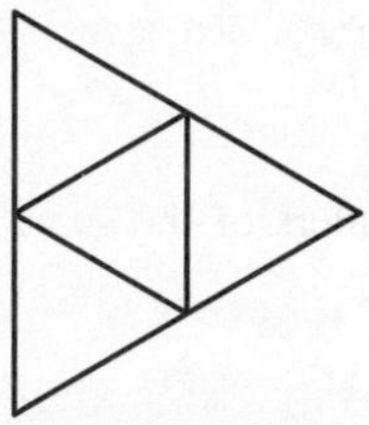

Fig. 16RQ.1

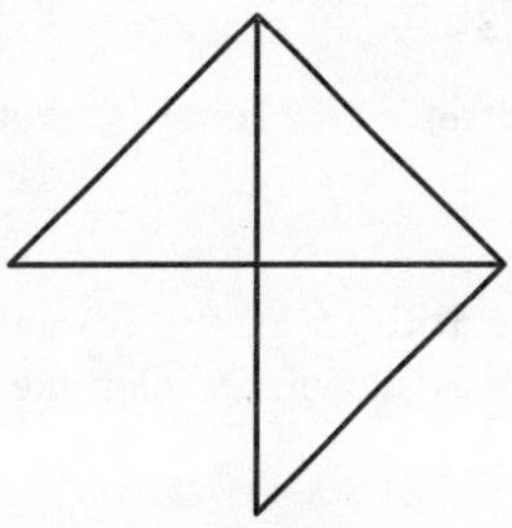

Fig. 16RQ.2

10. Figure 16RQ.2 shows the development of the lateral faces of a solid. All the triangles are right angled-isosceles triangles. Draw the two views of the solids. Name the solid.
11. Figure 16RQ.3(a), (b) and (c) show respectively a square prism, a pentagonal prism and a hexagonal prism, each resting on a corner on the ground. The base of each solid is inclined at 45° to the ground and perpendicular to the VP. The section planes cut the solids as shown. Develop the retained portion of each solid. Take side of base = 50 mm and length of axis = 100 mm.

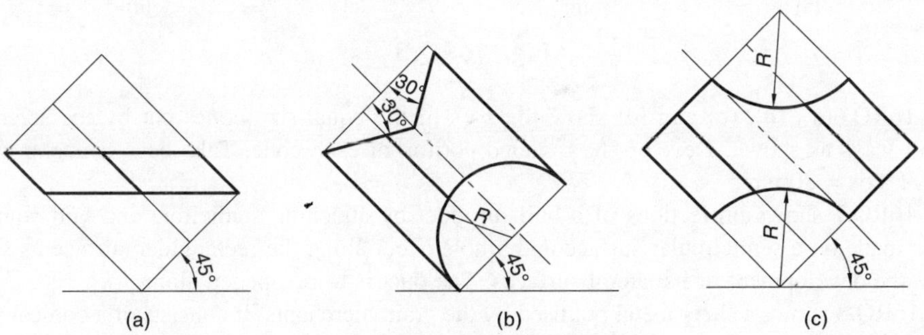

Fig. 16RQ.3

12. Figure 16RQ.4(a), (b), (c) and (d) show the two views of a triangular pyramid, a square pyramid, a pentagonal pyramid and a hexagonal pyramid respectively, each resting on its base on the VP. The solids are cut by the section planes as shown. Develop the lateral faces of the pyramids. Also, draw the sectional FV of each solid.

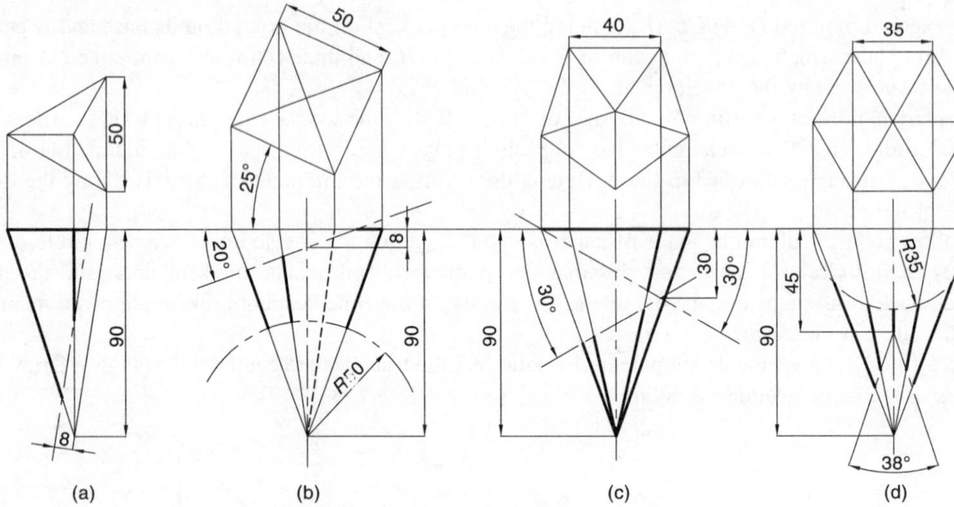

Fig. 16RQ.4

13. Figure 16RQ.5(a), (b), (c) and (d) show the FVs of the cylinders of the same sizes cut by the section planes as shown. Develop the retained portion in each case.

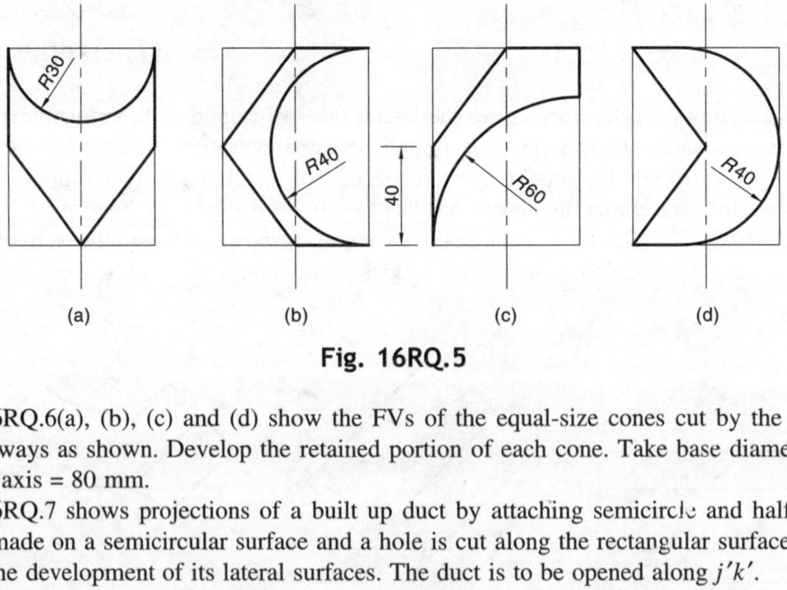

Fig. 16RQ.5

14. Figure 16RQ.6(a), (b), (c) and (d) show the FVs of the equal-size cones cut by the section planes in different ways as shown. Develop the retained portion of each cone. Take base diameter = 60 mm and length of axis = 80 mm.
15. Figure 16RQ.7 shows projections of a built up duct by attaching semicircle and half square. A notch $a'b'c'$ is made on a semicircular surface and a hole is cut along the rectangular surface as shown in FV. Prepare the development of its lateral surfaces. The duct is to be opened along $j'k'$.
16. Figure 16RQ.8 shows a sheet metal pot used by the grain merchants. It consists of a conical piece of base diameter 170 mm cut by an arched plane at the other end as shown. Develop the lateral surface of the pot.

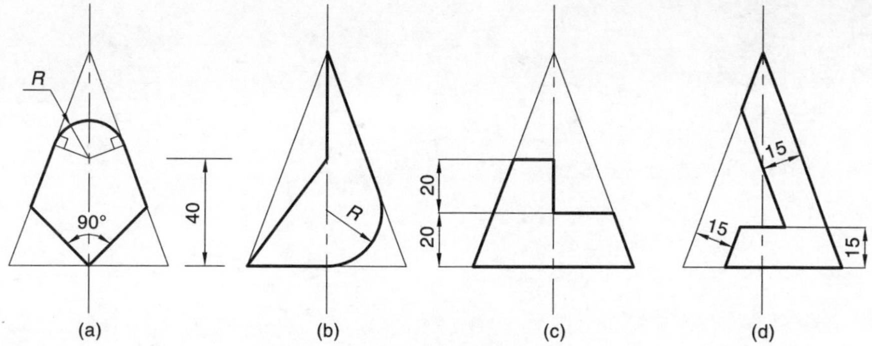

Fig. 16RQ.6

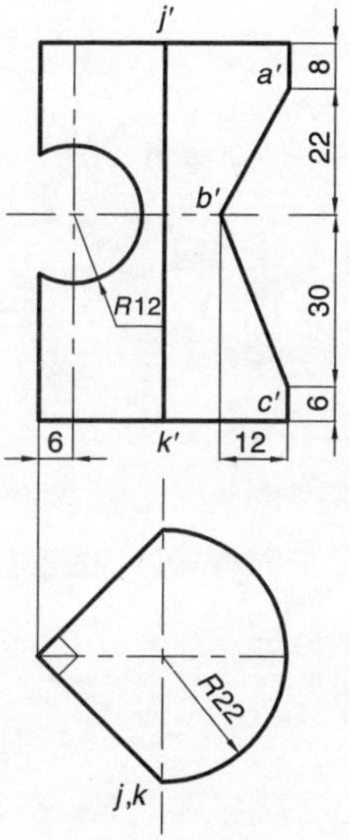

Fig. 16RQ.7

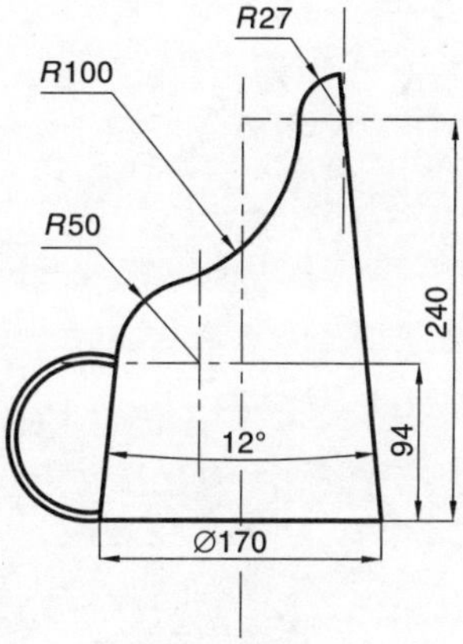

Fig. 16RQ.8

Chapter 17

INTERSECTION OF SURFACES OF SOLIDS

17.1 INTRODUCTION

Solids in the real world are obtained by a combination of two or more basic solids. Whenever two or more solids combine, a definite curve is seen at their intersection. This curve is called the *curve of intersection* (or *interpenetration*) (COI). Obviously, the COI is shared by both the solids. The COI is also visible when a hole or slot is created on a particular solid. The intersection of surfaces of solids plays an important role in designing and manufacturing of objects, especially sheet metal objects, wooden objects, automobile parts, moulding patterns, etc. A funnel, gardening spout, tee pipe joint, connecting rod, etc., are common examples of intersections of solids, *Illustration 17.1*.

Illustration 17.1

17.2 CASES OF INTERSECTION

The cases of intersection depend on the type of intersecting solids and the manner in which they intersect. Two intersecting solids may be of the same type (e.g., prism and prism) or of different types (e.g., prism and pyramid). The possible combinations are shown in Table 17.1.

Table 17.1 Cases of Intersection

		1st solid				
		Prism	*Pyramid*	*Cylinder*	*Cone*	*Sphere*
	Prism	Case 1				
	Pyramid	Case 2	Case 6			
2nd solid	*Cylinder*	Case 3	Case 7	Case 10		
	Cone	Case 4	Case 8	Case 11	Case 13	
	Sphere	Case 5	Case 9	Case 12	Case 14	Case 15

The two solids may intersect in different ways. The axes of the solids may be parallel, inclined or perpendicular to each other. The axes may be intersecting, offset or coinciding. Therefore, the following sub-cases exist:

(i) Axes perpendicular and intersecting
(ii) Axes perpendicular and offset
(iii) Axes inclined and intersecting
(iv) Axes inclined and offset
(v) Axes parallel and coinciding
(vi) Axes parallel and offset

17.3 THEORY OF INTERSECTION

When a solid penetrates another solid, it shows the COI at the intersecting surfaces. The COI may be a smooth curve or a segmented-line curve, depending on the type of the intersecting surfaces. The COI will be a smooth curve if any one or both of the intersecting surfaces are curved. If both the intersecting surfaces are flat surfaces, the COI will be a segmented-line curve. In such a case, the COI is often referred to as the *line of intersection* (or *interpenetration*) (LOI). Table 17.2 shows the nature of COI according to the types of intersecting surfaces.

Table 17.2 Nature of COI

		Intersecting Surface 1	
		Flat	*Curved*
Intersecting Surface 2	*Flat*	Segmented-line curve (Case 1, Case 2 and Case 6)	
	Curved	Smooth curve (Case 3, Case 4, Case 5, Case 7, Case 8 and Case 9)	Smooth curve (Case 10, Case 11,Case 12, Case 13, Case 14 and Case 15)

To draw the COI, the first step is to draw two or three views of the intersecting solids as per the given conditions. Then we locate POIs. In this case, POI is a point of intersection between two edges or an edge and a surface of the two intersecting solids. If any of the solids do not have edges along the intersecting surface (viz. cylinder, cone, sphere), POIs may be located at the intersections of imaginary generators drawn on the curved surface. All the POIs when joined in a proper sequence give the COI.

The two approaches used to locate POIs are discussed below.

17.3.1 Edge View Approach

This approach is preferred when the intersection of two edges (or an edge and a surface) is clearly seen in one view, i.e., when all the lateral faces of one solid are seen as edge views. Clearly, it is suitable for intersections involving prisms and cylinders. In case of cylinders and cones, a number of lines (generators) are drawn on the lateral surface in the region of intersection. The POIs obtained in one view are then transferred to other views.

17.3.2 Cutting Plane Approach

In this approach, two intersecting solids are assumed to be cut by a number of section planes. The section planes may be horizontal, vertical or inclined. Horizontal or vertical cutting planes are preferred since they show the true shape of the section in another view. The POIs between the sections are located and then transferred to other views. This approach can be adopted for any solid. However, it is more suitable when none of the intersecting solids shows the edge views of lateral faces, i.e., pyramids, cones and spheres.

Both these approaches are explained with the help of examples in the following sections.

REMEMBER THE FOLLOWING

- If both the intersecting surfaces are flat, COI is a segmented-line curve.
- If one of the intersecting surfaces is flat and the other is curved, COI is a smooth curve.
- If both the intersecting surfaces are curved, COI is a smooth curve.

17.4 INTERSECTION OF PRISM AND PRISM

Since both the prisms show an edge view in one of the three views the edge view approach should be preferred.

Example 17.1 A vertical square prism with a 60 mm base side and an 80 mm axis length, is completely penetrated by a horizontal square prism with a 40 mm side base and a 100 mm axis length such that their axes bisect each other. The faces of both the prisms are equally inclined to the VP. Draw the three views of the solids showing LOI.

Solution Refer Fig. 17.1.

1. Draw the three views of the two prisms as per the conditions given in the problem. The axes are intersecting at their midpoints. Note that the TV shows an edge view (*aa*1–*bb*1–*cc*1–*dd*1) of the vertical prism and the SV shows an edge view (*e*″*e*1″–*f*″*f*1″–*g*″*g*1″–*h*″*h*1″) of the horizontal prism.
2. Locate points 1, 2, 3, …, 8 in the TV at the intersections of the edges (or edge and surface) of the two solids. For example, locate 1 at the intersection of edge *e*–*e*1 and edge *b*–*b*1, 2 at the intersection of edge *f*–*f*1 and surface *b*–*b*1–*c*1–*c*, 3 at the intersection of edge *g*–*g*1 and edge *b*–*b*1, *4* at the intersection of edge *h*–*h*1 and surface *a*–*a*1–*b*1–*b*. Point 5, 6, 7 and 8 can be located in a similar way.
3. Locate the corresponding point 1″, 2″, 3″, …, 8″ in SV. (The points 1″, 2″, 3″ and 4″ will lie behind *e*″, *f*″, *g*″ and *h*″ respectively.)

4. Obtain 1′, 2′, 3′, ..., 8′ in FV by projecting 1, 2, 3, ..., 8 and 1″, 2″, 3″, ..., 8″.
5. Join 1′–2′(4′)–3′ and 5′–6′(8′)–7′ by line segments.
6. Draw hidden lines and remove unnecessary lines. The longer edges of the horizontal prism penetrate through the vertical prism. Therefore, part of these edges within the vertical prism will not be visible. So, in TV, 4–8, 1(3)–5(7), and 2–6 are hidden lines. Similarly, in FV, 1′–5′, 2′(4′) – 6′(8′) and 3′–7′ will be hidden lines.

The part of the edges and the surfaces of the vertical prism captured by the horizontal prism will fuse with the latter. Therefore, in FV, part 1′–3′ of *b*′–*b*1′ and part 5′–7′ of *d*′–*d*1′ will not be visible. Also, in SV, 1″(5″)–3″(7″) on *b*″ (*d*″) – *b*1″ (*d*1″) need to be removed.

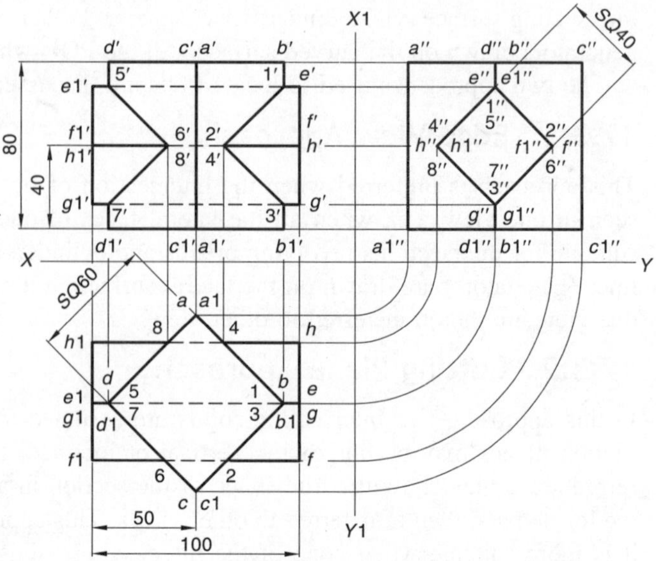

Fig. 17.1

Example 17.2 A square prism with a base side of 60 mm and an axis length of 100 mm stands vertically on the HP with its faces equally inclined to the VP. A horizontal square prism of base side 35 mm and axis length of 120 mm penetrates the vertical prism. The axis of the horizontal prism is parallel to both the RPs and 12 mm away from the midpoint of the axis of the vertical prism. A lateral face of the horizontal prism makes 30° with the HP. Draw the projections showing LOI.

Solution Refer Fig. 17.2.

1. Draw the three views of the prisms. The TV shows the edge view of the vertical prism and the SV shows the edge view of the horizontal prism. The distance between the axes of the two prisms is shown in the SV.
2. In the TV, locate points 1, 2, 3, ..., 12 at the intersections of edges or edge and surface. Locate the corresponding points 1″, 2″, 3″, ..., 12″ in SV.
3. Obtain 1′, 2′, 3′, ..., 12′ in FV by projecting 1, 2, 3, ..., 12 and 1″, 2″, 3″, ..., 12″.
4. Join 1′–2′–3′–4′–5′–6′ and 7′–8′–9′–10′–11′–12′ by line segments. Note that 2′–3′–4′–5′–6′ and 8′–9′–10′–11′–12′ will be hidden curves.
5. In FV 2′–8′, *g*–*g*1′, 1′–7′ and 6′–12′ will be hidden lines. In TV 4–10, *h*–*h*1, 2–8 and 1–7 will be hidden lines. In FV and SV 9′–11′, and 3′–5′ and 9″–11″ respectively will not be seen.

Note: To decide the hidden lines in FV, observe SV in the direction of arrow *A*. The points 1″, 2″, 6″, 7″, 8″ and 12″ fall on the visible faces, therefore lines joining them in FV (i.e., 2′–1′–6′ and 8′–7′–12′) will be visible. The lines joining the points falling on invisible faces should be hidden.

17.5 INTERSECTION OF PRISM AND PYRAMID

Example 17.3 A square pyramid with a base side of 55 mm and an axis length of 80 mm stands on its base on the HP with the sides of base equally inclined to the VP. A triangular prism with a base side of

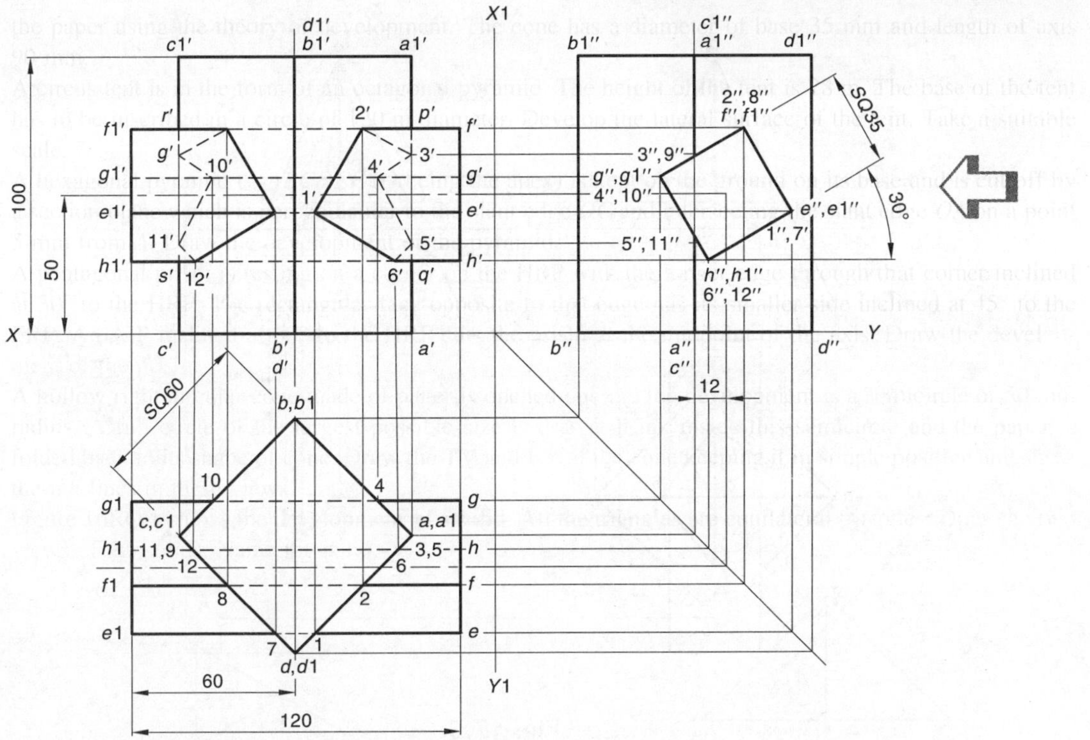

Fig. 17.2

34 mm and length of axis 100 mm, penetrates the pyramid completely. The axis of the prism is perpendicular to the VP and intersects the axis of pyramid at 24 mm from the HP. One of the lateral faces of the prism is perpendicular to the HP. Draw the three views of the solids showing LOI.

Solution Refer Fig. 17.3.

1. Draw the three views of the pyramid and the prism. FV shows an edge view of the prism.
2. Locate points 1′, 2′, 3′, …, 10′ in FV at the intersections of the edges/surfaces of the pyramid/ prism. (6′, 7′, …, 10′ lie on rear side.)
3. Draw lateral lines *o′–e′*(*j′*), *o′–f′*(*i′*) and *o′–g′*(*h′*) passing through the corners of the triangle.
4. Project *e′*(*j′*), *f′*(*i′*) and *g′*(*h′*) to TV to obtain *e, j, f, i, g* and *h*. Draw *o–e, o–j, …, o–h*.
5. Project 1′, 2′, 3′, …, 10′ on the corresponding line in TV. Join 1–2–3–4–5 and 6–7–8–9–10 by line segments. Note how 2′(7′) and 4′(9′) are projected. Draw the hidden lines properly.
6. Project 1′, 2′, 3′, …, 10′ and 1, 2, 3, …, 10 in SV to obtain the LOI. Draw the hidden lines and remove unnecessary lines.

Example 17.4 A hexagonal pyramid with a base side of 40 mm and an altitude of 90 mm is resting on the HP on its base with two opposite sides of the base parallel to the VP. It is penetrated by a square prism of base side of 35 mm such that the axis of the prism is perpendicular to the VP and the faces are equally inclined to the HP. Draw the three views of the assembly showing the LOI if the axes intersect at a point 35 mm from the base of the pyramid.

Solution Refer Fig. 17.4.

1. Draw the TV, FV and SV of the pyramid. Also, draw FV, TV and SV of the prism.
2. Locate 1′, 2′, …, 8′ at the intersections of the edges/surfaces of the two solids.

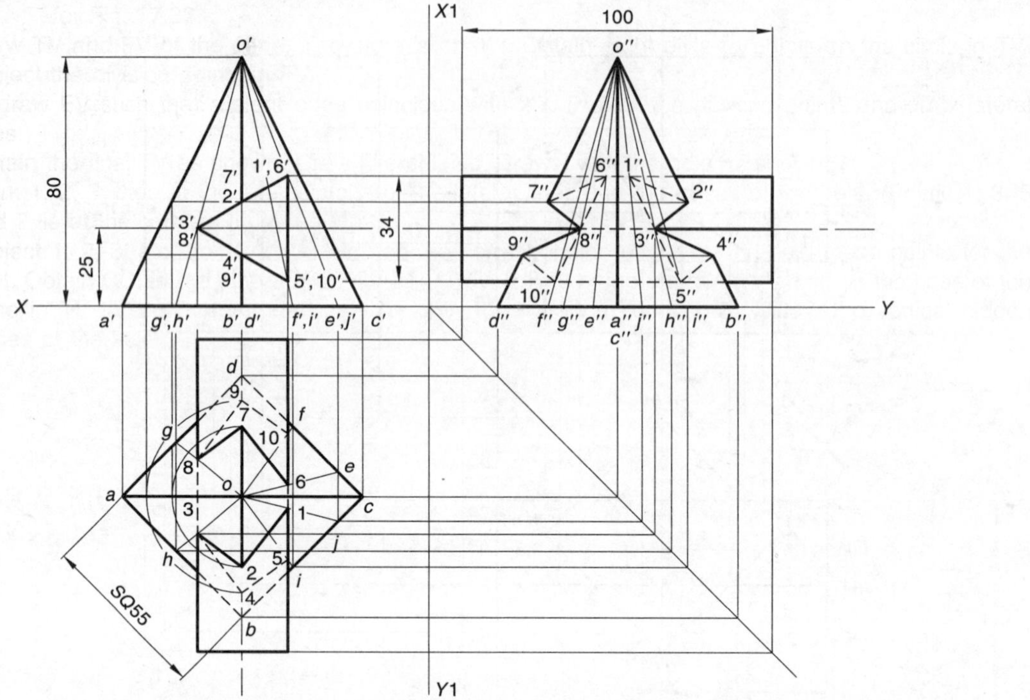

Fig. 17.3

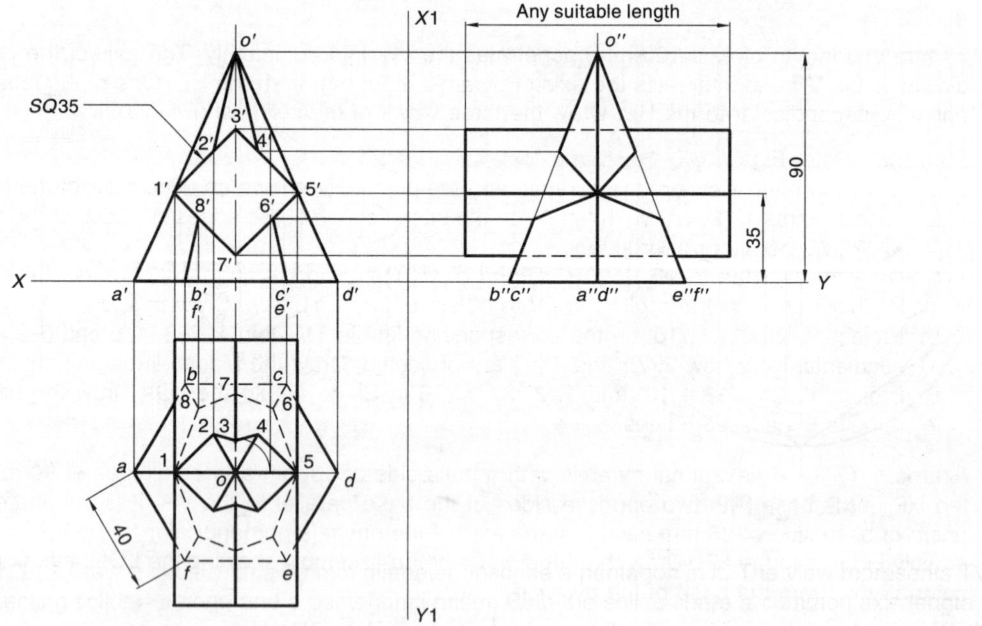

Fig. 17.4

3. Project 1′, 2′, …, 8′ in TV to locate 1, 2, …, 8 on corresponding edges. Note how 3′ is projected.
4. Join 1, 2, …, 8 for LOI. Draw the curve in other half in a similar way. Draw the hidden lines properly.
5. Project 1′, 2′, …, 8′ in SV to obtain LOI as shown.

17.6 INTERSECTION OF PRISM AND CYLINDER

Example 17.5 A vertical cylinder with a 60 mm diameter is penetrated by a horizontal square prism with a 40 mm base side, the axis of which is parallel to the VP and 10 mm away from the axis of the cylinder. A face of the prism makes an angle of 30° with the HP. Draw their projections showing COI.

Solution Refer Fig. 17.5.

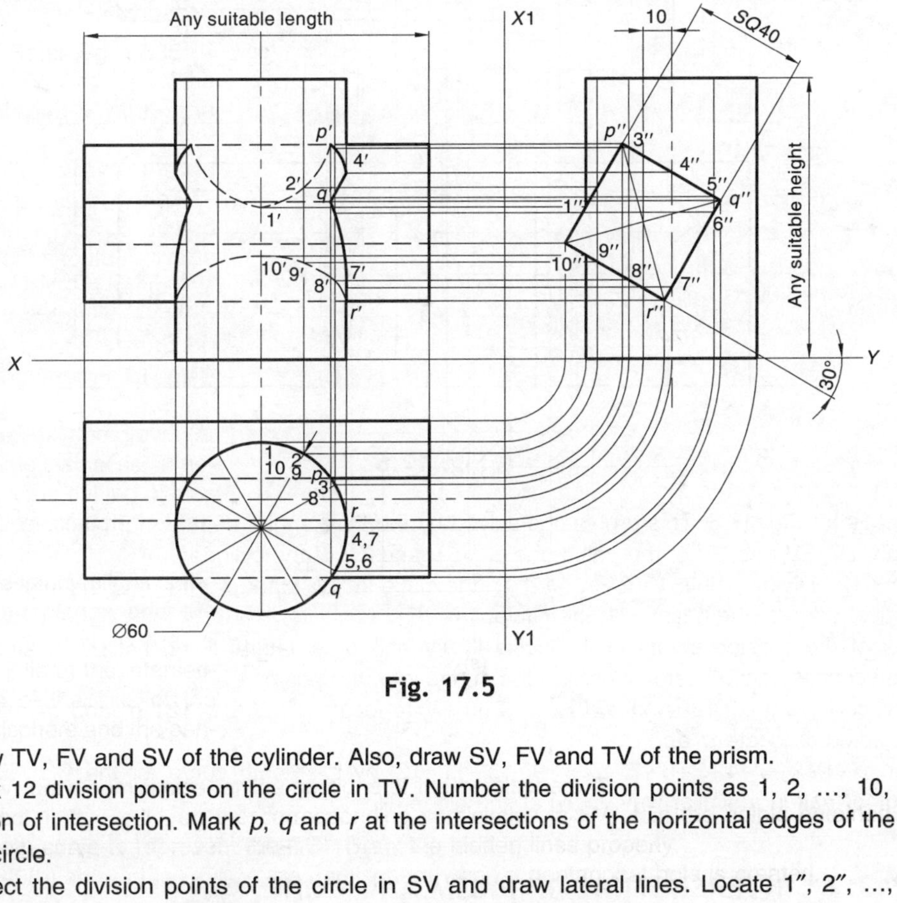

Fig. 17.5

1. Draw TV, FV and SV of the cylinder. Also, draw SV, FV and TV of the prism.
2. Mark 12 division points on the circle in TV. Number the division points as 1, 2, …, 10, only in the region of intersection. Mark *p*, *q* and *r* at the intersections of the horizontal edges of the prism with the circle.
3. Project the division points of the circle in SV and draw lateral lines. Locate 1″, 2″, …, 10″ at the intersections of the lateral lines and the surfaces of the prism.
4. Project 1, 2, …, 10 and 1″, 2″, …, 10″ in FV to locate 1′, 2′, …, 10′. *p*, *q* and *r* may be directly projected to locate *p*′, *q*′ and *r*′.
5. Join 1′–2′–*p*′–3′–4′–5′–*q*′–6′–7′–*r*′–8′–9′–10′ by a smooth curve for the COI. Obtain COI in another half in a similar way. Carefully draw all the hidden lines.

Example 17.6 A pentagonal prism with a 50 mm base side and a height of 80 mm, stands on the ground on its base. A vertical face of the prism is parallel to the VP and nearer to the observer. The prism is penetrated by a horizontal cylinder with a base diameter of 60 mm and a length of 100 mm. The axis of the cylinder is parallel to the VP and bisects the axis of the prism at right angles. Draw the projections of the solids showing COI.

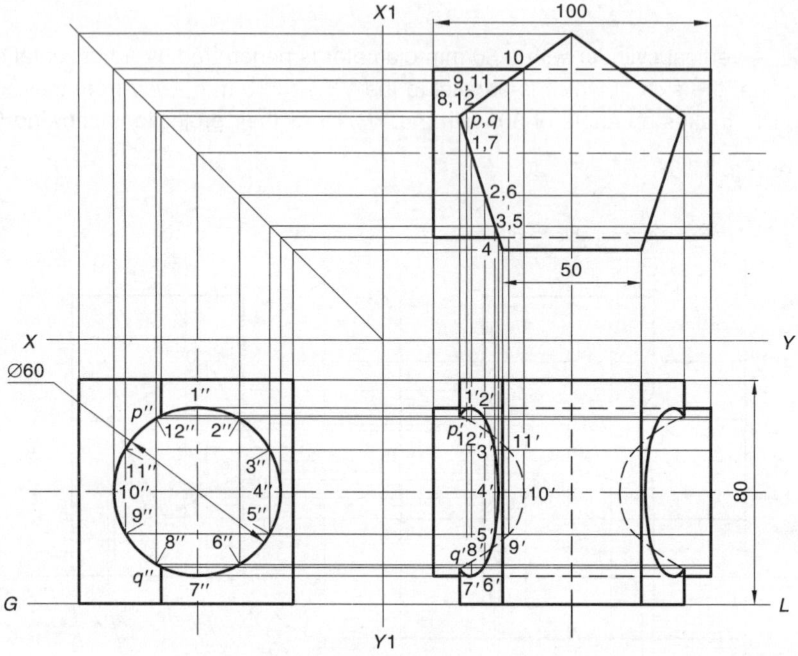

Fig. 17.6

Solution Refer Fig. 17.6. This problem is solved by the third angle method of projection.

1. Draw TV, FV and SV of the prism and SV, FV and TV of the cylinder.
2. Mark 12 division points 1″, 2″, ..., 12″ on the circle in SV. Mark *p*″ and *q*″ at the intersections of the vertical edge of the prism with the circle.
3. Project the division points of the circle in TV and draw lateral lines. Locate 1, 2, ..., 12 at the intersections of the lateral lines and the surfaces of the prism.
4. Project 1″, 2″, ..., 12″ and 1, 2, ..., 12 in FV to locate 1′, 2′, ..., 12′. *p*″ and *q*″ may be directly projected to locate *p*′ and *q*′.
5. Join *p*′–1′–2′–3′–4′–5′–6′–7′–*q*′–8′–9′–10′–11′–12′ by a smooth curve for the COI. Obtain COI in another half in a similar way. Draw all the hidden lines.

17.7 INTERSECTION OF PRISM AND CONE

Example 17.7 A square prism with base side of 20 mm and a length of 70 mm penetrates a cone with base diameter of 45 mm and a height of 60 mm. The axis of the cone is perpendicular to the HP while the axis of the prism is parallel to both the RPs. The axes intersect at a distance of 25 mm from the base of the cone. The lateral faces of the prism are equally inclined to the HP. Draw the projections showing COI.

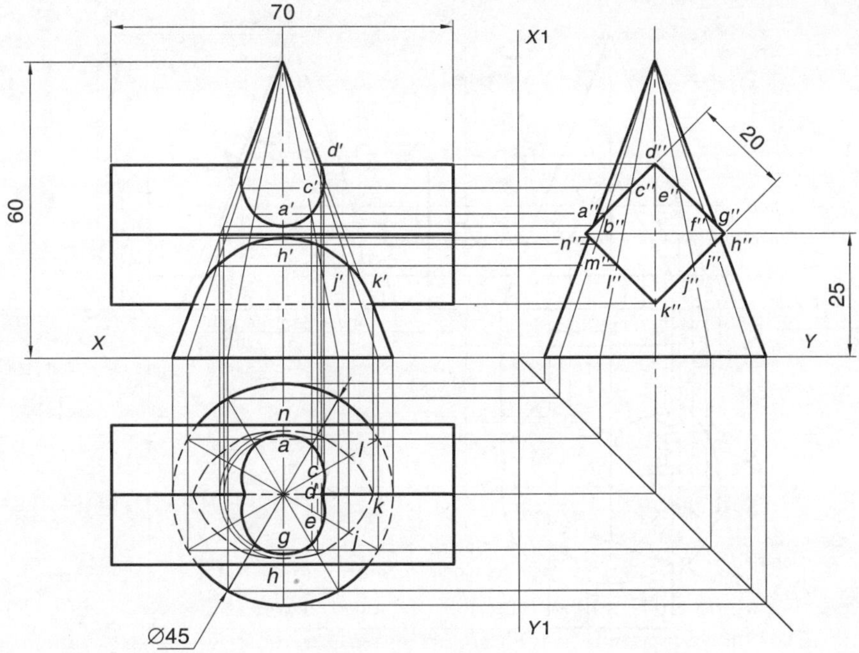

Fig. 17.7

Solution Refer Fig. 17.7.

1. Draw TV, FV and SV of the cone. Also, draw SV, FV and TV of the prism.
2. Obtain 12 division points on the circle in TV. Join them with the centre to draw lateral lines.
3. Project the division points in SV and TV and obtain lateral lines in those views.
4. In SV, mark *a″*, *b″*, ..., *n″* at the intersections of the lateral lines with the faces of the prism.
5. Project *a″*, *b″*, ..., *n″* to *a′*, *b′*, ..., *n′* in FV to obtain the COIs. Obtain the parts of COIs in the other half in a similar way.
6. Project *a′*, *b′*, ..., *n′* to *a*, *b*, ..., *n* on corresponding lateral lines. Draw smooth curves through them for the required COIs. Draw hidden lines in TV and FV.

Example 17.8 A cone with an 80 mm diameter and a 100 mm axis height is resting on its base. A triangular prism having 45 mm side of the triangular end penetrates the cone with their axes intersecting each other at 25 mm from the base of the cone. All the rectangular faces of the prism are perpendicular to the VP and two of its faces are equally inclined to the HP. Draw the projections showing the COI.

Solution Refer Fig. 17.8. The cutting plane approach is used in this problem.

1. Draw TV, FV and SV of the cone. Also, draw FV, TV and SV of the prism.
2. In FV, draw horizontal cutting planes *a–a*, *b–b*, *c–c* and *d–d*. The cutting planes are drawn in the region of intersection only. *a–a* and *d–d* pass through the corners 1′, 4′ and 5′ of the triangle. *b–b* and *c–c* are drawn between *a–a* and *d–d* at suitable distances. Mark 2′, 7′, 3′ and 6′ at the intersections of *b–b* and *c–c* with the edges of the triangle.
3. Draw the sections of the cone, i.e., *section a–a*, *section b–b*, *section c–c* and *section d–d* in TV as shown. These sections will be circles.
4. Project 1′, 2′, 3′, 4′, 5′, 6′ and 7′ to 1, 2, 3, 4, 5, 6, and 7 in TV on corresponding circles. Join these points by a smooth curve for the required COI. Obtain the COI in another half in a similar way.
5. Project 1′, 2′, 3′, 4′, 5′, 6′, 7′ and 1, 2, 3, 4, 5, 6, 7 in SV to locate 1″, 2″, 3″, 4″, 5″, 6″, 7″. Join them to obtain the COI. Draw hidden lines in TV.

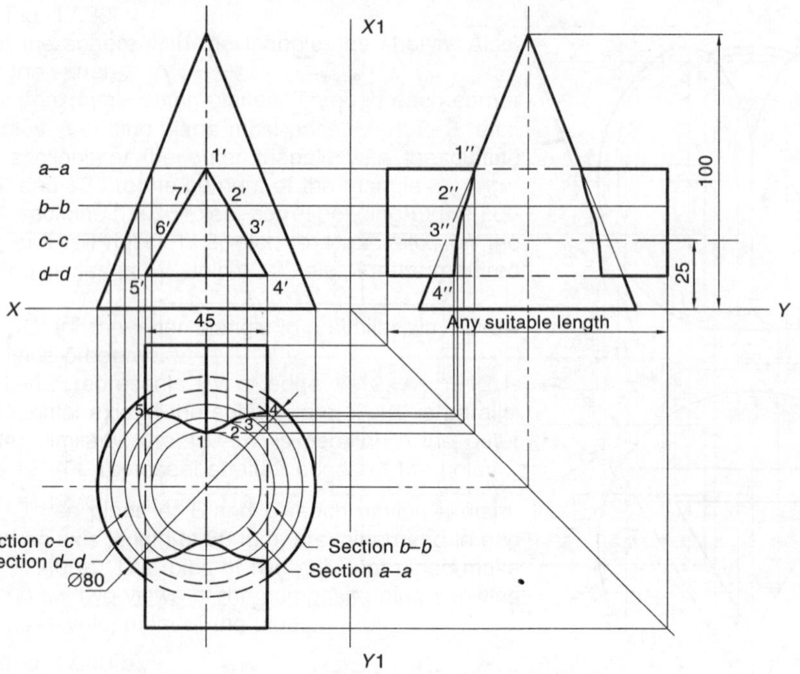

Fig. 17.8

17.8 INTERSECTION OF PRISM AND SPHERE

When any solid penetrates a sphere, the cutting plane approach should be used to draw the COI.

Example 17.9 A triangular prism of 60 mm base side and 100 mm length penetrates a sphere of diameter 80 mm. A lateral face of the prism is parallel to the HP and the edge opposite that face passes through the uppermost point on the sphere. The axis of the prism is perpendicular to the VP. The prism comes out equally from both the sides of the sphere. Draw the projections of the sphere and the prism showing COI.

Solution Refer Fig. 17.9.

1. Draw FVs, TVs and SVs of the sphere and the prism.
2. In FV, draw section circles, *section a–a* and *section b–b*, having centres at the centre of the sphere. *Section a–a* passes through corners 1′ and 9′ of the triangle and intersects at 4′ to the triangle. *Section b–b* intersects at 2′ and 3′ to the triangle. (2′ also lies on the axis of the sphere.) 5′ is marked at the corner of the triangle on the sphere. (*Alternatively*, pass horizontal cutting planes through 1′(9′), 2′, 3′, and 4′.
3. In TV, obtain cutting planes *a–a* and *b–b* by projecting *section a–a* and *section b–b*. (*Alternatively*, draw section circles in TV)
4. Project 1′, 2′, etc., to locate 1, 2, etc., on the corresponding cutting plane in TV. Join 1′, 2′, etc., by a smooth curve to obtain the part of COI. Draw the other part in a similar way. Draw COI in another half in a similar way. Arc 1–9 is parallel to the outer circle. *m* and *n* represent the apparent intersections of the edge of the prism with the sphere.

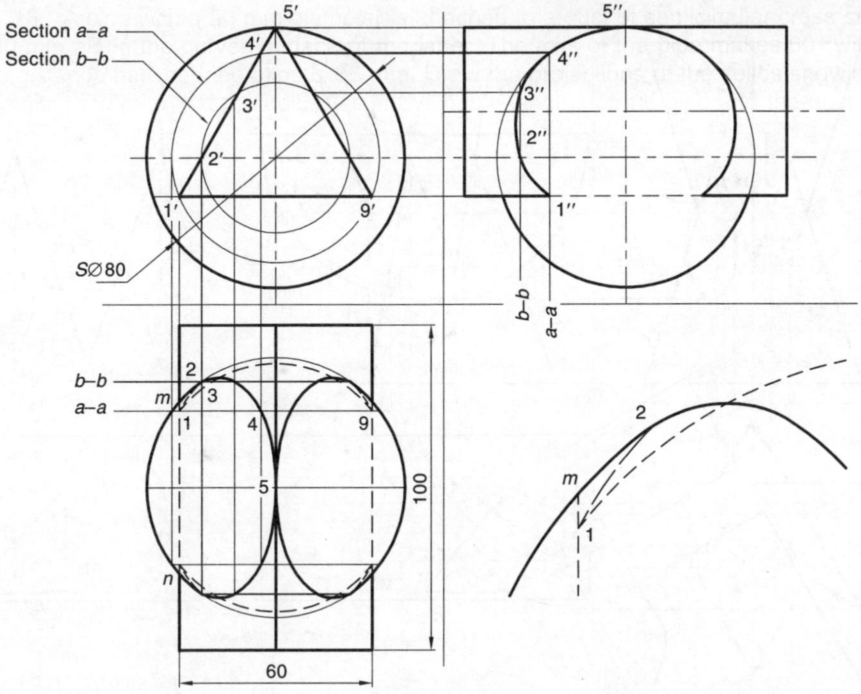

Fig. 17.9

5. In SV, draw cutting planes *a–a* and *b–b* by projecting *section a–a* and *section b–b*.
6. Project 1′, 2′, etc., to 1″, 2″, etc., on the corresponding cutting plane in SV. Complete the COI. Draw hidden lines in TV and SV.

17.9 INTERSECTION OF PYRAMID AND PYRAMID

As both the intersecting solids are pyramids, the cutting plane approach should be used.

Example 17.10 Two triangular pyramids of equal sizes penetrate each other. The axes of both the solids are vertical and coincident. The apex of each pyramid touches the base of the other. Two opposite sides of the bases of the pyramids are parallel to the VP. Draw three views of the pyramids showing the LOI. Side of base of pyramids = 45 mm and height of the pyramids = 70 mm.

Solution Refer Fig. 17.10.

1. Draw TVs, FVs and SVs of the pyramids.
2. In SV, draw horizontal cutting planes *a–a*, *b–b* and *c–c* in the region of intersection. *b–b* passes through the intersections of slant edges/surfaces in FV. Each of the cutting planes cuts both the solids.
3. Mark the points of intersections of *a–a*, *b–b* and *c–c* with the slant edges of the pyramids and project them in TV to obtain *Section a–a (1)*, *Section a–a (2) Section b–b (1)*, *Section b–b (2)*, *Section c–c (1)* and *Section c–c (2)*.

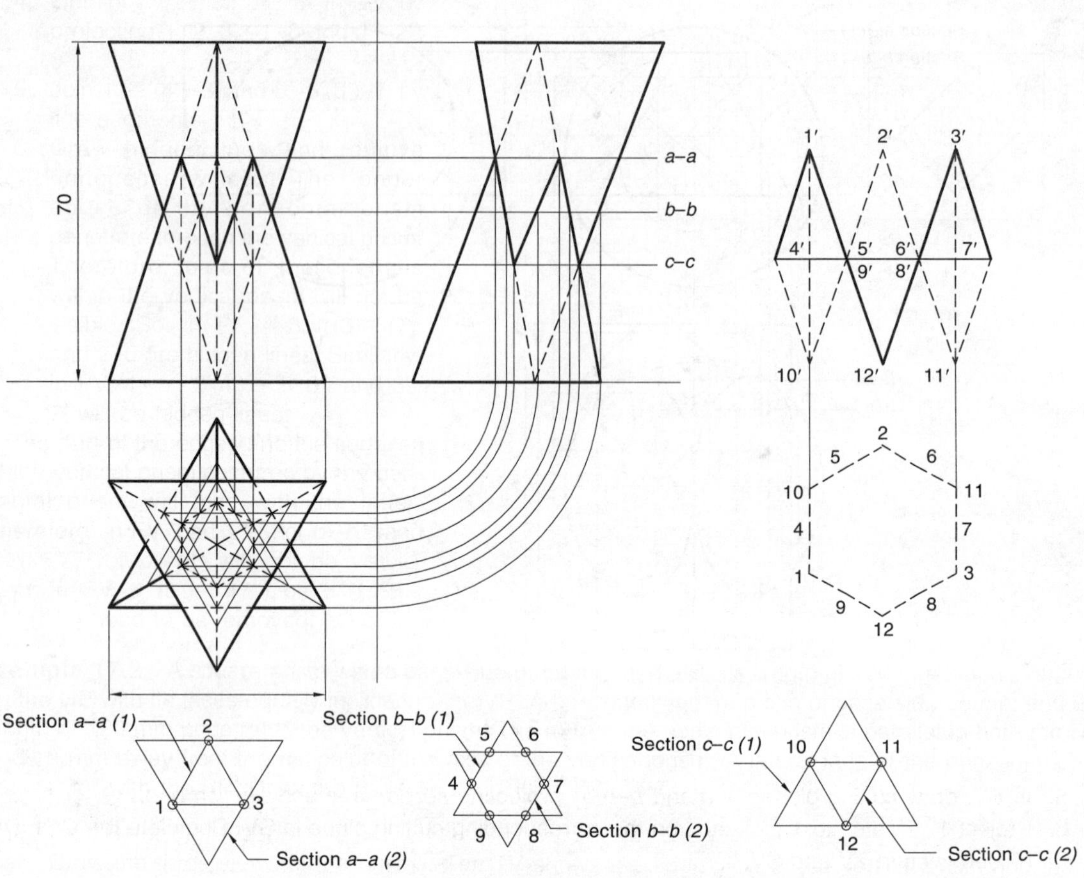

Fig. 17.10

4. Mark points 1, 2 and 3 at the intersection of *Section a–a (1)* and *Section a–a (2)*; points 4, 5, ..., 9 at the intersection of *Section b–b (1)* and *Section b–b (2)* and points 10, 11 and 12 at the intersection of *Section c–c (1)* and *Section c–c (2)*. Join 1–4–10–5–2–6–11–7–3–8–12–9–1 for the LOI.
5. Project 1, 2, ..., 12 in FV and SV on the corresponding cutting planes. Join the points obtained in proper sequence for the LOIs. Draw hidden lines properly.

17.10 INTERSECTION OF PYRAMID AND CYLINDER

Example 17.11 A triangular pyramid of 64 mm base side and an 80 mm long axis has its base in the VP with a side parallel to and away from the HP. A cylinder with a 36 mm diameter and a 90 mm length penetrates the pyramid. The axis of the cylinder is parallel to and 10 mm away, on opposite side of the HP, from the axis of the pyramid. Draw two views of the solids showing COI.

Solution Refer Fig. 17.11.

1. Draw FVs and TVs of the pyramid and the cylinder.

2. In FV, locate 1′, 2′ and 3′ at the intersections of the circle with the edges of the pyramid. Also, locate intermediate points *p*′ and *q*′ at suitable distances. Through *p*′ and *q*′, draw lateral lines joining the apex with the base edges.
3. In TV, obtain corresponding lateral lines. Project 1′, 2′ and 3′ to 1, 2 and 3 on the corresponding edges. Also, project *p*′ and *q*′ to *p* and *q* on the corresponding lateral lines. Note how 3′ is projected.
4. Join 1–*p*–2–*q*–3 for the required COI. Obtain COI in another half in a similar way. Draw hidden lines properly.

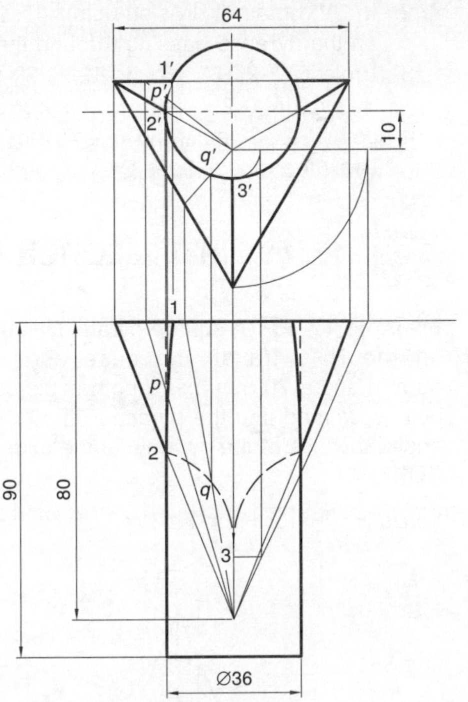

Fig. 17.11

Example 17.12 A square pyramid of 50 mm base side and slant height 75 mm is resting on its base on the HP with all the base sides equally inclined to the VP. A cylinder of diameter 34 mm and length 100 mm penetrates the pyramid completely. Axis of the cylinder is parallel to both the RPs and intersects the axis of the pyramid at a point 22 mm from the base of the pyramid. Draw the three views of the solid showing COI.

Solution Refer Fig. 17.12.

1. Draw TV, FV and SV of the pyramid. Also, draw SV, FV and TV of the cylinder.

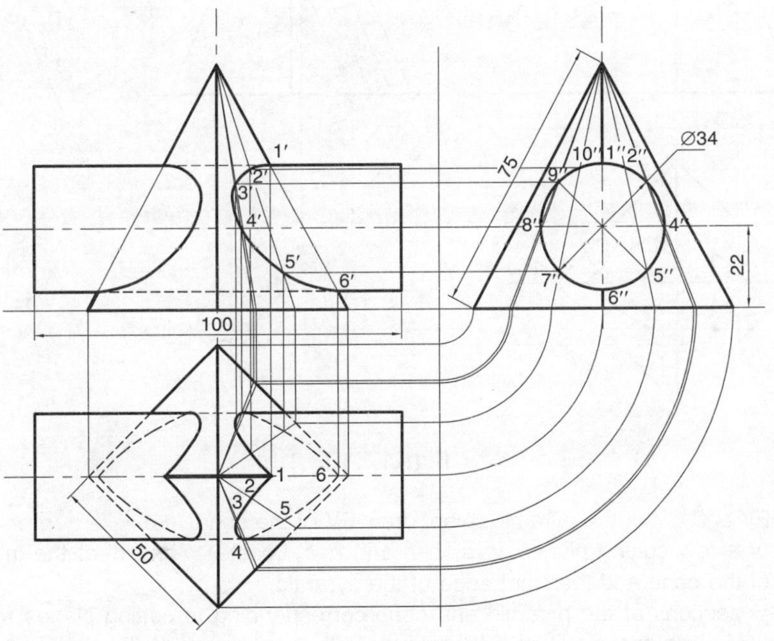

Fig. 17.12

2. In SV, obtain 8 division-points 1″, 2″, 3″, etc. Draw lateral lines (joining apex with the base edges) on the pyramid passing through these division points. Project these lateral lines in TV and FV.
3. Project 1″, 2″, 3″, etc., to 1′, 2′, 3′, etc., on the corresponding lateral lines in FV. Then, project 1′, 2′, 3′, etc., to 1, 2, 3, etc., on the corresponding lateral lines in TV.
4. Join 1′, 2′, 3′, etc., and 1, 2, 3, etc., for the required COIs. Draw the remaining COIs in a similar way. Draw the hidden lines.

17.11 INTERSECTION OF PYRAMID AND CONE

Example 17.13 A square pyramid with a 40 mm base side and a 64 mm long axis is resting on its base on the HP with all the base edges equally inclined to the VP. A cone of base diameter 40 mm and a 70 mm axis length is pierced into the pyramid. The cone is then removed so that a conical hole is created into the pyramid. The axis of the cone is parallel to both the RPs and intersects, at right angle, the axis of the pyramid at the midpoints. Draw the three views of the pyramid with the hole showing COI.

Solution Refer Fig. 17.13.

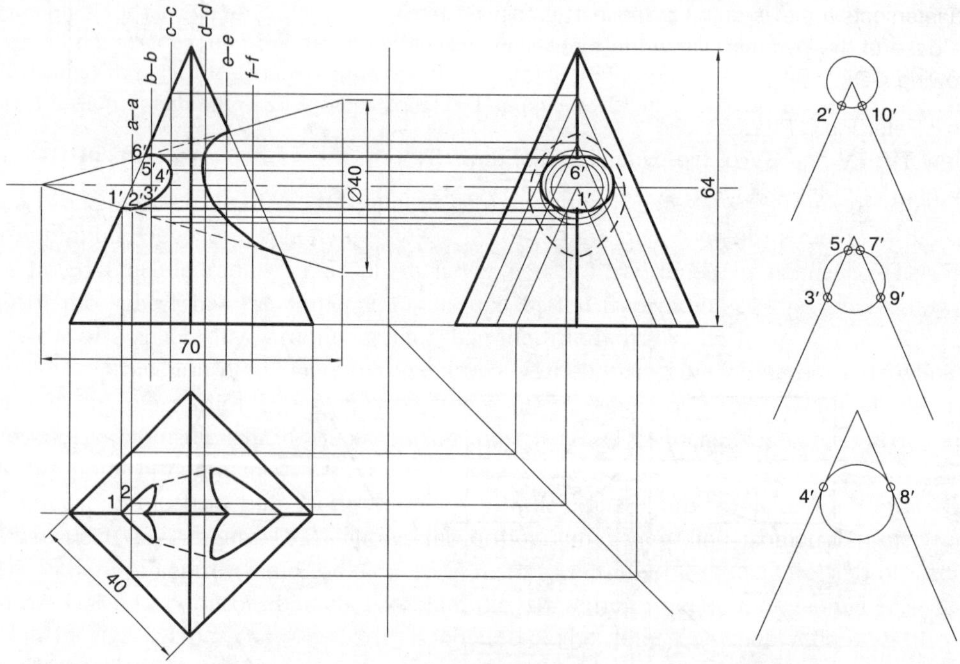

Fig. 17.13

1. Draw TV, FV and SV of the pyramid. Also, draw FV of the cone.
2. In FV, draw a few cutting planes, *a–a*, *b–b* and *c–c*. Locate 1′ and 6′ at the intersections of the generator of the cone and the slant edge of the pyramid.
3. In SV, draw sections of the pyramid and cone corresponding to cutting planes *a–a*, *b–b* and *c–c*. The section of the pyramid will be a triangle while that of the cone will be a circle. For each pair of

triangle and circle, mark points at their intersections, viz., 2″ and 10″, 3″, 5″, 7″ and 9″ and 4″ and 8″. Also, project 1′ and 6′ to 1″ and 2″ on the corresponding slant edges. Join 1″–2″ ... 10″ by a smooth curve for the required COI.

4. Project 2″, 3″, ..., 10″ to 2′, 3′, ..., 10′ on the corresponding cutting plane. Join 1′–2′ ... 10′ for the COI.
5. Project 1″, 2″, ..., 10″ and 1′, 2′, ..., 10′ to obtain 1, 2, ..., 10 in TV. Complete the COI.
6. Draw few more cutting planes *d–d*, *e–e* and *f–f* in the right half of the pyramid. Obtain corresponding COI in SV, FV and TV in a similar way. Draw the hidden lines properly.

17.12 INTERSECTION OF PYRAMID AND SPHERE

Example 17.14 A square pyramid of 45 mm base side and a height of 60 mm has its base parallel to the HP. All the sides of the base are equally inclined to the VP. A sphere of diameter 40 mm was partially penetrated into the pyramid and then removed from the latter. The centre of the sphere was at the midpoint of the slant edge parallel to the VP. Draw the three views of the pyramid showing the depression created by the sphere.

Solution Refer Fig. 17.14.

1. Draw the three views of the pyramid. Also, in FV, draw the sphere such that its centre is at the midpoint of a slant edge parallel to the VP.
2. In FV, locate 1′ and 5′ at the intersections of the slant edge of the pyramid with the circle.
3. In FV, draw a few cutting planes in between 1′ and 5′.
4. Project the cutting planes from FV to obtain sections in TV. The sections of the pyramid will be squares while that of the sphere are circles.
5. In TV, locate 1, 2, etc., at the intersections of the square section and circle section. Project 1′ and 5′ to 1 and 5 directly on the corresponding slant edge. Join 1, 2, etc., to obtain the COI in TV.
6. Project 1, 2, etc., to 1′, 2′, etc., on appropriate cutting planes. Join 1–2–3–4–5 by a smooth curve for the required COI.
7. Project 1′, 2′, etc., and 1″, 2″, etc., in SV. Join 1″–2″–3″–4″–5″ for the COI in FV. Draw the COI in another half in a similar way.

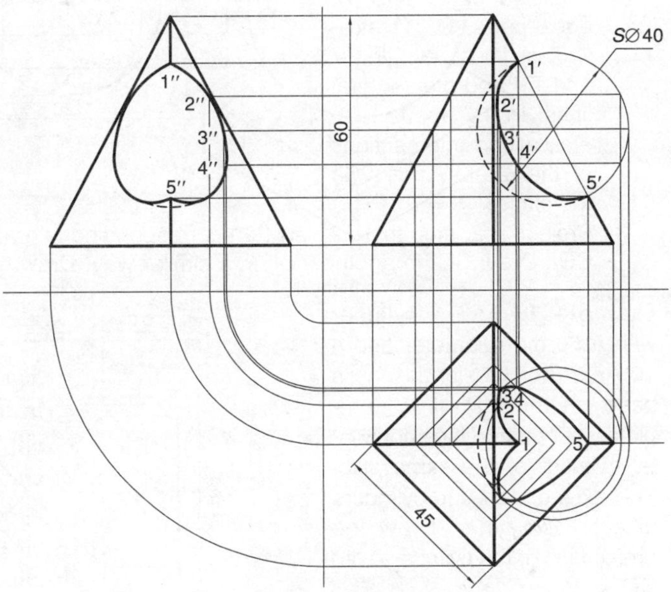

Fig. 17.14

17.13 INTERSECTION OF CYLINDER AND CYLINDER

Example 17.15 A vertical cylinder with a diameter of 70 mm and a height of 90 mm is penetrated by a horizontal cylinder with a diameter of 50 mm and a length of 120 mm. The axis of the horizontal cylinder is parallel to the VP. The axes of both the cylinders intersect at their midpoints. Draw three views of the cylinders showing COI.

Solution Refer Fig. 17.15.

1. Draw the three views of the cylinders. In SV, divide the circle into 12 equal parts, 1″, 2″, etc.
2. Project 1″, 2″, etc., in FV and TV and draw lateral lines. In TV, mark 1, 2, etc., at the intersections of the lateral lines with the circle.
3. Project 1, 2, etc., to 1′, 2′, etc., on corresponding lateral lines in FV. Join 1′, 2′, etc., for the required COI. Draw COI in another half in a similar way. Draw hidden lines properly.

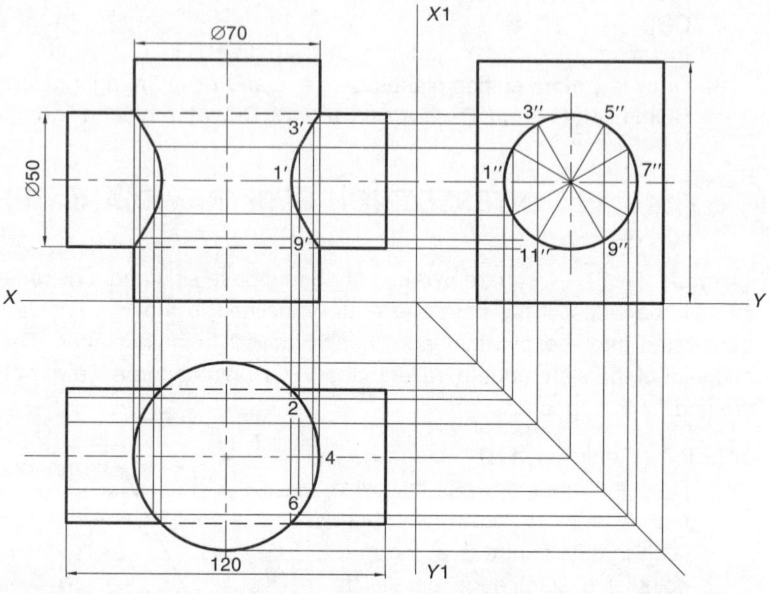

Fig. 17.15

Example 17.16 A cylinder with a 50 mm diameter and a 100 mm height stands on its base on the HP. It is completely penetrated by a horizontal cylinder of the same size. The axes of both the cylinders bisect each other. Draw the projections of the cylinders with COI.

Solution Refer Fig. 17.16.

1. Draw TVs and FVs of the cylinders. Also, draw the SV of the horizontal cylinder.
2. In the SV, obtain 12 division points on the circle. Project the division points in TV and FV and draw lateral lines.

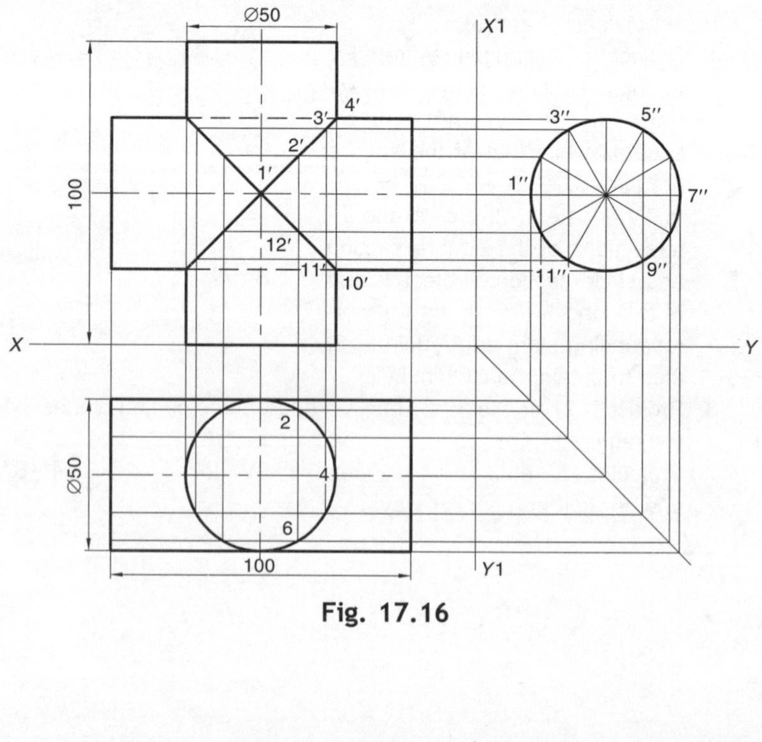

Fig. 17.16

3. In TV, mark POIs 1, 2, etc., between the lateral lines and the circle.
4. Project 1, 2, etc., to 1′, 2′, etc., on the corresponding lateral lines in FV. Join 1′, 2′, etc., for the required COI. Draw the hidden lines properly.

Note that, the COIs are seen as straight lines in this case.

Example 17.17 Two cylinders of equal sizes penetrate each other as shown in Fig. 17.17(a). The axes intersect at their midpoints. Draw the three views of the cylinders showing COI.

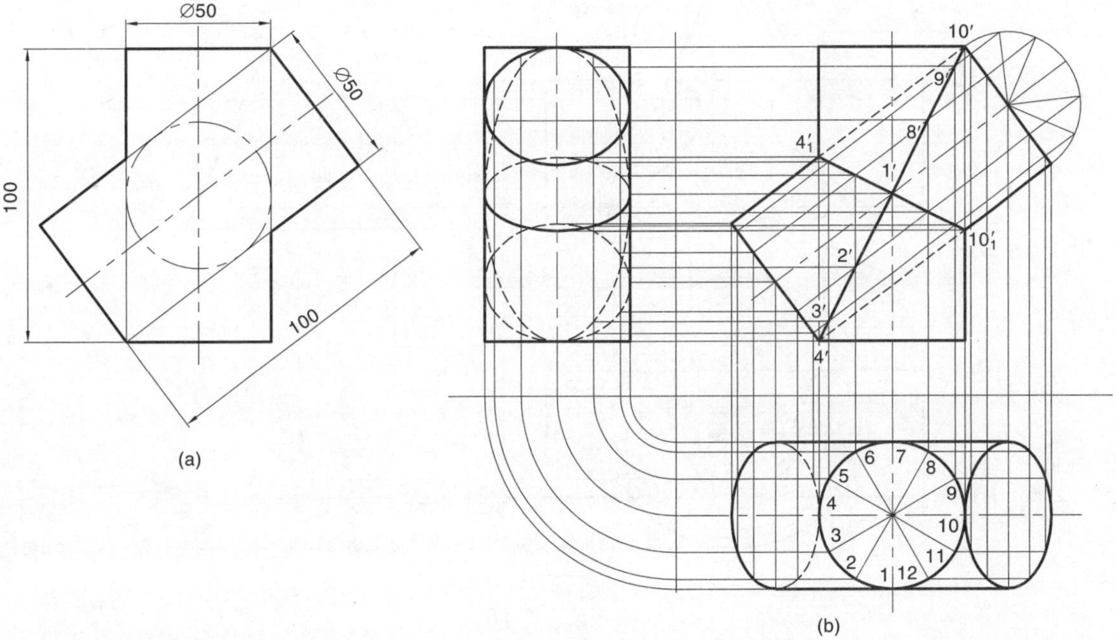

Fig. 17.17

Solution Refer Fig. 17.17(b).

1. Reproduce the given FVs. Draw the half-auxiliary view of the inclined cylinder. Obtain six division points on it and project them in FV to obtain lateral lines.
2. Draw TV of the vertical cylinder. Draw TV of the inclined cylinder by projecting the division points as shown. Draw lateral lines on the inclined cylinder in TV.
3. In TV, mark POIs 1, 2, etc., between the lateral lines and the circle.
4. Project 1, 2, etc., from TV to 1′, 2′, etc., on the corresponding lateral lines in FV. Join 4′–3′–2′–1′–8′–9′–10′ for the required COI. Draw $4_1-1'-10_1'$ in a similar way.
5. Project FV and TV with the POIs to obtain SV. Show the hidden lines properly.

Note: If the two intersecting cylinders have equal diameters and their axes intersect, then the COIs will be seen as straight lines in one view.

17.14 INTERSECTION OF CYLINDER AND CONE

Example 17.18 A cone with a base diameter of 64 mm and an axis length of 70 mm is kept on its base on the HP. A cylinder of diameter 30 mm and length 90 mm penetrates the cone horizontally. The axis of the cylinder is 20 mm above the base of the cone and 5 mm away from the axis of the latter. Draw the three views of the solids showing COI.

Solution Refer Fig. 17.18.

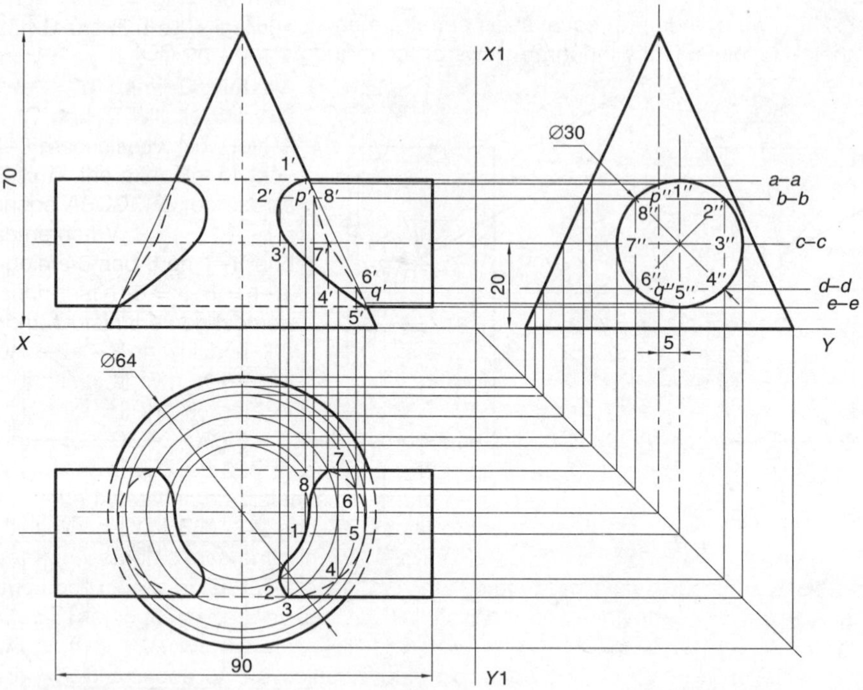

Fig. 17.18

1. Draw TV, FV and SV of the cone. Also, draw SV, FV and TV of the cylinder.
2. In SV, obtain 8 divisions 1″, 2″, etc., on the circle. Through 1″, 2″(8″), 3″(7″), 4″(6″) and 5″, draw horizontal cutting planes *a–a*, *b–b*, *c–c*, *d–d* and *e–e*. Also, mark *p*″ and *q*″ at the apparent intersections of the axis and the circle.
3. Project the cutting planes in TV to draw section circles. Project 1″, 2″, etc., to 1, 2, etc., on the corresponding sections in TV. Join 1, 2, etc., for the required COI. Obtain COI in another half in a similar way.
4. Project 1″, 2″, etc., and 1, 2, etc., in FV to obtain 1′, 2′, etc. Project *p*″ and *q*″ to *p*′ and *q*′ directly on the extreme generator. Join 1′, 2′, etc., to obtain the COI in FV. Draw the hidden lines properly.

Example 17.19 A cone with a base diameter of 80 mm and an axis length of 100 mm is penetrated by a cylinder with a diameter of 50 mm and a height of 114 mm. The axes of both the solids are vertical and 10 mm away from each other. The plane containing the two axes is parallel to the VP. Draw the three views showing COI. Also, draw an auxiliary FV on the AVP inclined at 60° to the VP.

Solution Refer Fig. 17.19.

1. Draw TVs, FVs and SVs of the cone and the cylinder.
2. In the TV, obtain 12 divisions on the base of the cone and draw lateral lines. Also, draw lateral lines on the cone in FV.
3. In TV, mark 1, 2, etc., at the intersections of the lateral lines and the circle.
4. Project 1, 2, etc., to 1′, 2′, etc., on the corresponding lateral lines in FV. Join 1′, 2′, etc., for the required COI.

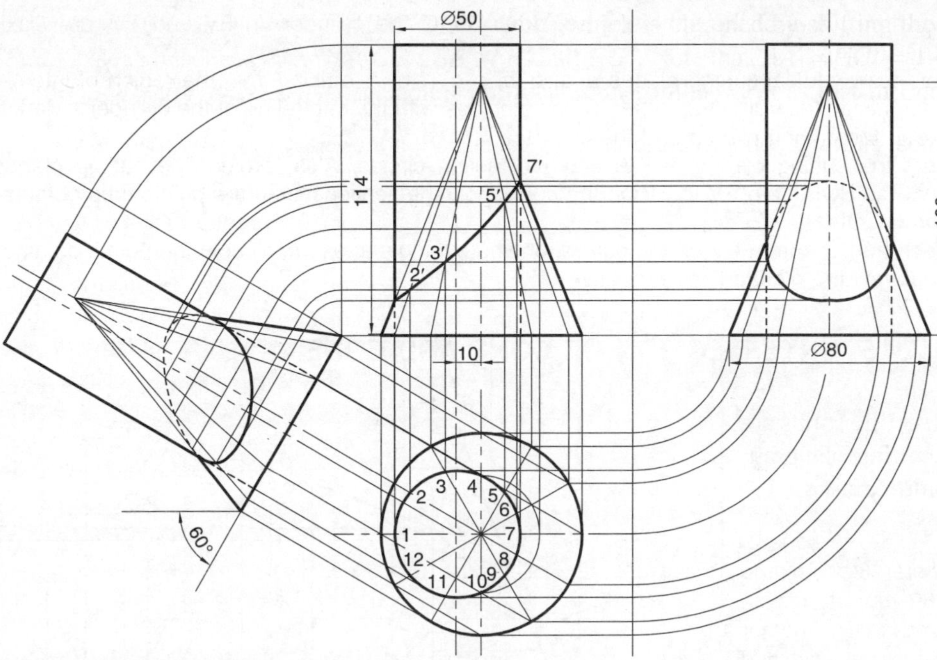

Fig. 17.19

5. Draw COI in SV by projecting 1, 2, etc., and 1′, 2′, etc.
6. Draw an auxiliary reference line at 60° to *XY*. Project FVs and TVs on it to obtain the required auxiliary FVs.

17.15 INTERSECTION OF CYLINDER AND SPHERE

Example 17.20 A through hole is created in a sphere by piercing a cylinder. The diameter of the sphere is 80 mm and that of the cylinder is 50 mm. The axis of the hole is parallel to both the RPs and 10 mm away from the centre of the sphere. The plane containing the centre of the sphere and the axis of the hole is inclined at 45° to the HP. Draw projections of the sphere with the hole.

Solution Refer Fig. 17.20.

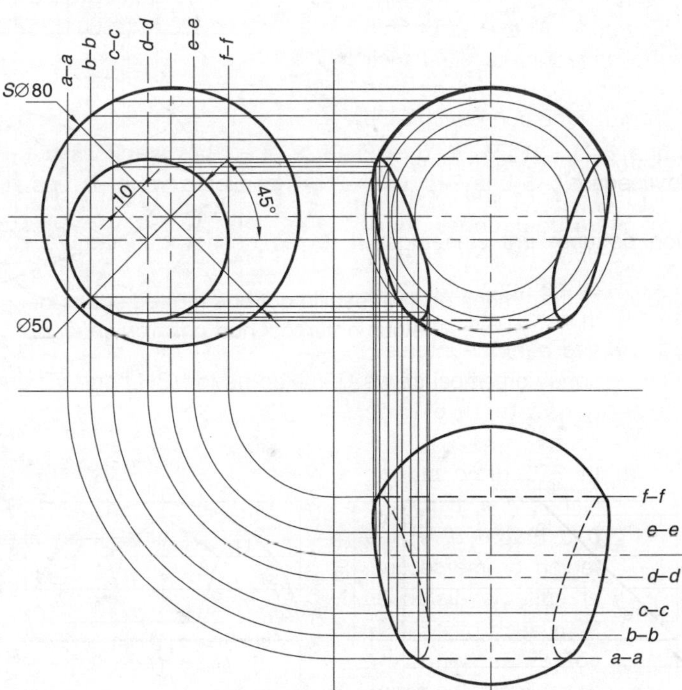

Fig. 17.20

1. Draw three views of the sphere. Also, draw SV of the cylinder. In FV and TV, draw axis of the cylinder (hole).
2. In SV, draw vertical cutting planes *a–a*, *b–b*, *c–c*, *d–d*, *e–e* and *f–f*, in the region of intersection, at suitable distances from each other. (*d–d* coincides with the centreline of the cylinder.) Mark the POIs between the cutting planes and the circle.
3. Project the cutting planes in FV to draw section circles. Also, project the cutting planes in TV. Project the POIs from SV to FV on the corresponding sections. Join the points thus obtained for the required COIs.
4. Project the POIs from FV on the corresponding cutting planes in TV. Join the points obtained for the COIs. Draw the hidden lines properly.

17.16 INTERSECTION OF CONE AND CONE

As the intersecting solids are cones, the cutting plane approach should be used.

Example 17.21 A cone of base diameter 60 mm and height of 80 mm stands on its base on the HP. Another cone of the same size and having its axis parallel to both the RPs penetrates the first cone. The axes of both the cones intersect at their midpoints. Draw the two views of the cones with COI.

Solution Refer Fig. 17.21.

1. Draw TV and FV of the vertical cone. Also, draw SV, FV and TV of the horizontal cone. In FV, mark *l′*, *m′*, *n′* and *o′* at the intersections of the extreme generators of the cones.
2. In FV, draw cutting planes *a–a*, *b–b*, *c–c*, *d–d* and *e–e*, in the region of intersection, at suitable distances from each other. (*c–c* coincides with the centreline of the cone.)
3. Project the cutting planes in TV to draw sections of both the

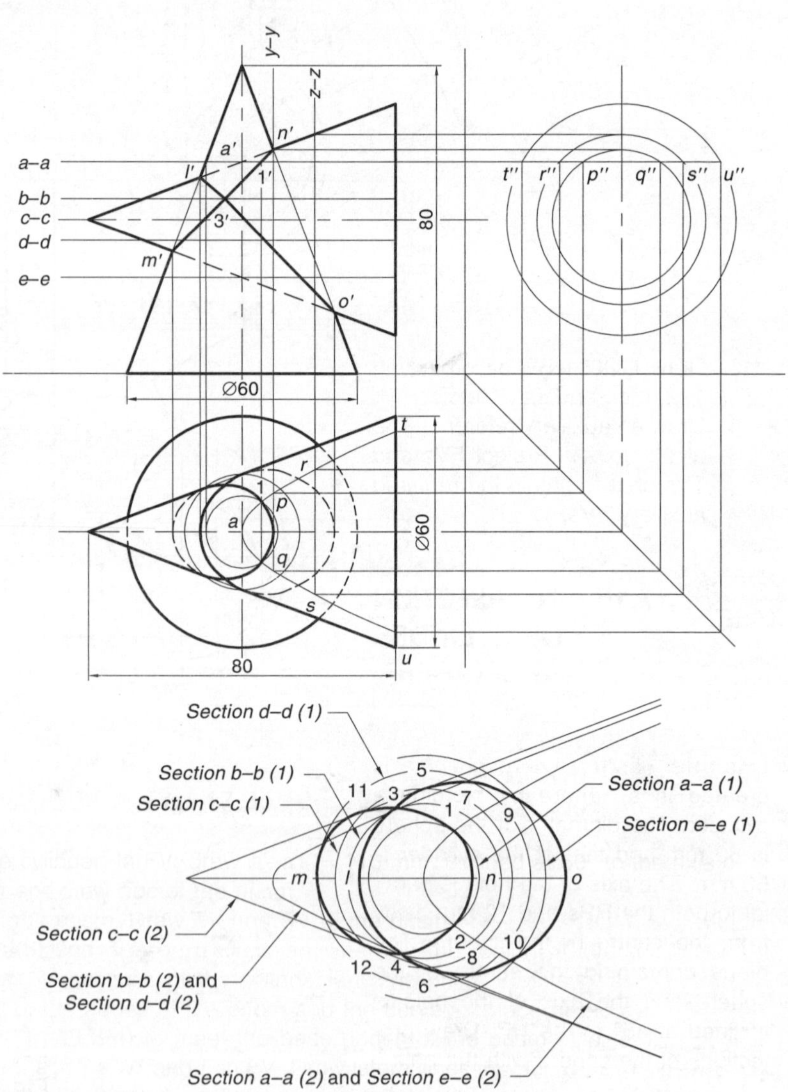

Fig. 17.21

cones. Sections of vertical cone will be circles. Sections of horizontal cone will be hyperbolas (since the cutting planes are parallel to the axis). To obtain the section hyperbolas, adopt the method as explained below:

Consider the cutting plane *a–a*. It cuts the generator at *a′* and the base at *t″* and *u″* (shown in SV). Project *a′* to *a* on the corresponding generator in TV. Also, project *t″* and *u″* to *t* and *u* on the base in TV. To locate more points for the hyperbola, draw the vertical cutting planes *y–y*, *z–z*, etc. Project *y–y* and *z–z* in SV to draw corresponding section circles. Mark points *p″*, *q″*, *r″* and *s″* at the intersections of the section circles with *a–a*. Project *p″*, *q″*, *r″* and *s″* to *p*, *q*, *r* and *s* on the *y–y* and *z–z*. Join *t–r–a–q–u* for the hyperbola, *Section a–a(2)*.

4. In TV, draw a section circle for the cutting plane *a–a*, i.e., *Section a–a(1)*. Mark 1 and 2 at the intersections of *Section a–a(1)* and *Section a–a(2)*.
5. Obtain section circles and section hyperbolas in TV for the cutting planes *b–b*, *d–d* and *e–e*. (For *c–c*, section will be seen as triangle in TV.)
6. In TV, mark POIs between the section circles and section hyperbolas (section triangle), i.e., 3 and 4 between *Section b–b(1)* and *Section b–b(2)*, 5 and 6 between *Section c–c(1)* and *Section c–c(2)*, 7 and 8 between *Section d–d(1)* and *Section d–d(2)*, and so on.
7. Project *l′*, *m′*, *n′* and *o′* to *l*, *m*, *n* and *o* on the corresponding generators in TV. Join *n*–1–3–5–7–9–*o*–10–8–6–4–2–*n* for the required COI. Also, join *l*–3–11–*m*–12–4–*l* for another COI.
8. Project 1, 2, etc., to 1′, 2′, etc., on the corresponding cutting planes in FV. Join the points for the COIs. Draw the hidden lines properly.

DRAWING TIP

Draw *a–a* and *e–e* and *b–b* and *d–d* at equal distances from *c–c*. The section hyperbolas for *a–a* and *e–e*, i.e., *Section a–a(2)* and *Section e–e(2)*, will be the same. Also, *Section b–b(2)* and *Section d–d(2)* will be the same. This reduces efforts of drawing different section hyperbolas.

17.17 INTERSECTION OF CONE AND SPHERE

Example 17.22 A cone ϕ70 mm × 80 mm, is intersected by a sphere of $S\phi$ 70 mm. The centre of the sphere is 40 mm from the base and 22 mm from the axis of cone. The plane containing the centre of the sphere and the axis of the cone is parallel to the VP. Draw the three views of the solids showing COI.

Solution Refer Fig. 17.22.

1. Draw TVs, FVs and SVs of the cone and the sphere. In FV, mark *p′* and *q′* at the intersections of the extreme generator of the cone and the sphere.
2. In FV, draw cutting planes *a–a*, *b–b*, *c–c*, *d–d* and *e–e*.

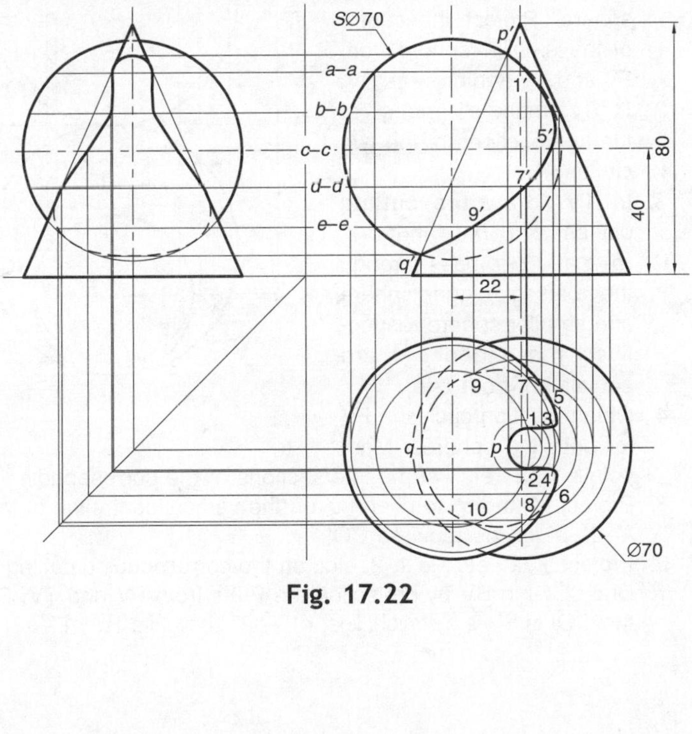

Fig. 17.22

(*c–c* passes through the axis of sphere.) *a–a* and *e–e* and *b–b* and *d–d* are drawn at equal distances from *c–c*.

3. Obtain section circles in TV for both the solids. Mark points 1, 2, etc., at the intersections of the corresponding section-circles.
4. Project *p′* and *q′* to *p* and *q* on the corresponding generators in TV. Join *p*–1–3–5–7–9–*q*–10–8–6–4–2–*p* for the required COI.
5. Project 1, 2, etc., to 1′, 2′, etc., on the corresponding cutting planes in FV. Join the points for the COI.
6. Draw COI in SV by projecting the POIs from FV and TV. Draw the hidden lines properly.

17.18 INTERSECTION OF SPHERE AND SPHERE

When a sphere penetrates another sphere, a flat circular face is created at the intersection. This face is perpendicular to the line joining the centres of two spheres. Obviously, when viewed perpendicular to the line joining the two centres, the face will be seen as a straight line, i.e., an edge view.

Example 17.23 A sphere with a diameter of 100 mm is so placed that it touches both the RPs. Another sphere with a diameter of 64 mm partially penetrates the first sphere. The centre of the smaller sphere is 90 mm above the HP and 68 mm in front of the VP. The line joining the centres of the spheres is parallel to the PP. Draw the three views of the spheres showing COI.

Solution Refer Fig. 17.23.

1. Draw FV, TV and SV of the bigger sphere. FV and TV must touch *XY*. Locate of the centre of the smaller sphere in FV and TV. Draw FV and TV of the smaller sphere. Project the centre of the smaller sphere from FV and TV and draw its SV.
2. In SV, mark *p″* and *q″* at the intersections of the two circles.
3. In TV, draw the cutting planes *a–a*, *b–b* and *c–c*. (*a–a* and *b–b* pass through the axes of bigger sphere and smaller sphere respectively.) *a–a* and *c–c* are equidistant from *b–b*.
4. Obtain section circles in FV for both the spheres. Mark points 1′, 2′, etc., at the intersections of the corresponding section circles.

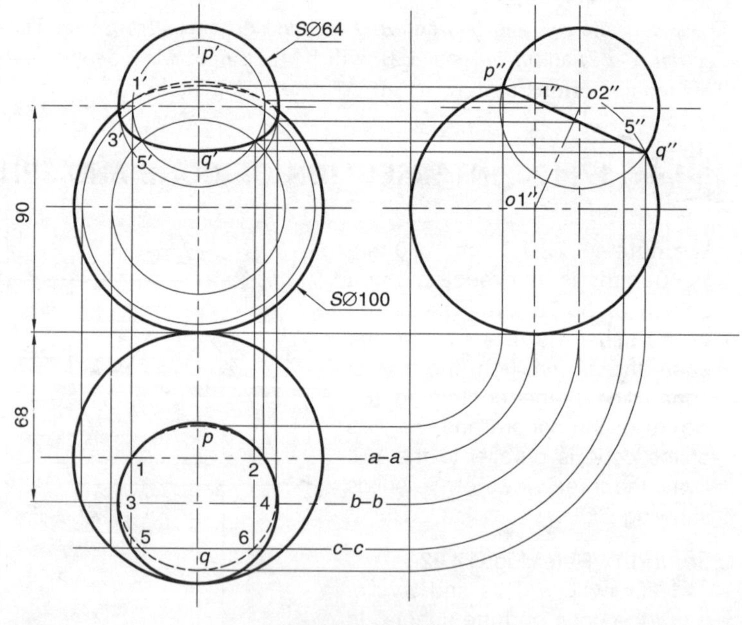

Fig. 17.23

5. Project *p″* and *q″* to *p′* and *q′* on the vertical centreline of the spheres in FV. Join *p′*–1′–3′–5′–*q′*–6′–4′–2′–*p′* for the required COI.
6. Project 1′, 2′, etc., to 1, 2, etc., on the corresponding cutting planes in TV. Join the points for the COI.
7. Draw COI in SV by projecting the POIs from FV and TV. Draw the hidden lines properly. Note that the COI in SV is a straight line. *o*1″–*o*2″ shows its TL. *o*1″–*o*2″ is perpendicular to *p″*–*q″*.

Remember the Following

- Whenever two cylinders of equal diameters penetrate (axes intersecting), the COIs are seen as straight lines in one view.
- The intersection of two spheres is a circle. It is seen as a straight line when viewed in the direction perpendicular to the line joining the centres of the two spheres.

Illustrative Problems

Problem 17.1 A square prism is intersected by a triangular prism, the axes bisecting at right angles. The square prism is vertical and its faces are equally inclined to the VP. A rectangular face of the triangular prism is inclined at 40° to the HP. Draw projections to show LOI. Side of base of square prism = side of base of triangular prism = 50 mm, and length of axis of square prism = length of axis of triangular prism = 100 mm.

Solution Refer Fig. 17.24.

1. Draw the three views of the prisms as shown.
2. In SV and TV, locate points 1, 2, ..., 5 and 1″, 2″, ..., 5″ at the intersections of the edges/surfaces of the prisms.
3. Project 1, 2, ..., 5 and 1″, 2″, ..., 5″ to locate 1′, 2′, ..., 5′ in FV. Join 1′, 2′, ..., 5′ for the LOI. Obtain another LOI on the left side in a similar way. Draw the hidden lines properly.
4. Draw the hidden edges of the triangular prism in FV and TV.

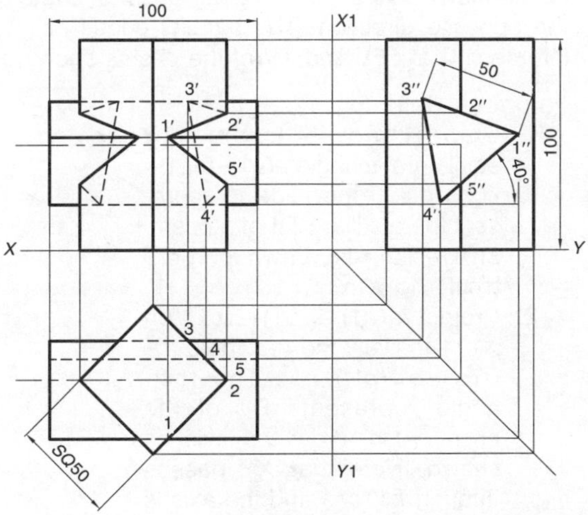

Fig. 17.24

Problem 17.2 A pentagonal prism with a base side of 50 mm and a height of 100 mm, stands on its base on the HP with a rectangular face nearer to the observer. A triangular hole of side edge 80 mm is cut through the prism. The axis of the hole is perpendicular and 6 mm offset to the axis of the prism and 44 mm above the HP. One of the rectangular faces of the hole makes 45° with the HP. Draw the three views of the prism with the hole.

Solution Refer Fig. 17.25.

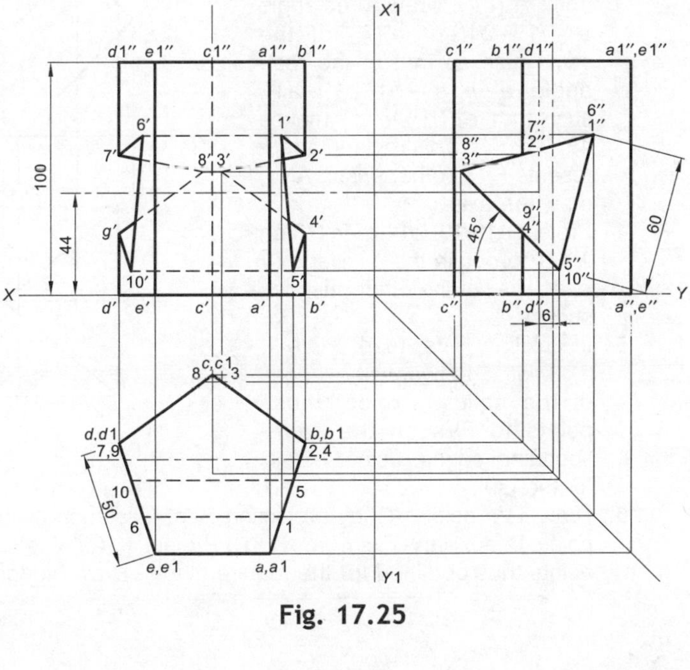

Fig. 17.25

1. Draw the three views of the pentagonal prism. Locate the triangle in SV as shown.
2. In SV, mark points 1″, 2″, 3″, ..., 10″. The points 6″, 7″, ..., 10″ lie at the back in SV.
3. Obtain the corresponding points 1, 2, 3, ..., 10 in TV.
4. Project 1″, 2″, 3″, ..., 10″ and 1, 2, 3, ..., 10 to obtain 1′, 2′, 3′, ..., 10′ in FV.
5. Join 1′–2′–3′ ... 10′ by observing their sequence in SV. Parts of lines 2′–3′, 3′–4′, 7′–8′ and 8′–9′ are shown by hidden lines since these are partly visible.
6. Join 1′–6′, 3′–8′ and 5′–10′ by dashed lines to indicate hidden edges of the hole.
7. In TV, also indicate the hidden edges of the hole properly.

Problem 17.3 A triangular prism with a base side of 50 mm and an axis length of 80 mm, rests on an edge of the base on the HP. The edge is perpendicular to the VP while the axis of the prism is inclined at 45° to the HP. Another triangular prism of same dimensions rests on the HP in a similar way but leans in the opposite direction. The parallel edges of the bases of the prisms are 30 mm apart and their axes intersect. Draw FV and TV of the prisms showing LOIs.

Solution Refer Fig. 17.26.

1. Draw *X*1*Y*1 at 45° to *XY*. Draw equilateral triangle *a*(*a*1)–*b*(*b*1)–*c*(*c*1) of 50 mm side to represent the auxiliary TV of a prism. *b*(*b*1)–*c*(*c*1) is drawn perpendicular to *X*1*Y*1.
2. Project *a*(*a*1)–*b*(*b*1)–*c*(*c*1) on *X*1*Y*1 to draw the rectangle *a*′–*b*′(*c*′)–*b*1′(*c*1′)–*a*1′. The rectangle represents FV of the prism. Also, draw the axis as shown. Note that *XY* passes through *b*1′(*c*1′) and the axis is at 45° to *XY*.
3. Locate *e*1′(*f*1′) on *XY* at 30 mm from *b*1′(*c*1′). Draw a rectangle *e*1′(*f*1′)–*d*1′–*d*′–*e*′(*f*′) of the same size as that of the rectangle *a*′–*b*′(*c*′)–*b*1′(*c*1′)–*a*1′, such that *e*1′(*f*1′)–*e*′(*f*′) makes 45° with *XY*. This rectangle represents FV of other prism. Also, draw the axis.
4. Project *e*1′(*f*1′)–*d*1′–*d*′–*e*′(*f*′) on *X*1*Y*1 to obtain the auxiliary TV *e*–*e*1–*f*1–*f* of the other prism as shown.
5. In auxiliary TVs, mark POIs 1, 2, 3, etc., between the edges of the solids. Project these points to FVs on the corresponding edges. Join 1′–2′(4′) for the LOI.

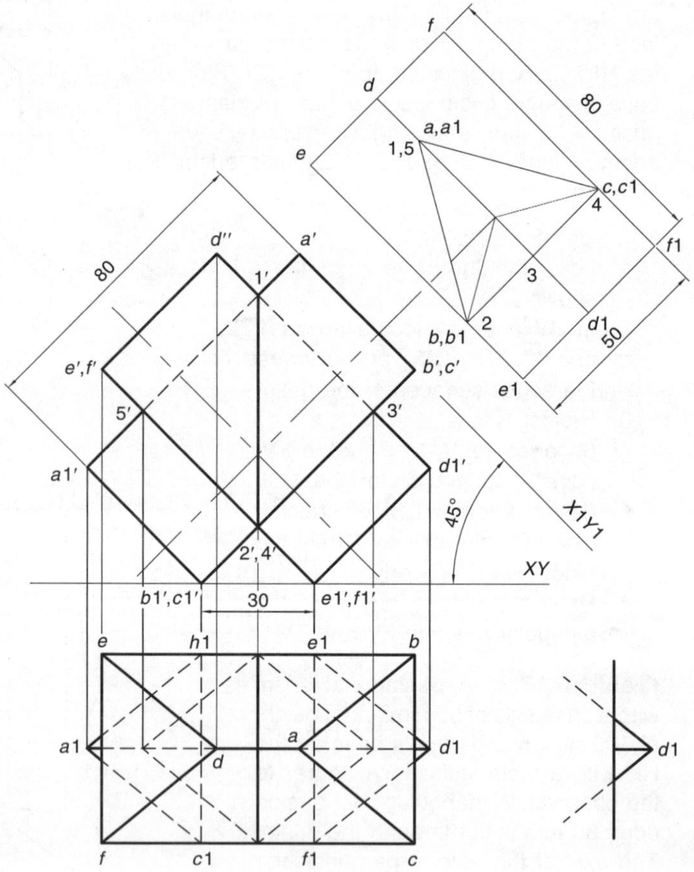

Fig. 17.26

6. Draw TVs below *XY* by projecting FVs. (Distance of the points in TVs from *XY* = distances of the points in auxiliary TVs from *X*1*Y*1.) Project 1′, 2′, 3′, etc., on the corresponding edges in TV. Join the points thus obtained for the required LOIs. Draw hidden lines properly.

Problem 17.4 A cube with a 40 mm side has a corner on the HP. The body diagonal through that corner is vertical. An edge through the corner on the HP is parallel to the VP. A square prism with a base side of 23 mm, penetrates the cube. The axis of the prism is equal to and coincides with the vertical body diagonal of the cube. The lateral faces of the prism are equally inclined to the VP. Draw the three views of the solids showing LOI.

Solution Refer Fig. 17.27.

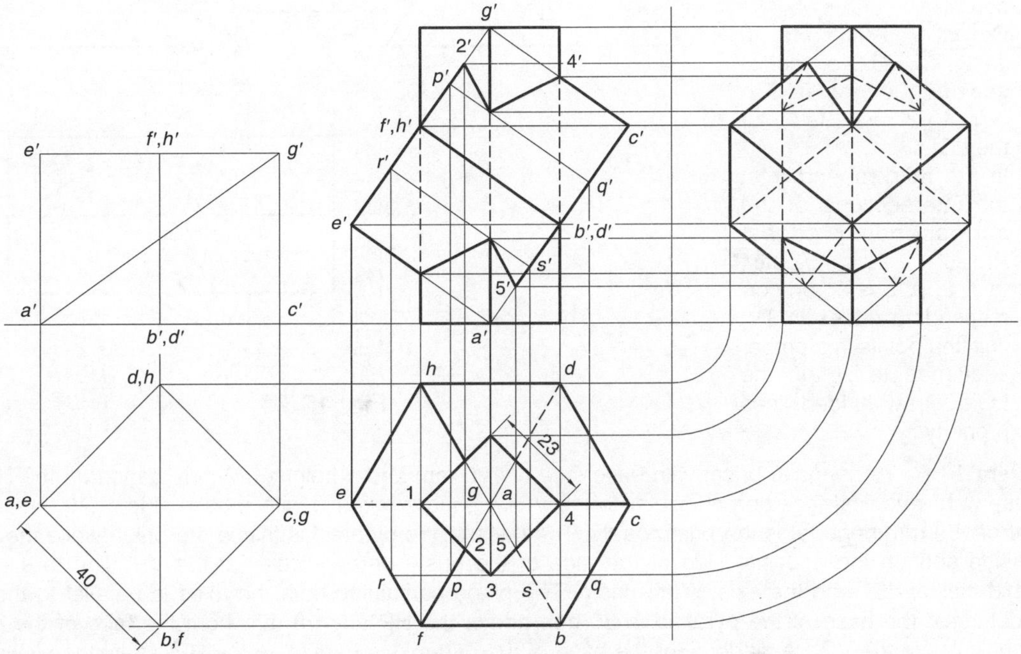

Fig. 17.27

1. Draw TV and FV of the cube as shown. Join *a′–g′* for the body diagonal.
2. Redraw FV with *a′–g′* vertical. Project TV and SV. Note that *a–e* is parallel to *XY*. As the body diagonal *AG* is vertical, it is seen as point view *a*(*g*) in TV.
3. Draw TV, FV and SV of the prism as shown.
4. In TV, locate points 1, 2, 4, etc., at the intersections of the edges of the solids. 3 represents a corner of the square. Draw a lateral line *pq* through 3 and project it in FV.
5. Project 1, 2, 3, etc., to 1′, 2′, 3′, etc., on the corresponding edges/lateral line in FV. Join them in a proper sequence for the required LOI. Obtain LOI in the other half in a similar way.
6. Project 1′, 2′, 3′, etc., to the corresponding edges in SV to obtain the LOIs. Note how the hidden lines are marked.

Problem 17.5 A tetrahedron with a side of 50 mm rests on one of its faces on the HP with a side of that face perpendicular to the VP. A square prism with a base side of 20 mm and a length of 60 mm, penetrates the tetrahedron. The axis of the prism is parallel to both the RPs. Both the axes intersect at their midpoints. The lateral faces of the prism are equally inclined to the HP. Draw the projections of the solids showing LOI.

Solution Refer Fig. 17.28.

1. Draw TV, FV and SV of the tetrahedron. Also, draw SV, FV and TV of the prism.
2. In SV, locate 1″, 2″, 3″, etc., at the intersections of the edges of the two solids.
3. Project 1″, 2″, 3″, etc., to 1′, 2′, 3′, etc., on corresponding edges in FV. Join 1′–2′ and 3′–4′ for the LOIs.
4. In FV, mark *p*′ and *q*′ at the intersections of the corresponding edges. Project 1′, 2′, *p*′, *q*′, etc., to 1, 2, *p*, *q*, etc., on corresponding edges in TV. Join the points in a proper sequence to obtain the LOIs. Draw hidden lines properly.

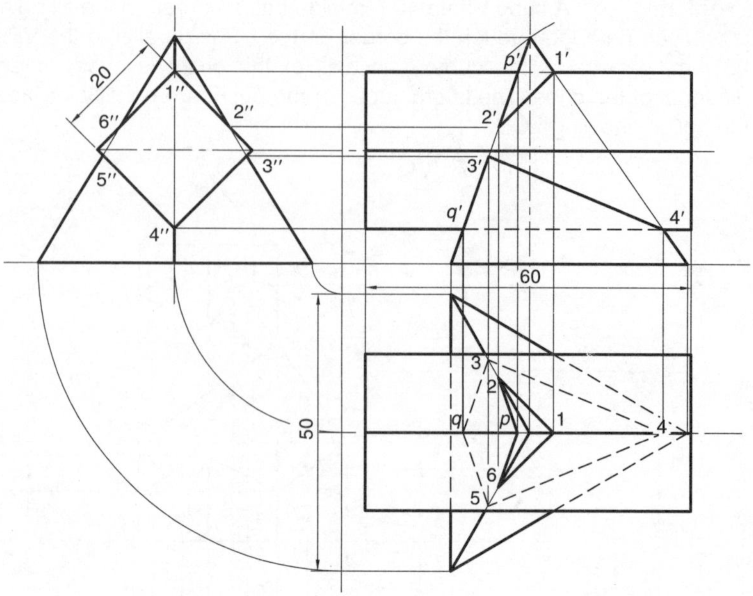

Fig. 17.28

Problem 17.6 A triangular prism with base side of 100 mm and a height 120 mm stands on the HP on its base with a vertical face perpendicular to the VP. A square pyramid with a base side of 40 mm and a height of 150 mm penetrates the prism partly. The base of the pyramid is inside the prism while the apex is outside and on the opposite side of the face of the prism perpendicular to the VP. The axis of the pyramid makes 45° with the axis of the prism. The plane containing both the axes is parallel to the VP. The centre of the base of the pyramid is 30 mm above the HP and 28 mm from the face of the prism perpendicular to the VP. A diagonal of the base of the pyramid is parallel to the HP. Draw the views and show LOI. Develop lateral surfaces of the prism and the pyramid.

Solution Refer Fig. 17.29.

1. Draw FV and TV of the prism. Locate o1′ 30 mm above *XY* and 28 mm left of the face *a*′*b*′–*a*1′*b*1′. Draw *o*1′–*o*′ = 150 mm, inclined at 45° to the axis of the prism.
2. Draw *X*1*Y*1 perpendicular to *o*1′–*o*′. Draw the auxiliary TV *d*1–*e*1–*f*1–*g*1–*o*1 of the pyramid. *d*1–*e*1–*f*1–*g*1 is a square of 50 mm side. (The auxiliary TV of the prism may also be drawn.)
3. Project *d*1–*e*1–*f*1–*g*1–*o*1 on *X*1*Y*1 to obtain FV *d*′–*e*′–*f*′–*g*′–*o*′ of the pyramid.
4. Project *d*′–*e*′–*f*′–*g*′–*o*′ on *XY* to obtain TV *d*–*e*–*f*–*g*–*o* of the pyramid. (Distances of *d*, *e*, *f*, *g* and *o* from *XY* = distances of *d*1, *e*1, *f*1, *g*1 and *o*1 from *X*1*Y*1.)
5. Locate 1′ and 3′ in FV and 2 and 4 in TV at the intersections of the corresponding edges/surfaces of the solids. Project 2 and 4 to 2′ and 4′ in FV. Join 1′–2′(4′)–3′ for the required LOI. 1′–2′(4′)–3′ may be projected to auxiliary TV to show LOI.
6. Draw the developments of the prism and the pyramid as shown.

Problem 17.7 A square prism with a base side of 40 mm and a height of 100 mm stands on the ground with a side of base inclined at 30° to the VP. It is completely penetrated by a cylinder having a 40 mm diameter and a 100 mm length whose axis is parallel to both the RPs and bisects the axis of the prism. Draw the projections showing COI.

Solution Refer Fig. 17.30.

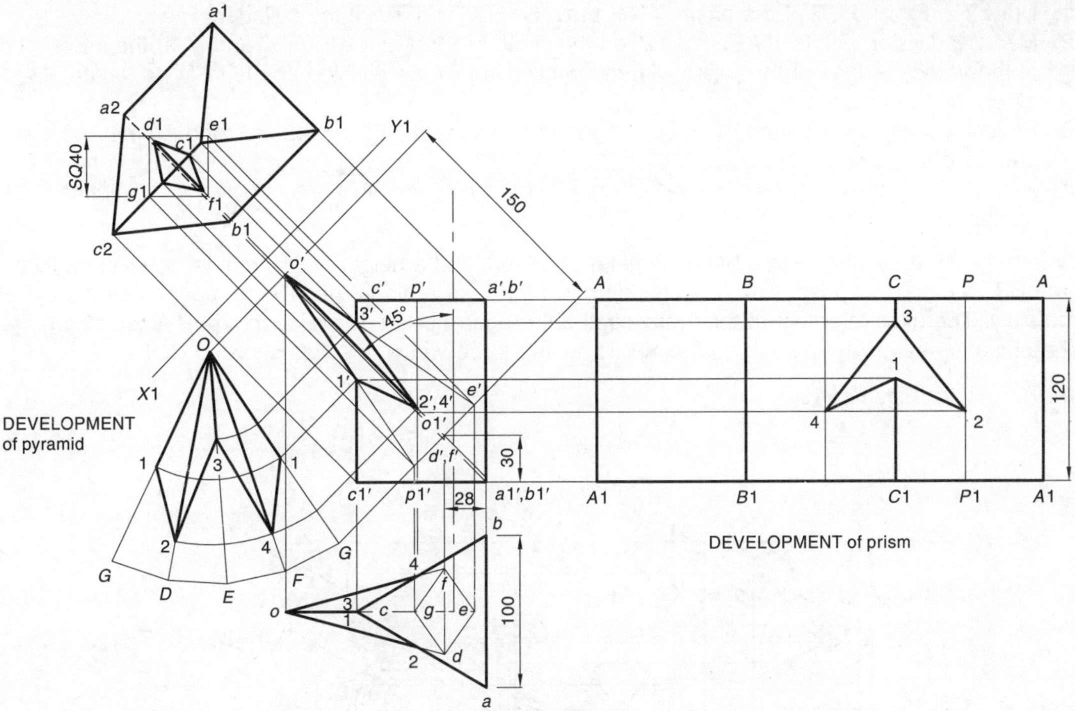

Fig. 17.29

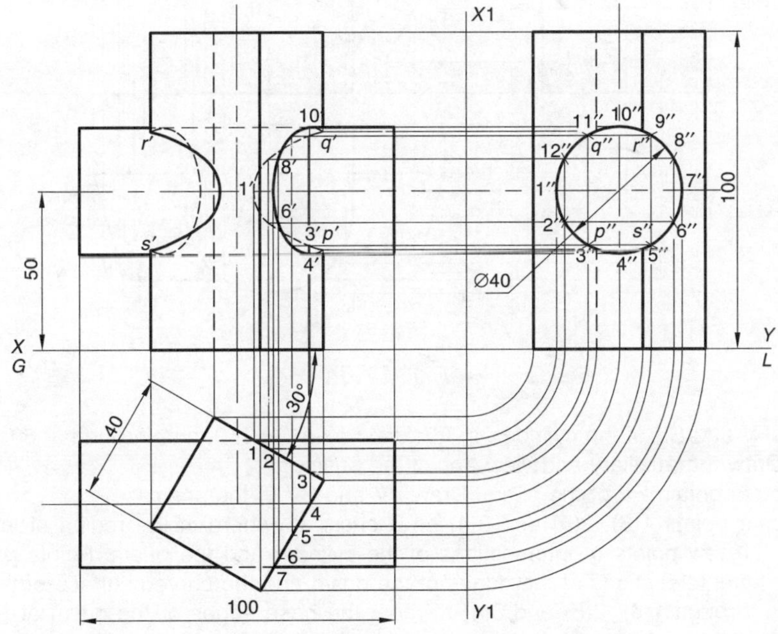

Fig. 17.30

1. Draw TV, FV and SV of the prism. Also, draw SV, FV and TV of the cylinder.
2. Mark 12 division points 1″, 2″, ..., 12″ on the circle in SV. Mark *p*″, *q*″, *r*″ and *s*″ at the intersections of the vertical edges of the prism with the circle. Project the division points in TV to locate 1, 2, ..., 12 on the surface of the prism.
3. Project 1″, 2″, ..., 12″ and 1, 2, ..., 12 in FV to locate 1′, 2′, ..., 12′. *p*″ and *q*″ may be directly projected to locate *p*′ and *q*′.
4. Join 1′–2′–3′–*p*′–4′–5′–6′–7′–8′–9′–10′–*q*′–11′–12′ by a smooth curve for the COI. Obtain COI in another half in a similar way.

Problem 17.8 A cylinder with a base diameter of 55 mm and a height of 110 mm is standing on its base on the HP. A triangular prism with a base side of 40 mm and a height of 110 mm penetrates the cylinder completely. The axes intersect at their midpoints but are inclined at 60° to each other. A rectangular face of the prism is nearer and parallel to the VP. Draw the three views of solids showing COI.

Solution Refer Fig. 17.31.

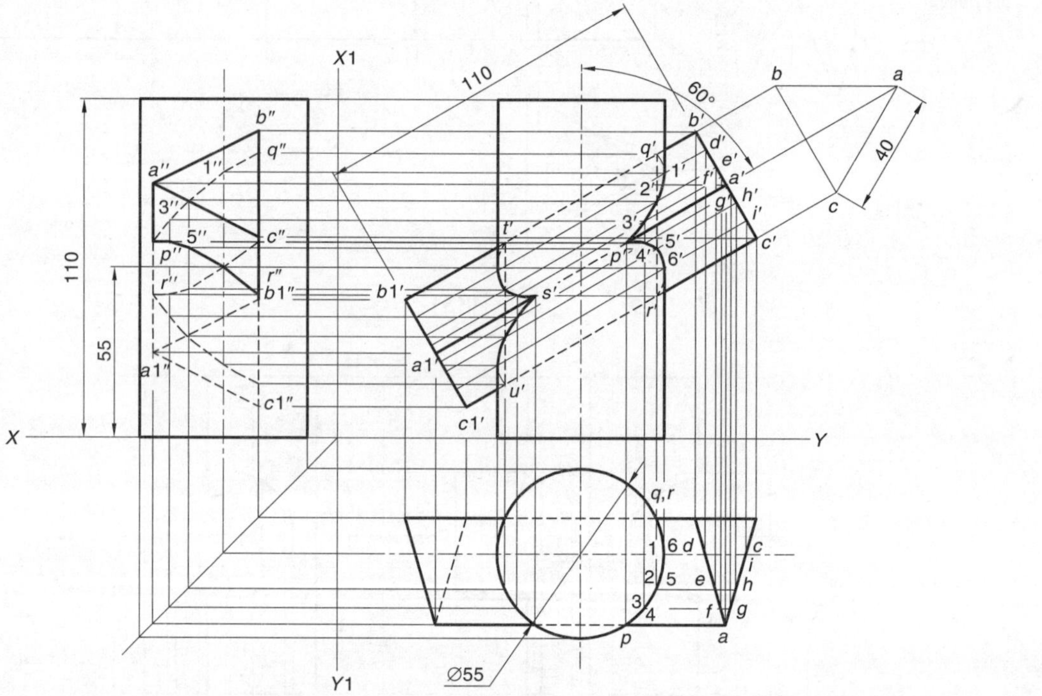

Fig. 17.31

1. Draw TV, FV and SV of the cylinder. In FV, draw *a*′–*a*1′ = 110 mm, inclined at 60° to the axis of the cylinder. Draw the auxiliary end view *abc* of the prism.
2. Project *abc* to obtain FV of the prism. Draw TV and SV of the prism.
3. In TV, locate points 1(6), 2(5) and 3(4) on a circle anywhere in the region of intersection. These represent the few points of intersections of the cylinder and the prism. Points *p*, *q* and *r* may be located at the intersections of the edges of the prism and the curved surface of the cylinder.
4. Draw lines through 1(6), 2(5) and 3(4) to meet the base edges of the prism at *d*, *e*, *f*, *g*, *h* and *i*. Project *d*, *e*, *f*, *g*, *h* and *i* to *d*′, *e*′, *f*′, *g*′, *h*′ and *i*′ in FV. Draw lateral lines through *d*′, *e*′, *f*′, *g*′, *h*′ and *i*′.
5. Project 1(6), 2(5) and 3(4) to 1′, 2′, 3′, 4′, 5′ and 6′ on corresponding lateral lines in FV. Also, project *p*, *q* and *r* on corresponding edges.

6. Join q'–$1'$–$2'$–$3'$–p'–$4'$–$5'$–$6'$–r' by a smooth curve for the COI. Obtain COI in another half in a similar way.
7. Project $1'$, $2'$, etc., and 1, 2, etc. to locate $1''$, $2''$, etc., in SV. Join $1''$, $2''$, etc., in a proper sequence to obtain COI in SV. Draw the hidden lines in all the views properly.

Problem 17.9 A pipe of hexagonal cross section is attached to a duct of semicircular cross section. The pipe intersects the duct at right angles along the curved surface of the duct. Two opposite faces of the pipe are inclined at 15° to a straight edge of the duct. Draw the three views of the pipe and the duct showing COI at their joint. Face width of the pipe = 75 mm and radius of the duct end = 90 mm.

Solution Refer Fig. 17.32.

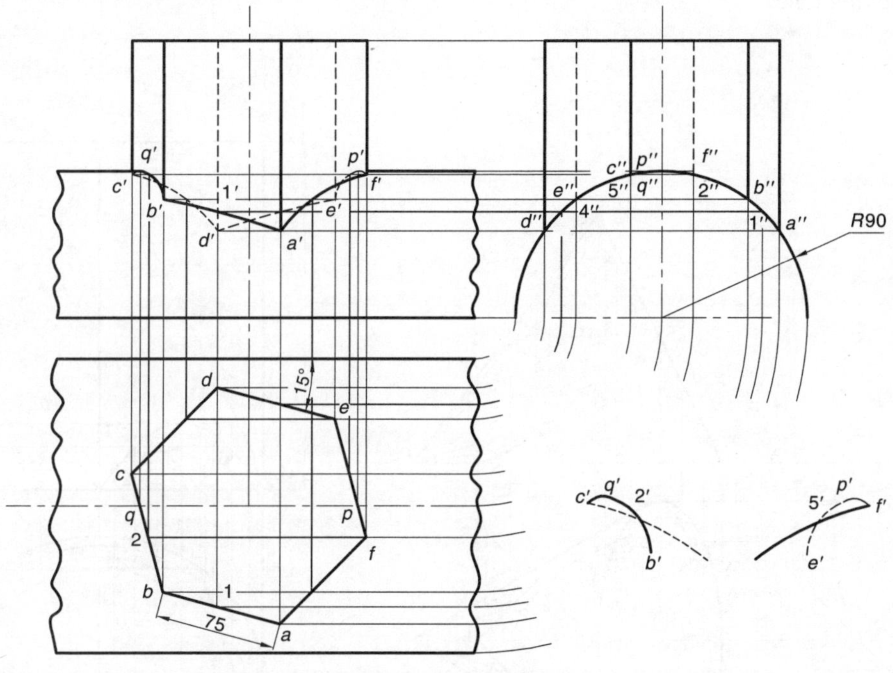

Fig. 17.32

1. Draw SV, partial FV and partial TV of the duct. Also, draw TV, FV and SV of the pipe. Assume a suitable height of the pipe.
2. In SV, locate a'', b'', c'', d'', e'' and f'' at the intersections of the edges of the pipe with the semicircle. Also, locate $1''$, $2''$, etc., in between a'' and b'', b'' and c'', etc. The points p'' and q'' represent the uppermost points (i.e., apparent intersection of the pipe axis with the semicircle) on the semicircle.
3. Project a'', b'', ..., $1''$, $2''$, ..., p'' and q'' to a, b, ..., 1, 2, ..., p and q in TV.
4. Project a'', b'', ..., $1''$, $2''$, ..., p'' and q'' and a, b, ..., 1, 2, ..., p and q to locate a', b', ..., $1'$, $2'$, ..., p' and q' in FV. Join all the points in a proper sequence by a smooth curve. Draw all the hidden line segments properly.

Problem 17.10 A cone with an 80 mm diameter and an 80 mm axis height is resting on its curved surface on the HP. Its axis is parallel to the VP. A through square hole of face width 24 mm is milled in the cone. The axis of the hole intersects the axis of the cone at midpoint. The faces of the hole are equally inclined to the VP. Draw the projections of the cone showing COI for the hole.

Solution Refer Fig. 17.33.

1. Draw TV and FV of the cone. The base is on *XY*. Obtain eight division points on the circle in TV. Project the division points in FV.
2. Redraw FV such that a slant edge coincides with *XY*. Project the division points and draw lateral lines.
3. Obtain the final TV as shown. Draw lateral lines. Draw TV of the hole as shown.
4. Mark 1, 2, 3, etc., at the intersections of the lateral lines and the edges of the hole. (Points 1, 3, 5 and 7 lie at the corners of the square.)
5. Project 1, 2, 3, etc., to 1′, 2′, 3′, etc., on the corresponding edges in FV. Join these points for the COI. Obtain COI in the other half in a similar way. Points *p* and *q* may be marked on the base of the cone in TV to draw lateral line *p′q′–o′* in FV. It will help in locating $3_1'$. Draw the vertical hidden edges of the hole.

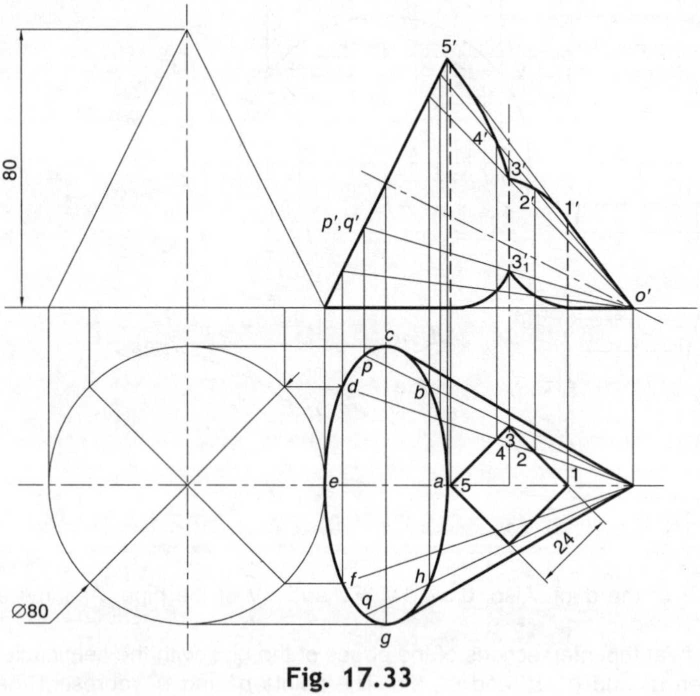

Fig. 17.33

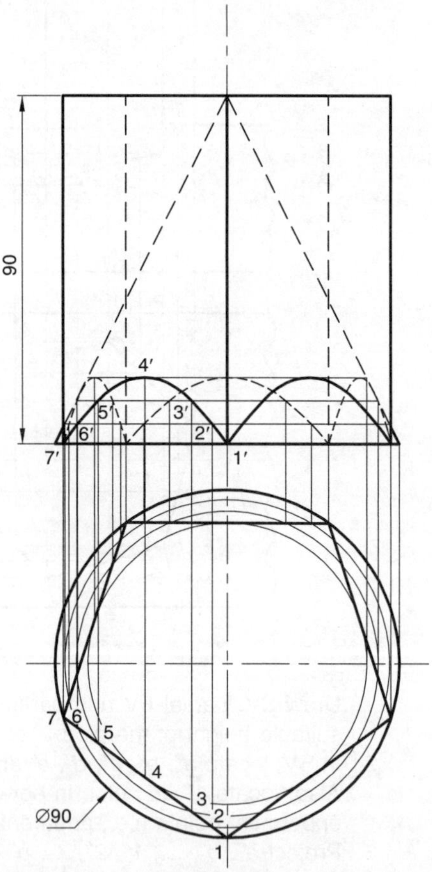

Fig. 17.34

Problem 17.11 Draw a circle with a 90 mm diameter. Inscribe a pentagon in it. The view represents TVs of two intersecting solids—a cone and a pentagonal prism. Both the solids share a common axis length of 90 mm. The base of the cone is on the HP and a rectangular face of the prism is parallel and nearer to the VP. Draw FVs of the solids showing COI.

Solution Refer Fig. 17.34.

1. Draw TVs of the solids as mentioned in the problem. (To inscribe a pentagon in a circle, see Example 4.20.) Draw one side of the pentagon parallel and nearer to *XY*. Draw FVs of the cone and the prism.
2. In TV, draw a few section circles. The innermost section circle is tangent to the pentagon. Mark POIs 1, 2, 3, etc., between the section circles and each edge of the pentagon.
3. Project the section circles to draw cutting planes in FV. Project 1, 2, 3, etc., to 1′, 2′, 3′, etc., on the corresponding cutting planes. Join these points for the COI. Draw COIs for the other faces of the prism in a similar way. Draw the hidden lines properly.

Problem 17.12 A hemisphere with a 30 mm radius rests on its flat face on the HP. A vertical pentagonal prism with a base side of 20 mm penetrates the hemisphere. The axis of the prism is 10 mm due south-east of the centre of the hemisphere. A rectangular face of the prism is parallel and nearer to the VP. Draw FV and TV of the combined solid showing the COI. Assume a suitable height of the prism.

If the prism was removed to create a pentagonal hole in the hemisphere, how would the hole and COI be seen?

Solution Refer Fig. 17.35.

1. Draw TVs and FVs of the hemisphere and the prism
2. In TV, draw cutting planes *a–a*, *b–b*, *c–c*, *d–d* and *e–e*. The cutting planes should only be drawn in the region of intersection. A cutting plane must pass through each corner of the pentagon. Few cutting planes may be drawn (at suitable distances) in between the cutting planes passing through the corners. Mark 1, 2, ..., 11 at the intersections of the cutting planes and the pentagon. Note that 5 and 8 lie at the intersections of the axis of the hemisphere and the pentagon.

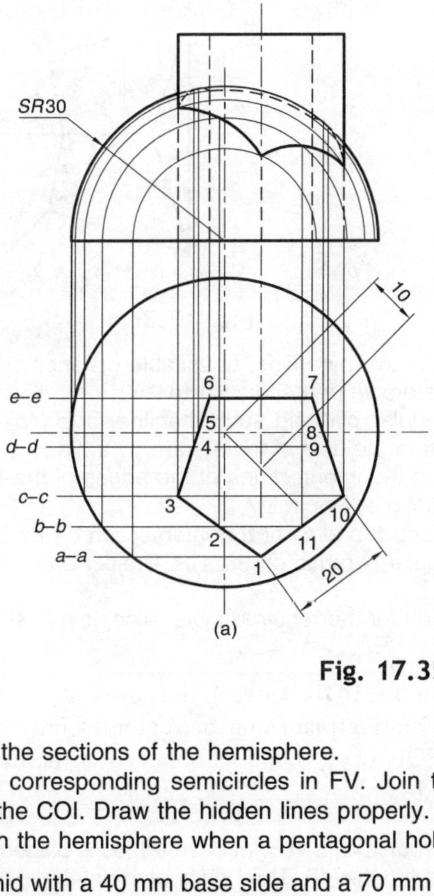

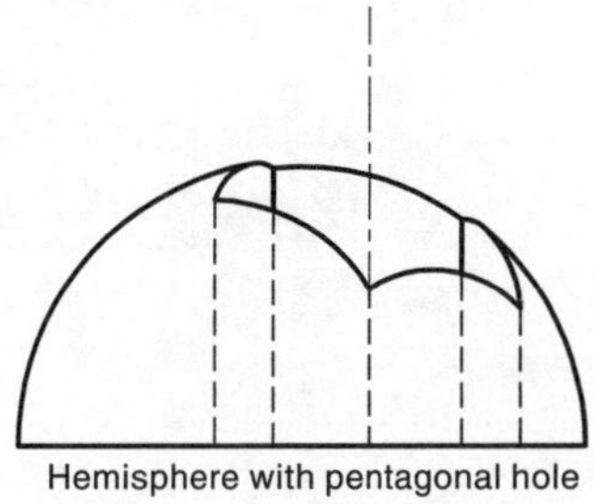

Fig. 17.35

3. In FV, draw semicircles for the sections of the hemisphere.
4. Project 1, 2, ..., 11 on the corresponding semicircles in FV. Join the points obtained in FV by a smooth curve to represent the COI. Draw the hidden lines properly.

Figure 17.40(b) shows the COI on the hemisphere when a pentagonal hole is created.

Problem 17.13 A square pyramid with a 40 mm base side and a 70 mm height, is resting on its base on the HP with all the sides equally inclined to the VP. A triangular pyramid with a 50 mm base side and an 80 mm axis length, penetrates the square pyramid. A lateral face of the triangular pyramid is on the HP. The axis of the triangular pyramid is parallel to the VP and intersects at its midpoint to the axis of the square pyramid. Draw two views of the solids showing LOI.

Solution Refer Fig. 17.36

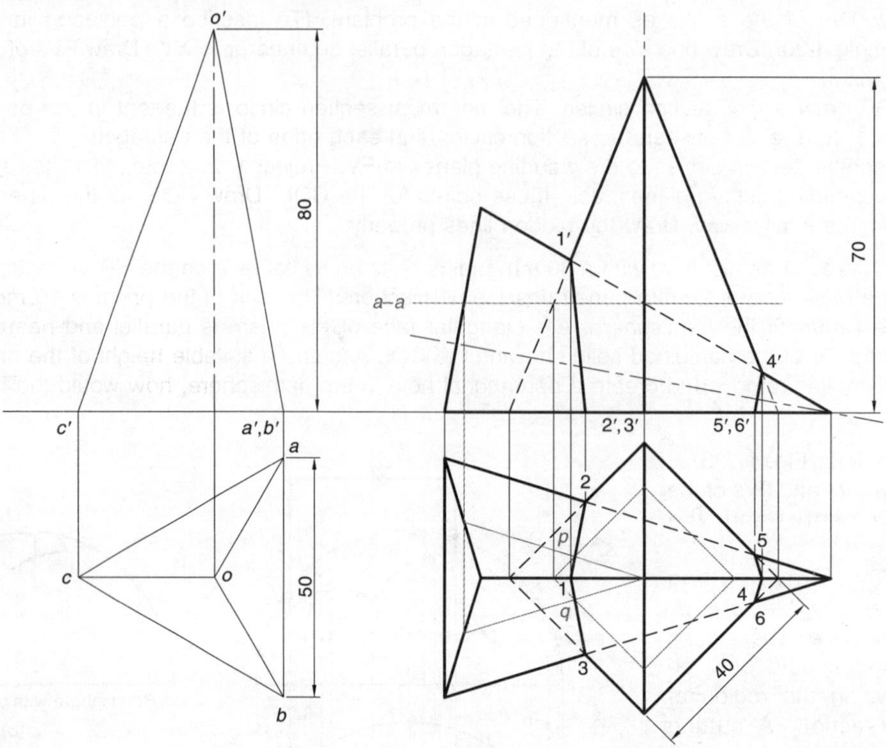

Fig. 17.36

1. Draw TVs and FVs of the two pyramids, at suitable distance apart, as shown. The base side *ab* of the triangular pyramid is drawn perpendicular to *XY*.
2. Redraw FV of the triangular pyramid such that the face *a′b′–o′* coincides with *XY* and the axis intersects at its midpoint to the axis of the square pyramid.
3. In FV, locate 1′ and 4′ at the intersections of the edges of the two pyramids. Project 1′ and 4′ to 1 and 4 on the corresponding edges in TV.
4. In TV, locate 2 and 3 (and 5 and 6) at the intersection of the base of the square pyramid and the lateral face of the triangular pyramid on the HP. Project 2 and 3, and 5 and 6 to 2′(3′) and 5′(6′) in FV.
5. Join 1′–2′(3′) and 4′–5′(6′) for the required LOIs. Also, join 2–1–3 and 5–4–6. Draw the hidden lines properly.

Note: In the above problem, the POIs between the edges of the pyramids are clearly seen. Hence, there is no need of drawing cutting planes in the region of intersection. If such cutting planes are drawn (e.g., *a–a*) then the POIs (e.g., *p* and *q*) obtained at the intersections of the sections in TV will lie along lines 1–2 and 1–3.

Problem 17.14 A square pyramid with 40 mm base edges is placed on its base on the HP, such that all base edges are equally inclined to the VP. The height of the pyramid is 75 mm. A circular hole of diameter 25 mm is drilled vertically, such that the axes of the pyramid and the hole coincide. Draw the elevation and plan of the solid showing COI. Draw the development of the lateral surfaces of the pyramid.

Solution Refer Fig. 17.37.

1. Draw TV and FV of the pyramid. In TV, draw the circle to represent the hole.
2. Divide the circle into 12 equal parts and number the divisions as 1, 2, …, 12. Through 1, 2, …, 12, draw lateral lines (joining apex with the base edges).

3. Project the lateral lines in FV and then project 1, 2, ..., 12 to 1′, 2′, ..., 12′ on the corresponding lateral lines.
4. Join 1′–2′, ..., 12′ for the required COI. Draw the hidden lines for the hole.
5. Draw the development of the pyramid as shown.

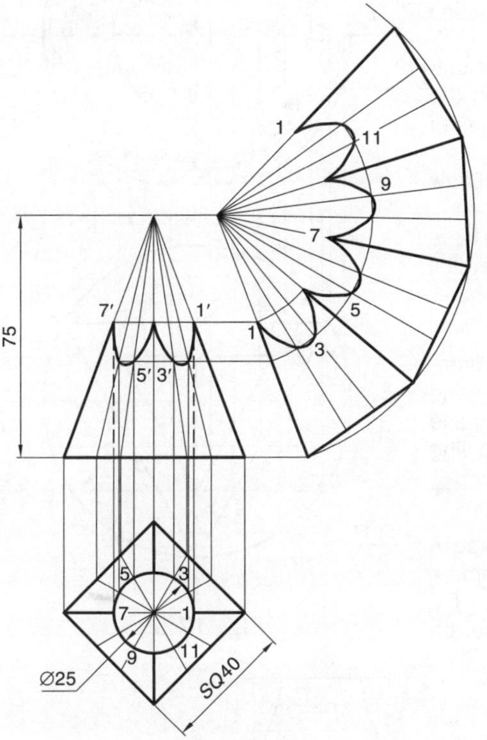

Fig. 17.37

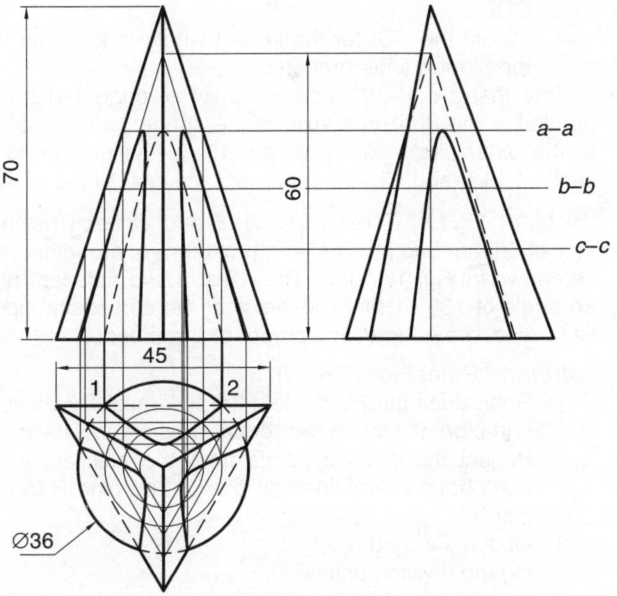

Fig. 17.38

Problem 17.15 A triangular pyramid (45 mm base side and 70 mm axis) stands on its base on the HP. A side of base is parallel to the VP. A cone (36 mm base diameter and length 60 mm of axis) penetrates the pyramid. The base of the cone is on the HP and the axes of both the solids coincide. Draw the three views of the solids to show COI.

Solution Refer Fig. 17.38.

1. Draw TVs, FVs and SVs of both the solids.
2. In SV, draw a few cutting planes, *a–a*, *b–b* and *c–c*. Extend the cutting planes in FV.
3. In TV, draw sections of the pyramid and cone corresponding to the cutting planes *a–a*, *b–b* and *c–c*. The section of the pyramid will be a triangle while that of the cone will be a circle. For each pair of triangle and circle, mark points at their intersections. Points 1 and 2 are located at the intersections of the bases of two solids. Join these points by a smooth curve for the required COI.
4. Project the points on COI from TV to FV and SV on the corresponding cutting planes. Join the points obtained to draw COIs.

Problem 17.16 Draw a circle with a 60 mm diameter. Inscribe an equilateral triangle in it. Draw another equilateral triangle with a 30 mm side having all sides parallel to and equidistant from the sides of the first triangle. The figure represents the TV of a sphere with a hole. The hole was created by piercing a triangular pyramid. Draw the FV of the sphere showing the COI for the hole.

Solution Refer Fig. 17.39.

1. Draw TV of the sphere with the triangles as shown. Also, draw FV of the sphere.
2. In TV, draw horizontal cutting planes. Through each corner of the triangles, a cutting plane must pass. Mark 2, 3, etc., at the intersections of the outer triangle with the cutting planes. 1, 7 and 12 are the corners of the triangle.
3. In FV, draw sections (i.e., circles) corresponding to the cutting planes in TV. Project 1, 2, etc., to 1′, 2′, etc., on the corresponding circles in FV. Join 1′, 2′, etc., for the required COI.
4. Obtain the COI for the inner triangle in a similar way. Draw the hidden lines properly.

Note that arc 1′–12′ represents FV of edge 1–12. As 1–12 is parallel to the horizontal axis of the sphere, arc 1′–12′ is parallel to the outer circle. Similarly, arc 13′–14′ is parallel to the outer circle. 1′–13′ and 12′–14′ represent straight edges of the hole.

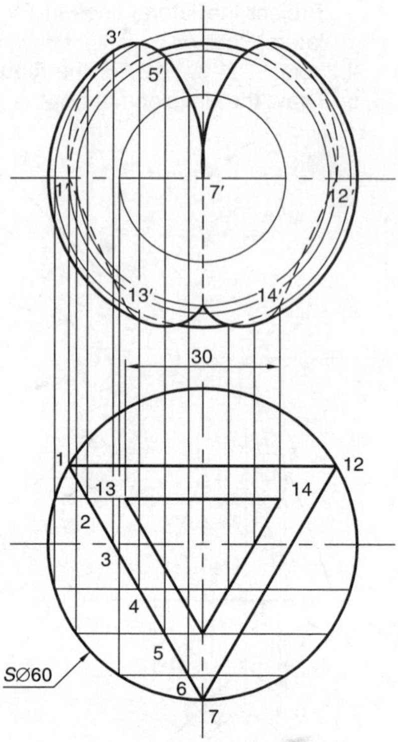

Fig. 17.39

Problem 17.17 Three pipes *A*, *B* and *C*, each having a diameter of 50 mm and an axis length of 80 mm, are joined end to end as shown in Fig. 17.40(a). The axes of two adjacent pipes make an angle of 135°. Draw two views of the composite pipe showing COI. Also, draw the development of the pipes.

Solution Refer Fig. 17.40(b).

1. Reproduce the FV. Obtain the half-auxiliary views of pipe *A* and pipe *B*. Obtain four equal divisions on each of them.
2. Project the division points from the auxiliary views to FV and obtain lateral lines on pipe *A* and pipe *B* (and, also, on pipe *C*).
3. Obtain TV by projecting the division points properly.
4. In FV, mark 1′, 2′, etc., at the intersections of the lateral lines and the mating ends of the pipe *A* and pipe *B*.
5. Project 1′, 2′, etc., to 1, 2, etc., on the corresponding lateral lines in TV. Join 1, 2, etc., for the COI. Obtain the COI for pipe *A* and pipe *C* in a similar way.
6. Draw SV by projecting FV and TV. Draw the hidden lines properly.
7. Develop pipe *A* and pipe *C* (or pipe *B*) as shown. The development of pipe *B* and pipe *C* is similar and need not be repeated.

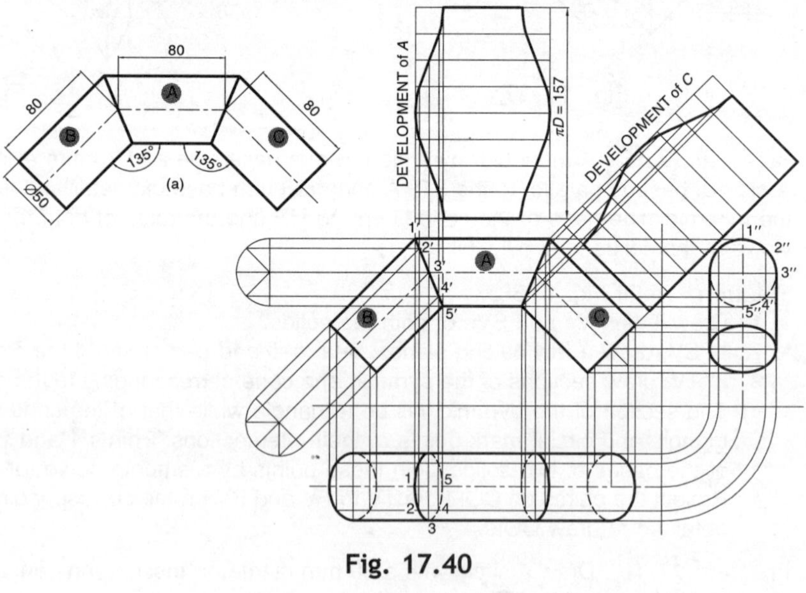

Fig. 17.40

Problem 17.18 A pipe with a 50 mm diameter is attached to a duct of semicircular cross section having a radius of 80 mm along the curved surface of the latter. The axis of the pipe makes 60° with the axis of the duct. The distance between the axes is 55 mm. Draw the projections of the solids showing COI at the joint. Also, develop the pipe and the duct. Assume suitable lengths of the pipe and the duct.

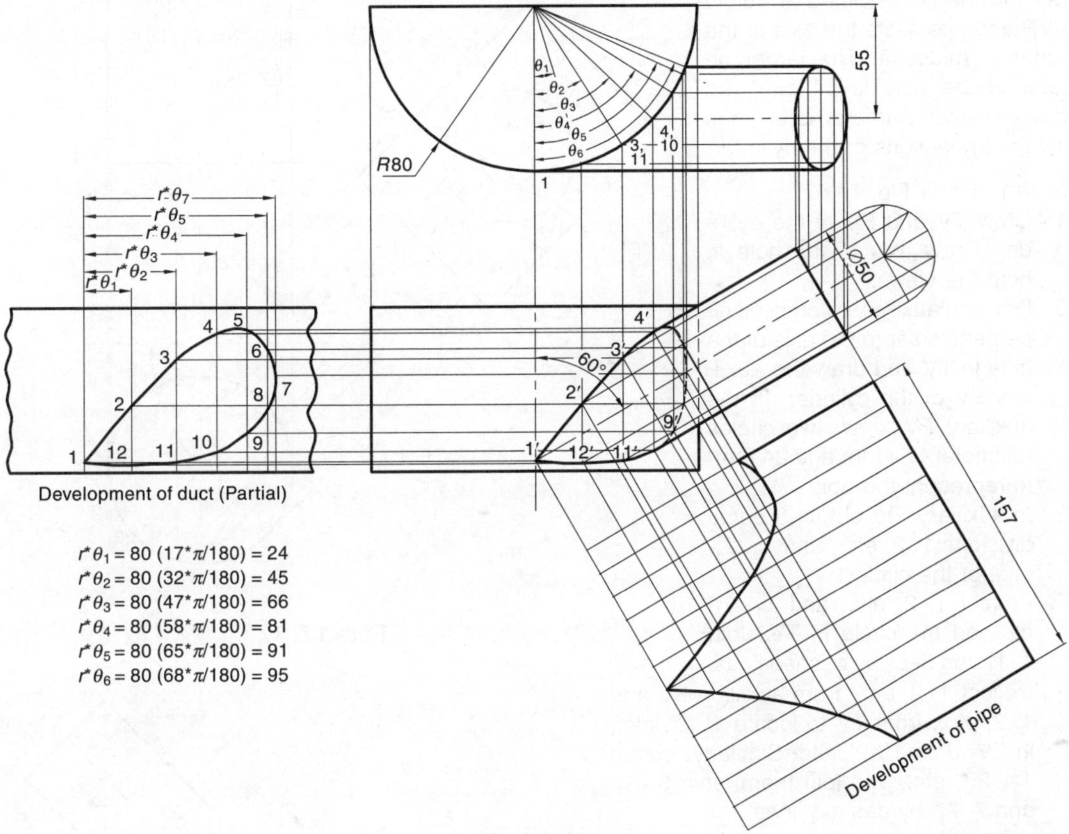

Fig. 17.41

Solution Refer Fig. 17.41. The problem is solved by the third angle method of projection.

1. Draw TV and FV of the duct. In TV, draw axis of the pipe as shown. Also, draw the FV of the pipe.
2. Draw the half-auxiliary view of the pipe, obtain six equal divisions on it and transfer the divisions to FV and TV to draw lateral lines on the pipe.
3. In TV, mark 1, 2, etc., at the intersections of the lateral lines and the semicircle.
4. Project 1, 2, etc., to 1′, 2′, etc., on the corresponding lateral lines in FV. Join 1′, 2′, etc., for the required COI. Draw the hidden lines properly.
5. Draw the development of the pipe as shown.
6. To draw the development of the duct, measure angles θ_1, θ_2, etc., i.e., the angle subtended by arc 1–2, arc 1–3, etc., at the centre of the semicircle. (In this case, $\theta_1 = 17°$, $\theta_2 = 32°$, $\theta_3 = 47°$, $\theta_4 = 58°$, $\theta_5 = 65°$ and $\theta_6 = 68°$). Then, find the lengths of arc 1–2, arc 1–3, etc. For example, arc 1–2 = $r^*\ \theta_1$ = 80*(17*/180) = 24 mm. (*r* is the radius of the semicircle).
7. In the development of the duct, draw parallel lines spaced at a distance of $r^*\ \theta_1$, $r^*\ \theta_2$, etc. Project 1′, 2′, etc., on the corresponding lines in the development. Join the points thus obtained.

Note: If *r* is reasonably small, then arc lengths may be taken equal to the corresponding chord lengths. For example, arc 1–2 ≈ chord 1–2.

Problem 17.19 A conical hole is created in a vertical cylinder with a base diameter of 76 mm and a height of 100 mm. The axis of the hole is parallel to the HP, inclined at 45° to the VP and intersects the axis of the cylinder at midpoint. The larger diameter of the hole is 54 mm and and the smaller diameter is 24 mm. Draw the projections of the cylinder.

Solution Refer Fig. 17.42.

1. Draw TV and FV of the cylinder. Draw axis of the hole in both the views.
2. Draw an auxiliary reference line perpendicular to the axis of the hole in TV and draw the auxiliary FV of the cylinder. In the auxiliary FV, draw two circles (diameters 54 mm and 24 mm) to represent the hole.
3. In auxiliary FV, obtain 8 equal divisions 1, 2, etc., and 1_1, 2_1, etc., of the circles.
4. Project 1, 2, etc., and 1_1, 2_1, etc., on the circle in TV. Join $1–1_1$ and $5–5_1$ by dashed lines.
5. Project 1, 2, etc., from auxiliary FV and 1, 2, etc., from TV to locate 1′, 2′, etc., in FV. Join 1′, 2′, etc. Similarly, obtain $1_1'$, $2_1'$, etc., and join them. Join $3'–3_1'$ and $7–7_1'$ by dashed lines.

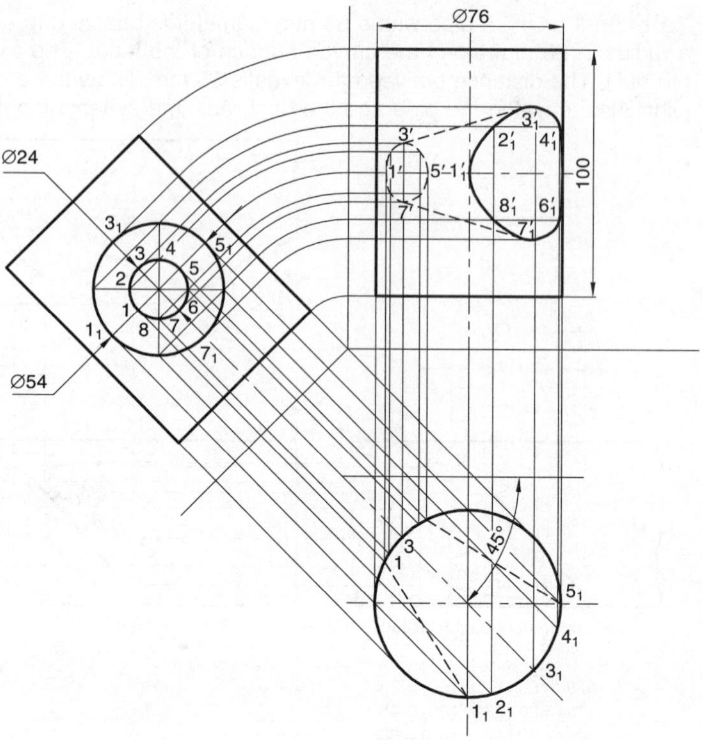

Fig. 17.42

Problem 17.20 A sphere of diameter 75 mm is intersected by a cylinder of diameter 50 mm. The axis of the cylinder is parallel to the VP, inclined at 45° to the HP and 25 mm from the centre of the sphere. The plane containing the axis of the cylinder and the centre of the sphere is vertical. Draw projections of the solids with COI. Assume a suitable length of the cylinder.

Solution Refer Fig. 17.43.

1. Draw FV and TV of the sphere. In FV, draw the axis of the cylinder inclined at 45° to *XY* and 25 mm from the centre of the circle. Also, draw FV of the cylinder. Mark *p*′ and *q*′ at the intersections of the edge of the rectangle and the circle.

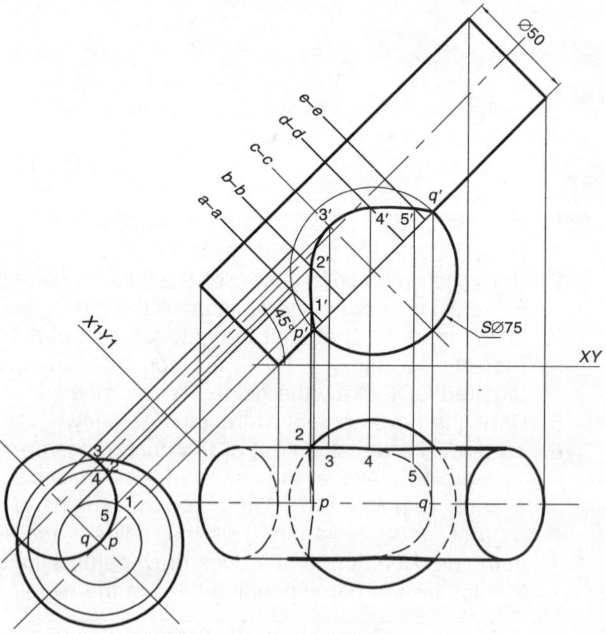

Fig. 17.43

2. Set $X1Y1$ perpendicular to the axis of the cylinder and draw the auxiliary views of the sphere and the cylinder.
3. In FV, draw cutting planes *a–a*, *b–b*, *c–c*, *d–d* and *e–e*, in the region of intersection, at suitable distances from each other. (*c–c* coincides with the centreline of the cylinder.) The cutting planes are perpendicular to the axis of the cylinder.
4. Project the cutting planes in the auxiliary view to draw sections of both the solids. Section circles of the cylinder will always be the same. Mark 1, 2, etc., at the intersections of the corresponding section circles.
5. Project 1, 2, etc., to 1′, 2′, etc., on the corresponding cutting planes in FV. Join 1′, 2′, etc., for the COI.
6. Obtain TV of the cylinder by the auxiliary plane projection method. In a similar way, obtain 1, 2, etc., in TV to draw COI. Draw the hidden lines.

Problem 17.21 Two cones of equal sizes (60 mm base diameter and 80 mm height) penetrate each other. The apex of one cone touches the base of the other. The axes are parallel and 15 mm apart. The plane containing the axes is parallel to the VP. Draw the three views of the cones showing COI.

Solution Refer Fig. 17.44.

1. Draw TVs, FVs and SVs of the cones. In FV, mark *p*′ and *q*′ at the intersections of the extreme generators of the cones.
2. In FV, draw cutting planes *a–a*, *b–b* and *c–c* in the region of intersection, at suitable distances from each other. (*b–b* passes through the point at which the axis of one cone intersects the generator of the other cone.)
3. Project the cutting planes in TV to draw section circles of both the cones.
4. In TV, mark POIs 1, 2, etc., between the corresponding section circles.
5. Project *p*′ and *q*′ to *p* and *q* on the corresponding generators in TV. Join *p*–1–3–5–*q*–6–4–2–*p* for the required COI.
6. Project 1, 2, etc., to 1′, 2′, etc, on the corresponding cutting planes in FV. Join the points for the COI.
7. Draw COI in SV by projecting the POIs from FV and TV. Draw the hidden lines properly.

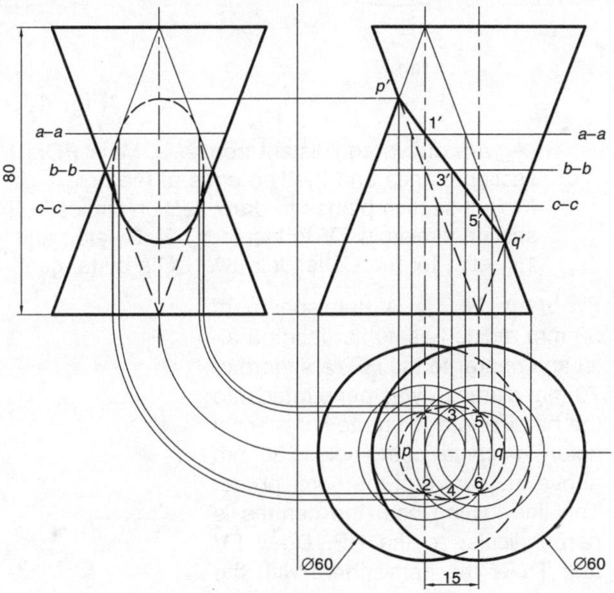

Fig. 17.44

DRAWING TIP

Draw *a–a* and *c–c* at equal distances from *b–b*. This gives the section circles of equal radii in TV.

Problem 17.22 Figure 17.45(a) shows RHSV of a sphere having a conical hole in it. Draw the FV of the sphere showing COI for the hole. Assume that the larger end of the hole is nearer to the PP.

Solution Refer Fig. 17.45(b).

1. Redraw given RHSV. Draw FV of the sphere.
2. In SV, draw section planes *a–a*, *b–b*, *c–c*, etc., in the region of intersection. *d–d* and *e–e* pass through the centrelines of the hole and the sphere respectively. *d–d* and *f–f* and *c–c* and

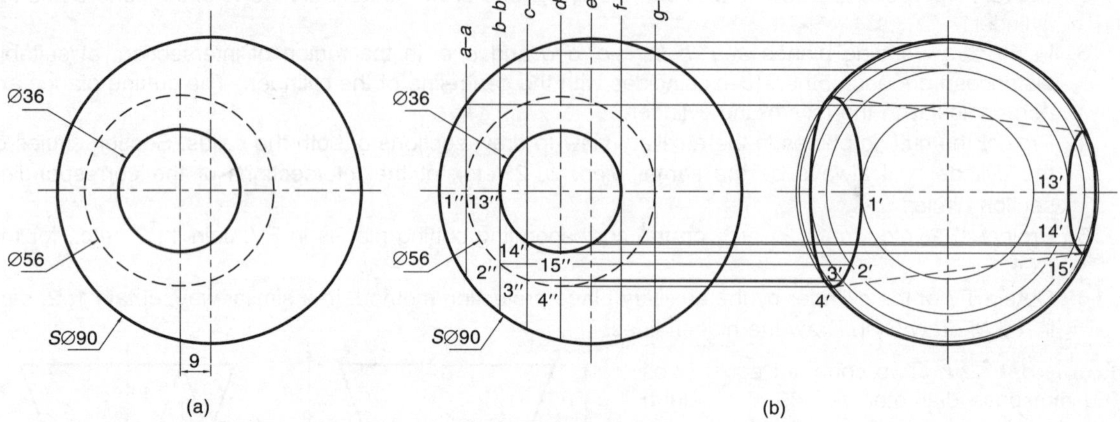

Fig. 17.45

g–g are drawn equidistant from *e–e*. Mark POIs 1″, 2″, 3″ etc., and 13″, 14″, 15″, etc., between the section planes and the two ends of the hole.

3. Project section planes to draw section circles in FV. Project the POIs from SV on the corresponding section circles in FV to locate 1′, 2′, 3′, etc., and 13′, 14′, 15′, etc. Join 1′, 2′, 3′, etc., and 13′, 14′, 15′, etc., for the COIs. Join two COIs by tangent dashed lines to represent the hole.

Problem 17.23 A hemisphere of 50 mm radius has its flat face parallel and nearer to the HP. A sphere of 70 mm diameter was penetrated into the hemisphere to create a spherical hole. The centre of the hole is 30 mm above the centre of the hemisphere. The line joining both the centres is perpendicular to the HP. Draw FV and TV of the hemisphere with the hole. Project FV on an AIP inclined at 50° to the HP to obtain the auxiliary TV of the hemisphere.

Solution Refer Fig. 17.46.

1. Draw FVs of the hemisphere and the sphere. Locate 1′, 2′, 3′ and 4′ at the intersections of the two solids. Join 1′–2′ to represent the flat face created at the intersection. Arcs 1′–3 and 2′–4′ represent the hidden surface of the hole.
2. Draw TV of the hemisphere. Project 1′, 2′, 3′ and 4′ to draw circles created due to intersection of the sphere with the hemisphere. The smallest

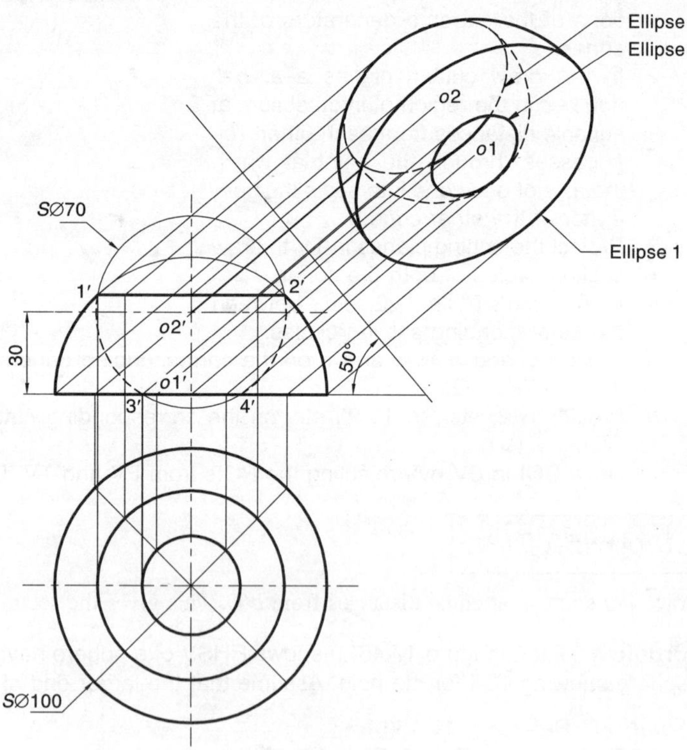

Fig. 17.46

circle represents the circle created at the flat face of the hemisphere. The middle circle represents the circle created at the curved face of the hemisphere.

3. In TV, obtain 8 equal divisions on the circles. Project the division points in FV.
4. Draw the auxiliary reference line inclined at 50° to *XY*. Project the division points from FV on this auxiliary reference line to obtain the auxiliary TV. Also, project the centres of the hemisphere and the sphere. The auxiliary TV shows three ellipses, one for each circle in the TV. Ellipses 1 and 3 are joined by tangent arcs (with *o*1 as centre). Ellipses 2 and 3 are joined by tangent arcs (with *o*2 as centre). Note how hidden lines are drawn.

REVIEW QUESTIONS

1. A square prism with a base side of 60 mm and a height of 100 mm rests on the base on the HP with a face inclined at 30° to the VP. Another horizontal square prism with a base side of 60 mm and a length of 130 mm, a face of which is inclined at 30° to the HP, penetrates the vertical prism completely. The axes of the two prisms are offset at 15 mm with their midpoints coinciding in FV. Draw the three views of the prisms showing LOI.
2. A vertical square prism, with a 60 mm base side is resting on its base on the ground, with its faces equally inclined to the VP. It is completely penetrated by a horizontal equilateral triangular prism with a 70 mm base side having a rectangular face parallel to the VP and 12 mm away from the axis of the square prism. Draw the projections showing LOI. Assume suitable lengths of prisms.
3. A hexagonal prism with a base side of 30 mm and a height of 110 mm stands on its base on the HP with two opposite rectangular faces perpendicular to the VP. A triangular prism with a base side of 50 mm and a length of 110 mm penetrates the vertical prism such that the axes of the two prisms bisect each other. A lateral face of the triangular prism is perpendicular to the VP and its axis makes 30° with the HP. Draw FVs, TVs and SVs of the prisms showing LOI.
4. A hexagonal prism with a 25 mm edge of base and a 110 mm height, is standing on its base on the ground with an edge of its base parallel to the VP. It is penetrated by a square prism of 30 mm base and 110 mm length. The axis of the penetrating prism is parallel to both the RPs and the two axes bisect each other. Draw the projections of the solids showing LOI. Take one of the faces of the square prism inclined at 30° to the VP.
5. Two equal triangular prisms with a base side of 45 mm and an axis length of 100 mm, intersect centrally at right angles. A rectangular face of each prism is on the VP. One of the prisms is vertical. Draw FV and SV of the prisms. Draw an auxiliary TV on an AIP inclined at 60° to the HP.
6. Figure 15RQ.1 shows the elevation of a vertical equilateral triangular prism of 70 mm base side and 80 mm height. A through trapezoidal hole is made in it as shown. Draw the plan and SV showing LOI. Obtain the development of the prism.
7. A regular hexagonal pyramid with a base side of 40 mm and a slant edge of 80 mm is resting on its base on the HP such that the opposite edges of its base are perpendicular to the VP. It is penetrated by a vertical square prism centrally. The sides of the prism are 35 mm and two of its opposite faces are parallel to the VP. Assume a suitable length for the prism. Draw the three views of this combination showing the LOI.
8. A vertical square pyramid with a 60 mm base side and 110 mm axis length, resting on the ground with all its edges of base equally inclined to the VP, has a horizontal square hole of 42 mm side cut through it. A face of the hole is inclined at 30° with the ground. The axis of the hole is parallel to the VP, 35 mm above the ground and 6 mm away from that of pyramid. Draw the projections of the pyramid with the hole.

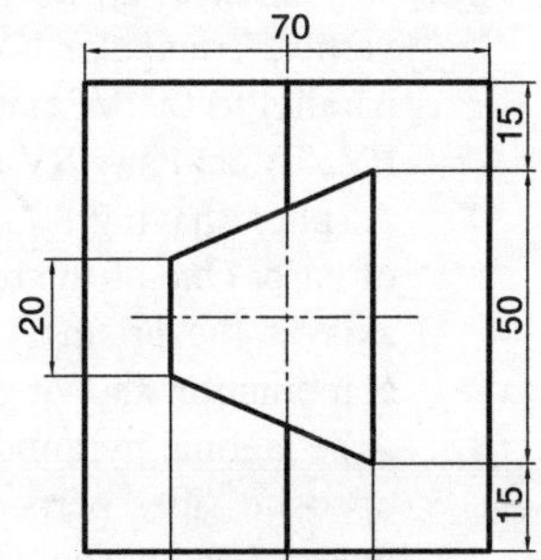

Fig. 15RQ.1

9. A square pyramid (base side of 50 mm and axis of 60 mm) is kept on the HP on its base with two of its sides of base parallel to the VP. An axial square hole of side 25 mm is cut through the pyramid, so that

the vertical faces of the hole are equally inclined to the VP. Draw projections of the solid and show the development of the lateral surface of the solid.

10. A hexagonal pyramid with a base edge of 40 mm and axis height of 90 mm is resting on its base with axis parallel to the VP and one edge of the base perpendicular to the VP. A square hole of 40 mm side is cut through the pyramid with the axis coinciding with the axis of the pyramid, such that two vertical faces of the hole are at 20° to the VP. Draw the projections of the pyramid showing LOI. Also, draw the development of the pyramid.
11. A cylinder with a 50 mm diameter base and a 70 mm height is resting on its base on the HP. It is intersected by a triangular prism of 35 mm sides whose axis is parallel to both the RPs and is offset by 5 mm from the cylinder's axis. Draw the three views and show COI.
12. A pentagonal prism (side of base = 60 mm and height = 100 mm) is kept on its base on the HP with a vertical face perpendicular to the VP. A circular hole (diameter = 90 mm) is drilled through the prism. The axis of the hole is perpendicular to the VP, 8 mm away from the axis of the prism and on the side opposite to the face perpendicular to the VP. Draw the projections of the prism showing COI for the hole. Develop the lateral faces of the prism.
13. Figure 15RQ.2 shows the plans of a horizontal cylinder and a vertical triangular prism. The axis of the cylinder is parallel to both the RPs. Draw the projections of the solids showing COI.

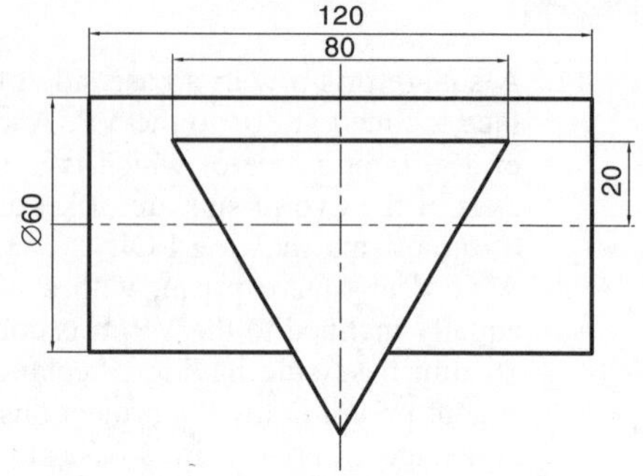

Fig. 15RQ.2

14. A vertical semicone with diameter 75 mm and a 75 mm long axis has its semicircular base on the HP with the straight edge of the base being parallel to the VP. It has a horizontal square hole of 30 mm side. The axis of the square hole is perpendicular to the VP and intersects the axis of the semicone at a point 25 mm above the base of the semicone. All the sides of the square hole are equally inclined to the HP. Draw the projections of the semicone with COI and develop its lateral surface.
15. A square prism with a 40 mm edge of base intersects a cone resting on its base on the ground. The diameter of the cone is 75 mm and its height is 90 mm. The axis of the prism cuts the axis of the cone normally and a rectangular face of the prism is parallel to a generator of the cone and 5 mm away from it. Draw the three views of the solids showing COI.
16. A cone with an 80 mm diameter of base and a 100 mm height is standing on its base on the HP. A vertical triangular hole of 35 mm sides is punched through the cone such that one face of the hole is parallel to the VP and away from the observer. The axis of the cone and that of the hole coincide. Draw FV, TV and any SV showing COI.
17. A sphere having 80 mm diameter is completely penetrated by a vertical triangular prism of 60 mm edge of base. One of the rectangular faces of the prism is parallel to the VP and away from the observer. The axis of the prism is 7 mm in front of the centre of the sphere. Draw the elevation and plan of the combination showing COI.
18. A hexagonal pyramid of 40 mm side of base and a 75 mm height stands on its base on the HP with two opposite sides perpendicular to the VP. An inverted square pyramid of base side and height equal to those of the hexagonal pyramid, penetrates the latter such that the axes are coincident. The sides of the base of the square pyramid are equally inclined to the VP. The base-to-base distance is 100 mm. Draw the three views of the solids showing the LOI.
19. A pentagonal pyramid of 40 mm base side and 90 mm height rests on an edge of base on the HP with its axis inclined at 45° to the HP and parallel to the VP. A triangular pyramid of the same dimensions rests on the HP in a similar way, but leans in the opposite direction. The distance between the base edges of the solids on the HP is 30 mm. The axes intersect. Draw the projections of the intersecting solids with LOI.

20. Figure 15RQ.3(a) shows FVs of a triangular pyramid (90 mm base side and 100 mm axis) and a cylinder (32 mm diameter and 150 mm length). The base of the pyramid is parallel to the HP with a side perpendicular to the VP. The axis of the cylinder intersects the axis of the pyramid as shown. Draw FVs and TVs of the solids to show COI.
21. A pentagonal pyramid having a base side of 40 mm and an axis length of 60 mm has a horizontal base. It is penetrated by a vertical cylinder with a 40 mm base diameter, so that their axes coincide with each other. Draw the projections of the solids showing COI. Assume the appropriate height of the cylinder.

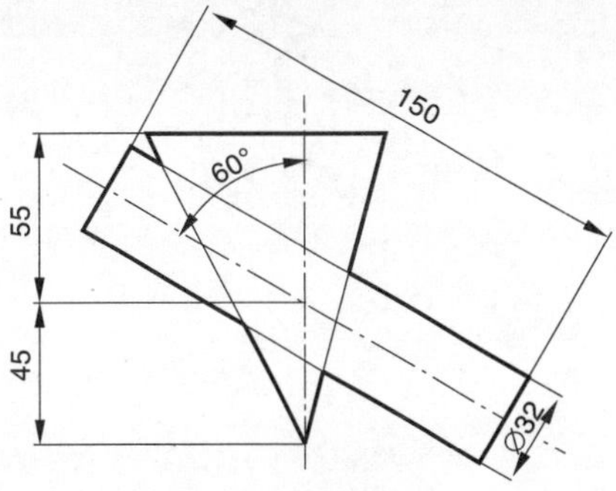

Fig. 15RQ.3

22. A cone with a base diameter of 60 mm and a slant height of 100 mm rests on its base on the HP. A square pyramid of 40 mm base side and an 80 mm long axis penetrates the cone. The axis of the pyramid is parallel to both the RPs and its base edges are equally inclined to the VP. Both the axes intersect at their midpoints. Draw the three views of the solids showing COI.
23. A hemisphere of diameter 75 mm has its circular face in the VP. A pentagonal pyramid, having its axis perpendicular to the VP and base nearer to the observer, penetrates the hemisphere. The midpoint of the axis of the pyramid coincides with the centre of the hemisphere. The base edge and axis of the pyramid are 40 mm and 100 mm respectively. Assume a base side of the pyramid parallel to the HP. Draw FV and TV of the solids showing COI.
24. A cylinder with a 60 mm diameter and a 100 mm length has axis perpendicular to the VP. Another cylinder with a 44 mm diameter and a 120 mm length penetrates the first cylinder. The axis of the penetrating cylinder is parallel to the HP, inclined at 150 to the VP and 8 mm away from the axis of the first cylinder. Draw the two views of the cylinders showing COI.
25. Two cylinders, each of 60 mm base diameter and 120 mm length of axis, intersect each other in such a way that an extreme generator of each passes through the midpoint of the other's axis. One of the cylinders is vertical while the other is horizontal. Draw the two views showing COI.
26. A vertical cone having an 80 mm base diameter and a 100 mm long axis is penetrated by a horizontal cylinder with a 45 mm diameter, the axis of which is 30 mm above the base of the cone, parallel to the VP and 5 mm away from the axis of the cone. Draw the three views showing the COI.
27. Fig. 15RQ.4 shows the plan of a hemisphere of 60 mm radius kept on its flat face on the HP. It is cut vertically by a plane and a semi-cylindrical surface as shown. Draw (i) plan (ii) elevation showing COI
28. A vertical cone with a 100 mm base diameter and 125 mm height is penetrated by another cone of 50 mm diameter and a 100 mm long axis. The axis of the penetrating cone is parallel to both the RPs, 6 mm away from the axis of the vertical cone and 40 mm above the base of the vertical cone. It comes out equally on both the sides of the vertical cone. Draw the projections showing COI.
29. A hemisphere of 90 mm diameter has its flat face parallel and nearer to the HP. A cone of 60 mm base diameter and 90 mm axis length penetrates the hemisphere. The base of the cone makes 60° to the HP (apex being above the flat face of the sphere) and centre of the base coincides with a point on the circumference of the flat face of the hemisphere. Draw two views of the solids showing COI.

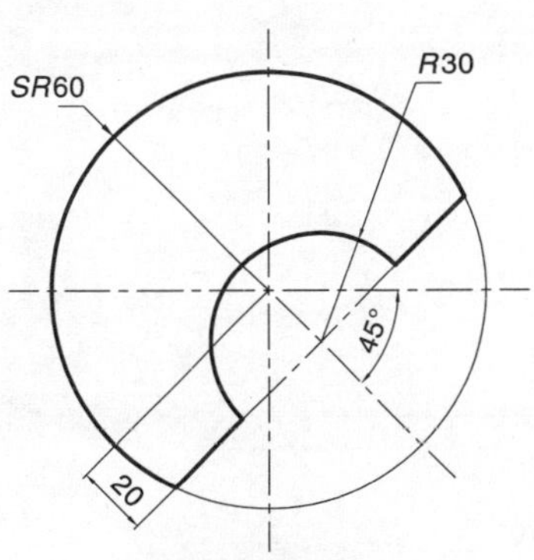

Fig. 15RQ.4

30. Two spheres, having diameters 80 mm and 50 mm, intersect each other. Their centres are 55 mm apart. The line joining the centres is inclined at 50° to the HP and 25° to the VP. The bigger sphere touches the HP. Draw the projections of the sphere showing COI.

Chapter 18

ISOMETRIC PROJECTION

18.1 INTRODUCTION

Isometric projection is a type of an axonometric projection (or pictorial projection). Isometric means 'equal measure'. As the name suggests, in isometric projection, all the mutually perpendicular plane surfaces of an object and the edges formed by these surfaces are equally inclined to a POP.

In multiview orthographic projections, two or three views are drawn on different RPs to understand the object fully. A minimum of two views are necessary to give information about the three dimensions of an object. When orthographic views are given, a good imagination is needed to visualize the object in 3D space. However, in isometric projection, only one view on a plane is drawn to represent the three dimensions of an object. This provides a pictorial view with a real appearance.

In isometric projection, unlike multiview projections, we use only one POP. Hence, it is also called *one-plane projection*.

18.2 PRINCIPLE OF ISOMETRIC PROJECTION

Consider a cube *ABCDEFGH* resting on one of its corners, say *A*, at origin '*O*' and the body diagonal through that corner, i.e., *AG*, equally inclined to the three axes—*X*, *Y* and *Z*, as shown in Fig. 18.1. The three edges of the cube through the corner *A* will lie along the three axes. The three faces of the cube formed by these edges will be coincident with the three RPs— the HP, the VP and the PP. Now, consider another plane *UVW* inclined equally to the three RPs and perpendicular to the body diagonal, *AG*. This plane makes approximately 54°44′ to each RP. The projection of cube *ABCDEFGH* obtained on the plane *UVW* is called an isometric projection. As *AG* is perpendicular to the plane *UVW*, it is seen as a point view in isometric projection. The three mutually perpendicular edges *AB*, *AD* and *AE* make equal angles, i.e., 120° to each other in isometric projection. The edges *CB* and *CD* make angles of 30° each with a horizontal line passing through *C*. The edges *AE*, *BF*, *CG* and *DH* are seen vertical. The edges *CB* and *CD* make angles of 60° each with *CA*.

It should be noted that, as all the edges of a cube are equally inclined to the POP, they get equally foreshortened in isometric projection. Thus, the isometric projection is smaller than the real object.

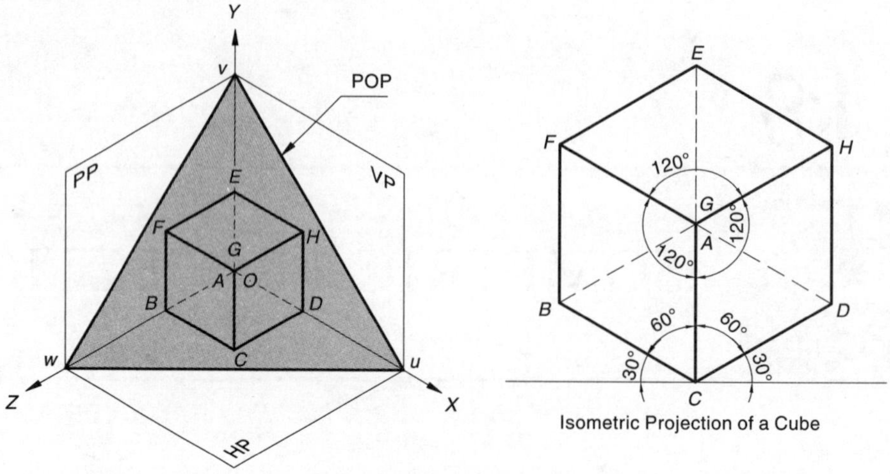

Isometric Projection of a Cube

Fig. 18.1

The isometric projection of a cube can also be obtained from orthographic views of the cube, as explained in Fig. 18.2. Stage I shows the TV and FV of a cube. It is resting on its base on the HP with two of its vertical faces coinciding with the VP and the PP. The FV and TV of body diagonal *AG*—*a′g′* and *ag* respectively will not show the TL. In Stage II, TV is redrawn such that *ag* will become

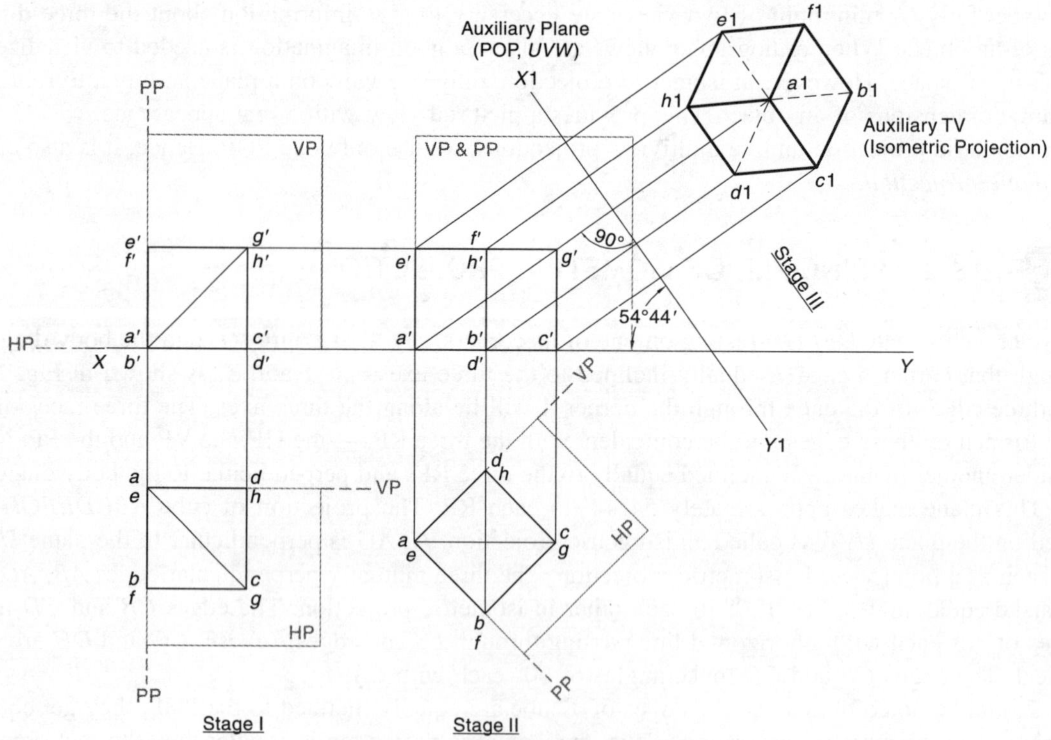

Fig. 18.2

parallel to XY. The corresponding FV $a'g'$ will show the TL of diagonal AG. In Stage III, an auxiliary plane $X1Y1$ is drawn perpendicular to $a'g'$. It represents the POP, i.e., UVW. Note that this plane makes an angle of 54°44′ to XY, i.e., the HP. The auxiliary TV $a1$–$b1$–$c1$–$d1$–$e1$–$f1$–$g1$–$h1$ obtained on auxiliary plane $X1Y1$ will represent the isometric projection of the cube. Note that $a1$–$g1$ represents the point view of the diagonal AG in isometric projection.

18.3 TERMINOLOGY

The following are the important terms used in isometric projection:

Isometric axes The three lines *GH, GF* and *GC* meeting at point *G* and making 120° angles with each other are termed *isometric axes*, Fig. 18.3(a). Isometric axes are often shown as in Fig. 18.3(b). The lines *CB, CG* and *CD* originate from point *C* and lie along *X*-, *Y*- and *Z*-axis respectively. The lines *CB* and *CD* make equal inclinations of 30° with the *horizontal reference line*. The line *CG* is vertical.

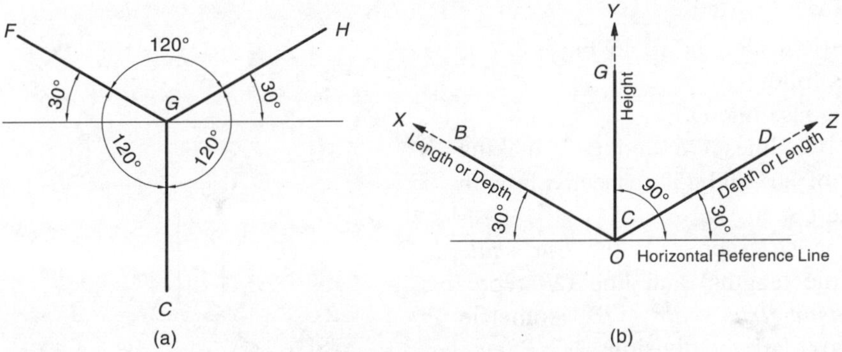

Fig. 18.3 Isometric Axes and Isometric Lines

In isometric, we show length (or width) of the object along the *X*-axis, height on the *Y*-axis and width (or length) on the *Z*-axis. It may be noted that the choice of axes is arbitrary and it depends on the direction of viewing the object.

Isometric lines The lines parallel to the isometric axes are called *isometric lines* or *isolines*. A line parallel to the *X*-axis may be called an *x-isoline*. So are the cases of *y-isoline* and *z-isoline*.

Non-Isometric lines The lines which are not parallel to isometric axes are called *non-isometric lines* or *non-isolines*. The face-diagonals and body diagonals of the cube shown in Fig. 18.1 and Fig. 18.2 are the examples of non-isolines.

Isometric planes The planes representing the faces of the cube as well as other faces parallel to these faces are called *isometric planes* or *isoplanes*. Note that isometric planes are always parallel to any of the planes formed by two isometric axes.

Non-Isometric planes The planes which are not parallel to isometric planes are called *non-isometric planes* or *non-isoplanes* (or *non-isometric faces*).

Origin or Pole Point The point on which a given object is supposed to be resting on the HP or ground such that the three isometric axes originating from that point make equal angles to POP is called an *origin* or *pole point*. It is marked as '*O*' as in Fig. 18.3(b). The origin is real if it lies at a corner of the object. The origin is imaginary if it lies outside the object, e.g., objects with polygonal, circular or spherical bases.

In isometric projection, all the faces of a cube are seen as rhombuses of the same size. The face *CGHD* in Fig. 18.1 falls on the right-hand side of the origin *O* and therefore it represents the right-hand vertical face of the cube. Similarly, the face *CBFG* represents left-hand vertical face of the cube. The face *GHEF* represents the top horizontal face of the cube.

18.4 ISOMETRIC SCALE

As explained earlier, the isometric projection appears smaller that the real object. This is because all the isometric lines get equally foreshortened. The proportion by which isometric lines get foreshortened in an isometric projection is called *isometric scale*. It is the ratio of the isometric length to the actual length.

The isometric scale, shown in Fig. 18.4, is constructed as follows:

1. Draw a base line *OA*.
2. Draw two lines *OB* and *OC*, making angles of 30° and 45° respectively with the line *OA*.
3. The line *OC* represents the *true scale* (i.e., true lengths) and line *OB* represents *isometric scale* (i.e., isometric lengths). Mark the divisions 1, 2, 3, etc., to show true distances, i.e., 1cm, 2cm, 3cm, etc., on line *OC*. Subdivisions may be marked to show distances in mm.
4. Through the divisions on the true scale, draw lines perpendicular to *OA* cutting the line *OB* at points 1, 2, 3, etc. The divisions thus obtained on *OB* represent the corresponding isometric distances.

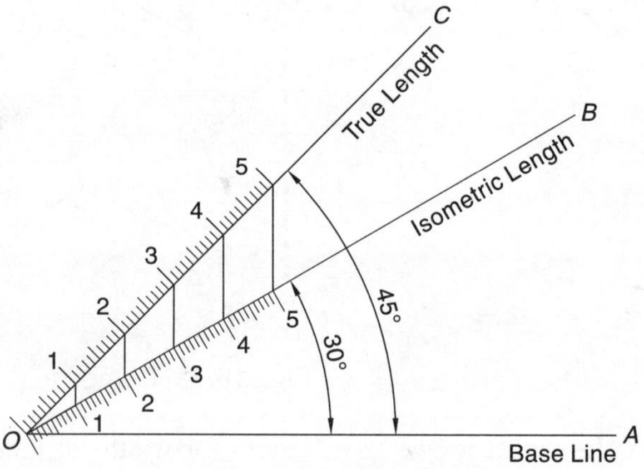

Fig. 18.4 Isometric Scale

To draw isometric projections from orthographic views, the true lengths in the orthographic view must be converted into isometric lengths using an isometric scale. Note that only lengths of isometric lines need to be converted. The lengths of non-isometric lines are obtained by using different methods as explained later in this chapter.

From the geometry of Fig. 18.4,

$$\text{Isometric scale} = (\text{Isometric length/True length}) = \frac{\cos 45°}{\cos 30°} = \frac{1}{\sqrt{2}} \div \frac{\sqrt{3}}{2} = \frac{\sqrt{2}}{\sqrt{3}} = 0.8165$$

$$= 82\% \text{ (approximately)}$$

i.e., Isometric length = 0.82* True length

18.5 ISOMETRIC PROJECTIONS AND ISOMETRIC VIEWS

At this point, a distinction must be made between isometric projection and isometric view. Isometric projection is often constructed using isometric scale which gives dimensions smaller than the true dimensions. However, to obtain isometric lengths from the isometric scale is always a cumbersome task. Therefore, the standard practice is to keep all dimensions as it is. The view thus obtained is called *isometric view* or *isometric drawing*. Obviously, one need not use an isometric scale to draw isometric view. As the isometric view utilises actual dimensions, the isometric view of the object is seen larger than its isometric projection.

Figure 18.5 shows the isometric projection and isometric view of a cube.

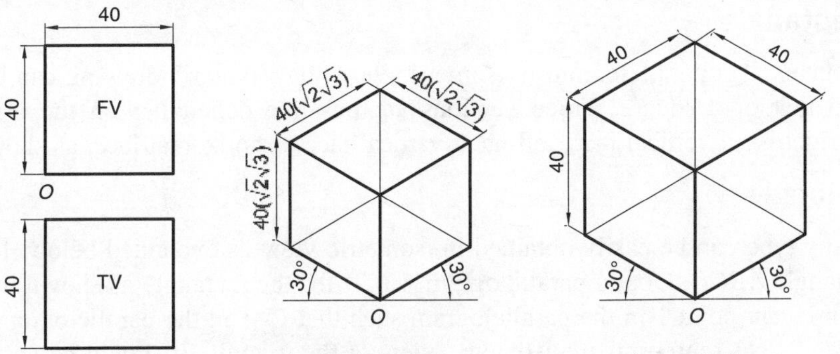

Orthographic Views | Isometric Projection (Lengths taken from Isometric Scale) | Isometric View

Fig. 18.5

18.6 ISOMETRIC VIEWS OF STANDARD SHAPES

18.6.1 Square

Consider a square *ABCD* with a 30 mm side as shown in Fig. 18.6. If the square lies in the vertical plane, it will appear as a rhombus with a 30 mm side in isometric view as shown in either Fig. 18.6(a) or (b), depending on its orientation, i.e., right-hand vertical face or left-hand vertical face. If the square lies in the horizontal plane (like the top face of a cube), it will appear as in Fig.18.6(c). The sides *AB* and *AD*, both, are inclined to the horizontal reference line at 30°.

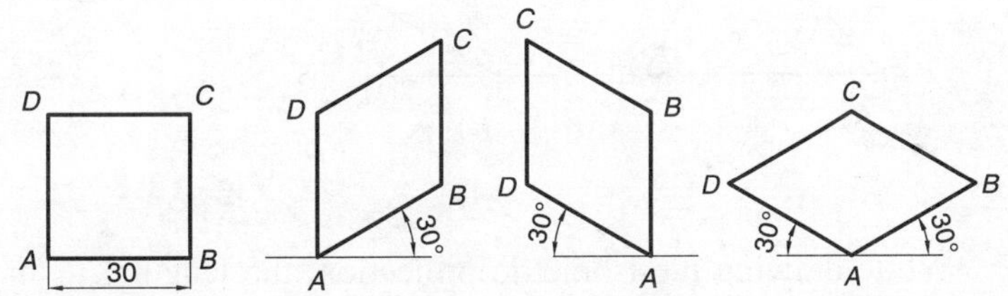

Square (a) (b) (c)

Fig. 18.6

As Fig. 18.7 shows isometric views, all the sides of the rhombuses are equal to the side of the square. In isometric projection, all the sides of the rhombuses will get reduced to isometric lengths. Therefore the rhombuses will appear to be of smaller size.

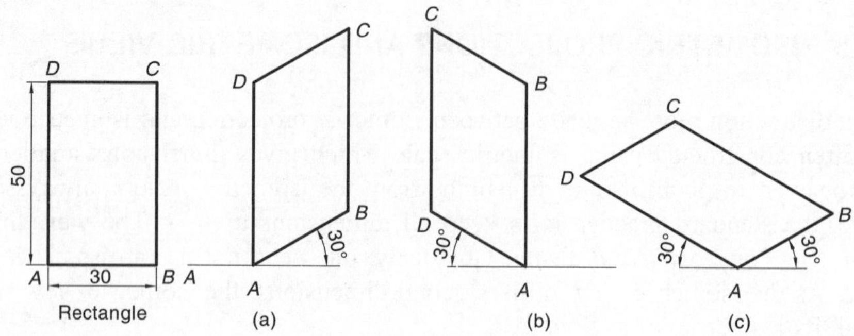

Fig. 18.7

18.6.2 Rectangle

A rectangle appears as a parallelogram in isometric view. Its isometric drawing can be obtained in a way similar to that of a square. Three versions are possible depending on the orientation of the rectangle, i.e., right-hand vertical face, left-hand vertical face or horizontal face, as shown in Fig. 18.7.

18.6.3 Triangle

A triangle of any type can be easily obtained in isometric view as explained below. First enclose the triangle in rectangle *ABCD*. Obtain parallelogram *ABCD* for the rectangle as shown in Fig. 18.8(a) or (b) or (c). Then locate point 1 in the parallelogram such that *C*–1 in the parallelogram is equal to *C*–1 in the rectangle. *A*–*B*–1 represents the isometric view of the triangle. It should be noted that the lines *A*–1 and *B*–1 are non-isolines. To draw such non-isolines in isometric view, their end points are located first. The end points are then joined to form the required lines.

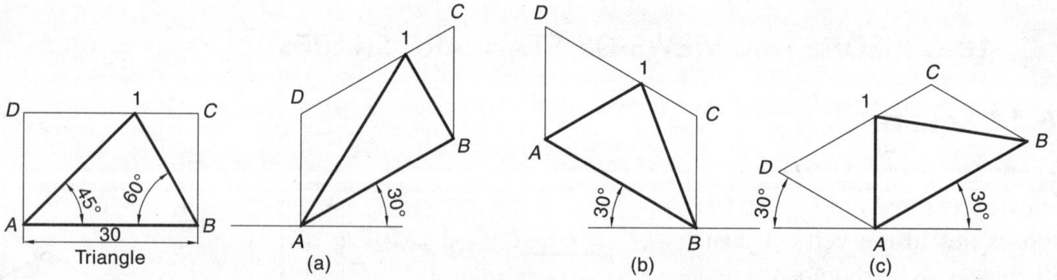

Fig. 18.8

While drawing the isometric projection, the length *C*–1 in isometric projection must be obtained from the isometric scale.

18.6.4 Pentagon

The isometric drawing of a pentagon can be obtained in the same manner as that of a triangle. Enclose the given pentagon in a rectangle and obtain the parallelogram as in Fig. 18.9(a) or (b) or (c). Locate points 1, 2, 3, 4 and 5 on the rectangle and mark them on the parallelogram. The distances *A*–1, *B*–2, *C*–3, *C*–4 and *D*–5 in isometric drawing are same as the corresponding distances on the pentagon enclosed in the rectangle.

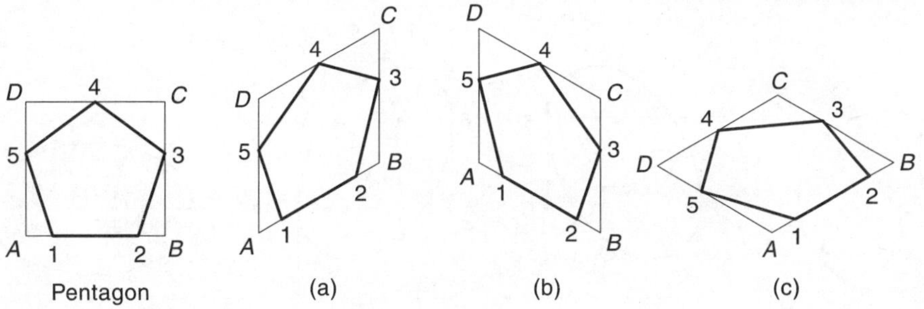

Fig. 18.9

The lines 2–3, 3–4, 4–5 and 5–1 are non-isolines. These lines are drawn by locating their end points.

18.6.5 Hexagon

The procedure for isometric drawing of a hexagon is the same as that for a pentagon. In Fig. 18.10, the lines 2–3, 3–4, 5–6 and 6–1 are non-isolines. Therefore, the points 1, 2, 3, 4, 5, 7 and 6 should be located properly as shown.

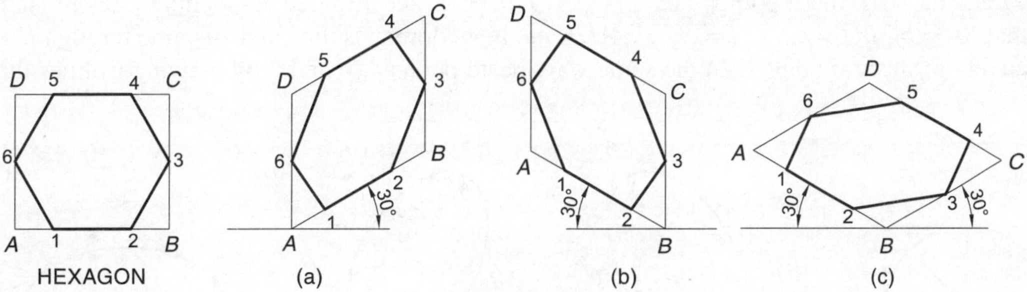

Fig. 18.10

18.6.6 Circle

The isometric view or isometric projection of a circle is an ellipse. It is obtained by using either of the two methods explained below.

Four-Centre Method It is explained in Fig. 18.11. First, enclose the given circle into a square *ABCD*. Draw rhombus *ABCD* as an isometric view of the square as shown. Join the farthest corners of the rhombus, i.e., *A* and *C* in Fig. 18.11(a) and (c). Obtain midpoints 3 and 4 of sides *CD* and *AD* respectively. Locate points 1 and 2 at the intersection of *AC* with *B*–3 and *B*–4 respectively. Now with 1 as a centre and radius 1–3, draw a small arc 3–5. Draw another arc 4–6 with same radius but 2 as a centre. With *B* as a centre and radius *B*–3, draw an arc 3–4. Draw another arc 5–6 with same radius but with *D* as a centre. Similar construction may be observed in relation to Fig. 18.11(b).

The above method is simple and easy for drawing the isometric view or isometric projection of the circle. However, it does not give the true ellipse. The ellipse obtained by this method consisted of four circular arcs.

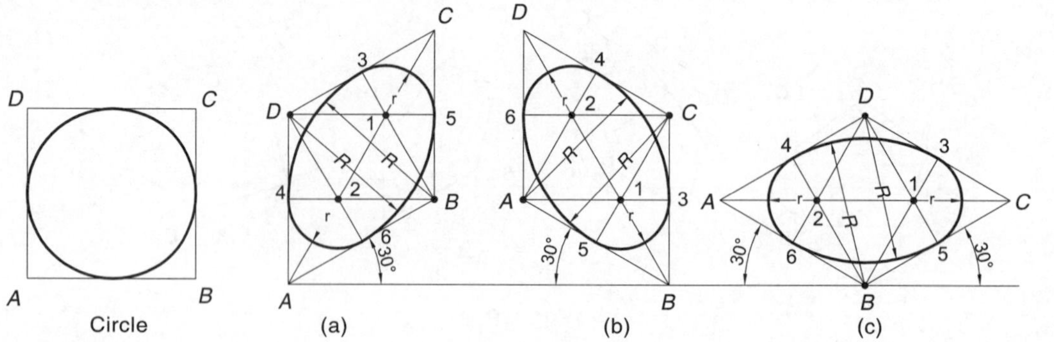

Fig. 18.11

Method of Points It is explained in Fig. 18.12. This method is an accurate method of obtaining an ellipse for the circle in isometric view. As shown in the figure, first enclose the circle in a square *abcd* and then obtain rhombus *ABCD* in isometric. Now divide the circle into eight equal parts and mark the divisions as 1, 2, 3, …, 8. The points 1, 3, 5 and 7 are the midpoints of sides *ab*, *bc*, *cd* and *da* respectively. From point 2 draw vertical and horizontal lines to meet *ab* and *bc* at *f* and *g* respectively. Similarly through points 4, 6 and 8 draw vertical and horizontal lines and mark points *h*, *i*, *j*, *k*, *l* and *e*. Mark these points, i.e., *F*, *G*, *H*, *I*, *J*, *K*, *L* and *E* on corresponding lines in isometric such that *BF* = *bf*, *BG* = *bg*, *CH* = *ch*, …, *AE* = *ae*. Now draw *y*-isoline and *z*-isoline through *F* and *G* respectively to meet at point 2. In the same way locate points 4, 6 and 8 by drawing isolines through

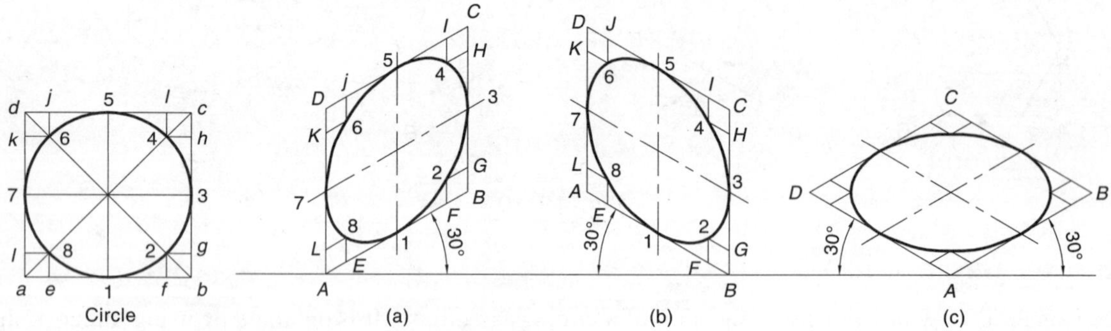

Fig. 18.12

H, *I*, *J*, *K*, *L* and *E*. Mark points 1, 3, 5 and 7 as midpoints of *AB*, *BC*, *CD* and *DA* respectively in the rhombus. Draw a smooth curve passing through points 1–2–3–4–5–6–7–8–1 to represents the required ellipse. The circle may be divided into more numbers of parts (say 12) to ensure the accuracy.

Figure 18.13 shows the difference between the ellipses drawn by two methods.

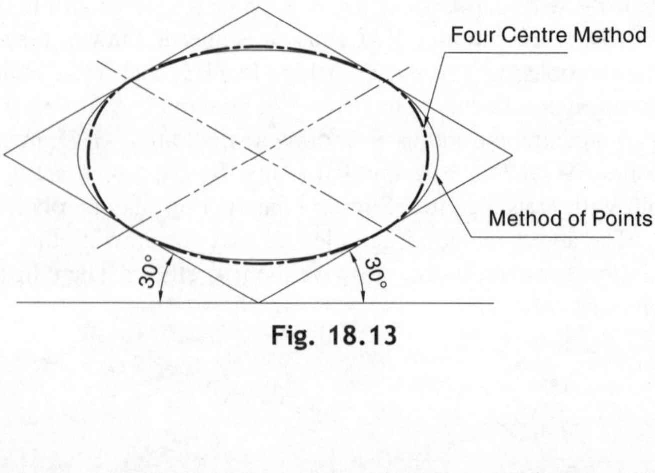

Fig. 18.13

18.6.7 Semicircle/Quadrant

The semicircle or quadrant will be seen as a half ellipse or a quarter of the ellipse in isometric. If the four-centre method is followed, only two arcs—one large and one small—will be seen, Fig. 18.14. In case of quadrant, only one arc—either large or small—will be seen, Fig. 18.15.

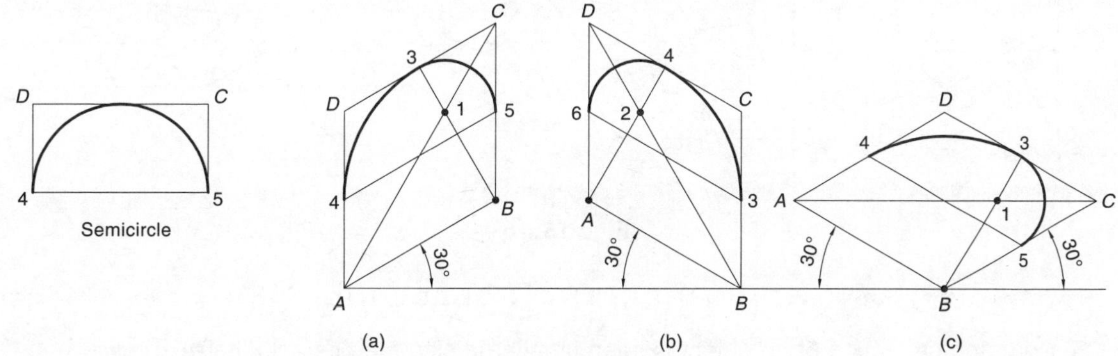

Fig. 18.14

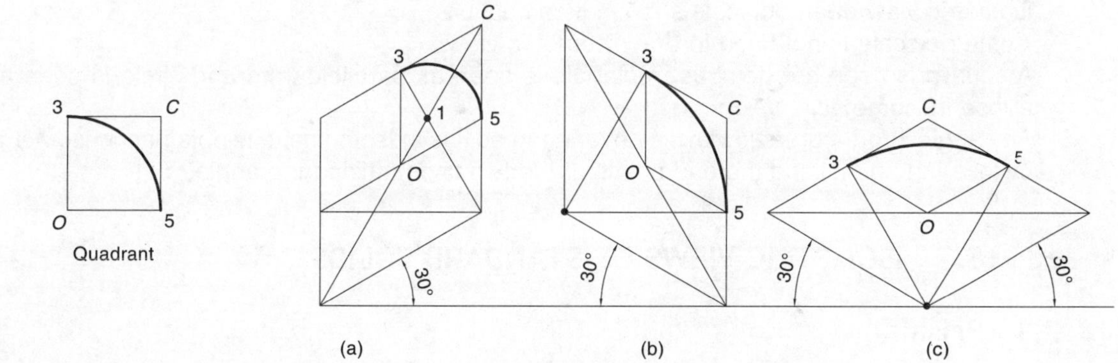

Fig. 18.15

18.6.8 Any Irregular Shape

Any irregular shape 1–2–3–4–5–6–7 can be drawn in isometric view as explained in Fig. 18.16. The figure is enclosed in a rectangle first. The parallelogram is obtained in isometric for the rectangle as shown. The isolines *B*–2, *D*–2, *C*–3, *E*–3, *G*–4, *F*–4, *H*–5, *H*–6 and *A*–7 has the same length as in original shape, e.g., *B*–2 in isometric = *B*–2 in irregular shape.

18.6.9 Angles in Isometric

The angle between two edges of the object, if one or both of them are non-isometric edges, does not have any meaning in isometric. Consider the irregular shape shown in Fig. 18.16. The angle between edges 7–1 and 1–2 is 31°. However this angle cannot be set off directly in isometric. Note that 1–2 is a non-isoline. It is drawn by locating its end points and not by measuring its angle with 7–1. Hence, the angles between 7–1 and 1–2 in Fig. 18.16(a) to (c) are different. The same is the case of edges 2–3 and 3–4 which make an angle of 107° with each other. Both these edges represent non-isometric lines and hence located with reference to their end points.

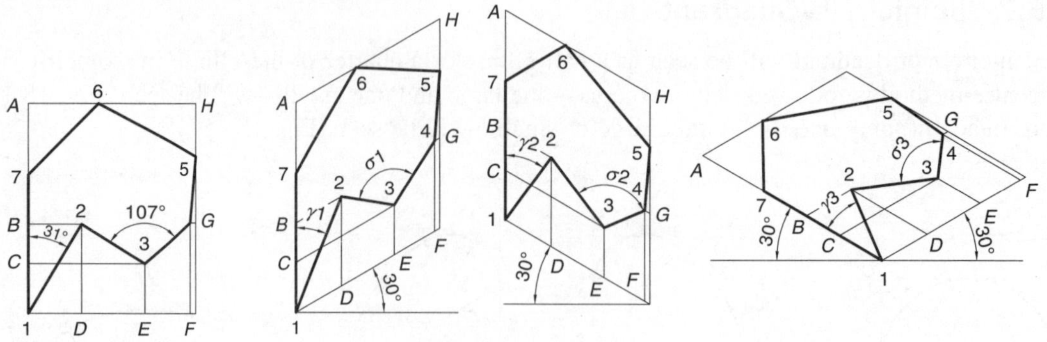

Irregular Shape (a) (b) (c)

Fig. 18.16

Remember the Following

- Isometric projection of an object is seen smaller in size than its actual size.
- Isometric scale is used to draw isometric projection.
- Isometric view of an object is seen in its actual size.
- Isometric scale is not used to draw isometric view.
- A square is seen as rhombus, rectangle is seen as parallelogram and circle is seen as ellipse in isometric.
- Any angle in orthographic view is never seen as it is in isometric. It is obtained in isometric by locating and joining the end points of the two lines making the angle.

18.7 ISOMETRIC VIEWS OF STANDARD SOLIDS

18.7.1 Prisms

The isometric view of a hexagonal prism is explained in Fig. 18.17. To obtain the isometric view from FV and SV, the FV is enclosed in rectangle *abcd*. This rectangle is drawn as a parallelogram *ABCD* in isometric view. The hexagon 1–2–3–4–5–6 is obtained to represent the front face of the prism in

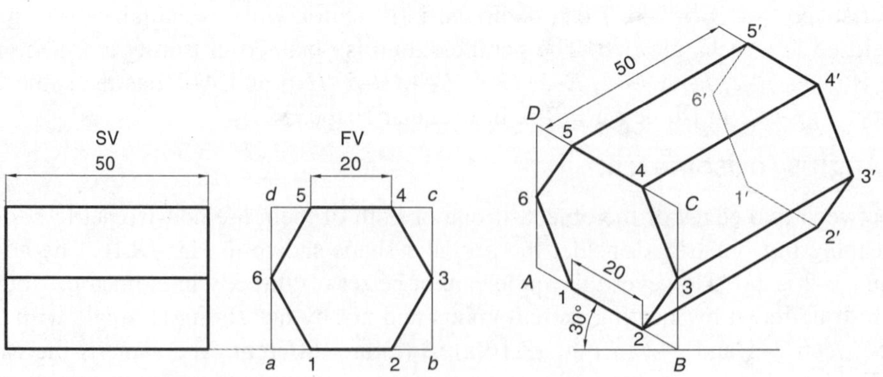

Fig. 18.17

isometric as explained in Section 18.6.5. The same hexagon is redrawn as 1′–2′–3′–4′–5′–6′ to represent the back face of the prism in such a way that 1–1′ = 2–2′ = 3–3′ = … = 6–6′ = 50 mm. The two faces are then joined together as shown. The lines 1–1′, 2–2′, 3–3′, 4–4′, 5–5′ and 6–6′ are isolines. The lines 5′–6′, 6′–1′ and 1′–2′ are invisible and need not be shown.

The isometric projection of other prisms can be drawn in a similar way using the isometric scale.

18.7.2 Pyramids

Figure 18.18 explains the isometric view of a pentagonal pyramid. The base is enclosed in a rectangle *abcd*, which is drawn as parallelogram *ABCD* in isometric. The points 1, 2, 3, 4 and 5 are marked in parallelogram as explained in Section 18.6.4. Mark point *O*1 in isometric such that 4–*O*1 in isometric is equal to 4–*o*1 in TV. Draw vertical *O*1–*O* = *o*1′–*o*′ to represent the axis in isometric projection. Finally join *O* with 1, 3, 4 and 5 to represent the slant edges of the pyramid. The edge *O*–2 is not seen and hence not drawn. Also, the edges 1–2 and 2–3 need not be drawn. The slant edges of the pyramid are non-isolines. It may be noted that the origin is at point *D* which lies outside the object.

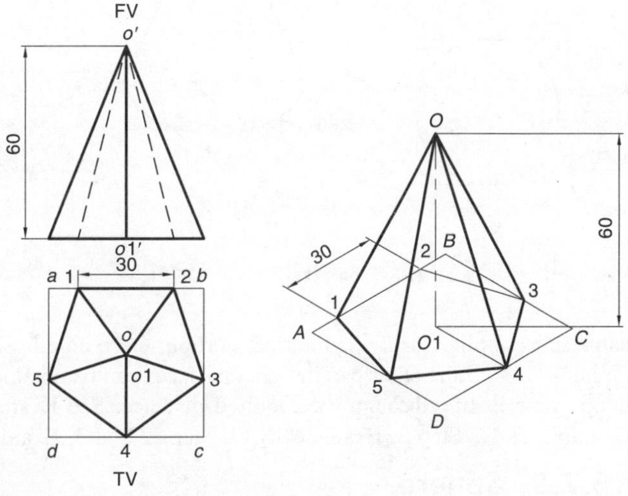

Fig. 18.18

18.7.3 Cone

The isometric view of the cone can be obtained easily from its FV and TV, as shown in Fig. 18.19. As already explained, the circle (i.e., base of cone) is seen as an ellipse in isometric and is drawn here by using the four-centre method. The point *O*1 is the centre of the ellipse. Through *O*1, draw *O*–*O*1 = Length of axis. Then, join *O* to the ellipse by two tangent lines which represent the slant edges of the cone.

18.7.4 Cylinder

The isometric view of a cylinder is shown in Fig. 18.20. The base is obtained as an ellipse with centre *O*. The same ellipse is redrawn (with *O*1 as a centre) for the top face at a distance equal to the height of the cylinder. The two ellipses are joined by two tangent lines, *A*–*A*1 and *B*–*B*1, which represent the two extreme generators of the cylinder.

DRAWING TIP

While drawing the isometric of prisms, the corners of one end may be directly transferred along the isoline through the distance equal to the length of the axis to obtain the other end. For example, in Fig. 18.17, corners 1, 2, 3, 4, 5 and 6 are transferred along *z*-isoline through 50 mm to obtain 1′, 2′, 3′, 4′, 5′ and 6′ respectively. The

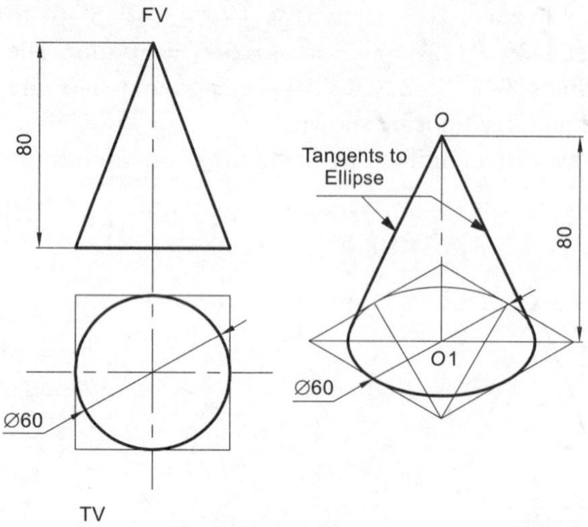

Fig. 18.19

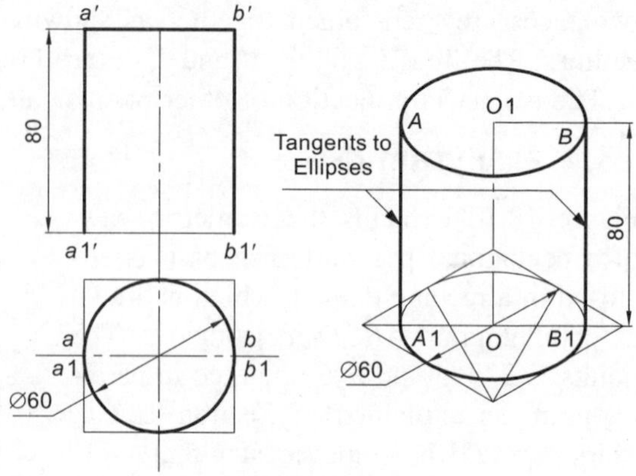

Fig. 18.20

same thing applies for the cylindrical portion. Once an ellipse is constructed by the four centre method for any circular face, all the other parallel circular faces can be obtained by shifting the centres of the first face along the appropriate isoline through the required distance. See Example 18.9, Step 3; Example 18.11, Steps 2 and 6; Example 18.12, Step 3; Example 18.13, Steps 2 and 3; Example 18.19; etc.

18.7.5 Sphere

The sphere is seen as a circle of radius equal to its own radius when viewed from any direction. That is why orthographic views of a sphere are the circles of radius equal to the true radius of the sphere. It should be noted that the radius of a sphere never gets foreshortened in isometric. The isometric projection of the sphere has the same radius as that of the true radius of the sphere; however the isometric view of a sphere has a radius greater than the true radius.

The isometric projection of a sphere may be drawn without using the isometric scale when it is not in contact with any other solid. However, when the point of contact of a sphere with any other solid or RPs or ground is given then the isometric scale must be used to locate the centre of the sphere in relation to the point of contact.

The isometric projection and isometric view of the sphere are explained in Fig. 18.21 and Fig. 18.22 respectively. Figure 18.21 shows the orthographic view and isometric projection of the sphere. The sphere of centre *O* and radius = 25 is resting centrally on the square slab of size 50 × 50 × 15 with point *P* as a point of contact. To obtain the isometric projection, an isometric scale is used and the slab of size *iso*50 × *iso*50 × *iso*15 is obtained. The point *P*, which represents the point of contact between the slab and the sphere, is located at the centre of the top parallelogram. The length of *PO* in isometric projection is equal to *iso*25, which is obtained from the isometric scale. Obviously, this length will be shorter than the length of *PO* in orthographic. Now, with *O* as a centre and radius equal to 25, a circle is drawn which represents the sphere in isometric. The radius of this sphere is same as that of the circle in orthographic. The slab is drawn using isometric scale, however, for the sphere, the radius is taken the same as in orthographic view. Obviously the sphere is seen larger compared to the slab in isometric projection.

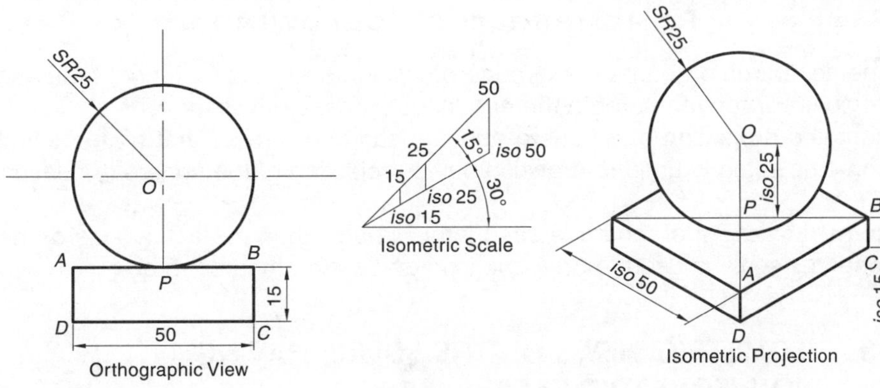

Fig. 18.21

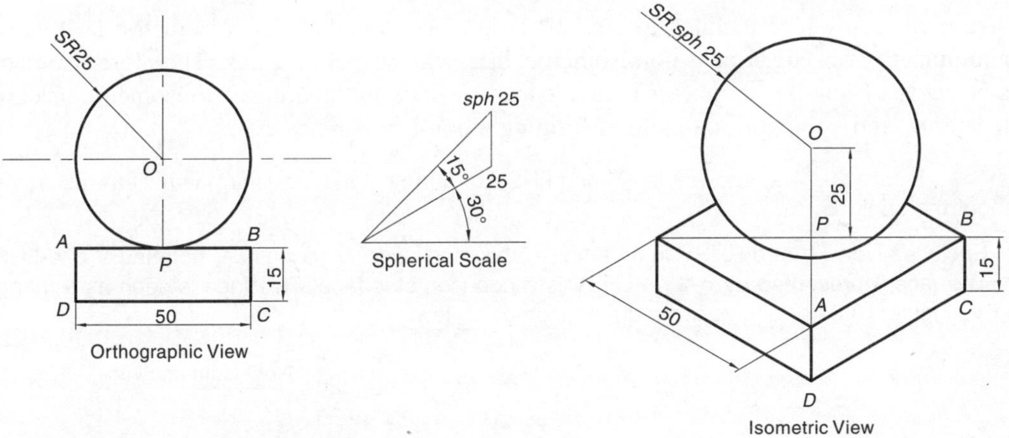

Fig. 18.22

The isometric view of the sphere is shown in Fig. 18.22. Spherical scale, shown in Fig. 18.23, is used to obtain the radius of the sphere in isometric view. The spherical scale is the reverse of the isometric scale. The actual radius of the sphere is taken on the true scale and then it is projected on the spherical scale. Obviously, the spherical length will be $(\sqrt{3}/\sqrt{2})$ times of the actual length.

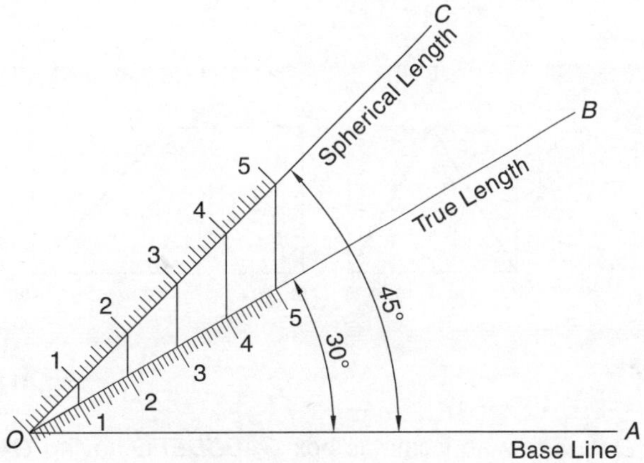

Fig. 18.23 Spherical Scale

To draw the isometric view of the sphere in contact with the slab, first draw the isometric view of the slab. Mark point of contact *P* at the centre of the top face of the slab. Now, through *P* draw vertical line *PO* = true radius of the sphere. Obtain the radius of the sphere in isometric view from the spherical scale, i.e., *sph*25. With *O* as a centre and radius = *sph*25, draw a circle to represent the sphere in isometric view.

REMEMBER THE FOLLOWING

- In isometric, extreme generators of cone or cylinders are drawn tangent to base face (in case of cone) or tangent to both the end faces (in case of cylinder).
- The isometric projection of a sphere appears same in size as that of the actual sphere. The isometric scale is used to draw isometric projection of the sphere in relation to other solids.
- The isometric view of a sphere is seen larger in size than the actual size of the sphere. The spherical scale is used to draw the isometric view of the sphere.

18.8 ISOMETRIC VIEWS OF THE SOLIDS HAVING NON-ISOMETRIC FACES

As mentioned earlier, any face inclined to the isometric plane is called a non-isometric face. Obviously, a minimum of two edges of a non-isometric face will be non-isolines. Therefore, isometric projections or views of non-isometric faces are obtained by drawing their edges in isometric. Clearly, one must locate the end points of non-isolines forming a non-isometric face.

Example 18.1 Figure 18.24(a) shows the FV and LHSV of a truncated triangular prism. Draw its isometric view about the origin *O*.

Solution Enclose given FV and RHSV in rectangles *abco* and *ocdg*. Mark point 1′ both in FV and LHSV as shown. The face represented by *o*–1′ in LHSV is a non-isometric face. This face is seen as a triangle *a*–1′–*o* in FV. Figure 18.24(b) shows the required isometric view.

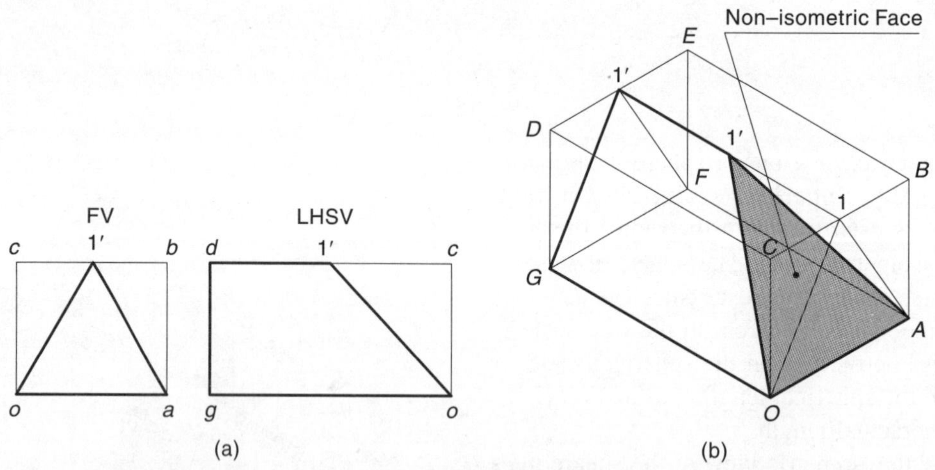

Fig. 18.24

1. Draw an isometric box *OABCDEFG* having *OA* = *oa*, *OC* = *oc* and *OG* = *og*. Mark point 1 on *CB* such that *C*–1 = *c*–1′. Join *O*–1–*A*. It shows a fictitious triangular face of the prism. In the figure it is drawn for the sake of understanding only. Note that *O*–1–*A* is an isometric face. In fact, the point 1 will not be seen on *CB*.

2. Draw *x*-isoline 1–1″ equal to *cd*. Mark 1′ on 1–1″ such that 1–1′ = *c*–1′. Join *O*–1′–*A*. The non-isometric triangular face *O*–1′–A represents the real face of the truncated prism. Note that we have located the end points of the non-isometric lines *O*–1' and *A*–1' to obtain this face.
3. Join *O*–*G*–1″–1′. The edges *GF*, *F*–1″ and *AF* will not be visible and hence need not be drawn.

Make all the visible edges of the object sufficiently thick to differentiate them from construction lines and other reference lines.

Example 18.2 Figure 18.25(a) shows the FV and TV of a cut pentagonal prism. Draw its isometric view.

Solution Enclose the TV in a rectangle *pqrs*. As shown in Fig. 18.25(b), obtain parallelogram *PQRS* in isometric and then mark points *ABCDE* to represent the base of the prism. Note that *PA* = *pa*, *QB* = *qb*, *QC* = *qc*, *PE* = *pe* and *SD* = *sd*. Lines *AE*, *ED*, *DC* and *CB* are non-isolines. Now, through each corner of base draw vertical lines and mark points *F*, *G*, 3, 4 and 5 on them such that *AF* = *BG* = *a′f′*, *C*–3 = *E*–5 = *c′*–3′ and *D*–4 = *d′*–4′. To mark points 1 and 2 in isometric, draw parallelogram *TUMN* to represent the rectangle *pqmn*. Mark points 1 and 2 on *MN* such that *N*–1 = *M*–2 = *n*–1 = *m*–2. Join points 1–2–3–4–5 to represent the cut face of the prism.

Note that, the points 1, 2, 3, 4 and 5 are located by measuring their distances along the isometric axes.

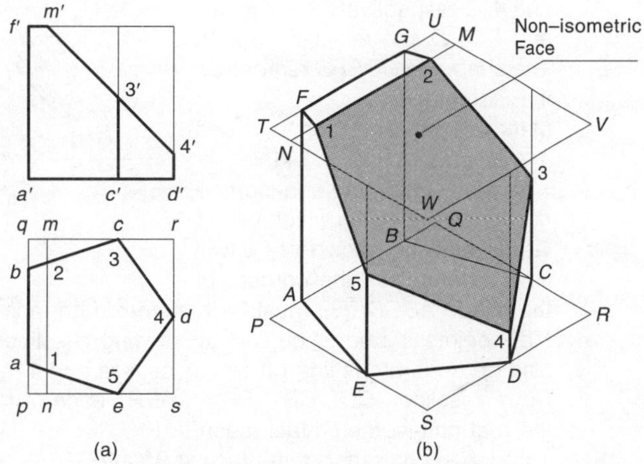

Fig. 18.25

Example 18.3 Figure 18.26 shows the FV and two RHSVs—RHSV-(a) and RHSV-(b), of an object. Draw its two isometric views, considering FV and each of the RHSVs.

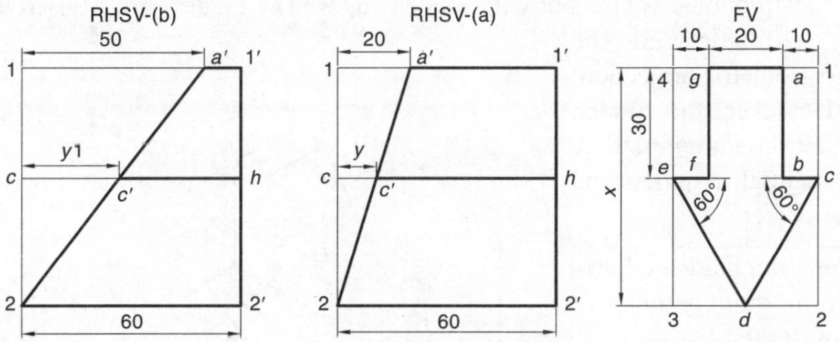

Fig. 18.26

Solution Figure 18.27(a) shows the isometric view of the object considering FV and RHSV-(a).

Enclose the given FV and RHSV-(a) into rectangles 1–2–3–4 and 1′–2′–2–1 respectively. The dimension '*x*' is not given. It is equal to (4–*e*) + (*e*–3). *e*–3 is height of triangle *ecd*. *d* is the midpoint of 2–3. The distance *c*–*c′* = *y* is unknown distance and can be found graphically as shown in RHSV-(a).

1. Draw an isometric box 2–2′–1′–1–4–4′–3′–3 such that 2–2′ = 2–2′ in RHSV, 2–3= 2–3 in FV and 2–1= 2–1 in FV.

2. Mark points *A* and *G* on 1–4 such that 1–*A* = 4–*G* = 1–*a* = 4–*g* = 10 mm. Through *A* and *G* draw *y*-isolines *AB* and *GF* such that *AB* = *GF* = *ab* = *gf* = 30 mm. Through *B* and *F*, draw *x*-isolines *BC* and *FE* such that *BC* = *FE* = *bc* = *fe* = 10 mm. Obviously, points *C* and *E* will lie on 1–2 and 4–3 respectively. Now join *C* and *E* to *D*, the midpoint of 2–3. The shape *ABCDEFG* represents the isometric-FV.
3. Mark points 5 and 6 on 1–1′ and 4–4′ such that 1–5 = 4–6 = 1–*a*′ = 20 mm. Obtain the non-isometric face 2–5–6–3 on which all the visible outlines shown in FV will lie. Therefore, all the corners of the shape *ABCDEFG* must be transferred on face 2–5–6–3 by drawing *z*-isolines through them.

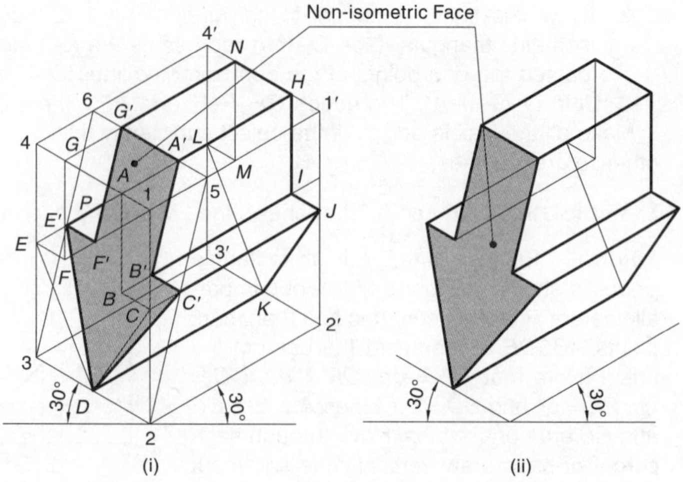

Fig. 18.27(a)

4. Mark points *A*′ and *G*′ on 5–6 by drawing *z*-isolines through *A* and *G*, each equal to 1–*a*′. (This can also be done by setting off distances 1–*a* and 4–*g* on 5–6 such that 5–*A*′ = 6–*G*′ = 1–*a* = 4–*g*.)
5. Draw *z*-isolines *CC*′, *BB*′, *FF*′ and *EE*′, each of them equal to *y*. Join *A*′*B*′*C*′*DE*′*F*′*G*′ to represent the real non-isometric face seen in FV.
6. Through each corner of the face *A*′*B*′*C*′*DE*′*F*′*G*′, draw *z*-isolines to show the back face *HIJKLMN* of the object. The edges *K–L–M–N* and *F*′*M* will not be visible. The edge *E*′*L* will be seen partially from *E*′ to *P*.

   All the visible edges of the object should be made sufficiently thick to differentiate them from construction and reference lines.

Figure 18.27(a)-(i) shows the object with all constructional details. Figure 18.27(a)-(ii) shows the object without constructional details but with hidden edges. The readers are advised to retain constructional details while drawing the isometric view (or isometric projection) of an object. However, the hidden edges need not be shown unless they are extremely essential to understand the shape of the object.

> **Note:** In isometric, hidden edges may be shown by thin continuous lines instead of dashed lines.

Figure 18.27(b) shows the isometric view of the object considering FV and RHSV-(b). The line 2–*a*′ is different in RHSV-(b) than that in RHSV-(a). Therefore, the non-isometric face in this case will be different.

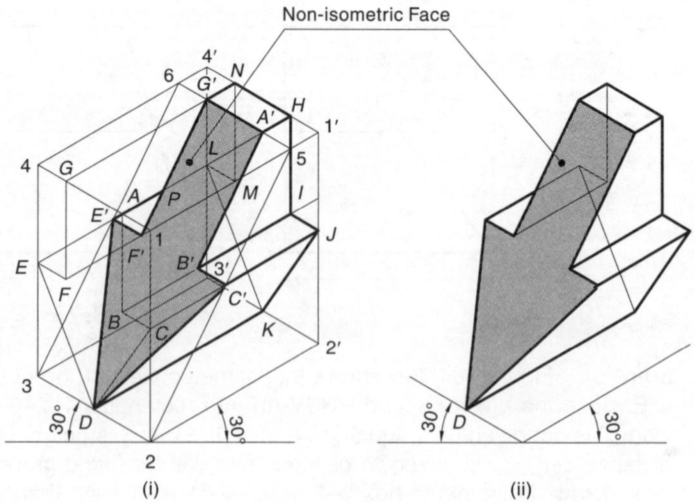

Fig. 18.27(b)

The non-isometric face is shown by $A'B'C'DE'F'G'A'$, which is obtained by shifting the points A, B, C, E, F and G along z-isolines AA', BB', CC', EE', FF' and GG'. Note that, $AA' = GG' = 1–a' = 50$ mm, $BB' = FF' = CC' = EE' = y1$. All other points are located in similar ways as that in Fig. 18.27(a).

Example 18.4 Figure 18.28(a) shows the FV and TV of a truncated cylinder. Draw its isometric view.

Solution Refer Fig. 18.28(b). To draw an isometric view of the base, the TV is enclosed in a square as usual. The rhombus is obtained for the square in isometric. The circle is obtained as an ellipse by the method of points as explained in Section 18.6.6, Fig. 18.12. The ellipse for the top face can be obtained in a similar way. Join the two ellipses by two tangent lines. In rhombus *JKLM*, locate point 1′ and 2′ such that *J*–1′ = *M*–2′ = *e*′–1′. Join 1′–2′ and mark its intersections with top ellipse as 1 and 2. 1–2 represents the edge formed at the top face of the cylinder. To draw a non-isometric elliptical face, adopt the following procedure:

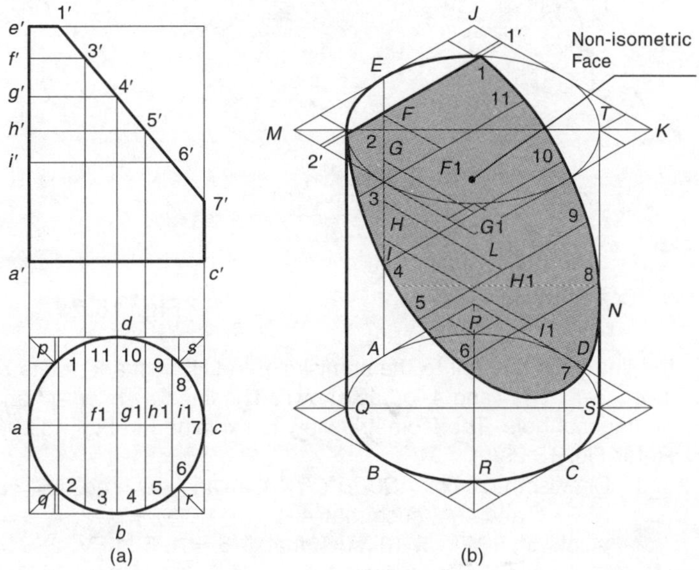

Fig. 18.28

1. Join *AE*. Locate points *F*, *G*, *H* and *I* on it in such a way that *EF* = *e*′*f*′, *EG* = *e*′*g*′, *EH* = *e*′*h*′ and *EI* = *e*′*i*′.
2. Draw x-isolines *F*–*F*1, *G*–*G*1, *H*–*H*1, *I*–*I*1 such that *F*–*F*1 = *f*′–3′, *G*–*G*1 = *g*′–4′, *H*–*H*1 = *h*′–5′ and *I*–*I*1 = *I*′–6′. Now, through *F*1, *G*1, *H*1 and *I*1, draw z-isolines 3–11, 4–10, 5–9 and 6–8 respectively taking their lengths from TV.
3. Join 2–3–4–5–6–7–8–9–10–11–1 by a smooth freehand curve. It represents the required non-isometric face.

   Note that the line *ST*, which is tangent to the bottom and top ellipses will be seen from *S* to *N* only. The point *N* represents the point of tangency with the non-isometric curve.

Example 18.5 Figure 18.29(a) shows the FV and LHSV of an object. Draw its isometric view.

Solution The FV and LHSV show that the object has a non-isometric face indicated by *a*–9′ in LHSV. Enclose FV and LHSV in rectangles *abcd* and *abb*′*a*′. In FV, draw unevenly spaced lines 1–1′, 2–2′, 3–3′ and 4–4′. Note that these lines pass through corners *e* and *i*, *f* and *h* and *g* respectively of pentagon. Mark points 5, 6, 7, …, 13 at the intersections of lines 1–1′, 2–2′, 3–3′ and 4–4′ with the semicircle. The point 9 is the point at which

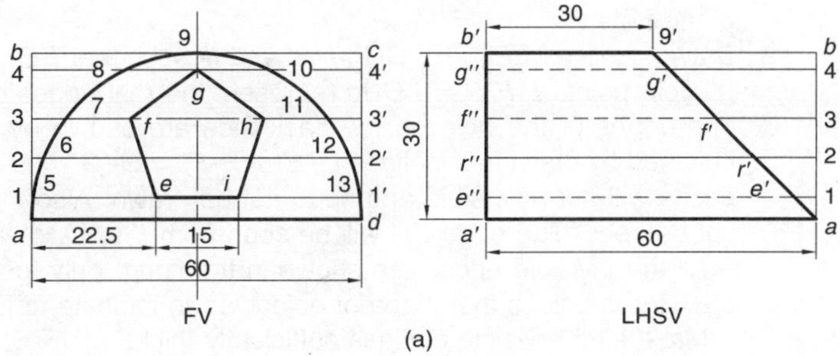

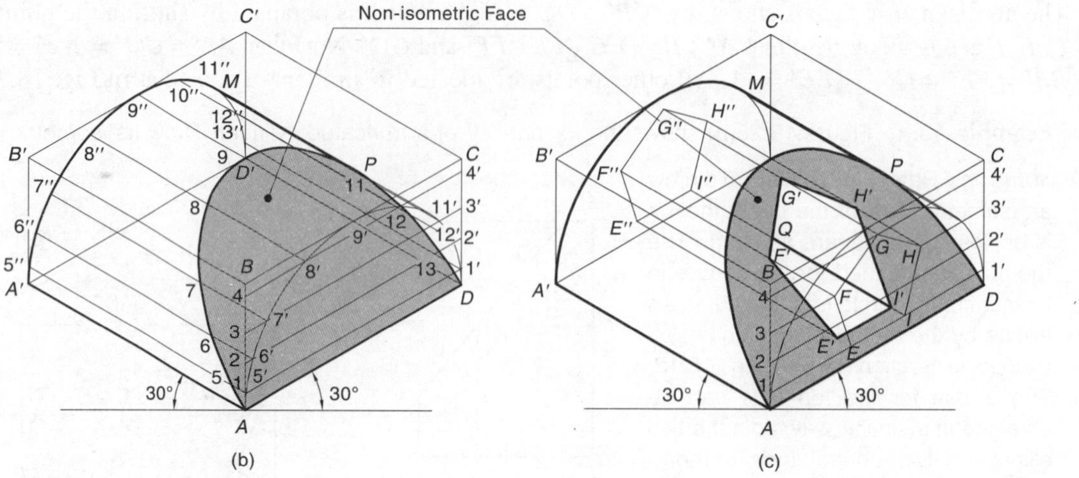

Fig. 18.29

the line *bc* is tangent to the semicircle. In LHSV, mark points *e*′, *r*′, *f*′ and *g*′ on *a*–9′ by drawing the lines 1–*e*″, 2–*r*″, 3–*f*″ and 4–*g*″ as shown. The lines *e*′–*e*″, *f*′–*f*″ and *g*′–*g*″ represent the hidden edges of the pentagonal hole. The isometric view is explained in Fig. 18.29(b) and Fig. 18.29(c).

Refer Fig. 18.29(b).

1. Draw isometric box *ADCBB′C′D′A′* having *AD* = *ad*, *AB* = *ab* and *AA′* = *aa′*. Obtain *z*-isolines 1–1′, 2–2′, 3–3′ and 4–4′ such that *A*–1 = *a*–1, *A*–2 = *a*–2, *A*–3 = *a*–3 and *A*–4 = *a*–4. On these lines locate points 5′, 6′, 7′ …, 13′ such that 1–5′ = 1–5 in FV, 2–6′ = 2–6 in FV, 3–7′ = 3–7 in FV, …, 1′–13′ = 1′–13 in FV (The points *A*–5′–6′–7′ … 13′–*D* may be joined by a thin semi-elliptical curve to show the non-existing face of the object.)
2. Draw *x*-isolines 5′–5, 6′–6, 7′–7, … 13′–13 such that 5′–5 = 13′–13 = 1–*e*′ in LHSV, 6′–6 = 12′–12 = 2–*r*′ in LHSV, 7′–7 = 11′–11 = 3–*f*′ in LHSV, 8′–8 = 10′–10 = 4–*g*′ in LHSV and *g*′–9 = *b*–9′ in LHSV. Join *A*–5–6–7 … 13–*D* by a smooth freehand curve. The non-isometric face thus obtained represents the front end of the object.
3. Draw *x*-isolines 5′–5″, 6″–6″, 7′–7″, …, 13′–13″, each equal to *a*–*a*′ in LHSV. Join points *A*′–5″–6″–7″–8″–9″–10″–11″–12″–13″–*D*′ by a smooth semi-elliptical curve to represent the back face (partly visible).
4. Draw a common tangent line MP to both the curves to represent the extreme right visible generator.

   Make all the visible outlines sufficiently thick.

Refer Fig.18.29(c). To draw the pentagonal hole, adopt the following steps:

1. Locate points *E*, *F*, *G*, *H* and *I* on 1–1′, 3–3′ and 4–4′ such that 1–*E* = 1′–*I* = 1–*e* in FV, 3–*F* = 3′–*H* = 3–*f* in FV and 4–*G* = 4–*g* in FV. The points *EFGHIE* may be joined to represent non-existing edges of the hole.
2. Draw *x*-isolines *EE*′, *FF*′, *GG*′, *HH*′ and *II*′ such that *EE*′ = *II*′ = 1–*e*′, *FF*′ = *HH*′ = 3–*f*′ and *GG*′ = 4–*g*′. Join points *E*′*F*′*G*′*H*′*I*′*E*′ to represent the real edges of the hole on the front non-isometric face.
3. The edges of the hole on the back face are shown by lines *E*″–*F*″–*G*″–*H*″–*I*″–*E*″. These can be obtained by drawing *x*-isolines *E*–*E*″ = *F*–*F*″ = *G*–*G*″ = *H*–*H*″ = *I*–*I*″ = *a*–*a*′ = 60 mm. However, these edges will not be visible and need not be drawn. Also the edges *E*′*E*″, *F*′*F*″, *G*′*G*″ and *H*′–*H*″ will not be seen. The edge *I*′*I*″ will be seen from *I*′ to *Q*.

   All the invisible edges are shown in the figure only for the sake of illustration. Students need not draw them unless the shape of object is too intricate to justify it.

   Make all the visible outlines sufficiently thick.

18.9 ISOMETRIC VIEWS: SYSTEMATIC APPROACH

The best way to learn isometric projection is to improve your imaginative powers. In this section, we are going to study the systematic way to obtain the isometric views or projections from two-dimensional views, i.e. orthographic views. The procedure is explained with the help of two sets of examples. The first set includes Examples 18.6 to 18.10 and the second set includes Examples 18.11 to 18.16. In each set, each higher numbered example is a modification of the object studied in the preceding example.

Example 18.6 Figure 18.30(a) shows the FV and LHSV of the object. Draw its isometric view assuming the origin *O* at a suitable corner.

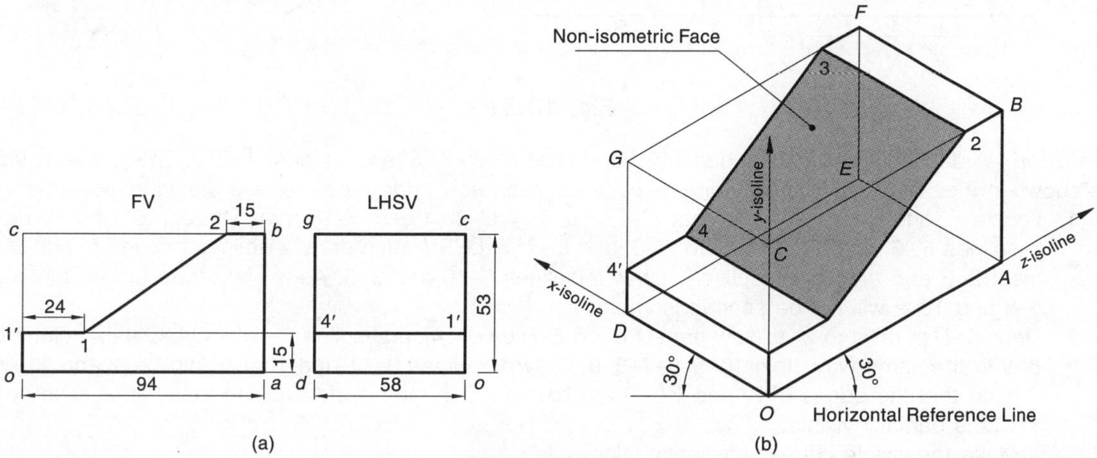

Fig. 18.30

Solution The isometric view is shown in Fig. 18.30(b).

1. Enclose the FV into a rectangle *oabc*. Name all the important points as 1′, 1 and 2 in FV. Name all the points as *o*, *c*, *g*, *d*, 1′ and 4′ LHSV.
2. Draw a horizontal reference line and mark the origin *O* on it.
3. Draw *OA* and *OD* making an angle of 30° each with the horizontal reference line. Draw *OC* perpendicular to the horizontal reference line. *OA*, *OD* and *OC* represent *z*-isoline, *x*-isoline and *y*-isoline respectively. As we are drawing isometric view, *OA* = *oa* = 94 mm, *OD* = *od* = 58 mm, *OC* = *oc* = 53 mm.
4. Construct an isometric box *OABCGFED* such that *OA* = *CB* = *GF* = *DE*, *OD* = *GC* = *FB* = *EA* and *OC* = *AB* = *EF* = *DG*.
5. Mark points 1′, 1 and 2 in isometric such that *O*–1′, 1′–1 and *B*–2 in isometric are equal to *o*–1′, 1′–1 and *b*–2 in FV. Note that 1–2 is a non-isometric line.
6. Draw equal *x*-isolines 1′–4′, 1–4 and 2–3. Join 4′–4–3–F. Make all visible edges of the object sufficiently thick. The face 1–2–3–4 is a non-isometric face.

Example 18.7 From the FV and LHSV shown in Fig. 18.31(a), draw the isometric view of the object.

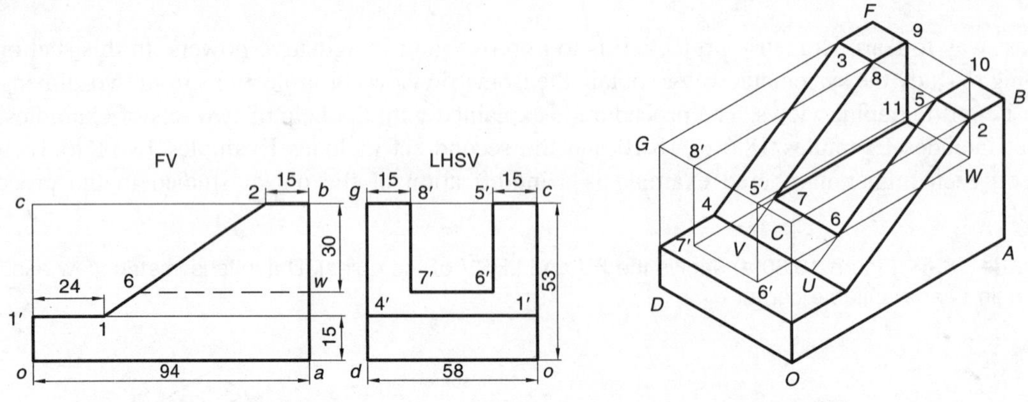

(a) (b)

Fig. 18.31

Solution A dashed line 6–*w* is added in FV and lines 5′–6′–7′–8′ are added in LHSV. The isometric view is shown in Fig. 18.31(b). The following steps will explain how added features are drawn in isometric.

1. Locate 5′ and 8′ on *CG* such that *C*–5′ = *c*–5′ = *G*–8′ = *g*–8′ = 15 mm. Through 5′ and 8′, draw *y*-isolines 5′–6′ and 8′–7′ equal to 5′–6′ and 8′–7′ in LHSV. Also draw *z*-isolines through 5′ and 8′ to meet 2–3 at 5 and 8 respectively. Draw *z*-isolines 5–10 and 8–9. As is clear from LHSV, the lines 5–8 and 10–9 will not be seen in isometric.
2. Draw 5–*U* parallel to 2–1. Now project 6′ on 5–*U* by drawing *z*-isoline 6′–*W* = *OA*. Obtain point 7 on 8–*V* in the same way. Join 10–5–6–7–8–9. Draw *y*-isolines 9–11 and 10–*W*. Join 7–11 and 11–*W*.

   Note that the edges 6–*W* and *W*–10 are hidden. One may avoid drawing these lines. The edge 11–*W* is partially visible.

   Make the visible edges sufficiently thick.

Example 18.8 Draw the isometric view of the object from the FV and LHSV shown in Fig. 18.32(a).

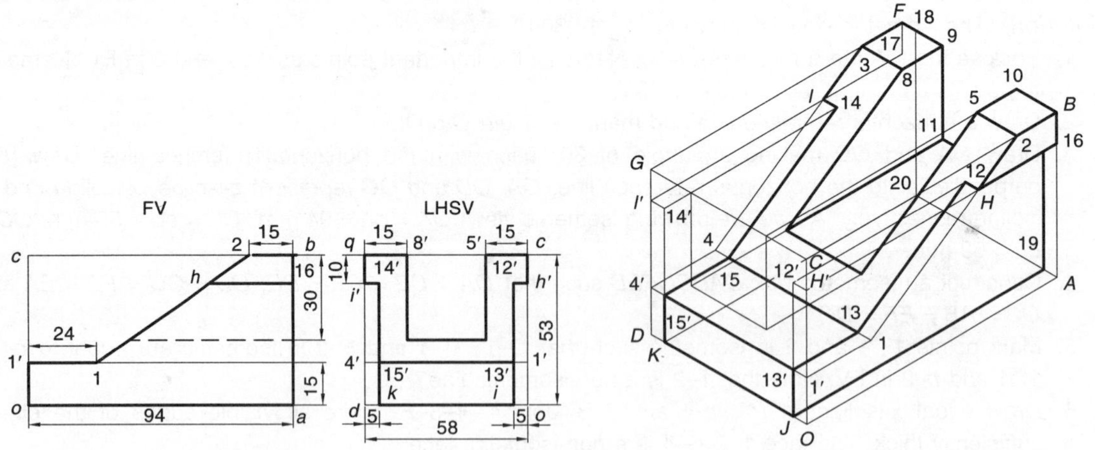

(a) (b)

Fig. 18.32

Solution In FV, line *h*–16 is added. In LHSV lines *h′*–12′–*j* and *i′*–14′–*k* are added. The modified isometric view is shown in Fig. 18.32(b).

1. Mark *H′* and *I′* on *CO* and *GD* respectively. *CH′* = *GI′* = *ch′* = 10 mm. Mark 12′ and 14′ by drawing *x*-isolines *H′*–12′ = *I′*–14′ = *h′*12′ = 5 mm.
2. Draw *z*-isolines *H′*–16 and *I′*–17′ and mark points *H* and *I* at their intersection with 1–2 and 4–3 respectively. Draw *z*-isolines 12′–12 and 14′–14 equal to *H′*–*H* and *I′*–*I* respectively. Join *H*–12 and *I*–14. The line *H*–16 represents the new visible edge formed on the front face.
3. Draw *y*-isolines 12′–*J* and14′–*K*. The points *J* and *K* will lie on *OD*. Mark 13′ and 15′ on 1′–4 such that 1′–13′ = 4′–15′ = 5 mm. Through 13′ and 15′ draw *z*-isolines to locate 13 and 15 on 1–4. Join 12–13–13′ and 15′–15–14.

   The origin *O* is now outside the object, which may be noted carefully. Make all visible outlines of the object sufficiently thick.

Example 18.9 Draw the isometric view of the object from the FV and LHSV shown in Fig. 18.33(a).

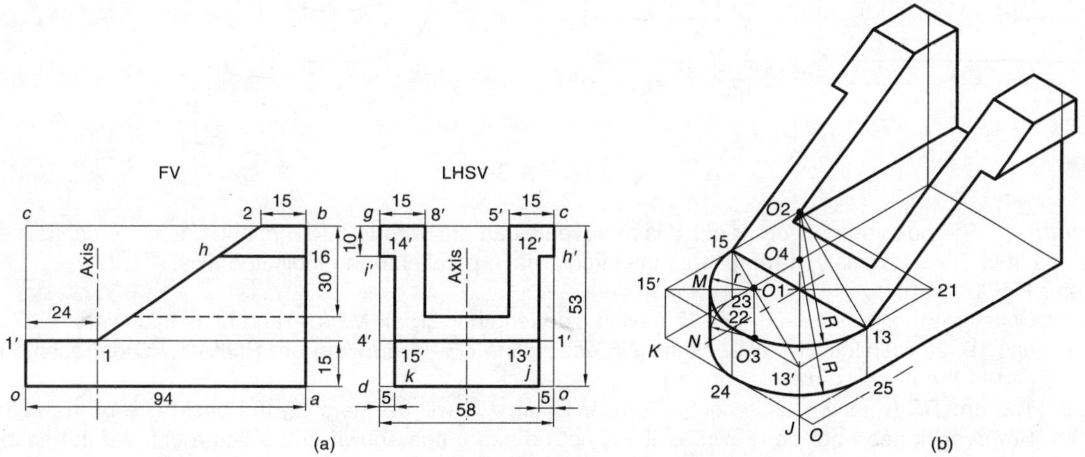

Fig. 18.33

Solution A centreline is added to FV and LHSV. It indicates the axis of some circular features. Careful observation will tell us that the leftmost portion of the object, i.e., block 13–13′–*J*–*K*–15′–15 in Fig. 18.32(b) is made semicircular.

Refer Fig. 18.33(b)

1. Construct a rhombus 13′–15′–*O*2–21. Join 15′–21, 13′–15 and *O*2–13. Mark centre *O*1 at the intersection of 15′–21 and 13′–15.
2. Draw an arc 15–22 with *O*1 as centre and *O*1–15 as a radius. (Point 22 is the midpoint of 13′–15′.) Draw another arc 13–22 with *O*2 as centre and *O*2–13 as a radius. The curve 15–22–13 represents semi-ellipse for the top face.
3. To draw the semi-ellipse for the bottom face, simply shift the centres *O*1 and *O*2 downward by the distance equal to the thickness of the semicircular portion, i.e., 15 mm. So, draw *y*- isolines *O*1–*O*3, *O*2–*O*4, 15–23 and 13–25, each equal to 15 mm. Now, with *O*3 as a centre and radius *O*1–15, draw an arc 23–24. (Point 24 is the midpoint of *KJ*). Draw another arc 24–25 with *O*4 as a centre and radius *O*2–13. The curve 22–24–25 represents semi-elliptical profile of bottom face.
4. Join both the semi-ellipses by a common tangent line *MN*. Note that the part *N*–23 of the semi ellipse 23–24–25 will not be visible.

   Make all visible edges and parts of the edges thick.

Example 18.10 Figure 18.34(a) shows the FV and LHSV of an object. Draw its isometric view.

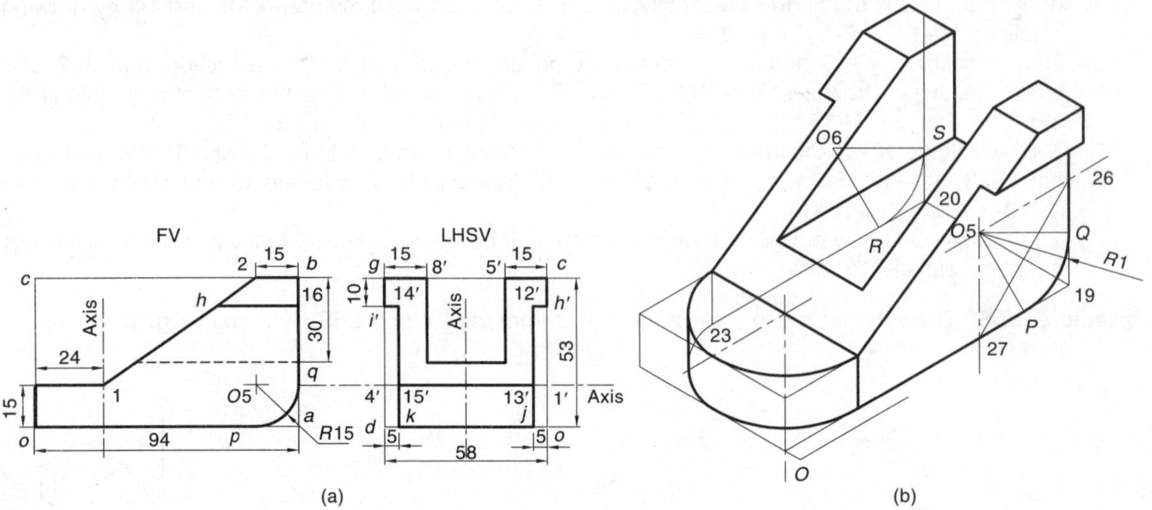

Fig. 18.34

Solution The bottom right corner of FV is removed by an arc of radius 15 mm and one more centreline is added in LHSV. Obviously, it represents the circular face parallel to the indicated axis.
Refer Fig. 18.34(b).

1. Construct rhombus 19–26–*O*5–27 having side length = 2(*pa*). Mark *P* and *Q* as midpoints of 27–19 and 19–26 respectively. With centre *O*5 and radius *O*5–*P*, draw an arc *PQ*. Arc *PQ* represents the part of the ellipse drawn for arc *pq*.
2. The arc *RS* (with *O*6 as a centre) similar to arc *PQ* will be there on the back face of the object. However, it need not be drawn as it will not be seen. It is shown in the figure only for the sake of understanding.

   The arcs *PQ* and *RS* remove corners 19 and 20 respectively and hence edge 19–20 will vanish. Note how axes of circular features are indicated by centrelines.

Example 18.11 Figure 18.35(a) shows the FV and SV of an object. Draw its isometric view.

Solution Enclose the given FV and SV into rectangles *abcd* and *adeh* respectively. Mark points 3, 4, 4′, 3′, 7, 8, *i*, *j*, 2 and 4 on them as shown. An axis in FV and the two intersecting axes with a circle in SV represent a cylinder. The bottom portion of the object is rectangular block. The small curves at 7 and 8 represent the intersection of flat surface with a curved surface.
Refer Fig. 18.35(b).

1. Draw an isometric box *ABCDEFGH* such that *AB* = *ab*, *AD* = *ad* and *AH* = *ah*. Draw *x*-isoline *JI* such that *DJ* = *dj*. In rhombus *DJIE*, draw an ellipse 1–2–3–4–1 (ellipse1) by the four-centre method. The points *O*1, *D*, *O*2 and *I* will serve as the centres.
2. Shift *O*1 and *O*2 along *z*-isoline to *O*1′ and *O*2′ through the distance equal to the length of cylinder, i.e., 90 mm. Now, using *O*1′, *C*, *O*2′ and *K* as centres, draw an ellipse 1′–2′–3′–4′–1′ (ellipse 2). This ellipse represents the right end of the cylinder.
3. Join both the ellipses by common tangent lines *MN* and *PS*. Draw the centrelines 2–4, 4–4′ and 2–2′.
4. Mark points 5 and 6 on *AB* such that *A*–5 = *B*–6 = *a*–5 = 15 mm. Draw *y*-isolines 5–7 and 6–8 by taking their lengths from FV, i.e., 60 mm. The points 7 and 8 will lie on the centreline 4–4′.

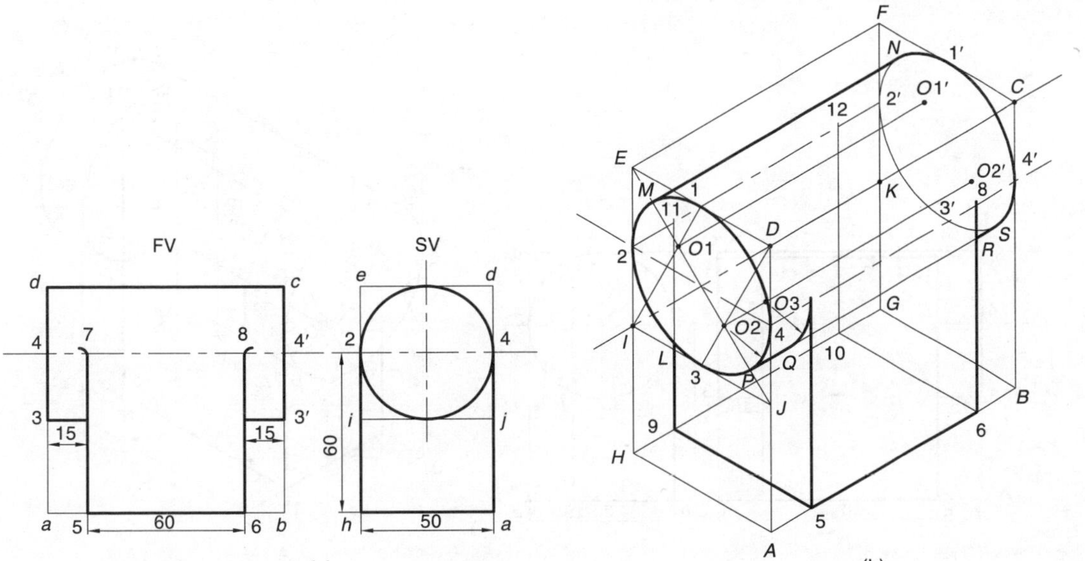

(a) (b)

Fig. 18.35

5. Draw *x*-isolines 5–9 and 6–10. Through 9 and 10, draw *y*-isolines 9–11 and 10–12 having lengths equal to 5–7 and 6–8. Note that the edges 6–10 and 10–12 are not visible and hence need not be drawn. These lines are drawn only for the sake of illustration. The line 9–11 will be seen partly, i.e., from 9 to *L*.
6. Draw an elliptical arc 7–*Q* parallel and equal to 4–*P*. This can be done by shifting the centre *O*2 to *O*3 along the *z*-isoline. The arc 7–*Q* has a radius equal to *O*2–3. Note that *PQ* is tangent to arc 7–*Q*. The arc 7–*Q* will be seen because it represents the curve of intersection of the cylinder with the rectangular block.

   The flat face 5–6–8–7 is tangent to the cylinder along 4–4′. Therefore the part of the edge *PS* from *Q* to *R* will not be visible.

Example 18.12 From the FV and SV of an object shown in Fig. 18.36(a), draw its isometric view.

Solution A line 15–*t* and a dashed line *t*–13′ is added in SV. In FV lines 7–13–14–8 are added. This clearly means that the width of the rectangular block is decreased from *ha* to *h*–15.

Refer Fig. 18.36(b).

1. Mark 15 on *AH* such that *A*–15 = *a*–15 = 15 mm. Through 15, draw *y*-isoline to meet the ellipse at *T* and 13′. From 13′, draw *z*-isoline 13′–14′ = length of cylinder.
2. Mark 13 and 14 on 13′–14′ by taking their distance from FV. Through 13 and 14, draw *y*-isolines to meet *x*-isolines from 5 and 6 at 15′ and 16′ respectively. Note that the new face 15′–16′–14–13 formed is cut across the cylinder and the block.
3. Draw an ellipse-arc 13–7 (ellipse 3) parallel and equal to 13′–4. This can be done by shifting centre *I* to *I*1 along *z*-isoline through distance 15 mm, i.e., *I*–*I*1 = 15 mm. Similarly, obtain another ellipse-arc 14–8–18 (ellipse 4) parallel and equal to 13′–4–*T*. The centres *I* and *O*2 may be shifted to *I*2 and *O*3 respectively through the distance 75 mm along *z*-isoline.

   The lines 15′–16′, 16′–14, 14–13 and 13–15′ represent newly formed edges of the object. The edges 5–6, 6–8 and 5–7 will not be there. Note that the edge 13–15′ is seen partly from 17–15′. Make all visible edges sufficiently thick.

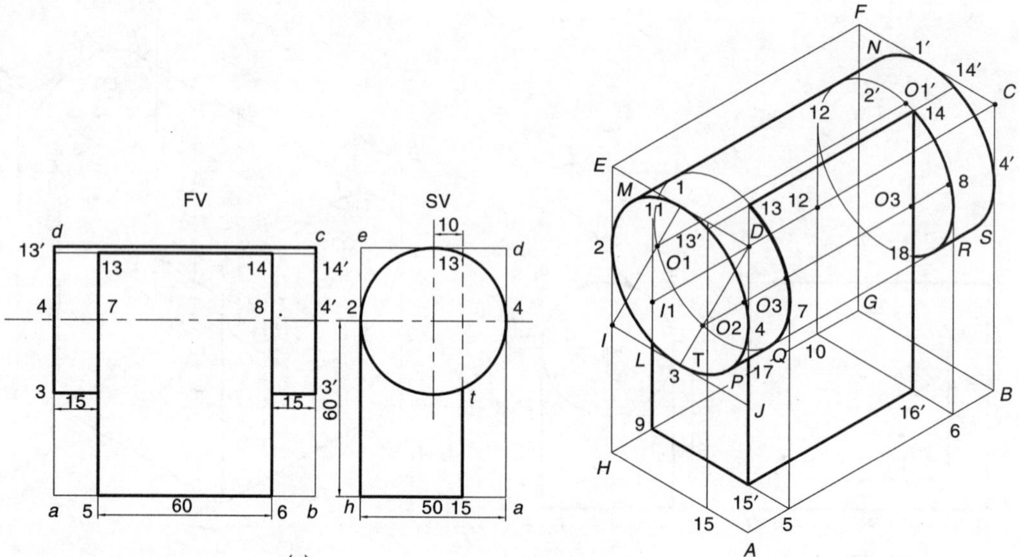

(a) (b)

Fig. 18.36

Example 18.13 From the FV and SV of an object shown in Fig. 18.37(a), draw its isometric view.

Solution A line *uv* is added in SV. The lines *v*–*v*1–17 and *v*3–*v*2–16 are added in FV. This clearly means that the top left and top right corners of the cylinder are removed.
Refer Fig. 18.37(b).

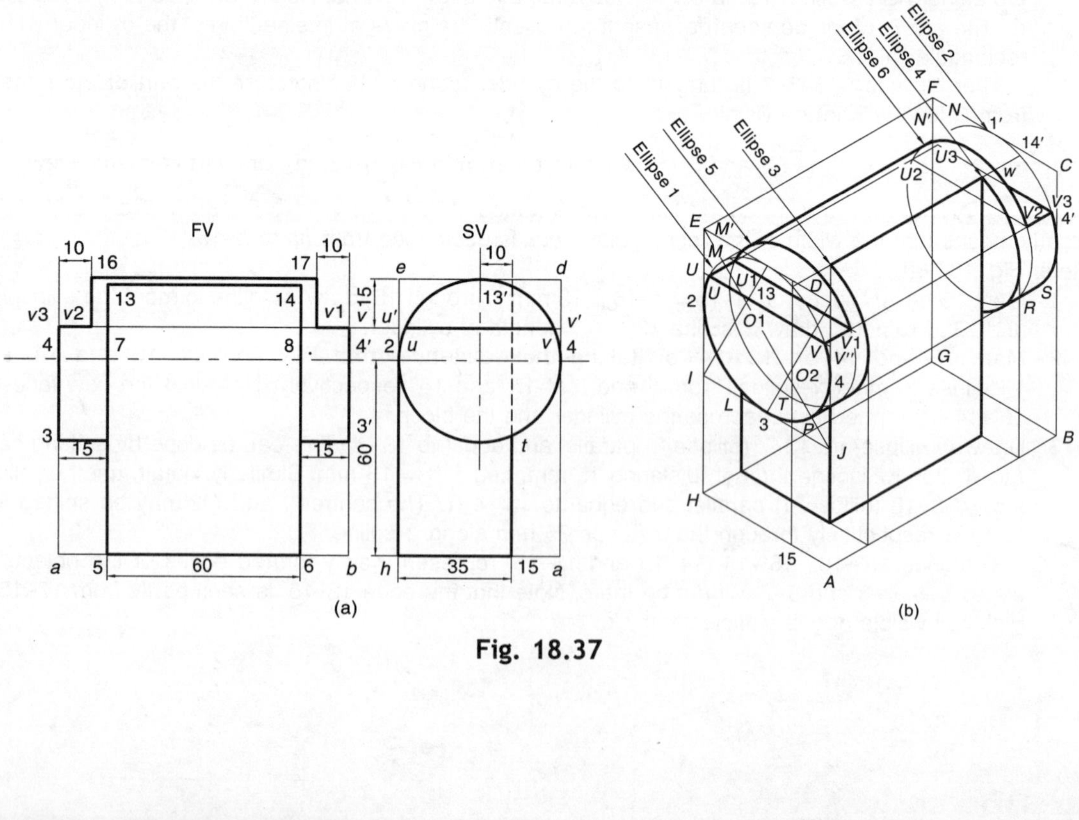

(a) (b)

Fig. 18.37

1. Mark V' and U' on DJ and EI respectively such that $DV' = EU' = dv' = 15$ mm. Join V'–U' intersecting ellipse 1 at V and U. VU represents the new edge formed on ellipse 1.
2. Draw z-isolines V–$V1$ and U–$U1$ each equal to v–$v1$. Join $V1$–$U1$. V–$V1$–$U1$–U represents the new isometric face formed. Now draw ellipse 5 passing through $V1$ and $U1$ as shown. For this, the centres of ellipse 1, i.e., $O1$, D, $O2$ and I may be shifted along respective z-isolines. The part of ellipse 5 above $U1$–$V1$ represent newly formed isometric face.

   Note that the part of ellipse 1 above UV and the part of ellipse 5 below $U1$–$V1$ do not represent the real edges and need not to be drawn.
3. The top right corner of the cylinder is also removed. It will also show a rectangular face $V2$–$V3$–$U3$–$U2$ and an elliptical face. To draw this, draw z-isoline V–$V3$ = U–$U3$ = v–$v3$ = 90 mm. Mark $V2$ and $U2$ such that $V3$–$V2$ = $U3$–$U2$ = $v3$–$v2$. Now draw ellipse 6 passing through $V2$–$U2$ by shifting the centres of ellipse 1 along z-isoline.

   Note that, only part of the ellipse 6 above $U2$–$V2$ will represent the real edge. A common tangent line $M'N'$ joining the ellipse 5 with the ellipse 6 will now represent the extreme visible generator of the cylinder. Obviously, MM' and NN' will not be visible as they are not the real edges. The part of edge $V3$–$U3$ from $V3$ to W will only be visible.

   Make all visible lines sufficiently thick.

Example 18.14 Figure 18.38(a) indicates the FV and SV of an object. Obtain its isometric view.

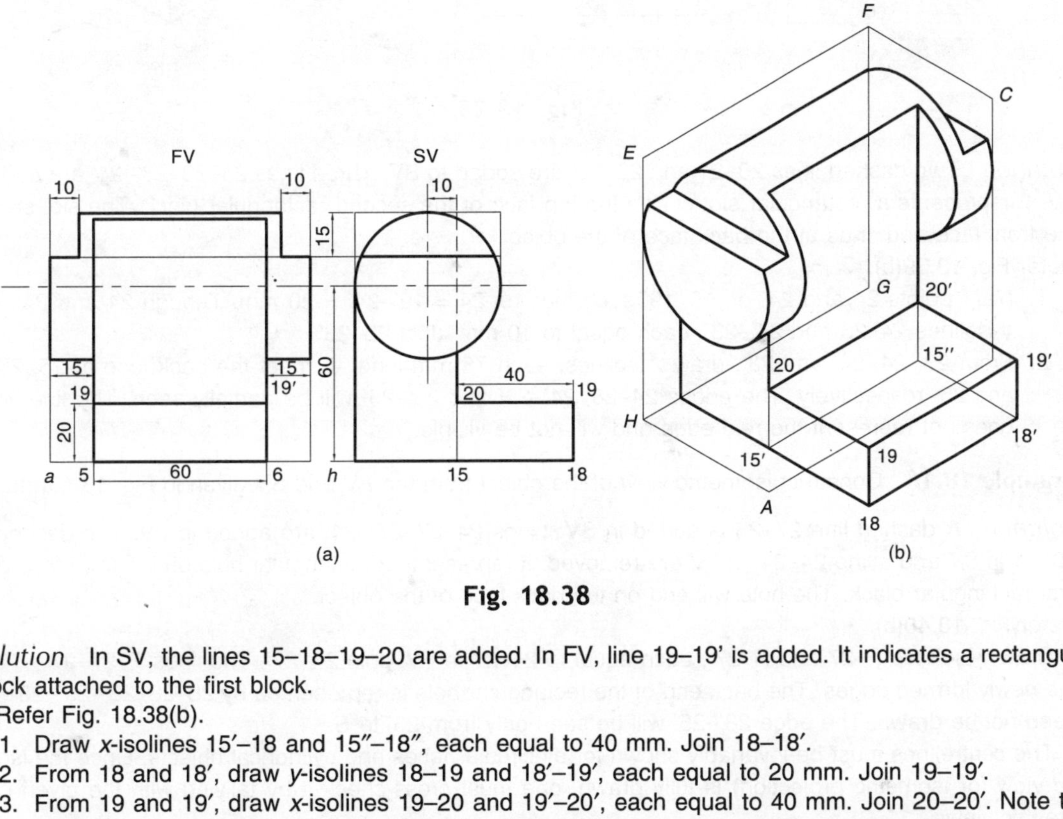

Fig. 18.38

Solution In SV, the lines 15–18–19–20 are added. In FV, line 19–19' is added. It indicates a rectangular block attached to the first block.

Refer Fig. 18.38(b).

1. Draw x-isolines 15′–18 and 15″–18″, each equal to 40 mm. Join 18–18′.
2. From 18 and 18′, draw y-isolines 18–19 and 18′–19′, each equal to 20 mm. Join 19–19′.
3. From 19 and 19′, draw x-isolines 19–20 and 19′–20′, each equal to 40 mm. Join 20–20′. Note that the edges 20–15′ and 20′–15″ will vanish since both the faces meeting at these edges are in the same plane. Same is the case of edge 15′–15″. The edge 15″–18′ will not be visible.

Example 18.15 Obtain isometric view of the object whose FV and SV are given in Fig. 18.39(a).

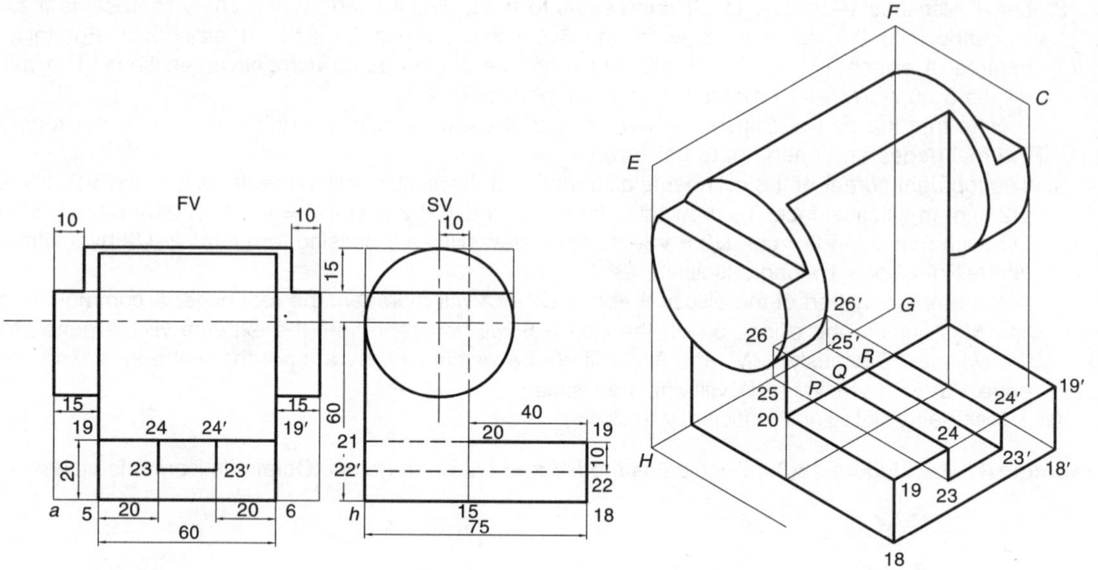

(a) (b)

Fig. 18.39

Solution Two dashed lines 20–21 and 22–22′ are added to SV. Three lines 24–23–23′–24′ are added to FV. It represents a rectangular slot cut on the top face of the second rectangular block. The slot starts at the front face and ends at the back face of the object.

Refer Fig. 18.39(b).

1. Mark points 24 and 24′ on 19–19′ such that 19–24 = 19′–24′ = 20 mm. Though 24 and 24′, draw *y*-isolines 24–23 and 24′–23′, each equal to 10 mm. Join 23–23′.
2. From 23, 24, 24′ and 23′, draw *x*-isolines, each 75 mm long, to meet the back face at 25, 26, 26′ and 25′ respectively. The edges 24–26, 24′–26′ and 23′–25′ will be partially seen. The line 24–24′ does not represent the real edge and will not be visible.

Example 18.16 Construct isometric view of the object from the FV and SV given in Fig. 18.40(a).

Solution A dashed line 27–28 is added in SV. Lines 24–27–27′–24′ are added in FV. The dashed line 20–21 in SV and a line 24–24′ in FV are removed. It represents a rectangular hole on the front face of the first rectangular block. The hole will end on the back face of the object.

Refer Fig. 18.40(b).

Draw *y*-isolines *P*–27 and *R*–27′, each equal to 24–27 in FV. Join 27–27′. The lines *P*–27–27′–*R* show the newly formed edges. The back end of the rectangular hole is represented by 25–28–28′–25′–25 which need not be drawn. The edge 23′–25′ will be seen only from 23′ to *S*.

The centrelines must be invariably shown for all circular faces and cylindrical objects. Once the isometric view (or isometric projection) is fully drawn, one must cross-check it by tallying with the given orthographic views.

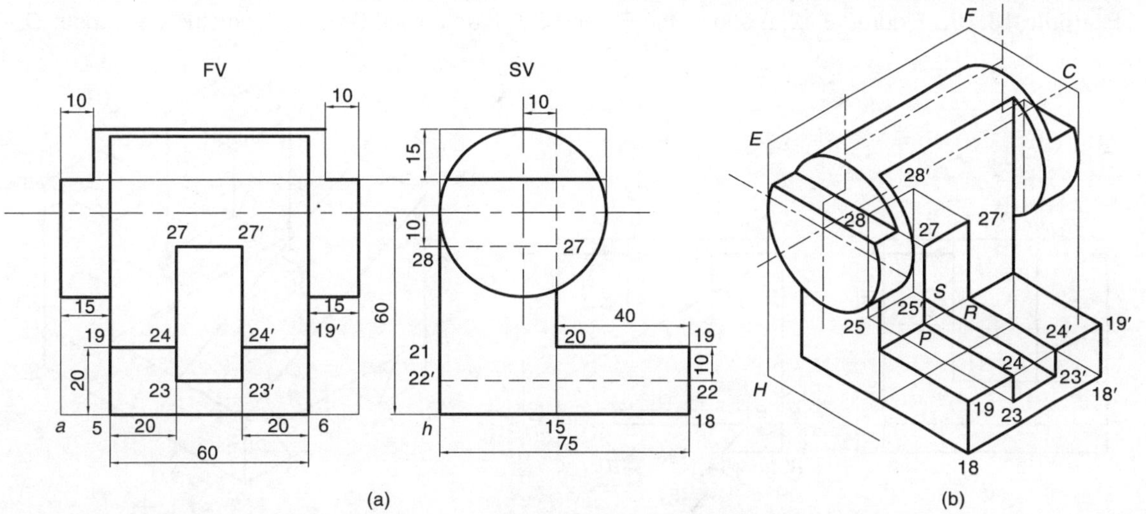

Fig. 18.40

Example 18.17 The TV and FV of an object are shown in Fig. 18.41(a). Draw its isometric projection about the origin *O*.

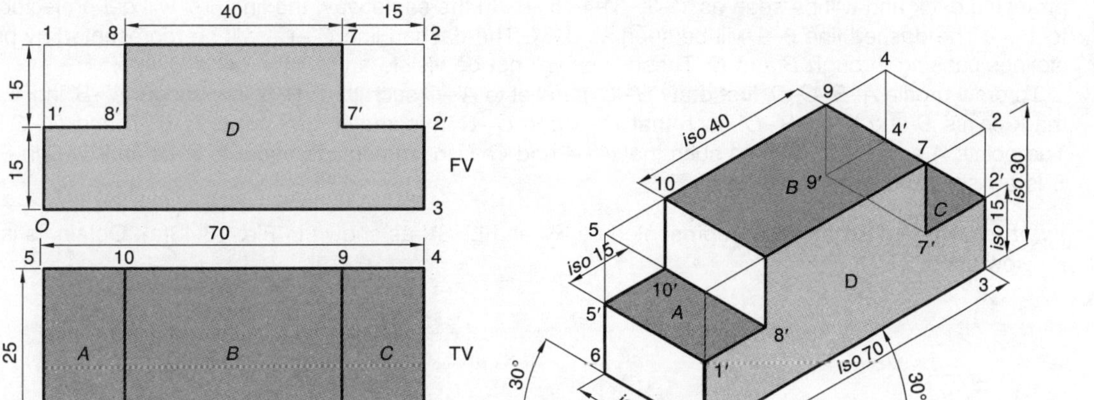

Fig. 18.41

Solution In this example, we have to draw the isometric projection. Therefore, isometric scale must be used to convert dimensions into isometric dimensions. Refer Fig. 18.41(b). Mark points 1, 2, 3, 1′, 8′, 8, 7 and 7′ in FV and 1, 2, 4, 5, 8, 7, 9 and 10 in TV.

Obtain the isometric block with isometric sides *O*–1, *O*–3 and *O*–6 as shown. The FV (i.e., face *D*) is drawn in isometric as *O*–1′–8′–8–7–7′–2′–3–*O* and TV (i.e., faces *A*, *B* and *C*) is drawn as 1–8–7–2–4–9–10–5–1. It should be noted that the faces *A* and *C* are at a lower level than face *B*, and hence, in isometric, the lines 1–5 and 2–4 are drawn as 1′–5′ and 2′–4′ respectively to obtain face 1′–8′–10′–5′ and face 7′–2′–4′–9′. The lines 7′–9′, 9–9′ and 9′–4′ need not to be shown. In Fig. 18.44(b), dimensions are shown only for the sake of illustration.

Example 18.18 Figure 18.42(a) shows the FV and SV of an object. Draw its isometric view about *O*.

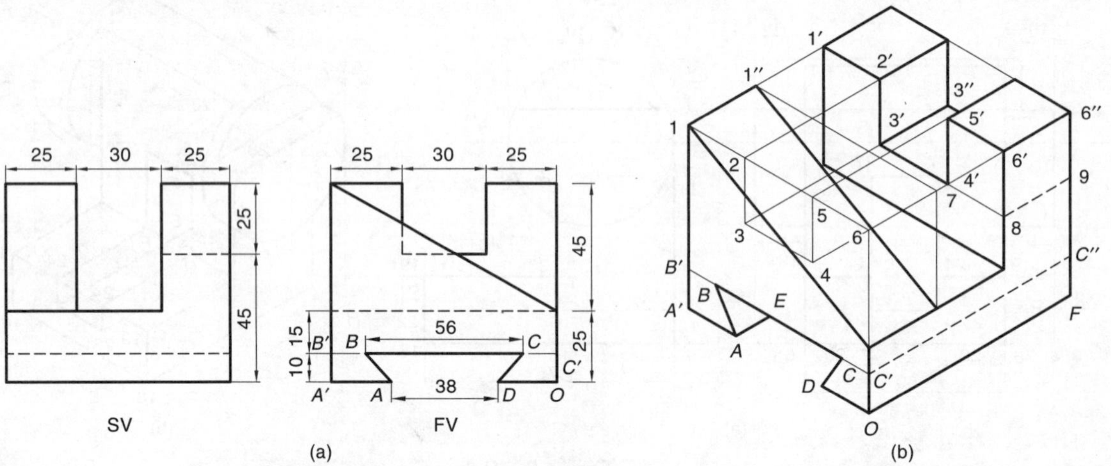

Fig. 18.42

Solution Refer Fig. 18.42(b). First, the isometric block is drawn. The FV and SV are drawn on the front and right face of the block, i.e., *O*–6–1–*A*′ and *O*–6–6″–*F* respectively. The profile 1–2–3–4–5–6 will get projected back and will be seen as 1′–2′–3′–4′–5′–6′. In the same way, the line 6–7 will get projected back to 1–1″. The dashed line 8–9 will be seen as 3–3″. The dashed line *C*′–*C*″ will be represented by parallel isolines passing through *B* and *C*. These lines will not be visible and hence not shown.

To draw profile *A*–*B*–*C*–*D*, first draw *B*′–*C*′ parallel to *A*′–*O* such that *A*′–*B*′ is same as *A*′–*B*′ in FV. Now, mark points *B* and *C* on *B*′–*C*′ such that *B*′–*B* and *C*′–*C* in isometric are same as *B*′–*B* and *C*′–*C* in FV. The points *A* and *D* are marked such that *A*′–*A* and *O*–*D* in isometric is equal to *A*′–*A* and *O*–*D* in FV. *A*–*E* is an isometric line parallel to *O*–*F*.

Example 18.19 An object is represented by FV and LHSV as shown in Fig. 18.43(a). Obtain its isometric view about *O*.

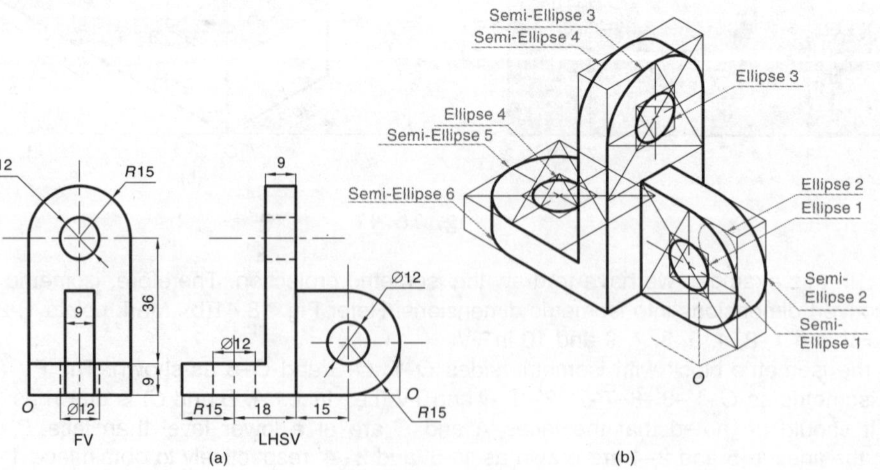

Fig. 18.43

Solution The isometric view of the object is shown in Fig. 18.43(b). There are three mutually perpendicular plates having semicircular ends. Each plate has a hole. The semicircular faces will be seen as semi-elliptical. The semi-ellipse 1 is drawn by the four-centre method. To draw the semi-ellipse 2, shift the two centres of the semi-ellipse 1 through the appropriate distances (i.e., 9 mm) along the *z*-isoline. In the same way, the semi-ellipse 4 can be drawn by shifting the two centres of the semi-ellipse 3. Similarly, obtain the semi-ellipse 6 from the semi-ellipse 5. The three circular holes, which are seen as ellipses, are drawn by the four-centre method. The ellipse 2 can be obtained by shifting the four centres of the ellipse 1 through distance = 9 mm along the *z*-isoline. The ellipse 2 is completely invisible.

Example 18.20 Figure 18.44(a) shows FV of an object symmetrical about its vertical axis. Draw its isometric view about *O*.

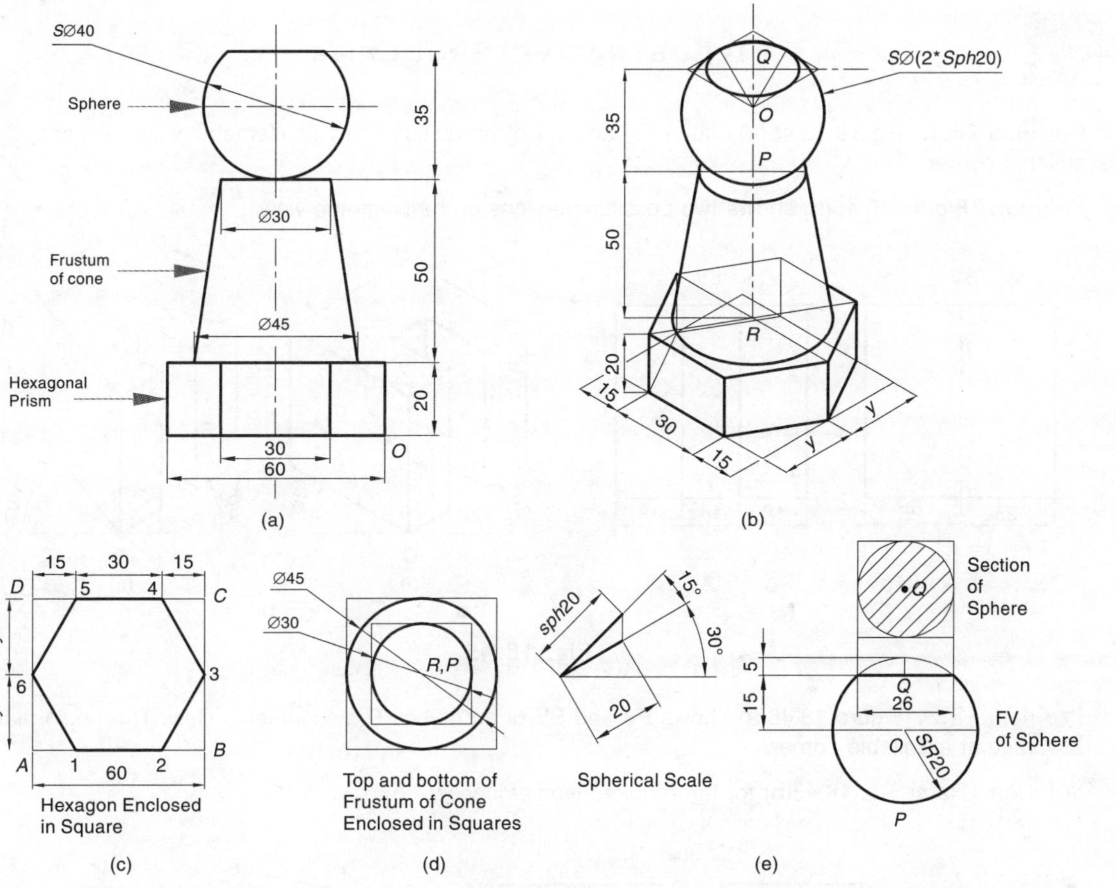

Fig. 18.44

Solution The object is a combination of a hexagonal prism, a frustum of a cone and a flattened sphere. As the FV alone is sufficient to fully describe the shape of the object, TV (or SV) is not given.

The isometric view is shown in Fig. 18.44(b). First, the TVs of the hexagonal prism and the frustum are drawn in Fig. 18.44(c) and (d) respectively. The isometric of the hexagon is drawn by enclosing it inside a rectangle as already mentioned. To obtain the isometric of the frustum, its top face and bottom face are enclosed in squares. Then two ellipses, one larger for bottom face and another smaller for top face, are drawn by the four-centre method. These two ellipses are joined together by two common tangent lines as shown in Fig. 18.44(b). The centre of the bottom face of the frustum and the centre of the top face of the prism are represented by point *R*. The sphere rests centrally on the top face of the frustum. Point *P* is the point of contact of the sphere and frustum. It is located at the centre of the top face of the frustum, Fig. 18.44(b). Through *P*, the vertical line *PO* of the length equal to the actual radius of the sphere (= 20 mm), is drawn. Point *O* represents the centre of the sphere. To draw the sphere in isometric, draw a circle of radius equal to its spherical radius (= *sph*20 mm) with point *O* as a centre.

The section of the flattened end of the sphere, which is a circle with centre *Q*, is shown in Fig. 18.44(e). It is drawn as an ellipse having the centre point at *Q* by the four-centre method. For this purpose, the section of the sphere is enclosed in a square, Fig. 18.44(e). The distance *OQ* is equal to the actual distance in the sphere, i.e., 15 mm.

Illustrative Problems

Problem 18.1 Figure 18.45(a) shows FV and SV of an object. Draw its isometric view. Assume *O* at a suitable corner.

Solution Figure 18.45(b) shows two possible versions of the isometric view.

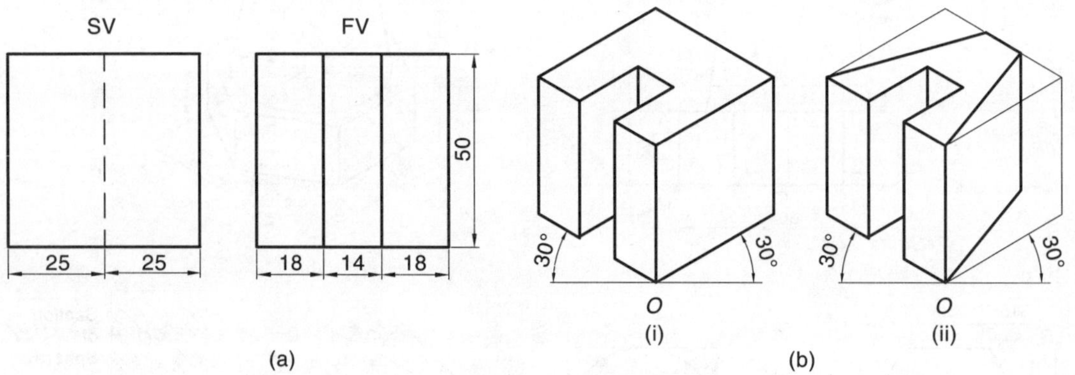

Fig. 18.45

Problem 18.2 Figure 18.46(a) shows FV and SV of an object. Draw isometric view. The origin may be assumed at a suitable corner.

Solution Refer Fig. 18.46(b) for the required isometric view.

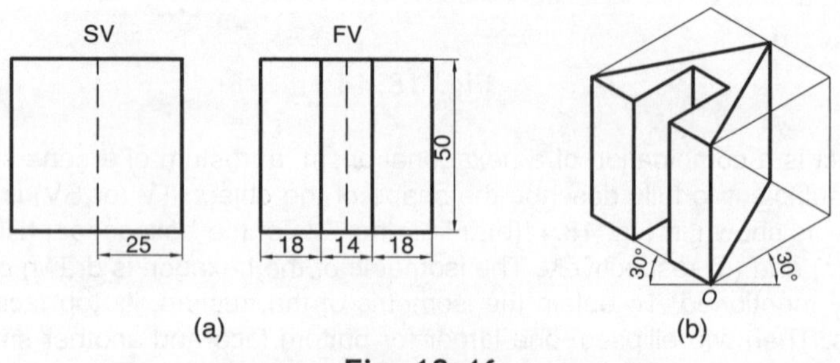

Fig. 18.46

Problem 18.3 Figure 18.47(a) shows the two views of an object. Draw the isometric view assuming origin at a suitable corner.

Solution The isometric view is shown in Fig. 18.47(b).

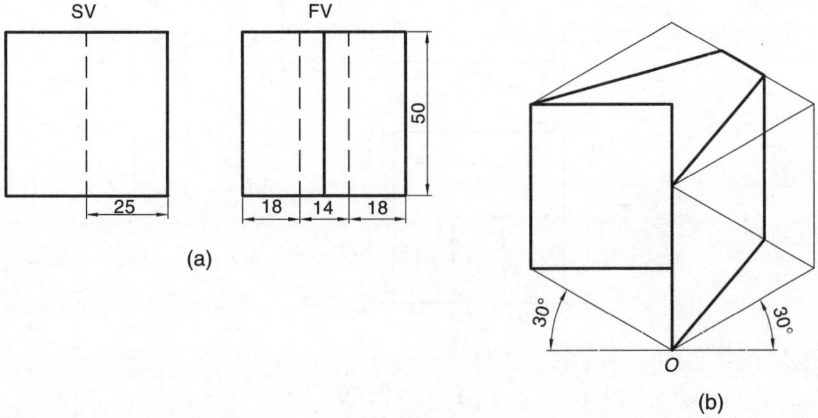

Fig. 18.47

Note: Observe the difference between FVs in Problems 18.2 and 18.3 and the corresponding isometric views.

Problem 18.4 FV and SV of an object are shown in Fig. 18.48(a). Draw the isometric view assuming *O* at suitable corner.

Solution Refer Fig. 18.48(b) for isometric view.

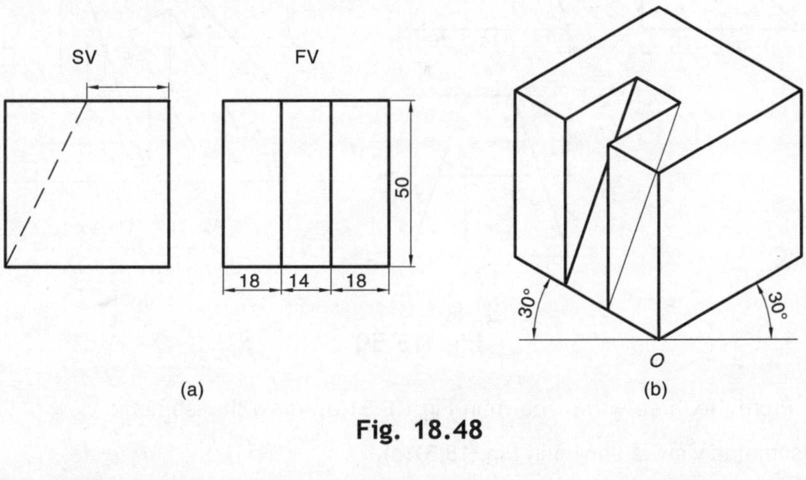

Fig. 18.48

Problem 18.5 Figure 18.49(a) shows FV, TV and SV of an object. Draw the isometric view.

Solution The required isometric view is shown in Fig. 18.49(b).

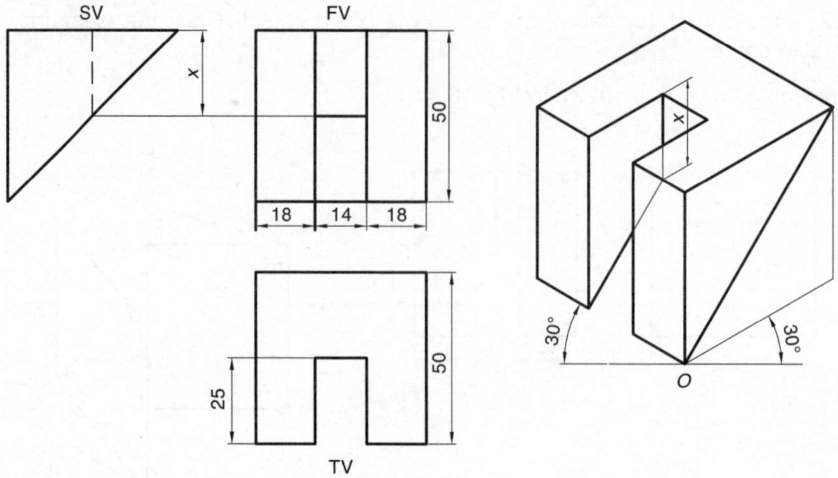

(a) (b)

Fig. 18.49

Problem 18.6 Figure 18.50(a) shows FV, TV and SV of an object. Draw the isometric view.

Solution Refer 18.50(b). Note how points *B*, *C*, *D*, *E* and *F* are marked in isometric view.

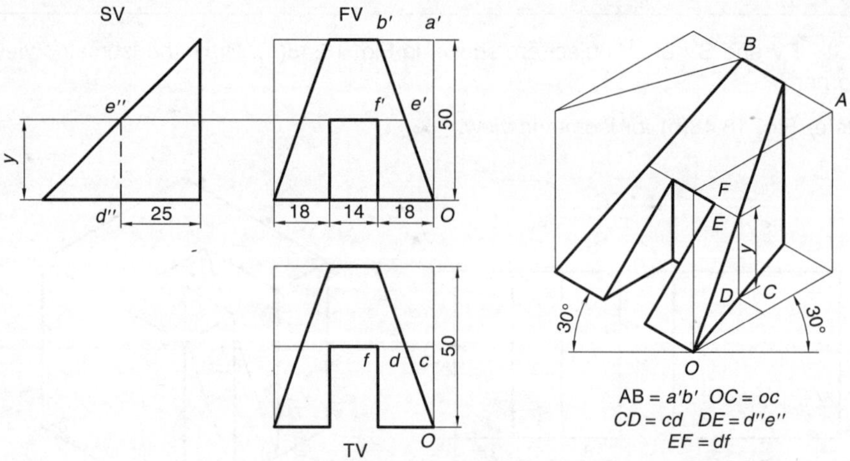

(a) (b)

Fig. 18.50

Problem 18.7 From the three views shown in Fig. 18.51(a), draw the isometric view of the object.

Solution The isometric view is shown in Fig. 18.51(b).

Problem 18.8 Draw the isometric view of an object, the three views of which are shown in Fig. 18.52(a). Assume the origin *O* at a suitable location.

Solution See Fig. 18.52(b) for the isometric view.

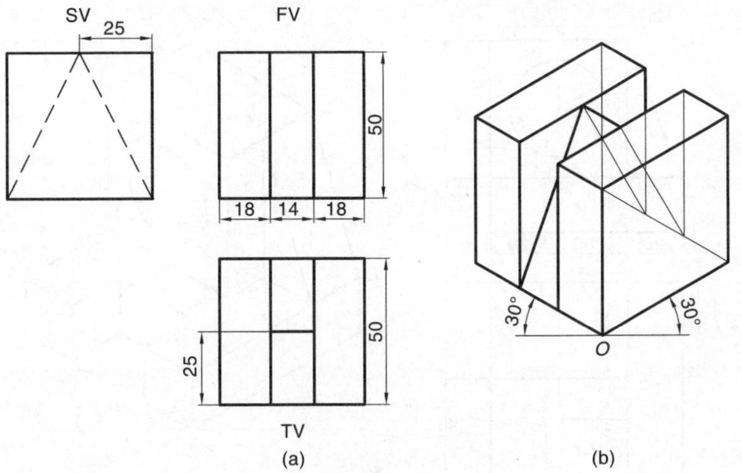

Fig. 18.51

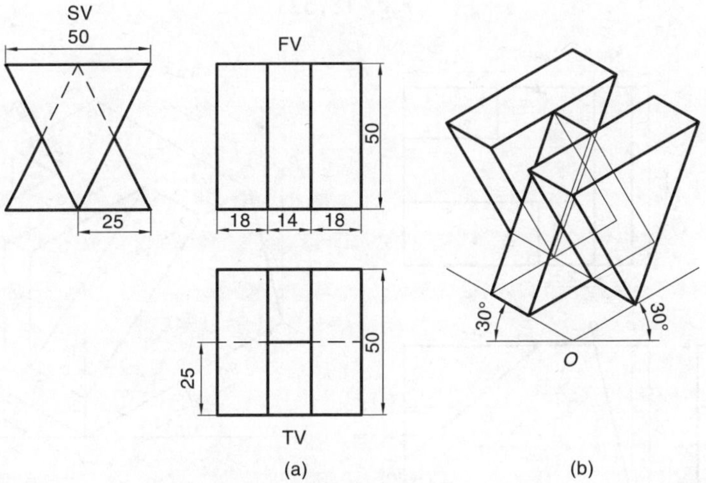

Fig. 18.52

Problem 18.9 Draw the isometric view from the orthographic projections shown in Fig. 18.53(a).

Solution Refer Fig. 18.53(b). Note how non-isolines *AB* and *CD* are drawn.

Problem 18.10 From the three views of the object shown in Fig. 18.54(a), draw its isometric view about *O*.

Solution The isometric view is shown in Fig. 18.54(b). The dimensions are shown only for the sake of understanding.

Problem 18.11 Draw the isometric projection of the object shown in Fig. 18.55(a).

Solution The isometric projection is shown in Fig. 18.55(b). As it is an isometric projection, the isometric scale should be used.

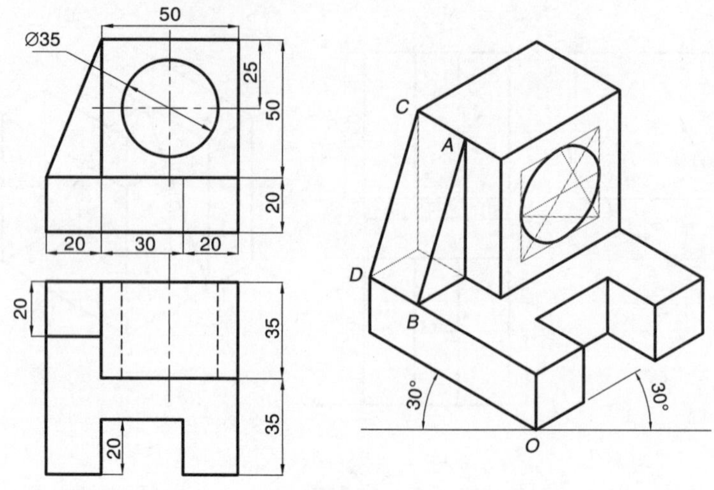

(a) (b)

Fig. 18.53

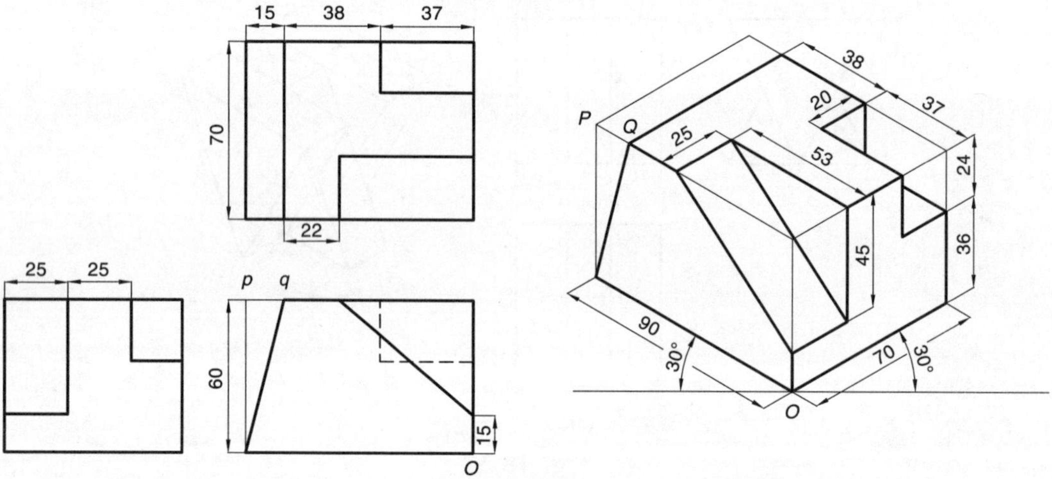

Fig. 18.54

Problem 18.12 Figure 18.56(a) shows the FV and TV of an object. Draw the isometric projection.

Solution Refer Fig. 18.56(b) for the required isometric projection. Note carefully how the edges *CD*, *GH*, *LM*, *CL*, etc., are drawn.

Problem 18.13 Draw the isometric view of the GATE LAMP shown in Fig. 18.57(a).

Solution The gate lamp consists of frustums of two square pyramids, a circular disc and a sphere. The isometric view of this assembly is shown in Fig. 18.57(b). Carefully observe how the base is drawn by locating the origin *O*. A spherical scale shall be used to draw the sphere. The point of contact of sphere *P* with the disc is located at the centre of the top face of the disc. The length *PC* is then equal to 20 mm, the actual radius of the sphere. With point *C* as a centre, a circle of radius equal to *sph* 20 is drawn.

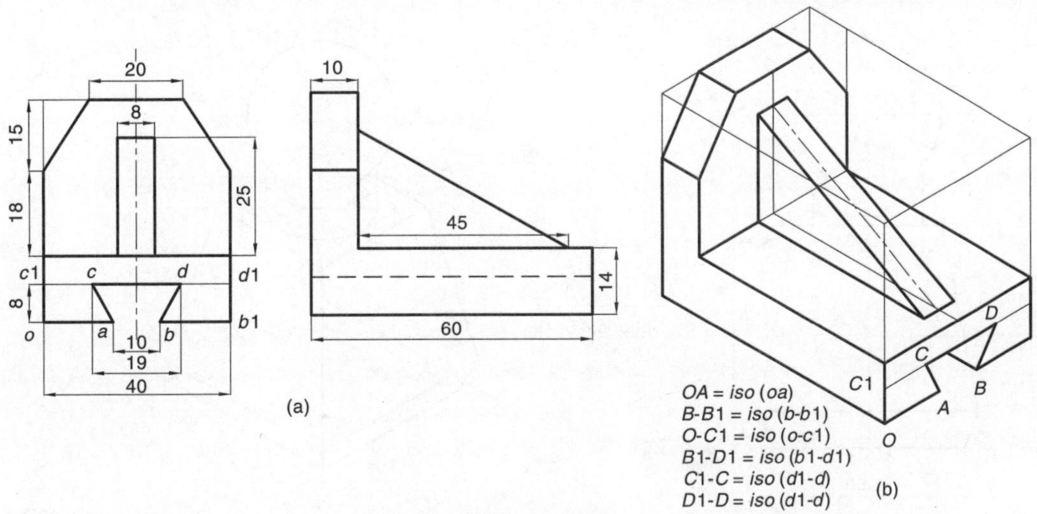

Fig. 18.55

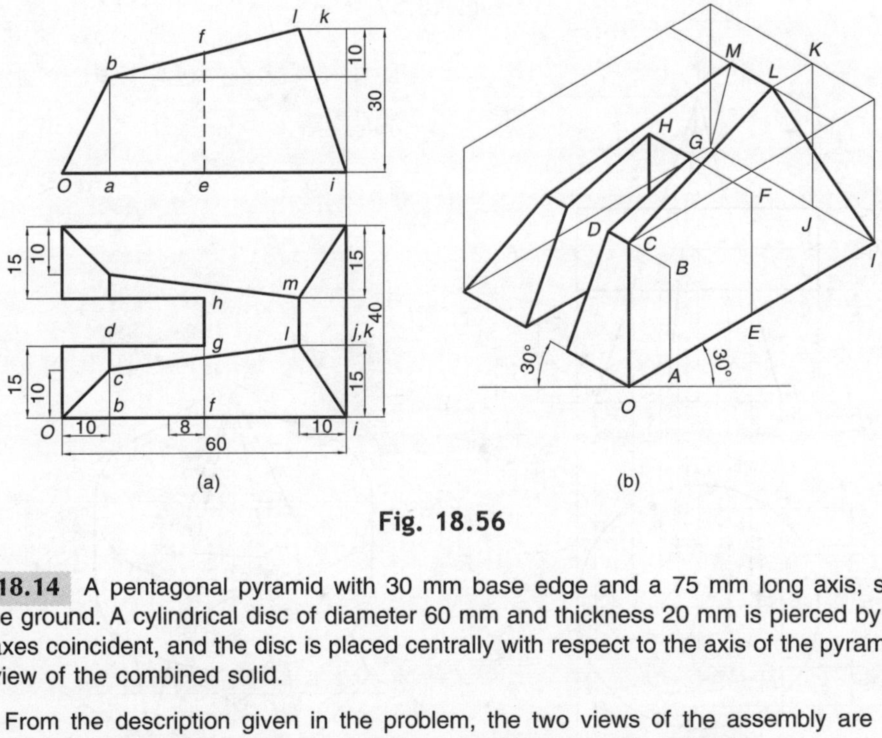

Fig. 18.56

Problem 18.14 A pentagonal pyramid with 30 mm base edge and a 75 mm long axis, stands on its base on the ground. A cylindrical disc of diameter 60 mm and thickness 20 mm is pierced by the pyramid with their axes coincident, and the disc is placed centrally with respect to the axis of the pyramid. Draw the isometric view of the combined solid.

Solution From the description given in the problem, the two views of the assembly are drawn as in Fig. 18.58(a). The required isometric view is then constructed as in Fig. 18.58(b).

Problem 18.15 From the two views shown in Fig. 18.59(a), draw the isometric view.

Solution Refer Fig. 18.59(b). Observe carefully how non-isometric face bounded by the curve *A–C–E–D–B* is drawn. Also note how points *M* and *N* are located.

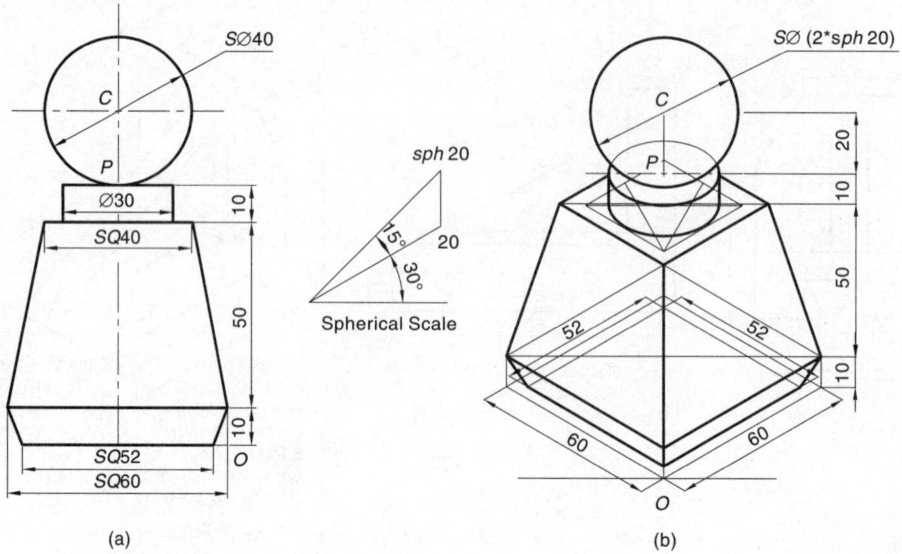

Fig. 18.57

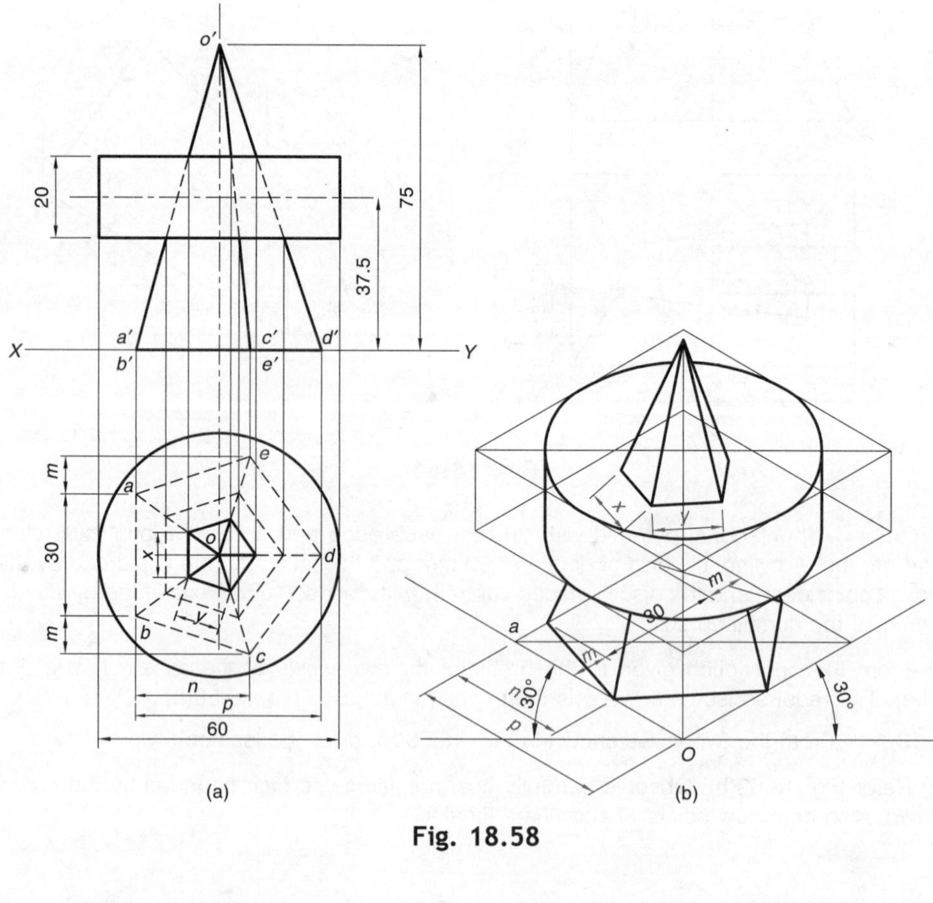

Fig. 18.58

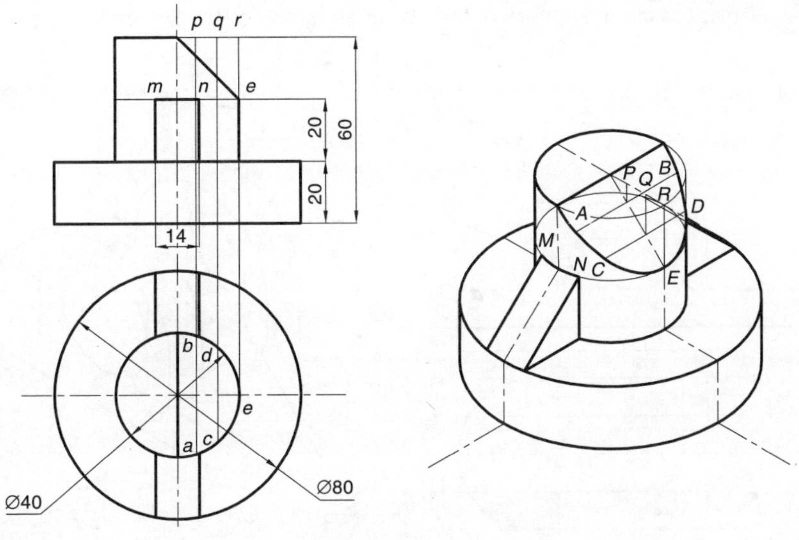

(a) (b)

Fig. 18.59

Problem 18.16 Figure 18.60(a) shows FV and TV of an object. Draw the isometric view that will show maximum details of the object.

Solution Refer Fig. 18.60(b) for the isometric view. Note, how edges of the internal hole are located by marking points 1, 2, 3, etc.

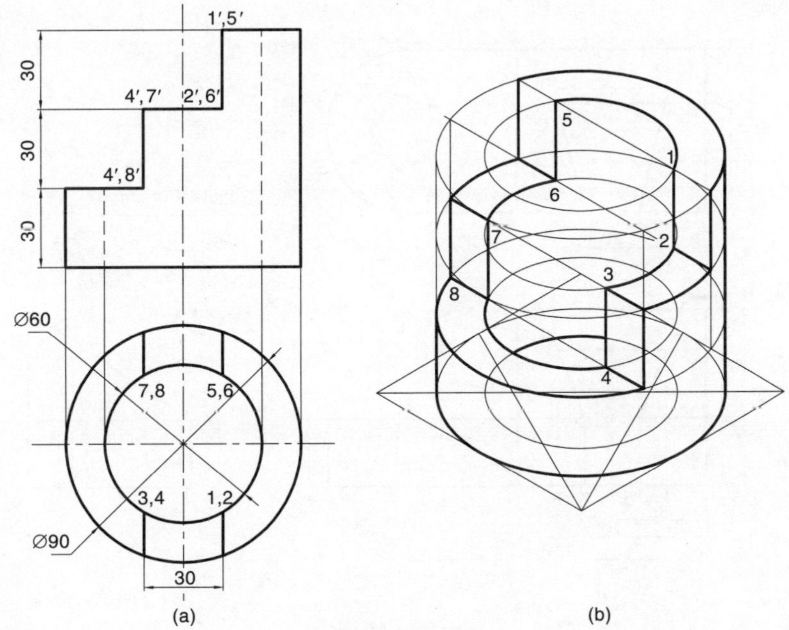

(a) (b)

Fig. 18.60

Problem 18.17 Draw the isometric view of the object about the origin *O* from the two views presented in Fig. 18.61(a).

Solution Refer Fig. 18.61(b). All the ellipses are drawn by off-setting the centres of first ellipse.

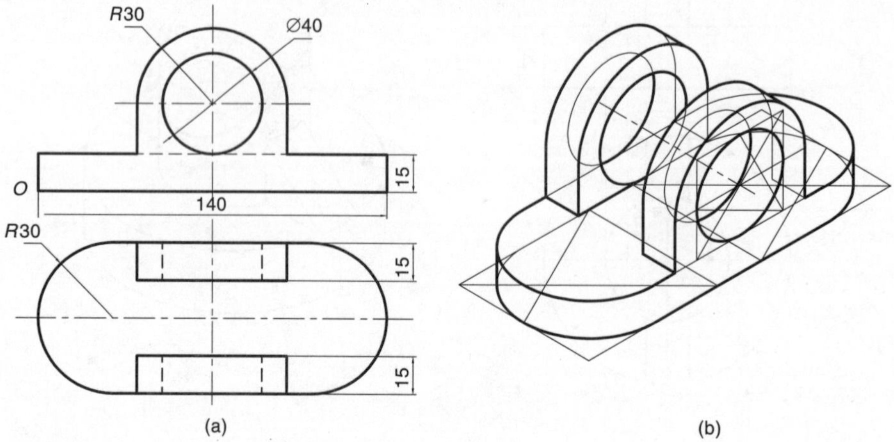

Fig. 18.61

Problem 18.18 Figure 18.62(a) shows the orthographic views of an object. Draw its isometric view about *O*.

Solution See Fig. 18.62(b) for the isometric view. The pentagon must be located properly as shown. The non-isolines *BC*, *EF*, *HI* and *GJ* should be drawn as shown.

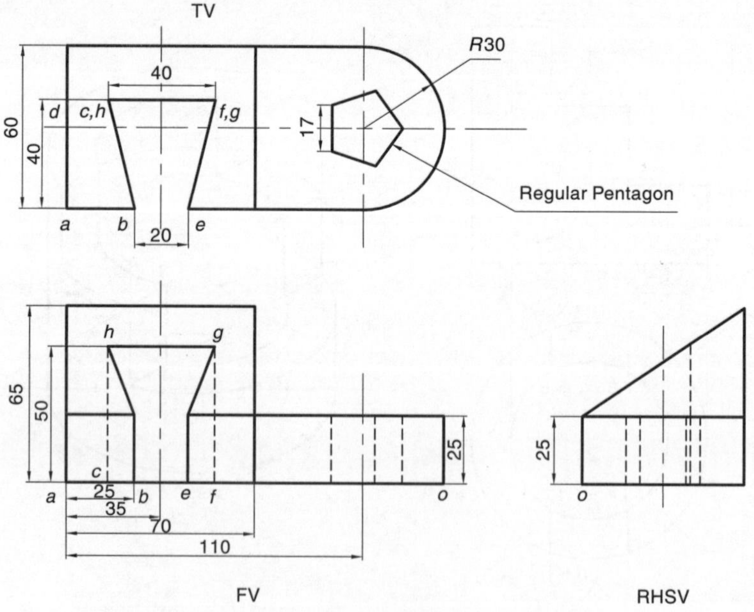

Fig. 18.62

Problem 18.19 Figure 18.63(a) shows FV and TV of an object. Draw its isometric view assuming *O* at a suitable location.

Solution The isometric view is shown in Fig. 18.63(b).

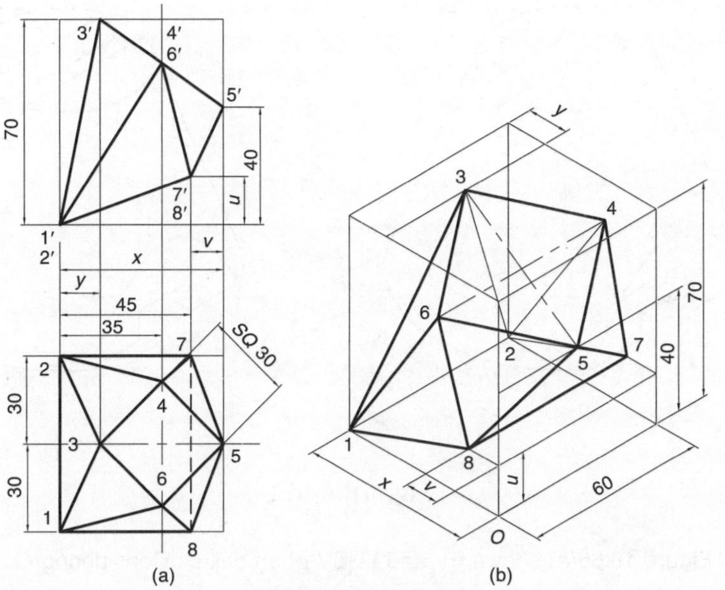

Fig. 18.63

Problem 18.20 Figure 18.64(a) shows FV and the TV of an object in the third-angle method of projection. Draw its isometric view assuming *O* at a suitable location.

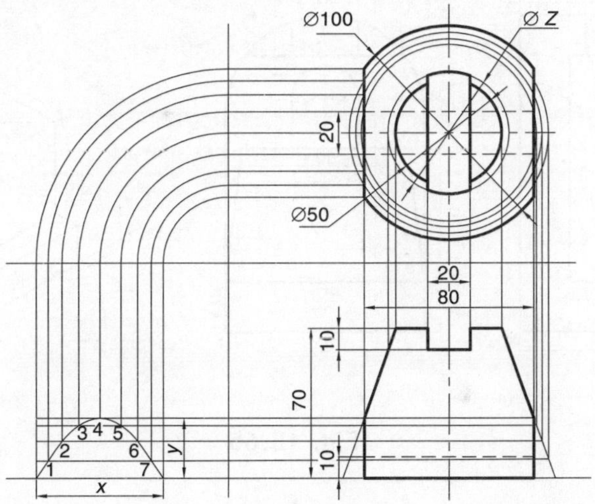

Fig. 18.64(a)

Solution Figure 18.64(b)-(i) shows the constructional details. Figure 18.64(b)-(ii) shows the isometric view without constructional details.

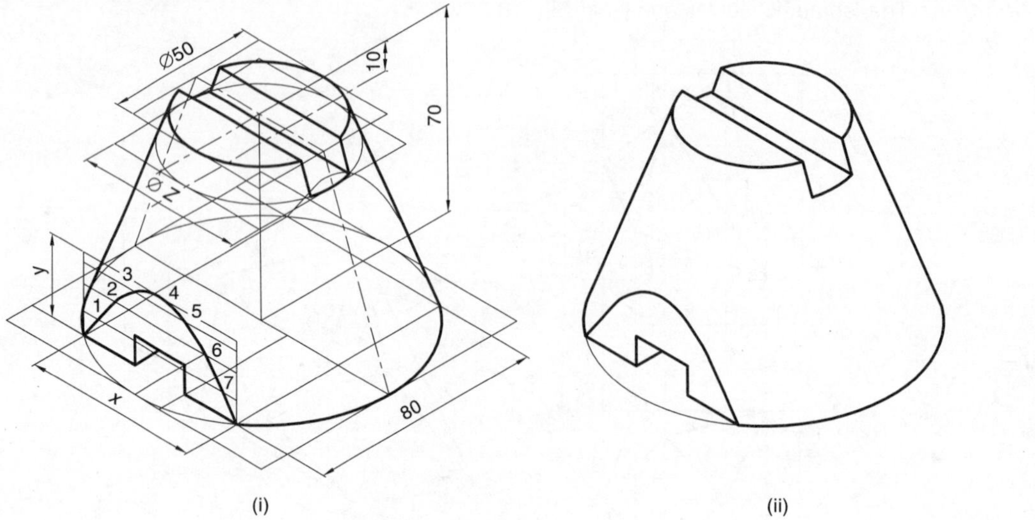

Fig. 18.64(b)

Problem 18.21 Figure 18.65(a) shows FV and LHSV of an object. Considering *O* as the origin, draw its isometric view.

Solution The isometric view is shown in Fig. 18.65(b).

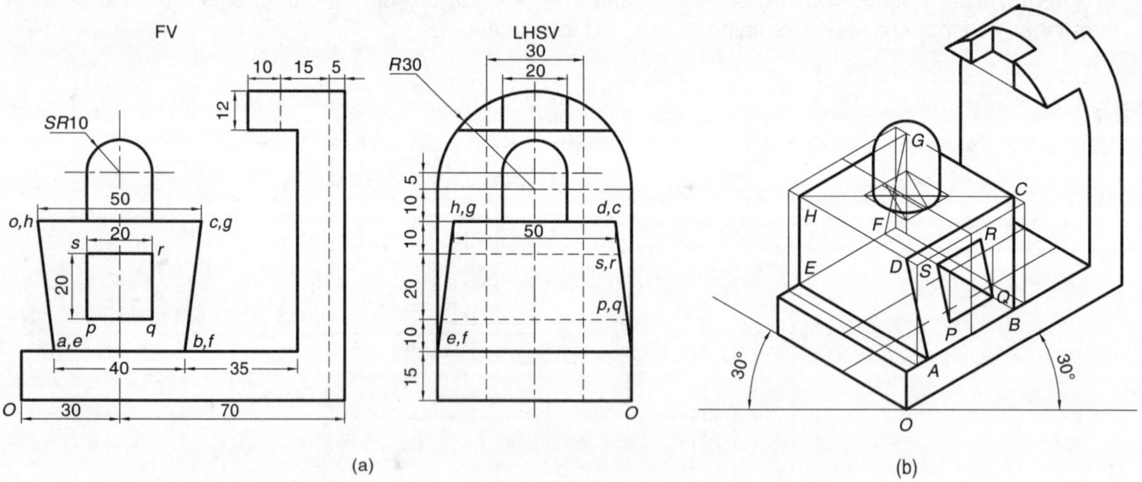

Fig. 18.65

REVIEW QUESTIONS

1. Draw the isometric projection of the object shown in Fig. 18RQ.1.

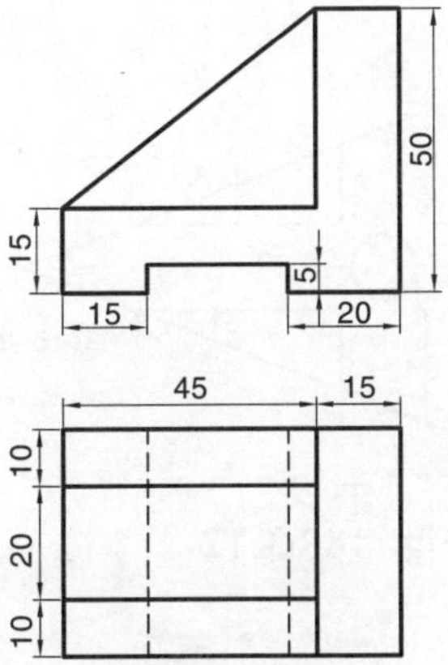

Fig. 18RQ.1

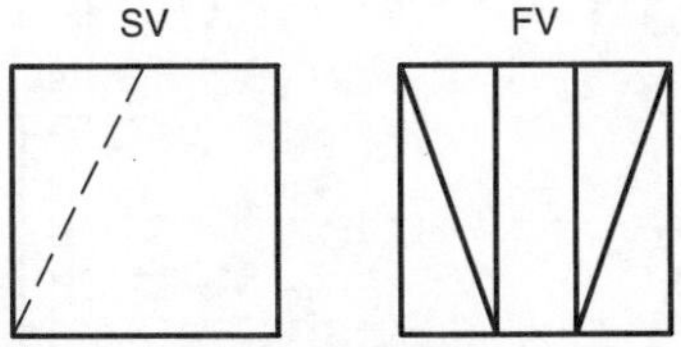

Fig. 18RQ.2

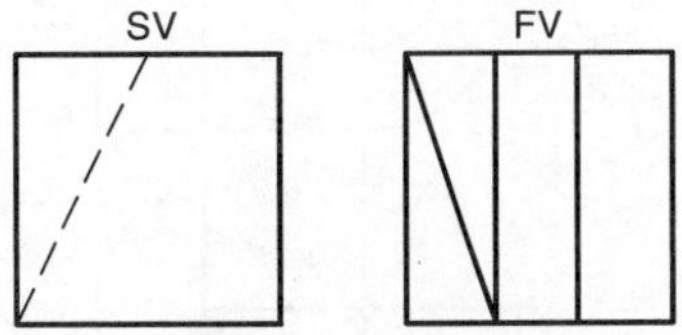

Fig. 18RQ.3

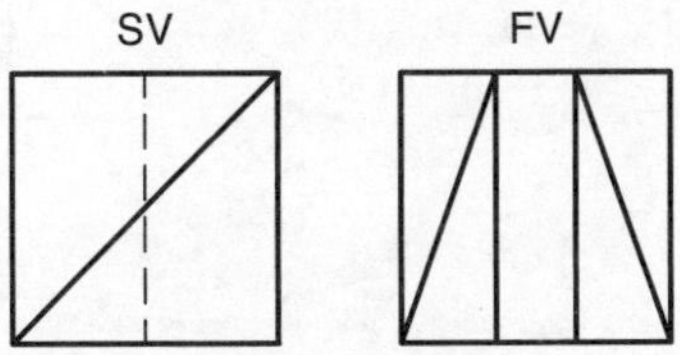

Fig. 18RQ.4

2. Figure 18RQ.2 to 18RQ.4 show the FVs and SVs of a cube 50 mm side cut in different ways. Obtain the corresponding isometric views.
3. Figure 18RQ.5 to 18RQ.9 show, in the first angle method of projection, the FVs and TVs of a cube of 50 mm side, cut in different ways. Obtain the isometric projections.

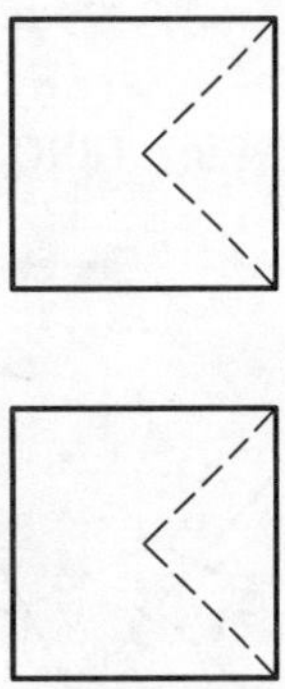

Fig. 18RQ.5

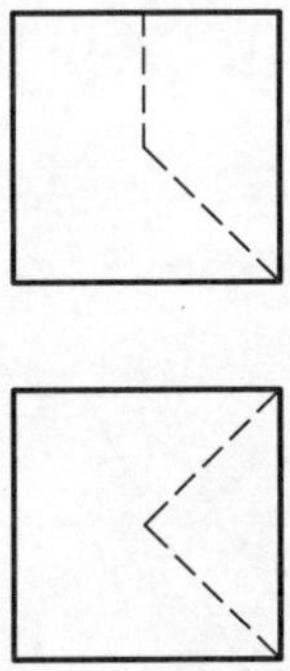

Fig. 18RQ.6

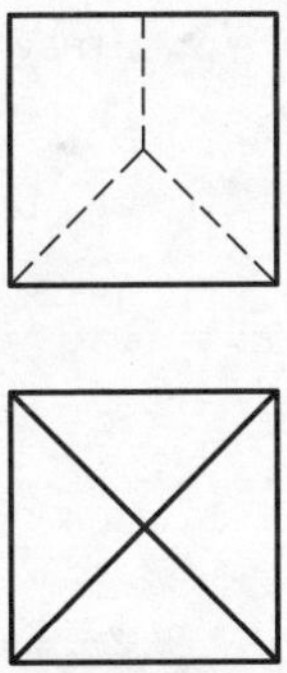

Fig. 18RQ.7

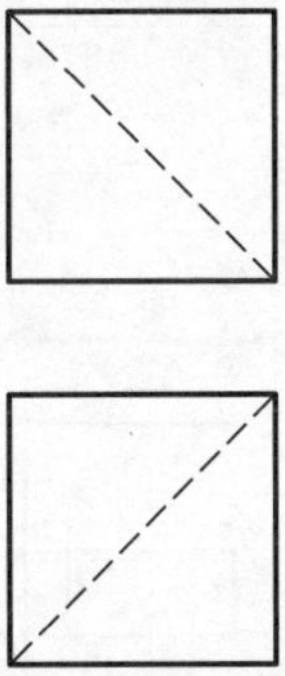

Fig. 18RQ.8

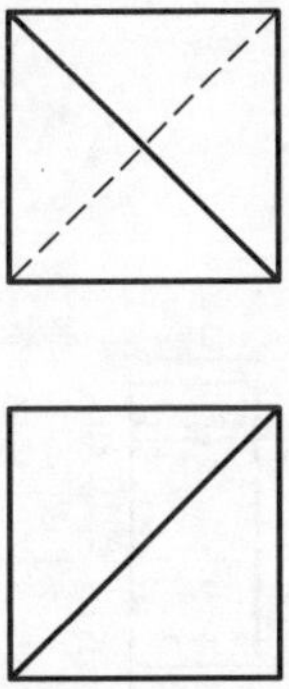

Fig. 18RQ.9

4. From the FVs and TVs (drawn in the first-angle method of projection) of the objects shown in Fig. 18RQ.10 to 18RQ.12, obtain their isometric views.
5. Figure 18RQ.13 to 18RQ.15 show the FVs and SVs of the objects. Draw their isometric views.

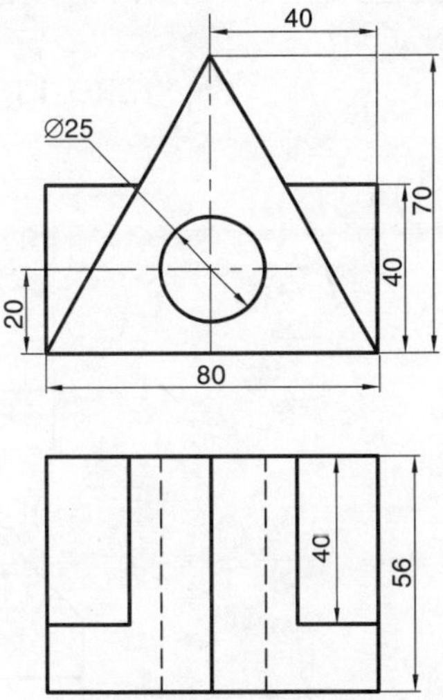

Fig. 18RQ.10

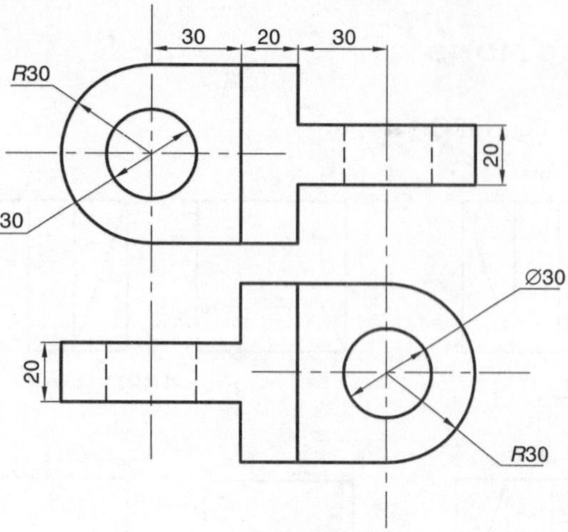

Fig. 18RQ.11

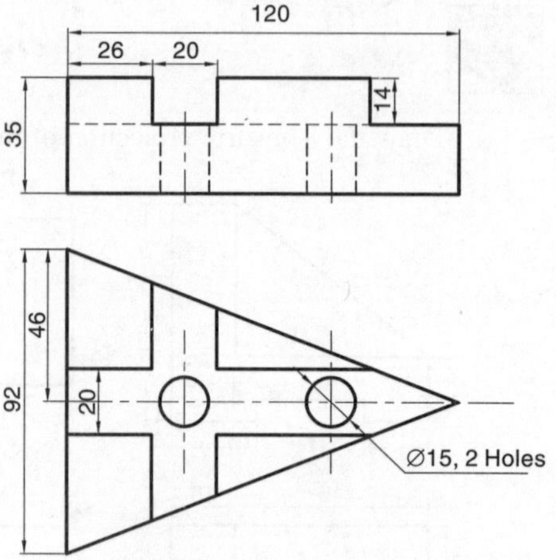

Fig. 18RQ.12

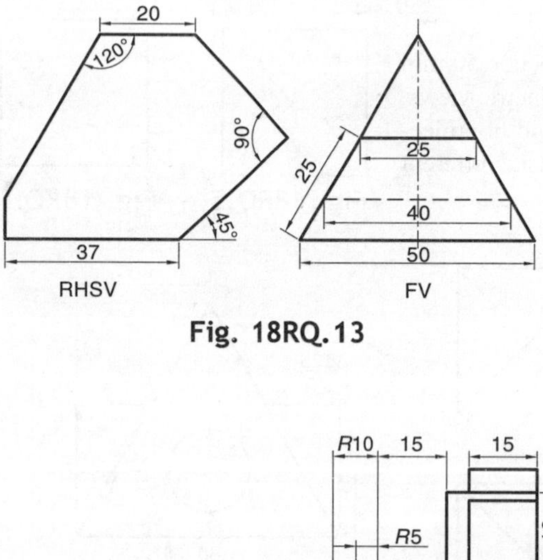

Fig. 18RQ.13

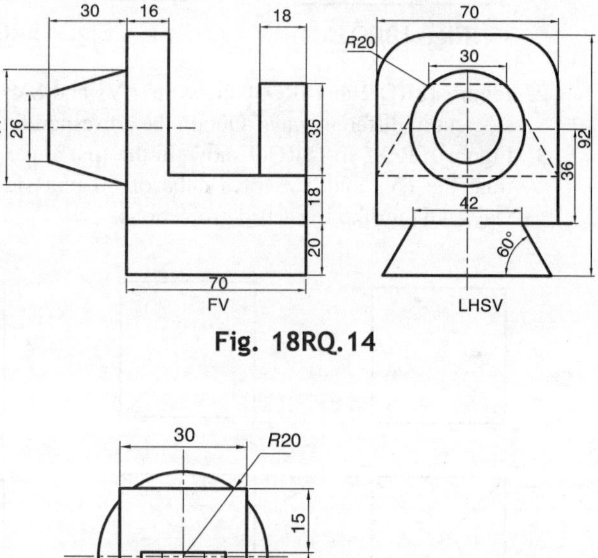

Fig. 18RQ.14

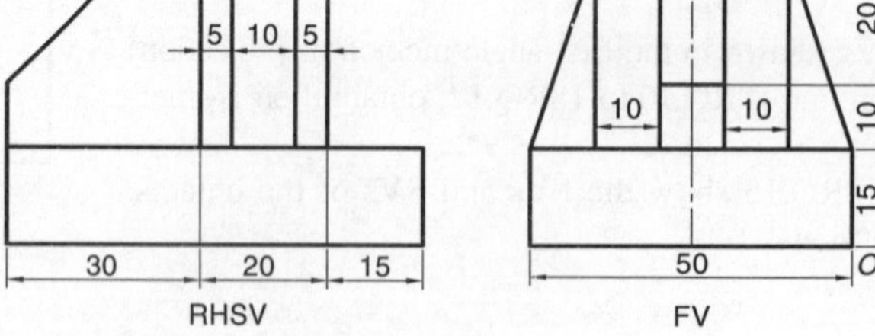

Fig. 18RQ.15

6. Figure 18RQ.16 and Fig. 18RQ.17 show the FVs and TVs of the objects. Draw their isometric projections.

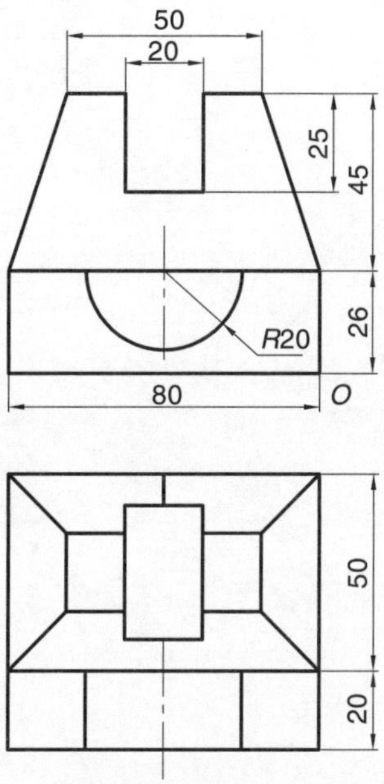

Fig. 18RQ.16

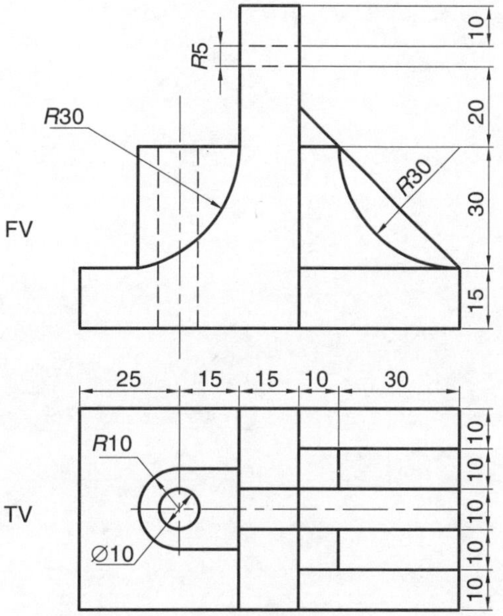

Fig. 18RQ.17

7. From the three views shown in Fig. 18RQ.18, draw the isometric view.

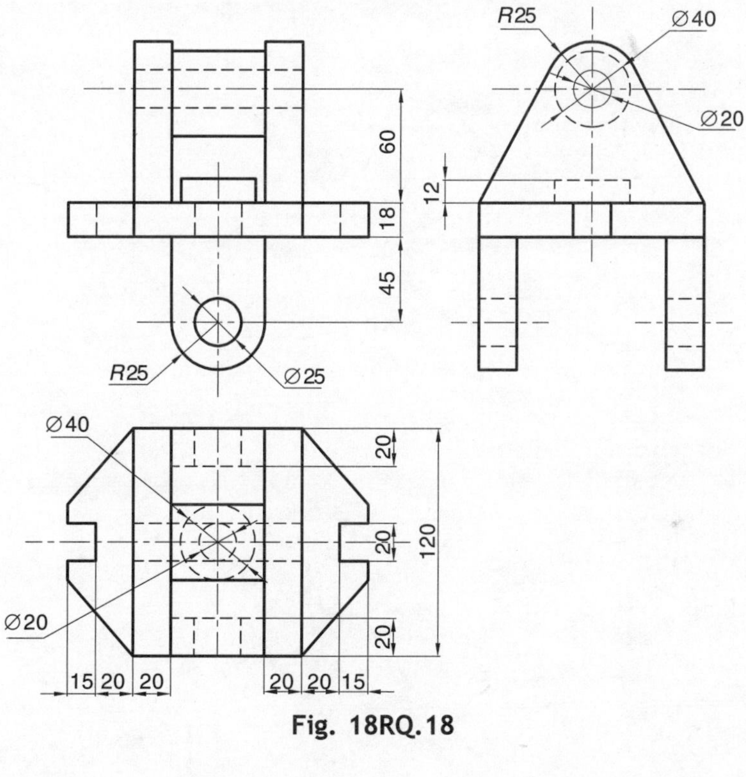

Fig. 18RQ.18

Chapter 19

PERSPECTIVE PROJECTION

19.1 INTRODUCTION

An object appears differently each time when viewed from different directions. Such a view of an object which changes with respect to the observer's location is called *perspective projection*. Perspective projection provides a realistic 3D view of an object. The perspective views are much similar to the images seen by human eyes or photographed by a camera. Hence, they are used in architectural and civil engineering drawings to indicate exteriors and interiors of the buildings. They are also used in advertisement campaigns to make it easier for a layperson to understand the features of the products. Perspective views are not used in manufacturing drawings.

This chapter deals with the theory of linear perspective projection. As mentioned in Chapter 8, in linear perspective, the size of the object's view decreases linearly as the distance of the object from the observer increases.

19.2 CONCEPT OF PERSPECTIVE PROJECTION

To understand the concept of perspective projection, let us consider an object, say a building, situated at approximately 50 m in front of you. Take a transparent glass of appropriate size through which a full view of the building is visible. Place the glass vertically on a stand at approximately 40 cm in front of you. Look at the building through the glass. Now, using a marker pen, sketch the lines on the glass along the edges of the building. You will get a perspective view of the building on the glass. If you change your position and look at the building through different directions, you will get another perspective.

19.3 TERMINOLOGY IN PERSPECTIVE PROJECTION

The following terms must be understood carefully for drawing the perspective views. See Fig. 19.1.

Station point (S) It is a point at which the eyes of the observer are located. *s* and *s*' indicate TV and FV of *S* respectively.

Perspective picture plane (PPP) It is a POP used to obtain the object's perspective. The transparent glass considered in the above section represents the PPP. The PPP is often assumed to be vertical.

Horizon plane (HP) It is an imaginary horizontal plane passing through the observer's eyes, i.e., *S*.

Horizon line (HL) It is the trace (i.e., intersection) of the HP on the PPP.

Ground plane (GP) It is the real ground or an imaginary plane parallel to the ground on which the object is assumed to be resting.

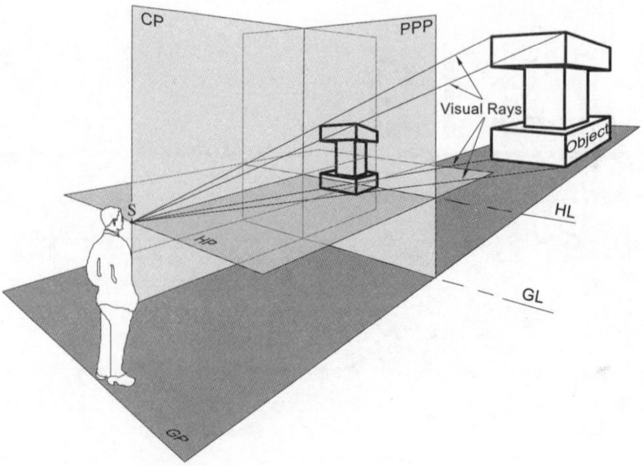

Fig. 19.1

Ground line (GL) It is the trace of the GP on the PPP.

Central plane (CP) It is vertical plane passing through *S* and perpendicular to the PPP.

Vanishing points (VPs) (Not shown in the figure) These are the points at which the edges of the object are seen to be converging. If you stand at the middle of a long straight road and look at its other end, the two parallel edges of the road are seen to be converging at a point. This point is the *VP* and is seen at eye level, i.e. on HL.

Visual rays These are the rays of sight emerging from *S* and ending at the object's corners. The intersections of the visual rays with the PPP are called the *piercing points*.

19.4 TYPES OF PERSPECTIVE PROJECTION

Linear perspective may use one or two or three *VP*s to obtain the perspective view of an object. Accordingly, there are three types of linear perspective.

One-Point Perspective, or Parallel Perspective In parallel perspective, one face of the object is kept parallel to the PPP. Obviously, this face will show the true shape. The edges perpendicular to this face are seen to be converging to a *VP*.

Two-Point Perspective, or Angular Perspective In angular perspective, one edge of the object is kept parallel to the PPP. Each of the edges perpendicular to this edge are seen to be converging to one of the two *VPs*.

Three-Point Perspective, or Oblique Perspective In oblique perspective, neither a face nor an edge of the object is kept parallel to the PPP. Each of the edges is seen to be converging to one of the three *VPs*.

19.5 METHODS OF PERSPECTIVE PROJECTION

To draw perspective projection, we need the TV and FV (or SV) of the object. As the PPP lies between the observer and the object, it is customary to use the third-angle method of projection. The second thing that we should know is the orientation and location of the object with respect to the PPP. The location of *S* with respect to the PPP and the GL is the third important requirement. As a standard practice, for big immovable objects like buildings, *S* is located at the normal eye level of human beings. For small objects, *S* is located at such a height that all the three dimensions of the object are appropriately visible. The distance of *S* from the PPP is usually taken twice of the greatest dimension of the object.

Two common methods followed in perspective projection are (i) vanishing point method and (ii) visual ray method.

19.5.1 Vanishing Point Method

Depending on the object's orientation with respect to the PPP, one or two or three the *VP*s may exist. All the corners of the object are joined with *S* by drawing visual rays. The points at which the visual rays cut the PPP, i.e., the piercing points, are then located. The piercing points when joined in a sequence give the perspective view of the object.

Parallel perspective The object is placed such that one of its principal faces is parallel to the PPP. The face shows the true shape. If the face is on the PPP, it will show the true size. It is seen reduced or enlarged if it lies behind or in front of the PPP. The edges perpendicular to this face will be seen converging to a *VP* on HL.

Example 19.1 Figure 19.2(a) shows TV and FV of a horizontal rectangular prism. The front face coincides with the PPP. The observer looks at the prism from a point *S* 70 mm above the ground and 60 mm in front of the PPP on the CP passing through the centre of the prism. Draw the perspective projection of the prism.

Solution Refer Fig. 19.2(b). The face *ab*–*b*1–*a*1 coincides with the PPP.

1. Draw GL and the PPP at sufficient distance from each other. Place FV and TV on GL and the PPP as shown. Draw the CP perpendicular to the PPP and passing through the centre of the prism.
2. Locate *s* and *s*′(*v*′) on the CP, 60 mm and 70 mm from the PPP and GL respectively. Join *a*(*a*1), *b*(*b*1), *c*(*c*1) and *d*(*d*1) with *s*. Locate the piercing points 1 and 2.
3. As the face *ab*–*b*1–*a*1 is in the PPP, *AB*–*B*1–*A*1 will show the true shape. Join *A*, *B*, *A*1 and *B*1 with *s*′.
4. Project the piercing points on the corresponding lines, i.e., 1 on *A*–*s*′ to locate *D*, 1 on *A*1–*s*′ to locate *D*1, 2 on *B*–*s*′ to locate *C* and 2 on *B*1–*s*′ to locate *C*1. Join *A*–*B*–

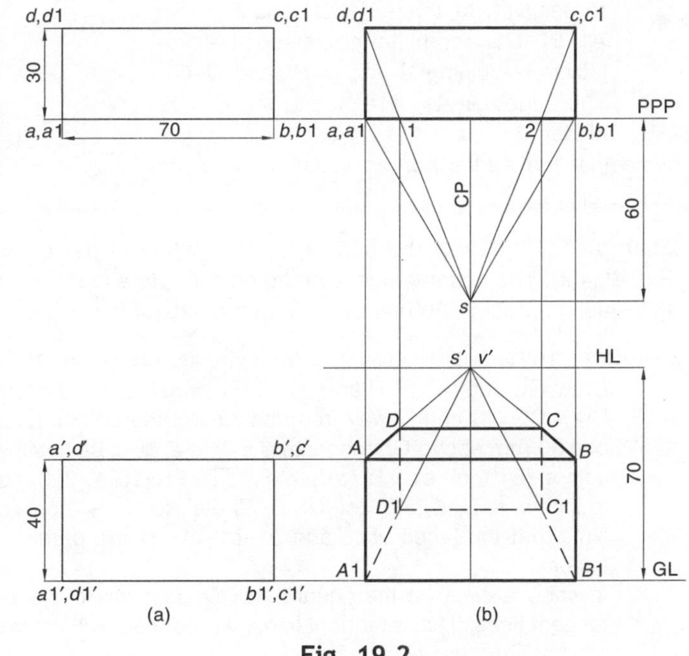

Fig. 19.2

C–D–A–A1–B1–B for the required perspective view. The edges D–D1–C1–C, A1–D1 and B1–C1 are hidden.

Note that the edges AD, BC, A1D1 and B1C1 which are perpendicular to AB–B1–A1 are converging to the VP v′.

Example 19.2 Figure 19.3(a) shows TV and FV of a triangular prism resting on its rectangular face on the ground. A triangular face is parallel to and 10 mm behind the PPP. The observer looks at the prism from a point 80 mm above ground and 40 mm in front of the PPP. The CP is 60 mm away from the axis of the prism. Draw the perspective projection of the prism.

Solution Refer Fig. 19.3(b). The face abc is parallel to the PPP.

1. Draw GL and the PPP at sufficient distance from each other. Place FV on GL and TV, 10 mm behind the PPP as shown.
2. Draw CP, 60 mm away from the axis of the prism. Locate s 40 mm below the PPP, and s′ (v′) 80 mm above GL on CP. Join a, b, c, a1, b1 and c1 with s. Locate the piercing points 1, 2, 3, 4, 5 and 6.
3. As the face abc is behind the PPP, it will be seen reduced in size.
   Join a′, b′ and c′ to s′. Project 1, 2, and 3 on a′s′, c′s′ and b′s′ respectively to locate A, B and C. Join A–B–C. ABC will show the perspective of the triangular face.
4. Project 4, 5 and 6 on a′s′, c′s′ and b′s′ respectively to locate A1, B1 and C1. Join A1–B1–C1. Complete the perspective projection by joining A–A1, B–B1 and C–C1. The edges A–A1, A1–B1 and A1–C1 are hidden.

Note that the edges perpendicular to ABC are converging to v′.

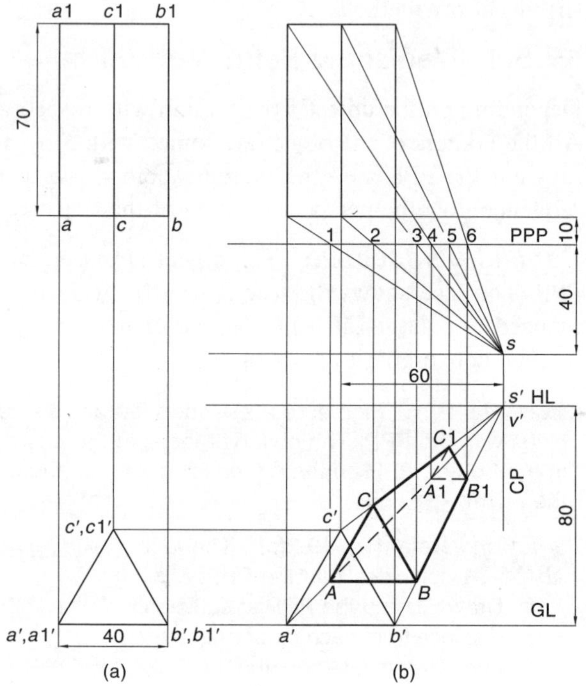

Fig. 19.3

Example 19.3 Draw the perspective projection of the object, the TV and FV of which are shown in Fig. 19.4(a). The observer looks at the object from a point 90 mm above ground and 60 mm in front of the PPP along the CP, 130 mm away from the axis of the object. The front end of the object is in the PPP.

Solution Refer Fig. 19.4(b). The front circular face is in the PPP.

1. Draw GL and the PPP and place FV on GL and TV on the PPP as shown.
2. Draw CP, 130 mm away from the axis of the object. Locate s and s′ on CP, 60 mm below the PPP and 90 mm above GL respectively. Join a, b, c, etc., with s and locate the piercing points 1, 2, 3, etc.
3. Join a′ (a1′), b′ (b1′), c′ (c1′), etc., to s′. Project 1, 2, 3, etc., on a′ (a1)–s′, b′ (b1′)–s′, c′ (c1′)–s′, etc., to locate A, B, C etc. Join A, B, C, etc., to show the perspective of the square block.
   Note that the faces abcd and a1–b1–c1–d1 are parallel to the PPP. Hence, they are seen as true shapes.
4. Inscribe a circle in the square ABCD. Join this circle with the circle on the front face by drawing tangent lines. These tangent lines, if produced, will converge to s′. Both the circles will show the true shape. The front circle will show the true size.

Angular perspective The object is so placed that one of its three mutually perpendicular edges is parallel to the PPP. The two faces sharing that edge are inclined to the PPP. The edges perpendicular to the edge parallel to the PPP will converge to two *VP*s on HL on either sides of the observer.

Angular perspectives are more realistic than parallel perspectives.

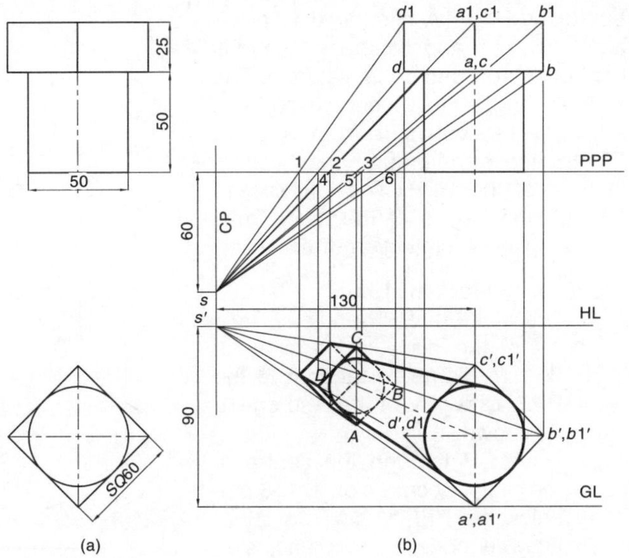

Fig. 19.4

Example 19.4 Figure 19.5(a) shows the two views of a square prism resting on the ground on its base with a vertical face inclined at 30° to the PPP. An edge of that face is in the PPP and is 30 mm to the right of *S*. Draw the perspective projection of the prism if *S* is 120 mm above the ground and 60 mm in front of the PPP.

Solution Refer Fig. 19.5(b). The edge *a*–*a*1 is in the PPP. The face *a*–*a*1–*b*1–*b* is inclined at 30° to the PPP.

1. Draw GL, the PPP and HL. Place TV on the PPP as shown. (GL passes through the base of the prism.)
2. Draw CP, 30 mm to the left of *a*(*a*1). Locate *s* and *s*′ on CP, 60 mm below the PPP and 120 mm above GL respectively.
3. Through *s*, draw lines parallel to *a*(*a*1)–*d*(*d*1) and *a*(*a*1)–*b*(*b*1), cutting PPP at *v*1 and *v*2 respectively. Project *v*1 and *v*2 on HL and locate *v*1′ and *v*2′.
4. Join *a*, *b*, *c*, etc., with *s* and locate the piercing points 1, 2 and 3.
5. Project *a*′–*a*1′ horizontally. Locate *A* and *A*1 at the intersections of a vertical projector through *a*(*a*1) and horizontal projectors through *a*′ and *a*1′. *AA*1 represents the perspective projection of the edge in the PPP. It shows the TL. All other edges will converge to *v*1′ and *v*2′.

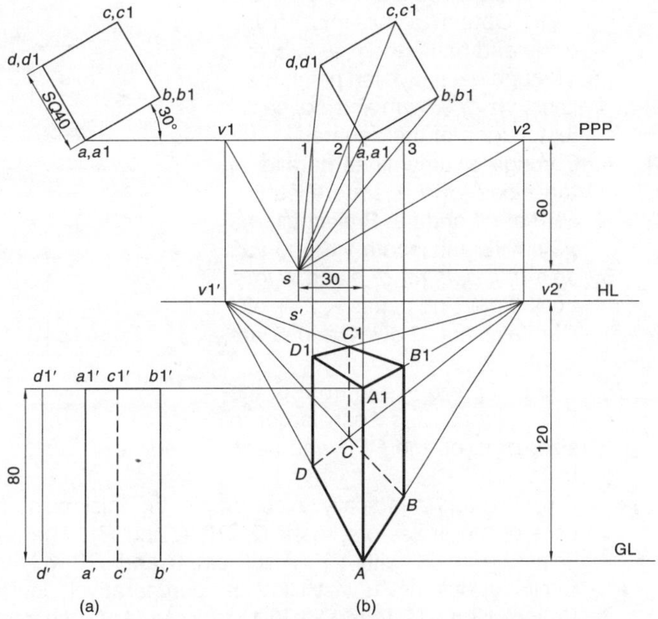

Fig. 19.5

6. Join *A* and *A*1 to *v*1′ and *v*2′ respectively. Project 1 on *A*–*v*1′ and *A*1–*v*1′ to locate *D* and *D*1 respectively. Project 3 on *A*–*v*2′ and *A*1–*v*2′ to locate *B* and *B*1 respectively.
7. Join *D* and *D*1 to *v*2′. Project 2 on *D*–*v*2′ and *D*1–*v*2′ to locate *C* and *C*1 respectively. *Alternatively*, join *B* and *B*1 to *v*1′ and locate *C* and *C*1 at the intersections of *D*–*v*2′ and *B*–*v*1′ and *D*1–*v*2′ and *B*1–*v*1′.
8. Join *A*, *B*, *C*, etc., for the required perspective projection.

Example 19.5 A circular disc of diameter 60 mm and thickness 10 mm is kept on the ground on its flat face. The PPP is tangent to its curved surface. An observer views it from a point 70 mm above the ground and 118 mm in front of the PPP. The CP passes through the centre of the disc. Draw the perspective projection of the disc.

Solution Refer Fig. 19.6.

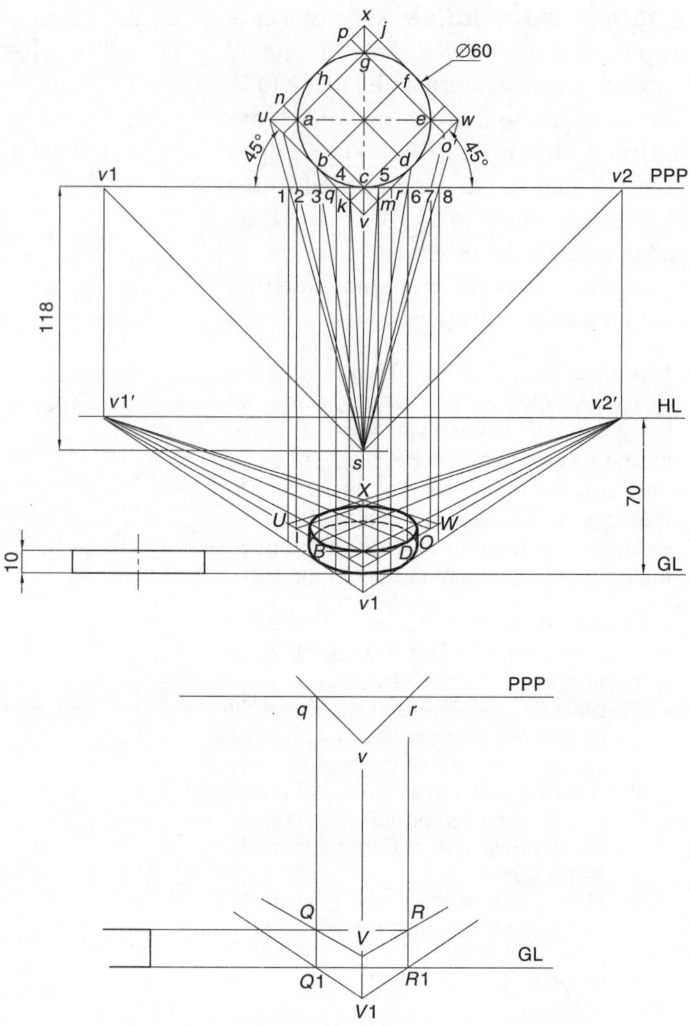

Fig. 19.6

1. Draw GL, the PPP and HL. Draw TV of the disc, i.e., a circle of 60 mm diameter, tangent to the PPP. Draw FV of the disc on GL as shown.
2. Draw CP through the centre of the circle. Locate *s* on it, 118 mm below the PPP.
3. Draw a square *uvwx* enclosing the circle as shown. Each side of the square makes 45° with the PPP. Obtain 8 divisions on the circle and name them *a*, *b*, *c*, etc. Through each division point, draw lines, viz, *ij*, *kl*, *mn* and *op*, parallel to sides of the square.
4. Through *s*, draw lines parallel to the sides of the square cutting PPP at *v*1 and *v*2. Project *v*1 and *v*2 on HL and locate *v*1′ and *v*2′.
5. Join *u*, *i*, *b*, *k*, *m*, *d*, *o* and *w* to *s*. Locate piercing points 1, 2, 3, etc. Carefully note how 4 and 5 are located.
6. The triangle *qrv* is in front of the PPP. Hence, it is seen larger in size. *qr* is on the PPP and seen to TL.
   Project *q* and *r* vertically. Also, project the thickness of the disc horizontally from FV. At the intersections of the projectors, mark *Q*, *Q*1, *R* and *R*1. The rectangle *Q*–*R*–*R*1–*Q*1 shows the true size.
7. Join *Q* and *Q*1 with *v*1′. Also, join *R* and *R*1 with *v*2′. Produce *v*1′–*Q* and *v*2′–*R* to meet at *V*. Similarly, obtain *V*1. *V*–*V*1 is seen comparatively longer since it lies in front of the PPP.
8. Project 1 on *v*1′–*V* and *v*1′–*V*1 to locate *U* and *U*1 respectively. Similarly, project 8 to obtain *W* and *W*1. Join *U* and *U*1 with *v*2′. Join *W* and *W*1 with *v*1′. Locate *X* and *X*1 at corresponding intersections.
9. *UVWX* represents the perspective of square *uvwx*. Obtain points *I*, *B*, *K*, *M*, *D* and *O* on it by projecting 2, 3, 4, 5, 6 and 7. Join *I*, *B* and *K* with *v*2′ and *K*, *D* and *O* with *v*1′. On the corresponding intersections, locate *A*, *B*, *C*, etc. Draw a smooth curve to represent the perspective of the top face of the disc.
10. Locate *A*1, *B*1, *C*1, etc., inside *U*1–*V*1–*W*1–*X*1 in a similar way and draw a smooth curve through them to represent the perspective of the bottom face of the disc. Join both the curves by tangent lines.

Oblique perspective When an object is placed in such a way that neither an edge nor a face is parallel to the PPP, the edges of the object will converge to three *VPs*. In case of parallel and angular perspectives, the vertical edges are parallel to the PPP. Hence, they do not converge. In oblique perspective, neither horizontal nor vertical edges are parallel to the PPP. Hence, the edges converge to three different *VPs*.

Oblique perspective shows distortions in all the three dimensions of the object. Hence, it is used to a limited extent.

Example 19.6 A cube with a 60 mm side is resting on a corner on the ground with an edge through that corner making 30° with the PPP. The other end of the edge is on the PPP. The other two edges emerging from the corner make equal inclinations with the PPP. Draw the perspective projection of the cube when viewed from a point 125 mm above the ground and 110 mm in front of the PPP. CP passes through the centre of the cube.

Solution The three mutually perpendicular edges of the cube are inclined to the PPP. Hence, the edges will converge to the three *VPs*.

Refer Fig. 19.7.

1. Draw GL and the PPP. Also, draw PPP″ perpendicular to the PPP.
2. Draw *a″–a1″* = 60 mm inclined at 30° with PPP″. *a″* is on PPP″ and *a1″* is on GL. Project *a″* (*a1″*) to draw auxiliary TV *a2b2c2d2* of the cube. Project auxiliary TV to complete SV *a″–a1″–c1″–c″*.
3. Project SV to obtain FV *abcd–d1–c1–b1–a1*. Note that *a* is on the PPP.
4. Locate *s* on CP, 110 mm from the PPP. Also, locate *s″*, 110 mm from PPP″ and 125 mm above GL.
5. Through *s*, draw *s–v1* and *s–v2* parallel to *ab* and *ad* respectively. Similarly, through *s″*, draw *s″–v2″* and *s″–v3″* parallel to *a″–c″* and *a″–a1″* respectively. Project *v1* and *v2* on HL to locate *v1′* and *v2′*. Project *v3″* on CP to locate *v3′*.
6. Join *a*, *b*, *c*, etc., with *s* and locate piercing points 1, 2, 3, etc. Join *a1″*, *b1″*, *c1″*, etc., with *s″* and locate piercing points 1″, 2″, 3″, etc.
7. Project *a*(*a1*) vertically and *a″* and 1″ horizontally to locate *A* and *A1*. Join *A* and *A1* with *v1′* and *v2′*. On *A–v1′* and *A–v2′*, project 1 and 4 to locate *B* and *D* respectively. Project 5″ on *A1–a* to locate *C*. Join *ABCD* for the top face of the cube.
8. Obtain *A1–B1–C1–D1* in a similar way. *B–B1* and *D–D1*, if produced, will converge to *v3′*.

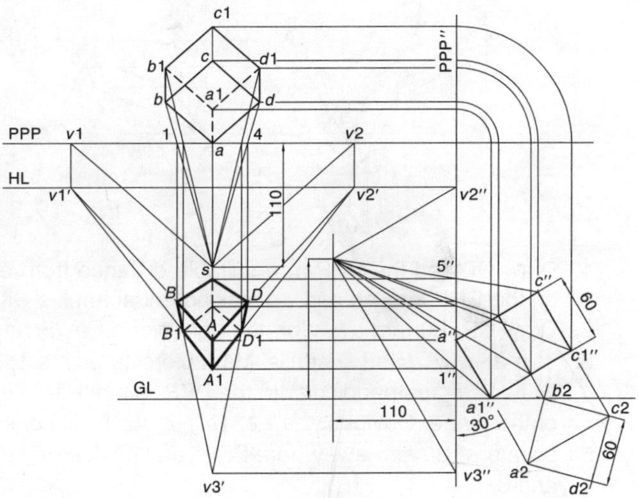

Fig. 19.7

19.5.2 Visual Ray Method

The visual ray method is a general method applicable to an object having any kind of orientation. Usually two views, i.e., TV and FV (or SV) of the object are given. Visual rays are then obtained by joining each point in TV with *s* and each point in FV (or SV) with *s′* (or *s″*). The points at which these rays intersect the PPP (i.e., piercing points) are projected vertically and horizontally to meet each other. The required points are located at the corresponding intersections.

The following example explains the visual ray method.

Example 19.7 A pentagonal plane of 50 mm side is lying on the ground with a corner on the PPP. The edges emerging from the corner make equal angles with the PPP. The plane is viewed from a point 50 mm above the ground and 30 mm in front of the PPP. The CP is 80 mm to the right side of the centre of the plane. Draw the perspective projection of the plane.

Solution **Method 1:** *Perspective from TV and SV*

Refer Fig. 19.8(a).

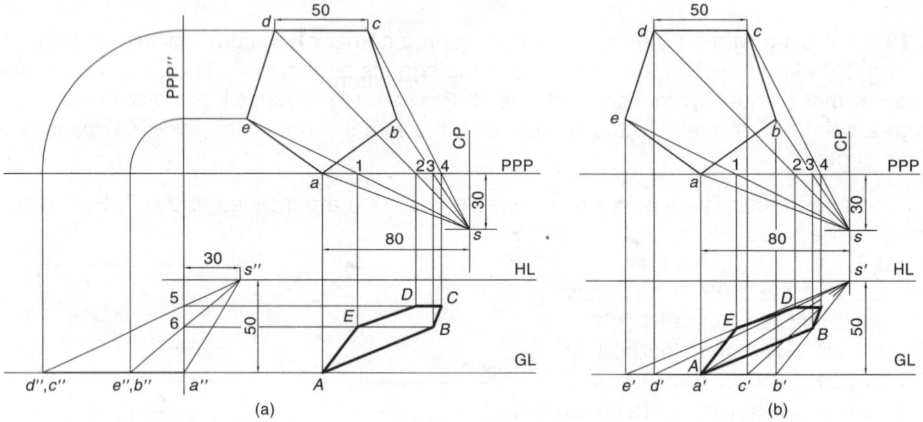

Fig. 19.8

1. Draw GL and the PPP at a suitable distance from each other. Draw TV, *abcde*, of the plane with *a* on the PPP and *ab* and *ae* making equal angles with the PPP. Also, draw HL, 50 mm above GL.
2. Draw CP, 80 mm away on the right side of *a*. Locate *s* on it, 30 mm below the PPP.
3. Join *a*, *b*, *c*, *d* and *e* with *s*. Mark piercing points 1, 2, 3, etc.
4. Draw PPP″ perpendicular to the PPP. Project *a*, *b*, *c*, etc., on PPP″ and obtain SV *a″–e″* (*b″*)–*d″* (*c″*) of the plane. Obviously, *a″–e″* (*b″*)–*d″* (*c″*) will coincide with GL.
5. Locate *s″* 30 mm away from PPP″ on HL. Join *a″*, *e″* (*b″*) and *d″* (*c″*) with *s″*. Mark piercing points 5 and 6.
6. Though 1, 2, 3 and 4, draw vertical projectors. Through 5 and 6, draw horizontal projectors. Locate *A*, *B*, *C*, *D* and *E* at the intersections of the corresponding projectors. Join *ABCDE* for the required perspective projection. Note that *CD* is parallel to GL.

Method 2: *Perspective from TV and FV*

Refer Fig. 19.8(b).

1. Follow steps 1 to 3 as explained in Method 1.
2. Project *a*, *b*, *c*, etc., on PPP and obtain FV, *e′d′a′c′b′* on GL. Project *s* to *s′* on HL. Join *a′*, *b′*, *c′*, *d′* and *e′* with *s′*.
3. Project 1 on *e′s′*, 2 on *d′s′*, 3 on *b′s′* and 4 on *c′s′* to locate *E*, *D*, *B* and *C* respectively. *A* will lie at *a′*. Join *ABCDE*.

Example 19.8 Figure 19.9 shows TV and SV of an object and the location of the station point in relation to the PPP and GL. Draw the perspective projection of the object.

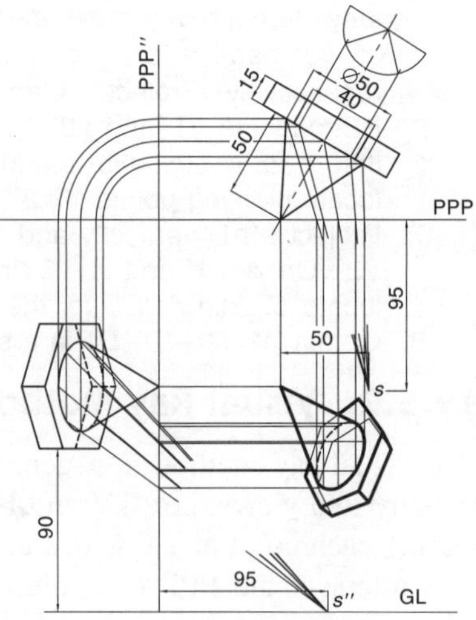

Fig. 19.9

Solution The station point is on GL and is 95 mm in front of the PPP.

1. In TV, obtain 8 division points on the base of the cone as shown. Project the division points in SV.
2. Join all the points in TV with *s* and the points in SV with *s″*. Locate the piercing points.
3. Project piercing points vertically from the PPP and horizontally from PPP″. Locate the desired points at the intersections of corresponding projectors.

19.6 LINE OF HEIGHTS

If a point lies on the PPP, its true height from ground is seen in its perspective view. However, if a point is behind or in front of the PPP, its perspective doesn't show its true height from the ground. If such a point is projected on the PPP, its projection on the PPP (i.e., FV) will show the true height from GL. Needless to say, all the points in an AVP can be projected to a single line on the PPP. That line is essentially the trace of the AVP on the PPP. As the line is vertical, it will show the true heights of all the points above the ground. Such a line is called the *line of heights* (LOH).

LOH helps to draw perspectives of the surfaces behind or in front of the PPP. Often, the vertical surfaces inclined to the PPP, are projected on the PPP to obtain LOHs for all the points on them. For the surfaces inclined to the ground, different LOHs are drawn for different points.

The following examples will explain the use of LOH.

Example 19.9 Figure 19.10(a) shows TVs and FVs of three vertical poles, *AB*, *CD* and *EF* of equal heights. Pole *AB* is in the PPP, *CD* is behind the PPP and *EF* is in front of the PPP. The observer views the pole from a point 30 m above the ground, 20 m in front of the PPP and 10 m on the right side of the pole *AB*. Draw the perspective projections of the poles.

Solution The three poles are in the same vertical plane. As *AB* is in the PPP, it will show TL. *CD* and *EF* will be seen smaller and larger respectively. Refer Fig. 19.10(b).

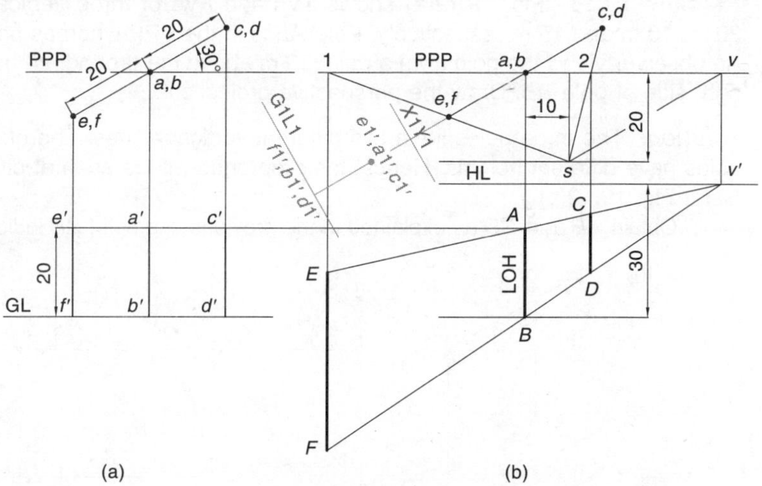

Fig. 19.10

1. Locate *s* as shown. Draw HL. Through *s*, draw *sv* parallel to *e*(*f*)–*c*(*d*). Project *v* to *v′* on HL.
2. Join *s* with *e*(*f*) and produce it to meet the PPP at 1. Join *s* with *c*(*d*) and locate 2.
3. Project *a*(*b*) vertically and *a′b′* horizontally to obtain *AB*. Join *A* and *B* with *v′*.
4. Project 1 on *v′*–*A* produced and *v′*–*B* produced to obtain *EF*. Similarly, project 2 on *v′*–*A* and *v′*–*B* for *CD*.

It should be noted that the perspectives of the three poles lie in the same triangular plane *EF*–*v′* (as the poles are in one plane). In this case, *AB* represents LOH. As *AB* = *c′d′* = *e′f′*, *AB* also gives the height of *C* and *D* above GL. *AB* represents the trace of the plane EFDC on the PPP.

If an auxiliary projection plane *X*1*Y*1 is set perpendicular to *c*(*d*)–*e*(*f*) to obtain auxiliary FVs of the poles, *e*1′(*a*1′,*c*1′)–*f*1′ (*b*1′,*d*1′) will represent LOH. Note that, *e*1′ (*a*1′,*c*1′)–*f*1′ (*b*1′,*d*1′) = *AB*.

Example 19.10 Figure 19.11(a) shows TVs and FVs of three vertical poles, *AB*, *CD* and *EF* of heights 20 m, 10 m and 15 m respectively. An observer views the pole from a point 30 m above the ground, 20 m in front of the PPP and 10 m on the right side of the pole *AB*. Draw the perspective projections.

Solution As the poles have different heights, points *A*, *C* and *E* will be seen at different heights on LOH. Refer Fig. 19.11(b).

1. Locate *s* and obtain the perspective projections as shown. Note that, *AB* represents LOH. Heights of points *C* and *E* are marked on it by projecting *c′* and *e′* to C_0 and E_0 respectively.
2. Join C_0–v'. Project 2 on it for *C*. Similarly, join E_0–v' and produce it to meet vertical projector through 1 at *E*. Points *F*, *B*, and *D* are on ground and they are seen on one line. Points *E*, *A* and *C* are at different heights and they are seen on different lines.

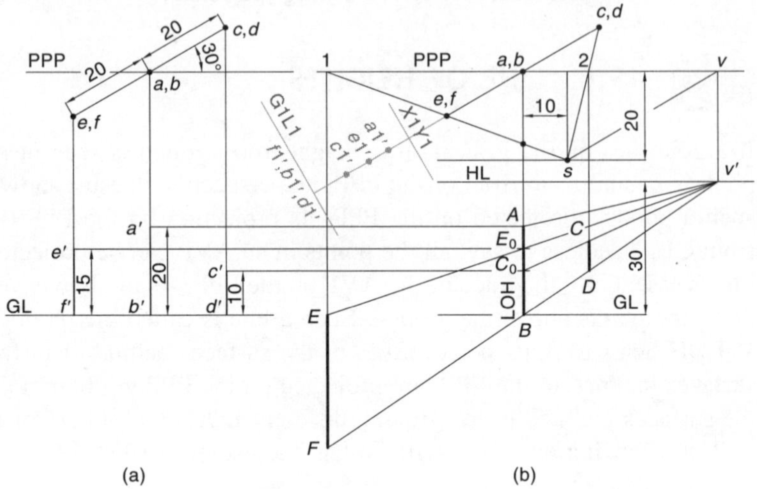

Fig. 19.11

The auxiliary view *a*1′–*f*1′ (*b*1′, *d*1′) represents LOH showing the heights of *e*1′ and *c*1′.

Example 19.11 Fig. 19.12(a) shows TVs and FVs of three vertical poles, *AB*, *CD* and *EF* of heights 20 m, 10 m and 15 m respectively. Pole *AB* is in the PPP whereas poles *CD* and *EF* are behind the PPP. An observer views the pole from a point 30 m above the ground, 20 m in front of the PPP and 10 m on the right side of pole *AB*. Draw the perspective projections.

Solution The three poles lie in two different vertical planes. Therefore, two LOHs are needed. Also, the poles have different heights. Hence, their top ends will be seen at different heights on the LOHs. Refer Fig. 19.12(b).

1. Obtain *AB* and *CD* as explained in the previous example. *AB* indicates LOH and shows the height of *C*.

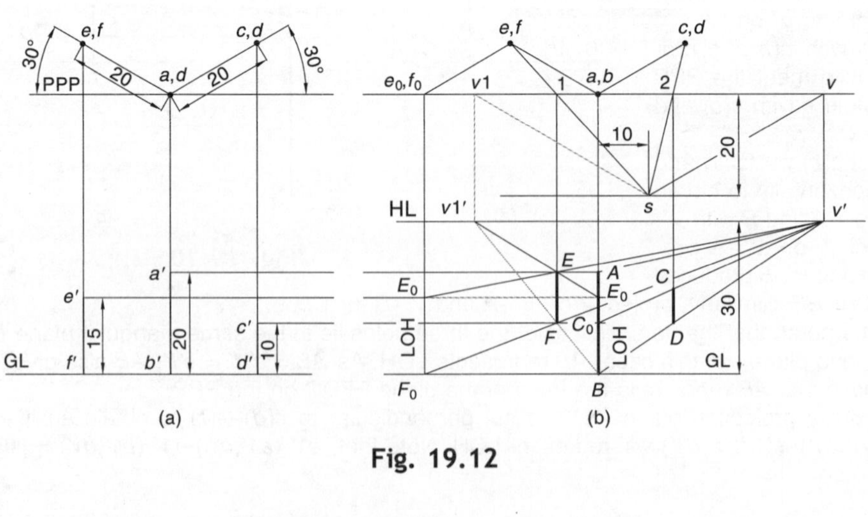

Fig. 19.12

2. Draw $e(f)$–$e_0(f_0)$ parallel to $c(d)$–$a(b)$. Project $e_0(f_0)$ vertically and e' and f' horizontally to obtain E_0F_0. E_0F_0 indicates LOH for point E. Join E_0–v' and F_0–v'. Project 1 on E_0–v' and F_0–v' to obtain EF.

Alternatively, draw s–$v1$ parallel to $a(b)$–$e(f)$. Project $v1$ to $v1'$ on HL. Project e' on AB to mark E_0. Join E_0–$v1'$ and B–$v1'$. Project 1 on E_0–$v1'$ and B–$v1'$ to obtain EF.

Example 19.12 Figure 19.13(a) shows TVs and FVs of two square blocks kept one above the other. A smaller edge of the larger block is in the PPP and a surface through that edge makes 30° with the PPP. The station point is 60 mm above the ground, 100 in front of the PPP and 50 mm to the right of the edge in the PPP. Draw the perspective projections of the blocks.

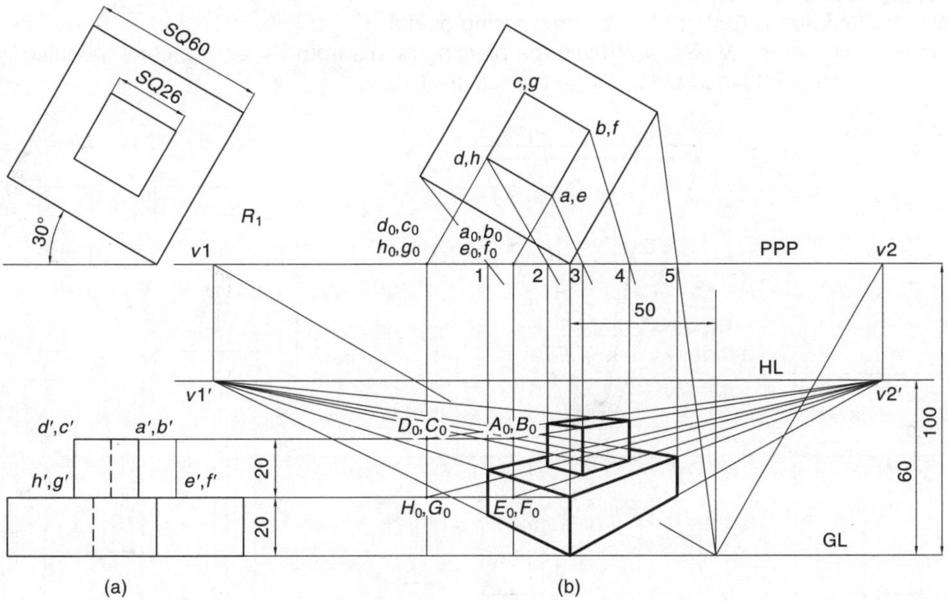

Fig. 19.13

Solution Refer Fig. 19.13(b).

1. Draw the PPP, GL and HL as shown. Locate s. Through s, draw s–$v1$ and s–$v2$ parallel to the two faces of the bigger block. Locate $v1'$ and $v2'$ on HL. Obtain the perspective of the bigger block as explained in Example 19.4.

   To draw the perspective of the smaller block, we need to draw LOHs for the points A, B, C, D, E, F, G and H.
2. Produce $c(g)$–$d(h)$ and $b(f)$–$a(e)$ to meet the PPP at $d_0(c_0)h_0(g_0)$ and $a_0(b_0)e_0(f_0)$ respectively. Project $d_0(c_0)h_0(g_0)$ vertically and a' (b') and e' (f') horizontally to obtain LOH, $D_0(C_0)$–$H_0(G_0)$. Obtain another LOH, $A_0(B_0)$–$E_0(F_0)$ in a similar way.
3. Join $D_0(C_0)$, $H_0(G_0)$, $A_0(B_0)$ and $E_0(F_0)$ with $v2'$. Project 2 on D_0–$v2'$ and H_0–$v2'$ to locate D and H respectively. Similarly, obtain A and E by projecting 3 on A_0–$v2'$ and E_0–$v2'$ and B and F by projecting 4 on B_0–$v2'$ and F_0–$v2'$.
4. Join B and F with $v1'$. Locate C and G at the intersections of D–$v2'$ and B–$v1'$ and H–$v2'$ and F–$v1'$ respectively. *Alternatively*, join $c(g)$ with s and project the piercing point to C_0–$v2'$ and G_0–$v2'$ to locate C and G.

Illustrative Problems

Problem 19.1 A hoarding of size 480 cm × 300 cm is supported by two pillars of 620 cm height each, as shown in Fig. 19.14(a). A person looks at it from a point, 240 cm above the top edge and 720 cm in front of the front surface. The PPP is horizontal and passes through the top edge of the hoarding. Draw the perspective view of the hoarding if the CP passes through its centre.

Solution Refer Fig. 19.14(b).

1. Draw PPP' passing through the top edge of the hoarding. Draw TV at suitable height from PPP'. Locate *s* and *s*′ as shown.
2. Join each corner in FV with *s*′. Locate piercing points.
3. Join each corner in TV with *s*. Project the piercing points from FV on the corresponding converging lines. Join the points thus obtained for the required view.

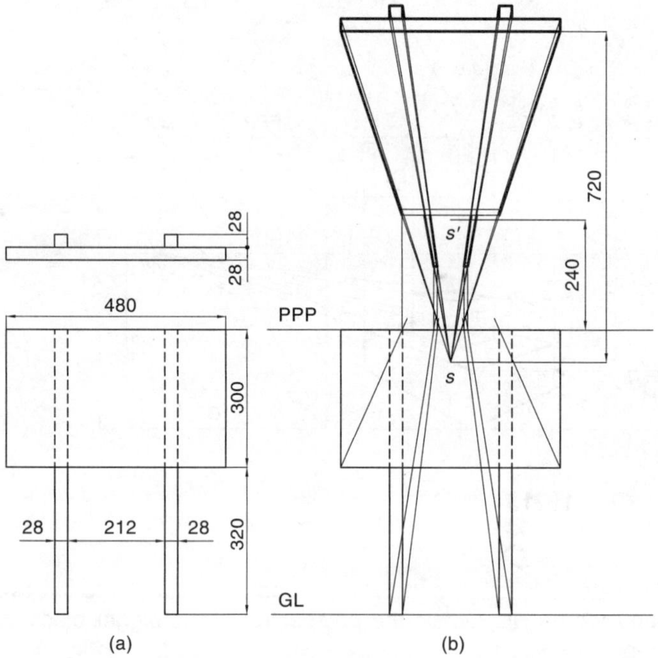

(a) (b)

Fig. 19.14

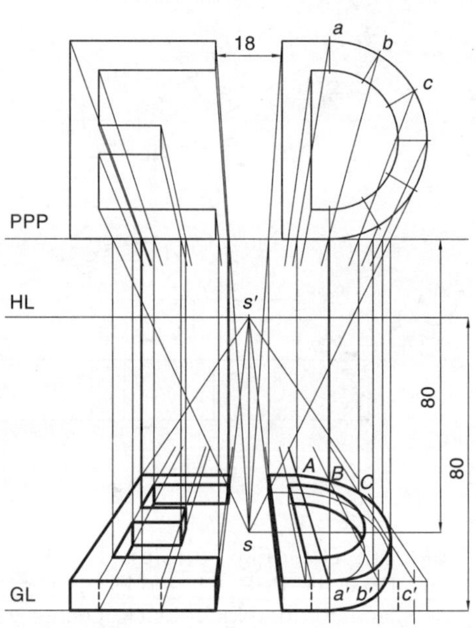

Fig. 19.15

Problem 19.2 Two steel letters, 'E' and 'D', are resting horizontally on the ground as shown in Fig. 19.15. The space between the letters is 18 cm. A camera situated midway between the two letters, at a height of 80 cm from GL and at a distance of 80 cm in front of the PPP, takes a shot of the letters. The PPP passes through the nearest vertical walls of the letters. Draw the picture as taken by the camera.

Solution

1. Draw the PPP through the vertical walls of the letters as shown in TV. Draw GL and HL as shown. Locate *s* and *s*′ at given distances.
2. Mark a few points, *a*, *b*, *c*, etc., on the arcs of letter 'D'. Join each point in TV with *s* to locate the piercing points.

3. FV rests on GL. Project *a*, *b*, *c*, etc., to *a*′, *b*′, *c*′, etc., in FV. Join each point in FV with *s*′. Project the piercing points on the corresponding converging lines to obtain the required view. Note carefully how the arcs in letter 'D' are obtained in perspective.

Problem 19.3 Figure 19.16(a) shows the profile of a concrete arch on a side of a window. The arch makes 45° with the PPP as shown in the TV in Fig. 19.16(b). The station point is 130 mm in front of the PPP and is on the CP passing through the edge of the arch on the PPP. HL is 32 mm above the top edge of the arch. Show the arch in perspective projection.

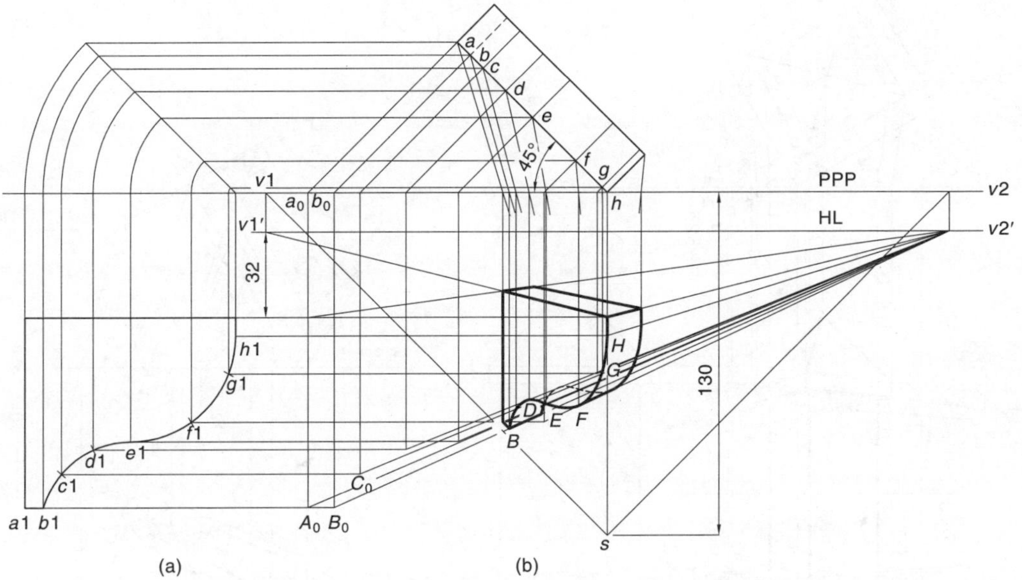

Fig. 19.16

Solution

1. Draw the PPP through the corner *h* in TV. Draw HL, 32 mm above the top edge of the arch. Locate *s*.
2. Through *s*, draw *s*–*v*1 and *s*–*v*2 parallel to the corresponding lines in TV. Project *v*1 and *v*2 on HL to locate *v*1′ and *v*2′.
3. Mark a few points *a*1, *b*1, *c*1, etc., on the profile of the arch. Project these points in TV to obtain *a*, *b*, *c*, etc. Join *a*, *b*, *c*, etc., with s and locate the piercing points.
4. Through *a*, *b*, *c*, etc., draw lines parallel to *s*–*v*2 to meet HL at a_0, b_0, c_0, etc. Project a_0, b_0, c_0, etc., vertically and *a*1, *b*1, *c*1, etc., horizontally to meet at A_0, B_0, C_0, etc., a_0–A_0, b_0–B_0, c_0–C_0, etc., represent LOHs for the points *A*, *B*, *C*, etc.
5. Join A_0, B_0, C_0, etc., to *v*2′. Project the piercing points on the corresponding converging lines. Draw a smooth curve through the points thus obtained. Draw another curve in a similar way. Other corners of the arch can be obtained in a usual way.

Problem 19.4 Figure 19.17 shows TV and front elevation of a traffic booth. A small edge of the base of the booth is in the PPP and a vertical surface from that edge makes 30° with the PPP. A motorcyclist looks at the booth from a point 115 cm above the ground and 525 cm in front of the edge in the PPP. Draw the perspective view of the booth as seen by the motorcyclist.

Solution

1. Draw the PPP, GL and HL as shown. Locate *s*. Through *s*, draw *s*–*v*1 and *s*–*v*2 parallel to the sides in TV. Locate *v*1′ and *v*2′ on HL (not shown in the figure). Complete the perspective of the base as explained in Example 19.4.
2. For the perspectives of the middle and top portions, draw LOHs as shown. Complete the perspectives as explained in Example 19.12.

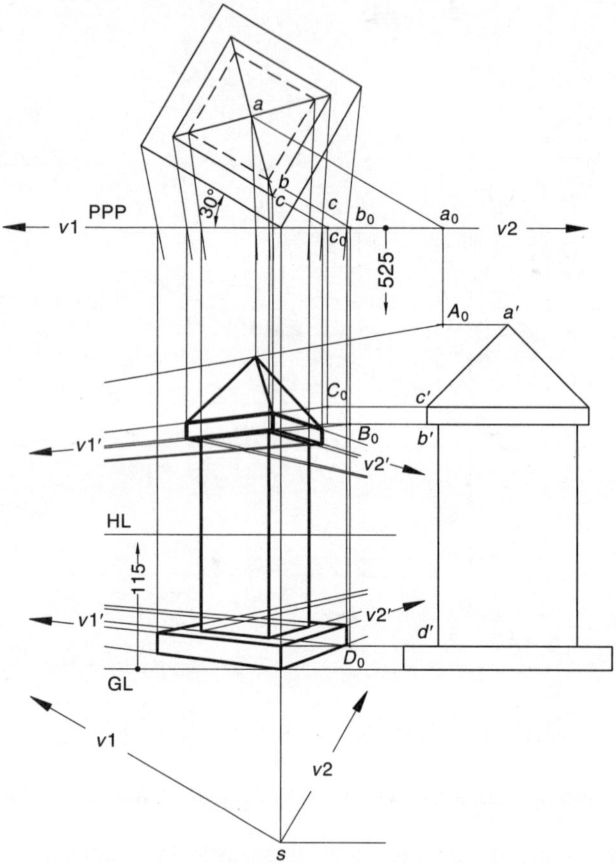

Fig. 19.17

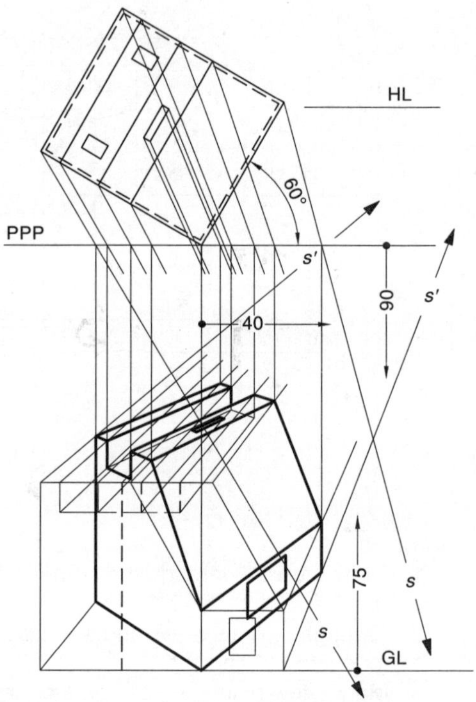

Fig. 19.18

Problem 19.5 Figure 19.18 shows TV and FV of the plastic body of a coin-operated telephone box. One of the vertical edges is in the PPP and a surface through that edge makes 60° with the PPP. An observer's eyes are 75 cm above the ground, 90 cm in front of the PPP and along the CP 40 cm on the right side of the edge in the PPP. Draw the perspective view of the box.

Solution

1. Draw the PPP, GL and HL as shown. Draw the CP and locate *s* and *s*′ (not shown in the figure).
2. Join all the corners in the TV with *s*. Locate piercing points.
3. Join all the corners in the FV with *s*′. Project the piercing points on the corresponding converging lines and complete the perspective view as explained in Example 19.7, Method 2.

Problem 19.6 Two square prisms of same base sizes are joined together to form a cross. The vertical prism is 95 mm long and the horizontal prism is 70 mm long. The base size of each prism is 20 mm × 20 mm. The axes intersect at a distance of 35 mm from the top of the vertical prism.

The cross rests on the ground with its front face making 30° with the *VP* and side faces 75° with ground. The lowest 40 mm edge is on the ground. Draw the three views of the cross.

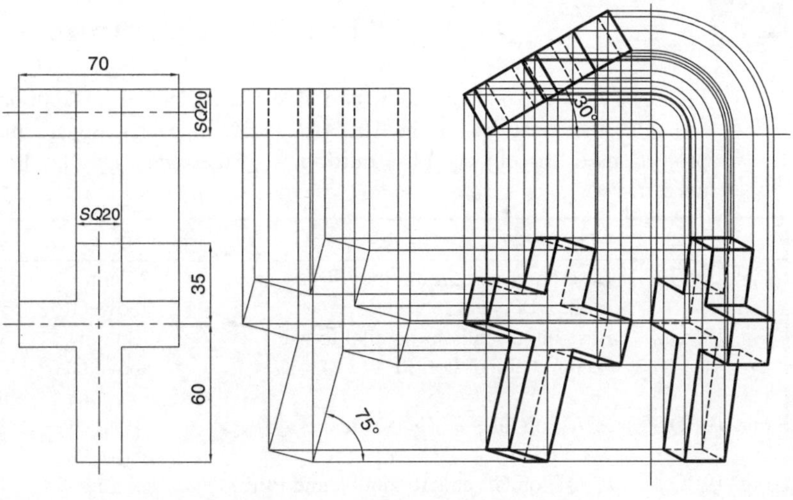

(a)

An observer looks at the cross from a point 60 mm above the ground, 250 mm in front of the PPP and along the CP 50 mm on the right side of the corner in the PPP. Draw the perspective view of the cross.

Solution Figure 19.19(a) shows FV, TV and SV of the cross. Note that the cross rests on an edge on the HP and a corner in the *VP*. The visual ray method is followed for the perspective.

Refer Fig. 19.19(b).

1. Redraw TV and SV. *XY* and *X*1 *Y*1 will serve as the PPP and PPP″ respectively. Draw GL, HL and CP and locate *s* and *s*″ at the given distances.
2. Join all the points in TV with *s* and mark the piercing points. Similarly, join all the points in SV with *s*″ and locate the piercing points.
3. Project the piercing points from the PPP vertically and the piercing points from the PPP″ horizontally. At the corresponding intersections, locate the desired points. Join these points for the perspective view.

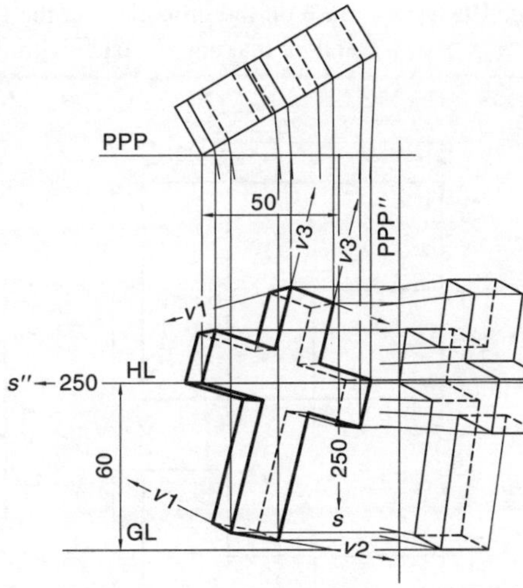

(b)

Fig. 19.19

If the edges of the cross are extended, they will meet at the three *VP*s. This is so because neither a face nor an edge of the cross is parallel to the PPP. Obviously, it is an oblique perspective.

REMEMBER THE FOLLOWING

- *VP*s are always seen on HL in FV.
- The third-angle method of projection is convenient in perspective projection.

REVIEW QUESTIONS

1. Figures 19RQ.1 to 19RQ.5 show two views of the objects. The orientation of the object with respect to the PPP, the locations of the HL, CP and *S* in each case are mentioned below. Draw perspective projections of the objects. (The third view of the object may be drawn, as per the given orientation, if necessary.)

	Orientation	*HL*	*CP*	*S*
Fig. 19RQ.1	Base on ground, *a* on the PPP, *ab* at 30° to the PPP	75 mm above GL	20 mm on the right side of *a*	100 mm in front of the PPP
Fig. 19RQ.2	Base on ground, *ab* parallel to and 20 mm behind the PPP	100 mm above GL	Through centreline of the object	80 mm in front of the PPP
Fig. 19RQ.3	*a″*(*b″*) on GL, *a″* (*b″*)–*c″* makes 40° with GL	40 mm above GL	Through *a*	110 mm in front of the PPP
Fig. 19RQ.4	*a″* (*b″*) on GL and 10 mm behind PPP', *c″* on PPP'	65 mm above GL	Through left edge of the object	140 mm in front of the PPP
Fig. 19RQ.5	Base on the ground, *a* on the PPP, *ab* and *ac* making 45° each with the PPP	40 mm above GL	Through *b*	200 mm in front of the PPP

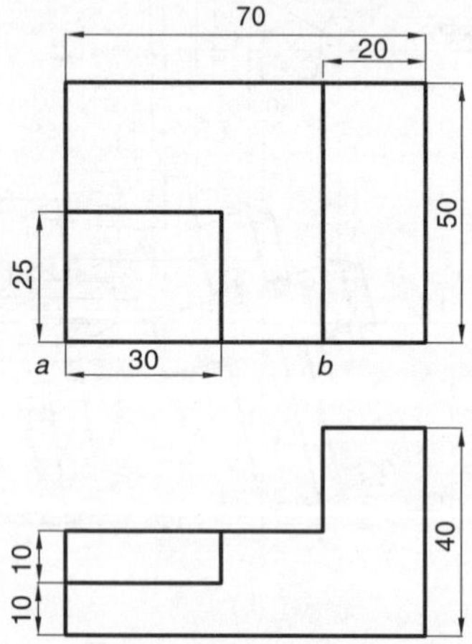

Fig. 19RQ.1

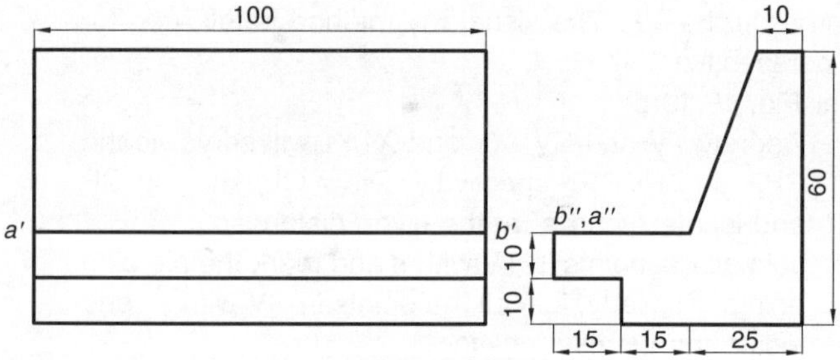

Fig. 19RQ.2

2. Figure 19RQ.6 shows the FV and SV of a balcony of a bungalow. The CP is 3 m on the left-hand side of *a*. Face *a′b′c′d′* is in the PPP. The station point is 8 m above the base of the balcony and 9 m in front of the PPP. Draw the perspective view of the exterior of the balcony.
3. Figure 19RQ.7 shows an elevation and plan of a water tank. The PPP is horizontal and 1 m above the tank. The CP is 1.5 m on the right-hand side of the centreline of the tank. The station point is 15 m above the ground and 17 m in front of the front face of the tank. Draw the view of the tank in perspective.

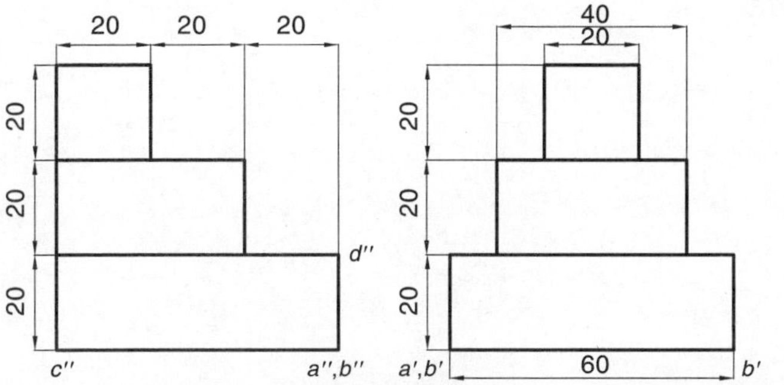

Fig. 19RQ.3

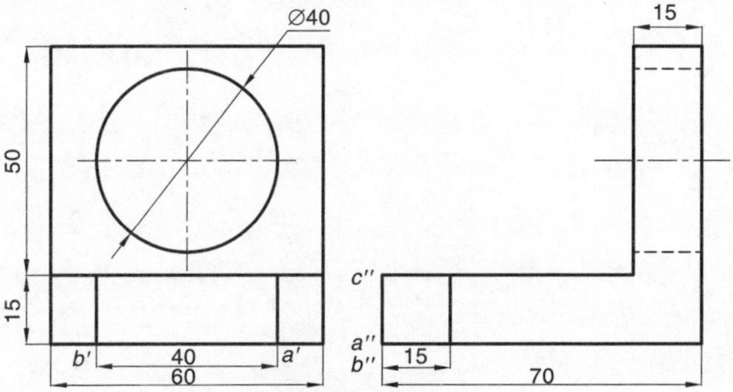

Fig. 19RQ.4

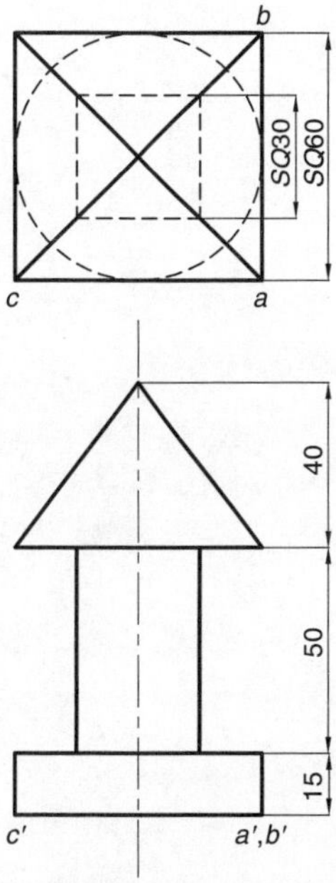

Fig. 19RQ.5

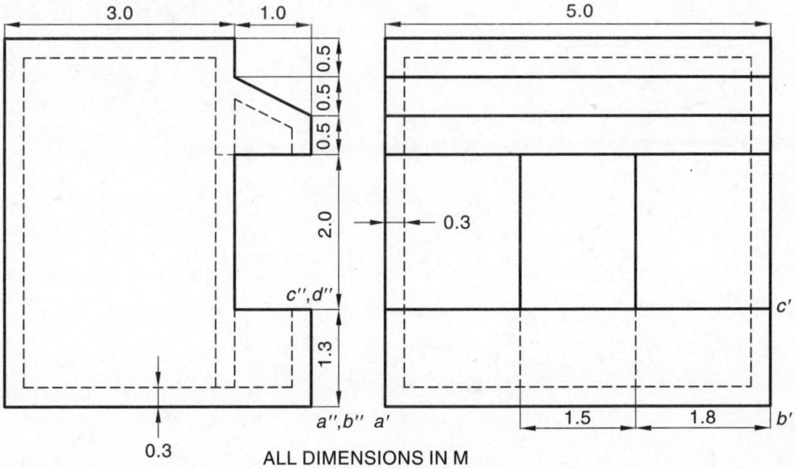

Fig. 19RQ.6

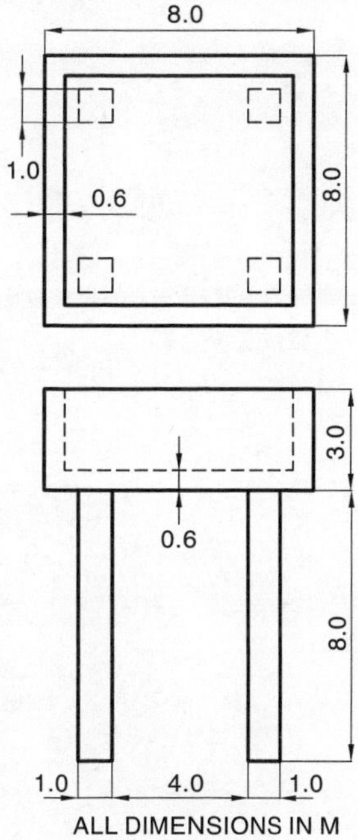

Fig. 19RQ.7

Chapter 20

INTERPRETATION OF THE VIEWS

20.1 INTRODUCTION

A language is said to be effective if it uses a minimum of words to convey thoughts. Similarly, a drawing is said to be effective if it contains a minimum of lines and views. Obviously, the views must be chosen in such a way that they will provide a complete and exact information about the object. The lines in all the views of an object should lead to one and only one interpretation. For this, one needs to have knowledge of drawing conventions, dimensioning techniques, sectioning methods, and use of notes and notation systems. Every engineer, must therefore, acquire the technique of constructing and interpreting a drawing with a minimum number of lines and views. This chapter explains how to read and interpret a given drawing correctly. It also provides the technique of constructing an additional view to ease the visualization.

20.2 INTERPRETATION FROM ONE VIEW

Many objects can be completely interpreted from one view only. Washers, gaskets, flat sheet metal objects, printed circuit boards (PCBs), etc., are the common examples. These objects have negligible thicknesses as compared to their surface areas. Hence, a view showing the details of the surface is sufficient to describe them fully. Similarly, cylindrical objects and bars of uniform cross sections can be correctly interpreted from one view only. When only one view is used to describe the object, use of appropriate dimensioning techniques, sectioning methods and notes should be made to clarify the features of the object, as illustrated in Fig. 20.1.

Standard solids, like right regular prisms, cylinders, spheres, etc., can be specified completely by one-line specifications, e.g., 'a sphere of 100 mm diameter'. Obviously, no drawing is needed to describe them.

20.3 INTERPRETATION FROM TWO VIEWS

A majority of the machine components require two views to specify their shapes completely. In such cases, if only one view is provided, it leads to misinterpretation. See Figs 20.2 to 20.4. Each (a) figure displays a TV of an object. The possible interpretations from the TV are shown in each (b) figure.

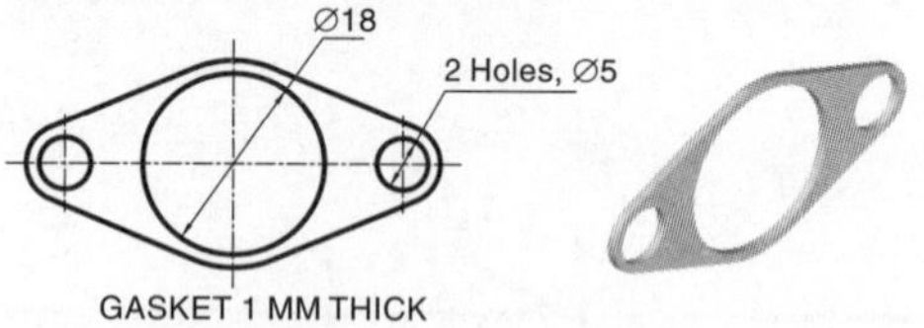

(a) Use of note 'GASKET 1 MM THICK' provides an idea about the thickness of the flat gasket.

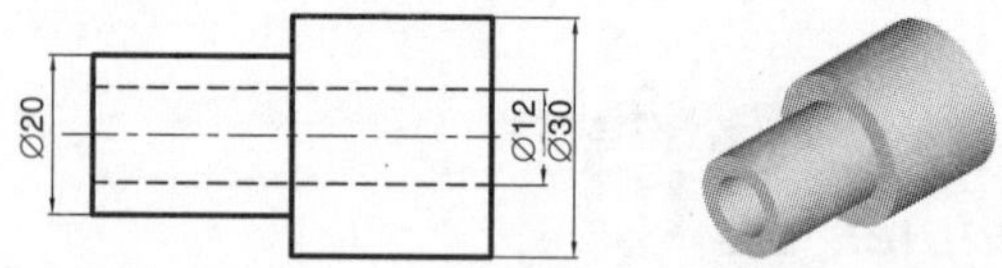

(b) Use of centerline and 'ϕ' symbol provide an idea about the cylindrical object.

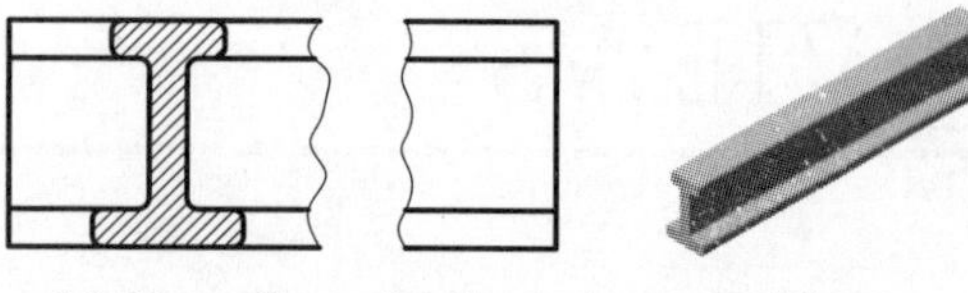

(c) Use of revolved section provides an idea about the cross section of the bar.

Fig. 20.1

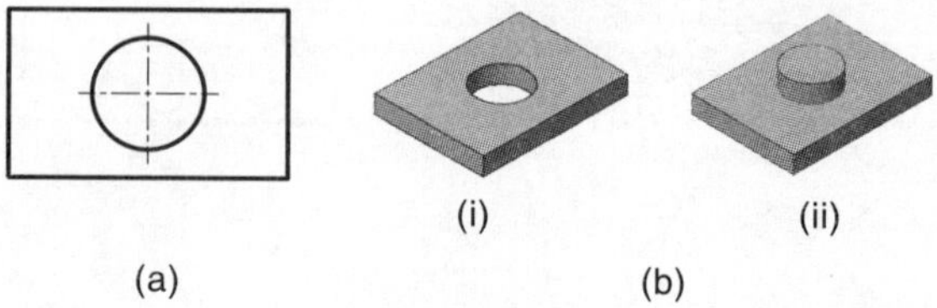

Fig. 20.2

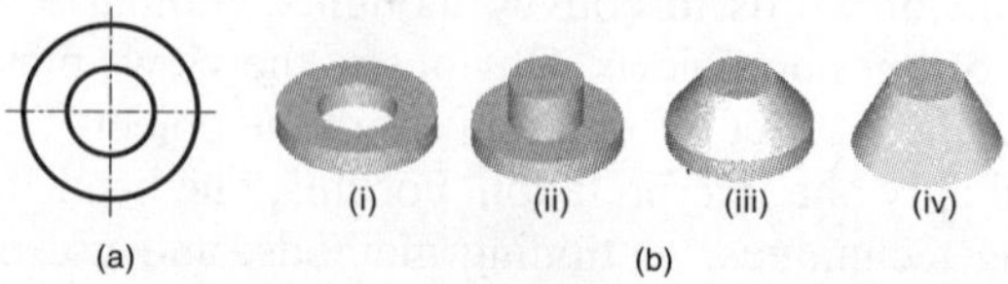

Fig. 20.3

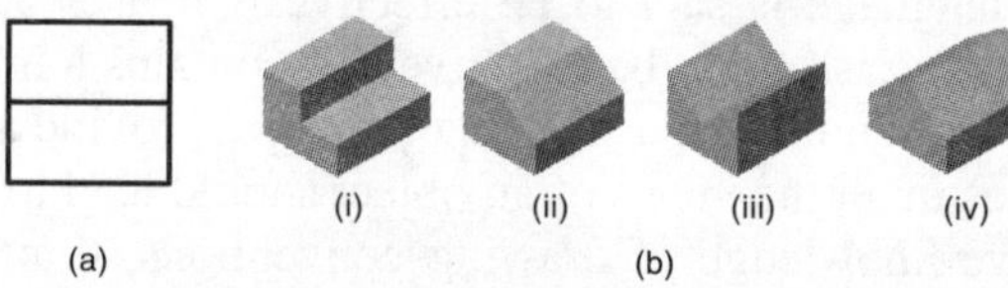

Fig. 20.4

It is clear that, a minimum of two views are necessary to decide the exact shape of the objects shown above. The second view often becomes necessary when a feature of the object protrudes from or pierces in a surface. If two similar features (say, holes) overlap in one view, another view becomes necessary.

In two-view drawings, the choice of the views plays an important role. As a standard practice, FV and TV or FV and SV are drawn. The view which displays the maximum details should be chosen as the FV or TV. For many objects, as a thumb rule, the view which has maximum dimensions (i.e., length × width) is chosen as the FV. Once the FV is decided, another view should be chosen in such a way that the two views together provide the complete information about the object. For illustration, consider an object shown in Fig. 20.5(a). When viewed in direction *X*, its FV, TV and SV are seen as in Fig. 20.5(b). For viewing direction *Y*, the three views will be as in Fig. 20.5(c). A little examination will show that only FV and SV in Fig. 20.5(b) are sufficient to provide a complete idea of the object. Also, FV and SV, or FV and TV in Fig. 20.5(c) will provide a complete idea. The third view is redundant and need not be drawn. If only FV

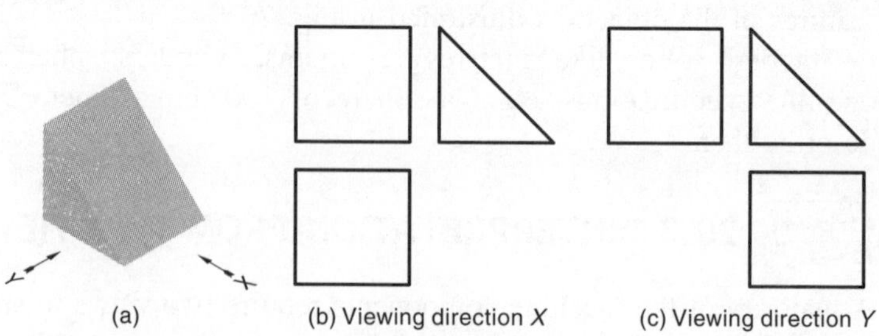

Fig. 20.5

and TV as in Fig. 20.5(b) are drawn, it will lead to three different interpretations as illustrated in Fig. 20.6.

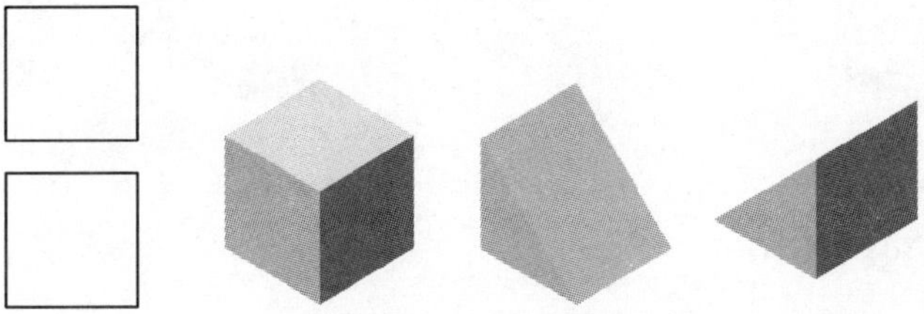

(i) (ii) (iii)

Fig. 20.6

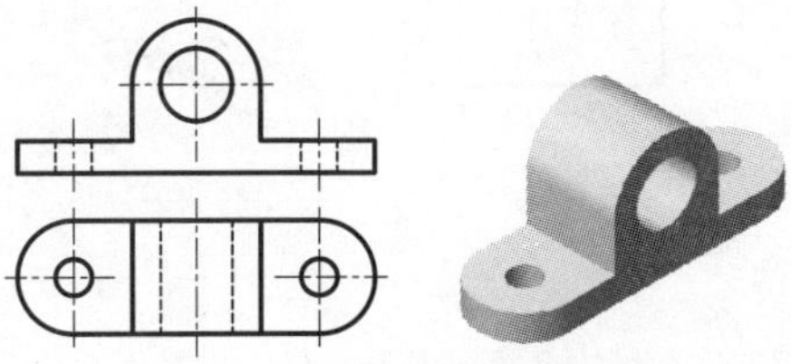

(a) (b)

Fig. 20.7

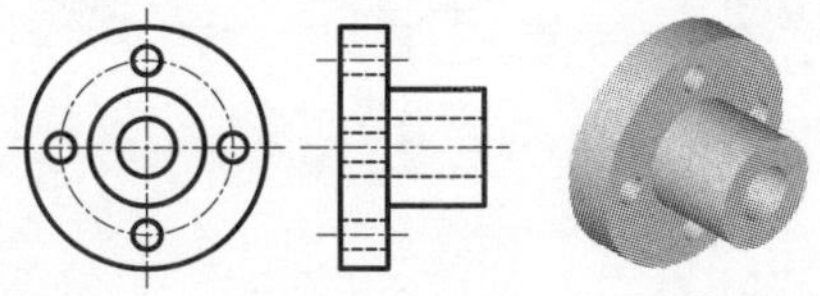

(a) (b)

Fig. 20.8

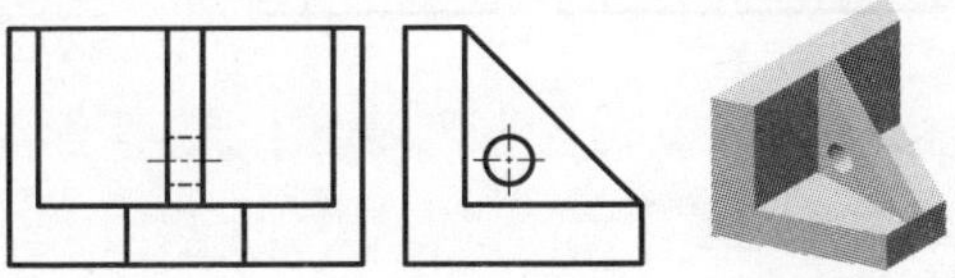

(a) (b)

Fig. 20.9

The objects shown in Fig. 20.7 to Fig. 20.9 represent examples of two-view drawings. In each case, only one interpretation is possible from the given two views.

In case of Fig. 20.7, the SV will not provide any additional information. In case of Fig. 20.8, TV will be similar to SV and hence need not be drawn. Similarly, in Fig. 20.9, the TV will not add to any information. If the TV would have been provided instead of the SV, the shape of the triangular rib would not have been clear. Hence, FV and SV is the best combination. In all these cases, two views are sufficient to describe the object completely.

20.4 INTERPRETATION FROM THREE VIEWS

There are a few objects which need three views for complete understanding. The third view becomes necessary if the object has different geometries in the three mutually perpendicular faces which cannot be identified by any two views. Figures 20.10 to 20.13 show the examples. All the objects, except those in Fig. 20.10(b)-(iv) and 20.11(b)-(iv), need three views to describe them fully. The objects in Fig. 20.10(b)-(iv) and 20.11(b)-(iv) can be interpreted by drawing their FV from the other direction and the corresponding TV.

If FV and TV of Fig. 20.10(a) are supplemented by SV of Fig. 20.11(a), we get a unique object as in Fig. 20.10(b)-(i) [or Fig. 20.11(b)-(i)]. Similarly, FV and SV of Fig. 20.12(a) together with TV of Fig. 20.13(a) will give a unique interpretation as in Fig. 20.12(b)-(iii) [or Fig. 20.13(b)-(i)].

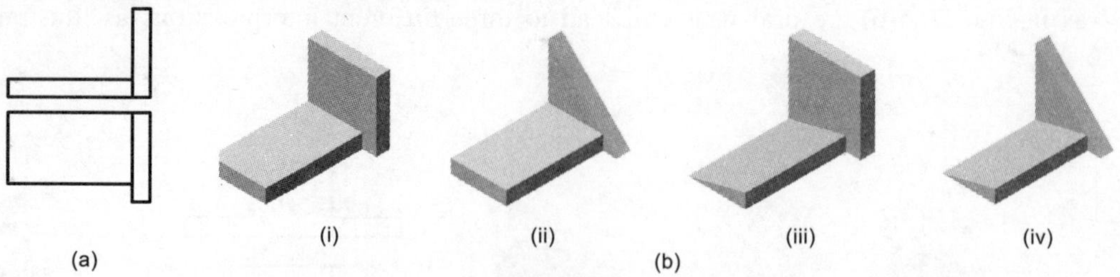

Fig. 20.10

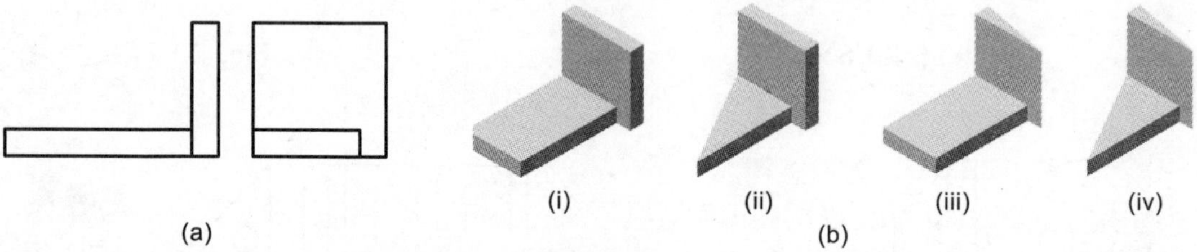

Fig. 20.11

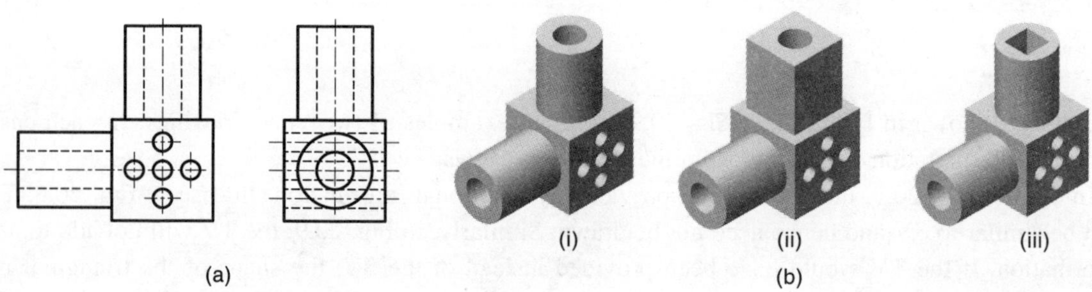

Fig. 20.12

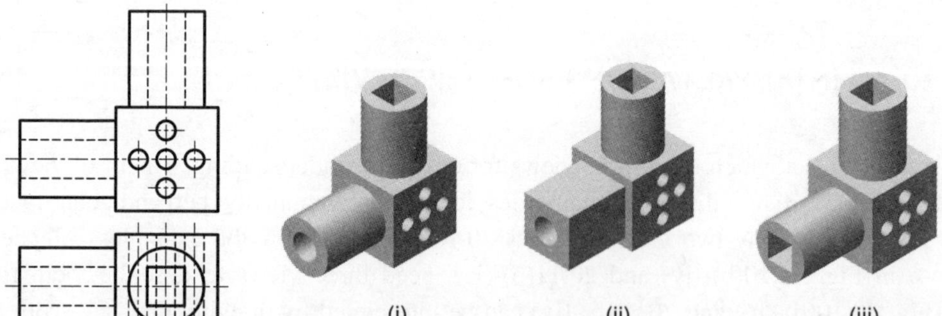

Fig. 20.13

Figure 20.14 to 20.17 explain the necessity of three views to explain some unique features of the objects. These objects cannot be visualized correctly with any two views. The third view is always necessary to determine the shape of some features of the object.

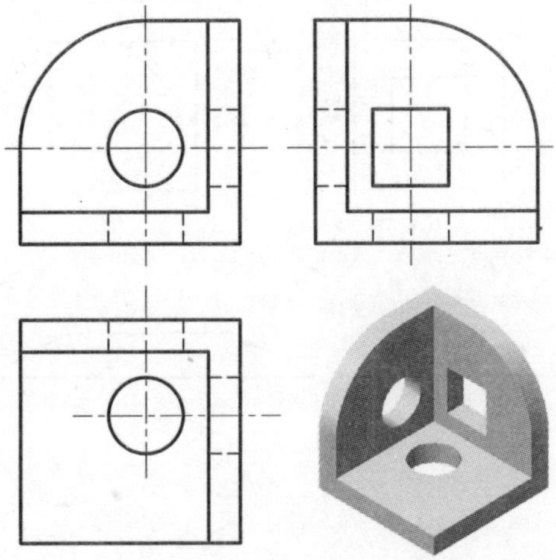

(a) (b)

Fig. 20.14

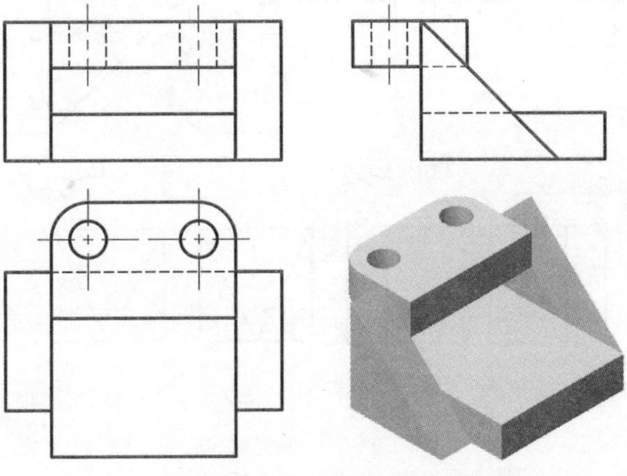

(a) (b)

Fig. 20.15

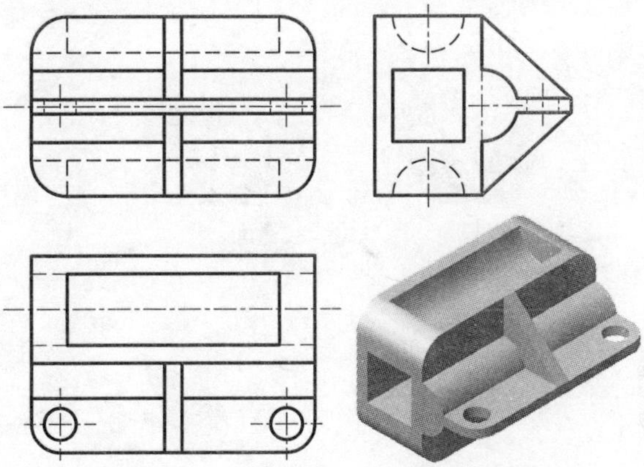

(a) (b)

Fig. 20.16

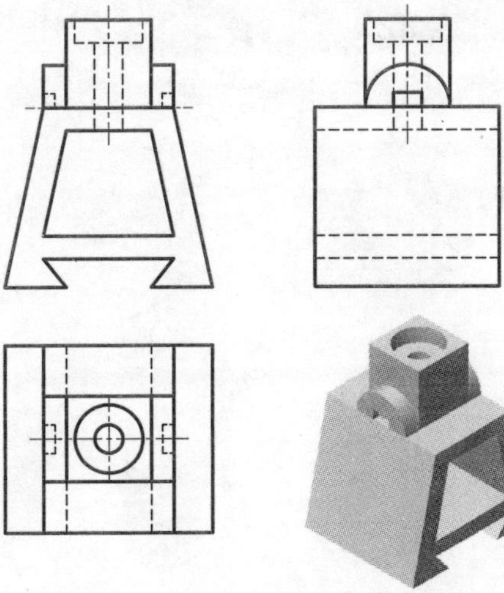

(a) (b)

Fig. 20.17

Example 20.1 Figure 20.18(a) to (g) show two views of the objects. Draw isometric view(s) of each object considering all possible interpretations.

Solution Refer Fig. 20.19(a) to (g) for possible interpretations.

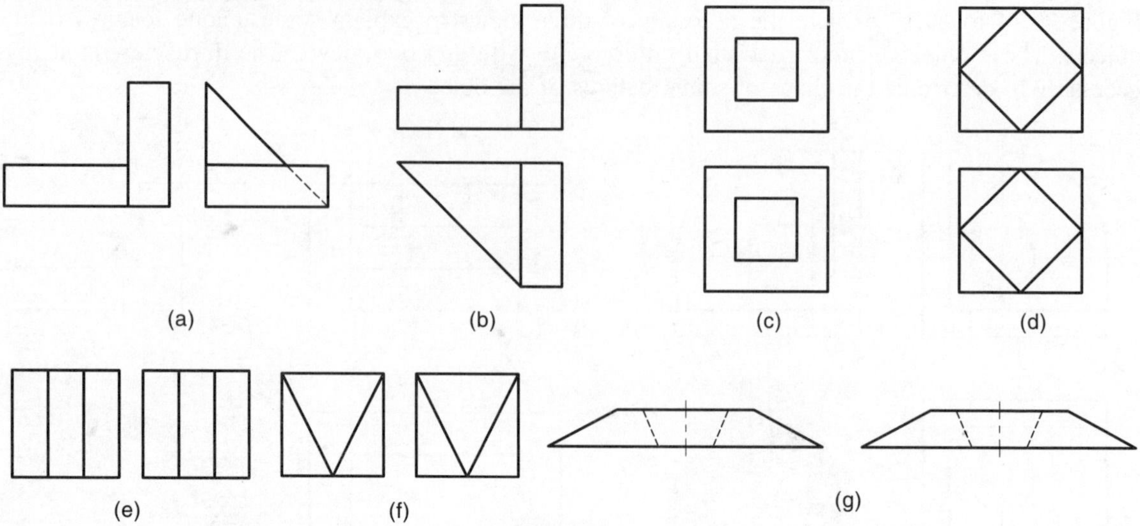

Fig. 20.18

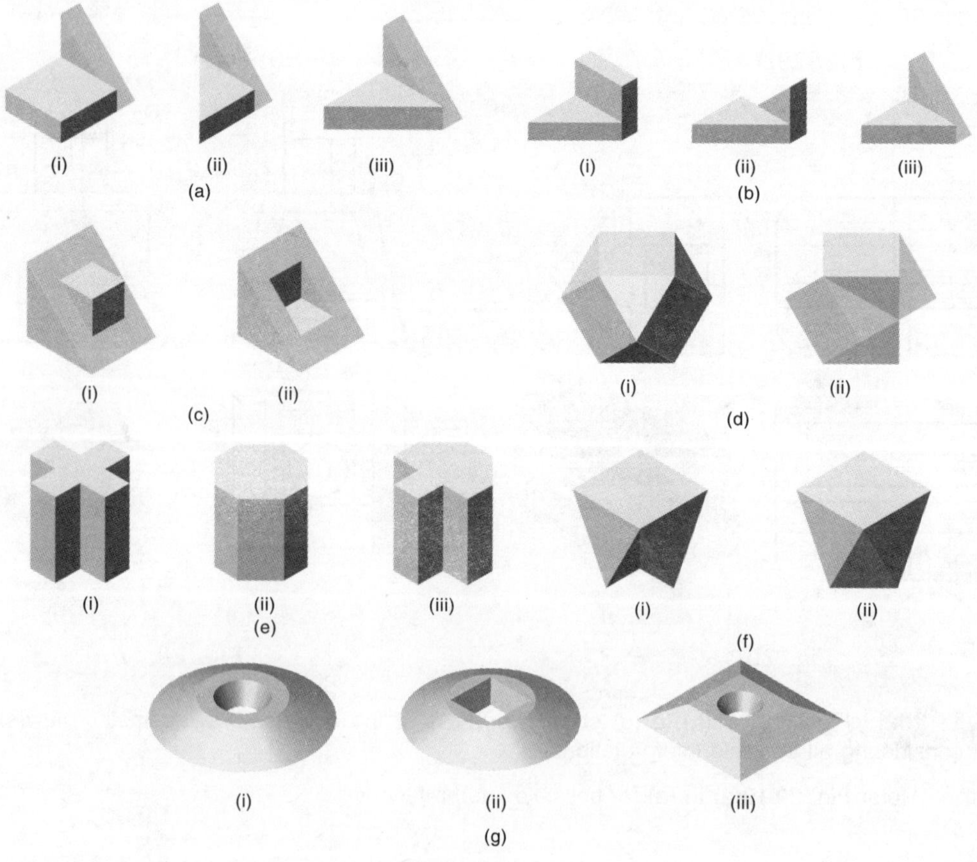

Fig. 20.19

Example 20.2 Figures 20.20 to 20.26 show pictorial views of the objects. For each object, state the minimum number of principal views needed to describe the object completely.

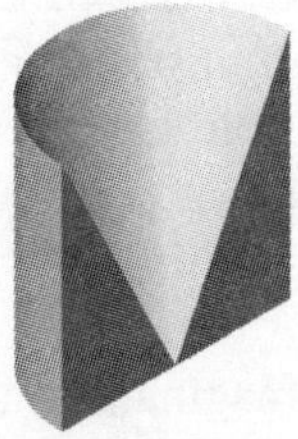
Fig. 20.20

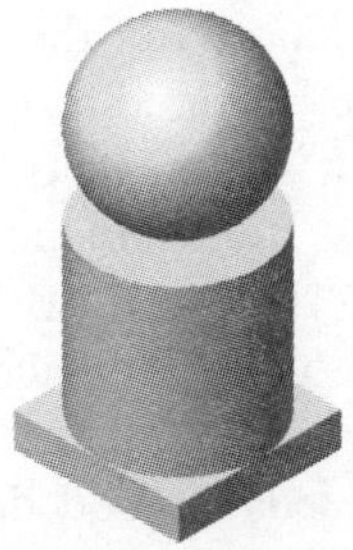
Fig. 20.21

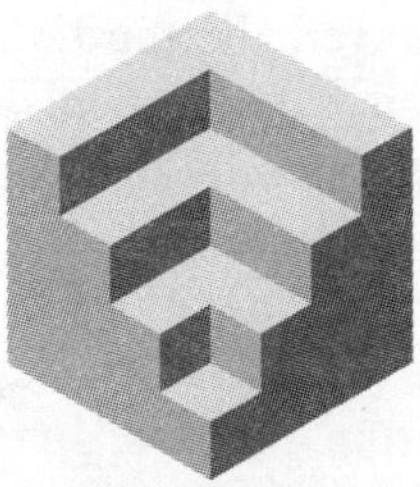
Fig. 20.22

Fig. 20.23

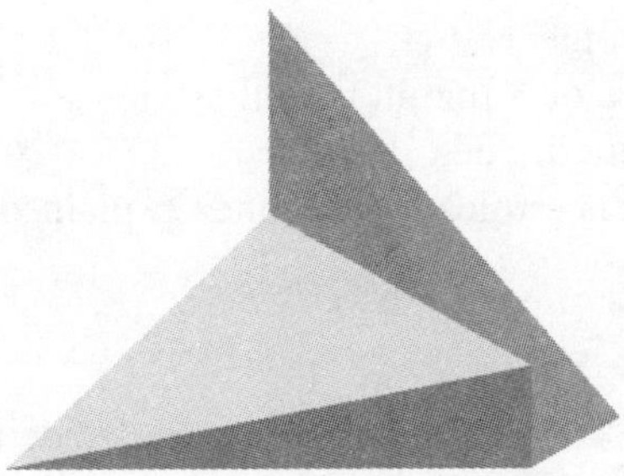
Fig. 20.24

Fig. 20.25

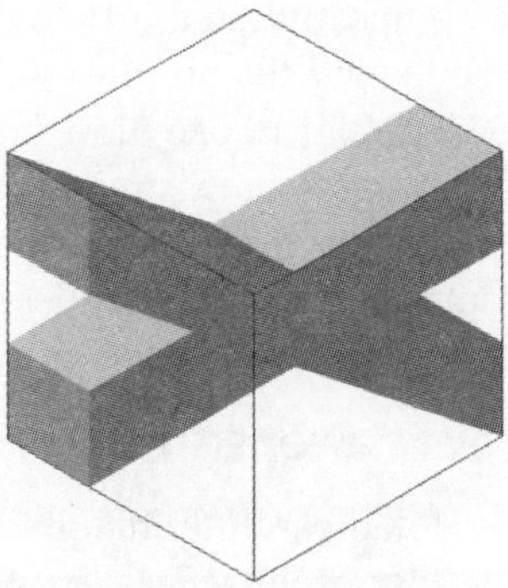
Fig. 20.26

Solution The minimum essential views are
Fig. 20.20: FV and TV   Fig. 20.21: FV   Fig. 20.22: FV and TV or FV and SV
Fig. 20.23: FV and SV   Fig. 20.24: FV and TV   Fig. 20.25: FV, TV and SV
Fig. 20.26: FV and SV
In each case, the direction for the FV must be chosen properly.

Remember the Following

- The view which displays maximum details should be chosen as the FV or TV.
- Each point/line/face in one view always has a correspondence with a point/line/face in the other view.
- A point in any view always indicates a corner or an edge of the object.
- A continuous straight line in any view always indicates an edge or a surface or a part of the surface of the object.
- A centerline always indicates the existence of a curved surface of a cylinder or a cylindrical hole. It also signifies the object's symmetry.
- The dashed lines (hidden lines) always form a closed area (except when they represent a flat surface tangent to a curved surface). One or more lines forming the area may be continuous thick lines.

20.5 MISSING VIEWS AND MISSING LINES

As is clear from the discussion and examples previously, a majority of the objects can be completely described from two views. However, the third view may be prepared to ease the visualization. The third (or fourth) unknown view is called the *missing view*. It should be noted that the missing view never adds to the information revealed by the existing views. It only reduces the multiple interpretations to one and only one interpretation. Just look at Figs 20.10, 20.11, 20.12, 20.13 and 20.18. Each of these figures reveals multiple interpretations from the two views. In each case, if the third view is added, only one interpretation is possible.

Drawing the missing view from the two given views needs a good degree of imagination and knowledge of drawing conventions. Sometimes, we may have three incomplete views of an object. There may be a few *missing lines* in each view. A careful reading of any two views will help draw the missing lines in the third view.

The following thumb rules will help draw missing views and missing lines.

1. A point in one view may represent a line or a point in the other view.
2. A continuous straight line in one view may represent a face or a line in the other view.
3. Follow the rules mentioned in Section 14.10 for deciding the hidden lines.

In addition to the above rules, readers should also use the precedence rules for the lines explained in Section 9.6.3.

20.5.1 Steps in Drawing Missing Views

1. Read carefully the given views. Draw projectors from one view to another view to decide the 'correspondences' between points/lines/faces in one view to points/lines/faces in other views.
   Also, draw projectors from both the views for the third view. The third view must be appropriately located in relation to the existing views.
2. Visualize the object. If multiple interpretations are possible, choose any one. A small freehand isometric sketch may be drawn if needed.
3. Draw the desired view by locating the required points at the intersections of the projectors. The visualization or the isometric sketch will help to draw hidden features.

To draw the missing lines, similar steps may be followed.

Example 20.3 From the FV and TV of an object shown in Fig. 20.27, draw the LHSV.

Solution Follow the steps explained in Fig. 20.28.

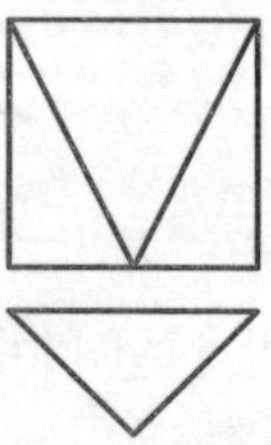

Fig. 20.27

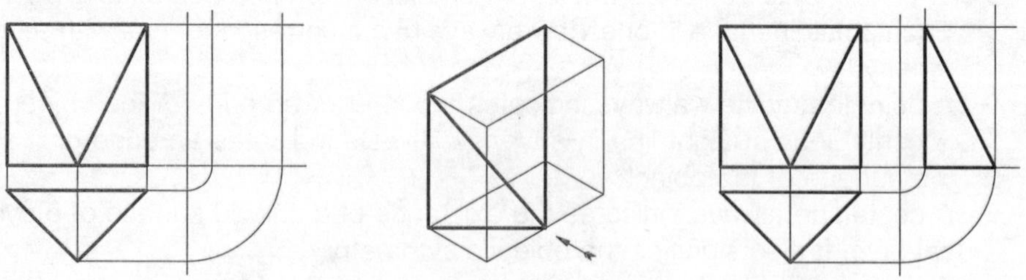

Step 1: Draw projectors. (a) **Step 2:** Prepare an isometric sketch. (b) **Step 3:** Draw the LHSV. (c)

Fig. 20.28

Example 20.4 From the TV and SV shown in Fig. 20.29, draw the FV.

Solution Refer Fig. 20.30 for the FV.

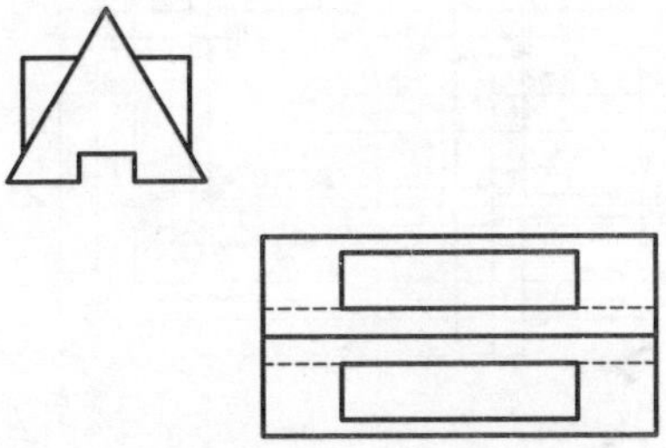

Fig. 20.29

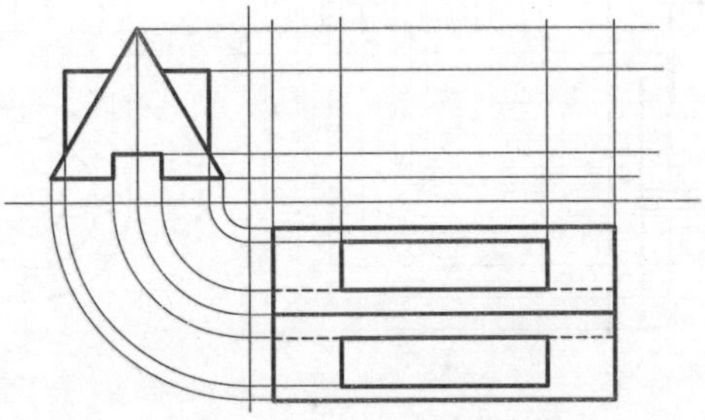

(a)

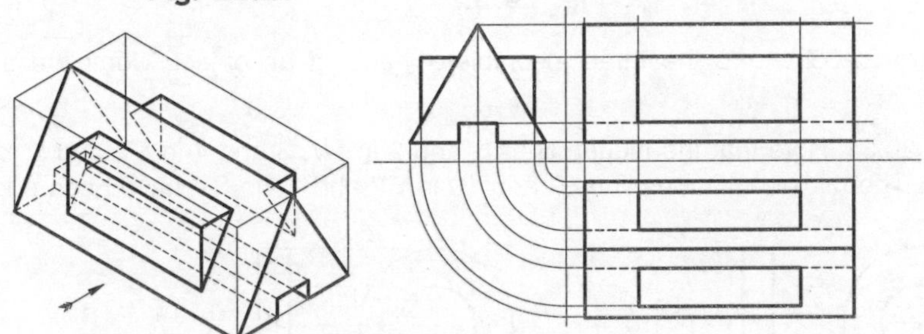

(b)

(c)

Fig. 20.30

Example 20.5 Figure 20.31 shows the FV and TV of an object. Draw

(i) Sectional FV (along given section)
(ii) TV
(iii) LHSV

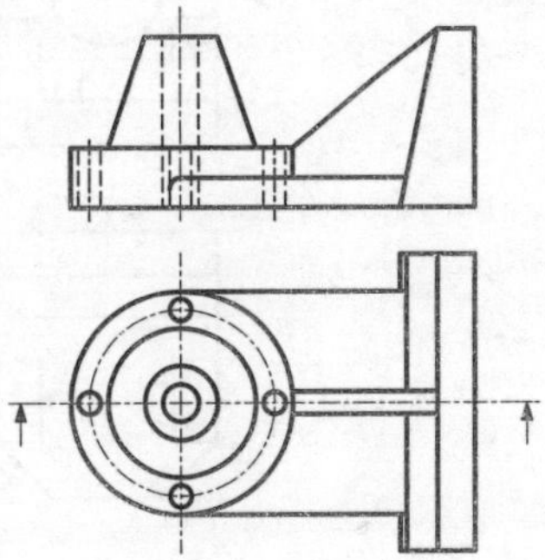

Fig. 20.31

Solution Refer Fig. 20.32. First, draw the LHSV as in (c) and then make the sectional FV as in (d). All the hidden lines and projectors should be removed from the FV before hatching.

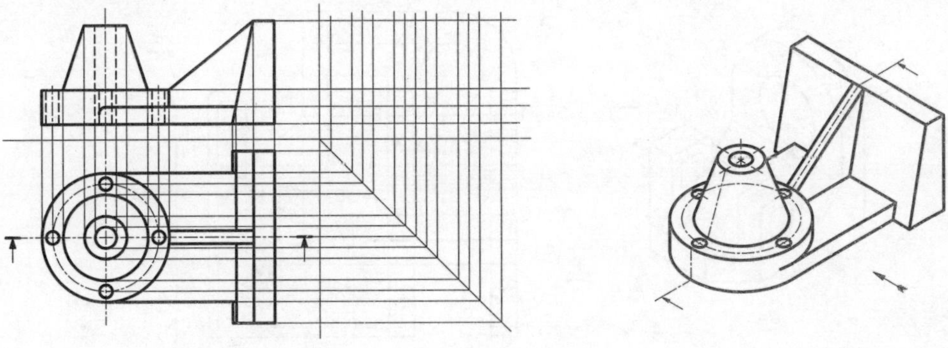

(a)

(b)

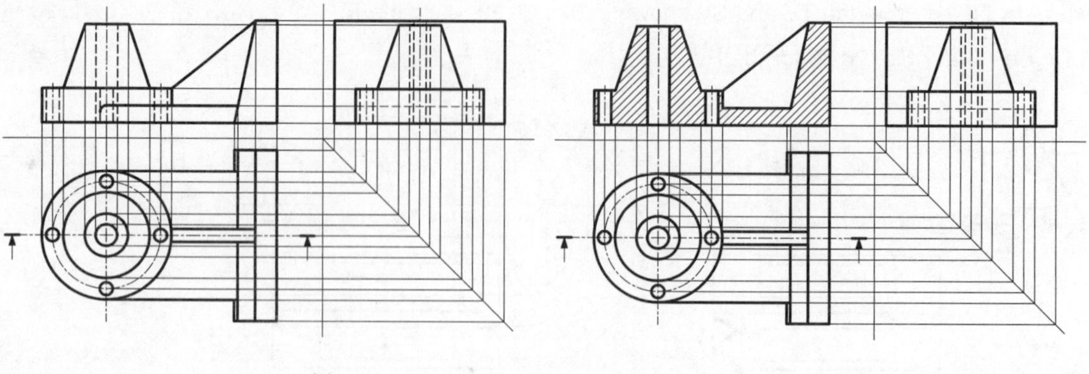

(c) (d)

Fig. 20.32

Example 20.6 Figure 20.33 shows the three incomplete views of an object. Complete the views by drawing missing lines.

Solution Refer Fig. 20.34. Note that the hidden lines 1 and 2 in FV, 3 and 4 in SV and 5, 6, 7 and 8 in TV have been added. The thick continuous lines 9 and 10 in FV and 11 in SV have been added.

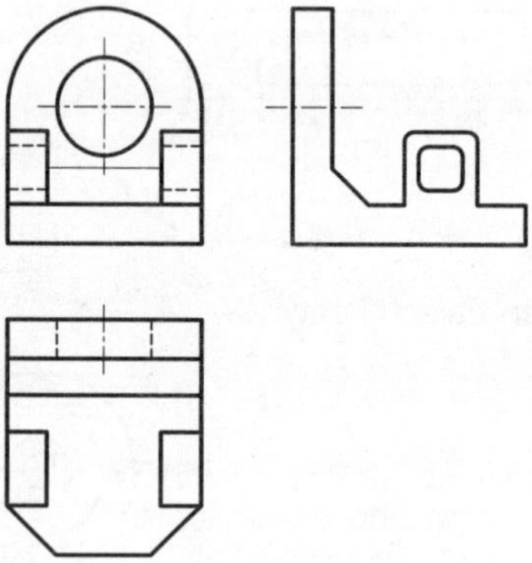

Fig. 20.33

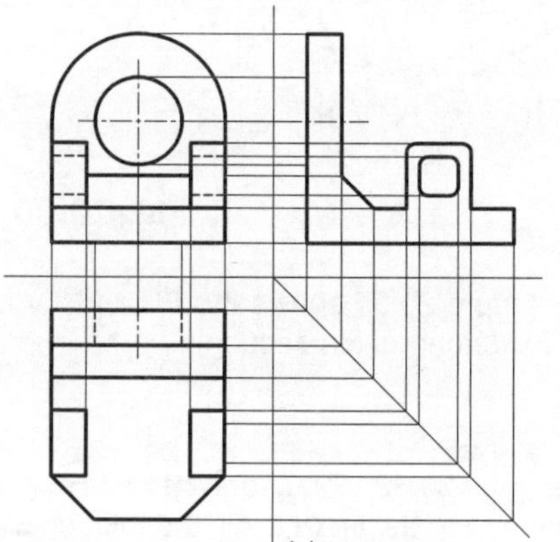

(a)

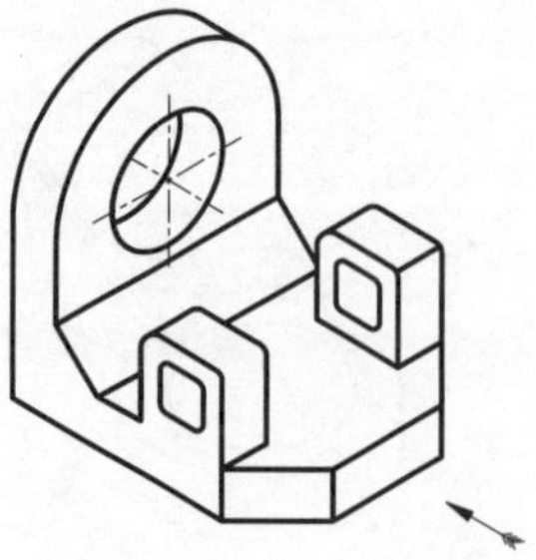

(b)

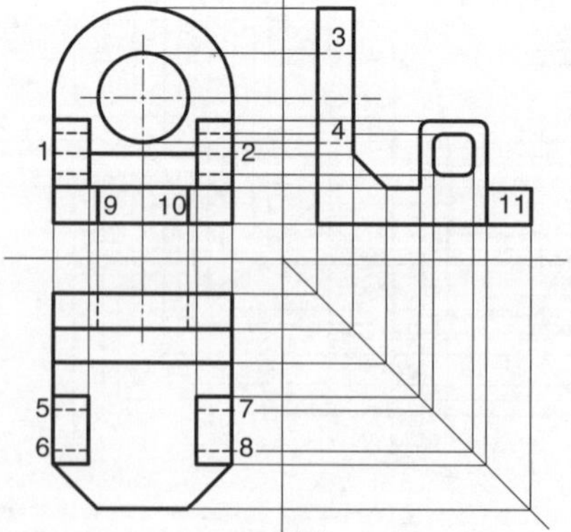

(c)

Fig. 20.34

Example 20.7 Complete the three views shown in Fig. 20.35 by drawing the missing lines.

Solution Refer Fig. 20.36. The thick continuous lines 1 in FV and 2 and 3 in SV have been added. The hidden lines 4, 5 and 6 in FV have been added. A centreline 7 has been drawn in SV.

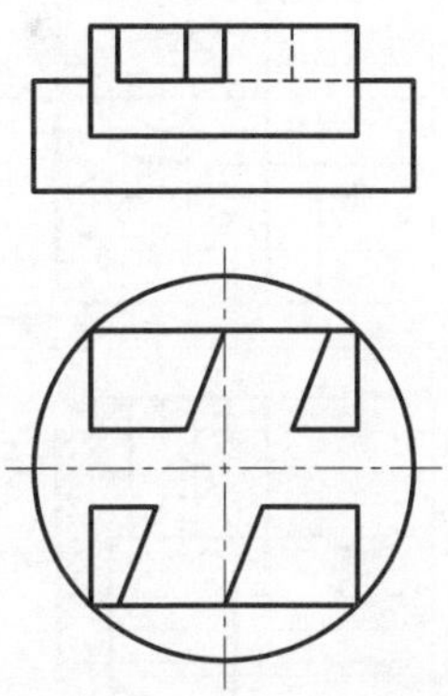

Fig. 20.35

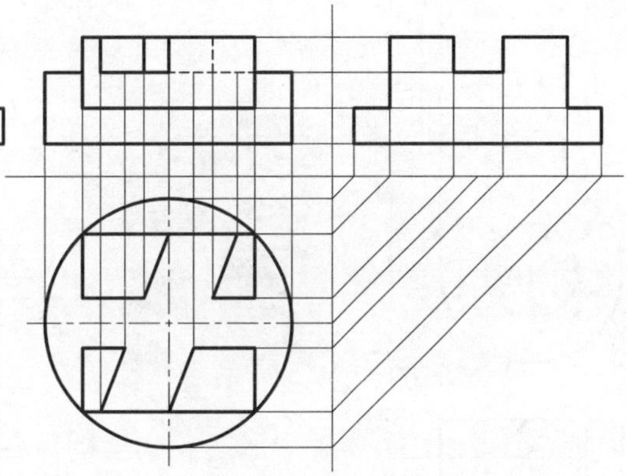

(a)

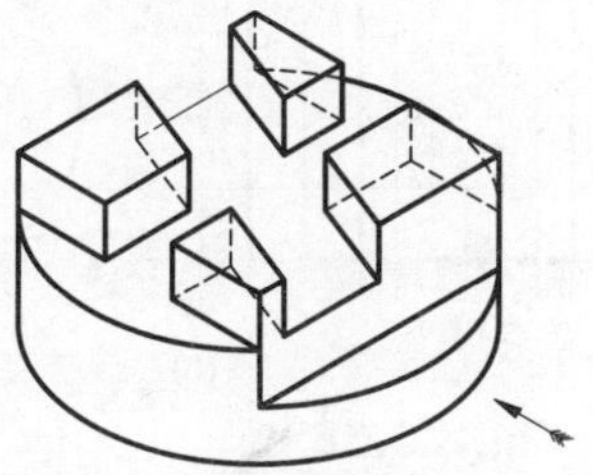

(b)

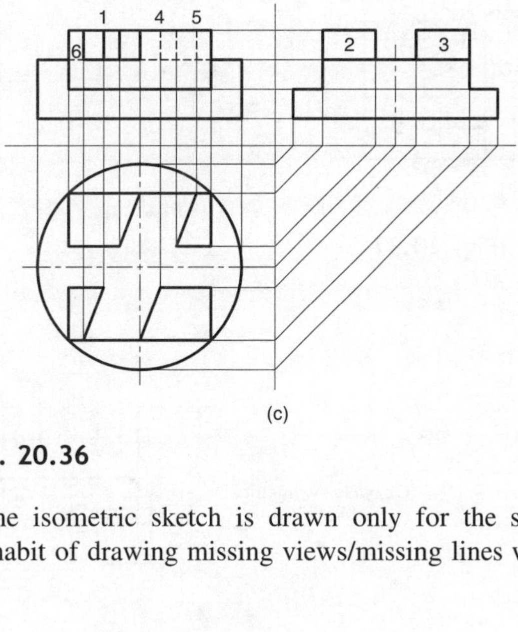

(c)

Fig. 20.36

Note that in all the examples given above, the isometric sketch is drawn only for the sake of understanding. The readers should develop the habit of drawing missing views/missing lines without constructing the pictorial sketches.

ILLUSTRATIVE PROBLEMS

Problem 20.1 Figure 20.37 shows the elevation and plan of an object. Using the third-angle method of projection, draw

(i) Sectional FV (section along *A–A*) (ii) LHSV (iii) TV

Solution Refer Fig. 20.38. The locations of the views are changed for the third-angle projection.

Problem 20.2 Figure 20.39 shows the FV, partial TV and partial SV. Using the first-angle method of projection, draw

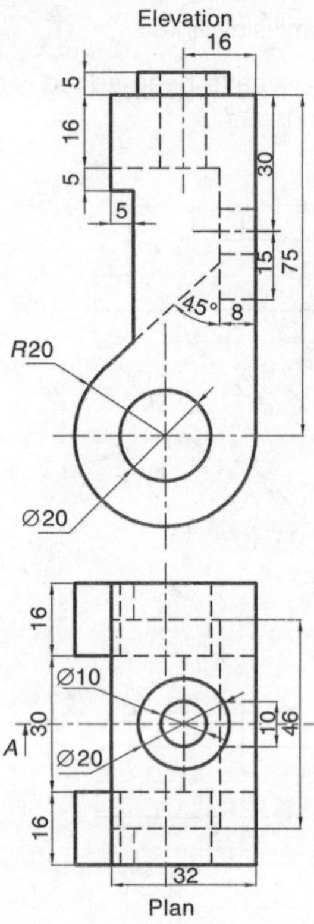

Fig. 20.37

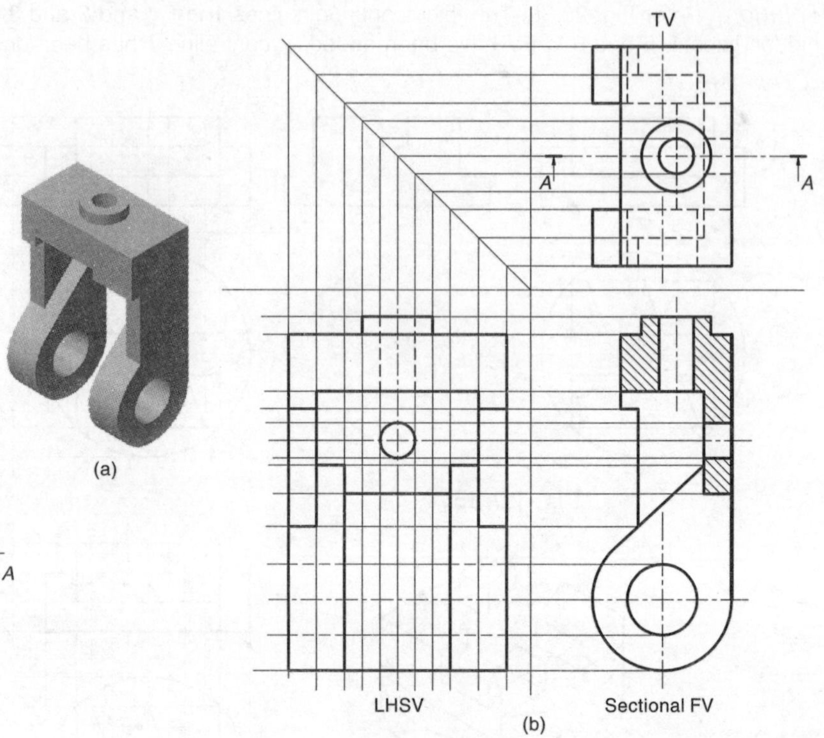

Fig. 20.38

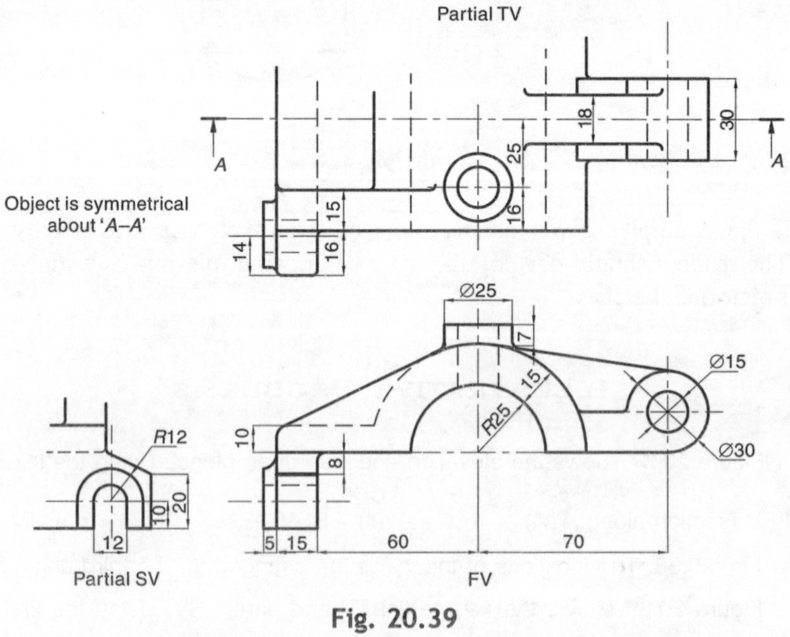

Fig. 20.39

(i) Sectional elevation (section along *A–A*)
(ii) Complete plan
(iii) LHSV

Solution Refer Fig. 20.40. Relocate the given views for the first-angle method of projection. As the object is symmetrical about *A–A*, first complete the TV. Then, visualize the object, draw the isometric sketch if necessary and complete the SV. Lastly, make the FV sectional.

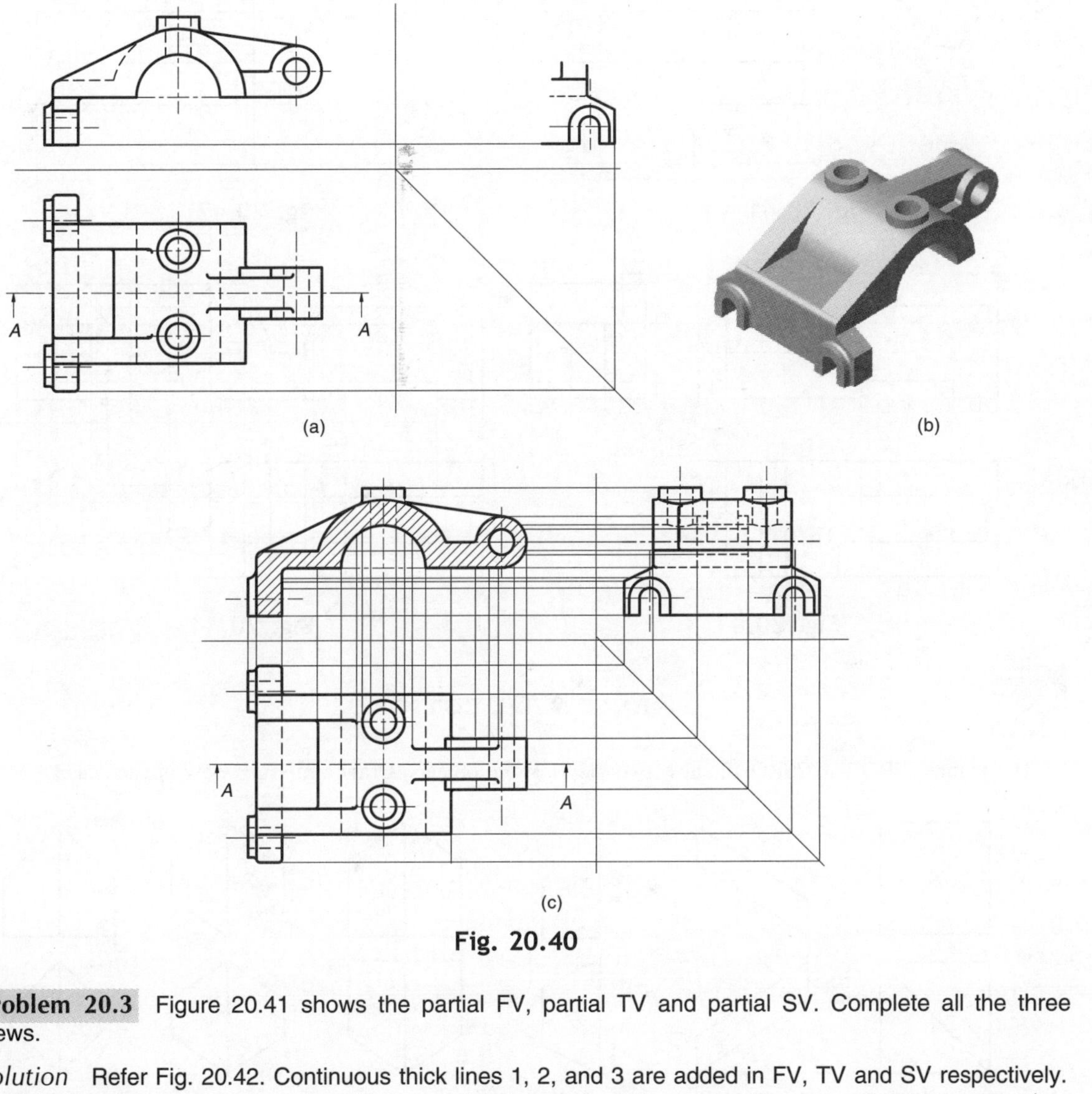

(a) (b)

(c)

Fig. 20.40

Problem 20.3 Figure 20.41 shows the partial FV, partial TV and partial SV. Complete all the three views.

Solution Refer Fig. 20.42. Continuous thick lines 1, 2, and 3 are added in FV, TV and SV respectively.

Problem 20.4 Complete the three views of an object shown in Fig. 20.43 by drawing the missing lines.

Solution Refer Fig. 20.44. Hidden lines 1, 2, 3, 4, 5 and a continuous line 6 are added.

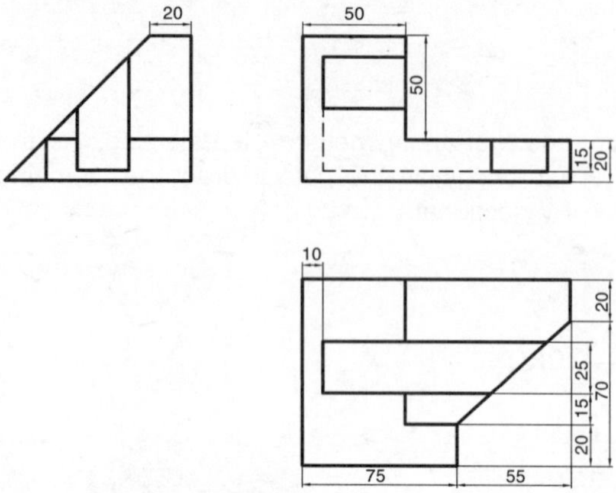

Fig. 20.41

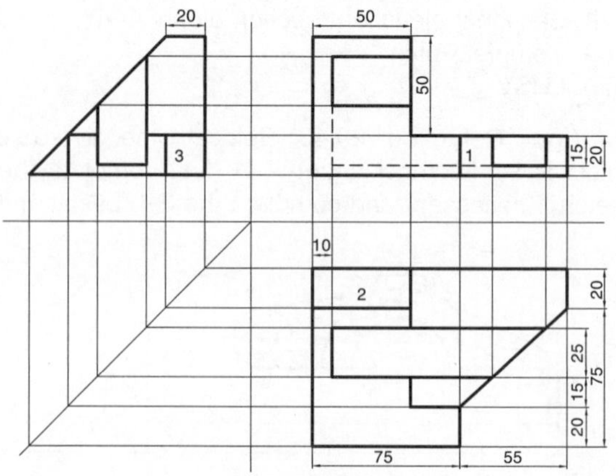

Fig. 20.42

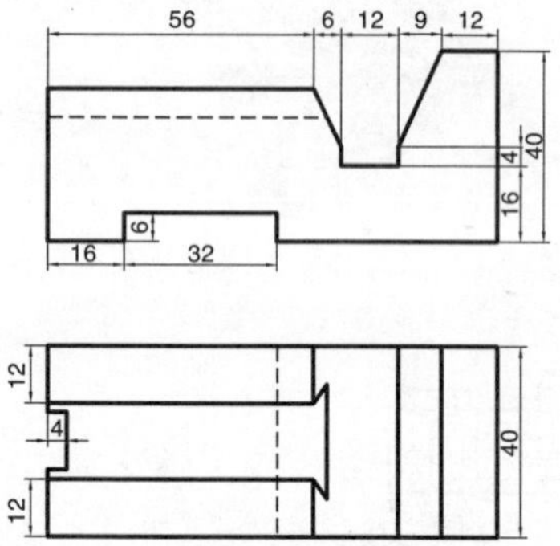

Fig. 20.43

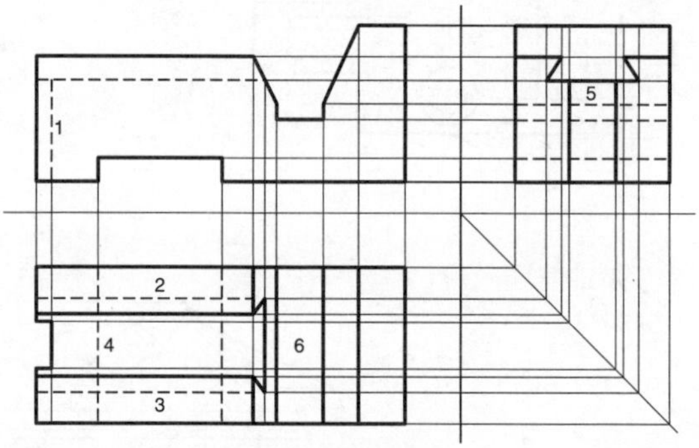

Fig. 20.44

Review Questions

1. Figure 20RQ.1 to 20RQ.12 show two views of the objects. Draw a missing view in each case.

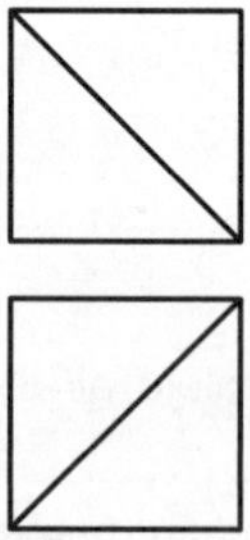

Fig. 20RQ.1

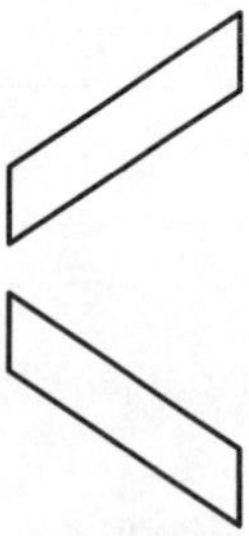

Fig. 20RQ.2

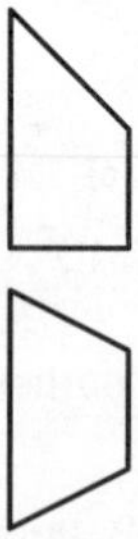

Fig. 20RQ.3

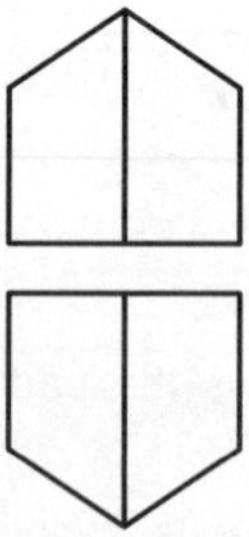

Fig. 20RQ.4

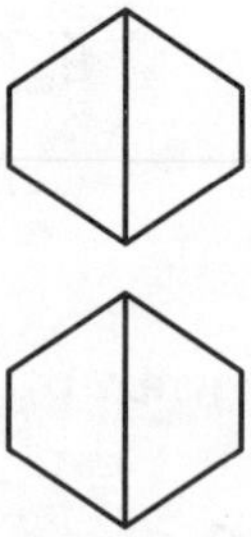

Fig. 20RQ.5

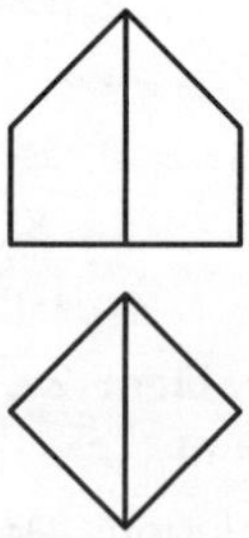

Fig. 20RQ.6

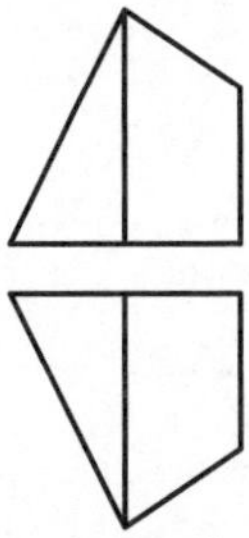

Fig. 20RQ.7

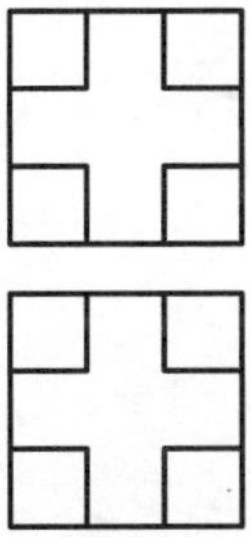

Fig. 20RQ.8

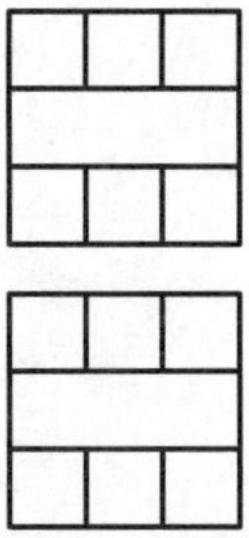

Fig. 20RQ.9

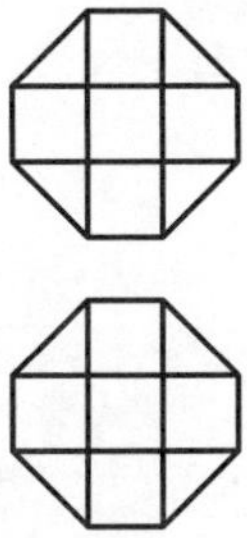

Fig. 20RQ.10

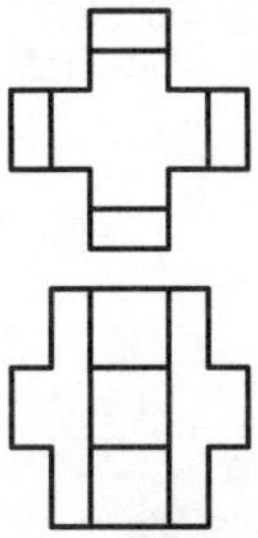

Fig. 20RQ.11

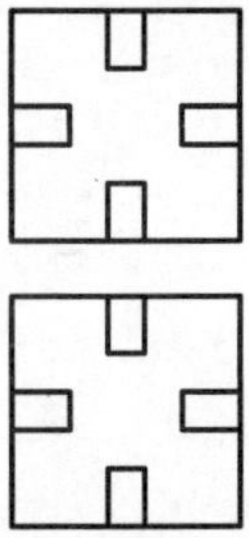

Fig. 20RQ.12

2. Figures 20RQ.13 to 20RQ.20 show three incomplete views of the objects. Complete them by drawing a minimum number of missing lines.

Fig. 20RQ.13

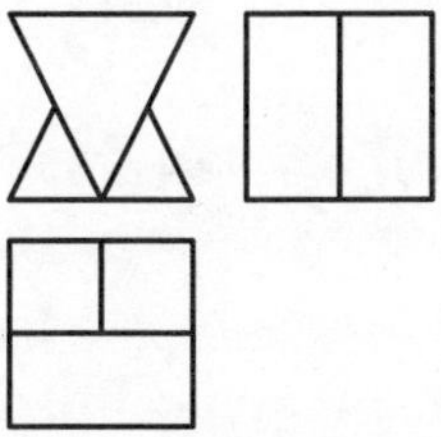

Fig. 20RQ.14

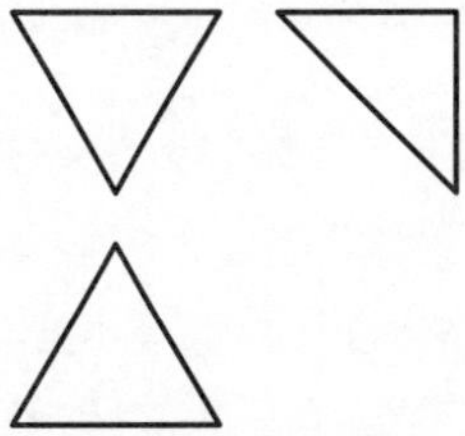

Fig. 20RQ.15

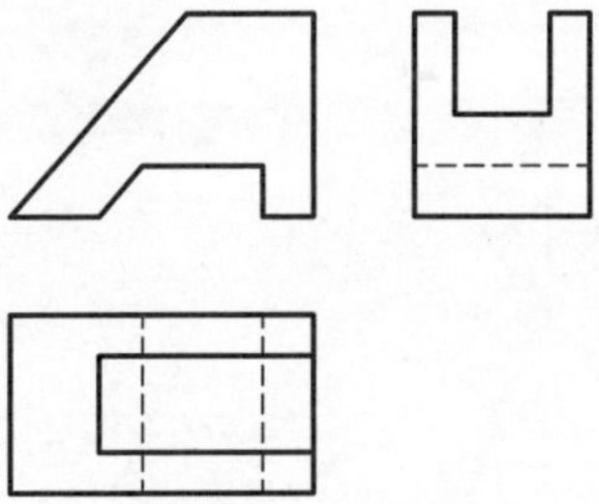

Fig. 20RQ.16

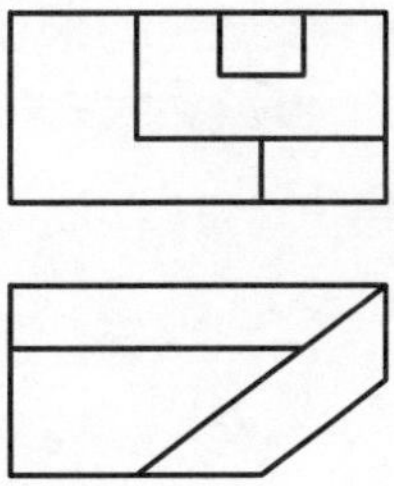

Fig. 20RQ.17

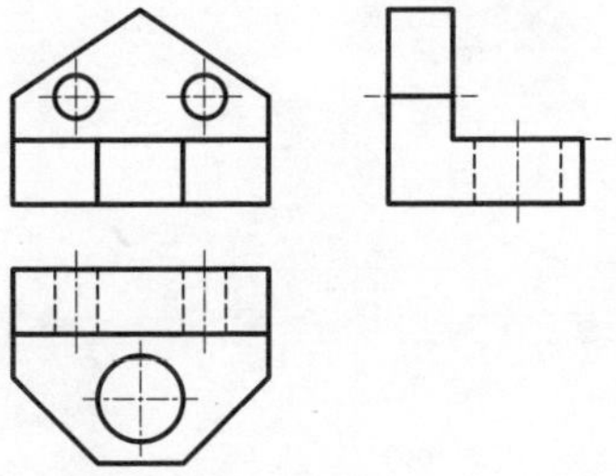

Fig. 20RQ.18

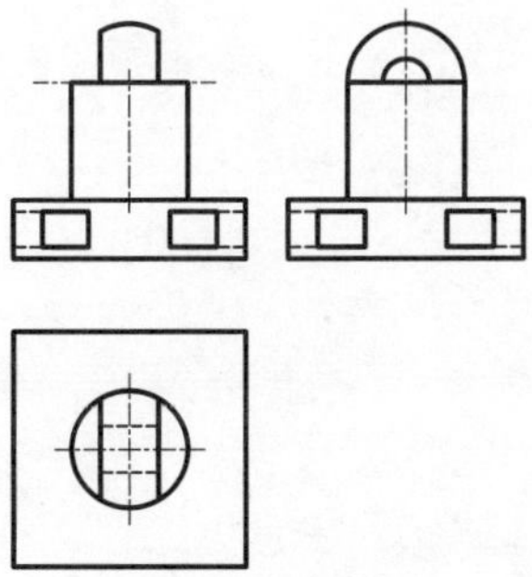

Fig. 20RQ.19

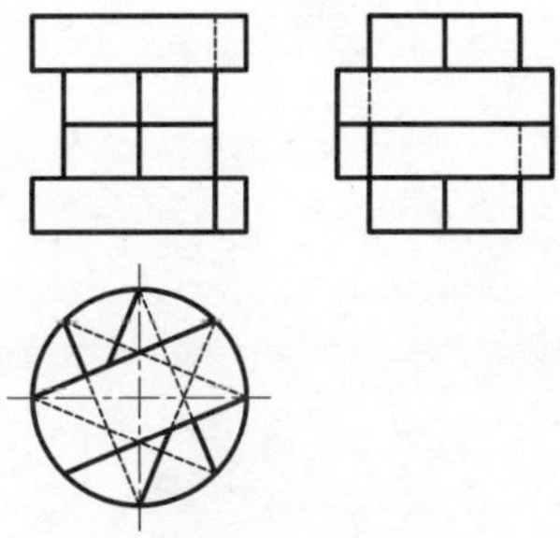

Fig. 20RQ.20

Chapter 21

FREEHAND DRAWING

21.1 INTRODUCTION

On many occassions, engineers have to work on shop floors or at sites. At such locations, they have to prepare drawings of objects without using any instrument. In such instances, engineers make use of freehand drawing. Freehand drawing refers to the act of drawing the views of the object without using a scale or instruments.

Though freehand sketches are drawn without exact dimensions, they should be proportionate. A good freehand drawing is one which resembles the scaled drawing. With little practice, it is possible to draw a fairly accurate freehand drawing. This chapter provides important tips and tricks for freehand drawing.

21.2 PREREQUISITES FOR FREEHAND DRAWING

21.2.1 Pencil Use

Freehand drawings are prepared using a pencil, a paper and an eraser. A soft grade pencil, preferably HB grade, with rounded lead tip (Section 1.4.2) will provide good results. The pencil shall be gripped at distance of approximately 30 mm from lead tip. The angle between pencil and paper should be smaller (preferably 45°) than that used in instrumental drawing. Unlike instrumental drawing, in freehand drawing, the pencil should slope up toward the wrist.

21.2.2 Hand Strokes

The next requirement is the practice of line strokes as explained in Section 2.2.5. In freehand sketching, maximum hand movement must be made about the wrist and elbow. The movement about the shoulder should be as minimum as possible. This will ensure fineness and accuracy in drawing.

While practicing hand strokes for straight lines, make movements about the elbow and shoulder keeping the wrist rigid. For circular hand strokes, make movements about the knuckle and wrist. Direction sense must be observed while making hand strokes. It should be noted that the palm rests on the paper slightly above the wrist which puts some limitations on the wrist movements.

21.2.3 Visual Judgement

Judgement about lengths and angles is very important in freehand sketching. It helps to draw proportionate drawings. Readers are advised to see closely the ruling edge of the scale. The spacing between centimetre marks should be observed carefully. This will enable the readers to know what 'distance' on a paper approximately corresponds to 1 cm. After sufficient practice, distances up to 15 cm can be drawn with fair accuracy.

Judgement about angles can be practiced in a similar way by observing the protractor scale. Some handy tips for drawing accurate angles are provided in the later section.

Readers are advised to use graph papers initially for practice purposes. Isometric grids (explained later) may be used for isometric drawings. After sufficient practice, plain white paper should be used.

Table 21.1 summarises the difference between instrumental drawing and freehand drawing.

Table 21.1 Instrumental Drawing versus Freehand Drawing

Instrumental Drawing	*Freehand Drawing*
• H/2H grade pencil is preferred. • The pencil is held at an angle of 60°–65° to the paper. The slope is toward the direction of the line being drawn. • The arm movement is more about elbow and shoulder and less about the wrist.	• HB grade pencil is preferred. • The pencil is held at an angle of 45° (approximately) to the paper. The slope is almost toward the wrist. • The arm movement is more about the wrist and elbow and less about the shoulder.

21.3 SKETCHING STRAIGHT LINES

Straight lines can be drawn in three steps as follows, Fig. 21.1:

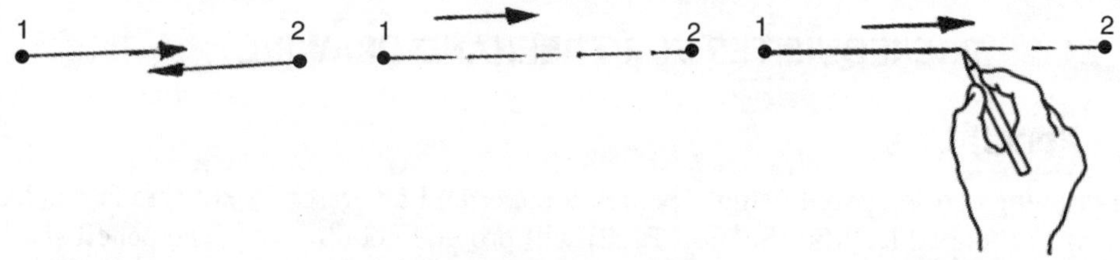

Fig. 21.1

Step 1

Locate the start point 1 and end point 2. Without touching the pencil to the paper, make trial movements from left to right and right to left.

Step 2

Sketch a very light segmented line starting from 1 and going on till 2.

Step 3

Draw a continuous thick line over the segmented line. The segments not aligned to the direction of the line should be discarded.

The vertical and inclined lines can be drawn in a similar way, Fig. 21.2 and Fig. 21.3. Follow the line strokes already mentioned, i.e., top to bottom for vertical lines and left to right or top to bottom (depending on the convenience) for inclined lines.

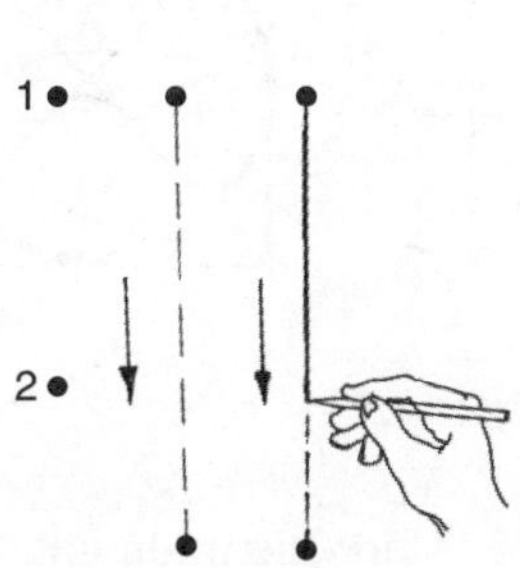

Fig. 21.2

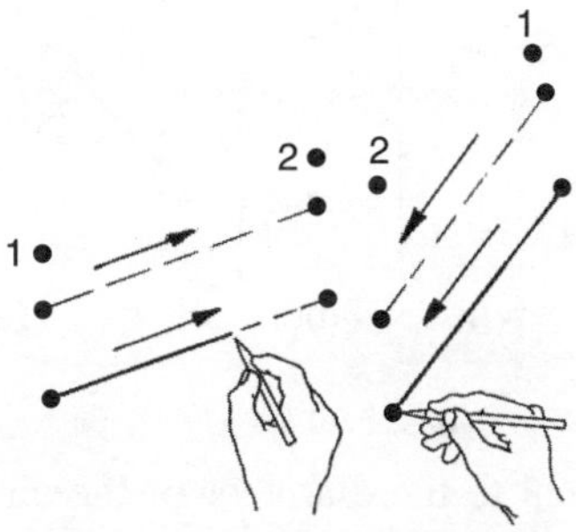

(a) Nearly horizontal inclined line (b) Nearly vertical inclined line

Fig. 21.3

21.4 SKETCHING CIRCLES

21.4.1 Small Circles

Small circle of given radius can be easily drawn by adopting one of the two methods.

Method I: Diagonal line method Adopt the following steps, Fig. 21.4.

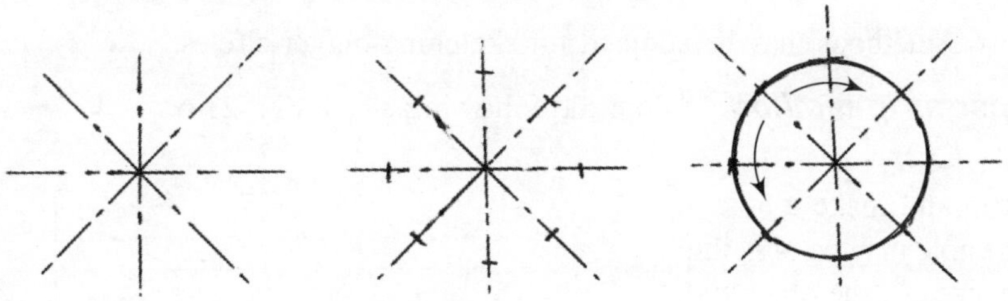

Fig. 21.4

Step 1

Draw two light centrelines—horizontal and vertical. Locate the centre at their intersection. Draw diagonal lines in each quadrant. These lines will approximately bisect the angle formed by the centrelines.

Step 2

Mark small perpendicular segments on each of the lines, at a distance equal to radius by the visual judgment. First, mark the segments on the centrelines and then on the diagonal lines.

Step 3

Draw a smooth freehand circle tangent to each segment. Follow direction sense. Make the circle sufficiently thick and uniform.

Note: For very small circles, only two centrelines are sufficient.

Method II: Square method Adopt the following steps, Fig. 21.5.

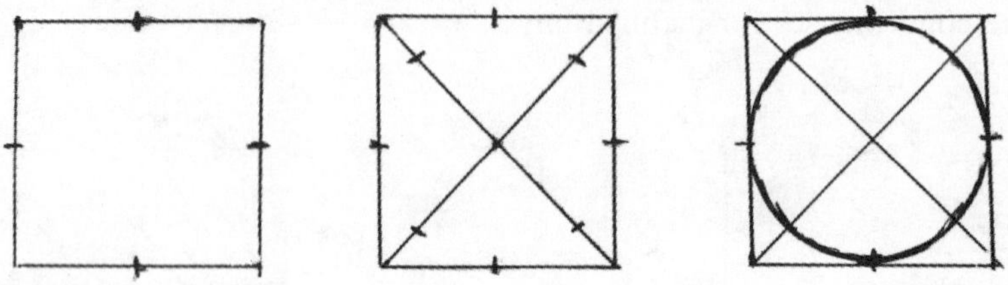

Fig. 21.5

Step 1
Draw a square of sides equal to the diameter of the circle. Mark the midpoint of each side.

Step 2
Draw two diagonals of the square. On each diagonal, locate points at a distance of radius from the centre.

Step 3
Draw tangent arcs to square sides at the midpoints. Draw perpendicular arcs at the points on diagonals. Join the arcs to complete the circle.

The construction lines may be erased after the circle is completed. Circular arcs may be drawn in a similar way.

21.4.2 Large Circles

Any one of the two methods may be adopted for sketching bigger circles.

Method I: Paper strip method Adopt the following steps, Fig. 21.6.

Step 1
Take a paper strip and make a hole at one end of it. The hole may be of nailtip size or fingertip size. At the other end, make a small V-notch. The perpendicular distance between the hole and V-notch will decide the radius of the circle.

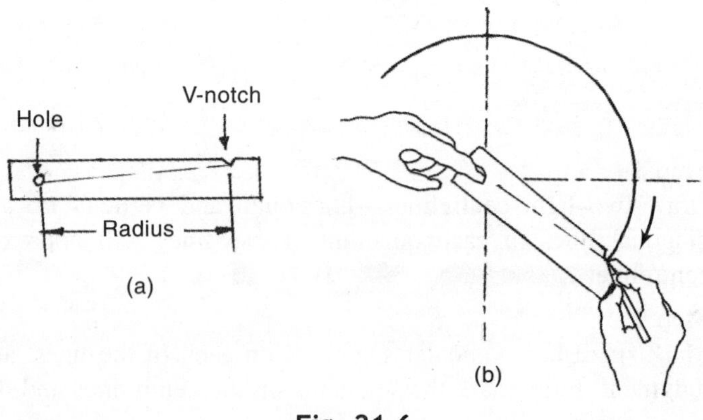

Fig. 21.6

Step 2
Locate the centre of the circle on paper. Place the paper strip such that the hole will match with the centre. Insert a finger of left hand (or a nail) in the hole and hold the finger firmly at the centre. Fix the pencil tip in the V-notch and rotate the strip clockwise with the help of the pencil about the centre to draw the circle.

Method 2: Hand Compass Adopt the following steps, Fig. 21.7.

Step 1

Form the hand compass as shown. The little finger will act as a needle leg. The pencil is to be held between the forefinger and the middle finger. The pencil tip should protrude the finger tips.

Step 2

Locate the centre of the circle on paper. Hold hand compass on the paper with the little fingertip on the centre and pencil tip touching the paper. By the other hand, rotate the paper gently in anticlockwise direction about the fingertip pivot, holding the hand compass rigidly.

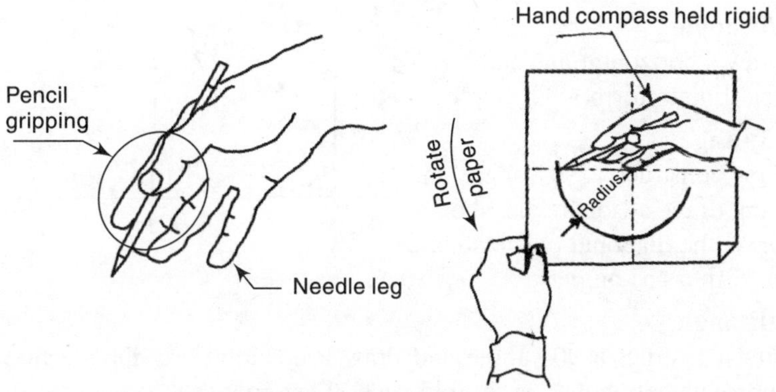

Fig. 21.7

21.5 SKETCHING ELLIPSES

Ellipses can be sketched by adopting the following steps, Fig. 21.8.

Step 1

Draw the major axis and minor axis perpendicular to each other.

Step 2

Complete the rectangle by drawing sides parallel to the axes.

Step 3

Draw tangent arcs to each sides of the rectangle.

Step 4

Join the arcs to each other to complete the ellipse. Make the curve sufficiently thick.

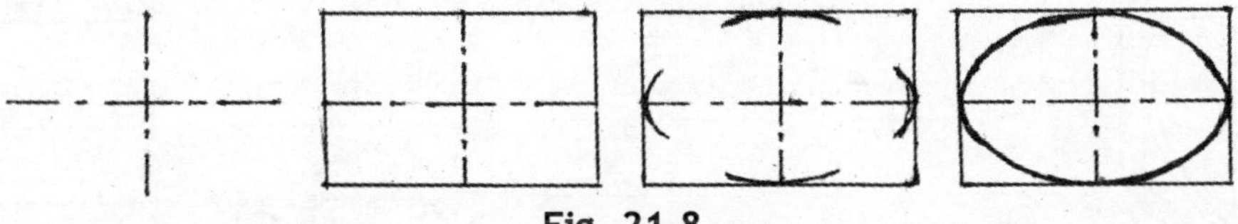

Fig. 21.8

Note: The readers may follow the Concentric Circle Method or Oblong Method explained in Sections 6.3.2 and 6.3.3 respectively for freehand sketching of the ellipse.

21.6 SKETCHING THE ANGLES

To sketch the angles accurately, a good degree of visual judgment is necessary. The angles of 90°,

45°, 30° and 10° can be sketched as explained in Fig. 21.9. A 5° angle can be obtained by dividing 10° angle equally.

90° angle

Draw a horizontal line and a vertical line to form a 90° angle.

45° angle

First construct a 90° angle and then draw a square as shown. Draw the diagonal of the square to form a 45° angle.

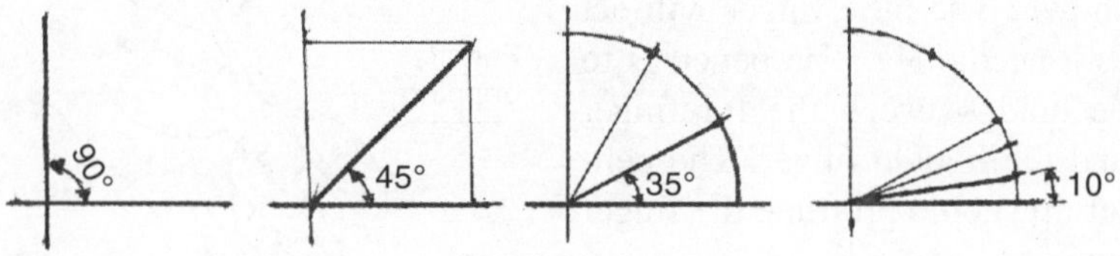

Fig. 21.9

30° angle

First construct a 90° angle and draw a quadrant arc. Divide the arc by trial and error in the three approximately equal parts. Join each division with the centre of the arc to form 30° angles.

10° angle

First construct 30° angle as explained. Divide the 30° arc into three approximate parts. Join each division with the centre of the angle to form 10° angles.

21.7 MULTIVIEW ORTHOGRAPHIC SKETCHING

The methods explained above will help prepare multiview sketches of an object. It is easy to maintain proportions in smaller orthographic drawings. Bigger drawings may get distorted when drawn freehand. To avoid distortions, bigger drawings are divided into smaller blocks. Each block is then drawn separately, considering its proportion in relation to the adjacent block. It is explained with the help of the following example.

Example 21.1 Figure 21.10(a) shows a pictorial view of a gasket. Sketch its FV.

Solution Refer Fig. 21.10(b). Complete the sketch stepwise as shown.

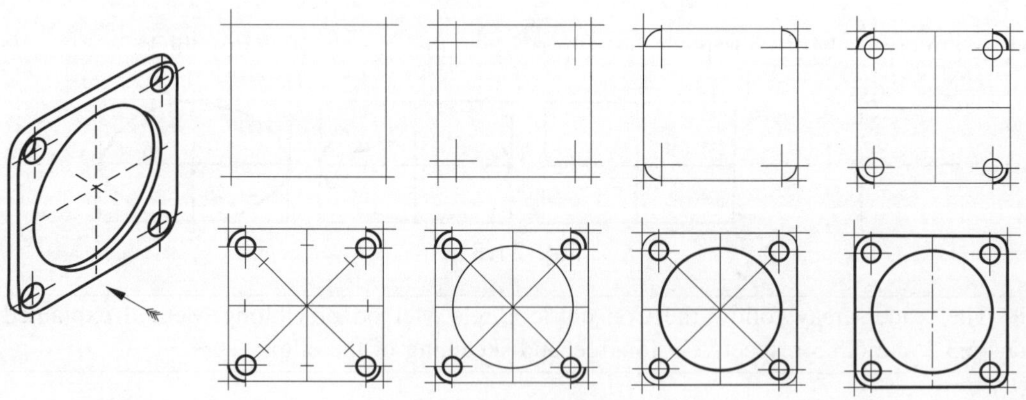

(a) (b)

Fig. 21.10

21.8 ISOMETRIC SKETCHING

The small isometric drawings, for example, the isometric view of a rectangular block may be constructed in three steps as shown in Fig. 21.11. In the first step, draw isometric axes. In the second step, mark the length, width and height of the block on the corresponding axes. In the third step, draw the edges of the block by drawing lines parallel to the isometric axes.

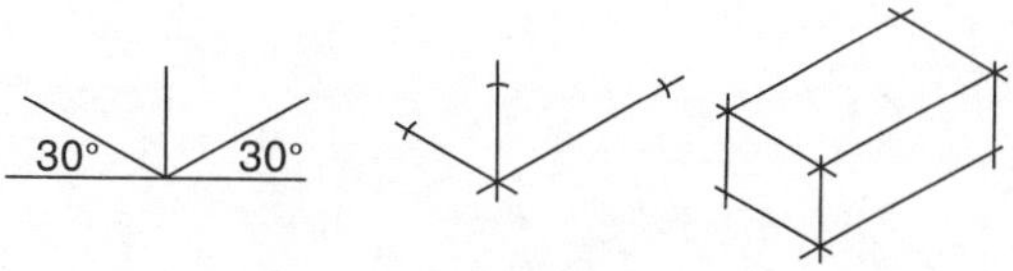

Fig. 21.11

For bigger drawings, isometric grid may be used initially. An isometric grid consists of a number of lines drawn parallel to three isometric axes, Fig. 21.12(b). Example 21.2 explains the use of an isometric grid. After sufficient practice, isometric views can be drawn without an isometric grid.

Example 21.2 Figure 21.12(a) shows FV and TV of an object. Sketch its isometric view.

Solution Refer Fig. 21.12(b). Complete the sketch stepwise as shown.

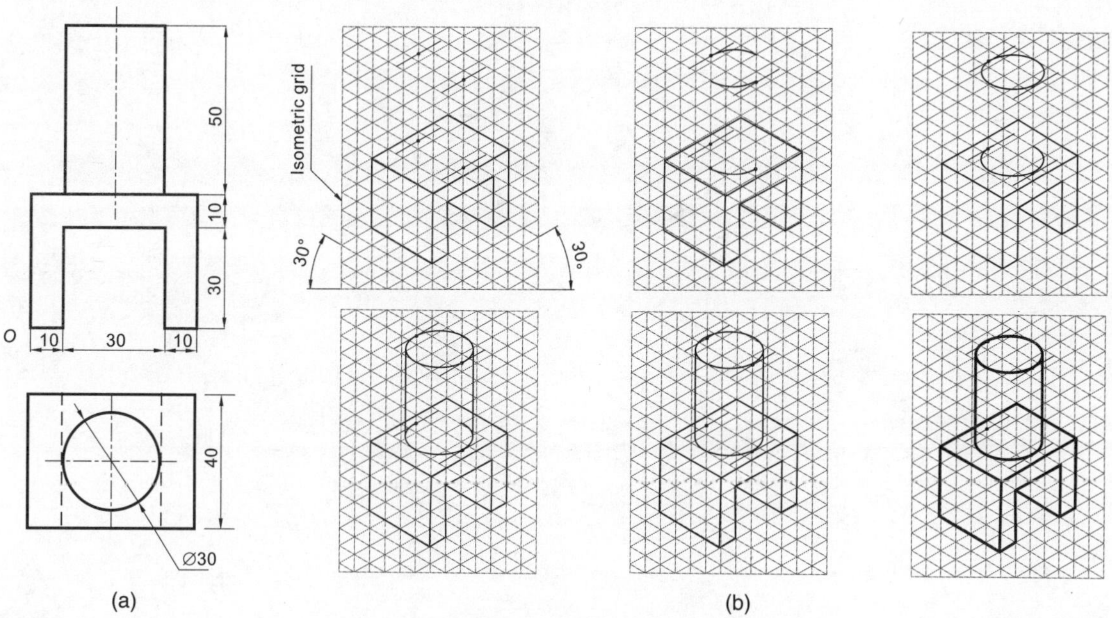

Fig. 21.12

REVIEW QUESTIONS

1. Sketch Fig. 4.47 freehand.
2. Sketch the isometric view of the object from the two views shown in Fig. 18RQ.11.

Chapter 22

COMPUTER AIDED DRAFTING

22.1 INTRODUCTION

In today's world, computers are used to perform many tasks which were done by human beings previously. Some common examples are accounting, typing, communicating, database management, etc. Computers use different softwares to perform these tasks. With the help of special softwares, computers can be advantageously used to do the work of drafting. The process of constructing the drawings on the computer screen with the help of specially developed softwares and hardwares is called *computer aided drafting* (CAD). The drawings in CAD are clearer and more exact than the manual drawings.

The CAD system is based on what is called *interactive computer graphics* (ICG). ICG helps to convert the data entered by the user in the form of graphics. The user enters the data in the form of commands by using hardwares (input devices) which is converted into graphics by the software. With CAD, the user can create new drawings, modify the existing ones, store the drawings and explore them further.

22.2 CAD WORKSTATION

A CAD workstation, in its simplest form, consists of a computer with a keyboard, mouse and monitor and loaded with CAD software, Fig. 22.1. The keyboard and mouse are essential input devices whereas the monitor is a real time output device. All the three are integral parts of the computer and are always connected to the central processing unit (CPU). For CAD applications, a computer with a reasonably good processing speed is recommended. The user must ensure their system's compatibility with the CAD software they are using.

Fig. 22.1 Basic CAD Workstation

The input and output devices (including keyboard, mouse and monitor) needed at CAD workstation are explained in the following sections.

22.2.1 Input Devices

The input devices are used to enter the numeric data and commands and to control cursor positions on the screen.

Keyboard and Mouse The keyboard and mouse, Fig. 22.1, are basic input devices for any computer. For CAD purposes, a standard 104-key keyboard is sufficient. Cursor control keys, function keys and number keys are frequently needed in CAD application. The keyboard with function keys on left end and number keys on the right end will ensure speed in drawing.

A two-button mouse with a scroll wheel is recommended for computerized drafting. An optical mouse ensures better positioning than roller mouse.

Joystick A joystick, Fig. 22.2, is a cursor control device consisting of a handheld stick pivoted at one end. The stick can be moved side to side or front to back. Moving the stick left to right, signals the cursor movement along the *X*-axis, and moving it front to back, signals the cursor movement along the *Y*-axis. A 3D joystick signals the cursor movement along the *Z*-axis by twisting the stick clockwise or anticlockwise.

Trackball A trackball, Fig. 22.3, can be treated as a mouse resting on its back. It has a ball that can be rolled inside a socket. The direction and speed of rotation of the ball will decide the direction and speed of cursor movement. One to three buttons are provided alongside the ball which can be used in a way similar to a mouse. Now a days, a mouse-cum-trackball, Fig. 22.4, is also available in the market.

Fig. 22.2 Joystick

Fig. 22.3 Trackball

Fig. 22.4 Mouse-cum-Trackball

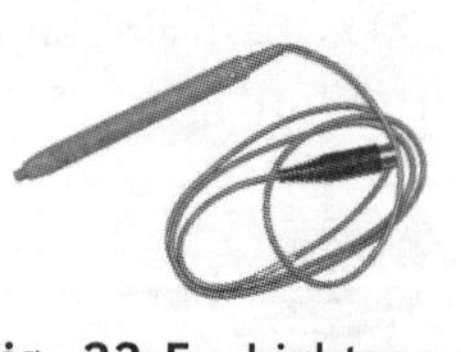

Fig. 22.5 Light pen

Light pen A light pen, Fig. 22.5, is a light-sensitive input device used directly on the computer's CRT monitor. The pen, when placed against the screen, detects light from the screen enabling the computer to identify the location of the pen on the screen. Thus, it can be used to select the menus or draw directly on the screen. A light pen can work with any CRT-based monitor, but not with LCD screens, projectors or other display devices.

Scanner The most common flatbed scanner, Fig. 22.6, is used to scan the manual drawings. It analyzes an image and processes it using *optical character recognition* (OCR) technology. The image may then be opened in CAD software and traced to obtain digital drawing.

Fig. 22.6 Scanner

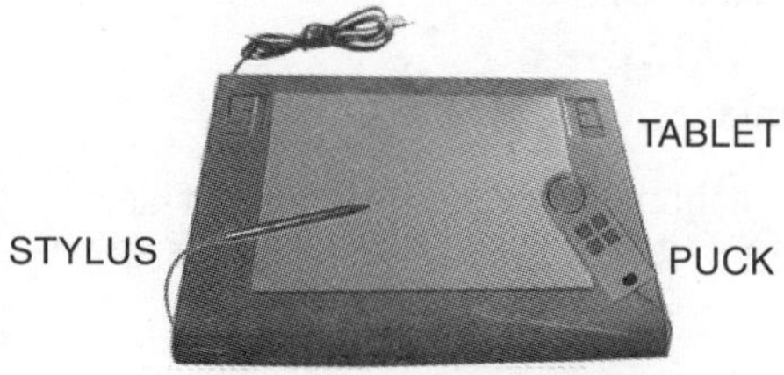

Fig. 22.7 Digitizer

Fig. 22.8 Printer

Digitizer* or *Pen Tablet Digitizer or Pen Tablet, Fig. 22.7, is an electromagnetic graphic input device. It is used to construct new drawing or convert an existing drawing into digital form. A digitizer consists of a flat tablet that resembles a drafting board, an electronic movable stylus and a puck. A drawing is constructed on a paper placed on the tablet (or directly on the tablet) by a stylus and puck. A puck helps to locate or enter specific points using the crosshair and the buttons. The drawing does not appear on the tablet but on the monitor screen.

22.2.2 Output Devices

The output devices show the numeric value, active commands, cursor positions and the drawing. These are used to take prints (hard copies) of the drawings.

Monitor A monitor, Fig. 22.1, provides a screen for visual display. It enables the real time control of the drafting activity. For better visibility, a 17" monitor may be preferred. Flat CRT or LCD monitors create minimum strain on the eyes of the user and are preferred for longer use. LCD monitors are compact but they pose a difficulty in using light pens.

Printer A printer, Fig. 22.8, is used to obtain print copies of the drawings. Two types of printers, namely, inkjet printer and laser printer, are in common use. Inkjet printers are cheaper but the cost per print is higher than that of laser printers. The initial cost of a laser printer is higher but it provides superior quality prints at a comparatively lower cost. Printers are used for prints up to A4 size of paper.

Plotter Plotter, Fig. 22.9, is a printing device used prominently for the prints of larger sizes, i.e., A3 to A0. Plotters print the drawing by moving a pen across the surface of a paper. Obviously, plotters are good at line art but incapable of drawing coloured objects with mixing and shadings. Further, they are very slow due to mechanical movement of the pens. As plotters can work on very large sizes of paper, they are extensively used in technical drawings and CAD applications.

Fig. 22.9 Plotter

In addition to input and output devices explained above, the user may need storage devices to store or transfer the digital drawings. The primary storage device used by a computer is the hard disk (HD). In addition, other storage devices like, compact disks (CDs), Digital Versatile Disks (DVDs), pen drives, memory cards, etc., may be used.

22.3 ADVANTAGES OF CAD

CAD offers the following advantages:

1. Accuracy CAD helps to achieve very high degree of accuracy that is impossible to achieve manually. For example, a line 22.532 mm long or an angle of 53.27° can be precisely drawn in CAD software.

2. Speed With sufficient practice, a user can create drawings speedily. Similar objects can be copied or mirrored or arrayed which saves time required for duplication. Automatic hatching, texting and dimensioning save time.

3. Easy Editing Drawings once constructed can be easily edited or modified as and when needed. Component drawings from one drawing file can be inserted in another drawing file.

4. Space Effectiveness A computer can store several thousand drawing files over a long period of time. Equal number of drawing sheets drawn manually will need a big godown to store!

5. Standard Libraries CAD softwares have libraries containing drawings of standard parts such as gears, valves, pulleys, electrical and electronics components, civil and architectural components that can be directly used.

6. Scaling A drawing can be enlarged or reduced by any scale factor. Dimensions change automatically. Further, printing can be made to any scale.

7. Better Visualization Use of different colours helps avoiding confusion. A 3D view of the object can be easily created to boost imagination.

8. Freedom from using Drawing Instruments A simple CAD system needs a computer with a mouse and keyboard to draw. The draftsmen need not use bulky drawing instruments like drawing board, drafter, set square, etc.

It should be noted that the CAD system does not possess intelligence to construct a drawing by itself. The users need to acquire skill and expertise in using CAD software to avail the advantages mentioned above. Further, CAD systems are costly. The cost of a CAD workstation is much higher than the cost of a manual drawing set-up.

22.4 CAD SOFTWARES

A big number of softwares are in use for 2D drawing and 3D modeling. A prominent few are listed in Table 22.1. Each of these softwares has specific applications and some advantages over others.

Table 22.1 CAD Softwares

Package	*Company*	*Application*	*First Version*	*Latest Version**
AutoCAD	Autodesk Inc. USA	2D and 3D Design and Drafting	MicroCAD/ AutoCAD R1 (1982)	AutoCAD 2007

(*Contd.*)

(*Contd.*)

Inventor	Autodesk Inc. USA	3D Parametric Solid Modeling	Inventor 1 'Mustang' (1999)	Inventor 2008 'Goddard'
Pro/ENGINEER	Parametric Technology Corporation, (PTC).	Mechanical Engineering 3D Modeling and Assembling and 2D Drawing	Pro/ENGINEER 1	Pro/ENGINEER Wildfire 3.0
NX Unigraphics)	UGS Corp.	3D Product Lifecycle Management	I-DEAS NX	NX5
IronCAD	IronCAD, Atlanta, G.A.	2D and 3D Design and Drafting	IronCAD (1998) (by Visionary Design Systems)	IronCAD *v*9.0
Catia	Dassault Systemes (Marketed by IBM)	3D Product Lifecycle Management	Catia V1 (1982)	Catia V5
Solid Edge	UGS group	Solid Modeling, Assembly Modeling and Drafting	Solid Edge V3 (1996) (by Intergraph)	Solid Edge V19
SolidWorks	Dassault Systemes, S. A.	3D CAD	SolidWorks (1995) (by SolidWorks Corporation)	Solid Works 2007
3ds Max	Autodesk Inc. USA	3D Modeling and Animation	3D Studio Max (1995)	3ds Max 9
Visio	Visio Corporation (previously Axon Corporation)	2D Drawing	Visio 1.0 (1992)	Visio 2007

*as in March 2007.

22.5 AutoCAD

AutoCAD is a very effective CAD software. It is used globally by CAD professionals. It supports 2D drafting and 3D modeling. This chapter is written for AutoCAD 2007. However, it is equally effective for previous versions of AutoCAD. AutoCAD is user friendly and easy to learn. The chapter explains, with the help of practice sessions, examples and assignments, the important commands needed to draw 2D drawings. Exploring AutoCAD in 3D environment is beyond the scope of this book. Interested readers may go through the advanced books on AutoCAD for this purpose.

22.6 AutoCAD WINDOW

When you start AutoCAD 2007 in AutoCAD Classic mode, the AutoCAD window shown in Fig. 22.10 appears on the screen. If opened for the first time, the window shows **SHEET SET MANAGER** palette and **TOOL PALETTES** palette, Fig. 22.10(a). The palettes can be closed to reveal maximum drawing area, Fig. 22.10(b). The main parts of the AutoCAD window are explained on the next page:

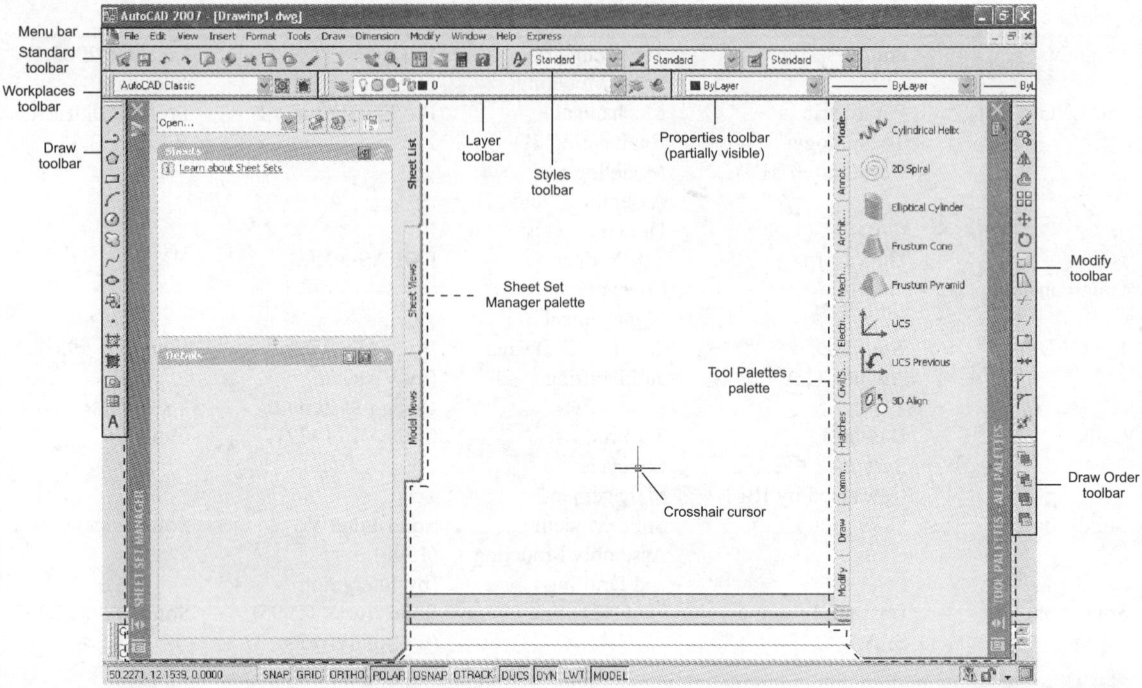

Fig. 22.10(a) AutoCAD Window* with Sheet Set Manager palette and Tool Palettes palette

Menu bar — Contains the default AutoCAD pull down menus:
File, Edit, View, Insert, Format, Tools, Draw, Dimension, Modify, Express, Window, Help

Standard toolbar — Contains standard and frequently used icons such as **Open, Save, Undo, Redo, Cut, Copy, Paste, Match Properties, Zoom,** etc.

Draw toolbar — Contains common draw commands: **Line, Polyline, Polygon, Rectangle, Arc, Circle, Spline, Ellipse, Hatch, Multiline Text,** etc.

Modify toolbar — Contains common modify commands: **Erase, Copy, Mirror, Offset, Array, Move, Rotate, Scale, Trim, Extend, Break, Chamfer, Fillet, Explode,** etc.

Properties toolbar — Sets object properties such as **Colour, Linetype** and **Lineweight**.

Drawing area — The space (called *Model Space*) on the screen used to compose/edit drawings. It shows a floating crosshair cursor and a user coordinate system (UCS) icon at the lower-left corner. By default, the colour of the model space is black. The drawing area may be divided into 2 to 4 rectangles (called *Viewports*) to draw/observe different views of the objects.

Layer toolbar — Used to make new layer, switch between layers and change layer properties

Crosshairs cursor — Helps to input points. The cursor is the 'crosshair' during draw commands. It changes to a square block (called *pickbox*) during modify commands (i.e., object selection mode). The crosshair movement is controlled by pointing devices (e.g., mouse).

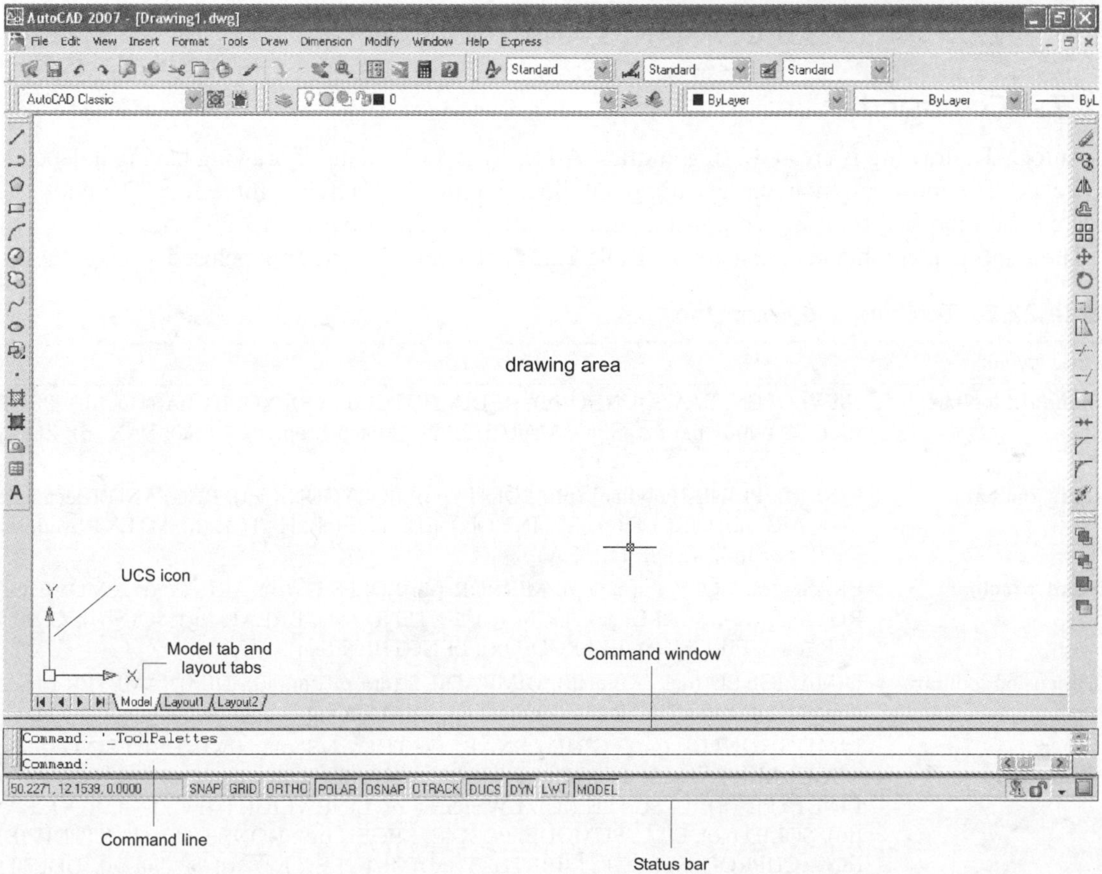

Fig. 22.10(b) AutoCAD Window* without Sheet Set Manager palette and Tool Palettes palette
*The colour of the drawing area, by default, is black. The users may change it to the desired colour (see Section 22.19, Practice Session 9). The colour of the drawing area shown in the window is white.

UCS icon — Shows the orientation of the *X*-axis and *Y*-axis for 2D drawing. The *Z*-axis is perpendicular to *XY* plane.

Model tab/ Layout tabs — Helps switching between **Model Space** and **Paper Space**. In **Model Space**, the drawing is drawn to 1:1 scale. In **Paper Space**, the drawing scale can be changed to fit on the paper of required size. **Layout tabs** are used for plotting and printing.

Command window — Provides the history of commands. The window can be increased or decreased in size. **AutoCAD Text Window**, showing history of commands, appears when function key F2 is activated.

Command line — Provides the interface between the user and the software. It helps entering commands, options, point inputs, etc. It also displays messages.

Status bar — Contains buttons like **SNAP, GRID, ORTHO, POLAR, OSNAP, OTRACK, DUCS, DYN, LWT** and **MODEL.** It also displays the **cursor coordinates** in the lower-left corner.

22.7 AutoCAD COMMANDS AND TOOLBARS

22.7.1 Commands

In AutoCAD, drawing is created using entities. An *entity* is an element of drawing having independent existence. The most common entities are: point, line, polyline, arc, circle, ellipse, etc. The entities are created and modified by using commands. Entities are termed as *objects* in AutoCAD.

The important commands are listed in Table 22.2. The abbreviations are enclosed in parenthesis ().

Table 22.2 Toolbars and Commands

Toolbar	*Commands**
Standard toolbar	NEW, OPEN, SAVE, UNDO (u), REDO, CUTCLIP, COPYCLIP, PASTECLIP, PROPERTIES (ch *or* mo *or* props), MATCHPROP [Match Properties] (ma), PAN (p), ZOOM (z).
Draw toolbar	LINE (l), PLINE [Polyline] (pl), POINT (po), POLYGON (pol), RECTANG [Rectangle] (rec), ARC (a), CIRCLE (c) , SPLINE (spl), ELLIPSE (el), HATCH (h), MTEXT [Multiline Text] (t *or* mt), XLINE (xl), RAY.
Modify toolbar	ERASE (e), COPY (co *or* cp), MIRROR (mi), OFFSET (o), ARRAY (ar), MOVE (m), ROTATE (ro), SCALE (sc), TRIM (tr), EXTEND (ex), BREAK (br), JOIN (j), CHAMFER (cha), FILLET (f), EXPLODE (x), LENGTHEN (len).
Dimension toolbar	DIMALIGNED (dal *or* dimali), DIMRADIUS (dra *or* dimrad), DIMDIAMETER (ddi *or* dimdia), DIMANGULAR (dan *or* dimang), LEADER (ql).
Other Commands:	LIMITS, UNITS (un), GRID, SNAP, ORTHO, OSNAP (os), DSETTINGS (ds), VSCURRENT, UCS, PEDIT (pe), ISOPLANE, LAYER (la), COLOR, LTYPE *or* LINETYPE (lt), LTSCALE (lts), LWEIGHT *or* LINEWEIGHT (lw), CUI, TOOLBAR (to), SOLID (so), FILL, PDMODE, PDSIZE, REGEN (re), DONUT (do), TEXT, DIVIDE (div), CHPROP, SELECT, MIRRTEXT, DIMSTYLE (d *or* dst *or* dimsty), DDEDIT, FIND, STYLE (st), SCALETEXT, JUSTIFYTEXT, OPTIONS (op), PLOT, CLOSE, QUIT, EXIT.

*Commands and their abbreviations are not case sensitive.

The commands can be given in one of the following ways:

1. Choose the command icon on a **Toolbar**.
2. Choose the command from a **Menu** of **Menu bar**.
3. Type the command in **Command line**.
4. Type the command near the **Crosshair** (Dynamic input).
5. Choose the command icon from **Tool Palettes**.
6. Choose the command from **Shortcut menu**.

When you enter a command in the **Command line**, you need to press ENTER↵ key to activate the command. Dynamic input works when **DYN** button on the **Status bar** is active. A shortcut menu is displayed when you right-click in the drawing area before entering any command.

Whichever the way you give the command, the command appears in the **Command line**. When a command is given by using way 1, way 2 or way 5 above, the underscore (_) appears before the command. Most of the commands are terminated by pressing ENTER. A few commands are self-terminating. Pressing ENTER after termination of a command will reactivate it. You may use UP/DOWN keys to scroll through commands and or point inputs used.

• Some commands work while some other command is active. Such commands are called *transparent commands,* e.g., zoom, pan, etc. To activate a transparent command when another command is active, type it in **Command line** by prefixing ', e.g., 'zoom, 'pan, etc.

Many commands have options in them. The options are enclosed in [ ]. To make a particular option active, simply enter capital letter(s) in that option in the **Command line**. The default value(s) or active option is enclosed in < >. Press ENTER to accept default values or active option.

22.7.2 Toolbars

A toolbar is a collection of similar types of commands. Each command is shown on the toolbar by a unique icon. In AutoCAD 2007, there are 35 predefined toolbars.

The important toolbars and the commands they contain are shown in Table 22.2.

Practice Session 1: Getting familiar with toolbars
In AutoCAD window, move each toolbar to the centre of the screen. A toolbar can be moved by holding and dragging it. To hold a toolbar, keep the pointer at **double bars** (or near to any edge of the toolbar) and then keep click pressed, Fig. 22.11. Move your mouse keeping click pressed to drag the toolbar. Toolbars will show **title bars** containing the names of the toolbars when moved to open space. Toolbars always appear horizontal when moved away from the sides of the screen.

Fig. 22.11

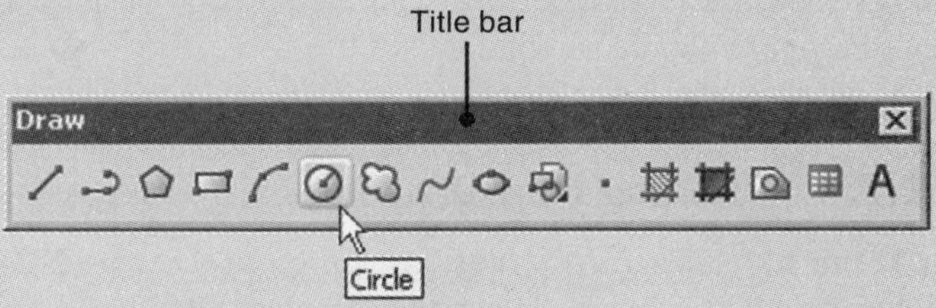

Fig. 22.12

Now move your mouse pointer slowly over the icons of each toolbar. The name of each icon (command) is displayed below the pointer, Fig. 22.12. The icon pictures tell about the commands they perform and can be remembered easily.

Move the toolbars, one by one, anywhere on the screen. Dock the **Draw toolbar** at the left and the **Modify toolbar** at the right side of the window. The other toolbars may be docked as shown in Fig. 22.10.

22.7.3 Displaying the Toolbars

Toolbars are the virtual drawing tools. They help you to draw and edit objects and write the dimensions and text. More toolbars may be made active on your screen. This can be done in one of the two ways:

1. Right-click on any existing toolbar. A list of toolbars will appear on the screen. Click on the desired toolbars name to display the toolbar on the screen.
2. From ***Tools*** menu, choose ***Customize » Interface...*** to open **Customize User Interface** dialog box. *Alternatively*, type CUI or TOOLBAR in **Command line**.

   In the **Customize User Interface** dialog box, ensure that **Customize** tab is active. In **Customizations in All CUI files** pane, see that the combo box shows **All Customization**

Files. Expand (if necessary) **Workspaces** node by clicking at the plus sign (+). Select **AutoCAD Classic Default (current)**. **Workspace Contents** pane will be visible on the right side. Click **Customize Workspace**. In **Customizations in All CUI files** pane, expand **Toolbars** node. Click the check boxes next to the toolbars you want to make active. In the **Workspace Contents** pane, click ***Done***. Click ***OK*** to finish.

The desired toolbars will appear on your screen.

Practice Session 2: Displaying the desired toolbars

Display the following toolbars on your screen:

Dimension, Modify II, Object Snap, Solid Editing, Text and **Zoom**

Get familiar with icons on these toolbars. Dock them to the desired locations.

Move all the toolbars existing on your screen to the middle of the window. Close all of them, one by one, by clicking ***Close*** ✕ button.

Now, display the following toolbars on your screen using way 2 mentioned in Section 22.7.3: **Standard, Properties, Layers, Draw** and **Modify**

Dock the **Standard toolbar** horizontally below the **Menu bar**. Dock the **Layers toolbar** and **Properties toolbar** side by side below the **Standard toolbar.**

Dock the **Draw toolbar** vertically on the left side of the window. Dock the **Modify toolbar** vertically on the right side of the window.

Use this window setting for all practice sessions ahead.

22.7.4 Opening New Drawing File

In **Menu bar** click ***File » New....*** *Alternatively*, type NEW in **Command line**. A **Select template** dialog box will appear. Select the template file. By default, the template file is **acad.dwt.** Click ***Open.*** Your new drawing file is now ready for work.

22.7.5 Opening Existing Drawing File

In **Menu bar** click ***File » Open....*** *Alternatively*, type OPEN in **Command line** *or* click the ***Open*** icon on **Standard toolbar**. A **Select File** dialog box will appear. Select the file to open. You may browse to locate the file on your drive by opening **Look in:** combo box for desired drive/folder. Click ***Open*** to open the selected file.

22.7.6 Saving the File

In **Menu bar** click ***File » Save***. *Alternatively*, type SAVE in **Command line** *or* click ***Save*** icon on **Standard toolbar**. A **Save Drawing As** dialog box will appear. Select the location you wish to save your file by opening **Save in:** combo box. Type the file name in **File name:** combo box. (By default, AutoCAD uses file names as Drawing1, Drawing2, etc.) Click ***Save.*** The file will be saved to selected location. By default, the file is saved in **Drawing (.dwg)** format. You may save it in **Drawing Standards (.dws)** or **Drawing Template (.dwt)** format. The **.dwg** format should be used for normal editable drawing.

The **Save Drawing As** dialog box is displayed the first time you save the file. At all subsequent save's, the changes are automatically saved in your file.

To change the file name or file format, click **Menu bar** » ***File*** » ***Save As...*** when the file is open.

22.7.7 Closing the Drawing File

Use **Menu bar** » ***File*** » ***Close*** *or* CLOSE in **Command line** *or* ***Close*** button on **Menu bar** to close your drawing. You may be prompted to save your drawing.

22.7.8 Exiting the AutoCAD

Use **Menu bar** » ***File*** » ***Exit*** *or* EXIT (or QUIT) in **Command line** *or* ***Close*** button on **AutoCAD Window** to exit the program. You may be prompted to save your drawing.

22.8 CREATING THE DRAWING ENVIRONMENT

The drawing environment refers to the initial settings needed for any drawing.

22.8.1 Units, Limits, Grid and Snap

AutoCAD uses 'drawing units' to measure the dimensions of the drawing. A drawing unit may be equal to one millimetre or one centimetre or one inch. Before you start your drawing, you must decide what one 'drawing unit' will represent. UNITS command serves this purpose.

Menu bar » ***Format*** » ***Units...*** *or*

Command line » **un** (for **Units**)

The **Drawing Units** dialog box, Fig. 22.13, is displayed. You may decide ***Type:*** and ***Precision:*** in **Length** and **Angle** area. The angles are measured in anticlockwise direction by default. In the **Insertion scale** area, choose the unit you wish to construct your drawing. By clicking ***Direction...*** tab, you can set directions for **Base Angle** in **Direction Control** dialog box.

Once you have chosen the units, the next task is to set the limits. The LIMITS command sets the size of the drawing area. Limits are specified by entering lower-left and upper-right corners of paper space. The lower-left corner usually coincides with UCS origin. Upper-right corner depends on the size of paper, e.g., A4 (210 mm × 297 mm), A3 (297 mm × 420 mm), A2 (420 mm × 594 mm), etc.

Menu bar » ***Format*** » ***Drawing Limits*** *or*
Command line » Limits

`Specify lower left corner or [ON/OFF] <0.0000,0.0000>:` ↵ to accept values in < >.
`Specify upper right corner <420.0000,297.0000>: 210,297` ↵ for A4 size paper (if the unit defined is millimeter).

The program does not accept any input outside the drawing area if LIMITS is turned **ON**.

> **Note:** The entire limits area will not be visible on the screen if it is larger than the screen. In such cases, **Zoom** » **All** is used (explained in Section 22.11).

Grid GRID command helps to create the rectangular pattern of dots or lines that covers the area specified by limits. The grid serves as a reference to align objects and visualize the distances between them. The grid does not appear in print or plot. Grid is more effective when used in conjunction with Snap.

Grid can be activated by ***GRID*** button on **Status bar** *or* **F7** key.

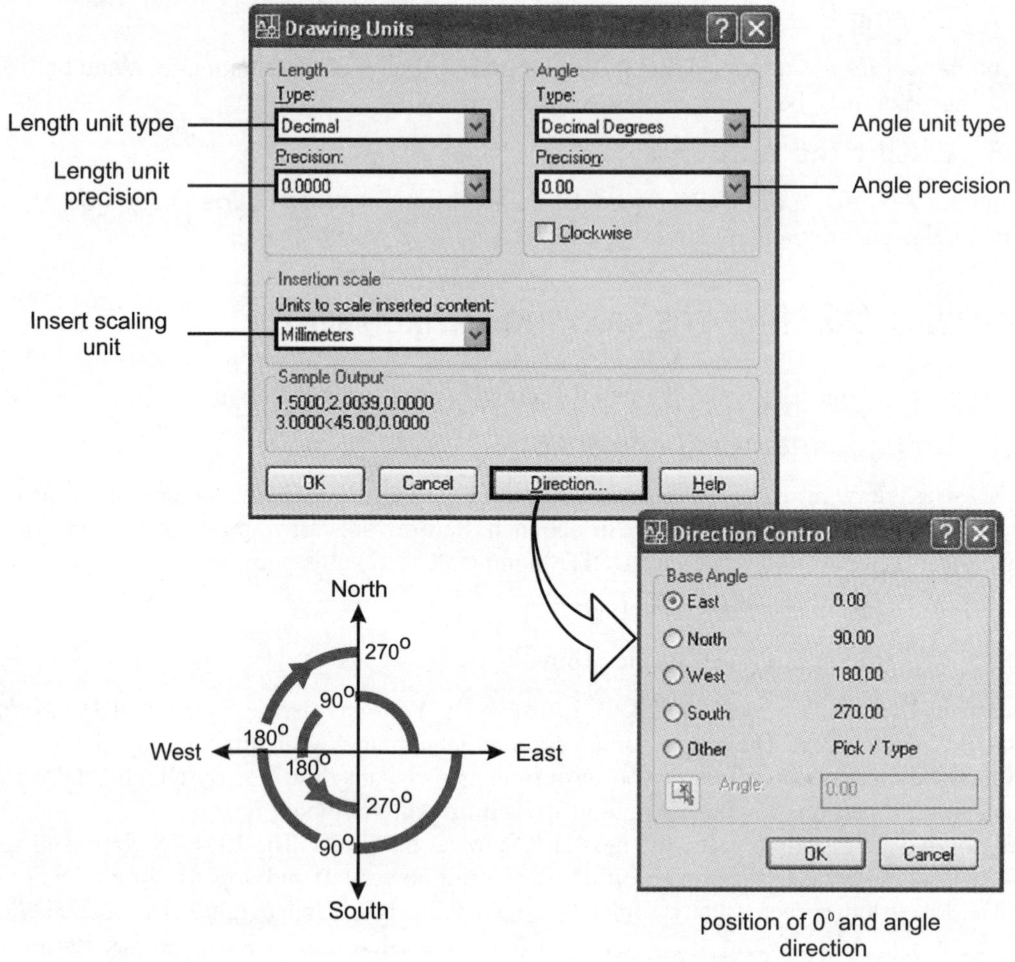

Fig. 22.13 Drawing Units Dialog Box with Direction Control Option

Snap SNAP command helps to choose an exact point. It enables the cursor to move through a 'specific' distance. When SNAP is ON, the cursor jumps from point to point located at a fixed distance.

Snap can be activated by ***SNAP*** button on the **Status bar** *or* **F9** key.

Grid and Snap settings Right-click ***GRID*** button (or ***SNAP*** button) on **Status bar** and choose ***Settings...*** option *or* chose **Menu bar » Tools » Drafting Settings...** *or* type DSETTINGS in **Command line**. **Drafting Settings** dialog box, Fig. 22.14, will appear (with ***Snap and Grid*** tab active). In **Grid spacing** area, enter the values for *X*-spacing and *Y*-spacing. The two values need not be same. If you want both the spacings to be the same, check mark the box in front of **Equal *X* and *Y* spacing** in **Snap spacing** area. Enter any integer value from 1 to 100 for major line spacing in **Major line every:** box. Major lines are the thick vertical lines in the grid. These are visible when the grid is in the form of lines. It should be noted that the grid or snap spacing is accepted in absolute units whereas major line spacing is accepted in terms of the numbers of grid-block.

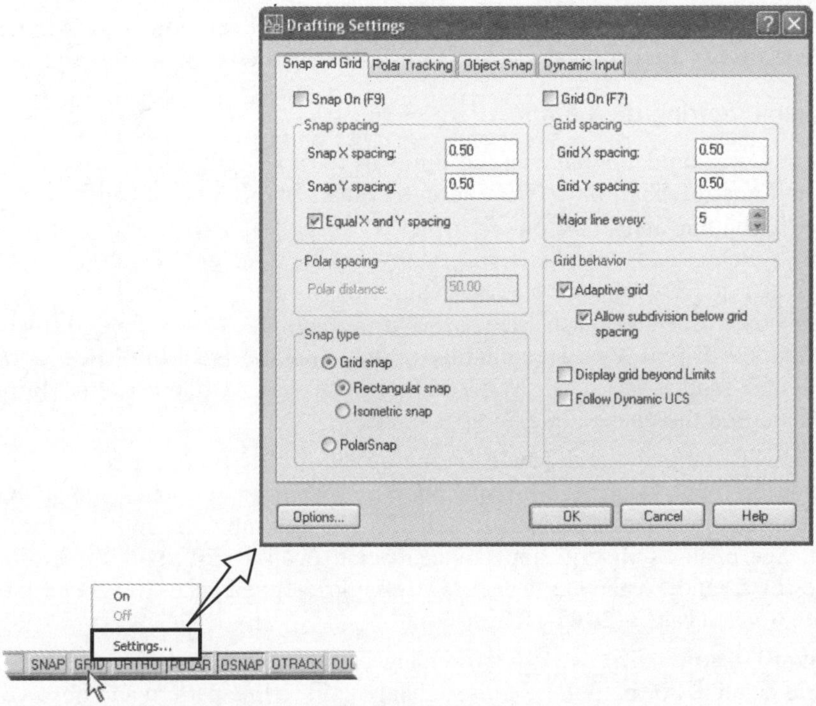

Fig. 22.14 Drafting Setting Dialog Box

In **Snap spacing** area, set the values for *X*-spacing and *Y*-spacing in a similar way. Note that when snap is turned on, your cursor will move along the *X*-axis and *Y*-axis exactly through the *X*-spacing and *Y*-spacing respectively. Click ***OK*** button to finish.

To change grid patterns from dots to lines, type VSCURRENT in **Command line.** Type **3** (for **3dwireframe** option) and press ENTER↵. For dotted grid pattern again, choose **Command line » vscurrent » 2** (for **2dwireframe** option) and press ENTER↵.

Practice Session 3: Setting the Units

Type UNITS in **Command line**. See various options available in the **Drawing Units** dialog box. In **Length** area, see options in **Type:** combo box (viz. Architectural, Decimal, Engineering, Fractional, Scientific). Choose each of them, one by one, and see what changes take place in **Precision:** combo box and **Sample Output** area. Now, choose various options in **Precision:** combo box and observe the corresponding changes in **Sample Output** area.

In a similar way, observe the changes in **Sample Output** area by using the various options in **Type:** combo box and **Precision:** combo box in **Angle** area.

In **Insertion scale** area, see various units available in **Units to scale inserted content:** combo box.

Click ***Direction...*** button to open **Direction Control** dialog box. Note the angle values marked ahead of East, North, West and South. Close **Direction Control** dialog box. Check in the box in front of **Clockwise**. Again open **Direction Control** dialog box. Note the changes in the angle values of East, North, West and South. Close **Direction Control** dialog box.

For engineering drawing, use setting: **Line: Type**-Decimal, **Precision**-0.00, **Angle: Type**-Decimal degree, **Precision**-0, **Insertion scale unit:** millimetre and **clockwise** unmarked.

Practice Session 4: Setting the Limits

Type LIMITS in **Command line** and set the limits as (0,0) to (210, 297) for A4 size paper. (The unit chosen is millimetre.) Turn on ***GRID*** button on **Status bar**. See what happens in drawing area. Right-click ***GRID*** button and click on ***Settings...*** to make the **Drafting Settings** dialog box visible. In **Grid spacing** area, enter new values of *X*- and *Y*-spacings, say 10 each. Click ***OK*** and see the change in grid. Try this for various values of *X*- and *Y*-spacings by opening **Drafting Settings** dialog box again and, each time, see corresponding changes in grid appearance. Now remove check mark at **Equal *X* and *Y* spacing** in **Snap spacing** area. In **Grid spacing** area, enter different values of *X*- and *Y*-spacings, say 1 and 2 respectively. Also, enter 5 in **Major line every:** box. Click ***OK*** and see the change in grid appearance.

Use VSCURRENT command and **3dwireframe** option to display line-grid pattern. Observe the relation between the input values (i.e., *X*-spacing = 1, *Y*-spacing = 2 and major line spacing = 5) and grid appearance. Open **Drafting Settings** dialog box and interchange the values of *X*-spacing and *Y*-spacing. See changes in grid appearance. Again open **Drafting Settings** dialog box and enter the values of *X*- and *Y*-spacings 1 each. Observe grid appearance. Revert to dot-grid pattern: **Command line » vscurrent » 2dwireframe.**

Set new limits (0,0) to (50,25) and observe change in grid. Now, set limits (50,25) to (100, 50) and observe grid change. For both these limits, change grid to line pattern and observe the changes. Revert to dot-grid and set original limits (0,0) to (210,297).

Practice Session 5: Setting the Snap

Move cursor slowly and freely in the drawing area. Now, turn on ***SNAP*** button on **Status bar**. Again move cursor slowly in the drawing area. Have you observed any difference between the two movements? The cursor moves through a fixed distance every time when snap is on.

Right-click ***SNAP*** button and click ***Settings...*** to open **Drafting Settings** dialog box. In **Snap spacing area**, enter *X*- and *Y*-spacings 5 each. Click ***OK*** to accept new settings. Now, move the cursor in drawing area and observe the difference.

Again open **Drafting Settings** dialog box. Enter *X*-spacing = 5 and *Y*-spacing = 10 in **Snap spacing** area (**Equal *X* and *Y* spacing** should be unmarked). Click ***OK***. Move the cursor vertically and horizontally and find the difference. Open **Drafting Settings** dialog box again and set *X*- and *Y*-spacings 1 each in **Snap spacing** area. Click ***OK*** to accept the changes and exit **Drafting Settings** dialog box.

22.8.2 Coordinate Systems

The coordinate systems help to locate/input points with the help of (*x*, *y*) coordinates. There are two coordinate systems: World Coordinate System (WCS) and User Coordinate System (UCS). When you begin a new drawing, you are automatically in WCS, i.e., *X*-axis horizontal, *Y*-axis vertical and *Z*-axis perpendicular to *XY* plane. The users may define UCS with a different origin and orientations of axes for their customized use. Beginners are advised to use only WCS. Coordinates are displayed in ***COORDINATE*** button located at left end of the **Status bar**.

22.8.3 Inputting the Points

We need to input the points frequently in AutoCAD. For example, to draw a line, two points need to be specified. To draw a circle, the centre needs to be mentioned. This can be done by using—(i) Cartesian coordinates (Absolute or Relative), (ii) Polar coordinate (Absolute or Relative), or (iii) Direct distance entry. This is explained in LINE command (Section 22.9.1).

22.8.4 Status bar

The ***SNAP*** and ***GRID*** buttons on the **Status bar** are already explained. Other buttons will be explained at appropriate places in the following sections. Most of the buttons on the **Status bar** are activated through function keys.

22.8.5 Use of Function Keys

The function keys help to activate a particular command or option or tool. The function keys, their uses and corresponding buttons on the **Status bar** are given below:

Function Key	*Use*	*Button on Status bar*
F1	Help	—
F2	AutoCAD Text Window (Command History)	—
F3	Osnap ON/OFF	OSNAP
F4	Tablet ON/OFF (To use digitizer's stylus as input device)	—
F5	Isoplane left/right/top	—
F6	Dynamic UCS ON/OFF	DUCS
F7	Grid ON/OFF	GRID
F8	Ortho ON/OFF	OTRHO
F9	Snap ON/OFF	SNAP
F10	Polar ON/OFF	POLAR
F11	Object Snap Tracking (Otrack) ON/OFF	OTRACK
F12	Dynamic Input ON/OFF	DYN
	To make lineweight visible	LWT
	To switch between Model and Paper space	MODEL [PAPER]
	Coordinates ON/OFF	COORDINATE (Left end of **Status bar**)

22.9 CREATING THE DRAWING

A drawing consists of lines, arcs, circles and curves. AutoCAD has commands for all these grouped under 'draw' head. The draw commands are located in **Draw toolbar** and ***Draw*** menu on **Menu bar**. We will see the important draw commands (with options) in this section. The settings used for all the Practice Sessions and Examples below is the same as mentioned in Practice Session 3 above. The limits are (0,0) to (210,297). The grid and snap may be set and activated as per the need.

22.9.1 Line

LINE command draws a line joining two points. It works in a sequence. The point input can be given by entering the Cartesian coordinates or the polar coordinates in absolute or relative mode. The coordinates and their modes are explained in Table 22.3.

Table 22.3 Point Input Mode

		Mode	
		Absolute	*Relative*
Coordinate	*Cartesian*	***x, y*** [x = distance of point from Y-axis y = distance of point from X-axis] 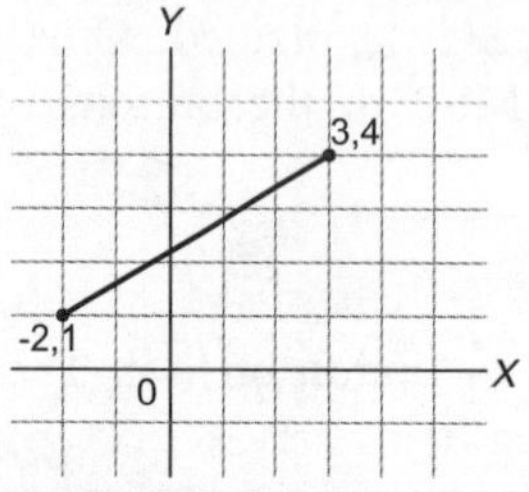	**@*x, y*** [at a distance of x (along X-axis) and y (along Y-axis) from the previous point] 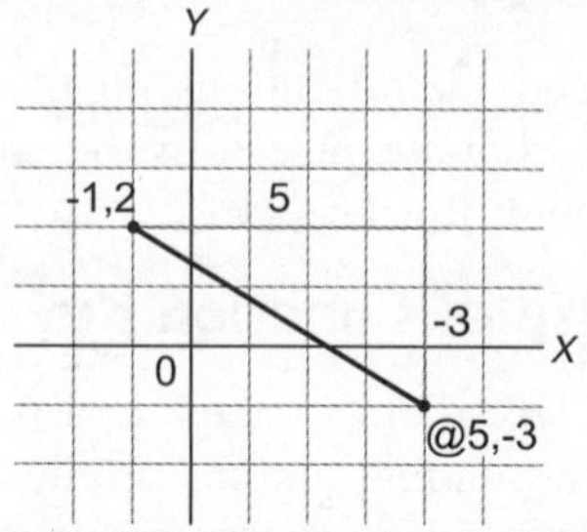
	Polar	***x* < *θ* at Command line** **# *x* < *θ* at Tooltip (Dynamic Input)** [at a distance of x from the previous point and at an angle of $\theta°$ to X-axis (θ measured in anticlockwise direction)] 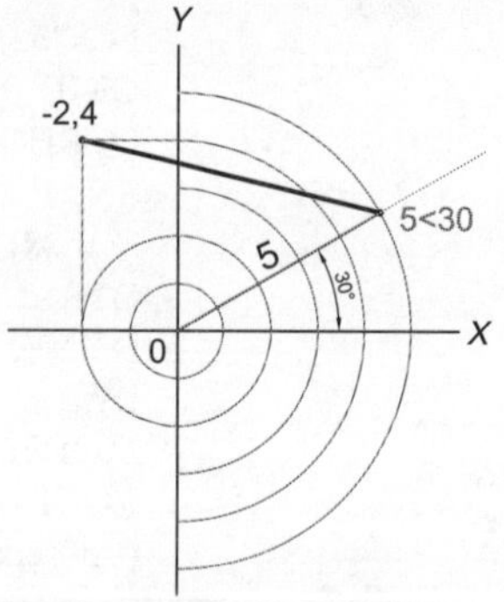	**@*x* < *θ*** [at a distance of x from origin and at an angle of $\theta°$ to X-axis (θ measured in anticlockwise direction)] 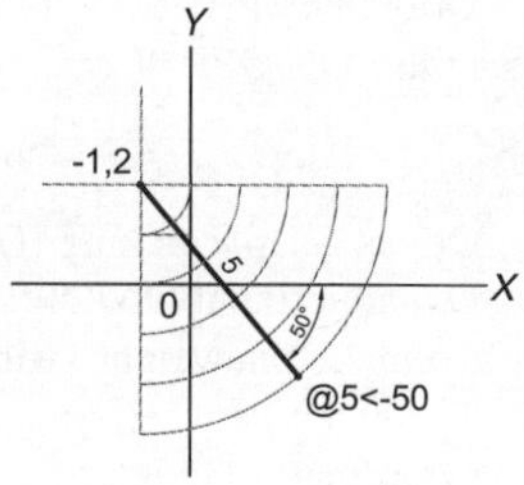

The coordinates of a point are displayed in ***COORDINATE*** button on **Status bar**. Click on ***COORDINATE*** button to turn it ON/OFF. While a command is active, the coordinate mode can be switched between **Absolute/Relative** by right-clicking ***COORDINATE*** button.

A point can be entered by *direct distance entry*, i.e., moving the cursor to indicate a direction and then entering the distance along that direction. For convenience, ***POLAR*** button on **Status bar** may be turned ON. It displays the cursor position in ($x < \theta$) format.

The LINE command is explained below with the help of examples.

> **Note:** For all the examples, save the drawing files by giving the name in the format: **Fig. 22.xx(y).dwg**. Create a folder **My drawings** on the desktop. Save all the files in the **My drawings** folder. Saving the file in Example 22.1 below is explained for the sake of illustration. For all other examples, the readers are supposed to save the files to: **C:\Desktop\My drawings**.

Example 22.1 Draw the following lines:

(i) (5,10) to (15,45).

(ii) (17.5,25.5) to a point 15 units on the right side and 21 units below (measured horizontally and vertically respectively) from the first point.

(iii) (52.55,32.55) to a point 38.55 units from origin at an angle of 45° to the *X*-axis.

(iv) Starting from (58.22,8.48), length 33.76 units and inclined at 75° to the *X*-axis.

Solution Set UNITS and LIMITS as already explained. Turn off ***DYN*** button on **Status bar** and execute LINE command in following way.

Draw toolbar » ***Line*** *or*
Menu bar » ***Draw*** » ***Line*** *or*
Command line » *l* (for **Line**)

(i)	`Command: l↵`	
	`LINE Specify first point: 5,10↵`	*Type 5,10 and press ENTER.*
	`Specify next point or [Undo]: 15,45↵`	*Type 15,45 and press ENTER*
	`Specify next point or [Undo]: ↵`	*Press ENTER to end LINE command.*
(ii)	`Command: ↵`	*Press ENTER to repeat LINE command.*
	`LINE Specify first point: 17.5,25.5↵`	*Type 17.5,25.5 and press ENTER.*
	`Specify next point or [Undo]: @15,-21↵`	*Type @15,-21 and press ENTER.*
	`Specify next point or [Undo]: ↵`	*Press ENTER to end LINE command.*
(iii)	`Command: ↵`	*Press ENTER to repeat LINE command.*
	`LINE Specify first point: 52.55,32.55↵`	*Type 52.55,32.55 and press ENTER.*
	`Specify next point or [Undo]: 38.55<45↵`	*Type 38.55<45 and press ENTER.*
	`Specify next point or [Undo]: ↵`	*Press ENTER to end LINE command.*
(iv)	`Command: ↵`	*Press ENTER to repeat LINE command.*
	`LINE Specify first point: 58.22,8.48↵`	*Type 58.22,8.48 and press ENTER.*
	`Specify next point or [Undo]: @33.76<75↵`	*Type 33.76<75 and press ENTER.*
	`Specify next point or [Undo]: ↵`	*Press ENTER to end LINE command.*

Choose ***Standard toolbar*** » **Save** (*or* **Menu bar** » ***File*** » ***Save***) » **Save Drawing As** dialog box. In ***Save in*:** Combo box, choose location–**Desktop**. In the list box, double-click **My drawings** folder. In **File name:** combo box, type **Fig. 22.15**. Ensure that **Files of type:** combo box shows **AutoCAD 2007 Drawing (*.dwg)**. Click at ***Save*** button.

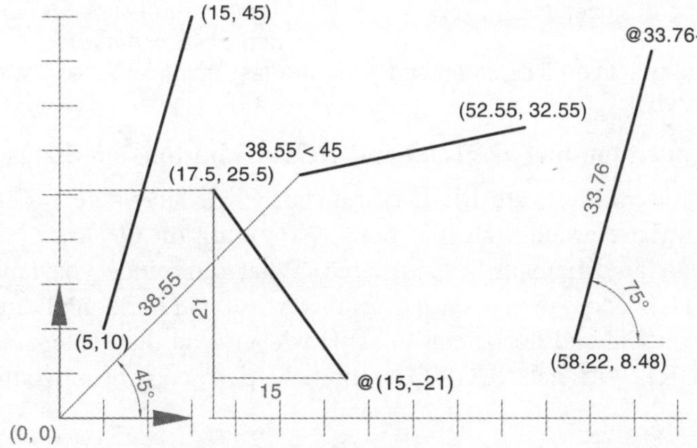

Fig. 22.15

Typing *u* (for Undo) during active LINE command will cancel the recent inputs one by one. The output is shown in Fig. 22.15.

Note: It is advised to keep ***DYN*** button on **Status bar** turned OFF for all the examples and concept assignments. It should be turned ON wherever mentioned to do so.

Example 22.2 Draw the line diagram shown in Fig. 22.16, start from (17,12).

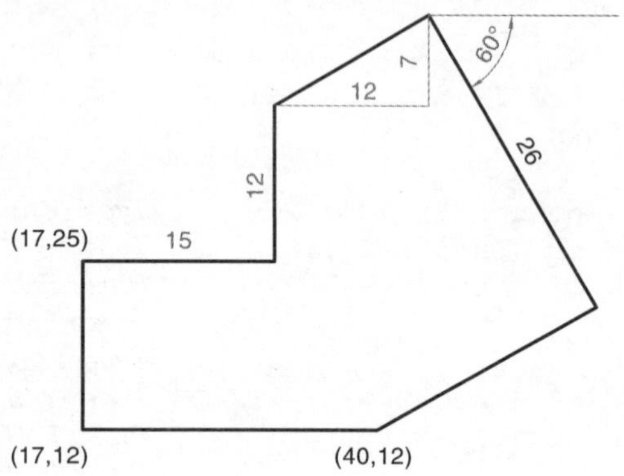

Fig. 22.16

Solution

`Command: l↵`	
`LINE Specify first point: 17,12↵`	*Type 17,12 and press ENTER.*
`Specify next point or [Undo]: 17,25↵`	*Type 17,25 and press ENTER.*
`Specify next point or [Undo]: @15,0↵`	*Type @15,0 and press ENTER.*
`Specify next point or [Close/Undo]: @0,12↵`	*Type @0,12 and press ENTER.*
`Specify next point or [Close/Undo]: @12,7↵`	*Type @12,7 and press ENTER.*
`Specify next point or [Close/Undo]: @26<-60↵`	*Type @26<-60 and press ENTER (Angle in clockwise direction).*
`Specify next point or [Close/Undo]: 40,12↵`	*Type 40,12 and press ENTER.*
`Specify next point or [Close/Undo]: c↵`	*Type c and press ENTER to Close and end LINE command.*

Typing c (for Close) during active LINE command joins the last point with the first point. It automatically terminates LINE command.

Practice Session 6: Understanding *ORTHO* and *POLAR* buttons on Status bar

Open a new drawing file and activate LINE command. Click anywhere for the first point. Just move the crosshair anywhere around the first point. Now, turn on ***ORTHO*** button on **Status bar** and then move crosshair anywhere in drawing area. What difference you have observed in the movement? When ORTHO is on, the cursor moves in vertical and horizontal directions only. It lets you to draw perfectly vertical and horizontal lines. However, you may enter relative polar coordinates, $@ \, x < \theta$, when ORTHO is active. ORTHO mode helps to copy or move the objects perfectly horizontal or vertical.

Turn on the ***POLAR*** button on the **Status bar**. (***ORTHO*** is automatically turned off.) Move the crosshair (LINE command is active) slowly anywhere in the drawing area. As you move through specific incremental distance, a message: **Polar:** $x < \theta$ is displayed in a rectangular block near the tooltip. The message indicates the dynamic location of the crosshair with respect to previous point. POLAR mode helps you to draw objects with direct distance entry. You may customize the POLAR setting using **Drafting Settings** dialog box (**Polar Tracking** tab).

Terminate LINE command and close the file without saving the changes.

22.9.2 Polyline

Polyline (or pline) is a curve consisting of line segments and or arcs of same or variable thicknesses. PLINE command operates in the same way as the LINE command. The difference is that it has more options: Arc, Halfwidth, Length, Undo, Width. The arc option has further more options. It helps to draw arcs in a variety of ways.

Example 22.3 Draw Fig. 22.17 using PLINE command. Start from appropriate point.

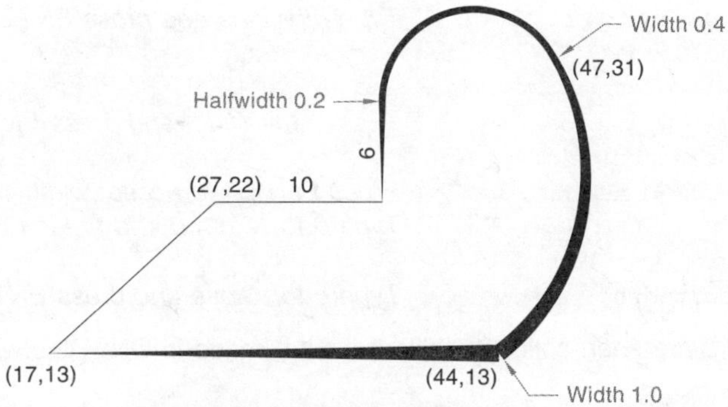

Fig. 22.17

Solution Execute PLINE command as follows.

Draw toolbar » ***Polyline*** or
Menu bar » ***Draw*** » ***Pline*** or
Command line » **pl** (for **Pline**)

`Command: pl↵`	
`PLINE`	
`Specify start point: 17,13↵`	*Type 17,13 and press ENTER.*
`Current line-width is 0.00`	
`Specify next point or [Arc/Halfwidth/ Length/Undo/Width]: 27,22↵`	*Type 27,22 and press ENTER.*
`Specify next point or [Arc/Close/ Halfwidth/Length/Undo/Width]:@10,0↵`	*Type @10,0 and press ENTER.*
`Specify next point or [Arc/Close/ Halfwidth/Length/Undo/Width]: h↵`	*Type h for Halfwidth and press ENTER.*
`Specify starting half-width <0.00>:↵`	*Press ENTER to accept halfwidth 0.*
`Specify ending half-width <0.00>:.2↵`	*Type .2 for halfwidth 0.2 and press ENTER.*
`Specify next point or [Arc/Close/ Halfwidth/Length/Undo/Width]: @0,6↵`	*Type @0,6 and press ENTER.*
`Specify next point or [Arc/Close/`	*Type a for Arc and press ENTER.*

`Halfwidth/Length/Undo/Width]: a↵`	
`Specify endpoint of arc or [Angle/Centre/CLose/Direction/ Halfwidth/Line/Radius/Second pt/Undo/Width]:47,31↵`	*Type 47,31 and press ENTER.*
`Specify endpoint of arc or [Angle/Centre/CLose/Direction/ Halfwidth/Line/Radius/Second pt/Undo/Width]: w↵`	*Type w for Width and press ENTER.*
`Specify starting width <0.40>:↵`	*Press ENTER to accept width 0.4.*
`Specify ending width <0.40>: 1↵`	*Type 1 for width 1 and press ENTER.*
`Specify endpoint of arc or [Angle/Centre/CLose/Direction/ Halfwidth/Line/Radius/Second pt/Undo/Width]:44,13↵`	*Type 44,13 and press ENTER.*
`Specify endpoint of arc or [Angle/Centre/CLose/Direction/ Halfwidth/Line/Radius/Second pt/Undo/Width]:l↵`	*Type l for Line and press ENTER.*
`Specify next point or [Arc/Close/ Halfwidth/Length/Undo/Width]: w↵`	*Type w for Width and press ENTER.*
`Specify starting width <1.00>:↵`	*Press ENTER to accept width 1.*
`Specify ending width <1.00>: 0↵`	*Type 0 for width 0 and press ENTER.*
`Specify next point or [Arc/Close/ Halfwidth/Length/Undo/Width]: c↵`	*Type c for Close and press ENTER.*

The widths of line or arc are seen solid (i.e., filled) if FILL mode is ON. Otherwise, the widths are seen hollow.

22.9.3 Arc

An arc is a part of a circle. There are many options to draw the arcs in ARC command. By default, arcs are drawn in anticlockwise direction. The options in ARC command (see Fig. 22.18 for illustration) are as follows.

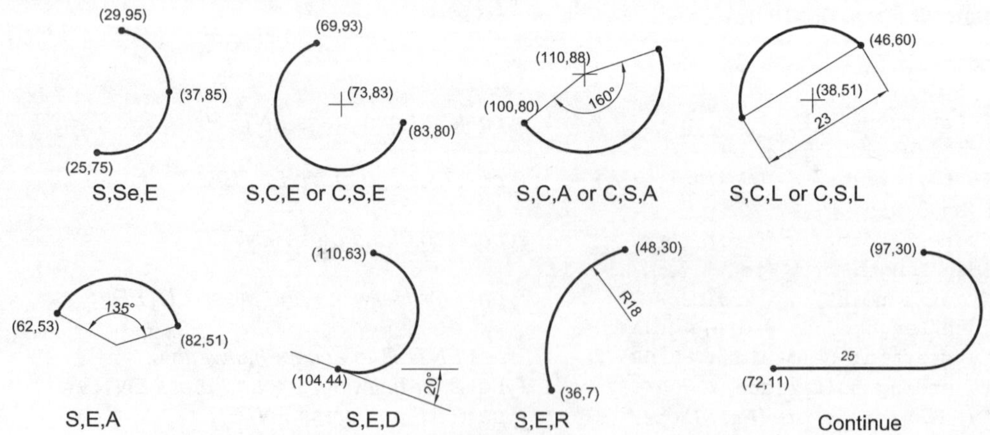

Fig. 22.18

Start point-Second point-End point (S, Se, E)
Start point-Centre-End point (S, C, E) or Centre-Start point-End point (C, S, E)
Start point-Centre-Included angle (S, C, A) or Centre-Start point-Included angle (C, S, A)
Start point-Centre-Chord length (S, C, L) or Centre-Start point-Chord length (C, S, L)
Start point-End point-Included angle (S, E, A)
Start point-End point-Direction of tangent at start point (S, E, D)
Start point-End point-Radius (S, E, R)
Continue (**Menu bar » *Draw* » *Arc* » *Continue***)

Example 22.4 Draw the arcs shown in Fig. 22.18 using ARC command.

Solution

Draw toolbar » ***Arc*** *or*
Menu bar » ***Draw*** » ***Arc*** *or*
Command line » **a** (for **Arc**)

`Command: a↵`	*Type a (for ARC command) and press ENTER.*
`ARC Specify start point of arc or [Centre]: 25,75↵`	*Type 25,75 and press ENTER.*
`Specify second point of arc or [Centre/End]: 37,85↵`	*Type 37,85 and press ENTER.*
`Specify end point of arc: 29,95↵`	*Type 39,95 and press ENTER.*
`Command: ↵`	*Press ENTER (or UP key) to repeat ARC command.*
`ARC Specify start point of arc or [Centre]: 69,93↵`	*Type 69,93 and press ENTER.*
`Specify second point of arc or [Centre/End]: c↵`	*Type c for Centre and press ENTER.*
`Specify centre point of arc: 73,83↵`	*Type 73,83 and press ENTER.*
`Specify end point of arc or [Angle/chord Length]: 83,80↵`	*Type 83,80 and press ENTER.*
`Command: ↵`	*Press ENTER (or UP key) to repeat ARC command.*
`ARC Specify start point of arc or [Centre]: 100,80↵`	*Type 100,80 and press ENTER.*
`Specify second point of arc or [Centre/End]: c↵`	*Type c for Centre and press ENTER.*
`Specify centre point of arc: 110,88↵`	*Type 110,88 and press ENTER.*
`Specify end point of arc or [Angle/chord Length]: a↵`	Type a for Angle and press ENTER.
`Specify included angle: 160↵`	*Type 160 (for anticlockwise angle) and press ENTER.*
`Command: ↵`	*Press ENTER (or UP key) to repeat ARC command.*
`ARC Specify start point of arc or [Centre]: c↵`	Type c for Centre and press ENTER.
`Specify centre point of arc: 38,51↵`	*Type 38,51 and press ENTER.*
`Specify start point of arc: 46,60↵`	*Type 46,60 and press ENTER.*
`Specify end point of arc or [Angle/chord Length]: l↵`	*Type l for chord Length and press ENTER.*
`Specify length of chord: 23↵`	*Type 23 and press ENTER.*

`Command: ↵`	*Press ENTER (or UP key) to repeat ARC command.*
`ARC Specify start point of arc or [Centre]: 82,51↵`	*Type 85,51 and press ENTER.*
`Specify second point of arc or [Centre/End]: e↵`	*Type e for End and press ENTER.*
`Specify end point of arc: 62,53↵`	*Type 62,53 and press ENTER.*
`Specify centre point of arc or [Angle/Direction/Radius]: a↵`	*Type a for Angle and press ENTER.*
`Specify included angle: 135↵`	*Type 135 (for anticlockwise angle) and press ENTER.*
`Command: ↵`	*Press ENTER (or UP key) to repeat ARC command.*
`ARC Specify start point of arc or [Centre]: 104,44↵`	*Type 104,44 and press ENTER.*
`Specify second point of arc or [Centre/End]: e↵`	*Type e for End and press ENTER.*
`Specify end point of arc: 110,63↵`	*Type 110,63 and press ENTER.*
`Specify centre point of arc or [Angle/Direction/Radius]: d↵`	*Type d for Direction and press ENTER.*
`Specify tangent direction for the start point of arc: -20↵`	*Type -20 (for clockwise angle direction) and press ENTER.*
`Command: ↵`	*Press ENTER (or UP key) to repeat ARC command.*
`ARC Specify start point of arc or [Centre]: 48,30↵`	*Type 48,30 and press ENTER.*
`Specify second point of arc or [Centre/End]: e↵`	*Type e for End and press ENTER.*
`Specify end point of arc: 36,7↵`	*Type 36,7 and press ENTER.*
`Specify centre point of arc or [Angle/Direction/Radius]: r↵`	*Type r for Radius and press ENTER.*
`Specify radius of arc: 18↵`	*Type 18 and press ENTER.*
`Command: l↵`	*Type l (for LINE command) and press ENTER.*
`LINE Specify first point: 72,11↵`	*Type 72,11 and press ENTER.*
`Specify next point or [Undo]: @25,0↵`	*Type @25,0 and press ENTER.*
`Specify next point or [Undo]: ↵`	*Press ENTER to end LINE command.*

Choose **Menu bar** » ***Draw*** » ***Arc*** » ***Continue***

`Command: _arc Specify start point of arc or [Centre]:`	
`Specify end point of arc: 97,30↵`	*Type 97,30 and press ENTER.*

22.9.4 Circle

A circle can be drawn in a variety of ways. The options in CIRCLE command (see Fig. 22.19) are as follows.

Centre-Radius, Centre-Diameter, 2 Points (2P), 3 Points (3P), Tangent Tangent Radius (Ttr), Tangent Tangent Tangent (**Menu bar** » ***Draw*** » ***Circle*** » ***Tan Tan Tan***)

In 2P option, two end points of a diameter need to be entered. 3P option draws a circle through any three non-collinear points. Ttr option enables us to draw a circle of given radius tangent to two objects, viz., line, circle, arc, etc. Using Tan Tan Tan option, a circle tangent to three objects can be drawn.

Example 22.5 Draw each of the following circles in a separate drawing file:

(i) Centre (95,52) and radius = 16 units
(ii) Passing through (100,60), (90.5,70.5) and (75,50.5)
(iii) Diameter = (79,35) to (95,60)
(iv) Radius = 12 units and tangent to lines through (97,75), (64,40) and (114,40)

Solution Open a new file each time, set units and limits as mentioned earlier and execute the CIRCLE command as follows.

Draw toolbar » ***Circle*** *or*
Menu bar » ***Draw*** » ***Circle*** *or*
Command line » **c** (for **Circle**)

(i)
```
Command: c↵
CIRCLE Specify centre point for circle or [3P/2P/Ttr (tan tan radius)]: 95,52↵
Specify radius of circle or [Diameter]: 16↵
```
The output is shown in Fig. 22.19(a).

(ii) Turn off ***DYN*** button on **Status bar.**
```
Command: c↵
CIRCLE Specify centre point for circle or [3P/2P/Ttr (tan tan radius)]: 3p↵
Specify first point on circle: 100,60↵
Specify second point on circle: 90.5,70.5↵
Specify third point on circle: 75,50.5↵
```
The output is shown in Fig. 22.19(b).

(iii)
```
Command: c↵
CIRCLE Specify centre point for circle or [3P/2P/Ttr (tan tan radius)]: 2p↵
Specify first end point of circle's diameter: 79,35↵
Specify second end point of circle's diameter: 95,60↵
```
The output is shown in Fig. 22.19(c).

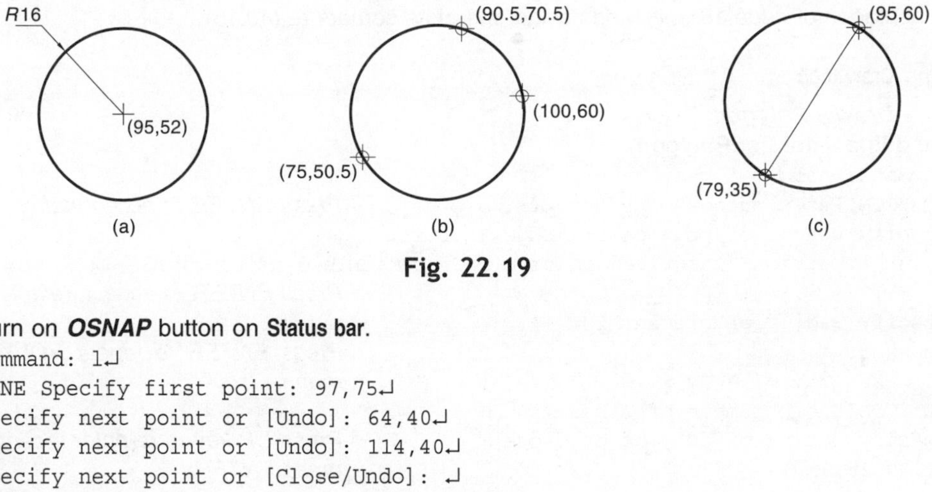

Fig. 22.19

(iv) Turn on ***OSNAP*** button on **Status bar.**
```
Command: l↵
LINE Specify first point: 97,75↵
Specify next point or [Undo]: 64,40↵
Specify next point or [Undo]: 114,40↵
Specify next point or [Close/Undo]: ↵
Command: c↵
```

```
CIRCLE Specify centre point for circle or [3P/2P/Ttr (tan tan radius)]: t↵
Specify point on object for first        Move cursor and click at line 1. The
tangent of circle:                       cursor will show floating tangent symbol.
Specify point on object for second       Move cursor and click at line 2.
tangent of circle:
Specify radius of circle<14.84>: 12↵
```

The output is shown in Fig. 22.19(d).

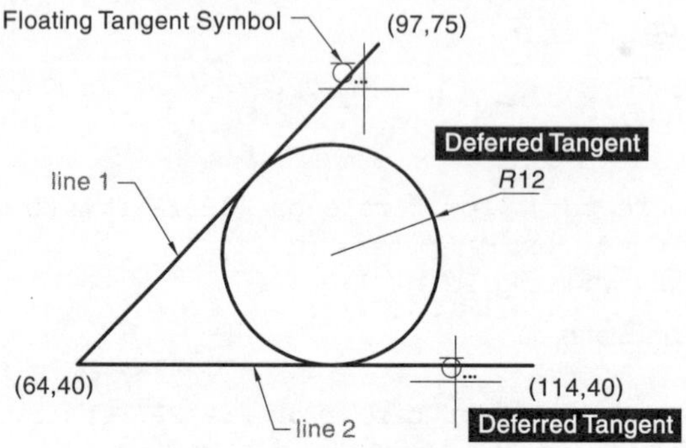

Fig. 22.19(d)

22.9.5 Polygon

The POLYGON command helps to draw regular polygons, like equilateral triangles, squares, pentagons, etc., quickly. It draws the polygon in one of the two ways—by inscribing in/circumscribing about a circle or by specifying the length of its edge.

Example 22.6 Draw each of the following in separate drawings:

(i) A square inscribed in a circle at centre (50,25) and radius = 20 units; a square circumscribed about the same circle.

(ii) A pentagon of edge 18 units and having one of its corners at (40,15).

Solution **Draw toolbar** » **Polygon** *or*
Menu bar » ***Draw*** » ***Polygon*** *or*
Command line » **pol** (for **Polygon**)

(i)
```
Command: pol↵
POLYGON Enter number of sides <4>:↵            Press ENTER to accept default input.
Specify centre of polygon or [Edge]: 50,25↵
Enter an option [Inscribed in circle/Circumscribed about circle] <I>:↵
                                               Press ENTER to accept default option.
Specify radius of circle: 20↵
Command: ↵                                     Press ENTER to repeat POLYGON command.

POLYGON Enter number of sides <4>:↵
Specify centre of polygon or [Edge]:           Press UP key to re-enter recent input and
50.00,25.00↵                                   press ENTER.
```

```
Enter an option [Inscribed in circle/Circumscribed about circle] <I>: c↵
Specify radius of circle: 20.00↵ Press UP key to re enter recent input and press ENTER.
```

The output is shown in Fig. 22.20(a).

(ii)
```
Command: pol↵
POLYGON Enter number of sides <4>: 5↵
Type 5 for pentagon and press ENTER.
Specify centre of polygon or [Edge]: e↵
Type e for Edge and press ENTER.
Specify first endpoint of edge: 40,15↵
Specify second endpoint of edge: @18,0↵
```

The output is shown in Fig. 22.20(b).

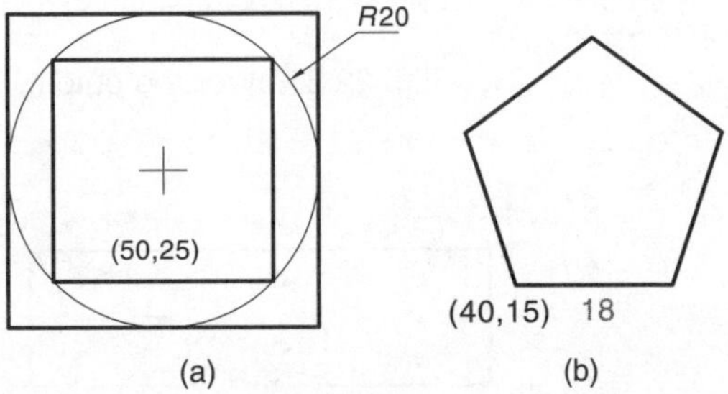

Fig. 22.20

22.9.6 Rectangle

A rectangle with right-angled or chamfered or filleted corners can be drawn by the RECTANG command. The two corner points to be entered are always the two ends of the diagonal of the rectangle. Various first-line options are: Chamfer/Elevation/Fillet/Thickness/Width. Chamfer and Fillet are used to draw rectangles with chamfered or filleted corners respectively. The width option is used to vary line thickness. Second line options—Area/Dimensions/Rotation—help to draw rectangle with area and length (or width)/ length and width/inclination of a side with *X*-axis respectively. Elevation and Thickness options are useful in 3D drawings.

Example 22.7 Draw following rectangles:

(i) Diagonal ends at (32,82) and (66,92)
(ii) Area = 84 unit^2, length = 12 units and a corner at (83,83)
(iii) Length = 10 units, width = 20 units and a corner at (120,90)

Solution **Draw toolbar** » ***Rectangle*** *or*
Menu bar » ***Draw*** » ***Rectangle*** *or*
Command line » **rec** (for **Rectang**)

(i)
```
Command: rec↵
RECTANG
Specify first corner point or [Chamfer/Elevation/Fillet/Thickness/Width]: 32,82↵
Specify other corner point or [Area/Dimensions/Rotation]: 66,92↵
```
See Fig. 22.21(a) for the output.

(ii)
```
Command: rec↵
RECTANG
Specify first corner point or [Chamfer/Elevation/Fillet/Thickness/Width]: 83,83↵
Specify other corner point or [Area/Dimensions/Rotation]: a↵
Enter area of rectangle in current units <100.00>: 84↵
Calculate rectangle dimensions based on [Length/Width] <Length>:↵
Enter rectangle length <10.00>: 12↵
```
See Fig. 22.21(b) for the output.

(iii)
```
Command: rec↵
RECTANG
Specify first corner point or [Chamfer/Elevation/Fillet/Thickness/Width]: 120,90↵
Specify other corner point or [Area/Dimensions/Rotation]: d↵
```

`Specify length for rectangles <10.00>:↵`
`Specify width for rectangles <10.00>: 20↵`
`Specify other corner point or [Area/Dimensions/Rotation]:` *Click anywhere on bottom-left side.*

See Fig. 22.21(c) for the output.

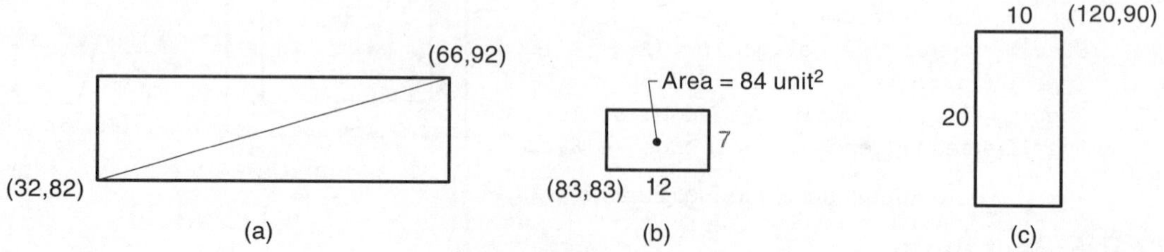

Fig. 22.21

It should be noted that the length of the rectangle is always drawn horizontal (even if it is smaller than the width).

22.9.7 Point

The POINT command is rarely used to draw any object. Rather, it is used to mark the points at particular locations on the objects. The point's appearance and size on the screen can be changed by using the **Point Style** dialog box, Fig. 22.22, activated through **Menu bar** » ***Format*** » ***Point Style...*** *or* by PDMODE and PDSIZE commands. PDMODE has values 0, 1, 2, 3, 4, 32, 33, 34, 35, 36, 64, 65, 66, 67, 68, 96, 97, 98, 99, 100. If PDMODE =1, the point will not be displayed on the screen. PDSIZE controls the size of the point (except for PDMODE values 0 and 1), i.e., relative to the screen (negative values) or absolute units (positive values).

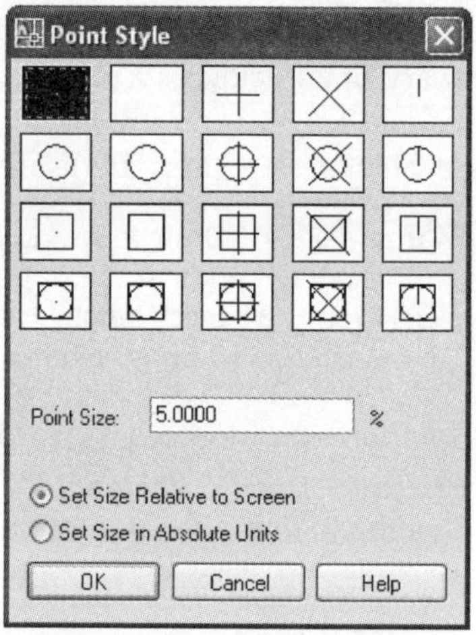

Fig. 22.22 Point Style Dialog Box

22.9.8 Ellipse

The ELLIPSE command is used to draw an ellipse or an elliptical arc or an isocircle. It draws the ellipse by accepting the length of one axis (axis endpoint and other endpoint of the same axis) and half-length of the other axis (distance to other axis). Rotation option enables to specify half-length of minor axis as (cos θ* half-length of major axis) where θ is the rotation about major axis. Arc option helps to draw elliptical arc. The parameter option defines the start parameter (i.e., start angle) and the end parameter (i.e., end angle) of the elliptical arc by using a parametric vector equation: p(u) = c + a* cos(u) + b* sin(u), where c is the centre of the ellipse and a and b are its major and minor axes, respectively.

Isocircle option is explained in Section 22.17.

Example 22.8 Draw the following entities:

(i) Ellipse: Major axis ends at (24,84) and (62,84); minor axis ends at (43,75).
(ii) Ellipse: Centre at (100,55); major axis = 50 units; minor axis = (½ major axis)*cos 60°.
(iii) Elliptical arc: Major axis = 30 units; minor axis = 12 units; start angle = 15°; end angle = 215°.

Solution

Draw toolbar » ***Ellipse*** *or*
Menu bar » ***Draw*** » ***Ellipse*** *or*
Command line » **el** (for **Ellipse**)

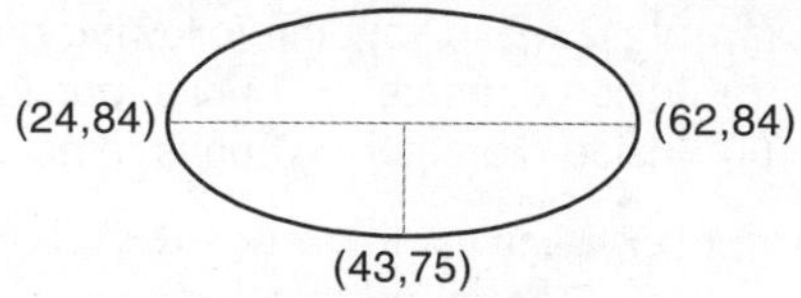

Fig. 22.23(a)

(i)
```
Command: el↵
ELLIPSE
Specify axis endpoint of ellipse or [Arc/Centre]: 24,84↵
Specify other endpoint of axis: 62,84↵
Specify distance to other axis or [Rotation]: 43,75↵
```
See Fig. 22.23(a) for the output.

(ii)
```
Command: ELLIPSE ↵
Press UP key and ENTER
Specify axis endpoint of ellipse or [Arc/Centre]: c↵
Specify centre of ellipse: 100,55↵
Specify endpoint of axis: @25<0↵
Specify distance to other axis or [Rotation]: r↵
Specify rotation around major axis: 60↵
```
See Fig. 22.23(b) for the output.

(iii)
```
Command: ELLIPSE ↵                    Press UP key and ENTER
Specify axis endpoint of ellipse or [Arc/Centre]: a↵
Specify axis endpoint of elliptical arc or [Centre]: Click at any suitable point
Specify other endpoint of axis: @30<0↵
Specify distance to other axis or [Rotation]: @6<90↵
Specify start angle or [Parameter]: 15↵
Specify end angle or [Parameter/Included angle]: 215↵
```
See Fig. 22.23(c) for the output.

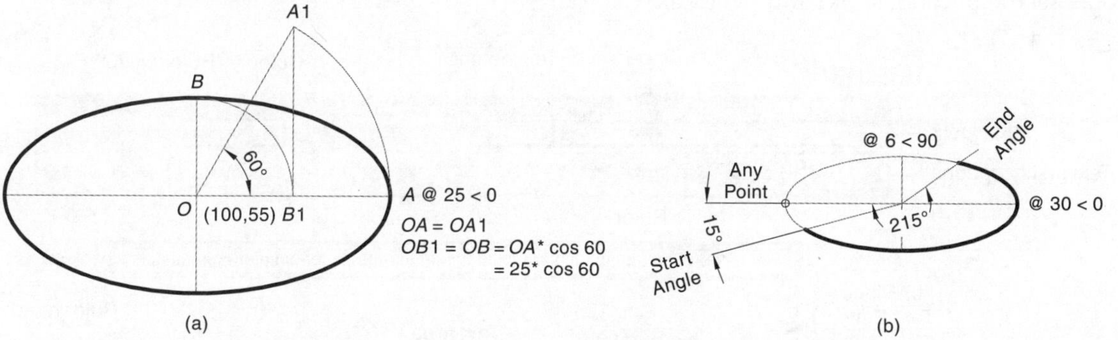

Fig. 22.23

The start angle and end angle are always measured in anticlockwise direction with respect to major axis.

22.9.9 Donut

DONUT command is used to draw filled circles or rings. The inside and outside diameters need to be specified for the rings. If the inside diameter is zero, filled circle is drawn.

Example 22.9 Draw the following donuts:

(i) Inside diameter = 5 units, outside diameter = 10 units, centres at (150,50).
(ii) Inside diameter = 0 units, outside diameter = 20 units, centre at (160,23).

Solution **Menu bar** » ***Draw*** » ***Donut*** *or*
Command line » **do** (for **Donut**)

(i)
```
Command: do↵
DONUT
Specify inside diameter of donut <0.50>: 5↵
Specify outside diameter of donut <1.00>: 10↵
Specify centre of donut or <exit>: 150,50↵
Specify centre of donut or <exit>:↵
```
Press UP key and ENTER (or only ENTER) to repeat DONUT command.

(ii)
```
Command: DONUT↵
Specify inside diameter of donut <5.00>: 0↵
Specify outside diameter of donut <10.00>: 20↵
Specify centre of donut or <exit>: 160,23↵
Specify centre of donut or <exit>:↵
```

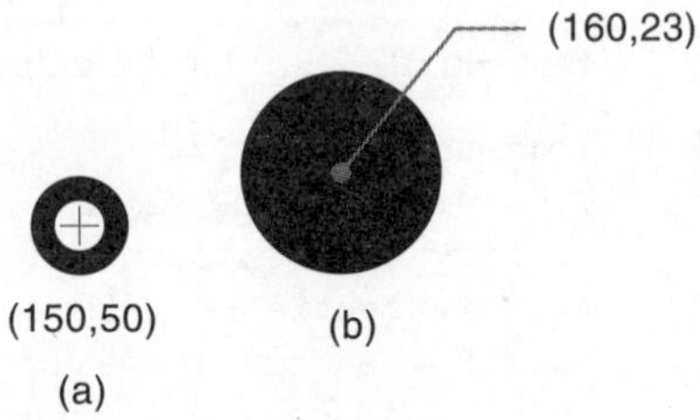

Fig. 22.24

See Fig. 22.24 for the outputs.

22.9.10 Text

To write text on the drawing, you can use either TEXT or MTEXT command. TEXT creates a single-line text using *bounding box*. You need to enter start point, height and rotation angle of the text.

MTEXT creates a multiline text paragraph using **Text Formatting** dialog box and In-Place Text Editor, Fig. 22.25. You can edit the font typeface, font style, font size, etc. Also, you can justify a paragraph to the left, right, centre, etc., and insert special symbols in your text. It enables to copy text from other applications, like MS Word or Notepad.

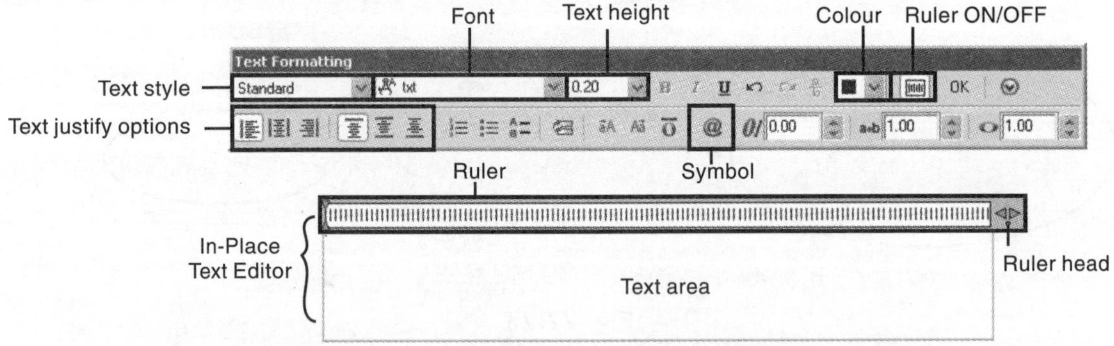

Fig. 22.25 Text Formatting Dialog Box and In-Place Text Editor

Example 22.10 Write the following sentences in the same file:

(i) 'I am OK with TEXT command.'
Use TEXT command. Start point (25,180), Text height = 10 units, Rotation angle = 0°.

(ii) 'I am OK with TEXT command.'
Use TEXT command. Text height = 15 units, Fit between (25,85) and (170,140).

(iii) '**MTEXT** command is <u>far better</u>.'
Use MTEXT command. Text height = 13 units, Font =Arial, Boldface 'MTEXT' and underline 'far better'.

Solution

Text toolbar » A ***Single Line Text*** *(Make* **Text toolbar** *active as mentioned in Section 22.7.3)*
or
Menu bar » ***Draw*** » ***Text*** » ***Single Line Text*** *or*
Command line » **Text**

(i)
```
Command: text↵
Current text style:  "Standard"  Text height:  0.20
Specify start point of text or [Justify/Style]: 25,180↵
Specify height <0.20>: 10↵
Specify rotation angle of text <0>:↵
```
Type the given sentence in Bounding box. Press ENTER twice when finished.

(ii)
```
Command: TEXT↵
```
Press UP key and ENTER (or only ENTER) to repeat TEXT command.
```
Current text style:  "Standard" Text height: 10.00
Specify start point of text or [Justify/Style]: j↵
Enter an option [Align/Fit/Centre/Middle/Right/TL/TC/TR/ML/MC/MR/BL/BC/BR]: f↵
Specify first endpoint of text baseline: 25,85↵
Specify second endpoint of text baseline: 170,140↵
Specify height <10.00>: 15↵
```
Type 15 and press ENTER. Type the given sentence. Press ENTER twice.

Draw toolbar or Text toolbar » A ***Multiline Text...*** *or*
Menu bar » ***Draw*** » ***Text*** » ***Multiline Text...*** *or*
Command line » **t** or **mt** (for **Mtext**)

(iii)
```
Command: t↵
MTEXT Current text style:  "Standard"  Text height:  15.00
Specify first corner:
```
Click at any suitable point.
```
Specify opposite corner or [Height/Justify/Line spacing/Rotation/Style/Width]:
```
Click at any other suitable point.

In **Text Formatting** *dialog box, choose* ***Font*** *as Arial and* ***Text Height*** *as 13. Type the given sentence in* ***In-Place Text Editor****. Select 'MTEXT' and make it bold using* ***B****old option on the* **Text Formatting** *dialog box. Similarly, select 'far better' and underline it using* ***U****nderline option. Click* ***OK*** *when finished. If the text does not appear in one line, select the text. Hold any blue grip and drag it horizontally till the text appears in one line. Alternatively, double-click the text to open* ***In-Place Text Editor****. Change the size of the text area by moving* ***ruler head****.*

See Fig. 22.26 for the output.

Practice Session 7: Copying the text from another application

Open Notepad (***start*** **» All Programs » Accessories » Notepad**). In Notepad window, type text- 'I am copying the text from Notepad to AutoCAD.' Select and copy the text (**Edit »Copy**). Minimize

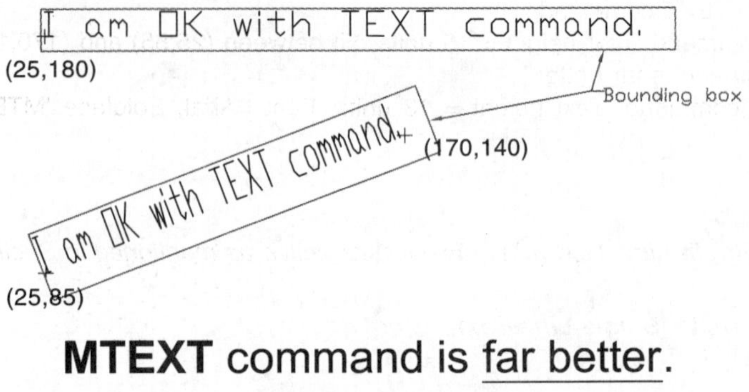

Fig. 22.26

Notepad window. In AutoCAD window, open **Text Formatting** dialog box. Right-click inside In-Place Text Editor and select ***Paste*** from shortcut menus. Click ***OK***.

The text typed in Notepad will appear in AutoCAD. You may edit it further.

22.9.11 Xline and Ray

XLINE command is used to draw construction line that extends infinitely in both the directions. Xlines are drawn for the purpose of reference. Hor (Horizontal), Ver (Vertical) and Ang (Angular) options help to draw, respectively, horizontal lines, vertical lines or lines inclined at specific angles to the *X*-axis through a desired point. The Bisect option enables to draw a line bisecting any angle. Offset options draw an xline parallel to and at a specific distance from a given line.

RAY command is similar to XLINE except that the line extends in only one direction. RAY command does not have Hor/Ver/Ang/Bisect/Offset options. Only two points need to be entered.

Example 22.11 Draw the following construction lines:
(i) From (130,160) and through (170, 120), (ii) Horizontal through (160,40), (iii) Vertical through (40,135), (iv) Inclined at 20° to *X*-axis and through (40,40).

Solution

Draw toolbar » ***Construction Line*** *or*
Menu bar » ***Draw*** » ***Construction Line*** *or*
Command line » **xl** (for **Xline**)

(i)
```
Command: xl↵
XLINE Specify a point or [Hor/Ver/Ang/Bisect/Offset]: 130,160↵
Specify through point: 170,120↵
Specify through point: ↵
```

(ii)
```
Command: XLINE↵                    Press UP key and ENTER.
Specify a point or [Hor/Ver/Ang/Bisect/Offset]: h↵
Specify through point: 160,40↵
Specify through point: ↵
```

(iii) `Command: XLINE↵` *Press UP key and ENTER.*

```
Specify a point or [Hor/Ver/Ang/Bisect/Offset]: v↵
Specify through point: 40,135↵
Specify through point: ↵
```

(iv) `Command: XLINE↵` *Press UP key and ENTER.*

```
Specify a point or [Hor/Ver/Ang/Bisect/Offset]: a↵
Enter angle of xline (0) or [Reference]:  20↵
Specify through point: 40,40↵
Specify through point: ↵
```

See Fig. 22.27 for the output.

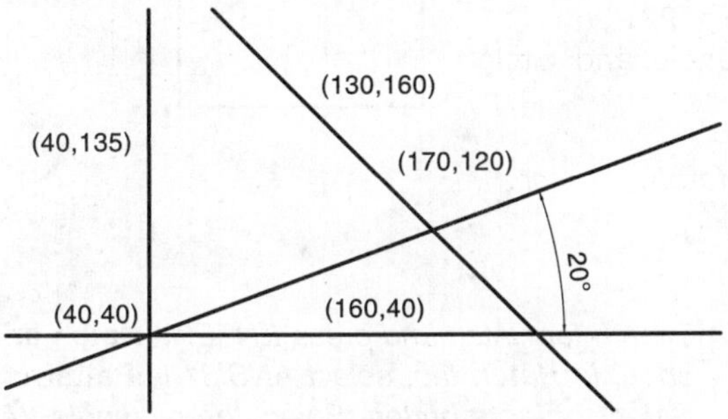

Fig. 22.27

22.9.12 Spline

SPLINE command is used to draw a freeform curve passing through or near given points. The curve is better known *nonuniform rational B-spline* (NURBS) *curve*. You can start spline from any point (start point) as pass through all given points (next points). After all the points are entered, you need to enter a point for start tangent and a point for end tangent.

Example 22.12 Draw a spline through (160,135)-(175,175)-(200,120)-(215,140) with start tangent through (170,110) and end tangent through (245,150).

Solution

Draw toolbar » ***Spline*** *or*
Menu bar » ***Draw*** » ***Spline*** *or*
Command line » **spl** (for **Spline**)

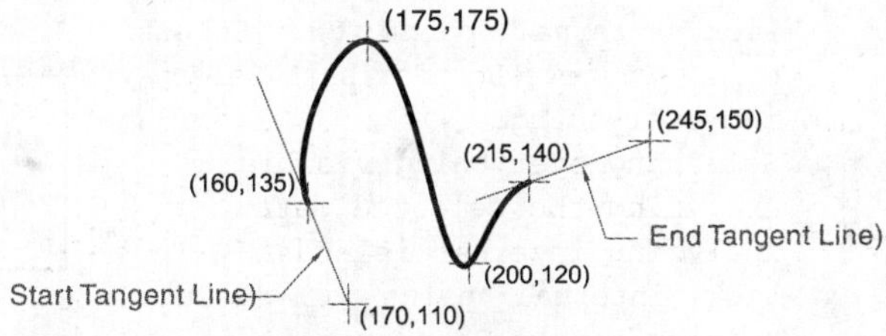

Fig. 22.28

```
Command: spl↵
SPLINE
Specify first point or [Object]: 160,135↵
Specify next point: 175,175↵
Specify next point or [Close/Fit tolerance] <start tangent>: 200,120↵
Specify next point or [Close/Fit tolerance] <start tangent>: 215,140↵
Specify next point or [Close/Fit tolerance] <start tangent>:↵
Specify start tangent: 170,110↵
Specify end tangent: 245,150↵
```

See Fig. 22.28 for the output

22.9.13 Hatch and Solid

HATCH command is used to hatch the closed area with the help of **Hatch and Gradient** dialog box.

If you choose SOLID hatch pattern (**Pattern:** combo box in **Hatch and Gradient** dialog box), the selected area is filled in by the colour shown in **Swatch:** box. (In this case, the box converts to combo box enabling the user to select the colours.)

SOLID command lets the user to fill the closed area by the desired colour. You need to select the points forming a polygonal area.

Example 22.13 Hatch (using ANSI31 hatch pattern),

(i) the rectangle shown in Fig. 22.29(a)

(ii) the area between rectangle and circle shown in Fig. 22.30(a).

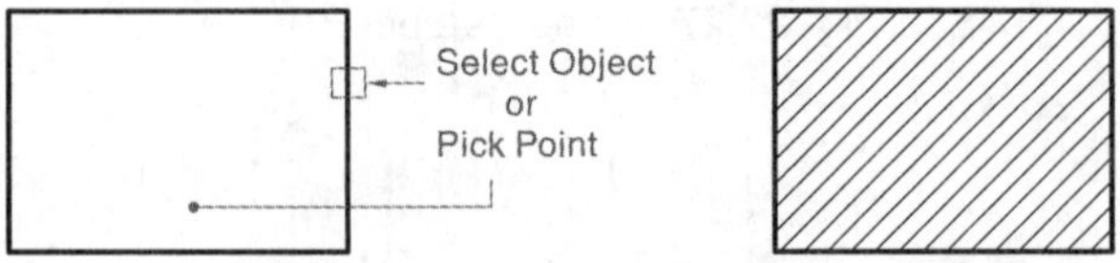

(a) (b)

Fig. 22.29

Solution **Draw toolbar** » ***Hatch...*** *or*
Menu bar » ***Draw*** » ***Hatch...*** *or*
Command line » **h** (for **Hatch**)

(i) `Command: h↵` *Type h for Hatch and press ENTER.* **Hatch and Gradient** *dialog box will open. In* ***Hatch*** *tab, select ANSI31 in* **Pattern:** *combo box. Click at* ***Add: Select objects*** *button. Select the rectangle. (Alternatively, you may click* ***Add: Pick points*** *button. Click inside the rectangle.) Press ENTER to return to* **Hatch and Gradient** *dialog box. Click* ***OK***.

```
HATCH
Select objects or [picK internal point/remove Boundaries]:1 found
Select objects or [picK internal point/remove Boundaries]:
```

See Fig. 22.29(b) for the output.

(ii) `Command: h↵` *Click at* ***Add: Pick points*** *button. Click at the area between rectangle and circle. (Alternatively, you may click at* ***Add: Select objects*** *button. Select the rectangle and circle.) Press ENTER and then click* ***OK***.

```
HATCH
Pick internal point or [Select objects/remove Boundaries]: Selecting everything...
Selecting everything visible...
Analyzing the selected data...
Analyzing internal islands...
Pick internal point or [Select objects/remove Boundaries]:
```

See Fig. 22.30(b) for the output.

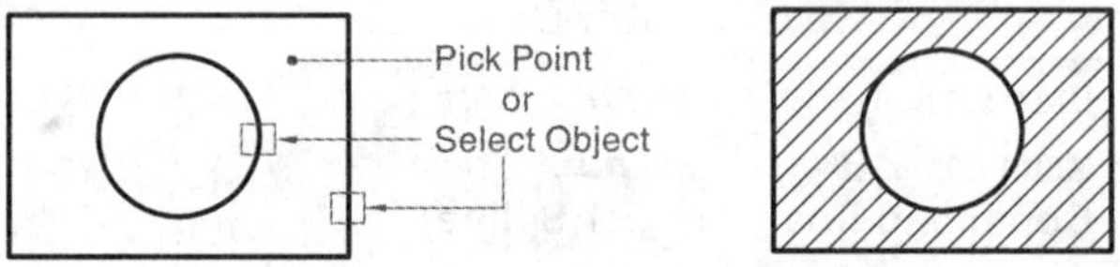

(a) (b)

Fig. 22.30

Example 22.14 Construct the arrowhead shown in Fig. 22.31(b) using SOLID command.

Solution Using LINE command, draw three lines- from (150,100) to (@20<90), from (150,110) to (210,110) and from (150,110) to (@30 < 180). The lines are shown in Fig. 22.31(a). Now, execute SOLID command as follows.

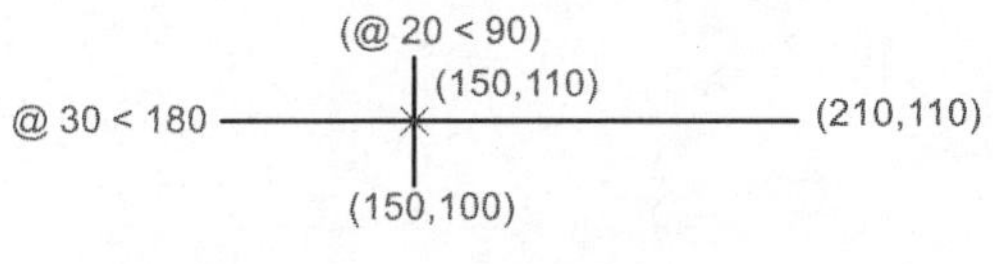

(a) (b)

Fig. 22.31

Surfaces toolbar » ***2D Solid*** *or*
Menu bar » ***Draw*** » ***Surfaces*** » ***2D Solid*** *or*
Command line » **so** (for **Solid**)

```
Command: so↵
SOLID Specify first point: 150,100↵
Specify second point: @20<90↵
Specify third point: 210,110↵
Specify fourth point or <exit>:↵
Specify third point: ↵
```

Note: Using OSNAP (explained in Section 22.10) will avoid the need of choosing the points for drawing the lines in Fig. 22.31(a).

22.10 DRAWING EXACTLY

AutoCAD draws exact figures. That is, it selects the points precisely while drawing. This is achieved by activating **AutoSnap**, i.e., turning on ***OSNAP*** (Object Snap) button on **Status bar**.

Open **Drafting Settings** dialog box (***OSNAP*** button (Right-click) » ***Settings...*** *or* **Command line » osnap**), Fig. 22.32, with ***Object Snap*** tab active. See various osnap modes available in **Object Snap modes** area. The osnaps are illustrated in Fig. 22.33. During active draw command, when you move the cursor over the existing object (with ***OSNAP*** button on), the appropriate snap markers are automatically displayed.

Note that osnap markers are visible only when any draw command (e.g., LINE) is active.

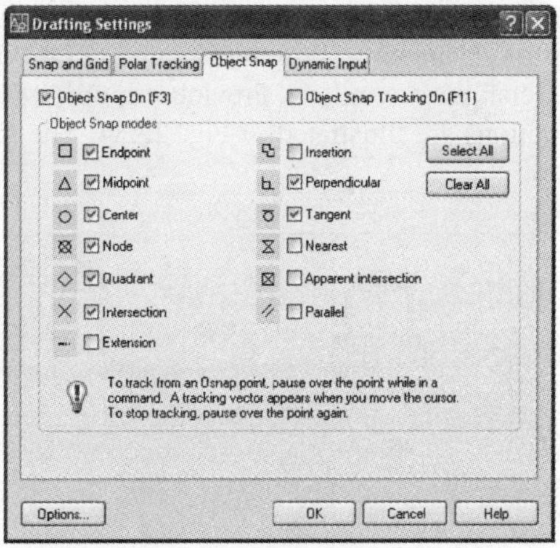

Fig. 22.32 Drafting Settings Dialog Box with Object Snap Modes

22.11 ZOOMING TO THE DRAWING

You may closely view a particular part of the drawing by zooming in. On the other hand, you may zoom out to see an overview of the drawing. ZOOM command can be activated as follows.

Zoom toolbar » **(Zoom-icons)** *or*
Menu bar » ***View*** » ***Zoom*** » **(Zoom-icons)** *or*
Command line » **z** (for **Zoom**)

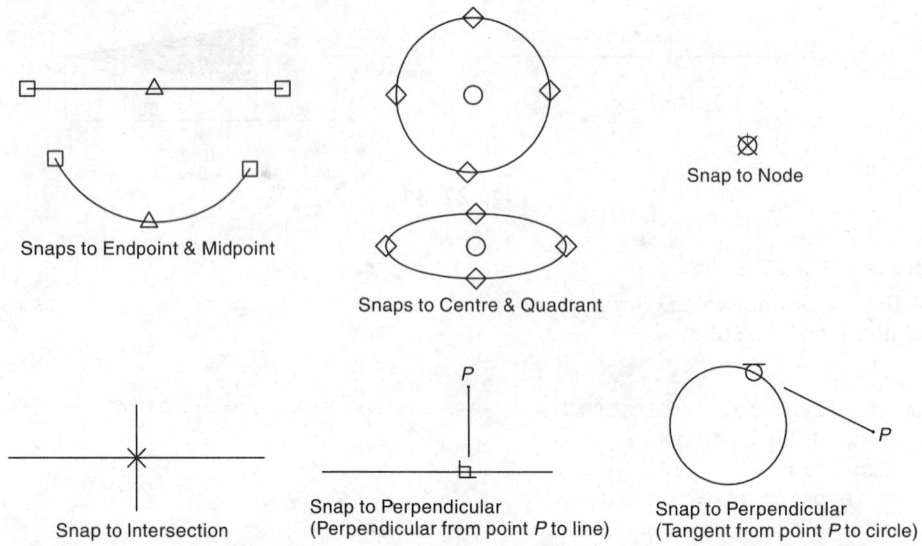

Fig. 22.33 Object Snap Modes

ZOOM command has various options: All/Centre/Dynamic/Extents/Previous/Scale/Window/Object. All option (**ZOOM »a**) displays grid limits or entire drawing, whichever is greater. It is advisable to use **ZOOM »a** after new limits are set. Extents option (**ZOOM »e**) provides the largest possible view of your drawing. Windows option (**ZOOM »w**) enables to enlarge a particular area by enclosing in a rectangular window. Previous option (**ZOOM »p**) returns you to previously zoomed view. The options are illustrated in Fig. 22.34. The scale of the object does not change while zooming.

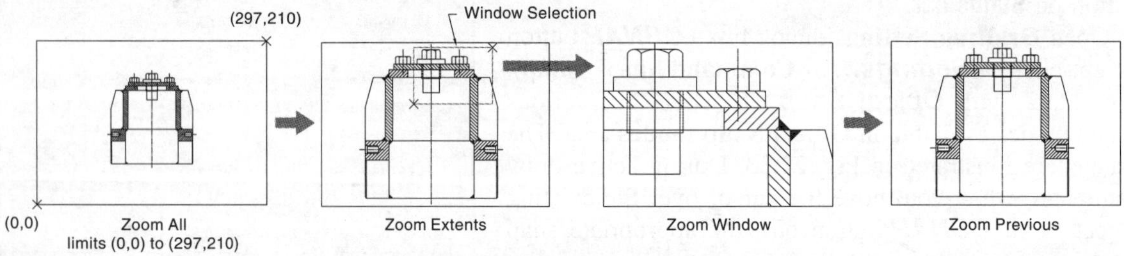

Fig. 22.34

22.12 REGEN, PAN AND UCS

REGEN command is used to regenerate the entire drawing and recompute the screen coordinates for all objects in the current viewport. It corrects the geometry of the zoomed circles/arc, removes marker blips (point marks) and restores the point sizes. REGEN command may be used after ZOOM command.

Menu bar »*View* » *Regen* *or*
Command line » re (for **Regen**)

Figure 22.35 explains the use of REGEN.

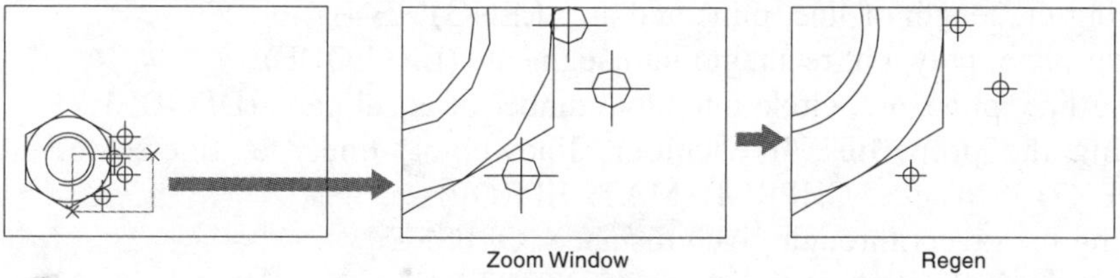

Fig. 22.35

PAN command is used to shift the location of the view. When activated, PAN command changes the crosshair cursor into the hand cursor. By holding and dragging the hand cursor, the view is moved in the direction of drag, Fig. 22.36. You may restore your original view by **ZOOM » a.**

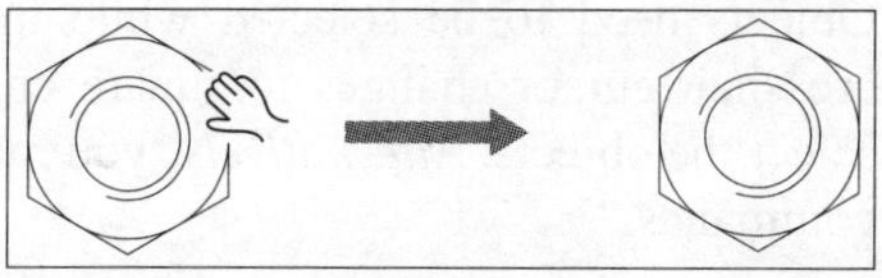

Fig. 22.36

Standard toolbar » ***Pan*** *or*
Command line » p (for **Pan**)

UCS command is used to relocate the user coordinate system for convenient coordinate entry. The origin can be shifted to any suitable point, Fig. 22.37. The coordinate entries are then accepted relative to the new origin.

UCS toolbar » (UCS-icons) *or*
Menu bar » ***Tools*** **»** ***New UCS*** **» (UCS-icons)** *or*
Command line » UCS

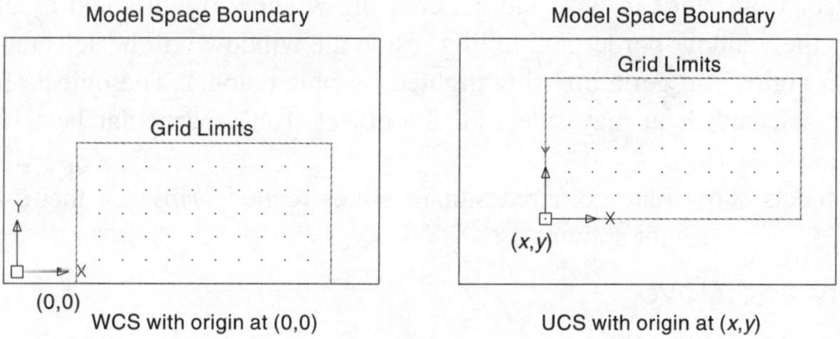

Fig. 22.37

22.13 MODIFYING THE DRAWING

Modifying the objects includes the following:

1. Copying/moving the object from one place to another place. (COPY, MOVE)
2. Copying the object in a particular pattern (ARRAY)
3. Mirroring the object about line of symmetry (MIRROR)
4. Erasing the object fully (ERASE)
5. Erasing the object partially (TRIM)
6. Extending the object to meet some reference (EXTEND)

7. Increasing the length of line, pline and arc (LENGTHEN)
8. Breaking pline, polygon, rectangle into segments (EXPLODE)
9. Dividing line, pline, arc, circle into any number of equal parts (DIVIDE)
10. Changing the properties, like colour, lineweight, linetype, line-scale, etc., of objects (PROPERTIES palette, CHPROP, MATCHPROP)
11. Offsetting the object through given distance (OFFSET)
12. Changing the inclination of the object (ROTATE)
13. Scaling the object (SCALE)
14. Chamfering/Filetting the corners (CHAMFER, FILLET)

22.13.1 Object Selection

Objects need to be selected while modifying them. When you apply any modify command, the crosshair cursor changes to square cursor (called *object selection target*) and you are prompted to select the objects. *Alternatively*, you may select objects by SELECT command and then apply modify commands.

`Command: select↵`	
`Select objects: n found`	*(where n is a number of objects selected). Select the object(s) in any one or more of the following ways.*
`Select objects: ↵`	*Press ENTER to terminate selection.*

There are many ways to select objects in AutoCAD. You can click on the objects, one by one, to select. You may select the objects by enclosing them in a window—clicking at a suitable point to fix a corner of *selection window* and then moving the cursor and clicking at another point to fix the opposite corner of the window. The selection windows are of two types—*crossing window* and *box*. If you move the cursor from **right to left**, you get crossing window (highlighted by green colour). The objects crossed by the window-border and falling inside the window will be selected. If you move the cursor from **left to right**, you get a box (highlighted by blue colour). The objects falling completely inside the box are selected. You may select all the objects (on a particular layer) by `Select objects: all` option.

The selected objects show blue coloured square boxes (called *grips*) on them. If more than 100 objects are selected, grips are not shown.

22.13.2 Copy and Move

Once you have drawn an object, it can be copied to a number of places. COPY command works in sequence. After you have selected the object to be copied, you need to enter base point. Base point can be any point serving as a reference. The second point is the point indicating a new location of the base point. Displacement option helps to copy the object through given distance.

MOVE command works in a similar way to COPY command. The object is removed from original location and permanently shifted to a new location.

> **Note:** From the Example 22.15 onwards, the commands are chosen from their respective toolbars or Menus.

Example 22.15 Copy the circle in Fig. 22.19(a).dwg taking the base point at its centre,
(i) to the points (115,85) and (135,52)
(ii) through the distances of 35 units along -*Y*-axis.

Solution Open file Fig. 22.19(a).dwg.

Modify toolbar » ***Copy*** *or*
Menu bar » ***Modify*** » ***Copy*** *or*
Command line » **co** (for **Copy**)

```
Command: _copy
Select objects: 1 found        Select the circle.
Select objects: ↵
Specify base point or [Displacement] <Displacement>:
Snap to Centre (95,52)
Specify second point or <use first point as displacement>:
115,85↵
Specify second point or [Exit/Undo] <Exit>: 135,52↵
Specify second point or [Exit/Undo] <Exit>: @35<-90↵
Specify second point or [Exit/Undo] <Exit>:↵
```

See Fig. 22.38 for the output.

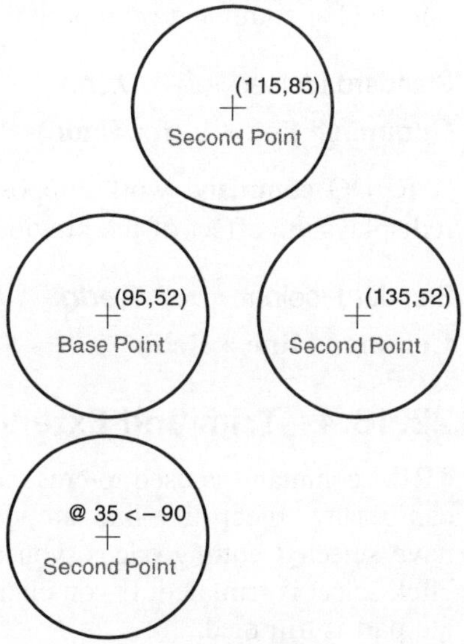

Fig. 22.38

Example 22.16 Move the circle in Fig. 22.19(a).dwg taking base point at (95,95) to (140,60).

Solution Open file Fig. 22.19(a).dwg.

Modify toolbar » ***Move*** *or*
Menu bar » ***Modify*** » ***Move*** *or*
Command line » **m** (for **Move**)

```
Command: _move
Select objects: 1 found        Select the circle.
Select objects: ↵
Specify base point or [Displacement] <Displacement>:
95,95↵
Specify second point or <use first point as displacement>:
140,60↵
```

See Fig. 22.39 for the output.

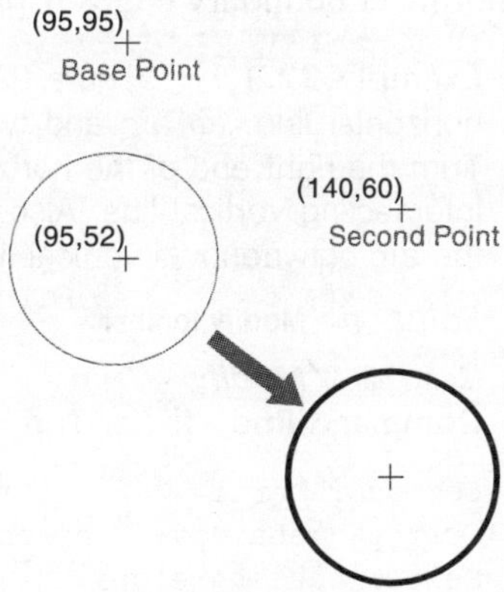

Fig. 22.39

22.13.3 Erase, Undo and Redo

ERASE command is used to delete the unwanted entities. The entities will be erased one by one or in a group depending on the selection mode. Once the entities are selected, you need to press ENTER to delete them.

Modify toolbar » ***Erase*** *or*
Menu bar » ***Modify*** » ***Erase*** *or*
Command line » **e** (for **Erase**) *or*
Select Object(s) » Press DELETE key

UNDO command is used to cancel the effect of the previous command. For example, if you have erased an entity, then applying UNDO command immediately will recover it. Undo also appears as an option [] at command prompt during many other commands. In such case, it cancels the recent input.

Standard toolbar » ***Undo*** *or*
Command line » u (for **Undo**)

REDO command works opposite of UNDO command. It cancels the effect of UNDO, i.e., it redisplays the effect of the previous command. Needless to say, REDO works only after UNDO.

Standard toolbar » ***Redo*** *or*
Command line » Redo

22.13.4 Trim and Extend

TRIM command is used to erase an entity partly. It trims the objects at *cutting edge(s)*. Cutting edge can be any object (like line, arc, circle, pline, etc.) that intersects the object to be trimmed. Once you have selected cutting edges, you are prompted to select objects to trim. The end of the object you click select is trimmed. If you click at the part of the object between two cutting edges, the intermediate part is trimmed.

EXTEND command is opposite of TRIM command. It extends an object to meet a particular reference object called *boundary edge*. Once the boundary edge is selected, you are prompted to select objects to extend. The object selected is extended to meet the boundary edge. If the object does not meet boundary edges if produced, it is not extended.

Example 22.17 Figure 22.40(a) shows a horizontal line, an arc and two vertical lines. Trim the right end of the horizontal line at the intersecting vertical line. Also, trim the part of the arc between two vertical lines.

Solution **Modify toolbar »** ***Trim*** *or*
Menu bar » ***Modify*** **»** ***Trim*** *or*
Command line » tr (for **Trim**)

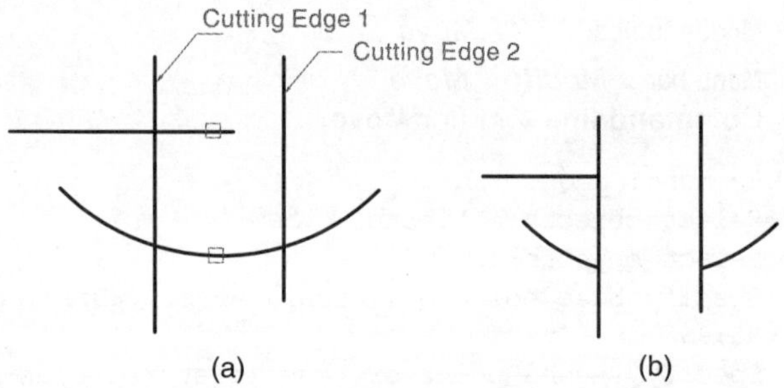

Fig. 22.40

```
Command: _trim
Current settings: Projection=UCS, Edge=None
Select cutting edges ...
Select objects or <select all>: 1 found     Select a vertical line
Select objects: 1 found, 2 total     Select another vertical line
Select objects: ↵     Press ENTER or right-click.
Select object to trim or shift-select to extend or
[Fence/Crossing/Project/Edge/eRase/Undo]:  Click at right end of the horizontal line
Select object to trim or shift-select to extend or
[Fence/Crossing/Project/Edge/eRase/Undo]:  Click at intermediate part of the arc
Select object to trim or shift-select to extend or
[Fence/Crossing/Project/Edge/eRase/Undo]: ↵
```

See Fig. 22.40(b) for the output.

Example 22.18 Fig. 22.41(a) shows a horizontal line and a vertical line. Extend the horizontal line to meet the vertical line.

Solution **Modify toolbar** » ***Extend*** *or*
Menu bar » ***Modify*** » ***Extend*** *or*
Command line » **ex** (for **Extend**)

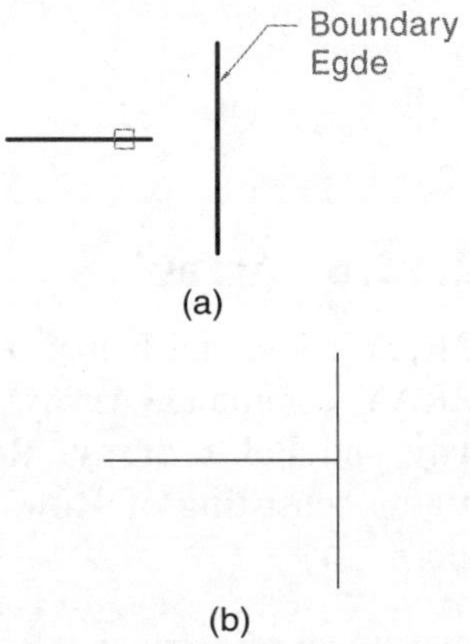

Fig. 22.41

`Command: _extend`
`Current settings: Projection=UCS, Edge=None`
`Select boundary edges...`
`Select objects or <select all>: 1 found`
Select the vertical line
`Select objects: ↵` *Press ENTER or right-click.*
`Select object to extend or shift-select to trim or`
`[Fence/Crossing/Project/Edge/Undo]:` *Click at the end of horizontal line nearer to boundary edge*
`Select object to extend or shift-select to trim or`
`[Fence/Crossing/Project/Edge/Undo]: ↵`

See Fig. 22.41(b) for the output.

22.13.5 Lengthen

LENGTHEN command is used to increase or decrease the length of lines, arcs, open plines, open splines, etc. DElta option enables to lengthen or shorten the object through incremental distance or angle. Percent option changes the length of an object by a specified percentage of its total length. Total option changes the length to total absolute length measured from an endpoint. DYnamic option turns on *dynamic dragging mode* that helps you change the length of a selected object by dragging one of its endpoints, keeping the other end fixed. Angle option is applicable to arc.

Example 22.19 Figure 22.42(a) shows a line that is 70 units long. (i) Increase its length by 20 units, (ii) Decrease its length to 50 units.

Solution **Menu bar** » ***Modify*** » ***Lengthen*** *or*
Command line » **len** (for **Lengthen**)

(i) `Command: _lengthen`
`Select an object or [DElta/Percent/Total/DYnamic]: de↵`
`Enter delta length or [Angle] <0.00>: 20↵`
`Select an object to change or [Undo]:` *Select the line near any end.*
`Select an object to change or [Undo]: ↵`

See Fig. 22.42(b) for the output.

(ii) `Command: _lengthen`
`Select an object or [DElta/Percent/Total/DYnamic]: t↵`
`Specify total length or [Angle] <1.0000)>: 50↵`
`Select an object to change or [Undo]:` *Select the line near any end.*
`Select an object to change or [Undo]: ↵`

See Fig. 22.42(c) for the output.

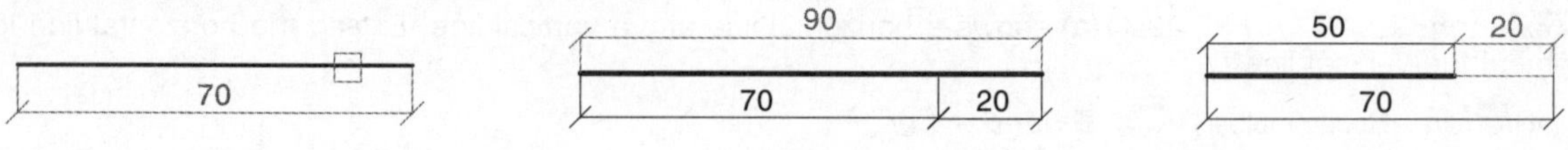

(a) (b) (c)

Fig. 22.42

22.13.6 Array

ARRAY command helps to copy object(s) in a rectangular or circular pattern. When you activate ARRAY command, **Array** dialog box, Fig. 22.43, appears. There are two options: **Rectangular array** and **Polar array**. **Rectangular array** helps to arrange the given object(s) in rectangular patterns consisting of **Rows** and **Columns**. **Polar array** arranges the given object(s) in a circular pattern.

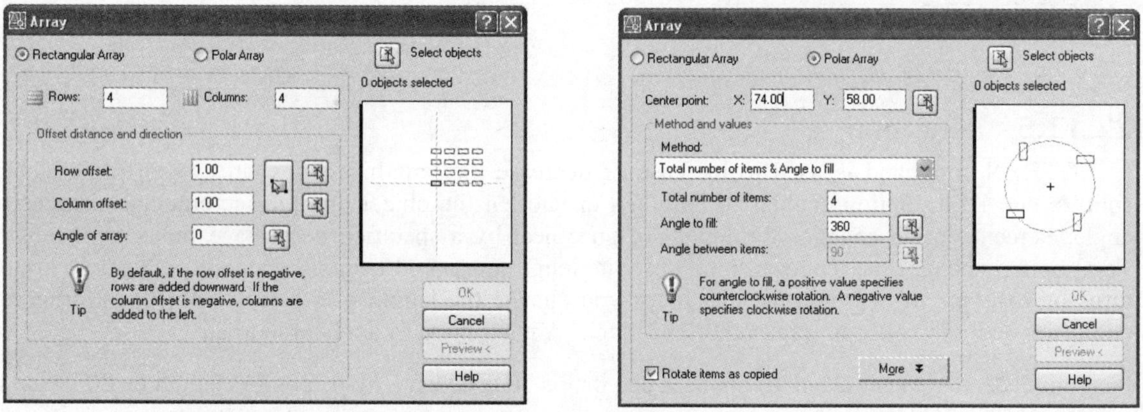

(a) Rectangular Array (b) Polar Array

Fig. 22.43 Array Dialog Box

Example 22.20 Obtain a rectangular array of two rows and three columns of the circle shown in Fig. 22.44(a). Take distance between rows = 40 units and distance between columns = 30 units.

Solution **Modify toolbar** » ***Array...*** *or*
Menu bar » ***Modify*** » ***Array...*** *or*
Command line » **ar** (for **Array**)

***Array** dialog box will appear. Choose **Rectangular array**. Click at **Select objects** button. The **Array** dialog box will close and you will be prompted for object selection. Select the given circle. Press ENTER or right-click. **Array** dialog box will reappear. In **Rows:** box, enter 2. In **Column:** box, enter 3. Enter 40 and 30 respectively in **Row offset:** box and **Column offset:** box. Enter 0 in **Angle of array:** box. Click **OK** to finish.*

```
Command: _array
Select objects: 1 found
Select objects:
```

See Fig. 22.44(b) for the output.

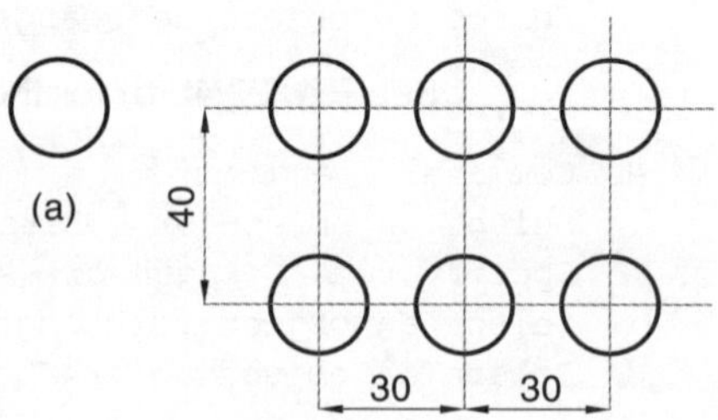

(b)

Fig. 22.44

Example 22.21 See Fig. 22.45(a). Obtain eight equispaced copies of the smaller circle along the circumference of bigger circle.

Solution **Modify toolbar** » ***Array...***

Choose ***Polar array*** *in* **Array** *dialog box. Click at* ***Select objects*** *button and select the smaller circle. Press ENTER or right-click to redisplay* **Array** *dialog box. To select the centre of array, click* **Pick Center Point** *button. Snap to Centre of bigger circle (Turn on* ***OSNAP*** *button on* **Status bar** *if it is off). In* **Method:** *combo box, choose* ***Total number of items & Angle to fill****. Enter 8 in* **Total number of items:** *box and enter 360 in* **Angle to fill:** *box. Click* ***OK****.*

```
Command: _array
Select objects: 1 found
Select objects:
Specify center point of array:
```

See Fig. 22.45(b) for the output.

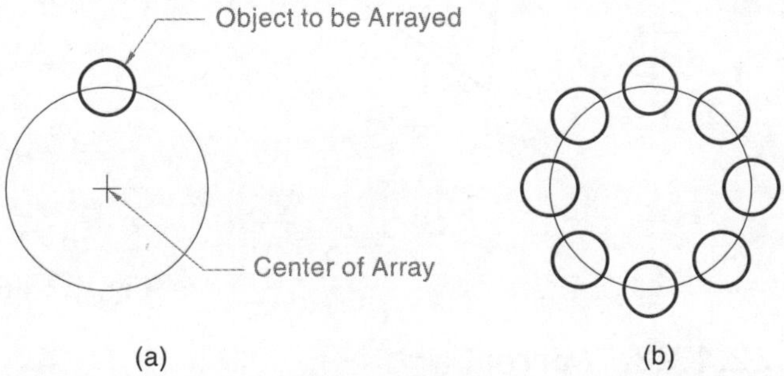

Fig. 22.45

22.13.7 Rotate

ROTATE command is used to rotate the objects about a specified base point through specified angle. The rotation, by default, is anticlockwise (if the angle values are positive). Copy option helps to obtain a rotated copy of an object. Reference option enables to rotate an object by entering reference angle and new angle. The rotation angle is calculated as (existing angle with *X*-axis + reference angle – new angle).

Example 22.22 Figure 22.46(a) shows an object.
(i) Rotate it through 75°,
(ii) Copy rotate it through –75°,

Solution **Modify toolbar** » ***Rotate*** *or*
Menu bar » ***Modify*** » ***Rotate*** *or*
Command line » **ro** (for **Rotate**)

(i)
```
Command: _rotate
Current positive angle in UCS:  ANGDIR=counterclockwise  ANGBASE=0
Select objects: Specify opposite corner: 4 found      Select the objects by box.
Select objects: ↵
Specify base point:      Snap to point 1.
Specify rotation angle or [Copy/Reference] <0>: 75↵
```

See Fig. 22.46(b) for the output.

(ii)
```
Command: _rotate
Current positive angle in UCS:  ANGDIR=counterclockwise  ANGBASE=0
Select objects: Specify opposite corner: 4 found      Select the objects by box.
Select objects: ↵
Specify base point:      Snap to point 1.
Specify rotation angle or [Copy/Reference] <75>: c↵
```

```
Rotating a copy of the selected objects.
Specify rotation angle or [Copy/Reference] <75>: -75↵
```

See Fig. 22.46(c) for the output.

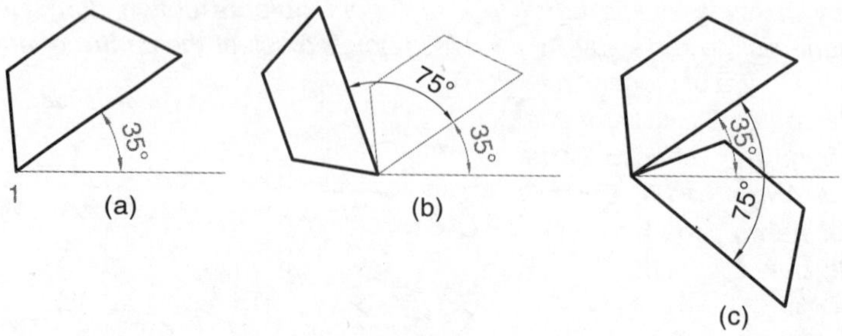

Fig. 22.46

22.13.8 Mirror

MIRROR command helps to create the mirror image of an object. It flips the objects about a specified axis (called *mirror line*) to create other symmetrical half. Mirror line may be the actual line or an imaginary line specified by two points.

Texts can also be mirrored. The texts are flipped (i.e., reversed or turned upside down) if MIRRTEXT = 1. The texts are not reversed if MIRRTEXT = 0.

Example 22.23 Mirror the objects shown in Fig. 22.47(a) about line 1–2.

Solution **Modify toolbar** » ***Mirror*** *or*
Menu bar » ***Modify*** » ***Mirror*** *or*
Command line » **mi** (for **Mirror**)

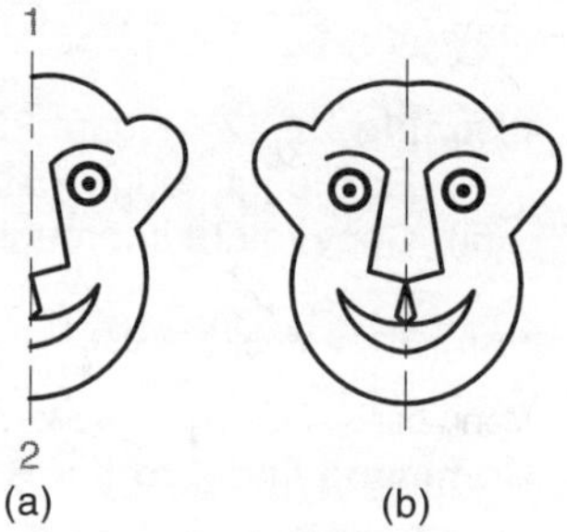

Fig. 22.47

```
Command: _mirror
Select objects: all↵
5 found
Select objects: ↵
Specify first point of mirror line: Snap to point 1.
Specify second point of mirror line:      Snap to point 2.
Erase source objects? [Yes/No] <N>:↵
```

See Fig. 22.47(b) for the output.

22.13.9 Offset

OFFSET command creates a new object parallel to the original object. The distance between the original object and the new object is called *offset distance*. When a closed curve (e.g., circle) is offset, a larger or smaller curve, depending on the side of the offset, is obtained.

Example 22.24 Offset the pline shown in Fig. 22.17 through 3 units on either side.

Solution Open file Fig. 22.17.dwg.

Modify toolbar » ***Offset*** *or*
Menu bar » ***Modify*** » ***Offset*** *or*
Command line » **o** (for **Offset**)

```
Command: _offset
Current settings: Erase source=No  Layer=Source OFFSETGAPTYPE=0
Specify offset distance or [Through/Erase/Layer] <Through>: 3↵
Select object to offset or [Exit/Undo] <Exit>:       Select the pline
Specify point on side to offset or [Exit/Multiple/Undo] <Exit>: Click outside the pline.
Select object to offset or [Exit/Undo] <Exit>:       Select the original pline
Specify point on side to offset or [Exit/Multiple/Undo] <Exit>: Click inside the pline.
Select object to offset or [Exit/Undo] <Exit>:↵
```

See Fig. 22.48 for the output.

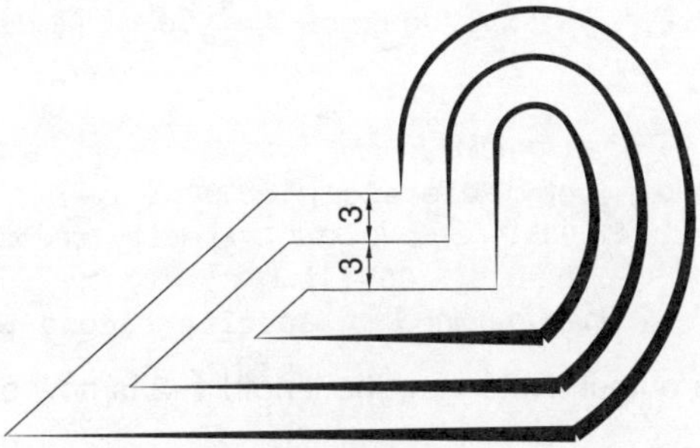

Fig. 22.48

22.13.10 Scale

SCALE command is used to reduce or enlarge the size of objects. A base point and a scale factor are needed to change the scale. To reduce the size of an object, scale factor should be less than 1. To enlarge, scale factor should be greater than 1. It also accepts the values in the form of 'x/y'. Copy option helps to create scaled copy of an object. Reference option helps to scale the object by entering reference length and new length.

Example 22.25 Scale the quadrilateral shown in Fig. 22.49(a) about base point 1,

(i) to 2:1 scale
(ii) with reference length 1–2 and new length 3–4

Solution **Modify toolbar** » ***Scale*** *or*
Menu bar » ***Modify*** » ***Scale*** *or*
Command line » **sc** (for **Scale**)

(i)
```
Command: _scale
Select objects: Specify opposite corner:        Select the quadrilateral by crossing
4 found                                         window.
Select objects: ↵
Specify base point:     Snap to point 1.
Specify scale factor or [Copy/Reference]        Type 2 for scale 2: 1 and press
<1.00>: 2↵                                      ENTER.
```

See Fig. 22.49(b) for the output.

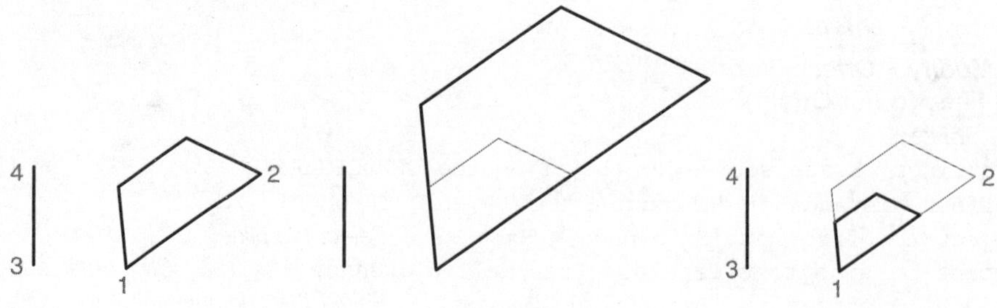

(a) (b) Scale 2:1 (c) Scale reference

Fig. 22.49

(ii)
```
Command: _scale
Select objects: Specify opposite corner:        Select the quadrilateral by crossing window.
4 found
Select objects: ↵
Specify base point:     Snap to point 1.
Specify scale factor or [Copy/Reference] <1.00>: r↵
Specify reference length <1.00>:   Snap to point 1. Specify second point: Snap to point 2.
Specify new length or [Points] <1.00>: p↵
Specify first point:     Snap to point 3.     Specify second point: Snap to point 4.
```

See Fig. 22.49(c) for the output. Note that, the length 1–2 is now equal to line 3–4.

22.13.11 Chamfer and Fillet

CHAMFER command is used to bevel the edges of the objects. It removes sharp corners by joining two objects with an angled line. Using Distance option, you can set chamfer lengths on two lines—First line and Second line. First chamfer distance is always taken on the first object you select for chamfer.

FILLET command is used to join two objects by a tangent arc. Radius option helps to set radius of the fillet.

Example 22.26 Figure 22.50(a) shows two lines.

(i) Chamfer the corner. Take first chamfer distance = 40 units and second chamfer distance = 20 units.
(ii) Fillet the corner. Take fillet radius = 30 units.

Solution **Modify toolbar** »  ***Chamfer*** *or*
Menu bar » ***Modify*** » ***Chamfer*** *or*
Command line » **cha** (for **Chamfer**)

```
Command: _chamfer
(TRIM mode) Current chamfer Dist1 = 0.00, Dist2 = 0.00
Select first line or [Undo/Polyline/Distance/Angle/Trim/mEthod/Multiple]: d↵
Specify first chamfer distance <0.00>: 40↵
Specify second chamfer distance <40.00>: 20↵
Select first line or [Undo/Polyline/Distance/Angle/Trim/   Select the horizontal line.
mEthod/Multiple]:
Select second line or shift-select to apply corner:        Select the vertical line.
```

See Fig. 22.50(b) for the output.

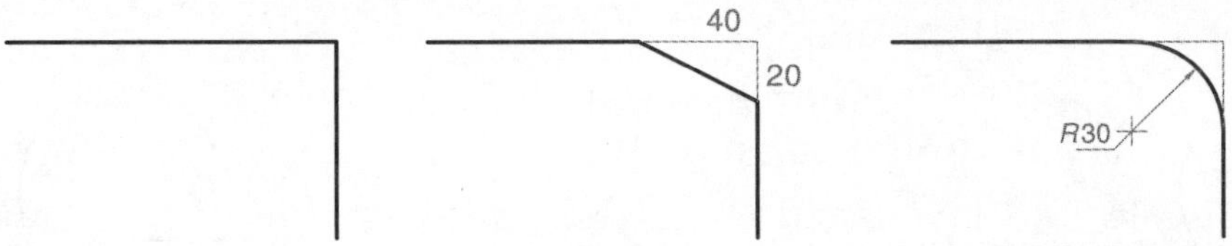

(a) (b) Chamfer (c) Fillet

Fig. 22.50

Modify toolbar » ***Fillet*** *or*
Menu bar » ***Modify*** » ***Fillet*** *or*
Command line » **f** (for **Fillet**)

```
Command: _fillet
Current settings: Mode = TRIM, Radius = 0.00
Select first object or [Undo/Polyline/Radius/Trim/Multiple]: r↵
Specify fillet radius <0.00>: 30↵
Select first object or [Undo/Polyline/Radius/Trim/Multiple]: Select the horizontal line.
Select second object or shift-select to apply corner: Select the vertical line.
```

See Fig. 22.50(c) for the output.

22.13.12 Break, Join and Explode

BREAK command is used to break an object with or without gap. The gap is created between two break points. The point at which you click to select the object is considered as the first break point. The second break point should be preferably on the object. If the gap is not expected, second break point should be chosen at the first break point.

JOIN command is used to join broken or separated similar objects. The object to which similar objects are to be joined is called *source object*. JOIN combines collinear line segments (with or without gaps); coplanar polylines (without gap) and arcs falling on same imaginary circle (with or without gaps). The arcs are joined in anticlockwise direction. The arc(s) may be converted into circle using cLose option.

EXPLODE command breaks the compound objects (drawn as a single entity, e.g., pline, dimensions, etc.) into component objects. Each component object may be then modified.

Modify toolbar » ***Explode*** *or*
Menu bar » ***Modify*** » ***Explode*** *or*
Command line » **x** (for **Explode**)

Example 22.27 Figure 22.51(a) shows an arc. Break the arc at any two points. Then, join the broken arc segments.

Solution **Modify toolbar** » ***Break*** *or*
Menu bar » ***Modify*** » ***Break*** *or*
Command line » **br** (for **Break**)

```
Command: _break Select object: Click at (or Snap to) any point 1 to select the arc.
Specify second break point or [First point]: Click at (or Snap to) any point 2.
```

See Fig. 22.51(b) for the output.

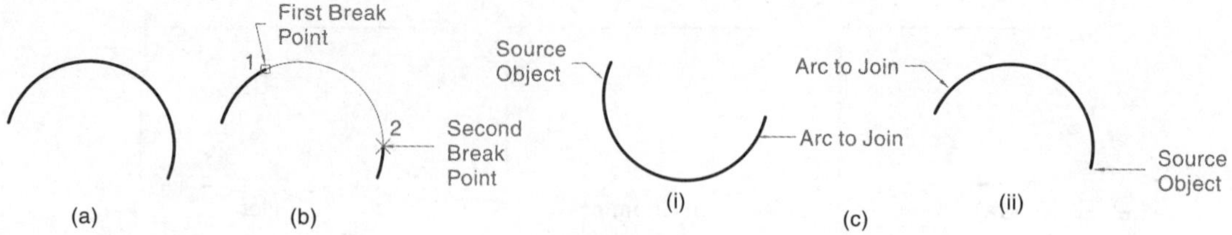

Fig. 22.51

Modify toolbar » ***Join*** *or*
Menu bar » ***Modify*** » ***Join*** *or*
Command line » **j** (for **Join**)

```
Command: _join Select source object:        Select any one arc.
Select arcs to join to source or [cLose]: Select another arc.
Select arcs to join to source: 1 found↵
1 arc joined to source
```

See Fig. 22.51(c) for the output. Any one of the two possible arcs, Fig. 22.52(c)-(i) and -(ii), will be obtained depending on the source object selection.

Practice Session 8: Exploding the objects

Open file Fig. 22.17.dwg. Choose **Modify toolbar** » ***Explode***. Select the pline. Press ENTER or right-click. See what happens to the polyline. The widths of pline have vanished. The segments are exploded, i.e., separated.

Click at any component object. It is selected independently.

Choose **Standard toolbar** » ***Undo*** (*or* **Command line** » **u**). The polyline will be restored with its original widths. Close the file without saving the changes.

22.13.13 Divide

DIVIDE command divides the objects (like, line, circle, etc.) into given number of equal parts (called *segments*). If PDMODE = 0 or 1, the divisions will not be visible. However, snap to node is detected at the division points during active draw command.

Example 22.28 Fig. 22.52(a) shows a circle. Divide it into 12 equal parts.

Solution Set PDMODE = 3 and PDSIZE = 5.
Menu bar » ***Draw*** » ***Point*** » ***Divide*** *or*
Command line » **div** (for **Divide**)

```
Command: _divide
Select object to divide:     Select the circle.
Enter the number of segments or [Block]: 12↵
```

See Fig. 22.52(b) for the output.

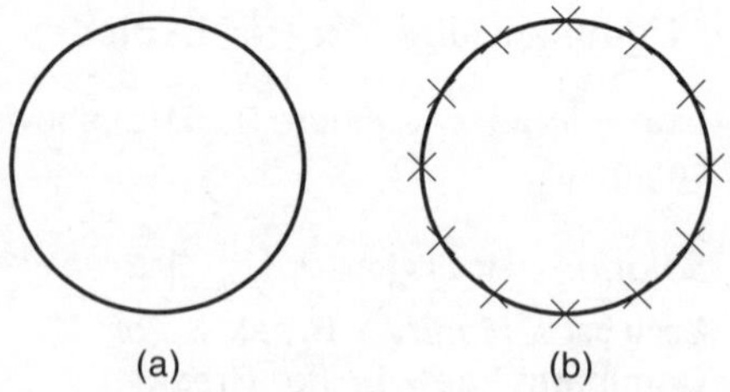

Fig. 22.52

22.13.14 Pedit

PEDIT (PolylineEDIT) command helps to edit polylines. Using PEDIT, you may convert a line or arc into pline. You may Join different adjoining lines, arcs and plines to form a pline. PEDIT enables to Fit curve passing through corner points (called *control points*) of pline. Spline option helps to pass B-spline curve through first and last control points of open polyline. Decurve option converts all arcs and curves into lines. Open option removes the last object from closed pline. Close option joins last point with the first point of open polyline.

Example 22.29 Edit the pline of Fig. 22.17 as mentioned below:
Fit curve through all control points. Undo it. Pass a Spline. Decurve the pline. Open the polyline. Close the pline.

Solution Open file Fig. 22.17.dwg.

Modify II toolbar » ***Edit Polyline*** *or*
Menu bar » ***Modify*** » ***Object*** » ***Polyline*** *or*
Command line » **pe** (for **Pedit**)

```
Command: _pedit Select polyline or [Multiple]:           Click at the polyline to select.
Enter an option [Open/Join/Width/Edit vertex/Fit/Spline/  See Fig. 22.53(a).
Decurve/Ltype gen/Undo]: f↵
Enter an option [Open/Join/Width/Edit vertex/Fit/
Spline/Decurve/Ltype gen/Undo]: u↵
Command has been completely undone.
Enter an option [Open/Join/Width/Edit vertex/Fit/         See Fig. 22.53(b).
Spline/Decurve/Ltype gen/Undo]: s↵
Enter an option [Open/Join/Width/Edit vertex/Fit/Spline/  See Fig. 22.53(c).
Decurve/Ltype gen/Undo]: d↵
Enter an option [Open/Join/Width/Edit vertex/Fit/Spline/  See Fig. 22.53(d).
Decurve/Ltype gen/Undo]: o↵
Enter an option [Close/Join/Width/Edit vertex/Fit/Spline/ See Fig. 22.53(e).
Decurve/Ltype  gen/Undo]: c↵
Enter an option [Open/Join/Width/Edit vertex/Fit/Spline/
Decurve/Ltype  gen/Undo]: ↵
```

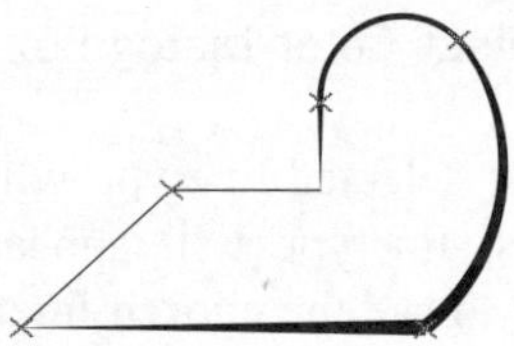

Fig. 22.17

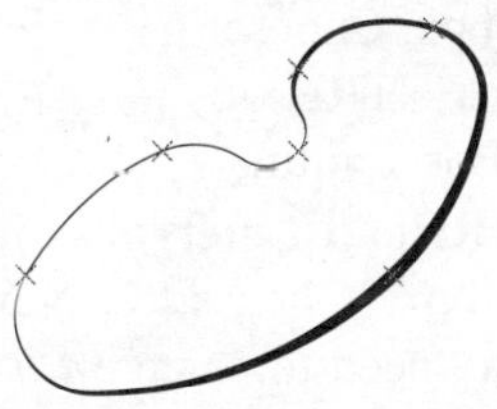

(a) Fit

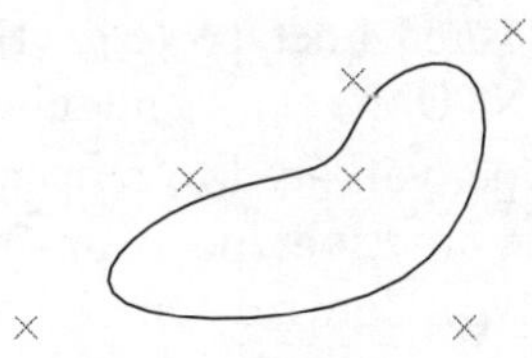

(b) Spline

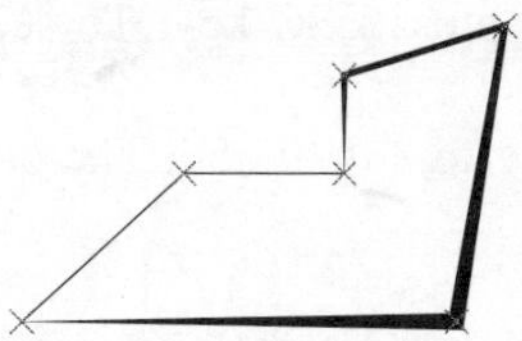

(c) Decurve

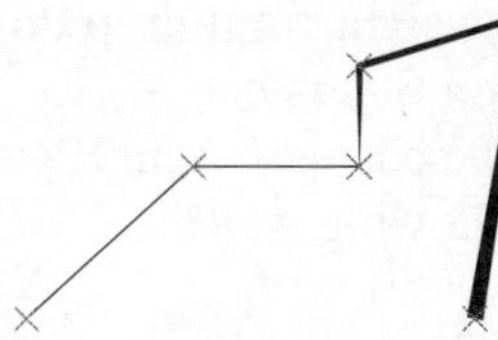

(d) Open

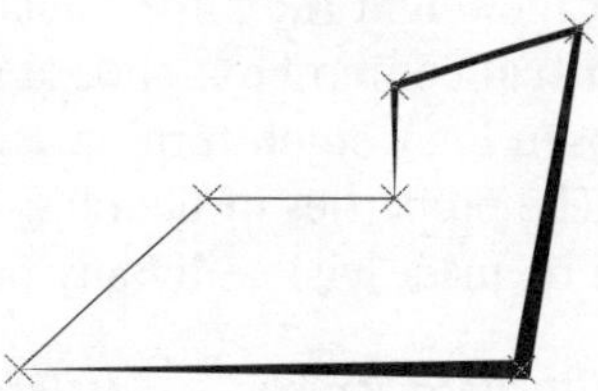

(e) Close

Fig. 22.53

22.14 CHANGING THE PROPERTIES

The properties (like, Color, Linetype, Lineweight, Linetype scale, etc.) of the object can be changed by PROPERTIES command. **Properties toolbar**, Fig. 22.54, is displayed at the top of the window.

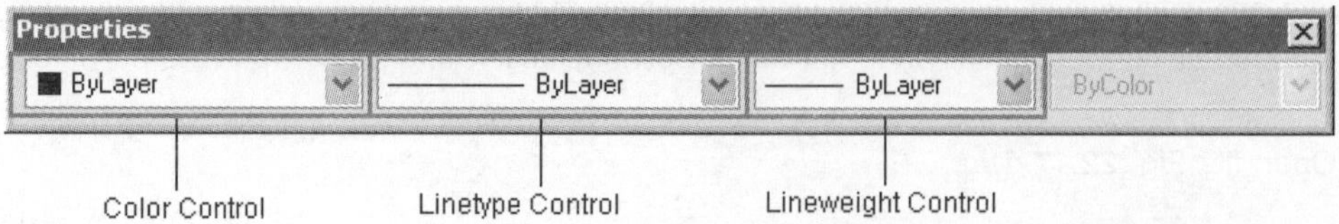

Fig. 22.54 Properties Toolbar

To change colour, select the object and then open **Color Control** combo box on **Properties toolbar.** Select the required colour and press ESC key. If you choose ***Select Color...*** option, **Select Color** dialog box, Fig. 22.55, is opened (*Alternatively*, you may use **Menu bar** » ***Format*** » ***Color...***). You may choose the desired colour from three option tabs—**Index Color**, **True Color** and **Color Books**.

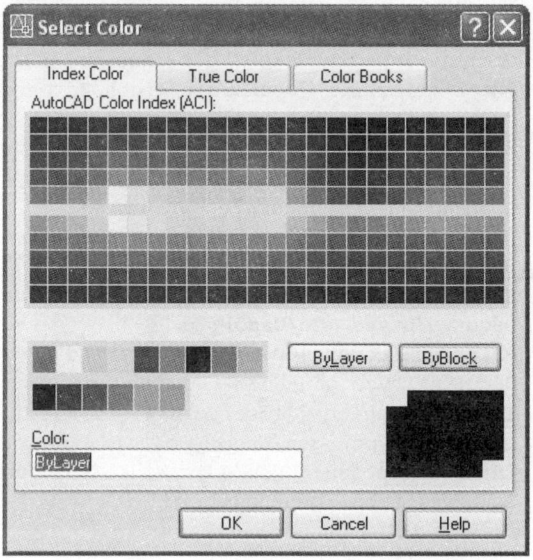

Fig. 22.55 Select Color Dialog Box

You may change continuous line to dashed line or centreline. Select the line, open **Linetype Control** combo box, choose the desired linetype and press ESC key. If the desired linetype is not visible in **Linetype Control** combo box, click ***Other...*** option (*Alternatively*, choose **Menu bar** » ***Format*** » ***Linetype...***) **Linetype Manager** dialog box, Fig. 22.56, will open. Click ***Load...*** button to display **Load or Reload Linetypes** dialog box. Choose the desired linetype (e.g., HIDDEN, CENTRE or PHANTOM, etc.) and click ***OK***. (For another linetype, you need to reopen **Load or Reload Linetypes** dialog box.). The selected linetype will be visible in **Linetype Manager** dialog box. Click ***OK***. Now, the selected linetype will appear in **Linetype Control** combo box. You may need to change ***Linetype scale*** to see the chosen linetype properly on the drawing.

Lineweight (i.e., line thickness) can be changed in a similar way. Select the line, open **Lineweight Control** combo box, choose desired lineweight from drop-down list and press ESC key. To see the chosen lineweight, turn on ***LWT*** button on **Status bar**.

The properties of the objects can also be changed using **Properties palette**, Fig. 22.57. The palette can be made visible by any one of the following ways:

Standard toolbar » ***Properties*** *or*
Menu bar » ***Tools*** » ***Properties*** *or*

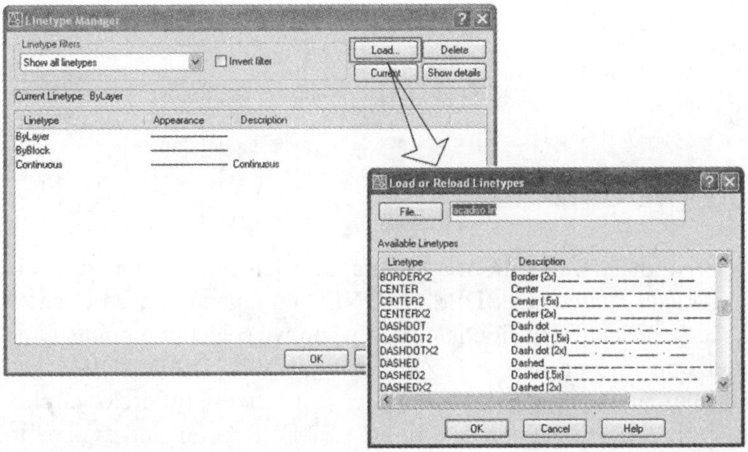

Fig. 22.56 Linetype Manager Dialog Box and Load or Reload Linetypes Dialog Box

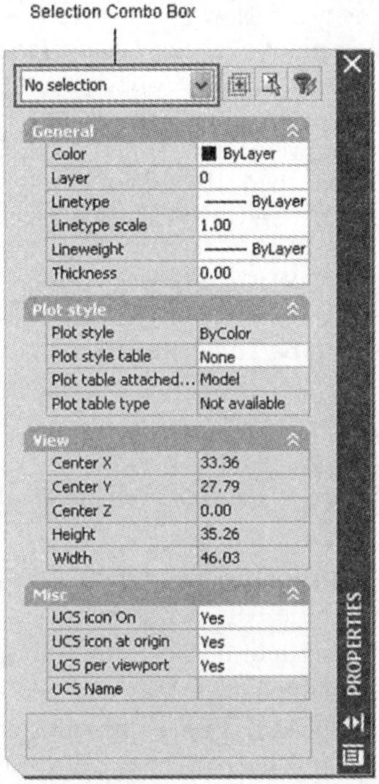

Fig. 22.57 Properties Palette

Command line » ch or **mo** or **props** (for **Properties**)

Double-click at the object

Click at the object » Right-click » *Properties* (Shortcut menu)

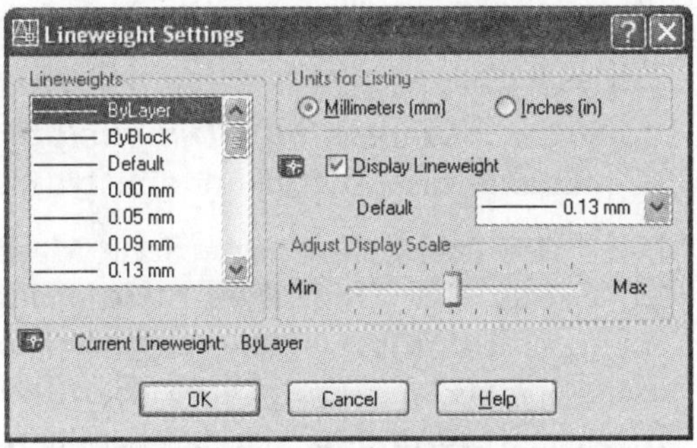

Fig. 22.58 Lineweight Settings Dialog Box

The properties like, Color, Linetype, Lineweight and Linetype scale may be changed using COLOR, LTYPE, LWEIGHT and LTSCALE commands respectively. COLOR opens **Select Color** dialog box, LTYPE opens **Linetype Manager** dialog box and LWEIGHT opens **Lineweight Settings** dialog box, Fig. 22.58. LTSCALE enables you to set a new linetype scale factor.

Example 22.30 Figure 22.59(a) shows five lines. Change the colour of the first line to grey (color 9). Change the thickness of the second line to 1 mm. Change third and fourth lines to centreline and dashed (hidden) lines respectively. Change fifth line to hidden line and set its scale to 2.

Solution Open **Linetype Control** combo box on **Properties toolbar**. Select ***Others...*** option to open **Linetype Manager** dialog box and further, click on ***Load...*** button to display **Load or Reload Linetypes** dialog box. Choose CENTER and HIDDEN (one at a time) and click ***OK***. Also, click ***OK*** on **Linetype Manager** dialog box.

Select first line, right-click and choose ***Properties*** to open **Properties palette**. In **General** pane, choose ***Color***. Open combo box and choose grey colour (color 9). Click in drawing area and press ESC key twice. Now select second line. In **Properties palette**, chose ***Lineweight***. Open combo box to show drop down list of various lineweight. Chose lineweight 1.00 mm. Click in drawing area and press ESC key twice. Select third line, open **Linetype** combo box and chose CENTER. Similarly, change fourth line to HIDDEN line. Select fifth line, change it to HIDDEN line and then choose ***Linetype scale*** option in **Properties palette**. Enter 2 in ***Linetype scale*** box. Click in drawing area and press ESC key twice.

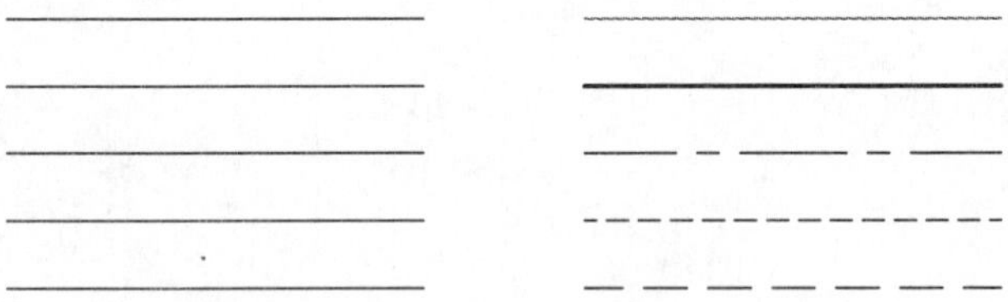

(a) (b)

Fig. 22.59

The output is shown in Fig. 22.59(b).

22.15 DIMENSIONING THE OBJECT

Dimensioning the object is very easy in AutoCAD. Length of a line, radius/diameter of an arc/a circle and angle between two lines are automatically calculated. DIMALIGNED command is used to show the length of a line parallel to the object line. The dimension is placed when we select two points (first extension line origin and second extension line origin) or the object line itself. DIMRADIUS and DIMDIAMETER commands are used to dimension radius and diameter respectively (of arc or circle). DIMANGULAR command dimensions the angle between two lines. LEADER command is used to attach notes with the help of leader line.

One may set the size and type of arrowheads, height of the dimension text and other parameters of dimensioning before or after giving the dimensions. DIMSTYLE command is used for this purpose. DIMSTYLE can be activated as:

Styles toolbar » ***Dimension Style...*** *or*
Menu bar » ***Dimension*** » ***Dimension Style...*** *or*
Command line » **d** or **dst** or **dimsty** (for Dimstyle)

DIMSTYLE opens **Dimension Style Manager** dialog box, Fig. 22.60. Click at ***New...*** button to open **Create New Dimension Style** dialog box which enables to set your own dimension style. Clicking at ***Modify...*** button will open **Modify Dimension Style: Standard** dialog box. Using the various options tabs, viz., ***Lines***, ***Symbols*** and ***Arrows***, ***Text***, ***Fit***, ***Primary Units***, ***Alternate Units*** and ***Tolerances***, you may set the required values/styles of various parameters.

Example 22.31 Dimension the horizontal line and the angle between two lines in Fig. 22.50(a). Dimension the arc of Fig. 22.51(a). Dimension the circle of Fig. 22.19(b).

Solution Open file Fig. 22.50(a).dwg.

Dimension toolbar » ***Aligned*** *or*
Menu bar » ***Dimension*** » ***Aligned*** *or*
Command line » **dal** or **dimali** (for **Dimaligned**)

```
Command: _dimaligned
Specify first extension line origin or <select object>:↵
```

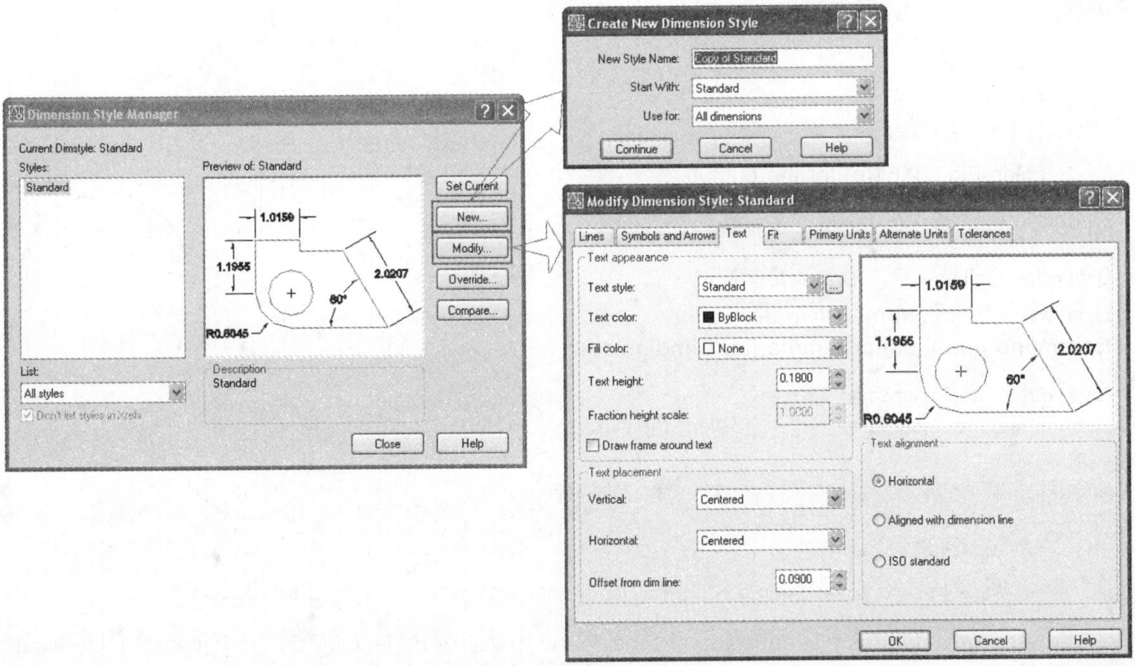

Fig. 22.60 Dimension Style Manager Dialog Box with Create New Dimension Style Dialog Box and Modify Dimension Style Dialog Box

```
Select object to dimension:            Select horizontal line.
Specify dimension line location or     Move cursor above object line at suitable point and click.
[Mtext/Text/Angle]:
Dimension text = 110
```

Dimension toolbar ***Angular*** *or*
Menu bar » ***Dimension*** » ***Angular*** *or*
Command line » **dan** or **dimang** (for **Dimangular**)

```
Command: _dimangular
Select arc, circle, line, or <specify vertex>:     Select any one line.
Select second line:     Select another line.
Specify dimension arc line location or             Move cursor at suitable point and click.
[Mtext/Text/Angle]:
Dimension text = 90
```

See Fig. 22.61(a) for the output.

Open file Fig. 22.51(a).dwg.

Dimension toolbar » ***Radius*** *or*
Menu bar » ***Dimension*** » ***Radius*** *or*
Command line » **dra** or **dimrad** (for **Dimradius**)

```
Command: _dimradius
Select arc or circle:        Select the arc.
Dimension text = 40
Specify dimension line location or        Move cursor at suitable point and click.
[Mtext/Text/Angle]:
```

See Fig. 22.61(b) for the output.

Open file Fig. 22.19(b).dwg.

Dimension toolbar » ***Diameter*** *or*
Menu bar » ***Dimension*** » ***Diameter*** *or*
Command line » **ddi** or **dimdia** (for **Dimdiameter**)

```
Command: _dimdiameter
Select arc or circle:        Select the circle.
Dimension text = 27
Specify dimension line location or  Move cursor at suitable point and click.
[Mtext/Text/Angle]:
```

See Fig. 22.61(c) for the output.

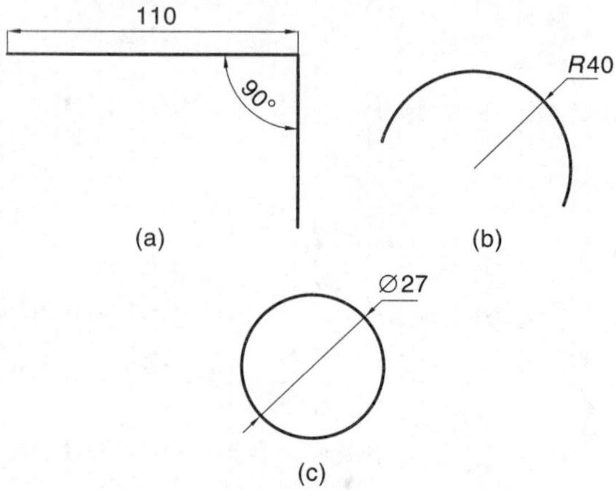

Fig. 22.61

The radius/diameter is placed inside or outside the arc/circle depending on the dimension line location point.

22.16 TEXT EDITING

Existing texts can be edited using DDEDIT, FIND, STYLE, SCALETEXT and JUSTIFYTEXT commands. All these commands are available in **Text toolbar**. Some of them are also available at **Menu bar** » ***Modify*** » ***Object*** » ***Text*** ».

The simple way to edit the texts is to double-click at them. If the texts were drawn by TEXT command, the bounding box opens and allows you to change the texts. **Text Formatting** dialog box (with In-Place Text Editor) will open if the texts were drawn by MTEXT command. The dialog box allows you to change the font size, font style, fontface, justification, etc.

22.17 ISOMETRIC DRAWING

Isometric drawing can be easily drawn by setting the grid snap to isometric snap (**Drafting Settings** dialog box » ***Snap and Grid*** tab » **Snap type and style** area » ***Grid snap*** » ***Isometric snap***). The crosshair is aligned to isometric axes. The direction of crosshair may change to Top (for top face), Left (for left face) or Right (for right face) by ISOPLANE command. If ***ORTHO*** button on **Status bar** is turned on, the cursor draws lines only along the isometric axes. Direct distance entry may be then used to draw the lines of desired length parallel to isometric axes. To draw ellipse for circular feature, you may use Isocircle option in ELLIPSE command.

The isometric lines can be drawn by inputting the coordinates in polar relative mode as explained in Concept Assignment 20.4. (The grid snap need not be set to isometric snap for this purpose).

22.18 WORKING IN LAYERS

You can draw objects with different properties in different layers. Layers are like transparent sheets placed one above others. You can make new layers or change the properties of existing layers by LAYER command. By default, you are in layer **0**. **Layer Properties Manager** dialog box can be opened by:

Layer toolbar » *Layer Properties Manager* *or*
Menu bar » *Format* » *Layer...* *or*
Command line » la (for **Layer**)

Right-click **List View** box (right side box) and click at ***New Layer*** to create new layer. You may set the desired properties for **Layer 1**, e.g., Colour—Red, Linetype—CENTRE, Lineweight—0.5 mm, etc. Right-click **Layer 1** and choose ***Set current*** to make it active. Click ***OK*** to close **Layer Properties Manager** dialog box. Now you are in **Layer 1**. The objects you draw are drawn with the properties defined in the layer.

If all the layers are ***ON***, the drawings drawn in different layers will be visible on the screen. Obviously, the drawings will be overlapped. You may edit any object on any layer. If a particular layer is turned ***OFF***, the drawing on that layer in neither visible nor printed. You must ***Set current*** and turned ***ON*** a particular layer so as to draw the objects with the properties defined in that layer. No drawing is drawn if current layer is turned ***OFF***.

Use of layer reduces confusion and helps to draw accurately. The readers are encouraged to use layers for complicated drawings.

22.19 CUSTOMIZING THE SETTINGS

By customizing the settings, you can let AutoCAD view and work as you wish. The OPTIONS command activates **Options** dialog box which enables user-specified settings.

Menu bar » *Tools* » *Options...* *or*
Command line » op (for **Options**)
Right-click in Command Window » *Options...* (Shortcut menu)
Right-click in Drawing Area (with no command active and no object selected) » *Options...* (Shortcut menu)

Practice Session 9: Customizing the AutoCAD Settings

Open **Options** dialog box.

Click at ***Display*** tab. In **Window Elements** area, click at ***Colors...*** button. **Color Options** dialog box appears. In **Window Element:** combo box, select ***Model tab background***. In **Color:** combo box, choose desired colour, say white. Click at ***Apply and Close*** button. The colour you have chosen is now displayed as the colour of the drawing area (i.e., model space). By default, the colour of the drawing area is black. The objects are drawn in white colours. If you choose white as a colour of drawing area, the objects are drawn in black colour. You may also change Crosshair size.

In ***User Preferences*** tab, you can customize right-click operation. In ***Drafting*** tab, you can change **AutoSnap marker color** and **AutoSnap Marker Size**.

In ***Selection*** tab, you may change **Pickbox Size**, **Grip Size** and other Grips settings (like, colour).

In ***Profile*** tab, you may save the settings under a profile name. Click ***Add to List...*** button to open **Add Profile** dialog box. Enter the profile name you wish to give (say, My profile) and then click at ***Apply & Close*** button. The profile name will appear in **Available profiles:** list. Select the name and click at ***Set Current*** button. The profile you created will become active.

Lastly, click ***OK*** in **Options** dialog box to accept the changes you made.

If you wish to revert back to default settings, click at ***Reset*** button on ***Profile*** tab.

22.20 CREATING YOUR TEMPLATE

A template is a file with some initial settings. When we start a new drawing, we usually adopt **acad.dwt** template. However, we may create our own template with required settings. Whenever a new drawing is started, this customized template may be used. This will save time in drawing. A template with the settings mentioned in Practice Session 10 below is recommended.

Practice Session 10: Creating the Customized Template

Open a new drawing file.

Activate UNITS command and set the values in **Drawing Units** dialog box as mentioned in Practice Session 3. Set LIMITS (0,0) to (297, 210). Choose **ZOOM » a**.

Open **Linetype Manager** dialog box and load CENTER, HIDDEN and PHANTOM linetypes.

Choose **Menu bar** » ***Format*** » ***Text Style...***. In **Font** area, select the font **Arial** using **Font Name:** combo box. Enter 4 in **Height:** box. Click at ***Apply*** button and ***Close*** the dialog box.

Save file. In **Save Drawing As** dialog box, choose AutoCAD Drawing Template (*.dwt) in **Files of type:** combo box. In **File name:** combo box, type My template. Click at ***Save*** button. **Template Description** dialog box will appear. In a box in **Description** area, type the description you want. In **Measurement** combo box, choose ***Metric***. Click ***OK***. Your new template is now saved in the **Template** folder.

Whenever you start a new drawing, choose **my template.dwt** (instead of **acad.dwt**) from **Select template** dialog box.

22.21 PRINTING AND PLOTTING

For printing or plotting your drawing, first switch to Paper Space (by clicking at ***Layout*** tab). Choose **Menu bar** » ***File*** » ***Plot...***. **Plot- Layout** dialog box will open. (If you are in Model Space and then use PLOT command, **Plot-Model** dialog box is opened. Both the boxes are same, but **Plot-Layout** dialog box automatically accepts settings of LIMITS and UNITS. Therefore, switching to Paper Space is recommended while printing the drawing.)

In **Printer/plotter area,** choose the printer or plotter in **Name:** combo box. (Printer's and or Plotter's names list will appear if the printers and plotters are installed on your system.) In **Plot area** area, choose ***Layout*** in **What to plot:** combo box. If you choose other options (**Display/Extend/Window**), you may ***Center the plot*** by check-marking the box in **Plot offset (origin set to printable area)** area. In **Plot scale** area, set the desired scale using **Scale:** combo box. For 1 drawing unit = 1 millimetre, choose scale 1:1. ***Fit to paper*** option is available, if you choose ***Display*** or ***Extend*** or ***Window*** option in **What to plot:** combo box. Other settings may be done as required.

You may preview the plot by clicking at ***Preview...*** button. (***Preview...*** button is inactive if printer/plotter is not chosen in **Name:** combo box.) Press ENTER (or ESC key) to return from preview to **Plot-Layout** dialog box. Click ***OK*** to print/plot.

CONCEPT ASSIGNMENTS

Assignment 22.1 Draw Fig. 4.47.

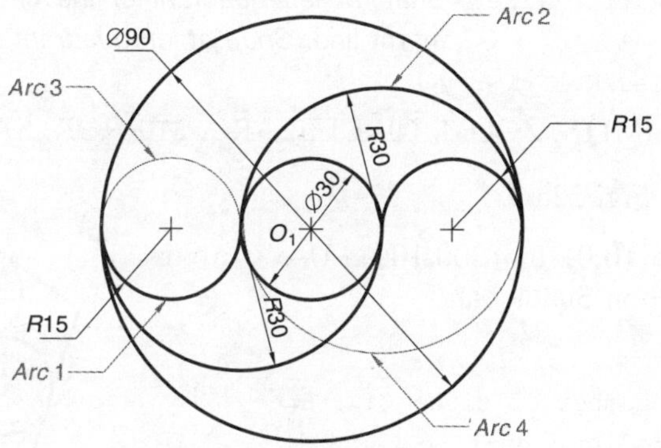

Fig. 4.47

Solution Set LIMITS to (0,0) to (200,100). Use ZOOM » a. Turn on ***SNAP*** on **Status bar**

Menu bar » *Draw* » *Circle* » *Centre, Diameter*

`Command: _circle Specify centre point for circle or [3P/2P/Ttr (tan tan radius)]:` *Click at O1 (anywhere at the middle of drawing area).*

`Specify radius of circle or [Diameter] <15.00>: _d Specify diameter of circle: 90↵`

Menu bar » *Draw* » *Arc* » *Start, Centre, Angle*

`Command: _arc Specify start point of arc or [Centre]:` *Snap at left quadrant of the circle.*

`Specify second point of arc or [Centre/End]: _c Specify centre point of arc: @15<0↵`

`Specify end point of arc or [Angle/chord Length]: _a Specify included angle: 180↵`

Menu bar » *Draw* »*Arc* » *Start, End, Radius*

`Command: _arc Specify start point of arc or [Centre]:` *Snap at right quadrant of the circle.*

Specify second point of arc or [Centre/End]: _e
Specify end point of arc: *Snap at right end of previous arc.*
Specify centre point of arc or [Angle/Direction/Radius]: _r Specify radius of arc: 30↵

Modify toolbar » *Mirror*

Command: _mirror
Select objects: 1 found *Select Arc1.*
Select objects: 1 found, 2 total *Select Arc2.*
Select objects: ↵
Specify first point of mirror line: *Snap at left quadrant of the circle.* Specify second point of mirror line: *Snap at right quadrant of the circle.*
Erase source objects? [Yes/No] <N>:↵
Command: MIRROR *Press UP key (or ENTER) to repeat MIRROR command.*
Select objects: 1 found *Select Arc3.*
Select objects: 1 found, 2 total *Select Arc4.*
Select objects: ↵
Specify first point of mirror line: *Snap at left quadrant of the circle.* Specify second point of mirror line: *Snap at left quadrant of the circle.*
Erase source objects? [Yes/No] <N>: y↵

Commands summary: LIMITS, ZOOM, CIRCLE, ARC, MIRROR, SAVE

Assignment 22.2 Draw Fig. 22.62.

Solution Set LIMITS to (0,0) to (200,100). Use **ZOOM » a**. Turn on ***SNAP*** on **Status bar**.

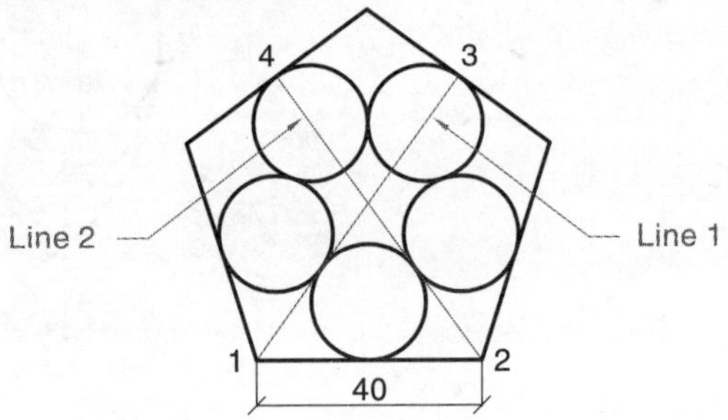

Fig. 22.62

Draw toolbar » *Polygon*

Command: _polygon Enter number of sides <4>: 5↵
Specify centre of polygon or [Edge]: e↵
Specify first endpoint of edge:
Click at any suitable point 1 Specify second endpoint of edge: @40,0↵

Draw toolbar » *Line*

Command: _line Specify first point: *Snap at corner 1.*
Specify next point or [Undo]: *Snap at midpoint 3 of opposite edge.*
Specify next point or [Undo]: ↵
Command: LINE
Specify first point: *Snap at corner 2.*
Specify next point or [Undo]: *Snap at midpoint 4 of opposite edge.*
Specify next point or [Undo]: ↵

Menu bar » *Draw* » *Circle* » *Tan, Tan, Tan*

Command: _circle Specify centre point for circle or [3P/2P/Ttr (tan tan radius)]:
_3p Specify first point on circle: _tan to *Click on edge1–2.*
Specify second point on circle: _tan to *Click at Line 1.*
Specify third point on circle: _tan to *Click at Line 2.*

Modify toolbar » *Array* » **Array** dialog box. *Choose* ***Polar Array****. Click* ***Select objects*** *button » Click at Circle 1 and press ENTER. Click* **Pick Centre Point** *button* [button] *» Snap at intersection of Line 1 and Line 2. In* **Method and values** *areas, type 5 in* **Total number of items:** *box and 360 in* **Angle to fill:** *box. Click* ***OK.***

```
Command: _erase
Select objects: 1 found                     Click at Line 1.
Select objects: 1 found, 2 total            Click at Line 2.
Select objects: ↵
```

Commands summary: LIMITS, ZOOM, POLYGON, LINE, CIRCLE, ARRAY, ERASE, SAVE

Assignment 22.3 Plot the graph for equation $PV^n = C$. The values of P vary from 10 N/m^2 to 60 N/m^2. The unit of V is m^3. Take n =1.4 and C = 100. Show P on X-axis and V on Y-axis.

Solution Take P = 10 N/m^2, 20 N/m^2, 30 N/m^2, …, 60 N/m^2 and find out the corresponding values of V using the given equation, i.e., $PV^{(1.4)} = 100$.

P (N/m^2)	10	20	30	40	50	60
V (m^3)	5.18	3.16	2.36	1.92	1.64	1.44

Choose scale: X-axis = 10 mm = 1 m^3; Y-axis = 10 mm = 10 N/m^2.

Set LIMITS (0,0) to (297,210). Use **ZOOM » a**↵.

UCS toolbar » [icon] *Origin*

```
Command: _ucs
Current ucs name: *WORLD*
Specify origin of UCS or [Face/NAmed/OBject/Previous/View/World/X/Y/Z/ZAxis]  <World>: _o
Specify new origin point <0,0,0>: 50,50↵ Type 50,50 and press ENTER to shift origin to (50,50).
```

Draw toolbar » *Line*

```
Command: _line Specify first point:          Snap at (0,70).
Specify next point or [Undo]:                Snap at (0,0).
Specify next point or [Undo]:                Snap at (60,0).
Specify next point or [Close/Undo]: ↵
```

Draw toolbar » *Pline*

```
Command: _pline
Specify start point: 51.8,10↵       Point A
Current line-width is 0.00
Specify next point or [Arc/Halfwidth/Length/Undo/Width]: 31.6,20↵          Point B
Specify next point or [Arc/Close/Halfwidth/Length/Undo/Width]: 23.6,30↵    Point C
Specify next point or [Arc/Close/Halfwidth/Length/Undo/Width]: 19.2,40↵    Point D
Specify next point or [Arc/Close/Halfwidth/Length/Undo/Width]: 16.4,50↵    Point E
Specify next point or [Arc/Close/Halfwidth/Length/Undo/Width]: 14.4,60↵    Point F
Specify next point or [Arc/Close/Halfwidth/Length/Undo/Width]: ↵
```

Menu bar » *Draw* » *Point* » *Divide*

```
Command: _divide
```

Select object to divide: *Select vertical line.*

Enter the number of segments or [Block]: 7↵ *Type 7 for 7 equal parts and press ENTER. Set PDMODE at suitable value (say, 3) for visibility of the division points 1, 2, 3, ..., 6.*

Draw toolbar » *Line*

Command: _line Specify first point: <Osnap on> *Turn on **SNAP** button on* **Status bar** *and snap to node 1 (point 1).*

Specify next point or [Undo]: *Snap at point A.*

Specify next point or [Undo]: ↵

... Repeat LINE command and draw lines 2–B, 3–C, 4–D, 5–E and 6–F...

Command: *Press ENTER to repeat line command.*

LINE Specify first point: *Snap at point A.*

Specify next point or [Undo]: *Snap to perpendicular to horizontal line (point 7).*

Specify next point or [Undo]:

...Repeat LINE command and draw lines B–8, C–9, D–10, E–11 and F–12.

The output is shown in Fig. 22.63(a).

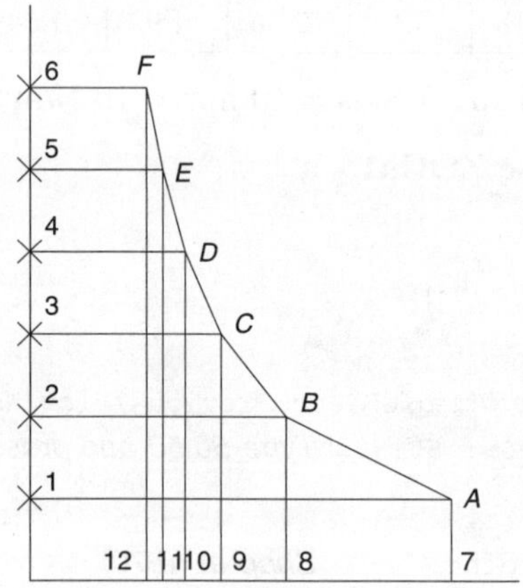

Fig. 22.63(a)

UCS toolbar » *Origin*

Command: _ucs

Current ucs name: *NO NAME*

Specify origin of UCS or [Face/NAmed/OBject/Previous/View/World/X/Y/Z/ZAxis] <World>: _o

Specify new origin point <0,0,0>: -50,-50↵ *Type -50,-50 and press ENTER to shift origin to original place.*

Menu bar » *Modify* » *Object* » *Polyline*

Command: _pedit Select polyline or [Multiple]: *Select the polyline.*

Enter an option [Close/Join/Width/Edit vertex/Fit/Spline/Decurve/Ltype gen/Undo]: f↵

Enter an option [Close/Join/Width/Edit vertex/Fit/Spline/Decurve/Ltype gen/Undo]: ↵

Open drawing file: Fig. 22.31(b) for arrowhead.

Standard toolbar » *Copy* (*or* Command line » Copyclip)

```
Command: _copyclip
Select objects: all↵
6 found
Select objects: ↵
```

Minimise or close drawing file: Fig. 22.31(b).

In cuurent drawing file, paste the arrow.

Standard toolbar » *Paste* (*or* Command line » Pasteclip)

```
Command: _pasteclip Specify insertion point:
```
Click anywhere in model space. The arrow will be pasted at that point.

Modify toolbar » *Scale*

```
Command: _scale
Select objects: Specify opposite corner: 6 found
```
Select the arrow by window.

```
Select objects: ↵
Specify base point:
```
Click at the arrow tip.

```
Specify scale factor or [Copy/Reference] <1.00>: .25↵
```
Type .25 for scale 1:4 and press ENTER.

Modify toolbar » *Copy*

```
Command: _copy
Select objects: Specify opposite corner: 6 found
```
Select the arrow by window.

```
Select objects: ↵
Specify base point or [Displacement] <Displacement>: Specify second point or <use first point as displacement>:
```
Click at the arrow tail for base point. Click at free end of the horizontal line for second point.

```
Specify second point or [Exit/Undo] <Exit>:↵
```

Modify toolbar » *Rotate*

```
Command: _rotate
Current positive angle in UCS:  ANGDIR=counterclockwise  ANGBASE=0
Select objects: Specify opposite corner: 6 found
```
Select the original arrow by window.

```
Select objects: ↵
Specify base point:
```
Click at the arrow tail.

```
Specify rotation angle or
[Copy/Reference] <0>: 90↵
```
Type 90 and press ENTER to rotate the arrow through 90°.

Modify toolbar » *Move*

```
Command: _move
Select objects: Specify opposite corner: 6 found
```
Select the original arrow by window.

```
Select objects: ↵
```

`Specify base point or [Displacement] <Displacement>: Specify second point or <use first point as displacement>:` *Click at the arrow tail for base point. Click at free end of the horizontal line for second point.*

Using **Properties toolbar**, change lineweight of pline to 0.50mm. Turn on ***LWT*** button on **Status bar**. Change PDMODE to 1 to vanish the point marks. Using MTEXT command, type the values along *X*-axis and *Y*-axis and the other texts. Fontface, size, etc., may be changed using **Text Formatting** dialog box. The values along *X*-axis may be rotated through 90° for vertical appearance.

The final output is shown in Fig. 22.63(b).

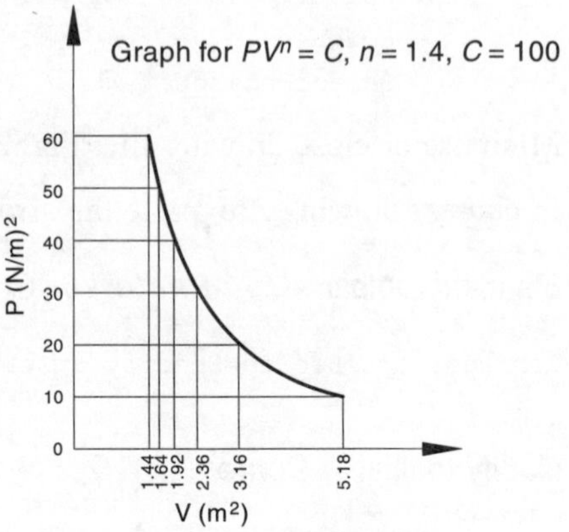

Fig. 22.63(b)

Commands summary: LIMITS, ZOOM, UCS, LINE, PLINE, DIVIDE, PEDIT, COPYCLIP, PASTECLIP, SCALE, COPY, ROTATE, MOVE, PDMODE, MTEXT, SAVE

Assignment 22.4 Draw the isometric view as shown in Fig. 22.64(c).

Solution Set LIMITS (0,0) to (297,210). Use **ZOOM » a**. Assume that origin '*O*' is at (150,25).

Draw toolbar » *Line*

`Command: _line Specify first point: 150,25 ↵` *Type 150,25 and press ENTER for origin.*
`Specify next point or [Undo]: @80<30↵`
`Specify next point or [Undo]: @60<90↵`
`Specify next point or [Close/Undo]: @80<210↵`
`Specify next point or [Close/Undo]: 150.00,50.00↵` *Press UP key four times for the recent input and press ENTER.*
`Specify next point or [Close/Undo]: @50<150↵`
`Specify next point or [Close/Undo]: @60<90↵`
`Specify next point or [Close/Undo]: @50<-30↵`
`Specify next point or [Close/Undo]: ↵`
`Command: ↵`
`LINE Specify first point: <Osnap on>` *Turn on **OSNAP** button on **Status bar**. Click at point 1.*
`Specify next point or [Undo]: @50<150↵`
`Specify next point or [Undo]:` *Click at point 2.*
Specify next point or [Close/Undo]: ↵
`Command: ↵`
`LINE Specify first point:` *Click at point 2.*
`Specify next point or [Undo]:` *Click at point 1.*
`Specify next point or [Undo]:` *Click at point O.*
`Specify next point or [Close/Undo]: ↵`

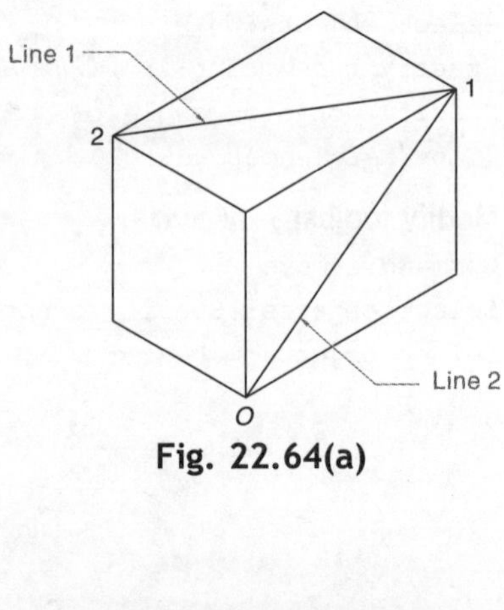

The output is shown in Fig. 22.64(a).

Fig. 22.64(a)

Right-click ***SNAP*** button on **Status bar** and open **Drafting Settings** dialog box. In **Snap type** area, choose ***Isometric snap***. Click ***OK*** and observe the change in crosshair.

Command line » Isoplane

Command: isoplane↵ *Type isoplane and press ENTER. Alternatively, you may press F5 key to change isoplane to Left/Top/Right*

Current isoplane: Left

Enter isometric plane setting [Left/Top/Right] <Top>:↵

Current isoplane: Top *Observe the change in crosshair.*

Draw toolbar » *Ellipse*

Command: _ellipse

Specify axis endpoint of ellipse or [Arc/Centre/Isocircle]: i↵

Specify centre of isocircle: *Snap at midpoint of line 1.*

Specify radius of isocircle or [Diameter]: 20↵

Modify toolbar » *Copy*

Command: _copy

Select objects: 1 found *Select the ellipse*

Select objects: ↵

Specify base point or [Displacement] <Displacement>: Specify second point or *Snap at midpoint of line 1 for base point.*

<use first point as displacement>: @60<90↵

Specify second point or [Exit/Undo] <Exit>:↵

Draw toolbar » *Line*

Command: _line Specify first point: *Snap at left quadrant of top ellipse.*

Specify next point or [Undo]: *Snap at left quadrant of bottom ellipse.*

Specify next point or [Undo]: ↵

Command: ↵

LINE Specify first point: *Snap at right quadrant of top ellipse.*

Specify next point or [Undo]: *Snap at right quadrant of bottom ellipse.*

Specify next point or [Undo]: ↵

Command: <Isoplane Right> *Press F5 to change isoplane to Right. Obseve the change in crosshair.*

Draw toolbar » *Ellipse*

Command: _ellipse

Specify axis endpoint of ellipse or [Arc/Centre/Isocircle]: i↵

Specify centre of isocircle: *Snap at midpoint of line 2.*

Specify radius of isocircle or [Diameter]: 18↵

The output is shown in Fig. 22.64(b).

Modify toolbar » *Trim*

Command: _trim

Current settings: Projection=UCS, Edge=None

Select cutting edges ...

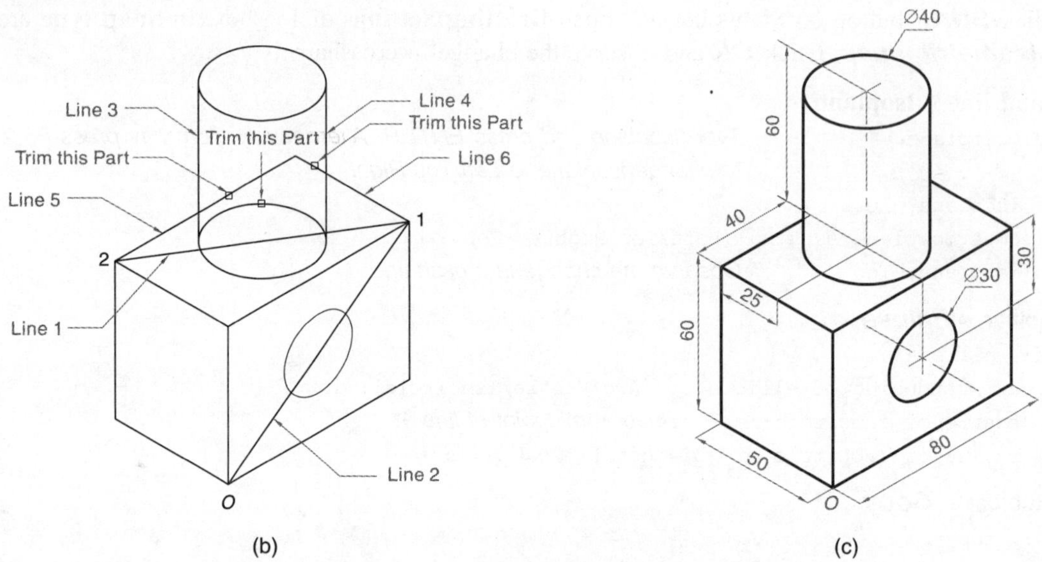

Fig. 22.64

```
Select objects or <select all>: 1 found        Select line 3.
Select objects: 1 found, 2 total               Select line 4.
Select objects: ↵
Select object to trim or shift-select to extend or
[Fence/Crossing/Project/Edge/eRase/Undo]:                Select right end of line 5.
Select object to trim or shift-select to extend or
[Fence/Crossing/Project/Edge/eRase/Undo]:                Select left end of line 6.
Select object to trim or shift-select to extend or
[Fence/Crossing/Project/Edge/eRase/Undo]:          Select upper part of bottom ellipse.
Select object to trim or shift-select to extend or
[Fence/Crossing/Project/Edge/eRase/Undo]: ↵
```

Select line 1 and line 2 and press DELETE key. Using **Properties toolbar**, change lineweight to 0.5 mm. Turn on ***LWT*** button on **Status bar**.

The output is shown in Fig. 22.64(c).

Commands summary: LIMITS, ZOOM, LINE, ISOPLANE, ELLIPSE, COPY, TRIM, ERASE, SAVE

Assignment 22.5 Draw the object shown in Fig. 4RQ.5.

Solution Set LIMITS to (0,0) to (210,297). Use **ZOOM » a** and execute the commands in sequence as shown in Fig. 22.65.

Commands summary: LIMITS, ZOOM, CIRCLE, XLINE, LINE, OFFSET, ERASE, TRIM, MIRROR, PROPERTIES, DIMALIGNED, DIMRADIUS, DIMDIAMETER, DIMANGULAR, SAVE.

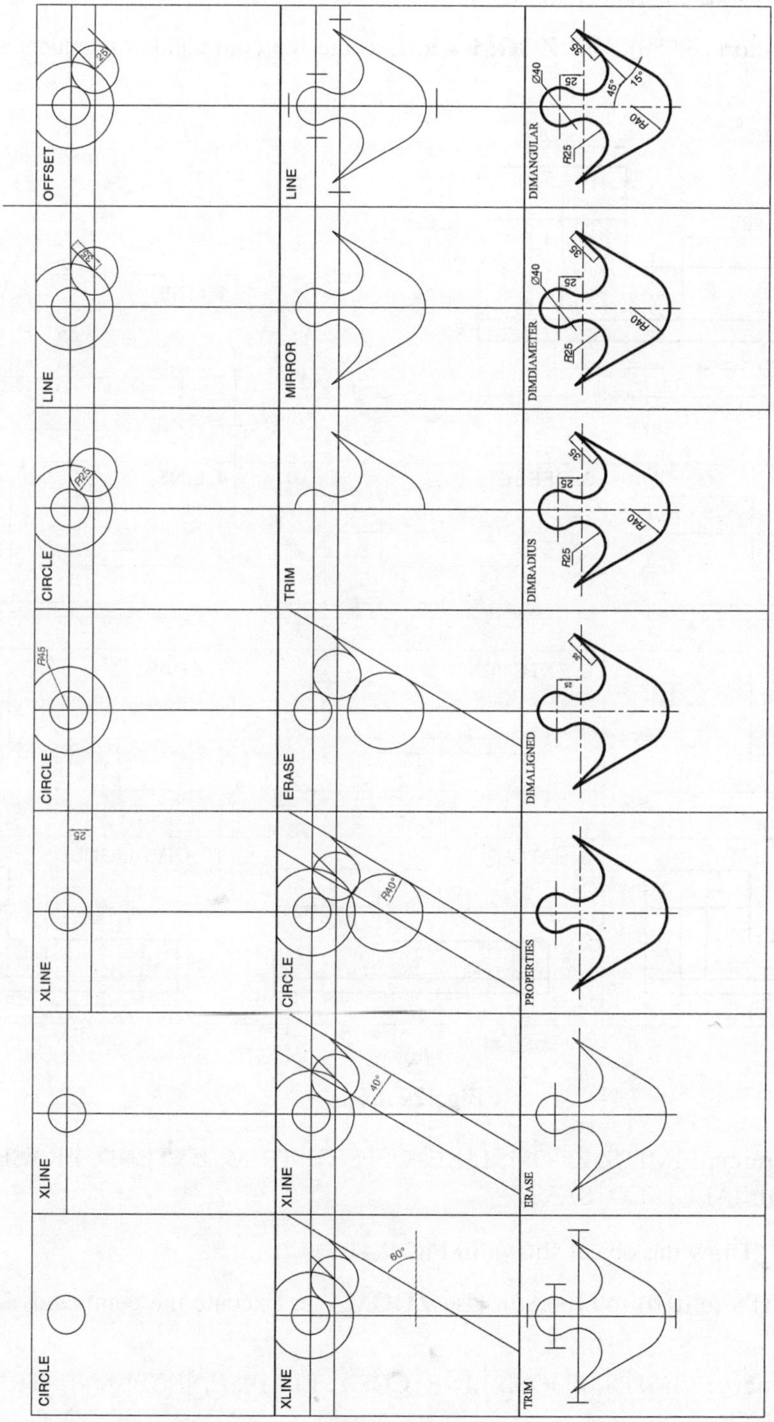
CIRCLE
XLINE
XLINE
CIRCLE
CIRCLE
LINE
OFFSET
XLINE
XLINE
CIRCLE
ERASE
TRIM
MIRROR
LINE
TRIM
ERASE
PROPERTIES
DIMALIGNED
DIMRADIUS
DIMDIAMETER
DIMANGULAR

Fig. 22.65

Assignment 22.6 Draw the object shown in Fig. 22.66(a).

Set LIMITS to (0,0) to (100,50). Use **ZOOM » a**. Execute the commands in sequence as shown in Fig. 22.66(b).

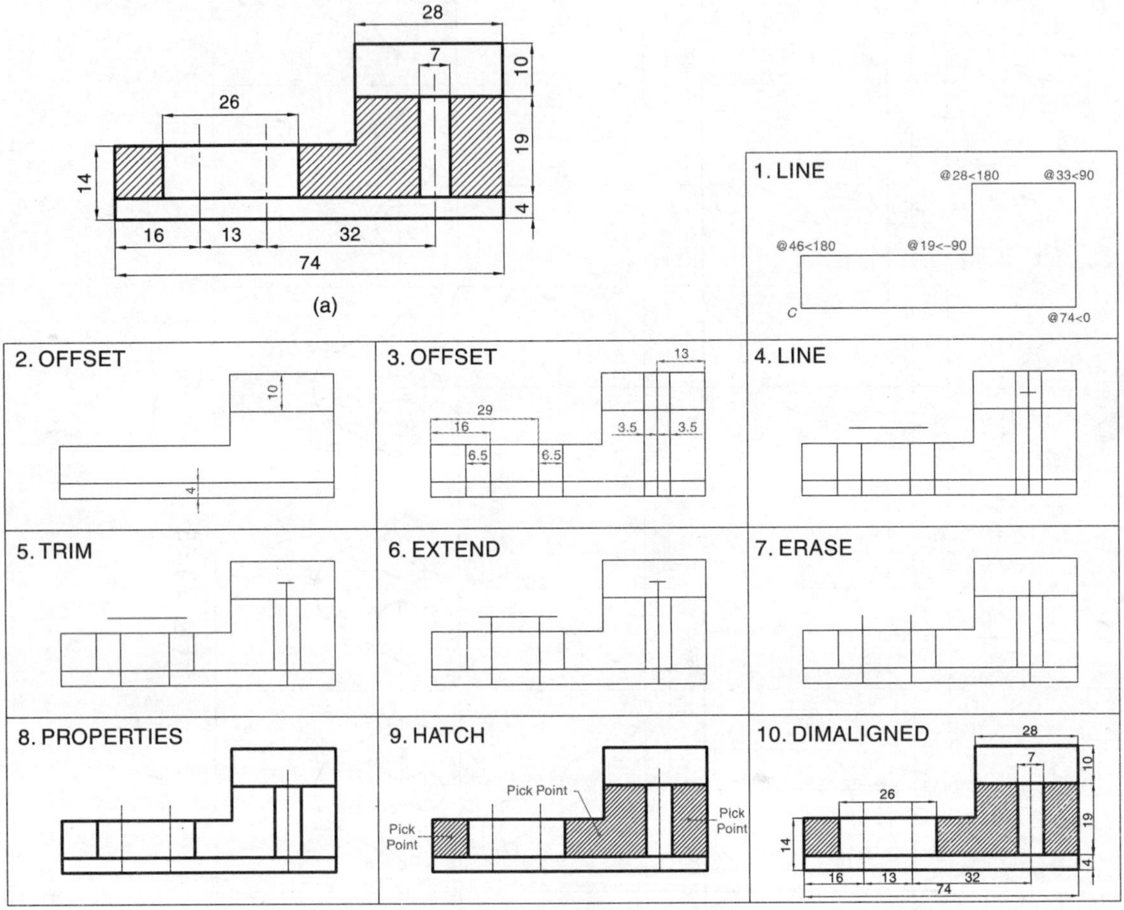

(b)

Fig. 22.66

Commands summary: LIMITS, ZOOM, LINE, OFFSET, TRIM, EXTEND, ERASE, PROPERTIES, HATCH, DIMALIGNED, SAVE.

Assignment 22.7 Draw the object shown in Fig. 9.41(a).

Solution Set LIMITS to (0,0) to (160,80). Use **ZOOM » a**. Execute the commands in sequence as shown in Fig. 22.67.

Commands summary: LIMITS, ZOOM, LINE, COPY, ELLIPSE, ISOPLANE, TRIM, ERASE, PROPERTIES, SAVE.

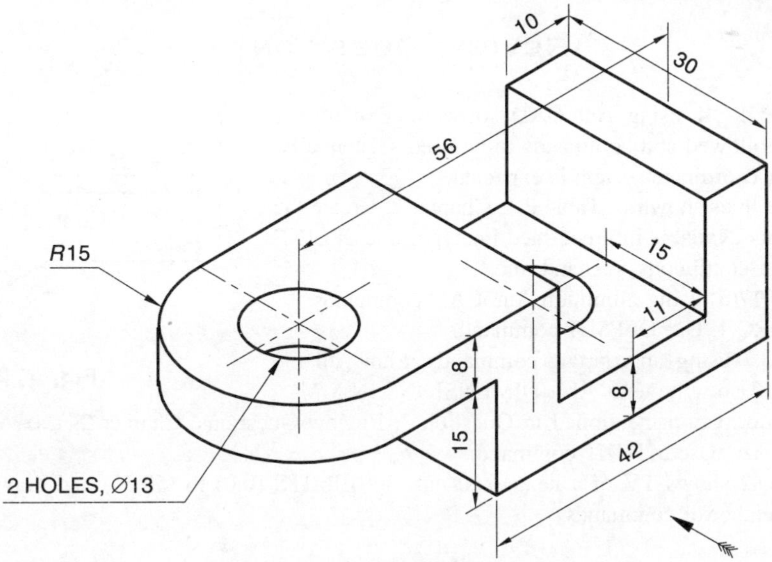

Fig. 9.41

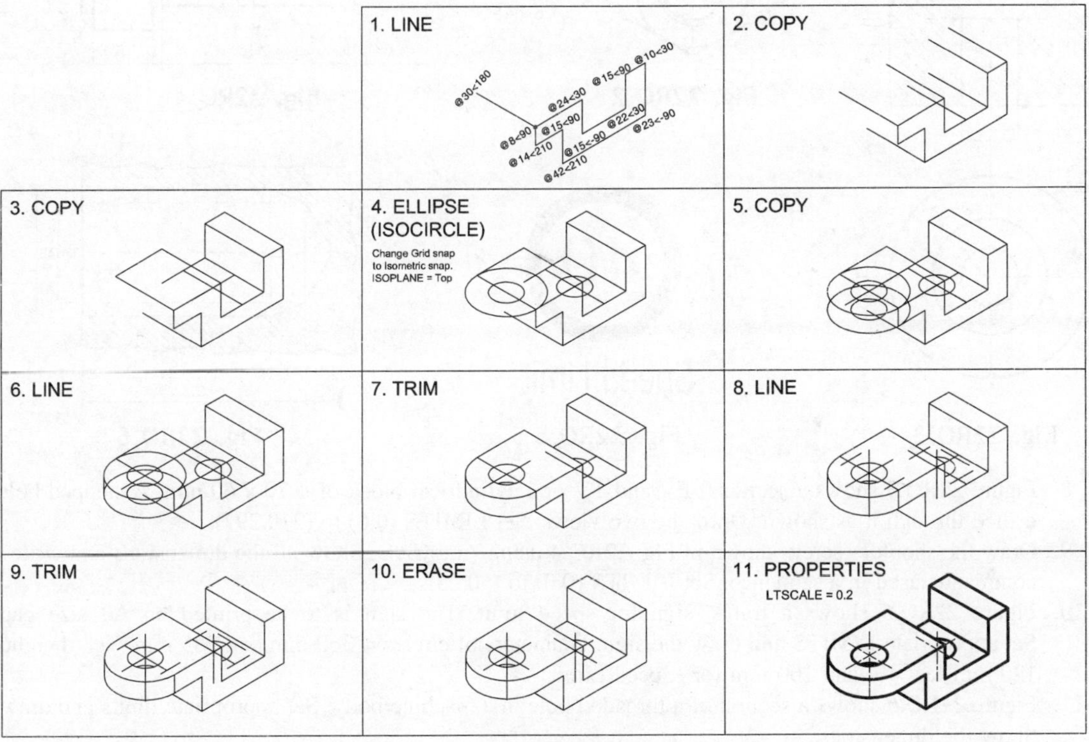

Fig. 22.67

Review Questions

1. Draw Fig. 22RQ.1 using AutoCAD software. Explain the steps to be followed and commands to be used sequentially. Use of polar coordinate system is expected.
2. Draw all the lines shown in Table 2.1, Chapter 2. Create the line if it is not available in predefined linetype. Use SPLINE command for continuous freehand line.
3. Draw Fig. 3.17(d) using minimum AutoCAD commands.
4. Draw Fig. 4RQ.1. Use OFFSET command.
5. Draw Fig. 3.7 using appropriate commands. Show all the dimensions. Also write text 'ALL DIMENSIONS IN MM'.

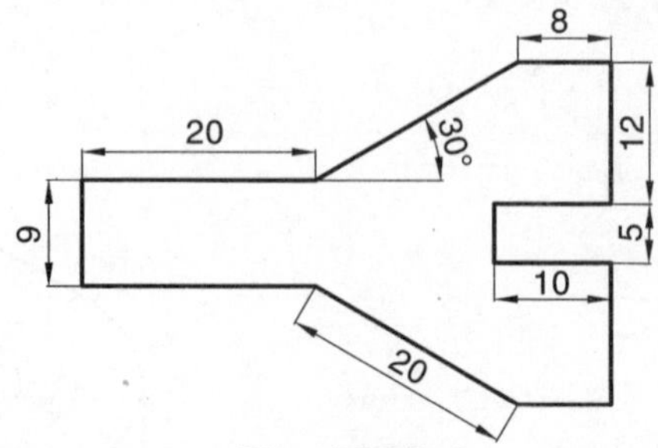

Fig. 22RQ.1

6. Write the information mentioned in Question 3, Review Questions, Chapter 2. Use Arial Narrow font and 7 point size. Use MTEXT command.
7. Figure 22RQ.2 shows TV of a hexagonal nut. Set LIMITS (0,0) to (50,50) and draw the TV using a minimum number of commands.

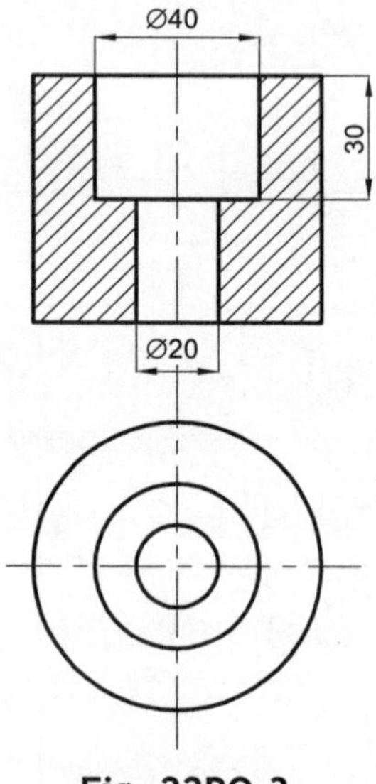

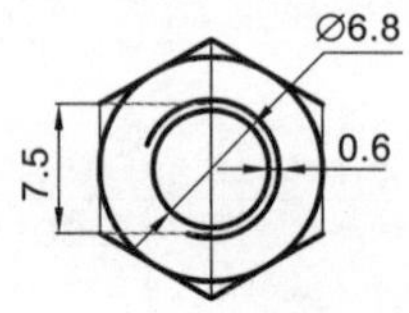

Fig. 22RQ.2

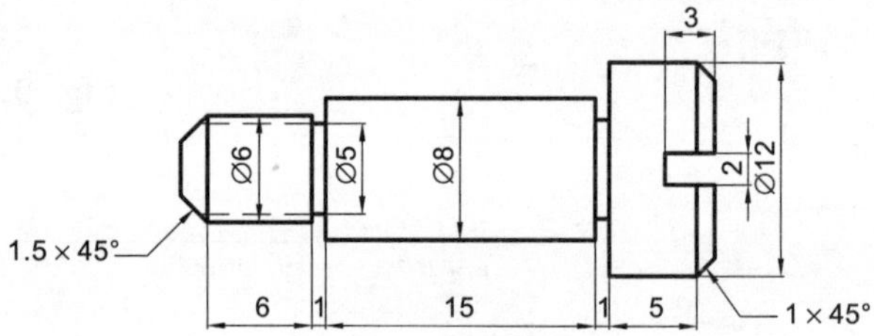

Fig. 22RQ.4

Fig. 22RQ.3

Fig. 22RQ.5

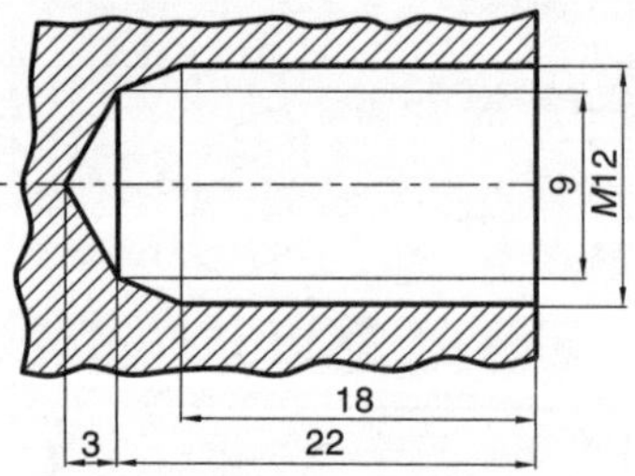

Fig. 22RQ.6

8. Figure 22RQ.3 shows a sectional FV and TV of a cylindrical block of ϕ 70 × 60 mm. A stepped hole is drilled through it as shown. Draw the two views. Set LIMITS (0,0) to (210,297).
9. Draw the shoulder screw shown in Fig. 22RQ.4 using AutoCAD. Show all the dimensions and write the commands used in a sequence. Set LIMITS (0,0) to (50,25).
10. Figure 22RQ.5 shows a traffic sign for speed limit. The sign is to be printed on A2 size paper. Set appropriate LIMITS and draw the sign. Diameters of circles = 360 mm and 285 mm. Text heights = 120 mm for '40' and 100 mm for 'Speed Limit'.
11. Figure 22RQ.6 shows a section of a threaded hole in a machine body. Set appropriate limits and draw it. Show the dimensions.
12. Draw isometric view shown in Fig. 9RQ.9 using AutoCAD. Set appropriate LIMITS. Write all the commands in sequence.

OBJECTIVE QUESTION BANK

There are ten tests of 20 questions each. In each test, the first ten questions are TRUE/FALSE type. For next ten questions, choose the most correct alternative from the four alternatives available. Tally your answers with the ANSWER KEYS given at the end of the question bank.

TEST I: INTRODUCTION TO ENGINEERING DRAWING/LINES AND LETTERING

1. The length of A2 size drawing sheet is equal to the width of A1 size drawing sheet.
2. For technical drawing, harder grades of pencils are preferred.
3. A D2 size drawing board has dimensions of 920 mm × 650 mm.
4. A title block is placed at bottom right corner of the drawing frame.
5. Dashed lines are used to show outlines of the adjacent part.
6. A phantom line is used to indicate alternate positions of the part.
7. The width of all the letters in one line is kept same.
8. Thick lines in line group 0.25 are drawn 0.75 mm thick.
9. To draw section lines, continuous thin lines are used.
10. Gothic letters have a uniform line width for all the parts of a letter.
11. A2 size sheet has the dimensions
    (a) 297 mm × 210 mm (b) 420 mm × 297 mm (c) 594 mm × 420 mm (d) 841 mm × 594 mm
12. To draw a circle of diameter 20 mm, the most preferred instrument is
    (a) large compass (b) bow pencil compass (c) circle template (d) any of the above
13. A French curve is used to draw
    (a) polygons (b) circles (c) ellipses (d) smooth freeform curves
14. IS 10714: 2001 refers to
    (a) scales (b) lines (c) lettering (d) projection methods
15. Which of the following ISs provides the guidelines for dimensioning on technical drawings?
    (a) IS 10714: 1983 (b) IS 11669: 1986 (c) IS 10711: 2001 (d) IS 1444: 1989
16. Use of lettering template is recommended for
    (a) freehand lettering (b) single stroke lettering (c) double stroke lettering (d) cursive lettering
17. Centreline is used to indicate
    (a) axis of cylinder (b) centreline of the hole (c) axis of symmetry (d) all of the above
18. A short break line is used to indicate a
    (a) broken part (b) part to be broken (c) long part of uniform cross section
    (d) short part of non-uniform cross section
19. The preferred line width for letter group of 7 mm is
    (a) 1 mm (b) 0.7 mm (c) 0.5 mm (d) 0.25 mm
20. The type of line used to indicate a cutting plane is
    (a) dashed (b) long dashed dotted (c) long dashed double dotted (d) continuous freehand

TEST II: DIMENSIONING/GEOMETRICAL CONSTRUCTIONS

1. In the aligned system of dimensioning, the dimensions are placed near the middle of a dimension line by interrupting it.

2. Dimension lines should not cross each other and other lines of the object.
3. The note '5 × ϕ10' means five holes of diameter 10 units each.
4. To indicate the metric threads, the nominal diameter should be preceded by '*M*'.
5. Knowledge of geometrical constructions is essential in designing the specific profiles on the objects.
6. The internal angle of pentagon is 120°.
7. Any given angle can be divided into 6 equal parts.
8. The perpendicular bisector of any chord of a circle passes through the centre of the circle.
9. A regular pentagon cannot be inscribed exactly in a given circle.
10. The shortest distance between the centres of two circles tangent to each other is always equal to the sum of their radii.
11. If all the horizontal or vertical dimensions of the object start from a common extension line situated at one end, the way of dimensioning is called
    (a) chain dimensioning (b) parallel dimensioning (c) combined dimensioning (d) none of the above
12. The line used to write a note pertaining to a specific feature of an object is
    (a) extension line (b) dimension line (c) leader line (d) oblique stroke
13. The symbol '*S*ϕ' indicates
    (a) sectional diameter (b) spherical diameter (c) squared diameter (d) straight diameter
14. The note '2 × 45°' means
    (a) two angles of 45° each (b) two chamfers of 45^0 each
    (c) a chamfer of width 2 units and 45° angle (d) none of the above
15. Which of the following notes indicates the hole of 40 unit diameter and 60 unit depth?
    (a) ϕ 40 × 60 (b) DEEP 60, ϕ 40 (c) ϕ 40,DEEP 60 (d) 60 × ϕ 40
16. The abbreviation CSK stands for
    (a) conical shaft (b) cylindrical shaft (c) counterbore (d) countersunk
17. A keyway is specified by providing the dimensions of
    (a) width only (b) depth only (c) either width or depth (d) width and depth both
18. The abbreviation 'SF' stands for
    (a) spot face (b) spherical face (c) spot finish (d) spherical finish
19. In a big circle, three small circles of equal size are drawn. Each of the small circles is tangent to the big circle and the other two circles. Which of the following sentences is correct?
    (a) The centres of the small circles lie along a diagonal of big circle.
    (b) The centres of the small circles lie at the corner of an equilateral triangle.
    (c) The distance between the centre of any two small circles is equal to the radius of the big circle.
    (d) One of the small circles will be concentric with the big circle.
20. If two circles are tangent to each other and to a line, then there exists
    (a) three different points of the tangency (b) two different points of the tangency
    (c) one common point of the tangency (d) either (a) or (c) above depending on the condition of tangency

TEST III: SCALES

1. To draw the drawing of a multistoried building, the RF of 1:200 would be appropriate.
2. LOS is equal to the product of RF and LC.
3. A plain scale gives distances in a unit and its immediate two sub-units.
4. A diagonal scale is based on the similarity of triangles.
5. For backward vernier scale, LC = MSD – VSD.
6. All the divisions on the base of a scale of chords (i.e., linear degree scale) are equal.
7. Scale of chords measures the angles based on the length of chords of a circle.
8. Reducing scales are expressed in the format *Y*: 1, *Y* being greater than 1.
9. Measurement of the distances is simpler in a diagonal scale than in a vernier sale.

10. In a diagonal scale, a horizontal subdivision represents *y* cm. If there are *n* vertical divisions, then LC of the scale is equal to *y*/*n* cm.
11. In a scale, 1 cm represents 1 m. Its RF is
    (a) 1/1000 (b) 1/100 (c) 1/10 (d) 1/10000
12. The size of the drawing drawn to scale 2:1 will be ________ the actual size of the object.
    (a) same as (b) twice of (c) half of (d) can't tell
13. To draw a small gear in wrist watch, the RF would be
    (a) 1:20 (b) 20:1 (c) 1:1 (d) none of the above
14. The information needed to construct any scale (except the scale of chords) is
    (a) RF of the scale (b) unit of measurement
    (c) maximum distance to be represented (d) all of the above
15. If an area of Y^2 is represented by an area of X^2 on a drawing, then the RF is equal to
    (a) X/Y (b) X^2/Y^2 (c) $\sqrt{X}/\sqrt{Y}$ (d) $\sqrt{X^2}/\sqrt{Y^2}$
16. The scale used for angular measurement is
    (a) plain scale (b) vernier scale (c) diagonal scale (d) none of the above
17. Which one of the following is not a reduction scale?
    (a) 1:200 (b) 5: 6 (c) 1:1 (d) 3/250
18. Which of the following sentences is CORRECT about comparative scales?
    (a) RF of both the scales is same (b) LOS for both the scales is same
    (c) LC of both the scales is same (d) All of the above
19. Which of the following sentences is WRONG about the forward vernier scale?
    (a) LC = MSD – VSD
    (b) MSDs and VSDs are numbered in the same direction.
    (c) The 0th mark is on the left end of the main scale.
    (d) Length of vernier > length of a main division
20. A diagonal scale of RF 10 is constructed to measure maximum distance of 10 mm. The LC of this scale would be
    (a) 0.01 mm (b) 0.1 mm (c) 1 mm (d) 10 mm

TEST IV: ENGINEERING CURVES/LOCI OF POINTS

1. The locus traced by a point in such a way that the sum of its distances from two fixed points is always constant is called an ellipse.
2. The eccentricity of parabola is less than the eccentricity of a hyperbola.
3. In case of an ellipse, the distance of an end of the major axis from any focus is equal to half of the minor axis.
4. A helix is a 2D locus.
5. A line joining the midpoint of any two parallel chords of a parabola is parallel to its axis.
6. An oblique hyperbola will have the angle between its asymptotes less than 90°.
7. Two normals can be drawn at any point on an Archimedean spiral.
8. The locus of a point equidistant from a fixed line is a line perpendicular to the fixed line.
9. The study of loci of points is needed in designing electronic circuits.
10. The engine of your motorbike is an example of slider crank mechanism.
11. The of ratio of the distance of a point on a conic from the focus to the distance of the point from the directrix is known as
    (a) asymptote (b) minor axis (c) pitch (d) eccentricity
12. Boyle's law, *PV* = constant generates a curve which is a
    (a) hyperbola (b) rectangular hyperbola (c) parabola (d) rectangular parabola

13. The line joining any point on an Archimedean spiral with the pole is called the
    (a) shortest radius (b) radius vector (c) vectorial angle (d) convolution
14. If the radius of a generating circle which is moving inside the directing circle is ½ of the radius of the directing circle, the curve generated by a point on the circumference of the generating circle is a
    (a) circle (b) ellipse (c) straight line (d) spiral
15. If the generating point is on the generating circle and the generating circle is outside the directing circle, the curve obtained is
    (a) hypocycloid (b) superior trochoid (c) epicycloid (d) inferior hypotrochoid
16. A gear tooth profile is in the form of
    (a) parabola (b) involute (c) spiral (d) helix
17. The sum of distances of any point on the ellipse from the foci is equal to
    (a) minor axis (b) major axis (c) ½ major axis (d) ½ minor axis
18. The curve traced out by an end of a string unwound from a circle or polygon, keeping it always tight, is a
    (a) cycloid (b) ellipse (c) helix (d) none of the above
19. The locus traced by a point moving along a pendulum, from one end to another, when the pendulum oscillates about an end, is a
    (a) spiral (b) involute (c) cycloid (d) helix
20. A four-bar mechanism consists of
    (a) 4 links (b) 2 cranks (c) 1 connecting rod (d) all of the above

TEST V: THEORY OF PROJECTION/ORTHOGRAPHIC PROJECTIONS

1. The plane on which an object's view is obtained is called the POP.
2. A multiview orthographic projection is a type of convergent projection.
3. In cabinet projection, the receding lines are drawn to half of their actual lengths.
4. A horizontal reference line, *XY*, is an intersection of an object's surface with the HP.
5. To draw the TV of an object, the HP is always rotated in a clockwise direction.
6. In the first-angle method of projection, the FV is always drawn below *XY*.
7. If a face is parallel to the direction of viewing, it is seen as edge view.
8. Sectional views are drawn to reveal internal details of an object.
9. A horizontal section plane will create a sectional FV.
10. A Half-sectional view is obtained by cutting a quarter part by two perpendicular cutting planes.
11. An axonometric projection in which three perpendicular edges of the object make different angles with the POP is called
    (a) isometric projection (b) diametric projection (c) trimetric projection (d) none of the above
12. Which one of the following is not a principal plane of projection?
    (a) HP (b) VP (c) PP (d) Auxiliary plane
13. In orthographic projections, the FV is projected on
    (a) HP (b) VP (c) *XY* (d) GL
14. In the first-angle projection method, the view seen from the left is placed on
    (a) Left of FV (b) right of FV (c) above FV (d) below FV
15. In the first-angle projection method, the direction of arrows on the cutting plane line is
    (a) away from the POP (b) towards the POP
    (c) away from the base of the solid (d) towards the base of the solid
16. Which of the following is a symbol of the first-angle method of projection?

(a) 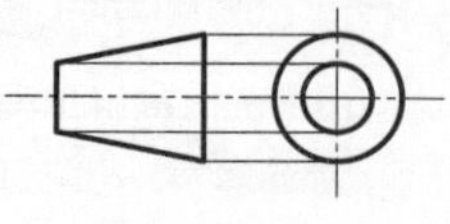 (b) 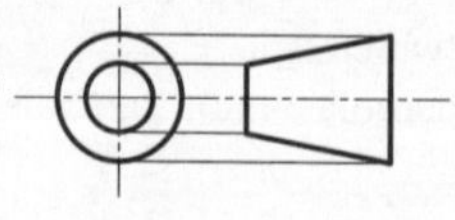 (c) 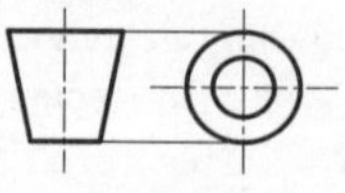 (d) 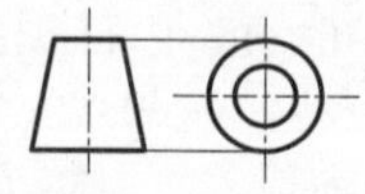

17. The location of LHSV in the third-angle method of projection is on the
    (a) left-hand side of FV (b) left-hand side of TV
    (c) right-hand side of FV (d) right-hand side of TV
18. The TV of a rectangular shaped room will show
    (a) length and height (b) length and width (c) width and height (d) none of the above
19. Which of the following relationships is true for the first-angle method of projection?
    (a) Object–POP- observer (b) Object–observer–POP
    (c) POP–observer–object (d) Observer–object–POP
20. If an object is cut by an AVP, then it will show
    (a) sectional FV (b) sectional TV (c) sectional FV and SV (d) sectional SV

TEST VI: PROJECTIONS OF POINTS/ PROJECTIONS OF LINES/ AUXILIARY PLANE PROJECTION METHOD

1. If a point is in the VP, its FV is seen on *XY*.
2. If a point is on the HP, its SV will be on *XY*.
3. If FV of a line is parallel to *XY*, its TV gives TL.
4. PL of a line would be constant if angle ϕ is constant.
5. HT of a line is seen on TV or extension of TV.
6. If TV and FV both are parallel to $X1Y1$, then the line is parallel to the PP.
7. If TV of a line is a point view, then the line is perpendicular to the VP.
8. The plane perpendicular to the VP and inclined to the HP is called AVP.
9. The projection on an AVP is called the auxiliary FV.
10. The distances of all the TVs of a point from the respective reference lines are not equal.
11. If SV of a point is seen on $X1Y1$, the point lies on
    (a) the HP (b) the VP (c) the PP (d) any one of the above
12. If a line is inclined to the HP and parallel to the VP, it will have
    (a) only HT (b) only VT (c) both HT and VT (d) neither HT nor VT
13. If a line is parallel to both the RPs, then which of the following statements is WRONG?
    (a) TL = PL (b) TL = EL (c) TL > EL (d) $\alpha = \beta$
14. If a line is inclined to the VP and parallel to the HP, then which of the following statements is always CORRECT?
    (a) TL = PL (b) TL = EL (c) TL > EL (d) VT is above *XY*
15. The projection of VT on *XY*, i.e., *v* is seen on
    (a) TV or extension of TV (b) FV or extension of FV (c) either TV or FV (d) none of the above
16. If $\theta + \phi = 90°$, then which of the following statements is CORRECT?
    (a) $\alpha = \beta = 90°$ (b) SV = TL (c) FV is perpendicular to *XY* (d) All of the above
17. To obtain the point view of a line, the auxiliary plane is set
    (a) perpendicular to TL (b) parallel to TL
    (c) inclined at an angle $\phi°$ to TL (d) inclined at an angle $\theta°$ to TL
18. To find θ, auxiliary plane is set
    (a) parallel to FV (b) perpendicular to FV (c) parallel to TV (d) perpendicular to TV
19. To obtain the TL of a line, auxiliary plane is set
    (a) perpendicular to FV or TV (b) parallel to FV or TV
    (c) inclined at an angle β to FV (d) inclined at an angle α to TV
20. The distance between two skew lines is equal to the length of the perpendicular from the
    (a) point view of one line to *XY*
    (b) point view of one line to $X1Y1$
    (c) point view of one line to the corresponding view of another line
    (d) any of the above

TEST VII: PROJECTIONS OF PLANES/PROJECTIONS OF SOLIDS/ SECTIONS OF SOLIDS

1. If a corner of a pentagonal plate is in the VP, then its TV has one point on *XY*.
2. If a plane is parallel to an RP, its projection on that RP shows the true shape and size.
3. The trace of a plane is a line.
4. If an edge view of a plane is projected on the auxiliary plane parallel to the edge view, then the auxiliary view obtained gives the true shape of the plane.
5. To obtain θ_p, a line is drawn parallel to an auxiliary plane in the final TV.
6. A tetrahedron has four equal square faces.
7. A cylinder is a solid of revolution.
8. If a body diagonal of a cube is vertical, the three edges emerging from an end of the body diagonal make equal angles with the HP.
9. A parabola can be obtained by cutting a cylinder.
10. If a cutting plane cuts all the generators of a cone then the section is always an ellipse.
11. If an edge of a pentagonal plate is making an angle of 40° with the VP and surface is making an angle of 30° with HP, the TV in the first step will be as in

(a) 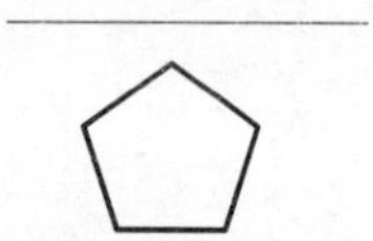

(b) 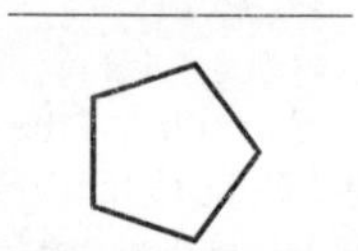

(c) 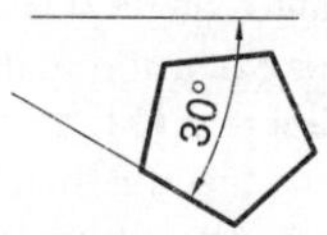

(d) 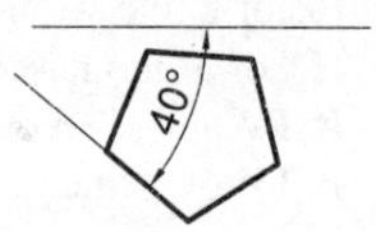

12. If an edge of an oblique pentagonal plane is parallel to the HP and the VP, then which of the following sentences is WRONG?
    (a) FV will show TL of the edge. (b) TV will show TL of the edge.
    (c) FV will show TL of the plane. (d) SV will show edge view.
13. A regular pentagonal plane *ABCDE* makes an angle of 40° to the HP. The edge *AB* is on the ground and makes an angle of 55° with the VP. The point *D* is in the VP. To obtain the final FV, auxiliary plane is set
    (a) inclined at 40° to *ab* (b) inclined at 40° to *ab* and passing through *d*
    (c) inclined at 55° to *ab* (d) inclined at 55° to *ab* and passing through *d*
14. A hexahedron consists of
    (a) four equal square faces (b) six equal square faces
    (c) four equal triangular faces (d) six equal triangular faces
15. A pentagonal pyramid is resting on its trianglular face on the HP with its axis parallel to the VP. Which of the following sentences is CORRECT?
    (a) FV shows TL of axis. (b) SV of axis is perpendicular to *XY*.
    (c) TV of axis is parallel to *XY*. (d) All of the above.
16. A hexagonal prism has its axis inclined at 30° to the HP and 60° to the VP. Which of the following sentences is CORRECT?
    (a) The axis will be seen at 30° to *XY* in FV. (b) The axis will be seen at 60° to *XY* in FV.
    (c) The base will make 60° with the HP. (d) The base will make 30° with the HP.
17. The largest possible section of a pentagonal prism will have
    (a) five edges (b) six edges (c) seven edges (d) eight edges
18. Which one of the following cannot be a section of a tetrahedron?
    (a) Isosceles triangle (b) Equilateral triangle (c) Trapezium (d) Pentagon
19. To obtain the true shape of the section of a solid, an auxiliary plane is set
    (a) inclined at an angle of 45° to a cutting plane (b) perpendicular to a cutting plane
    (c) parallel to a cutting plane (d) parallel to *XY*
20. If the cutting plane includes the axis of a cylinder, the section obtained is a
    (a) rectangle (b) circle (c) ellipse (d) any of the above

TEST VIII: THEORY OF DEVELOPMENT/INTERSECTIONS OF SOLIDS

1. The radial line development method is used for cylinder.
2. The development of tetrahedron is four equal-sized equilateral triangles.
3. The development of a cone is always a sector having included angle less than 180°.
4. A semicircle represents the development of a sphere.
5. If two cutting planes cut a solid, its development is always obtained in two parts.
6. If a cutting plane cuts only the lateral edges of a prism, then the development of top face or bottom face need not to be shown.
7. A common household funnel is an example of intersection of a cone and a cylinder.
8. Intersection of two square prisms shows a straight line segmented curve.
9. If a horizontal cylinder penetrates a vertical cylinder, the COI is seen in the TV.
10. Intersection of two equal-sized cylinders when their axes meet perpendicularly is seen as straight line in one view.
11. The theory of development is used in manufacturing of
    (a) plastic moulded parts (b) cast iron parts (c) sheet metal parts (d) electronic components
12. Parallel line development method is not suitable for the development of a
    (a) tetrahedron (b) hexahedron (c) pentagonal prism (d) cylinder
13. The included angle, θ of the sector development of a cone of base radius r and slant height R is given by,
    (b) $\theta° = 360\ (R/r)$ (b) $\theta° = 360\ (r/R)$ (c) $\theta° = 180\ (R/r)$ (d) $\theta° = 180\ (r/R)$
14. If a thread is wound around a cone, starting from a point on the base, and brought back to the same point, then the shortest possible length of the thread is equal to the
    (a) slant height of the cone (b) diameter of the base of the cone
    (c) longest chord of the development sector
    (d) length of a perpendicular from a corner of the development sector to the opposite edge
15. The development of all the surfaces of a cube will be
    (a) 4 squares (b) 5 squares (c) 6 squares (d) 8 squares
16. The development of a curved surface of a cylinder will be a
    (a) rectangle (b) sector (c) triangle (d) circle
17. Whenever a prism and a pyramid intersect, the curve seen at their intersection is a
    (a) smooth curve (b) segmented-line curve
    (c) either smooth curve or segmented-line curve (d) none of the above
18. A cone is resting on the base on the HP. A horizontal square prism penetrates the cone. Which of the following sentences is CORRECT?
    (a) TV will not show COI (b) Neither FV nor SV will show COI
    (c) TV will show COI (d) None of the view will show COI
19. To obtain the COI between a cone and a sphere, the approach used is
    (a) edge view approach (b) cutting plane approach
    (c) solid intersection approach (d) any of the above
20. Which of the following sentences is WRONG about the intersections of two spheres?
    (a) Cutting plane approach is used. (b) COI is a circle.
    (c) Flat face is created at the intersection. (d) None of the above

TEST IX: ISOMETRIC PROJECTION/PERSPECTIVE PROJECTION/ INTERPRETATION OF THE VIEWS

1. In an isometric view of a prism, no two lines are seen parallel to each other.
2. An isometric view of any object is drawn to actual size.
3. An isometric projection is a one- plane projection.

4. Three concurrent edges of a cube originating from origin 'O', will make 30° each with the HP.
5. Isometric lines are always parallel to isometric axes.
6. In perspective projection the station point coincides with the eyes of the observer.
7. The HP always passes over the head of an observer in perspective projection.
8. A centreline denotes cylindrical features.
9. A sphere is completely specified by only one view indicating the spherical diameter.
10. Three views are always necessary to indicate any regular prism.
11. Compared to the actual diameter, the isometric diameter of a sphere is
    (a) equal (b) smaller (c) greater (d) none
12. The real angle made by isometric axes with each other is
    (a) 120° (b) 90° (c) 60° (d) 30°
13. In isomeric projection, the length or width of the object is drawn at ___ to the horizontal reference line.
    (a) 30° (b) 45° (c) 90° (d) 120°
14. While drawing the isometric view of the sphere, its diameter is taken
    (a) 11/9 times of the actual diameter (b) 9/11 times of the actual diameter
    (c) equal to the actual diameter (d) none of the above
15. Perspective projections are mostly used in
    (a) architectural drawings(b) advertising drawings
    (c) artistic drawings (d) all of the above
16. If a principal face of an object is parallel to the picture plane, the perspective projection is called
    (a) parallel perspective (b) angular perspective (c) oblique perspective (d) any of the above
17. Which of the following sentences is WRONG about three-point perspective?
    (a) All the three principal edges of the object are inclined to the picture plane.
    (b) There are three vanishing points.
    (c) Vertical edges are seen parallel.
    (d) Some of the dimensions represents the true dimension.
18. A continuous straight line in FV of an object may represent
    (a) an edge of the object (b) a face of the object
    (c) either an edge or a face of the object (d) a corner on the object
19. A rectangle drawn by a dashed line in FV will represent a
    (a) Rectangular depression on the back side (b) Rectangular projection on the front side
    (c) Rectangular depression on the front side (d) none of above
20. Which of the following sentences is WRONG?
    (a) A hidden edge may emerge from the intersection of two visible edges.
    (b) A hidden edge may emerge from the intersection of two hidden edges.
    (c) A visible edge may emerge from the intersection of two visible edges.
    (d) A visible edge may emerge from the intersection of two hidden edges.

TEST X: FREEHAND DRAWING/CAD

1. For freehand drawing, an HB grade pencil is preferred.
2. In freehand drawing, proportion is not important.
3. Plotting is recommended for the drawing on an A3 or larger size sheet.
4. A digitizer is used to convert manual drawings into digital drawings.
5. The LINE command can be used to draw curved lines.
6. The ARC command can also be used to draw circles.
7. The ARRAY command copies the object in a particular pattern.
8. The DONUT command gives a filled-in circle.
9. The Isocircle option is always available in the ELLIPSE command.

10. The F7 key activates grid.
11. A freehand vertical line should always be drawn from
    (a) bottom to top (b) top to bottom
    (c) midpoint to top (d) midpoint to bottom
12. The advantages offered by CAD are
    (a) accuracy and speed (b) easy editing and scaling
    (c) space effectiveness and better visualization (d) all of the above
13. Which one of the following is not an output device?
    (a) Printer (b) Plotter (c) Joystick (d) Monitor
14. Which one the following is an input device?
    (a) Mouse (b) Monitor (c) Plotter (d) Pen drive
15. Which one the following is not a toolbar in AutoCAD?
    (a) Draw (b) Edit (c) Standard (d) Properties
16. The command used to erase the object partly is
    (a) ERASE (b) EXPLODE (c) TRIM (d) EXTEND
17. The most effective command used to draw symmetrical objects is
    (a) COPY (b) ARRAY (c) LENGTHEN (d) MIRROR
18. Which of the following commands is not included in the Modify I toolbar?
    (a) TEXT (b) SCALE (c) BREAK (d) MOVE
19. The 'Tan Tan Tan' option in CIRCLE command is available at
    (a) **Command line** » **c** (b) **Menu bar** » ***Draw*** » ***circle***
    (c) **Draw toolbar** » ***circle*** (d) any of the above
20. Which of the following do not represent a button on the Status bar?
    (a) COLOR (b) DYN (c) OSNAP (d) POLAR

Answer Keys

Questions	Test I	II	III	IV	V	VI	VII	VIII	IX	X
1	T	F	T	T	T	F	T	F	F	T
2	T	T	F	T	F	T	T	T	F	F
3	F	T	F	F	T	T	T	F	T	T
4	T	T	T	F	F	F	T	F	F	T
5	F	T	F	T	T	T	F	F	T	F
6	T	F	F	T	F	T	F	T	T	F
7	F	F	T	F	T	F	T	T	F	T
8	F	T	F	F	T	F	T	T	T	T
9	T	F	T	F	F	T	F	F	T	F
10	T	F	T	T	T	F	F	T	F	T
11	c	b	b	d	c	b	b	c	a	b
12	b	c	b	b	d	a	c	a	b	d
13	d	b	b	b	b	c	d	b	a	c
14	b	c	d	c	b	a	b	c	a	a
15	b	c	d	c	b	a	d	c	d	b
16	c	d	d	b	a	d	c	a	a	c
17	d	d	c	b	a	a	c	b	c	d
18	c	a	a	d	b	c	d	c	c	a
19	c	b	d	a	d	b	c	b	a	b
20	b	d	a	d	c	c	a	d	d	a

INDEX